OUR NATIONAL INCOME ACCOUNTS AND CHAIN WEIGHTED REAL GDP SINCE 1929*

In this table we see historical data for the various components of nominal GDP. These are given in the first four columns. We then show the rest of the national income accounts going from GDP to NDP to NI to PI to DPI. The last column gives chain-weighted real GDP.

Krislo Geremia

	The Sum of These Expenditures			Equals	Less	Equals	Plus	Less	Equals	Less		Plus	Equals	Less	Equals	
Year	Personal Consumption Expenditures	Gross Private Domestic Investment	Government Purchases of Goods and Services	Net Exports	Gross Domestic Product	Depreciation	Net Domestic Product	Net U.S. Income Earned Abroad	Indirect Business Taxes and Transfers	National Income	Undistributed Corporate Profits	Social Security Taxes	Corporate Income Taxes	Transfer Payments and Net Interest Earnings	Personal Income	Personal Income Taxes and Nontax Payments	Disposable Personal Income	Chain-Weighted Real GDP (1992 dollars)
1975	1029.1	225.4	362.6	13.6	1630.6	200.1	1430.5	13.3	148.3	1295.5	59.4	121.1	50.9	251.5	1315.6	156.4	1159.2	3865.1
1976	1148.8	286.6	385.9	−2.3	1819.0	218.9	1600.1	17.2	169.8	1447.5	73.7	137.7	64.2	283.5	1455.4	182.3	1273.0	4081.1
1977	1277.1	356.6	416.9	−23.7	2026.9	251.1	1775.8	20.7	180.2	1616.3	89.6	155.4	73.0	313.1	1611.4	210.0	1401.4	4279.3
1978	1428.8	430.8	457.9	−26.1	2291.4	281.8	2009.6	22.1	192.5	1839.2	108.6	177.0	83.5	350.1	1820.2	240.1	1580.1	4493.7
1979	1593.5	480.9	507.1	−24.0	2557.5	322.3	2235.2	32.9	214.8	2053.3	121.3	204.2	88.0	409.9	2049.7	280.2	1769.5	4624.0
1980	1760.4	465.9	572.8	−14.0	2784.2	368.0	2416.2	35.3	235.4	2216.1	97.3	225.0	84.8	476.7	2285.7	312.4	1973.3	4611.9
1981	1941.3	556.2	633.4	−15.0	3115.9	419.9	2696.0	34.7	260.5	2470.2	79.1	261.6	81.1	512.0	2560.4	360.2	2200.2	4724.9
1982	2076.8	501.1	684.8	−20.5	3242.1	456.3	2785.8	31.1	247.7	2569.2	43.8	280.6	63.1	537.0	2718.7	371.4	2347.3	4623.5
1983	2283.4	547.1	735.7	−51.7	3514.5	477.9	3036.6	32.0	307.2	2761.4	54.8	301.9	77.2	564.2	2891.7	369.3	2522.4	4810.0
1984	2492.3	715.6	796.6	−102.0	3902.4	494.0	3408.4	31.1	306.8	3132.7	66.9	345.5	94.0	579.2	3205.5	395.5	2810.0	5138.2
1985	2704.8	715.1	875.0	−114.2	4180.7	519.5	3661.2	20.4	330.1	3351.5	40.6	375.9	96.5	601.1	3439.6	437.7	3002.0	5329.5
1986	2892.7	722.5	938.5	−131.5	4422.2	552.8	3869.4	12.9	365.8	3516.5	5.8	402.0	106.5	645.3	3647.5	459.9	3187.6	5489.9
1987	3094.5	747.2	992.8	−142.1	4692.3	581.9	4110.4	8.9	341.2	3778.1	59.5	423.3	127.1	709.1	3877.3	514.2	3363.1	5648.4
1988	3349.7	773.9	1032.0	−106.1	5049.6	620.2	4429.4	13.0	333.8	4108.6	100.5	462.8	137.0	764.5	4172.8	532.0	3640.8	5862.9
1989	3594.8	829.2	1095.1	−80.4	5438.7	662.2	4776.5	14.2	428.6	4362.1	67.9	491.2	141.3	827.6	4489.3	594.9	3894.5	6060.4
1990	3839.3	799.7	1176.1	−71.3	5743.8	693.1	5050.7	21.1	459.9	4611.9	79.4	518.5	140.5	918.1	4791.6	624.8	4166.8	6138.7
1991	3975.1	736.2	1225.9	−20.5	5916.7	723.1	5193.6	15.7	489.6	4719.7	77.7	543.5	133.4	1003.4	4968.5	624.8	4343.7	6079.0
1992	4219.8	790.4	1263.8	−29.5	6244.4	754.2	5490.2	11.1	550.5	4950.8	93.9	571.4	143.0	1121.7	5264.2	650.5	4613.7	6244.4
1993	4454.1	871.1	1289.9	−64.9	6550.2	773.8	5776.4	9.8	591.8	5194.4	103.3	592.9	163.8	1144.8	5479.2	689.9	4789.3	6383.8
1994	4698.7	1014.4	1314.7	−96.4	6931.4	818.8	6112.6	−8.9	608.6	5495.1	121.9	628.3	195.3	1200.6	5750.2	731.4	5018.8	6604.2
1995	4923.4	1067.5	1358.6	−108.4	7241.1	855.6	6387.7	−9.3	636.0	5742.4	127.4	656.6	204.1	1254.6	6009.0	764.3	5244.6	6786.2
1998[a]	5659.4	1329.8	1466.4	−123.4	8332.2	951.3	7380.9	−25.1	730.8	6625.0	140.0	711.1	220.1	1573.1	7126.9	1032.4	6094.5	7356.0

*Note: Except for real GDP, all figures in billions of dollars. Some rows may not add up due to rounding errors.
[a]Estimates based on preliminary data.

MACROECONOMIC PRINCIPLES

NOMINAL VERSUS REAL INTEREST RATE

$$i_n = i_r + \text{expected rate of inflation}$$

where i_n = nominal rate

i_r = real rate of interest

MARGINAL VERSUS AVERAGE TAX RATES

$$\text{Marginal tax rate} = \frac{\text{change in taxes due}}{\text{change in taxable income}}$$

$$\text{Average tax rate} = \frac{\text{total taxes due}}{\text{total taxable income}}$$

GDP–THE EXPENDITURE AND INCOME APPROACHES

$$\text{GDP} = C + I + G + X$$

where C = consumption expenditures

I = investment expenditures

G = government expenditures

X = net exports

$$\text{GDP} = \text{wages} + \text{rent} + \text{interest} + \text{profits}$$

SAY'S LAW

Supply creates its own demand, or *desired* aggregate expenditures will equal *actual* aggragate expenditures

SAVING, CONSUMPTION, AND INVESTMENT

$$\text{Consumption} + \text{saving} = \text{disposable income}$$
$$\text{Saving} = \text{disposable income} - \text{consumption}$$
$$\text{Actual saving} = \text{actual investment}$$

AVERAGE AND MARGINAL PROPENSITIES

$$\text{APC} = \frac{\text{consumption}}{\text{real disposable income}}$$

$$\text{APS} = \frac{\text{saving}}{\text{real disposable income}}$$

$$\text{MPC} = \frac{\text{change in consumption}}{\text{change in real disposable income}}$$

$$\text{MPS} = \frac{\text{change in saving}}{\text{change in real disposable income}}$$

THE MULTIPLIER FORMULA

$$\text{Multiplier} = \frac{1}{\text{MPS}} = \frac{1}{1 - \text{MPC}}$$

$$\text{Multiplier} \times \begin{array}{c} \text{change in} \\ \text{autonomous} \\ \text{spending} \end{array} = \begin{array}{c} \text{change in} \\ \text{equilibrium level} \\ \text{of national income} \end{array}$$

RELATIONSHIP BETWEEN BOND PRICES AND INTEREST RATES

The market price of existing (old) bonds is inversely related to "the" rate of interest prevailing in the economy.

GOVERNMENT SPENDING AND TAXATION MULTIPLIERS

$$M_g = \frac{1}{\text{MPS}}$$

$$M_t = -\text{MPC} \times \frac{1}{\text{MPS}}$$

GRESHAM'S LAW

Bad money drives good money out of circulation.

Economics Today

1999–2000 EDITION

THE ADDISON-WESLEY SERIES IN ECONOMICS

To Jeff and Sandra LeSage:

*Thanks for your advice and friendship
throughout the years. Good luck in
your new environment.*

R.L.M.

CONTENTS IN BRIEF

CONTENTS IN DETAIL

Economics Today

1999–2000 EDITION

ROGER LeROY MILLER

INSTITUTE FOR UNIVERSITY STUDIES, ARLINGTON, TEXAS

▲▲ ADDISON-WESLEY

An imprint of Addison Wesley Longman, Inc.

Reading, Massachusetts • Menlo Park, California • New York • Harlow, England
Don Mills, Ontario • Sydney • Mexico City • Madrid • Amsterdam

Photo Credits

Pages 3 and 13, Merritt Vincent/PhotoEdit; pages 17 and 33, Richard Heinzen/SuperStock, Inc.; pages 45 and 68, Courtesy of Egghead.com; pages 73 and 89, © Syracuse Newspapers/Li-Hua Lan/The Image Works; pages 94 and 111, Michael Newman/PhotEdit; pages 116 and 134, Paul Conklin/Monkmeyer; pages 141 and 159, Jeff Greenberg/Omni-Photo; pages 163 and 182, PN/The Slide File; page 165 left, Frank Siteman/The Picture Cube; page 165 right, Bernsau/The Image Works; pages 187 and 202, Alex Farnsworth/The Image Works; pages 207 and 224, AP/Wide World Photos; pages 227 and 242, Spencer Grant/PhotoEdit; pages 245 and 267, David Young-Wolff/PhotoEdit; pages 275 and 289, Terry Ashe/Gamma Liaison; pages 297 and 312, Stephen Jaffe/The Image Works; page 302, Topham/The Image Works; pages 319 and 335, Ilkka Uimonen/Sygma; pages 339 and 359, Reuters/Carlos Hernandez/Archive Photos; pages 364 and 382, SuperStock, Inc.; pages 388 and 408, Richard R. Renaldi/Impact Visuals; pages 413 and 425, R. Lord/The Image Works; pages 439 and 457, J and M Studios/Gamma Liaison; pages 461 and 474, Stephen Ferry/Gamma Liaison; pages 481 and 503, Reprinted with the permission of America Online, Inc. © 1998 America Online, Inc. All Rights Reserved.; pages 508 and 528, PhotoEdit; pages 533 and 552, Lee Snider/The Image Works; pages 557 and 578, Mark Ide; pages 583 and 598, Michael A. Schwarz/The Image Works; pages 605 and 623, Steven Rubin/The Image Works; pages 628 and 644, Jonathan Elderfield/Gamma Liaison; page 631, Skjold/The Image Works; pages 649 and 663, Frozen Images/The Image Works; pages 666 and 689, Daemmrich/The Image Works; page 679, Bob Kramer/The Picture Cube; pages 694 and 707, Reuters/Archive Photos; pages 711 and 726, Michael Newman/PhotoEdit; pages 733 and 748, Walter Bibikow/The Picture Cube; pages 753 and 770, Edouard Berne/Tony Stone Images; page 761, © Chappatte in Le Temps (Switzerland)/www.globecartoon.com; pages 775 and 788, Andy Hernandez/Gamma Liaison.

Executive Editor: Denise Clinton
Senior Editor: Andrea Shaw
Developmental Editor: Mary Draper
Supplements Editor: Deb Kiernan
Senior Production Supervisor: Nancy Fenton
Marketing Manager: Amy Cronin
Senior Project Manager: Melissa Honig
Designer: Regina Hagen
Cover illustration: Photomosaic™ ©1997 Robert Silvers, www.photomosaic.com
Art Studio: ElectraGraphics, Inc.
Photo Researcher: Billie Porter
Print Buyer: Sheila Spinney
Media Buyer: Sue Ward
Composition: WestWords, Inc.
Printer and Binder: R.R. Donnelley & Sons Company
Cover Printer: Coral Graphic Services, Inc.

Library of Congress Cataloging-in-Publication Data
Miller, Roger LeRoy.
    Economics today / Roger LeRoy Miller. — 10th ed.
      p.   cm. — (The Addison-Wesley series in economics)
    Includes index.
    ISBN (invalid) 0-201-36189-7
    1. Economics. 2. Microeconomics. 3. Macroeconomics. I. Title.
  II. Series.
  HB171.5.M642   1998
  330—dc21
                                          98-22980
                                          CIP

Reprinted with corrections, December 1998

ISBN 0-201-31689-7
345678910—DOW—02010099

COURSE OUTLINE

The 1999–2000 Edition of *Economics Today* presents economic principles within the context of sweeping changes occurring in the economic landscape. These changes, including the "wiring" of the economy, have prompted me to revise this market-leading textbook in two years instead of the usual three. Alongside changes in the economy are the dramatic new approaches to teaching and learning introductory economics. The 1999–2000 Edition responds to these changes with significant revisions to the text and supplements.

In the textbook you will find all new contemporary issues presented in a hallmark feature, Issues and Applications, at the start and end of each chapter. Because economic problems are being influenced by today's "wired world," I have also added new Cyberspace Examples throughout the text and a new Chapter 35, "Cybernomics." In addition, every chart, table, and graph has been revised to reflect the most recent data available.

This new edition also responds to the latest teaching methods to enhance your lectures and aid student learning. Many of you have been asking for PowerPoint slides. Accompanying this text is a comprehensive, dynamic PowerPoint Lecture Presentation system of key terms and concepts and animated graphs from the text. In addition, the 1999–2000 Edition is accompanied by a rich variety of economic experiments to involve students in testing economic theory.

To explore economic theory and real-world applications, students will receive the Economics in Action, 1999–2000 Edition, CD-ROM with every purchase of a text. This interactive software uses dynamic graphs, sound effects, and step-by-step tutorials to guide students in their understanding of economic concepts.

In addition, Internet exercises and a Web site featuring practice quizzes will get students on line to test and expand their knowledge.

I am grateful for the extensive feedback received from reviewers, focus groups, and students, which continues to shape and enhance *Economics Today*. You may reach me at **www.econtoday.com** to share your feedback and suggestions for improving the text and supplements package.

Roger LeRoy Miller

ACKNOWLEDGMENTS

I feel that I am one of the luckiest textbook writers around, for I get the benefit of continuous feedback from professors who use *Economics Today*. I am grateful for the constructive criticisms that you continue to send me. Below I list those of you who generously offered your time to participate in the reviewing process for this edition. Please accept my sincere appreciation.

Mohammed Akacem, Metropolitan State College
John Allen, Texas A&M University
Ann AlYasiri, University of Wisconsin, Platteville
Abraham Bertisch, Nassua Community College
Steffany Ellis, University of Michigan–Dearborne
Sandy Evans, St. John's River Community College
Arthur Friedberg, Mohawk Valley Community College

Edward Greenberg, Washington University
Nick Grunt, Tarrant City Junior College
Kwabena Gyimah-Brempong, University of Southern Florida
Grover A. Howard, Rio Hondo College
Mark Jensen, Southern Illinois University
Faik Koray, Louisiana State University
Akbar Marvasti, University of Houston–Downtown
Michael Metzger, University of Central Oklahoma
Margaret Moore, Franklin University
Randy Parker, East Carolina University

Norm Paul, San Jacinto College
Mannie Poen, Houston Community College
Henry Ryder, Gloucester County College
David Schorow, Richland College
Columbus Stephens, Brevard Community College
Kay Unger, University of Montana
Mark Wilkening, Blinn Community College
Pete Wyman, Spokane Falls Community College
Paul Zarembka, SUNY Buffalo

Those who reviewed previous editions:

Esmond Adams
John Adams
John R. Aidem
M. C. Alderfer
Leslie J. Anderson
Fatima W. Antar
Aliakbar Ataiifar
Leonard Atencio
Glen W. Atkinson
Thomas R. Atkinson
James Q. Aylesworth
Charlie Ballard
Maurice B. Ballabon
G. Jeffrey Barbour
Daniel Barszcz
Robin L. Bartlett
Kari Battaglia
Robert Becker
Charles Beem
Glen Beeson
Charles Berry
Scott Bloom
M. L. Bodnar
Mary Bone
Karl Bonnhi
Thomas W. Bonsor
John M. Booth
Wesley F. Booth
Thomas Borcherding
Tom Boston
Barry Boyer
Maryanna Boynton
Ronald Brandolini
Fenton L. Broadhead
Elba Brown

William Brown
Michael Bull
Maureen Burton
Ralph T. Byrns
Conrad P. Caligaris
Kevin Carey
Dancy R. Carr
Doris Cash
Thomas H. Cate
Richard J. Cebula
Richard Chapman
Young Back Choi
Carol Cies
Joy L. Clark
Gary Clayton
Marsha Clayton
Warren L. Coats
Ed Coen
Pat Conroy
James Cox
Stephen R. Cox
Eleanor D. Craig
Joanna Cruse
John P. Cullity
Thomas Curtis
Andrew J. Dane
Mahmoud Davoudi
Edward Dennis
Carol Dimamro
William Dougherty
Barry Duman
Diane Dumont
Floyd Durham
G. B. Duwaji
James A. Dyal

Ishita Edwards
Robert P. Edwards
Alan E. Ellis
Mike Ellis
Frank Emerson
Zaki Eusufzai
John L. Ewing-Smith
Frank Falero
Frank Fato
Grant Ferguson
David Fletcher
James Foley
John Foreman
Ralph G. Fowler
Arthur Friedberg
Peter Frost
E. Gabriel
Steve Gardner
Peter C. Garlick
Alexander Garvin
Joe Garwood
J. P. Gilbert
Otis Gilley
Frank Glesber
Jack Goddard
Allen C. Goodman
Richard J. Gosselin
Gary Greene
Nicholas Grunt
William Gunther
Demos Hadjiyanis
Martin D. Haney
Mehdi Haririan
Ray Harvey
E. L. Hazlett

Sanford B. Helman
John Hensel
Robert Herman
Gus W. Herring
Charles Hill
John M. Hill
Morton Hirsch
Benjamin Hitchner
R. Bradley Hoppes
James Horner
Grover Howard
Nancy Howe-Ford
R. Jack Inch
Christopher Inya
Tomotaka Ishimine
E. E. Jarvis
Parvis Jenab
S. D. Jevremovic
J. Paul Jewell
Frederick Johnson
David Jones
Lamar B. Jones
Paul A. Joray
Daniel A. Joseph
Craig Justice
Septimus Kai Kai
Devajyoti Kataky
Timothy R. Keely
Ziad Keilany
Norman F. Keiser
Randall G. Kesselring
E. D. Key
M. Barbara Killen
Bruce Kimzey
Philip G. King

Terrence Kinal
E. R. Kittrell
David Klingman
Charles Knapp
Jerry Knarr
Janet Koscianski
Peter Kressler
Michael Kupilik
Larry Landrum
Margaret Landman
Keith Langford
Anthony T. Lee
George Lieu
Stephen E. Lile
Lawrence W. Lovick
Warren T. Matthews
Robert McAuliffe
Howard J. McBride
Bruce McClung
John McDowell
E. S. McKuskey
James J. McLain
John L. Madden
Mary Lou Madden
Glen Marston
John M. Martin
Paul J. Mascotti
James D. Mason
Paul M. Mason
Tom Mathew
Warren Matthews
G. Hartley Mellish
Mike Melvin
Dan C. Messerschmidt

Herbert C. Milikien
Joel C. Millonzi
Glenn Milner
Thomas Molloy
Margaret D. Moore
William E. Morgan
Stephen Morrell
Irving Morrissett
James W. Moser
Martin F. Murray
George L. Nagy
Jerome Neadly
James E. Needham
Claron Nelson
Douglas Nettleton
Gerald T. O'Boyle
Lucian T. Orlowski
Diane S. Osborne
Jan Palmer
Gerald Parker
Randall E. Parker
Raymond A. Pepin
Martin M. Perline
Timothy Perri
Jerry Petr
Maurice Pfannesteil
James Phillips
Raymond J. Phillips
I. James Pickl
Dennis Placone
William L. Polvent
Reneé Prim
Robert W. Pulsinelli
Rod D. Raehsler
Kambriz Raffiee

Sandra Rahman
John Rapp
Gautam
 Raychaudhuri
Ron Reddall
Mitchell Redlo
Charles Reichhelu
Robert S. Rippey
Ray C. Roberts
Richard Romano
Duane Rosa
Richard Rosenberg
Larry Ross
Barbara Ross-Pfeiffer
Philip Rothman

John Roufagalas
Patricia Sanderson
Thomas N. Schaap
William A. Schaeffer
William Schaniel
David Schauer
A. C. Schlenker
Scott J. Schroeder
William Scott
Dan Segebarth
Robert Sexton
Augustus Shackelford
Richard Sherman Jr.
Liang-rong Shiau
David Shorow

Vishwa Shukla
R. J. Sidwell
David E. Sisk
Alden Smith
Howard F. Smith
Lynn A. Smith
Phil Smith
Steve Smith
William Doyle Smith
Lee Spector
George Spiva
Richard L. Sprinkle
Herbert F. Steeper
William Stine
Allen D. Stone

Osman Suliman
J. M. Sullivan
Rebecca Summary
Joseph L. Swaffar
Frank D. Taylor
Daniel Teferra
Gary Theige
Robert P. Thomas
Deborah Thorsen
Richard Trieff
George Troxler
William T. Trulove
William N. Trumbull
Arianne K. Turner
John Vahaly

Jim VanBeek
Lee J. Van Scyoc
Roy Van Til
Robert F. Wallace
Henry C. Wallich
Milledge Weathers
Robert G. Welch
Terence West
Wylie Whalthall
Everett E. White
Michael D. White
Mark A. Wilkening
Raburn M. Williams
James Willis
George Wilson

Travis Wilson
Ken Woodward
Peter R. Wyman
Whitney Yamamura
Donald Yankovic
Alex Yguado
Alex A. Yguado
Paul Young
Shik Young
Mohammed Zaheer
Ed Zajicek
William J. Zimmer Jr.

No author alone can complete a new large-scale revision of a textbook. I was helped by a hard-working group of people, from start to finish. My editor at Addison Wesley, Denise Clinton, provided assistance in all aspects of this project. My developmental editor, Mary Draper, helped me make many important decisions about the direction of this revision. She also managed many of the new supplements and the revisions of old. Deborah Kiernan saw to the production details for each and every print supplement, as did Melissa Honig for all of the multimedia supplements, including the major task of getting the CD-ROM out on time and without errors. My production editor, Nancy Fenton, probably spent more time talking, faxing, and e-mailing me than she would have preferred, but the results are certainly worth all of her efforts, I believe. My long-time copy editor, Bruce Emmer, came through again and made my prose as smooth as possible. To the above-mentioned Addison-Wesley team members and all of the others who have helped me, I thank you and look forward to working with you again.

Many of my colleagues worked with me intimately in redoing or providing new important supplements. Dan Benjamin updated the *Internet Activities* as well as added ones for each of the 35 new *Issues and Applications*. David VanHoose worked tirelessly on the new interactive CD-ROM and finished it on time in the face of time-consuming technical issues. Andy Dane again made masterful changes in the *Instructor's Manual* and the *Lecture Outlines with Transparency Masters.* Steve Smith, Jeff Caldwell, and Mark Mitchell came up with an incredibly useful PowerPoint presentation system for this edition. Randall Parker worked tirelessly on new test questions and revisions of old. Denise Hazlett provided a state-of-the-art active learning guide to go along with this edition. To these professors I extend a special note of appreciation.

As always, I wish to thank Sue Jasin of K&M Consulting for her expert manuscript preparation as well as camera-ready copy for some of the supplements.

Keeping with the cyberage, and because I always enjoy reading suggestions about what to do in future editions, you and your students can contact me directly via my Web site at: **www.econtoday.com**

Roger LeRoy Miller

ECONOMIC PRINCIPLES IN PRACTICE

Chapter-Opening Issues. Each Chapter-Opening Issue motivates student interest in the key chapter concepts with student-friendly examples.

CHAPTER 26
REGULATION AND ANTITRUST POLICY

By now, most of you reading this text will have used a Web browser on the Internet. There are basically two competing Web browsers today: one developed by Netscape Communications Corporation, called Navigator, and the other developed by Microsoft Corporation, called Internet Explorer. A few years ago, when Netscape practically "owned" the Internet browser market, Microsoft decided to compete. The initial versions of Internet Explorer were not so good as Navigator. Little by little, though, Microsoft began to catch up, resulting in two browsers that are more or less equally easy to use and have similar features. Most of the world's computers use the Microsoft-owned Windows operating system. If Microsoft decided to "bundle" a new version of its Internet Explorer with its Windows operating system, could that destroy competition in the browser market? Before you answer this question, you need to know about regulation and antitrust policy.

PREVIEW QUESTIONS

1. What is a natural monopoly, and how does one arise?
2. If natural monopolies are required to price at marginal cost, what problem emerges?
3. What are some means of regulating a natural monopoly?
4. Why have economists been reevaluating the government's role as an economic regulator?

583

Issues and Applications. Each Issues and Applications feature is linked to the Chapter-Opening Issue and is designed to encourage students to apply economic concepts and think critically about those concepts. Each begins with the concepts being applied and is followed by several critical thinking questions that may be used to prompt in-class discussion. You will find suggested answers to the critical thinking questions in the Instructor's Manual.

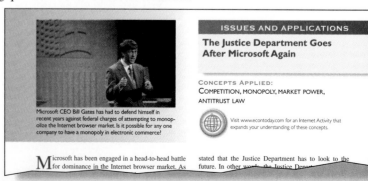

ISSUES AND APPLICATIONS
The Justice Department Goes After Microsoft Again

CONCEPTS APPLIED:
COMPETITION, MONOPOLY, MARKET POWER, ANTITRUST LAW

Visit www.econtoday.com for an Internet Activity that expands your understanding of these concepts.

Microsoft CEO Bill Gates has had to defend himself in recent years against federal charges of attempting to monopolize the Internet browser market. Is it possible for any one company to have a monopoly in electronic commerce?

Microsoft has been engaged in a head-to-head battle for dominance in the Internet browser market. As stated that the Justice Department has to look to the future. In other words, the Justice Depar...

From cover to cover, you'll find current, provocative examples that expand your students' understanding of economic principles and problems.

Thinking Critically About the Media. Thinking Critically About the Media offers a twist on typical news reporting and encourages students to think critically about what they hear reported in the news. These boxed features also keep students abreast of recent news-making issues. See page 48.

Policy Examples. Many of the economic discussions presented by the media involve important policy issues. In the 1999–2000 Edition, students are exposed to important policy questions on both the domestic and international fronts in over 30 Policy Examples.

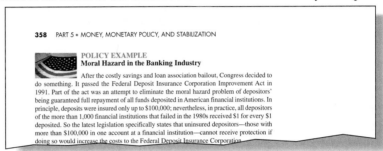

358   PART 5 • MONEY, MONETARY POLICY, AND STABILIZATION

POLICY EXAMPLE
Moral Hazard in the Banking Industry

After the costly savings and loan association bailout, Congress decided to do something. It passed the Federal Deposit Insurance Corporation Improvement Act in 1991. Part of the act was an attempt to eliminate the moral hazard problem of depositors' being guaranteed full repayment of all funds deposited in American financial institutions. In principle, deposits were insured only up to $100,000; nevertheless, in practice, all depositors of the more than 1,000 financial institutions that failed in the 1980s received $1 for every $1 deposited. So the latest legislation specifically states that uninsured depositors—those with more than $100,000 in one account at a financial institution—cannot receive protection if doing so would increase the costs to the Federal Deposit Insurance Corporation.

A World Of Global Examples. Over 50 international examples emphasize today's global economy.

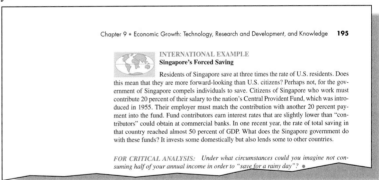

Chapter 9 • Economic Growth: Technology, Research and Development, and Knowledge   195

INTERNATIONAL EXAMPLE
Singapore's Forced Saving

Residents of Singapore save at three times the rate of U.S. residents. Does this mean that they are more forward-looking than U.S. citizens? Perhaps not, for the government of Singapore compels individuals to save. Citizens of Singapore who work must contribute 20 percent of their salary to the nation's Central Provident Fund, which was introduced in 1955. Their employer must match the contribution with another 20 percent payment into the fund. Fund contributors earn interest rates that are slightly lower than "contributors" could obtain at commercial banks. In one recent year, the rate of total saving in that country reached almost 50 percent of GDP. What does the Singapore government do with these funds? It invests some domestically but also lends some to other countries.

FOR CRITICAL ANALYSIS: Under what circumstances could you imagine not consuming half of your annual income in order to "save for a rainy day"? •

Examples Closer to Home. More than 50 thought-provoking and relevant examples highlight U.S. current events and demonstrate economic principles.

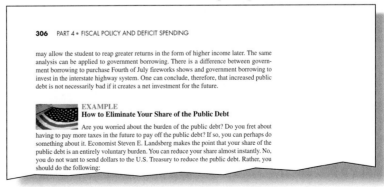

306   PART 4 • FISCAL POLICY AND DEFICIT SPENDING

may allow the student to reap greater returns in the form of higher income later. The same analysis can be applied to government borrowing. There is a difference between government borrowing to purchase Fourth of July fireworks shows and government borrowing to invest in the interstate highway system. One can conclude, therefore, that increased public debt is not necessarily bad if it creates a net investment for the future.

EXAMPLE
How to Eliminate Your Share of the Public Debt

Are you worried about the burden of the public debt? Do you fret about having to pay more taxes in the future to pay off the public debt? If so, you can perhaps do something about it. Economist Steven E. Landsberg makes the point that your share of the public debt is an entirely voluntary burden. You can reduce your share almost instantly. No, you do not want to send dollars to the U.S. Treasury to reduce the public debt. Rather, you should do the following:

WHAT'S NEW IN THE 1999-2000 EDITION?

ALL NEW! Issues and Applications. Continuing a hallmark tradition, the 1999–2000 Edition of *Economics Today* includes 35 new Issues and Applications features, one at the end of each chapter. These features encourage students to apply economic concepts and to think critically about how they apply those concepts in everyday life. Each is supported by new suggested Internet Activities that will permit students to continue their exploration.

NEW! Full Chapter on Cybernomics. How do technological innovations change economic theory? The new Chapter 35, beginning on page 775, explores how the Information Age affects our study of economics.

NEW! Internet Activities. In every chapter, students have the option of going online to build research skills and reinforce their understanding of economics concepts. The Internet Activities were written by Daniel K. Benjamin of Clemson University. When you see this icon in the margin of the text, go to **www.econtoday.com** to gain more insights into related issues.

Exercise 7.2
Visit www.econtoday.com for more about the CPI.

NEW! Cyberspace Examples. Today's "wired" students learn and benefit from advances in technology. New Cyberspace Examples demonstrate the significant impact of technology on our economic choices.

---

334   PART 5 • MONEY, MONETARY POLICY, AND STABILIZATION

7. *The Fed regulates the money supply.* Perhaps the Fed's most important task is its ability to regulate the nation's money supply. To understand how the Fed manages the money supply, we must examine more closely its reserve-holding function and the way in which depository institutions aid in expansion and contraction of the money supply. We will do this in Chapter 16.

FORCED INTO ELECTRONIC BANKING BY THE GOVERNMENT

The federal government is making cyberbanking, or at least a small part of it, a reality for millions of Americans. In an attempt to save on transaction costs, it is trying to force all recipients of federal funds to receive payments electronically, rather than by paper checks. For example, it is attempting to force military contractors who receive millions of dollars, as well as Social Security recipients who receive only thousands of dollars, to have those deposits made directly into their bank accounts. The goal is to eliminate all paper checks, at an estimated savings of over $500 million during the period 1999 to 2004.

Consider that the federal government makes over 850 million individual payments a year. Until recently, about half were made with paper checks, which cost 42 cents each to process, compared to electronic direct deposits, which cost only 2 cents. To achieve some of these savings, the federal government is turning to the E-Pay network of Visa U.S.A. Companies that receive federal payments must install software that they obtain from Visa. When many companies have the same software, they will surely start settling private

The 1999–2000 Edition of *Economics Today* highlights the dramatic changes technology has made to the economic landscape. Fresh, new examples throughout the chapters bring relevance to the changing world of economics.

Current Data.   Every chart, table, and graph in the book has been updated to reflect the most recent data available.

NEW!   **www.econtoday.com.**   The *Economics Today* web site provides on-line access to innovative teaching and learning tools.

- The Weekly Student Quiz tests students' understanding of key concepts. After completing each multiple-choice quiz, students quickly receive quiz results and are guided to appropriate sections of the text if they need further study.
- The Practice Exam is designed to test students' readiness for a midterm or final exam. The Practice Exam offers immediate test results and suggestions for students on how to improve their grades.
- Nearly 100 Internet Activities, organized by chapter and referenced with an icon in the margins of the text, will build students' research skills and reinforce key concepts. The Internet Activities can be accessed from the PowerPoint Lecture Presentations for in-class or group discussion.
- Ask the Author gives professors and students immediate access to Roger L. Miller to ask questions and give feedback on the text or supplements.
- All the URLs from Interacting with the Internet are kept current and organized by chapter.

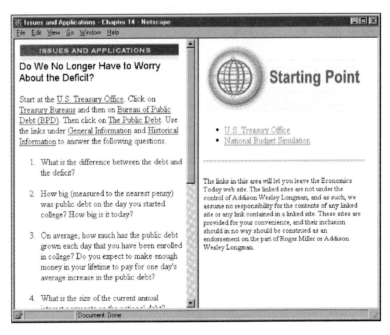

NEW! Economics in Action 1999–2000 CD-ROM. This interactive tutorial software has been developed by Michael Parkin and Robin Bade of the University of Western Ontario and adapted by David VanHoose of the University of Alabama for use with *Economics Today*. Already used by thousands of introductory economics students, Economics in Action uses dynamic graphs, sound effects, and step-by-step tutorials to guide students in their discovery of relationships between economic theory and real-world applications.

- Graphs from the textbook are re-created for more in-depth exploration and analysis.
- Economic data are presented in shifting curves and dynamic graphical output.
- Detailed, customizable quizzes help students prepare for exams and test their knowledge.

PEDAGOGY WITH PURPOSE

The 1999–2000 Edition of *Economics Today* is loaded with time-tested pedagody that helps students apply what they learn.

For Critical Analysis. At the end of each example, students are asked to "think like economists" and answer the "For Critical Analysis" questions. The answers to all questions are found in the Instructor's Manual. See page 53.

Did You Know That...? Each chapter starts with a provocative question to engage students and lead them into the content of the chapter.

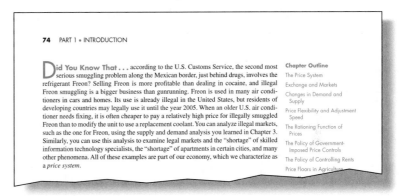

74 PART 1 • INTRODUCTION

Did You Know That . . . according to the U.S. Customs Service, the second most serious smuggling problem along the Mexican border, just behind drugs, involves the refrigerant Freon? Selling Freon is more profitable than dealing in cocaine, and illegal Freon smuggling is a bigger business than gunrunning. Freon is used in many air conditioners in cars and homes. Its use is already illegal in the United States, but residents of developing countries may legally use it until the year 2005. When an older U.S. air conditioner needs fixing, it is often cheaper to pay a relatively high price for illegally smuggled Freon than to modify the unit to use a replacement coolant. You can analyze illegal markets, such as the one for Freon, using the supply and demand analysis you learned in Chapter 3. Similarly, you can use this analysis to examine legal markets and the "shortage" of skilled information technology specialists, the "shortage" of apartments in certain cities, and many other phenomena. All of these examples are part of our economy, which we characterize as a *price system*.

Chapter Outline

The Price System

Exchange and Markets

Changes in Demand and Supply

Price Flexibility and Adjustment Speed

The Rationing Function of Prices

The Policy of Government-Imposed Price Controls

The Policy of Controlling Rents

Price Floors in Agriculture

Preview Questions. On the first page of each chapter, several questions are posed and then fully answered at the end of the chapter. See page 733.

Graphs. Articulate and precise, the four-color graphs illustrate key concepts.

Key Terms. Key terms are printed in bold type and defined in the margin of the text the first time they appear.

Concepts in Brief. At the end of each major section, Concepts in Brief summarizes the main points of the section to reinforce and test learning.

Chapter Summary. Every chapter ends with a concise but thorough summary of the important ideas of the chapter.

Problems. A variety of problems support each chapter, and answers for all odd-numbered problems are provided at the back of the textbook.

EXPANSIVE, INNOVATIVE TEACHING/LEARNING PACKAGE

NEW! **Instructor's Resource Disk (IRD) with PowerPoint Lecture Presentation.** The PowerPoint Lecture Presentation is available for Windows 95 and Macintosh computers—all on one IRD. The Power-Point Lecture Presentation was developed by Jeff Caldwell, Steve Smith, and Mark Mitchell of Rose State College. With nearly 100 slides per chapter, the PowerPoint Lecture Presentation animates graphs from the text; outlines key terms, concepts, and figures; and provides direct links to **www.econtoday.com** for in-class Internet Activities. The IRD also includes the Instructor's Manual in a Word file.

NEW! **Economic Experiments in the Classroom.** These economic experiments were developed by Denise Hazlett of Whitman College to involve students in actively testing economic theory. In addition to providing a variety of micro and macro experiments, this new supplement offers step-by-step guidelines for successfully running experiments in the classroom.

NEW! **www.econtoday.com.** The *Economics Today* Web site provides on-line access to innovative teaching and learning tools. The Weekly Student Quiz and Practice Midterm Exams test students' understanding of key concepts and directs them to appropriate sections of the text for further study. Students and professors have instant access to the author to share feedback, offer suggestions, and ask questions. Internet Activities, organized by chapter, are designed to build student research skills and reinforce key concepts.

Pocket Guide to Economics Today for Printed and Electronic Supplements. This pocket guide is designed to coordinate the extensive teaching/learning package that accompanies the 1999–2000 Edition of *Economics Today.* For each chapter heading, the author has organized a list of print and electronic ancillaries with page references to help organize lectures, develop class assignments, and prepare examinations.

Instructor's Manual. Prepared by Andrew J. Dane of Angelo State University, the Instructor's Manual provides the following instructor materials, three-hole-punched for easy insertion into the Instructor's Binder.

- Chapter overviews, objectives, and outlines
- Points to emphasize for those who wish to stress theory
- Answers to Issues and Applications critical thinking questions
- Further questions for class discussion
- Answers to even-numbered end-of-chapter problems
- Detailed step-by-step analysis of end-of-chapter problems
- Annotated answers to selected Student Learning Questions
- Selected references

Lecture Outlines with Transparency Masters. Prepared by Andrew J. Dane of Angelo State University, this lecture system features more than 500 pages of lecture outlines and text illustrations, including numerous tables taken from the text. Its pages can be made into transparencies or handouts to assist student note taking.

Four-color Overhead Transparencies. One hundred of the most important tables and graphs from the textbook are reproduced as full-color transparency acetates. Many contain multiple overlays.

Test Bank One. This test bank provides over 3,000 multiple-choice questions with answers. It has been developed by Susan G. Mason. The questions have been extensively classroom-tested for a number of years. Randall Parker of East Carolina University enhanced each of the three test banks with questions that cover the new Cybernomics chapter.

Test Bank Two. John Lunn of Hope College developed Test Bank Two, which includes over 3,000 multiple-choice questions. These questions have been class-tested by many professors, including Clark G. Ross, coauthor of the National Competency Test for economics majors for the Educational Testing Service in Princeton, New Jersey.

Short Essay Test Bank. As an alternative to the multiple-choice questions presented in the Test Banks One and Two, this completely separate test bank, developed by John Lunn of Hope College, provides short-answer essay questions.

NEW! Computerized Test Banks. The test banks are also available in Test Generator Software (TestGen-EQ with QuizMaster-EQ). Fully networkable, this software is available for Windows and Macintosh. TestGen-EQ's friendly graphical interface enables instructors to easily view, edit, and add questions; transfer questions to tests; and print tests in a variety of fonts and forms. Search and sort features let the instructor quickly locate questions and arrange them in a preferred order. QuizMaster-EQ automatically grades the exams, stores results on disk, and allows the instructor to view or print a variety of reports. Ask your publisher's representative for information about our test preparation service.

Economic Video Series. A series of micro and macro videotapes are available based on the award-winning MacNeil/Lehrer business reports. Each segment is reported by Paul Solman, MacNeil/Lehrer's special business correspondent.

The macroeconomics videotapes include	The microeconomics videotapes include
• Numbers Crunching	• Trade-Off: NAFTA
• Balance Act	• Heated Up
• Productivity: Man or Machine	• Second Look: Prices and Profits
• Boom or Bust	• Taxing or Energizing?
• Budget Scoring	• Beer Wars?
• The S&L Crisis: In Irreverent History	• Special Delivery: Attempt to Unionize Bicycle Messengers in New York
• Making Sense of the Sanctum	• Factory Fight
• European Currency Crisis	• Tax Cutters: Report on Middle Income Americans
• Steering the Course	• A Fish Story
• What's the Dollar Worth: The Pros and Cons of Devaluation	

Additional Homework Problems.   For each chapter of the text, more than 20 additional homework problems are provided for homework or in-class assignments in two separate and distinct sets of reproducible homework assignments, Set A and Set B. Many problems involve working with graphs. Written by Eirik Evenhouse and Siobhan Reilly, both of Vanderbilt University, each homework problem is accompanied by suggested answers and is three-hole-punched for insertion into the Instructor's Binder.

Regional Case Studies for the East Coast, Texas, and California.   Additional case studies, available in either East Coast, Texas, or California versions, can be used for in-class team exercises or for additional homework assignments.

FOR THE STUDENT

NEW! Student Study Notes for PowerPoint Lecture Presentation.   Developed by Jeff Caldwell of Rose State College, the Student Study Notes provide students with an individualized note-taking and study device designed to be used in conjunction with the PowerPoint Lecture Presentation.

Study Guide.   Available in micro, macro, and complete versions, the Study Guide has been written by the author and includes the following sections:

- Putting the chapter into perspective
- Learning objectives
- Chapter outlines
- Key terms
- Key concepts
- Completion questions
- True-or-false questions
- Multiple-choice questions
- Problems
- Matching questions
- Further notes on working with graphs
- Case studies
- Glossary of terms defined exactly as in the textbook
- Answers to problems and questions

Your Economic Life.   This free booklet is provided with every purchase of *Economics Today*. It is a student guide to economics' practical applications. In this guide, the author takes students through practical problems in the world today to help them see the application of economics to everyday life and to help them analyze economic news.

ET Computer-Assisted Instruction.   Prepared by Daniel K. Benjamin of Clemson University, this free student software presents additional problems and learning modules for nearly all chapters in the text. The software contains interactive problems and computer-assisted instruction as indicated by the following icon in each chapter. Check out **www.econtoday.com** for more details.

PART 1

INTRODUCTION

Woody Allen once said, "Money is better than poverty, if only for financial reasons." Yet who has not heard or even said that "money cannot buy happiness"? Such a statement seems to pose problems for the study of economics. As you will see, economics does deal with people's quest for money or, more correctly, for wealth. Is it possible to study economics even if "money doesn't buy happiness"? You will find out as you read about the nature of economics in this introductory chapter.

PREVIEW QUESTIONS

1. What is the difference between microeconomics and macroeconomics?

2. What role does rational self-interest play in economic analysis?

3. Why is the study of economics a science?

4. What is the difference between positive and normative economics?

Did You Know That . . . since 1989, the number of fax machines in U.S. offices and homes has increased by over 10,000 percent? During the same time period, the number of bike messengers in downtown New York City *decreased* by over 65 percent. The world around us is definitely changing. Much of that change is due to the dramatically falling cost of communications and information technology. By 2002, the computers inside video games will cost only about $100 yet will have 50 times the processing power that a $10 million IBM mainframe had in 1975. Not surprisingly, since the start of the 1990s, American firms have been spending more on communications equipment and computers than on new construction and heavy machinery.

Cyberspace, the Internet, the World Wide Web—call it what you want, but your next home (if not your current one) will almost certainly have an address on it. The percentage of U.S. households that have at least one telephone is close to 100 percent, and those that have video game players is over 50 percent. Over 42 percent of homes have personal computers, and more than half of those machines are set up to receive and access information via phone lines. Your decisions about such things as when and what type of computer to buy, whether to accept a collect call from a friend traveling in Europe, and how much time you should invest in learning to use the latest Web browser involve an untold number of variables: where you live, the work your parents do, what your friends think, and so on. But, as you will see, there are economic underpinnings for nearly all the decisions you make.

THE POWER OF ECONOMIC ANALYSIS

Knowing that an economic problem exists every time you make a decision is not enough. You also have to develop a framework that will allow you to analyze solutions to each economic problem—whether you are trying to decide how much to study, which courses to take, whether to finish school, or whether America should send troops abroad or raise tariffs. The framework that you will learn in this text is based on the *economic way of thinking*.

This framework gives you power—the power to reach informed conclusions about what is happening in the world. You can, of course, live your life without the power of economic analysis as part of your analytical framework. Indeed, most people do. But economists believe that economic analysis can help you make better decisions concerning your career, your education, financing your home, and other important areas. In the business world, the power of economic analysis can help you increase your competitive edge as an employee or as the owner of a business. As a voter, for the rest of your life you will be asked to make judgments about policies that are advocated by a particular political party. Many of these policies will deal with questions related to international economics, such as whether the U.S. government should encourage or discourage immigration, prevent foreigners from investing in domestic TV stations and newspapers, or restrict other countries from selling their goods here. Finally, just as taking an art, music, or literature appreciation class increases the pleasure you receive when you view paintings, listen to concerts, or read novels, taking an economics course will increase your understanding when watching the news on TV or reading the newspaper.

DEFINING ECONOMICS

What is economics exactly? Some cynics have defined *economics* as "common sense made difficult." But common sense, by definition, should be within everyone's grasp. You will encounter in the following pages numerous examples that show that economics is, in fact, pure and simple common sense.

Economics
The study of how people allocate their limited resources to satisfy their unlimited wants.

Economics is part of the social sciences and as such seeks explanations of real events. All social sciences analyze human behavior, as opposed to the physical sciences, which generally analyze the behavior of electrons, atoms, and other nonhuman phenomena.

> **Economics is the study of how people allocate their limited resources in an attempt to satisfy their unlimited wants. As such, economics is the study of how people make choices.**

To understand this definition fully, two other words need explaining: *resources* and *wants*. **Resources** are things that have value and, more specifically, are used to produce things that satisfy people's wants. **Wants** are all of the things that people would consume if they had unlimited income.

Resources
Things used to produce other things to satisfy people's wants.

Wants
What people would buy if their incomes were unlimited.

Whenever an individual, a business, or a nation faces alternatives, a choice must be made, and economics helps us study how those choices are made. For example, you have to choose how to spend your limited income. You also have to choose how to spend your limited time. You may have to choose how much of your company's limited funds to spend on advertising and how much to spend on new-product research. In economics, we examine situations in which individuals choose how to do things, when to do things, and with whom to do them. Ultimately, the purpose of economics is to explain choices.

MICROECONOMICS VERSUS MACROECONOMICS

Economics is typically divided into two types of analysis: **microeconomics** and **macroeconomics.**

Microeconomics
The study of decision making undertaken by individuals (or households) and by firms.

> **Microeconomics is the part of economic analysis that studies decision making undertaken by individuals (or households) and by firms. It is like looking through a microscope to focus on the small parts of our economy.**

> **Macroeconomics is the part of economic analysis that studies the behavior of the economy as a whole. It deals with economywide phenomena such as changes in unemployment, the general price level, and national income.**

Macroeconomics
The study of the behavior of the economy as a whole, including such economywide phenomena as changes in unemployment, the general price level, and national income.

Microeconomic analysis, for example, is concerned with the effects of changes in the price of gasoline relative to that of other energy sources. It examines the effects of new taxes on a specific product or industry. If price controls were reinstituted in the United States, how individual firms and consumers would react to them would be in the realm of microeconomics. The raising of wages by an effective union strike would also be analyzed using the tools of microeconomics.

By contrast, issues such as the rate of inflation, the amount of economywide unemployment, and the yearly growth in the output of goods and services in the nation all fall into the realm of macroeconomic analysis. In other words, macroeconomics deals with **aggregates,** or totals—such as total output in an economy.

Aggregates
Total amounts or quantities; aggregate demand, for example, is total planned expenditures throughout a nation.

Be aware, however, of the blending of microeconomics and macroeconomics in modern economic theory. Modern economists are increasingly using microeconomic analysis—the study of decision making by individuals and by firms—as the basis of macroeconomic analysis. They do this because even though in macroeconomic analysis aggregates are being examined, those aggregates are made up of individuals and firms.

THE ECONOMIC PERSON: RATIONAL SELF-INTEREST

Economists assume that individuals act *as if* motivated by self-interest and respond predictably to opportunities for gain. This central insight of economics was first clearly articulated by Adam Smith in 1776. Smith wrote in his most famous book, *An Inquiry into the*

Exercise 1.1
Visit www.econtoday.com for more about the national economy.

Nature and Causes of the Wealth of Nations, that "it is not from the benevolence of the butcher, the brewer, or the baker that we expect our dinner, but from their regard to their own interest." Otherwise stated, the typical person about whom economists make behavioral predictions is assumed to look out for his or her own self-interest in a rational manner. Because monetary benefits and costs of actions are often the most easily measured, economists most often make behavioral predictions about individuals' responses to ways to increase their wealth, measured in money terms. Let's see if we can apply the theory of rational self-interest to explain an anomaly concerning the makeup of the U.S. population.

Exercise 1.2
Visit www.econtoday.com
for more about your home state.

EXAMPLE
The Increasing Native American Population

Look at Figure 1-1. You see that the proportion of Native Americans increased quite dramatically from 1970 to 1990. Can we use Adam Smith's ideas to understand why so many Native Americans have decided to rejoin their tribes? Perhaps. Consider the benefits of being a member of the Mdewakanton *(bday-WAH-kan-toon),* a tribe of about 100 that runs a casino in which in a recent year gamblers wagered over $500 million. Each member of the tribe received over $400,000. There is now a clear economic reason for Native Americans to return home. Over 200 of the nation's 544 tribes have introduced gambling of some sort, and almost half of those have big-time casinos. Reservations are grossing almost $6 billion a year from gaming. Tribe members sometimes get direct payments and others get the benefits of better health care, subsidized mortgages, and jobs. Self-identified Native Americans increased in number by 137 percent between 1970 and 1990.

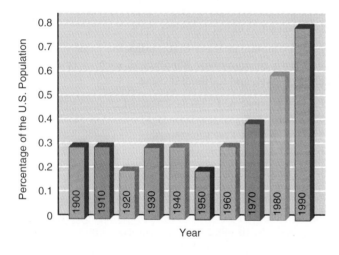

FIGURE 1-1

Native American Population of the United States, 1900–1990
The percentage of the U.S. population identifying itself as Native American has increased substantially in recent decades. Is there an economic explanation for this demographic trend?

FOR CRITICAL ANALYSIS: *What nonmonetary reasons are there for Native Americans to rejoin their tribes?* ●

The Rationality Assumption

The **rationality assumption** of economics, simply stated, is as follows:

We assume that individuals do not intentionally make decisions that would leave them worse off.

Rationality assumption
The assumption that people do not intentionally make decisions that would leave them worse off.

The distinction here is between what people may think—the realm of psychology and psychiatry and perhaps sociology—and what they do. Economics does *not* involve itself in analyzing individual or group thought processes. Economics looks at what people actually do in life with their limited resources. It does little good to criticize the rationality assumption by stating, "Nobody thinks that way" or "I never think that way" or "How unrealistic! That's as irrational as anyone can get!"

Take the example of driving. When you consider passing another car on a two-lane highway with oncoming traffic, you have to make very quick decisions: You must estimate the speed of the car that you are going to pass, the speed of the oncoming cars, the distance between your car and the oncoming cars, and your car's potential rate of acceleration. If we were to apply a model to your behavior, we would use the laws of calculus. In actual fact, you and most other drivers in such a situation do not actually think of using the laws of calculus, but to predict your behavior, we could make the prediction *as if* you understood the laws of calculus.

In any event, when you observe behavior around you, what may seem irrational often has its basis in the rationality assumption, as you can see by the following example.

EXAMPLE
When It Is Rational *Not* to Learn New Technology

The standard young person's view of older people (particularly one's parents) is that they're reluctant to learn new things. The saying "You can't teach an old dog new tricks" seems to apply. Young people, in contrast, seem eager to learn about new technology—mastering computers and multimedia, playing interactive games, surfing the Internet. But there is a rational reason for older people's reduced willingness to learn new technologies. If you are 20 years old and learn a new skill, you will be able to gain returns from your investment in learning over the course of many decades. If you are 60, however, and invest the same amount of time and effort learning the same skill, you will almost certainly not be able to reap those returns for as long a time period. Hence it is perfectly rational for "old dogs" not to want to learn new tricks.

FOR CRITICAL ANALYSIS: Some older people do learn to use new technologies as they emerge. What might explain this behavior? ●

Responding to Incentives

If it can be assumed that individuals never intentionally make decisions that would leave them worse off, then almost by definition they will respond to different incentives. We define **incentives** as the potential rewards available if a particular activity is undertaken. Indeed, much of human behavior can be explained in terms of how individuals respond to changing incentives over time.

Incentives
Rewards for engaging in a particular activity.

Schoolchildren are motivated to do better by a variety of incentive systems, ranging from gold stars and certificates of achievement when they are young to better grades with accompanying promises of a "better life" as they get older. There are, of course, negative incentives that affect our behavior, too. Children who disrupt the class are given after-school detention or sent to the vice principal for other punishment.

Implicitly, people react to changing incentives after they have done some sort of rough comparison of the costs and benefits of various courses of action. In fact, making rational choices invariably involves balancing costs and benefits.

The linked concepts of incentive and costs and benefits can be used to explain seeming anomalies in the world around us.

INTERNATIONAL EXAMPLE
Why Are There So Few Whiplash Complaints in Lithuania?

Rear-end car collisions occur about as frequently in the country of Lithuania as they do in the rest of the world. Curiously, chronic whiplash, or whiplash syndrome, appears to be unknown there. In the United States, auto accident victims commonly complain of whiplash, sometimes years after the accidents. In Norway, which has a population of only 4.2 million, over 70,000 people currently claim chronic disability because of whiplash.

What accounts for such differences in whiplash rate across countries? One answer relates to the potential payoff to auto accident victims from claiming such injuries. In Lithuania, personal injury insurance is virtually nonexistent. As a result, no money can be won from an insurance company because of a diagnosis of whiplash. By contrast, in Norway, in the United States, and elsewhere, significant financial settlements can be obtained through such claims.

FOR CRITICAL ANALYSIS: Does the fact that there are few reported claims of whiplash in Lithuania necessarily mean that headaches and lingering neck pains after being rear-ended do not occur in that country? ●

Defining Self-Interest

Self-interest does not always mean increasing one's wealth measured in dollars and cents. We assume that individuals seek many goals, not just increased wealth measured in monetary terms. Thus the self-interest part of our economic-person assumption includes goals relating to prestige, friendship, love, power, helping others, creating works of art, and many other matters. We can also think in terms of enlightened self-interest whereby individuals, in the pursuit of what makes them better off, also achieve the betterment of others around them. In brief, individuals are assumed to want the right to further their goals by making decisions about how things around them are used. The head of a charitable organization usually will not turn down an additional contribution, because accepting it lets that person control how that money is used, even if it is always for other people's benefit.

Otherwise stated, charitable acts are not ruled out by self-interest. Giving gifts to relatives can be considered a form of charity that is nonetheless in the self-interest of the giver. But how efficient is such gift giving?

EXAMPLE
The Perceived Value of Gifts

Every holiday season, aunts, uncles, grandparents, mothers, and fathers give gifts to their college-aged loved ones. Joel Waldfogel, an economist at Yale University, surveyed several thousand college students after Christmas to find out the value of holiday gifts. He found that compact discs and outerwear (coats and jackets) had a perceived intrinsic value about equal to their actual cash equivalent. By the time he got down the list to socks, underwear, and cosmetics, the students' valuation was only about 85 percent of the cash value of the gift. He found out that aunts, uncles, and grandparents gave the "worst" gifts and friends, siblings, and parents gave the "best."

FOR CRITICAL ANALYSIS: What argument could you use against the idea of substituting cash or gift certificates for physical gifts? ●

CONCEPTS IN BRIEF

- Economics is a social science that involves the study of how individuals choose among alternatives to satisfy their wants, which are what people would buy if their incomes were unlimited.

- Microeconomics, the study of the decision-making processes of individuals (or households) and firms, and macroeconomics, the study of the performance of the economy as a whole, are the two main branches into which the study of economics is divided.

- In economics, we assume that people do not intentionally make decisions that will leave them worse off. This is known as the rationality assumption.

- Self-interest is not confined to material well-being but also involves any action that makes a person feel better off, such as having more friends, love, power, affection, or providing more help to others.

ECONOMICS AS A SCIENCE

Models, or theories
Simplified representations of the real world used as the basis for predictions or explanations.

Economics is a social science that makes use of the same kinds of methods used in other sciences, such as biology, physics, and chemistry. Similar to these other sciences, economics uses models, or theories. Economic **models, or theories,** are simplified representations of the real world that we use to help us understand, explain, and predict economic phenomena in the real world. There are, of course, differences between sciences. The social sciences—especially economics—make little use of laboratory methods in which changes in variables can be explained under controlled conditions. Rather, social scientists, and especially economists, usually have to examine what has already happened in the real world in order to test their models, or theories.

Models and Realism

At the outset it must be emphasized that no model in *any* science, and therefore no economic model, is complete in the sense that it captures *every* detail or interrelationship that exists. Indeed, a model, by definition, is an abstraction from reality. It is conceptually impossible to construct a perfectly complete realistic model. For example, in physics we cannot account for every molecule and its position and certainly not for every atom and subparticle. Not only is such a model impossibly expensive to build, but working with it would be impossibly complex.

The nature of scientific model building is such that the model should capture only the *essential* relationships that are sufficient to analyze the particular problem or answer the particular question with which we are concerned. *An economic model cannot be faulted as unrealistic simply because it does not represent every detail of the real world.* A map of a city that shows only major streets is not necessarily unrealistic if, in fact, all you need to know is how to pass through the city using major streets. As long as a model is realistic in terms of shedding light on the *central* issue at hand or forces at work, it may be useful.

A map is the quintessential model. It is always a simplified representation. It is always unrealistic. But it is also useful in making (refutable) predictions about the world. If the model—the map—predicts that when you take Campus Avenue to the north, you always run into the campus, that is a (refutable) prediction. If our goal is to explain observed behavior, the simplicity or complexity of the model we use is irrelevant. If a simple model can explain observed behavior in repeated settings just as well as a complex one, the simple model has some value and is probably easier to use.

Assumptions

Every model, or theory, must be based on a set of assumptions. Assumptions define the set of circumstances in which our model is most likely to be applicable. When scientists predicted that sailing ships would fall off the edge of the earth, they used the *assumption* that the earth was flat. Columbus did not accept the implications of such a model. He assumed that the world was round. The real-world test of his own model refuted the flat-earth model. Indirectly, then, it was a test of the assumption of the flat-earth model.

EXAMPLE
Getting Directions

Assumptions are a shorthand for reality. Imagine that you have decided to drive from your home in San Diego to downtown San Francisco. Because you have never driven this route, you decide to get directions from the local office of the Automobile Association of America (AAA).

When you ask for directions, the travel planner could give you a set of detailed maps that shows each city through which you will travel—Oceanside, San Clemente, Irvine, Anaheim, Los Angeles, Bakersfield, Modesto, and so on—and then, opening each map, show you exactly how the freeway threads through each of these cities. You would get a nearly complete description of reality because the AAA travel planner will not have used many simplifying assumptions. It is more likely, however, that the travel planner will simply say, "Get on Interstate 5 going north. Stay on it for about 500 miles. Follow the signs for San Francisco. After crossing the toll bridge, take any exit marked 'Downtown.'" By omitting all of the trivial details, the travel planner has told you all that you really need and want to know. The models you will be using in this text are similar to the simplified directions on how to drive from San Diego to San Francisco—they focus on what is relevant to the problem at hand and omit what is not.

FOR CRITICAL ANALYSIS: In what way do small talk and gossip represent the use of simplifying assumptions? ●

The *Ceteris Paribus* Assumption: All Other Things Being Equal. Everything in the world seems to relate in some way to everything else in the world. It would be impossible to isolate the effects of changes in one variable on another variable if we always had to worry about the many other variables that might also enter the analysis. As in other sciences, economics uses the **ceteris paribus** assumption. *Ceteris paribus* means "other things constant" or "other things equal."

Consider an example taken from economics. One of the most important determinants of how much of a particular product a family buys is how expensive that product is relative to other products. We know that in addition to relative prices, other factors influence decisions about making purchases. Some of them have to do with income, others with tastes, and yet others with custom and religious beliefs. Whatever these other factors are, we hold them constant when we look at the relationship between changes in prices and changes in how much of a given product people will purchase.

THINKING CRITICALLY ABOUT THE MEDIA

Cancer and Smoking

You read it in the newspaper and hear about it on TV—smoking imposes higher costs on all Americans. The American Cancer Society has convinced the media that smoking is costly due to patients' lengthy hospital stays for treatment of lung cancer. As a result, life insurance premiums go up. But we also have to look at the other side of the ledger. Premature death due to smoking saves Americans billions of dollars in pension and medical payments as well as billions of dollars in nursing home expenses. All things considered, according to Duke University economist Kip Viscusi, smoking does not impose higher costs on all Americans. (That does not, to be sure, mean that we should encourage more smoking!)

Ceteris paribus [KAY-ter-us PEAR-uh-bus] assumption
The assumption that nothing changes except the factor or factors being studied.

Deciding on the Usefulness of a Model

We generally do not attempt to determine the usefulness, or "goodness," of a model merely by evaluating how realistic its assumptions are. Rather, we consider a model good if it yields usable predictions and implications for the real world. In other words, can we use the model to predict what will happen in the world around us? Does the model provide useful implications of how things happen in our world?

Once we have determined that the model does predict real-world phenomena, the scientific approach to the analysis of the world around us requires that we consider evidence. Evidence is used to test the usefulness of a model. This is why we call economics an **empirical** science, *empirical* meaning that evidence (data) is looked at to see whether we are right. Economists are often engaged in empirically testing their models.

Consider two competing models for the way students act when doing complicated probability problems to choose the best gambles. One model predicts that, based on the assumption of rational self-interest, students who are paid more money for better performance will in fact perform better on average during the experiment. A competing model might be that students whose last names start with the letters *A* through *L* will do better than students with last names starting with *M* through *Z,* irrespective of how much they are paid. The model that consistently predicts more accurately is the model that we would normally choose. In this example, the "alphabet" model did not work well: The first letter of the last name of the students who actually did the experiment at UCLA was irrelevant in predicting how well they would perform the mathematical calculations necessary to choose the correct gambles. On average, students who received higher cash payments for better gambles did choose a higher percentage of better gambles. Thus the model based on rational self-interest predicted well.

Empirical
Relying on real-world data in evaluating the usefulness of a model.

Models of Behavior, Not Thought Processes

Take special note of the fact that economists' models do not relate to the way people *think;* they relate to the way people *act,* to what they do in life with their limited resources. Models tend to generalize human behavior. Normally, the economist does not attempt to predict how people will think about a particular topic, such as a higher price of oil products, accelerated inflation, or higher taxes. Rather, the task at hand is to predict how people will act, which may be quite different from what they say they will do (much to the consternation of poll takers and market researchers). The people involved in examining thought processes are psychologists and psychiatrists, not typically economists.

EXAMPLE
Incentives Work for Pigeons and Rats, Too

Researchers at Texas A&M University did a series of experiments with pigeons and rats. They allowed them to "purchase" food and drink by pushing various levers. The "price" was the number of times a lever had to be pushed. A piece of cheese required 10 pushes, a drop of root beer only one. The "incomes" that the animals were given equaled a certain number of total pushes per day. Once the income was used up, the levers did not work. The researchers discovered that when the price of cheese went down, the animals purchased more cheese. Similarly, they found that when the price of root beer was increased, the animals purchased less root beer. These are exactly the predictions that we make about human behavior.

FOR CRITICAL ANALYSIS: "People respond to incentives." Is this assumption also usable in the animal world? ●

POSITIVE VERSUS NORMATIVE ECONOMICS

Economics uses *positive analysis,* a value-free approach to inquiry. No subjective or moral judgments enter into the analysis. Positive analysis relates to statements such as "If A, then B." For example, "If the price of gasoline goes up relative to all other prices, then the amount of it that people will buy will fall." That is a positive economic statement. It is a statement of *what is.* It is not a statement of anyone's value judgment or subjective feelings. For many problems analyzed in the hard sciences such as physics and chemistry, the analyses are considered to be virtually value-free. After all, how can someone's values enter into a theory of molecular behavior? But economists face a different problem. They deal with the behavior of individuals, not molecules. That makes it more difficult to stick to what we consider to be value-free or **positive economics** without reference to our feelings.

When our values are interjected into the analysis, we enter the realm of **normative economics,** involving *normative analysis.* A positive economic statement is "If the price of gas rises, people will buy less." If we add to that analysis the statement "so we should not allow the price to go up," we have entered the realm of normative economics—we have expressed a value judgment. In fact, any time you see the word *should,* you will know that values are entering into the discussion. Just remember that positive statements are concerned with *what is,* whereas normative statements are concerned with *what ought to be.*

Each of us has a desire for different things. That means that we have different values. When we express a value judgment, we are simply saying what we prefer, like, or desire. Because individual values are diverse, we expect—and indeed observe—people expressing widely varying value judgments about how the world ought to be.

A Warning: Recognize Normative Analysis

It is easy to define positive economics. It is quite another matter to catch all unlabeled normative statements in a textbook such as this one (or any other), even though an author goes over the manuscript many times before it is printed. Therefore, do not get the impression that a textbook author will be able to keep all personal values out of the book. They will slip through. In fact, the very choice of which topics to include in an introductory textbook involves normative economics. There is no value-free, or objective, way to decide which topics to use in a textbook. The author's values ultimately make a difference when choices have to be made. But from your own standpoint, you might want to be able to recognize when you are engaging in normative as opposed to positive economic analysis. Reading this text will help equip you for that task.

Positive economics
Analysis that is strictly limited to making either purely descriptive statements or scientific predictions; for example, "If A, then B." A statement of *what is.*

Normative economics
Analysis involving value judgments about economic policies; relates to whether things are good or bad. A statement of *what ought to be.*

CONCEPTS IN BRIEF

- A model, or theory, uses assumptions and is by nature a simplification of the real world. The usefulness of a model can be evaluated by bringing empirical evidence to bear on its predictions.

- Models are not necessarily deficient simply because they are unrealistic and use simplifying assumptions, for every model in every science requires simplification compared to the real world.

- Most models use the *ceteris paribus* assumption, that all other things are held constant, or equal.

- Positive economics is value-free and relates to statements that can be refuted, such as "If A, then B." Normative economics involves people's values, and normative statements typically contain the word *should.*

The very rich often buy expensive "toys," such as this Rolls-Royce. But do such goods bring happiness?

Does Money Buy Happiness?

CONCEPTS APPLIED:
RATIONAL SELF-INTEREST, THE RATIONALITY
ASSUMPTION, INCENTIVES, MODELS, REALISM

Visit www.econtoday.com for an Internet Activity that expands your understanding of these concepts.

One of the major criticisms of economics is that it seems to posit that more money (wealth) is better than less. In other words, economic theory appears to assume that people act in such a way as to make higher and higher incomes. People are assumed always to act so as to maximize their incomes, even if "money cannot buy happiness." A recent study in the *Journal of Personality and Social Psychology* presents evidence to support the notion that seeking ever-higher wealth does not lead to any greater level of happiness.

What Researchers Have Found

The researchers of this study randomly selected 100 of America's wealthiest individuals identified as such in popular business magazines. Each wealthy American in the study filled out a detailed inquiry, which included the question "How do you feel about how happy you are?" to which the answer choices ranged from "delighted" to "terrible." The same questionnaire was given to a randomly selected set of individuals who were not rich. The average happiness score for the rich was only slightly above the nonrich. Indeed, one-third of the superrich scored below the average group.

The conclusion the researchers reached was that an increase in income is like a martini: It induces optimism and raises the spirits, but only temporarily. The researchers argued that only recent life events (occurring within the past three months) have any influence on one's feelings of subjective well-being.

International Confirmation

The researchers discovered that international data confirmed their findings. Only residents of the poorest countries (India and Bangladesh) had below-average happi-

ness ratings. Happiness in all the others appeared about the same. Moreover, neither U.S. nor Japanese residents showed any rising trend in reported subjective well-being over the past few decades despite rising average household incomes.

But Asking Gets You Nowhere

Do the research results summarized here contradict the methodology we use in economics? Hardly. Economics is a science of *revealed* preferences. We find out virtually no useful information by asking people to rate their happiness on a scale of 1 to 10. We assume that people act rationally. In other words, they will not knowingly do things that make them worse off. We can predict that given the choice between a lower-paying job and an otherwise identical yet higher-paying job, people will choose the latter. We make no assumptions about their thought processes.

One Can Always Become Poorer

Finally, if indeed income does not buy happiness, the rich and the very rich always have an option—they can dispose of their wealth at any time. No one is forced to keep wealth. Because we rarely see individuals routinely giving away all of their wealth, we can infer that higher income is preferred to lower income.

FOR CRITICAL ANALYSIS

1. Even if you choose not to spend income that you earn on yourself, what other options do you have?
2. Are we making a value judgment when we assume that an individual prefers higher income over lower income?

CHAPTER SUMMARY

1. Economics as a social science is the study of how individuals make choices to satisfy wants. Wants are defined as what people would buy if their incomes were unlimited.
2. Economics is usually divided into microeconomic analysis, which is the study of individual decision making by households and firms, and macroeconomics, which is the study of nationwide phenomena, such as inflation and unemployment.
3. The rationality assumption is that individuals never intentionally make decisions that would leave them worse off.
4. We use models, or theories, to explain and predict behavior. Models, or theories, are never completely realistic because by definition they are simplifica-

tions using assumptions that are not directly testable. The usefulness of a theory, or model, is determined not by the realism of its assumptions but by how well it predicts real-world phenomena.
5. An important simplifying assumption is that all other things are held equal, or constant. This is sometimes known as the *ceteris paribus* assumption.
6. No model in economics relates to individuals' thought processes; all models relate to what people do, not to what they think or say they will do.
7. Much economic analysis involves positive economics; that is, it is value-free. Whenever statements embodying values are made, we enter the realm of normative economics, or how individuals and groups think things ought to be.

DISCUSSION OF PREVIEW QUESTIONS

1. What is the difference between microeconomics and macroeconomics?
Microeconomics is concerned with the choice-making processes of individuals, households, and firms, whereas macroeconomics focuses on the performance of the economy as a whole.

2. What role does rational self-interest play in economic analysis?
Rational self-interest is the assumption that individuals behave in a reasonable (rational) way in making choices to further their interests. In other words, we assume that individuals' actions are motivated primarily by their self-interest, keeping in mind that self-interest can relate to monetary and nonmonetary objectives, such as love, prestige, and helping others.

3. Why is the study of economics a science?
Economics is a science in that it uses models, or theories, that are simplified representations of the real world to analyze and make predictions about the real world. These predictions are then subjected to empirical tests in which real-world data are used to decide whether or not to reject the predictions.

4. What is the difference between positive and normative economics?
Positive economics deals with *what is*, whereas normative economics deals with *what ought to be*. Positive economic statements are of the "if . . . then" variety; they are descriptive and predictive and are not related to what "should" happen. Normative economics, by contrast, is concerned with what ought to be and is intimately tied to value judgments.

PROBLEMS

(Answers to the odd-numbered problems appear at the back of the book.)

1-1. Construct four separate models to predict the probability that a person will die within the next five

years. Include only one determining factor in each of your models.

1-2. Does it matter whether all of a model's assumptions are "realistic"? Why or why not?

1-3. Give a refutable implication (one that can be dis-proved by evidence from the real world) for each of the following models:

   a. The accident rate of drivers is inversely related to their age.

   b. The rate of inflation is directly related to the rate of change in the nation's money supply.

   c. The wages of professional basketball players are directly related to their high school grade point averages.

   d. The rate at which bank employees are promot-ed is inversely related to their frequency of absenteeism.

1-4. Is gambling an example of rational or irrational behavior? What is the difference between gam-bling and insurance?

1-5. Over the past 20 years, first-class mail rates have more than tripled, while prices of long-distance phone calls, televisions, and sound systems have decreased. Over a similar period, it has been reported that there has been a steady decline in the ability of high school graduates to communicate effectively in writing. Do you feel that this increase in the relative price of written communi-cation (first-class mail rates) is related to the alleged decline in writing ability? If so, what do you feel is the direction of causation? Which is causing which?

1-6. If there is no way to test a theory with real-world data, can we determine if it is a good theory? Why is empirical evidence used to validate a theory?

1-7. Identify which of the following statements use positive economic analysis and which use norma-tive economic analysis.

   a. The government should not regulate the bank-ing system because recent problems have demonstrated that it does not know what it is doing.

   b. The elimination of barriers to the free move-ment of individuals across European borders has caused wages to become more equal in many industries.

   c. Paying members of Congress more provides them with less incentive to commit wrongful acts.

   d. We need more restrictions on companies that pollute because air pollution is destroying our way of life.

COMPUTER-ASSISTED INSTRUCTION

Key elements of the scientific way of thinking are illustrated by applying them to everyday situations.

Complete problem and answer appear on disk.

INTERACTING WITH THE INTERNET

The Internet is a worldwide network of computers; it includes the computer on which you will do the exercises in this book. Three types of computers are involved: servers, routers, and clients. Servers are the machines that contain and dispense the information you are looking for. Routers direct your request to the correct server and make sure the information gets back to you. The com-puter on which you are working is the client, because it (and you) are being served by the other two types of machines.

   The information available on the Internet is staggering in both volume and variety—not to men-tion the speed with which it changes, appearing and disappearing in a manner that even the White Rabbit would find astonishing. Just a few years ago, most of the information moving on the Internet was scientific and of interest chiefly to academics and members of the military and defense community. Increasingly, however, the Internet is being transformed into a combination giant shopping mall, meeting hall, publishing frontier, and entertainment center. It also has some sites that offer vast amounts of information about the economy, the environment, and the world—indeed information about almost any question you can ask. It is in search of information such as this that we will be headed in this book.

Searching Through the Internet

Besides sending and receiving electronic mail (e-mail), the most common usage of the Internet is searching for and retrieving information. This is done through a variety of Internet *browsers.*

The most popular Internet browsers are Netscape Navigator and Microsoft Explorer. By using one of these browsers, you can also access numerous *search engines,* which help you find the information you want if you do not know the exact address. Some search engines are Yahoo!, WebCrawler, HotBot, Lycos, Infoseek, and Excite.

Addresses

Each site on the Internet has an address. Many of the ones that you access will have somewhere in the address the letters *edu* or *gov,* indicating educational institutions or government organizations, respectively. All addresses that start with *www* indicate that they are part of the World Wide Web. This means that the site has the capacity to display photographs, animated icons, and elaborate graphics, in addition to routine text. Today, many sites dispense with the *www* and can be reached without this prefix.

In any event, successful navigation requires that you type the correct address into your browser. These addresses are called *uniform resource locators* (URLs). Although most URLs start with *http://* (which stands for *hypertext transfer protocol*), the latest browsers allow you to omit these initials.

Getting Started

If you want to "surf" (browse) economics resources immediately, use your browser to go directly to Resources for Economists by typing in

http://econwpa.wustl.edu/EconFAQ/EconFAQ.html

You can also access the World Wide Web Resources for Economics at WebEc at

netec.wustl.edu/WebEc.html

In URLs in this text, we will dispense with *http://* before the actual address.
By the way, if you want to look up some jokes about economists, go to

netec.wustl.edu/JokEc.html

Happy surfing!

CHAPTER 2

SCARCITY AND THE WORLD OF TRADE-OFFS

What seems to be the scarcest thing around? For a lot of people, it is time. You can be the richest person on earth and still not have "enough time." When you are driving, you are ordinarily aware of time—how long it takes for you to get to your destination. When traffic lanes are congested, you lose time. And that time is valuable to you. Why? Because you could be doing something else instead of sitting in your car waiting for traffic to clear. In this chapter, you will learn about how to put a value on that time.

PREVIEW QUESTIONS

1. Do affluent people face the problem of scarcity?

2. Fresh air may be consumed at no charge, but is it free of cost to society?

3. Why does the scarcity problem force individuals to consider opportunity costs?

4. Can a "free" college education ever be truly free?

Did You Know That . . . Chris Van Horn, president of CVK Group in Washington, D.C., grosses over $200,000 a year for having people wait in line? Adam Goldin loves working as a "line waiter" because he gets paid for "doing nothing." His job is to arrive early in the morning on Capitol Hill to hold places for lobbyists who must attend congressional hearings. Van Horn charges his more than 100 lobbyists and law firm clients $27 an hour and pays his part-time line waiters like Mr. Goldin $10 an hour. For example, when Congress was going to hold hearings for the proposed 1997 tax cut, $10-an-hour professional standees arrived to hold places for $300-an-hour lobbyists who would not show up until hours later. After all, lobbyists do not have an unlimited amount of time. Their time is scarce. It is worth more than what they are charged to "save" it.

SCARCITY

Whenever individuals or communities cannot obtain everything they desire simultaneously, choices occur. Choices occur because of *scarcity*. **Scarcity** is the most basic concept in all of economics. Scarcity means that we do not and cannot have enough income or wealth to satisfy our *every* desire. Scarcity exists because human wants always exceed what can be produced with the limited resources and time that nature makes available.

Scarcity
A situation in which the ingredients for producing the things that people desire are insufficient to satisfy all wants.

What Scarcity Is Not

Scarcity is not a shortage. After a hurricane hits and cuts off supplies to a community, TV newscasts often show people standing in line to get minimum amounts of cooking fuel and food. A news commentator might say that the line is caused by the "scarcity" of these products. But cooking fuel and food are always scarce—we cannot obtain all that we want at a zero price. Therefore, do not confuse the concept of scarcity, which is general and all-encompassing, with the concept of shortages as evidenced by people waiting in line to obtain a particular product.

Scarcity is not the same thing as poverty. Scarcity occurs among the poor and among the rich. Even the richest person on earth faces scarcity because available time is limited. Low income levels do not create more scarcity. High income levels do not create less scarcity.

Scarcity is a fact of life, like gravity. And just as physicists did not invent gravity, economists did not invent scarcity—it existed well before the first economist ever lived. It exists even when we are not using all of our resources.

Scarcity and Resources

The scarcity concept arises from the fact that resources are insufficient to satisfy our every desire. Resources are the inputs used in the production of the things that we want. **Production** can be defined as virtually any activity that results in the conversion of resources into products that can be used in consumption. Production includes delivering things from one part of the country to another. It includes taking ice from an ice tray to put it in your soft-drink glass. The resources used in production are called *factors of production*, and some economists use the terms *resources* and *factors of production* interchangeably. The total quantity of all resources that an economy has at any one time determines what that economy can produce.

Factors of production can be classified in many ways. Here is one such classification:

1. **Land. Land** encompasses all the nonhuman gifts of nature, including timber, water, fish, minerals, and the original fertility of land. It is often called the *natural resource*.

Production
Any activity that results in the conversion of resources into products that can be used in consumption.

Land
The natural resources that are available from nature. Land as a resource includes location, original fertility and mineral deposits, topography, climate, water, and vegetation.

Labor
Productive contributions of humans who work, involving both mental and physical activities.

Physical capital
All manufactured resources, including buildings, equipment, machines, and improvements to land that is used for production.

Human capital
The accumulated training and education of workers.

Entrepreneurship
The factor of production involving human resources that perform the functions of raising capital, organizing, managing, assembling other factors of production, and making basic business policy decisions. The entrepreneur is a risk taker.

2. **Labor. Labor** is the human resource, which includes all productive contributions made by individuals who work, such as steelworkers, ballet dancers, and professional baseball players.

3. **Physical capital. Physical capital** consists of the factories and equipment used in production. It also includes improvements to natural resources, such as irrigation ditches.

4. **Human capital. Human capital** is the economic characterization of the education and training of workers. How much the nation produces depends not only on how many hours people work but also on how productive they are, and that, in turn, depends in part on education and training. To become more educated, individuals have to devote time and resources, just as a business has to devote resources if it wants to increase its physical capital. Whenever a worker's skills increase, human capital has been improved.

5. **Entrepreneurship.** The factor of production known as **entrepreneurship** (actually a subdivision of labor) involves human resources that perform the functions of organizing, managing, and assembling the other factors of production to make business ventures. Entrepreneurship also encompasses taking risks that involve the possibility of losing large sums of wealth on new ventures. It includes new methods of doing common things and generally experimenting with any type of new thinking that could lead to making more money income. Without entrepreneurship, virtually no business organization could operate.

Goods Versus Economic Goods

Goods
All things from which individuals derive satisfaction or happiness.

Economic goods
Goods that are scarce, for which the quantity demanded exceeds the quantity supplied at a zero price.

Goods are defined as all things from which individuals derive satisfaction or happiness. Goods therefore include air to breathe and the beauty of a sunset as well as food, cars, and CD players.

Economic goods are a subset of all goods—they are goods derived from scarce resources about which we must constantly make decisions regarding their best use. By definition, the desired quantity of an economic good exceeds the amount that is directly available at a zero price. Virtually every example we use in economics concerns economic goods—cars, CD players, computers, socks, baseball bats, and corn. Weeds are a good example of *bads*—goods for which the desired quantity is much *less* than what nature provides at a zero price.

Services
Mental or physical labor or help purchased by consumers. Examples are the assistance of doctors, lawyers, dentists, repair personnel, housecleaners, educators, retailers, and wholesalers; things purchased or used by consumers that do not have physical characteristics.

Sometimes you will see references to "goods and services." **Services** are tasks that are performed for someone else, such as laundry, cleaning, hospital care, restaurant meal preparation, car polishing, psychological counseling, and teaching. One way of looking at services is thinking of them as *intangible goods*.

WANTS AND NEEDS

Wants are not the same as needs. Indeed, from the economist's point of view, the term *needs* is objectively undefinable. When someone says, "I need some new clothes," there is no way to know whether that person is stating a vague wish, a want, or a life-saving necessity. If the individual making the statement were dying of exposure in a northern country during the winter, we might argue that indeed the person does need clothes—perhaps not new ones, but at least some articles of warm clothing. Typically, however, the term *need* is used very casually in most conversations. What people mean, usually, is that they want something that they do not currently have.

Humans have unlimited wants. Just imagine if every single material want that you might have were satisfied. You can have all of the clothes, cars, houses, CDs, tickets to concerts, and other things that you want. Does that mean that nothing else could add to your total level of happiness? Probably not, because you might think of new goods and services that you could obtain, particularly as they came to market. You would also still be lacking in fulfilling all of your wants for compassion, friendship, love, affection, prestige, musical abilities, sports abilities, and so on.

In reality, every individual has competing wants but cannot satisfy all of them, given limited resources. This is the reality of scarcity. Each person must therefore make choices. Whenever a choice is made to do or buy something, something else that is also desired is not done or not purchased. In other words, in a world of scarcity, every want that ends up being satisfied causes one or more other wants to remain unsatisfied or to be forfeited.

CONCEPTS IN BRIEF

- Scarcity exists because human wants always exceed what can be produced with the limited resources and time that nature makes available.

- We use scarce resources, such as land, labor, physical and human capital, and entrepreneurship, to produce economic goods—goods that are desired but are not directly obtainable from nature to the extent demanded or desired at a zero price.

- Wants are unlimited; they include all material desires and all nonmaterial desires, such as love, affection, power, and prestige.

- The concept of need is difficult to define objectively for every person; consequently, we simply consider that every person's wants are unlimited. In a world of scarcity, satisfaction of one want necessarily means nonsatisfaction of one or more other wants.

SCARCITY, CHOICE, AND OPPORTUNITY COST

The natural fact of scarcity implies that we must make choices. One of the most important results of this fact is that every choice made (or not made, for that matter) means that some opportunity had to be sacrificed. Every choice involves giving up another opportunity to do or use something else.

Consider a practical example. Every choice you make to study one more hour of economics requires that you give up the opportunity to do any of the following activities: study more of another subject, listen to music, sleep, browse at a local store, read a novel, or work out at the gym. Many more opportunities are forgone also if you choose to study economics an additional hour.

Because there were so many alternatives from which to choose, how could you determine the value of what you gave up to engage in that extra hour of studying economics? First of all, no one else can tell you the answer because only you can *subjectively* put a value on the alternatives forgone. Only you know what is the value of another hour of sleep or of an hour looking for the latest CDs. That means that only you can determine the highest-valued, next-best alternative that you had to sacrifice in order to study economics one more hour. It is you who come up with the *subjective* estimate of the expected value of the next-best alternative.

The value of the next-best alternative is called **opportunity cost.** The opportunity cost of any action is the value of what is given up—the next-highest-ranked alternative—

Opportunity cost
The highest-valued, next-best alternative that must be sacrificed to attain something or to satisfy a want.

because a choice was made. When you study one more hour, there may be many alternatives available for the use of that hour, but assume that you can do only one thing in that hour—your next-highest-ranked alternative. What is important is the choice that you would have made if you hadn't studied one more hour. Your opportunity cost is the *next-highest-ranked* alternative, not *all* alternatives.

In economics, cost is always a forgone opportunity.

One way to think about opportunity cost is to understand that when you choose to do something, you lose. What you lose is being able to engage in your next-highest-valued alternative. The cost of your choice is what you lose, which is by definition your next-highest-valued alternative. This is your opportunity cost.

Let's consider opportunity cost in cyberspace—on the Web, and particularly for Web browsers such as Navigator and Explorer and search engines such as Yahoo! and Excite.

AD SPACE AND PLACEMENT DECISIONS ON THE WEB

When you access the Internet, your home page is typically either your Internet service provider's page, Netscape's or Explorer's home page, or a search engine's home page. Each time you access the Net, you see advertising—banners, buttons, keywords, cobranded ads, or other promotions or links. Some of the biggest advertisers on the Web are Microsoft, Toyota, General Motors, Disney, IBM, AT&T, and American Express. All in all, these advertisers will spend almost $100 million on the Web in the year 2001. The owner of any Web page that carries an ad faces an opportunity cost. For example, the opening page of the Yahoo! search engine is considered "prime real estate" because so many people see it every day. But there is relatively little space on the screen. Thus Yahoo! faces an opportunity cost. Any space that it uses to promote its own services and products, it cannot sell it to, say, IBM or Microsoft. And if it fills up too much of the screen with ads, some users will switch to a less cluttered search engine. Thus there is an opportunity cost for literally every square centimeter on a Web page.

FOR CRITICAL ANALYSIS: How does a Web home page owner decide how to use the "real estate"? ●

THE WORLD OF TRADE-OFFS

Whenever you engage in any activity using any resource, even time, you are *trading off* the use of that resource for one or more alternative uses. The value of the trade-off is represented by the opportunity cost. The opportunity cost of studying economics has already been mentioned—it is the value of the next-best alternative. When you think of any alternative, you are thinking of trade-offs.

Let's consider a hypothetical example of a one-for-one trade-off between the results of spending time studying economics and accounting. For the sake of this argument, we will assume that additional time studying either economics or accounting will lead to a higher grade in the subject studied more. One of the best ways to examine this trade-off is with a graph. (If you would like a refresher on graphical techniques, study Appendix A at the end of this chapter before going on.)

Exercise 2.1
Visit www.econtoday.com
for more about shopping trade-offs.

Graphical Analysis

In Figure 2-1, the expected grade in accounting is measured on the vertical axis of the graph, and the expected grade in economics is measured on the horizontal axis. We simplify the world and assume that you have a maximum of 10 hours per week to spend studying these two subjects and that if you spend all 10 hours on economics, you will get an A in the course. You will, however, fail accounting. Conversely, if you spend all of your 10 hours studying accounting, you will get an A in that subject, but you will flunk economics. Here the trade-off is a special case: one-to-one. A one-to-one trade-off means that the opportunity cost of receiving one grade higher in economics (for example, improving from a C to a B) is one grade lower in accounting (falling from a C to a D).

The Production Possibilities Curve (PPC)

The graph in Figure 2-1 illustrates the relationship between the possible results that can be produced in each of two activities, depending on how much time you choose to devote to each activity. This graph shows a representation of a **production possibilities curve (PPC).**

Consider that you are producing a grade in economics when you study economics and a grade in accounting when you study accounting. Then the graph in Figure 2-1 can be related to the production possibilities you face. The line that goes from A on one axis to A on the other axis therefore becomes a production possibilities curve. It is defined as the maximum quantity of one good or service that can be produced, given that a specific quantity of another is produced. It is a curve that shows the possibilities available for increasing the output of one good or service by reducing the amount of another. In the example in Figure 2-1, your time for studying was limited to 10 hours per week. The two possible outputs were grades in accounting and grades in economics. The particular production possibilities curve presented in Figure 2-1 is a graphical representation of the opportunity cost of studying one more hour in one subject. It is a *straight-line production possibilities curve,* which is a special case. (The more general case will be discussed next.) If you decide to be at point *x* in Figure 2-1, 5 hours of study time will be spent on accounting and 5 hours will be spent on economics. The expected grade in each course will be a C. If you are more interested in getting a B in economics, you will go to point *y* on the production possibilities curve, spending only 2.5 hours on accounting but 7.5 hours on economics. Your expected grade in accounting will then drop from a C to a D.

Exercise 2.2

Visit www.econtoday.com for more about trade-offs concerning cars.

Production possibilities curve (PPC)

A curve representing all possible combinations of total output that could be produced assuming (1) a fixed amount of productive resources of a given quality and (2) the efficient use of those resources.

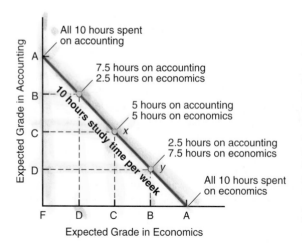

FIGURE 2-1

Production Possibilities Curve for Grades in Accounting and Economics (Trade-offs)

We assume that only 10 hours can be spent per week on studying. If the student is at point *x*, equal time (5 hours a week) is spent on both courses and equal grades of C will be received. If a higher grade in economics is desired, the student may go to point *y*, thereby receiving a B in economics but a D in accounting. At point *y*, 2.5 hours are spent on accounting and 7.5 hours on economics.

Note that these trade-offs between expected grades in accounting and economics are the result of *holding constant* total study time as well as all other factors that might influence a student's ability to learn, such as computerized study aids. Quite clearly, if you wished to spend more total time studying, it would be possible to have higher grades in both economics and accounting. In that case, however, we would no longer be on the specific production possibilities curve illustrated in Figure 2-1. We would have to draw a new curve, farther to the right, to show the greater total study time and a different set of possible trade-offs.

CONCEPTS IN BRIEF

- Scarcity requires us to choose. When we choose, we lose the next-highest-valued alternative.
- Cost is always a forgone opportunity.
- Another way to look at opportunity cost is the trade-off that occurs when one activity is undertaken rather than the next-best alternative activity.
- A production possibilities curve (PPC) graphically shows the trade-off that occurs when more of one output is obtained at the sacrifice of another. The PPC is a graphical representation of, among other things, opportunity cost.

THE CHOICES SOCIETY FACES

The straight-line production possibilities curve presented in Figure 2-1 can be generalized to demonstrate the related concepts of scarcity, choice, and trade-offs that our entire nation faces. As you will see, the production possibilities curve is a simple but powerful economic model because it can demonstrate these related concepts. The example we will use is the choice between the production of M-16 semiautomatic rifles and CD-ROM players. We assume for the moment that these are the only two goods that can be produced in the nation. Panel (a) of Figure 2-2 on page 24 gives the various combinations of M-16s and CD-ROM players that are possible. If all resources are devoted to M-16 production, 10 billion per year can be produced. If all resources are devoted to CD-ROM player production, 12 billion per year can be produced. In between are various possible combinations. These combinations are plotted as points *A, B, C, D, E, F,* and *G* in panel (b) of Figure 2-2. If these points are connected with a smooth curve, the nation's production possibilities curve is shown, demonstrating the trade-off between the production of M-16 semiautomatic rifles and CD-ROM players. These trade-offs occur *on* the production possibilities curve.

Notice the major difference in the shape of the production possibilities curves in Figures 2-1 and 2-2. In Figure 2-1, there is a one-to-one trade-off between grades in economics and in accounting. In Figure 2-2, the trade-off between CD-ROM production and M-16 production is not constant, and therefore the production possibilities curve is a *bowed* line. To understand why the production possibilities curve for a society is typically bowed outward, you must understand the assumptions underlying the PPC.

Assumptions Underlying the Production Possibilities Curve

When we draw the curve that is shown in Figure 2-2, we make the following assumptions:

1. That resources are fully employed
2. That we are looking at production over a specific time period—for example, one year

	Panel (a)	
Combination	M-16 Rifles (billions of units per year)	CD-ROM Players (billions of units per year)
A	10.0	0
B	9.6	2
C	9.0	4
D	8.0	6
E	6.6	8
F	4.5	10
G	0	12

FIGURE 2-2

Society's Trade-off Between M-16 Rifles and CD-ROM Players

Both the production of M-16 semiautomatic rifles and the production of CD-ROM players are measured in billions of units per year. The various combinations are given in panel (a) and plotted in panel (b). Connecting the points *A–G* with a relatively smooth line gives the society's production possibilities curve for M-16 rifles and CD-ROM players. Point *R* lies outside the production possibilities curve and is therefore unattainable at the point in time for which the graph is drawn. Point *S* lies inside the production possibilities curve and therefore represents an inefficient use of available resources.

3. That the resource inputs, in both quantity and quality, used to produce M-16 rifles or CD-ROM players are fixed over this time period
4. That technology does not change over this time period

Technology is defined as society's pool of applied knowledge concerning how goods and services can be produced by managers, workers, engineers, scientists, and craftspeople, using land and capital. You can think of technology as the formula (or recipe) used to combine factors of production. (When better formulas are developed, more production can be obtained from the same amount of resources.) The level of technology sets the limit on the amount and types of goods and services that we can derive from any given amount of resources. The production possibilities curve is drawn under the assumption that we use the best technology that we currently have available and that this technology doesn't change over the time period under study.

Technology
Society's pool of applied knowledge concerning how goods and services can be produced.

Being off the Production Possibilities Curve

Look again at panel (b) of Figure 2-2. Point *R* lies *outside* the production possibilities curve and is *impossible* to achieve during the time period assumed. By definition, the production possibilities curve indicates the *maximum* quantity of one good given some quantity of the other.

It is possible, however, to be at point *S* in Figure 2-2. That point lies beneath the production possibilities curve. If the nation is at point *S*, it means that its resources are not being fully utilized. This occurs, for example, during periods of unemployment. Point *S* and all such points within the production possibilities curve are always attainable but usually not desirable.

Efficiency

The production possibilities curve can be used to define the notion of efficiency. Whenever the economy is operating on the PPC, at points such as *A, B, C,* or *D,* we say that its production is efficient. Points such as *S* in Figure 2-2, which lie beneath the production possibilities curve, are said to represent production situations that are not efficient.

Efficiency can mean many things to many people. Even within economics, there are different types of efficiency. Here we are discussing efficiency in production, or productive efficiency. An economy is productively efficient whenever it is producing the maximum output with given technology and resources.

A simple commonsense definition of efficiency is getting the most out of what we have as an economy. Clearly, we are not getting the most that we have if we are at point *S* in panel (b) of Figure 2-2. We can move from point *S* to, say, point *C,* thereby increasing the total quantity of M-16s produced without any decrease in the total quantity of CD-ROM players produced. We can move from point *S* to point *E,* for example, and have both more M-16s and more CD-ROM players. Point *S* is called an **inefficient point,** which is defined as any point below the production possibilities curve.

The concept of economic efficiency relates to how goods are distributed among different individuals and entities. An efficient economy is one in which people who value specific goods relatively the most end up with those goods. If you own a vintage electric Fender guitar, but I value it more than you, I can buy it from you. Such trading benefits you and me mutually. In the process, the economy becomes more efficient. The maximum efficiency an economy can reach is when all such mutual benefits through trade have been exhausted.

Efficiency
The case in which a given level of inputs is used to produce the maximum output possible. Alternatively, the situation in which a given output is produced at minimum cost.

Inefficient point
Any point below the production possibilities curve at which resources are being used inefficiently.

The Law of Increasing Relative Cost

In the example in Figure 2-1, the trade-off between a grade in accounting and a grade in economics is one-to-one. The trade-off ratio was fixed. That is to say, the production possibilities curve was a straight line. The curve in Figure 2-2 is a more general case. We have re-created the curve in Figure 2-2 as Figure 2-3. Each combination, *A* through *G,* of M-16s and CD-ROM players is represented on the production possibilities curve. Starting with the production of zero CD-ROM players, the nation can produce 10 billion units of M-16s with its available resources and technology. When we increase production of CD-ROM players from zero to 2 billion units per year, the nation has to give up in M-16s that first vertical arrow, *Aa.* From panel (a) of Figure 2-2 you can see that this is .4 billion M-16s a

FIGURE 2-3

The Law of Increasing Relative Cost
Consider equal increments of CD-ROM player production, as measured on the horizontal axis. All of the horizontal arrows—*aB, bC,* and so on—are of equal length (2 billion units). The opportunity cost of going from 10 billion CD-ROM players per year to 12 billion (*Ff*) is much greater than going from zero units to 2 billion units (*Aa*). The opportunity cost of each additional equal increase in CD-ROM production rises.

year (10.0 billion − 9.6 billion). Again, if we increase production of CD-ROM players by 2 billion units per year, we go from *B* to *C*. In order to do so, the nation has to give up the vertical distance *Bb,* or .6 billion M-16s a year. By the time we go from 10 billion to 12 billion CD-ROM players, to obtain that 2 billion unit increase, we have to forgo the vertical distance *Ff,* or 4.5 billion M-16s. In other words, we see an increase in the opportunity cost of the last 2 billion units of CD-ROM players—4.5 billion M-16s—compared to an equivalent increase in CD-ROM players when we started with none being produced at all—.4 billion M-16s.

What we are observing is called the **law of increasing relative cost.** When society takes more resources and applies them to the production of any specific good, the opportunity cost increases for each additional unit produced. The reason that, as a nation, we face the law of increasing relative cost (which causes the production possibilities curve to bow outward) is that certain resources are better suited for producing some goods than they are for other goods. Resources are generally not *perfectly* adaptable for alternative uses. When increasing the output of a particular good, producers must use less efficient resources than those already used in order to produce the additional output. Hence the cost of producing the additional units increases. With respect to our hypothetical example here, at first the electronic technicians in the armed services would shift over to producing CD-ROM players. After a while, though, janitors and army cooks would be asked to help. Clearly, they would be less effective in making CD-ROM players.

As a rule of thumb, *the more specialized the resources, the more bowed the production possibilities curve.* At the other extreme, if all resources are equally suitable for CD-ROM player production or M-16 production, the curves in Figures 2-2 and 2-3 would approach the straight line shown in our first example in Figure 2-1.

Law of increasing relative cost

The observation that the opportunity cost of additional units of a good generally increases as society attempts to produce more of that good. This accounts for the bowed-out shape of the production possibilities curve.

CONCEPTS IN BRIEF

- Trade-offs are represented graphically by a production possibilities curve showing the maximum quantity of one good or service that can be produced, given a specific quantity of another, from a given set of resources over a specified period of time—for example, one year.

- A PPC is drawn holding the quantity and quality of all resources fixed over the time period under study.

- Points outside the production possibilities curve are unattainable; points inside are attainable but represent an inefficient use or underuse of available resources.

- Because many resources are better suited for certain productive tasks than for others, society's production possibilities curve is bowed outward, following the law of increasing relative cost.

ECONOMIC GROWTH AND THE PRODUCTION POSSIBILITIES CURVE

Over any particular time period, a society cannot be outside the production possibilities curve. Over time, however, it is possible to have more of everything. This occurs through economic growth (why economic growth occurs will be discussed in a later chapter). Figure 2-4 shows the production possibilities curve for M-16 rifles and CD-ROM players shifting outward. The two additional curves shown represent new choices open to an economy that has experienced economic growth. Such economic growth occurs because of

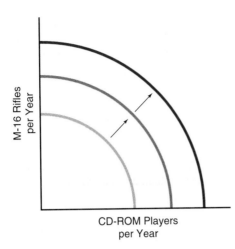

FIGURE 2-4

Economic Growth Allows for More of Everything

If the nation experiences economic growth, the production possibilities curve between M-16 rifles and CD-ROM players will move out, as is shown. This takes time, however, and it does not occur automatically. This means, therefore, that we can have more M-16s and more CD-ROM players only after a period of time during which we have experienced economic growth.

many things, including increases in the number of workers and productive investment in equipment.

Scarcity still exists, however, no matter how much economic growth there is. At any point in time, we will always be on some production possibilities curve; thus we will always face trade-offs. The more we want of one thing, the less we can have of others.

If a nation experiences economic growth, the production possibilities curve between M-16 rifles and CD-ROM players will move outward, as is shown in Figure 2-4. This takes time and does not occur automatically. One reason it will occur involves the choice about how much to consume today.

THE TRADE-OFF BETWEEN THE PRESENT AND THE FUTURE

Consumption
The use of goods and services for personal satisfaction.

The production possibilities curve and economic growth can be used to examine the trade-off between present **consumption** and future consumption. When we consume today, we are using up what we call consumption or consumer goods—food and clothes, for example. And we have already defined physical capital as the manufactured goods, such as machines and factories, used to make other goods and services.

Why We Make Capital Goods

Why would we be willing to use productive resources to make things—capital goods—that we cannot consume directly? For one thing, capital goods enable us to produce larger quantities of consumer goods or to produce them less expensively than we otherwise could. Before fish are "produced" for the market, equipment such as fishing boats, nets, and poles are produced first. Imagine how expensive it would be to obtain fish for market without using these capital goods. Catching fish with one's hands is not an easy task. The price per fish would be very high if capital goods weren't used.

Forgoing Current Consumption

Whenever we use productive resources to make capital goods, we are implicitly forgoing current consumption. We are waiting for some time in the future to consume the fruits that will be reaped from the use of capital goods. In effect, when we forgo current consumption to invest in capital goods, we are engaging in an economic activity that is forward-looking—we do not get instant utility or satisfaction from our activity. Indeed, if we were to produce only consumer goods now and no capital goods, our capacity to produce consumer goods in the future would suffer. Here we see a trade-off situation.

The Trade-off Between Consumption Goods and Capital Goods

To have more consumer goods in the future, we must accept fewer consumer goods today. In other words, an opportunity cost is involved here. Every time we make a choice for more goods today, we incur an opportunity cost of fewer goods tomorrow, and every time we make a choice of more goods in the future, we incur an opportunity cost of fewer goods today. With the resources that we don't use to produce consumer goods for today, we invest in capital goods that will produce more consumer goods for us later. The trade-off is shown in Figure 2-5. On the left in panel (a), you can see this trade-off depicted as a production possibilities curve between capital goods and consumption goods.

Assume that we are willing to give up $1 trillion worth of consumption today. We will be at point A in the left-hand diagram of panel (a). This will allow the economy to grow. We will have more future consumption because we invested in more capital goods today. In the right-hand diagram of panel (a), we see two goods represented, food and recreation. The production possibilities curve will move outward if we collectively decide to restrict consumption each year and invest in capital goods.

In panel (b), we show the results of our willingness to forgo more current consumption. We move to point C, where we have many fewer consumer goods today but produce a lot

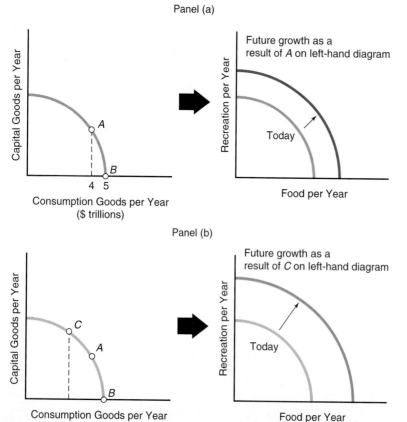

Panel (a)

Panel (b)

FIGURE 2-5

Capital Goods and Growth
In panel (a), the nation chooses not to consume $1 trillion, so it invests that amount in capital goods. In panel (b), it chooses even more capital goods. The PPC moves even more to the right on the right-hand diagram in panel (b) as a result.

more capital goods. This leads to more future growth in this simplified model, and thus the production possibilities curve in the right-hand side of panel (b) shifts outward more than it did in the right-hand side of panel (a).

In other words, the more we give up today, the more we can have tomorrow, provided, of course, that the capital goods are productive in future periods and that society desires the consumer goods produced by this additional capital.

INTERNATIONAL EXAMPLE
Consumption Versus Capital Goods in the United States and Japan

The trade-off represented in Figure 2-5 on the production possibilities curve of capital versus consumption goods can be observed in real life when we compare different countries. The Japanese, for example, have chosen to devote more than twice the amount of resources each year to the production of capital goods than we have in the United States. Not surprisingly, the Japanese have until recently experienced economic growth at a much higher rate than the United States has. In effect, then, Japan is represented by panel (b) in Figure 2-5—choosing more capital goods—and America by panel (a)—choosing fewer capital goods.

FOR CRITICAL ANALYSIS: Does this analysis apply to the trade-off between consumption and human capital for you as an individual? If so, how? ●

CONCEPTS IN BRIEF

- The use of capital requires using productive resources to produce capital goods that will later be used to produce consumer goods.

- A trade-off is involved between current consumption and capital goods or, alternatively, between current consumption and future consumption because the more we invest in capital goods today, the greater the amount of consumer goods we can produce in the future and the smaller the amount of consumer goods we can produce today.

SPECIALIZATION AND GREATER PRODUCTIVITY

Specialization
The division of productive activities among persons and regions so that no one individual or one area is totally self-sufficient. An individual may specialize, for example, in law or medicine. A nation may specialize in the production of coffee, computers, or cameras.

Specialization involves working at a relatively well-defined, limited endeavor, such as accounting or teaching. It involves a division of labor among different individuals and regions. Most individuals, in fact, do specialize. For example, you could change the oil in your car if you wanted to. Typically, though, you take your car to a garage and let the mechanic change the oil. You benefit by letting the garage mechanic specialize in changing the oil and in doing other repairs on your car. The specialist will get the job finished sooner than you could and has the proper equipment to make the job go more smoothly. Specialization usually leads to greater productivity, not only for each individual but also for the nation.

Absolute Advantage

Absolute advantage
The ability to produce a good or service at an "absolutely" lower cost, usually measured in units of labor or resource input required to produce one unit of the good or service.

Specialization occurs because different individuals and different nations have different skills. Sometimes it seems that some individuals are better at doing everything than anyone else. A president of a large company might be able to type better than any of the typists, file better than any of the file clerks, and wash windows better than any of the window washers. The president has an **absolute advantage** in all of these endeavors—he uses fewer labor hours for each task than anyone else in the company. The president does not, however, spend his time doing those other activities. Why not? Because he is being paid the most for undertaking the president's managerial duties. The president specializes in one particular task in spite of having an absolute advantage in all tasks. Indeed, absolute advantage is irrelevant in predicting how he uses his time; only *comparative advantage* matters.

Comparative Advantage

Comparative advantage is the ability to perform an activity at the lowest opportunity cost. You have a comparative advantage in one activity whenever you have the lowest opportunity cost of performing that activity. Comparative advantage is always a *relative* concept. You may be able to change the oil in your car; you might even be able to change it faster than the local mechanic. But if the opportunity cost you face by changing the oil exceeds the mechanic's opportunity cost, the mechanic has a comparative advantage in changing the oil. The mechanic faces a lower opportunity cost for that activity.

> **Comparative advantage**
> The ability to produce a good or service at a lower opportunity cost compared to other producers.

You may be convinced that everybody can do everything better than you. In this extreme situation, do you still have a comparative advantage? The answer is yes. What you need to do to discover your comparative advantage is to find a job in which your *disadvantage* relative to others is the smallest. You do not have to be a mathematical genius to figure this out. The market tells you very clearly by offering you the highest income for the job for which you have the smallest disadvantage compared to others. Stated differently, to find your comparative advantage no matter how much better everybody else can do the jobs that you want to do, you simply find which job maximizes your income.

The coaches of sports teams are constantly faced with determining each player's comparative advantage. Babe Ruth was originally one of the best pitchers in professional baseball when he played for the Boston Red Sox. After he was traded to the New York Yankees, the owner and the coach decided to make him an outfielder, even though he was a better pitcher than anyone else on the team roster. They wanted "The Babe" to concentrate on his hitting. Good pitchers do not bring in as many fans as home-run kings. Babe Ruth's comparative advantage was clearly in hitting homers rather than practicing and developing his pitching game.

Scarcity, Self-Interest, and Specialization

In Chapter 1, you learned about the assumption of rational self-interest. To repeat, for the purposes of our analyses we assume that individuals are rational in that they will do what is in their own self-interest. They will not consciously carry out actions that will make them worse off. In this chapter, you learned that scarcity requires people to make choices. We assume that they make choices based on their self-interest. When they make these choices, they attempt to maximize benefits net of opportunity cost. In so doing, individuals choose their comparative advantage and end up specializing. Ultimately, when people specialize, they increase the money income they make and therefore become richer. When all individuals and businesses specialize simultaneously, the gains are seen in greater material well-being. With any given set of resources, specialization will result in higher output.

 INTERNATIONAL EXAMPLE
Why Foreign Graduate Students Specialize When Studying in the United States

Specialization is evident in the fields of endeavor that foreign students choose when they come to the United States for graduate studies. Consider the following statistics: More than

60 percent of U.S. doctorates in engineering and 55 percent of those in mathematics, computer science, and the physical sciences are earned by foreign-born students. Yet foreign nationals are awarded relatively few advanced degrees in business, law, or medicine. The reason has nothing to do with intelligence or giftedness; it is simply that many more of the best American students choose schools in these professional fields rather than ones offering science and engineering programs.

Why does this specialization occur? For American students, the greatest returns for about the same effort come from business, law, and medicine. In contrast, foreign-born graduate students face fewer language and cultural obstacles (and hence better job prospects) if they choose technical subjects.

When students from foreign countries come to American graduate schools to obtain their Ph.D. degrees, more than 70 percent of them remain in the United States after graduation, thereby augmenting America's supply of engineers and scientists. Such specialization has helped the United States maintain its leadership in both the technoscientific and sociocultural areas.

FOR CRITICAL ANALYSIS: What type of capital do foreign-born students bring with them to the United States? ●

THE DIVISION OF LABOR

Division of labor
The segregation of a resource into different specific tasks; for example, one automobile worker puts on bumpers, another doors, and so on.

In any firm that includes specialized human and nonhuman resources, there is a **division of labor** among those resources. The best-known example of all time comes from one of the earliest and perhaps most famous economists, Adam Smith, who in *The Wealth of Nations* (1776) illustrated the benefits of a division of labor in the making of pins, as depicted in the following example:

> One man draws out the wire, another straightens it, a third cuts it, a fourth points it, a fifth grinds it at the top for receiving the head; to make the head requires two or three distinct operations; to put it on is a peculiar business, to whiten the pins is another; it is even a trade by itself to put them into the paper.

Making pins this way allowed 10 workers without very much skill to make almost 48,000 pins "of a middling size" in a day. One worker, toiling alone, could have made perhaps 20 pins a day; therefore, 10 workers could have produced 200. Division of labor allowed for an increase in the daily output of the pin factory from 200 to 48,000! (Smith did not attribute all of the gain to the division of labor according to talent but credited also the use of machinery and the fact that less time was spent shifting from task to task.)

What we are discussing here involves a division of the resource called labor into different kinds of labor. The different kinds of labor are organized in such a way as to increase the amount of output possible from the fixed resources available. We can therefore talk about an organized division of labor within a firm leading to increased output.

COMPARATIVE ADVANTAGE AND TRADE AMONG NATIONS

Though most of our analysis of absolute advantage, comparative advantage, and specialization has dealt with individuals, it is equally applicable to nations. First consider the United States. The Plains states have a comparative advantage in the production of grains and other agricultural goods. The states to the north and east tend to specialize in industrialized production, such as automobiles. Not surprisingly, grains are shipped from the

Plains states to the northern states, and automobiles are shipped in the reverse direction. Such specialization and trade allow for higher incomes and standards of living. If both the Plains states and the northern states were politically defined as separate nations, the same analysis would still hold, but we would call it international trade. Indeed, Europe is comparable to the United States in area and population, but instead of one nation, Europe has 15. What in America we call *interstate* trade, in Europe they call *international* trade. There is no difference, however, in the economic results—both yield greater economic efficiency and higher average incomes.

Political problems that do not normally arise within a particular nation often do between nations. For example, if California avocado growers develop a cheaper method than growers in southern Florida to produce a tastier avocado, the Florida growers will lose out. They cannot do much about the situation except try to lower their own costs of production or improve their product. If avocado growers in Mexico, however, develop a cheaper method to produce better-tasting avocados, both California and Florida growers can (and likely will) try to raise political barriers that will prevent Mexican avocado growers from freely selling their product in America. U.S. avocado growers will use such arguments as "unfair" competition and loss of American jobs. In so doing, they are only partly right: Avocado-growing jobs may decline in America, but jobs will not necessarily decline overall. If the argument of U.S. avocado growers had any validity, every time a region in the United States developed a better way to produce a product manufactured somewhere else in the country, employment in America would decline. That has never happened and never will.

When nations specialize where they have a comparative advantage and then trade with the rest of the world, the average standard of living in the world rises. In effect, international trade allows the world to move from inside the global production possibilities curve toward the curve itself, thereby improving worldwide economic efficiency.

CONCEPTS IN BRIEF

- With a given set of resources, specialization results in higher output; in other words, there are gains to specialization in terms of greater material well-being.
- Individuals and nations specialize in their areas of comparative advantage in order to reap the gains of specialization.
- Comparative advantages are found by determining which activities have the lowest opportunity cost—that is, which activities yield the highest return for the time and resources used.
- A division of labor occurs when different workers are assigned different tasks. Together, the workers produce a desired product.

When you're stuck in traffic, you pay an opportunity cost. How is this driver reducing that cost?

Fast Lanes for a Fee

CONCEPTS APPLIED:
SCARCITY, OPPORTUNITY COST, TRADE-OFFS

Visit www.econtoday.com for an Internet Activity that expands your understanding of these concepts.

"Time is money." Translated into the economic terminology you have learned in this chapter, time represents an opportunity cost. Highway planners ignored this reality for many years. Then they started to add high-occupancy vehicle lanes, sometimes called carpool lanes or diamond lanes. At rush hour, only cars carrying at least two (or in some places three) passengers can use this special fast lane.

Using a carpool lane imposes a cost on the driver. The driver has to arrange for there to be a passenger in the car (we will ignore the cheaters who have tried to get away with putting lifelike dummies in the passenger seat). The benefit, of course, is saving time by avoiding the more congested normal lanes on freeways and expressways. The rational driver is assumed, therefore, to compare the opportunity cost of time saved with the "cost" of picking up someone with whom to carpool. The opportunity cost is the highest-valued use of the time saved. It may be measured by extra pay for working more, which may be a proxy for the value of extra time spent with one's family, going to the gym, and the like.

Direct Payments for Using Fast Lanes—an Alternative

Some people may value their time highly yet be unwilling always to try to find a carpooler with whom to drive to work. Some of these individuals would be willing to pay for the ability to drive in less congested lanes on freeways and expressways.

In San Diego, California, highway planners decided to let drivers do just that. The experiment started in December 1996 and continues to this day. In the first seven hours, 500 express passes were sold at $50 per month each. The price has now been increased to $70 per month. As the process becomes more popular, officials plan to raise the price even higher. By March 1997, over $70,000 had been collected. That money was destined to be used to build a new bus route along the Interstate 15 corridor.

By the time you read this, overhead antennas should have been installed to deduct tolls electronically from a coaster-sized transponder inside each car. That way, motorists can pay on a trip-by-trip basis rather than by the month.

Did Fast Lanes Become "Lexus Lanes"?

At the beginning of the San Diego experiment, critics argued that the fast lanes would simply become "Lexus lanes," meaning that well-to-do drivers would be the only ones purchasing the right to use those fast lanes without carrying additional passengers. That has turned out to be inaccurate. Certainly drivers of luxury cars have purchased the rights to drive those lanes, but so have owners of plain old Fords, Chevrolets, and Toyotas. A priori, we cannot be certain how individuals value their time. While in general those with higher earning abilities face a higher opportunity cost of time, many with lower earnings place a high value on free time in order to engage in, say, sports, theater, meditation, or movies. Those lower-income individuals may be willing to sacrifice a relatively larger percentage of their incomes to drive in the fast lanes because of the high value they place on time.

But Is It Fair?

The first thought that comes to some people's minds when they see lone drivers in the fast lane is that it "isn't fair." Why should people, just because they paid for the right, be able to drive in the fast lane? The issue of fairness cannot be answered by economics. Remember that economics is a positive science.

We can point out, though, that for virtually all goods and services, people who are willing to pay more generally get more in both quantity and quality. Is it fair that people who are willing to pay a relatively high price for hothouse-grown strawberries in the middle of winter get to buy them? Is it fair that people who are willing to pay a higher price for luxury cars get to buy them? Is it fair that people who want to pay higher prices for more sophisticated five-channel surround-sound home theater systems get to buy them? Economists cannot answer such questions. Suffice it to say that all of us make choices all the time about how to use our limited incomes. No value judgment can be reached about the choices other individuals make.

Montana's Answer to Reducing Driving Time

Montana, a relatively unpopulated state, has chosen another way to reduce driving time. It changed its speed limit to whatever is "reasonable and prudent." Some 85 percent of traffic now moves at around 74 miles an hour. Driving speeds tend to be higher where there are long stretches of straight, flat road. For interstate truckers, who are generally paid 23 to 25 cents a mile, the higher highway speeds translate directly into increased pay. On these roads, truckers can specifically estimate the opportunity cost of time. For example, a trucker paid 25 cents per mile for a 480-mile trip would earn $120. At 60 miles an hour, the trip would take eight hours, yielding an hourly wage of $15. But the same trip made at 80 miles an hour would take six hours, and the trucker's wage would jump to $20 an hour. Is it any wonder that long-distance truckers favor higher speed limits . . . or none at all?

FOR CRITICAL ANALYSIS

1. What is the relationship between paying a fee for fast lane use and giving a tip to maître d' to be seated more quickly at a crowded restaurant? Does the question of fairness enter into either of these practices?
2. Many bridges in major cities are extremely congested at rush hour. How could traffic planners reduce such congestion?
3. Under what circumstances would relatively poor individuals be willing to pay to drive in fast lanes?
4. How do potential purchasers of express lane passes determine whether the pass is worth the money they have to pay each month?

CHAPTER SUMMARY

1. All societies at all times face the universal problem of scarcity because we cannot obtain everything we want from nature without sacrifice. Thus scarcity and poverty are not synonymous. Even the richest persons face scarcity because they also have to make choices among alternatives.
2. The resources we use to produce desired goods and services can be classified into land, labor, physical and human capital, and entrepreneurship.
3. Goods are all things from which individuals derive satisfaction. Economic goods are those for which the desired quantity exceeds the amount that is directly available from nature at a zero price. The goods that we want are not necessarily those that we need. The term *need* is undefinable in economics, whereas humans have unlimited *wants,* which are defined as the goods and services on which we place a positive value.

4. We measure the cost of anything by what has to be given up in order to have it. This cost is called opportunity cost.

5. The trade-offs we face as individuals and those we face as a society can be represented graphically by a production possibilities curve (PPC). This curve shows the maximum quantity of one good or service that can be produced, given a specific quantity of another, from a given set of resources over a specified period of time, usually one year.

6. Because resources are specialized, production possibilities curves bow outward. This means that each additional increment of one good can be obtained only by giving up more and more of the other goods. This is called the law of increasing relative cost.

7. It is impossible to be outside the production possibilities curve, but we can be inside it. When we are, we are in a situation of unemployment, inefficiently organized resources, or some combination of the two.

8. There is a trade-off between consumption goods and capital goods. The more resources we devote to capital goods, the more consumption goods we can normally have in the future (and less currently). This is because more capital goods allow the economy to grow, thereby moving the production possibilities curve outward.

9. One finds one's comparative advantage by looking at the activity that has the lowest opportunity cost. That is, one's comparative advantage lies in the activity that generates the highest income. By specializing in one's comparative advantage, one is assured of reaping the gains of specialization.

10. Division of labor occurs when workers are assigned different tasks.

DISCUSSION OF PREVIEW QUESTIONS

1. Do affluent people face the problem of scarcity?

Scarcity is a relative concept and exists because wants are great relative to the means of satisfying those wants (wealth or income). Even though affluent people have relatively and absolutely high levels of income or wealth, they nevertheless typically want more than they can have (in luxury goods, power, prestige, and so on).

2. Fresh air may be consumed at no charge, but is it free of cost to society?

Individuals are not charged a price for the use of air. Yet truly fresh air is not free to society. If a good were free to society, every person would be able to use all that he or she wanted to use; no one would have to sacrifice anything in order to use that good, and people would not have to compete for it. In the United States, different groups compete for air; for example, environmentalists and concerned citizens compete with automobile drivers and factories for clean air.

3. Why does the scarcity problem force people to consider opportunity costs?

Individuals have limited incomes; as a consequence, an expenditure on an automobile necessarily pre- cludes expenditures on other goods and services. The same is true for society, which also faces the scarcity problem; if society allocates specific resources to the production of a steel mill, those same resources can- not be allocated elsewhere. Because resources are limited, society is forced to decide how to allocate its available resources; scarcity means that the cost of allocating resources to produce specific goods is ulti- mately assessed in terms of other goods that are nec- essarily sacrificed. Because there are millions of ways in which the resources allocated to a steel mill might otherwise be allocated, one is forced to consider the *highest-valued* alternative. We define the oppor- tunity cost of a good as its highest-valued alternative; the opportunity cost of the steel mill to society is the highest-valued output that those same resources could otherwise have produced.

4. Can a "free" college education ever be truly free?

Suppose that you were given a college education without having to pay any fees whatsoever. You could say that you were receiving a free education. But someone is paying for your education because you are using scarce resources—buildings, professors' time, electricity for lighting, etc. The opportunity cost of your education is certainly not zero, so in that sense it is not free. Furthermore, by going to college, you are giving up the ability to earn income during that time period. Therefore, there is an opportunity cost to your attending classes and studying. You can approximate that opportunity cost by estimating what your current after-tax income would be if you were working instead of going to school.

PROBLEMS

(Answers to the odd-numbered problems appear at the back of the book.)

2-1. The following sets of numbers represent hypothetical production possibilities for a nation in 1998. Plot these points on graph paper.

Butter	Guns
4	0
3	1.6
2	2.4
1	2.8
0	3.0

Does the law of increasing relative cost seem to hold? Why? On the same graph, plot and draw the production possibilities curve that will represent 10 percent economic growth.

2-2. There are 150,000 conscripts (draftees) in the French army, each paid $2,000 a year. The average salary of each conscript prior to military service was $18,500 per year. What does it cost for conscripts in France each year?

2-3. Answer the questions using the following information.

Employee	Daily Work Effort	Production
Ann Jones	4 hours	8 jackets
	4 hours	12 ties
Ned Lopez	4 hours	8 jackets
	4 hours	12 ties
Total daily output		16 jackets
		24 ties

a. Who has an absolute advantage in jacket production?
b. Who has a comparative advantage in tie production?
c. Will Jones and Lopez specialize?
d. If they specialize, what will total output equal?

2-4. Two countries, Workland and Playland, have similar populations and identical production possibilities curves but different preferences. The production possibilities combinations are as follows:

Point	Capital Goods	Consumption Goods
A	0	20
B	1	19
C	2	17
D	3	14
E	4	10
F	5	5
G	7	0

Playland is located at point *B* on the PPC, and Workland is located at point *E*. Assume that this situation continues into the future and that all other things remain the same.

a. What is Workland's opportunity cost of capital goods in terms of consumption goods?
b. What is Playland's opportunity cost of capital goods in terms of consumption goods?
c. How would the PPCs of Workland and Playland be expected to compare to each other 50 years in the future?

2-5. Which of the following are part of the opportunity cost of going to a football game in town instead of watching it on TV at home? Explain why.

a. The expense of lunch in a restaurant prior to the football game.

b. The value of one hour of sleep lost because of a traffic jam after the game.

c. The expense of a babysitter for your children if they are too young to go to a football game.

2-6. Assume that your economics and English exams are scheduled for the same day. How would you determine how much time you should spend study-ing for each exam? Does the grade you are cur-rently receiving in each course affect your deci-sion? Why or why not?

2-7. Some people argue that air is not an economic good. If you agree with this statement, explain why. If you disagree, explain why. (Hint: Is all air the same?)

COMPUTER-ASSISTED INSTRUCTION

If you are given a production possibilities table, can you calculate the opportunity cost of successive units of one good in terms of forgone units of the other? By requiring specific calculations, the concept of opportunity cost is revealed.

Complete problem and answer appear on disk.

INTERACTING WITH THE INTERNET

What Happens When You Are Lost in Cyberspace?

All of the Internet addresses that you will find in this text were active at the time of publication. Beware, though: The saying "Here today, gone tomorrow" is especially true with reference to Inter-net sites.

If an address does not work, the first thing you should do is check the spelling, punctuation, and capitalization of your URL to make sure it corresponds exactly to what is printed in the book. Your Internet browser may still tell you that it is "unable to locate the server" or that "the server does not have DNS entry." Don't despair; even if a particular link or page no longer exists, there might be something of value hidden somewhere.

The trick is to start "trimming" the URL, one slash at a time. If your first destination is not found, click on the URL shown in your browser and delete all of the information to the right of the forward slash that is farthest to the right. Then press Enter and see where you go. If you still cannot find what you want, trim back to the next forward slash, and so forth. Eventually, you will get to the home page and can restart your investigation. (A temporary problem you might encounter at any time and for any location is the message "This server is not responding" or the like. This simply means that there is a temporary problem with the server you are trying to access; another attempt later in the day or the next day will probably be successful.)

Let's say you wanted to get information on the economic status of the United States. You might go to the Federal Reserve Board's "Beige Book" at the following Web site:

www.bog.frb.fed.us/fomc/bb/current/

You could start trimming this URL by deleting *current/* . Then if that did not work, you would delete *bb/*. And if that did not work, you would delete *fomc/*. You would end up at the home page of the Fed-eral Reserve Board.

APPENDIX A

READING AND WORKING WITH GRAPHS

A graph is a visual representation of the relationship between variables. In this appendix, we'll stick to just two variables: an **independent variable,** which can change in value freely, and a **dependent variable,** which changes only as a result of changes in the value of the independent variable. For example, if nothing else is changing in your life, your weight depends on the amount of food you eat. Food is the independent variable and weight the dependent variable.

A table is a list of numerical values showing the relationship between two (or more) variables. Any table can be converted into a graph, which is a visual representation of that list. Once you understand how a table can be converted to a graph, you will understand what graphs are and how to construct and use them.

Consider a practical example. A conservationist may try to convince you that driving at lower highway speeds will help you conserve gas. Table A-1 shows the relationship between speed—the independent variable—and the distance you can go on a gallon of gas at that speed—the dependent variable. This table does show a pattern of sorts. As the data in the first column get larger in value, the data in the second column get smaller.

Now let's take a look at the different ways in which variables can be related.

DIRECT AND INVERSE RELATIONSHIPS

Two variables can be related in different ways, some simple, others more complex. For example, a person's weight and height are often related. If we measured the height and weight of thousands of people, we would surely find that taller people tend to weigh more than shorter people. That is, we would discover that there is a **direct relationship** between height and weight. By this we simply mean that an *increase* in one variable is usually associated with an *increase* in the related variable. This can easily be seen in panel (a) of Figure A-1.

Let's look at another simple way in which two variables can be related. Much evidence indicates that as the price of a specific commodity rises, the amount purchased decreases—there is an **inverse relationship** between the variable's price per unit and quantity purchased. A table listing the data for this relationship would indicate that for higher and higher prices, smaller and smaller quantities would be purchased. We see this relationship in panel (b) of Figure A-1.

TABLE A-1
Gas Mileage as a Function of Driving Speed

Miles per Hour	Miles per Gallon
45	25
50	24
55	23
60	21
65	19
70	16
75	13

FIGURE A-1
Relationships

Panel (a)
Direct Relationship

(Height vs. Weight)

Panel (b)
Inverse Relationship

(Price vs. Quantity Purchased)

CONSTRUCTING A GRAPH

Let us now examine how to construct a graph to illustrate a relationship between two variables.

A Number Line

Number line
A line that can be divided into segments of equal length, each associated with a number.

FIGURE A-3
Vertical Number Line

The first step is to become familiar with what is called a **number line.** One is shown in Figure A-2. There are two things that you should know about it.

1. The points on the line divide the line into equal segments.
2. The numbers associated with the points on the line increase in value from left to right; saying it the other way around, the numbers decrease in value from right to left. However you say it, what we're describing is formally called an *ordered set of points.*

On the number line, we have shown the line segments—that is, the distance from 0 to 10 or the distance between 30 and 40. They all appear to be equal and, indeed, are equal to $\frac{1}{2}$ inch. When we use a distance to represent a quantity, such as barrels of oil, graphically, we are *scaling* the number line. In the example shown, the distance between 0 and 10 might represent 10 barrels of oil, or the distance from 0 to 40 might represent 40 barrels. Of course, the scale may differ on different number lines. For example, a distance of 1 inch could represent 10 units on one number line but 5,000 units on another. Notice that on our number line, points to the left of 0 correspond to negative numbers and points to the right of 0 correspond to positive numbers.

Of course, we can also construct a vertical number line. Consider the one in Figure A-3. As we move up this vertical number line, the numbers increase in value; conversely, as we descend, they decrease in value. Below 0 the numbers are negative, and above 0 the numbers are positive. And as on the horizontal number line, all the line segments are equal. This line is divided into segments such that the distance between -2 and -1 is the same as the distance between 0 and 1.

Combining Vertical and Horizontal Number Lines

By drawing the horizontal and vertical lines on the same sheet of paper, we are able to express the relationships between variables graphically. We do this in Figure A-4.

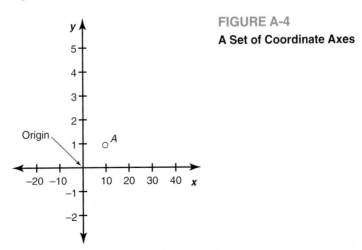

FIGURE A-4
A Set of Coordinate Axes

We draw them (1) so that they intersect at each other's 0 point and (2) so that they are perpendicular to each other. The result is a set of coordinate axes, where each line is called an *axis.* When we have two axes, they span a plane.

For one number line, you need only one number to specify any point on the line; equivalently, when you see a point on the line, you know that it represents one number or one value. With a coordinate value system, you need two numbers to specify a single point in the plane; when you see a single point on a graph, you know that it represents two numbers or two values.

The basic things that you should know about a coordinate number system are that the vertical number line is referred to as the **y axis,** the horizontal number line is referred to as the **x axis,** and the point of intersection of the two lines is referred to as the **origin.**

Any point such as *A* in Figure A-4 represents two numbers—a value of *x* and a value of *y.* But we know more than that; we also know that point *A* represents a positive value of *y* because it is above the *x* axis, and we know that it represents a positive value of *x* because it is to the right of the *y* axis.

Point *A* represents a "paired observation" of the variables *x* and *y;* in particular, in Figure A-4, *A* represents an observation of the pair of values *x* = 10 and *y* = 1. Every point in the coordinate system corresponds to a paired observation of *x* and *y,* which can be simply written (*x, y*)—the *x* value is always specified first, then the *y* value. When we give the values associated with the position of point *A* in the coordinate number system, we are in effect giving the coordinates of that point. *A*'s coordinates are *x* = 10, *y* = 1, or (10, 1).

GRAPHING NUMBERS IN A TABLE

Consider Table A-2. Column 1 shows different prices for T-shirts, and column 2 gives the number of T-shirts purchased per week at these prices. Notice the pattern of these numbers. As the price of T-shirts falls, the number of T-shirts purchased per week increases. Therefore, an inverse relationship exists between these two variables, and as soon as we represent it on a graph, you will be able to see the relationship. We can graph this relationship using a coordinate number system—a vertical and horizontal number line for each of these two variables. Such a graph is shown in panel (b) of Figure A-5.

y axis
The vertical axis in a graph.

x axis
The horizontal axis in a graph.

Origin
The intersection of the *y* axis and the *x* axis in a graph.

TABLE A-2
T-Shirts Purchased

(1) Price of T-Shirts	(2) Number of T-Shirts Purchased per Week
$10	20
9	30
8	40
7	50
6	60
5	70

FIGURE A-5
Graphing the Relationship Between T-Shirts Purchased and Price

Panel (a)

Price per T-Shirt	T-Shirts Purchased per Week	Point on Graph
$10	20	I (20, 10)
9	30	J (30, 9)
8	40	K (40, 8)
7	50	L (50, 7)
6	60	M (60, 6)
5	70	N (70, 5)

Panel (b)

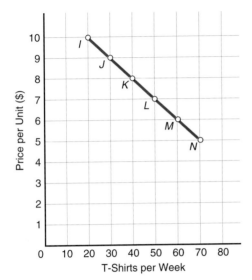

FIGURE A-6

Connecting the Observation Points

In economics, it is conventional to put dollar values on the *y* axis. We therefore construct a vertical number line for price and a horizontal number line, the *x* axis, for quantity of T-shirts purchased per week. The resulting coordinate system allows the plotting of each of the paired observation points; in panel (a), we repeat Table A-2, with a column added expressing these points in paired-data (*x*, *y*) form. For example, point *J* is the paired observation (30, 9). It indicates that when the price of a T-shirt is $9, 30 will be purchased per week.

If it were possible to sell parts of a T-shirt ($\frac{1}{2}$ or $\frac{1}{20}$ of a shirt), we would have observations at every possible price. That is, we would be able to connect our paired observations, represented as lettered points. Let's assume that we can make T-shirts perfectly divisible. We would then have a line that connects these points, as shown in the graph in Figure A-6.

In short, we have now represented the data from the table in the form of a graph. Note that an inverse relationship between two variables shows up on a graph as a line or curve that slopes *downward* from left to right. (You might as well get used to the idea that economists call a straight line a "curve" even though it may not curve at all. Much of economists' data turn out to be curves, so they refer to everything represented graphically, even straight lines, as curves.)

THE SLOPE OF A LINE (A LINEAR CURVE)

An important property of a curve represented on a graph is its *slope*. Consider Figure A-7 on page 42, which represents the quantities of shoes per week that a seller is willing to offer at different prices. Note that in panel (a) of Figure A-7, as in Figure A-5, we have expressed the coordinates of the points in parentheses in paired-data form.

Slope

The change in the *y* value divided by the corresponding change in the *x* value of a curve; the "incline" of the curve.

The **slope** of a line is defined as the change in the *y* values divided by the corresponding change in the *x* values as we move along the line. Let's move from point *E* to point *D* in panel (b) of Figure A-7. As we move, we note that the change in the *y* values, which is the change in price, is +$20, because we have moved from a price of $20 to a price of $40 per pair. As we move from *E* to *D*, the change in the *x* values is +80; the number of pairs of shoes willingly offered per week rises from 80 to 160 pairs. The slope calculated as a change in the *y* values divided by the change in the *x* values is therefore

$$\frac{20}{80} = \frac{1}{4}$$

FIGURE A-7

A Positively Sloped Curve

Panel (a)

Price per Pair	Pairs of Shoes Offered per Week	Point on Graph
$100	400	A (400,100)
80	320	B (320, 80)
60	240	C (240, 60)
40	160	D (160, 40)
20	80	E (80, 20)

Panel (b)

It may be helpful for you to think of slope as a "rise" (movement in the vertical direction) over a "run" (movement in the horizontal direction). We show this abstractly in Figure A-8. The slope is measured by the amount of rise divided by the amount of run. In the example in Figure A-8, and of course in Figure A-7, the amount of rise is positive and so is the amount of run. That's because it's a direct relationship. We show an inverse relationship in Figure A-9. The slope is still equal to the rise divided by the run, but in this case the rise and the run have opposite signs because the curve slopes downward. That means that the slope will have to be negative and that we are dealing with an inverse relationship.

Now let's calculate the slope for a different part of the curve in panel (b) of Figure A-7. We will find the slope as we move from point B to point A. Again, we note that the slope, or rise over run, from B to A equals

$$\frac{20}{80} = \frac{1}{4}$$

A specific property of a straight line is that its slope is the same between any two points; in other words, the slope is constant at all points on a straight line in a graph.

We conclude that for our example in Figure A-7, the relationship between the price of a pair of shoes and the number of pairs of shoes willingly offered per week is *linear,* which simply means "in a straight line," and our calculations indicate a constant slope. Moreover, we calculate a direct relationship between these two variables, which turns out to be an

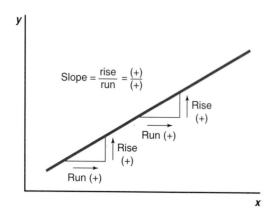

FIGURE A-8

Figuring Positive Slope

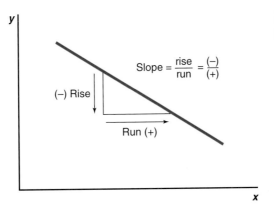

FIGURE A-9
Figuring Negative Slope

upward-sloping (from left to right) curve. Upward-sloping curves have positive slopes—in this case, it is $+\frac{1}{4}$.

We know that an inverse relationship between two variables shows up as a downward-sloping curve—rise over run will be a negative slope because the rise and run have opposite signs as shown in Figure A-9. When we see a negative slope, we know that increases in one variable are associated with decreases in the other. Therefore, we say that downward-sloping curves have negative slopes. Can you verify that the slope of the graph representing the relationship between T-shirt prices and the quantity of T-shirts purchased per week in Figure A-6 is $-\frac{1}{10}$?

Slopes of Nonlinear Curves

The graph presented in Figure A-10 indicates a *nonlinear* relationship between two variables, total profits and output per unit of time. Inspection of this graph indicates that at first, increases in output lead to increases in total profits; that is, total profits rise as output increases. But beyond some output level, further increases in output cause decreases in total profits.

Can you see how this curve rises at first, reaches a peak at point *C,* and then falls? This curve relating total profits to output levels appears mountain-shaped.

Considering that this curve is nonlinear (it is obviously not a straight line), should we expect a constant slope when we compute changes in *y* divided by corresponding changes in *x* in moving from one point to another? A quick inspection, even without specific numbers, should lead us to conclude that the slopes of lines joining different points in this curve, such as between *A* and *B, B* and *C,* or *C* and *D,* will *not* be the same. The curve slopes upward (in a positive direction) for some values and downward (in a negative direction) for

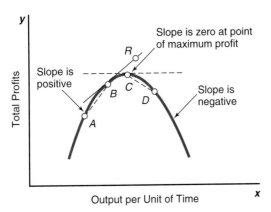

FIGURE A-10
The Slope of a Nonlinear Curve

other values. In fact, the slope of the line between any two points on this curve will be different from the slope of the line between any two other points. Each slope will be different as we move along the curve.

Instead of using a line between two points to discuss slope, mathematicians and economists prefer to discuss the slope *at a particular point*. The slope at a point on the curve, such as point *B* in the graph in Figure A-10, is the slope of a line *tangent* to that point. A tangent line is a straight line that touches a curve at only one point. For example, it might be helpful to think of the tangent at *B* as the straight line that just "kisses" the curve at point *B*.

To calculate the slope of a tangent line, you need to have some additional information besides the two values of the point of tangency. For example, in Figure A-10, if we knew that the point *R* also lay on the tangent line and we knew the two values of that point, we could calculate the slope of the tangent line. We could calculate rise over run between points *B* and *R*, and the result would be the slope of the line tangent to the one point *B* on the curve.

APPENDIX SUMMARY

1. Direct relationships involve a dependent variable changing in the same direction as the change in the independent variable.
2. Inverse relationships involve the dependent variable changing in the opposite direction of the change in the independent variable.
3. When we draw a graph showing the relationship between two economic variables, we are holding all other things constant (the Latin term for which is *ceteris paribus*).
4. We obtain a set of coordinates by putting vertical and horizontal number lines together. The vertical line is called the *y* axis; the horizontal line, the *x* axis.

5. The slope of any linear (straight-line) curve is the change in the *y* values divided by the corresponding change in the *x* values as we move along the line. Otherwise stated, the slope is calculated as the amount of rise over the amount of run, where rise is movement in the vertical direction and run is movement in the horizontal direction.
6. The slope of a nonlinear curve changes; it is positive when the curve is rising and negative when the curve is falling. At a maximum or minimum point, the slope of the nonlinear curve is zero.

PROBLEMS

(The answer to Problem A-1 appears at the back of the book.)

A-1. Complete the schedule and plot the following function:

$y = 3x$

y	x
	4
	3
	2
	1
	0
	-1
	-2
	-3
	-4

A-2. Complete the schedule and plot the following function:

$y = x^2$

y	x
	4
	3
	2
	1
	0
	-1
	-2
	-3
	-4

CHAPTER 3

DEMAND AND SUPPLY

Auctions have been around for centuries. Farmers first used auctions to sell their grains to people who would use the grains to make flour and other food products. Today, some of the best-publicized auctions involve fine art at Sotheby's and Christie's. In addition to the normal auction scene, however, a whole new revolution in auction-eering is taking place. Hundreds, if not thousands, of auctions are taking place on the Internet as you read this sentence. To understand better how auctions work, whether on-line or elsewhere, you will need the tools of supply and demand analysis.

PREVIEW QUESTIONS

1. Why are relative prices important in understanding the law of demand?

2. How can we distinguish between a change in *demand* and a change in *quantity demanded*?

3. Why is there normally a direct relationship between price and quantity supplied (other things being equal)?

4. Why will the market clearing price occur at the intersection of the supply and demand curves rather than at a higher or lower price?

Did You Know That . . . more than 60 million people currently own portable cellular phones? This is a huge jump from the mere 200,000 who owned them in 1985. Since 1992, two out of every three new telephone numbers have been assigned to cellular phones. There are several reasons for the growth of cellular phones, not the least being the dramatic reduction in both price and size due to improved and cheaper computer chips that go into making them. There is something else at work, though. It has to do with crime. In a recent survey, 46 percent of new cellular phone users said that personal safety was the main reason they bought a portable phone. In Florida, for example, most cellular phone companies allow users simply to dial *FHP to reach the Florida Highway Patrol. The rush to cellular phones is worldwide. Over the past decade, sales have grown by nearly 50 percent every year outside the United States.

We could attempt to explain the phenomenon by saying that more people like to use portable phones. But that explanation is neither satisfying nor entirely accurate. If we use the economist's primary set of tools, *demand and supply,* we will have a better understanding of the cellular phone explosion, as well as many other phenomena in our world. Demand and supply are two ways of categorizing the influences on the price of goods that you buy and the quantities available. As such, demand and supply form the basis of virtually all economic analysis of the world around us.

As you will see throughout this text, the operation of the forces of demand and supply take place in *markets*. A **market** is an abstract concept referring to all the arrangements individuals have for exchanging with one another. Goods and services are sold in markets, such as the automobile market, the health market, and the compact disc market. Workers offer their services in the labor market. Companies, or firms, buy workers' labor services in the labor market. Firms also buy other inputs in order to produce the goods and services that you buy as a consumer. Firms purchase machines, buildings, and land. These markets are in operation at all times. One of the most important activities in these markets is the setting of the prices of all of the inputs and outputs that are bought and sold in our complicated economy. To understand the determination of prices, you first need to look at the law of demand.

THE LAW OF DEMAND

Demand has a special meaning in economics. It refers to the quantities of specific goods or services that individuals, taken singly or as a group, will purchase at various possible prices, other things being constant. We can therefore talk about the demand for microprocessor chips, French fries, compact disc players, children, and criminal activities.

Associated with the concept of demand is the **law of demand,** which can be stated as follows:

> **When the price of a good goes up, people buy less of it, other things being equal. When the price of a good goes down, people buy more of it, other things being equal.**

The law of demand tells us that the quantity demanded of any commodity is inversely related to its price, other things being equal. In an inverse relationship, one variable moves up in value when the other moves down. The law of demand states that a change in price causes a change in the quantity demanded in the *opposite* direction.

Notice that we tacked onto the end of the law of demand the statement "other things being equal." We referred to this in Chapter 1 as the *ceteris paribus* assumption. It means, for example, that when we predict that people will buy fewer DVD (digital videodisc) play-

Market
All of the arrangements that individuals have for exchanging with one another. Thus we can speak of the labor market, the automobile market, and the credit market.

Demand
A schedule of how much of a good or service people will purchase at any price during a specified time period, other things being constant.

Law of demand
The observation that there is a negative, or inverse, relationship between the price of any good or service and the quantity demanded, holding other factors constant.

ers if their price goes up, we are holding constant the price of all other goods in the economy as well as people's incomes. Implicitly, therefore, if we are assuming that no other prices change when we examine the price behavior of DVD players, we are looking at the *relative* price of DVD players.

The law of demand is supported by millions of observations of people's behavior in the marketplace. Theoretically, it can be derived from an economic model based on rational behavior, as was discussed in Chapter 1. Basically, if nothing else changes and the price of a good falls, the lower price induces us to buy more over a certain period of time because we can enjoy additional net gains that were unavailable at the higher price. For the most part, if you examine your own behavior, you will see that it generally follows the law of demand.

Relative Prices Versus Money Prices

Relative price
The price of one commodity divided by the price of another commodity; the number of units of one commodity that must be sacrificed to purchase one unit of another commodity.

Money price
The price that we observe today, expressed in today's dollars. Also called the *absolute, nominal,* or *current price.*

The **relative price** of any commodity is its price in terms of another commodity. The price that you pay in dollars and cents for any good or service at any point in time is called its **money price.** Consider an example that you might hear quite often around parents and grandparents. "When I bought my first new car, it cost only fifteen hundred dollars." The implication, of course, is that the price of cars today is outrageously high because the average new car might cost $19,000. But that is not an accurate comparison. What was the price of the average house during that same year? Perhaps it was only $12,000. By comparison, then, given that houses today average about $145,000, the price of a new car today doesn't sound so far out of line, does it?

The point is that money prices during different time periods don't tell you much. You have to find out relative prices. Consider an example of the price of CDs versus cassettes from last year and this year. In Table 3-1, we show the money price of CDs and cassettes for two years during which they have both gone up. That means that we have to pay out in today's dollars and cents more for CDs and more for cassettes. If we look, though, at the relative prices of CDs and cassettes, we find that last year, CDs were twice as expensive as cassettes, whereas this year they are only $1\frac{3}{4}$ times as expensive. Conversely, if we compare cassettes to CDs, last year they cost only half as much as CDs, but today they cost about 57 percent as much. In the one-year period, while both prices have gone up in money terms, the relative price of CDs has fallen (and, equivalently, the relative price of cassettes has risen).

TABLE 3-1

Money Price Versus Relative Price

The money price of both compact discs (CDs) and cassettes has risen. But the relative price of CDs has fallen (or conversely, the relative price of cassettes has risen).

	Money Price		Relative Price	
	Price Last Year	Price This Year	Price Last Year	Price This Year
CDs	$12	$14	$\frac{\$12}{\$6} = 2.0$	$\frac{\$14}{\$8} = 1.75$
Cassettes	$ 6	$ 8	$\frac{\$6}{\$12} = 0.5$	$\frac{\$8}{\$14} = 0.57$

Exercise 3.1
Visit www.econtoday.com for more about currency exchange rates.

INTERNATIONAL EXAMPLE
Cross-Border Shopping for Pharmaceuticals

Throughout the world, cross-border shopping has increased as individuals respond to changing relative prices. For example, for some Americans, it is worth an 800-mile car ride from northern California to travel to Los Algodones, Mexico. This tiny border town of 5,000 people offers prescription drugs at much lower prices than in the United States. An inhaler for asthmatics priced at $83.70 in the States costs only $15.60 in Mexico. Shoppers may legally purchase other prescription drugs at similarly low prices. So it's not surprising that between 7,000 and 10,000 Americans line up at pharmacy counters in this small Mexican town every day. A few years ago, there were 10 drugstores in Los Algodones; today there are over 30. People who purchase Prozac pay less than half the price in the United States. A bottle of ninety 10-mg tablets of Valium is priced below $10—less than one-tenth the cost north of the border.

Realizing the potential business that exists, Mexican dentists and optometrists have flocked to Los Algodones. They offer discount services as well.

FOR CRITICAL ANALYSIS: The average age of the Americans traveling to Los Algodones is over 60. Why is there a disproportionate share of senior citizens among the American clientele of Los Algodones drugstores? (Hint: What important concept did you learn in Chapter 2?) ●

THINKING CRITICALLY ABOUT THE MEDIA

The Real Price of Stamps

The press is fond of pointing out the rise in the price of a particular good, such as a stamp for first-class mail. In the 1940s, a first-class stamp cost only 3 cents, but by the mid-1990s, it had climbed to 32 cents. That is the absolute price of postage, however. What about the relative price, the price relative to the average of all other prices? The relative price of postage is actually lower today than when it reached its peak in 1975. Many other relative prices have fallen over the years, ranging from gasoline prices to the president's salary. Indeed, relatively speaking, the president's current $200,000-a-year salary is peanuts compared to what President Truman earned in 1947. In relative terms (dollars in 1947), the current president only earns about $30,000, even though in absolute terms, the current president makes more. Remember, everything is relative.

CONCEPTS IN BRIEF

- The law of demand posits an inverse relationship between the quantity demanded of a good and its price, other things being equal.

- The law of demand applies when other things, such as income and the prices of all other goods and services, are held constant.

THE DEMAND SCHEDULE

Let's take a hypothetical demand situation to see how the inverse relationship between the price and the quantity demanded looks (holding other things equal). We will consider the quantity of diskettes demanded *per year*. Without stating the *time dimension,* we could not make sense out of this demand relationship because the numbers would be different if we were talking about the quantity demanded per month or the quantity demanded per decade.

In addition to implicitly or explicitly stating a time dimension for a demand relationship, we are also implicitly referring to *constant-quality* units of the good or service in question. Prices are always expressed in constant-quality units in order to avoid the problem of comparing commodities that are in fact not truly comparable.

In panel (a) of Figure 3-1, we see that if the price were $1 per diskette, 50 of them would be bought each year by our representative individual, but if the price were $5 per diskette,

FIGURE 3-1

The Individual Demand Schedule and the Individual Demand Curve

In panel (a), we show combinations *A* through *E* of the quantities of diskettes demanded, measured in constant-quality units at prices ranging from $5 down to $1 per disk. In panel (b), we plot combinations *A* through *E* on a grid. The result is the individual demand curve for diskettes.

Panel (a)

Combination	Price per Constant-Quality Diskette	Quantity of Constant-Quality Diskettes per Year
A	$5	10
B	4	20
C	3	30
D	2	40
E	1	50

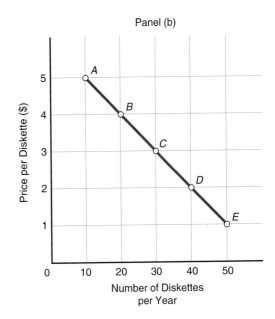

Panel (b)

only 10 diskettes would be bought each year. This reflects the law of demand. Panel (a) is also called simply demand, or a *demand schedule,* because it gives a schedule of alternative quantities demanded per year at different possible prices.

The Demand Curve

Tables expressing relationships between two variables can be represented in graphical terms. To do this, we need only construct a graph that has the price per constant-quality diskette on the vertical axis and the quantity measured in constant-quality diskettes per year on the horizontal axis. All we have to do is take combinations *A* through *E* from panel (a) of Figure 3-1 and plot those points in panel (b). Now we connect the points with a smooth line, and *voilà,* we have a **demand curve.**[1] It is downward-sloping (from left to right) to indicate the inverse relationship between the price of diskettes and the quantity demanded per year. Our presentation of demand schedules and curves applies equally well to all commodities, including toothpicks, hamburgers, textbooks, credit, and labor services. Remember, the demand curve is simply a graphical representation of the law of demand.

Individual Versus Market Demand Curves

The demand schedule shown in panel (a) of Figure 3-1 and the resulting demand curve shown in panel (b) are both given for an individual. As we shall see, the determination of price in the marketplace depends on, among other things, the **market demand** for a particular commodity. The way in which we measure a market demand schedule and derive a

Demand curve

A graphical representation of the demand schedule; a negatively sloped line showing the inverse relationship between the price and the quantity demanded (other things being equal).

Market demand

The demand of all consumers in the marketplace for a particular good or service. The summing at each price of the quantity demanded by each individual.

---

[1]Even though we call them "curves," for the purposes of exposition we often draw straight lines. In many real-world situations, demand and supply curves will in fact be lines that do curve. To connect the points in panel (b) with a line, we assume that for all prices in between the ones shown, the quantities demanded will be found along that line.

market demand curve for diskettes or any other commodity is by summing (at each price) the individual demand for all those in the market. Suppose that the market demand for diskettes consists of only two buyers: buyer 1, for whom we've already shown the demand schedule, and buyer 2, whose demand schedule is displayed in column 3 of panel (a) of Figure 3-2. Column 1 shows the price, and column 2 shows the quantity demanded by buyer 1 at each price. These data are taken directly from Figure 3-1. In column 3, we show the quantity demanded by buyer 2. Column 4 shows the total quantity demanded at each price, which is obtained by simply adding columns 2 and 3. Graphically, in panel (d) of Figure 3-2, we add the demand curves of buyer 1 [panel (b)] and buyer 2 [panel (c)] to derive the market demand curve.

There are, of course, literally tens of millions of potential consumers of diskettes. We'll simply assume that the summation of all of the consumers in the market results in a demand schedule, given in panel (a) of Figure 3-3, and a demand curve, given in panel (b). The quantity demanded is now measured in billions of units per year. Remember, panel (b) in Figure 3-3 shows the market demand curve for the millions of users of diskettes. The "market" demand curve that we derived in Figure 3-2 was undertaken assuming that there were only two buyers in the entire market. That's why the "market" demand curve for two

FIGURE 3-2

The Horizontal Summation of Two Demand Schedules

Panel (a) shows how to sum the demand schedule for one buyer with that of another buyer. In column 2 is the quantity demanded by buyer 1, taken from panel (a) of Figure 3-1. Column 4 is the sum of columns 2 and 3. We plot the demand curve for buyer 1 in panel (b) and the demand curve for buyer 2 in panel (c). When we add those two demand curves horizontally, we get the market demand curve for two buyers, shown in panel (d).

Panel (a)

(1) Price per Diskette	(2) Buyer 1 Quantity Demanded	(3) Buyer 2 Quantity Demanded	(4) = 2 + 3 Combined Quantity Demanded per Year
$5	10	10	20
4	20	20	40
3	30	40	70
2	40	50	90
1	50	60	110

Panel (b)

Buyer 1

Panel (c)

Buyer 2

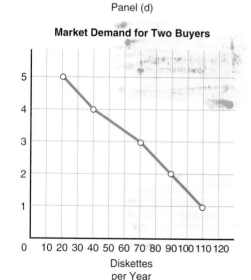

Panel (d)

Market Demand for Two Buyers

FIGURE 3-3

The Market Demand Schedule for Diskettes

In panel (a), we add up the millions of existing demand schedules for diskettes. In panel (b), we plot the quantities from panel (a) on a grid; connecting them produces the market demand curve for diskettes.

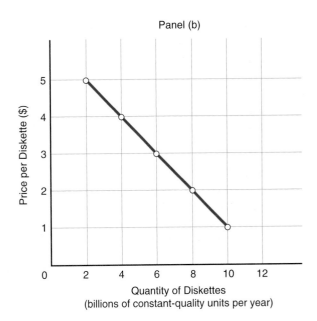

Panel (b)

Panel (a)	
Price per Constant-Quality Diskette	Total Quantity Demanded of Constant-Quality Diskettes per Year (billions)
$5	2
4	4
3	6
2	8
1	10

buyers in panel (d) of Figure 3-2 is not a smooth line, whereas the true market demand curve in panel (b) of Figure 3-3 is a smooth line with no kinks.

Now consider some special aspects of the market demand curve for compact discs.

Exercise 3.2
Visit www.econtoday.com for more about purchasing CDs.

EXAMPLE
Garth Brooks, Used CDs, and the Law of Demand

A few years ago, country singer Garth Brooks tried to prevent his latest album from being sold to any chain or store that also sells used CDs. His argument was that the used-CD market deprived labels and artists of earnings. His announcement came after Wherehouse Entertainment, Inc., a 339-store retailer based in Torrance, California, started selling used CDs side by side with new releases, at half the price. Brooks, along with the distribution arms of Sony, Warner Music, Capitol-EMI, and MCA, was trying to quash the used-CD market. By so doing, it appears that none of these parties understands the law of demand.

Let's say the price of a new CD is $15. The existence of a secondary used-CD market means that to people who choose to resell their CDs for $5, the cost of a new CD is in fact only $10. Because we know that quantity demanded is inversely related to price, we know that more of a new CD will be sold at a price of $10 than of the same CD at a price of $15. Taking only this force into account, eliminating the used-CD market tends to reduce sales of new CDs.

But there is another force at work here, too. Used CDs are substitutes for new CDs. If used CDs are not available, some people who would have purchased them will instead purchase new CDs. If this second effect outweighs the incentive to buy less because of the higher effective price, then Brooks is behaving correctly in trying to suppress the used market.

FOR CRITICAL ANALYSIS: Can you apply this argument to the used-book market, in which both authors and publishers have long argued that used books are "killing them"? ●

SHIFTS IN DEMAND

Assume that the federal government gives every student registered in a college, university, or technical school in the United States a personal computer that uses diskettes. The demand curve presented in panel (b) of Figure 3-3 would no longer be an accurate representation of total market demand for diskettes. What we have to do is shift the curve outward, or to the right, to represent the rise in demand. There will now be an increase in the number of diskettes demanded *at each and every possible price.* The demand curve shown in Figure 3-4 will shift from D_1 to D_2. Take any price, say, \$3 per diskette. Originally, before the federal government giveaway of personal computers, the amount demanded at \$3 was 6 billion diskettes per year. After the government giveaway, however, the new amount demanded at \$3 is 10 billion diskettes per year. What we have seen is a shift in the demand for diskettes.

The shift can also go in the opposite direction. What if colleges uniformly outlawed the use of personal computers by any of their students? Such a regulation would cause a shift inward—to the left—of the demand curve for diskettes. In Figure 3-4, the demand curve would shift to D_3; the amount demanded would now be less at each and every possible price.

The Other Determinants of Demand

The demand curve in panel (b) of Figure 3-3 is drawn with other things held constant, specifically all of the other factors that determine how much will be bought. There are many such determinants. The major other determinants are income; tastes and preferences; the prices of related goods; expectations regarding future prices, future incomes, and future product availability; and population (market size). Let's examine each determinant more closely.

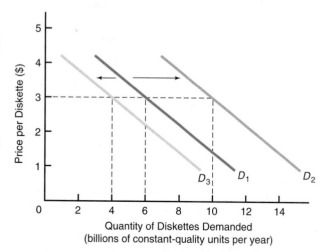

FIGURE 3-4

A Shift in the Demand Curve
If some factor other than price changes, the only way we can show its effect is by moving the entire demand curve, say, from D_1 to D_2. We have assumed in our example that the move was precipitated by the government's giving a free personal computer to every registered college student in America. That meant that at *all* prices, a larger number of diskettes would be demanded than before. Curve D_3 represents reduced demand compared to curve D_1, caused by a law prohibiting computers on campus.

Income. For most goods, an increase in income will lead to an increase in demand. The phrase *increase in demand* always refers to a comparison between two different demand curves. Thus for most goods, an increase in income will lead to a rightward shift in the position of the demand curve from, say, D_1 to D_2 in Figure 3-4. You can avoid confusion about shifts in curves by always relating a rise in demand to a rightward shift in the demand curve and a fall in demand to a leftward shift in the demand curve. Goods for which the demand rises when income rises are called **normal goods.** Most goods, such as shoes, computers, and CDs, are "normal goods." For some goods, however, demand *falls* as income rises. These are called **inferior goods.** Beans might be an example. As households get richer, they tend to spend less and less on beans and more and more on meat. (The terms *normal* and *inferior* are merely part of the economist's terminology; no value judgments are associated with them.)

Remember, a shift to the left in the demand curve represents a fall in demand, and a shift to the right represents a rise, or increase, in demand.

Normal goods
Goods for which demand rises as income rises. Most goods are considered normal.

Inferior goods
Goods for which demand falls as income rises.

Tastes and Preferences. A change in consumer tastes in favor of a good can shift its demand curve outward to the right. When Frisbees® became the rage, the demand curve for them shifted outward to the right; when the rage died out, the demand curve shifted inward to the left. Fashions depend to a large extent on people's tastes and preferences. Economists have little to say about the determination of tastes; that is, they don't have any "good" theories of taste determination or why people buy one brand of product rather than others. Advertisers, however, have various theories that they use to try to make consumers prefer their products over those of competitors.

KIDS ARE TURNING OFF THE TV

CYBERSPACE EXAMPLE

Suppliers of children's television programs are finding out what happens when there is a shift in demand for their commodity. The average number of hours that children aged 2 to 11 spend watching television has dropped by about 20 percent since 1984.

Preteens are spending relatively more time sitting in front of a computer screen. The amount of interactive children's software, particularly on CD-ROM, is staggering today compared to what it was a few years ago. Perhaps more important, computers and TV sets hooked into the Internet now offer preteens thousands of games that can be played, some with other people anywhere in the world. A typical interactive Web game search on the Internet yields literally thousands of games. Preteens also chat with other preteens on the Net and "surf" the World Wide Web.

FOR CRITICAL ANALYSIS: What happened to the demand curve for traditional preteen TV programs? ●

Prices of Related Goods: Substitutes and Complements. Demand schedules are always drawn with the prices of all other commodities held constant. That is to say, when deriving a given demand curve, we assume that only the price of the good under study changes. For example, when we draw the demand curve for butter, we assume that the price of margarine is held constant. When we draw the demand curve for stereo speakers, we assume that the price of stereo amplifiers is held constant. When we refer to *related goods,* we are talking about goods for which demand is interdependent. If a change in the price of one good shifts the demand for another good, those two goods are related. There are two types of related goods: *substitutes* and *complements*. We can define and distinguish between substitutes and complements in terms of how the change in price of one commodity affects the demand for its related commodity.

Butter and margarine are **substitutes.** Let's assume that each originally cost $2 per pound. If the price of butter remains the same and the price of margarine falls from $2 per pound to $1 per pound, people will buy more margarine and less butter. The demand curve for butter will shift inward to the left. If, conversely, the price of margarine rises from $2 per pound to $3 per pound, people will buy more butter and less margarine. The demand curve for butter will shift outward to the right. In other words, an increase in the price of margarine will lead to an increase in the demand for butter, and an increase in the price of butter will lead to an increase in the demand for margarine. For substitutes, a price change in the substitute will cause a change in demand *in the same direction*.

For **complements,** the situation is reversed. Consider stereo speakers and stereo amplifiers. We draw the demand curve for speakers with the price of amplifiers held constant. If the price per constant-quality unit of stereo amplifiers decreases from, say, $500 to $200, that will encourage more people to purchase component stereo systems. They will now buy more speakers, at any given speaker price, than before. The demand curve for speakers will shift outward to the right. If, by contrast, the price of amplifiers increases from $200 to $500, fewer people will purchase component stereo systems. The demand curve for speakers will shift inward to the left. To summarize, a decrease in the price of amplifiers leads to an increase in the demand for speakers. An increase in the price of amplifiers leads to a decrease in the demand for speakers. Thus for complements, a price change in a product will cause a change in demand *in the opposite direction*.

Are new learning technologies complements or substitutes for college instructors? Read on.

Substitutes
Two goods are substitutes when either one can be used for consumption to satisfy a similar want—for example, coffee and tea. The more you buy of one, the less you buy of the other. For substitutes, the change in the price of one causes a shift in demand for the other in the same direction as the price change.

Complements
Two goods are complements if both are used together for consumption or enjoyment—for example, coffee and cream. The more you buy of one, the more you buy of the other. For complements, a change in the price of one causes an opposite shift in the demand for the other.

GETTING YOUR DEGREE VIA THE NET

In this class and in others, you have most likely been exposed to such instructional technologies as films, videos, and interactive CD-ROM learning systems. The future for some of you, or at least the next few generations, may be quite different. All of the instructional technology that your professor provides may be packaged in the form of on-line courses. Many institutions of higher learning are now using the Internet to provide full instruction. It is called *distance learning* or *distributive learning*. And it is worldwide. For example, the University of Michigan, in conjunction with companies in Hong Kong, South Korea, and Europe, offers a global M.B.A. through the Internet. A professor teaches a course "live" via video and uses the software program Lotus Notes, which allows course information to be sent via the Internet. Students submit their homework assignments the same way. Duke University runs the Global Executive M.B.A. program, in which students "attend" CD-ROM video lectures, download additional video and audio materials, and receive interactive study aids, all via the Internet.

Virtually all major college publishers now have projects to develop distance learning via the Internet. In addition, a consortium of over 100 universities has put in place what is called Internet II. Internet II permits full-motion video and virtually instantaneous interactivity for participating universities. The age of fully interactive distance learning with full-motion video is not far off. Certainly, even better technology, as yet undeveloped, will speed up this process.

FOR CRITICAL ANALYSIS: What do you predict will happen to the demand curve for college professors in the future? ●

Expectations. Consumers' expectations regarding future prices, future incomes, and future availability may prompt them to buy more or less of a particular good without a change in its current money price. For example, consumers getting wind of a scheduled 100 percent price increase in diskettes next month may buy more of them today at today's prices. Today's demand curve for diskettes will shift from D_1 to D_2 in Figure 3-4 on page 52. The opposite would occur if a decrease in the price of diskettes were scheduled for next month.

Expectations of a rise in income may cause consumers to want to purchase more of everything today at today's prices. Again, such a change in expectations of higher future income will cause a shift in the demand curve from D_1 to D_2 in Figure 3-4.

Finally, expectations that goods will not be available at any price will induce consumers to stock up now, increasing current demand.

Population. An increase in the population in an economy (holding per capita income constant) often shifts the market demand outward for most products. This is because an increase in population leads to an increase in the number of buyers in the market. Conversely, a reduction in the population will shift most market demand curves inward because of the reduction in the number of buyers in the market.

Changes in Demand Versus Changes in Quantity Demanded

We have made repeated references to demand and to quantity demanded. It is important to realize that there is a difference between a *change in demand* and a *change in quantity demanded.*

Demand refers to a schedule of planned rates of purchase and depends on a great many nonprice determinants. Whenever there is a change in a nonprice determinant, there will be a change in demand—a shift in the entire demand curve to the right or to the left.

A quantity demanded is a specific quantity at a specific price, represented by a single point on a demand curve. When price changes, quantity demanded changes according to the law of demand, and there will be a movement from one point to another along the same demand curve. Look at Figure 3-5 on page 56. At a price of $3 per diskette, 6 billion diskettes per year are demanded. If the price falls to $1, quantity demanded increases to 10 billion per year. This movement occurs because the current market price for the product changes. In Figure 3-5, you can see the arrow pointing down the given demand curve D.

When you think of demand, think of the entire curve itself. Quantity demanded, in contrast, is represented by a single point on the demand curve.

A change or shift in demand causes the *entire* curve to move. The *only* thing that can cause the entire curve to move is a change in a determinant *other than its own price.*

In economic analysis, we cannot emphasize too much the following distinction that must constantly be made:

A change in a good's own price leads to a change in quantity demanded, for any given demand curve, other things held constant. This is a movement *on* the curve.

A change in any other determinant of demand leads to a change in demand. This causes a movement *of* the curve.

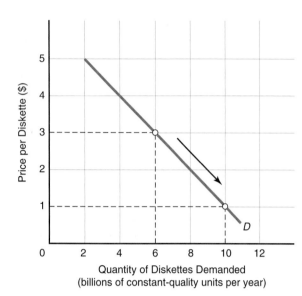

FIGURE 3-5

Movement Along a Given Demand Curve

A change in price changes the quantity of a good demanded. This can be represented as movement along a given demand schedule. If, in our example, the price of diskettes falls from $3 to $1 apiece, the quantity demanded will increase from 6 billion to 10 billion units per year.

CONCEPTS IN BRIEF

- Demand curves are drawn with determinants other than the price of the good held constant. These other determinants are (1) income; (2) tastes and preferences; (3) prices of related goods; (4) expectations about future prices, future incomes, and future availability of goods; and (5) population (number of buyers in the market). If any one of these determinants changes, the demand schedule will shift to the right or to the left.

- A change in demand comes about only because of a change in the other determinants of demand. This change in demand shifts the demand curve to the left or to the right.

- A change in the quantity demanded comes about when there is a change in the price of the good (other things held constant). Such a change in quantity demanded involves a movement along a given demand curve.

THE LAW OF SUPPLY

The other side of the basic model in economics involves the quantities of goods and services that firms will offer for sale to the market. The **supply** of any good or service is the amount that firms will offer for sale under certain conditions during a specified time period. The relationship between price and quantity supplied, called the **law of supply,** can be summarized as follows:

> **At higher prices, a larger quantity will generally be supplied than at lower prices, all other things held constant. At lower prices, a smaller quantity will generally be supplied than at higher prices, all other things held constant.**

There is generally a direct relationship between quantity supplied and price. For supply, as the price rises, the quantity supplied rises; as price falls, the quantity supplied also falls. Producers are normally willing to produce and sell more of their product at a higher price than at a lower price, other things being constant. At $5 per diskette, 3M, Sony, Maxell, Fuji, and other manufacturers would almost certainly be willing to supply a larger quantity than at $1 per unit, assuming, of course, that no other prices in the economy had changed.

Supply
A schedule showing the relationship between price and quantity supplied for a specified period of time, other things being equal.

Law of supply
The observation that the higher the price of a good, the more of that good sellers will make available over a specified time period, other things being equal.

As with the law of demand, millions of instances in the real world have given us confidence in the law of supply. On a theoretical level, the law of supply is based on a model in which producers and sellers seek to make the most gain possible from their activities. For example, as a diskette manufacturer attempts to produce more and more diskettes over the same time period, it will eventually have to hire more workers, pay overtime wages (which are higher), and overutilize its machines. Only if offered a higher price per diskette will the diskette manufacturer be willing to incur these higher costs. That is why the law of supply implies a direct relationship between price and quantity supplied.

THE SUPPLY SCHEDULE

Just as we were able to construct a demand schedule, we can construct a *supply schedule*, which is a table relating prices to the quantity supplied at each price. A supply schedule can also be referred to simply as *supply*. It is a set of planned production rates that depends on the price of the product. We show the individual supply schedule for a hypothetical producer in panel (a) of Figure 3-6. At $1 per diskette, for example, this producer will supply 20 million diskettes per year; at $5, this producer will supply 55 million diskettes per year.

The Supply Curve

Supply curve
The graphical representation of the supply schedule; a line (curve) showing the supply schedule, which generally slopes upward (has a positive slope), other things being equal.

We can convert the supply schedule in panel (a) of Figure 3-6 into a **supply curve,** just as we earlier created a demand curve in Figure 3-1. All we do is take the price-quantity combinations from panel (a) of Figure 3-6 and plot them in panel (b). We have labeled these combinations *F* through *J*. Connecting these points, we obtain an upward-sloping curve that shows the typically direct relationship between price and quantity supplied. Again, we have to remember that we are talking about quantity supplied *per year,* measured in constant-quality units.

FIGURE 3-6

The Individual Producer's Supply Schedule and Supply Curve for Diskettes

Panel (a) shows that at higher prices, a hypothetical supplier will be willing to provide a greater quantity of diskettes. We plot the various price-quantity combinations in panel (a) on the grid in panel (b). When we connect these points, we find the individual supply curve for diskettes. It is positively sloped.

Panel (a)

Combination	Price per Constant-Quality Diskette	Quantity of Diskettes Supplied (millions of constant-quality units per year)
F	$5	55
G	4	40
H	3	35
I	2	25
J	1	20

Panel (b)

The Market Supply Curve

Just as we had to sum the individual demand curves to get the market demand curve, we need to sum the individual producers' supply curves to get the market supply curve. Look at Figure 3-7, in which we horizontally sum two typical diskette manufacturers' supply curves. Supplier 1's data are taken from Figure 3-6; supplier 2 is added. The numbers are presented in panel (a). The graphical representation of supplier 1 is in panel (b), of supplier 2 in panel (c), and of the summation in panel (d). The result, then, is the supply curve for diskettes for suppliers 1 and 2. There are many more suppliers of diskettes, however. The total market supply schedule and total market demand curve for diskettes are represented in Figure 3-8, with the curve in panel (b) obtained by adding all of the supply curves such as those shown in panels (b) and (c) of Figure 3-7. Notice the difference between the

Panel (a)

(1) Price per Diskette	(2) Supplier 1 Quantity Supplied (millions)	(3) Supplier 2 Quantity Supplied (millions)	(4) = (2) + (3) Combined Quantity Supplied per Year (millions)
$5	55	35	90
4	40	30	70
3	35	20	55
2	25	15	40
1	20	10	30

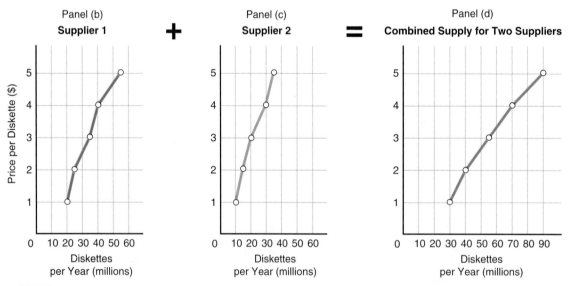

FIGURE 3-7

Horizontal Summation of Supply Curves
In panel (a), we show the data for two individual suppliers of diskettes. Adding how much each is willing to supply at different prices, we come up with the combined quantities supplied in column 4. When we plot the values in columns 2 and 3 on grids in panels (b) and (c) and add them horizontally, we obtain the combined supply curve for the two suppliers in question, shown in panel (d).

FIGURE 3-8

The Market Supply Schedule and the Market Supply Curve for Diskettes

In panel (a), we show the summation of all the individual producers' supply schedules; in panel (b), we graph the resulting supply curve. It represents the market supply curve for diskettes and is upward-sloping.

Panel (a)

Price per Constant-Quality Diskette	Quantity of Diskettes Supplied (billions of constant-quality units per year)
$5	10
4	8
3	6
2	4
1	2

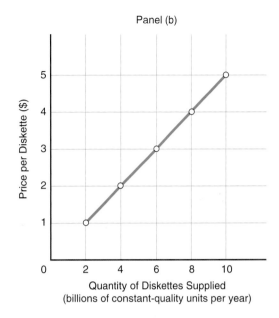

Panel (b)

market supply curve with only two suppliers in Figure 3-7 and the one with a large number of suppliers—the entire true market—in panel (b) of Figure 3-8. There are no kinks in the true total market supply curve because there are so many suppliers.

Notice what happens at the market level when price changes. If the price is $3, the quantity supplied is 6 billion diskettes. If the price goes up to $4, the quantity supplied increases to 8 billion per year. If the price falls to $2, the quantity supplied decreases to 4 billion diskettes per year. Changes in quantity supplied are represented by movements along the supply curve in panel (b) of Figure 3-8.

CONCEPTS IN BRIEF

- There is normally a direct, or positive, relationship between price and quantity of a good supplied, other things held constant.

- The supply curve normally shows a direct relationship between price and quantity supplied. The market supply curve is obtained by horizontally adding individual supply curves in the market.

SHIFTS IN SUPPLY

When we looked at demand, we found out that any change in anything relevant besides the price of the good or service caused the demand curve to shift inward or outward. The same is true for the supply curve. If something relevant changes besides the price of the product or service being supplied, we will see the entire supply curve shift.

Consider an example. A new method of putting magnetic material on diskettes has been invented. It reduces the cost of producing a diskette by 50 percent. In this situation, diskette producers will supply more product at *all* prices because their cost of so doing has fallen dramatically. Competition among diskette manufacturers to produce more at each and

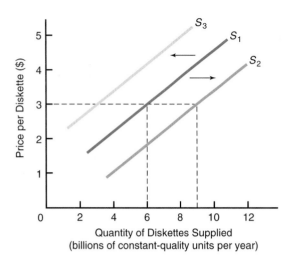

FIGURE 3-9

A Shift in the Supply Schedule
If the cost of producing diskettes were to fall dramatically, the supply schedule would shift rightward from S_1 to S_2 such that at all prices, a larger quantity would be forthcoming from suppliers. Conversely, if the cost of production rose, the supply curve would shift leftward to S_3.

every price will shift the supply schedule of diskettes outward to the right from S_1 to S_2 in Figure 3-9. At a price of $3, the quantity supplied was originally 6 billion diskettes per year, but now the quantity supplied (after the reduction in the costs of production) at $3 a diskette will be 9 billion diskettes a year. (This is similar to what has happened to the supply curve of personal computers and fax machines in recent years as computer memory chip prices have fallen.)

Consider the opposite case. If the cost of the magnetic material needed for making diskettes doubles, the supply curve in Figure 3-9 will shift from S_1 to S_3. At each and every price, the number of diskettes supplied will fall due to the increase in the price of raw materials.

The Other Determinants of Supply

When supply curves are drawn, only the price of the good in question changes, and it is assumed that other things remain constant. The other things assumed constant are the costs of resources (inputs) used to produce the product, technology and productivity, taxes and subsidies, producers' price expectations, and the number of firms in the industry. These are the major nonprice determinants of supply. If *any* of them changes, there will be a shift in the supply curve.

Cost of Inputs Used to Produce the Product. If one or more input prices fall, the supply curve will shift outward to the right; that is, more will be supplied at each and every price. The opposite will be true if one or more inputs become more expensive. For example, when we draw the supply curve of new cars, we are holding the cost of steel (and other inputs) constant. When we draw the supply curve of blue jeans, we are holding the cost of cotton fabric fixed.

Technology and Productivity. Supply curves are drawn by assuming a given technology, or "state of the art." When the available production techniques change, the supply curve will shift. For example, when a better production technique for diskettes becomes available, the supply curve will shift to the right. A larger quantity will be forthcoming at each and every price because the cost of production is lower.

INTERNATIONAL EXAMPLE
Changing Technology and the Supply of Salmon

One example of how changes in technology can shift the supply curve out to the right involves salmon. In 1980, the total worldwide catch of salmon (wild and farmed) was just over 10,000 metric tons. Since 1980, new technology has been developed in what is called aquaculture, or the farm-raising of fish and related products. Aquaculture currently generates over $30 billion in worldwide revenues and is one of the world's fastest-growing industries. Farmed salmon from Chile, Scotland, Canada, Norway, and Iceland now exceeds 240,000 metric tons a year. Thus it is not surprising that despite a depletion of many wild salmon fishing grounds and a worldwide increase in the consumer demand for salmon, the retail price of salmon today (corrected for inflation) is about 50 percent of what it was in 1980.

FOR CRITICAL ANALYSIS: What might slow down the growth in salmon farming throughout the world? •

Taxes and Subsidies. Certain taxes, such as a per-unit tax, are effectively an addition to production costs and therefore reduce the supply. If the supply curve were S_1 in Figure 3-9, a per-unit tax increase would shift it to S_3. A **subsidy** would do the opposite; it would shift the curve to S_2. Every producer would get a "gift" from the government of a few cents for each unit produced.

Subsidy
A negative tax; a payment to a producer from the government, usually in the form of a cash grant.

Price Expectations. A change in the expectation of a future relative price of a product can affect a producer's current willingness to supply, just as price expectations affect a consumer's current willingness to purchase. For example, diskette suppliers may withhold from the market part of their current supply if they anticipate higher prices in the future. The current amount supplied at each and every price will decrease.

Number of Firms in the Industry. In the short run, when firms can only change the number of employees they use, we hold the number of firms in the industry constant. In the long run, the number of firms (or the size of some existing firms) may change. If the number of firms increases, the supply curve will shift outward to the right. If the number of firms decreases, it will shift inward to the left.

Changes in Supply Versus Changes in Quantity Supplied

We cannot overstress the importance of distinguishing between a movement along the supply curve—which occurs only when the price changes for a given supply curve—and a shift in the supply curve—which occurs only with changes in other nonprice factors. A change in price always brings about a change in quantity supplied along a given supply curve. We move to a different coordinate on the existing supply curve. This is specifically called a *change in quantity supplied.* When price changes, quantity supplied changes, and there will be a movement from one point to another along the same supply curve.

When you think of *supply,* think of the entire curve itself. Quantity supplied is represented by a single point on the supply curve.

A change or shift in supply causes the entire curve to move. The *only* thing that can cause the entire curve to move is a change in a determinant *other than price.*

Consequently,

> **A change in the price leads to a change in the quantity supplied, other things being constant. This is a movement *on* the curve.**

> **A change in any other determinant of supply leads to a change in supply. This causes a movement *of* the curve.**

CONCEPTS IN BRIEF

- If the price changes, we *move along* a curve—there is a change in quantity demanded or supplied. If some other determinant changes, we *shift* a curve—there is a change in demand or supply.

- The supply curve is drawn with other things held constant. If other determinants of supply change, the supply curve will shift. The other major determinants are (1) input costs, (2) technology and productivity, (3) taxes and subsidies, (4) expectations of future relative prices, and (5) the number of firms in the industry.

PUTTING DEMAND AND SUPPLY TOGETHER

In the sections on supply and demand, we tried to confine each discussion to supply or demand only. But you have probably already realized that we can't view the world just from the supply side or just from the demand side. There is an interaction between the two. In this section, we will discuss how they interact and how that interaction determines the prices that prevail in our economy. Understanding how demand and supply interact is essential to understanding how prices are determined in our economy and other economies in which the forces of supply and demand are allowed to work.

Let's first combine the demand and supply schedules and then combine the curves.

Demand and Supply Schedules Combined

Let's place panel (a) from Figure 3-3 (the market demand schedule) and panel (a) from Figure 3-8 (the market supply schedule) together in panel (a) of Figure 3-10. Column 1 shows the price; column 2, the quantity supplied per year at any given price; and column 3, the quantity demanded. Column 4 is merely the difference between columns 2 and 3, or the difference between the quantity supplied and the quantity demanded. In column 5, we label those differences as either excess quantity supplied (a surplus) or excess quantity demanded (a shortage). For example, at a price of $1, only 2 billion diskettes would be supplied, but the quantity demanded would be 10 billion. The difference would be −8 billion, which we label excess quantity demanded (a shortage). At the other end of the scale, a price of $5 per diskette would elicit 10 billion in quantity supplied, but quantity demanded would drop to 2 billion, leaving a difference of +8 billion units, which we call excess quantity supplied (a surplus).

Panel (a)

(1) Price per Constant-Quality Diskette	(2) Quantity Supplied (diskettes per year)	(3) Quantity Demanded (diskettes per year)	(4) Difference (2) − (3) (diskettes per year)	(5) Condition
$5	10 billion	2 billion	8 billion	Excess quantity supplied (surplus)
4	8 billion	4 billion	4 billion	Excess quantity supplied (surplus)
3	6 billion	6 billion	0	Market clearing price—equilibrium (no surplus, no shortage)
2	4 billion	8 billion	−4 billion	Excess quantity demanded (shortage)
1	2 billion	10 billion	−8 billion	Excess quantity demanded (shortage)

Panel (b)

FIGURE 3-10

Putting Demand and Supply Together

In panel (a), we see that at the price of $3, the quantity supplied and the quantity demanded are equal, resulting in neither an excess in the quantity demanded nor an excess in the quantity supplied. We call this price the equilibrium, or market clearing, price. In panel (b), the intersection of the supply and demand curves is at *E,* at a price of $3 per constant-quality diskette and a quantity of 6 billion per year. At point *E,* there is neither an excess in the quantity demanded nor an excess in the quantity supplied. At a price of $1, the quantity supplied will be only 2 billion disks per year, but the quantity demanded will be 10 billion. The difference is excess quantity demanded at a price of $1. The price will rise, so we will move from point *A* up the supply curve and point *B* up the demand curve to point *E.* At the other extreme, $5 elicits a quantity supplied of 10 billion but a quantity demanded of only 2 billion. The difference is excess quantity supplied at a price of $5. The price will fall, so we will move down the demand curve and the supply curve to the equilibrium price, $3 per diskette.

Now, do you notice something special about the price of $3? At that price, both the quantity supplied and the quantity demanded per year are 6 billion diskettes. The difference then is zero. There is neither excess quantity demanded (shortage) nor excess quantity supplied (surplus). Hence the price of $3 is very special. It is called the **market clearing price**—it clears the market of all excess supply or excess demand. There are no willing consumers who want to pay $3 per diskette but are turned away by sellers, and there are no willing suppliers who want to sell diskettes at $3 who cannot sell all they want at that price. Another term for the market clearing price is the **equilibrium price,** the price at which there is no tendency for change. Consumers are able to get all they want at that price, and suppliers are able to sell the amount that they want at that price.

Market clearing, or **equilibrium, price**
The price that clears the market, at which quantity demanded equals quantity supplied; the price where the demand curve intersects the supply curve.

Equilibrium

We can define **equilibrium** in general as a point from which there tends to be no movement unless demand or supply changes. Any movement away from this point will set into motion certain forces that will cause movement back to it. Therefore, equilibrium is a stable point. Any point that is not at equilibrium is unstable and cannot be maintained.

Equilibrium
The situation when quantity supplied equals quantity demanded at a particular price.

The equilibrium point occurs where the supply and demand curves intersect. The equilibrium price is given on the vertical axis directly to the left of where the supply and demand curves cross. The equilibrium quantity demanded and supplied is given on the horizontal axis directly underneath the intersection of the demand and supply curves. Equilibrium can change whenever there is a *shock.*

A shock to the supply-and-demand system can be represented by a shift in the supply curve, a shift in the demand curve, or a shift in both curves. Any shock to the system will result in a new set of supply-and-demand relationships and a new equilibrium; forces will come into play to move the system from the old price-quantity equilibrium (now a disequilibrium situation) to the new equilibrium, where the new demand and supply curves intersect.

Panel (b) in Figure 3-3 and panel (b) in Figure 3-8 are combined as panel (b) in Figure 3-10 on page 63. The only difference now is that the horizontal axis measures both the quantity supplied and the quantity demanded per year. Everything else is the same. The demand curve is labeled D, the supply curve S. We have labeled the intersection of the supply curve with the demand curve as point E, for equilibrium. That corresponds to a market clearing price of $3, at which both the quantity supplied and the quantity demanded are 6 billion units per year. There is neither excess quantity supplied nor excess quantity demanded. Point E, the equilibrium point, always occurs at the intersection of the supply and demand curves. This is the price toward which the market price will automatically tend to gravitate.

EXAMPLE
Dinosaurs and the Price of Amber

When there is a shift in either supply or demand, there is a movement toward equilibrium that usually involves a change in the equilibrium quantity and the equilibrium price. A good example is found in the market for amber, a semiprecious stone that often preserves fossil plants and animals from millions of years ago. In Figure 3-11, you see the original supply and demand curves for amber, labeled S and D_1. The equilibrium price is P_1, and the equilibrium quantity is Q_1. Then along came a book, and later a movie, called *Jurassic Park,* written by Michael Crichton. In the story, million-year-old mosquitoes that had feasted on dinosaurs were trapped in amber. Scientists were able to clone

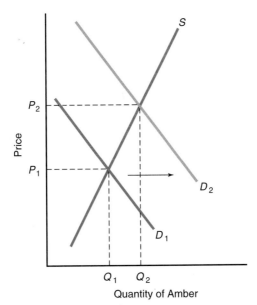

FIGURE 3-11
The Changing Price of Amber
With stable supply, a shift in the demand curve for amber from D_1 to D_2 will cause the equilibrium price of amber to rise from P_1 to P_2 and the equilibrium quantity to increase from Q_1 to Q_2.

various dinosaurs by removing the DNA from the dinosaur blood inside the mosquitoes. (The technique remains in the realm of science fiction.) The success of the book and the movie in the early 1990s made amber suddenly popular; in economic terms, the demand curve for amber shifted outward to D_2. Very quickly, the price rose to P_2 and the equilibrium quantity increased to Q_2.

FOR CRITICAL ANALYSIS: The sequel to Jurassic Park *came out in 1997. Assuming that there is no* Jurassic Park III, *what would you expect to happen to the demand curve for amber over the next few years?* ●

Shortages

The demand and supply curves depicted in Figure 3-10 represent a situation of equilibrium. But a non-market-clearing, or disequilibrium, price will put into play forces that cause the price to change toward the market clearing price at which equilibrium will again be sustained. Look again at panel (b) in Figure 3-10 on page 63. Suppose that instead of being at the market clearing price of $3 per diskette, for some reason the market price is $1 per diskette. At this price, the quantity demanded exceeds the quantity supplied, the former being 10 billion diskettes per year and the latter, 2 billion per year. We have a situation of excess quantity demanded at the price of $1. This is usually called a **shortage.** Consumers of diskettes would find that they could not buy all that they wished at $1 apiece. But forces will cause the price to rise: Competing consumers will bid up the price, and suppliers will raise the price and increase output, whether explicitly or implicitly. (Remember, some buyers would pay $5 or more rather than do without diskettes. They do not want to be left out.) We would move from points *A* and *B* toward point *E*. The process would stop when the price again reached $3 per diskette.

At this point, it is important to recall a distinction made in Chapter 2:

Shortages and scarcity are not the same thing.

Shortage
A situation in which quantity demanded is greater than quantity supplied at a price below the market clearing price.

A shortage is a situation in which the quantity demanded exceeds the quantity supplied at a price *below* the market clearing price. Our definition of scarcity was much more general and all-encompassing: a situation in which the resources available for producing output are insufficient to satisfy all wants. Any choice necessarily costs an opportunity, and the opportunity is lost. Hence we will always live in a world of scarcity because we must constantly make choices, but we do not necessarily have to live in a world of shortages.

Surpluses

Now let's repeat the experiment with the market price at $5 per diskette rather than at the market clearing price of $3. Clearly, the quantity supplied will exceed the quantity demanded at that price. The result will be an excess quantity supplied at $5 per unit. This excess quantity supplied is often called a **surplus.** Given the curves in panel (b) in Figure 3-10, however, there will be forces pushing the price back down toward $3 per diskette: Competing suppliers will attempt to reduce their inventories by cutting prices and reducing output, and consumers will offer to purchase more at lower prices. Suppliers will want to reduce inventories, which will be above their optimal level; that is, there will be an excess over what each seller believes to be the most profitable stock of diskettes. After all, inventories are costly to hold. But consumers may find out about such excess inventories and see the possibility of obtaining increased quantities of diskettes at a decreased price. It behooves consumers to attempt to obtain a good at a lower price, and they will therefore try to do so. If the two forces of supply and demand are unrestricted, they will bring the price back to $3 per diskette.

Shortages and surpluses are resolved in unfettered markets—markets in which price changes are free to occur. The forces that resolve them are those of competition: In the case of shortages, consumers competing for a limited quantity supplied drive up the price; in the case of surpluses, sellers compete for the limited quantity demanded, thus driving prices down to equilibrium. The equilibrium price is the only stable price, and all (unrestricted) market prices tend to gravitate toward it.

What happens when the price is set below the equilibrium price? Here come the scalpers.

Surplus
A situation in which quantity supplied is greater than quantity demanded at a price above the market clearing price.

POLICY EXAMPLE
Should Shortages in the Ticket Market Be Solved by Scalpers?

If you have ever tried to get tickets to a playoff game in sports, a popular Broadway play, or a superstar's rock concert, you know about "shortages." The standard ticket situation for a Super Bowl is shown in Figure 3-12. At the face-value price of Super Bowl tickets (P_1), the quantity demanded (Q_2) greatly exceeds the quantity supplied (Q_1). Because shortages last only so long as prices and quantities do not change, markets tend to exhibit a movement out of this disequilibrium toward equilibrium. Obviously, the quantity of Super Bowl tickets cannot change, but the price can go as high as P_2.

Enter the scalper. This colorful term is used because when you purchase a ticket that is being resold at a price that is higher than face value, the seller is skimming an extra profit off the top. Every time an event sells out, ticket prices by definition have been lower than

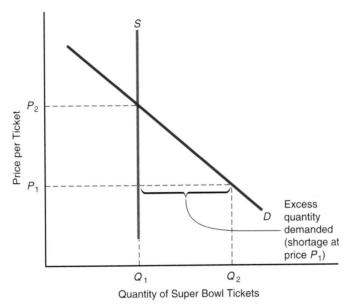

Shortages of Super Bowl Tickets

The quantity of tickets for any one Super Bowl is fixed at Q_1. At the price per ticket of P_1, the quantity demanded is Q_2, which is greater than Q_1. Consequently, there is an excess quantity demanded at the below–market clearing price. Prices can go as high as P_2 in the scalpers' market.

market clearing prices. Sellouts indicate that the event is very popular and that there may be people without tickets willing to buy high-priced tickets because they place a greater value on the entertainment event than the actual face value of the ticket. Without scalpers, those individuals would not be able to attend the event. In the case of the Super Bowl, various forms of scalping occur nationwide. Tickets for a seat on the 50-yard line have been sold for more than $2,000 a piece. In front of every Super Bowl arena, you can find ticket scalpers hawking their wares.

In most states, scalping is illegal. In Pennsylvania, convicted scalpers are either fined $5,000 or sentenced to two years behind bars. For an economist, such legislation seems strange. As one New York ticket broker said, "I look at scalping like working as a stockbroker, buying low and selling high. If people are willing to pay me the money, what kind of problem is that?"

FOR CRITICAL ANALYSIS: *What happens to ticket scalpers who are still holding tickets after an event has started?* ●

CONCEPTS IN BRIEF

- The market clearing price occurs at the intersection of the market demand curve and the market supply curve. It is also called the equilibrium price, the price from which there is no tendency to change unless there is a change in demand or supply.

- Whenever the price is greater than the equilibrium price, there is an excess quantity supplied (a surplus).

- Whenever the price is less than the equilibrium price, there is an excess quantity demanded (a shortage).

This is the home page for one of many Internet-based auction companies. How do they affect the marketplace?

On-Line Auctions: Reaching the Equilibrium Price on the Web

CONCEPTS APPLIED:

DEMAND AND SUPPLY, SHIFTS IN DEMAND AND SUPPLY, EQUILIBRIUM

Visit www.econtoday.com for an Internet Activity that expands your understanding of these concepts.

In the absence of constraints, the equilibrium price of just about anything tends toward where the demand curve intersects the supply curve. Notice the word *tends*. As with everything, reaching an equilibrium price takes time. A shift in demand or supply normally does not immediately result in a change in price to its equilibrium level. Where we see the equilibrium price determined rapidly, though, is at auctions. Certain commodities in certain quantities are offered for sale at auctions, typically to the highest bidder. The equilibrium price becomes obvious when the auctioneer pounds the gavel and says something like "Going once, going twice, gone."

Enter the Internet Auction

Nowadays, just about anything in the world can be auctioned off on the Internet. Indeed, one of the fastest-growing activities on the Internet is the on-line auction. For example, the Web-based auctioneer company OnSale, Inc., of Palo Alto, California, recently cut a deal with America Online (AOL) to be featured on its "shopping channel." That gave OnSale instant access to AOL's 12 million members.

OnSale started out as an on-line auction company for computer equipment. Visitors to OnSale's Web site can still bid on a wide range of new and refurbished computer equipment that OnSale buys from manufacturers. OnSale lists items with minimum prices. Visitors to the site post their offers over a short time period, usually two days. The highest bidder gets the product. Today OnSale also auctions off microwave ovens, Omaha steaks, and beachfront rentals, among a great many other commodities.

As of 1998, there were over 200 on-line auctions. Auction seekers can gain access by using BidFind (**www.vsn.net/af/**). This is a search engine that allows you to type in the item you would like to purchase.

BidFind will display for you a list of matches on the product or service and the names of on-line auctioneers who have it for sale. There are "hot links" (instant transfers) directly to those sites.

On-line Auctions Are Different, Though

Notice the difference between on-line auctions and traditional auctions. At a traditional auction, you have to go or send a representative who is physically present (although for fine art auctions, you can sometimes do your bidding over the phone). The auction process for each item takes only a few minutes. On the Internet, in contrast, auctions may last from a day to a week or longer.

Reverse, or Dutch, Auctions

Rather than the normal "selling to the highest bidder" type of auction, there are also so-called reverse, or Dutch, auctions on the Internet. Klik-Klok OnLine Dutch Auction (**www.klik-klok.com**) reverses the normal bidding process. Klik-Klok's gardening tools and jewelry are offered with a clock ticking and prices dropping every few seconds. Registered users who click their computer's mouse get the product at the currently displayed price.

A very successful reverse auction system has been used by Internet Liquidators, which is co-owned by America Online. Every five minutes, the prices of offered goods decline. Bidders time their move to get the best price before the goods they wish to buy sell out.

Buying and Selling Electronics Parts over the Internet

One of the fastest-growing on-line auction markets involves electronics parts. Electronics manufacturing managers routinely end up with too few or too many parts. They do not want to disclose anything about their business to rivals, however. Therefore, they need an anonymous way to auction parts. Today they use FastParts, which started in 1996. About 300 electronics firms trade their excess parts at an Internet auction that FastParts holds three times a week. Prices typically average about two-thirds of the original manufacturing cost of the parts.

Getting a Cheap Round Trip to Anywhere

Airlines often find themselves with excess inventory, just as electronics companies do. Many airlines have turned to the Internet to auction off their excess seats. They offer silent auctions and also last-minute fare deals handled via e-mail.

American Airlines was one of the first companies to start electronic auctions on a regular basis a few years ago. American Airlines usually runs its auctions for 24 to 48 hours. The company periodically posts the highest bid during each round of bidding. American also sends last-minute deals by e-mail each Wednesday, offering discounted travel on the following weekend. Table 3-2 highlights some of the auction deals that American has provided.

One airline, Cathay Pacific, has even held on-line auctions for use with its frequent-flier mileage. A typical first-class round-trip ticket normally requires 125,000 frequent-flier miles, but some lucky on-line bidders got them for 60,000 frequent-flier miles. When Cathay Pacific inaugurated its first New York–Hong Kong flights, it held an on-line auction for all 387 seats on one of its flights.

TABLE 3-2

Buying a Cheap Round-Trip Ticket on the Internet
Here you see the prices of a pair of first-class tickets obtained via different American Airlines Internet auctions compared with the estimated value of the tickets.

Route	List Price	Internet Price
Amarillo, Tex., to Seattle	$3,496	$ 895
Carlsbad, Calif., to Washington, D.C.	$4,176	$ 800
Los Angeles to New York	$2,916	$1,020
San Antonio to Miami	$2,976	$ 865
Washington, D.C., to San Diego	$4,176	$ 680

Source: American Airlines.

The Future of On-Line Auctioning

The future of on-line auctions is limited. Not everyone wants to purchase overstocked, discontinued, and reconditioned items. Even for airline flights and holiday offers, many on-line auctions attract no bids at all. Nonetheless, some people enjoy the "thrill of the chase" that an auction provides. On-line auctions have found their niche.

FOR CRITICAL ANALYSIS
1. Increased on-line security in the form of better encryption systems is being developed. How will this affect the use of on-line auctions?
2. What goods or services might never be sold on-line? Why not?

CHAPTER SUMMARY

1. The law of demand says that at higher prices, individuals will purchase less of a commodity and at lower prices, they will purchase more, other things being equal.
2. Relative prices must be distinguished from absolute, or money, prices. During periods of rising prices, almost all prices go up, but some rise faster than others.

3. All references to the laws of supply and demand refer to constant-quality units of a commodity. A time period for the analysis must also be specified.
4. The demand schedule shows the relationship between various possible prices and their respective quantities purchased per unit time period. Graphically, the demand schedule is a demand curve and is downward-sloping.

5. The determinants of demand other than price are (a) income, (b) tastes and preferences, (c) the prices of related goods, (d) expectations, and (e) population, or market, size. Whenever any of these determinants of demand changes, the demand curve shifts.

6. The supply curve is generally upward-sloping such that at higher prices, more will be forthcoming than at lower prices. At higher prices, suppliers are willing to incur the increasing costs of higher rates of production.

7. The determinants of supply other than price are (a) input costs, (b) technology and productivity, (c) taxes and subsidies, (d) price expectations, and (e) entry and exit of firms.

8. A movement along a demand or supply curve is not the same thing as a shift in the curve. A change in price causes movement along the curve. A change in any other determinant of supply or demand shifts the entire curve.

9. The demand and supply curves intersect at the equilibrium point, marking the market clearing price, where quantity demanded just equals quantity supplied. At that point, the plans of buyers and sellers mesh exactly.

10. When the price of a good is greater than its market clearing price, an excess quantity is supplied at that price; it is called a surplus. When the price is below the market clearing price, an excess quantity is demanded at that price; it is called a shortage.

DISCUSSION OF PREVIEW QUESTIONS

1. Why are relative prices important in understanding the law of demand?

People respond to changes in relative prices rather than absolute prices. If the price of CDs rises by 50 percent next year, while at the same time the prices of everything else, including your wages, also increase by 50 percent, the relative price of CDs has not changed. If nothing else has changed in your life, your normal quantity demanded of CDs will remain about the same. In a world of generally rising prices (inflation), you have to compare the price of one good with the average of all other goods in order to decide whether the relative price of that one good has gone up, gone down, or stayed the same.

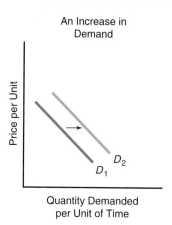

An Increase in Demand

2. How can we distinguish between a change in *demand* and a change in *quantity demanded*?

Use the accompanying graphs to aid you. Because demand is a curve, a change in demand is equivalent to a *shift* in the demand curve. Changes in demand result from changes in the other determinants of demand, such as income, tastes and preferences, expectations, prices of related goods, and population. A change in quantity demanded, given demand, is a movement along a demand curve and results only from a change in the price of the commodity in question.

An Increase in Quantity Demanded

3. Why is there generally a direct relationship be-tween price and quantity supplied (other things being equal)?

In general, businesses experience increasing *extra* costs as they expand output in the short run. This means that additional units of output, which may be quite similar in physical attributes to initial units of output, actually cost the firm more to produce. Consequently, firms often require a higher and higher price (as an incentive) in order to produce more in the short run; this "incentive" effect implies that higher prices, other things being constant, lead to increases in quantity supplied.

4. Why will the market clearing price occur at the intersection of the supply and demand curves rather than at a higher or lower price?

Consider the accompanying graph. To demonstrate that the equilibrium price will be at P_e, we can eliminate all other prices as possibilities. Consider a price above P_e, $8 per unit. By inspection of the graph, we can see that at that price, the quantity supplied exceeds the quantity demanded for this product ($B > A$). Clearly, sellers cannot sell all they wish at $8, and they therefore find it profitable to lower price and decrease output. In fact, this surplus situation exists at *all* prices above P_e. Sellers, competing for sales, will reduce prices if a surplus exists.

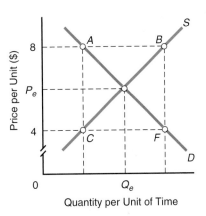

Quantity per Unit of Time

Consider a price of $4 per unit, where the quantity demanded exceeds the quantity supplied ($F > C$); a shortage of this commodity exists at a price of $4 per unit. Buyers will not be able to get all they want at that relatively low price. Because buyers are competing for this good, buyers who are willing to give up more of other goods in order to get this one will offer higher and higher prices. By doing so, they eliminate buyers who are not willing to give up more of other goods. An increase in price encourages sellers to produce and sell more. A shortage exists at *any* price below P_e, and therefore price will rise if it is below P_e.

At P_e, the quantity supplied equals the quantity demanded, Q_e, and both buyers and sellers are able to realize their intentions. Because neither group has an incentive to change its behavior, equilibrium exists at P_e.

PROBLEMS

(Answers to the odd-numbered problems appear at the back of the book.)

3-1. Construct a demand curve and a supply curve for skateboards, based on the data provided in the following tables.

Price per Skateboard	Quantity Demanded per Year
$75	3 million
50	6 million
35	9 million
25	12 million
15	15 million
10	18 million

Price per Skateboard	Quantity Supplied per Year
$75	18 million
50	15 million
35	12 million
25	9 million
15	6 million
10	3 million

What is the equilibrium price? What is the equilibrium quantity at that price?

3-2. "Drugs are obviously complementary to physicians' services." Is this statement always correct?

3-3. Five factors, other than price, that affect the demand for a good were discussed in this chapter. Place each of the following events in its proper category, and state how it would shift the demand curve in parentheses.

　a. New information is disclosed that large doses of vitamin C prevent common colds. (Demand for vitamin C)

　b. A drop in the price of educational interactive CD-ROMs occurs. (Demand for teachers)

　c. A fall in the price of pretzels occurs. (Demand for beer)

3-4. Examine the following table, and then answer the questions.

	Price per Unit Last Year	Price per Unit Today
Heating oil	$1.00	$2.00
Natural gas	.80	3.20

What has happened to the absolute price of heating oil? Of natural gas? What has happened to the price of heating oil relative to the price of natural gas? What has happened to the relative price of heating oil? Will consumers, through time, change their relative purchases? If so, how?

3-5. Suppose that the demand for oranges remains constant but a frost occurs in Florida that could potentially destroy one-third of the orange crop. What will happen to the equilibrium price and quantity for Florida oranges?

3-6. "The demand has increased so much in response to our offering of a $75 rebate that our inventory of portable laptop computers is now running very low." What is wrong with this assertion?

3-7. Analyze the following statement: "Federal farm price supports can never achieve their goals because the above-equilibrium price floors that are established by Congress and the Department of Agriculture invariably create surpluses (quantities supplied in excess of quantities demanded), which in turn drive the price right back down toward equilibrium."

3-8. Suppose that an island economy exists in which there is no money. Suppose further that every Sunday morning, at a certain location, hog farmers and cattle ranchers gather to exchange live pigs for cows. Is this a market, and if so, what do the supply and demand diagrams use as a price? Can you imagine any problems arising at the price at which cows and pigs are exchanged?

3-9. Here is a supply and demand schedule for rain in an Amazon jungle settlement where cloud seeding or other scientific techniques can be used to coax rainfall from the skies.

Price (cruzeiros per yearly centimeter of rain)	Quantity Supplied (centimeters of rain per year)	Quantity Demanded (centimeters of rain per year)
0	200	150
10	225	125
20	250	100
30	275	75
40	300	50
50	325	25
60	350	0
70	375	0
80	400	0

What are the equilibrium price and the equilibrium quantity? Explain.

COMPUTER-ASSISTED INSTRUCTION

By examining the consequence of a specific price change, we examine the roles of the substitution effect and the income effect in producing the law of demand.

Complete problem and answer appear on disk.

CHAPTER 4

EXTENSIONS OF DEMAND AND SUPPLY ANALYSIS

They are big, they are fat, and they are smelly. But for the people who love them—who call themselves *aficionados*—they are heavenly. The commodity in question is the handrolled Cuban cigar. Recently, the prices of Cuban cigars in the United States have increased dramatically to double or triple what they were a few years ago. Even if you do not like cigar smoke, you might wonder why the prices of Cuban cigars could increase so dramatically. To understand why, you need to understand some extensions of supply and demand analysis, which are presented in this chapter. Many of them have to do with government restrictions on the market.

PREVIEW QUESTIONS

1. Does an increase in demand always lead to a rise in price?
2. Can there ever be shortages in a market with no restrictions?
3. How are goods rationed?
4. When would you expect to encounter black markets?

Did You Know That . . . according to the U.S. Customs Service, the second most serious smuggling problem along the Mexican border, just behind drugs, involves the refrigerant Freon? Selling Freon is more profitable than dealing in cocaine, and illegal Freon smuggling is a bigger business than gunrunning. Freon is used in many air conditioners in cars and homes. Its use is already illegal in the United States, but residents of developing countries may legally use it until the year 2005. When an older U.S. air conditioner needs fixing, it is often cheaper to pay a relatively high price for illegally smuggled Freon than to modify the unit to use a replacement coolant. You can analyze illegal markets, such as the one for Freon, using the supply and demand analysis you learned in Chapter 3. Similarly, you can use this analysis to examine legal markets and the "shortage" of skilled information technology specialists, the "shortage" of apartments in certain cities, and many other phenomena. All of these examples are part of our economy, which we characterize as a *price system*.

THE PRICE SYSTEM

A **price system,** otherwise known as a *market system,* is one in which relative prices are constantly changing to reflect changes in supply and demand for different commodities. The prices of those commodities are the signals to everyone within the system as to what is relatively scarce and what is relatively abundant. Indeed, it is the *signaling* aspect of the price system that provides the information to buyers and sellers about what should be bought and what should be produced. In a price system, there is a clear-cut chain of events in which any changes in demand and supply cause changes in prices that in turn affect the opportunities that businesses and individuals have for profit and personal gain. Such changes influence our use of resources.

Price system
An economic system in which relative prices are constantly changing to reflect changes in supply and demand for different commodities. The prices of those commodities are signals to everyone within the system as to what is relatively scarce and what is relatively abundant.

EXCHANGE AND MARKETS

The price system features **voluntary exchange,** acts of trading between individuals that make both parties to the trade subjectively better off. The **terms of exchange**—the prices we pay for the desired items—are determined by the interaction of the forces underlying supply and demand. In our economy, the majority of exchanges take place voluntarily in markets. A market encompasses the exchange arrangements of both buyers and sellers that underlie the forces of supply and demand. Indeed, one definition of a market is a low-cost institution for facilitating exchange. A market in essence increases incomes by helping resources move to their highest-valued uses by means of prices. Prices are the providers of information.

Voluntary exchange
An act of trading, done on a voluntary basis, in which both parties to the trade are subjectively better off after the exchange.

Terms of exchange
The terms under which trading takes place. Usually the terms of exchange are equal to the price at which a good is traded.

Transaction Costs

Individuals turn to markets because markets reduce the cost of exchanges. These costs are sometimes referred to as **transaction costs,** which are broadly defined as the costs associated with finding out exactly what is being transacted as well as the cost of enforcing contracts. If you were Robinson Crusoe and lived alone on an island, you would never incur a transaction cost. For everyone else, transaction costs are just as real as the costs of produc-

Transaction costs
All of the costs associated with exchanging, including the informational costs of finding out price and quality, service record, and durability of a product, plus the cost of contracting and enforcing that contract.

tion. High-speed large-scale computers have allowed us to reduce transaction costs by increasing our ability to process information and keep records.

Consider some simple examples of transaction costs. The supermarket reduces transaction costs relative to your having to go to numerous specialty stores to obtain the items you desire. Organized stock exchanges, such as the New York Stock Exchange, have reduced transaction costs of buying and selling stocks and bonds. In general, the more organized the market, the lower the transaction costs. One group of individuals who constantly attempt to lower transaction costs are the much maligned middlemen.

The Role of Middlemen

As long as there are costs to bringing together buyers and sellers, there will be an incentive for intermediaries, normally called middlemen, to lower those costs. This means that middlemen specialize in lowering transaction costs. Whenever producers do not sell their products directly to the final consumer, there are, by definition, one or more middlemen involved. Farmers typically sell their output to distributors, who are usually called wholesalers, who then sell those products to supermarkets.

Recently, technology has changed the way middlemen work.

MIDDLEMEN FIND WAYS TO SURVIVE ON-LINE SHOPPING

Will the Internet eliminate intermediaries? Or will it just change the identity and activities of middlemen? Though it is true that on-line information about air travel and the on-line purchasing of tickets are shifting the demand curve for travel agents inward, such is not the case for all intermediaries. Middleman sites are popping up everywhere on the Web. People wishing to buy a car can access Auto-By-Tel Corp., which acts as an Internet intermediary to find the best price on a car. Other sites are available for buying computers, books, wine, and insurance. InsWeb Corp. has such a Web site, which allows users to compare quotes from several insurance companies. In any event, because total revenues from on-line retail shopping are projected to exceed $25 billion by 2001, electronic middlemen are certain to proliferate.

FOR CRITICAL ANALYSIS: *Anybody connected to the Internet can find the same information that an Internet intermediary can. Why, then, would someone pay for the intermediary's services?* •

CHANGES IN DEMAND AND SUPPLY

It is in markets that we see the results of changes in demand and supply. In certain situations, it is possible to predict what will happen to equilibrium price and equilibrium quantity when a change occurs in demand or supply. Specifically, whenever one curve is stable while the other curve shifts, we can tell what will happen to price and quantity. Consider the four possibilities in Figure 4-1 on page 76. In panel (a), the supply curve remains stable but demand increases from D_1 to D_2. Note that the result is both an increase in the market clearing price from P_1 to P_2 and an increase in the equilibrium quantity from Q_1 to Q_2.

In panel (b), there is a decrease in demand from D_1 to D_3. This results in a decrease in both the relative price of the good and the equilibrium quantity. Panels (c) and (d) show the

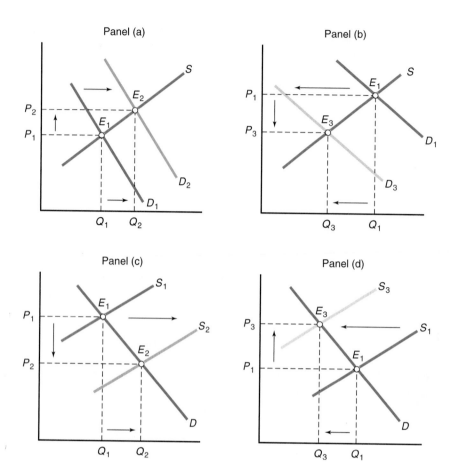

Panel (a)

Panel (b)

Panel (c)

Panel (d)

FIGURE 4-1

Shifts in Demand and in Supply: Determinate Results
In panel (a), the supply curve is stable at S. The demand curve shifts outward from D_1 to D_2. The equilibrium price and quantity rise from P_1, Q_1 to P_2, Q_2, respectively. In panel (b), again the supply curve remains stable at S. The demand curve, however, shifts inward to the left, showing a decrease in demand from D_1 to D_3. Both equilibrium price and equilibrium quantity fall. In panel (c), the demand curve now remains stable at D. The supply curve shifts from S_1 to S_2. The equilibrium price falls from P_1 to P_2. The equilibrium quantity increases, however, from Q_1 to Q_2. In panel (d), the demand curve is stable at D. Supply decreases as shown by a leftward shift of the supply curve from S_1 to S_3. The market clearing price increases from P_1 to P_3. The equilibrium quantity falls from Q_1 to Q_3.

effects of a shift in the supply curve while the demand curve is stable. In panel (c), the supply curve has shifted rightward. The relative price of the product falls; the equilibrium quantity increases. In panel (d), supply has shifted leftward—there has been a supply decrease. The product's relative price increases; the equilibrium quantity decreases.

When Both Demand and Supply Shift

The examples given in Figure 4-1 each showed a theoretically determinate outcome of a shift in either the demand curve holding the supply curve constant or the supply curve holding the demand curve constant. When both supply and demand curves change, the outcome is indeterminate for either equilibrium price or equilibrium quantity.

When both demand and supply increase, all we can be certain of is that equilibrium quantity will increase. We do not know what will happen to equilibrium price until we determine whether demand increased relative to supply (equilibrium price will rise) or supply increased relative to demand (equilibrium price will fall). The same analysis applies to decreases in both demand and supply, except that in this case equilibrium quantity falls.

We can be certain that when demand decreases and supply increases, the equilibrium price will fall, but we do not know what will happen to the equilibrium quantity unless we actually draw the new curves. If supply decreases and demand increases, we can be sure that equilibrium price will rise, but again we do not know what happens to equilibrium quantity without drawing the curves. In every situation in which both supply and demand change, you should always draw graphs to determine the resulting change in equilibrium price and quantity.

PRICE FLEXIBILITY AND ADJUSTMENT SPEED

We have used as an illustration for our analysis a market in which prices are quite flexible. Some markets are indeed like that. In others, however, price flexibility may take the form of indirect adjustments such as hidden payments or quality changes. For example, although the published price of bouquets of flowers may stay the same, the freshness of the flowers may change, meaning that the price per constant-quality unit changes. The published price of French bread might stay the same, but the quality could go up or down, thereby changing the price per constant-quality unit. There are many ways to change prices without actually changing the published price for a *nominal* unit of a product or service.

We must also consider the fact that markets do not return to equilibrium immediately. There must be an adjustment time. A shock to the economy in the form of an oil embargo, a drought, or a long strike will not be absorbed overnight. This means that even in unfettered market situations, in which there are no restrictions on changes in prices and quantities, temporary excess quantities supplied and excess quantities demanded may appear. Our analysis simply indicates what the market clearing price ultimately will be, given a demand curve and a supply curve. Nowhere in the analysis is there any indication of the speed with which a market will get to a new equilibrium if there has been a shock. The price may overshoot the equilibrium level. Remember this warning when we examine changes in demand and in supply due to changes in their nonprice determinants.

Now consider how long it takes the labor market to adjust to changes in supply and demand.

EXAMPLE
If You Are a Wired "Techie," There Is a Job for You

At the end of 1997, the Information Technology Association of America claimed that there were over 200,000 unfilled jobs available for skilled computer professionals. Those numbers did not include openings at small companies, government agencies, or nonprofit institutions. Information technology (IT) specialists are in demand because they help companies "tweak" software so that different computers can communicate with each other in what is know as a client-server network. IT specialists also create Web sites (home pages) and staff so-called help desks.

So what is happening here? Why are there so many unfilled job openings for IT specialists? One of the reasons has to do with a 43 percent drop in bachelor's degrees awarded in computer sciences during the period from 1986 to 1994. But on the demand side of the picture, by the mid-1990s, the demand curve for IT specialists had shifted outward to the right. The supply curve was unable to shift outward at the same swift pace. Consequently, even though salaries for software engineers increased more than 30 percent between 1995 and 1997, the equilibrium salary has still not been reached. There continues to be an excess quantity demanded of information technology specialists at current salaries.

You can see what might have happened using the supply and demand curves in Figure 4-2. The supply curve shift from S_1 to S_2 represents the period 1986–1994, reflecting

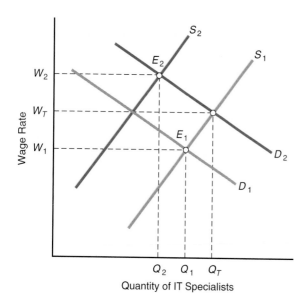

FIGURE 4-2

Rising Wages for Information Technology (IT) Specialists
Prior to the shift in supply and demand for IT specialists, the equilibrium wage rate was W_1. During the period from 1986 to 1994, the supply curve shifted to S_2. From the mid-1990s onward, the demand increased, as shown by a shift in the curve to D_2. Wages have increased somewhat to, say, W_T but not yet to the full equilibrium level of W_2. In the meantime, there is a "shortage" of skilled IT specialists at W_T.

the decrease in the number of computer science bachelor's degrees awarded. From the mid-1990s on, the demand curve has, in contrast, shifted outward from D_1 to D_2, reflecting the increase in the demand for information technology specialists. At the initial equilibrium E_1, the wage rate was W_1 and the equilibrium quantity of software engineers was Q_1. When the supply curve shifted to S_1 and the demand curve shifted to D_2, there was an excess quantity demanded at wage rate W_1. Though the wage rate has increased to, say, W_T (T for temporary), it has not yet reached the new equilibrium level at W_2. Until it gets to that level, there will continue to be an excess quantity demanded of skilled computer professionals.

FOR CRITICAL ANALYSIS: Why do you think so few university students chose to seek computer science degrees from 1986 to 1994? •

CONCEPTS IN BRIEF

• The terms of exchange in a voluntary exchange are determined by the interaction of the forces underlying demand and supply. These forces take place in markets, which tend to minimize transaction costs.

• When the demand curve shifts outward or inward with a stable supply curve, equilibrium price and quantity increase or decrease, respectively. When the supply curve shifts outward or inward given a stable demand curve, equilibrium price moves in the direction opposite of equilibrium quantity.

• When there is a shift in demand or supply, the new equilibrium price is not obtained instantaneously. Adjustment takes time.

THE RATIONING FUNCTION OF PRICES

A shortage creates a situation that forces price to rise toward a market clearing, or equilibrium, level. A surplus brings into play forces that cause price to fall toward its market clearing level. The synchronization of decisions by buyers and sellers that creates a situa-

THINKING CRITICALLY ABOUT THE MEDIA

Water "Rationing"

More and more these days, we hear about the lack of water in some city, state, or country. For seven successive years in the 1980s and 1990s, California suffered droughts and was "forced" to "ration" water. Puerto Rico suffered a drought when rainfall dropped to 35 percent below normal; residents of San Juan were subjected to water cutoffs every other day. These stories about "running out of water" always focus on the supply of water, never on the demand. The demand curve for water slopes downward, just like that for any other good or service. When the supply of strawberries increases in the summer, their prices go down; when the supply decreases, their prices go up. When the supply of water falls because of a drought, one way to ration a smaller supply is to increase the price. For some reason, politicians and media announcers reject this possibility, implying that water is different. Beware when you see the word *rationing* in the media; it typically means that the price of a good or service has not been allowed to reach equilibrium.

tion of equilibrium is called the *rationing function of prices*. Prices are indicators of relative scarcity. An equilibrium price clears the market. The plans of buyers and sellers, given the price, are not frustrated.[1] It is the free interaction of buyers and sellers that sets the price that eventually clears the market. Price, in effect, rations a commodity to demanders who are willing and able to pay the highest price. Whenever the rationing function of prices is frustrated by government-enforced price ceilings that set prices below the market clearing level, a prolonged shortage situation is not allowed to be corrected by the upward adjustment of the price.

There are other ways to ration goods. *First come, first served* is one method. *Political power* is another. *Physical force* is yet another. Cultural, religious, and physical differences have been and are used as rationing devices throughout the world.

Consider first come, first served as a rationing device. In countries that do not allow prices to reflect true relative scarcity, first come, first served has become a way of life. We call this *rationing by queues,* where *queue* means "line," as in Britain. Whoever is willing to wait in line the longest obtains meat that is being sold at less than the market clearing price. All who wait in line are paying a higher *total* price than the money price paid for the meat. Personal time has an opportunity cost. To calculate the total price of the meat, we must add up the money price plus the opportunity cost of the time spent waiting.

Lotteries are another way to ration goods. You may have been involved in a rationing-by-lottery scheme during your first year in college when you were assigned a university-provided housing unit. Sometimes for popular classes, rationing by lottery is used to fill the available number of slots.

Rationing by *coupons* has also been used, particularly during wartime. In the United States during World War II, families were allotted coupons that allowed them to purchase specified quantities of rationed goods, such as meat and gasoline. To purchase such goods, you had to pay a specified price *and* give up a coupon.

Rationing by waiting may occur in situations in which entrepreneurs are free to change prices to equate quantity demanded with quantity supplied but choose not to do so. This results in queues of potential buyers. The most obvious conclusion seems to be that the price in the market is being held below equilibrium by some noncompetitive force. That is not true, however.

The reason is that queuing may also arise when the demand characteristics of a market are subject to large or unpredictable fluctuations, and the additional costs to firms (and ultimately to consumers) of constantly changing prices or of holding sufficient inventories or providing sufficient excess capacity to cover these peak demands are greater than the costs to consumers of waiting for the good. This is the usual case of waiting in line to purchase a fast-food lunch or to purchase a movie ticket a few minutes before the next show.

[1]There is a difference between frustration and unhappiness. You may be unhappy because you can't buy a Rolls Royce, but if you had sufficient income, you would not be frustrated in your attempt to purchase one at the current market price. By contrast, you would be frustrated if you went to your local supermarket and could get only two cans of your favorite soft drink when you had wanted to purchase a dozen and had the necessary income.

The Essential Role of Rationing

In a world of scarcity, there is, by definition, competition for what is scarce. After all, any resources that are not scarce can be had by everyone at a zero price in as large a quantity as everyone wants, such as air to burn in internal combustion engines. Once scarcity arises, there has to be some method to ration the available resources, goods, and services. The price system is one form of rationing; the others that we mentioned are alternatives. Economists cannot say which system of rationing is best. They can, however, say that rationing via the price system leads to the most efficient use of available resources. This means that generally in a price system, further trades could not occur without making somebody worse off. In other words, in a freely functioning price system, all of the gains from mutually beneficial trade will be exhausted.

CONCEPTS IN BRIEF

- Prices in a market economy perform a rationing function because they reflect relative scarcity, allowing the market to clear. Other ways to ration goods include first come, first served; political power; physical force; lotteries; and coupons.

- Even when businesspeople can change prices, some rationing by waiting will occur. Such queuing arises when there are large unexpected changes in demand coupled with high costs of satisfying those changes immediately.

THE POLICY OF GOVERNMENT-IMPOSED PRICE CONTROLS

The rationing function of prices is often not allowed to operate when governments impose price controls. **Price controls** typically involve setting a **price ceiling**—the maximum price that may be allowed in an exchange. The world has had a long history of price ceilings applied to some goods, wages, rents, and interest rates, among other things. Occasionally a government will set a **price floor**—a minimum price below which a good or service may not be sold. These have most often been applied to wages and agricultural products. Let's consider price controls in terms of price ceilings.

Price controls
Government-mandated minimum or maximum prices that may be charged for goods and services.

Price ceiling
A legal maximum price that may be charged for a particular good or service.

Price floor
A legal minimum price below which a good or service may not be sold. Legal minimum wages are an example.

Price Ceilings and Black Markets

As long as a price ceiling is below the market clearing price, imposing a price ceiling creates a shortage, as can be seen in Figure 4-3. At any price below the market clearing, or equilibrium, price of P_e, there will always be a larger quantity demanded than quantity supplied, that is, a shortage. This was discussed initially in Chapter 3. Normally, whenever a shortage exists, there is a tendency for price and output to rise to equilibrium levels. This is exactly what we pointed out when discussing shortages in the labor market. But with a price ceiling, this tendency cannot be fully realized because everyone is forbidden to trade at the equilibrium price.

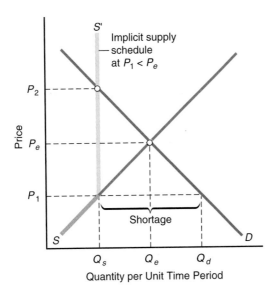

FIGURE 4-3
Black Markets
The demand curve is *D*. The supply curve is *S*. The equilibrium price is P_e. The government, however, steps in and imposes a maximum price of P_1. At that lower price, the quantity demanded will be Q_d, but the quantity supplied will only be Q_s. There is a "shortage." The implicit price (including time costs) tends to rise to P_2. If black markets arise, as they generally will, the equilibrium black market price will end up somewhere between P_2 and P_e.

Nonprice rationing devices
All methods used to ration scarce goods that are price-controlled. Whenever the price system is not allowed to work, nonprice rationing devices will evolve to ration the affected goods and services.

Black market
A market in which goods are traded at prices above their legal maximum prices or in which illegal goods are sold.

The result is fewer exchanges and **nonprice rationing devices.** In Figure 4-3, at an equilibrium price of P_e, the equilibrium quantity demanded and supplied (or traded) is Q_e. But at the price ceiling of P_1, the equilibrium quantity offered is only Q_s. What happens if there is a shortage? The most obvious nonprice rationing device to help clear the market is queuing, or long lines, which we have already discussed.

Typically, an effective price ceiling leads to a **black market.** A black market is a market in which the price-controlled good is sold at an illegally high price through various methods. For example, if the price of gasoline is controlled at lower than the market clearing price, a gas station attendant may take a cash payment on the side in order to fill up a driver's car (as happened in the 1970s in the United States during price controls on gasoline). If the price of beef is controlled at below its market clearing price, the butcher may give special service to a customer who offers the butcher great seats at an upcoming football game. Indeed, the number of ways in which the true implicit price of a price-controlled good or service can be increased is infinite, limited only by the imagination. (Black markets also occur when goods are made illegal—their legal price is set at zero.)

Whenever a nation attempts to freeze all prices, a variety of problems arise. Many of them occurred a few years ago in one African country, Sierra Leone.

INTERNATIONAL EXAMPLE
Price Controls in Sierra Leone

Lisa Walker spent a year as a Peace Corps volunteer in Sierra Leone, West Africa, and she kept a diary of her experiences. One thing she wrote about was what happened when the government imposed price controls on many common items: "For the last five days," she wrote, "nobody has sold cigarettes, kerosene, Maggi [bouillon] cubes, or rice here. . . . This is the result of the government's new order. The government says that Maggi cubes have to be sold for 30 cents, but sellers bought them for 50 cents, so when military men enter the village to enforce the government price, those with Maggis hide them. Same story for cigarettes and kerosene. The rice supplies are now hidden because of government prices. Unless one is willing to pay an outrageous price, it is impossible to buy rice in the marketplace. The only way to get rice legally is to buy it from the government. This means standing in long lines for many hours to get a rationed amount. I don't know how Sierra Leoneans are managing or how long this artificial rice shortage will last."

FOR CRITICAL ANALYSIS: How would you graphically illustrate the market for rice in Sierra Leone in the presence of price controls? •

CONCEPTS IN BRIEF

• Government policy can impose price controls in the form of price ceilings and price floors.

• An effective price ceiling is one that sets the legal price below the market clearing price and is enforced. Effective price ceilings lead to nonprice rationing devices and black markets.

THE POLICY OF CONTROLLING RENTS

Over 200 American cities and towns, including Santa Monica, Berkeley, and New York City, operate under some kind of rent control. **Rent control** is a system under which the local government tells building owners how much they can charge their tenants in rent. In the United States, rent controls date back to at least World War II. The objective of rent control is to keep rents below levels that would be observed in a freely competitive market.

Rent control
The placement of price ceilings on rents in particular cities.

The Functions of Rental Prices

In any housing market, rental prices serve three functions: (1) to promote the efficient maintenance of existing housing and stimulate the construction of new housing, (2) to allocate existing scarce housing among competing claimants, and (3) to ration the use of existing housing by current demanders.

Rent Controls and Construction. Rent controls have discouraged the construction of new rental units. Rents are the most important long-term determinant of profitability, and rent controls have artificially depressed them. Consider some examples. In a recent year in Dallas, Texas, with a 16 percent rental vacancy rate but no rent control laws, 11,000 new rental housing units were built. In the same year in San Francisco, California, only 2,000 units were built. The major difference? San Francisco has only a 1.6 percent vacancy rate but stringent rent control laws. In New York City, until a change in the law in 1997, the only rental units being built were luxury units, which were exempt from controls. In Santa Monica, California, new apartments were not being constructed at all until 1996 when that city's rent control law was softened by the state legislature. New office rental space and commercial developments have always been exempt from rent controls.

Effects on the Existing Supply of Housing. When rental rates are held below equilibrium levels, property owners cannot recover the cost of maintenance, repairs, and capital improvements through higher rents. Hence they curtail these activities. In the extreme situation, taxes, utilities, and the expenses of basic repairs exceed rental receipts. The result is abandoned buildings. Numerous buildings have been abandoned in New York City. Some owners have resorted to arson, hoping to collect the insurance on their empty buildings before the city claims them for back taxes.

In Santa Monica, the result is bizarre contrasts: Run-down rental units sit next to homes costing more than $500,000, and abandoned apartment buildings share the block with luxury car dealerships. With the new law, such an anomaly should gradually disappear.

Rationing the Current Use of Housing. Rent controls also affect the current use of housing because they restrict tenant mobility. Consider the family whose children have gone off to college. That family might want to live in a smaller apartment. But in a rent-controlled environment, there can be a substantial cost to giving up a rent-controlled unit. In most rent-controlled cities, rents can be adjusted only when a tenant leaves. That means that a move from a long-occupied rent-controlled apartment to a smaller apartment can involve a hefty rent hike. This artificial preservation of the status quo became known in New York as "housing gridlock."

Attempts at Evading Rent Controls

The distortions produced by rent controls lead to efforts by both property owners and tenants to evade the rules. This leads to the growth of expensive government bureaucracies whose job it is to make sure that rent controls aren't evaded. In New York City, property owners have had an incentive to make life unpleasant for tenants to drive them out or to evict them on the slightest pretense as the only way to raise the rent. The city has responded by making evictions extremely costly for property owners. Eviction requires a tedious and expensive judicial proceeding. Tenants, for their part, routinely try to sublet all or part of their rent-controlled apartments at fees substantially above the rent they pay to the owner. Both the city and the property owners try to prohibit subletting and typically end up in the city's housing courts—an entire judicial system developed to deal with disputes involving rent-controlled apartments. The overflow and appeals from the city's housing courts is now clogging the rest of New York's judicial system. Santa Monica has a similar rent control board. Its budget grew 500 percent in less than a decade. The property owners pay for it through a special annual assessment of more than $150 per rental unit per year.

Who Gains and Who Loses from Rent Controls?

The big losers from rent controls are clearly property owners. But there is another group of losers—low-income individuals, especially single mothers, trying to find their first apartment. Some observers now believe that rent controls have worsened the problem of homelessness in such cities as New York.

Typically, owners of rent-controlled apartments often charge "key money" before a new tenant is allowed to move in. This is a large up-front cash payment, usually illegal but demanded nonetheless—just one aspect of the black market in rent-controlled apartments. Poor individuals cannot afford a hefty key money payment, nor can they assure the owner that their rent will be on time or even paid each month. Because controlled rents are usually below market clearing levels, there is little incentive for apartment owners to take any risk on low-income-earning individuals as tenants. This is particularly true when a prospective tenant's chief source of income is a welfare check. Indeed, a large number of the litigants in the New York housing courts are welfare mothers who have missed their rent payments due to emergency expenses or delayed welfare checks. Often their appeals end in evictions and a new home in a temporary public shelter—or on the streets.

Who benefits from rent control? Ample evidence indicates that upper-income professionals benefit the most. These are the people who can use their mastery of the bureaucracy and their large network of friends and connections to exploit the rent control system. Consider that in New York, actresses Mia Farrow and Cicely Tyson live in rent-controlled apartments, paying well below market rates. So do State Senate Democratic leader Manfred Ohrenstein, the director of the Metropolitan Museum of Art, the chairman of Pathmark Stores, and writer Alistair Cooke.

The average subsidy from rent regulation in New York City has been about $345 a month for tenant households with annual incomes above $75,000 but only $176 a month for households with incomes between $10,000 and $20,000. The results of a study by the Pacific Legal Foundation concerning rent controls in Santa Monica and Berkeley are instructive. Since the institution of rent controls in those two communities, they have become more exclusive in terms of median income and average education level compared to surrounding communities. In other words, both Santa Monica and Berkeley have experienced significant declines in the populations that the legislation was intended to protect.

INTERNATIONAL EXAMPLE
Rent Controls in Bombay

In the mid-1990s, the most expensive capital in the world with respect to rents was Bombay, India. The annual rent per square foot for *available* unleased space was estimated at about $177, compared to $45 in midtown Manhattan. In addition, most landlords insist on receiving a year's rent in advance plus an additional security deposit equal to two years' rent. For major businesses, this can add up to millions of dollars, which are usually returned, but in three to five years and without payment of any interest.

One reason why Bombay rents are so high is the existence of rent controls and other laws intended to protect tenants. These controls and restrictions have kept out real estate developers and even scared owners of rentable property from renting that property, be it commercial or residential. One rent control law makes it almost impossible for a landlord to evict a tenant or to raise rents. Tenants can obtain what is called *statutory tenancy,* which allows them and their descendents to remain without a lease in any property they currently rent. There are situations in Bombay in which renters from 50 years ago still live in the same apartment, paying approximately the same rent as they originally did. Not surprisingly, unleased rental space is hard to find and hence quite expensive.

FOR CRITICAL ANALYSIS: *What effect do you think Bombay's high rents might have on foreign firms' desire to operate in that city?* •

CONCEPTS IN BRIEF

- Rental prices perform three functions: (1) allocating existing scarce housing among competing claimants, (2) promoting efficient maintenance of existing houses and stimulating new housing construction, and (3) rationing the use of existing houses by current demanders.

- Effective rent controls reduce or alter the three functions of rental prices. Construction of new rental units is discouraged. Rent controls decrease spending on maintenance of existing ones and also lead to "housing gridlock."

- There are numerous ways to evade rent controls; key money is one.

PRICE FLOORS IN AGRICULTURE

Another way that government can affect markets is by imposing price floors or price supports. In the United States, price supports are most often associated with agricultural products.

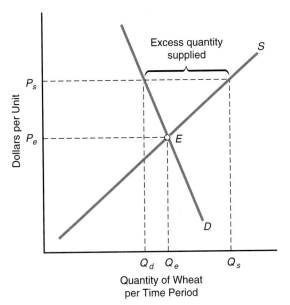

FIGURE 4-4

Agricultural Price Supports
Free market equilibrium occurs at E, with an equilibrium price of P_e and an equilibrium quantity of Q_e. When the government set a support price at P_s, the quantity demanded was Q_d, and the quantity supplied was Q_s. The difference was the surplus, which the government bought. Note that farmers' total income was from consumers ($P_s \times Q_d$) plus taxpayers [$(Q_s - Q_d) \times P_s$].

Price Supports

During the Great Depression, the federal government swung into action to help farmers. In 1933, it established a system of price supports for many agricultural products. Until recently there were price supports for wheat, feed grains, cotton, rice, soybeans, sorghum, and dairy products. The nature of the supports was quite simple: The government simply chose a *support price* for an agricultural product and then acted to ensure that the price of the product never fell below the support level. Figure 4-4 shows the market demand and supply of wheat. Without a price support program, competitive forces would yield an equilibrium price of P_e and an equilibrium quantity of Q_e. Clearly, if the government sets the support price at P_e or below, nothing will happen, because farmers can sell all they want at the market clearing price of P_e.

Until 1996, however, the government set the support price *above* P_e, at P_s. At a support price of P_s, the quantity demanded is only Q_d, but the quantity supplied is Q_s. The difference between them is called the *excess quantity supplied*, or *surplus*. As simple as this program seems, two questions arise: (1) How did the government decide on the level of the support price P_s? (2) How did it prevent market forces from pushing the actual price down to P_e?

If production exceeded the amount consumers wanted to buy at the support price, what happened to the surplus? Quite simply, the government had to buy the surplus—the difference between Q_s and Q_d—if the price support program was to work. As a practical matter, the government acquired the quantity $Q_s - Q_d$ indirectly through a government agency. The government either stored the surplus or sold it to foreign countries at a greatly reduced price (or gave it away free of charge) under the Food for Peace program.

Who Benefited from Agricultural Price Supports?

Traditionally advocated as a way to guarantee a decent wage for low-income farmers, most of the benefits of agricultural price supports were skewed toward owners of very large farms. Price supports were made on a per-bushel basis, not on a per-farm basis. Thus traditionally, the larger the farm, the bigger the benefit from agricultural price supports. In addition, *all* of the benefits from price supports ultimately accrued to *landowners* on whose land price-supported crops could grow. Except for peanuts, tobacco, and sugar, the price-support program was eliminated in 1996.

PRICE FLOORS IN THE LABOR MARKET

The **minimum wage** is the lowest hourly wage rate that firms may legally pay their workers. Proponents want higher minimum wages to ensure low-income workers a "decent" standard of living. Opponents claim that higher minimum wages cause increased unemployment, particularly among unskilled minority teenagers.

The federal minimum wage started in 1938 at 25 cents an hour, about 40 percent of the average manufacturing wage at the time. Typically, its level has stayed at about 40 to 50 percent of average manufacturing wages. It was increased to $4.25 in 1991 and may be higher by the time you read this. Many states and cities have their own minimum wage laws that sometimes exceed the federal minimum.

What happens when the government passes a floor on wages? The effects can be seen in Figure 4-5. We start off in equilibrium with the equilibrium wage rate of W_e and the equilibrium quantity of labor demanded and supplied equal to Q_e. A minimum wage, W_m, higher than W_e, is imposed. At W_m, the quantity demanded for labor is reduced to Q_d, and some workers now become unemployed. Note that the reduction in employment from Q_e to Q_d, or the distance from *B* to *A,* is less than the excess quantity of labor supplied at wage rate W_m. This excess quantity supplied is the distance between *A* and *C,* or the distance between Q_d and Q_s. The reason the reduction in employment is smaller than the excess supply of labor at the minimum wage is that the latter also includes a second component that consists of the additional workers who would like to work more hours at the new, higher minimum wage. Some workers may become unemployed as a result of the minimum wage, but others will move to sectors where minimum wage laws do not apply; wages will be pushed down in these uncovered sectors.

In the long run (a time period that is long enough to allow for adjustment by workers and firms), some of the reduction in labor demanded will result from a reduction in the number of firms, and some will result from changes in the number of workers employed by each firm. Economists estimate that a 10 percent increase in the real minimum wage decreases total employment of those affected by 1 to 2 percent.[2]

QUANTITY RESTRICTIONS

Governments can impose quantity restrictions on a market. The most obvious restriction is an outright ban on the ownership or trading of a good. It is presently illegal to buy and sell human organs. It is also currently illegal to buy and sell certain psychoactive drugs such as cocaine, heroin, and marijuana. In some states, it is illegal to start a new hospital without obtaining a license for a particular number of beds to be offered to patients. This licensing requirement effectively limits the quantity of hospital beds in some states. From 1933 to

Minimum wage
A wage floor, legislated by government, setting the lowest hourly rate that firms may legally pay workers.

Exercise 4.2
Visit www.econtoday.com for more about minimum wage.

---

[2]Because we are referring to a long-run analysis here, the reduction in labor demanded would be demonstrated by an eventual shift inward to the left of the short-run demand curve, *D,* in Figure 4-5.

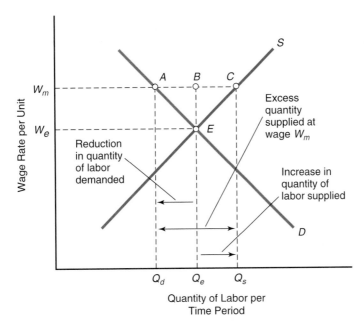

FIGURE 4-5
The Effect of Minimum Wages
The market clearing wage rate is W_e. The market clearing quantity of employment is Q_e, determined by the intersection of supply and demand at point E. A minimum wage equal to W_m is established. The quantity of labor demanded is reduced to Q_d; the reduction in employment from Q_e to Q_d is equal to the distance between B and A. That distance is smaller than the excess quantity of labor supplied at wage rate W_m. The distance between B and C is the increase in the quantity of labor supplied that results from the higher minimum wage rate.

1973, it was illegal for U.S. citizens to own gold except for manufacturing, medicinal, or jewelry purposes.

Some of the most common quantity restrictions exist in the area of international trade. The U.S. government, as well as many foreign governments, imposes import quotas on a variety of goods. An **import quota** is a supply restriction that prohibits the importation of more than a specified quantity of a particular good in a one-year period. The United States has had import quotas on tobacco, sugar, and immigrant labor. For many years, there were import quotas on oil coming into the United States. There are also "voluntary" import quotas on certain goods. Japanese automakers have agreed since 1981 "voluntarily" to restrict the amount of Japanese cars they send to the United States.

Import quota
A physical supply restriction on imports of a particular good, such as sugar. Foreign exporters are unable to sell in the United States more than the quantity specified in the import quota.

POLICY EXAMPLE
Should the Legal Quantity of Cigarettes Supplied Be Set at Zero?

Nicotine has been used as a psychoactive drug by the native people of the Americas for approximately 8,000 years. Five hundred years ago, Christopher Columbus introduced tobacco to the Europeans, who discovered that once they overcame the nausea and dizziness produced by chewing, snorting, or smoking the tobacco, they simply could not get along without it. Nicotine quickly joined alcohol and caffeine as one of the world's principal psychoactive drugs of choice.

In the century after Columbus returned from the Americas with tobacco, the use of and addiction to nicotine spread quickly around the world. There followed numerous efforts to quash what had become known as the "evil weed." In 1603, the Japanese prohibited the use of tobacco and repeatedly increased the penalties for violating the ban, which wasn't lifted until 1625. By the middle of the seventeenth century, similar bans on tobacco were in place in Bavaria, Saxony, Zurich, Turkey, and Russia, with punishments ranging from confiscation of property to execution. Even in the early twentieth century, several state governments in the United States attempted to ban the use of tobacco.

A proposed quantity restriction—outright prohibition—was in the news again a few years ago when the head of the Food and Drug Administration announced that his agency had finally determined that nicotine is addictive. He even argued that it should be classified with marijuana, heroin, and cocaine.

What can we predict if tobacco were ever completely prohibited today? Because tobacco is legal, the supply of illegal tobacco is zero. If the use of tobacco were restricted, the supply of illegal tobacco would not remain zero for long. Even if U.S. tobacco growers were forced out of business, the production of tobacco in other countries would increase to meet the demand. Consequently, the supply curve of illegal tobacco products would shift outward to the right as more foreign sources determined they wanted to enter the illegal U.S. tobacco market. The demand curve for illegal tobacco products would emerge almost immediately after the quantity restriction. The price people pay to satisfy their nicotine addiction would go up.

If you do not believe that cigarette smuggling would become big business after any type of ban on cigarettes in the United States, consider what has happened in Europe. In Germany, there are currently gang wars similar to those that occurred between rival bootleggers in the United States during Prohibition and in recent years between rival gangs selling crack cocaine. In Germany, the gangs are Vietnamese, and their stock in trade is cigarettes. They import the cigarettes illegally by buying them in Eastern European countries or at free ports, such as Rotterdam, without paying taxes or customs duties and then smuggling them into Germany. The gangs distribute the cigarettes to thousands of Vietnamese street sellers, who sell the cigarettes to German smokers for 50 to 65 percent of the normal retail price. German authorities estimate that 300 million packages of cigarettes are sold this way every year. In Italy, criminal organizations allegedly even sign "contracts" with tobacco companies to supply them directly, again without payment of taxes or customs duties. The agreements supposedly specify that the tobacco company not sell to any of the gang's competitors. All tobacco companies maintain, of course, that they do not knowingly sell to smugglers.

FOR CRITICAL ANALYSIS: What other goods or services follow the same analysis as the one presented here? •

CONCEPTS IN BRIEF

- With a price support system, the government sets a minimum price at which, say, qualifying farm products can be sold. Any farmers who cannot sell at that price can "sell" their surplus to the government. The only way a price support system can survive is for the government or some other entity to buy up the excess quantity supplied at the support price.

- When a floor is placed on wages at a rate that is above market equilibrium, the result is an excess quantity of labor supplied at that minimum wage.

- Quantity restrictions may take the form of import quotas, which are limits on the quantity of specific foreign goods that can be brought into the United States for resale purposes.

These smokers might like Cuban cigars, but imports from Cuba are illegal. Does that mean Cuban cigars can't be bought in America?

You Can Smoke a Big Cuban If You Are Willing to Pay a Big Price

CONCEPTS APPLIED:

SUPPLY, DEMAND, GOVERNMENT RESTRICTIONS, SHIFT IN SUPPLY, SHIFT IN DEMAND, EQUILIBRIUM

Visit www.econtoday.com for an Internet Activity that expands your understanding of these concepts.

"**H**ey, mister! How would you like to buy a box of big Cubans—8 inches long?"
"How much?"
"Only $700."
"Really?"

This hypothetical conversation between a seller of big Cuban cigars and a cigar *aficionado* is only partly hypothetical. The price is about right. Compared with other cigars, big Cubans are quite expensive. The reason is not hard to find: It is illegal to import them into the United States.

The Trade Embargo

In July 1963, President John F. Kennedy imposed a trade embargo on the Cuban regime. Since then, products of Cuban origin cannot be imported legally into the United States. Cigar *aficionados* in the United States did not, however, lose their desire to smoke big Cubans overnight. Look at Figure 4-6. There you see the demand curve for Cubans. The supply curve prior to the embargo ($S_{pre-embargo}$) intersected the demand curve at price P_e. After the embargo, the supply curve for legal imports became the vertical axis (labeled S_{legal}). Because of illegal imports, the true supply curve is $S_{illegal}$. The equilibrium price increased to P_1.

Explaining Recent Price Increases

During the past few years, the price of illegally imported Cubans has doubled or even tripled. There are two reasons why this has occurred. For one thing, cigar demand in America is smokin'. The demand curve for premium cigars—handmade with long, not chopped, filler leaf—has been surging outward. Consolidated Cigar Holdings, Inc., the largest domestic manufacturer, started off the year 1996 with a backlog of 4.3 million

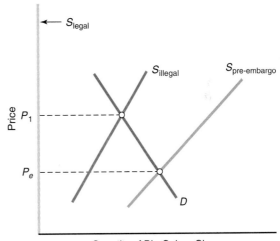

FIGURE 4-6

Cigar Prices Rise for a Reason
When the embargo was placed on Cuban goods, the supply curve for legal imports became the vertical axis. The supply curve shifted to $S_{illegal}$. The equilibrium price rose from P_e to P_1.

cigars. By 1997, it had 18 million on backorder. Because premium cigars use tobacco leaves aged for two to five years, increases in demand cannot be met with immediate increases in quantity supplied.

The second reason for the surge in price is that the market for Cuban cigars changed abruptly. After the collapse of the Soviet Union in 1991, Cuba was no longer able to obtain big subsidies from the Soviets. Island tobacco farmers subsequently saw their supplies of fuel, fertilizer, and even twine and boxes fall dramatically. The result was higher costs of producing cigars and a reduction in their supply. In 1990, Cuba was producing 90 million cigars per year; five years later, production had dropped to 50 million per year.

89

1. According to the marketing director of Hunters & Frankau, the distributor of Cuban cigars in Britain, "The worldwide demand for these cigars is still around 100 million." What is wrong with this statement?

2. What do you think has happened to the supply of fake Cuban cigars? Why?

CHAPTER SUMMARY

1. A price system, otherwise called a market system, allows prices to respond to changes in supply and demand for different commodities. Consumers and business managers' decisions on resource use depend on what happens to prices.

2. Exchanges take place in markets. The terms of exchange—prices—are registered in markets that tend to minimize transaction costs.

3. With a stable supply curve, a rise in demand leads to an increase in equilibrium price and quantity; a decrease in demand leads to a reduction in equilibrium price and quantity. With a stable demand curve, a rise in supply leads to a decrease in equilibrium price and an increase in equilibrium quantity; a fall in supply leads to an increase in equilibrium price and a decrease in equilibrium quantity.

4. When both demand and supply shift at the same time, indeterminate results occur. We must know the direction and degree of each shift in order to predict the change in equilibrium price and quantity.

5. When there is a shift in demand or supply, it takes time for markets to adjust to the new equilibrium. During that time, there will be temporary shortages or surpluses.

6. In a market system, prices perform a rationing function—they ration scarce goods and services. Other ways of rationing include first come, first served; political power; physical force; lotteries; and coupons.

7. Government-imposed price controls can take the form of price ceilings and price floors. Effective price ceilings—ones that are set below the market clearing price and enforced—lead to nonprice rationing devices and black markets.

8. Rent controls interfere with many of the functions of rental prices. For example, effective rent controls discourage the construction of new rental units. They also encourage "housing gridlock." Landlords lose during effective rent controls. Other losers are typically low-income individuals, especially single mothers, trying to find their first apartments.

9. A price floor can take the form of a government-imposed price support for agricultural products. This creates an excess quantity supplied at the supported price. To maintain that price, the government must buy up the surplus agricultural products. A price floor can apply to wages. When the government-imposed minimum wage exceeds the equilibrium wage rate, an excess quantity of labor is supplied. The result is higher unemployment for the affected group of workers.

10. Quantity restrictions can take the form of import quotas, under which there is a limit to the quantity of the affected good that can be brought into the United States and sold.

DISCUSSION OF PREVIEW QUESTIONS

1. **Does an increase in demand always lead to a rise in price?**

   Yes, provided that the supply curve doesn't shift also. If the supply is stable, every rise in demand will cause a shift outward to the right in the demand curve. The new equilibrium price will be higher than the old equilibrium price. If, however, the supply curve shifts at the same time, you have to know in which direction and by how much. If the supply curve shifts outward, indicating a rise in supply, the equilibrium price can rise if the shift is not as great as in demand. If the increase in supply is greater than in demand, the price can actually fall. We can be sure, though, that if demand increases and supply decreases, the equilibrium price will rise. This can be seen in the accompanying graph.

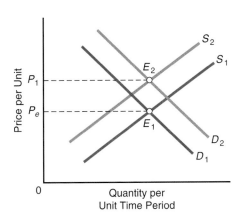

2. **Can there ever be shortages in a market with no restrictions?**

   Yes, there can, because adjustment is never instantaneous. It takes time for the forces of supply and demand to work. In all our graphs, we draw new equilibrium points where a new supply curve meets a new demand curve. That doesn't mean that in the marketplace buyers and sellers will react immediately to a change in supply or demand. Information is not perfect. Moreover, people are often slow to adapt to higher or lower prices. Suppliers may require months or years to respond to an increase in the demand for their product. Consumers take time to respond to new information about changing relative prices.

3. **How are goods rationed?**

   In a pure price system, prices ration goods. Prices are the indicators of relative scarcity. Prices change so that quantity demanded equals quantity supplied. In the absence of a price system, an alternative way to ration goods is first come, first served. In many systems, political power is another method. In certain cultures, physical force is a way to ration goods. Cultural, religious, and physical differences among individuals can be used as rationing devices. The fact is that given a world of scarcity, there has to be some method to ration goods. The price system is only one alternative.

4. **When would you expect to encounter black markets?**

   Black markets occur in two situations. The first occurs whenever a good or service is made illegal by legislation. There are black markets in the United States for prostitution, gambling, and drugs. Second, there are black markets whenever a price ceiling (one type of price control) is imposed on any good or service. The price ceiling has to be below the market clearing price and enforced for a black market to exist, however. Price ceilings on rents in cities in the United States have created black markets for rental units.

PROBLEMS

(Answers to the odd-numbered problems appear at the back of the book.)

4-1. This is a graph of the supply and demand for oranges.

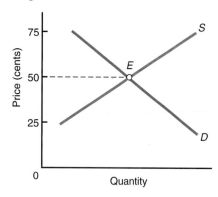

Explain the effect on this graph of each of the following events.

a. It is discovered that oranges can cure acne.
b. A new machine is developed that will automatically pick oranges.
c. The government declares a price floor of 25 cents.
d. The government declares a price floor of 75 cents.
e. The price of grapefruits increases.
f. Income decreases.

4-2. What might be the long-run results of price controls that maintained a good's money price below its equilibrium price? Above its equilibrium price?

4-3. Here is a demand schedule and a supply schedule for scientific hand calculators.

Price	Quantity Demanded	Quantity Supplied
$10	100,000	0
20	60,000	0
30	20,000	0
40	0	0
50	0	100,000
60	0	300,000
70	0	500,000

What are the equilibrium price and the equilibrium quantity? Explain.

4-4. This is a graph of the supply and demand for raisins.

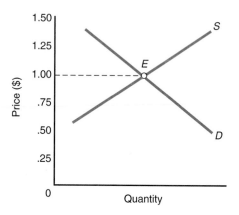

The following series of events occurs. Explain the result of the occurrence of each event.

a. An advertising campaign for California raisins is successful.
b. A fungus wipes out half the grape crop (used to make raisins) in California.
c. The price of bran flakes (a complement) increases.
d. The price of dried cranberries (a substitute) increases.
e. The government declares a price floor of 75 cents.
f. The government imposes and enforces a price ceiling of 75 cents.
g. Income increases (assume that raisins are an inferior good).

4-5. Below is a demand schedule and a supply schedule for lettuce.

Price per Crate	Quantity Demanded (crates per year)	Quantity Supplied (crates per year)
$1	100 million	0 million
2	90 million	10 million
3	70 million	30 million
4	50 million	50 million
5	20 million	80 million

What are the equilibrium price and the equilibrium quantity? At a price of $2 per crate, what is the quantity demanded? The quantity supplied? What is this disequilibrium situation called? What is the magnitude of the disequilibrium, expressed in terms of quantities? Now answer the same questions for a price of $5 per crate.

4-6. What is wrong with the following assertion? "The demand has increased so much in response to our offering of a $500 rebate that our inventory of cars is now running very low."

4-7. Rent control is a price ceiling. There are also legislated price floors. Assume that the equilibrium price for oranges is 10 cents each. Draw the supply and demand diagram to show the effect of a government-imposed price floor, or minimum price, of 15 cents per orange. Be sure to label any shortages or surpluses that result. Then show the effect of a price floor of 5 cents per orange.

COMPUTER-ASSISTED INSTRUCTION

A set of price ceiling and price floor situations is presented. You are asked to predict different outcomes for each situation in both the short and the long run.

Complete problem and answer appear on disk.

INTERACTING WITH THE INTERNET

If you enter "price controls" in the Yahoo! search engine, you will be directed to more than 6,000 Web sites. (Put the phrase in quotation marks so that the entire phrase is used in the search procedure.) You will find articles on all types of price controls, ranging from those on health care to those on gasoline and agricultural products.

Here's a hint: If you use the Yahoo! search engine, at the end of the of the list of the first 20 sites found, you will see the heading "Other Search Engines." Click on one of them, such as Lycos, HotBot, or Excite, and you will get a variation on Yahoo!'s search of the subject requested.

CHAPTER 5

THE PUBLIC SECTOR

After Congress got through completing the tax legislation of 1997—touted as the "great middle-class tax reduction"—the average American family was to see its taxes decline by all of $70 per year. The new legislation will actually cause some households that apply for new tax credits for children to be worse off! Nonetheless, two groups of individuals are now definitely better off—tax attorneys and accountants. The federal income tax is currently so complicated that more and more households feel that they must turn to professionals to calculate the taxes they owe. Is there an alternative way for government to raise revenues? Before you can answer that question, you must learn some details about the public sector in America.

PREVIEW QUESTIONS

1. What problems will you encounter if you refuse to pay a portion of your income tax because you oppose national defense spending?
2. Will you benefit from many so-called tax loopholes when you first start working?
3. In what ways do regressive, proportional, and progressive tax structures differ?
4. Who pays the corporate income tax?

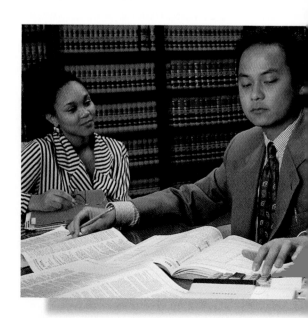

Did You Know That . . . the average American works from January 1 through May 7 each year to pay for all local, state, and federal taxes? The average New York resident works approximately three weeks longer to pay for all of the taxes owed each year. Looked at another way, the average American in a typical eight-hour day works about 2 hours and 42 minutes to pay for government at all levels. Every citizen, including children, averages about $8,000 a year in taxes of all kinds. The total amount paid exceeds $2 trillion. What is a trillion dollars? It is a million times a million. Thus it would take more than 2 million millionaires to have as much money as is spent each year by government. So we cannot ignore the presence of government in our society. Government exists, at a minimum, to take care of what the price system does not do well.

WHAT A PRICE SYSTEM CAN AND CANNOT DO

Throughout the book so far, we have alluded to the benefits of a price system. High on the list is economic efficiency. In its most ideal form, a price system allows resources to move from lower-valued uses to higher-valued uses through voluntary exchange. The supreme point of economic efficiency occurs when all mutually advantageous trades have taken place. In a price system, consumers are sovereign; that is to say, they have the individual freedom to decide what they wish to purchase. Politicians and even business managers do not ultimately decide what is produced; consumers decide. Some proponents of the price system argue that this is its most important characteristic. A market organization of economic activity generally prevents one person from interfering with another in respect to most of his or her activities. Competition among sellers protects consumers from coercion by one seller, and sellers are protected from coercion by one consumer because other consumers are available.

Sometimes the price system does not generate these results, with too few or too many resources going to specific economic activities. Such situations are called **market failures.** Market failures prevent the price system from attaining economic efficiency and individual freedom, as well as other social goals. Market failures offer one of the strongest arguments in favor of certain economic functions of government, which we now examine.

CORRECTING FOR EXTERNALITIES

In a pure market system, competition generates economic efficiency only when individuals know the true opportunity cost of their actions. In some circumstances, the price that someone actually pays for a resource, good, or service is higher or lower than the opportunity cost that all of society pays for that same resource, good, or service.

Consider a hypothetical world in which there is no government regulation against pollution. You are living in a town that until now has had clean air. A steel mill moves into town. It produces steel and has paid for the inputs—land, labor, capital, and entrepreneurship. The price it charges for the steel reflects, in this example, only the costs that the steel mill incurred. In the course of production, however, the mill gets one input—clean air—by simply taking it. This is indeed an input because in the making of steel, the furnaces emit smoke. The steel mill doesn't have to pay the cost of using the clean air; rather, it is the people in the community who pay that cost in the form of dirtier clothes, dirtier cars and houses, and more respiratory illnesses. The effect is similar to what would happen if the steel mill could take coal or oil or workers' services free. There has been an **externality,** an external cost. Some of the costs associated with the production of the steel have "spilled over" to affect **third parties,** parties other than the buyer and the seller of the steel.

Market failure
A situation in which an unrestrained market economy leads to too few or too many resources going to a specific economic activity.

Externality
A consequence of an economic activity that spills over to affect third parties. Pollution is an externality.

Third parties
Parties who are not directly involved in a given activity or transaction.

External Costs in Graphical Form

Look at panel (a) in Figure 5-1. Here we show the demand curve for steel to be D. The supply curve is S_1. The supply curve includes only the costs that the firms have to pay. The equilibrium, or market clearing, situation will occur at quantity Q_1. Let us take into account the fact that there are externalities—the external costs that you and your neighbors pay in the form of dirtier clothes, cars, and houses and increased respiratory disease due to the air pollution emitted from the steel mill; we also assume that all other suppliers of steel use clean air without having to pay for it. Let's include these external costs in our graph to find out what the full cost of steel production really is. This is equivalent to saying that the price of an input used in steel production increased. Recall from Chapter 3 that an increase in input prices shifts the supply curve. Thus in panel (a) of the figure, the supply curve shifts from S_1 to S_2; the external costs equal the vertical distance between A and E_1. If the external costs were somehow taken into account, the equilibrium quantity would fall to Q_2 and the price would rise to P_2. Equilibrium would shift from E to E_1. If the price does not account for external costs, third parties bear those costs—represented by the distance between A and E_1—in the form of dirtier clothes, houses, and cars and increased respiratory illnesses.

External Benefits in Graphical Form

Externalities can also be positive. To demonstrate external benefits in graphical form, we will use the example of inoculations against communicable disease. In panel (b) of Figure

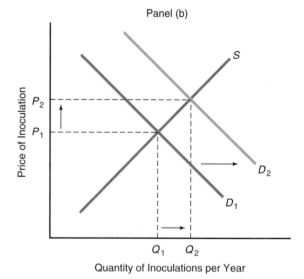

Panel (a)

Panel (b)

FIGURE 5-1

External Costs and Benefits
In panel (a), we show a situation in which the production of steel generates external costs. If the steel mills ignore pollution, at equilibrium the quantity of steel will be Q_1. If the mills had to pay for the additional cost borne by nearby residents that is caused by the steel mill's production, the supply curve would shift the vertical distance A–E_1, to S_2. If consumers were forced to pay a price that reflected the spillover costs, the quantity demanded would fall to Q_2. In panel (b), we show the situation in which inoculations against communicable diseases generate external benefits to those individuals who may not be inoculated but who will benefit because epidemics will not occur. If each individual ignores the external benefit of inoculations, the market clearing quantity will be Q_1. If external benefits are taken into account by purchasers of inoculations, however, the demand curve would shift to D_2. The new equilibrium quantity would be Q_2 and the price would be higher, P_2.

5-1, we show the demand curve as D_1 (without taking account of any external benefits) and the supply curve as S. The equilibrium price is P_1, and the equilibrium quantity is Q_1. We assume, however, that inoculations against communicable diseases generate external benefits to individuals who may not be inoculated but will benefit nevertheless because epidemics will not break out. If such external benefits were taken into account, the demand curve would shift from D_1 to D_2. The new equilibrium quantity would be Q_2, and the new equilibrium price would be P_2. With no corrective action, this society is not devoting enough resources to inoculations against communicable diseases.

When there are external costs, the market will tend to *overallocate* resources to the production of the good or service in question, for those goods or services will be deceptively low-priced. With the example of steel, too much will be produced because the steel mill owners and managers are not required to take account of the external cost that steel production is imposing on the rest of society. In essence, the full cost of production is unknown to the owners and managers, so the price they charge the public for steel is lower than it would be otherwise. And of course, the lower price means that buyers are willing and able to buy more. More steel is produced and consumed than is socially optimal.

When there are external benefits, the market *underallocates* resources to the production of that good or service because the good or service is relatively too expensive (because the demand is relatively too low). In a market system, too many of the goods that generate external costs are produced and too few of the goods that generate external benefits are produced.

How the Government Corrects Negative Externalities

The government can in theory correct externality situations in a variety of ways in all cases that warrant such action. In the case of negative externalities, at least two avenues are open to the government: special taxes and legislative regulation or prohibition.

Effluent fee
A charge to a polluter that gives the right to discharge into the air or water a certain amount of pollution. Also called a *pollution tax*.

Special Taxes. In our example of the steel mill, the externality problem originates from the fact that the air as a waste disposal place is costless to the firm but not to society. The government could make the steel mill pay a tax for dumping its pollutants into the air. The government could attempt to tax the steel mill commensurate with the cost to third parties from smoke in the air. This, in effect, would be a pollution tax or an **effluent fee.** The ultimate effect would be to reduce the supply of steel and raise the price to consumers, ideally making the price equal to the full cost of production to society.

Regulation. To correct a negative externality arising from steel production, the government could specify a maximum allowable rate of pollution. This action would require that the steel mill install pollution abatement equipment within its facilities, that it reduce its rate of output, or some combination of the two. Note that the government's job would not be that simple, for it still would have to determine the level of pollution and then actually measure its output from steel production in order to enforce such regulation.

How the Government Corrects Positive Externalities

What can the government do when the production of one good spills *benefits* over to third parties? It has several policy options: financing the production of the good or producing the good itself, subsidies (negative taxes), and regulation.

Government Financing and Production. If the positive externalities seem extremely large, the government has the option of financing the desired additional production facilities so that the "right" amount of the good will be produced. Again consider inoculations against communicable diseases. The government could—and often does—finance campaigns to inoculate the population. It could (and does) even produce and operate centers for inoculation in which such inoculations would be free.

Subsidies. A subsidy is a negative tax; it is a payment made either to a business or to a consumer when the business produces or the consumer buys a good or a service. In the case of inoculations against communicable diseases, the government could subsidize everyone who obtains an inoculation by directly reimbursing those inoculated or by making payments to private firms that provide inoculations. If you are attending a state university, taxpayers are helping to pay the cost of providing your education; you are being subsidized by as much as 80 percent of the total cost. Subsidies reduce the net price to consumers, thereby causing a larger quantity to be demanded.

Regulation. In some cases involving positive externalities, the government can require by law that a certain action be undertaken by individuals in the society. For example, regulations require that all school-age children be inoculated before entering public and private schools. Some people believe that a basic school education itself generates positive externalities. Perhaps as a result of this belief, we have regulations—laws—that require all school-age children to be enrolled in a public or private school.

CONCEPTS IN BRIEF

- External costs lead to an overallocation of resources to the specific economic activity. Two possible ways of correcting these spillovers are taxation and regulation.

- External benefits result in an underallocation of resources to the specific activity. Three possible government corrections are financing the production of the activity, subsidizing private firms or consumers to engage in the activity, and regulation.

THE OTHER ECONOMIC FUNCTIONS OF GOVERNMENT

Besides compensating for externalities, the government performs many other functions that affect the way in which exchange is carried out in the economy. In contrast, the political functions of government have to do with deciding how income should be redistributed among households and selecting which goods and services have special merits and should therefore be treated differently. The economic and political functions of government can and do overlap.

Let's look at four more economic functions of government.

Providing a Legal System

The courts and the police may not at first seem like economic functions of government (although judges and police personnel must be paid). Their activities nonetheless have important consequences on economic activities in any country. You and I enter into contracts constantly, whether they be oral or written, expressed or implied. When we believe that we have been wronged, we seek redress of our grievances within our legal institutions. Moreover, consider the legal system that is necessary for the smooth functioning of our system. Our system has defined quite explicitly the legal status of businesses, the rights of private ownership, and a method for the enforcement of contracts. All relationships among consumers and businesses are governed by the legal rules of the game. We might consider the government in its judicial function, then, as the referee when there are disputes in the economic arena.

Much of our legal system is involved with defining and protecting *property rights*. **Property rights** are the rights of an owner to use and to exchange his or her property. One might say that property rights are really the rules of our economic game. When property rights are well defined, owners of property have an incentive to use that property efficiently. Any mistakes in their decision about the use of property have negative consequences that the owners suffer. Furthermore, when property rights are well defined, owners of property have an incentive to maintain that property so that if those owners ever desire to sell it, it will fetch a better price.

Establishing and maintaining an independent constitutional judiciary, a familiar activity in the United States, is relatively new to Central and Eastern European countries.

Property rights
The rights of an owner to use and to exchange property.

INTERNATIONAL EXAMPLE
Post-Communist Rule of Law

Prior to the collapse of the Soviet empire, Central and Eastern European nations did not have an independent constitutional judiciary. Today that has changed. As a result, there is more of an institutional climate favorable for both domestic and foreign businesses.

The new constitutional frameworks in Central and Eastern European countries are based in large part on the U.S. Constitution. They emphasize the doctrines of separation of powers and checks and balances. They even allow for the courts to have the power of judicial review. (In the United States, this power allows the courts to declare laws unconstitutional.) A good case in point is Hungary. There, legislators passed laws providing for restitution of nationalized land to pre-Communist owners. The court ruled that such laws were retroactive and thus invalid. The Hungarian court further stated that the only basis for returning land to former owners was through the transition to a market economy.

Bulgaria's constitutional court has consistently angered politicians. The court curbed government efforts to control radio and television. In Poland, the constitutional court voided a law passed by Parliament that would have lowered pensions of former state employees. This legal decision alone created a government obligation to pay almost $3 billion in compensation to almost 10 million Poles. This forced the government to sell bonds to pay for those pensions.

The trend toward highly independent court systems continues throughout Central and Eastern Europe.

FOR CRITICAL ANALYSIS: Why would an independent constitutional judiciary be important to someone who wished to invest in a new business in a Central or Eastern European country? ●

Promoting Competition

Many people believe that the only way to attain economic efficiency is through competition. One of the roles of government is to serve as the protector of a competitive economic system. Congress and the various state governments have passed **antitrust legislation.** Such legislation makes illegal certain (but not all) economic activities that might, in legal terms, restrain trade—that is, prevent free competition among actual and potential rival firms in the marketplace. The avowed aim of antitrust legislation is to reduce the power of **monopolies**—firms that have great control over the price of the goods they sell. A large number of antitrust laws have been passed that prohibit specific anticompetitive business behavior. Both the Antitrust Division of the Department of Justice and the Federal Trade Commission attempt to enforce these antitrust laws. Various state judicial agencies also expend efforts at maintaining competition.

Antitrust legislation
Laws that restrict the formation of monopolies and regulate certain anticompetitive business practices.

Monopoly
A firm that has great control over the price of a good. In the extreme case, a monopoly is the only seller of a good or service.

Providing Public Goods

The goods used in our examples up to this point have been **private goods.** When I eat a cheeseburger, you cannot eat the same one. So you and I are rivals for that cheeseburger, just as much as rivals for the title of world champion are. When I use a CD-ROM player, you cannot use the same player. When I use the services of an auto mechanic, that person cannot work at the same time for you. That is the distinguishing feature of private goods—their use is exclusive to the people who purchase or rent them. The **principle of rival consumption** applies to all private goods by definition. Rival consumption is easy to understand. With private goods, either you use them or I use them.

There is an entire class of goods that are not private goods. These are called **public goods.** The principle of rival consumption does not apply to them. That is, they can be consumed *jointly* by many individuals simultaneously. National defense, police protection, and the legal system, for example, are public goods. If you partake of them, you do not necessarily take away from anyone else's share of those goods.

Characteristics of Public Goods. Several distinguishing characteristics of public goods set them apart from all other goods.[1]

1. **Public goods are often indivisible.** You can't buy or sell $5 worth of our ability to annihilate the world with bombs. Public goods cannot usually be produced or sold very easily in small units.
2. **Public goods can be used by more and more people at no additional cost.** Once money has been spent on national defense, the defense protection you receive does not reduce the amount of protection bestowed on anyone else. The opportunity cost of your receiving national defense once it is in place is zero.
3. **Additional users of public goods do not deprive others of any of the services of the goods.** If you turn on your television set, your neighbors don't get weaker reception because of your action.
4. **It is difficult to design a collection system for a public good on the basis of how much individuals use it.** It is nearly impossible to determine how much any person uses or values national defense. No one can be denied the benefits of national defense for failing to pay for that public good. This is often called the **exclusion principle.**

One of the problems of public goods is that the private sector has a difficult, if not impossible, time in providing them. There is little or no incentive for individuals in the private sector to offer public goods because it is so difficult to make a profit in so doing. Consequently, a true public good must necessarily be provided by government.

INTERNATIONAL EXAMPLE
Are Lighthouses a Public Good?

One of the most common examples of a public good is a lighthouse. Arguably, it satisfies all the criteria listed in points 1 through 4. In one instance, however, a lighthouse was not a public good in that a collection system was devised and enforced on the basis of how much individuals used it. In the thirteenth century, the city of Aigues-Mortes, a French southern port, erected a tower, called the King's Tower, designed to assert

---

Private goods
Goods that can be consumed by only one individual at a time. Private goods are subject to the principle of rival consumption.

Principle of rival consumption
The recognition that individuals are rivals in consuming private goods because one person's consumption reduces the amount available for others to consume.

Public goods
Goods to which the principle of rival consumption does not apply; they can be jointly consumed by many individuals simultaneously at no additional cost and with no reduction in quality or quantity.

Exclusion principle
The principle that no one can be excluded from the benefits of a public good, even if that person hasn't paid for it.

---

[1]Sometimes the distinction is made between pure public goods, which have all the characteristics we have described here, and quasi- or near-public goods, which do not. The major feature of near-public goods is that they are jointly consumed, even though nonpaying customers can be, and often are, excluded—for example, movies, football games, and concerts.

the will and power of Louis IX (Saint Louis). The 105-foot tower served as a lighthouse for ships. More important, it served as a lookout so that ships sailing on the open sea, but in its view, did not escape paying for use of the lighthouse. Those payments were then used for the construction of the city walls.

FOR CRITICAL ANALYSIS: Explain how a lighthouse satisfies the characteristics of public goods described in points 1, 2, and 3. ●

Free-rider problem
A problem that arises when individuals presume that others will pay for public goods so that, individually, they can escape paying for their portion without causing a reduction in production.

Free Riders. The nature of public goods leads to the **free-rider problem,** a situation in which some individuals take advantage of the fact that others will take on the burden of paying for public goods such as national defense. Free riders will argue that they receive no value from such government services as national defense and therefore really should not pay for it. Suppose that citizens were taxed directly in proportion to how much they tell an interviewer that they value national defense. Some people will probably tell interviewers that they are unwilling to pay for national defense because they don't want any of it—it is of no value to them. Many of us may end up being free riders when we assume that others will pay for the desired public good. We may all want to be free riders if we believe that someone else will provide the commodity in question that we actually value.

The free-rider problem is a definite problem among nations with respect to the international burden of defense and how it should be shared. A country may choose to belong to a multilateral defense organization, such as the North American Treaty Organization (NATO), but then consistently attempt not to contribute funds to the organization. The nation knows it would be defended by others in NATO if it were attacked but would rather not pay for such defense. In short, it seeks a "free ride."

Ensuring Economywide Stability

The government attempts to stabilize the economy by smoothing out the ups and downs in overall business activity. Our economy sometimes faces the problems of unemployment and rising prices. The government, especially the federal government, has made an attempt to solve these problems by trying to stabilize the economy. The notion that the federal government should undertake actions to stabilize business activity is a relatively new idea in the United States, encouraged by high unemployment rates during the Great Depression of the 1930s and subsequent theories about possible ways by which government could reduce unemployment. In 1946, the government passed the Employment Act, a landmark law concerning government responsibility for economic performance. It established three goals for government accountability: full employment, price stability, and economic growth. These goals have provided the justification for many government economic programs during the post–World War II period.

CONCEPTS IN BRIEF

- The economic activities of government include (1) correcting for externalities, (2) providing a judicial system, (3) promoting competition, (4) producing public goods, and (5) ensuring economywide stability.
- Public goods can be consumed jointly. The principle of rival consumption does not apply as it does with private goods.
- Public goods have the following characteristics: (1) They are indivisible; (2) once they are produced, there is no opportunity cost when additional consumers use them; (3) your use of a public good does not deprive others of its simultaneous use; and (4) consumers cannot conveniently be charged on the basis of use.

THE POLITICAL FUNCTIONS OF GOVERNMENT

At least two areas of government are in the realm of political, or normative, functions rather than that of the economic ones discussed in the first part of this chapter. These two areas are (1) the regulation and/or provision of merit and demerit goods and (2) income redistribution.

Merit and Demerit Goods

Certain goods are considered to have special merit. A **merit good** is defined as any good that the political process has deemed socially desirable. (Note that nothing inherent in any particular good makes it a merit good. It is a matter of who chooses.) Some examples of merit goods in our society are museums, ballets, plays, and concerts. In these areas, the government's role is the provision of merit goods to the people in society who would not otherwise purchase them at market clearing prices or who would not purchase an amount of them judged to be sufficient. This provision may take the form of government production and distribution of merit goods. It can also take the form of reimbursement for payment on merit goods or subsidies to producers or consumers for part of the cost of merit goods. Governments do indeed subsidize such merit goods as concerts, ballets, museums, and plays. In most cases, such merit goods would rarely be so numerous without subsidization.

Demerit goods are the opposite of merit goods. They are goods that, through the political process, are deemed socially undesirable. Heroin, cigarettes, gambling, and cocaine are examples. The government exercises its role in the area of demerit goods by taxing, regulating, or prohibiting their manufacture, sale, and use. Governments justify the relatively high taxes on alcohol and tobacco by declaring them demerit goods. The best-known example of governmental exercise of power in this area is the stance against certain psychoactive drugs. Most psychoactives (except nicotine, caffeine, and alcohol) are either expressly prohibited, as is the case for heroin, cocaine, and opium, or heavily regulated, as in the case of prescription psychoactives.

Merit good
A good that has been deemed socially desirable through the political process. Museums are an example.

Demerit good
A good that has been deemed socially undesirable through the political process. Heroin is an example.

Income Redistribution

Another relatively recent political function of government has been the explicit redistribution of income. This redistribution uses two systems: the progressive income tax (described later in this chapter) and *transfer payments*. **Transfer payments** are payments made to individuals for which in return no services or goods are concurrently rendered. The three key money transfer payments in our system are welfare, Social Security, and unemployment insurance benefits. Income redistribution also includes a large amount of income **transfers in kind,** as opposed to money transfers. Some income transfers in kind are food stamps, Medicare and Medicaid, government health care services, and low-cost public housing.

The government has also engaged in other activities as a form of redistribution of income. For example, the provision of public education is at least in part an attempt to redistribute income by making sure that the very poor have access to education.

Transfer payments
Money payments made by governments to individuals for which in return no services or goods are concurrently rendered. Examples are welfare, Social Security, and unemployment insurance benefits.

Transfers in kind
Payments that are in the form of actual goods and services, such as food stamps, low-cost public housing, and medical care, and for which in return no goods or services are rendered concurrently.

CONCEPTS IN BRIEF

- Political, or normative, activities of the government include the provision and regulation of merit and demerit goods and income redistribution.

- Merit and demerit goods do not have any inherent characteristics that qualify them as such; rather, collectively, through the political process, we make judgments about which goods and services are "good" for society and which are "bad."

> • Income redistribution can be carried out by a system of progressive taxation, coupled with transfer payments, which can be made in money or in kind, such as food stamps and Medicare.

PAYING FOR THE PUBLIC SECTOR

Jean-Baptiste Colbert, the seventeenth-century French finance minister, said the art of taxation was in "plucking the goose so as to obtain the largest amount of feathers with the least possible amount of hissing." In the United States, governments have designed a variety of methods of plucking the private-sector goose. To analyze any tax system, we must first understand the distinction between marginal tax rates and average tax rates.

Marginal and Average Tax Rates

If somebody says, "I pay 28 percent in taxes," you cannot really tell what that person means unless you know if he or she is referring to average taxes paid or the tax rate on the last dollars earned. The latter concept has to do with the **marginal tax rate.**[2]

The marginal tax rate is expressed as follows:

$$\text{Marginal tax rate} = \frac{\text{change in taxes due}}{\text{change in taxable income}}$$

It is important to understand that the marginal tax rate applies only to the income in the highest **tax bracket** reached, where a tax bracket is defined as a specified level of taxable income to which a specific and unique marginal tax rate is applied.

The marginal tax rate is not the same thing as the **average tax rate,** which is defined as follows:

$$\text{Average tax rate} = \frac{\text{total taxes due}}{\text{total taxable income}}$$

Taxation Systems

No matter how governments raise revenues—from income taxes, sales taxes, or other taxes—all of those taxes can fit into one of three types of taxation systems—proportional, progressive, and regressive, expressing a relationship between the percentage tax, or tax rate, paid and income. To determine whether a tax system is proportional, progressive, or regressive, we simply ask the question, What is the relationship between the average tax rate and the marginal tax rate?

Proportional Taxation. **Proportional taxation** means that regardless of an individual's income, his or her taxes comprise exactly the same proportion. In terms of marginal versus average tax rates, in a proportional taxation system, the marginal tax rate is always equal to the average tax rate. If every dollar is taxed at 20 percent, then the average tax rate is 20 percent, as is the marginal tax rate.

A proportional tax system is also called a *flat-rate tax.* Taxpayers at all income levels end up paying the same *percentage* of their income in taxes. If the proportional tax rate were 20 percent, an individual with an income of $10,000 would pay $2,000 in taxes, while an individual making $100,000 would pay $20,000, the identical 20 percent rate being levied on both.

Marginal tax rate
The change in the tax payment divided by the change in income, or the percentage of additional dollars that must be paid in taxes. The marginal tax rate is applied to the highest tax bracket of taxable income reached.

Tax bracket
A specified interval of income to which a specific and unique marginal tax rate is applied.

Average tax rate
The total tax payment divided by total income. It is the proportion of total income paid in taxes.

Proportional taxation
A tax system in which regardless of an individual's income, the tax bill comprises exactly the same proportion. Also called a *flat-rate tax.*

---

[2]The word *marginal* means "incremental" (or "decremental") here.

Progressive Taxation. Under **progressive taxation,** as a person's taxable income increases, the percentage of income paid in taxes increases. In terms of marginal versus average tax rates, in a progressive system, the marginal tax rate is above the average tax rate. If you are taxed 5 percent on the first $10,000 you make, 10 percent on the next $10,000 you make, and 30 percent on the last $10,000 you make, you face a progressive income tax system. Your marginal tax rate is always above your average tax rate.

Progressive taxation
A tax system in which as income increases, a higher percentage of the additional income is taxed. The marginal tax rate exceeds the average tax rate as income rises.

EXAMPLE
The Most Progressive Tax System of All: College Financial Aid

Strangely enough, it is not a government agency that imposes the most progressive tax system in the United States but rather colleges and universities. Through their financial aid programs, they severely punish parents who earn progressively more income during the years that their children are attending college and receiving financial aid. Starting at very low annual parents' income, most college financial aid departments begin reducing financial aid as parents' incomes rise. This constitutes an implicit additional marginal income tax. In Figure 5-2, you see that federal marginal tax rates start at zero, rise to 19 percent, and then rise again to 32 percent at about $60,000. When one adds the effective impact of the reduction in financial aid for parents in these different tax brackets, the actual marginal tax rate reaches as high as 79 percent. This is because the effective marginal tax rate of losing financial aid as income rises is between 22 and 47 percent, all added on top of local, state, and federal income taxes.

FOR CRITICAL ANALYSIS: What effect do you think this system of college financial aid has on parents' incentive to earn more income while their children are in college? •

FIGURE 5-2

College Financial Aid and High Implicit Marginal Income Tax Rates for Parents
Because most college and university financial aid officers decrease aid to students whose families earn more, parents of college-enrolled children face relatively high implicit marginal income tax rates. At an income of $60,000 the actual rate faced is almost 80 percent.
Source: Data from *Forbes,* January 17, 1994, p. 74.

Regressive taxation

A tax system in which as more dollars are earned, the percentage of tax paid on them falls. The marginal tax rate is less than the average tax rate as income rises.

Regressive Taxation. With **regressive taxation,** a smaller percentage of taxable income is taken in taxes as taxable income increases. The marginal rate is *below* the average rate. As income increases, the marginal tax rate falls, and so does the average tax rate. The U.S. Social Security tax is regressive. Once the legislative maximum taxable wage base is reached, no further Social Security taxes are paid. Consider a simplified hypothetical example: Every dollar up to $50,000 is taxed at 10 percent. After $50,000 there is no Social Security tax. Someone making $100,000 still pays only $5,000 in Social Security taxes. That person's average Social Security tax is 5 percent. The person making $50,000, by contrast, effectively pays 10 percent. The person making $1 million faces an average Social Security tax rate of only .5 percent in our simplified example.

> **CONCEPTS IN BRIEF**
>
> - Marginal tax rates are applied to marginal tax brackets, defined as spreads of income over which the tax rate is constant.
>
> - Tax systems can be proportional, progressive, or regressive, depending on whether the marginal tax rate is the same as, greater than, or less than the average tax rate as income rises.

THE MOST IMPORTANT FEDERAL TAXES

The federal government imposes income taxes on both individuals and corporations and collects Social Security taxes and a variety of other taxes.

The Federal Personal Income Tax

The most important tax in the U.S. economy is the federal personal income tax, which accounts for about 46 percent of all federal revenues. All American citizens, resident aliens, and most others who earn income in the United States are required to pay federal income taxes on all taxable income. The rates that are paid rise up to a specified amount, depending on marital status, and then fall, as can be seen in Table 5-1. Marginal income tax rates at the federal level have varied from as low as 1 percent after the passage of the Sixteenth Amendment to as high as 94 percent (reached in 1944). There were 14 separate tax brackets prior to the Tax Reform Act of 1986, which reduced the number to three. Advocates of a more progressive income tax system in the United States argue that such a system redistributes income from the rich to the poor, taxes people according to their ability to pay, and

TABLE 5-1

Federal Marginal Income Tax Rates

These rates became effective in 1998. The highest rate includes a 10 percent surcharge on taxable income above $278,450.

Single Persons		Married Couples	
Marginal Tax Bracket	Marginal Tax Rate	Marginal Tax Bracket	Marginal Tax Rate
$0–$25,350	15%	$0–$42,350	15%
$25,351–$61,400	28%	$42,351–$102,300	28%
$61,401–$128,100	31%	$102,301–$155,950	31%
$128,101–$278,450	36%	$155,951–$278,450	36%
$278,451 and up	39.6%	$278,451 and up	39.6%

Source: U.S. Department of the Treasury.

taxes people according to the benefits they receive from government. Although there is much controversy over the redistributional nature of our progressive tax system, there is no strong evidence that in fact the tax system has never done much income redistribution in this country. Currently, about 85 percent of all Americans, rich or poor, pay roughly the same proportion of their income in federal income taxes.

The Treatment of Capital Gains

The difference between the buying and selling price of an asset, such as a share of stock or a plot of land, is called a **capital gain** if it is a profit and a **capital loss** if it is not. As of 1998, there were several capital gains tax rates.

Capital gains are not always real. If you pay $100,000 for a house in one year and sell it for 50 percent more 10 years later, your nominal capital gain is $50,000. But what if, during those 10 years, there had been inflation such that average prices had also gone up by 50 percent? Your *real* capital gain would be zero. But you still have to pay taxes on that $50,000. To counter this problem, many economists have argued that capital gains should be indexed to the rate of inflation. This is exactly what is done with the marginal tax brackets in the federal income tax code. Tax brackets for the purposes of calculating marginal tax rates each year are expanded at the rate of inflation, or the rate at which the average of all prices is rising. So if the rate of inflation is 10 percent, each tax bracket is moved up by 10 percent. The same concept could be applied to capital gains. Thus far, Congress has refused to enact such a measure.

Capital gain
The positive difference between the purchase price and the sale price of an asset. If a share of stock is bought for $5 and then sold for $15, the capital gain is $10.

Capital loss
The negative difference between the purchase price and the sale price of an asset.

The Corporate Income Tax

Corporate income taxes account for about 12 percent of all federal taxes collected and almost 8 percent of all state and local taxes collected. Corporations are generally taxed on the difference between their total revenues (or receipts) and their expenses. The federal corporate income tax structure is given in Table 5-2.

Double Taxation. Because individual stockholders must pay taxes on the dividends they receive, paid out of *after-tax* profits by the corporation, corporate profits are taxed twice. If you receive $1,000 in dividends, you have to declare them as income, and you must pay taxes at your marginal tax rate. Before the corporation was able to pay you those dividends, it had to pay taxes on all its profits, including any that it put back into the company or did not distribute in the form of dividends. Eventually the new investment made possible by those **retained earnings**—profits not given out to stockholders—along with borrowed funds will be reflected in the increased value of the stock in that company. When you sell your stock in that company, you will have to pay taxes on the difference between

Retained earnings
Earnings that a corporation saves, or retains, for investment in other productive activities; earnings that are not distributed to stockholders.

Corporate Taxable Income	Corporate Tax Rate
$0–$50,000	15%
$50,001–$75,000	25%
$75,001–$10,000,000	34%
$10,000,000 and up	35%

TABLE 5-2
Federal Corporate Income Tax Schedule
The rates were in effect through 1999.

Source: Internal Revenue Service.

what you paid for the stock and what you sold it for. In both cases, dividends and retained earnings (corporate profits) are taxed twice.

Who Really Pays the Corporate Income Tax? Corporations can exist only as long as consumers buy their products, employees make their goods, stockholders (owners) buy their shares, and bondholders buy their bonds. Corporations per se do not do anything. We must ask, then, who really pays the tax on corporate income. This is a question of **tax incidence.** (The question of tax incidence applies to all taxes, including sales taxes and Social Security taxes.) There remains considerable debate about the incidence of corporate taxation. Some economists say that corporations pass their tax burdens on to consumers by charging higher prices. Other economists believe that it is the stockholders who bear most of the tax. Still others believe that employees pay at least part of the tax by receiving lower wages than they would otherwise. Because the debate is not yet settled, we will not hazard a guess here as to what the correct conclusion should be. Suffice it to say that you should be cautious when you advocate increasing corporation income taxes. You may be the one who ultimately ends up paying the increase, at least in part, if you own shares in a corporation, buy its products, or work for it.

Tax incidence
The distribution of tax burdens among various groups in society.

CONCEPTS IN BRIEF

- Because corporations must first pay an income tax on most earnings, the personal income tax shareholders pay on dividends received (or realized capital gains) constitutes double taxation.

- The corporate income tax is paid by one or more of the following groups: stockholder-owners, consumers of corporate-produced products, and employees in corporations.

Social Security and Unemployment Taxes

An increasing percentage of federal tax receipts is accounted for each year by taxes (other than income taxes) levied on payrolls. These taxes are for Social Security, retirement, survivors' disability, and old-age medical benefits (Medicare). As of 1998, the Social Security tax was imposed on earnings up to $68,400 at a rate of 6.2 percent on employers and 6.2 percent on employees. That is, the employer matches your "contribution" to Social Security. (The employer's contribution is really paid, at least in part, in the form of a reduced wage rate paid to employees.) A Medicare tax is imposed on all wage earnings at a combined rate of 2.9 percent. These taxes and the base on which they are levied will rise in the next decade. Social Security taxes came into existence when the Federal Insurance Contributions Act (FICA) was passed in 1935.

There is also a federal unemployment tax, which obviously has something to do with unemployment insurance. This tax rate is .8 percent on the first $7,000 of annual wages of each employee who earns more than $1,500. Only the employer makes the tax payment. This tax covers the costs of the unemployment insurance system and the costs of employment services. In addition to this federal tax, some states with an unemployment system impose an additional tax of up to about 3 percent, depending on the past record of the particular employer. An employer who frequently lays off workers will have a slightly higher state unemployment tax rate than an employer who never lays off workers.

It has been argued that Social Security is a system in which current workers subsidize already retired workers. It is also argued that the system is not an insurance system because Social Security benefits are legislated by Congress; they are not part of the original Federal Insurance Contributions Act. Therefore, future generations may decide that they do not want to give large Social Security benefits to retired workers. Even if workers had paid large amounts into Social Security, they could conceivably be denied the benefits of a Social Security retirement income.

INTERNATIONAL EXAMPLE
Chile's Privatized Social Security System

Since 1981, Chile has gradually transformed its government-sponsored social security system into a private pension plan. Entrants into the labor force have been required to contribute 10 percent of their gross monthly earnings to private pension fund accounts that they own outright. During this time period, and even today, virtually anyone still in the public social security system can decide to leave it. Those who choose to leave the public system are given a type of bond that is deposited in their new private pension account to be redeemed at retirement. Fully 94 percent of Chile's labor force is enrolled in 20 competing private pension plans.

FOR CRITICAL ANALYSIS: Under what circumstances might American workers choose to "opt out" of the current federal Social Security system if they were offered the same options as Chilean workers? ●

SPENDING, GOVERNMENT SIZE, AND TAX RECEIPTS

The size of the public sector can be measured in many different ways. One way is to count the number of public employees. Another is to look at total government outlays. Government outlays include all of its expenditures on employees, rent, electricity, and the like. In addition, total government outlays include transfer payments, such as welfare and Social Security. In Figure 5-3, you see that government outlays prior to

THINKING CRITICALLY ABOUT THE MEDIA

Social Security

Countless articles have been written about the problem with the Social Security system in America. They all make reference to the employer and employee "contributions" to the Social Security trust fund. One gets the impression that Social Security payments by employees go into a special government account and that employees do not pay for their employers' "contribution" to this account. Both concepts are not merely flawed but grossly misleading. Though there may be an official Social Security trust fund in the accounts of the U.S. government, "contributing" employees simply have no legal claim on the assets of that trust fund. Indeed, they are just commingled with the rest of government taxes collected and spent every year. Social Security "contributions" are not contributions at all; they are merely taxes paid to the federal government. The so-called employer contribution, which matches the employee payments, is not in fact paid for by employers but rather by employees because of the lower wages that they are paid. Anybody who quits a job and becomes self-employed finds this out when the time comes to pay one's self-employment taxes (Social Security "contributions"), which effectively double the payments previously being made as an employee.

FIGURE 5-3
Total Government Outlays over Time
Here you see that total government outlays (federal, state, and local combined) remained small until the 1930s, except during World War I. Since World War II, government outlays have not fallen back to their historical average.
Sources: Facts and Figures on Government Finance and Economic Indicators, various issues.

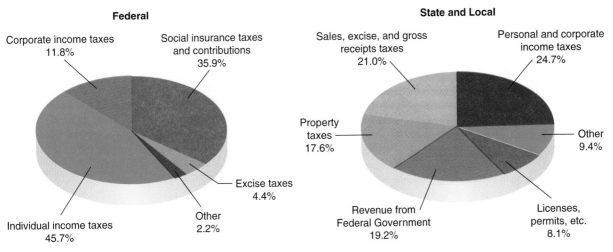

FIGURE 5-4
Sources of Government Tax Receipts
Over 80 percent of federal revenues come from income and Social Security taxes, whereas state government revenues are spread more evenly across sources, with less emphasis on taxes based on individual income.
Source: U.S. Department of Commerce, Bureau of Economic Analysis.

World War I did not exceed 10 percent of annual national income. There was a spike during World War I, a general increase during the Great Depression, and then a huge spike during World War II. Contrary to previous postwar periods, since World War II government outlays as a percentage of total national income have not gradually fallen but rather have risen fairly regularly.

Government Receipts

The main revenue raiser for all levels of government is taxes. We show in the two pie diagrams in Figure 5-4 the percentage of receipts from various taxes obtained by the federal government and by state and local governments.

The Federal Government. The largest source of receipts for the federal government is the individual income tax. It accounts for 45.7 percent of all federal revenues. After that come social insurance taxes and contributions (Social Security), which account for 35.9 percent of total revenues. Next come corporate income taxes and then a number of other items, such as taxes on imported goods and excise taxes on such things as gasoline and alcoholic beverages.

State and Local Governments. As can be seen in Figure 5-4, there is quite a bit of difference between the origin of receipts for state and local governments and for the federal government. Personal and corporate income taxes account for only 24.7 percent of total state and local revenues. There are even a number of states that collect no personal income tax. The largest sources of state and local receipts (other than from the federal government) are personal and corporate income taxes, sales taxes, and property taxes.

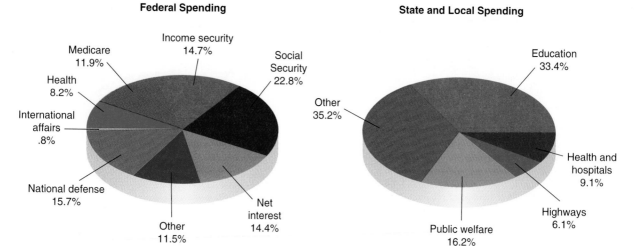

FIGURE 5-5

Federal Government Spending Compared to State and Local Spending
The federal government's spending habits are quite different from those of the states and cities. On the left you can see that the categories of most importance in the federal budget are defense, income security, and Social Security, which make up 53.2 percent. The most important category at the state and local level is education, which makes up 33.4 percent. "Other" includes expenditures in such areas as waste treatment, garbage collection, mosquito abatement, and the judicial system.
Sources: Budget of the United States Government; Government Finances.

Comparing Federal with State and Local Spending. A typical federal government budget is given in Figure 5-5. The largest three categories are defense, income security, and Social Security, which together constitute 53.2 percent of the total federal budget.

The makeup of state and local expenditures is quite different. Education is the biggest category, accounting for 33.4 percent of all expenditures.

CONCEPTS IN BRIEF

- Total government outlays including transfers have continued to grow since World War II and now account for about 40 percent of yearly total national output.

- Government spending at the federal level is different from that at the state and local levels. At the federal level, defense, income security, and Social Security account for about 53 percent of the federal budget. At the state and local levels, education comprises 33 percent of all expenditures.

Every year, Americans spend time worth about $70 billion figuring out their taxes. Many also pay tax specialists. Why is calculating taxes so difficult?

Scrap the Income Tax—Switch to a National Sales Tax

CONCEPTS APPLIED:

MARGINAL TAX RATE, FEDERAL INCOME TAX, INCENTIVES, OPPORTUNITY COST

Visit www.econtoday.com for an Internet Activity that expands your understanding of these concepts.

When Congress got done with the Tax Act of 1997, it made 824 changes to the 3,570-page Internal Revenue Code. Previously, there was one long-term capital gains rate. Now there are four rates (or even more, depending on how you count). One part of the law allows a $400 to $500 child credit. The only problem is that many taxpayers will have to use the so-called alternative minimum tax tables. As a consequence, if they try to reduce their normal taxes owed with child credits, they will find that they actually owe *more* because their taxes under the alternative minimum tax will be higher.

So 45 days after the 1997 Tax Act was signed, Congress started working on a "technical corrections" tax act. When you make 824 tax code changes, you cannot get all of them right, can you?

The Cost of the Current Federal Income Tax System

Because our tax system is so complicated, individuals who fill in their own tax returns must spend many hours doing so. These hours have an opportunity cost. Economist Joel Slemrod has estimated that this opportunity cost is currently about $70 billion a year. In addition, the amount of resources devoted to tax lawyers and accountants probably adds another $70 billion a year. Yet another cost to society of our tax code derives from the fact that it alters individual and business behavior. People respond to incentives. When marginal tax rates are relatively high, some individuals will change their behavior to avoid those high marginal rates. In particular, at high marginal income tax rates, some individuals will work less, retire earlier, not take on a second job, enter the labor market later, and so on. With respect to saving, if the income from saving is taxed at a relatively high marginal rate, some people will be induced to save less than they would otherwise.

The Federal Income Tax, Then and Now

Although the United States first enacted an income tax in 1861 to help pay for the Civil War, it was not until the Sixteenth Amendment was ratified in 1913 that the modern federal income tax came into being. Then, however, very few Americans had to pay it. Look at Table 5-3. It shows the tax rates imposed on various income brackets in 1913 and those same brackets expressed in 1998 dollars. A 1 percent tax rate would be in effect on incomes up to around $300,000. The highest rate, 7 percent, would take effect on incomes over $7.5 million measured in 1998 dollars. Obviously, that is not the situation today—look again at Table 5-1.

Clearly, the federal income tax system as initiated in 1913 was a quite different animal than it is today. If you go back to Table 5-1, you will see that current tax rates are considerably higher than they were in 1913, and they affect virtually all Americans. (Note also that inflation-adjusted federal expenditures increased more than 13,000 percent between 1913 and 1998.)

A National Sales Tax—A Viable Alternative?

Every few years, there is public debate on "simplifying" the federal income tax system. Numerous suggestions have been made, including a "flat tax." But not everyone who wants to change our complicated system agrees that a flat tax is the best alternative. Some critics want to scrap the federal income tax completely. They point out that even when tax rates were simplified in 1986, Congress and the president gradually made them more and more complicated. Thus even if we were to legislate a "flat" income tax rate, it would not last very long, according to these critics.

Tax Rate	Income Level in 1913	Income Level in 1998 Dollars	TABLE 5-3
1%	Up to $20,000	Up to $298,507	**1913 U.S. Income Tax Rates and Brackets**
2%	$20,000–$50,000	$298,507–746,269	
3%	$50,000–$75,000	$746,269–$1,119,403	
4%	$75,000–$100,000	$1,119,403–$1,492,537	
5%	$100,000–$250,000	$1,492,537–$3,731,343	
6%	$250,000–$500,000	$3,731,343–$7,462,687	
7%	Over $500,000	Over $7,462,687	

Source: *U.S. Department of the Treasury*

What they want to see put in place is a national sales tax. This is not just pie-in-the-sky theorizing—proposed legislation was actually introduced in 1996. Some politicians take it seriously. Proponents of a national sales tax want it to replace the personal income tax, the corporate income tax, and estate and gift taxes.

The Proposed Rate

Proponents of a national sales tax argue that it could replace all of the above-mentioned federal taxes using a rate of 15 percent on all *final* purchases of goods and services at the retail level. Many poor people would effectively be exempt from the taxes, however, because there would be a universal rebate for every household up to the poverty level of around $20,000 for a family of four. That would mean that the first $20,000 of consumption each year for a family of four would be tax-free. In addition, the federal government would reimburse states and retailers for the cost of collecting the national sales tax.

Adios IRS

Obviously, the replacement of a current complicated federal tax system with a simple national sales tax could mean the abolition or dramatic downsizing of the Internal Revenue Service. The states would bear the primary responsibility for administrating the national sales tax. Thus most Americans would be freed from the scrutiny of the IRS. More than 100 million Americans who file personal tax returns would no longer have to file them. The number of tax returns filed would fall by as much as 80 percent.

Businesses would find their paperwork burden reduced dramatically. Business-to-business purchases would be exempt from the tax because it would apply only to final purchases of goods and services from retailers. Retailers would have to determine which sales they made to consumers, but they already do that in most states in order to remit state sales taxes.

An Increased Reward for Saving

Because a national sales tax would be assessed only on final purchases of goods and services, individuals would be rewarded more for saving. They would pay no tax on the income they put into savings or on the earnings of those savings. According to some economists, this would increase the rate of saving in America and be beneficial to the economy. Proponents of the national sales tax even argue that because the economy would grow so much faster under the new system, the national sales tax rate could drop from 15 percent to 12 or even 10 percent over time.

Not Universally Favored

To be sure, some groups in society would be hurt by a switch from our current federal tax system to a national sales tax. Tax and estate attorneys, as well as accountants, would find dramatic reductions in their incomes. The employees of the Internal Revenue Service would have to look for other work. Tax preparation companies such as H&R Block would suffer large reductions in revenues.

Another group would be hurt by the switch to a national sales tax: current members of Congress. Even if the national sales tax generated exactly the same amount of government revenues for Congress to spend, members of that body will have lost an effective means of raising campaign reelection funds. Currently, many members of Congress receive campaign contributions from individuals and lobbyists who wish to obtain special exemptions from the income tax system. The abolition of the current system would eliminate this source of campaign contributions.

FOR CRITICAL ANALYSIS
1. What types of businesses would most easily be able—albeit illegally—to evade a national sales tax?
2. How would you calculate whether to fill out your own tax returns or to pay a consulting firm such as H&R Block to do them?

CHAPTER SUMMARY

1. Government can correct external costs through taxation, legislation, and prohibition. It can correct external benefits through financing or production of a good or service, subsidies, and regulation.
2. Government provides a legal system in which the rights of private ownership, the enforcement of contracts, and the legal status of businesses are provided. In other words, government sets the legal rules of the game and enforces them.
3. Public goods, once produced, can be consumed jointly by additional individuals at zero opportunity cost.
4. If users of public goods know that they will be taxed on the basis of their expressed valuation of those public goods, their expressed valuation will be low. They expect to get a free ride.
5. Merit goods (chosen as such, collectively, through the political process) may not be purchased at all or not in sufficient quantities at market clearing prices. Therefore, government subsidizes or provides such

merit goods at a subsidized or zero price to specified classes of consumers.
6. When it is collectively decided that something is a demerit good, government taxes, regulates, or prohibits the manufacture, sale, and use of that good.
7. Marginal tax rates are those paid on the last dollars of income, whereas average taxes rates are determined by the proportion of income paid in income taxes.
8. With a proportional income tax system, marginal rates are constant. With a regressive system, they go down as income rises, and with a progressive system, they go up as income rises.
9. Total government outlays including transfers have continued to grow since World War II and now account for about 40 percent of yearly total national output.
10. Government spending at the federal level is different from that at the state and local levels. Defense, income security, and Social Security account for about 55 percent of the federal budget.

DISCUSSION OF PREVIEW QUESTIONS

1. What problems will you encounter if you refuse to pay a portion of your income tax because you oppose national defense spending?

You must share in national defense collectively with the rest of the country. Unlike private goods, national defense is a public good and must be consumed collectively. You receive national defense benefits whether you choose to or not; the exclusion principle does not work for public goods, such as national defense. The government could make the exclusion principle work better by deporting you to foreign shores if you don't wish to pay for national defense. This is typically not done. If you were allowed to forgo taxes allocated to national defense, the IRS would be swamped with similar requests. Everyone would have an incentive to claim no benefits from national defense (whether true or not) because it must be consumed collectively. So, if you refuse, you may go to jail.

2. Will you benefit from many so-called tax loopholes when you first start working?

Probably not, for you will not be making enough income to put you into the highest marginal income tax bracket. Tax loopholes are more beneficial the more they save you in taxes. At low incomes, your marginal tax rate is low, so each dollar in tax saved because of your use of a tax loophole yields you very little additional after-tax income. If you're in the 15 percent marginal tax bracket, you only benefit by 15 cents for every dollar in tax loopholes you find. Compare this to the benefit for someone in the 39.6 percent marginal tax bracket.

3. In what ways do regressive, proportional, and progressive tax structures differ?

Under a regressive tax structure, the average tax rate (the percentage of income paid in taxes) falls as income rises. The marginal tax rate is below the average tax rate. Proportional tax structures are those in which the average tax rate remains constant as income rises; the marginal tax rate equals the average tax rate. Under a progressive tax structure, the average tax rate rises as income rises; the marginal tax rate is above the average tax rate. Our federal personal income tax system is an example of a progressive system.

4. **Who pays the corporate income tax?**

Ultimately, only people can be taxed. As a consequence, corporate taxes are ultimately paid by people: corporate owners (in the form of reduced dividends and less stock appreciation for stockholders), consumers of corporate products (in the form of higher prices for goods), and/or employees working for corporations (in the form of lower wages).

PROBLEMS

(Answers to the odd-numbered problems appear at the back of the book.)

5-1. Consider the following system of taxation, which has been labeled *degressive*. The first $5,000 of income is not taxed. After that, all income is assessed at 20 percent (a proportional system). What is the marginal tax rate on $3,000 of taxable income? $10,000? $100,000? What is the average tax rate on $3,000? $10,000? $100,000? What is the maximum average tax rate?

5-2. You are offered two possible bonds to buy as part of your investing program. One is a corporate bond yielding 9 percent. The other is a tax-exempt municipal bond yielding only 6 percent. Assuming that you are certain you will be paid your interest and principal on these two bonds, what marginal tax bracket must you be in to decide in favor of the tax-exempt bond?

5-3. Consider the following tax structure:

Income Bracket	Marginal Tax Rate
$0–$1,500	0%
$1,501–$2,000	14%
$2,001–$3,000	20%

Mr. Smith has an income of $2,500 per annum. Calculate his tax bill for the year. What is his average tax rate? His highest marginal tax rate?

5-4. Assume that Social Security tax payments on wages are 7.65 percent of wages, on wages up to $51,300. No *further* Social Security payments are made on earnings above this figure. Calculate the *average* Social Security tax rate for annual wages of (a) $4,000, (b) $51,300, (c) $56,000, (d) $100,000. Is this Social Security system a progressive, proportional, or regressive tax structure?

5-5. Briefly, what factors could be included as part of the requirements for a "good" tax structure?

5-6. What is meant by the expression "market failure"?

5-7. Is local police protection a public good? Explain.

5-8. TV signals have characteristics of public goods, yet TV stations and commercial networks are private businesses. Analyze this situation.

5-9. Assume that you live in a relatively small suburban neighborhood called Parkwood. The Parkwood Homeowners' Association collects money from homeowners to pay for upkeep of the surrounding stone wall, lighting at the entrances to Parkwood, and mowing the lawn around the perimeter of the area. Each year you are asked to donate $50. No one forces you to do it. There are 100 homeowners in Parkwood.

a. What percentage of the total yearly revenue of the homeowners' association will you account for?

b. At what level of participation will the absence of your $50 contribution make a difference?

c. If you do not contribute your $50, are you really receiving a totally free ride?

5-10. Assume that the only textile firm that exists has created a negative externality by polluting a nearby stream with the wastes associated with production. Assume further that the government can measure the external costs to the community with accuracy and charges the firm for its pollution, based on the social cost of pollution per unit of textile output. Show how such a charge will lead to a higher selling price for textiles and a reduction in the equilibrium quantity of textiles.

5-11. Label two columns on your paper "Private Goods" and "Public Goods." List each of the following under the heading that describes it better.

a. Sandwich
b. Public television
c. Cable television
d. National defense
e. Shirt
f. Elementary education
g. College education
h. Health clinic flu shots
i. Opera
j. Museum
k. Automobile

COMPUTER-ASSISTED INSTRUCTION

The decisions made by people in the government (bureaucrats) and people in the private sector often differ because of the different constraints they face. We show the impact of this on innovation in the ethical drug industry.

Complete problem and answer appear on disk.

INTERACTING WITH THE INTERNET

To get information on the federal budget, go to

www.access.gpo.gov/su_docs/budget/index.html

If you would like more information about Social Security, go to

www.ssa.gov/

There you can find hypothetical personal earnings and benefits estimate statements as well as facts and figures on the Social Security system. A history of Social Security can also be found there.

To get the latest information on taxes, go to the Internal Revenue Service's site at

www.irs.ustreas.gov/cover.html

CHAPTER 6

ECONOMIES IN TRANSITION

Today you are studying economics and many other subjects. By the time you finish your studies, you will probably have made a decision about what type of work to seek. When you look for your first job (or a better one after completing your degree), you and only you decide which job you will take. Imagine a world in which, just before graduation, someone else—a government official—tells you what job you will have and where you will live to do that job. That is exactly the world in which college and university students in the People's Republic of China have lived for decades. The job assignment system is changing, though. Before you read about the implications of the changes, you need to understand how resource use is determined in a market economy such as that of the United States.

PREVIEW QUESTIONS

1. Why does the scarcity problem force all societies to answer the questions *what, how,* and *for whom*?

2. How can economies be classified?

3. Why do we say that *all* economies are mixed economies?

4. What are the "three *P*s" of pure capitalism?

116

Economic system
The institutional means through which resources are used to satisfy human wants.

Resource allocation
The assignment of resources to specific uses by determining what will be produced, how it will be produced, and for whom it will be produced.

Did You Know That . . . there used to be a country called the Soviet Union whose chief of state in 1960 took off his shoe at the United Nations and pounded it on the desk while shouting, "We will bury you"? That person was Nikita Khrushchev; he died in 1971. It took quite a few more years for his country to die, but die it did. The Soviet Union is no more. The 74-year experiment in trying to run an economy without using the price, or market, system will go down in history as one of the greatest social and economic failures of all time. Just because the Soviet Union dissolved itself at the end of 1991 does not mean that the entire world economy automatically became like that of the United States. In particular, the 15 republics of the former Soviet Union, the Soviet "satellite" countries of Eastern Europe, and other nations, including China, are what we call *economies in transition.*

At any point in time, every nation has its own **economic system,** which can be defined as the institutional means through which resources are used to satisfy human wants. No matter what institutional means—marketplace or government—a nation chooses to use, three basic economic questions must always be answered.

THE THREE BASIC ECONOMIC QUESTIONS

In every nation, no matter what the form of government, what the type of economic system, who is running the government, or how poor or rich it is, three basic economic questions must be answered. They concern the problem of **resource allocation,** which is simply how resources are to be allocated. As such, resource allocation answers the three basic economic questions of *what, how,* and *for whom* goods and services will be produced.

1. *What and how much will be produced?* Literally billions of different things could be produced with society's scarce resources. Some mechanism must exist that causes some things to be produced and others to remain as either inventors' pipe dreams or individuals' unfulfilled desires.
2. *How will it be produced?* There are many ways to produce a desired item. It is possible to use more labor and less capital or vice versa. It is possible to use more unskilled labor and fewer units of skilled labor. Somehow, in some way, a decision must be made as to the particular mix of inputs, the way they should be organized, and how they are brought together at a particular place.
3. *For whom will it be produced?* Once a commodity is produced, who should get it? In a market economy, individuals and businesses purchase commodities with money income. The question then is what mechanism there is to distribute income, which then determines how commodities are distributed throughout the economy.

THE PRICE SYSTEM AND HOW IT ANSWERS THE THREE ECONOMIC QUESTIONS

As explained in Chapter 4, a price (or market) system is an economic system in which (relative) prices are constantly changing to reflect changes in supply and demand for different commodities. In addition, the prices of those commodities are the signals to everyone within the system as to what is relatively scarce and what is relatively abundant. Indeed, it is the *signaling* aspect of the price system that provides the information to buyers and sellers about what should be bought and what should be produced. The price system, which is characteristic of a market economy, is only one possible way to organize society.

What and How Much Will Be Produced?

In a price system, the interaction of demand and supply for each good determines what and how much to produce. Note, however, that if the highest price that consumers are willing to pay is less than the lowest cost at which a good can be produced, output will be zero. That doesn't mean that the price system has failed. Today consumers do not purchase their own private space shuttles. The demand is not high enough in relation to the supply to create a market. But it may be someday.

How Will It Be Produced?

The question of how output will be produced in a price system relates to the efficient use of scarce inputs. Consider the possibility of using only two types of resources, capital and labor. A firm may have the options given in Table 6-1. It can use various combinations of labor and capital to produce the same amount of output. Two hypothetical combinations are given in the table. How, then, is it decided which combination should be used? In the price system, the **least-cost combination** (technique B in our example) will in fact be chosen because it maximizes profits. We assume that the owners of business firms act as if they are maximizing profits. Recall from Chapter 1 that we assume that individuals act *as if* they are rational.

Least-cost combination
The level of input use that produces a given level of output at minimum cost.

In a price system, competition *forces* firms to use least-cost production techniques. Any firm that fails to employ the least costly technique will find that other firms can undercut its price. In other words, other firms that choose the least-cost production technique will be able to offer the product at a lower price and still make a profit. This lower price will induce consumers to shift purchases from the higher-priced firm to the lower-priced firm. Inefficient firms will be forced out of business.

For Whom Will It Be Produced?

This last question that every economic system must answer involves who gets what. In a market system, the choice about what is purchased is made by individuals, but that choice is determined by the ability to pay. Who gets what is determined by the distribution of money income.

Determination of Money Income. In a price system, a consumer's ability to pay for consumer products is based on the size of that consumer's money income. That in turn depends on the quantities, qualities, and types of the various human and nonhuman resources that the individual owns and supplies to the marketplace. It also depends on the prices, or payments, for those resources. When you are selling your human resources as labor

TABLE 6-1

Production Costs for 100 Units of Product X
Technique A or B can be used to produce the same output. Obviously, B will be used because its total cost is less than A's. Using production technique B will generate a $2 savings for every 100 units produced.

Inputs	Input Unit Price	Production Technique A (input units)	Cost	Production Technique B (input units)	Cost
		A		B	
Labor	$10	5	$50	4	$40
Capital	8	4	32	5	40
Total cost of 100 units			82		80

services, your money income is based on the wages you can earn in the labor market. If you own nonhuman resources—physical capital and land, for example—the level of interest and rents that you are paid for your physical capital and land will clearly influence the size of your money income and thus your ability to buy consumer products.

Which Consumers Get What? In a price system, the distribution of finished products to consumers is based on consumers' ability and willingness to pay the market price for the product. If the market price of compact discs is $9, consumers who are able and willing to pay that price will get those CDs. All others won't.

Here we are talking about the *rationing* function of market prices in a price system. Rather than have a central political figure or agency decide which consumers will get which goods, those consumers who are willing and able to pay the market price obtain the goods. That is to say, relative prices ration the available resources, goods, and services at any point in time among those who place the highest value on those items. If scarcity didn't exist, we would not need any system to ration available resources, goods, and services. All of us could have all of everything that we wanted without taking away from what anyone else obtained.

CONCEPTS IN BRIEF

- Any economic system must answer three questions: (1) *What* will be produced? (2) *How* will it be produced? (3) *For whom* will it be produced?
- In a price system, supply and demand determine the prices at which exchanges take place.
- In a price system, firms choose the least-cost combination use of inputs to produce any given output. Competition forces firms to do so.
- In a price system, who gets what is determined by consumers' money income and choices about how to use that money income.

TODAY'S INCREASINGLY ALL-CAPITALIST WORLD

Not long ago, textbooks presented a range of economic systems, usually capitalism, socialism, and communism. **Communism** was intended as a system in which the state disappeared and individuals contributed to the economy according to their productivity and received income according to their needs. Under **socialism,** the state owned a major share of productive resources except labor. **Capitalism** has been defined as a system under which individuals hold government-protected private property rights to all goods, including those used in production, and their own labor.

Pure Capitalism in Theory

In its purest theoretical form, market capitalism, or pure capitalism, has the following attributes:

1. Private property rights exist and are upheld by the judicial system.
2. Prices are allowed to seek their own level as determined by the forces of supply and demand. In this sense, pure capitalism is a price system.
3. Resources, including human labor, are free to move in and out of industries and geographic locations. The movement of resources follows the lure of profits—higher expected profits create an incentive for more resources to go where those profits might occur.

Communism
In its purest form, an economic system in which the state has disappeared and individuals contribute to the economy according to their productivity and are given income according to their needs.

Socialism
An economic system in which the state owns the major share of productive resources except labor. Socialism also usually involves the redistribution of income.

Capitalism
An economic system in which individuals own productive resources; these individuals can use the resources in whatever manner they choose, subject to common protective legal restrictions.

4. Risk takers are rewarded by higher profits, but those whose risks turn out to be bad business decisions suffer the consequences directly in terms of reduced wealth.

5. Decisions about what and how much should be produced, how it should be produced, and for whom it should be produced are left to the market. In a pure market capitalist system, all decisions are decentralized and made by individuals in a process of *spontaneous coordination* throughout the economy.

One way to remember the attributes of pure capitalism is by thinking of the three *P*s: prices, profits, and private property.

The role of government is limited to provision of certain public goods, such as defense, police protection, and a legal framework within which property rights and contracts are enforced.

Pure capitalism has also been called a **laissez-faire** system. The French term means "leave [it] alone" or "let [it] be." A pure capitalist system is one in which the government lets the economic actors in the economy make their own decisions without government constraints.

Laissez-faire
French for "leave [it] alone"; applied to an economic system in which the government minimizes its interference with the economy.

The Importance of Incentives

Though it is doubtful that full-blown communism ever really existed or could survive in a whole economy, various forms of socialism, in which the state owned important parts of the economy, have existed. Indeed, one can argue that the most important distinguishing feature between capitalist countries and everywhere else is the lack of private property rights. Economics predicts that, for example, when an apartment building is owned by no one (that is, owned by the "state"), there is less incentive for anyone to take care of it. This analysis has predicted well with respect to public housing in the United States. Just imagine an entire country for which all housing is public housing. That is what the former Soviet Union was like. (Note that we are not passing judgment on a system that has few private property rights. Rather, we are simply pointing out the predictions that economists can make with respect to how individuals treat such property.)

We pointed out in Chapter 4 that in a world of scarcity, resources must always be rationed. In economic systems in which prices were not allowed to be the rationing device, other methods had to be used. In the former Soviet Union, rationing by queuing (waiting) was one of the most prevalent. Some economists estimated that the average Russian spent as many hours a week waiting in lines as the average American spends watching television.

Today one might say that the collapse of communism has left the world with one system only, the **mixed economy,** in which decisions about how resources are used are made partly by the private sector and partly by the public sector—capitalism with government. Figure 6-1 represents the size of government relative to annual national output. You can see that even among the traditional capitalist countries of the world, there are great variations. These can be regarded as the different faces of capitalism.

Exercise 6.1
Visit www.econtoday.com for more about alternative systems.

Mixed economy
An economic system in which decisions about how resources should be used are made partly by the private sector and partly by the government, or the public sector.

CONCEPTS IN BRIEF

• Communism is an economic system in which, in theory, individuals would produce according to their abilities and consume according to their needs. Under socialism, the state owns most major capital goods and attempts to redistribute income.

• Pure capitalism allows for the spontaneous coordination of millions of individuals by allowing the free play of the three *P*s—prices, profits, and property rights. Often, pure capitalism is called a laissez-faire system.

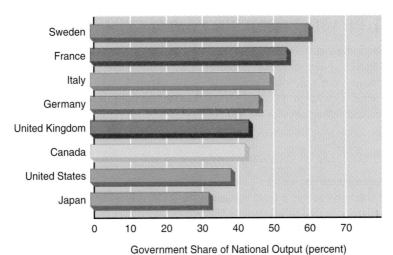

FIGURE 6-1

Percentage of National Yearly Output Accounted for by Government in Various Countries
Even among countries that have embraced capitalism for a long time, government plays an important, but widely different, role. It constitutes over 60 percent of the economy in Sweden, but less than 40 percent in the United States.

Government Share of National Output (percent)

- Incentives matter in any economic system; therefore, in countries that have had few or unenforced property rights, individuals lacked the incentives to take care of most property that wasn't theirs.

- Most economies today can be viewed as mixed in that they combine private decisions and government controls.

THE DIFFERENT FACES OF CAPITALISM

The world is left with a single economic system that, thanks to the diversity of human cultures, has a variety of faces. Table 6-2 presents one way to categorize today's economic systems.

TABLE 6-2

Four Faces of Capitalism

Type of Capitalism	Examples	Characteristics	Problem Areas
Consumer	Canada, United States, New Zealand, Australia, United Kingdom	Borders are relatively open; focus is on profit maximization and laissez-faire.	Low saving and investment rates; income inequality
Producer	Japan, France, Germany	Production is emphasized over consumption; employment is a major policy issue; state controls a relatively large part of the economy.	Consumer dissatisfaction; potential slow future growth rates; inertia within the economy
Family	Indonesia, Malaysia, Thailand, Taiwan	Extended clans dominate business and capital flows.	Lack of modern corporate organizations; lack of money markets
Frontier	Russia, China, Ukraine, Romania, Albania	Many government enterprises pursue for-profit activities; new entrepreneurs emerge every day.	Difficulty of crossing borders; rising criminal activity

Source: Based, in part, on "21st Century Capitalism," *Business Week,* February 23, 1995, p. 19.

THE TRANSITIONAL PHASE: FRONTIER CAPITALISM

Frontier capitalism describes economies in transition from state ownership and control of most of the factors of production to a system of private property rights in which the price system is used to answer the basic economic questions. Table 6-3 presents theoretical stages in the development of frontier capitalism. Two aspects appear to be the most important: developing the legal system and selling off state-owned businesses.

Development of the Legal System

In the United States and many other countries, we take a well-established legal system as a given. That does not imply the total absence of a legal system in countries where we are now seeing frontier capitalism. To be sure, the former Soviet Union had a legal system, but virtually none of it had to do with economic transactions, which were carried out by state dictates. Individuals could not own the factors of production, and therefore, by definition, there were no legal disputes over property rights involving them. Consequently, the legal system in the former Soviet Union and its Eastern European satellites consisted of many volumes of criminal codes—laws against robbery, murder, rape, and theft as well as so-called economic crimes.

Enter the new world of private property rights and unfettered exchange of those rights among buyers and sellers. Now what happens when a buyer claims that a seller breached a particular agreement? In the United States, lawyers, courts, and the Uniform Commercial Code can be used to settle the dispute. Yet until recently in the frontier economies of the former Soviet Union, there was nothing even vaguely comparable. The rule of law in the United States and Great Britain has developed over hundreds of years; we cannot expect that in countries in transition toward full capitalism, an entire body of law and procedure can be developed overnight.

Privatization

The transition toward capitalism requires that the government lessen its role in the economy. This transition involves what has become known as *privatization*. **Privatization** is the transfer of ownership or responsibility for businesses run by the government, so-called *state enterprises,* to individuals and companies in the private sector. Even in capitalist countries, the government has owned and run various parts of the economy. During and after World War II, it became fashionable for many European governments to "nationalize" different industries. This was particularly prevalent in the United Kingdom, where the steel industry was nationalized, for example. In the early 1980s, France nationalized the banking industry. The opposite of nationalization is privatization.

In the early 1980s, Turkey and Chile were the first capitalist countries to start carrying out mass privatization of government-owned businesses. Under Margaret Thatcher, the United Kingdom pioneered the mass privatization of state industry, including the huge road haulage company (NFC), a health care group (Amersham International), British Telecom, British Petroleum, and British Aerospace.

A country must employ some method to put government-owned businesses into the hands of the private sector; government-owned businesses are not simply given away to the first party who asks. Imagine if the U.S. government said that it wanted to sell the United States Postal Service. How would it do so? One way is to sell it outright, but there might not be any buyers who would be willing to pay to take over such a giant money-losing corporation. An alternative would involve selling shares of stock to anyone who wanted to buy

Privatization
The sale or transfer of state-owned property and businesses to the private sector, in part or in whole. Also refers to *contracting out*—letting private business take over government-provided services such as trash collection.

Stage	Characteristics
I	The central government, as the controller of all economic activities, collapses and starts to disappear. The black market, typically involving government enterprises still owned by the state, expands enormously. Many former state factory managers and other bosses become involved in criminal activities using the state's resources. Government corruption flourishes more than before.
II	Small businesses start to flourish. Families pool funds in order to become entrepreneurs. The rules of commerce are not well understood because there is not yet a well-established commercial law system, nor are property rights well defined or protected by the state.
III	The economy is growing, but much of its growth is not measured by government statisticians. Small financial markets, such as stock markets, begin to develop. Foreigners cautiously invest in the new stock markets. The government attempts to develop a clear set of commercial laws.
IV	Foreign corporations are more willing to invest directly in new factories and stores. The state gets serious about selling all businesses that it owns. More resources are devoted to suppressing criminal activity. Commercial law becomes better established and better understood.

TABLE 6-3
How Frontier Capitalism Develops

them at the stated price. This latter technique is indeed the way in which most privatizations have been carried out in established capitalist countries throughout the world over the past 15 or 20 years.

In the former Soviet Union and in Eastern Europe, alternative systems have been devised. For example, citizens, at various times, have been given vouchers granting them the right to purchase a specified number of shares in particular government-owned companies that were being sold off.

The trend in privatization versus nationalization can be seen in panel (a) of Figure 6-2 on page 124. The cumulative worldwide sales of state-owned enterprises can be seen in panel (b). In Europe, privatization will probably continue at the rate of over $50 billion a year into the next century. Privatization in Latin America will continue much longer. Finally, because privatization in the former Soviet Union and Eastern Europe has in a sense just begun, such wholesale privatization may take a long time indeed.

Political Opposition to Privatization

There is often strong political pressure to slow down or even prevent privatization of state-owned businesses. The political pressure to prevent privatization is derived from simple economics: Managers of state-owned businesses typically have had lifetime job security, better working conditions than they could obtain elsewhere, and little threat of competition. In other words, life for a manager is typically better in a state-owned firm than in that same firm once it has been privatized.

Workers in state-run firms also believe, often rightly, that their lot in life will not be quite so good if the state-owned firm is sold to the private sector. State-owned firms tend to pay their workers higher wages and give them better fringe benefits, including much better pension plans, than similar firms that are privately owned. For example, an examination of state-owned phone companies in France and Germany shows that they have two to three

Panel (a)

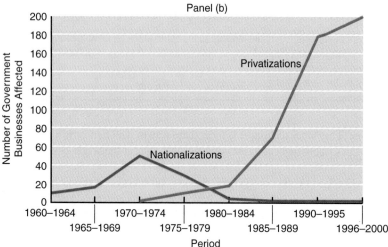

Panel (b)

FIGURE 6-2

The Trend Toward Privatization
Privatization worldwide has been on the upswing since 1985, as shown in panel (a). Nationalizations (the opposite of privatizations) reached their peak in about 1970 as is shown in panel (b).

Source: OECD and *The Economist*, August 21, 1993, p. 19; United Nations.

times as many workers per telephone customer as the private telephone companies in the United States. This comparative overuse of labor in state-owned firms is even more obvious in the republics of the former Soviet Union and in Eastern Europe.

Economists cannot say whether privatization of state-owned firms is good or bad. Rather, economists can simply state that the rigors of a competitive market will generally cause resources to be used more efficiently after privatization occurs. In the process, however, some managers and workers may be made worse off.

Is There a Right Way to Go About the Transition?

Ever since the fall of the Berlin Wall in 1989, economists have debated whether there is a "right" way for former socialist and communist countries to move toward capitalist systems. The once-communist nations have, indeed, embarked on a social experiment in how to move toward a market economy. Basically, they have chosen two methods—a slow one and a fast one. Romania, Belarus, and Ukraine have only gradually privatized their economies, whereas the Czech Republic and, to a lesser extent, Poland and Estonia opted for a "shock treatment."

The rapid move toward a market economy, though not free of problems, has seemed to work better than the go-slow approach. The slower the transition occurs, the more the former entrenched bureaucrats in the state-owned businesses have been able to maintain their power over the use of resources. In the meantime, the state-owned businesses continue to use valuable resources inefficiently in these developing countries.

In contrast, a country like the Czech Republic used a voucher system to privatize over 2,000 state-owned enterprises. All citizens were given vouchers—legal rights evidenced on printed certificates—which could be used to purchase shares of stock in state-owned businesses. A stock market quickly developed in which shares of hundreds of companies are now traded every day. After an initial period of transition to a market economy, the Czech Republic has now achieved one of the lowest unemployment rates in Europe.

We will next examine the current situation of two of the largest countries in the world that are in the throes of frontier capitalism. Both are grappling with the problems of the transition from communism to capitalism.

CONCEPTS IN BRIEF

- Today there are four types of capitalism: consumer, producer, family, and frontier. The last begins when a centralized economy starts collapsing and black markets thrive. Eventually small businesses flourish, and then financial markets develop. Finally, foreign investment is attracted, and state-owned businesses are privatized.

- The development of a well-functioning legal system is one of the most difficult problems for an economy in the frontier capitalism stage. Such economies do not have the laws or courts to handle the new system of property right transfers.

- Privatization, or the turning over to the private sector of state-owned and state-run businesses, is occurring all over the world in all types of economies. There is much political opposition, however, whenever managers in soon-to-be privatized businesses realize that they may face harder times in a private setting.

RUSSIA AND ITS FORMER SATELLITES, YESTERDAY AND TODAY

Russia was the largest republic in the former Soviet Union. The economic system in place was at times called communism and at other times called command socialism. There is no question that it was a command economy in which there was centralized economic leadership and planning. All economies involve planning, of course; the difference is that in capitalist societies, most of the planning is done by private businesses rather than the government. Leaders in the former Soviet Union somehow believed that its economic planners in Moscow could micromanage an economy spanning 11 time zones, involving millions and millions of consumers and producers, and affecting vast quantities of goods and services.

Imagine trying to run a single business that big! No one can. Perhaps more important, state ownership in such a large country resulted in perverse incentives throughout the economy. For example, when the government issued production quotas for glass based on the number of panes, they ended up being almost paper thin and shattering easily. When the government then changed its quotas to weight, the glass panes were so thick that they were useless. In short, former Soviet citizens responded appropriately every time central planners figured out a new way to set production quotas. In the process, untold resources were inefficiently used or completely wasted.

By the time the Soviet Union collapsed in 1991, it consisted of a society in which perhaps 1 or 2 percent of the population (the communists, privileged bureaucrats, athletes, and artists) enjoyed a nice lifestyle and the rest of the citizens were forced to scrape by. The same was true perhaps to an even greater degree in the former East Germany, Romania, Poland, Hungary, Czechoslovakia (now the Czech Republic and Slovakia), and Albania. The standard of living of the average citizen prior to the Soviet Union's breakup was at best a quarter but more realistically one-tenth of that in the United States.

Rapid Privatization

One of the most dramatic privatization movements in history has occurred in Russia. Since 1992, about 18,000 state-owned companies have been privatized. Two-thirds of Russia's economy is now in private hands, and the private sector currently accounts for more than half of Russian output. The switch to privatization was Russia's decisive step into capitalism. Although official government statistics do not show much or any economic growth, they do not reflect reality (see the accompanying Thinking Critically About the Media box). The underground economy represents at least 40 percent and perhaps 50 percent of officially measured total economic activity. The standard of living has also improved because price controls (see Chapter 4) were abandoned in 1992. Prior to 1992, shortages at the officially controlled prices were common, and many consumer goods were constantly unavailable. That is no longer true today.

Russian housing has also been privatized for the most part. Some observers argue that the privatization of virtually all businesses and housing has been one of the most remarkable achievements of the post-Soviet era.

One Major Problem: Business Wars

The quick switch to a capitalist economy has not been without problems in Russia. Because of the lack of both a well-established legal system and an adequate police force, crimes against business people have shocked much of the Western world. Indeed, some observers argue that the breakdown of law enforcement and the proliferation of private armies and protection rackets prone to ruthless gangland tactics may be a threat to this new free market economy. Sergei Concharov, head of a group of former KGB (Soviet security) troops who now runs a protection agency for Russian businesses, stated that the power of bandits is important. He puts the power of bandits as perhaps the most important governing business power today. The International Institute of Strategic Studies in London estimates that over 80 percent of Russian enterprises pay an average of 10 to 20 percent of their profits as protection money. From 1994 through 1997, almost 130 bankers were murdered. Russia's Interior Ministry contends that criminal gangs control 40,000 enterprises, 500 of which are banks.

The judiciary is surely corrupt and underpaid. Anyone in business eventually has to hire the services of a *krysha*—a "fixer." The fixer will sort out disputes. Resorting to such extralegal intermediaries is the only way to survive in a system in which the law does not count.

The massive transfer of property to private hands has led to a steady struggle for wealth made even riskier in the absence of the rule of law. The Russian economy currently has a

THINKING CRITICALLY ABOUT THE MEDIA

Taking Russia's Pulse

When economists and journalists discuss the transition from the centralized Soviet economy to its current market orientation, they lament the tremendous reduction in national output. Official estimates for the period 1989 to 1995, for example, claim that national output dropped by over 50 percent. True though it may be that output dropped during this time, it is not clear what the actual value of that output was to the population. Much of the reduction was in military hardware, such as missiles. How much did the average citizen lose when that output shrank? Also, fewer television sets and radios were produced during this time period—but the ones produced earlier either never worked properly or tended to explode. Steel mills have been shut down in Russia but they had been using technology that was 45 years old. Further, the official Russian state agency that measures the economy, Goskomstat, has none of the sophistication that the U.S. Department of Commerce and the Bureau of Labor Statistics have for measuring a nation's output. Even if Goskomstat had better computers and more refined techniques, it would still miss a vast off-the-books economy that won't be counted by government statisticians for years to come. All in all, Russia's 150 million people earn more and live better than what Goskomstat statistics say.

small cadre of "business barons," who are often allied with powerful politicians. These business barons frequently enter into deals with state officials that prevent free competition from occurring. Many observers of the economic scene in Russia are not particularly worried, though. They point out that because Russia has opened its borders to competitors from other countries, industrial concentration will not be a serious problem. If foreign goods are available domestically, they provide a competitive check that will prevent excessive prices or poor quality. Today one sees foreign goods in virtually all Russian stores.

The Nightmare They Call Their Tax System

A major problem preventing Russia from truly entering a modern era is its bizarre and exceedingly complex tax system. Many tax rates are so high that if enforced, they would amount to a confiscation of wealth, and that situation has led to a culture of tax evasion and a huge underground economy. The problem is so serious that the Russian government collects less than half the taxes it is owed.

Exchanging Goods for Goods   In modern economies, most transactions are completed using money. When goods are instead exchanged directly for other goods, the process is called *barter* (discussed in more detail in Chapter 15). Not surprisingly, to avoid the tax collector, many industrial sales are done without using money and hence are not recorded conventionally. Figure 6-3 shows the share of barter in industrial sales in Russia from 1992 to the present. The percentage is starting to fall, but it still exceeds that in any other modern industrial economy today by a wide margin.

Is There a Solution?   Clearly, one solution is to simplify the tax system. Cutting the number of different taxes from over 200 to, say, a half a dozen at much lower rates would reduce the incentive for evasion and bring the underground economy back into official statistics. A sensible and nonconfiscatory tax system would eliminate the need for private businesses to bribe government tax collectors. And more foreign investment would be drawn into Russia under a reformed system. To reduce criminal activities in that country, more resources need to be devoted to the development of a true judiciary and a noncorrupt police force.

FIGURE 6-3

The Share of Barter in Industrial Sales in Russia

INTERNATIONAL EXAMPLE
Capitalism May Start Early in Russia

A growing number of grammar school children in Russia are learning about capitalism as part of their official school curriculum. What they learn now is quite different from what they learned under communism. The textbook they use, published in 1997, is called *Economics for Little Ones, or How Misha Became a Businessman*. The text involves an industrious bear who opens a honey, berry, and nut store. His only competitor is Winnie the Pooh's overpriced Golden Beehive Cooperative. Textbooks for older students bear such titles as *Enterprise for Everyone*, and *Tales of Queen Economy, Evil Inflation, the Magical Computer, and Their Trusty Friends*. A computer game called *100 Steps to the Market Economy* is proving to be very popular as well.

FOR CRITICAL ANALYSIS: Little teaching of capitalism occurs in grammar schools in the United States. Why would Russian educators wish to teach more about capitalism than we do in the United States? ●

CONCEPTS IN BRIEF

- Russia and its former satellite states in Eastern Europe operated under a system of command socialism with much centralized economic planning. The end result was a declining economy in which a small percentage of the population lived extremely well and the rest very poorly.

- Russia and Eastern Europe are privatizing at varying speeds, depending on the level of political opposition.

- Russia has experienced a crime wave during its transition to capitalism. One can compare this period to America's Wild West and to our period of Prohibition. As property rights and the legal system become more efficient, much of the crime associated with illegal economic activities will probably disappear.

THE PEOPLE'S REPUBLIC OF CHINA

The People's Republic of China remains the largest nation on earth and hence the largest with some form of command socialism. However, a decreasing share of the nation's activity is being guided by government. In fact, China started introducing market reforms in various sectors of the economy well before Russia did.

In 1978, the commune system that had been implemented in the 1950s was replaced by what was known as the *household responsibility system*. Each peasant household became responsible for its own plot of land. Whatever was produced in excess of the minimum obligation to the state remained the property of the household. So the incentives for peasant farmers were quite different from those prior to 1978. Peasants were also encouraged to enrich themselves further by engaging in a variety of economic activities. The results were impressive. Between 1979 and 1984, virtually millions of jobs were created in the urban and rural private sector, and farm productivity increased dramatically.

In the 1980s, the highly centralized planning from Beijing, the capital, was relaxed. Decision-making powers were given to state-owned enterprises at the local level. Indeed,

Incentive structure
The motivational rewards and costs that individuals face in any given situation. Each economic system has its own incentive structure. The incentive structure is different under a system of private property than under a system of government-owned property, for example.

China had embarked on a gradual sell-off of state-owned enterprises so that the size of the state-run sector, which accounted for 70 percent of industrial production in the mid-1980s, dropped to less than 40 percent in 1998. The result was an increase in output. The problem with state-run factories was the **incentive structure.** Managers of those factories never had much incentive to maximize the equivalent of profits. Rather, managers of state-run factories attempted to maximize incomes and benefits for their workers because workers constituted a political constituency that was more important than the politicians at the national level.

Two Decades of Economic Reform

Another major economic reform in China began in 1979, when the central government created a special economic zone in Guangdong province, bordering the then separate nation of Hong Kong. In that special zone, the three *P*s of pure capitalism—prices, profits, and private property—have now prevailed for nearly two decades. The result has been economic growth rates that have exceeded those in virtually any other part of the world. Within an area housing less than 1.5 percent of the population, Guangdong province now accounts for about 7 percent of the entire country's industrial output.

Transition Problems in Farming

Even though the Chinese central government was able to increase agricultural production dramatically when it gave peasants the household responsibility system, the agricultural sector has been lagging well behind the industrial sector in recent years. In effect, China has been undergoing an industrial revolution but not an agricultural one. One of the major problems is that peasants do not have legal title to their land. In other words, farmers cannot obtain legal property rights. As a result, the techniques used by agribusiness companies elsewhere in the world cannot be used by most of China's farmers. Peasants, in effect, have their land on loan from the state. The average size of a peasant farm is less than an acre for a family of six. It takes this family about 60 workdays to cultivate this amount of land, whereas a single American farmer can cultivate the same amount of land in about two hours.

Changes are occurring, though. At the Communist Party's 15th Congress in 1997, party leader Deng Xiaoping introduced market reforms into agriculture.

A Major Problem: The Rule of Law

As with virtually all countries experiencing frontier capitalism, China faces the perennial issue of how to establish the rule of law. When no specific property rights exist because resources are owned by "the people," the inevitable result is corruption. As with Russia, there is a sense of the Wild West in China, an atmosphere of lawlessness and unpredictability for anyone doing business. Both the government and the

THINKING CRITICALLY ABOUT THE MEDIA

268 Million Chinese Unemployed?

"China Sees 268 Million Unemployed in 2000." This was the headline a few years ago, reportedly based on statements by mainland Chinese officials in the Labor Ministry. Imagine that—the number of unemployed in China equaling the entire population of men, women, and children in the United States! A frightening prospect, no doubt, but also pure nonsense. Such a large number of unemployed presupposes that there is no way for them to find jobs of any sort. As China shifts toward a market economy, however, many of the unemployed will be able to find jobs in businesses that the current Chinese leadership cannot even conceive of today. That is what happens in a country in transition toward market capitalism. Of course, during the transition, there will be social and human costs associated with higher-than-normal unemployment rates, but that is statistically a temporary blip, not a long-term trend.

army continue to seek bribes and other favors because those two institutions still control many of the resources and influence the way business is conducted in China.

Only very slowly is China becoming a nation of laws, rather than of men and women. Otherwise stated, only gradually is the institution of a strong legal system being built up in China. The notion of property rights is slow to take in a nation where the communist dogma has denied their legitimacy. A good example is the state-supported bootleg compact disc factories that were first shut down because of international pressure and then reopened a few years ago. That American singers and musicians are being denied royalties seems not to bother some mainland Chinese government officials.

Exercise 6.2
Visit www.econtoday.com for more about the Chinese economy.

INTERNATIONAL EXAMPLE
The Rule of Law Is Still Precarious in China

In Imperial China, Mandarins were members of any of the nine ranks of high public officials. They exercised absolute and arbitrary powers. They often acted unpredictably. Apparently that is still how the final arbiters of what is legal today—Communist Party officials—still behave. In China, according to American-trained Chinese lawyers, there is not yet any true rule of law. In legal disputes, references to laws typically lead nowhere. An official may simply say, "It may be the law, but it is not our policy." Judges are normally under the control of local businesspersons. Consider the following: If a person from province A sues a business in province B, the case is handled in the court of province B. The local court's professional expenses, wages, and welfare benefits all depend on the local tax administration. Consequently, the local court will rarely defend the rights of an outside party. Also, the Chinese Supreme Court will hear only criminal cases; economic cases have no true "court of last resort" as they do in the United States. There is not even an unbiased intermediate court system for businesses from different provinces to use.

Foreign investors try to avoid China's court system altogether. They know that judges serve the needs of local Communist Party leaders and that many judges are former military officers who lack legal experience. So to safeguard their own interests, most non-Chinese businesses now insist on clauses in their contracts that provide for at least one foreign arbitrator.

FOR CRITICAL ANALYSIS: Which groups in China would be against the rule of law, and why? ●

The Slow Pace of Privatization

Virtually all state-run companies in China have provided cradle-to-grave social welfare benefits to their workers. The process of privatization, which started gradually years ago, first requires that these companies slowly eliminate many of these social welfare programs. Such programs are one of the reasons why over 50 percent of state-run enterprises are losing money every year. You can see from Figure 6-4 which state-run industrial enterprises are most prevalent. It clearly will be many years before the Chinese government is completely (if ever) out of the petroleum and tobacco businesses. But as Figure 6-5 shows, a growing percentage of firms are escaping from state control.

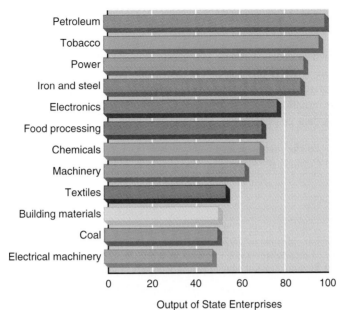

FIGURE 6-4
Relative Importance of Government in China's Industry
The government in China owns most of the oil, tobacco, and power industries, but is shedding itself of other industries.

The trend toward privatization in China is inevitably leading to labor dislocations. As state-run enterprises become privatized, new technology will be introduced that will require fewer labor hours per unit of output. Workers have been and will continue to be laid off in recently privatized firms. Laid-off workers will have to seek employment elsewhere, and in the process unemployment rates will rise, at least temporarily.

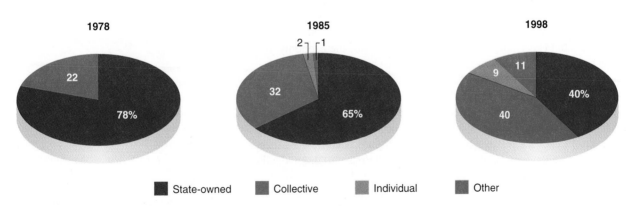

FIGURE 6-5

The Changing Face of China's Business Ownership
State ownership of all industries in China has fallen from 78 percent in 1978 to only 40 percent in 1998.

INTERNATIONAL EXAMPLE
Town- and Village-Owned Enterprises in China

In the past two decades, China's per capita income has quadrupled. According to Rudiger Dornbush of MIT, this success is due to the nation's 1.5 million town- and village-owned enterprises (TVEs). TVEs have been at the core of the Chinese economic performance. What is remarkable is that there are 7 million industrial companies in China; TVEs account for less than 20 percent.

FOR CRITICAL ANALYSIS: In the past, who has owned and operated the other millions of industrial companies in China? •

CONCEPTS IN BRIEF

- China started instituting market reforms in 1979 when it created special economic zones in which the three *P*s of capitalism were allowed to work. Problems remain in agriculture because peasant farmers cannot obtain property rights in land.

- The rule of law as capitalist countries know it is coming slowly to China. Government officials sometimes break contract agreements with foreign investors.

- The process of privatization started years ago but is proceeding slowly. The state still owns most of the businesses in oil, tobacco, power, and iron and steel.

FUTURE ECONOMIC POWER SHIFTS

The fact that there are so many economies in transition today is not just a momentary curiosity. It has implications for the future with respect to which nations will become economic powerhouses. Look at the three panels of Figure 6-6. You see in panel (a) that in the mid-1990s, the United States was clearly the world's largest economy. Japan and China were not even half its size. Now look at panel (b), which shows the World Bank's prediction of the largest economies in the year 2020. The leading economic powerhouse then is predicted to be China, with the United States a distant second. (These numbers reflect the total size of the economy, not how rich the average citizen is.) Japan will still be among the top three, but India and Indonesia will have expanded dramatically relative to 1995. Indeed, Asia, including India, will be a major economic power in the year 2020. These developments are reflected in panel (c) of Figure 6-6, where we show the projected shares of world output of today's industrial countries relative to today's developing countries. Realize, however, that the fact that developing Asian countries will dramatically increase the size of their economies does not mean that westerners will be worse off. Rather, the incomes of most westerners will also increase, but not as rapidly. Given that per-person incomes are generally higher in the West than in Asia, westerners will still remain rich by historical standards. The rest of the world is simply catching up with us.

THINKING CRITICALLY ABOUT THE MEDIA

Rich Industrial Nations—Really?

Virtually all news commentators and research organizations continue to classify countries such as the United States, the United Kingdom, and France as the industrial economies. Such an appellation today is a misnomer. In the industrial economies of today, less than one-third of the output is from "industry." Two-thirds of the jobs in so-called industrial economies are from services—doctors, lawyers, computer programmers, and Internet facilitators. Indeed, it might be more appropriate to call the richer countries *knowledge economies* because that is where the primary source of growth will lie—the storage, processing, and distribution of knowledge.

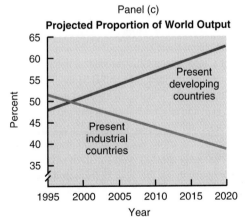

FIGURE 6-6

World Economic Powerhouses, 1995–2020

While the United States is the largest economy today, by 2020, China may be the world's greatest economic power. In any event, the share of world output from developing countries will increase steadily during that same time period.

Source: World Bank, *Global Economic Prospects.*

These mainland Chinese university students may be receiving their education free of charge. If so, a government official can tell them what job to take and where to live.

China Abandons Its Job Assignment System

CONCEPTS APPLIED:
INCENTIVES, MARKETS, CAPITALISM, LAISSEZ-FAIRE

Visit www.econtoday.com for an Internet Activity that expands your understanding of these concepts.

You know firsthand about how unrestricted labor markets work. Most of you reading this text have already had some type of job or might even be working full time. In so doing, you became part of the supply of labor. You reacted to the demand for labor. The laws of supply and demand apply to labor markets as they do to all other markets. You cannot help hearing about sectors in the economy in which wages are falling and unemployment is high, just as you cannot help hearing about sectors in which wages are rising and unemployment is low—such as telecommunications, software, engineering, and multimedia. No central planner in the United States has ever decided how many college graduates will go into any particular occupation. The choice has been decided by each graduate.

In China, every student who was given a free education had to agree to allow a state planner to tell him or her where to work. Consequently, many graduates ended up with jobs they never wanted, and many ended up living in cities that they never would have chosen. Such state-planned decisions usually lasted a lifetime.

The Problem with Mandatory Job Assignments

Perhaps state planners were capable of predicting changes in the demand for different types of labor in the past, when virtually all industry was owned and operated by the state. Gradually, though, state-owned enterprises have become a less important part of the Chinese economy (particularly because 50 percent of them run at a loss). The ever more market-oriented Chinese economy is becoming as dynamic as other market economies throughout the world. Changes in the demand for specific labor skills can no longer be well predicted by state planners. Consequently, the planners have failed to provide the right mix of job skills for today's labor market.

The Gradual Shift to Freedom of Choice

A few years ago, the Chinese government started a new system. Students who choose to pay their own way to colleges and universities can then choose an occupation and where they want to work. The tuition of $180 a year may seem small, but it represents about one-third of a Chinese citizen's annual income. To help students who choose the fee system, arrangements for student loans have been made, and many students have been able to borrow money from their families.

The new system has attracted the best students in the major cities of Shanghai and Beijing. They know that after graduation, they will easily find relatively high-paying jobs, particularly with foreign-owned companies and joint ventures, which tend to concentrate in China's largest cities. Of the more than 900,000 students who graduated in 1998, only 20,000 paid for their schooling—but that is twice as many as the year before, and their numbers continue to rise.

FOR CRITICAL ANALYSIS
1. So far, relatively few students in the less developed parts of China have chosen to pay for their own studies. Why do you think that they are less interested in the new system?
2. What were the benefits, if any, of the old-style, centrally planned job assignment system in China?

CHAPTER SUMMARY

1. The price system answers the resource allocation and distribution questions relating to what and how much will be produced, how it will be produced, and for whom it will be produced. The question of what to produce is answered by the value people place on a good—the highest price they are willing to pay for it. How goods are produced is determined by competition, which inevitably results in least-cost production techniques. Finally, goods and services are distributed to the individuals who are willing and able to pay for them. This answers the question about for whom goods are produced.

2. Pure capitalism can be defined by the three *P*s: prices, profits, and private property.

3. Communism is an economic system in which, theoretically, individuals would produce according to their abilities and consume according to their needs. Under socialism, the state owns most major capital goods and attempts to redistribute income. Most economies today can be viewed as mixed in that they rely on a combination of private decisions and government controls.

4. Incentives matter in any economic system; consequently, in countries that have had few or unenforced property rights, individuals lacked the incentives to take care of property that wasn't theirs.

5. Today there are four types of capitalism: consumer, producer, family, and frontier. The last emerges when a centralized economy starts collapsing and black markets thrive. Eventually, small businesses flourish and financial markets develop. Finally, foreign investment is attracted, and state-owned businesses are privatized.

6. The development of a well-functioning legal system is one of the most difficult problems for an economy in the frontier capitalism stage. Such economies do not have the laws or courts to handle property right protection and transfers.

7. Privatization, or turning over state-owned or state-run businesses to the private sector is occurring all over the world in all types of economies. There is much political opposition, however, whenever managers in soon-to-be-privatized businesses realize that they may face harder times in a private setting.

8. Russia and its former satellite states in Eastern Europe operated under a system of command socialism with much centralized economic planning. The end result was a declining economy in which a small percentage of the population lived extremely well and the rest very poorly.

9. Russia has experienced a crime wave during its transition to capitalism. One can compare this period to America's Wild West and to our period of Prohibition. As property rights and the legal system become more efficient, much of the crime associated with illegal economic activities probably will disappear.

10. China started instituting true market reforms in 1979, when it created special economic zones in which the three *P*s of capitalism—prices, profits, and private property—were allowed to work. Problems remain in agriculture because peasant farmers cannot obtain property rights to land.

11. The process of privatization in China started years ago but is proceeding slowly. The state still owns most of the businesses in oil, tobacco, power, and iron and steel.

12. The United States and Japan will remain economic powerhouses, but China could take the lead over the next 25 years. Other Asian countries, including Indonesia, India, Taiwan, South Korea, and Thailand, will become economically much stronger than they are today.

DISCUSSION OF PREVIEW QUESTIONS

1. **Why does the scarcity problem force all societies to answer the questions *what, how,* and *for whom?*** Scarcity exists for a society because people want more than their resources will allow them to have.

Society must decide *what* to produce because of scarcity. But if wants are severely restricted and resources are relatively superabundant, the question of *what* to produce is trivial—society simply produces *everything* that everyone wants. Superabundant resources relative to restricted wants also make the question of *how* to produce trivial. If scarcity doesn't exist, superabundant resources can be combined in *any* manner; waste and efficiency have no meaning without scarcity. Similarly, without scarcity, *for whom* is meaningless; *all* people can consume *all* they want.

2. How can economies be classified?

All societies must resolve the three fundamental economic problems: what, how, and for whom? One way to classify economies is according to the manner in which they answer these questions. In particular, we can classify them according to the degree to which *individuals* privately are allowed to make these decisions. Under pure command socialism, practically all economic decisions are made by a central authority; under pure capitalism, practically all economic decisions are made by private individuals pursuing their own economic self-interest.

3. Why do we say that *all* economies are mixed economies?

No economy in the real world is purely capitalistic. Resource allocation decisions in all economies are made by some combination of private individuals and governments. Even under an idealized capitalistic economy, important roles are played by the government; it is generally agreed that government is required for some income redistribution, national defense, protection of property rights, and so on.

4. What are the "three *P*s" of pure capitalism?

They are prices, profits, and property rights. In a pure capitalist economic system, prices are allowed to change when supply or demand changes. Prices are the signals to all about the relative scarcity of different resources. Profits are not constrained. When profits are relatively great in an industry, more resources flow to it. The converse is also true. Finally, property rights exist and are supported by the legal system.

PROBLEMS

(Answers to the odd-numbered problems appear at the back of the book.)

6-1. Suppose that you are an economic planner and you have been told by your country's political leaders that they want to increase automobile production by 10 percent over last year. What other industries will be affected by this decision?

6-2. Some argue that prices and profits automatically follow from well-established property rights. Explain how this might occur.

6-3. A business has found that it makes the most profits when it produces $172 worth of output of a particular product. It can choose from three possible techniques, A, B, and C, to produce the desired level of output. The table gives the amount of inputs these techniques use along with each input price.

a. Which technique will the firm choose, and why?

b. What would the firm's maximum profit be?

c. If the price of labor increases to $4 per unit, which technique will be chosen, and why? What will happen to profits?

| | | Production Technique | | |
Input	Input Unit Price	A (units)	B (units)	C (units)
Land	$10	7	4	1
Labor	2	6	7	18
Capital	15	2	6	3
Entrepreneurship	8	1	3	2

6-4. Answer the questions on the basis of the accompanying graph.

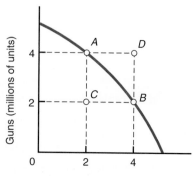

Butter (millions of barrels)

a. A switch to a decentralized, more market-oriented economy might do what to the production possibilities curve, and why?

b. What point on the graph represents an economy with unemployment?

6-5. The table gives the production techniques and input prices for 100 units of product X.

Input	Input Unit Price	Production Technique		
		A (units)	B (units)	C (units)
Labor	$10	6	5	4
Capital	8	5	6	7

a. In a market system, which techniques will be used to produce 100 units of product X?

b. If the market price of a unit of X is $1, which technique will lead to the greatest profit?

c. The output of X is still $1, but the price of labor and capital changes so that labor is $8 and capital is $10. Which production technique will be used?

d. Using the information in (c), what is the potential profit of producing 100 units of X?

6-6. The table gives the production techniques and input prices for one unit of product Y.

Input	Input Unit Price	Production Technique		
		A (units)	B (units)	C (units)
Labor	$10	1	3	2
Capital	5	2	2	4
Land	4	3	1	1

a. If the market price of a unit of product Y is $50, which technique generates the greatest potential profit?

b. If input unit prices change so that labor is $10, capital is $10, and land is $10, which technique will be chosen?

c. Assuming that the unit cost of each input is $10 and the price of a unit of Y is $50, which technique generates the greatest profit?

COMPUTER-ASSISTED INSTRUCTION

The role of prices in communicating information and allocating goods and services are illustrated by examining the ongoing transformation of the economies of Russia and China.

Complete problem and answer appear on disk.

INTERACTING WITH THE INTERNET

Extensive information on Eastern European economic conditions, with an emphasis on financial matters, can be found (for a fee) at

www.securities.com/

You can obtain general information on the countries studied in this chapter as well as other countries in the CIA's *World Fact Book*, which you can access at

www.odci.gov/cia/publications/pubs.html

You can also access the *Handbook of International Economic Statistics* for the latest year. Information on different countries' economic and trade policies can be found at

gopher://gopher.umsl.edu/11/library/govdocs/crpt

A very nice guide with extensive links to trade, economic, and business information for Eastern Europe and the former Soviet Union can be obtained from REESweb: Russian and East European

Studies, sponsored by the University Center for Russian and East European Studies of the University of Pittsburgh. It is located at

www.pitt.edu/~cjp/Econ/econind.html

If you would like to find out what is happening in the 15 member nations of the European Union (EU), you can access the European Commission's extensive Web site at

www.europa.eu.int

There you will start at the *Europa* home page for the European Union. Click on *Welcome*, then *News*, then *Eurostat* to obtain a menu of keywords from which you can choose.

You can get information about China from China's home page at

www.ihep.ac.cn/china.html

To find Internet resources on the economics of doing business in Russia and the other nations of the former Soviet Union, go to

dylee.keel.econ.ship.edu/INTNTL/INTDEV/Russia.htm

A great page of links on the economy of China can be found at

www.mindspring.com/~gsecondi/china.html

PART 2

INTRODUCTION TO MACROECONOMICS AND ECONOMIC GROWTH

CHAPTER 7

THE MACROECONOMY: Unemployment and Inflation

You know that you are affected by changes in the prices of the goods and services that you buy and by what happens to your wage rate or salary. To determine whether you are better off this year than you were last year, you have to compare the average percentage increase in all prices in the United States with the percentage increase in your income. For many decades, there have been increases, but no decreases, in the average price level in the United States. Thus you have had to worry about inflation and how it affected your real standard of living. The inflation rate has been dropping in recent years. So now some people are worried that the average of all prices may fall in the future. If this occurs, will you be better off or worse off? Before you can answer that question, you need to learn more about two important aspects of the macroeconomy: unemployment and inflation.

PREVIEW QUESTIONS

1. Why is frictional unemployment not necessarily harmful?

2. Does it matter whether inflation is anticipated or not?

3. Who is hurt by inflation?

4. How do we describe the phases of national business fluctuations?

141

Did You Know That... although the United States is considered a highly advanced industrialized nation, less and less of its employment is involved in manufacturing? The same is true of Japan, Germany, France, Italy, and the United Kingdom, where the number of manufacturing workers has been dropping steadily since 1970, despite significant increases in total adult population. Yet the result has *not* been workers permanently out of jobs. Even so, work is a major policy issue facing many countries today. At the core of macroeconomics—the study of the performance and structure of the national economy—are the issues of employment and, more important, unemployment.

UNEMPLOYMENT

Unemployment is normally defined as adults actively looking for work, but without a job. Unemployment creates a cost to the entire economy in terms of loss of output. One researcher estimated that at the beginning of the 1990s when unemployment was about 7 percent and factories were running at 80 percent of their capacity, the amount of output that the economy lost due to idle resources was almost 4 percent of the total production throughout the United States. (In other words, we were somewhere inside the production possibilities curve that we talked about in Chapter 2.) That was the equivalent of almost $275 billion of schools, houses, restaurant meals, cars, and movies that *could have been* produced. It is no wonder that policymakers closely watch the unemployment figures published by the Department of Labor's Bureau of Labor Statistics.

On a more personal level, the state of being unemployed often results in hardship and failed opportunities as well as a lack of self-respect. Psychological researchers believe that being fired creates at least as much stress as the death of a close friend. The numbers that we present about unemployment can never fully convey its true cost to this or any other nation.

Unemployment
The total number of adults (aged 16 years or older) who are willing and able to work and who are actively looking for work but have not found a job.

Historical Unemployment Rates

The unemployment rate, defined as a proportion of the measured **labor force** that is unemployed, reached a low of 1.2 percent of the labor force at the end of World War II after having exceeded 25 percent during the Great Depression in the 1930s. You can see in Figure 7-1 what happened to unemployment in the United States over the past century. The highest level ever was reached in the Great Depression, but unemployment was also very high during the Panic of 1893.

Labor force
Individuals aged 16 years or older who either have jobs or are looking and available for jobs; the number of employed plus the number of unemployed.

REDUCING UNEMPLOYMENT USING CYBERSPACE

As you will find out later in the chapter, one reason there is unemployment is that there is a continuous flow of individuals from job to job and in and out of employment. People do not always wait until they have another job lined up before they quit the one they currently have. Also, some people are newly entering the labor force and are looking for a job. Others have been fired and are looking for a job. Information about job openings is not, however, free for the asking—at a minimum, it takes time to find out what "appropriate" jobs are available. The standard way to look for a new job involves some combination of the following:

1. Asking friends for contacts
2. Looking at the "help wanted" ads
3. Submitting résumés "cold" to prospective employers

FIGURE 7-1

A Century of Unemployment

Unemployment reached lows during World Wars I and II of less than 2 percent and highs during the
Great Depression of more than 25 percent.

Source: U.S. Department of Labor, Bureau of Labor Statistics.

    4. Using the services of a private employment agency

    5. Using the services of a government employment agency

    6. Knocking on business doors

    Now there's the cyberspace job market. Newspaper employment ads have started to instruct job seekers to send their résumés to a particular e-mail address. Electronic résumés are relatively new and becoming more important. One of the reasons is that electronic résumés allow prospective employers to scan for keywords. In so doing, employers can more rapidly locate qualified candidates for unfilled jobs. A big company like Intel (the chip maker for most of the world's computers) receives thousands of résumés electronically each year via the Internet, and the many more that it receives by conventional means it scans into a database using optical character recognition (OCR) technology. In both cases, the company can then search electronically for key candidate qualifications.

    Employment agencies on the Internet are a growing phenomenon. Consider the Professional Job Network on the Web, which lets you select from over 1 million openings each month on-line, 24 hours a day. Some of these are jobs advertised in more than 1,000 newspapers and 500 trade journals; others are unadvertised opportunities with an additional 200,000 employers. There is also a listing from 200 professional job banks worldwide. In addition, the Internet Business Network specializes in electronic recruiting. Among other things, it offers information on the top 100 electronic recruiters.

    There is an extensive jobs database at a Web site called CareerMosaic. You can search according to the type of job you want and the region in which you wish to work. Looking for a job will never be the same.

FOR CRITICAL ANALYSIS: What types of jobs do you think are most heavily advertised on the Web? •

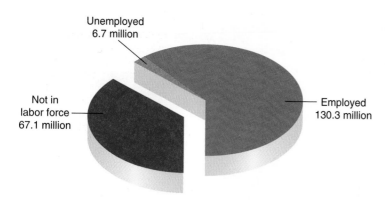

FIGURE 7-2

Adult Population

The population aged 16 and older can be broken down into three groups: people who are employed, those who are unemployed, and those not in the labor force.

Source: U.S. Department of Labor, Bureau of Labor Statistics.

Employment, Unemployment, and the Labor Force

Figure 7-2 presents the population of individuals 16 years of age or older broken into three segments: (1) employed, (2) unemployed, and (3) not in the labor force (a category that includes homemakers, full-time students, and retired persons). Those who are employed and those who are unemployed, added together, make up the labor force. (In 1998, the labor force amounted to 130.3 million + 6.7 million = 137.0 million Americans.) To calculate the unemployment rate, we simply divide the number of unemployed by the number of people in the labor force and multiply by 100: 6.7 million/137.0 million × 100 = 4.9 percent.

The Arithmetic Determination of Unemployment

Because there is a transition between employment and unemployment at any point in time—people are leaving jobs and others are finding jobs—there is a simple relationship between the employed and the unemployed, as can be seen in Figure 7-3. People departing jobs are shown at the top of the diagram, and people taking new jobs are shown at the bottom. If job leavers and job finders are equal, the unemployment rate stays the same. If departures exceed new hires, the unemployment rate rises.

The number of unemployed is some number at any point in time. It is a **stock** of individuals who do not have a job but are actively looking for one. The same is true for the number of employed. The number of people departing jobs, whether voluntarily or

Stock
The quantity of something, measured at a given point in time—for example, an inventory of goods or a bank account. Stocks are defined independently of time, although they are assessed at a point in time.

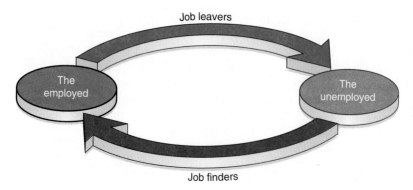

FIGURE 7-3

The Logic of the Unemployment Rate

Job leavers are individuals who are no longer employed and add to the unemployed (except for those who permanently leave the labor force such as new retirees.) When the unemployed find a job, they add to the employed. When both flows are equal, the unemployment rate is stable. If more people leave jobs than find them, the unemployment rate increases, and vice versa.

Stock of
unemployment

Flow of people
leaving jobs

Flow of people
finding jobs

FIGURE 7-4

Visualizing Stocks and Flows
Unemployment at any point in time is
some number that represents a
stock, such as the amount of water
in a bathtub. People who lose their
job constitute a new flow into the
bathtub. Those who find a job can be
thought of as the water that flows out
by the drain.

Flow
A quantity measured per unit of
time; something that occurs
over time, such as the income
you make per week or per year
or the number of individuals
who are fired every month.

Job loser
An individual in the labor force
who was employed and whose
employment was involuntarily
terminated or who was laid off.

Reentrant
An individual who used to work
full time but left the labor force
and has now reentered it looking for a job.

Job leaver
An individual in the labor force
who quits voluntarily.

New entrant
An individual who has never
held a full-time job lasting two
weeks or longer but is now in
the labor force.

involuntarily, is a **flow,** as is the number of people finding jobs. Picturing a bathtub, as illustrated in Figure 7-4, is a good way of remembering how stocks and flows work.

Unemployment Categories. According to the Bureau of Labor Statistics, an unemployed individual may fall into any of four categories:

1. A **job loser,** whose employment was involuntarily terminated or who was laid off
(varies between 40 and 60 percent of the unemployed)
2. A **reentrant,** having worked a full-time job before but having been out of the labor
force (varies from 20 to 30 percent of the unemployed)
3. A **job leaver,** who voluntarily ended employment (varies between less than 10 to
around 15 percent of the unemployed)
4. A **new entrant,** who has never worked a full-time job for two weeks or longer (varies
from 10 to 13 percent of the unemployed)

Duration of Unemployment. If you are out of a job for a week, your situation is typically much less serious than if you are out of a job for 14 weeks. An increase in the duration of unemployment can increase the unemployment rate because workers stay unemployed longer, thereby creating a greater number of them at any given time. The most
recent information on duration of unemployment paints the following picture: 37.1 percent of those who become unemployed find a new job by the end of one month, an additional 31.8 percent find a job by the end of two months, and only 16.3 percent are still
unemployed after six months. The average duration of unemployment for all unemployed
has been 15.2 weeks over the past decade.

When overall business activity goes into a downturn, the duration of unemployment
tends to rise, thereby causing much of the increase in the estimated unemployment rate. In
a sense, then, it is the increase in the duration of unemployment during a downturn in
national economic activity that generates the bad news that concerns policymakers in
Washington, D.C. Furthermore, the 16.3 percent who stay unemployed longer than six

months are the ones who create the pressure on Congress to "do something." What Congress does typically is extend and supplement unemployment benefits.

The Discouraged Worker Phenomenon. Critics of the published unemployment rate calculated by the federal government believe that there exist numerous **discouraged workers** and "hidden unemployed." Though there is no exact definition or way to measure discouraged workers, the Department of Labor defines them as people who have dropped out of the labor force and are no longer looking for a job because they believe that the job market has little to offer them. To what extent do we want to include in the measured labor force individuals who voluntarily choose not to look for work or those who take but only two minutes a day to scan the want ads and then decide that there are no jobs?

Some economists argue that people who work part time but are willing to work full time should be classified as "semihidden" unemployed. Estimates range as high as 6 million workers at any one time. Offsetting this factor, though, is *overemployment.* An individual working 50 or 60 hours a week is still counted as only one full-time worker.

Labor Force Participation. The way in which we define unemployment and membership in the labor force will affect what is known as the **labor force participation rate.** It is defined as the proportion of working-age individuals who are employed or seeking employment. (If there are discouraged, or hidden, unemployed within any particular group, the labor force participation rate for that particular group will drop.)

Figure 7-5 illustrates the labor force participation rates since 1950. The major change has been the increase in female labor force participation. If we take into account only married women aged 25 to 34, this increase is even more striking because it occurred over a shorter period of time. In 1960, about 29 percent of such women participated in the labor force outside of the home, compared with over 70 percent today. Is there an economic explanation for this increase?

Declining Job Security?

The decade of the 1990s has been labeled by the media as the one during which Americans by the millions lost job security. We have been told that corporate downsizing and global competition have resulted in American workers having to accept job changes as a regular part of their lives. Princeton economist Henry Farber looked at the actual numbers and came up with an entirely different picture. In 1973, some 54 percent of men aged 45 to 54 had been in their jobs for more than ten years, compared with 52 percent today. For workers with less than a high school degree, job tenure has definitely eroded, but for women, job tenure has been steadily rising because more women have career jobs than in the past. Indeed, the latest data show that workers in America stay with the same employer for an average of 5.1 years, longer than at almost any time since 1951.

Discouraged workers
Individuals who have stopped looking for a job because they are convinced that they will not find a suitable one. Typically, they become convinced after unsuccessfully searching for a job.

Labor force participation rate
The percentage of noninstitutionalized working-age individuals who are employed or seeking employment.

FIGURE 7-5

Labor Force Participation Rates by Sex
The combined labor force participation rate has increased in recent years. However, over the same period, the male participation rate has fallen, and the female rate has risen markedly.

Source: U.S. Department of Labor, Bureau of Labor Statistics.

Overworked Americans

Data show that the average American spends more time today working for pay than in the past. Since 1976, household surveys report that the average number of hours worked per week increased from 42.5 to 46.5 for working husbands and from 39 to 41.5 for working wives. Does this mean that Americans are overworked? Not necessarily. One has to include the total amount of work that American family members perform, such as cooking, doing laundry, and handling other household tasks. Since 1976, the number of hours that couples spend doing work in the home has fallen by almost exactly the same number of hours that working couples have increased work for pay. Thus, American couples are not forgoing additional leisure hours in order to work for more pay. Rather, Americans are simply substituting work for pay for work in the home without pay. This substitution has been possible because of increased labor-saving appliances and smaller families.

EXAMPLE
No-Fault Divorce and Increased Female Labor Force Participation

It is possible to explain the increased female labor participation rate by simply stating that there has been a change in attitudes. But there may be an economic reason behind the dramatic increase in the labor force participation rate of married females. In most states prior to the 1970s, both parties in a marriage had to consent to a divorce, which would normally be granted for a specific legally recognized cause, such as adultery. Specifically, one party or the other had to be found at fault. In most states, wives who did not want a divorce could remain married. Changes in the law in the 1970s saw the advent of no-fault divorce in which only one party had to want the divorce. The other party could not successfully oppose it. The result was less of a guarantee to married women that their financial support would remain intact. As a consequence, a larger percentage of young married women have chosen to enter and remain in the labor market, even while raising a family. For these women, no-fault divorce has created too high a risk if they choose to specialize in at-home work only.

FOR CRITICAL ANALYSIS: Has anything in particular made it more convenient for married women to work outside the home? ●

CONCEPTS IN BRIEF

- Unemployed persons are adults who are willing and able to work and are actively looking for a job but have not found one. The unemployment rate is computed by dividing the number of unemployed by the total labor force, which is equal to those who are employed plus those who are unemployed.

- The unemployed are job losers, reentrants, job leavers, and new entrants to the labor force. The flow of people leaving jobs and people finding jobs determines the stock of unemployed as well as the stock of employed.

- The duration of unemployment affects the unemployment rate. The number of unemployed workers can remain the same, but if the duration of unemployment increases, the measured unemployment rate will go up.

- Whereas overall labor force participation has risen only a bit since World War II, there has been a major increase in female labor force participation, particularly among married women between the ages of 25 and 34.

The Major Types of Unemployment

Unemployment has been categorized into four basic types: frictional, seasonal, structural, and cyclical.

Frictional Unemployment. Of the more than 137 million Americans in the labor force, more than 12 million will have either changed jobs or taken new jobs during the year;

every single month about 1 in 20 workers will have quit, been laid off (told that they will be rehired later), or been permanently fired; another 6 percent will have gone to new jobs or returned to old ones. In the process, more than 20 million persons will have reported themselves unemployed at one time or another. What we call **frictional unemployment** is the continuous flow of individuals from job to job and in and out of employment. There will always be some frictional unemployment as resources are redirected in the market because transaction costs are never zero. To eliminate frictional unemployment, we would have to prevent workers from leaving their present jobs until they had already lined up other jobs at which they would start working immediately and we would have to guarantee first-time job seekers a job *before* they started looking.

Frictional unemployment
Unemployment due to the fact that workers must search for appropriate job offers. This takes time, and so they remain temporarily ("frictionally") unemployed.

Seasonal Unemployment. **Seasonal unemployment** comes and goes with seasons of the year in which the demand for particular jobs rises and falls. In northern states, construction workers can often work only during the warmer months; they are seasonally unemployed during the winter. Summer resort workers can usually get jobs in resorts only during the summer season. They, too, become seasonally unemployed during the winter; the opposite is true for ski resort workers.

Seasonal unemployment
Unemployment resulting from the seasonal pattern of work in specific industries. It is usually due to seasonal fluctuations in demand or to changing weather conditions, rendering work difficult, if not impossible, as in the agriculture, construction, and tourist industries.

Structural Unemployment. Structural changes in our economy cause some workers to become unemployed permanently or for very long periods of time because they cannot find jobs that use their particular skills. This is called **structural unemployment.** Structural unemployment is not caused by general business fluctuations, although business fluctuations may affect it. And unlike frictional unemployment, structural unemployment is not related to the movement of workers from low-paying to high-paying jobs. Structural unemployment results when the consuming public no longer wants to buy an individual's services in that location.

Structural unemployment
Unemployment resulting from fundamental changes in the structure of the economy. It occurs, for example, when the demand for a product falls drastically so that workers specializing in the production of that product find themselves out of work.

Cyclical Unemployment. **Cyclical unemployment** is related to business fluctuations. It is defined as unemployment associated with changes in business conditions—primarily recessions and depressions. The way to lessen cyclical unemployment would be to reduce the intensity, duration, and frequency of ups and downs of business activity. Economic policymakers attempt, through their policies, to reduce cyclical unemployment by keeping business activity on an even keel.

Cyclical unemployment
Unemployment resulting from business recessions that occur when aggregate (total) demand is insufficient to create full employment.

Full Employment

Does full employment mean that everybody has a job? Certainly not, for not everyone is looking for a job—full-time students and full-time homemakers, for example, are not. Is it possible for everyone who is looking for a job always to find one? No, because transaction costs in the labor market are not zero. Transaction costs include any activity whose goal is to enter into, carry out, or terminate contracts. In the labor market, these costs involve time spent looking for a job, being interviewed, negotiating the pay, and so on.

We will always have some frictional unemployment as individuals move in and out of the labor force, seek higher-paying jobs, and move to different parts of the country. **Full employment** is therefore a vague concept implying some sort of balance or equilibrium in an ever-shifting labor market. Of course, this general notion of full employment must somehow be put into numbers so that economists and others can determine whether the economy has reached the full-employment point. In 1986, the President's Council of Economic Advisers, which generates the *Economic Report of the President* each year (published in February), estimated that full employment in 1986 was at 6.5 percent unemployed. Using this definition, the economy was running at more than full employment from 1987 through the first few months of 1991 and from 1994 until today!

Full employment
As presented by the Council of Economic Advisers, an arbitrary level of unemployment that corresponds to "normal" friction in the labor market. In 1986, the council declared that 6.5 percent unemployment was full employment. Today, it is less than 5.0 percent.

Full Employment, Wage Rigidity, and Wait Unemployment

The official definition of full employment has changed over the years. This should not be a surprise because since World War II, the rate of unemployment has changed often. In 1948, it was only 3.8 percent, whereas in 1983, it was 9.9 percent. For a while, government economists argued that the level of unavoidable unemployment was growing in the U.S. economy. They therefore kept raising their estimate of the full-employment rate of unemployment—all the way up to 6.5 percent. That high number was shown to be far off the mark during the 1990s, when the unemployment rate dipped to 4.6 percent. But even that figure was greater than in 1948 and even in 1956, when unemployment stood at only 4.1 percent.

Nonetheless, this slight rise in the full-employment rate of unemployment seems at odds with the standard supply and demand analysis presented in Chapters 3 and 4. There we showed that if prices are allowed to adjust, there will be neither surpluses nor shortages. A certain portion of unemployment- ran be defined as a surplus of workers at a particular wage rate that is clearly above equilibrium. It must be, then, that there are wage rigidities (because wages are the price of labor) in the labor market. These result in a situation in which workers are waiting. Workers are unemployed because, at the going wage rate, the quantity of labor supplied exceeds the quantity demanded. This is called **wait unemployment,** and it is due to firms' inability to reduce wages in the face of an excess quantity supplied of labor—by wage rigidities. You already examined one cause of wait unemployment in Chapter 4—minimum wage laws. There are others, including the setting of minimum wages for a firm or an industry because of union power, and a variety of other reasons, some of which you will examine in other chapters in this macroeconomic part of your text.

Wait unemployment
Unemployment that is caused by wage rigidities resulting from minimum wages, unions, and other factors.

CONCEPTS IN BRIEF

- Frictional unemployment occurs because of transaction costs in the labor market. For example, workers do not have all the information necessary about vacancies. Structural unemployment occurs when the demand for a commodity permanently decreases so that workers find that the jobs that they are used to doing are no longer available.

- The level of frictional unemployment is used in part to determine our (somewhat arbitrary) definition of full employment.

- When wage rigidities exist because of minimum wage laws, union contracts, and other reasons, wait unemployment may result.

INFLATION

Inflation
The situation in which the average of all prices of goods and services in an economy is rising.

Deflation
The situation in which the average of all prices of goods and services in an economy is falling.

During World War II, you could buy bread for 8 to 10 cents a loaf and have milk delivered fresh to your door for about 25 cents a half gallon. The average price of a new car was less than $700, and the average house cost less than $3,000. Today bread, milk, cars, and houses all cost more—a lot more. Prices in the late 1990s are more than 10 times what they were in 1940. Clearly, this country has experienced quite a bit of *inflation* since then. We define **inflation** as an upward movement in the average level of prices. The opposite of inflation is **deflation,** defined as a downward movement in the average level of prices. Notice that these definitions depend on the *average* level of prices. This means that even during a period of inflation, some prices can be falling if other prices are rising at a faster rate. The price of computers and computer-related equipment has dropped dramatically since the 1960s even though there has been general inflation.

To discuss what has happened to inflation in this and other countries, we have to know how to measure it.

Inflation and the Purchasing Power of Money

A rose may be a rose may be a rose, but a dollar is not always a dollar. The value of a dollar does not stay constant when there is inflation. The value of money is usually talked about in terms of the **purchasing power** of money. A dollar's purchasing power is the real goods and services that it can buy. Consequently, another way of defining inflation is as a decline in the purchasing power of money. The faster the rate of inflation, the greater the drop in the purchasing power of money.

One way to think about inflation and the purchasing power of money is to discuss dollar values in terms of *nominal* versus *real* values. The nominal value of anything is simply its price expressed in today's dollars. In contrast, the real value of anything is its value expressed in purchasing power, which varies with the rate of inflation. Let's say that you received a $100 bill from your grandparents this year. One year from now, the nominal value of that bill will still be $100. The real value will depend on what the purchasing power of money is after one year's worth of inflation. Obviously, if there has been a lot of inflation in one year, the real value of that $100 bill will have dropped.

Measuring the Rate of Inflation

How do we come up with a measure of the rate of inflation? This is indeed a thorny problem for government statisticians. It is easy to determine how much the price of an individual commodity has risen: If last year a light bulb cost 50 cents and this year it costs 75 cents, there has been a 50 percent rise in the price of that light bulb over a one-year period. We can express the change in the individual light bulb price in one of several ways: The price has gone up 25 cents; the price is one and a half (1.5) times as high; the price has risen by 50 percent. An *index number* of this price rise is simply the second way (1.5) multiplied by 100, meaning that the index number would be 150. We multiply by 100 to eliminate decimals because it is easier to think in terms of percentage changes using integers. This is the standard convention adopted for convenience in dealing with index numbers or price levels.

Purchasing power
The value of money for buying goods and services. If your money income stays the same but the price of one good that you are buying goes up, your effective purchasing power falls, and vice versa.

THINKING CRITICALLY ABOUT THE MEDIA

Super Bowl Advertising

Each year, the popular press makes sure that everyone knows how much it costs to advertise a 30-second spot during the Super Bowl. A favorite comparison is what it cost for the same 30-second spot during the first Super Bowl in 1967. Back then it cost $50,000, whereas today it costs $1.25 million, or 25 times more. Two problems arise with such a comparison (and all others like it): (1) The price level has increased more than fourfold since 1967, thereby reducing the real (inflation-corrected) increase in Super Bowl advertising prices to only eight times what they were in 1967, and (2) the number of TV game viewers has more than doubled since 1967, further reducing the real advertising cost per viewer to less than four times what it was in 1967.

Computing a Price Index. The measurement problem becomes more complicated when it involves a large number of goods, some of whose prices have risen faster than others and some that have even fallen. What we have to do is pick a representative bundle, a so-called market basket, of goods and compare the cost of that market basket of goods over time. When we do this, we obtain a **price index,** which is defined as the cost of a market basket of goods today, expressed as a percentage of the cost of that identical market basket of goods in some starting year, known as the **base year.**

$$\text{Price index} = \frac{\text{cost today of market basket}}{\text{cost of market basket in base year}} \times 100$$

Price index
The cost of today's market basket of goods expressed as a percentage of the cost of the same market basket during a base year.

Base year
The year that is chosen as the point of reference for comparison of prices in other years.

In the base year the price index will always be 100, because the year in the numerator and in the denominator of the above fraction is the same; therefore, the fraction equals 1, and when we multiply it by 100, we get 100. A simple numerical example is given in Table

TABLE 7-1

Calculating a Price Index for a Two-Good Market Basket

In this simplified example, there are only two goods—corn and micro-computers. The quantities and base-year prices are given in columns 2 and 3. The cost of the 1986 market basket, calculated in column 4, comes to $1,400. The 2000 prices are given in column 5. The cost of the market basket in 2000, calculated in column 6, is $1,700. The price index for 2000 compared with 1986 is 121.43.

(1) Commodity	(2) Market Basket Quantity	(3) 1986 Price per Unit	(4) Cost of Market Basket in 1986	(5) 2000 Price per Unit	(6) Cost of Market Basket at 2000 Prices
Corn	100 bushels	$ 4	$ 400	$ 8	$ 800
Microcomputers	2	500	1,000	450	900
Totals			$1,400		$1,700

$$\text{Price index} = \frac{\text{cost of market basket in 2000}}{\text{cost of market basket in base year 1986}} \times 100 = \frac{\$1,700}{\$1,400} \times 100 = 121.43$$

Consumer Price Index (CPI)
A statistical measure of a weighted average of prices of a specified set of goods and services purchased by wage earners in urban areas.

Producer Price Index (PPI)
A statistical measure of a weighted average of prices of commodities that firms purchase from other firms.

GDP deflator
A price index measuring the changes in prices of all new goods and services produced in the economy.

7-1. In the table there are only two goods in the market basket—corn and microcomputers. The *quantities* in the basket remain the same between the base year, 1986, and the current year, 2000; only the *prices* change. Such a *fixed-quantity* price index is the easiest to compute because the statistician need only look at prices of goods and services sold every year rather than actually observing how much of these goods and services consumers actually purchase each year.

Real-World Price Indexes. Government statisticians calculate a number of price indexes. The most often quoted are the **Consumer Price Index (CPI)**, the **Producer Price Index (PPI)**, and the **GDP deflator.** The CPI attempts to measure changes only in the level of prices of goods and services purchased by wage earners. The PPI attempts to show what has happened to the price level for commodities that firms purchase from other firms. The GDP deflator attempts to show changes in the level of prices of all new goods and services produced in the economy. The most general indicator of inflation is the GDP deflator because it measures the changes in the prices of everything produced in the economy.

The CPI. The Bureau of Labor Statistics (BLS) has the task of identifying a market basket of goods and services of the typical consumer. It uses a survey from 1982–1984 to come up with its estimates. For example, during this base period, out of every consumer dollar spent, almost 17 cents was spent on food and almost 4 cents on transportation. Entertainment got a little more than 10 cents and clothing 6 cents. The largest item was housing, taking about 16 cents of every consumer dollar.

Economists have known for years that the way the BLS measures changes in the Consumer Price Index is flawed. Specifically, the BLS has been unable to account for the way consumers substitute less expensive items for higher-priced items. The reason is that the CPI is a fixed-quantity price index, meaning that each month the BLS samples only prices, rather than relative quantities purchased by consumers. In addition, the BLS has been unable to take account of quality changes as they occur. Even if the BLS captures the dramatically falling price of personal computers, it has been unable to reflect the dramatic improvement in personal computers. Finally, the CPI ignores the introduction of new products.

EXAMPLE
New Product Bias in the CPI: The Case of Cellular Phones

Any new product that is successful, by definition, makes those people better off who choose to purchase it. Successful new products should therefore reduce the cost of maintaining a given standard of living, and so successful new product introductions should reduce the CPI or at least lessen increases in it. Nevertheless, the government is often slow to recognize this fact when it calculates the CPI. Consider the research done by economist Jerry Hausman of MIT. He looked at cellular phones. Since the late 1980s, cell phone prices have dropped by 90 percent and quality has improved greatly. As of 1998, however, the price of cellular phones was still not included in the government's CPI calculations. Hausman estimated that Americans are $24 billion to $50 billion better off because cellular phones exist. That is about .5 percent of the nation's annual national output.

FOR CRITICAL ANALYSIS: *"When people don't know about a new product, they don't miss it, and therefore they are not worse off." Analyze this statement.* ●

Exercise 7.2
Visit www.econtoday.com for more about the CPI.

The PPI.   There are a number of Producer Price Indexes, including one for food materials, another for intermediate goods (goods used in the production of other goods), and one for finished goods. Most of the producer prices included are in mining, manufacturing, and agriculture. The PPIs can be considered general-purpose indexes for nonretail markets.

Although in the long run the various PPIs and the CPI generally show the same rate of inflation, such is not the case in the short run. Most often the PPIs increase before the CPI because it takes time for producer price increases to show up in the prices that consumers pay for final products. Often changes in the PPIs are watched closely as a hint that inflation is going to increase or decrease.

The GDP Deflator.   The broadest price index reported in the United States is the GDP deflator, where GDP stands for gross domestic product, or annual total national income. Unlike the CPI and the PPIs, the GDP deflator is not based on a fixed market basket of goods and services. The basket is allowed to change with people's consumption and investment patterns. In this sense, the changes in the GDP deflator reflect both price changes and the public's market responses to those price changes. Why? Because new expenditure patterns are allowed to show up in the GDP deflator as people respond to changing prices.

Historical Changes in the CPI. The Consumer Price Index has shown a fairly dramatic trend upward since about World War II. Figure 7-6 shows the annual rate of change in the Consumer Price Index since 1860. Prior to World War II, there were numerous periods of deflation along with periods of inflation. Persistent year-in and year-out inflation seems to be a post–World War II phenomenon, at least in this country. As far back as before the American Revolution, prices used to rise during war periods but then would fall back to more normal levels afterward. This occurred after the Revolutionary War, the War of 1812, the Civil War, and World War I. Consequently, the overall price level in 1940 wasn't much different from 150 years earlier.

POLICY EXAMPLE
The Labor Department Quietly Reduces Its Inflation Statistics

The Consumer Price Index has been inaccurate because it ignores many changes in quality, increased discount shopping at club warehouses, and other developments in the consumer market. The statisticians responsible for computing the CPI each month know this. As a result, they have made changes in the index. Without much fanfare, the Labor Department has modified the way it calculates the CPI. It altered its sampling procedure for food and nonfood items, and it made its treatment of rent, hospital prices, and generic drugs more accurate. After those adjustments, government-estimated inflation rates dropped by .2 to .3 percent. Further calculation changes in 1998 and 1999 will reduce estimated inflation by another .75 percent.

FOR CRITICAL ANALYSIS: The government has not changed past published data on the CPI. Why is this fact important to a policymaker today? ●

CONCEPTS IN BRIEF

- Once we pick a market basket of goods, we can construct a price index that compares the cost of that market basket today with the cost of the same market basket in a base year.

- The Consumer Price Index (CPI) is the most often used price index in the United States. The Producer Price Index (PPI) is the second most mentioned.

- The GDP deflator measures what is happening to the average price level of *all* new, domestically produced final goods and services in our economy.

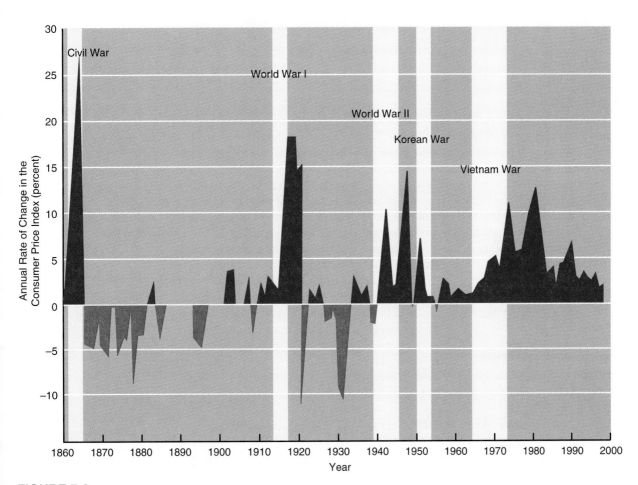

FIGURE 7-6

Inflationary Periods in U.S. History

Since the Civil War, there have been numerous periods of inflation in the United States. Here we show them as reflected by changes in the Consumer Price Index. Since World War II, the periods of inflation have not been followed by periods of deflation; that is, even during peacetime, the price index has continued to rise. The yellow areas represent wartime.

Source: U.S. Department of Labor, Bureau of Labor Statistics.

Anticipated Versus Unanticipated Inflation

Before examining who is hurt by inflation and what the effects of inflation are in general, we have to distinguish between anticipated and unanticipated inflation. We will see that the effects on individuals and the economy are vastly different, depending on which type of inflation exists.

Anticipated inflation is the rate of inflation that the majority of individuals believe will occur. If the rate of inflation this year turns out to be 10 percent, and that's about what most people thought it was going to be, we are in a situation of fully anticipated inflation.

Unanticipated inflation is inflation that comes as a surprise to individuals in the economy. For example, if the inflation rate in a particular year turns out to be 10 percent when on average people thought it was going to be 5 percent, there will have been unanticipated inflation—inflation greater than anticipated.

Some of the problems caused by inflation arise when it is unanticipated, for when it is anticipated, many people are able to protect themselves from its ravages. With the distinction in mind between anticipated and unanticipated inflation, we can easily see the relationship between inflation and interest rates.

Anticipated inflation
The inflation rate that we believe will occur; when it does, we are in a situation of fully anticipated inflation.

Unanticipated inflation
Inflation at a rate that comes as a surprise, either higher or lower than the rate anticipated.

Inflation and Interest Rates

Let's start in a hypothetical world in which there is no inflation and anticipated inflation is zero. In that world, you may be able to borrow money—to buy a computer or a car, for example—at a **nominal rate of interest** of, say, 10 percent. If you borrow the money to purchase a computer or a car and your anticipation of inflation turns out to be accurate, neither you nor the lender will have been fooled. The dollars you pay back in the years to come will be just as valuable in terms of purchasing power as the dollars that you borrowed.

What you ordinarily need to know when you borrow money is the *real rate of interest* that you will have to pay. The **real rate of interest** is defined as the nominal rate of interest minus the anticipated rate of inflation. If you are able to borrow money at 10 percent and you anticipated an inflation rate of 10 percent, your real rate of interest would be zero—lucky you, particularly if the actual rate of inflation turned out to be 10 percent. In effect, we can say that the nominal rate of interest is equal to the real rate of interest plus an *inflationary premium* to take account of anticipated inflation. That inflationary premium covers depreciation in the purchasing power of the dollars repaid by borrowers.[1] Consider the purchase of a home. In 1982, mortgage rates for the purchase of new homes were around 15 percent. By 1998, they had fallen to around 6.5 percent. Why would anyone have paid 15 percent in 1982 to borrow money to buy a home? Well, home prices in much of the country had been rising for several years at 25 percent per year, so at 15 percent, mortgage rates seemed like a good deal. By the mid- to late-1990s, home prices in most places were holding steady.

Nominal rate of interest
The market rate of interest expressed in today's dollars.

Real rate of interest
The nominal rate of interest minus the anticipated rate of inflation.

There is fairly strong evidence that inflation rates and nominal interest rates move in parallel fashion. Periods of rapid inflation create periods of high interest rates. In the early 1970s, when the inflation rate was between 4 and 5 percent, average interest rates were around 8 to 10 percent. At the beginning of the 1980s, when the inflation rate was near 9 percent, interest rates had risen to between 12 and 14 percent. By the early 1990s, when the inflation rate was about 3 percent, nominal interest rates had again fallen to between 4 and 8 percent.

---

[1]Whenever there are relatively high rates of anticipated inflation, we must add an additional factor to the inflationary premium—the product of the real rate of interest times the anticipated rate of inflation. Usually this last term is omitted because the anticipated rate of inflation is not high enough to make much of a difference.

INTERNATIONAL EXAMPLE
Deflation and Real Interest Rates in Japan

Wholesale prices in Japan have been falling for several years. In the past few years, consumer prices also have been falling, which means that Japan has been experiencing *deflation*. What does this have to do with real interest rates in Japan? Real interest rates are roughly equivalent to nominal, or market, rates minus the expected rate of inflation. Market interest rates are rarely negative. If the nominal interest rate a Japanese person has to pay for a mortgage is 4 percent and the expected rate of *deflation* is 3 percent, then the expected real rate of interest is 7 percent, which is extremely high by historical standards. (In the United States, for example, real interest rates have hovered around 3 percent for most of its history.) The point is that in the United States, where we have learned to expect some inflation, we subtract that anticipated inflation from nominal interest rates to obtain real interest rates. In Japan, with expectations of deflation, the Japanese end up *adding* the expected deflationary rate to the nominal rate of interest to get real rates of interest.

FOR CRITICAL ANALYSIS: Why can't nominal interest rates be negative? •

Does Inflation Necessarily Hurt Everyone?

Most people think that inflation is bad. After all, inflation means higher prices, and when we have to pay higher prices, are we not necessarily worse off? The truth is that inflation affects different people differently. Its effects also depend on whether it is anticipated or unanticipated.

Unanticipated Positive Inflation: Creditor Loses, Debtor Gains. Creditors lose and debtors gain with unanticipated positive inflation. In most situations, unanticipated inflation benefits borrowers because they are not charged a nominal interest rate that fully covers the rate of inflation that actually occurred. Why? Because the lender did not anticipate inflation correctly. Whenever inflation rates are underestimated for the life of a loan, creditors lose and debtors gain. The past several decades have known periods of considerable unanticipated (higher than anticipated) inflation—the late 1960s, the early 1970s, and the late 1970s. During those years, creditors lost and debtors gained.

Protecting Against Inflation. Banks attempt to protect themselves against inflation by raising nominal interest rates to reflect anticipated inflation. Adjustable-rate mortgages in fact do just that: The interest rate varies according to what happens to interest rates in the economy. Workers can protect themselves by **cost-of-living adjustments (COLAs)**, which are automatic increases in wage rates to take account of increases in the price level.

Cost-of-living adjustments (COLAs)
Clauses in contracts that allow for increases in specified nominal values to take account of changes in the cost of living.

To the extent that you hold non-interest-bearing cash, you will lose because of inflation. If you have put $100 in a mattress and the inflation rate is 10 percent for the year, you will have lost 10 percent of the purchasing power of that $100. If you have your funds in a non-interest-bearing checking account, you will suffer the same fate. Individuals attempt to reduce the cost of holding cash by putting it into interest-bearing accounts, a wide variety of which often pay nominal rates of interest that reflect anticipated inflation.

The Resource Cost of Inflation. Some economists believe that the main cost of unanticipated inflation is the opportunity cost of resources used to protect against inflation and the distortions introduced as firms attempt to plan for the long run. Individuals have to spend time and resources to figure out ways to cover themselves in case inflation is different from what it has been in the past. That may mean spending a longer time working out more complicated contracts for employment, for purchases of goods in the future, and for purchases of raw materials.

Inflation requires that price lists be changed. This is called the **repricing, or menu, cost of inflation.** The higher the rate of inflation, the higher the repricing cost of inflation. Imagine the repricing cost of inflation in Argentina in 1989 with its rapid inflation compared to that in the United States, where the average inflation rate has rarely reached double digits.

Another major problem with inflation is that usually it does not proceed perfectly evenly. Consequently, the rate of inflation is not exactly what people anticipate. When this is so, the purchasing power of money changes in unanticipated ways. Because money is what we use as the measuring rod of the value of transactions we undertake, we have a more difficult time figuring out what we have really paid for things. As a result, resources tend to be misallocated in such situations because people have not really valued them accurately.

Think of any period during which you have to pay a higher price for something that was cheaper before. You are annoyed. But every time you pay a higher price, that represents the receipt of higher income for someone else. Therefore, it is impossible for all of us to be worse off because of rising prices. There are numerous costs to inflation, but they aren't the ones commonly associated with inflation. One way to think of inflation is that it is simply a *change in the accounting system.* One year the price of fast-food hamburgers averages $1; 10 years later the price of fast-food hamburgers averages $2. Clearly, $1 doesn't mean the same thing 10 years later. If we changed the name of our unit of accounting each year so that one year we paid $1 for fast-food hamburgers and 10 years later we paid, say, 1 peso, this lesson would be driven home.

Repricing, or menu, cost of inflation
The cost associated with recalculating prices and printing new price lists when there is inflation.

CONCEPTS IN BRIEF

- Whenever inflation is greater than anticipated, creditors lose and debtors gain. Whenever the rate of inflation is less than anticipated, creditors gain and debtors lose.

- Holders of cash lose during periods of inflation because the purchasing power of their cash depreciates at the rate of inflation.

- Households and businesses spend resources in attempting to protect themselves against unanticipated inflation, thus imposing a resource cost on the economy whenever there is unanticipated inflation.

CHANGING INFLATION AND UNEMPLOYMENT: BUSINESS FLUCTUATIONS

Some years unemployment goes up, some years it goes down. Some years there is a lot of inflation, other years there isn't. We have fluctuations in all aspects of our macroeconomy. The ups and downs in economywide economic activity are sometimes called **business fluctuations.** When business fluctuations are positive, they are called **expansions—** speedups in the pace of national economic activity. The opposite of an expansion is a **contraction,** which is a slowdown in the pace of national economic activity. The top of an expansion is usually called its *peak,* and the bottom of a contraction is usually called its *trough.* Business fluctuations used to be called *business cycles,* but that term no longer seems appropriate because *cycle* implies predetermined or automatic recurrence, and we certainly haven't had automatic recurrent fluctuations in general business and economic activity. What we have had are contractions and expansions that vary greatly in length. For example, nine post–World War II expansions averaged 48 months, but three of those exceeded 55 months, and two lasted less than 25 months.

Business fluctuations
The ups and downs in overall business activity, as evidenced by changes in national income, employment, and the price level.

Expansion
A business fluctuation in which overall business activity is rising at a more rapid rate than previously or at a more rapid rate than the overall historical trend for the nation.

Contraction
A business fluctuation during which the pace of national economic activity is slowing down.

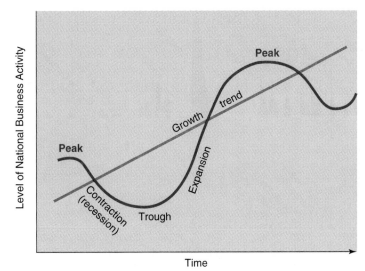

Recession
A period of time during which the rate of growth of business activity is consistently less than its long-term trend or is negative.

Depression
An extremely severe recession.

If the contractionary phase of business fluctuations becomes severe enough, we call it a **recession.** An extremely severe recession is called a **depression.** Typically, at the beginning of a recession, interest rates rise, and as the recession gets worse, they fall. At the same time, people's income starts to fall and the duration of unemployment increases, so that the unemployment rate increases. In times of expansion, the opposite occurs.

In Figure 7-7, you see that typical business fluctuations occur around a growth trend in overall national business activity shown as a straight upward-sloping line. Starting out at a peak, the economy goes into a contraction (recession). Then an expansion starts that moves up to its peak, higher than the last one, and the sequence starts over again.

The official dating of business recessions is done by the National Bureau of Economic Research in New York City; Cambridge, Massachusetts; and Palo Alto, California.

A Historical Picture of Business Activity in the United States

Figure 7-8 on page 158 traces U.S. business activity from 1880 to the present. Note that the long-term trend line is shown as horizontal, so all changes in business activity focus around that trend line. Major changes in business activity in the United States occurred during the Great Depression and World War II. Note that none of the business fluctuations that you see in Figure 7-8 exactly mirror the idealized typical course of a business fluctuation shown in Figure 7-7.

Explaining Business Fluctuations: External Shocks

As you might imagine, because changes in national business activity affect everyone, economists for decades have attempted to understand and explain business fluctuations. For years, one of the most obvious explanations has been external events that tend to disrupt the economy. In many of the graphs in this chapter, you have seen that World War II was a critical point in this nation's economic history. A war is certainly an external shock—something that originates outside of our economy.

Other examples of external shocks, particularly for an agrarian nation, have to do with abrupt changes in the weather. Long-term drought tended to create downturns in national business activity when the majority of Americans worked on farms. Today, major droughts or floods usually affect specific regions of the U.S. economy. Even a hurricane or an earthquake that dramatically affects one area rarely causes a national economic downturn.

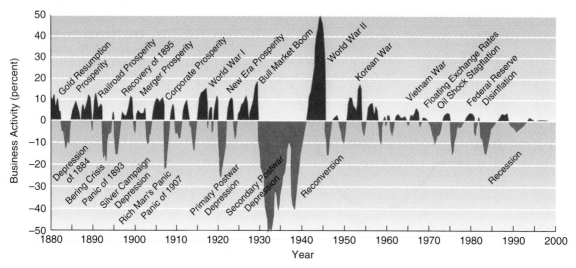

FIGURE 7-8

National Business Activity, 1880 to the Present

Variations around the trend of U.S. business activity have been frequent since 1880.

Sources: American Business Activity from 1790 to Today, 67th ed., AmeriTrust Co., January 1996, plus author's projections.

In the 1970s, due to actions on the part of certain countries in the Middle East, the United States received an "oil shock." The price of oil increased dramatically then, and some economists argue that this had a major effect on national economic activity.

It is not enough for us to say simply that business downturns are caused by external shocks. In the first place, if that were the only determinant of recessions, there would be little reason to study macroeconomics. Second, we know that historically we have had business recessions in the absence of any external shocks. We therefore need a theory of why national economic activity changes. The remainder of the macro chapters in this book develop a series of models that will help you understand the ups and downs of our business fluctuations.

CONCEPTS IN BRIEF

- The ups and downs in economywide business activity are called business fluctuations, which consist of expansions and contractions in overall business activity.

- The lowest point of a contraction is called the trough; the highest point of an expansion is called the peak.

- A recession is a downturn in business activity for some length of time.

- One possible explanation for business fluctuations relates to external shocks, such as wars, dramatic increases in the price of oil, earthquakes, floods, and droughts.

The rate of price increase for cars has slowed. Some analysts predict that new car prices may even fall. Does this mean that there is deflation in the economy?

Do We Need to Worry About Deflation?

CONCEPTS APPLIED:
INFLATION, DEFLATION, REAL INCOME

Visit www.econtoday.com for an Internet Activity that expands your understanding of these concepts.

Just when you thought everything was getting better—the inflation rate has been relatively low for a decade—a sudden spate of articles is telling you to be worried. Why? Because there is the prospect of the opposite of inflation—*deflation*. Deflation is defined as a consistent decline in a weighted average of all prices in the economy over time. The last time deflation occurred in the United States was during the Great Depression, when prices fell by 10 percent annually from 1929 to 1933. That was a period when the economy suffered from high unemployment and falling standards of living.

A current example of deflation can be found in Japan. Its price level has been falling every year since 1994. Its economy has been in a depressed state during that time period. The conclusion, of course, is that deflation can be accompanied by recessions and depressions.

Who Would Benefit from Deflation?

Obviously, if you hold cash, you are better off during a period of deflation. If prices drop by 5 percent during the next year, the dollar that you hold for a year would buy 5 percent more goods and services. Retired individuals on fixed incomes would find themselves richer each year during a deflation. Moreover, if the deflation was unanticipated, creditors would benefit. They would be paid back the same amount of dollars as before, but those dollars would have greater purchasing power. Therein lies the main problem with *unanticipated* deflation.

Debtors Lose Out

If deflation is unanticipated, creditors gain, but debtors lose out. They pay back their debts in dollars that are worth more and more. Certain companies in particular are highly susceptible to unanticipated deflation. They are the companies that are "leveraged"—that have borrowed heavily to purchase other companies or to expand rapidly. An unanticipated deflation would trigger a wave of business and personal bankruptcies. Investment and economic growth might collapse.

Don't Confuse Deflation with Falling Relative Prices

Even during a period of low or nonexistent inflation, some prices rise and some prices fall. Some of the popular press has focused on price decreases in the goods sector, particularly in computers, telecommunications, and imported items. But at the same time, in the services sector, many prices have been rising—this is simple arithmetic, for if the Consumer Price Index is still going up, albeit at a relatively slow rate, some prices have to be rising. Remember that deflation is defined as a *consistent* decline in the average of all prices. In the United States, prices, on average, have been rising, but at a decreasing rate. This is called *disinflation*, not deflation. And even if there were deflation, the key to understanding deflation's impact is to determine whether or not it was anticipated. Anticipated deflation would be reflected in lower nominal interest rates, reduced labor requests for salary increases, and other market phenomena.

FOR CRITICAL ANALYSIS
1. Describe a situation in which you personally would be better off during a period of unanticipated deflation.
2. How could you protect yourself against deflation?

159

CHAPTER SUMMARY

1. The labor force consists of all persons who are employed plus those who are unemployed. Those over age 16 who are not in the labor force are full-time students, homemakers, and retired persons. The rate of unemployment is obtained by dividing the number of unemployed by the size of the labor force. If the duration of unemployment increases, the rate of unemployment also increases. Labor force participation rates have increased dramatically for women since World War II.

2. There are four types of unemployment in the United States: frictional, seasonal, structural, and cyclical. There is also wait unemployment, which is caused by wage rigidities, such as minimum wage laws and union contracts.

3. Frictional unemployment is caused by the temporary inability of workers to match their skills and talents with available jobs.

4. Structural unemployment occurs when the demand for a particular skill falls off abruptly.

5. Inflation occurs when the average of all prices of goods and services is rising; deflation occurs when the average of all prices is falling. During periods of inflation, the purchasing power of money falls (by definition).

6. The most commonly used measures of changes in general prices are the Consumer Price Index (CPI), the Producer Price Index (PPI), and the GDP deflator.

7. The nominal rate of interest includes the anticipated rate of inflation. Therefore, when anticipated inflation increases, nominal rates of interest will rise.

8. Whenever the actual rate of inflation turns out to exceed the anticipated rate of inflation, creditors lose and debtors gain because the latter are able to repay debts in cheaper dollars. Of course, if everybody anticipates rising prices, nominal interest rates will rise to take account of this future expected reduction in the purchasing power of the dollar.

9. Workers can protect themselves against inflation by having cost-of-living adjustment (COLA) clauses in their employment contracts.

10. Business fluctuations consist of expansions and contractions. Long contractions are called recessions, and a severe recession is called a depression. One explanation for changes in national economic activity relates to external shocks, such as earthquakes, droughts, floods, wars, and dramatic increases in the price of oil.

DISCUSSION OF PREVIEW QUESTIONS

1. Why is frictional unemployment not necessarily harmful?

Because imperfect information exists in the real world, at any given time some people seeking jobs won't be matched with job vacancies. Given imperfect information, frictional unemployment indicates that the economy is reacting to changes in relative demands and supplies in different sectors. Moreover, frictional unemployment occurs when people climb up the occupational ladder. Thus frictional unemployment is not necessarily harmful to society (or to the individuals involved), and hence the overall unemployment percentage may be a misleading statistic.

2. Does it matter whether inflation is anticipated or not?

Whether inflation is anticipated or not is important to households and firms. When everyone fully and cor-

rectly anticipates the rate of future inflation, all contracts will take account of the declining purchasing power of the dollar. Debtors will not be able to gain at the expense of creditors, and employers will not be able to fool employees into agreeing to accept wage increases that do not have an inflationary factor built in. Only when inflation is not anticipated can it have unexpected negative effects on households and firms.

3. Who is hurt by inflation?

In periods of inflation, fixed-income groups are obviously hurt; however, because most retired people collect Social Security payments (which have increased more rapidly than the price level for the past quarter century), this point is easily overstressed. In periods of unanticipated inflation (or when the rate of inflation is more than that anticipated), creditors are hurt at the expense of borrowers, who gain. Also, people locked into long-term contracts to receive fixed nominal-money amounts (bondholders and other moneylenders, and some pensioners) are hurt if the rate of inflation is greater than they had anticipated. People who hold cash are also hurt by inflation; as prices rise, a given amount of cash buys less.

4. How do we describe the phases of national business fluctuations?
When business fluctuations are positive, they are called expansions, and when they are negative, they

are called contractions. The top of the expansion is the peak, and the bottom is the trough. A long-lasting trough is called a recession. If a recession gets very serious, it is called a depression. Recessions are officially dated by the National Bureau of Economic Research.

PROBLEMS

(Answers to the odd-numbered problems appear at the back of the book.)

7-1. Assume that your taxable income is $30,000 per year. Assume further that you are in the 15 percent tax bracket applied to all income from $0 to $30,000. If your taxable income increases to $30,001 per year, you will move into the 28 percent marginal tax bracket. Your boss gives you a raise equal to 4 percent. How much better off are you?

7-2. Assume that you are receiving unemployment benefits of $100 a week. You are offered a job that will pay you $150 a week before taxes. Assume further that you would have to pay 7 percent Social Security taxes plus federal income taxes equal to 15 percent of your salary. What is the opportunity cost of remaining unemployed—that is, how much will it cost you to refuse the job offer?

7-3. Assume that the labor force consists of 100 people and that every month five people become unemployed and five others who were unemployed find jobs.
   a. What is the frictional unemployment rate?
   b. What is the average duration of unemployment?

   Now assume that the only type of unemployment in this economy is frictional.

   c. What is the unemployment rate?

   Suppose that a system of unemployment compensation is instituted, and the average duration of unemployment rises to two months.

   d. What will the unemployment rate for this economy be now?

e. Does a higher unemployment rate necessarily mean that the economy is sicker or that laborers are worse off?

7-4. Suppose that a country has a labor force of 100 people. In January, Miller, Pulsinelli, and Hooper are unemployed; in February, those three find jobs but Stevenson, Conn, and Romano become unemployed. Suppose further that every month the previous three that were unemployed find jobs and three different people become unemployed.
   a. What is this country's unemployment rate?
   b. What is its frictional unemployment rate?
   c. What is the average duration of unemployment?

7-5. a. Suppose that the nominal interest rate is currently 12 percent. If the anticipated inflation rate is zero, what is the real interest rate?
   b. The anticipated inflation rate rises to 13 percent while the nominal interest rate remains at 12 percent. Does it make sense to lend money under these circumstances?

7-6. An economic slump occurs and two things happen:
   a. Many people stop looking for jobs because they know that the probability of finding a job is low.
   b. Many people who become laid off start doing such work at home as growing food and painting and repairing their houses and autos.

   Which of these events implies that the official unemployment rate overstates unemployment, and which implies the opposite?

7-7. Columns 1 and 3 in the table show employment and the price level in the economy.

(1) Employment (millions of workers)	(2) Unemployment Rate (%)	(3) Price Level	(4) Rate of Inflation (%)
90	_____	1.00	N.A.
91	_____	1.08	_____
92	_____	1.17	_____
93	_____	1.28	_____
94	_____	1.42	_____
95	_____	1.59	_____
96	_____	1.81	_____
97	_____	2.10	_____

a. Assume that the labor force in the economy is 100 million. Compute and enter in column 2 the unemployment rate at each level of employment. (Hint: Divide the number of workers unemployed by the labor force.)

b. For each row (except the first), compute and enter in column 4 the rate of inflation.

COMPUTER-ASSISTED INSTRUCTION

In this problem, a consumer spends all of her income on pizza, jeans, and wine. Over time, the price of each of these goods changes, and the consumer changes the quantities that she buys. The problem requires step-by-step calculations to derive a Consumer Price Index for specific price-quantity values in specific years.

Complete problem and answer appear on disk.

INTERACTING WITH THE INTERNET

It can be confusing to access U.S. macroeconomic data because they are published and placed on the Internet by several different agencies. However, many of them place each other's data on the Internet, so you can often run across summary and press releases by chance. One major site is the Bureau of Labor Statistics,

stats.bls.gov/

Its "Economy at a Glance" section,

stats.bls.gov/eag.table.html

and "Most Requested Series,"

stats.bls.gov/top20.html

are likely to be of most interest. The BLS covers employment and price data.

The Commerce Department's Electronic Bulletin Board (part of its STAT-USA program) provides a large amount of macroeconomic data as well. It is available in two places: at the Commerce Department itself,

www.stat-usa.gov

and at the University of Michigan,

gopher://una.hh.lib.umich.edu:70/11/ebb

under the name "Department of Commerce Economic Data (UMICH)." The former is a fee-based service (with significant free guest access), while the information in the latter is freely available (this odd arrangement occurs because U.S. government data are not copyrighted). The Michigan site has almost all of the data from the Commerce Department.

CHAPTER 8

MEASURING THE ECONOMY'S PERFORMANCE

If you watch the evening news, read newspapers and newsmagazines, or listen to news on the radio, you cannot miss hearing about the economy. One of the most eagerly awaited statistics, often touted in the media, concerns the federal government's quarterly estimate of how fast the economy is growing. Much is at stake here. Federal government policy aimed at stabilizing the economy hinges on these numbers. If the economy appears to be slowing down, that may indicate one policy; if the economy appears to be "overheating," that may lead to a different policy. A whole industry has developed to predict what will happen to the overall economy—and hence what the next policy change will be. How successful are those economic soothsayers? Before we can address this issue, you need to learn how the government derives its estimates of national economic performance.

PREVIEW QUESTIONS

1. What is gross domestic product (GDP), and what does it measure?

2. Why are only *final* goods and services evaluated in deriving GDP?

3. Why must depreciation and indirect taxes be added to national income at factor cost in order to derive GDP via the income approach?

4. How does correcting GDP for changes in the price level and population improve the usefulness of GDP estimates?

Did You Know That... whenever a single person who is currently paying a housekeeper marries that housekeeper, government statistics show that the economy's performance has declined? The reason for this seeming anomaly is that government statisticians do not yet consider unpaid housework as contributing to the total annual national income of the country (even though the same services would have to be purchased if not provided free of charge). In spite of such measurement problems, the statistics about the nation's economic performance are watched closely throughout the year by investors, bankers, businesspeople, and macroeconomic policymakers. After all, most people like to know where they stand financially at the end of each month or year. Why shouldn't we have similar information about the economy as a whole? The way we do this is by using what has become known as **national income accounting,** the main focus of this chapter.

But first we need to look at the flow of income within an economy, for it is the flow of goods and services from businesses to consumers and payments from consumers to businesses that constitutes economic activity.

THE SIMPLE CIRCULAR FLOW

The concept of a circular flow of income (ignoring taxes) involves two principles:

1. **In every economic exchange, the seller receives exactly the same amount that the buyer spends.**
2. **Goods and services flow in one direction and money payments flow in the other.**

In the simple economy shown in Figure 8-1, there are only businesses and households. It is assumed that businesses sell their *entire* output *immediately* to households and that households spend their *entire* income *immediately* on consumer products. Households receive their income by selling the use of whatever factors of production they own, such as labor services.

Profits Explained

We have indicated in Figure 8-1 that profit is a cost of production. You might be under the impression that profits are not part of the cost of producing goods and services; but profits are indeed a part of this cost because entrepreneurs must be rewarded for providing their services or they won't provide them. Their reward, if any, is profit. The reward—the profit—is included in the cost of the factors of production. If there were no expectations of profit, entrepreneurs would not incur the risk associated with the organization of productive activities. That is why we consider profits a cost of doing business.

Total Income or Total Output

The arrow that goes from businesses to households at the bottom of Figure 8-1 is labeled "Total income." What would be a good definition of **total income?** If you answered "the total of all individuals' income," you would be right. But all income is actually a payment for something, whether it be wages paid for labor services, rent paid for the use of land, interest paid for the use of capital, or profits paid to entrepreneurs. It is the amount paid to the resource suppliers. Therefore, total income is also defined as the annual *cost* of producing the entire output of **final goods and services.**

The arrow going from households to businesses at the top of the figure represents the dollar value of output in the economy. This is equal to the total monetary value of all final goods

Chapter Outline

The Simple Circular Flow

National Income Accounting

Two Main Methods of Measuring GDP

Other Components of National Income Accounting

Distinguishing Between Nominal and Real Values

Comparing GDP Throughout the World

National income accounting
A measurement system used to estimate national income and its components; one approach to measuring an economy's aggregate performance.

Total income
The yearly amount earned by the nation's resources (factors of production). Total income therefore includes wages, rent, interest payments, and profits that are received, respectively, by workers, landowners, capital owners, and entrepreneurs.

Final goods and services
Goods and services that are at their final stage of production and will not be transformed into yet other goods or services. For example, wheat is normally not a final good because usually it is used to make bread, which is a final good.

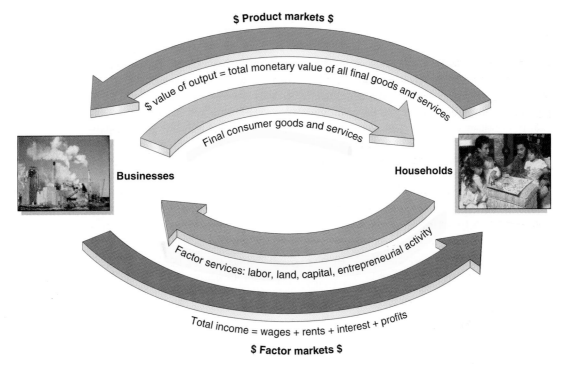

$ Product markets $

$ value of output = total monetary value of all final goods and services

Final consumer goods and services

Businesses

Households

Factor services: labor, land, capital, entrepreneurial activity

Total income = wages + rents + interest + profits

$ Factor markets $

FIGURE 8-1

The Circular Flow of Income and Product
Businesses provide final goods and services to households (upper clockwise loop), who in turn pay for them with money (upper counterclockwise loop). Money flows in a counterclockwise direction and can be thought of as a circular flow. The dollar value of output is identical to total income because profits are defined as being equal to total business receipts minus business outlays for wages, rents, and interest.

and services for this simple economy. In essence, it represents the total business receipts from the sale of all final goods and services produced by businesses and consumed by households. Business receipts are the opposite side of household expenditures. When households purchase goods and services with money, that money becomes a *business receipt*. Every transaction, therefore, simultaneously involves an expenditure as well as a receipt.

Product Markets. Transactions in which households buy goods take place in the product markets—that's where households are the buyers and businesses are the sellers of consumer goods. *Product market* transactions are represented in the upper loops in Figure 8-1. Note that consumer goods and services flow to household demanders, while money flows in the opposite direction to business suppliers.

Factor Markets. *Factor market* transactions are represented by the lower loops in Figure 8-1. In the factor market, households are the sellers; they sell resources such as labor, land, capital, and entrepreneurial ability. Businesses are the buyers in factor markets; business expenditures represent receipts or, more simply, income for households. Also, in the lower loops of Figure 8-1, factor services flow from households to businesses, while the money paid for these services flows in the opposite direction from businesses to households. Observe also the circular flow of money (counterclockwise) from households to businesses and back again from businesses to households; it is an endless circular flow.

Why the Dollar Value of Total Output Must Equal Total Income

Total income represents the income received by households in payment for the production of goods and services. Why must total income be identical to the dollar value of total output? First, as Figure 8-1 shows, spending by one group is income to another. Second, it is a matter of simple accounting and the economic definition of profit as a cost of production. Profit is defined as what is *left over* from total business receipts after all other costs—wages, rents, interest—have been paid. If the dollar value of total output is $1,000 and the total of wages, rent, and interest for producing that output is $900, profit is $100. Profit is always the *residual* item that makes total income equal to the dollar value of total output.

CONCEPTS IN BRIEF

- In the circular flow model of income and output, households sell factor services to businesses that pay for those factor services. The receipt of payments is total income. Businesses sell goods and services to households that pay for them.

- The dollar value of total output is equal to the total monetary value of all final goods and services produced.

- The dollar value of final output must always equal total income.

NATIONAL INCOME ACCOUNTING

We have already mentioned that policymakers need information about the state of the national economy. Historical statistical records on the performance of the national economy aid economists in testing their theories about how the economy really works. National income accounting is therefore important. Let's start with the most commonly presented statistic on the national economy.

Gross Domestic Product

Gross domestic product (GDP) represents the total market value of the nation's annual final product, or output, produced per year by factors of production located within national borders. We therefore formally define GDP as the total market value of all final goods and services produced in an economy during a year. We are referring here to a *flow of production.* A nation produces at a certain rate, just as you receive income at a certain rate. Your income flow might be at a rate of $5,000 per year or $50,000 per year. Suppose you are told that someone earns $500. Would you consider this a good salary? There is no way to answer that question unless you know whether the person is earning $500 per month or per week or per day. Thus you have to specify a time period for all flows. Income received is a flow. You must contrast this with, for example, your total accumulated savings, which are a stock measured at a point in time, not across time. Implicit in just about everything we deal with in this chapter is a time period—usually one year. All the measures of domestic product and income are specified as rates measured in dollars per year.

Gross domestic product (GDP)
The total market value of all final goods and services produced by factors of production located within a nation's borders.

Stress on Final Output

GDP does not count **intermediate goods** (goods used up entirely in the production of final goods) because to do so would be to count them twice. For example, even though grain that

Intermediate goods
Goods used up entirely in the production of final goods.

a farmer produces may be that farmer's final product, it is not the final product for the nation. It is sold to make bread. Bread is the final product.

We can use a numerical example to clarify this point further. Our example will involve determining the value added at each stage of production. **Value added** is the amount of dollar value contributed to a product at each stage of its production. In Table 8-1 we see the difference between total value of all sales and value added in the production of a donut. We also see that the sum of the values added is equal to the sale price to the final consumer. It is the 15 cents that is used to measure GDP, not the 32 cents. If we used the 32 cents, we would be double-counting from stages 2 through 5, for each intermediate good would be counted at least twice—once when it was produced and again when the good it was used in making was sold. Such double counting would grossly exaggerate GDP.

Exclusion of Financial Transactions, Transfer Payments, and Secondhand Goods

Remember that GDP is the measure of the value of all final goods and services produced in one year. Many more transactions occur that have nothing to do with final goods and services produced. There are financial transactions, transfers of the ownership of preexisting goods, and other transactions that should not and do not get included in our measure of GDP.

Value added

The dollar value of an industry's sales minus the value of intermediate goods (for example, raw materials and parts) used in production.

TABLE 8-1

Sales Value and Value Added at Each Stage of Donut Production

(1) Stage of Production	(2) Dollar Value of Sales	(3) Value Added
Stage 1: Fertilizer and seed	$.01	$.01
Stage 2: Growing	.02	.01
Stage 3: Milling	.04	.02
Stage 4: Baking	.10	.06
Stage 5: Retailing	.15	.05
Total dollar value of all sales	$.32	Total value added $.15

Stage 1: A farmer purchases a penny's worth of fertilizer and seed, which are used as factors of production in growing wheat.

Stage 2: The farmer grows the wheat, harvests it, and sells it to a miller for 2 cents. Thus we see that the farmer has added 1 cent's worth of value. That 1 cent represents income paid to the farmer.

Stage 3: The miller purchases the wheat for 2 cents and adds 2 cents as the value added; that is, there is 2 cents for the miller as income. The miller sells the ground wheat flour to a donut-baking company.

Stage 4: The donut-baking company buys the flour for 4 cents and adds 6 cents as the value added. It then sells the donut to the final retailer.

Stage 5: The donut retailer sells fresh hot donuts at 15 cents apiece, thus creating an additional value of 5 cents.

We see that the total value of sales resulting from the production of one donut was 32 cents, but the total value added was 15 cents, which is exactly equal to the retail price. The total value added is equal to the sum of all income payments.

Financial Transactions. There are three general categories of purely financial transactions: (1) the buying and selling of securities, (2) government transfer payments, and (3) private transfer payments.

1. **Securities.** When you purchase a share of existing stock in Microsoft Corporation, someone else has sold it to you. In essence, there was merely a *transfer* of ownership rights. You paid $100 to obtain the stock certificate. Someone else received the $100 and gave up the stock certificate. No producing activity was consummated at that time. Hence the $100 transaction is not included when we measure gross domestic product.

2. **Government transfer payments.** Transfer payments are payments for which no productive services are concurrently provided in exchange. The most obvious government transfer payments are Social Security benefits, veterans' payments, and unemployment compensation. The recipients make no contribution to current production in return for such transfer payments (although they may have made contributions in the past to receive them). Government transfer payments are not included in GDP.

3. **Private transfer payments.** Are you receiving money from your parents in order to live at school? Has a wealthy relative ever given you a gift of money? If so, you have been the recipient of a private transfer payment. This is merely a transfer of funds from one individual to another. As such, it does not constitute productive activity and is not included in gross domestic product.

Transfer of Secondhand Goods. If I sell you my two-year-old stereo, no current production is involved. I transfer to you the ownership of a sound system that was produced years ago; in exchange, you transfer to me $550. The original purchase price of the stereo was included in GDP in the year I purchased it. To include it again when I sell it to you would be counting the value of the stereo a second time.

Other Excluded Transactions. Many other transactions are not included in GDP for practical reasons:

1. Household production—home cleaning, child care, and other tasks performed by people within their *own* households and for which they are not paid through the marketplace
2. Otherwise legal underground transactions—those that are legal but not reported and hence not taxed, such as paying housekeepers in cash that is not declared as income
3. Illegal underground activities—these include prostitution, illegal gambling, and the sale of illicit drugs

Many economists criticize measured GDP statistics because the underground economy is not included. Right now, let's consider some suggestions for measuring unpaid household production.

Exercise 8.1
Visit www.econtoday.com for more about garage sales.

INTERNATIONAL POLICY EXAMPLE
Measuring Household Production in France and Norway

In the 1980s, the Decade for Women World Conference passed a resolution calling for all nations to include the unpaid contributions of women in GDP calculations. At least two countries, France and Norway, have started to release "satellite" GDP figures that incorporate estimates of unpaid household production. Australia, Canada, and Germany are studying a similar procedure. Of course, any estimate of unremunerated household work has serious problems. Does one add up the market cost of each activity that an unpaid homemaker provides to the family? If so, the figure turns out to be quite large, in excess of $30,000 a year. Another problem concerns the quality of household work. Some homemakers serve fabulous gourmet meals while others warm up canned and frozen foods. Should they be valued equally? Yet another problem lies in knowing where to *stop* counting: A person can hire a valet to help him or her get dressed in the morning. Should we therefore count the time spent getting dressed as part of unpaid household work? Both men and women perform services around the house every day of the year. Should all of these unremunerated services be included in a new measure of GDP?

FOR CRITICAL ANALYSIS: In general, which countries would have the smallest amount of unpaid household production? (Hint: Think about labor force participation rates.) ●

CONCEPTS IN BRIEF

- GDP is the total market value of final goods and services produced in an economy during a one-year period by factors of production within the nation's borders. It represents the flow of production over a one-year period.

- To avoid double counting, we look only at final goods and services produced or, alternatively, at value added.

- In measuring GDP, we must exclude (1) purely financial transactions, such as the buying and selling of securities; (2) government transfer payments and private transfer payments; and (3) the transfer of secondhand goods.

- Many other transactions are excluded from GDP, among them household services rendered by homemakers, underground economy transactions, and illegal economic activities.

TWO MAIN METHODS OF MEASURING GDP

If the definition of GDP is the total value of all final goods and services produced during a year, then to measure GDP we could add up the prices times the quantities of every individual commodity produced. But this would involve a monumental, if not impossible, task for government statisticians.

The circular flow diagram presented in Figure 8-1 gives us a shortcut method for calculating GDP. We can look at the *flow of expenditures,* which consists of consumption, investment, government purchases of goods and services, and net expenditures in the foreign sector (net exports). This is called the **expenditure approach** to measuring GDP, in which we add the dollar value of all final goods and services. We could also use the *flow of income,* looking at the income received by everybody producing goods and services. This is called the **income approach,** in which we add the income received by all factors of production.

Deriving GDP by the Expenditure Approach

To derive GDP using the expenditure approach, we must look at each of the separate components of expenditures and then add them together. These components are consumption expenditures, investment, government expenditures, and net exports.

Consumption Expenditures. How do we spend our income? As households or as individuals, we spend our income through consumption expenditure (*C*), which falls into

Expenditure approach
A way of computing national income by adding up the dollar value at current market prices of all final goods and services.

Income approach
A way of measuring national income by adding up all components of national income, including wages, interest, rent, and profits.

three categories: **durable consumer goods, nondurable consumer goods,** and **services.** Durable goods are *arbitrarily* defined as items that last more than three years; they include automobiles, furniture, and household appliances. Nondurable goods are all the rest, such as food and gasoline. Services are intangible commodities: medical care, education, and so on.

Housing expenditures constitute a major proportion of anybody's annual expenditures. Rental payments on apartments are automatically included in consumption expenditure estimates. People who own their homes, however, do not make rental payments. Consequently, government statisticians estimate what is called the *implicit rental value* of owner-occupied homes. It is equal to the amount of rent you would have to pay if you did not own the home but were renting it from someone else.

Gross Private Domestic Investment. We now turn our attention to **gross private domestic investment** (*I*) undertaken by businesses. When economists refer to investment, they are referring to additions to productive capacity. **Investment** may be thought of as an activity that uses resources today in such a way that they allow for greater production in the future and hence greater consumption in the future. When a business buys new equipment or puts up a new factory, it is investing; it is increasing its capacity to produce in the future.

The layperson's notion of investment often relates to the purchase of stocks and bonds. For our purposes, such transactions simply represent the *transfer of ownership* of assets called stocks and bonds. Thus you must keep in mind the fact that in economics, investment refers *only* to additions to productive capacity, not to transfers of assets.

In our analysis, we will consider the basic components of investment. We have already mentioned the first one, which involves a firm's buying equipment or putting up a new factory. These are called **producer durables,** or **capital goods.** A producer durable, or a capital good, is simply a good that is purchased not to be consumed in its current form but to be used to make other goods and services. The purchase of equipment and factories—capital goods—is called **fixed investment.**

The other type of investment has to do with the change in inventories of raw materials and finished goods. Firms do not immediately sell off all their products to consumers. Some of this final product is usually held in inventory waiting to be sold. Firms hold inventories to meet future expected orders for their products. When a firm increases its inventories of finished products, it is engaging in **inventory investment.** Inventories consist of all finished goods on hand, goods in process, and raw materials.

The reason that we can think of a change in inventories as being a type of investment is that an increase in such inventories provides for future increased consumption possibilities. When inventory investment is zero, the firm is neither adding to nor subtracting from the total stock of goods or raw materials on hand. Thus if the firm keeps the same amount of inventories throughout the year, inventory *investment* has been zero.

In estimating gross private domestic investment, government statisticians also add consumer expenditures on *new* residential structures because new housing represents an addition to our future productive capacity in the sense that a new house can generate housing services in the future.

Government Expenditures. In addition to personal consumption expenditures, there are government purchases of goods and services (*G*). The government buys goods and services from private firms and pays wages and salaries to government employees. Generally, we value goods and services at the prices at which they are sold. But many government goods and services are not sold in the market. Therefore, we cannot use their market value when computing GDP. The value of these goods is considered equal to their *cost.* For

Durable consumer goods
Consumer goods that have a life span of more than three years.

Nondurable consumer goods
Consumer goods that are used up within three years.

Services
Mental or physical labor or help purchased by consumers. Examples are the assistance of doctors, lawyers, dentists, repair personnel, housecleaners, educators, retailers, and wholesalers; things purchased or used by consumers that do not have physical characteristics.

Gross private domestic investment
The creation of capital goods, such as factories and machines, that can yield production and hence consumption in the future. Also included in this definition are changes in business inventories and repairs made to machines or buildings.

Investment
Any use of today's resources to expand tomorrow's production or consumption.

Producer durables, or **capital goods**
Durable goods having an expected service life of more than three years that are used by businesses to produce other goods and services.

Fixed investment
Purchases by businesses of newly produced producer durables, or capital goods, such as production machinery and office equipment.

Inventory investment
Changes in the stocks of finished goods and goods in process, as well as changes in the raw materials that businesses keep on hand. Whenever inventories are decreasing, inventory investment is negative; whenever they are increasing, inventory investment is positive.

example, the value of a newly built road is considered equal to its construction cost and is included in the GDP for the year it was built.

Net Exports (Foreign Expenditures). To get an accurate representation of gross domestic product, we must include the foreign sector. As Americans, we purchase foreign goods called *imports*. The goods that foreigners purchase from us are our *exports*. To get an idea of the *net* expenditures from the foreign sector, we subtract the value of imports from the value of exports to get net exports (X) for a year:

$$\text{Net exports } (X) = \text{total exports} - \text{total imports}$$

To understand why we subtract imports rather than ignoring them altogether, consider that we are using the expenditures approach. If we want to estimate *domestic* output, we have to subtract U.S. expenditures on the goods of other nations.

Mathematical Representation Using the Expenditure Approach

We have just defined the components of GDP using the expenditure approach. When we add them all together, we get a definition for GDP, which is as follows:

$$GDP = C + I + G + X$$

where

C = consumption expenditures
I = investment expenditures
G = government expenditures
X = net exports

The Historical Picture. To get an idea of the relationship among C, I, G, and X, look at Figure 8-2 on page 172, which shows gross domestic product, personal consumption expenditures, government purchases, and gross private domestic investment plus net exports from 1929 to 1996. When we add up the expenditures of the household, business, government, and foreign sectors, we get GDP.

Depreciation and Net Domestic Product. We have used the terms *gross domestic product* and *gross private domestic investment* without really indicating what *gross* means. The dictionary defines it as "without deductions," as opposed to *net*. Deductions for what? you might ask. The deductions are for something we call **depreciation.** In the course of a year, machines and structures wear out or are used up in the production of domestic product. For example, houses deteriorate as they are occupied, and machines need repairs or they will fall apart and stop working. Most capital, or durable, goods depreciate. An estimate of this is subtracted from gross domestic product to arrive at a figure called **net domestic product (NDP),** which we define as follows:

$$NDP = GDP - \text{depreciation}$$

Depreciation is also called **capital consumption allowance** because it is the amount of the capital stock that has been consumed over a one-year period. In essence, it equals the amount a business would have to put aside to repair and replace deteriorating machines. Because we know that

$$GDP = C + I + G + X$$

Depreciation
Reduction in the value of capital goods over a one-year period due to physical wear and tear and also to obsolescence; also called *capital consumption allowance.*

Net domestic product (NDP)
GDP minus depreciation.

Capital consumption allowance
Another name for depreciation, the amount that businesses would have to save in order to take care of the deterioration of machines and other equipment.

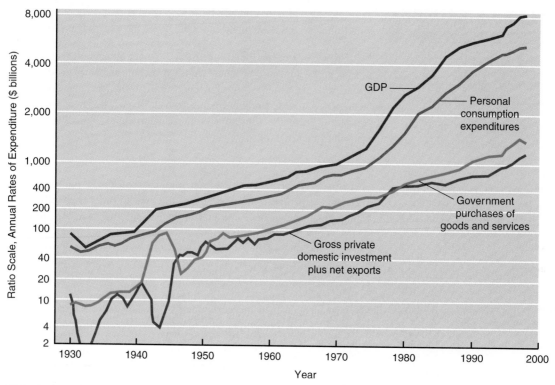

FIGURE 8-2

GDP and Its Components

Here we see a display of gross domestic product, personal consumption expenditures, government purchases, and gross private domestic investment plus net exports for the years 1929–1998. Actually, during the Great Depression of the 1930s, gross private domestic investment *plus* net exports was negative because we were investing very little at that time.

we know that the formula for NDP is

$$\text{NDP} = C + I + G + X - \text{depreciation}$$

Alternatively, because net $I = I - \text{depreciation}$,

$$\text{NDP} = C + \text{net } I + G + X$$

Net investment measures *changes* in our capital stock over time and is positive nearly every year. Because depreciation does not vary greatly from year to year as a percentage of GDP, we get a similar picture of what is happening to our national economy by looking at either NDP or GDP data.

Net investment
Gross private domestic investment minus an estimate of the wear and tear on the existing capital stock. Net investment therefore measures the change in capital stock over a one-year period.

CONCEPTS IN BRIEF

• The expenditure approach to measuring GDP requires that we add up consumption expenditures, gross private investment, government purchases, and net exports. Consumption expenditures include consumer durables, consumer nondurables, and services.

- Gross private domestic investment *excludes* transfers of asset ownership. It includes only additions to the productive capacity of a nation, repairs on existing capital goods, and changes in business inventories.
- We value government expenditures at their cost because we do not usually have market prices at which to value government goods and services.
- To obtain net domestic product (NDP), we subtract from GDP the year's depreciation of the existing capital stock.

Deriving GDP by the Income Approach

Gross domestic income (GDI)
The sum of all income—wages, interest, rent, and profits—paid to the four factors of production.

If you go back to the circular flow diagram in Figure 8-1, you see that product markets are at the top of the diagram and factor markets are at the bottom. We can calculate the value of the circular flow of income and product by looking at expenditures—which we just did—or by looking at total factor payments. Factor payments are called income. We calculate **gross domestic income (GDI),** which we will see is identical to gross domestic product (GDP). Using the income approach, we have four categories of payments to individuals: wages, interest, rent, and profits.

1. *Wages.* The most important category is, of course, wages, including salaries and other forms of labor income, such as income in kind and incentive payments. We also count Social Security taxes (both the employees' and the employers' contributions).
2. *Interest.* Here interest payments do not equal the sum of all payments for the use of funds in a year. Instead, interest is expressed in *net* rather than in gross terms. The interest component of total income is only net interest received by households plus net interest paid to us by foreigners. Net interest received by households is the difference between the interest they receive (from savings accounts, certificates of deposit, and the like) and the interest they pay (to banks for mortgages, credit cards, and other loans).
3. *Rent.* Rent is all income earned by individuals for the use of their real (nonmonetary) assets, such as farms, houses, and stores. As stated previously, we have to include here the implicit rental value of owner-occupied houses. Also included in this category are royalties received from copyrights, patents, and assets such as oil wells.
4. *Profits.* Our last category includes total gross corporate profits plus *proprietors' income.* Proprietors' income is income earned from the operation of unincorporated businesses, which include sole proprietorships, partnerships, and producers' cooperatives. It is unincorporated business profit.

All of the payments listed are *actual* factor payments made to owners of the factors of production. When we add them together, though, we do not yet have gross domestic income. We have to take account of two other components: **indirect business taxes,** such as sales and business property taxes, and depreciation, which we have already discussed.

Indirect business taxes
All business taxes except the tax on corporate profits. Indirect business taxes include sales and business property taxes.

Indirect Business Taxes. Indirect taxes are the (nonincome) taxes paid by consumers when they buy goods and services. When you buy a book, you pay the price of the book plus any state and local sales tax. The business is actually acting as the government's agent in collecting the sales tax, which it in turn passes on to the government. Such taxes therefore represent a business expense and are included in gross domestic income.

Depreciation. Just as we had to deduct depreciation to get from GDP to NDP, so we must *add* depreciation to go from net domestic income to gross domestic income. Depreci-

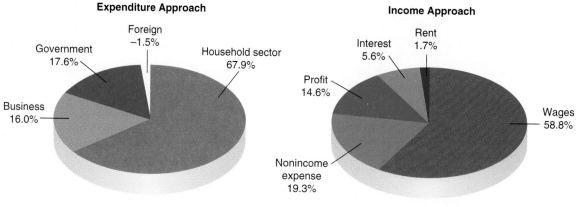

Expenditure Point of View—Product Flow		Income Point of View—Cost Flow	
Expenditures by Different Sectors:		Domestic Income (at Factor Cost):	
Household sector		*Wages*	
Personal consumption expenses	$5,659.4	All wages, salaries, and supplemental employee compensation	$4,901.4
Government sector		*Rent*	
Purchase of goods and services	1,466.4	All rental income of individuals plus implicit rent on owner-occupied dwellings	142.8
Business sector		*Interest*	
Gross private domestic investment (including depreciation)	1,329.8	Net interest paid by business	464.7
Foreign sector		*Profit*	
Net exports of goods and services	−123.4	Proprietorial income	519.7
		Corporate profits before taxes deducted	701.3
		Nonincome expense items	
		Indirect business taxes and other adjustments	730.8
		Depreciation	951.3
		Statistical discrepancy	−79.8
Gross domestic product	$8,332.2	Gross domestic income	$8,332.2

FIGURE 8-3

Gross Domestic Product and Gross Domestic Income, 1998 (in billions of 1998 dollars per year)

By using the two different methods of computing the output of the economy, we come up with gross domestic product and gross domestic income, which are by definition equal. One approach focuses on expenditures, or the flow of product; the other approach concentrates on income, or the flow of costs.

Source: U.S. Department of Commerce. First quarter preliminary data annualized.

ation can be thought of as the portion of the current year's GDP that is used to replace physical capital consumed in the process of production. Because somebody has paid for the replacement, depreciation must be added as a component of gross domestic income.

The last two components of GDP—indirect business taxes and depreciation—are called **nonincome expense items.**

Figure 8-3 shows a comparison between gross domestic product and gross domestic income for 1998. Whether you decide to use the expenditure approach or the income approach, you will come out with the same number. There are sometimes statistical discrepancies, but they are usually relatively small.

Nonincome expense items
The total of indirect business taxes and depreciation.

OTHER COMPONENTS OF NATIONAL INCOME ACCOUNTING

Gross domestic income or product does not really tell how much income people have access to for spending purposes. To get to those kinds of data, we must make some adjustments, which we now do.

National Income (NI)

We know that net domestic product (NDP) represents the total market value of goods and services available for both consumption, used in a broader sense here to mean "resource exhaustion," and net additions to the economy's stock of capital. NDP does not, however, represent the income available to individuals within that economy because it includes indirect business taxes, such as sales taxes. We therefore deduct these indirect business taxes from NDP to arrive at the figure for all factor income of resource owners. The result is what we define as **national income (NI)**—income *earned* by the factors of production.

National income (NI)
The total of all factor payments to resource owners. It can be obtained by subtracting indirect business taxes from NDP.

Personal Income (PI)

National income does not actually represent what is available to individuals to spend because some people obtain income for which they have provided no concurrent good or service and others earn income but do not receive it. In the former category are mainly recipients of transfer payments from the government, such as Social Security, welfare, and food stamps. These payments represent shifts of funds within the economy by way of the government, where no good or service is concurrently rendered in exchange. For the other category, income earned but not received, the most obvious examples are corporate retained earnings that are plowed back into business, contributions to social insurance, and corporate income taxes. When transfer payments are added and when income earned but not received is subtracted, we end up with **personal income (PI)**—income *received* by the factors of production prior to the payment of personal income taxes.

Personal income (PI)
The amount of income that households actually receive before they pay personal income taxes.

Disposable Personal Income (DPI)

Everybody knows that you do not get to take home all your salary. To get **disposable personal income (DPI),** we subtract all personal income taxes from personal income. This is the income that individuals have left for consumption and saving.

Disposable personal income (DPI)
Personal income after personal income taxes have been paid.

Deriving the Components of GDP

Table 8-2 takes you through the steps necessary to derive the various components of GDP. It shows how you go from gross domestic product to net domestic product to national

	Billions of Dollars
Gross domestic product (GDP)	8,332.2
Minus depreciation	−951.3
Net domestic product (NDP)	7,380.9
Minus indirect business taxes and other adjustments	−755.9
National income (NI)	6,625.0
Minus corporate taxes, Social Security contributions, corporate retained earnings	−1,071.2
Plus government and business transfer payments	+1,573.1
Personal income (PI)	7,126.9
Minus personal income tax and nontax payments	−1,032.4
Disposable personal income (DPI)	6,094.5

TABLE 8-2

Going from GDP to Disposable Income, 1998

Source: U.S. Department of Commerce.

income to personal income and then to disposable personal income. On the endpapers of your book, you can see the historical record for GDP, NDP, NI, PI, and DPI for selected years since 1929.

We have completed our rundown of the different ways that GDP can be computed and of the different variants of national income and product. What we have not yet touched on is the difference between national income measured in this year's dollars and national income representing real goods and services.

CONCEPTS IN BRIEF

- To obtain national income, we subtract indirect business taxes from net domestic product. National income gives us a measure of all factor payments to resource owners.

- To obtain personal income, we must add government transfer payments, such as Social Security benefits and food stamps. We must subtract income earned but not received by factor owners, such as corporate retained earnings, Social Security contributions, and corporate income taxes.

- To obtain disposable personal income, we subtract all personal income taxes from personal income. Disposable personal income is income that individuals actually have for consumption or saving.

DISTINGUISHING BETWEEN NOMINAL AND REAL VALUES

So far we have shown how to measure *nominal* income and product. When we say "nominal," we are referring to income and product expressed in the current "face value" of today's dollar. Given the existence of inflation or deflation in the economy, we must also be able to distinguish between the **nominal values** that we will be looking at and the **real values** underlying them. Nominal values are expressed in current dollars. Real income involves

Nominal values
The values of variables such as GDP and investment expressed in current dollars, also called *money values*; measurement in terms of the actual market prices at which goods are sold.

Real values
Measurement of economic values after adjustments have been made for changes in the average of prices between years.

our command over goods and services—purchasing power—and therefore depends on money income and a set of prices. Thus real income refers to nominal income corrected for changes in the weighted average of all prices. In other words, we must make an adjustment for changes in the price level. Consider an example. Nominal income *per person* in 1960 was only about $2,800 per year. In 1996, nominal income per person was close to $28,000. Were people really that bad off in 1960? No, for nominal income in 1960 is expressed in 1960 prices, not in the prices of today. In today's dollars, the per-person income of 1960 would be closer to $10,000, or almost 40 percent of today's income per person. This is a meaningful comparison between income in 1960 and income today. (The uncorrected 1960 data show per-person income to be only 10 percent of today's income.) Next we will show how we can translate nominal measures of income into real measures by using an appropriate price index, such as the CPI or the GDP deflator discussed in Chapter 7.

Correcting GDP for Price Changes

If a compact disc (CD) costs $15 this year, 10 CDs will have a market value of $150. If next year they cost $20 each, the same 10 CDs will have a market value of $200. In this case, there is no increase in the total quantity of CDs, but the market value will have increased by one-third. Apply this to every single good and service produced and sold in the United States and you realize that changes in GDP, measured in *current* dollars, may not be a very useful indication of economic activity. If we are really interested in variations in the *real* output of the economy, we must correct GDP (and just about everything else we look at) for changes in the average of overall prices from year to year. Basically, we need to generate an index that approximates the changes in average prices and then divide that estimate into the value of output in current dollars to adjust the value of output to what is called **constant dollars,** or dollars corrected for general price level changes. This price-corrected GDP is called *real GDP.*

Constant dollars
Dollars expressed in terms of real purchasing power using a particular year as the base or standard of comparison, in contrast to current dollars.

EXAMPLE
Correcting GDP for Price Level Changes, 1987–1997

Let's take a numerical example to see how we can adjust GDP for changes in prices. We must pick an appropriate price index in order to adjust for these price level changes. We mentioned the Consumer Price Index, the Producer Price Index, and the GDP deflator in Chapter 7. Let's use the GDP deflator to adjust our figures. Table 8-3 gives 11 years of GDP figures. Nominal GDP figures are shown in column 2. The price level index (GDP deflator) is in column 3, with base year of 1992 when the GDP deflator equals 100. Column 4 shows real (inflation-adjusted) GDP in 1992 dollars.

The formula for real GDP is

$$\text{Real GDP} = \frac{\text{nominal GDP}}{\text{price level}} \times 100$$

The step-by-step derivation of real (constant-dollar) GDP is as follows: The base year is 1992, so the price index must equal 100. In 1992, nominal GDP was $6,020.2 billion, and so too was real GDP expressed in 1992 dollars. In 1993, the price level increased to 102.2. Thus to correct 1993's nominal GDP for inflation, we divide the price index, 102.2, into the nominal GDP figure of $6,343.3 billion and then multiply it by 100. The result is $6,206.8 billion, which is 1993 GDP expressed in terms of the purchasing power of dollars in 1992. What about a situation when the price level is lower than in 1992? Look at 1987. Here the price index shown in column 3 is only 82.7. That means that in 1987, the average of all prices was

(1) Year	(2) Nominal GDP (billions of dollars per year)	(3) Price Level Index (base year 1992 = 100)	(4) = [(2) ÷ (3)] × 100 Real GDP (billions of dollars per year in constant 1992 dollars)
1987	4,539.9	82.7	5,489.6
1988	4,900.4	85.9	5,704.8
1989	5,250.8	89.7	5,853.7
1990	5,546.1	93.7	5,919.0
1991	5,724.8	97.3	5,883.6
1992	6,020.2	100.0	6,020.2
1993	6,343.3	102.2	6,206.8
1994	6,738.4	104.3	6,460.6
1995	7,007.9	106.3	6,592.6
1996	7,636.0	110.6	6,928.4
1997	8,079.9	112.4	7,188.8

Source: U.S. Department of Commerce, Bureau of Economic Analysis.

TABLE 8-3

Correcting GDP for Price Changes
To correct GDP for price changes, we first have to pick a price level index (the GDP deflator) with a specific year as its base. In our example, the base level is 1992 prices; the price level index for that year is 100% = 1.00. To obtain 1992 constant-dollar GDP, we divide the price level index into nominal GDP. In other words, we divide column 3 into column 2 (and multiply by 100). This gives us column 4, which is a measure of real GDP expressed in 1992 purchasing power.

about 83 percent of prices in 1992. To obtain 1987 GDP expressed in terms of 1992 purchasing power, we divide nominal GDP, $4,539.9 billion, by 82.7 and then multiply by 100. The result is a larger number—$5,489.6 billion. Column 4 in Table 8-3 is a better measure of how the economy has performed than column 2, which shows nominal GDP changes.

FOR CRITICAL ANALYSIS: A few years ago, the base year for the GDP deflator was 1982. What does a change in the base year for the price level index affect? •

Plotting Nominal and Real GDP

Nominal GDP and real GDP from 1970 to 1998 are plotted in Figure 8-4. Notice that there is quite a big gap between the two GDP figures, reflecting the amount of inflation that has occurred. Note, further, that the choice of a base year is arbitrary. We have chosen 1992 as the base year in our example. This happens to be the base year that will be used by the government.

Per Capita GDP

Looking at changes in real gross domestic product may be deceiving, particularly if the population size has changed significantly. If real GDP over a 10-year period went up 100 percent, you might jump to the conclusion that the material well-being of the economy had increased by that amount. But what if during the same period population increased by 200 percent? Then what would you say? Certainly, the amount of real GDP per person, or *per capita real GDP,* would have fallen, even though total deflated (or real) GDP had risen. What we must do to account not only for price changes but also for population changes is first deflate GDP and then divide by the total population, doing this for each year. If we

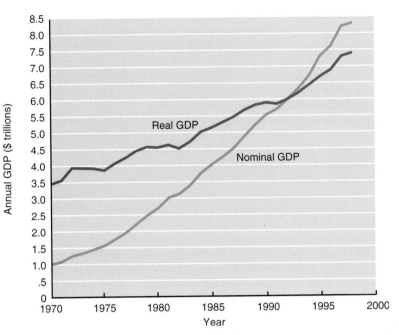

FIGURE 8-4

Nominal and Real GDP

Here we plot both nominal and real GDP. Real GDP is expressed in the purchasing power of 1992 dollars. The gap between the two represents price level changes.

Source: U.S. Department of Commerce.

were to look at certain less developed countries, we would find that in many cases, even though real GDP has risen over the past several decades, per capita real GDP has remained constant or fallen because the population has grown just as rapidly or more quickly.

The difficulties of using GDP as an indicator of social well-being do not end here. In fact, there has been a running battle over the use of GDP statistics because, according to its critics, such numbers do not capture the true overall well-being of a nation. How do we take account of changes in leisure time? How do our national income accounts recognize increased traffic congestion, air pollution in our cities, crime in the streets, and so on? And housework, which constitutes a major amount of the labor performed in the United States, isn't even counted in GDP.

A New Chain-Weighted Measure of the Growth in Real GDP

In December 1995, the Commerce Department's Bureau of Economic Analysis (BEA) made a fundamental change in the way it computes real gross domestic product. Remember that real GDP consists of consumer spending, business investment, government expenditures on goods and services, and net foreign trade. To calculate real GDP, the BEA has used a weighted sum of 1,100 components of these four categories. Until 1996, these 1,100 components were fixed in weight, and their relative importance changed only periodically. For example, the last revision was made in 1987. Otherwise stated, the BEA has been using a *fixed-weight* measure of changes in real GDP.

Now the BEA will change the weights of the different components of real GDP depending on how their relative prices have changed and how their relative shares in the overall economy's output change. The new measure is called *chain-weighted real GDP.* Rather than a specific number, an index is used. Thus to calculate a year's *change* in real GDP, it is necessary to compare one year's index with the previous year's index. For a while, the BEA plans to publish both the chain-weighted real GDP index and its dollar equivalent. You can find chain-weighted real GDP statistics on the endpapers of this book, which show our national income accounts.

CONCEPTS IN BRIEF

- To correct nominal GDP for price changes, we first use a base year for our price index and assign it the number 100 percent (or 1.00). Then we construct an index based on how a weighted average of the price level has changed relative to that base year. For example, if in the next year a weighted average of the price level indicates that prices have increased by 10 percent, we would assign it the number 110 (or 1.10). We then divide each year's price index, so constructed, into its respective nominal GDP figure (and multiply by 100).

- We can divide the population into real GDP to obtain per capita real GDP.

COMPARING GDP THROUGHOUT THE WORLD

It is relatively easy to compare the standard of living of a family in Los Angeles with that of one living in Boston. Both families get paid in dollars and can buy the same goods and services at Kmart, McDonald's, and Price Costco. It is not so easy, however, to make a similar comparison between a family living in the United States and one in, say, India. The first problem concerns money. Indians get paid in rupees, their national currency, and buy goods and services with those rupees. That means that just as we can compare families in Los Angeles and Boston, we can compare the living standards of a family in Delhi with one in Bombay. But how do we compare the average standard of living in India with that in the United States?

Exercise 8.2
Visit www.econtoday.com for more about foreign currencies.

Foreign Exchange Rates

In earlier chapters, you have encountered international examples that involved local currencies, but the dollar equivalent always has been given. The dollar equivalent is calculated by looking up the **foreign exchange rate** that is published daily in major newspapers throughout the world. If you know that you can exchange $1 for 5 francs, the exchange rate is 5 to 1 (or otherwise stated, a franc is worth 20 cents). So if French incomes per capita are, say, 100,000 francs, that translates at an exchange rate of 5 francs to $1, to $20,000. For years, statisticians calculated relative GDP by simply adding up each country's GDP in its local currency and dividing by each respective dollar exchange rate.

Foreign exchange rate
The price of one currency in terms of another.

True Purchasing Power

The problem with simply using foreign exchange rates to convert other countries' GDP and per capita GDP into dollars is that not all goods and services are bought and sold in a world market. Restaurant food, housecleaning services, and home repairs do not get exchanged across countries. In countries that have very low wages, those kinds of services are much cheaper than foreign exchange rate computations would imply. Government statistics claiming that per capita income in some poor country is only $300 a year seems shocking. But such a statistic does not tell you the true standard of living of people in that country. Only by looking at what is called **purchasing power parity** can you determine other countries' true standards of living compared to ours.

Purchasing power parity
Adjustment in exchange rate conversions that takes into account differences in the true cost of living across countries.

TABLE 8-4

Comparing GDP Internationally

Country	Annual GDP Based on Purchasing Power Parity (billions of U.S. dollars)	Per Capita GDP Based on Purchasing Power Parity (U.S. dollars)	Per Capita GDP Based on Foreign Exchange Rates (U.S. dollars)
United States	6,897.2	26,528	26,528
Japan	2,493.8	19,399	26,424
China	2,490.1	1,692	375
Germany	2,007.4	19,870	24,421
France	1,421.6	18,450	23,489
Russia	1,101.8	6,903	2,640
India	1,100.4	1,155	379
Italy	1,099.0	17,050	17,990
United Kingdom	1,088.0	16,352	16,804
Brazil	980.4	5,251	2,794

Sources: International Monetary Fund; World Bank; Organization for Economic Cooperation and Development.

INTERNATIONAL EXAMPLE
Purchasing Power Parity Comparisons of World Incomes

A few years ago, the International Monetary Fund accepted the purchasing power parity approach as the correct one. It started presenting international statistics on each country's GDP relative to every other's based on purchasing power parity. The results were surprising. As you can see from Table 8-4, China has a higher per capita GDP compared to what was measured at market foreign exchange rates.

FOR CRITICAL ANALYSIS: What percentage increase is there in per capita GDP in China when one switches from foreign exchange rates to purchasing power parity? •

CONCEPTS IN BRIEF

- The foreign exchange rate is the price of one currency in terms of another.
- Statisticians often calculate relative GDP by adding up each country's GDP in its local currency and dividing by the dollar exchange rate.
- Because not all goods and services are bought and sold in the world market, we must correct exchange rate conversions of other countries' GDP figures in order to take into account differences in the true cost of living across countries.

How Well Do Economists Predict GDP?

Many forecasting economists use large-scale models to predict economywide changes. Here a group is also consulting with an expert from the Middle East. Why?

CONCEPTS APPLIED:

NATIONAL INCOME ACCOUNTING, GDP, REAL GDP

Visit www.econtoday.com for an Internet Activity that expands your understanding of these concepts.

A joke among economists is that they have been able to forecast nine of the last seven recessions. Underlying this joke is a reality: The people who make their living forecasting changes in real GDP do not have a stellar track record. Actually, this unflattering assessment is a little too harsh. Forecasting economists have done a pretty good job predicting *long-run* trends in real GDP. Where they go wrong is in predicting downturns, otherwise known as recessions. In Table 8-5, you can see that forecasters missed four of the five past downturns in our economy since the 1960s. The best that can be said about typical economic forecasts of downturns is that they are usually late. In other words, downturns seemed to be recognized only after they have begun.

How the Forecasters Do It

Most forecasters use large-scale computer models to develop their estimates of changes in real GDP. These computer models attempt to make sense of how our multitrillion-dollar economy works. Sometimes these models involve hundreds of sectors. A sector, such as automobiles, may be shown to depend on a wide range of variables—interest rates, price changes, and so on. Some experts argue that even the largest-scale computer models of our economy can no longer handle its changing nature. Furthermore, the U.S. economy is increasingly part of an interconnected world. Little long-term research has been done to discover how changes in the rest of the world's economies ultimately affect the U.S. economy.

Other Difficulties in Predicting Downturns

The globalization of the American economy cannot be used as an excuse for missing the downturn that started in December 1969. The 1960s was a decade of sustained good times (similar to the 1990s). A year before the downturn started, economic forecasters as a group pegged the probability of recession in the coming year at less than 15 percent. Their excuse for missing this downturn was that they did not foresee federal government defense

Start of Recession	Date of Forecast	Forecasted Growth over the Next Year (%)	Actual Growth in Real GDP(%)
December 1969	December 1969	1.5	-.6
November 1973	December 1973	1.5	-1.8
January 1980	December 1979	-.7	-.3
July 1990	December 1989	2.1	-.1
July 1991	December 1990	2.2	.7

Source: Business Week, September 30, 1996, p. 92.

TABLE 8-5

Economic Forecasts: Missing the Mark

The forecasts given in the table are taken from *Business Week* surveys through the years. Only the recession that started at the beginning of 1980 was correctly anticipated by the economic forecasters surveyed. They missed the other four downturns completely.

spending cuts and rising interest rates caused by contractionary government policies.

The forecasters' reasons for missing the 1973 downturn was that they could not predict the embargo imposed by oil-producing countries at that time. The recession of 1990 arrived without much warning at all. Indeed, virtually no economic model predicted that recession.

Economic forecasters defend themselves by stating that recessions that happen quickly are virtually impossible to predict. Those that commence slowly are countered by government policy and presumably do not actually occur. So, according to these forecasters, only when policymakers are caught by surprise do we have recessions.

The Raw Data

No matter who is making a prediction about changes in real GDP, the prediction must be based on data. Those data typically come from government agencies. Government data are notoriously unreliable in their preliminary form. For example, the Commerce Department said that the economy was growing at 2.2 percent per year in the second quarter of 1997. About a month later, it stated that the economy actually grew at about 3.6 percent per year.

Many critics of government statistics argue that American economic policy is being made in the dark. Everybody knows that the Consumer Price Index is biased and that this bias has inflated cost-of-living increases given to Social Security recipients and some private pensioners.

There is a conceptual problem today. Before the age of information—our new cyberage—counting was a lot easier. Goods could be added up. Today it is difficult to measure the benefits of recent technological improvements. Software spending is not even counted as an investment, though it clearly is.

Part of the problem stems from the way statistics are obtained by the government. The government still estimates exports and inventories on the basis of surveys filled out by hand on pieces of paper. The government's collection of data has to go electronic, particularly in our computerized, just-in-time inventory control age. But so far, Congress has turned a deaf ear to requests by the Bureau of Labor Statistics and the Department of Commerce to increase funding to improve our economic statistics.

FOR CRITICAL ANALYSIS
1. Explain how a business could be hurt by relying on an inaccurate forecast of changes in real GDP.
2. Computing power is relatively cheap and incredibly massive today compared to the 1960s. Nonetheless, large-scale computer economic models have done no better in predicting economic downturns? Why?

CHAPTER SUMMARY

1. Households provide labor services, land, capital, and entrepreneurship, for which they are paid wages, rent, interest, and profits. Profits are considered a factor cost—they are the reward for entrepreneurship or risk taking. Profits are a residual payment.
2. In the simplest representation of our economy, there are only households and businesses. The circular flow goes from households to factor markets to businesses and from businesses to product markets to households.
3. National income accounting is the method by which economists attempt to measure statistically the variables with which they are concerned in their study of macroeconomics.
4. One of the concepts most often used in national income accounting is gross domestic product, which is defined as the total market value of all *final* goods and services produced annually by domestic factors of production. The stress on *final* is important to avoid the double counting of intermediate goods used in the production of other goods.
5. We can compute GDP using the expenditure approach or the income approach. In the former, we merely add up the dollar value of all final goods and services; in the latter, we add up the payments generated in producing all those goods and services, or wages, interest, rent, and profits, plus indirect business taxes and depreciation.

6. It is difficult to measure the market value of government expenditures because generally government-provided goods are not sold at a market clearing price. We therefore value government expenditures at their cost for inclusion in our measure of GDP.

7. Investment does not occur when there is merely a transfer of assets among individuals; rather, it occurs only when new productive capacity, such as a machine tool, is built.

8. Part of our capital stock is worn out or becomes obsolete every year. To take account of the expenditures made merely to replace such capital equipment, we subtract depreciation from GDP to yield net domestic product.

9. To correct for price changes, we deflate GDP with a price index to come up with real GDP. To take account of rising population, we divide by population to come up with per capita real GDP.

10. To compare GDP across countries, we must first apply the foreign exchange rate to GDP expressed in the local currency and then adjust the exchange rate to take account of the purchasing power of that income. This is called the purchasing power parity approach.

DISCUSSION OF PREVIEW QUESTIONS

1. What is gross domestic product (GDP), and what does it measure?

Gross domestic product is defined as the market value of all final goods and services produced during one year by domestic factors of production. Because GDP is measured per unit of time, it is a flow concept. Economists try to estimate GDP in order to evaluate the productive performance of an economy during the year; economists also use GDP estimates to aid them in judging overall economic well-being.

2. Why are only *final* goods and services evaluated in deriving GDP?

Because GDP estimates are an attempt to evaluate an economy's performance and to generalize about group well-being, we must be careful to evaluate only final goods and services; otherwise GDP would be exaggerated. For example, because an automobile uses plastic, steel, coke, rubber, coal, and other products in its manufacture, to count each of these *and* the value of the automobile would be double counting. Thus to count steel *and* the automobile when it is sold is to count steel twice and hence to exaggerate the economy's performance and the group's economic well-being. Steel in this instance would not be a final good; it would be an intermediate good.

3. Why must depreciation and indirect business taxes be added to national income at factor cost in order to derive GDP via the income approach?

The expenditure approach to GDP counts expenditures on all final goods and services; in particular, expenditures on *all* investment goods amount to gross investment. The income approach to GDP estimation, by contrast, sums the wages, interest, rent, and profit receipts of income earners. Because depreciation is not a wage, rent, interest, or profit, the expenditure approach would yield a higher number. In order to compare correctly, we must add depreciation to national income at factor cost to calculate GDP via the income approach. Similarly, indirect business taxes (excise, sales, and property taxes) are automatically reflected in the expenditure approach, whereas indirect business taxes are not wages, interest, rent, or profit receipts to factors of production.

4. How does correcting GDP for changes in the price level and population improve the usefulness of GDP estimates?

When the price level is rising (during periods of inflation), GDP estimates would overstate true productive activity and group economic well-being. Similarly, when the general price level is falling (during periods of deflation), GDP estimates would understate productive activity and group economic well-being. If population is rising more rapidly than real output, real GDP estimates would rise, but living standards might well be falling. Dividing by population corrects for such cases. Per capita real GDP is a better clue to productive activity and overall economic well-being than nominal GDP.

PROBLEMS

(Answers to the odd-numbered problems appear at the back of the book.)

8-1. The following are a year's data for a hypothetical economy.

	Billions of Dollars
Consumption	400
Government spending	350
Gross private domestic investment	150
Exports	150
Imports	100
Depreciation	50
Indirect business taxes	25

    a. Based on the data, what is the value of GDP? NDP? NI?

    b. Suppose that in the next year exports increase to $175 billion, imports increase to $200 billion, and consumption falls to $350 billion. What will GDP be in that year?

    c. If the value of depreciation (capital consumption allowance) should ever exceed that of gross private domestic investment, how would this affect the future productivity of the nation?

8-2. Look back at Table 8-3, which explains how to correct GDP for price level changes. Column 4 of that table gives real GDP in terms of 1992 constant dollars. Change the base year to 1987. Recalculate the price level index and then recalculate real GDP—that is, express column 4 in terms of 1987 dollars instead of 1992 dollars.

8-3. Study the following table; then answer the questions.

Stage of Production	Sales Receipts	Intermediate Costs	Value Added
Coal	$2	$0	$2
Steel	5	2	3
Manufactured autos	8	5	3
Sold autos	9	8	1

    a. What is the intermediate good for steel production? How much did it cost?

    b. What is the value added resulting from auto manufacturing?

    c. If automobiles are the only final goods produced in this economy, what would GDP via the expenditures approach be equal to?

    d. If automobiles are the only final goods produced in this economy, what would GDP via the income approach be equal to?

8-4. At the top of a piece of paper, write the headings "Production Activity" and "Nonproduction Activity." List each of the following under one of these headings by determining which would go into our measure of GDP.

    a. Mr. X sells his used car to Mr. Y.

    b. Joe's used car lot sells a car to Mr. Z and receives a $50 profit for doing so.

    c. Merrill Lynch receives a brokerage commission for selling stocks.

    d. Mr. Arianas buys 100 shares of AT&T stock.

    e. Mrs. Romano cooks and keeps house for her family.

    f. Mr. Gonzalez mows his own lawn.

    g. Mr. Gonzalez mows lawns for a living.

    h. Mr. Smith receives a welfare payment.

    i. Mr. Johnson sends his daughter $500 for a semester of studies at College U.

8-5. What happens to the official measure of GDP in each of the following situations?

    a. A man marries his housekeeper, who then quits working for wages.

    b. A drug addict marries her supplier.

    c. Homemakers perform the same jobs but switch houses and charge each other for their services.

8-6. Construct a value-added table for various stages in the production and sale of bread.

8-7. Consider the following table for an economy that produces only four goods.

Good	1992 Price	1992 Quantity	1997 Price	1997 Quantity
Pizza	$ 4	10	$ 8	12
Cola	12	20	36	15
T-shirts	6	5	10	15
Business equipment	25	10	30	12

Assuming a 1992 base year:

a. What is nominal GDP for 1992 and 1997?

b. What is real GDP for 1992? For 1997?

8-8. Examine the following figures for a hypothetical year; then calculate GDP, NDP, NI, PI, and DPI.

	Billions of Dollars
Consumption	400
Net exports	−20
Transfer payments	20
Gross investment	100
Social Security contributions	10
Government purchases	120
Net investment	50
Dividends	20
Indirect business taxes	10
Corporate income taxes	30
Personal income taxes	60
Undistributed corporate profits	20

COMPUTER-ASSISTED INSTRUCTION

Coal is transformed into steel, steel is turned into a manufactured auto, and a manufactured auto is sold to a final buyer. You are required to calculate value added at various stages; in the process, it is revealed that the expenditure approach and the income approach to national income accounting yield identical estimates of GDP.

Complete problem and answer appear on disk.

INTERACTING WITH THE INTERNET

The Federal Reserve Bank of St. Louis's FRED (Federal Reserve Economic Data) gives you quarterly updates on GDP and its components. Go to

www.stls.frb.org/fred/

For information on the Consumer Price Index, look at the home page of the Bureau of Labor Statistics. Go to

stats.bls.gov/eag.table.html

CHAPTER 9

ECONOMIC GROWTH: Technology, Research and Development, and Knowledge

Let there be no doubt about it: Without economic growth, our standard of living would never rise. In other words, increases in the measured standard of living are the result of positive economic growth. What determines how fast a nation's economy grows? There are many theories and at least some evidence to support those theories. Among the purported determinants of the rate of economic growth are the rate of saving, the existence of well-defined and enforced property rights, free trade, and a fertile terrain for innovation and invention. Some economists and politicians also believe that the tax system can influence the rate of economic growth. Do taxes matter? Before you answer this question, you need to know how to measure a nation's economic growth.

PREVIEW QUESTIONS

1. What is economic growth?
2. What does economic growth measure?
3. What are some of the ways in which you can experience economic growth for yourself or for your family?
4. What are the determinants of economic growth?

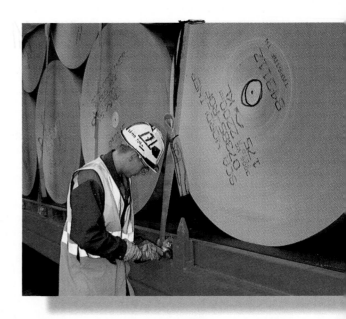

Did You Know That . . . at the turn of the twentieth century, Argentina had the sixth highest per capita income in the world, whereas it is now around fortieth, somewhat below Iran? Consider also that 100 years ago, Hong Kong was basically a barren rock, whereas today its per capita income exceeds that of France and the United Kingdom. How can we explain such dramatic changes in relative living standards? From an arithmetic point of view, the answer is simple: Argentina experienced little and in some cases negative economic growth over the past century, whereas Hong Kong had significant economic growth. That answer, though, does not tell us why economic growth rates differed in these two countries. That is the task of this chapter. Should you care about the rate of economic growth in the United States? The answer is yes, if you care about your future standard of living and that of your children and grandchildren. You have already demonstrated that you care about your future standard of living; otherwise, you would not be bothering to obtain a higher education. Obviously, you want to make sure that you experience economic growth as an individual. Now it is time to consider the nation as a whole.

HOW DO WE DEFINE ECONOMIC GROWTH?

Remember from Chapter 2 that we can show economic growth graphically as an outward shift of a production possibilities curve, as is seen in Figure 9-1. If there is economic growth between 1998 and 2025, the production possibilities curve will shift outward toward the red line. The distance that it shifts represents the amount of economic growth, defined as the increase in the productive capacity of a nation. Although it is possible to come up with a measure of a nation's increased productive capacity, it would not be easy. Therefore, we turn to a more readily obtainable definition of economic growth.

Most people have a general idea of what economic growth means. When a nation grows economically, its citizens must be better off in at least some ways, usually in terms of their material well-being. Typically, though, we do not measure the well-being of any nation solely in terms of its total output of real goods and services or in terms of real GDP without making some adjustments. After all, India has a GDP about three times as large as that in Switzerland. The population in India, though, is about 125 times greater than that in Switzerland. Consequently, we view India as a relatively poor country and Switzerland as a relatively rich country. That means that to measure how much a country is growing in terms of annual increases in real GDP, we have to adjust for population growth. Our formal definition becomes this: **Economic growth** occurs when there are increases in per capita real GDP; it is measured by the rate of change in per capita real GDP per year.

Economic growth
Increases in per capita real GDP measured by its rate of change per year.

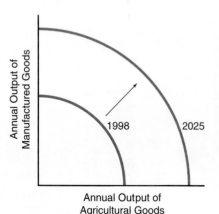

Annual Output of
Manufactured Goods

1998   2025

Annual Output of
Agricultural Goods

FIGURE 9-1

Economic Growth
If there is growth between 1998 and 2025, the production possibilities curve for the entire economy will shift outward from the blue line labeled 1998 to the red line labeled 2025. The distance that it shifts represents an increase in the productive capacity of the nation.

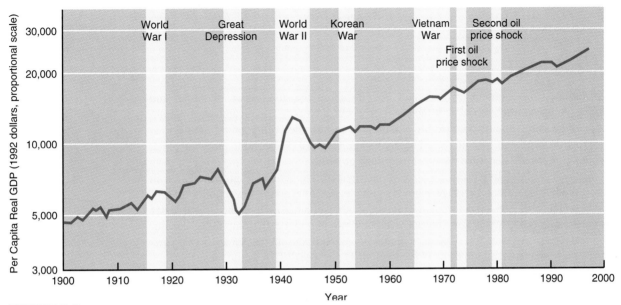

FIGURE 9-2

The Historical Record of U.S. Economic Growth

The graph traces per capita real GDP in the United States since 1900. Data are given in 1992 dollars.

Source: U.S. Department of Commerce.

Figure 9-2 presents the historical record of real GDP per person in the United States.

INTERNATIONAL EXAMPLE

Growth Rates Around the World

Table 9-1 shows the annual average rate of growth of income per person in selected countries. Notice that the United States during the time period under study is positioned about midway in the pack. In other words, even though we are one of the world's richest countries, our recent rate of economic growth is not particularly high.

TABLE 9-1

Per Capita Growth Rates in Various Countries

Country	Average Annual Rate of Growth of Income Per Capita, 1970–1997 (%)	Country	Average Annual Rate of Growth of Income Per Capita, 1970–1997 (%)
Sweden	1.8	Italy	2.9
Switzerland	1.8	Spain	2.9
Germany	2.2	United States	2.9
Netherlands	2.3	Japan	4.4
France	2.4	Turkey	5.5
United Kingdom	2.4	China	6.2
Canada	2.7		

Sources: World Bank; International Monetary Fund.

FOR CRITICAL ANALYSIS: *"The largest change is from zero to one." Does this statement have anything to do with relative growth rates in poorer versus richer countries?* ●

Problems in Definition

Our definition of economic growth says nothing about the *distribution* of output and income. A nation might grow very rapidly in terms of increases in per capita real output, while at the same time its poor people remain poor or become even poorer. Therefore, in assessing the economic growth record of any nation, we must be careful to pinpoint which income groups have benefited the most from such growth.

Real standards of living can go up without any positive economic growth. This can occur if individuals are, on average, enjoying more leisure by working fewer hours but producing as much as they did before. For example, if per capita real GDP in the United States remained at $20,000 a year for a decade, we could not automatically jump to the conclusion that Americans were, on average, no better off. What if, during that same 10-year period, average hours worked fell from 37 per week to 33 per week? That would mean that during the 10 years under study, individuals in the labor force were "earning" four hours more leisure a week. Actually, nothing so extreme has occurred in this country, but something similar has. Average hours worked per week fell steadily until the 1960s, at which time they leveled off. That means that during much of the history of this country, the increase in per capita real GDP *understated* the actual economic growth that we were experiencing because we were enjoying more and more leisure as things progressed.

Is Economic Growth Bad?

Some commentators on our current economic situation believe that the definition of economic growth ignores its negative effects. Some psychologists even contend that we are made worse off because of economic growth. They say that the more we grow, the more "needs" are created so that we feel worse off as we become richer. Our expectations are rising faster than reality, so we presumably always suffer from a sense of disappointment. Clearly, the measurement of economic growth cannot take into account the spiritual and cultural aspects of the good life. As with all activities, there are costs and benefits. You can see some of those listed in Table 9-2.

In any event, any measure of economic growth that we use will be imperfect. Nonetheless, the measures that we do have allow us to make comparisons across countries and over time and, if used judiciously, can enable us to gain important insights. Per-capita real GDP, used so often, is not always an accurate measure of economic well-being, but it is a serviceable measure of productive activity.

Benefits	Costs
Reduction in illiteracy	Environmental pollution
Reduction in poverty	Breakdown of the family
Improved health	Isolation and alienation
Longer lives	Urban congestion
Political stability	

TABLE 9-2

Costs and Benefits of Economic Growth

The Importance of Growth Rates

Notice back in Table 9-1 that the growth rates in real per capita income for most countries differ by very little—generally, only a few percentage points. You might want to know why such small differences in growth rates are important. What would it matter if we grew at 3 percent rather than at 4 percent per year?

It matters a lot—not for next year or the year after but for the more distant future. The power of compound interest is impressive. Let's see what happens with three different annual rates of growth: 3 percent, 4 percent, and 5 percent. We start with $1 trillion per year, which is approximately equal to the gross domestic product of the United States in 1971. We then compound this $1 trillion, or allow it to grow, into the future at these three different growth rates. The difference is huge. In 50 years, $1 trillion per year becomes $4.38 trillion per year if compounded at 3 percent per year. Just one percentage point more in the growth rate, 4 percent, results in a real GDP of $7.11 trillion per year in 50 years, almost double the previous amount. Two percentage points difference in the growth rate—5 percent per year—results in a real GDP of $11.5 trillion per year in 50 years, or nearly three times as much. Obviously, there is a great difference in the results of economic growth for very small differences in annual growth rates. That is why nations are concerned if the growth rate falls even a little in absolute percentage terms.

Compound Interest. When we talk about growth rates, we are basically talking about compound interest. In Table 9-3, we show how $1 compounded annually grows at different interest rates. We see in the 3 percent column that $1 in 50 years grows to $4.38. We merely multiplied $1 trillion times 4.38 to get the growth figure in our earlier example. In the 5 percent column, $1 grows to $11.50 after 50 years. Again, we multiplied $1 trillion times 11.50 to get the growth figure for 5 percent in the preceding example.

TABLE 9-3

One Dollar Compounded Annually at Different Interest Rates
Here we show the value of a dollar at the end of a specified period during which it has been compounded annually at a specified interest rate. For example, if you took $1 today and invested it at 5 percent per year, it would yield $1.05 at the end of one year. At the end of 10 years, it would equal $1.63, and at the end of 50 years, it would equal $11.50.

Number of Years	Interest Rate						
	3%	4%	5%	6%	8%	10%	20%
1	1.03	1.04	1.05	1.06	1.08	1.10	1.20
2	1.06	1.08	1.10	1.12	1.17	1.21	1.44
3	1.09	1.12	1.16	1.19	1.26	1.33	1.73
4	1.13	1.17	1.22	1.26	1.36	1.46	2.07
5	1.16	1.22	1.28	1.34	1.47	1.61	2.49
6	1.19	1.27	1.34	1.41	1.59	1.77	2.99
7	1.23	1.32	1.41	1.50	1.71	1.94	3.58
8	1.27	1.37	1.48	1.59	1.85	2.14	4.30
9	1.30	1.42	1.55	1.68	2.00	2.35	5.16
10	1.34	1.48	1.63	1.79	2.16	2.59	6.19
20	1.81	2.19	2.65	3.20	4.66	6.72	38.30
30	2.43	3.24	4.32	5.74	10.00	17.40	237.00
40	3.26	4.80	7.04	10.30	21.70	45.30	1,470.00
50	4.38	7.11	11.50	18.40	46.90	117.00	9,100.00

EXAMPLE
What If the United States Had Grown a Little Bit Less or More Each Year?

In 1870, the per-person real GDP expressed in 1996 dollars was $3,276. That figure had grown to $26,718 by the beginning of 1996. The average economic growth rate was therefore about 1.75 percent per year. What if the U.S. growth rate over the same century and a quarter had been simply 1 percent less—only .75 percent per year? Per capita real GDP in 1996 would have been only 30 percent of what it actually was. The United States would have ranked somewhere around thirty-fifth on the scale of per capita income throughout the world. We would be poorer than Greece or Portugal.

Consider a rosier scenario: What if the U.S. economic rate of growth had been one point higher, or 2.75 percent per year? Today's per capita real GDP would be more than three times its actual value, or about $90,000!

FOR CRITICAL ANALYSIS: Can you relate this example to anything in your own life? *(Hint: Use the compound interest rates in Table 9-3 to make various predictions about your future standard of living.)* ●

CONCEPTS IN BRIEF

- Economic growth can be defined as the increase in real per capita output measured by its rate of change per year.
- The benefits of economic growth are reductions in illiteracy, poverty, and illness and increases in life spans and political stability. The costs of economic growth may include environmental pollution, alienation, and urban congestion.
- Small percentage-point differences in growth rates lead to large differences in real GDP over time. These differences can be seen by examining a compound interest table such as the one in Table 9-3.

PRODUCTIVITY INCREASES: THE HEART OF ECONOMIC GROWTH

Let's say that you are required to type 10 term papers and homework assignments a year. You have a word processor to do so, but you do not know how to touch-type. You end up spending an average of two hours per typing job. The next summer, you buy a touch-typing tutorial to use on your word processor and spend a few minutes a day improving your typing speed. The following term, you spend only one hour per typing assignment, thereby saving 10 hours a semester. You have become more productive. This concept of productivity relates to your ability (and everyone else's) to produce the same output with fewer labor hours. Thus **labor productivity** is normally measured by dividing the total real domestic output (real GDP) by the number of workers or the number of labor hours. Labor productivity increases whenever average output produced per worker during a specified time period increases. Clearly, there is a relationship between economic growth and increases in labor productivity. If you divide all resources into just capital and labor, economic growth can be defined simply as follows:

Economic growth = rate of growth of capital + rate of growth of labor +
rate of growth in the productivity of capital and of labor

Exercise 9.1
Visit www.econtoday.com for more about productivity.

Labor productivity
Total real domestic output (real GDP) divided by the number of workers (output per worker).

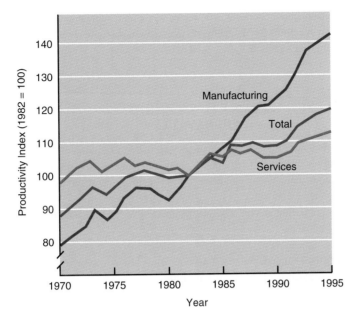

FIGURE 9-3
Nonfarm U.S. Productivity Growth
Whereas productivity growth in the services sector started increasing only in the early 1980s, productivity in the manufacturing sector has been increasing almost consistently since 1970.
Sources: U.S. Department of Commerce; U.S. Department of Labor, Bureau of Labor Statistics.

If everything else remains constant, improvements in labor productivity ultimately lead to economic growth and higher living standards.

Although productivity growth seemed to lag in the United States from the mid-1970s through the mid-1980s, there is quite a bit of evidence that it has been on the rise since then. Figure 9-3 traces productivity growth in the manufacturing and service sectors of the economy as well as total productivity growth.

THINKING CRITICALLY ABOUT THE MEDIA

Productivity as a Prerequisite for International Competitiveness

The recurring major story about the American economy relates to the rate of growth of productivity—or more generally, the lack thereof. The claim in the media is that if the United States fails to sustain high productivity, it will lose out in the competitive race among nations. The fallacy in such media stories is that the benefit of high productivity is somehow related to allowing the United States to compete with other countries. The reality is that with the benefit of high productivity, *any* country can produce more with the same amount of resources. That means that all its residents can consume more, which in turn means a higher standard of living because of higher productivity. As a nation, we would want higher productivity even if no other country in the world existed!

INTERNATIONAL EXAMPLE
How Does U.S. Productivity Stack Up?

Productivity is important because increases in productivity determine the standard of living of a country. For years, statisticians attempted to show that the growth in labor productivity in the United States was less than in Germany, Japan, and the United Kingdom. Indeed, from 1950 to the early 1990s, U.S. labor productivity growth was below that of many other countries. A recent study by the McKenzie Global Institute, however, shows a different result.

The McKenzie consultants examined productivity in various manufacturing industries. In five of the nine industries—automobiles, automobile parts, consumer electronics, metalworking, and steel—Japanese workers are more productive than American workers. In contrast, American workers are more productive than the Japanese in food and beer, computers, and soap and detergents. Because these latter industries are more important overall in terms of percentage of total national output, Japanese workers are only 83 percent as productive as American workers. In steel and metalworking, German workers are as productive as American workers, but in all other sectors, they are less productive. On average, German workers are 79 percent as productive as American workers.

FOR CRITICAL ANALYSIS: Should we care how productive American workers are in relation to those in the rest of the world? (Be careful—see the accompanying Thinking Critically About the Media box on page 193). ●

ONE FUNDAMENTAL DETERMINANT OF THE RATE OF ECONOMIC GROWTH: THE RATE OF SAVING

Economic growth does not occur in a vacuum. It is not some predetermined fate of a nation. Rather, economic growth depends on certain fundamental factors. One of the most important factors that affect the rate of economic growth and hence long-term living standards is the rate of saving.

A basic proposition in economics is that if you want more tomorrow, you have to take less today.

To have more consumption in the future, you have to consume less today and save the difference between your consumption and your income.

On a national basis, this implies that higher saving rates eventually mean higher living standards in the long run, all other things held constant. Concern has been growing in America that we are not saving enough, which means that our rate of saving may be too low. Saving is important for economic growth because without saving, we cannot have investment. If all income is consumed each year, there is nothing left over for saving, which could be used by business for investment. If there is no investment in our capital stock, there could be little hope of much economic growth.

The relationship between the rate of savings and per capita real GDP is shown in Figure 9-4. A nation with one of the highest rates of saving is Japan. Why?

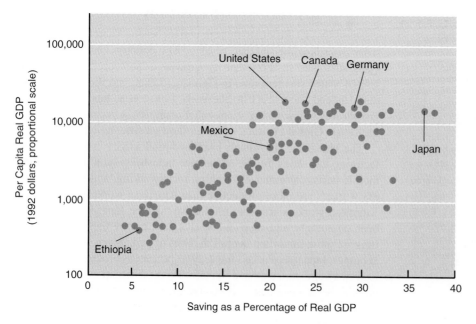

FIGURE 9-4

Relationship Between Rate of Saving and Per Capita Real GDP

This diagram shows the combination of per capita real GDP and the rate of saving expressed as the average percentage of annual real GDP for many nations since 1960. Centrally planned economies and major oil-producing countries are not shown.

Source: After Robert Summers and Alan Heston, "A New Set of International Comparisons of Real Product and Price Level," *Review of Income and Wealth,* March 1988.

INTERNATIONAL EXAMPLE
Singapore's Forced Saving

Residents of Singapore save at three times the rate of U.S. residents. Does this mean that they are more forward-looking than U.S. citizens? Perhaps not, for the government of Singapore compels individuals to save. Citizens of Singapore who work must contribute 20 percent of their salary to the nation's Central Provident Fund, which was introduced in 1955. Their employer must match the contribution with another 20 percent payment into the fund. Fund contributors earn interest rates that are slightly lower than "contributors" could obtain at commercial banks. In one recent year, the rate of total saving in that country reached almost 50 percent of GDP. What does the Singapore government do with these funds? It invests some domestically but also lends some to other countries.

FOR CRITICAL ANALYSIS: *Under what circumstances could you imagine not consuming half of your annual income in order to "save for a rainy day"?* ●

CONCEPTS IN BRIEF

- Economic growth is numerically equal to the rate of growth of capital plus the rate of growth of labor plus the rate of growth in the productivity of capital and of labor. Improvements in labor productivity, all other things being equal, lead to greater economic growth and higher living standards.

- One fundamental determinant of the rate of growth is the rate of saving. To have more consumption in the future, we have to save rather than consume. In general, countries that have had higher rates of saving have had higher rates of growth in real GDP.

NEW GROWTH THEORY AND WHAT DETERMINES GROWTH

A simple arithmetic definition of economic growth has already been given. Growth rates of capital and labor plus the growth rate in their productivity are simply defined as the components of economic growth. Economists have had good data on the growth of the physical capital stock in the United States as well as on the labor force. But when you add those two growth rates together, you still do not get the total economic growth rate in the United States. The difference has to be due to improvements in productivity. Economists typically labeled this "improvements in technology," and that was that. More recently, proponents of what is now called the **new growth theory** argue that technology cannot simply be looked at as an outside factor without explanation. Technology must be examined from what drives it. What are the forces that make productivity grow in America and elsewhere?

New growth theory
A relatively modern theory of economic growth that examines the factors that determine why technology, research, innovation, and the like are undertaken and how they interact.

Growth in Technology

Consider some startling statistics about the growth in technology. Look at Figure 9-5 on page 196 to learn what may happen to computers in the future. Microprocessor speeds may increase from 350 megahertz to 800 megahertz by the year 2011. By that same year, the size of the thinnest circuit line within a transistor will decrease by 77 percent. The typical memory capacity of computers will jump from 64 megabytes, or about the equivalent text

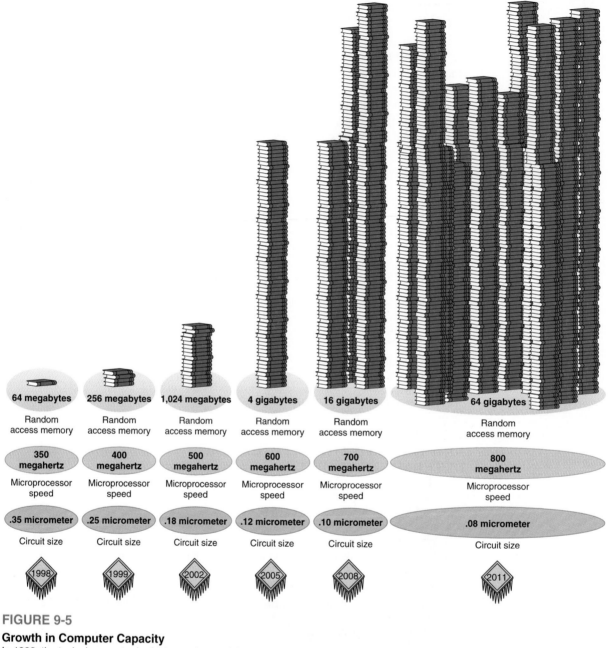

FIGURE 9-5

Growth in Computer Capacity

In 1998, the typical computer had 64 megabytes of dynamic random access memory. By the year 2002, that will increase to over 1,000 megabytes, or a gigabyte. By 2011, it will be 64 gigabytes. Similarly dramatic increases in microprocessor speed and reductions in transistor circuit thinness will also occur.

Source: Semiconductor Industry Association.

Do New Technologies Signal the End of Work?

Throughout the world, the media as well as numerous "experts" have painted a gloomy picture for the average working person. They point out that the newest technologies have led to a reduction in the percentage of workers who devote their time to manufacturing. Efficient production lines certainly do require fewer workers, and sophisticated telecommunications have reduced the need for physical offices. During one recent talk show in England, the commentator stated that "the rich no longer need the poor. More and more goods can be produced with fewer and fewer workers. Therefore, permanent unemployment will grow." Such commentaries have been popular since the weaving machine with a single operator replaced the work that 10 people did previously. The idea is that the other nine workers were unemployed forever. Both theory and data render such media analyses basically meaningless. In the United States, in spite of dramatic increases in technology, the number of new jobs created has averaged 2.5 million per year since 1975. In the same time period, the population increased over 40 million, but the number of unemployed remained relatively stable at around 8 million. And theoretically, there is no limit to employment. Labor employment is a function of the supply and demand for labor. Demand is not a fixed constant somehow based on a mechanical relationship between the number of widgets produced and the number of workers needed to produce them. Workers released from industries that are more productive because of new technologies must—and do—find employment elsewhere, often in other industries that are expanding. (After all, wants *are* unlimited.)

Patent
A government protection that gives an inventor the exclusive right to make, use, or sell an invention for a limited period of time (currently, 17 years).

in the *Encyclopaedia Britannica,* to 64 gigabytes—a thousandfold increase.

By 2005, new microchip plants will produce 1,000 transistors a week for every person on earth. Predictions are that computers may become as powerful as the human brain by 2020.

EXAMPLE
Our High-Tech Economy

Four decades ago, one in six American businesses was automotive-related. Today, autos and light trucks account for about 3.5 percent of GDP. So does spending on computers and related equipment. The automobile's share of GDP has remained stable, but high-tech's share has doubled in the past decade. Nonetheless, government statisticians have yet to use chip inventories and personal computer sales as economic indicators. The reason is that the economic welfare created by high-tech industries is much harder to measure than tons of steel or bushels of corn.

FOR CRITICAL ANALYSIS: When software is distributed free on the Internet, does that contribute to the economy? •

Technology: A Separate Factor of Production

We now recognize that technology must be viewed as a separate factor of production that is sensitive to rewards. Otherwise stated, one of the major foundations of new growth theory is this:

The greater the rewards, the more technological advances we will get.

Let's consider several aspects of technology here, the first one being research and development.

Research and Development

A certain amount of technological advance results from research and development (R&D) activities that have as their goal the development of specific new materials, new products, and new machines. How much spending a nation devotes to R&D can have an impact on its long-term economic growth. Part of how much a nation spends depends on what businesses decide is worth spending. That, in turn, depends on their expected rewards from successful R&D. If your company develops a new way to produce computer memory chips, how much will it be rewarded? The answer depends on whether others can freely copy the new technique.

Patents. To protect new techniques developed through R&D, we have a system of **patents,** protections whereby the federal government gives the patent holder the exclusive right to make, use, and sell an invention for a period of 20 years. One can argue that this special position given owners of patents increases expenditures on R&D and therefore adds to long-term economic growth.

Positive Externalities and R&D. As we discussed in Chapter 5, positive externalities are benefits from an activity that do not spill over to the instigator of the activity. In the case of R&D spending, a certain amount of the benefits go to other companies that do not have to pay for them. In particular, according to economists David Coe of the International Monetary Fund and Elhanan Helpman of Tel Aviv University, about a quarter of the global benefits of R&D investment in the top seven industrialized countries goes to foreigners. For every 1 percent rise in the stock of research and development in America alone, for example, productivity in the rest of the world increases by about .04 percent. One country's R&D expenditures benefit foreigners because foreigners are able to import goods from technologically advanced countries and then use them as inputs in making their own industries more efficient. In addition, countries that import high-tech goods are able to imitate the technology.

The Open Economy and Economic Growth

People who study economic growth today tend to emphasize the importance of the openness of the economy. Free trade encourages a more rapid spread of technology and industrial ideas. Moreover, open economies may experience higher rates of economic growth because their own industries have access to a bigger market. When trade barriers are erected in the form of tariffs and the like, domestic industries become isolated from global technological progress. This occurred for many years in former communist countries and in many developing countries in Latin America and elsewhere. Figure 9-6 shows the relationship between economic growth and the openness as measured by the level of protectionism of a given economy.

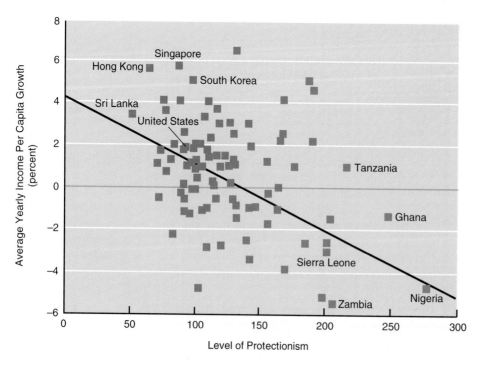

FIGURE 9-6

The Relationship Between Protectionism and Economic Growth
Closed economies are ones in which the government prevents imports from entering the country and sometimes exports from leaving the country. Such protectionism closes off the economy to new technologies. Here you see the relationship between the level of protectionism and economic growth rates measured on a per capita basis. The data seem to indicate that the more closed an economy, the lower its rate of growth, all other things held constant.

Source: Economic Review, Fourth Quarter 1993, p. 3.

Innovation and Knowledge

Innovation
Transforming an invention into something that is useful to humans.

We tend to think of technological progress as, say, the invention of the transistor. But invention means nothing by itself; **innovation** is required. Innovation involves the transformation of something new, such as an invention, into something that benefits the economy either by lowering production costs or providing new goods and services. Indeed, the new growth theorists believe that real wealth creation comes from innovation and that invention is but a facet of innovation.

Historically, technologies have moved relatively slowly from invention to innovation to widespread use, and the dispersion of new technology remains for the most part slow and uncertain. The inventor of the transistor thought it might be used to make better hearing aids. At the time it was invented, the *New York Times*'s sole reference to it was in a small weekly column called "News of Radio." When the laser was invented, no one really knew what it could be used for. It was initially used to help in navigation, measurement, and chemical research. Today, it is used in the reproduction of music, printing, surgery, and telecommunications. Tomorrow, who knows?

Much innovation involves small improvements in the use of an existing technology. Such improvements develop from experimentation and discovery, which has been fostered in the Japanese automobile market, for example.

INTERNATIONAL EXAMPLE
Innovation in the Japanese Auto Industry

The automobile has been around for a century. By the 1950s, U.S. automobile manufacturers were fairly well convinced that they had developed the best and most efficient assembly-line operation in the world. They did so through what were called time-and-motion studies. A "final" set of directions were given to each worker on the assembly line, and that worker adhered to those directions. The Japanese decided to improve on this through a process of experimentation and discovery. In Japanese automobile plants, workers were encouraged to experiment with small changes in how they assembled a car—should the door molding go on before or after the door is put on the car? Gradually, Japanese automobile workers became more efficient than their American counterparts. The process came about through small innovative changes, not one great invention.

FOR CRITICAL ANALYSIS: How many ways are there to put together a car? ●

The Importance of Ideas and Knowledge

Economist Paul Romer has added at least one important factor that determines the rate of economic growth. He contends that production and manufacturing knowledge is just as important as the other determinants and perhaps even more so. He considers knowledge a factor of production that, like capital, has to be paid for by forgoing current consumption. Economies must therefore invest in knowledge just as they invest in machines. Because past investment in capital may make it more profitable to acquire more knowledge, there exists the possibility of an investment-knowledge cycle in which investment spurs knowledge and knowledge spurs investment. A once-and-for-all increase in a country's rate of investment may permanently raise that country's growth rate. (According to traditional theory, a once-and-for-all increase in the rate of saving and therefore in the rate of investment simply leads to a new steady-state standard of living but not one that continues to increase.)

Another way of looking at knowledge is that it is a store of ideas. According to Romer, ideas are what drive economic growth. We have become, in fact, an idea economy. Consider

Microsoft Corporation. A relatively small percentage of that company's labor force is involved in actually producing diskettes. Rather, a majority of Microsoft workers are attempting to discover new ideas that can be translated to computer code that can then be placed on diskettes. The major conclusion that Romer and other new growth theorists draw is this:

> Economic growth can continue as long as we keep coming up with new ideas.

The Importance of Human Capital

Knowledge, ideas, and productivity are all tied together. One of the threads is the quality of the labor force. Increases in the productivity of the labor force are a function of increases in human capital, the fourth factor of production discussed in Chapter 2. Recall that human capital is the knowledge and skills that people in the workforce acquire through education, on-the-job training, and self-teaching. To increase your own human capital, you have to invest by forgoing income-earning activities while you attend school. Society also has to invest in the form of libraries and teachers. According to the new growth theorists, human capital is at least as important as physical capital, particularly when trying to explain international differences in living standards.

As you will see in Chapter 35, one of the most effective ways that developing countries can become developed is by investing in secondary schooling.

One can argue that policy changes that increase human capital will lead to more technological improvements. One of the reasons why concerned citizens, policymakers, and politicians are looking for a change in America's schooling system is that our educational system seems to be falling behind that of other countries. This lag is greatest in science and mathematics—precisely the areas that are required for developing better technology.

CONCEPTS IN BRIEF

- New growth theory argues that the greater the rewards, the more rapid the pace of technology. And greater rewards spur research and development.

- The openness of an economy seems to correlate with its economic rate of growth.

- Invention and innovation are not the same thing. Inventions are useless until innovation transforms them into things that people find valuable.

- According to the new growth economists, economic growth can continue as long as we keep coming up with new ideas.

- Increases in human capital can lead to greater rates of economic growth. These come about by increased education, on-the-job training, and self-teaching.

POPULATION AND IMMIGRATION AS THEY AFFECT ECONOMIC GROWTH

There are several ways to view population growth as it affects economic growth. On the one hand, population growth means an increase in the amount of labor, which, as we have previously learned, is one component of economic growth. On the other hand, population growth can be seen as a drain on the economy because for any given amount of GDP, more population means lower per capita GDP. According to Massachusetts Institute of Technology economist Michael Kremer, the first view is historically correct. His conclusion is that

Exercise 9.2
Visit www.econtoday.com for more
about immigration policy.

population growth drives technological progress, which then increases economic growth. The theory is simple: If there are 50 percent more people in the United States, there will be 50 percent more geniuses. And with 50 percent more people, the rewards for creativity are commensurately greater. Otherwise stated, the larger the potential market, the greater the incentive to become ingenious.

Does the same argument apply to immigration? Yes, according to economist Julian Simon, whose research points out that "every time our system allows in one more immigrant, on average, the economic welfare of American citizens goes up. . . . Additional immigrants, both the legal and the illegal, raise the standard of living of U.S. natives and have little or no negative impact on any occupational or income class." He further argues that immigrants do not displace natives from jobs but rather create jobs through their purchases and by starting new businesses. Immigrants' earning and spending simply expand the economy.

Not all researchers agree with Simon, and few studies exist to back up the theories advanced here. The area is currently the focus of much research.

PROPERTY RIGHTS AND ENTREPRENEURSHIP

If you were in a country where bank accounts and businesses were periodically expropriated by the government, how willing would you be to leave your money in a savings account or to invest in a business? Certainly you would be less willing than if such things never occurred. In general, the more certain private property rights are, the more capital accumulation there will be. People will be willing to invest their savings in endeavors that will increase their wealth in future years. They have property rights in their wealth that are sanctioned and enforced by the government. In fact, some economic historians have attempted to show that it was the development of well-defined private property rights that allowed Western Europe to increase its growth rate after many centuries of stagnation. The ability and certainty with which they can reap the gains from investing also determine the extent to which business owners in other countries will invest capital in developing countries. The threat of nationalization that hangs over some developing nations probably prevents the massive amount of foreign investment that might be necessary to allow these nations to develop more rapidly.

The property rights, or legal structure, in a nation are closely tied to the degree with which individuals use their own entrepreneurial skills. In Chapter 2, we identified entrepreneurship as the fifth factor of production. Entrepreneurs are the risk takers who seek out new ways to do things and create new products. To the extent that entrepreneurs are allowed to capture the rewards from their entrepreneurial activities, they will seek to engage in those activities. In countries where such rewards cannot be captured because of a lack of property rights, there will be less entrepreneurship. Typically, this results in fewer investments and a lower rate of growth.

CONCEPTS IN BRIEF

- While some economists argue that population growth stifles economic growth, others contend that empirically the opposite is true. The latter economists consequently believe that immigration should be encouraged rather than discouraged.

- Well-defined and protected property rights are important for fostering entrepreneurship. In the absence of well-defined property rights, individuals have less incentive to take risks, and economic growth rates usually suffer.

Increased saving may lead to higher industrial output. Some economists believe that reducing marginal income tax rates will affect business behavior. How?

How Important Are Tax Cuts in Promoting Economic Growth?

CONCEPTS APPLIED:

MARGINAL TAX RATE, INCENTIVES, RATE OF SAVING, INVESTMENT

Visit www.econtoday.com for an Internet Activity that expands your understanding of these concepts.

On a personal level, you can easily understand why changes in marginal tax rates might influence your behavior. If the marginal tax rate on income is 95 percent, you have relatively little incentive to work for extra income. In addition, you have little incentive to save if your earned interest will be taxed at 95 percent. So it is logical that reducing marginal tax rates might encourage people to work harder and to save more. The results should be an increase in the labor supply, an increase in productivity, and hence higher economic growth rates.

What Does the Evidence Say?

There is much controversy over the impact of lower marginal income tax rates on the rate of economic growth. Most reductions in tax rates have been short-lived. So any increase in the rate of economic growth during those periods might not be due solely to a reduction in marginal tax rates. Moreover, at least in the United States, many tax reductions have had different effects on earners at different income levels. Nevertheless, the maximum federal marginal income tax rates fell from 70 percent in 1980 to 28 percent in 1988, and according to Federal Reserve Board Governor Lawrence Lindsey, somewhere between 40 and 90 percent of the reported increase in the earnings of high-income individuals during the 1980s was the result of people working harder, spurred by the lower rates.

International Comparisons

The graph in Figure 9-7 shows tax revenues as a percentage of GDP compared to average annual increases in per capita GDP (economic growth rates) for nine industrialized countries over the past three decades. Japan had the lowest tax revenues as a percentage of GDP; the United

States was not far behind but had only half the economic growth rate. Although Switzerland and Sweden had approximately the same economic growth rate, Sweden's tax burden was much greater than Switzerland's.

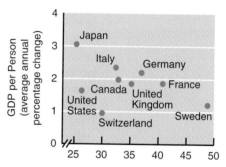

Tax Revenues as a Percentage of GDP (average 1970 to present)

FIGURE 9-7

Tax Takes and Economic Growth Rates
Sources: Organization for Economic Cooperation and Development; *Economist*, August 24, 1996.

What's Wrong with This Picture?

Of course, Figure 9-7 does not tell the whole story. The data relate to *average* taxes. But incentives depend on changes in *marginal* tax rates. In many countries in that graph, marginal income tax rates are extremely high. If such punitive rates were reduced, more economic growth would surely follow.

FOR CRITICAL ANALYSIS

1. Might economic growth depend on how tax revenues are spent by the collecting governments?
2. Why does information on average tax rates not tell us much about the effect of taxes on work effort?

CHAPTER SUMMARY

1. Economic growth is defined as the rate of increase in per capita real GDP. It can be shown graphically as an outward shift in the production possibilities curve. Small changes in rates of growth lead to large differences in GDP over time because of compounding.

2. Economic growth can be defined as numerically equal to the rate of growth of capital plus the rate of growth of labor plus the rate of growth in the productivity of capital and of labor.

3. To consume more in the future, you have to not consume—save—today. The rate of saving is a key determinant of a nation's rate of economic growth.

4. The new growth theorists argue that advances in technology are a function of the rewards to those advances. In particular, research and development will increase the more it is rewarded.

5. The more open an economy, the faster its rate of economic growth.

6. Although inventions are important, they have no value until they are made useful by innovation. Innovations may be slow to occur and may involve small improvements in the use of existing technologies. Economic growth can continue as long as we keep coming up with new ideas.

7. Increases in human capital can occur because of schooling and on-the-job training. Schooling requires a personal investment by the student—giving up consumption that would otherwise be available through for-pay work—as well as investment by society in teachers and libraries. Differences in standards of living across countries can, to some extent, be explained by differences in the level of human capital investment.

8. Empirically, increased population size has been associated with higher rates of economic growth. Consequently, immigration can be viewed as good rather than bad.

9. Well-defined property rights and resulting entrepreneurship may explain differences in rates of economic growth. Increased certainty about property rights may lead to more capital accumulation and higher rates of economic growth in nations in which property rights have been uncertain in the past.

DISCUSSION OF PREVIEW QUESTIONS

1. What is economic growth?

By economic growth, economists are referring to the rate of increase in an economy's real level of output over time. It is generally agreed that the rate of changes in per capita (corrected for population change) real (corrected for price level changes) GDP is a good measure of an economy's economic growth. The very long-run economic growth rate for the United States is approximately 1.75 percent per year—with much deviation around this trend line, of course.

2. What does economic growth measure?

Many people try to make inferences about changes in economic well-being from a nation's economic growth rate; presumably, higher growth rates imply more rapid increases in living standards. Others have argued that increased income inequality may accompany rapid economic growth, as a relatively small percentage of the population may benefit from economic growth while the majority experiences little economic improvement. Critics also point out that rapid economic growth is not necessarily consistent with increases in the spiritual, cultural, and environmental quality of life. However, because per capita increases in real GDP do not measure the increased leisure that usually accompanies economic growth, this measure may *understate* economic well-being. Economic growth is therefore a rather crude measure of changes in a nation's well-being and is perhaps a better indicator of its productive activity.

3. What are some of the ways in which you can experience economic growth for yourself or for your family?

You can experience economic growth only if you are willing to sacrifice something. When you continue to go to school, you are sacrificing your current ability to earn and consume income. But in exchange for that sacrifice, you are developing skills and talents that will allow you to have a higher income in the future. You are investing in yourself (human capital) by sacrificing current consumption now.

If you wish to accumulate much wealth during your lifetime, you must be willing to sacrifice current consumption. You do this by not consuming all of your income—that is, by saving part of it. The more you save, the more you can accumulate. In particular, if you invest your accumulated savings in wise savings outlets, you will be rewarded by a compounded rate of growth so that in the future you will have accumulated larger amounts of wealth.

4. What are the determinants of economic growth?
One obvious determinant of economic growth is the quantity and quality of a nation's natural resources—

although this determinant can easily be exaggerated. Hence many slowly developing nations have bountiful natural resources, and some rapidly developing areas have very few. The quality and quantity of labor and capital are also important determinants of economic growth, as is a nation's rate of technological progress. A decidedly underrated determinant of economic growth is the industriousness and willingness of people to be productive—which is surely related to personal incentives related to property rights. The certainty of property rights may also affect a nation's growth rate.

PROBLEMS

(Answers to the odd-numbered problems appear at the back of the book.)

9-1. The graph shows the production possibilities frontier for an economy. Which of the labeled points would be associated with the highest feasible growth rate for this economy?

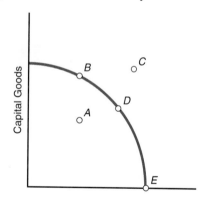

9-2. Why might an economy be operating inside its production possibilities curve?

9-3. Consider the following table, which describes growth rate data for four countries between 1989 and 1998.

a. Which country has the largest rate of output growth per capita?
b. Which country has the smallest rate of output growth per capita?

		Annual Growth Rate (%)		
Country	J	K	L	M
Nominal GDP	20	15	10	5
Price level	5	3	6	2
Population	5	8	2	1

9-4. Use Table 9-3 (page 191) to answer the following questions.

a. Country A has a growth rate of 3 percent, and country B has a growth rate of 4 percent. Assume that they both start off with equal incomes. How much richer will country A be after 10 years? After 50 years?
b. Assume that country A has twice the income per capita of country B. Country A is growing at 3 percent, and country B is growing at 4 percent. Will country B ever catch up? If so, when?

COMPUTER-ASSISTED INSTRUCTION

The links among global integration, markets, and economic growth are explored.

Complete problem and answer appear on disk.

PART 3

NATIONAL INCOME DETERMINATION

CHAPTER 10

MICRO FOUNDATIONS: Aggregate Demand and Aggregate Supply

Throughout the 1980s and most of the 1990s, the "miracle" economies seemed all to be in Southeast Asia. Economists even gave one group of these nations—Hong Kong, Singapore, Taiwan, and South Korea—a special nickname: the Four Tigers. In the region, Japan began to lose some of its luster in the mid-1990s but the Four Tigers and their Southeast Asian neighbors continued to grow. Then it hit—a massive currency depreciation and a stock market sell-off that started in Thailand and then spread to Malaysia, Indonesia, and the Philippines. It hit South Korea hard. The Southeast Asian economies were wounded. To understand how the stock market collapse that hit these nations affected the economies of Southeast Asia, you must know how aggregate demand and aggregate supply work together to create the equilibrium level of real GDP.

PREVIEW QUESTIONS

1. Why does the aggregate demand curve slope downward?

2. Why does the short-run aggregate supply curve slope upward?

3. Why is the long-run aggregate supply curve vertical?

4. How can we show improvements in technology using aggregate demand and aggregate supply analysis?

207

Did You Know That . . . the U.S. Department of Commerce provides a monthly publication of over 100 pages of statistics on the economy called *Survey of Current Business,* but prior to the 1970s, the same publication was called *Business Cycle Digest?* Purportedly, the Department of Commerce changed the name of this publication because government economists in the 1960s thought that the "business cycle" was dead because the American economy had experienced a relatively long period of expansion. Today, no one believes that national business fluctuations are obsolete. Since the time the Department of Commerce changed the name of its statistical publication, the economy has experienced five recessions. So we still need to understand why national business activity fluctuates. In this chapter you will learn about one way to explain changes in output, unemployment, and the price level in our economy.

SPENDING AND TOTAL EXPENDITURES

As explained in Chapters 7 and 8, GDP is the dollar value of total expenditures on domestically produced final goods and services. Because all expenditures are made by individuals, firms, or governments, the total value of these expenditures must be what each of these market participants decides it shall be. The decisions of individuals, managers of firms, and government officials determine the annual dollar value of total expenditures. You can certainly see this in your role as an individual. You decide what the total value of your expenditures will be in a year. You decide how much you want to spend and how much you want to save. Thus if we want to know what determines the total value of GDP, the answer would be clear: the spending decisions of individuals like you; firms; and local, state, and national governments. In an open economy, we must also include foreign individuals, firms, and governments (foreigners, for short) that decide to spend their money income in the United States.

Simply stating that the dollar value of total expenditures in this country depends on what individuals, firms, governments, and foreigners decide to do really doesn't tell us much, though. Two important issues remain:

1. What determines the total amount that individuals, firms, governments, and foreigners want to spend?
2. What determines whether this spending will result in a higher output of goods and services (quantities) or higher prices (inflation)?

The way we will answer these questions in this chapter is by developing the concepts of *aggregate demand* and *aggregate supply.* **Aggregate demand** is the total of all planned expenditures in the economy. **Aggregate supply** is the total of all planned production in the economy. Given these definitions, we can now proceed to construct an aggregate demand curve and an aggregate supply curve.

Aggregate demand
The total of all planned expenditures for the entire economy.

Aggregate supply
The total of all planned production for the entire economy.

THE AGGREGATE DEMAND CURVE

The **aggregate demand curve,** *AD,* gives the various quantities of all final commodities demanded at various price levels, all other things held constant. Recall the components of GDP that you studied in Chapter 8: consumption spending, investment expenditures, government purchases, and net foreign demand for domestic production. They are all components of aggregate demand. Throughout this chapter and the next, whenever you see the aggregate demand curve, realize that it is a shorthand way of talking about the components

Aggregate demand curve
A curve showing planned purchase rates for all goods and services in the economy at various price levels, all other things held constant.

of GDP that are measured by government statisticians when they calculate total economic activity each year. In Chapter 12 you will look more closely at the relationship between these components and in particular how consumption spending depends on income.

Aggregate Demand Curve

The aggregate demand curve gives the total amount of *real* domestic income that will be purchased at each price level. Real domestic income consists of the output of final goods and services in the economy—everything produced for final use by either businesses or households. This includes stereos, socks, shoes, medical and legal services, computers, and millions of other goods and services that people buy each year. A graphic representation of the aggregate demand curve is seen in Figure 10-1. On the horizontal axis is measured real gross domestic output, or real GDP. For our measure of the price level, we use the GDP price deflator on the vertical axis. The aggregate demand curve is labeled *AD*. If the GDP deflator is 100, aggregate quantity demanded is $8 trillion per year (point *A*). At price level 120 it is $7 trillion per year (point *B*). At price level 140 it is $6 trillion per year (point *C*). The higher the price level, the lower will be the total real output demanded by the economy, everything else remaining constant, as shown by the arrow along *AD* in Figure 10-1. Conversely, the lower the price level, the higher will be the total real output demanded by the economy, everything else staying constant.

Let's take the year 1996. Looking at U.S. Department of Commerce preliminary statistics will reveal the following information:

- GDP was $7,566.9 billion.
- The price level as measured by GDP deflator was 109.21 (base year 1992, when the index equals 100).
- Real GDP (output) was $6,928.8 billion in 1992 dollars.

What can we say about 1996? Given the dollar cost of buying goods and services and all of the other factors that go into spending decisions by individuals, firms, governments, and foreigners, the total amount of real domestic output demanded by firms, individuals, governments, and foreigners was $6,928.8 billion in 1996 (in terms of 1992 dollars).

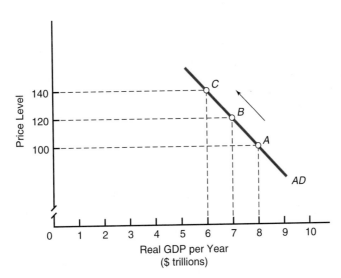

FIGURE 10-1

The Aggregate Demand Curve

Because of the real-balance, interest rate, and open economy effects, the aggregate demand curve, *AD*, slopes downward. If the price level is 100, we will be at point *A* with $8 trillion of real GDP demanded per year. As the price level increases to 120 and 140, we will move up the aggregate demand curve to points *B* and *C*.

What Happens When the Price Level Rises?

What if the price level in the economy rose to 160 tomorrow? What would happen to the amount of real goods and services that individuals, firms, governments, and foreigners wish to purchase in the United States? When we asked that question about individual commodities in Chapter 3, the answer was obvious: The quantity demanded would fall if the price went up. Now we are talking about the *price level*—the average price of *all* goods and services in the economy. The answer is still that the total quantities of real goods and services demanded would fall, but the reasons are different. Remember that in Chapter 3, when the price of one good or service went up, the consumer would substitute other goods and services. For the entire economy, when the price level goes up, the consumer doesn't simply substitute one good for another, for now we are dealing with the demand for all goods and services in the entire nation. There are *economywide* reasons that cause the aggregate demand curve to slope downward. They involve at least three distinct forces: the *real-balance effect,* the *interest rate effect,* and the *open economy effect.*

The Direct Effect: The Real-Balance Effect. A rise in the price level will have a direct effect on spending. Individuals, firms, governments, and foreigners carry out transactions using money. Money in this context only consists of currency and coins that you have in your pocket (or stashed away) right now. Because people use money to purchase goods and services, the amount of money that people have influences the amount of goods and services they want to buy. For example, if you found a $10 bill on the sidewalk, the amount of money you had would rise. This would likely have a *direct* effect on the amount of spending in which you would engage. Given your greater level of money balances—currency in this case—you would almost surely increase your spending on goods and services. Similarly, if while on a trip downtown you had your pocket picked, there would be a direct effect on your desired spending. For example, if your wallet had $30 in it when it was stolen, the reduction in your cash balances—in this case currency—would no doubt cause you to reduce your planned expenditures. You would ultimately buy fewer goods and services. This response is sometimes called the **real-balance effect** (or *wealth effect*) because it relates to the real value of your cash balances. While your nominal cash balances may remain the same, any change in the price level will cause a change in the real value of those cash balances—hence the real-balance effect on the quantity of aggregate goods and services demanded.

Real-balance effect
The change in the real value of money balances when the price level changes, all other things held constant. Also called the *wealth effect.*

When you think of the real-balance effect, just think of what happens to your real wealth if you have, say, a $100 bill hidden under your mattress. If the price level increases by 10 percent, the purchasing power of that $100 bill drops by 10 percent, so not only may you feel less wealthy, you actually are. This will reduce your spending on all goods and services by some small amount.

The Indirect Effect: The Interest Rate Effect. There is a more subtle, but equally important, *indirect* effect on your desire to spend. As we said before, when the price level goes up, the real value of your money balances declines. You end up with too few real money balances relative to other things that you own. After all, we all own a bit of many things—clothes, money balances, bicycles, cars, CD players, and perhaps houses and stocks and bonds. If, because of the price level increase, you find out that you have too few real money balances, you might actually go out to borrow to replenish them. When there are more people going in the front door of lending institutions to borrow money than there are people coming in the back door, as it were, to lend the money, the price of borrowing is going to go up. The price you pay to borrow money is the interest rate you have to pay. Because more people want to borrow now to replenish their real cash balances, interest rates will rise, and this is where the indirect effect—the **interest rate effect**—on total spending comes in.

Higher interest rates make it less attractive for people to buy houses and cars. Higher interest rates also make it less profitable for firms to install new equipment and to erect new office buildings. Whether we are talking about individuals or firms, the indirect effect of a rise in the price level will cause a higher level of interest rates, which in turn reduces the amount of goods and services that people are willing to purchase when the price level rises. Therefore, an increase in the price level will tend to reduce the quantity of aggregate goods and services demanded. (The opposite occurs if the price level declines.)

The Open Economy Effect: The Substitution of Foreign Goods. Remember from Chapter 8 that GDP includes net exports—the difference between exports and imports. In an open economy, we buy imports from other countries and ultimately pay for them through the foreign exchange market. The same is true for foreigners who purchase our goods (exports). Given any set of exchange rates between the U.S. dollar and other currencies, an increase in the price level in the United States makes American goods more expensive relative to foreign goods. Foreigners have downward-sloping demand curves for American goods. When the relative price of American goods goes up, foreigners buy fewer American goods and more of their own. In America, the cheaper-priced foreign goods now result in Americans wanting to buy more foreign goods rather than American goods. The result is a fall in exports and a rise in imports when the domestic price level rises. That means that a price level increase tends to reduce net exports, thereby reducing the amount of real goods and services purchased in the United States. This is known as the **open economy effect.**

What Happens When the Price Level Falls?

What about the reverse? Suppose now that the GDP deflator falls to 100 from an initial level of 120. You should be able to trace the three effects on desired purchases of goods and services. Specifically, how do the real-balance, interest rate, and open economy effects cause people to want to buy more? You should come to the conclusion that the lower the price level, the greater the quantity of output of goods and services demanded.

The aggregate demand curve, *AD,* shows the quantity of aggregate output that will be demanded at alternative price levels. It is downward-sloping, as is the demand curve for individual goods. The higher the price level, the lower the quantity of aggregate output demanded, and vice versa.

Aggregate Demand Versus *Individual* Demand

Even though the aggregate demand curve, *AD,* in Figure 10-1 on page 209 looks quite similar to the individual demand curve, *D,* to which you were introduced in Chapters 3 and 4, it is not the same. When we derive the aggregate demand curve, we are looking at the entire economic system. The aggregate demand curve, *AD,* differs from an individual demand curve, *D,* because we are looking at the *entire* circular flow of income and product when we construct *AD.*

Interest rate effect
One of the reasons that the aggregate demand curve slopes downward is because higher price levels indirectly increase the interest rate, which in turn causes businesses and consumers to reduce desired spending due to the higher cost of borrowing.

Open economy effect
One of the reasons that the aggregate demand curve slopes downward is because higher price levels result in foreigners' desiring to buy fewer American-made goods while Americans now desire more foreign-made goods, thereby reducing net exports, which is equivalent to a reduction in the amount of real goods and services purchased in the United States.

SHIFTS IN THE AGGREGATE DEMAND CURVE

In Chapter 3 you learned that any time a nonprice determinant of demand changed, the demand curve shifted inward to the left or outward to the right. The same analysis holds for the aggregate demand curve, except we are now talking about the non-price-level determinants of aggregate demand. So when we ask the question, "What determines the position of the aggregate demand curve?" the fundamental proposition is as follows:

Any non-price-level change that increases aggregate spending (on domestic goods) shifts _AD_ to the right. Any non-price-level change that decreases aggregate spending (on domestic goods) shifts _AD_ to the left.

The list of potential determinants of the position of the aggregate demand curve is virtually without limit. Some of the most important "curve shifters" with respect to aggregate demand are presented in Table 10-1.

Changes That Cause an Increase in Aggregate Demand	Changes That Cause a Decrease in Aggregate Demand
A drop in the foreign exchange value of the dollar	A rise in the foreign exchange value of the dollar
Increased security about jobs and future income	Decreased security about jobs and future income
Improvements in economic conditions in other countries	Declines in economic conditions in other countries
A reduction in real interest rates (nominal interest rates corrected for inflation) not due to price level changes	A rise in real interest rates (nominal interest rates corrected for inflation) not due to price level changes
Tax decreases	Tax increases
An increase in the amount of money in circulation	A decrease in the amount of money in circulation

TABLE 10-1

Determinants of Aggregate Demand
Aggregate demand consists of the demand for domestically produced consumption goods, investment goods, government purchases, and net exports. Consequently, any change in the demand for any one of these components of real GDP will cause a change in aggregate demand. Here are listed some possibilities.

CONCEPTS IN BRIEF

- Aggregate demand is the total of all planned expenditures in the economy, and aggregate supply is the total of all planned production in the economy. The aggregate demand curve shows the various quantities of all commodities demanded at various price levels; it is downward-sloping.

- There are three reasons why the aggregate demand curve is downward-sloping: the direct effect, the indirect effect, and the open economy effect.

- The direct effect, sometimes called the real-balance effect, occurs because price level changes alter the real value of cash balances, thereby directly causing people to desire to spend more or less, depending on whether the price level decreases or increases.

- The indirect, or interest rate, effect is caused via interest rate changes that mimic price level changes. At higher interest rates, people desire to buy fewer houses and cars, and vice versa.

- The open economy effect occurs because of the substitution toward foreign goods when the domestic price level increases and a shift away from foreign goods when the domestic price level decreases.

THE AGGREGATE SUPPLY CURVE

The aggregate demand curve tells us how much output will be demanded given the price level. It also indicates the point toward which the price level will gravitate for any *given* total output. Knowing the position and shape of the aggregate demand curve does not tell us anything about how the *total* dollar value of spending will ultimately be divided between output—real goods and services—and prices. To determine this and thus the equilibrium level of real GDP, we must introduce supply conditions.

When we talk about aggregate supply, we have to distinguish between the long run, when all adjustments to changes in the price level can be made, and the short run, when all adjustments to changes in the price level cannot be made. Therefore, we must derive two different aggregate supply curves.

Long-Run Aggregate Supply Curve

In Chapter 2 we showed the derivation of the production possibilities curve. At any point in time, the economy can be inside or on the production possibilities curve but never outside it. The only way we can have more of everything is through economic growth—the production possibilities curve moves outward as shown in panel (a) of Figure 10-2. The idea behind the production possibilities curve can be translated into what we call the **long-run aggregate supply curve** *(LRAS).*

Put yourself in a world in which nothing has been changing, year in and year out. The price level has not changed. Technology has not changed. The prices of inputs that firms must purchase have not changed. Labor productivity has not changed. This is a world that is fully adjusted and in which people have all the information they are ever going to get about that world. The long-run aggregate supply curve in this world is some amount of output of real goods and services, say, $7 trillion of real GDP. We can show long-run aggregate supply simply by a vertical line at $7 trillion of real GDP. This is what you see in

Long-run aggregate supply curve
A vertical line representing real output of goods and services based on full information and after full adjustment has occurred. Can also be viewed as representing the real output of the economy under conditions of full employment—the full-employment level of real GDP.

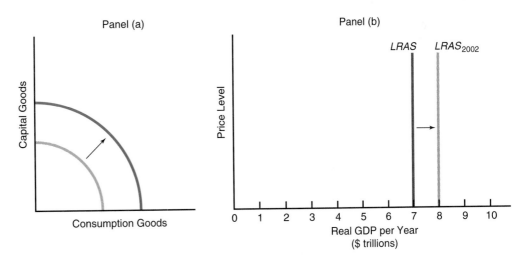

FIGURE 10-2

The Long-Run Aggregate Supply Curve and Shifts in It
In panel (a), we repeat a diagram that we used in Chapter 2 to show the meaning of economic growth. Over time, the production possibilities curve shifts outward. In panel (b), we demonstrate the same principle by showing the long-run aggregate supply curve as initially a vertical line at *LRAS* at $7 trillion of real GDP per year. As our endowments increase, the *LRAS* moves outward to *LRAS*$_{2002}$.

panel (b) of Figure 10-2. That curve, labeled *LRAS,* is a vertical line determined by tastes, technology, and the **endowments** of resources that exist in our economy. It is the full-information and full-adjustment level of real output of goods and services. It is the level of real output that will continue being produced year after year, forever, if nothing changes.

Another way of viewing the *LRAS* is to think of it as the full-employment level of real GDP. When the economy reaches full employment, no further adjustments will occur unless a fundamental change occurs.

To understand why the long-run aggregate supply curve is vertical, think about the long run. The price level has no effect on real output (real GDP per year) because higher output prices will be accompanied by comparable changes in input prices, and suppliers will therefore have no incentive to increase or decrease output. Remember that in the long run, everybody has full information and there is full adjustment to price level changes.

What If Non-Price-Level Variables Change? Clearly, as the years go by, things do change. Population increases, we discover more resources, and we improve technology. That means that over time, at least in a growing economy such as ours, *LRAS* will shift outward to the right, as in Figure 10-2. We have drawn *LRAS* for the year 2002 to the right of our original *LRAS* of $7 trillion of real GDP. The number we attached to $LRAS_{2002}$ is $8 trillion of real GDP, but that is only a guess; the point is that it is to the right of today's *LRAS.*

Aggregate Demand and Long-Run Output. Because *LRAS* depends on technology and endowments, aggregate demand in the long run has no bearing on the level of output of real goods and services. Draw any *AD* curve on $LRAS_{2002}$ in panel (b) of Figure 10-2, and you will see that the only thing that changes will be the price level. In the long run, the output of real goods and services is supply-side determined. Only shifts in *LRAS* will change long-run levels of output of real goods and services.

Short-Run Aggregate Supply Curve

The **short-run aggregate supply curve,** *SRAS,* represents the relationship between the price level and the real output of goods and services in the economy *without* full adjustment and full information. Just as we drew the supply curve for an individual good or service in Chapter 3 holding everything constant except the price of the good or service, we will do the same here. The short-run aggregate supply curve will be drawn under the assumption that all determinants of aggregate supply other than the price level will be held constant. Most notably, we hold constant the prices of the inputs used in the production of real goods and services. Now, what does this mean? It means that when we hold the prices of the factors of production constant in the short run, as the price level rises, it becomes profitable for all firms to expand production. Otherwise stated, changes in the price level in the short run can affect real output because some production costs might be relatively fixed in nominal terms. Therefore, an increase in the price level increases expected profits.

Why Can Output Be Expanded in the Short Run? In the short run, if the price level rises, output can be expanded (even beyond the economist's notion of the normal capacity of a firm). That is to say, the overall economy can temporarily produce beyond its normal limits or capacity, for a variety of reasons:

1. In the short run, most labor contracts implicitly or explicitly call for flexibility in hours of work at the given wage rate. Therefore, firms can use existing workers more intensively in a variety of ways: They can get them to work harder. They can get them to

Endowments
The various resources in an economy, including both physical resources and such human resources as ingenuity and management skills.

Short-run aggregate supply curve
The relationship between aggregate supply and the price level in the short run, all other things held constant; the curve is normally positively sloped.

work more hours per day. And they can get them to work more days per week. Workers can also be switched from *uncounted* production, such as maintenance, to *counted* production, which generates counted output. The distinction between counted and uncounted is simply what is measured in the marketplace, particularly by government statisticians and accountants. If a worker cleans a machine, there is no measured output. But if that worker is put on the production line and helps increase the number of units produced each day, measured output will go up. That worker's production has then been counted.

2. Existing capital equipment can be used more intensively. Machines can be worked more hours per day. Some can be made to work at a faster speed. Maintenance can be delayed.

3. Finally, and just as important, if wage rates are held constant, a higher price level means that profits go up, which induces firms to hire more workers. The duration of unemployment falls, and thus the unemployment rate falls. And people who were previously not in the labor force (homemakers and younger or older workers) can be induced to enter.

All these adjustments cause national output to rise as the price level increases.

The Shape of the Short-Run Supply Curve. Even if firms want to continue increasing production because the price level has risen, they cannot do this forever. That means that when we hold input prices constant, the extra output that will be forthcoming for the three reasons just listed must eventually come to an end. Individual workers get tired. Workers are more willing to work one extra weekend than they are eight extra weekends in a row. Machines cannot go forever without maintenance. Finally, as all firms are hiring more workers from the pool of unemployed, it gets harder (more costly) to find workers at the existing level of wages.

What does all this mean? Simply that the short-run aggregate supply curve at some point must get steeper and steeper.

Graphing the Short-Run Aggregate Supply Curve. Look at Figure 10-3. There you see the short-run aggregate supply curve, *SRAS*. As we have drawn it, after a real GDP of $7 trillion, it starts to become steeper and steeper, and by the time it gets close to $8 trillion,

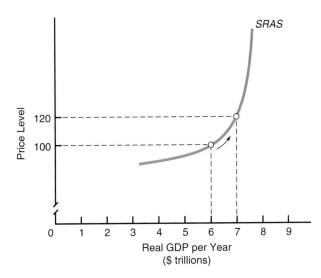

FIGURE 10-3

The Short-Run Aggregate Supply Curve

The short-run aggregate supply curve, *SRAS,* slopes upward because with fixed input prices, at a higher price level firms make more profits and desire more output. They use workers and capital more intensively. At price level 100, $6 trillion of real GDP per year is supplied. If the price level rises to 120, $7 trillion of real GDP per year will be supplied.

it is very steep indeed.[1] If the price index, as represented by the GDP deflator, is 100, the economy will supply $6 trillion per year of real GDP in Figure 10-3. If the GDP deflator increases to 120, the economy will move up the *SRAS* to $7 trillion of real GDP per year.

The Difference Between Aggregate and Individual Supply. Although the aggregate supply curve tends to look like the supply curve for an individual commodity, the two curves are not exactly the same. A commodity supply curve reflects a change in the price of an individual commodity *relative* to the prices of goods, whereas the aggregate supply curve shows the effects of changes in the price *level* for the entire economy.

SHIFTS IN THE AGGREGATE SUPPLY CURVE

Just as there were non-price-level factors that could cause a shift in the aggregate demand curve, there are non-price-level factors that can cause a shift in the aggregate supply curve. The analysis here is not quite so simple as the analysis for the non-price-level determinants for aggregate demand, for here we are dealing with both the short run and the long run— *SRAS* and *LRAS*. Still, anything other than the price level that affects supply will shift aggregate supply curves.

Shifts in Both Short- and Long-Run Aggregate Supply

There is a core class of events that causes a shift in both the short-run aggregate supply curve and the long-run aggregate supply curve. These include any change in our endowments of the factors of production.[2] Any change in land, labor, or capital will shift *SRAS* and *LRAS*. Furthermore, any change in the level of our technology or knowledge will also shift *SRAS* and *LRAS*. Look at Figure 10-4. Initially, the two curves are $SRAS_1$ and $LRAS_1$. Now consider a big oil discovery in Tennessee in an area where no one thought oil existed.

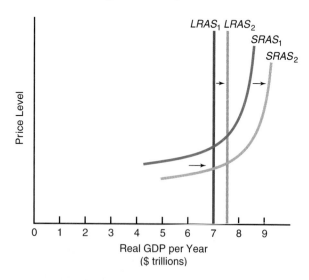

FIGURE 10-4

Shifts in Both Short- and Long-Run Aggregate Supply
Initially, the two supply curves are $SRAS_1$ and $LRAS_1$. Now consider a big oil find in Tennessee in an area where no one thought oil existed. This shifts $LRAS_1$ to $LRAS_2$ at $7.5 trillion of real GDP. $SRAS_1$ also shifts outward horizontally to $SRAS_2$.

---

[1]If there is a maximum short-run amount of output, at some point the *SRAS* becomes vertical. However, there is always some way to squeeze a little bit more out of an economic system, so the *SRAS* does not necessarily have to become vertical, just extremely steep.

[2]There is a complication here. A big enough increase in natural resources not only shifts aggregate supply outward but also affects aggregate demand. Aggregate demand is a function of people's wealth, among other things. A big oil discovery in America will make enough people richer that desired total spending will increase. For the sake of simplicity, we ignore this complication.

This shifts $LRAS_1$ to $LRAS_2$ at $7.5 trillion of real GDP. $SRAS_1$ also shifts outward horizontally to $SRAS_2$.

Shifts in *SRAS* Only

Some events, particularly those that are short-lived, will temporarily shift *SRAS* but not *LRAS*. One of the most obvious is a temporary shift in input prices, particularly those caused by external events that are not expected to last forever. Consider the possibility of an announced 90-day embargo of oil from the Middle East to the United States. Oil is an important input in many production activities. The 90-day oil embargo will cause at least a temporary increase in the price of this input. You can see what happens in Figure 10-5. *LRAS* remains fixed, but $SRAS_1$ shifts to $SRAS_2$ reflecting the increase in input prices—the higher price of oil. This is because the rise in costs at each level of real GDP per year requires a higher price level to cover those costs.

We summarize the possible determinants of aggregate supply in Table 10-2 on page 218. These determinants will cause a shift in either the short-run or the long-run aggregate supply curve, or both, depending on whether they are temporary or permanent.

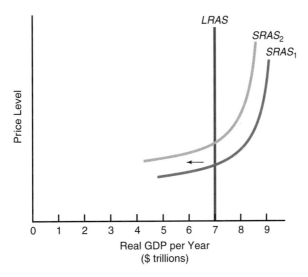

FIGURE 10-5

Shifts in *SRAS* Only

A temporary increase in an input price will shift the short-run aggregate supply curve from $SRAS_1$ to $SRAS_2$.

CONCEPTS IN BRIEF

- The long-run aggregate supply curve, *LRAS*, is a vertical line determined by technology and endowments of natural resources in an economy. It is the full-information and full-adjustment level of real output of goods and services.

- If population increases, more resources are discovered, or technology improves, *LRAS* will shift outward to the right.

- The short-run aggregate supply curve, *SRAS*, shows the relationship between the price level and the real output of goods and services in the economy without full adjustment or full information. It is upward-sloping.

- Output can be expanded in the short run because firms can use existing workers and capital equipment more intensively. Also, in the short run, when input prices are fixed, a higher price level means higher profits, which induces firms to hire more workers.

- Any change in land, labor, or capital will shift both *SRAS* and *LRAS*. A temporary shift in input prices, however, will shift only *SRAS*.

Changes That Cause an Increase in Aggregate Supply	Changes That Cause a Decrease in Aggregate Supply
Discoveries of new raw materials	Depletion of raw materials
Increased competition	Decreased competition
A reduction in international trade barriers	An increase in international trade barriers
Fewer regulatory impediments to business	More regulatory impediments to business
An increase in labor supplied	A decrease in labor supplied
Increased training and education	Decreased training and education
A decrease in marginal tax rates	An increase in marginal tax rates
A reduction in input prices	An increase in input prices

TABLE 10-2

Determinants of Aggregate Supply
The determinants listed here can affect short-run or long-run aggregate supply (or both), depending on whether they are temporary or permanent.

EQUILIBRIUM

As you discovered in Chapter 3, equilibrium occurs where demand and supply curves intersect. It is a little more complicated here because we have two types of aggregate supply curves, long-run and short-run. Let's look first at short-run equilibrium. It occurs at the intersection of aggregate demand, *AD,* and short-run aggregate supply, *SRAS,* as shown in Figure 10-6. The equilibrium price level is 120, and the equilibrium annual level of real GDP is $7 trillion. If the price level increased to 140, there would be an excess quantity of real goods and services supplied in the entire economy, and the price level would tend to fall. If the price level were 100, aggregate quantity demanded would be greater than aggregate quantity supplied, and buyers would bid up prices so that the price level would move toward 120.

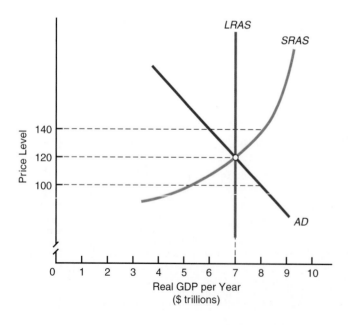

FIGURE 10-6

Equilibrium
Equilibrium will occur where the aggregate demand curve intersects the short-run aggregate supply curve and the long-run aggregate supply curve. In this diagram it is at price level 120 and a real GDP of $7 trillion per year.

In Figure 10-6 you see that we have drawn the long-run aggregate supply curve, *LRAS*, so that there is full equilibrium in both the short run and the long run at price level 120. At price level 120 this economy can operate forever at $7 trillion without the price level changing.

In the short run, it is possible for us to be on *SRAS* to the right and above the intersection with *AD* and *LRAS*. Why? Because more can be squeezed out of the economy in the short run than would occur in the long-run, full-information, full-adjustment situation. Although in this economy a real GDP greater than $7 trillion per year is possible, it is not consistent with long-run aggregate supply. Firms would be operating beyond long-run desired capacity, and inputs would be working too long and too hard for too little money. Input prices would begin to rise. When this happens, we can no longer stay with the same *SRAS*, because it was drawn with input prices held constant.

If the economy finds itself on *SRAS* below and to the left of the intersection of *AD* and *LRAS*, the opposite will occur. Firms are operating well below long-run capacity, and there are too many unemployed inputs. Input prices will begin to fall. We can no longer stay with the same *SRAS*, because it was drawn with constant input prices. *SRAS* will shift down.

CONSEQUENCES OF CHANGES IN AGGREGATE SUPPLY AND DEMAND

We now have a basic model of the entire economy. We can trace the movement of the equilibrium price level and the equilibrium real GDP when there are shocks to the economy. Whenever there is a shift in our economy's curves, the equilibrium price level or real GDP level (or both) may change. These shifts are called **aggregate demand shocks** on the demand side and **aggregate supply shocks** on the supply side.

In Chapter 4 you learned what happened to the equilibrium price and quantity when there was a shift in demand, then a shift in supply, and then shifts in both curves. In the analysis that follows, we will be using the same basic analysis, but you should remember that we are now talking about changes in the overall price level and changes in the equilibrium level of real GDP per year.

Aggregate Demand Shifts While Aggregate Supply Is Stable

Now we can show what happens when aggregate supply remains stable but aggregate demand falls. The outcome may be the possible cause of a recession and can under certain circumstances explain a rise in the unemployment rate. In Figure 10-7 on the next page you see that with AD_1, both long-run and short-run equilibrium are at $7 trillion of real GDP per year (because *SRAS* and *LRAS* also intersect AD_1 at that level of real GDP). The long-run equilibrium price level is 120. A reduction in aggregate demand shifts the aggregate demand curve to AD_2. The new intersection with *SRAS* is at $6.8 trillion per year, which is below the economy's long-run aggregate supply. The difference between $7 trillion and $6.8 trillion is called the **contractionary gap,** which is defined as the difference between the short-run equilibrium level of real GDP and how much the economy could be producing if it were operating at full employment on its *LRAS*.

Aggregate demand shock
Any shock that causes the aggregate demand curve to shift inward or outward.

Aggregate supply shock
Any shock that causes the aggregate supply curve to shift inward or outward.

Contractionary gap
The gap that exists whenever the equilibrium level of real national income per year is less than the full-employment level as shown by the position of the long-run aggregate supply curve.

FIGURE 10-7

The Effects of Stable Aggregate Supply and a Decrease in Aggregate Demand: The Contractionary Gap

If the economy is at equilibrium at E_1, with price level 120 and real GDP per year of $7 trillion, a shift inward of the aggregate demand curve to AD_2 will lead to a new short-run equilibrium at E_2. The equilibrium price level will fall to 115, and the short-run equilibrium level of real GDP per year will fall to $6.8 trillion. There will be a contractionary gap.

Exercise 10.1

Visit www.econtoday.com for more about shifts in aggregate demand.

Effect on the Economy of an Increase in Aggregate Demand

We can reverse the situation and have aggregate demand increase to AD_2, as is shown in Figure 10-8. The initial equilibrium conditions are exactly the same as in Figure 10-7. The move to AD_2 increases the short-run equilibrium from E_1 to E_2 such that the economy is operating at $7.2 trillion of real GDP per year, which exceeds *LRAS*. This is a condition of an overheated economy, typically called an **expansionary gap.**

Expansionary gap

The gap that exists whenever the equilibrium level of real national income per year is greater than the full-employment level as shown by the position of the long-run aggregate supply curve.

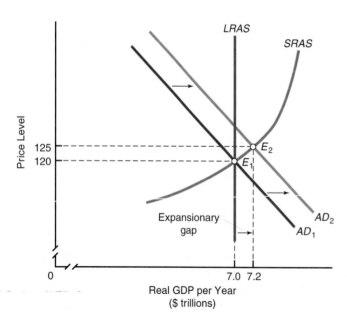

FIGURE 10-8

The Effects of Stable Aggregate Supply with an Increase in Aggregate Demand: The Expansionary Gap

The economy is at equilibrium at E_1. An increase in aggregate demand of AD_2 leads to a new short-run equilibrium at E_2 with the price level rising from 120 to 125 and the equilibrium level of real GDP per year rising from $7 trillion to $7.2 trillion. The difference is called the expansionary gap.

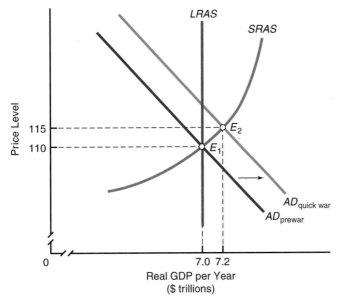

FIGURE 10-9

The Effects of War on Equilibrium

A quick temporary war will shift aggregate demand to $AD_{\text{quick war}}$. Equilibrium will move from E_1 to E_2 temporarily.

EXAMPLE

The Effects of a Short-Lived War

One way we can show what happens to the equilibrium price level and the equilibrium real GDP level with an aggregate demand shock is to consider a short-lived war (we actually had one in the Persian Gulf from August 1990 to early 1991). In Figure 10-9 you see the equilibrium price level of 110 and the equilibrium real GDP level of $7 trillion at the long-run aggregate supply curve. The quick war shifts aggregate demand from AD_{prewar} to $AD_{\text{quick war}}$. Equilibrium moves from E_1 to E_2, and the price level moves from 110 to 115. The short-run equilibrium real GDP increases to $7.2 trillion per year. The government's spending for the short-lived war caused AD to shift outward to the right. Also notice that the quick war temporarily pushed the economy above its long-run aggregate supply curve.

FOR CRITICAL ANALYSIS: What would happen if the short-lived war became permanent? How would you show it in Figure 10-9? ●

EXPLAINING INFLATION: DEMAND-PULL OR COST-PUSH?

When you first examined inflation in Chapter 7, no theory was given for why the general level of prices might rise. You can use the *AD-AS* framework to explain inflation. Indeed, Figure 10-8 is what is known as a theory of demand-side inflation, sometimes called *demand-pull inflation*. Whenever the general level of prices rises because of continual increases in aggregate demand, we say that the economy is experiencing **demand-pull inflation**—inflation caused by increases in aggregate demand. (Some economists argue that generally economywide increases in demand—increased aggregate demand—often

Demand-pull inflation
Inflation caused by increases in aggregate demand not matched by increases in aggregate supply.

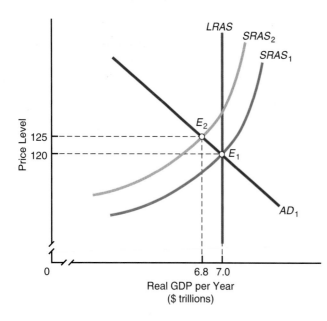

FIGURE 10-10

The Effects of Stable Aggregate Demand and a Decrease in Aggregate Supply: Supply-Side Inflation

If aggregate demand remains stable but $SRAS_1$ shifts to $SRAS_2$, equilibrium changes from E_1 to E_2. The price level rises from 120 to 125. If there are continual decreases in aggregate supply of this nature, the situation is called cost-push inflation.

occur when the amount of money in circulation increases faster than the growth in the economy. You will read more about this subject in Chapter 17.)

An alternative explanation comes from the supply side. Look at Figure 10-10. The initial equilibrium conditions are the same as in Figures 10-8 and 10-9. Now, however, there is a decrease in the aggregate supply curve, from $SRAS_1$ to $SRAS_2$. Equilibrium shifts from E_1 to E_2. The price level has increased from 120 to 125, too, while the equilibrium level of real GDP per year decreased from $7 trillion to $6.8 trillion. If there are continual decreases in aggregate supply, the situation is called **cost-push inflation.**

As the example of cost-push inflation shows, if the economy is initially in equilibrium on its *LRAS*, a decrease in *SRAS* will lead to a rise in the price level. Thus any abrupt change in one of the factors that determine aggregate supply will shift the equilibrium level of real GDP and the equilibrium price level. If the economy for some reason is operating to the left of its *LRAS*, an increase in *SRAS* will lead to a simultaneous *increase* in the equilibrium level of real GDP per year and a *decrease* in the price level. You should be able to show this in a graph similar to Figure 10-10.

The Real Price of Gas

Since the 1970s, the media have made references to the "high price of gas." A typical comment by some senior citizens interviewed on TV might be, "When I was a kid, gas cost only 25 cents a gallon." The interviewee is obviously referring to the *nominal* price of gasoline. References to nominal prices during periods of inflation are virtually meaningless. Only after a nominal price is corrected for general price level changes can we make a meaningful comparison to the price of the same product or service today. In the case of gas, the price of a gallon in the late 1990s, in real terms, is about where it was a few years after World War II.

Cost-push inflation
Inflation caused by a continually decreasing short-run aggregate supply curve.

EXAMPLE
The Oil Price Shock of the 1970s

One of the best examples of an aggregate supply shock occurred in the 1970s. During several instances, the supply of crude oil to the United States was restricted.

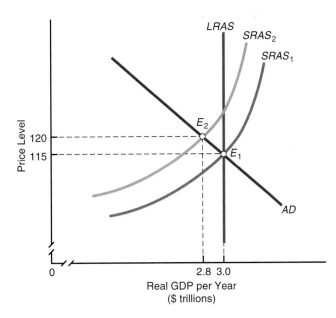

FIGURE 10-11

The Effects of Oil Price Shocks on the Economy
In the 1970s, the supply of crude oil to the United States was restricted. Higher oil prices raised the cost of production. $SRAS_1$ shifted to $SRAS_2$, and equilibrium went from E_1 to E_2 with a higher price level and a lower equilibrium real GDP per year.

Exercise 10.2
Visit www.econtoday.com for more about the shock of an earthquake.

These restrictions were the result of actions taken by the Organization of Petroleum Exporting Countries (OPEC). The oil embargo had an almost immediate impact on the price of oil and petroleum products, mainly gasoline and heating oil. Higher oil prices raised the cost of production in many U.S. industries that relied on petroleum. The result was a shift in the aggregate supply curve as shown in Figure 10-11. The equilibrium shifted from E_1—$3 trillion of real GDP per year and a price level of 115—to E_2—equilibrium real GDP of $2.8 trillion and a price level of 120.

FOR CRITICAL ANALYSIS: If the price of oil had remained permanently high, what would have happened to LRAS in Figure 10-11? ●

CONCEPTS IN BRIEF

- Short-run equilibrium occurs at the intersection of the aggregate demand curve, *AD,* and the short-run aggregate supply curve, *SRAS.* Long-run equilibrium occurs at the intersection of AD and the long-run aggregate supply curve, *LRAS.* Any unanticipated shifts in aggregate demand or supply are called aggregate demand shocks or aggregate supply shocks.

- When aggregate demand shifts while aggregate supply is stable, a contractionary gap can occur, defined as the difference between the equilibrium level of real GDP and how much the economy could be producing if it were operating on its *LRAS.* The reverse situation leads to an expansionary gap.

- With stable aggregate supply, an abrupt shift in *AD* may lead to what is called demand-pull inflation. With a stable aggregate demand, an abrupt shift inward in *SRAS* may lead to what is called cost-push inflation.

These Indonesian students are demonstrating for political reform after the economic crisis that hit Indonesia in 1997 and 1998. Most countries in Southeast Asia were experiencing similar crises at that time.

A Demand Shock Hits Southeast Asia, and the World Holds Its Breath

CONCEPTS APPLIED:

AGGREGATE DEMAND, AGGREGATE SUPPLY, DEMAND SHOCKS

 Visit www.econtoday.com for an Internet Activity that expands your understanding of these concepts.

Economic growth rates in Southeast Asia have been the envy of most countries in the world for many years. Growth of real GDP in China, Taiwan, Singapore, Thailand, South Korea, and Malaysia have averaged twice the rate in the United States for at least 15 years. Except in Japan, suffering from a recession since the early 1990s, stock markets in the countries in that region continued to rise year after year. Southeast Asian economies appeared to be so strong that many articles were written about the "Asian way" to long-term growth and prosperity. Some analysts predicted that Southeast Asia would come to dominate the world economy and push the United States into second place.

Setbacks in Stock Markets and Currencies

From October 22 through October 29, 1997, major stock markets in Southeast Asia took a beating. Hong Kong's dropped 22.15 percent, South Korea's 17.63 percent, Malaysia's 11.46 percent, Singapore's 13.55 percent, and Japan's 7.77 percent. Many currencies had already started to lose value in world foreign exchange markets. Thailand's baht dropped by about 25 percent from June to the beginning of 1998. South Korea's won lost about half its value during the same time period. Indonesia's rupiah fell by even more. Forecasts of real GDP growth in most Southeast Asian countries for 1998 were less than one-third their actual growth rates in 1996.

Understanding the Shocks Using *AD-AS* Analysis

Look at Figure 10-12. For simplicity, we lump all of the Southeast Asian countries affected by the stock and currency market shocks into one economy. Its long-run aggregate

supply curve is represented by $LRAS_{\text{Southeast Asia}}$. Before the shock, the aggregate demand curve is AD_1. The short-run aggregate supply curve remains $SRAS_1$. Prior to the shock, the equilibrium was at E_1. Real GDP per year was y_1 and rising (that is, the $LRAS$ curve was shifting outward at a healthy clip). The price level is assumed to be at 100 before the shock. When the demand shock occurs, the aggregate demand curve shifts to AD_2, and the equilibrium real GDP per year falls to y_2. At E_2, the intersection of the $SRAS_1$ and AD_2, the price level has now fallen to 90—there is deflation.

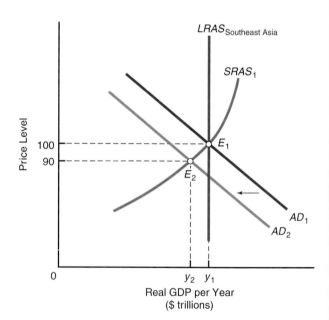

FIGURE 10-12

A Demand Shock Hits Southeast Asia

After the demand shock in Southeast Asia, the aggregate demand curve shifts to AD_2 and intersects the short-run aggregate supply curve at E_2. Real GDP per year falls to y_2, and the price level decreases from 100 to 90.

A Rescue Package

To cushion the shock of the abrupt shift in aggregate demand AD_2, other nations, through the International Monetary Fund, put together a rescue package. It involved a line of credit for various countries in Southeast Asia that totaled $100 billion by the beginning of 1998. South Korea alone received $57 billion.

FOR CRITICAL ANALYSIS

1. Has there ever been a similar scenario in the history of the U.S. economy?
2. Some observers say that a stock market crash should not have had much effect on the real economy of Southeast Asia. After all, the same amount of physical real goods, factories, and the like existed after the crash. Why was the stock market crash important nonetheless?

CHAPTER SUMMARY

1. Aggregate demand is the total of all planned expenditures on final goods and services, and aggregate supply is the total of all planned production.
2. The aggregate demand curve gives the various quantities of all commodities demanded at various price levels. It slopes downward due to the real-balance effect, the interest rate effect, and the open economy effect.
3. Aggregate demand is not the same thing as individual demand because individual demand curves are drawn holding income, among other things, constant. The aggregate demand curve reflects the entire circular flow of income and product.
4. Any non-price-level change that increases aggregate spending on domestic goods shifts the aggregate demand curve to the right. Any non-price-level change that decreases aggregate spending on domestic goods shifts the aggregate demand curve to the left.
5. There are two aggregate supply curves. The long-run aggregate supply curve is a vertical line, the location of which depends on tastes, technology, and endowments of natural resources; it assumes full information and full adjustment. The short-run aggregate sup-

ply curve is drawn without full information and full adjustment and slopes upward, but it is not vertical.
6. Output can be expanded in the short run because firms can work both capital and labor more intensively and because firms with fixed input prices experience higher profits as the price level increases and therefore desire to hire more workers. The closer to capacity the economy is running, the steeper the short-run aggregate supply curve becomes.
7. There are events that shift both the long-run and short-run aggregate curves simultaneously. These include any change in the endowments of factors of production (land, labor, or capital). A temporary change in an input price, by contrast, shifts only the short-run aggregate supply curve.
8. Equilibrium occurs at the intersection of aggregate demand, short-run aggregate supply, and long-run aggregate supply.
9. The economy may experience shifts in aggregate demand and supply, called aggregate demand shocks and aggregate supply shocks. The impacts of such shocks on the equilibrium level of real output depend on the time period under study and other factors.

DISCUSSION OF PREVIEW QUESTIONS

1. Why does the aggregate demand curve slope downward?

There are three reasons for believing that the quantity demanded for real output rises as the price level falls, and vice versa. A decrease in the price level leads to higher *real* money balances, all other things held constant. This increased real wealth causes a direct effect on consumers' spending decisions.

There is an indirect effect via interest rates, which move with price level changes. As the price level falls, the interest rate will fall, and consumers will want to spend more on houses and cars. Finally, in an open economy, if the price level falls, people will want domestic goods rather than imports, and foreigners will want to buy more of our goods.

2. **Why does the short-run aggregate supply curve slope upward?**

As the price level increases, firms presumably face fixed input prices in the short run. Their profits go up, and will rise even more if they increase production. They do so by working their labor force and their capital equipment more intensively, thereby generating more output.

3. **Why is the long-run aggregate supply curve vertical?**

The definition of the long-run aggregate supply curve is the amount of real output of goods and services that will be produced in the long run with full infor-mation and full adjustment. With full information and full adjustment, changes in the price level do not affect real output. Real output in the long run is solely a function of tastes, technology, and endowments of land, labor, and capital. Hence the long-run aggregate supply curve is a vertical line.

4. **How can we show improvements in technology using aggregate demand and aggregate supply analysis?**

Improvements in technology shift both the long-run aggregate supply curve and the short-run aggregate supply curve outward. Essentially, you can show this using aggregate supply and aggregate demand analysis by drawing the curves that are shown in Figure 10-4.

PROBLEMS

(Answers to the odd-numbered problems appear at the back of the book.)

10-1. Given the curves in the accompanying graph, discuss why the equilibrium price level will be at P_e and not at P_1 or P_2.

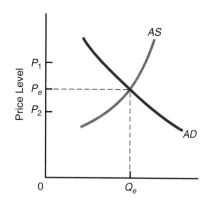

10-2. In the discussion of why the *AD* curve slopes downward from left to right, notice that nothing was said about what happens to the quantity of real output demanded when the price level rises and causes wealth to fall for people in businesses who own mortgages on houses and buildings. Why not? (Hint: What is the *net* effect to the whole economy when the price level rises and causes a wealth loss to lenders who get paid back in fixed nominal dollars?)

10-3. Distinguish between short-run and long-run supply curves.

10-4. How is aggregate demand affected when the price level in *other* economies decreases? What happens to aggregate demand when the price level in *this* economy falls?

10-5. Suppose that aggregate supply decreases while aggregate demand is held constant.

   a. What happens to the price level?
   b. What happens to national output?

COMPUTER-ASSISTED INSTRUCTION

When the price level falls, what happens to (1) mortgage owners and (2) holders of $1,000 bills? The differential impact of a lower price level on these two groups helps explain the real-balance effect. That effect can in turn help explain a negatively sloped aggregate demand curve.

Complete problem and answer appear on disk.

CHAPTER 11

CLASSICAL AND KEYNESIAN MACRO ANALYSES

The Great Depression, which lasted from 1929 through much of the 1930s, was probably the worst period in U.S. economic history. During the 1920s, stock prices rose almost 500 percent before the Crash of 1929. Only in 1931 did stock prices recover to their 1921 level. Officially measured unemployment peaked at almost 25 percent in 1933. By then more than 5,000 banks—one out of every five—had failed and their customers' deposits had vanished. One out of every 215 Americans filed for bankruptcy. Today, as the 1990s come to a close, at least one person in 10 percent of U.S. households will have declared bankruptcy at some point over the past decade. Does that mean that we have been in a great depression and did not realize it? Or has some other factor been at work? As background for evaluating this issue, you need to learn the classical and Keynesian views of macroeconomics.

PREVIEW QUESTIONS

1. What are the assumptions of the classical macro model?
2. What determines the rate of interest in the classical model?
3. Why do Keynesian economists believe that the short-run aggregate supply curve is horizontal?
4. Why is real GDP said to be demand-determined when the short-run aggregate supply curve is horizontal?

Did You Know That . . . in spite of continuing general inflation, magazine publishers tend to keep the same magazine prices for more than a year? According to one study by economist Stephen G. Cecchetti, the typical magazine publisher lets inflation eat away at a fourth of the magazine's price before a new price is printed on the magazine. This common example of "sticky" prices gives just a hint that our economy may not instantaneously adapt itself to changes in macroeconomic variables such as an increase in the rate of inflation. Economists want to know what causes fluctuations in employment, output, and the price level. The fact that magazine prices are sticky is just one empirical observation that would lead researchers to develop macroeconomic models that somehow reflect the less flexible nature of certain prices. Such was not the case with the classical economists, who had a different view of how the macroeconomy operated. We will start this chapter with a look at the classical model of the economy and then examine a model developed in the twentieth century.

THE CLASSICAL MODEL

The classical model, which traces its origins to the 1770s, was the first systematic attempt to explain the determinants of the price level and the national levels of output, income, employment, consumption, saving, and investment. The term *classical model* was coined by John Maynard Keynes (pronounced "kainz"), a Cambridge University economist, who used the term to refer to the way in which earlier economists had analyzed economic aggregates. Classical economists—Adam Smith, J. B. Say, David Ricardo, John Stuart Mill, Thomas Malthus, and others—wrote from the 1770s to the 1870s. They assumed, among other things, that all wages and prices were flexible and that competitive markets existed throughout the economy. Starting in the 1870s, so-called neoclassical economists, including Alfred Marshall, introduced a mathematical approach that allowed them to refine earlier economists' models.

Say's Law

Every time you produce something for which you receive income, you generate the income necessary to make expenditures on other goods and services. That means that an economy producing $7 trillion of GDP (final goods and services) simultaneously produces the income with which these goods and services can be supplied. As an accounting identity, *actual* aggregate income always equals *actual* aggregate expenditures. Classical economists took this accounting identity one step further by arguing that total national supply creates its own demand. They asserted what has become known as **Say's law:**

> **Supply creates its own demand; hence it follows that *desired* expenditures will equal *actual* expenditures.**

What does Say's law really mean? It states that the very process of producing specific goods (supply) is proof that other goods are desired (demand). People produce more goods than they want for their own use only if they seek to trade them for other goods. Someone offers to supply something only because he or she has a demand for something else. The implication of this, according to Say, is that no general glut, or overproduction, is possible in a market economy. From this reasoning, it seems to follow that full employment of labor and other resources would be the normal state of affairs in such an economy.

Say's law
A dictum of economist J. B. Say that supply creates its own demand; producing goods and services generates the means and the willingness to purchase other goods and services.

Underlying Say's law is the premise that wants are unlimited and, further, that the primary goal of economic activity is consumption for oneself or one's family, either in the present or in the future. If a more or less self-sufficient family wants to increase its consumption, it can do so by producing more and trading its surplus of one good to get more of another good.

Say indicated that an oversupply of some goods might occur in particular markets. He argued that such surpluses would simply cause prices to fall, thereby decreasing production in the long run. The opposite would occur in markets in which shortages temporarily appeared.

All this seems reasonable enough in a simple barter economy in which households produce most of the goods they need and trade for the rest. This is shown in Figure 11-1, where there is a simple circular flow. But what about a more sophisticated economy in which people work for others and there is no barter but rather the use of money? Can these complications create the possibility of unemployment? And does the fact that laborers receive money income, some of which can be saved, lead to unemployment? No, said the classical economists to these last two questions. They based their reasoning on a number of key assumptions.

Assumptions of the Classical Model

The classical model makes four major assumptions:

1. *Pure competition exists.* No single buyer or seller of a commodity or an input can affect its price.
2. *Wages and prices are flexible.* The assumption of pure competition leads to the notion that prices, wages, interest rates, and the like are free to move to whatever level supply and demand dictate (in the long run). Although no *individual* buyer can set a price, the community of buyers or sellers can cause prices to rise or to fall to an equilibrium level.
3. *People are motivated by self-interest.* Businesses want to maximize their profits, and households want to maximize their economic well-being.
4. *People cannot be fooled by money illusion.* Buyers and sellers react to changes in relative prices. That is to say, they do not suffer from **money illusion.** For example, a worker will not be fooled into thinking that he or she is better off by a doubling of wages if the price level has also doubled during the same time period.

Money illusion
Reacting to changes in money prices rather than relative prices. If a worker whose wages double when the price level also doubles thinks he or she is better off, the worker is suffering from money illusion.

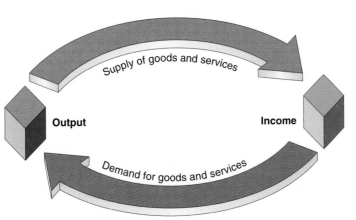

FIGURE 11-1

Say's Law and the Circular Flow
Here we show the circular flow of income and output. The very act of supplying a certain level of goods and services necessarily equals the level of goods and services demanded, in Say's simplified world.

The classical economists concluded, after taking account of the four major assumptions, that the role of government in the economy should be minimal. If all prices, wages, and markets are flexible, any problems in the macroeconomy will be temporary. The market will come to the rescue and correct itself.

The Problem of Saving

When income is saved, it is not reflected in product demand. It is a type of *leakage* in the circular flow of income and output because saving withdraws funds from the income stream. Consumption expenditures can fall short of total output now. In such a situation, it does not appear that supply necessarily creates its own demand.

The classical economists did not believe that the complicating factor of saving in the circular flow model of income and output was a problem. They contended that each dollar saved would be invested by businesses so that the leakage of saving would be matched by the injection of business investment. *Investment* here refers only to additions to the nation's capital stock. The classical economists believed that businesses as a group would intend to invest as much as households wanted to save. Equilibrium between the saving plans of consumers and the investment plans of businesses comes about, in the classical economists' world, through the working of the credit market. In the credit market, the *price* of credit is the interest rate. At equilibrium, the price of credit—the interest rate—is such that the quantity of credit demanded equals the quantity of credit supplied. Planned investment just equals planned saving, for saving represents the supply of credit and investment represents the demand for credit.

The Interest Rate: Equating Desired Saving and Investment. In Figure 11-2, the vertical axis measures the rate of interest in percentage terms; on the horizontal axis are the

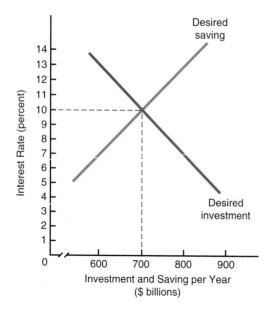

FIGURE 11-2

Equating Desired Saving and Investment in the Classical Model
The demand curve for investment is labeled "Desired investment." The supply of resources used for investment occurs when individuals do not consume but save instead. The desired saving curve is shown as an upward-sloping supply curve of saving. The equilibrating force here is, of course, the interest rate. At higher interest rates, people desire to save more. But at higher interest rates, businesses demand less investment because it is more expensive to invest. In this model, at an interest rate of 10 percent, the quantity of investment desired just equals the quantity of saving desired (supply), which is $700 billion per year.

Exercise 11.1
Visit www.econtoday.com for more about historical saving rates.

quantities of desired saving and desired investment per unit time period. The desired saving curve is really a supply curve of saving. It shows how much individuals and businesses wish to save at various interest rates. People wish to save more at higher interest rates than at lower interest rates.

Investment, primarily desired by businesses, responds in a predictable way. The higher the rate of interest, the more expensive it is to invest and the lower the level of desired investment. The desired investment curve slopes downward. In this simplified model, the equilibrium rate of interest is 10 percent, and the equilibrium quantity of saving and investment is $700 billion per year.

POLICY EXAMPLE
Should We Be Worried About Our Falling Saving Rate?

The net national rate of saving in the United States was 9.1 percent in the 1950s and 1960s but less than 3 percent in the 1990s. Policymakers are concerned because low rates of saving tend to reduce rates of investment.

Some researchers contend that part of the problem is with the elderly, whose rate of saving is lower than it has ever been. For example, in the early 1960s, the typical 70-year-old consumed only about 70 percent as much as a 30-year-old. By the beginning of the 1990s, the typical 70-year-old was consuming 20 percent more than the 30-year-old! Part of the reason has to do with the amount of income, such as Social Security, and Medicare benefits, that the elderly are receiving from the government. Because Social Security benefits are paid regardless of how long you live, today's elderly have less fear of running out of money. Consequently, they have reduced their rate of saving. Also, because the elderly's medical payments are covered by Medicare, they no longer have to save to protect against medical emergencies. Researchers at the Federal Reserve Bank of Cleveland believe that without such disincentives to saving, the national rate of saving would be more than three times higher than it is.

FOR CRITICAL ANALYSIS: What would happen to the rate of saving if taxes on interest earned from savings were reduced? •

Equilibrium in the Labor Market

Now consider the labor market. If an excess quantity of labor is supplied at a particular wage level, the wage level is above equilibrium. By accepting lower wages, unemployed workers will quickly be put back to work. We show equilibrium in the labor market in Figure 11-3 on page 232.

Equilibrium of $12 per hour and 135 million workers employed represents full-employment equilibrium. If the wage rate were $14 an hour, there would be unemployment—145 million workers would want to work, but businesses would want to hire only 125 million. In the classical model, this unemployment is eliminated rather rapidly by wage rates dropping back to $12 per hour. As you will see in the Issues and Applications section at the end of this chapter, there are forces that may prevent workers from offering to work at the lower wage rates that would lead to full employment.

Exercise 11.2
Visit www.econtoday.com for more about the labor market.

The Relationship Between Employment and Real GDP. Employment is not to be regarded simply as some isolated figure that government statisticians estimate. Rather, the level of employment in an economy determines its real GDP (output), other things held

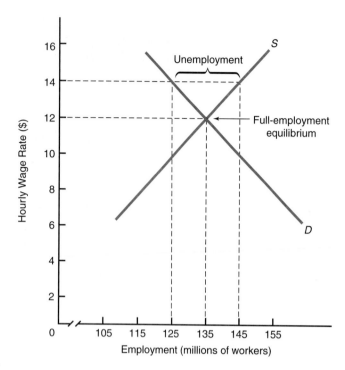

FIGURE 11-3

Equilibrium in the Labor Market
The demand for labor is downward-sloping; at higher wage rates, firms will employ fewer workers. The supply of labor is upward-sloping; at higher wage rates, more workers will work longer and more people will be willing to work. The equilibrium wage rate is $12 with an equilibrium employment per year of 135 million workers.

constant. A hypothetical relationship between input (number of employees) and output (rate of real GDP per year) is shown in Table 11-1. We have highlighted the row that has 135 million workers per year as the labor input. That might be considered a hypothetical level of full employment, and it is related to a rate of real GDP of $7 trillion per year.

Classical Theory, Vertical Aggregate Supply, and the Price Level

In the classical mold of reasoning, long-term unemployment is impossible. Say's law, coupled with flexible interest rates, prices, and wages, would always tend to keep workers fully employed so that the aggregate supply curve, as shown in Figure 11-4, is vertical at Q_0. We

TABLE 11-1

The Relationship Between Employment and Real GDP

Labor Input per Year (millions of workers)	Real GDP per Year ($ trillions)
98	4
104	5
120	6
135	7
145	8
160	9

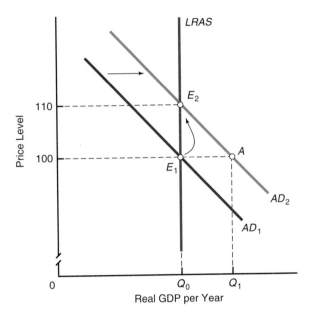

FIGURE 11-4

Classical Theory and Increases in Aggregate Demand

The classical theorists believed that Say's law, flexible interest rates, prices, and wages would always lead to full employment at Q_0 along the vertical aggregate supply curve, $LRAS$, was vertical. With aggregate demand, AD_1, the price level is 100. An increase in aggregate demand shifts AD_1 to AD_2. At price level 100, the quantity of real GDP per year demanded is A on AD_2, or Q_1. But this is greater than at full employment. Prices rise, and the economy quickly moves from E_1 to E_2 at the higher price level of 110.

have labeled the supply curve *LRAS,* consistent with the long-run aggregate supply curve introduced in Chapter 10. It was defined there as the quantity of output that would be produced in an economy with full information and full adjustment of wages and prices year in and year out. In the classical model, this happens to be the *only* aggregate supply curve that exists in equilibrium. Everything adjusts so fast that we are essentially always on or quickly moving toward *LRAS.* Furthermore, because the labor market is working well, Q_0 is always at, or soon to be at, full employment. Full employment is defined as the amount of employment that would exist year in and year out if all parties in the labor market fully anticipated any inflation or deflation that was occurring. Full employment does not mean zero unemployment because there is always some frictional unemployment (discussed in Chapter 7), even in the classical world.

Effect of an Increase in Aggregate Demand in the Classical Model. In this model, any change in aggregate demand will soon cause a change in the price level. Consider starting at E_1, at price level 100. If the aggregate demand shifts to AD_2, at price level 100, output would increase to Q_1. But that is greater than the full-employment level of output of real GDP, Q_0. The economy will attempt to get to point A, but because this is beyond full employment, prices will rise, and the economy will find itself back on the vertical *LRAS* at point E_2 at a higher price level, 110. The price level will increase at output rates in excess of the full-employment level of output because employers will end up bidding up wages for now more relatively scarce workers. In addition, factories will be bidding up the price of other inputs at this greater-than-full-employment rate of output.

The level of real GDP per year clearly does not depend on any changes in aggregate demand. Hence we say that in the classical model, the equilibrium level of real GDP per year is completely *supply-determined.* Changes in aggregate demand affect only the price level, not the output of real goods and services.

FIGURE 11-5

Effect of a Decrease in Aggregate Demand in the Classical Model

Effect of a Decrease in Aggregate Demand in the Classical Model. The effect of a decrease in aggregate demand in the classical model is the converse of the analysis just presented for an increase in aggregate demand. You can simply reverse AD_2 and AD_1 in Figure 11-4. To help you see how this analysis works, consider the flowchart in Figure 11-5.

CONCEPTS IN BRIEF

• Say's law states that supply creates its own demand and therefore *desired* expenditures will equal *actual* expenditures.

• The classical model assumes that (1) pure competition exists, (2) wages and prices are completely flexible, (3) individuals are motivated by self-interest, and (4) they cannot be fooled by money illusion.

• When saving is introduced into the model, equilibrium occurs in that market through changes in the interest rate such that desired saving equals desired investment at the equilibrium rate of interest.

• In the labor market, full employment occurs at a wage rate at which quantity demanded equals quantity supplied. That particular level of employment is associated with a certain value of real GDP per year.

• In the classical model, because the *LRAS* is vertical, the equilibrium level of real GDP is supply-determined. Any changes in aggregate demand simply change the price level.

KEYNESIAN ECONOMICS AND THE KEYNESIAN SHORT-RUN AGGREGATE SUPPLY CURVE

The classical economists' world was one of fully utilized resources. There would be no unused capacity and no unemployment. However, post–World War I Europe entered a period of long-term economic decline that could not be explained by the classical model. John Maynard Keynes developed an explanation that has since become known as the Keynesian model, which presented an explanation of the Great Depression in the 1930s. Keynes argued that if we are in a world in which there are large amounts of excess capacity and unemployment, a positive aggregate demand shock will not raise prices and a negative aggregate demand shock will not cause firms to lower prices. This situation is depicted in Figure 11-6. The short-run aggregate supply curve is labeled as the horizontal line *SRAS*. If we start out in equilibrium with aggregate demand at AD_1, the equilibrium level of real

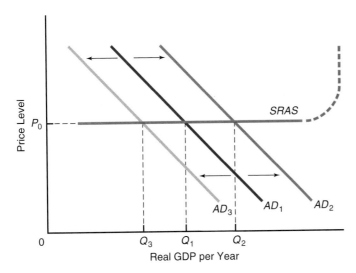

FIGURE 11-6
Demand-Determined Income Equilibrium
If we assume that prices will not fall when aggregate demand falls and that there is excess capacity so that prices will not rise when aggregate demand increases, the short-run aggregate supply curve is simply a horizontal line at the given price level, P_0, represented by SRAS. An aggregate demand shock that increases aggregate demand to AD_2 will increase the equilibrium level of real national income per year to Q_2. An aggregate demand shock that decreases aggregate demand to AD_3 will decrease the equilibrium level of real national income to Q_3. The equilibrium price level will not change.

GDP per year will be Q_1 and the equilibrium price level will be P_0. If there is an aggregate demand shock such that the aggregate demand curve shifts outward to the right to AD_2, the equilibrium price level will not change; only the equilibrium level of real GDP per year will increase, to Q_2. Conversely, if there is an aggregate demand shock that shifts the aggregate demand curve to AD_3, the equilibrium price level will again remain at P_0, but the equilibrium level of real GDP per year will fall to Q_3.

Under such circumstances, the equilibrium level of real GDP per year is completely *demand-determined*.

The horizontal short-run aggregate supply curve represented in Figure 11-6 is often called the **Keynesian short-run aggregate supply curve.** It is so named because Keynes hypothesized that many prices, especially the price of labor (wages), are "sticky downward." According to Keynes, the existence of unions and of long-term contracts between workers are real-world factors that can explain the downward inflexibility of *nominal* wage rates. Such "stickiness" of wages makes *involuntary* unemployment of labor a distinct possibility. The classical assumption of everlasting full employment no longer holds.

Further, even in situations of excess capacity and large amounts of unemployment, we will not necessarily see the price level falling; rather, all we will see is continuing unemployment and a reduction in the equilibrium level of real GDP per year. Thus general economywide equilibrium can occur and endure even if there is excess capacity. Keynes and his followers argued that capitalism was therefore not necessarily a self-regulating system sustaining full employment. At the time, Keynes was attacking the classical view of the world, which argued that markets would all eventually be in equilibrium—prices and wages would adjust—so that full employment would never be far away.

A pretty good example of a horizontal short-run aggregate supply curve can be seen by examining data from the aftermath of the Great Depression of the 1930s. Look at Figure 11-7 on page 236, where you see real GDP in billions of 1992 dollars on the horizontal axis and the price level index on the vertical axis. From the early days of recovery from the Great Depression to the outbreak of World War II, real GDP increased without much rise in the price level. During this period the economy experienced neither supply

Keynesian short-run aggregate supply curve
The horizontal portion of the aggregate supply curve in which there is unemployment and unused capacity in the economy.

FIGURE 11-7

Real GDP and the Price Level, 1934–1940

In a depressed economy, increased aggregate spending can increase output without raising prices. This is what John Maynard Keynes believed, and the data for the United States's recovery from the Great Depression seem to bear this out. In such circumstances, the level of real output is demand-determined.

constraints nor any dramatic changes in the price level. The most simplified Keynesian model in which prices do not change is essentially an immediate post-Depression model that fits the data very well during this period.

INCOME DETERMINATION USING AGGREGATE DEMAND AND AGGREGATE SUPPLY: FIXED VERSUS CHANGING PRICE LEVELS

The underlying assumption of the simplified Keynesian model is that the relevant range of the short-run aggregate supply schedule *(SRAS)* is horizontal, as depicted in panel (a) of Figure 11-8. There you see that short-run aggregate supply is fixed at price level 120. If

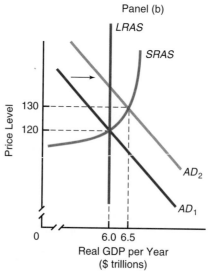

FIGURE 11-8

Income Determination with Fixed Versus Flexible Prices

In panel (a), the price level index is fixed at 120. An increase in aggregate demand from AD_1 to AD_2 moves the equilibrium level of real GDP from $6 trillion per year to $7 trillion per year. In panel (b), *SRAS* is upward-sloping. The same shift in aggregate demand yields an equilibrium level of real GDP of only $6.5 trillion per year and a higher price level index at 130.

aggregate demand is AD_1, the equilibrium level of real GDP is at $6 trillion per year. If aggregate demand increases to AD_2, the equilibrium level of real GDP increases to $7 trillion per year. Compare this situation with the standard upward-sloping short-run aggregate supply curve presented in Chapter 10. In panel (b) of Figure 11-8, *SRAS* is upward-sloping, with its slope becoming steeper and steeper after it crosses long-run aggregate supply, *LRAS*. Recall that *LRAS* is the level of real GDP that the economy would produce year in and year out with full information and full adjustment. It is sometimes called the full-employment level of real GDP because, presumably, full employment occurs when there is full information and full adjustment possible in the economy. If aggregate demand is AD_1, the equilibrium level of real GDP in panel (b) is also $6 trillion per year, also at a price level of 120. A similar increase in aggregate demand to AD_2 as occurred in panel (a) produces a different equilibrium, however. Equilibrium real GDP increases to $6.5 trillion per year, which is less than in panel (a) because part of the increase in *nominal* GDP has occurred through an increase in the price level to 130.

EXAMPLE
Keynesian Analysis of the Great Depression

At the beginning of 1929, the American economy was doing quite well, with the unemployment rate hovering around 3 percent. A year later it was almost 9 percent, and by 1933 it had reached an astonishing 25 percent. The real GDP of 1929 was not reached again until 1937, when another business downturn hit the economy. We can use the Keynesian analysis presented in Figure 11-9 to describe what happened. Aggregate demand to start with is AD_{1929}. According to Keynes and his followers, the economy experienced a dramatic reduction in aggregate demand, represented by a shift to AD_{1933}. To prevent massive unemployment, wages and prices would have to have fallen such that a new equilibrium would have been at point A on *LRAS*. Even though many wages and prices did fall, they didn't fall sufficiently. Consequently, a new equilibrium was established at E_2.

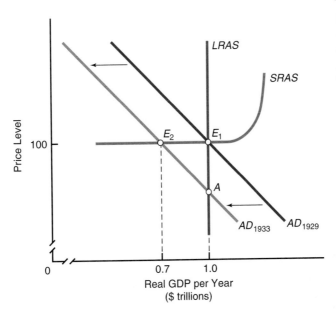

FIGURE 11-9

Keynesian Analysis of the Great Depression
Aggregate demand dropped from AD_{1929} to AD_{1933}. The price level would have had to drop to point A on *LRAS* in order to avoid unemployment. In reality, it did not, so that the new equilibrium shifted from E_1 to E_2. By 1933, the economy was operating at 30 percent below its potential output.

Real GDP fell from about $1 trillion dollars to $700 billion (expressed in 1992 dollars). By 1933, the economy was operating at 30 percent below its potential output represented by *LRAS*.

FOR CRITICAL ANALYSIS: *If the equilibrium stayed at E_2, what do you expect would eventually happen to LRAS?* •

CONCEPTS IN BRIEF

- If we assume that we are operating on a horizontal short-run aggregate supply curve, the equilibrium level of real GDP per year is completely demand-determined.
- The horizontal short-run aggregate supply curve has been called the Keynesian short-run aggregate supply curve because Keynes believed that many prices, especially wages, would not be reduced even when aggregate demand decreased.

AGGREGATE DEMAND AND SUPPLY IN AN OPEN ECONOMY

In many of the international examples in the preceding chapters, we had to translate foreign currencies into dollars when the open economy was discussed. We used the exchange rate, or the price of the dollar relative to other currencies. In Chapter 10 you also discovered that the open economy effect was one of the reasons why the aggregate demand curve slopes downward. When the domestic price level rises, Americans want to buy cheaper-priced foreign goods. The opposite occurs when the American domestic price level falls. Currently, the foreign sector of the American economy constitutes over 12 percent of all economic activities.

How a Stronger Dollar Affects Aggregate Supply

Assume that the dollar becomes stronger in international foreign exchange markets. If last week the dollar could buy 4 francs but this week it now buys 5 francs, it has become stronger. To the extent that American companies import raw and partially processed goods from abroad, a stronger dollar can lead to lower input prices. This will lead to a shift outward to the right in the short-run aggregate supply curve as shown in panel (a) of Figure 11-10. In that simplified model, equilibrium GDP would rise and the price level would fall. The result might involve increased employment and lower inflation.

How a Stronger Dollar Affects Aggregate Demand

There is another effect of a stronger dollar that we must consider. Foreigners will find that American goods are now more expensive, expressed in their own currency. After all, a $10 compact disc before the stronger dollar cost a French person 40 francs when the exchange rate was 4 to 1. After the dollar became stronger and the exchange rate increased to 5 to 1, that same $10 compact disc would cost 50 francs. Conversely, Americans will find that the stronger dollar makes imported goods cheaper. The result for Americans is fewer exports

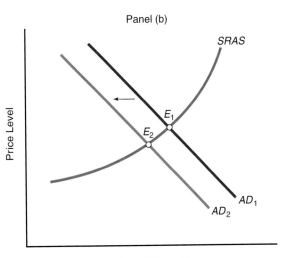

FIGURE 11-10

The Effects of a Stronger Dollar

When the dollar increases in value in the international currency market, lower prices for imported inputs result, causing a shift outward to the right in the short-run aggregate supply schedule from $SRAS_1$ to $SRAS_2$ in panel (a). If nothing else changes, equilibrium shifts from E_1 to E_2 at a lower price level and a higher equilibrium real GDP per year. A stronger dollar can also affect the aggregate demand curve because it will lead to fewer net exports and cause AD_1 to fall to AD_2 in panel (b). Equilibrium would move from E_1 to E_2, a lower price level, and a lower equilibrium real GDP per year.

and more imports, or lower net exports (exports minus imports). If net exports fall, employment in export industries will fall: This is represented in panel (b) of Figure 11-10. After the dollar becomes stronger, the aggregate demand curve shifts inward from AD_1 to AD_2. The result is a tendency for equilibrium real GDP and the price level to fall, and unemployment to rise.

The Net Effect

We have learned, then, that a stronger dollar *simultaneously* leads to an increase in *SRAS* and a decrease in *AD*. Remember from Chapter 4 that in such situations, the result depends on which curve shifts more. If the aggregate demand curve shifts more than the short-run aggregate supply curve, equilibrium real GDP will fall. Conversely, if the aggregate supply curve shifts more than the aggregate demand curve, equilibrium real GDP will rise.

You should be able to redo this entire analysis for a weaker dollar.

ECONOMIC GROWTH IN AN AGGREGATE DEMAND AND SUPPLY FRAMEWORK

Much (not all) of the Keynesian macroeconomic analysis to which you have been introduced in this chapter, and which you will examine in the next chapter, relates to short-run fluctuations in unemployment, inflation, and other macroeconomic variables. Whether one

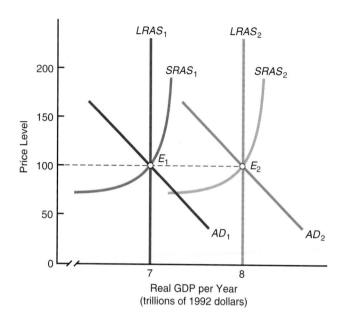

FIGURE 11-11

Economic Growth, Aggregate Demand, and Aggregate Supply
Economic growth can be shown using short-run and long-run aggregate demand and supply curves. Aggregate demand, AD_1, intersects short-run aggregate supply, $SRAS_1$, at E_1, yielding $7 trillion of real GDP per year at a price level of 100. This yearly real GDP is consistent with full employment. The long-run aggregate supply curve is vertical at $7 trillion and is labeled $LRAS_1$. With economic growth, $LRAS_1$ moves outward to $8 trillion per year. Short-run aggregate supply shifts to $SRAS_2$, and aggregate demand increases to AD_2. New equilibrium is at E_2, still at a price level of 100. There is no inflation.

uses some variant of classical macroeconomic analysis or the Keynesian analysis, over time, short-term business fluctuations tend to iron out. We are left with economic growth, which can occur with or without inflation.

Economic Growth Without Inflation

Look at Figure 11-11. We start in equilibrium with AD_1 and $SRAS_1$ intersecting at the long-run aggregate supply curve, $LRAS_1$, at a price level of 100. Real GDP per year is $7 trillion. Economic growth occurs due to labor force expansion, capital investments, and other occurrences. The result is a rightward shift in the long-run aggregate supply curve to $LRAS_2$. As the long-run productive capacity of the nation grows, the economy doesn't stay on its short-run aggregate supply curve, $SRAS$. Rather, $SRAS$ shifts along with shifts in aggregate demand due to population increases and rising per capita income. It is thus possible for us to achieve real GDP of $8 trillion without any increase in the price level. The short-run aggregate supply curve moves outward to $SRAS_2$ and intersects AD_2 at E_2 where the new long-run aggregate supply curve, $LRAS_2$, has moved.

In the world just hypothesized, aggregate demand shifts outward so that at the same price level, 100, it intersects the new short-run aggregate supply curve, $SRAS_2$ at the rate of real GDP that is consistent with more or less full employment (on $LRAS_2$). Firms sell all the output produced at the new level without changing prices. In some situations, however, inflation may accompany growth.

EXAMPLE
The U.S. Record over the Past Few Decades

What has been the United States's experience regarding economic growth and the rate of inflation over the past few decades? Has it resembled Figure 11-11? The answer can be seen in Figure 11-12, which reflects the U.S. experience from 1970 to 1996. In essence, each of the points represents the intersection of aggregate supply and aggregate demand for that year. Since 1970, the price level has clearly risen. So, too, has real GDP.

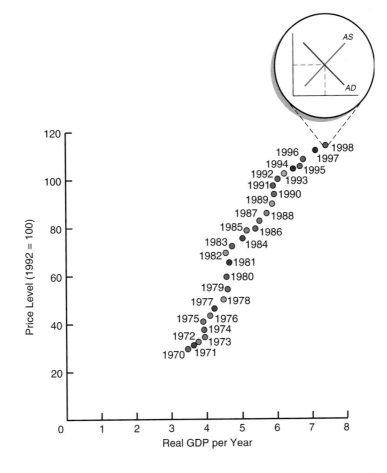

FIGURE 11-12

Economic Growth and Inflation in the United States

This figure shows the points where aggregate demand and aggregate supply have intersected each year from 1970 to the present. The United States has experienced economic growth over this period, but not without inflation.

Sources: Economic Report of the President; Economic Indicators, various issues.

Apparently, the American economy has been unable to experience economic growth without inflation.

FOR CRITICAL ANALYSIS: As an individual, should you care whether the United States has economic growth with or without inflation? Explain your answer. •

CONCEPTS IN BRIEF

- A change in the international value of the dollar can affect both the *SRAS* and aggregate demand.

- A stronger dollar will reduce the cost of imported inputs, thereby causing the *SRAS* to shift outward to the right, leading to a lower price level and a higher equilibrium real GDP per year, given no change in aggregate demand.

- In contrast, a stronger dollar will lead to lower net exports, causing the aggregate demand curve to shift inward, leading to a lower price level and a lower equilibrium real GDP per year. The net effect depends on which shift is more important. The opposite analysis applies to a weakening dollar in international currency markets.

- It is possible to have economic growth with and without inflation. If the aggregate demand curve shifts outward to the right at the same speed as the aggregate supply curve, there will be no inflation accompanying economic growth.

The 1990s saw an increasing number of bankruptcies despite employment rates that fell and incomes that rose. Why are so many Americans unable to pay off their debts?

Even During a Booming Economy, Bankruptcies Are Rising

CONCEPTS APPLIED:

RECESSION, DEPRESSION, AGGREGATE DEMAND, AGGREGATE SUPPLY, BUSINESS CYCLE

Visit www.econtoday.com for an Internet Activity that expands your understanding of these concepts.

The Great Depression was a period that many people associate with terrible economic times—and rightly so. Aggregate demand decreased so much that what might have been just a severe recession turned into a depression. The hallmark of serious economic downturns is a spate of bankruptcies.

A Long History

At one time, debtors who could not pay their debts as they came due faced harsh consequences, including imprisonment and involuntary servitude. That is no longer true. Article I, Section 8, of the U.S. Constitution gives Congress the power to establish uniform laws on bankruptcy throughout the United States. Modern bankruptcy law is based on the Bankruptcy Reform Act of 1978, as amended. Bankruptcy law in the United States has two goals—to protect a debtor by giving the person a fresh start and

to ensure fair treatment to creditors who are competing for the debtor's assets.

Historical Record of Bankruptcies

In panel (a) of Figure 11-13, you can see that total bankruptcy filings per year grew as we came out of the recession of 1990. They started to fall in 1992 but have increased steadily since 1994. In panel (b), you can see that bankruptcy filings during the decade of the 1990s continued to rise, approaching 40 per 1,000 Americans.

So at least in recent years, there seems to be little correlation between bankruptcies and the state of the economy. During much of the 1990s, unemployment has been historically low. Consider just one year. In 1996, over 1.1 million Americans declared personal bankruptcy. That was a 29 percent increase from 1995. In 1997, personal bankruptcy filings grew at 21 percent compared to 1996.

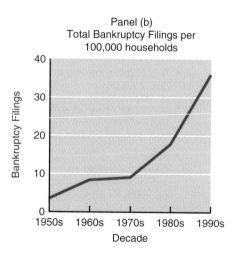

FIGURE 11-13

The Rising Tide of Bankruptcies

Source: Administrative Office of the United States Courts.

Yet during that same two-year period, the unemployment rate fell to a low of 4.6 percent.

By the end of the decade, at least one person in 10 percent of America's 100 million households will have declared personal bankruptcy at one point or another during the 1990s. What is wrong with this picture?

Some Reasons Why

There is little correlation between bankruptcy filings and the business cycle. One of the reasons there were so few bankruptcies in the Great Depression, compared to today, was that credit was harder to get. Today, credit is much more readily available. Households are scored on the basis of their income—rather than assets—to determine

whether credit should be extended to them. Moreover, most creditors do not keep track of a borrower's changing circumstances. Further, credit card companies rarely check on the self-reported income of a credit applicant. Consequently, with more people obtaining credit, more people will overextend themselves. And because filing for bankruptcy has become easier and the penalties have become less severe, the result is more bankruptcy filings.

FOR CRITICAL ANALYSIS

1. What do you think will happen to bankruptcy rates during the next recession?
2. What circumstances might cause a person to declare bankruptcy?

CHAPTER SUMMARY

1. The classical model was developed in the 1770s by such economists as Adam Smith, David Ricardo, John Stuart Mill, and Thomas Malthus. It attempted to explain the determinants of the price level and national income and employment.

2. Say's law holds that supply creates its own demand. A more complete classical model assumes (a) pure competition, (b) wage and price flexibility, (c) self-interest motivation throughout the population, and (d) no money illusion. With the introduction of saving, the classical economists believed, the market economy would still reach full employment of resources because planned saving would be met by planned investment. Saving is the supply of credit, and investment is the demand for credit. The interest rate in the credit market was assumed to be flexible, like all other prices, so equilibrium would always prevail, and therefore planned saving would always equal planned investment.

3. Because the classical model posits a vertical long-run aggregate supply curve, any changes in aggregate demand simply change the equilibrium price level. The equilibrium level of real GDP per year is completely supply-determined.

4. Whenever we are operating on a horizontal short-run aggregate supply curve, the equilibrium level of real GDP is completely demand-determined by the position of the aggregate demand curve. The Keynesian short-run aggregate supply curve is typically given as horizontal because Keynes assumed that wages and

prices would not be reduced even if aggregate demand decreased substantially.

5. If we relax the assumption of a fixed price level, we are then operating on the upward-sloping portion of the short-run aggregate supply curve. Hence an increase in aggregate demand will lead to some increase in the price level. This increase in the price level will have an offsetting effect on equilibrium total planned expenditures because of wealth, interest rate, and foreign goods substitution effects. Under such circumstances, any increase in aggregate demand will lead to both an increase in the price level and an increase in output.

6. A stronger dollar will reduce the cost of imported inputs, thereby causing the *SRAS* to shift outward to the right, leading to a lower price level and a higher equilibrium real GDP per year, given no change in aggregate demand.

7. In contrast, a stronger dollar will lead to lower net exports, causing the aggregate demand curve to shift inward, leading to a lower price level and a lower equilibrium real GDP per year. The net effect depends on which shift is more important. The opposite analysis applies to a weakening dollar in international currency markets.

8. It is possible to have economic growth with or without inflation. If the aggregate demand curve shifts outward to the right at the same speed as the aggregate supply curve, there will be no inflation accompanying economic growth.

DISCUSSION OF PREVIEW QUESTIONS

1. **What are the assumptions of the classical macro model?**

   In the classical model, the following four assumptions are made: (a) the existence of pure competition, (b) complete wage and price flexibility, (c) individuals motivated by self-interest, and (d) individuals not fooled by money illusion.

2. **What determines the rate of interest in the classical model?**

   In the classical model, the interaction between desired investment and desired saving determines the equilibrium rate of interest in the economy. Otherwise stated, the equilibrium rate of interest is determined at the intersection of the desired investment curve and the desired saving curve.

3. **Why do Keynesian economists believe that the short-run aggregate supply curve is horizontal?**

   In the horizontal range of the *SRAS* curve, changes in real GDP (output) occur without changes in the price level. This pure quantity response (no price response) to changes in *AD* reflects Keynes's assumption that during a depression or a very deep recession, businesses have so much excess capacity that *increases* in *AD* will elicit only an increase in output; businesses

that try to increase prices in such a situation discover that they lose sales to competitors. Similarly, a *reduction* in *AD* will lead only to a reduction in output; businesses won't reduce prices. Keynes assumed that in modern economies the existence of unions and contracts to support the unemployed imply that wages are "sticky downward"—wages aren't likely to fall even during periods of significant unemployment. Businesses have a certain control over prices and, confronting wages that are sticky, prefer to reduce output instead of price.

4. **Why is real GDP said to be demand-determined when the short-run aggregate supply curve is horizontal?**

   When the *SRAS* curve is horizontal, real GDP will change only in response to a change in *AD*. If *AD* increases, real GDP rises; if *AD* decreases, real GDP falls. Therefore, real GDP merely responds to changes in *AD,* which is therefore the primary mover in the economy. According to Keynes, businesses are prepared to produce *any* output level; the output level that they do produce is the most profitable one, and that depends on *AD*. This theory says that if you want to predict what real GDP and national employment will be in the future, discover what is happening to *AD* now.

PROBLEMS

(Answers to the odd-numbered problems appear at the back of the book.)

11-1. The desired investment curve intersects the desired saving curve in the economy at an interest rate of 8 percent. The current market rate of interest is 9 percent. Outline what will now take place in the economy so that the saving and investment market is in equilibrium.

11-2. Look at Figure 11-3 on page 232 again. At a wage rate of $12 per hour, 135 million workers are employed. This is called full-employment equilibrium. Does that mean there is no unemployment?

11-3. Show the effects of a decrease in aggregate demand in the classical model.

11-4. On one graph, show economic growth with concomitant increases in the price level.

COMPUTER-ASSISTED INSTRUCTION

The sharp contrast between the classical and Keynesian models is illustrated.

CHAPTER 12
CONSUMPTION, INCOME, AND THE MULTIPLIER

You have two choices when you earn income—you can either consume it or save it. What you do not consume is, by definition, what you save. Saving is important because investment is impossible without it. In the United States, the rate of personal saving has dropped significantly over the past several decades. Some economists argue, nonetheless, that the rate of saving may not be as low as government statisticians have estimated. To understand the role of saving in our economy, you need to know more about the relationship between income, consumption (and saving), and the multiplier, the subject of this chapter.

PREVIEW QUESTIONS

1. What does the total planned expenditures curve indicate?

2. How do we interpret the 45-degree reference line?

3. What is the concept of the multiplier, how does it work, and what is its main determinant?

4. What might cause shifts in the total planned expenditures curve?

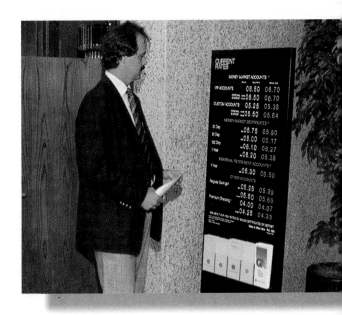

Did You Know That . . . personal consumption expenditures in the United States have averaged about two-thirds of gross domestic product for decades? Each year, Americans purchase millions of television sets, millions of pairs of shoes, millions of compact discs, and billions of stress-reducing pills, among other products and services. We are a nation of spenders, and our personal consumption expenditures keep the American economic machine moving day in and day out. As it turns out, John Maynard Keynes focused much of his research on what determines how much you and I decide to spend each year. Remember that aggregate demand consists of consumption expenditures, plus expenditures for investment purposes, what the government spends, and what foreigners spend on domestically produced output. As you will learn in this chapter, Keynes focused on the relationship between how much people earn and their willingness to engage in personal consumption expenditures. In this chapter you will learn about that relationship as well as the influence of investment, government, and the foreign sector on the economy's equilibrium level of real output per year.

SOME SIMPLIFYING ASSUMPTIONS IN A KEYNESIAN MODEL

Continuing in the Keynesian tradition, we will assume that the short-run aggregate supply curve within the relevant range is horizontal. That is to say, we assume that it is similar to Figure 11-6 on page 235, meaning that the equilibrium level of real GDP is demand-determined. That is why Keynes wished to examine the elements of desired aggregate expenditures.

Also, for the time being we will not be concerned with the problem of inflation, because by definition, along the Keynesian short-run aggregate supply curve, inflation is impossible. Finally, given that the price level is assumed to be unchanging, all of the variables with which we will be dealing will be expressed in real terms. After all, with no change in the price level, any change in the magnitude of an economic variable, such as income, will be equivalent to a real change in terms of purchasing power. Hence we will be examining Keynes's income-expenditure model of real GDP determination in a world of inflexible prices.

To simplify the income determination model that follows, a number of assumptions are made:

1. Businesses pay no indirect taxes (for example, sales taxes).
2. Businesses distribute all of their profits to shareholders.
3. There is no depreciation (capital consumption allowance), so gross private domestic investment equals net investment.
4. The economy is closed—that is, there is no foreign trade.

Given all these simplifying assumptions, real disposable income will be equal to real national income minus taxes.[1]

Definitions and Relationships Revisited

You can do only two things with a dollar of income (in the absence of taxes): consume it or save it. If you consume it, it is gone forever. If you save the entire dollar, however, you will

---

[1]Strictly speaking, we are referring here to net taxes—that is, the difference between taxes paid and transfer payments received. If taxes are $1 trillion but individuals receive transfer payments—Social Security, unemployment benefits, and so forth—of $300 billion, net taxes are equal to $700 billion.

Consumption
Spending on new goods and services out of a household's current income. Whatever is not consumed is saved. Consumption includes such things as buying food and going to a concert.

Saving
The act of not consuming all of one's current income. Whatever is not consumed out of spendable income is, by definition, saved. *Saving* is an action measured over time (a flow), whereas *savings* are a stock, an accumulation resulting from the act of saving in the past.

Consumption goods
Goods bought by households to use up, such as food, clothing, and movies.

Investment
The spending by businesses on things such as machines and buildings, which can be used to produce goods and services in the future. The investment part of total income is the portion that will be used in the process of producing goods in the future.

Capital goods
Producer durables; nonconsumable goods that firms use to make other goods.

be able to consume it (and perhaps more if it earns interest) at some future time. That is the distinction between **consumption** and **saving.** Consumption is the act of using income for the purchase of consumption goods. **Consumption goods** are goods purchased by households for immediate satisfaction. Consumption goods are such things as food, clothing, and movies. By definition, whatever you do not consume you save and can consume at some time in the future.

Stocks and Flows: The Difference Between Saving and Savings. It is important to distinguish between *saving* and *savings. Saving* is an action that occurs at a particular rate—for example, $10 a week or $520 a year. This rate is a flow. It is expressed per unit of time, usually a year. Implicitly, then, when we talk about saving, we talk about a *flow* or rate of saving. *Savings,* by contrast, is a *stock* concept, measured at a certain point or instant in time. Your current *savings* are the result of past *saving.* You may presently have *savings* of $2,000 that are the result of four years' *saving* at a rate of $500 per year. Consumption, being related to saving, is also a flow concept. You consume from after-tax income at a certain rate per week, per month, or per year.

Relating Income to Saving and Consumption. Obviously, a dollar of take-home income can be either consumed or not consumed. Realizing this, we can see the relationship among saving, consumption, and disposable income:

$$Consumption + saving \equiv disposable\ income$$

This is called an *accounting identity.* It has to hold true at every moment in time. From it we can derive the definition of saving:

$$Saving \equiv disposable\ income - consumption$$

Recall that disposable income is what you actually have left to spend after you pay taxes.

Investment

Investment is also a flow concept. *Investment* as used in economics differs from the common use of the term, as we have already pointed out. In common speech, it is often used to describe putting money into the stock market or real estate. In economic analysis, investment is defined as expenditures by firms on new machines and buildings—**capital goods**—that are expected to yield a future stream of income. This we have already called *fixed investment.* We also included changes in business inventories in our definition. This we have already called *inventory investment.*

CONCEPTS IN BRIEF

- If we assume that we are operating on a horizontal short-run aggregate supply curve, the equilibrium level of real GDP per year is completely demand determined.
- *Saving* is a flow, something that occurs over time. It equals disposable income minus consumption. *Savings* are a stock. They are the accumulation resulting from saving.
- Investment is also a flow. It includes expenditures on new machines, buildings, and equipment and changes in business inventories.

DETERMINANTS OF PLANNED CONSUMPTION AND PLANNED SAVING

In the classical model, the supply of saving was determined by the rate of interest: The higher the rate of interest, the more people wanted to save and therefore the less people wanted to consume. According to Keynes, the interest rate is not the primary determinant of an individual's saving and consumption decisions.

> **Keynes argued that saving and consumption decisions depend primarily on an individual's real current income.**

The relationship between planned consumption expenditures of households and their current level of real income has been called the **consumption function.** It shows how much all households plan to consume per year at each level of real disposable income per year. Using for the moment only columns 1, 2, and 3 of Table 12-1, we will present a consumption function for a hypothetical household.

We see from Table 12-1 that as real disposable income rises, planned consumption also rises, but by a smaller amount, as Keynes suggested. Planned saving also increases with disposable income. Notice, however, that below an income of $10,000, the planned saving of this hypothetical family is actually negative. The further that income drops below that

Consumption function
The relationship between amount consumed and disposable income. A consumption function tells us how much people plan to consume at various levels of disposable income.

TABLE 12-1

Real Consumption and Saving Schedules: A Hypothetical Case
Column 1 presents real disposable income from zero up to $20,000 per year; column 2 indicates planned consumption per year; column 3 presents planned saving per year. At levels of disposable income below $10,000, planned saving is negative. In column 4, we see the average propensity to consume, which is merely planned consumption divided by disposable income. Column 5 lists average propensity to save, which is planned saving divided by disposable income. Column 6 is the marginal propensity to consume, which shows the proportion of *additional* income that will be consumed. Finally, column 7 shows the proportion of *additional* income that will be saved, or the marginal propensity to save.

Combination	(1) Real Disposable Income per Year (Y_d)	(2) Planned Real Consumption per Year (C)	(3) Planned Real Saving Per Year $(S \equiv Y_d - C)$ (1) − (2)	(4) Average Propensity to Consume $(APC \equiv C/Y_d)$ (2) ÷ (1)	(5) Average Propensity to Save $(APS \equiv S/Y_d)$ (3) ÷ (1)	(6) Marginal Propensity to Consume $(MPC \equiv \Delta C/\Delta Y_d)$	(7) Marginal Propensity to Save $(MPS \equiv \Delta S/\Delta Y_d)$
A	$ 0	$ 2,000	$−2,000	—	—	—	—
B	2,000	3,600	− 1,600	1.8	−.8	.8	.2
C	4,000	5,200	−1,200	1.3	−.3	.8	.2
D	6,000	6,800	− 800	1.133	−.133	.8	.2
E	8,000	8,400	− 400	1.05	−.05	.8	.2
F	10,000	10,000	0	1.0	.0	.8	.2
G	12,000	11,600	400	.967	.033	.8	.2
H	14,000	13,200	800	.943	.057	.8	.2
I	16,000	14,800	1,200	.925	.075	.8	.2
J	18,000	16,400	1,600	.911	.089	.8	.2
K	20,000	18,000	2,000	.9	.1	.8	.2

Dissaving

Negative saving; a situation in which spending exceeds income. Dissaving can occur when a household is able to borrow or use up existing owned assets.

level, the more the family engages in **dissaving,** either by going into debt or by using up some of its existing wealth.

Graphing the Numbers

When we constructed demand and supply curves in Chapter 3, we merely plotted the points from a table showing price-quantity pairs onto a diagram whose axes were labeled "Price" and "Quantity." We will graph the consumption and saving relationships presented in Table 12-1 in the same manner. In the upper part of Figure 12-1, the vertical axis measures the level of planned real consumption per year, and the horizontal axis measures the level of real disposable income per year. In the lower part of the figure, the horizontal axis is again real disposable income per year, but now the vertical axis is planned real saving per year. All of these are on a dollars-per-year basis, which emphasizes the point that we are measuring flows, not stocks.

As you can see, we have taken income-consumption and income-saving combinations A through K and plotted them. In the upper part of Figure 12-1, the result is called the

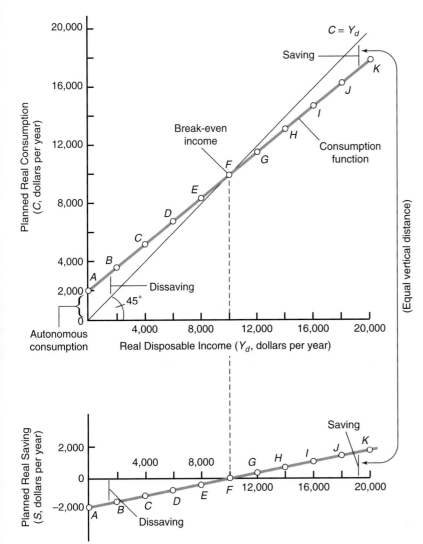

FIGURE 12-1

The Consumption and Saving Functions

If we plot the combinations of real disposable income and planned real consumption from columns 1 and 2 in Table 12-1, we get the consumption function. At every point on the 45-degree line, a vertical line drawn to the income axis is the same distance from the origin as a horizontal line drawn to the consumption axis. Where the consumption function crosses the 45-degree line at *F*, we know that consumption equals real disposable income and there is zero saving. The vertical distance between the 45-degree line and the consumption function measures the rate of saving or dissaving at any given income level. If we plot the relationship between column 1, real disposable income, and column 3, planned real saving, from Table 12-1, we arrive at the saving function shown in the lower part of this diagram. It is the complement of the consumption function presented above it.

consumption function. In the lower part, the result is called the *saving function.* Mathematically, the saving function is the *complement* of the consumption function because consumption plus saving always equals disposable income. What is not consumed is, by definition, saved. The difference between actual disposable income and the planned level of consumption per year *must* be the planned level of saving per year.

How can we find the rate of saving or dissaving in the upper part of Figure 12-1? We draw a line that is equidistant from both the horizontal and the vertical axes. This line is 45 degrees from either axis and is often called the **45-degree reference line.** At every point on the 45-degree reference line, a vertical line drawn to the income axis is the same distance from the origin as a horizontal line drawn to the consumption axis. Thus at point *F,* where the consumption function intersects the 45-degree line, real disposable income equals planned consumption. Point *F* is sometimes called the *break-even income point* because there is neither positive nor negative saving. This can be seen in the lower part of Figure 12-1 as well. The planned annual rate of saving at a real disposable income level of $10,000 is indeed zero.

45-degree reference line
The line along which planned real expenditures equal real national income per year.

Dissaving and Autonomous Consumption

To the left of point *F* in either part of Figure 12-1, this hypothetical family engages in dissaving, either by going into debt or by consuming existing assets, including savings. The amount of saving or dissaving in the upper part of the figure can be found by measuring the vertical distance between the 45-degree line and the consumption function. This simply tells us that if our hypothetical family starts above $10,000 of real disposable income per year and then temporarily finds its real disposable income below $10,000, it will not cut back its consumption by the full amount of the reduction. It will instead go into debt or consume existing assets in some way to compensate for part of the loss.

Now look at the point on the diagram where real disposable income is zero but planned consumption per year is $2,000. This amount of planned consumption, which does not depend at all on actual disposable income, is called **autonomous consumption.** The autonomous consumption of $2,000 is *independent* of the level of disposable income. That means that no matter how low the level of income of our hypothetical family falls, the family will always attempt to consume at least $2,000 per year. (We are, of course, assuming here that the family's real disposable income does not equal zero year in and year out. There is certainly a limit to how long our hypothetical family could finance autonomous consumption without any income.) That $2,000 of yearly consumption is determined by things other than the level of income. We don't need to specify what determines autonomous consumption; we merely state that it exists and that in our example it is $2,000 per year. Just remember that the word *autonomous* means "existing independently." In our model, autonomous consumption exists independently of the hypothetical family's level of real disposable income. (Later we will review some of the non-real-disposable-income determinants of consumption.) There are many possible types of autonomous expenditures. Hypothetically, we can consider that investment is autonomous—independent of income. We can assume that government expenditures are autonomous. We will do just that at various times in our discussions to simplify our analysis of income determination.

Autonomous consumption
The part of consumption that is independent of (does not depend on) the level of disposable income. Changes in autonomous consumption shift the consumption function.

Average Propensity to Consume and to Save

Let's now go back to Table 12-1, and this time let's look at columns 4 and 5: **average propensity to consume (APC)** and **average propensity to save (APS).** They are defined as follows:

Average propensity to consume (APC)
Consumption divided by disposable income; for any given level of income, the proportion of total disposable income that is consumed.

Average propensity to save (APS)
Saving divided by disposable income; for any given level of income, the proportion of total disposable income that is saved.

Exercise 12.1

Visit www.econtoday.com for more about average propensity to consume and save.

$$APC \equiv \frac{consumption}{real\ disposable\ income}$$

$$APS \equiv \frac{saving}{real\ disposable\ income}$$

Notice from column 4 in Table 12-1 that for this hypothetical family, the average propensity to consume decreases as real disposable income increases. This decrease simply means that the fraction of the family's real disposable income going to saving rises as income rises. The same fact can be found in column 5. The average propensity to save (APS), which at first is negative, finally hits zero at an income level of $10,000 and then becomes positive. In this example, the APS reaches a value of .1 at income level $20,000. This means that the household saves 10 percent of a $20,000 income.

It's quite easy for you to figure out your own average propensity to consume or to save. Just divide your total real disposable income for the year into what you consumed and what you saved. The result will be your personal APC and APS, respectively, at your current level of income. This gives the proportions of total income that are consumed and saved.

Marginal Propensity to Consume and to Save

Now we go to the last two columns in Table 12-1: **marginal propensity to consume (MPC)** and **marginal propensity to save (MPS).** We have used the term *marginal* before. It refers to a small incremental or decremental change (represented by Δ in Table 12-1). The marginal propensity to consume, then, is defined as

$$MPC \equiv \frac{change\ in\ consumption}{change\ in\ real\ disposable\ income}$$

The marginal propensity to save is defined similarly as

$$MPS \equiv \frac{change\ in\ saving}{change\ in\ real\ disposable\ income}$$

Marginal propensity to consume (MPC)

The ratio of the change in consumption to the change in disposable income. A marginal propensity to consume of .8 tells us that an additional $100 in take-home pay will lead to an additional $80 consumed.

Marginal propensity to save (MPS)

The ratio of the change in saving to the change in disposable income. A marginal propensity to save of .2 indicates that out of an additional $100 in take-home pay, $20 will be saved. Whatever is not saved is consumed. The marginal propensity to save plus the marginal propensity to consume must always equal 1, by definition.

What do MPC and MPS tell you? They tell you what percentage of a given increase or decrease in income will go toward consumption and saving, respectively. The emphasis here is on the word *change*. The marginal propensity to consume indicates how much you will change your planned rate of consumption if there is a change in your real disposable income. If your marginal propensity to consume is .8, that does not mean that you consume 80 percent of *all* disposable income. The percentage of your real disposable income that you consume is given by the average propensity to consume, or APC, which is not, in Table 12-1, equal to .8. In contrast, an MPC of .8 means that you will consume 80 percent of any *increase* in your disposable income. In general, we assume that the marginal propensity to consume is between zero and one. We assume that individuals increase their planned consumption by more than zero and less than 100 percent of any increase in real disposable income that they receive.

Consider a simple example in which we show the difference between the average propensity to consume and the marginal propensity to consume. Assume that your consumption behavior is exactly the same as our hypothetical family's behavior depicted in Table 12-1. You have an annual real disposable income of $18,000. Your planned consumption rate, then, from column 2 of Table 12-1 is $16,400. So your average propensity to consume is $16,400 ÷ $18,000 = .911. Now suppose that at the end of the year your boss gives you an after-tax bonus of $2,000. What would you do with that additional

$2,000 in real disposable income? According to the table, you would consume $1,600 of it and save $400. In that case, your *marginal* propensity to consume would be $1,600 ÷ $2,000 = .8, and your marginal propensity to save would be $400 ÷ $2,000 = .2. What would happen to your *average* propensity to consume? To find out, we add $1,600 to $16,400 of planned consumption, which gives us a new consumption rate of $18,000. The average propensity to consume is then $18,000 divided by the new higher salary of $20,000. Your APC drops from .911 to .9. By contrast, your MPC remains in our simplified example .8 all the time. Look at column 6 in Table 12-1. The MPC is .8 at every level of income. (Therefore, the MPS is always equal to .2 at every level of income.) Underlying the constancy of MPC is the assumption that the amount that you are willing to consume out of additional income will remain the same in percentage terms no matter what level of real disposable income is your starting point.

Some Relationships

Consumption plus saving must equal income. Both your total real disposable income and the change in total real disposable income are either consumed or saved. The proportions of either measure must equal 1, or 100 percent. This allows us to make the following statements:

$$APC + APS = 1 \ (= 100 \text{ percent of total income})$$

$$MPC + MPS = 1 \ (= 100 \text{ percent of the } \textit{change} \text{ in income})$$

The average propensities as well as the marginal propensities to consume and save must total 1, or 100 percent. Check the two statements by adding the figures in columns 4 and 5 for each level of real disposable income in Table 12-1. Do the same for columns 6 and 7.

Causes of Shifts in the Consumption Function

A change in any other relevant economic variable besides real disposable income will cause the consumption function to shift. There is a virtually unlimited number of such non-income determinants of the position of the consumption function. When population increases or decreases, for example, the consumption function will shift up or down, respectively. Changes in expectations can also shift the consumption function. If the average household believes that the rate of inflation is going to fall dramatically in the years to come, the current consumption function will probably shift down: Planned consumption would be less at every level of real disposable income than before this change in expectations. Real household **wealth** is also a determinant of the position of the consumption function. An increase in real wealth of the average household will cause the consumption function to shift upward. A decrease in real wealth will cause it to shift downward.

Wealth
The stock of assets owned by a person, household, firm, or nation. For a household, wealth can consist of a house, cars, personal belongings, bank accounts, and cash.

CONCEPTS IN BRIEF

- The consumption function shows the relationship between planned rates of consumption and real disposable income per year. The saving function is the complement of the consumption function because saving plus consumption must equal real disposable income.

- The average propensity to consume (APC) is equal to consumption divided by real disposable income. The average propensity to save (APS) is equal to saving divided by real disposable income.

- The marginal propensity to consume (MPC) is equal to the change in planned consumption divided by the change in real disposable income. The marginal propensity to save (MPS) is equal to the change in planned saving divided by the change in real disposable income.

- Any change in real disposable income will cause the planned rate of consumption to change; this is represented by a movement along the consumption function. Any change in a nonincome determinant of consumption will shift the consumption function.

DETERMINANTS OF INVESTMENT

Investment, you will remember, is defined as expenditures on new buildings and equipment and changes in business inventories. Real gross private domestic investment in the United States has been extremely volatile over the years relative to real consumption. If we were to look at net private domestic investment (investment after depreciation has been deducted), we would see that in the depths of the Great Depression and at the peak of the World War II effort, the figure was negative. In other words, we were eating away at our capital stock—we weren't even maintaining it by completely replacing depreciated equipment.

If we compare real investment expenditures historically with real consumption expenditures, we find that the latter are relatively less variable over time than the former. Why is this so? The answer is that the real investment decisions of businesspeople are based on highly variable, subjective estimates of how the economic future looks. We just discussed the role of expectations in determining the position of the consumption function. Expectations play an even greater role in determining the position of the investment function. This could account for much of the instability of investment over time.

The Planned Investment Function

Consider that at all times, businesses perceive an array of investment opportunities. These investment opportunities have rates of return ranging from zero to very high, with the number (or dollar value) of all such projects inversely related to the rate of return. Because a project is profitable only if its rate of return exceeds the opportunity cost of the investment—the rate of interest—it follows that as the interest rate falls, planned investment spending increases, and vice versa. Even if firms use retained earnings (internal financing) to fund an investment, the higher the market rate of interest, the greater the *opportunity cost* of using those retained earnings. Thus it does not matter in our analysis whether the firm must seek financing from external sources or can obtain such financing by using retained earnings. Just consider that as the interest rate falls, more investment opportunities will be profitable, and planned investment will be higher.

It should be no surprise, therefore, that the investment function is represented as an inverse relationship between the rate of interest and the value of planned investment. A hypothetical investment schedule is given in panel (a) of Figure 12-2 on page 254 and plotted in panel (b). We see from this schedule that if, for example, the rate of interest is 13 percent, the dollar value of planned investment will be $400 billion per year. Notice, by the way, that planned investment is also given on a per-year basis, showing that it represents a flow, not a stock. (The stock counterpart of investment is the stock of capital in the economy measured in dollars at a point in time.)

Panel (a)

Rate of Interest (percent per year)	Planned Investment per Year ($ trillions)
15	.2
14	.3
13	.4
12	.5
11	.6
10	.7
9	.8
8	.9
7	1.0
6	1.1

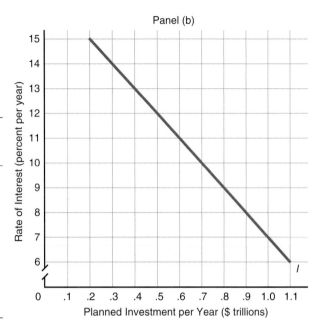

FIGURE 12-2

Planned Investment

In the hypothetical planned investment schedule in panel (a), the rate of planned investment is asserted to be inversely related to the rate of interest. If we plot the data pairs from panel (a), we obtain the investment function, *I*, in panel (b). It is negatively sloped.

What Causes the Investment Function to Shift?

Because planned investment is assumed to be a function of the rate of interest, any non-interest-rate variable that changes can have the potential of shifting the investment function. Expectations of businesspeople is one of those variables. If higher future sales are expected, more machines and bigger plants will be planned for the future. More investment will be undertaken because of the expectation of higher future profits. In this case the investment schedule, *I*, would shift outward to the right, meaning that more investment would be desired at all rates of interest. Any change in productive technology can potentially shift the investment function. A positive change in productive technology would stimulate demand for additional capital goods and shift the investment schedule, *I*, outward to the right. Changes in business taxes can also shift the investment schedule. If they increase, we predict a leftward shift in the planned investment function.

Exercise 12.2

Visit www.econtoday.com for more about housing as investment.

CONCEPTS IN BRIEF

- The planned investment schedule shows the relationship between investment and the rate of interest; it slopes downward.

- The non-interest-rate determinants of planned investment are expectations, innovation and technological changes, and business taxes.

- Any change in the non-interest-rate determinants of planned investment will cause the planned investment function to shift so that at each and every rate of interest a different amount of planned investment will be obtained.

CONSUMPTION AS A FUNCTION OF REAL NATIONAL INCOME

We are interested in determining the equilibrium level of real national income per year. But when we examined the consumption function earlier in this chapter, it related planned consumption expenditures to the level of real disposable income per year. We have already shown where adjustments must be made to GDP in order to get real disposable income (see Table 8-2 in Chapter 8). Real disposable income turns out to be less than real national income because net taxes (taxes minus government transfer payments) are usually about 11 to 18 percent of national income. A representative average in the 1990s is about 15 percent, so disposable income, on average, has in recent years been around 85 percent of national income.

If we are willing to assume that real disposable income, Y_d, differs from real national income by an amount T every year, we can relatively easily substitute real national income for real disposable income in the consumption function.

We can now plot any consumption function on a diagram in which the horizontal axis is no longer real disposable income but rather real national income, as in Figure 12-3. Notice that there is an autonomous part of consumption that is so labeled. The difference between this graph and the graphs presented earlier in this chapter is the change in the horizontal axis from real disposable income to real national income per year. For the rest of this chapter, assume that this calculation has been made, and the result is that the MPC out of real national income equals .8, suggesting that 20 percent of changes in real national income are either saved or paid in taxes: In other words, of an additional $100 earned, an additional $80 will be consumed.

The 45-Degree Reference Line

Like the earlier graphs, Figure 12-3 shows a 45-degree reference line. The 45-degree line bisects the quadrant into two equal spaces. Thus along the 45-degree reference line, planned consumption expenditures, C, equal real national income per year, Y. One can see, then, that at any point where the consumption function intersects the 45-degree reference line, planned consumption expenditures will be exactly equal to real national income per year, or $C = Y$. Note that in this graph, because we are looking only at planned consumption on the vertical axis, the 45-degree reference line is where planned consumption, C, is always equal to real

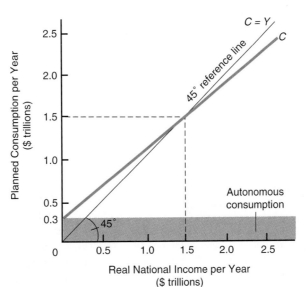

FIGURE 12-3

Consumption as a Function of Real National Income
This consumption function shows the rate of planned expenditures for each level of real national income per year. There is an autonomous component in consumption equal to $0.3 trillion. Along the 45-degree reference line, planned consumption expenditures per year, C, are identical to real national income per year, Y. The consumption curve intersects the 45-degree reference line at a value of $1.5 trillion per year.

national income per year, *Y.* Later, when we add investment, government spending, and net exports to the graph, the 45-degree reference line with respect to *all* planned expenditures will be labeled as such on the vertical axis. In any event, consumption and real national income are equal at $1.5 trillion per year. That is where the consumption curve, *C,* intersects the 45-degree reference line. At that income level, all income is consumed.

Adding the Investment Function

Another component of private aggregate demand is, of course, investment spending, *I.* We have already looked at the planned investment function, which related investment to the rate of interest. You see that as the downward-sloping curve in panel (a) of Figure 12-4. Recall from Figure 11-2 that the equilibrium rate of interest is determined at the intersection of the desired savings schedule, which is labeled *S* and is upward-sloping. The equilibrium rate of interest is 10 percent, and the equilibrium rate of investment is $700 billion per year. The $700 billion of real investment per year is *autonomous* with respect to real national income—that is, it is independent of real national income. In other words, given that we have a determinant investment level of $700 billion at a 10 percent rate of interest, we can treat this level of investment as constant, regardless of the level of national income. This is shown in panel (b) of Figure 12-4. The vertical distance of investment spending is $700 billion. Businesses plan on investing a particular amount—$700 billion per year— and will do so no matter what the level of real national income.

How do we add this amount of investment spending to our consumption function? We simply add a line above the *C* line that we drew in Figure 12-3 that is higher by the vertical distance equal to $700 billion of autonomous investment spending. This is shown by the arrow in panel (c) of Figure 12-4. Our new line, now labeled *C + I,* is called the *consumption plus investment line.* In our simple economy without government expenditures and net exports, the *C + I* curve represents total planned expenditures as they relate to different levels of real national income per year. Because the 45-degree reference line shows all

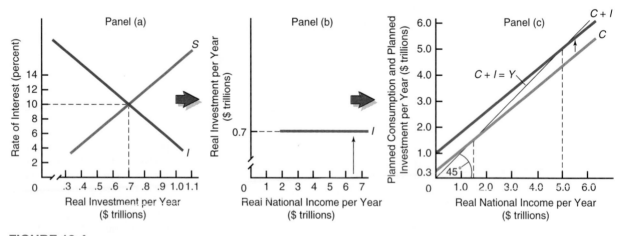

FIGURE 12-4

Combining Consumption and Investment

In panel (a), we show the determination of real investment in trillions of dollars per year. It occurs where the investment schedule intersects the saving schedule at an interest rate of 10 percent and is equal to $700 billion per year. In panel (b), investment is a constant $700 billion per year. When we add this amount to the consumption line, we obtain in panel (c) the *C + I* line, which is vertically higher than the *C* line by exactly $700 billion. Real national income is equal to *C + I* at $5 trillion per year where total planned expenditure, *C + I,* is equal to actual real national income, for this is where the *C + I* line intersects the 45-degree reference line, on which *C + I* is equal to *Y* at every point.

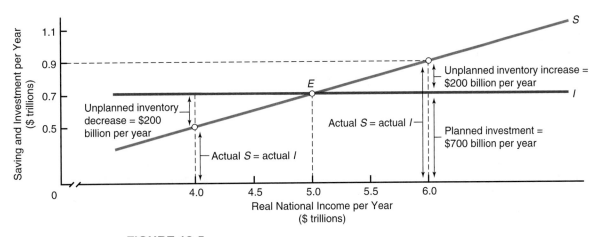

FIGURE 12-5

Planned and Actual Rates of Saving and Investment

Only at the equilibrium level of real national income of $5 trillion per year will planned saving equal actual saving, planned investment equal actual investment, and hence planned saving equal planned investment.

the points where planned expenditures (now $C + I$) equal real national income, we label it $C + I = Y$. Equilibrium Y equals $5 trillion per year. Equilibrium occurs when total planned expenditures equal total planned production (given that any amount of production in this model in the short run can occur without a change in the price level).

SAVING AND INVESTMENT: PLANNED VERSUS ACTUAL

Figure 12-5 shows the planned investment curve as a horizontal line at $700 billion per year. Investment is completely autonomous in this simplified model—it does not depend on the level of income.

The planned saving curve is represented by S. Because in our model whatever is not consumed is, by definition, saved, the planned saving schedule is the complement of the planned consumption schedule, represented by the C line in Figure 12-3. For better exposition, we look at only a small part of the saving and investment schedules—real national incomes between $4 and $6 trillion per year.

Why does equilibrium have to occur at the intersection of the planned saving and planned investment schedules? If we are at E in Figure 12-5, planned saving equals planned investment. All anticipations are validated by reality. There is no tendency for businesses to alter the rate of production or the level of employment because they are neither increasing nor decreasing their inventories in an unplanned way.

If we are producing at a real national income level of $6 trillion instead of $5 trillion, planned investment, as usual, is $700 billion per year, but it is exceeded by planned saving, which is $900 billion per year. This means that consumers will purchase less of total output than businesses had anticipated. Unplanned business inventories will now rise at the rate of $200 billion per year, bringing actual investment into line with actual saving because the $200 billion increase in inventories is included in actual investment. But this rate of output cannot continue for long. Businesses will respond to this unplanned increase in inventories by cutting back production and employment, and we will move toward a lower level of real national income.

Conversely, if the real national income is $4 trillion per year, planned investment continues annually at $700 billion; but at that output rate, planned saving is only $500 billion. This means that households and businesses are purchasing more of real national income than businesses had planned. Businesses will find that they must draw down their inventories below the planned level by $200 billion (business inventories will fall now at the unplanned rate of $200 billion per year), bringing actual investment into equality with actual saving because the $200 billion decline in inventories is included in actual investment (thereby decreasing it). But this situation cannot last forever either. In their attempt to increase inventories to the desired previous level, businesses will increase output and employment, and real national income will rise toward its equilibrium value of $5 trillion per year. Figure 12-5 demonstrates the necessary equality between actual saving and actual investment. Inventories adjust so that saving and investment, after the fact, are *always* equal in this simplified model. (Remember that changes in inventories count as part of investment.)

Every time the saving rate planned by households differs from the investment rate planned by businesses, there will be a shrinkage or an expansion in the circular flow of income and output (introduced in Chapter 8) in the form of unplanned inventory changes. Real national income and employment will change until unplanned inventory changes are again zero—that is, until we have attained the equilibrium level of real national income.

CONCEPTS IN BRIEF

- We assume that the consumption function has an autonomous part that is independent of the level of real national income per year. It is labeled "autonomous consumption."

- For simplicity, we assume that investment is autonomous with respect to real national income and therefore unrelated to the level of real national income per year.

- The equilibrium level of real national income can be found where planned saving equals planned investment.

- Whenever planned saving exceeds planned investment, there will be unplanned inventory accumulation, and national income will fall as producers reduce output. Whenever planned saving is less than planned investment, there will be unplanned inventory depletion, and national income will rise as producers increase output.

THINKING CRITICALLY ABOUT THE MEDIA

Small Businesses and New Jobs

One of the darlings of both politicians and the media is small businesses. According to a common explanation of job creation, small businesses are the source of all new jobs. In recent years, there has been a lot of talk concerning major corporate "restructuring" and the subsequent laying off of thousands of workers. Yet an examination of all of the available data does not support the conclusion that only small firms are hiring. Although it is true that small businesses hire at twice the rate, relative to their total employment, as midsized and big businesses, small businesses also *eliminate* jobs at a far higher rate. In other words, hiring is not the same as job creation because we have to look at the difference between hirings and firings. Indeed, while some big businesses are in the news because of layoffs, others are hiring and are not getting news coverage. For instance, one year, the media reported that Sears and Woolworth had laid off 80,000 workers; that same year, however, Wal-Mart quietly created almost 90,000 new jobs. The moral of the story is that headlines are not always based on the overall economic picture.

KEYNESIAN EQUILIBRIUM WITH GOVERNMENT AND THE FOREIGN SECTOR ADDED

Government

We have to add government spending, *G,* to our macroeconomic model. We assume that the level of resource-using government purchases of goods and services (federal, state, and local), *not* including transfer payments, is determined by the political process. In other words, *G* will be considered autonomous, just like investment (and a certain component of consumption). In the United States, resource-using government expenditures are around 25 percent of real national income. The other side of the coin, of course, is that there are taxes, which are used to pay for much of government spending. We will simplify our model greatly

Lump-sum tax
A tax that does not depend on income or the circumstances of the taxpayer. An example is a $1,000 tax that every family must pay, irrespective of its economic situation.

by assuming that there is a constant **lump-sum tax** of $1 trillion a year to finance $1 trillion of government spending. This lump-sum tax will reduce disposable income and consumption by the same amount. We show this in Table 12-2 (column 2), where we give the numbers for a complete model.

The Foreign Sector

Not a week goes by without a commentary in the media about the problem of our foreign trade deficit. For many years, we have been buying merchandise from foreigners—imports—the value of which exceeds the value of the exports we have been selling to them and service. The difference between exports and imports is *net exports,* which we label X in our graphs. The level of exports depends on international economic conditions, especially in the countries that buy our products. Imports depend on economic conditions here at home. For simplicity, let us assume that exports exceed imports (net exports, X, is positive) and furthermore that the level of net exports is autonomous—independent of national income. Assume a level of X of $100 billion per year. In Table 12-2, net exports is shown in column 8 as $100 billion per year.

Determining the Equilibrium Level of Real National Income per Year

We are now in a position to determine the equilibrium level of real national income per year under the continuing assumptions that the short-run aggregate supply curve is horizontal; that investment, government, and the foreign sector are autonomous; and that planned consumption expenditures are determined by the level of real national income. As can be seen in Table 12-2, total planned expenditures of $6.5 trillion per year equal real national income of $6.5 trillion per year, and this is where we reach equilibrium.

Remember that equilibrium *always* occurs when total planned expenditures equal total production (given that any amount of production in this model in the short run can occur without a change in the price level).

TABLE 12-2
The Determination of Equilibrium Real National Income with Net Exports
Figures are trillions of dollars.

(1) Real National Income	(2) Taxes	(3) Real Disposable Income	(4) Planned Consumption	(5) Planned Saving	(6) Planned Investment	(7) Government Spending	(8) Net Exports (exports − imports)	(9) Total Planned Expenditures (4) + (6) + (7) + (8)	(10) Unplanned Inventory Changes	(11) Direction of Change in Real National Income
2.0	1.0	1.0	1.1	−.1	.7	1.0	.1	2.9	−.9	Increase
2.5	1.0	1.5	1.5	0	.7	1.0	.1	3.3	−.8	Increase
3.0	1.0	2.0	1.9	.1	.7	1.0	.1	3.7	−.7	Increase
4.0	1.0	3.0	2.7	.3	.7	1.0	.1	4.5	−.5	Increase
5.0	1.0	4.0	3.5	.5	.7	1.0	.1	5.3	−.3	Increase
6.0	1.0	5.0	4.3	.7	.7	1.0	.1	6.1	−.1	Increase
6.5	1.0	5.5	4.7	.8	.7	1.0	.1	6.5	0	Neither (equilibrium)
7.0	1.0	6.0	5.1	.9	.7	1.0	.1	6.9	+.1	Decrease
8.0	1.0	7.0	5.9	1.1	.7	1.0	.1	7.7	+.3	Decrease

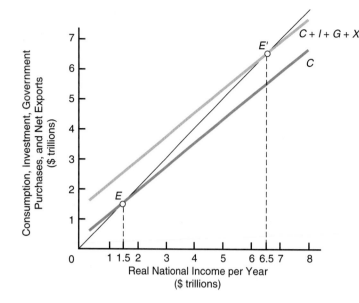

FIGURE 12-6

The Equilibrium Level of Real National Income
The consumption function, with no government and thus no taxes, is shown as C. When we add autonomous investment, government, taxes, and net exports, we obtain $C + I + G + X$. We move from E_1 to E_2. The equilibrium level of real national income is $6.5 trillion per year.

Now look at Figure 12-6, which shows the equilibrium level of real national income. There are two curves, one showing the consumption function, which is the exact duplicate of the one shown in Figure 12-3, and the other being the $C + I + G + X$ curve, which intersects the 45-degree reference line (representing equilibrium) at $6.5 trillion per year.

Whenever total planned expenditures differ from real national income, there are unplanned inventory changes. When total planned expenditures are greater than real national income, inventory levels drop in an unplanned manner. To get them back up, firms seek to expand their production, which increases real national income. Real national income rises toward its equilibrium level. Whenever total planned expenditures are less than real national income, the opposite occurs. There are unplanned inventory increases, causing firms to cut back on their production. The result is a drop in real national income toward the equilibrium level.

CONCEPTS IN BRIEF

- When we add autonomous investment, *I*, and autonomous government spending, *G*, to the consumption function, we obtain the $C + I + G$ curve, which represents total planned expenditures for a closed economy. In an open economy, we add the foreign sector, which consists of exports minus imports, or net exports, *X*. Total planned expenditures are thus represented by the $C + I + G + X$ curve.

- The equilibrium level of real national income can be found by locating the intersection of the total planned expenditures curve with the 45-degree reference line. At that level of real national income per year, planned consumption plus planned investment plus government expenditures plus net exports will equal real national income.

- Whenever total planned expenditures exceed real national income, there will be unplanned decreases in inventories; the size of the circular flow of income will increase, and a higher level of equilibrium real national income will prevail. Whenever planned expenditures are less than real national income, there will be unplanned increases in inventories; the size of the circular flow will shrink, and a lower equilibrium level of real national income will prevail.

THE MULTIPLIER

Look again at panel (c) of Figure 12-4. Assume for the moment that the only expenditures included in real national income are consumption expenditures. Where would the equilibrium level of income be in this case? It would be where the consumption function *(C)* intersects the 45-degree reference line, which is at $1.5 trillion per year. Now we add the autonomous amount of planned investment, or $700 billion, and then determine what the new equilibrium level of income will be. It turns out to be $5 trillion per year. Adding $700 billion per year of investment spending increased the equilibrium level of income by *five* times that amount, or by $3.5 trillion per year.

What is operating here is the multiplier effect of changes in autonomous spending. The **multiplier** is the number by which a permanent change in autonomous investment or autonomous consumption is multiplied to get the change in the equilibrium level of real national income. Any permanent increases in autonomous investment or in any autonomous component of consumption will cause an even larger increase in real national income. Any permanent decreases in autonomous spending will cause even larger decreases in the equilibrium level of real national income per year. To understand why this multiple expansion (or contraction) in the equilibrium level of real national income occurs, let's look at a simple numerical example.

We'll use the same figures we used for the marginal propensity to consume and to save. MPC will equal .8, or $\frac{4}{5}$, and MPS will equal .2, or $\frac{1}{5}$. Now let's run an experiment and say that businesses decide to increase planned investment permanently by $100 billion a year. We see in Table 12-3 that during what we'll call the first round in column 1, investment is

Multiplier
The ratio of the change in the equilibrium level of real national income to the change in autonomous expenditures; the number by which a change in autonomous investment or autonomous consumption, for example, is multiplied to get the change in the equilibrium level of real national income.

TABLE 12-3

The Multiplier Process
We trace the effects of a permanent $100 billion increase in autonomous investment spending on the equilibrium level of real national income. If we assume a marginal propensity to consume of .8, such an increase will eventually elicit a $500 billion increase in the equilibrium level of real national income per year.

(1) Round	(2) Annual Increase in Real National Income ($ billions per year)	(3) Annual Increase in Planned Consumption ($ billions per year)	(4) Annual Increase in Planned Saving ($ billions per year)
1 ($100 billion per year increase in *I*)	100.00	80.000	20.000
2	80.00	64.000	16.000
3	64.00	51.200	12.800
4	51.20	40.960	10.240
5	40.96	32.768	8.192
⋮	⋮	⋮	⋮
All later rounds	163.84	131.072	32.768
Totals (*C* + *I* + *G*)	500.00	400.000	100.000

Assumption: MPC = .8, or $\frac{4}{5}$

increased by $100 billion; this also means an increase in real national income of $100 billion, because the spending by one group represents income for another, shown in column 2. Column 3 gives the resultant increase in consumption by households that received this additional $100 billion in real income. This is found by multiplying the MPC by the increase in real income. Because the MPC equals .8, consumption expenditures during the first round will increase by $80 billion.

But that's not the end of the story. This additional household consumption is also spending, and it will provide $80 billion of additional real income for other individuals. Thus during the second round, we see an increase in real income of $80 billion. Now, out of this increased real income, what will be the resultant increase in consumption expenditures? It will be .8 times $80 billion, or $64 billion. We continue these induced expenditure rounds *ad infinitum* and find that because of an initial increase in autonomous investment expenditures of $100 billion, the equilibrium level of real national income has increased by $500 billion. A permanent $100 billion increase in autonomous investment spending has induced an additional $400 billion increase in consumption spending, for a total increase in real national income of $500 billion. In other words, the equilibrium level of real national income has changed by an amount equal to five times the change in investment.

The Multiplier Formula

It turns out that the autonomous spending multiplier is equal to the reciprocal of the marginal propensity to save. In our example, the MPC was $\frac{4}{5}$; therefore, because MPC + MPS = 1, the MPS was equal to $\frac{1}{5}$. The reciprocal is 5. That was our multiplier. A $100 billion increase in planned investment led to a $500 billion increase in the equilibrium level of real income. Our multiplier will always be the following:

$$\text{Multiplier} \equiv \frac{1}{1 - \text{MPC}} \equiv \frac{1}{\text{MPS}}$$

You can always figure out the multiplier if you know either the MPC or the MPS. Let's take some examples. If MPS = $\frac{1}{4}$,

$$\text{Multiplier} = \frac{1}{\frac{1}{4}} = 4$$

Repeating again that MPC + MPS = 1, then MPS = 1 − MPC. Hence we can always figure out the multiplier if we are given the marginal propensity to consume. In this example, if the marginal propensity to consume were given as $\frac{3}{4}$,

$$\text{Multiplier} = \frac{1}{1 - \frac{3}{4}} = \frac{1}{\frac{1}{4}} = 4$$

By taking a few numerical examples, you can demonstrate to yourself an important property of the multiplier:

The smaller the marginal propensity to save, the larger the multiplier.

Otherwise stated:

The larger the marginal propensity to consume, the larger the multiplier.

Demonstrate this to yourself by computing the multiplier when the marginal propensities to save equal $\frac{3}{4}$, $\frac{1}{2}$, and $\frac{1}{4}$. What happens to the multiplier as the MPS gets smaller?

When you have the multiplier, the following formula will then give you the change in the equilibrium level of real national income due to a permanent change in autonomous spending:

$$\text{Multiplier} \times \text{change in autonomous spending} =$$
$$\text{change in equilibrium level of real national income}$$

The multiplier, as we have mentioned, works for a permanent increase or permanent decrease in autonomous spending. In our earlier example, if the autonomous component of consumption had fallen by $100 billion, the reduction in the equilibrium level of real national income per year would have been $500 billion per year.

Significance of the Multiplier

Depending on the size of the multiplier, it is possible that a relatively small change in planned investment or autonomous consumption can trigger a much larger change in the equilibrium level of real national income per year. In essence, the multiplier magnifies the fluctuations in the equilibrium level of real national income initiated by changes in autonomous spending.

As was just stated, the larger the marginal propensity to consume, the larger the multiplier. If the marginal propensity to consume is $\frac{1}{2}$, the multiplier is 2. In that case, a $1 billion decrease in (autonomous) investment will elicit a $2 billion decrease in the equilibrium level of real national income per year. Conversely, if the marginal propensity to consume is $\frac{9}{10}$, the multiplier will be 10. That same $1 billion decrease in planned investment expenditures with a multiplier of 10 will lead to a $10 billion decrease in the equilibrium level of real national income per year.

EXAMPLE
Changes in Investment and the Great Depression

Changes in autonomous spending lead to shifts in the total expenditures $(C + I + G + X)$ curve and, as you have seen, cause a multiplier effect on the equilibrium level of real GDP per year. A classic example apparently occurred during the Great Depression. Indeed, some economists believe that it was an autonomous downward shift (collapse) in the investment function that provoked the Great Depression. Look at panel (a) of Figure 12-7 on page 264. There you see the net investment in the United States from 1929 to 1941 (expressed in 1992 dollars). Clearly, during business contractions, decision makers in the business world can and do decide to postpone long-range investment plans for buildings and equipment. This causes the business recovery to be weak unless those business plans are revised. If you examine real GDP in panel (b) of Figure 12-7, you see that the contraction that started in 1929 reached its trough in 1933. The expansion was relatively strong for the following four years, and then there was another contraction from 1937 to 1938. Some researchers argue that even though the 1937–1938 contraction was more severe than the initial one that started in 1929, it was short-lived because long-range investment plans were revised upward by the end of 1938.

FOR CRITICAL ANALYSIS: Relatively speaking, how healthy was the national economy in 1941? [Hint: Look at panel (b) of Figure 12-7.] ●

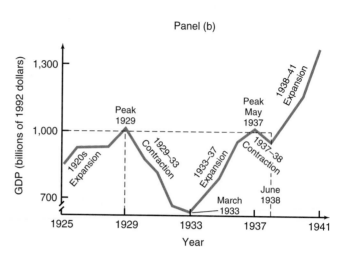

Panel (a)	
Year	Net Private Domestic Investment (billions of 1992 dollars)
1929	85.96
1930	24.48
1931	−26.89
1932	−83.34
1933	−80.20
1934	−43.51
1935	− 6.13
1936	18.39
1937	54.20
1938	− 9.54
1939	24.27
1940	66.89
1941	107.71

FIGURE 12-7

Net Private Domestic Investment and Real GDP During the Great Depression

In panel (a), you see how net private investment expressed in billions of 1992 dollars became negative starting in 1931 and stayed negative for several years. It became positive in 1936 and 1937, only to become negative again in 1938. Look at panel (b). There you see how changes in GDP seem to mirror changes in net private domestic investment.

Source: U.S. Bureau of the Census.

THE MULTIPLIER EFFECT WHEN THE PRICE LEVEL CAN CHANGE

Clearly, the multiplier effect on the equilibrium overall level of *real* national income will not be as great if part of the increase in *nominal* national income occurs because of increases in the price level. We show this in Figure 12-8. The intersection of AD_1 and *SRAS* is at a price level of 120 with equilibrium real national income of $5 trillion per year. An increase in autonomous spending shifts the aggregate demand curve outward to the right to AD_2. If price level remained at 120, the short-run equilibrium level of real GDP would increase to $5.5 trillion per year because, for the $100 billion increase in autonomous spending, the multiplier would be 5, as it was in Table 12-3. But the price level does not stay fixed because ordinarily *SRAS* is positively sloped. In this diagram, the new short-run equilibrium level of real national income is hypothetically $5.3 trillion of real national income per year. Instead of the multiplier being 5, the multiplier with respect to the equilibrium changes in the output of real goods and services—real national income—is only 3. The multiplier is smaller because part of the additional income is used to pay higher prices; not all is spent on increased output, as is the case when the price level is fixed.

If the economy is at an equilibrium level of real national income that is greater than *LRAS,* the implications for the multiplier are even more severe. Look again at Figure 12-8. The *SRAS* curve starts to slope upward more dramatically after $5 trillion of real national income per year. Therefore, any increase in aggregate demand will lead to a proportionally greater increase in the price level and a smaller increase in the equilibrium level of real national income per year. The multiplier effect of any increase in autonomous spending will be relatively small because most of the changes will be in the price level. Moreover,

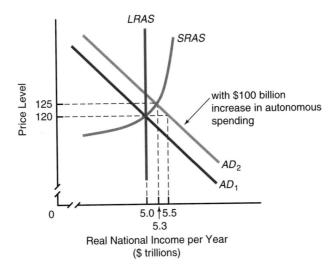

FIGURE 12-8

Multiplier Effect on Equilibrium of Real National Income

A $100 billion increase in autonomous spending (investment, government, or net exports), which moves AD_1 to AD_2, will yield a full multiplier effect only if prices are constant. If the price index increases from 120 to 125, the multiplier effect is less, and the equilibrium level of real national income goes up only to, say, $5.3 trillion per year instead of $5.5 trillion per year.

any increase in the short-run equilibrium level of real national income will tend to be temporary because the economy is temporarily above *LRAS*—the strain on its productive capacity will raise prices.

THE RELATIONSHIP BETWEEN AGGREGATE DEMAND AND THE $C + I + G + X$ CURVE

There is clearly a relationship between the aggregate demand curves that you studied in Chapters 10 and 11 and the $C + I + G + X$ curve developed in this chapter. After all, aggregate demand consists of consumption, investment, and government purchases, plus the foreign sector of our economy. There is a major difference, however, between the aggregate demand curve, *AD,* and the $C + I + G + X$ curve: The latter is drawn with the price level held constant, whereas the former is drawn, by definition, with the price level changing. In other words, the $C + I + G + X$ curve shown in Figure 12-6 on page 260 is drawn with the price level fixed. To derive the aggregate demand curve, we must now allow the price level to change. Look at the upper part of Figure 12-9 on page 266. Here we show the $C + I + G + X$ curve at a price level equal to 100 and equilibrium at $8 trillion of income per year. This gives us point *A* in the lower graph, for it shows what real income would be at a price level of 100.

Now let's assume that in the upper graph, the price level doubles to 200. What are the effects?

1. A higher price level can decrease the purchasing power of any cash that people hold (the real-balance effect). This is a decrease in real wealth, and it causes consumption expenditures, *C,* to fall, thereby putting downward pressure on the $C + I + G + X$ curve.
2. Because individuals attempt to borrow more to replenish their real cash balances, interest rates will rise, which will make it more costly for people to buy houses and cars (the interest rate effect). Higher interest rates make it more costly, for example, to install new equipment and to erect new buildings. Therefore, the rise in the price level indirectly causes a reduction in the quantity of aggregate goods and services demanded.
3. In an open economy, our higher price level causes the foreign demand for our goods to fall (the open economy effect). Simultaneously, it increases our demand for others' goods. If the foreign exchange price of the dollar stays constant for a while, there will

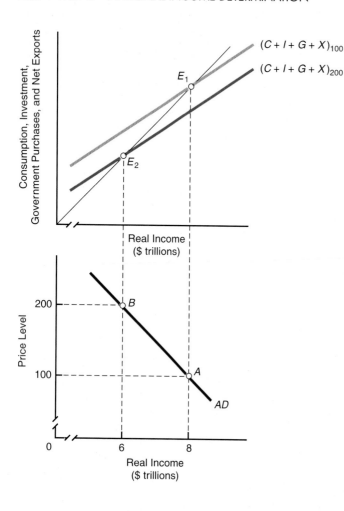

FIGURE 12-9

The Relationship Between *AD* and the *C* + *I* + *G* + *X* curve

In the upper graph, the *C* + *I* + *G* + *X* curve at a price level equal to 100 intersects the 45-degree reference line at E_1, or $8 trillion of real income per year. That gives us point *A* (price level = 100; real income = $8 trillion) in the lower graph. When the price level increases to 200, the *C* + *I* + *G* + *X* curve shifts downward, and the new equilibrium level of real income is at E_2 at $6 trillion per year. This gives us point *B* in the lower graph. Connecting points *A* and *B*, we obtain the aggregate demand curve.

be an increase in imports and a decrease in exports, thereby reducing the size of *X*, again putting downward pressure on the *C* + *I* + *G* + *X* curve.

The result is that a new *C* + *I* + *G* + *X* curve at a price level equal to 200 generates an equilibrium at E_2 at $6 trillion of real income per year. This gives us point *B* in the lower part of Figure 12-9. When we connect points *A* and *B*, we obtain the aggregate demand curve, *AD*.

CONCEPTS IN BRIEF

- Any change in autonomous spending shifts the expenditure curve and causes a multiplier effect on the equilibrium level of real national income per year.

- The multiplier is equal to the reciprocal of the marginal propensity to save.

- The smaller the marginal propensity to save, the larger the multiplier. Otherwise stated, the larger the marginal propensity to consume, the larger the multiplier.

- The *C* + *I* + *G* + *X* curve is drawn with the price level held constant, whereas the *AD* curve allows the price level to change. Each different price level generates a new *C* + *I* + *G* + *X* curve.

Higher yields on savings accounts may induce people to save more. If actual increases in real household net worth are taken into account, people are already saving more than the government has been saying.

CONCEPTS APPLIED:
CONSUMPTION, SAVING, INCOME, WEALTH

Visit www.econtoday.com for an Internet Activity that expands your understanding of these concepts.

Y ou learned in Chapter 11 that the rate of saving in the United States has fallen dramatically over the past few decades. As a percentage of GDP, net national saving is down to a mere 3 or 4 percent, a third or less of what it was in the 1960s. This is troublesome because saving is how we accumulate capital, which is needed for technological innovations and development.

Are We Measuring Saving Incorrectly?

Some economists do not accept the standard government definition of saving. They argue that looking at the portion of income that people do not consume tells us little about the increase in wealth in our society. Consider two households. One earns $50,000 and also consumes $50,000. By our standard definition, that household's saving is zero. But what if that household had an investment portfolio that increased in market value by $50,000 during the same year? Hasn't that household in effect "saved" $50,000? The household has accumulated additional assets worth $50,000, which could then be used to purchase machines or buildings.

Consider another household. It, too, earns $50,000. It spends only $25,000, however. By conventional accounting, it has saved $25,000. But what if it took that $25,000 not consumed and undertook an investment that turned out to be worth zero by the end of the year? At the end of the year, that household will have added zero to its wealth.

Thus perhaps the notion of "increase in wealth" is a more important concept when considering the state of our national economy and the likely course of its future. If individuals place their savings into terrible investments—perhaps encouraged by the sort of government-sanctioned tax shelters that were prevalent in the 1960s and

1970s—the nation is not better off, even though its official rate of saving might be high.

What Do the Data Show?

Figure 12-10 presents the real increase in household net wealth as a percentage of disposable income. Notice that it actually became negative during part of the 1970s and reached its peak at about 1985.

Perhaps we are not so bad off as we thought we were.

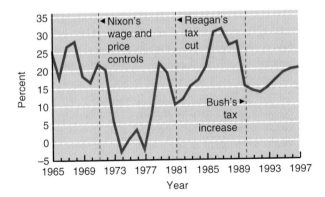

FIGURE 12-10

Increases in Real Wealth as a Ratio of GDP
This graph shows saving as a percentage of GDP. Here, though, saving is the real increase in household net worth at current market prices.
Source: Federal Reserve Board.

FOR CRITICAL ANALYSIS
1. "The rate of saving is not as important as what is done with those savings." Analyze this statement.
2. Why is your wealth position so important?

CHAPTER SUMMARY

1. If we assume that there are large amounts of excess capacity and labor unemployment, we can use the horizontal portion of the short-run aggregate supply curve. Therefore, prices are assumed to be constant, and nominal values are equivalent to real values.

2. A consumption function, in its simplest form, shows that current real consumption is directly related to current real disposable income. The complement of a consumption function is a saving function. A saving function shows the relationship between current real saving and current real disposable income.

3. The marginal propensity to consume shows how much additional income is devoted to consumption. The marginal propensity to save is the difference between 1 and the marginal propensity to consume. Otherwise stated, the marginal propensity to save plus the marginal propensity to consume must equal 1.

4. We must be careful to distinguish between average and marginal propensities. The average propensity to consume is the amount of total real consumption divided by total real disposable income. The average propensity to save is the total amount of real saving divided by total real disposable income. The marginal propensities relate to changes in consumption and saving resulting from changes in income.

5. Some nonincome determinants of planned consumption are wealth, expectations, and population.

6. Investment is made by the business sector of the economy. Investment is the spending by businesses on such things as new machines and buildings that can be used later in the production of goods and services. Investment is the use of resources to provide for future production. There are numerous determinants of investment, including the rate of interest, changes in expectations, innovation and technology, and business taxes.

7. When we add the consumption function, autonomous investment, autonomous government spending, and the autonomous net exports function, we obtain the $C + I + G + X$ curve, which gives us total planned expenditures per year. The equilibrium level of real national income occurs where the $C + I + G + X$ curve intersects the 45-degree reference line, or where total planned expenditures exactly equal real national income (total production).

8. When total planned expenditures exceed real national income, inventories will be drawn down more rapidly than planned. As a result, firms will expand production and, in the process, hire more workers, thus leading to an increase in output and employment. The opposite occurs when total planned expenditures are less than real national income.

9. Planned saving and planned investment must be equal at the equilibrium rate of real national income (ignoring government and foreign transactions). Whenever the actual level of real national income exceeds the equilibrium level, an unplanned inventory increase will trigger production cuts and layoffs. Whenever actual real national income is less than the equilibrium level of real national income, an unplanned inventory decrease will cause increased production and employment.

10. A key aspect of simplified Keynesian analysis is that a change in investment will result in a multiple change in equilibrium income. The size of the multiplier effect of a change in autonomous investment is positively related to the marginal propensity to consume. The higher the marginal propensity to consume, the greater the autonomous investment multiplier. We find the autonomous investment multiplier by first finding the marginal propensity to save (1 minus the marginal propensity to consume), expressed as a fraction, and taking the inverse of that fraction. A marginal propensity to consume of .8 means that the marginal propensity to save is .2 or $\frac{1}{5}$. The inverse of $\frac{1}{5}$ is 5; thus the investment multiplier is 5.

DISCUSSION OF PREVIEW QUESTIONS

1. What does the total planned expenditures curve indicate?

The total planned expenditures curve indicates what the community intends to spend at every level of real national income. In a closed (omitting international transactions), private (omitting government transactions) economy, the total planned expenditures curve equals the value of consumption expenditures plus the value of investment expenditures at every level of real national income.

2. How do we interpret the 45-degree reference line?

Because the 45-degree reference line bisects the total planned expenditures/real national income quadrant, total planned expenditures *exactly* equal real national income at all points on this line. Hence equilibrium is possible at any point on the 45-degree reference line.

3. What is the concept of the multiplier, how does it work, and what is its main determinant?

The multiplier concept says, simply, that a $1 shift in the total planned expenditures curve will cause the equilibrium level of national income to change by more than $1. In particular, a $1 increase (shift upward) in the total planned expenditures curve will cause the equilibrium level of national income to rise by more than $1; a $1 decrease (shift downward) in the total planned expenditures curve will cause the equilibrium level of national income to fall by more than $1. In a closed, private economy, changes (shifts) in the total planned expenditures curve are caused by changes (shifts) in autonomous consumption and autonomous investment.

Let's take an example. Suppose that we start from an equilibrium position and then autonomous net investment rises by $1 due to an increase in the output and sale of one machine priced at $1. The people who produced this machine receive an extra $1 in income (above last year's income). Thus income already rises by $1 in the first round. The people who produced the machine will spend some of the increase in their income and save some of it. Because one person's expenditure is another's income, income will rise again.

Thus if the MPC is $\frac{3}{4}$, the group that produced the machine (and received a $1 increase in income) will spend 75 cents on goods and services and will save 25 cents. The 75 cents spent becomes income for the people who produced the 75 cents' worth of consumer goods. Note that after two rounds, national income has already increased by $1.75 ($1 + $.75); we already have a multiplier effect. Moreover, there is no reason why this process should stop here; the people who just received an increase in income of 75 cents will spend some and save some. The amount they spend becomes income for others. Thus the multiplier effect exists because increases in income lead to increases in consumption expenditures, which in turn lead to further income increases. Because one person's expenditure is another's income, it follows that the higher the MPC, the more the equilibrium level of income will change for given changes in autonomous expenditures.

4. What might cause shifts in the total planned expenditures curve?

In our model, total planned expenditures equal consumption *(C)*, investment *(I)*, government purchases of goods and services *(G)*, and net exports *(X)*. For simplicity, we have made the last three components of total planned expenditures autonomous—that is, independent of the level of real disposable income. Consumption also has an autonomous component. Therefore, any change in the nonincome determinants of consumption—for example, changes in expectations—will shift the $C + I + G + X$ curve. Furthermore, because *I*, *G*, and *X* are all considered autonomous, any change in those functions will also shift the $C + I + G + X$ curve.

PROBLEMS

(Answers to the odd-numbered problems appear at the back of the book.)

12-1. Complete the accompanying table.
   a. Plot the consumption and saving schedules on graph paper.
   b. Determine the marginal propensity to consume and the marginal propensity to save.
   c. Determine the average propensity to consume and the average propensity to save for each level of income.

Disposable Income	Consumption	Saving
$ 500	$510	$_____
600	600	_____
700	690	_____
800	780	_____
900	870	_____
1,000	960	_____

Real National Income	Consumption Expenditures	Saving	Investment	APC	APS	MPC	MPS
$1,000	$1,100	$_____	$100	_____	_____	_____	_____
2,000	2,000	_____		_____	_____	_____	_____
3,000		_____		_____	_____	_____	_____
4,000		_____		_____	_____	_____	_____
5,000		_____		_____	_____	_____	_____
6,000		_____		_____	_____	_____	_____

12-2. Make a list of determinants, other than income, that might affect your personal MPC.

12-3. List each of the following under the heading "Stock" or "Flow."

a. The Chens have $100 of savings in the bank.
b. Smith earns $200 per week.
c. General Electric owns 2,000 autos.
d. Inventories rise at 400 units per year.
e. Lopez consumes $80 per week out of income.
f. The equilibrium quantity is 1,000 per day.
g. The corporation spends $1 billion per year on investments.

12-4. The rate of return on an investment on new machinery is 9 percent.

a. If the market interest rate is 9.5 percent, will the investment be carried out?
b. If the interest rate is 8 percent, will the machinery be purchased?
c. If the interest rate is 9 percent, will the machinery be purchased?

12-5. The data in the table above apply to a hypothetical economy. Assume that the marginal propensity to consume is constant at all levels of income. Further assume that investment is autonomous.

a. Draw a graph of the consumption function. Then add the investment function, giving you $C + I$.
b. Right under the first graph, draw in the saving and investment curves. Does the $C + I$ curve intersect the 45-degree line in the upper graph at the same level of real national income as where saving equals investment in the lower graph? (If not, redraw your graphs.)
c. What is the multiplier effect from the inclusion of investment?
d. What is the numerical value of the multiplier?
e. What is the equilibrium level of real national income and output without investment? With investment?
f. What will happen to income if autonomous investment increases by $100?
g. What will the equilibrium level of real national income be if autonomous consumption increases by $100?

12-6. Assume a closed, private economy.

a. If the MPC = 0, what is the multiplier?
b. What is the multiplier if the MPC = $\frac{1}{2}$? If the MPC = $\frac{3}{4}$? If the MPC = $\frac{9}{10}$? If the MPC = 1?
c. What happens to the multiplier as the MPC rises?
d. In what range does the multiplier fall?

12-7. Calculate the multiplier for the following cases.

a. MPC = .9
b. MPS = .3
c. MPS = .15
d. $C = \$100 + .65Y$

COMPUTER-ASSISTED INSTRUCTION

Consumption spending is the single most important component of desired aggregate demand. This computer session examines the determinants of consumption spending and saving, as well as the link between the marginal and average propensities to consume. In addition, a blend of numerical and graphical exercises is used to examine the basics of income determination, emphasizing the central role of the multiplier.

Complete problem and answer appear on disk.

THE KEYNESIAN CROSS AND THE MULTIPLIER

We can see the multiplier effect more clearly if we look at Figure B-1, in which we see only a small section of the graphs that we used in Chapter 12. We start with an equilibrium level of real national income of $6.5 trillion per year. This equilibrium occurs with total planned expenditures represented by $C + I + G + X$. The $C + I + G + X$ curve intersects the 45-degree reference line at $6.5 trillion per year. Now we increase investment, I, by $100 billion. This increase in investment shifts the entire $C + I + G + X$ curve vertically to $C + I' + G + X$. The vertical shift represents that $100 billion increase in autonomous investment. With the higher level of planned expenditures per year, we are no longer in equilibrium at E. Inventories are falling. Production will increase. Eventually, planned production will catch up with total planned expenditures. The new equilibrium level of real national income is established at E' at the intersection of the new $C + I' + G + X$ curve and the 45-degree reference line, along which $C + I + G + X = Y$ (total planned expenditures equal real national income). The new equilibrium level of real national income is $7 trillion per year. Thus the increase in equilibrium real national income is equal to five times the permanent increase in planned investment spending.

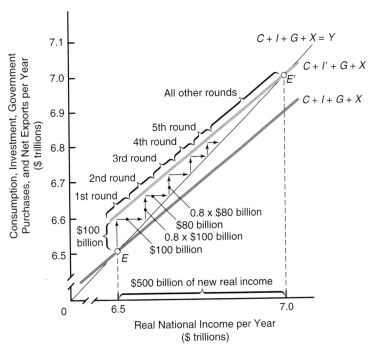

FIGURE B-1

Graphing the Multiplier

We can translate Table 12-3 on page 261 into graphic form by looking at each successive round of additional spending induced by an autonomous increase in planned investment of $100 billion. The total planned expenditures curve shifts from $C + I + G + X$, with its associated equilibrium level of real national income of $6.5 trillion, to a new curve labeled $C + I' + G + X$. The new equilibrium level of real national income is $7 trillion. Equilibrium is again established.

PART 4

FISCAL POLICY AND DEFICIT SPENDING

CHAPTER 13

FISCAL POLICY

One major government policy tool is fiscal policy, which involves changes in government spending, changes in taxes, or both. During periods when the economy is doing poorly, policymakers in Washington, D.C., have at times recommended and enacted tax cuts. At other times, when the federal government was spending much more than it was receiving in taxes, policymakers have recommended and enacted tax increases. How individuals and businesses react to such fiscal policy changes is a critical question. Is it possible, for example, that reductions in marginal tax rates cause individuals to work harder and businesses to invest more so that the economy will grow faster in the future? Before you can answer such a question, you need to know more about how fiscal policy works.

PREVIEW QUESTIONS

1. What is fiscal policy?

2. What is automatic fiscal policy, and how does it lend stability to an economy?

3. How does the crowding-out effect offset expansionary fiscal policy?

4. What types of time lags exist between the need for fiscal stimulus and the time when such stimulus actually affects the national economy?

Did You Know That . . . the first type of income tax was probably established in the 1200s and 1300s during times of war in the Italian city-states? America's first income tax, enacted in 1861 to help pay for the Civil War, was 3 percent on incomes over $800 a year. The following year it was raised to 5 percent on incomes over $10,000 a year. It was not until the Sixteenth Amendment to the Constitution was ratified in 1913 that most Americans came to know of the federal income tax, and even then very few had to pay it. Today, federal income taxes are taken for granted. More important for this chapter, the federal tax system is now viewed as being capable of affecting the equilibrium level of real GDP. On the spending side of the budget, changes in the federal government's expenditures are also viewed as potentially capable of changing the equilibrium level of real GDP.

FISCAL POLICY

Deliberate, discretionary changes in government expenditures and/or taxes in order to achieve certain national economic goals is the realm of **fiscal policy.** Some national goals are high employment (low unemployment), price stability, economic growth, and improvement in the nation's international payments balance. Fiscal policy can be thought of as a deliberate attempt to cause the economy to move to full employment and price stability more quickly than it otherwise might.

Fiscal policy has typically been associated with the economic theories of John Maynard Keynes and what is now called *traditional* Keynesian analysis. Recall from Chapter 11 that Keynes's explanation of the Great Depression was that there was insufficient aggregate demand. Because he believed that wages and prices were "sticky downward," he argued that the classical economists' view of the economy automatically moving toward full employment was inaccurate. To Keynes and his followers, government had to step in to increase aggregate demand. In other words, expansionary fiscal policy initiated by the federal government was the way to ward off recessions and depressions.

Traditional Keynesian economics dominated academic and government policymaking debates (and often actions) in the 1960s and 1970s. Perhaps the best-known policy action based on traditional Keynesian theory was the Kennedy-Johnson tax cut of 1964. When John Kennedy took office in 1961 with the claim that he wanted to "get the country moving again," his advisers recommended a tax cut. The tax cut did not occur until after Kennedy's death, when Lyndon Johnson was in office. In 1964, federally collected taxes were cut by $11 billion. From 1964 to 1965, the unemployment rate fell from 5.2 percent to 4.5 percent.

As you will see in Chapter 18, modern-day variants of Keynesian analysis are now taking center stage in policymaking discussions.

Fiscal policy
The discretionary changing of government expenditures and/or taxes in order to achieve national economic goals, such as high employment with price stability.

Changes in Government Spending

Recall that in Chapter 10 (Figures 10-8 and 10-9 on pages 220 and 221), we looked at the contractionary gap and the expansionary gap. The former was defined as the amount by which the current level of real GDP fell short of how much the economy could be producing if it were operating on its *LRAS.* The latter was defined as the amount by which the equilibrium level of real GDP exceeds the long-run equilibrium level as given by *LRAS.* In this section we examine fiscal policy in the context of a contractionary gap.

When There Is a Contractionary Gap. The government, along with firms, individuals, and foreigners, is one of the spending agents in the economy. When the government

Exercise 13.1
Visit www.econtoday.com for more about the federal budget.

Panel (a)

Panel (b)

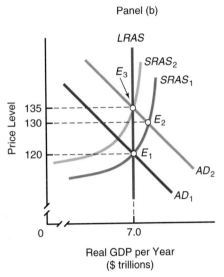

FIGURE 13-1

Expansionary Fiscal Policy: Two Scenarios

If there is a contractionary gap and equilibrium is at E_1 in panel (a), fiscal policy can presumably increase aggregate demand to AD_2. The new equilibrium is at E_2 at higher real GDP per year and a higher price level. If, though, we are already on *LRAS* as in panel (b), expansionary fiscal policy will simply lead to a temporary equilibrium at E_2 and a final equilibrium at E_3, again at *LRAS* of $7 trillion of real GDP per year but at a higher price level of 135.

decides to spend more, all other things held constant, the dollar value of total spending must rise. Look at panel (a) of Figure 13-1. We start at short-run equilibrium with AD_1 intersecting *SRAS* at $6.5 trillion of real GDP per year. There is a contractionary gap of $500 billion of real GDP per year—the difference between *LRAS* (the economy's long-run potential) and the short-run equilibrium level of real GDP per year. When the government decides to spend more, the aggregate demand curve shifts to the right to AD_2. Here we assume that the government knows exactly how much more to spend so that AD_2 intersects *SRAS* at $7 trillion, or at *LRAS*. Because of the upward-sloping *SRAS*, the price level has risen from 120 to 130. Real GDP has gone to $7 trillion per year. (Nominal GDP has gone up by even more because it consists of the price level index times real GDP. Here the GDP deflator has gone up by $10 \div 120 = 8.33$ percent.)[1]

When the Economy Is Operating on Its *LRAS.*   Suppose that the economy is operating on *LRAS*, as in panel (b) of Figure 13-1. An increase in government spending shifts the aggregate demand curve from AD_1 to AD_2. Both prices and real output of goods and services begin to rise toward the intersection of E_2. But this rate of real GDP per year is untenable in the long run because it exceeds *LRAS*. In the long run, expectations of input owners—workers, owners of capital and raw materials, and so on—are revised. The short-run aggregate supply curve shifts from $SRAS_1$ to $SRAS_2$ because of higher prices and higher resource costs. Real GDP returns to the *LRAS* level of $7 trillion per year. The full impact of the increased government expenditures is on the price level only, which increases to 135. Therefore, an attempt to increase real GDP above its long-run equilibrium can be accomplished only in the short run.

Reductions in Government Spending.   The entire process shown in Figure 13-1 can be reversed. Government can reduce spending, thereby shifting the aggregate demand curve inward. You should be able to show how this affects the equilibrium level of the price index and the real output of goods and services (real GDP) on similar diagrams.

---

[1]Percent change in price index $= \dfrac{\text{change in price index}}{\text{price index}} = \dfrac{130 - 120}{120} = 8.33$ percent

Changes in Taxes

The spending decisions of firms, individuals, and foreigners depend on the taxes levied on them. Individuals in their role as consumers look to their disposable (after-tax) income when determining their desired rate of consumption. Firms look at their after-tax profits when deciding on the level of investment to undertake. Foreigners look at the tax-inclusive cost of goods when deciding whether to buy in the United States or elsewhere. Therefore, holding all other things constant, a rise in taxes causes a reduction in aggregate demand for three reasons: (1) It reduces consumption, (2) it reduces investment, and (3) it reduces net exports. What actually happens depends, of course, on whom the taxes are levied.

When the Current Short-Run Equilibrium Is Greater than *LRAS*. Assume that aggregate demand is AD_1 in panel (a) of Figure 13-2. It intersects *SRAS* at E_1, which is at a level greater than *LRAS*. In this situation, an increase in taxes shifts the aggregate demand curve inward to the left. For argument's sake, assume that it intersects *SRAS* at E_2, or exactly where *LRAS* intersects AD_2. In this situation, the equilibrium level of real GDP falls from $7.5 trillion per year to $7 trillion per year. The price level index falls from 120 to 100.

If the Economy Is in Long-Run Equilibrium. Assume that the economy is already at short-run and long-run equilibrium as shown in panel (b) of Figure 13-2. The aggregate demand curve, AD_1, intersects both *LRAS* and *SRAS* at $7 trillion of real GDP per year. If aggregate demand decreases to AD_2, a new temporary equilibrium will occur at E_2 with the price level at 110 and real equilibrium GDP at $6.5 trillion per year. That means that in the short run, prices and the real output of goods and services fall. Input suppliers revise their expectations downward. The short-run aggregate supply curve shifts to $SRAS_2$. The real level of equilibrium GDP returns to the *LRAS* level of $7 trillion per year. The full *long-run* impact of fiscal policy in this situation is solely on the price level, which falls to 100.

Effects of a Reduction in Taxes. The effects of a reduction in taxes are exactly the reverse of the effects of an increase in taxes. Figure 13-1 on page 277 and the accompanying discussion of the effects of an increase in government expenditures provide the full analysis.

Panel (a)

Panel (b)

FIGURE 13-2

Contractionary Fiscal Policy: Two Scenarios
In panel (a), the economy is initially at E_1, which exceeds *LRAS*. Contractionary fiscal policy can move aggregate demand to AD_2 so the new equilibrium is at E_2 at a lower price level and now at *LRAS*. In panel (b), similar contractionary fiscal policy initially moves equilibrium from E_1 to E_2, but then it goes to E_3 at *LRAS*. The only long-run effect is to lower the price level to 100.

Tax Rates and Tax Revenues

Every time the federal government—or state and local governments, for that matter—announces a change in tax rates, the media are quick to pick up on projected increases or decreases in tax revenues. The arithmetic is simple: If the Treasury obtains $100 billion from the highest-earning individuals, it will garner $120 billion if their tax rates are increased by 20 percent. But tax revenues received after the tax rate increase are nowhere near those projected. Why? Because individuals and businesses are not static—they respond to higher marginal tax rates by retiring earlier, entering the job market later, engaging in the off-the-books underground economy, quitting second jobs, and compensating in other ways. The rule must be this: Never assume a static economy.

POLICY EXAMPLE
Did the New Deal Really Provide a Stimulus?

Many researchers have pointed out that Roosevelt's New Deal was influenced by Keynes's view that government had to increase "effective" aggregate demand. To be sure, Roosevelt's New Deal included what appeared on the surface to be large federal government expenditures and numerous government jobs programs. We have to look at the total picture, however. During the Great Depression, taxes were raised repeatedly. The Revenue Act of 1932, for example, passed during the depths of the Depression, brought the largest percentage increase in federal taxes in the history of the United States in peacetime—it almost doubled total federal tax revenues. Federal government deficits during the Depression years were small. In fact, in 1937 the total government budget—including federal, state, and local levels—was in surplus by $300 million. That means that at the same time that the federal government was increasing expenditures, local and state governments were decreasing them. If we measure the total of federal, state, and local fiscal policies, we find that they were truly expansive only in 1931 and 1936 compared to what the government was doing prior to the Great Depression. These two years were expansive only because of large veterans' payments, passed by Congress in both years over the vigorous opposition of the president.

FOR CRITICAL ANALYSIS: What other aspects of Roosevelt's New Deal might be studied to see if they had expansionary effects on the national economy? •

CONCEPTS IN BRIEF

- Fiscal policy is defined as the discretionary change in government expenditures and/or taxes in order to achieve such national goals as high employment or reduced inflation.
- If there is a contractionary gap and the economy is operating at less than long-run average supply (LRAS), an increase in government spending can shift the aggregate demand curve to the right and perhaps lead to a higher equilibrium level of real GDP per year. If the economy is already operating on LRAS, in contrast, expansionary fiscal policy in the long run simply leads to a higher price level.
- Changes in taxes can have similar effects on the equilibrium rate of real GDP and the price level. A decrease in taxes can lead to an increase in real GDP, but if the economy is already operating on its LRAS, eventually such decreases in taxes will lead only to increases in the price level.

POSSIBLE OFFSETS TO FISCAL POLICY

Fiscal policy does not operate in a vacuum. Important questions have to be answered: If government expenditures increase, how are those expenditures financed, and by whom? If taxes are increased, what does the government do with the taxes? What will happen if individuals worry about increases in *future* taxes because there is more government spending today with no increased taxes? All of these questions involve *offsets* to the effects of fiscal policy. We will look at each of them and others in detail.

Indirect Crowding Out

Let's take the first example of fiscal policy in this chapter, an increase in government expenditures. If government expenditures rise and taxes are held constant, something has to give. Our government does not simply take goods and services when it wants them. It has to pay for them. When it pays for them and does not simultaneously collect the same amount in taxes, it must borrow. That means that an increase in government spending without raising taxes creates additional government borrowing from the private sector (or from foreigners).

The Interest Rate Effect. Holding everything else constant, if the government attempts to borrow more from the private sector to pay for its increased budget deficit, it is not going to have an easy time selling its bonds. If the bond market is in equilibrium, when the government tries to sell more bonds, it is going to have to offer a better deal in order to get rid of them. A better deal means offering a higher interest rate. This is the interest rate effect of expansionary fiscal policy financed by borrowing from the public. In this sense, when the federal government finances increased spending by additional borrowing, it may push interest rates up. When interest rates go up, it is more expensive for firms to finance new construction, equipment, and inventories. It is also more expensive for individuals to finance their cars and homes. Thus a rise in government spending, holding taxes constant (in short, deficit spending), tends to crowd out private spending, dampening the positive effect of increased government spending on aggregate demand. This is called the **crowding-out effect.** In the extreme case, the crowding out may be complete, with the increased government spending having no net effect on aggregate demand. The final result is simply more government spending and less private investment and consumption. Figure 13-3 shows how the crowding-out effect occurs.

The Firm's Investment Decision. To understand the interest rate effect better, consider a firm that is contemplating borrowing $100,000 to expand its business. Suppose that the interest rate is 9 percent. The interest payments on the debt will be 9 percent times $100,000, or $9,000 per year ($750 per month). A rise in the interest rate to 12 percent will push the payments to 12 percent of $100,000, or $12,000 per year ($1,000 per month). The extra $250 per month in interest expenses will discourage some firms from making the investment. Consumers face similar decisions when they purchase houses and cars. An increase in the interest rate causes their monthly payments to go up, thereby discouraging some of them from purchasing cars and houses.

Graphical Analysis. You see in Figure 13-4 that the initial equilibrium, E_1, is below *LRAS*. But suppose that government expansionary fiscal policy in the form of increased

Crowding-out effect
The tendency of expansionary fiscal policy to cause a decrease in planned investment or planned consumption in the private sector; this decrease normally results from the rise in interest rates.

FIGURE 13-3
The Crowding-out Effect in Words

FIGURE 13-4

The Crowding-out Effect
Expansionary fiscal policy that causes deficit financing initially shifts AD_1 to AD_2. Equilibrium initially moves toward E_2. But because of crowding out, the aggregate demand curve shifts inward to AD_3, and the new short-run equilibrium is at E_3.

government spending (without increasing taxes) shifts aggregate demand from AD_1 to AD_2. In the absence of the crowding-out effect, the real output of goods and services would increase to \$7 trillion per year, and the price level would rise to 120 (point E_2). With the (partial) crowding-out effect, however, as investment and consumption decline, partly offsetting the rise in government spending, the aggregate demand curve shifts inward to the left to AD_3. The new equilibrium is now at E_3, with real GDP of \$6.75 trillion per year at a price level of 115.

Planning for the Future: The New Classical Economics

Economists have implicitly assumed that people look at changes in taxes or changes in government spending only in the present. What if people actually think about the size of *future* tax payments? Does this have an effect on how they react to an increase in government spending with no tax increases? Some economists, who call themselves the *new classical economists,* believe that the answer is yes. What if people's horizons extend beyond this year? Don't we then have to take into account the effects of today's government policies on the future?

Consider an example. If the government wants to spend \$1 today, it can raise tax revenues by \$1 and the public's responsibility to the government for that particular dollar has now been met and will never return. Alternatively, the government can borrow \$1 today and the public will owe \$1 plus interest later. Realizing that \$1 today is mathematically equivalent to \$1 plus interest next year, people may save the \$1 to meet the future tax liabilities. Therefore, whether the \$1 spending is financed by taxation or by borrowing, the two methods of finance are equivalent.

Increased government spending without an increase in taxes, according to the new classical economists, will not necessarily have a large impact on aggregate demand. In terms of Figure 13-4, the aggregate demand curve will shift inward from AD_2 to AD_3. In the extreme case, if consumers fully compensate for a higher tax liability in the future by saving more, the aggregate demand curve shifts all the way back to AD_1 in Figure 13-4. This is the case of individuals fully discounting their increased tax liabilities. The result is that an increased budget deficit created entirely by a current tax cut has literally no effect on the economy. This is known as the **Ricardian equivalence theorem,** after the nineteenth-century economist David Ricardo, who first developed the argument publicly.

Ricardian equivalence theorem
The proposition that an increase in the government budget deficit has no effect on aggregate demand.

Though the Ricardian equivalence theorem has generated much theoretical excitement, recent empirical studies cast some doubt on its relevance. During the 1980s, government spending exceeded government taxes by over $100 billion every year. There is little evidence that, in response, private saving rates increased during that same time period.

Direct Crowding Out

Government has a distinct comparative advantage over the private sector in certain activities such as diplomacy and national defense. Otherwise stated, certain resource-using activities in which the government engages do not compete with the private sector. In contrast, some of what government does competes directly with the private sector, such as education. When government competes with the private sector, **direct expenditure offsets** to fiscal policy may occur. For example, if the government starts providing milk at no charge to students who are already purchasing milk, there is a direct expenditure offset. Households spend less directly on milk, but government spends more.

The normal way to analyze the impact of an increase in government spending on aggregate demand is implicitly to assume that government spending is *not* a substitute for private spending. This is clearly the case for an ICBM missile. Whenever government spending is a substitute for private spending, however, a rise in government spending causes a direct reduction in private spending to offset it.

Direct expenditure offsets
Actions on the part of the private sector in spending money that offset government fiscal policy actions. Any increase in government spending in an area that competes with the private sector will have some direct expenditure offset.

The Extreme Case. In the extreme case, the direct expenditure offset is dollar for dollar, so we merely end up with a relabeling of spending from private to public. Assume that you have decided to spend $100 on groceries. Upon your arrival at the checkout counter, you are met by a U.S. Department of Agriculture official. She announces that she will pay for your groceries—but only the ones in the cart. Here increased government spending is $100. You leave the store in bliss. But just as you are deciding how to spend the $100, an Internal Revenue Service agent meets you. He announces that as a result of the current budgetary crisis, your taxes are going to rise by $100. You have to pay right now. Increases in taxes have now been $100. We have a balanced-budget increase in government spending. Under the assumption of a complete direct expenditure offset, there would be no change in total spending. We simply end up with higher government spending, which directly crowds out exactly the same amount of consumption. Aggregate demand and GDP are unchanged. Otherwise stated, if there is a full direct expenditure offset, the government spending multiplier is zero.

The Less Extreme Case. Much government spending has a private-sector substitute. When government expenditures increase, there is a tendency for private spending to decline somewhat (but not in proportion), thereby mitigating the upward impact on total aggregate demand. To the extent that there are some direct expenditure offsets to expansionary fiscal policy, predicted changes in aggregate demand will be lessened. Consequently, real output and the price level will be less affected.

POLICY EXAMPLE
Crowding-out Effects During World War II

Most American history books point to World War II as a clear-cut example of beneficial expansionary fiscal policy in action. The U.S. economy was pulled out of the Great Depression by enormous governmental outlays for the war effort—or so the story goes. The actual situation was a little more complex, though. The U.S. economy's growth rate from 1933 to 1941 was already higher than that of any other recorded peace-time period of the same length. Moreover, the increase in military expenditures during World War II was not matched by a similar increase in total output. In fact, it looks as if the crowding-out effect was relatively great, at least much greater than the history books indicate. This can be readily observed in terms of what happened to per capita personal consumption expenditures. They dropped by 3.5 percent in real terms from 1941 and 1942 and did not rebound to 1941 levels until after 1944. In other words, the average American saw no real increase in living standards during the war, in spite of massive military expenditures.

FOR CRITICAL ANALYSIS: *Given the information presented here, what could you say about the government's spending multiplier during World War II?* ●

The Open Economy Effect

The last offset to fiscal policy that we will discuss involves the open economy effect. It is a variant of the crowding-out effect, but one that now works its way through changes in net exports. If government spending is increased without a rise in taxes or if taxes are decreased without a reduction in government spending, the federal government must borrow more. As we pointed out, the government has to offer more attractive interest rates, so overall interest rates go up. When interest rates go up in the United States, foreigners demand more securities such as U.S. government bonds. When they do this, they have to pay for the bonds with dollars. After all, the typical Japanese stock and bond firm cannot buy more U.S. government bonds without getting its hands on more U.S. dollars. This increases the demand for dollars at the same time that it increases the supply of yen. The value of the yen falls relative to the value of the dollar in international transactions. When this occurs, Japanese-made goods become cheaper in America, and American-made goods become more expensive in Japan. Americans want to buy more Japanese goods, and the Japanese want to buy fewer American goods. This causes a reduction in net exports *(X)* and cuts into any increase in aggregate demand. In sum, to the extent that federal deficit spending reduces net exports, the effect of expansionary fiscal policy will be less.

The Supply-Side Effects of Changes in Taxes

We have talked about changing taxes and changing government spending, the traditional tools of fiscal policy. We have not really talked about the possibility of changing marginal tax rates. Recall from Chapter 5 that the marginal tax rate is the rate applied to the last bracket of taxable income. In our federal tax system, rising marginal tax rates are applied to rising income. In that sense, the United States has a progressive federal individual income tax system. Expansionary fiscal policy might involve reducing marginal tax rates. Advocates of such changes argue that (1) lower tax rates will lead to an increase in productivity because individuals will work harder and longer, save more, and invest more; and (2) increased productivity will lead to more economic growth, which will lead to higher real GDP. The government, by applying lower marginal tax rates, will not necessarily lose tax revenues, for the lower marginal tax rates will be applied to a growing tax base because of economic growth—after all, tax revenues are the product of a tax rate times a tax base.

People who support this notion are called supply-side economists. **Supply-side economics** involves changing the tax structure to create incentives to increase productivity. Due to a shift outward to the right in the aggregate supply curve, there can be greater output without upward pressure on the price level.

Effect of Changes in Tax Rates on Labor. Consider the supply-side effects of taxes on labor. An increase in tax rates reduces the opportunity cost of leisure, thereby inducing individuals (at least on the margin) to reduce their work effort and to consume more leisure. But an increase in tax rates will also reduce spendable income, thereby shifting the demand for leisure curve inward to the left. Here a reduction in real spendable income shifts the demand curve for all goods and services, including leisure, inward to the left. The outcome of these two effects depends on which of them is stronger. Supply-side economists argue that in the 1970s and 1980s the first effect dominated: increases in marginal tax rates caused workers to work less and decreases in marginal tax rates caused workers to work more.

> **Supply-side economics**
> The notion that creating incentives for individuals and firms to increase productivity will cause the aggregate supply curve to shift outward.

INTERNATIONAL EXAMPLE
Islam and Supply-Side Economics

Supply-side economics has a long history, dating back to at least the fourteenth century. The greatest of medieval Islamic historians, Abu Zayd Abd-Ar-Rahman Ibn Khaldun (1332–1406) included an Islamic view of supply-side economics in his monumental book, *The Muqaddimah* (1377). He pointed out that "When tax assessments . . . upon the subjects are low, the latter have the energy and desire to do things. Cultural enterprises grow and increase. . . . [Therefore] the number of individual imposts [taxes] and assessments mounts." If taxes are increased both in size and rates, "the result is that the interest of subjects in cultural enterprises disappears, because when they compare expenditures and taxes with their income and gain and see little profit they make, they lose all hope." Ibn Khaldun concluded that "At the beginning of a dynasty, taxation yields a large revenue from small assessments. At the end of a dynasty, taxation yields a small revenue from large assessments."

FOR CRITICAL ANALYSIS: How do this Islamic scholar's economic theories apply to the modern world? •

CONCEPTS IN BRIEF

- Indirect crowding out occurs because of an interest effect in which the government's efforts to finance its deficit spending cause interest rates to rise, thereby crowding out private investment and spending, particularly on cars and houses. This is called the crowding-out effect.

- Many new classical economists believe in the Ricardian equivalence theorem, which argues that an increase in the government budget deficit has no effect on aggregate demand because individuals correctly perceive their increased future taxes and therefore save more today to pay for them.

- Direct crowding out occurs when government spending competes with the private sector and is increased. Direct expenditure offsets to fiscal policy may occur.

- There is an open economy effect that offsets fiscal policy. Like the crowding-out effect, it occurs because the government's increased deficit causes interest rates to rise. This encourages foreigners to invest more in American securities. When they do so, they demand more dollars, thereby increasing the international value of the dollar. As a result, American-made goods become more expensive abroad and foreign goods cheaper here, so America exports fewer goods and imports more.

- Changes in marginal tax rates may cause supply-side effects if a reduction in marginal tax rates induces enough additional work, saving, and investing. Government tax receipts can actually increase. This is called supply-side economics.

DISCRETIONARY FISCAL POLICY IN PRACTICE

We can discuss fiscal policy in a relatively precise way. We draw graphs with aggregate demand and supply curves to show what we are doing. We could even in principle estimate the offsets that were just discussed. However, even if we were able to measure all of these offsets exactly, would-be fiscal policymakers still face problems: which fiscal policy mix to choose and the various time lags involved in conducting fiscal policy.

Fiscal Policy Mix

Exercise 13.2

Visit www.econtoday.com for more about playing the budget game.

Suppose that it is agreed that fiscal policy is desirable. What is the proper mix of taxes and government expenditures? Let's say that policymakers decide that a change in taxes is desirable. At least seven options are available:

1. Permanent change in personal income taxes
2. Permanent change in corporate income taxes
3. Temporary change in personal income taxes
4. Temporary change in corporate income taxes
5. Change in employment subsidies
6. Change in depreciation allowance on investment expenditures
7. Change in specific consumption tax, such as on oil

Note that all of these are tax changes, but their effects on individual groups will be different, and special-interest groups will be lobbying powerful politicians to protect specific interests.

Alternatively, assume that policymakers decide that a change in government expenditures is desirable. There are disadvantages to these changes. Political wrangling will arise over the amount, type, and geographic location of the expenditure change ("spend more in my district or state, less in someone else's"). Furthermore, if the expenditure is to be made on a capital goods project, such as a highway, a dam, or a public transportation system, the problem of timing arises. If started during a recession, should or could such a project be abandoned or delayed if inflation emerges before the project is finished? Are delays or reversals politically feasible, even if they are economically sensible?

Time Lags

Recognition time lag

The time required to gather information about the current state of the economy.

Policymakers must be concerned with various time lags. Quite apart from the fact that it is difficult to measure economic variables, it takes time to collect and assimilate such data. Thus policymakers must be concerned with the **recognition time lag,** the period of months that may elapse before economic problems can be identified.[2]

---

[2]Final annual data for GDP, after various revisions, are not forthcoming for three to six months after the year's end.

After an economic problem is recognized, a solution must be formulated; thus there will be an **action time lag,** the period between the recognition of a problem and the implementation of policy to solve it. For fiscal policy, the action time lag is particularly long. It must be approved by Congress, and much political wrangling and infighting accompany congressional fiscal policy decision making. It is not at all unusual for the action time lag to last a year or two. Then it takes time to put the policy into effect. After Congress enacts a fiscal policy as legislation, it takes time to decide, for example, who gets the new federal construction contract, and so on.

When we add the recognition time lag to the action time lag, we get what is known as the *inside lag.* That is how long it takes to get a policy from inside the institutional structure of our federal government.

Finally, there is the **effect time lag:** After fiscal policy is enacted, it takes time for it to affect the economy. Multiplier effects take more time to work through the economy than it takes an economist to shift a curve on a chalkboard.

Because the various fiscal policy time lags are long, a policy designed to combat a recession might not produce results until the economy is experiencing inflation, in which case the fiscal policy would worsen the situation. Or a fiscal policy designed to eliminate inflation might not produce effects until the economy is in a recession; in that case, too, fiscal policy would make the economic problem worse rather than better.

Furthermore, because fiscal policy time lags tend to be *variable* (anywhere from one to three years), policymakers have a difficult time fine-tuning the economy. Clearly, fiscal policy is more an art than a science.

AUTOMATIC STABILIZERS

Not all changes in taxes (or in tax rates) or in government spending (including government transfers) constitute discretionary fiscal policy. There are several types of automatic (or nondiscretionary) fiscal policies. Such policies do not require new legislation on the part of Congress. Specific automatic fiscal policies—called **automatic,** or **built-in, stabilizers**—include the progressive federal income tax system itself and the government transfer system; the latter includes unemployment compensation.

The Progressive Income Tax

We have in the United States a progressive income tax that reaches a maximum rate of around 40 percent. For an individual, as taxable income rises, the marginal tax rate rises, and as taxable income falls, so does the marginal tax rate. Think about this now in terms of the entire economy. If the nation is at full employment, personal income taxes may yield the government, say, $600 billion per year. Now suppose that, for whatever reason, business activity suddenly starts to slow down. Workers are not allowed to put in as much overtime as before. Some workers are laid off, and some must change to jobs that pay less. Some workers and even some executives might take voluntary pay cuts. What happens to federal income taxes when wages and salaries go down? Taxes are still paid, but at a lower marginal rate than before, because the tax schedule is progressive. As a result of these decreased taxes, disposable income—the amount remaining after taxes—doesn't fall by the same percentage as before-tax income. In other words, the individual doesn't feel the pinch of recession as much as we might think if we ignored the progressive nature of our tax schedule. The *average* tax rate falls when less is earned.

Conversely, when the economy suddenly comes into a boom period, people's incomes tend to rise. They can work more overtime and can change to higher-paying jobs. Their *disposable* income does not, however, go up as rapidly as their total income because their

Action time lag
The time required between recognizing an economic problem and putting policy into effect. The action time lag is short for monetary policy but quite long for fiscal policy, which requires congressional approval.

Effect time lag
The time that elapses between the onset of policy and the results of that policy.

Automatic, or **built-in, stabilizers**
Special provisions of the tax law that cause changes in the economy without the action of Congress and the president. Examples are the progressive income tax system and unemployment compensation.

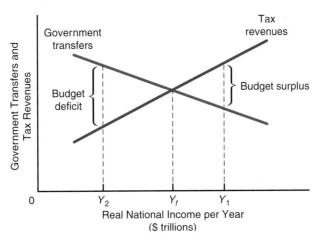

FIGURE 13-5
Automatic Stabilizers
Here we assume that as real national income rises, tax revenues rise and government transfers fall, other things remaining constant. Thus as the economy expands from Y_f to Y_1, a budget surplus automatically arises; as the economy contracts from Y_f to Y_2, a budget deficit automatically arises. Such automatic changes tend to drive the economy back toward its full-employment output level.

average tax rates are rising at the same time. Uncle Sam ends up taking a bigger bite. In this situation, the progressive income tax system tends to stabilize any abrupt changes in economic activity. (Actually, the progressive tax structure simply magnifies any stabilization effect that might exist.)

Unemployment Compensation

Like the progressive income tax, unemployment compensation stabilizes aggregate demand. Throughout the business cycle, it reduces changes in people's disposable income. When business activity drops, most laid-off workers automatically become eligible for unemployment compensation from their state governments. Their disposable income therefore remains positive, although certainly it is less than when they were employed. During boom periods there is less unemployment, and consequently fewer unemployment payments are made to the labor force. Less purchasing power is being added to the economy because fewer unemployment checks are paid out. Historically, the relationship between the unemployment rate and unemployment compensation payments has been strongly positive.

Stabilizing Impact

The key stabilizing impact of the progressive income tax and unemployment compensation is their ability to mitigate changes in disposable income, consumption, and the equilibrium level of national income. If disposable income is prevented from falling as much as it would during a recession, the downturn will be moderated. In contrast, if disposable income is prevented from rising as rapidly as it would during a boom, the boom will not get out of hand. The progressive income tax and unemployment compensation thus provide automatic stabilization to the economy. We present the argument graphically in Figure 13-5.

WHAT DO WE REALLY KNOW ABOUT FISCAL POLICY?

There are two ways of looking at fiscal policy, one that prevails during normal times and the other during abnormal times.

Fiscal Policy During Normal Times

During normal times (without "excessive" unemployment, inflation, or problems in the national economy), we know that given the time lag between the recognition of the need to increase aggregate demand and the impact of any expansionary fiscal policy, and given the very modest size of any fiscal policy action that Congress actually will take, discretionary fiscal policy is probably not very effective. Congress ends up doing too little too late to help in a minor recession. Moreover, fiscal policy that generates repeated tax changes (as it has done) creates uncertainty, which may do more harm than good. To the extent that fiscal policy has any effect during normal times, it probably achieves this by way of automatic stabilizers rather than by way of discretionary policy.

Fiscal Policy During Abnormal Times

During abnormal times, fiscal policy can be effective. Consider some classic examples: the Great Depression and war periods.

The Great Depression. When there is a substantial catastrophic drop in real GDP, as there was during the Great Depression, fiscal policy probably can do something to stimulate aggregate demand. Because so many people are cash-constrained, government spending is a good way during such periods to get cash into their hands.

Wartime. Wars are in fact reserved for governments. War expenditures are not good substitutes for private expenditures—they have little or no direct expenditure offsets. Consequently, war spending as part of expansionary fiscal policy usually has noteworthy effects, such as occurred while we were waging World War II, during which real GDP increased dramatically. (There was excess capacity, and so little crowding out.)

The "Soothing" Effect of Keynesian Fiscal Policy

One view of traditional Keynesian fiscal policy does not relate to its being used on a regular basis. As you have learned in this chapter, there are many problems associated with attempting to use fiscal policy. But if we should encounter a severe downturn, fiscal policy is available. Knowing this may reassure consumers and investors. After all, the ability of the federal government to prevent another great depression—given what we know about how to use fiscal policy today—may take some of the large risk out of consumers' and particularly investors' calculations. This may induce more buoyant and stable expectations of the future, thereby smoothing investment spending.

CONCEPTS IN BRIEF

- Time lags of various sorts reduce the effectiveness of fiscal policy. These include the recognition time lag, the action time lag, and the effect time lag.

- Two automatic, or built-in, stabilizers are the progressive income tax and unemployment compensation.

- Built-in stabilizers tend automatically to moderate changes in disposable income resulting from changes in overall business activity.

- Though discretionary fiscal policy may not necessarily be a useful policy tool in normal times because of time lags, it may work well during abnormal times, such as depressions and wartime. In addition, the existence of fiscal policy may have a soothing effect on consumers and investors.

When taxes are less than government spending, Congress goes into hot debate. A seemingly safe way to raise more taxes is to increase marginal tax rates on the rich. But does that always work?

Does "Soaking the Rich" Make Sense?

CONCEPTS APPLIED:
INCENTIVES, MARGINAL TAX RATE, FISCAL POLICY, SUPPLY OF LABOR AND INVESTMENT

 Visit www.econtoday.com for an Internet Activity that expands your understanding of these concepts.

Whenever government revenues are less than government expenditures—a problem that has occurred on numerous occasions in the United States and elsewhere in the world—the immediate response seems to be "soak the rich." That type of fiscal policy has populist backing—after all, people reason, the rich are rich, so they can afford to pay more taxes. This reasoning makes it relatively easy for a president to propose, especially during "good times," a "tax reform" that involves raising marginal income tax rates on high-income-earning individuals. But how effective is such fiscal policy in actually raising more revenues for the U.S. Treasury? Before we examine some actual historical episodes, let's first look at a few bits of relevant information.

Who Pays What Percentage of Federal Taxes?

According to the U.S. Treasury, the richest 5 percent of Americans now pay about 47 percent of all income taxes. According to the Census Bureau, the richest 5 percent of American households receive about 21 percent of aggregate income. Clearly, the top 5 percent are paying more than their "fair share" of income taxes.

Let's look at the superrich—the top .5 percent of income earners. During all of the 1980s, for example, the richest .5 percent of income recipients paid about 20 percent of all income taxes. In other words, during this period, the average person in this group of superrich paid 40 times as much federal income taxes as the average American.

The share of all taxes paid by the top .5 percent was less than 20 percent in the 1970s and has been falling in the 1990s. There appears to be a reason for this, and it has to do with fiscal policy.

The Effect of Changing Marginal Tax Rates on the Superrich

Figure 13-6 shows the share of income taxes paid by the top .5 percent of income recipients. The average for the 1960s was about 17 percent. The average for the 1970s was about 14.5 percent. The lowest level was reached in 1981, when it was only 13.5 percent. The increase thereafter correlates nicely with the change in tax laws in 1981.

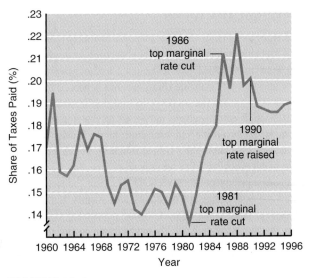

FIGURE 13-6

Share of Income Taxes Paid by the Superrich
Here we plot the share of income taxes paid by the top .5 percent of income recipients from 1960 to the late 1990s. The trough occurred just prior to the reduction in marginal tax rates in 1981, and the peak was reached just before Congress raised marginal tax rates in 1990.

Sources: U.S. Bureau of the Census; U.S. Department of the Treasury.

289

In that year, the highest marginal tax rate on so-called unearned income (dividends, interest, and the like) was dropped from 70 percent to 50 percent. In 1986, marginal tax rates were again reduced, dropping to 28 percent on all forms of income, including capital gains. The conclusion that some economists draw is that at least at the top, the superrich do in fact respond to the incentive of higher after-tax rewards for working, saving, and investing. The share of income taxes paid by the top .5 percent of income earners reached its peak in modern times, 22 percent, in 1988.

Responding to Tax Increases

In 1990, tax legislation increased the top marginal tax rate from 28 percent to an effective 31 percent. In 1993, fiscal policy legislation signed into law by President Clinton increased marginal tax rates on the superrich to around 40 percent (or higher under special circumstances). Since those marginal tax rate increases, the share of total tax revenues paid by the superrich has stayed below what it was during its peak in the latter half of the 1980s.

Some Undesirable Results of High Marginal Tax Rates

One thing is certain: People respond to incentives. Very high marginal tax rates can, if they are high enough, actually lead to reduced tax revenues for the government. How can this be? For one thing, no one is forced to work as much as before the increase in marginal rates. Also, at high enough rates, people may turn to the underground economy to avoid paying such high taxes. Under certain circumstances, taxing the rich at much higher rates yields little or no additional tax revenues.

From a policy point of view, if "soaking the rich" produces no additional tax revenues and simply harms the superrich, what is the benefit? Some people say the benefit is that the superrich are "brought down a notch."

The Bigger Picture

Let's remove ourselves from the world of the superrich and turn now to overall tax revenues during periods of marginal tax rate changes. Consider the period from 1982 to 1989, when marginal tax rates fell sharply. Despite a serious recession in the early 1980s, federal tax receipts grew from $618 billion in 1982 to $991 billion in 1989, an inflation-corrected increase of about 24 percent.

Now look at the period from 1990 to 1997, when taxes were increased first from 28 to 31 percent and then from 31 to over 40 percent. Total federal tax collections rose from $1.03 trillion to $1.55 trillion; after inflation adjustment, this was a little less than 22 percent. So tax revenues increased in the 1990s pursuant to marginal tax rate increases. But tax revenues also increased during a similar period in the 1980s, when there were dramatic reductions in the marginal tax rates. In other words, policymakers may sometimes have two choices: They can obtain increased tax revenues by increasing marginal tax rates, or they might also increase tax revenues in the long run by *decreasing* marginal tax rates. From an overall efficiency point of view, reductions in marginal tax rates might be the more appropriate choice.

Another Piece of Evidence

Consider just one special tax rate—that on capital gains, the difference between the purchase price of assets and the sale price of those same assets. In 1978, top capital gains rates were 35 percent. In 1981, they were reduced to 20 percent. Tax revenues received by the U.S. Treasury increased by 90 percent in real dollars during that period.

Contrast this with what occurred after capital gains rates were increased from 20 percent to 28 percent as part of the Tax Reform Act of 1986. Tax revenues from capital gains declined by 20 percent by 1990. In other words, a 40 percent increase in the capital gains tax rate produced no new tax revenues for the U.S. Treasury.

Tax Rate and Investment—International Comparisons

There also appears to be some effect on investment growth rates when there is a reduction in marginal tax rates. Consider the 1980s again. Marginal tax rates dropped from 70 percent to 28 percent in the United States. In Britain, they were decreased from 83 percent to 40 percent (10 years earlier, they were 98 percent on investment income).

Look at investment growth rates during that period in Figure 13-7. In the United States, the investment growth rate was 5 percent, and in the United Kingdom, over 6 percent. The rate in Germany and France, however, was 3 percent or less. During that period, both Germany and France increased marginal tax rates.

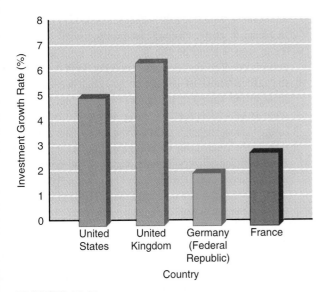

FIGURE 13-7

Relevant Investment Growth in Four Selected Countries During a Period of Marginal Tax Rate Changes

The data shown are for the 1980s. During that period, marginal tax rates were reduced in the United States and the United Kingdom but increased in Germany and France.

Sources: Organization for Economic Cooperation and Development; World Bank.

Evidence from the States

Economists Dean Stansel and Steven Moore looked at 10 states that increased taxes between 1990 and 1996 and 10 states that cut them during the same period. The results are consistent with much of the foregoing discussion. The 10 tax-cutting states ended up with healthier balanced budgets—reserves at 7.1 percent of state expenditures, versus less than 2 percent in the states that raised taxes. The average gross state product was 6 percent higher in the tax-reducing states than in the tax-raising states. Furthermore, 1.8 million jobs were gained in the tax-cutting states, double the national average, while almost no net new jobs were generated in the tax-raising states.

FOR CRITICAL ANALYSIS

1. Taken to its logical extreme, some of the preceding analysis might lead to the conclusion that the most effective marginal tax rate is close to zero. What is wrong with this conclusion?

2. Why does the "soak the rich" mentality remain popular in spite of the fact that higher marginal tax rates on the superrich rarely, if ever, increase tax revenues to the U.S. Treasury?

CHAPTER SUMMARY

1. Fiscal policy involves deliberate discretionary changes in government expenditures and personal income taxes. Typically, policymakers argue in favor of fiscal policy during a contractionary gap.

2. Increased government spending when there is a contractionary gap can lead to a shift outward in the aggregate demand curve such that the equilibrium level of real GDP per year increases. If, however, the economy is already operating on its long-run aggregate supply curve *(LRAS)*, the increase in aggregate demand will simply lead in the long run to a rise in the price level, all other things held constant.

3. Individuals respond to changes in after-tax profits, after-tax (disposable) income, and the tax-inclusive cost of foreign goods. Consequently, changes in taxes will change aggregate demand by changing consumption, investment, and net exports.

4. A decrease in taxes can lead to an increase in aggregate demand and in the equilibrium level of real GDP per year, provided that the economy is not already on

its long-run aggregate supply curve. If it is, such tax decreases will simply lead to a higher price level.

5. There are numerous possible offsets to any fiscal policy. Indirect crowding out occurs when increased deficit spending requires the government to borrow more and drives interest rates up. Increased interest rates cause private firms to undertake fewer investments. This is called the crowding-out effect.

6. The new classical economists believe in the Ricardian equivalence theorem, a proposition stating that an increase in the government budget deficit has no effect on aggregate demand because individuals properly discount increased future tax liabilities and therefore increase saving when the government engages in new deficit spending.

7. Direct crowding out occurs when the government competes with the private sector and then increases spending in those areas of competition. There is a direct expenditure offset. This occurs, for example, when the government increases direct payments for

school lunches that students' parents have been paying for anyway.
8. There is a possible open economy effect offsetting fiscal policy. Deficit spending that leads to increased interest rates causes foreigners to invest more in the United States. To do so, they demand more dollars, thereby increasing the international price of our currency. Our goods become more expensive to foreigners, they buy less, and the result is a reduction in net exports that offsets the fiscal policy stimulus.
9. If marginal tax rates are lowered, individuals and firms may react by increasing work, saving, and investing. People who believe this favor supply-side

economics, which involves changing the tax structure to create incentives to increase productivity.
10. Time lags, including the recognition time lag, the action time lag, and the effect time lag, tend to reduce the effectiveness of fiscal policy. When we add the recognition time lag to the action time lag, we get what is known as the inside lag, because this is how long it takes to get a policy from inside the institutional structure of our federal government.
11. Automatic stabilizers include personal and corporate income taxes and unemployment insurance. Automatic stabilizers counter ups and downs in fiscal activity without the necessity for legislative action.

DISCUSSION OF PREVIEW QUESTIONS

1. What is fiscal policy?

Fiscal policy refers to the changing of governmental expenditures and/or taxes in order to eliminate expansionary and contractionary gaps. Proponents of fiscal policy make the value judgment that price stability and full employment are worthwhile goals. Proponents also assume that our knowledge of positive economics is sufficient to achieve these normative goals.

2. What is automatic fiscal policy, and how does it lend stability to an economy?

With discretionary fiscal policy, government spending and taxing policies are consciously applied to stabilize an economy. Automatic fiscal policy, by contrast, does not require conscious policy or congressional legislation; automatic fiscal policy results from institutional characteristics in the economy. Thus a progressive tax structure and an unemployment compensation system (which are already in force) automatically change taxes and government outlays as national income changes. In particular, as national income falls in a recession, government outlays for unemployment automatically increase, and tax revenues fall as lower incomes push people into lower marginal tax brackets. These automatic stabilizers counteract declining national income. Similarly, in an expansionary period, tax revenues automatically rise (as people are forced into higher marginal tax brackets), and unemployment compensation out-

lays fall. Thus aggregate demand is automatically counteracted by higher tax revenues and decreased government outlays. Because income increases or decreases are automatically countered to a certain extent by a progressive tax system and an unemployment compensation program, we say that automatic fiscal policy lends stability to the U.S. economy.

3. How does the crowding-out effect tend to offset expansionary fiscal policy?

When the government spends more without increasing taxes or taxes less without reducing spending, it increases the government budget deficit. When the government attempts to sell more bonds to finance the increased deficit, it may end up increasing interest rates. Higher interest rates induce private businesses to reduce investment projects and also cause consumers to reduce their purchases of houses and cars. Therefore, expansionary fiscal policy tends to crowd out private investment and spending.

4. What types of time lags exist between the need for fiscal stimulus and the time when such stimulus actually affects the national economy?

There is a lag between the start of a recession and the availability of relevant data—the recognition time lag. There is a lag between the recognition of a need for a fiscal policy and putting one in motion—the action time lag. And there is a lag between policy implementation and tangible results—the effect time lag.

PROBLEMS

(Answers to the odd-numbered problems appear at the back of the book.)

13-1. What is *discretionary fiscal policy?* What are *automatic stabilizers?* Give examples of each.

13-2. Assume that you are a new member of Congress. You believe that expansionary government fiscal policy will pull the country rapidly out of its recession. What are some of the possible tax and spending changes you could recommend? What are the possible mixes?

13-3. Given the existence of automatic stabilizers, a recession is expected to generate a budget deficit, and an expansion is expected to generate a budget surplus. If the generation of such budget deficits or surpluses is to be countercyclical, what assumptions must be made about how consumers react to such budget deficits or surpluses?

13-4. How do economists distinguish between budget deficits or surpluses that occur automatically and those that are the result of discretionary policy?

COMPUTER-ASSISTED INSTRUCTION

Key elements of successful and unsuccessful fiscal policy are illustrated in a series of exercises that examine the implications of changes in both taxes and government expenditures.

Complete problem and answer appear on disk.

INTERACTING WITH THE INTERNET

A nice description of the U.S. federal budget (with both detailed and summary information) can be found at

gopher://sunny.stat-usa.gov/11/BudgetFY98

(future budgets should have a similar name). The University of California at Berkeley's Center for Community Economic Research (CCER) sponsors a good simulation of the effects of changing government spending. It can be found at

garnet.berkeley.edu:3333/budget/budget.html

APPENDIX C

FISCAL POLICY: A KEYNESIAN PERSPECTIVE

The traditional Keynesian approach to fiscal policy differs in three ways from that presented in Chapter 13. First, it emphasizes the underpinnings of the components of aggregate demand. Second, it assumes that government expenditures are not substitutes for private expenditures and that current taxes are the only taxes taken into account by consumers and firms. Third, the traditional Keynesian approach focuses on the short run and so assumes that as a first approximation, the price level is constant.

CHANGES IN GOVERNMENT SPENDING

Figure C-1 measures real national income along the horizontal axis and total planned expenditures (aggregate demand) along the vertical axis. The components of aggregate demand are consumption *(C)*, investment *(I)*, government spending *(G)*, and net exports *(X)*. The height of the schedule labeled $C + I + G + X$ shows total planned expenditures (aggregate demand) as a function of income. This schedule slopes upward because consumption depends positively on income. Everywhere along the 45-degree reference line, planned spending equals income. At the point Y^*, where the $C + I + G + X$ line intersects the 45-degree line, planned spending is consistent with real national income. At any income less than Y^*, spending exceeds income, and so income and thus spending will tend to rise. At any level of income greater than Y^*, planned spending is less than income, and so income and thus spending will tend to decline. Given the determinants of *C, I, G,* and *X*, total spending (aggregate demand) will be Y^*.

    The Keynesian approach assumes that changes in government spending cause no direct offsets in either consumption or investment spending because *G* is not a substitute for *C, I,* or *X*. Hence a rise in government spending from *G* to *G'* causes the $C + I + G + X$ line to shift upward by the full amount of the rise in government spending, yielding the line $C + I + G' + X$. The rise in government spending causes income to rise, which in turn causes consumption spending to rise, which further increases income. Ultimately, aggregate demand rises to Y^{**}, where spending again equals income. A key conclusion of the Keynesian analysis is that total spending rises by *more* than the original rise in government spending because consumption spending depends positively on income.

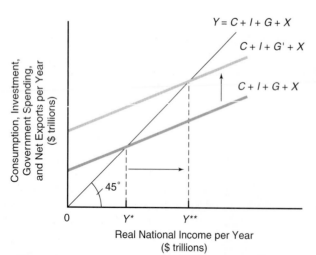

FIGURE C-1

The Impact of Higher Government Spending on Aggregate Demand
Government spending increases, causing $C + I + G + X$ to move to $C + I + G' + X$. Equilibrium increases to Y^{**}.

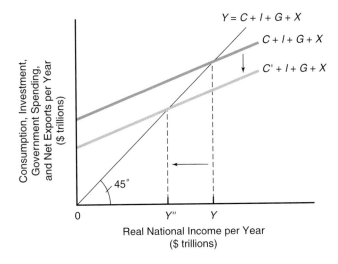

FIGURE C-2

The Impact of Higher Taxes on Aggregate Demand
Higher taxes cause consumption to fall to C'. Equilibrium decreases to Y''.

CHANGES IN TAXES

According to the Keynesian approach, changes in current taxes affect aggregate demand by changing the amount of disposable (after-tax) income available to consumers. A rise in taxes reduces disposable income and thus reduces consumption; conversely, a tax cut raises disposable income and thus causes a rise in consumption spending. The effects of a tax increase are shown in Figure C-2. Higher taxes cause consumption spending to decline from C to C', causing total spending to shift downward to $C' + I + G + X$. In general, the decline in consumption will be less than the increase in taxes because people will also reduce their saving to help pay the higher taxes. Thus although aggregate demand declines to Y'', the decline is *smaller* than the tax increase.

THE BALANCED-BUDGET MULTIPLIER

One interesting implication of the Keynesian approach concerns the impact of a balanced-budget change in government spending. Suppose that the government increases spending by $1 billion and pays for it by raising current taxes by $1 billion. Such a policy is called a *balanced-budget increase in spending.* Because the higher spending tends to push aggregate demand *up* by *more* than $1 billion while the higher taxes tend to push aggregate demand *down* by *less* than $1 billion, a most remarkable thing happens: A balanced-budget increase in G causes total spending to rise by *exactly* the amount of the rise in G—in this case, $1 billion. We say that the *balanced-budget multiplier* is equal to 1. Similarly, a balanced-budget reduction in spending will cause total spending to fall by exactly the amount of the spending cut.

THE FIXED PRICE LEVEL ASSUMPTION

The final key feature of the Keynesian approach is that it typically assumes that as a first approximation, the price level is fixed. Recall that nominal income equals the price level multiplied by real output. If the price level is fixed, an increase in government spending that causes nominal income to rise will show up exclusively as a rise in *real* output. This will in turn be accompanied by a decline in the unemployment rate because the additional output can be produced only if additional factors of production, such as labor, are utilized.

PROBLEMS

C-1. In this problem, equilibrium income is $1.1 trillion and full-employment equilibrium is $1.45 trillion. The marginal propensity to save is $\frac{1}{7}$. Answer the questions using the data in the following graph.

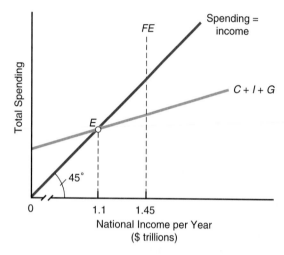

a. What is the marginal propensity to consume?
b. By how much must new investment or government spending increase to bring the economy up to full employment?
c. By how much must government cut personal taxes to stimulate the economy to the full-employment equilibrium?

C-2. Consider the following model; then answer the questions.

If $C = 30 + \frac{3}{4}Y$ and $I_n = 25$, equilibrium $Y = \$220$.

a. If government expenditures equal $5, what will be the new equilibrium level of national income? (Hint: Aggregate spending $\equiv C + I + G$.)
b. What was the government spending multiplier in this example?

C-3. Assume that MPC $= \frac{9}{10}$; then answer the following questions.

a. If government expenditures fall by $500, by how much will the aggregate expenditure curve shift downward? By how much will equilibrium income change?
b. If taxes fall by $500, by how much will the aggregate expenditure curve shift upward? By how much will equilibrium income change?

C-4. Assume that MPC $= \frac{3}{4}$; then answer the following questions.

a. If government expenditures rise by $1 billion, by how much will the aggregate expenditure curve shift upward?
b. If taxes rise by $1 billion, by how much will the aggregate expenditure curve shift downward?
c. If both taxes and government expenditures rise by $1 billion, by how much will the aggregate expenditure curve shift? What will happen to the equilibrium level of income?
d. How does our conclusion in the second part of (c) change if MPC $= \frac{9}{10}$? If MPC $= \frac{1}{2}$?

CHAPTER 14

DEFICIT SPENDING AND THE PUBLIC DEBT

Almost everybody has gone into debt. Even if you have never borrowed money, you probably will in the future. You may want to buy a house or something else for which you do not have funds readily available. Most individuals and households are comfortable having a certain amount of debt, provided they believe they will earn sufficient income to be able to pay off the debt without hardship. For decades, the federal government has been going into debt. (Indeed, it started doing so shortly after its founding.) Every once in a while, the president and Congress show concern about the growing public debt. Recently, though, there has not been much talk about deficits and the public debt. Does that mean that we no longer have to worry about our government "spending too much"? To answer this question, you will need to know more about deficit financing and the public debt.

PREVIEW QUESTIONS

1. By what methods can the U.S. federal government obtain purchasing power?

2. What are some suggested ways to reduce the federal government deficit?

3. What is the difference between the gross public debt and the net public debt?

4. What is the burden of the public debt?

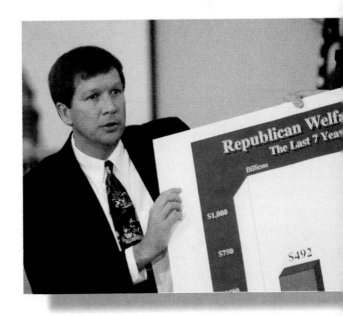

Did You Know That . . . every year your federal government has so consistently spent more than it receives that by the time you read this, the total accumulated net public debt will be almost $4 trillion! Here is what $4 trillion could buy: about 1.4 trillion dozen Dunkin Donuts or 3.7 trillion cheeseburgers or 450 textbooks for every man, woman, and child in the United States. Your individual share of what the federal government owes is around $15,000. Should you be worried? The answer is both yes and no, as you will see in this chapter. First, let's examine what the government actually does when it spends more than it receives.

GOVERNMENT FINANCE: FILLING THE GAP

When the government spends more than it receives, its spending exceeds its tax revenues. Life must go on, though, so the government has to finance this shortfall somehow. Barring any resort to money creation (the subject matter of Chapters 15, 16, and 17), the U.S. Treasury sells IOUs on behalf of the U.S. government, in the form of securities that are normally called bonds. In effect, the federal government asks Americans and others to lend money to the government to cover its deficit. For example, if the federal government spends $100 billion more than it receives in revenues, the Treasury will raise that $100 billion by selling $100 billion of new Treasury bonds. The people who buy the Treasury bonds (lend money to the U.S. government) will receive interest payments over the life of the bond. In return, the Treasury receives immediate purchasing power.

The Historical Record of Deficit Financing

The process of how the government finances the deficit is relatively straightforward. So, too, are the data that show the historical record of deficit financing in the United States. In panel (a) of Figure 14-1, you can see that while federal government tax revenues have crept up to a little over 20 percent of GDP, federal government expenditures in recent years have consistently been greater. The difference in the two curves in panel (a) represents the federal budget deficit expressed as a percentage of GDP since 1950. In panel (b), you see the absolute growth in federal government tax revenues and expenditures. The shaded red area represents the actual dollar size of the deficit since 1975.

Deficits Versus Debt: The Distinction Between Stocks and Flows

You have already learned the distinction between stocks and flows. The same analysis can be applied to the difference between the federal budget deficit and the total accumulated **public debt.** The public debt is a stock. At any point in time, it is some number, such as $4 trillion. The federal budget deficit, in contrast, is a flow. If it is $200 billion, that means that the federal government is spending at a rate of $200 billion per year more than it is receiving in taxes and other revenues. Hence if this year the public debt is $4 trillion and each year the federal government has a deficit of $200 billion, then next year the public debt will be $4.2 trillion, the year after that it will be $4.4 trillion, and so on.

Public debt
The total value of all outstanding federal government securities.

The Relative Size of the Federal Deficit

The problem with looking at panel (b) of Figure 14-1 is that the annual deficit is expressed as a current dollar figure. In a growing economy (both through real output increases and

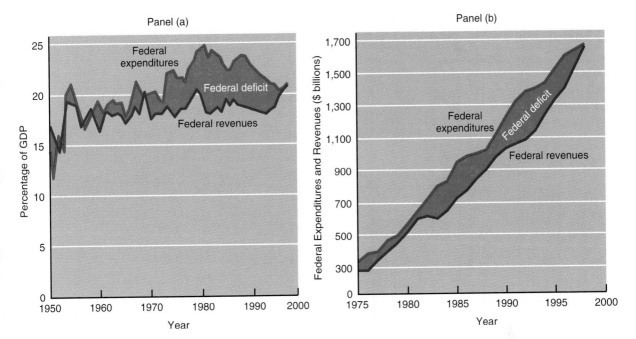

Panel (a)

Panel (b)

FIGURE 14-1

Two Ways of Viewing the Historical Record of Federal Deficit Financing
In panel (a), federal expenditures and revenues are expressed as a percentage of GDP. The difference is the federal deficit, also expressed as a percentage of GDP. Since the 1980s, the federal deficit has averaged about 3 percent of GDP. In panel (b), we express federal expenditures and federal revenues in nominal dollar terms. The difference is, of course, the nominal dollar deficit.

Sources: Economic Report of the President; Economic Indicators, various issues.

inflation), what is perhaps more important is the relative size of the federal budget deficit expressed as a percentage of GDP. This is shown in Figure 14-2. You can see that the federal budget deficit expressed as a percentage of GDP reached its most recent peak of nearly 6 percent early in the Reagan administration before falling back, again rose substantially during the Bush administration, and has been falling ever since.

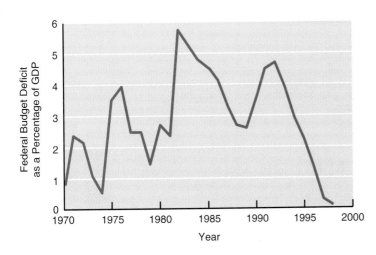

FIGURE 14-2

The Federal Budget Deficit Expressed as a Percentage of GDP
The budget deficit reached its peak during the Reagan administration and hit another peak during the Bush administration, but has fallen ever since.

Sources: Economic Report of the President; Economic Indicators, various issues.

INTERNATIONAL POLICY EXAMPLE
Will the European Union Have Its Way?

The European Union has outlined a policy strategy that requires all of its 15 members to have government deficits that do not exceed 3 percent of GDP. Each country must reach this goal by the year 1999 in order for all EU countries to adopt a common currency. As you see in Figure 14-3, by 1996, only 7 of the 15 EU countries had met that goal.

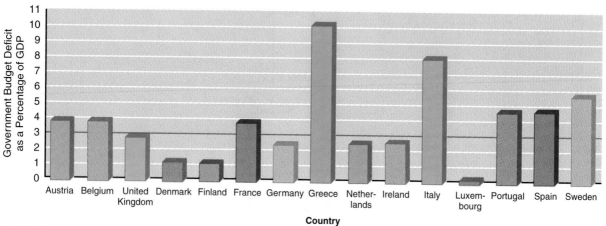

FIGURE 14-3

European Union Budget Deficits
Only 7 of the 15 EU countries have deficits that fall below 3 percent of GDP.

Source: European Commission.

FOR CRITICAL ANALYSIS: *If the United States were part of the European Union, how would its annual government budget deficit stack up against the deficits of other members?* ●

CONCEPTS IN BRIEF

- Whenever the federal government spends more than it receives, it runs a budget deficit.

- The budget deficit is a flow, whereas the accumulated budget deficits are a stock, called the public debt.

- The federal deficit expressed as a percentage of GDP hit a peak of around 6 percent in the Reagan administration in the 1980s, fell back, rose to another peak during the Bush administration, and has been falling ever since.

ACCUMULATED DEFICITS: THE PUBLIC DEBT AND INTEREST PAYMENTS ON IT

As you have already learned, every time the federal government runs a deficit, it must borrow from the private sector and foreigners, thereby increasing its debt.

The Public Debt

Gross public debt
All federal government debt irrespective of who owns it.

Net public debt
Gross public debt minus all government interagency borrowing.

All federal public debt, taken together, is called the **gross public debt.** When we subtract from the gross public debt the portion that is held by government agencies (what the federal government owes to itself), we arrive at the **net public debt.** The net public debt normally increases whenever the federal government runs a budget deficit—that is, whenever total government outlays are greater than total government revenues. Look at column 3 in Table 14-1. The total net public debt has been growing continuously for many years.

TABLE 14-1
The Federal Deficit, Our Public Debt, and the Interest We Pay on It
Net public debt in column 3 is defined as total federal debt excluding all loans between federal government agencies. Per capita net public debt is obtained by dividing population into the net public debt. A surplus occurred in 1998.

(1) Year	(2) Federal Budget Deficit (billions of current dollars)	(3) Net Public Debt (billions of current dollars)	(4) Per Capita Net Public Debt (current dollars)	(5) Net Interest Costs (billions of current dollars)	(6) Net Interest as a Percentage of GDP
1940	3.9	42.7	323.2	.9	.90
1945	53.9	235.2	1,681.2	3.1	1.45
1950	3.1	219.0	1,438.0	4.8	1.68
1955	3.0	226.6	1,365.9	4.9	1.23
1960	.3	237.2	1,312.7	6.9	1.37
1965	1.6	261.6	1,346.4	8.6	1.26
1970	2.8	284.9	1,389.1	14.4	1.47
1975	45.1	396.9	1,837.5	23.3	1.52
1980	73.8	709.3	3,140.5	52.5	1.92
1981	78.9	804.7	3,501.7	68.7	2.25
1982	127.9	929.3	4,003.9	85.0	2.68
1983	207.8	1,141.8	4,875.3	89.8	2.63
1984	185.3	1,312.6	5,538.4	111.1	2.94
1985	212.3	1,499.4	6,322.9	129.4	3.22
1986	221.2	1,736.2	7,357.2	136.0	3.21
1987	149.7	1,888.1	7,867.8	138.6	3.06
1988	155.1	2,050.2	8,473.6	151.7	3.23
1989	152.5	2,189.3	8,941.3	169.1	3.23
1990	221.4	2,410.4	9,641.6	175.6	3.23
1991	269.5	2,687.4	10,664.2	173.0	3.22
1992	290.2	2,998.6	11,759.2	177.9	3.21
1995	163.9	3,603.7	13,711.1	232.2	3.19
1996	107.4	3,733.0	14,204.2	241.1	3.16
1997	22.6	3,771.1	14,611.4	244.1	2.98
1998	−39.0	3,731.1	14,465.3	241.7	2.85

Sources: U.S. Department of the Treasury; Office of Management and Budget. Data for 1998 are estimates.

FIGURE 14-4

Net U.S. Public Debt as a Percentage of GDP

During World War II, the net public debt grew dramatically. It fell until the 1970s, then started rising again.

Source: U.S. Department of the Treasury.

Expressed in terms of per capita figures, however, it has not grown so rapidly. (We should also take account of inflation.) Perhaps a better way to look at the U.S. national debt is to examine it as a percentage of GDP, which we do in Figure 14-4. We see that after World War II, this ratio fell steadily until the early 1970s (except for a small rise in the late 1950s) and then leveled off until the 1980s. Since then, the ratio of net public debt to annual income continued to rise until the late 1990s, when it started to fall.

Exercise 14.1

Visit www.econtoday.com for more about the national debt.

INTERNATIONAL EXAMPLE
Public Debt Around the World

Whereas our net public debt as a percentage of GDP now exceeds 50 percent, many other industrialized nations have a much greater debt ratio. Figure 14-5 shows predicted public debt as a percentage of GDP for several of the United States's important trading partners. It is clear from the graph that none of the countries depicted plans to reduce the size of its public debt-to-annual GDP ratio.

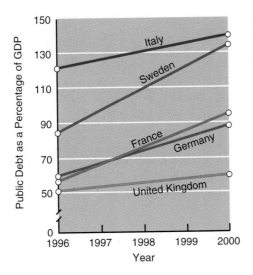

FIGURE 14-5
Rising Debt in Europe
Over the next few years, the public debt of many EU countries is expected to rise.
Source: European Commission.

FOR CRITICAL ANALYSIS: What does Figure 14-5 tell you about projected annual budget deficits in Italy, Sweden, France, Germany, and the United Kingdom? •

Annual Interest Payments on the Public Debt

Exercise 14.2
Visit www.econtoday.com for more about interest on the debt.

Consider the size of interest payments on the public debt as shown in column 5 of Table 14-1. Those interest payments started rising dramatically around 1975. Expressed as a percentage of GDP, today they are more than twice what they were a half century ago. The true size of the government deficit each year has not fallen as planned. Therefore, it is possible that interest payments expressed as a percentage of national income will rise, as is apparent in column 6 in Table 14-1. As long as the government borrows from Americans, the interest payments will be made to Americans. In other words, we owe the debt to ourselves; some people are taxed so that the government can pay interest to others (or themselves). The share of the public debt owned by foreigners started to rise in the 1970s, when it reached a high of 22 percent in 1978. That percentage declined into the late 1980s, but rose to over 38 percent in 1998. We don't just owe the debt to ourselves.

INTERNATIONAL POLICY EXAMPLE
Belgium's Diminishing Policy Options

Belgium's public debt is approaching 150 percent of GDP. This figure has little meaning until one examines its effect on the Belgian government's policy options. Today in the United States, the interest cost of our public debt is about 17 percent of the federal government budget; in Belgium, it exceeds 40 percent. This increasing net interest cost of the public debt in Belgium is steadily crowding out everything else the government wants to do. Recently, it stopped maintaining its national road system. If Belgium continues to add to its public debt through annual budget deficits the way it has done in the past, the net interest payment on that public debt will eventually crowd out every other government expenditure!

FOR CRITICAL ANALYSIS: What policy options are available to the Belgian government to prevent the doomsday prediction just mentioned from coming true? •

The Burden of the Public Debt

From 1984 to 1998, the net public debt of the United States almost tripled, to nearly $4 trillion. The public debt is the total of all the outstanding debt owed by the Treasury to its individual and institutional lenders. Whenever the federal government is in deficit, the public debt rises; for example, in fiscal 1996, the federal government deficit was about $107 billion, so the public debt increased by that amount in that fiscal year. Because of the large deficits incurred by the federal government in the 1980s and 1990s, the public debt rose dramatically—at least in nominal values. We shall now analyze whether federal deficits, and the accompanying increase in the public debt that they generate, impose a burden on future generations or are irrelevant.

As you read the remainder of this chapter, try to keep two things in mind. First, given the level of government expenditures, the main alternative to the deficit is higher taxes; therefore, the costs of a deficit should be compared to the costs of higher taxes, not to zero. Second, it is important to distinguish between the effects of deficits when full employment exists and when substantial unemployment exists.

Federal Budget Deficits: A Burden on Future Generations?

Assume that the federal government decides to increase government expenditures on final goods and services by $100 billion and that it can finance such expenditures either by raising taxes by $100 billion or by selling $100 billion of bonds. Many economists maintain that the second option, deficit spending, would lead to a higher level of national consumption and a lower level of national private saving than the first option.

The reason this is so, say these economists, is that if people are taxed, they will have to forgo private consumption now as they substitute government goods for private goods. Suppose that taxes are not raised, but instead the public buys bonds to finance the $100 billion in government expenditures. The community's disposable income is the same, and it has increased its assets by $100 billion in the form of bonds. The community will either (1) fail to realize that its liabilities (in the form of future taxes due to an increased public debt that must eventually be paid) have *also* increased by $100 billion or (2) believe that it can consume the governmentally provided goods and simultaneously purchase the same quantity of privately provided consumer goods because the bill for the currently governmentally provided goods will be paid by *future* taxpayers.

If full employment exists, then as people raise their present consumption (the same quantity of private consumption goods, but more public consumption goods), something must be crowded out. In a closed economy, investment (spending on capital goods) is crowded out. The mechanism by which this crowding out occurs is an increase in the interest rate: Deficit spending increases the total demand for credit but leaves the total supply of credit unaltered. The rise in interest rates that causes a reduction in the growth of investment and capital formation in turn slows the growth of productivity and improvement in the community's living standard.

The foregoing analysis suggests that deficit spending can impose a burden on future generations in two ways. First, unless income grows dramatically, future generations will have to be taxed at a higher rate to retire the higher public debt resulting from the present generation's increased consumption of governmentally provided goods. Second, the increased level of consumption by the present generation crowds out investment and reduces the growth of capital goods; this leaves future generations with a smaller capital stock and thereby reduces their wealth.

Paying Off the Public Debt in the Future. Suppose that after 50 years of running deficits, the public debt becomes so large that each adult person's tax liability is $50,000. Suppose further that the government chooses (or is forced) to pay off the debt at that time. Will that generation be burdened with our generation's overspending? The debt is, after all, owed (mostly) to ourselves. It's true that every adult will have to come up with $50,000 in taxes to pay off the debt; but then the government will use that money to pay off bondholders, who are (mostly) the same people. Thus *some* people will be burdened because they owe $50,000 and own less than $50,000 in government bonds. But others will receive more than $50,000 for the bonds they own. As a generation or a community, they will pay and receive about the same amount of money.

Of course, there could be a burden on some low-income adults who will find it difficult or impossible to obtain $50,000 to pay the tax liability. Still, nothing says that taxes to pay off the debt must be assessed equally; it seems likely that a special tax would be levied, based on the ability to pay.

Our Debt to Foreigners. We have been assuming that most of the debt is owed to ourselves. What about the 38 percent of our public debt that is owned by foreigners?

It is true that if foreigners buy U.S. government bonds, we do not owe that debt to ourselves, and a potential burden on future generations may result. But not necessarily. Foreigners will buy our government's debt if the inflation-adjusted, risk-adjusted, after-tax rate of return on such bonds exceeds what the investors can earn in their own country or some other country. If they buy U.S. bonds voluntarily, they perceive a benefit in doing so.

It is important to realize that not all government expenditures can be viewed as consumption; government expenditures on such things as highways, bridges, dams, research and development, and education might properly be perceived as investments. If the rate of return on such investments exceeds the interest rate paid to foreign investors, both foreigners and future Americans will be economically better off. What really matters is on what the government spends its money. If government expenditures financed by foreigners are made on wasteful projects, a burden may well be placed on future generations.

We can use the same reasoning to examine the problem of current investment and capital creation being crowded out by current deficits. If deficits lead to slower growth rates, future generations will be poorer. But if the government expenditures are really investments, and if the rate of return on such public investments exceeds the interest rate paid on the bonds, both present and future generations will be economically richer.

The Effect of Unemployment. If the economy is operating at a level substantially below full-employment real GDP, crowding out need not take place. In such a situation, an expansionary fiscal policy via deficit spending can increase current consumption (of governmentally provided goods) without crowding out investment. Indeed, if some government spending is in the form of high-yielding public investments, both present and future generations can be economically richer; such public investments will provide positive benefits in the future.

Not All Borrowing Is Bad. Don't get the impression that the government should never borrow. After all, borrowing is not always bad. Consider an example of a student who has a choice of borrowing money for one of two purposes: the purchase of a home entertainment center or tuition payments to attend college. Borrowing for the first purpose may prove to be burdensome; borrowing for the second purpose—building human capital—

may allow the student to reap greater returns in the form of higher income later. The same analysis can be applied to government borrowing. There is a difference between government borrowing to purchase Fourth of July fireworks shows and government borrowing to invest in the interstate highway system. One can conclude, therefore, that increased public debt is not necessarily bad if it creates a net investment for the future.

EXAMPLE
How to Eliminate Your Share of the Public Debt

Are you worried about the burden of the public debt? Do you fret about having to pay more taxes in the future to pay off the public debt? If so, you can perhaps do something about it. Economist Steven E. Landsberg makes the point that your share of the public debt is an entirely voluntary burden. You can reduce your share almost instantly. No, you do not want to send dollars to the U.S. Treasury to reduce the public debt. Rather, you should do the following:

1. Calculate how much you owe. If you are the average American, you owe about $15,000.
2. Lend $15,000 to the federal government by buying a $15,000 Treasury bond.

Presto! You owe $15,000 to yourself. Every year, you will pay taxes to cover your share on the interest on the debt, but every year, you will receive those taxes back as interest on your $15,000 Treasury bond.

What if you do not have the money to buy the $15,000 bond? The same question would arise, in any event, if politicians decided to raise taxes to pay off the public debt. You would still have to come up with the $15,000 to pay your share of those taxes. Hence the purchase of a $15,000 Treasury bond is no more or less attractive than being taxed $15,000 for debt reduction. In effect, the purchase of the $15,000 bond is a way to tax yourself. It is hard to imagine that buying bonds is more painful than paying taxes to eliminate the debt.

FOR CRITICAL ANALYSIS: You can opt out of your share of the public debt, but you cannot opt out of your share of government spending. Why is that so? ●

CONCEPTS IN BRIEF

- When we subtract the money government agencies borrow from each other from the gross public debt, we obtain the net public debt.
- There may be a burden of the public debt on future generations if they have to be taxed at higher rates to pay for the current generation's increased consumption of governmentally provided goods; also there may be a burden if there is crowding out of current investment, resulting in less capital formation and hence a lower economic growth rate.
- If a significant part of our public debt is bought by foreigners, then we no longer "owe it to ourselves." If the rate of return on the borrowed funds is higher than the interest to be paid, future generations can be made better off by government borrowing, but will be worse off if the opposite is true.

FEDERAL BUDGET DEFICITS IN AN OPEN ECONOMY

Many economists, and most noneconomists, believe that the U.S. trade deficit (a situation in which the value of the nation's imports of goods and services exceeds the value of its exports) is just as serious a problem as its government budget deficit. The U.S. trade deficit went from a surplus of $32 billion in 1980 to a deficit of $119.9 billion in 1987; in 1997 the U.S. trade deficit was an estimated $166.4 billion.

By virtue of such trade deficits, foreigners have accumulated U.S. dollars and purchased U.S. assets (real estate, corporate stocks, bonds, and so on). If this country continues to incur huge trade deficits, foreigners will continue to purchase assets here.

Let us examine the link between federal budget deficits and trade deficits.

What the Evidence Says

Figure 14-6 shows U.S. international trade deficits and surpluses compared to federal budget deficits and surpluses. The year 1983 appears to be a watershed year, for that is when imports began to consistently exceed exports on an annual basis in the United States. Concurrently, the federal budget fiscal deficit moved progressively into new territory.

On the basis of the evidence presented in Figure 14-6, it appears that a somewhat close relationship between trade and fiscal deficits occurred until the 1990s. Since then this relationship has broken down.

Why the Two Deficits Are Related

Intuitively, there is a reason why we would expect federal budget deficits to lead to trade deficits. You might call this the unpleasant arithmetic of trade and federal budget deficits.

Assume that the federal government runs a budget deficit. Assume further that domestic consumption and domestic investment haven't decreased relative to GDP. Where, then, does the money come from to finance the federal government deficit? Part of it must come from abroad. That is to say, dollar holders abroad are buying our newly created federal government–issued bonds. If that's the case, dollar holders abroad have fewer dollars to spend on our goods, that is, our exports. Hence when we run large federal government deficits, we should expect to see foreign dollar holders spending more on U.S. government securities (bonds) and less on U.S.-produced goods and services (exports).

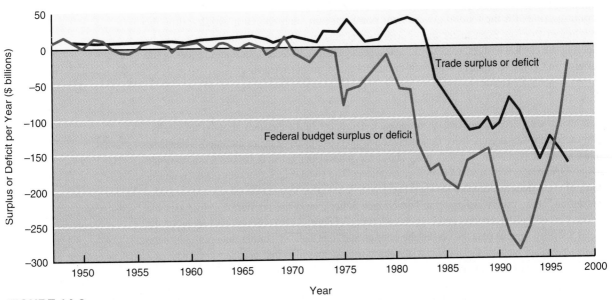

FIGURE 14-6

America's Twin Deficits
The United States exported more than it imported until 1983. Then it started running large trade deficits, as shown in this diagram. The federal budget has been in deficit for many years, starting in earnest in the late 1960s. The question is, has the federal budget deficit created the trade deficit?

Source: Economic Indicators, various issues.

The reason that foreign dollar holders are induced to buy U.S. government securities is that domestic U.S. interest rates will normally rise, all other things held constant, whenever there is an increase in government deficits financed by increased borrowing.

HAS THE DEFICIT BEEN MEASURED CORRECTLY?

Part of the problem, according to some economists, is that we are measuring the deficit incorrectly. One such economist is Robert Eisner of Northwestern University, who claims that we need to change the government accounting system to come up with a better measure of the deficit.

Capital Budgeting Theory

The federal government has only one budget to guide its spending and taxing each fiscal year. It does not distinguish between current spending for upkeep on the White House, for example, and spending for a new park that's going to last for many years to come. By contrast, businesses, as well as state and local governments, have two budgets. One, called the *operating budget,* includes expenditures for current operations, such as salaries and interest payments. The other is called a *capital budget,* which includes expenditures on investment items, such as machines, buildings, roads, and dams. With municipal governments, for example, expenditures on the capital budget may be paid for by long-term borrowing.

The Office of Management and Budget (OMB) estimated that in fiscal 1996, investment-type outlays such as military equipment and loans for research and development exceeded $150 billion. Given an estimated budget deficit of over $170 billion, then, if a capital budgeting system were used, we would simply see that most of the deficit was being used to finance activities or assets yielding long-term returns.

Eisner and others recommend that Congress should set up a capital budget, thereby removing investment outlays from its operating budget. Opponents of such a change in the accounting rules for the federal government point out that such an action would allow the government to grow even faster than currently because many new expenditures could be placed in the capital budget, thereby reducing the operating budget deficit and reducing the pressure on Congress to cut the growth in federal government spending.

Pick a Deficit, Any Deficit

Even using standard accounting techniques, the federal budget deficit that is "officially" announced can vary dramatically, depending on what is included or is not included. The OMB comes up each year with its predictions about the federal budget deficit. The Congressional Budget Office has its own set of deficit calculations. The two budget agencies produce a minimum of eight deficit estimates for each fiscal year. They give them such names as the "baseline deficit," the "policy deficit," the "on-budget deficit," and the "deficit that includes the bailout to save failing savings and loan associations." There is also a deficit that includes the Social Security surplus plus the cost of the savings and loan bailout. Rather than going into the details to explain each of these deficits, the point to understand is that no one number gives a complete picture of how much the government is spending over and above what it is receiving.

Liabilities That Aren't Showing Up

Even the highest figures shown for the federal budget deficit do not include liabilities that the federal government is incurring each year. In particular, the federal government has increasingly become liable for civilian and military employee pension plans. These are as much an obligation as a formal bond contract that is sold to finance the federal budget deficit. One estimate by economist Henning Bohn of the University of California, Santa Barbara, shows that the federal government is liable for over $1.2 trillion for just the pension obligations for government employees. The federal government is also incurring liabilities for private pension plans, savings and loan and bank deposits, and shareholders' brokerage accounts. Economist Jean-Michel Paul of the University of California, Berkeley, has estimated that the net pension liabilities of the U.S. government amount to almost 70 percent of GDP.

INTERNATIONAL EXAMPLE
Pension Liabilities Around the World

Table 14-2 shows net pension liabilities for various countries expressed as a percentage of GDP.

If you add a country's net pension liabilities to its existing public debt, you come up with some impressive numbers. In Italy, the combined liabilities of the government equal 350 percent of GDP.

TABLE 14-2

Net Pension Liabilities of the National Government as a Percentage of GDP

Country	Net Pension Liabilities as a Percentage of GDP
United States	66
Germany	160
Belgium	165
United Kingdom	186
France	216
Japan	218
Italy	233
Canada	250

Sources: Organization of Economic Cooperation and Development; Jean-Michel Paul, "Belgium's Debt Crisis Is Europe's Too," *Wall Street Journal Europe,* May 22, 1995, p. A-17.

FOR CRITICAL ANALYSIS: Does it matter what the government's net pension liabilities are relative to its GDP? Why or why not? •

SUGGESTIONS FOR REDUCING THE DEFICIT

There have been many suggestions about how to reduce the government deficit. The most obvious way to reduce the deficit is to increase taxes.

Increasing Taxes

From an arithmetic point of view, a federal budget deficit can be wiped out by simply increasing the amount of taxes collected. Let's see what this would require. The data for 1996 are instructive. The Office of Management and Budget estimated the 1996 federal budget deficit at about $170 billion. This is as much as Americans paid in total individual income taxes to the federal government in all of 1978. That deficit in 1996 shows that for the year, the federal government spent about $700 more than it had in tax revenues for every person in the country. To eliminate the deficit by raising taxes, we need $1400 more in taxes every year from *every worker* in America just to balance the budget. In 1996, Americans paid about $600 billion in personal income taxes. Every taxpayer would have to pay 30 percent more in income taxes to balance the budget. Needless to say, reality is such that we will never see a simple tax increase that will wipe out the annual federal budget deficit.

Taxing the Rich. Some people suggest that the way to eliminate the deficit is to raise taxes on the rich. Currently, over 70 percent of all federal income taxes are already being paid by the top 20 percent of families. The entire bottom 60 percent of families (those earning below $45,000 per year) pay only slightly more than 11 percent of federal income taxes. Families earning below $30,000 pay less than 3 percent of federal income taxes. Currently, families whose income are in the top 5 percent pay about 45 percent of all federal income taxes paid. The richest 1 percent pay about 25 percent of all income taxes paid. What does it mean to tax the rich more? If you talk about taxing "millionaires," you are referring to those who pay taxes on more than $1 million income per year. There are only around 57,000 of them. Even if you doubled the taxes they paid, the reduction in the deficit would be relatively trivial. Changing marginal tax rates at the upper end will show similarly unimpressive results. An increase in the top marginal tax rate from 39.6 percent to 45 percent will raise, at best, only about $20 billion in additional taxes (assuming that people do not figure out a way to avoid the higher tax rate). This $20 billion per year in extra tax revenues represented only 12 percent of the estimated 1996 federal budget deficit.

The Historical Reality. The data do not support the notion that tax increases can reduce deficits. Though it is possible arithmetically, politically just the opposite has occurred. Since World War II, for every dollar increase in taxes legislated, federal government spending has increased $1.59.

Reducing Expenditures, Particularly on Entitlements

Reducing expenditures is another way to reduce the federal budget deficit. Figure 14-7 shows spending on the military as a percentage of GDP. There you see that the military budget will be shrinking in real terms at least through 1997.

THINKING CRITICALLY ABOUT THE MEDIA

Proposed Government Spending "Cuts"

Every year the budget battle occurs in Congress. Spending cuts are proposed by one group, maybe even by the president, and opposed by others, who claim that all sorts of horrors will occur. The statements from Congress and released by the media have little to do with what you and I think of as true spending cuts. The government uses baseline budgeting. This means that a certain trend in spending is already included in its projections. For example, increases on school lunch programs were to be 5.1 percent. Some members of Congress wanted to have a 4.5 percent increase instead. The press picked it up as a spending cut! So be careful when you see the words *spending cuts* in the media today. They usually refer to smaller increases in government spending than were planned before. They rarely refer to actual reductions in spending.

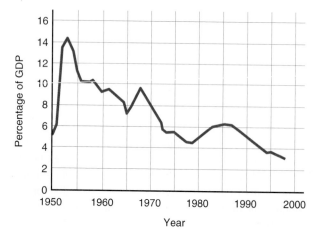

FIGURE 14-7

Defense Outlays as a Percentage of GDP
Defense spending as a percentage of GDP continues to fall.
Source: Office of Management and Budget.

TABLE 14-3
Federal Domestic Spending

Year	Social Security, Medicare, and Medicaid (billions of 1992 dollars)	All Other Domestic Programs (billions of 1992 dollars)
1953	17.93	87.82
1963	74.01	136.52
1973	183.65	255.63
1983	325.29	340.95
1995	544.27	423.81
1998	643.23	491.24

Entitlements
Guaranteed benefits under a government program such as Social Security, Medicare, or Medicaid.

During the Cold War, the military budget was the most important aspect of the federal budget; it no longer is. **Entitlements** are now the most important aspect of the federal budget. These include payments for Social Security, welfare, Medicare, and Medicaid. Entitlements are legislated federal government payments; anybody who qualifies is entitled to them. They are consequently often called noncontrollable expenditures. They represent about 50 percent of the total federal budget today. In 1960, they represented only 10 percent. Let's look at Social Security, Medicaid, and Medicare in Table 14-3. In constant 1992 dollars, in 1998 Social Security, Medicaid, and Medicare represented about $643 billion of federal government expenditures, compared to almost $491 billion of other domestic federal government expenditures. (These exclude military and international payments and interest on the public debt.)

Entitlement payments on Social Security, Medicaid, and Medicare now exceed all other domestic spending. Entitlements are growing faster than any other part of the federal government budget. In the past two decades, real spending on entitlements (adjusted for inflation) grew between 6 and 7 percent a year, while the economy grew by less than 3 percent per year. Social Security payments are growing in real terms at about 6 percent a year, but Medicare and Medicaid are growing at double-digit rates.

Entitlement programs are believed to be necessary. Interest on the public debt must be paid, but just about every other federal expenditure that is labeled necessary can be changed by Congress. The federal deficit is not expected to drop in the near future because entitlement programs are not likely to be eliminated. It is difficult to cut government benefits once they are established.

CONCEPTS IN BRIEF

- Some people argue that the federal budget deficit is measured incorrectly because it lumps together spending on capital and spending on consumption. It is therefore argued that there should be an operating budget and a capital budget.
- Some observers see a close correlation between foreign trade deficits and federal budget deficits.
- There are many deficits measured and announced by various government offices. Also, there are many liabilities that are not shown, such as future pension obligations.
- Suggested ways to reduce the deficit are to increase taxes, particularly on the rich, and to reduce expenditures, particularly on entitlements, defined as guaranteed benefits under a government program such as Social Security or Medicare.

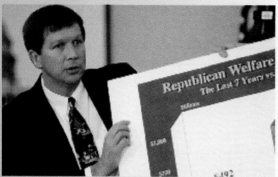

Congressional committee hearings on government spending are less heated than they used to be because of the expected elimination of the deficit. Medicare spending may spoil such projections, though.

Do We No Longer Have to Worry About the Deficit?

CONCEPTS APPLIED:
DEFICIT, DEFICIT FINANCING, PUBLIC DEBT, MEDICARE, ENTITLEMENTS

Visit www.econtoday.com for an Internet Activity that expands your understanding of these concepts.

In February 1997, some 1,100 prominent economists, including 11 Nobel laureates, signed a public statement that appeared in the *Wall Street Journal*, the *New York Times*, and elsewhere. Among other things, they stated, "We condemn the proposed 'balanced-budget' amendment to the federal Constitution. It is unsound and unnecessary. . . . There is no need to put the nation in an economic straitjacket. Let the President and Congress make fiscal policies in response to national needs and priorities as the authors of our Constitution wisely provided."

These economists were referring to legislation that had been proposed in Congress for several years running. That legislation, had it passed, would have been a proposed amendment to the Constitution to require the federal government to balance its budget every year.

There is much less talk about a balanced-budget amendment today. An important reason is that the fiscal 1998 budget ended up in surplus for the first time in decades. How did this happen?

Tax Revenues on the Rise

The reason the government deficit declined so much in the 1990s is that federal tax receipts were running higher than predicted. Figure 14-8 shows what has happened to federal tax receipts as a share of GDP since the middle of World War II. Recently, tax receipts hit a record 21 percent of GDP, a level not reached even during World War II. The postwar average has been 18.5 percent. When President Clinton took office, the figure was 19 percent.

How Long Can It Last?

The question remains, for how long can federal tax receipts be roughly equal to federal expenditures? Even if we assume that federal tax receipts will remain a relatively high percentage of GDP, we cannot assume that federal expenditures will stay in line. The problem lies in the so-called babyboom generation. In about a decade, the baby boomers will start turning 65. There are 80 million of them, and they are going to be consuming medical care, most of which will be paid for by the federal Medicare program. Currently, Medicare expenses constitute about 2.5 percent of GDP. According to the consulting firm of Watson Wyatt Worldwide, by the year 2030, Medicare expenditures will equal 14 percent of GDP (see Figure 14-9).

The Clinton administration has set up a national commission to examine the hard choices that have to be made.

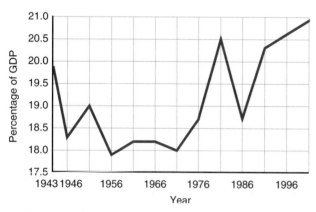

FIGURE 14-8

Federal Tax Receipts as a Share of GDP Since World War II

Sources: Joint Economic Committee of Congress; Department of Commerce; *Economic Indicators*, various issues.

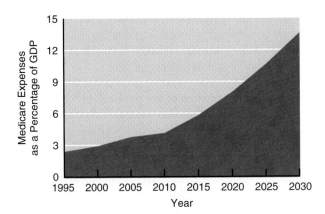

Medicare Expenses as a Percentage of GDP

Year

FIGURE 14-9
Medicare Expenses on the Rise
Sources: Watson Wyatt Worldwide; *Business Week*, June 2, 1997.

FOR CRITICAL ANALYSIS

1. As an individual, does it matter to you how the government pays for its spending—through taxation or through deficit financing?
2. "The federal government can't run in the red forever." Is this statement correct? Explain your answer.

CHAPTER SUMMARY

1. Whenever government expenditures exceed government revenues, a budget deficit occurs. Federal deficit spending as a share of GDP reached its peak right after World War II. In recent years, it has been running at about 50 percent of GDP.
2. The federal government will not go bankrupt just because the public debt is rising, for it has its taxing authority to cover interest payments on the debt, which is constantly rolled over.
3. Government use of resources today must be paid for by people living today, because there is a trade-off between private use of resources and government use of resources in any one year.
4. To the extent that the existence of the federal deficit encourages foreigners to purchase American assets, there is a potential problem that we no longer owe the public debt to ourselves. To the extent that the capital invested by foreigners in the United States has been

productively used, however, future generations will be no worse off and in fact may be better off by the fact that foreigners have invested in this country.
5. If all taxpayers perfectly anticipate increased future tax liabilities due to higher deficits, saving will increase to cover those tax liabilities. Future productivity will therefore not be affected, nor will interest rates rise; there will be no crowding-out effect.
6. Some people argue that the federal budget deficit is measured incorrectly because it lumps together spending on capital and spending on consumption. It is therefore argued that there should be an operating budget and a capital budget.
7. Suggested ways to reduce the deficit are to increase taxes, particularly on the rich, and to reduce expenditures, particularly on entitlements, defined as guaranteed benefits under a government program such as Social Security or Medicare.

DISCUSSION OF PREVIEW QUESTIONS

1. **By what methods can the U.S. federal government obtain purchasing power?**
   In the United States, the federal government is able to obtain purchasing power by selling bonds, taxing, or creating money. State and local governments can also obtain purchasing power by selling bonds and by taxing, but only the federal government has the power to create money in the United States. Perhaps surprisingly, regardless of how government expenditures are financed, most of the burden of government expendi-

tures falls on the present generation; the effects of government money creation and bond sales are similar to the effects of taxation. All of the methods of financing government expenditures require the present generation to consume fewer consumer goods now in order to get more governmentally provided goods. Taxation does so in an obvious way; government bond sales compete with private industry bond sales, thereby contracting the private sector.

2. **What are some suggested ways to reduce the federal government deficit?**

The two most obvious ways to reduce the federal budget deficit are increasing taxes and reducing expenditures. Historically, though, for every dollar increase in federal taxes there has been $1.59 increase in federal government spending. Reductions in federal spending face political problems because of the difficulty of reducing entitlements.

3. **What is the difference between the gross public debt and the net public debt?**

The gross public debt is all federal government debt irrespective of who owns it. The net public debt eliminates all government interagency borrowing. In other words, if we subtract what government agencies borrow from each other from the gross public debt, we obtain the net public debt.

4. **What is the burden of the public debt?**

If federal spending that increases the public debt crowds out private investment, future generations will be burdened with a lower capital stock and lower incomes. If the Ricardian equivalence theorem holds—if people in fact increase saving today to pay for higher tax liabilities in the future when there is deficit spending—crowding out is not inevitable, and this burden may not be as great as presumed.

PROBLEMS

(Answers to the odd-numbered problems appear at the back of the book.)

14-1. In 1999, government spending is $8 trillion and taxes collected are $7.7 trillion. What is the federal budget deficit in that year?

14-2. Look at the accompanying table showing federal budget spending and federal budget receipts. Calculate the federal budget deficit as a percentage of GDP for each year.

Year	Federal Budget Receipts ($ billions)	Federal Budget Spending ($ billions)	GDP ($ trillions)
1988	972.3	1,109.0	4,900.4
1989	1,059.3	1,181.6	5,250.8
1990	1,107.4	1,273.6	5,522.2
1991	1,122.2	1,332.7	5,677.5

14-3. It may be argued that the effects of a higher public debt are the same as the effects of higher taxes. Why?

14-4. To reduce the size of the deficit (and reduce the growth in the net public debt), a politician suggests that "we should tax the rich." The politician makes a simple arithmetic calculation in which he applies the increased tax rate to the total income reported by "the rich" in a previous year. He says that this is how much the government could receive from the increased taxes on "the rich." What is the major fallacy in such calculations?

14-5. Proponents of capital budgeting theory argue that whenever the government invests in capital expenditures, such as roads and dams, such government spending should be put in a separate budget called the capital budget. In doing so, the federal government's budget deficit would thereby be reduced by the amount of government capital spending. Would such a change in measuring the government deficit change anything? Explain.

14-6. What is the relationship between the gross public debt and the net public debt? What is the relationship between the annual federal government budget deficit and the net public debt?

COMPUTER-ASSISTED INSTRUCTION

A series of conceptual and numerical exercises illustrates the links among taxation, government spending, and the size of the public debt.

Complete problem and answer appear on disk.

INTERACTING WITH THE INTERNET

You can visit the U.S. Treasury at

www.ustreas.gov

You can keep up with the federal government's budget by going to the White House homepage at

www.whitehouse.gov

When you get there, select *Interactive Citizen's Handbook* and click on *White House Offices and Agencies.* Select *Office of Management and Budget,* and click on *Budget of the United States Government, Fiscal Year 1998.* Select *Search Documents, On-Line* and download individual sections of documents.

You can also find out what the Council of Economic Advisers has to say about the government budget deficit by going to

www.whitehouse.gov/WH/EOP/CEA/html/CEA.html

You can find out information on the Federal Reserve's function by going to the home page of the Federal Reserve Bank of San Francisco at

www.frbsf.org

PART 5

MONEY, MONETARY POLICY, AND STABILIZATION

CHAPTER 15

MONEY AND THE BANKING SYSTEM

If you live in any major city, you probably know what it is like to stand in line at your local bank, waiting for a teller to become free. A lot of people have stopped going to their local bank, however. They find it more convenient to deal with their bank via the Internet. This is called *cyberbanking*, and it is done on your computer. With relatively simple software, virtually anybody with a phone line and a computer can do his or her banking with such well-known institutions as Wells Fargo and Citibank. At the same time, electronic commerce is booming. People make payments for goods and services not through regular banking channels but over the Internet. (You will read more about "e-commerce" in Chapter 35.) What about security risks? Could someone steal money from you via the Internet? And what about the possibility of drug traffickers and others being able to launder money more easily through the Internet? To answer these questions, we must first look at money and the banking system in the United States.

PREVIEW QUESTIONS

1. What is money?
2. What "backs" the U.S. dollar?
3. What are the functions of the Federal Reserve System?
4. Who is involved in the process of transferring funds from savers to investors?

Did You Know That . . . the typical dollar bill changes hands 50 times a year? Cash, of course, is not the only thing we use as money. As you will see in this chapter, our definition of money is much broader. Money has been important to society for thousands of years. In 300 B.C., Aristotle claimed that everything had to "be accessed in money, for this enables men always to exchange their services, and so makes society possible." Money is indeed a part of our everyday existence. We have to be careful, though, when we talk about money because it means two different things. Most of the time when people say "I wish I had more money," they mean that they want more income. Thus the normal use of the term *money* implies the ability to purchase goods and services. In this chapter, in contrast, you will use the term **money** to mean anything that people generally accept in exchange for goods and services. Most people think of money as the paper bills and coins they carry. But as you will see in this chapter, the concept of money is normally more inclusive. Table 15-1 provides a list of the types of money that have been used throughout the history of civilization. The best way to understand money is to examine its functions.

THE FUNCTIONS OF MONEY

Money traditionally serves four functions. The one that most people are familiar with is money's function as a *medium of exchange*. Money also serves as a *unit of accounting,* a *store of value* or *purchasing power,* and a *standard of deferred payment.* Anything that serves these four functions is money. Anything that could serve these four functions could be considered money.

Money as a Medium of Exchange

When we say that money serves as a **medium of exchange,** what we mean is that sellers will accept it as payment in market transactions. Without some generally accepted medium of exchange, we would have to resort to *barter.* In fact, before money was used, transactions took place by means of barter. **Barter** is simply a direct exchange—no intermediary

Money
Any medium that is universally accepted in an economy both by sellers of goods and services as payment for those goods and services and by creditors as payment for debts.

Medium of exchange
Any asset that sellers will accept as payment.

Barter
The direct exchange of goods and services for other goods and services without the use of money.

Iron	Boar tusk	Playing cards
Copper	Red woodpecker scalps	Leather
Brass	Feathers	Gold
Wine	Glass	Silver
Corn	Polished beads (wampum)	Knives
Salt	Rum	Pots
Horses	Molasses	Boats
Sheep	Tobacco	Pitch
Goats	Agricultural implements	Rice
Tortoise shells	Round stones with centers removed	Cows
Porpoise teeth	Crystal salt bars	Paper
Whale teeth	Snail shells	Cigarettes

TABLE 15-1

Types of Money
This is a partial list of things that have been used as money. Native Americans used wampum, beads made from shells. Fijians used whale teeth. The early colonists in North America used tobacco. And cigarettes were used in prisoner-of-war camps during World War II and in post–World War II Germany.

Source: Roger LeRoy Miller and David D. VanHoose, *Modern Money and Banking,* 3d ed. (New York: McGraw-Hill, 1993), p. 13.

good called money is used. In a barter economy, the shoemaker who wants to obtain a dozen water glasses must seek out a glassmaker who at exactly the same time is interested in obtaining a pair of shoes. For this to occur, there has to be a *double coincidence of wants.* If there isn't, the shoemaker must go through several trades in order to obtain the desired dozen glasses—perhaps first trading shoes for jewelry, then jewelry for some pots and pans, and then the pots and pans for the desired glasses.

Money facilitates exchange by reducing the transaction costs associated with means-of-payment uncertainty—that is, with regard to goods that the partners in any exchange are willing to accept. The existence of money means that individuals no longer have to hold a diverse collection of goods as an exchange inventory. As a medium of exchange, money allows individuals to specialize in any area in which they have a comparative advantage and to receive money payments for their labor. Money payments can then be exchanged for the fruits of other people's labor. The use of money as a medium of exchange permits more specialization and the inherent economic efficiencies that come with it (and hence greater economic growth). Money is even more important when used for large amounts of trade.

Money as a Unit of Accounting

Unit of accounting
A measure by which prices are expressed; the common denominator of the price system; a central property of money.

A **unit of accounting** is a way of placing a specific price on economic goods and services. Thus as a unit of accounting, the monetary unit is used to measure the value of goods and services *relative to* other goods and services. It is the common denominator, or measure, the commonly recognized unit of value measurement. The dollar is the monetary unit in the United States. It is the yardstick that allows individuals easily to compare the relative value of goods and services. Accountants at the U.S. Department of Commerce use dollar prices to measure national income and domestic product, a business uses dollar prices to calculate profits and losses, and a typical household budgets regularly anticipated expenses using dollar prices as its unit of accounting.

Another way of describing money as a unit of accounting is to say that it serves as a *standard of value* that allows economic actors to compare the relative worth of various goods and services. It allows for comparison shopping, for example.

Exercise 15.1
Visit www.econtoday.com for more about barter.

Money as a Store of Value

Store of value
The ability to hold value over time; a necessary property of money.

One of the most important functions of money is that it serves as a **store of value** or purchasing power. The money you have today can be set aside to purchase things later on. In the meantime, money retains its nominal value, which you can apply to those future purchases. If you have $1,000 in your checking account, you can either spend it today on goods and services, spend it tomorrow, or spend it a month from now. In this way, money provides a way to transfer value (wealth) into the future.

Money as a Standard of Deferred Payment

Standard of deferred payment
A property of an asset that makes it desirable for use as a means of settling debts maturing in the future; an essential property of money.

The fourth function of the monetary unit is as a **standard of deferred payment.** This function involves the use of money both as a medium of exchange and as a unit of accounting. Debts are typically stated in terms of a unit of accounting; they are paid with a monetary

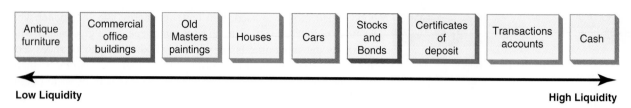

FIGURE 15-1

Degrees of Liquidity
The most liquid asset is, of course, cash. Liquidity decreases as you move from right to left.

medium of exchange. That is to say, a debt is specified in a dollar amount and paid in currency (or by check). A corporate bond, for example, has a face value—the dollar value stated on it, which is to be paid upon maturity. The periodic interest payments on that corporate bond are specified and paid in dollars, and when the bond comes due (at maturity), the corporation pays the face value in dollars to the holder of the bond.

Not all countries, or the firms and individuals in those countries, will specify that debts owed must be paid in their own national monetary unit. For example, individuals, private corporations, and governments in other countries incur debts in terms of the U.S. dollar, even though the dollar is neither the medium of exchange nor the monetary unit in those countries. Also, contracts for some debts specify repayment in gold rather than in a nation's currency.

Liquidity

Money is an asset—something of value—that accounts for part of personal wealth. Wealth in the form of money can be exchanged later for some other asset. Although it is not the only form of wealth that can be exchanged for goods and services, it is the one most widely and readily accepted. This attribute of money is called **liquidity.** We say that an asset is liquid when it can easily be acquired or disposed of without high transaction costs and with relative certainty as to its value. Money is by definition the most liquid asset there is. Just compare it, for example, with a share of stock listed on the New York Stock Exchange. To buy or sell that stock, you usually call a stockbroker, who will place the buy or sell order for you. This generally must be done during normal business hours. You have to pay a commission to the broker. Moreover, there is a distinct probability that you will get more or less for the stock than you originally paid for it. This is not the case with money. Money can be easily converted to other asset forms. Therefore, most individuals hold at least a part of their wealth in the form of the most liquid of assets, money. You can see how assets rank in liquidity relative to one another in Figure 15-1.

When we hold money, however, we pay a price for this advantage of liquidity. That price is the interest yield that could have been obtained had the asset been held in another form—for example, in the form of stocks and bonds.

> **The cost of holding money (its opportunity cost) is measured by the alternative interest yield obtainable by holding some other asset.**

MONETARY STANDARDS, OR WHAT BACKS MONEY

Today in the United States, all of us accept coins, paper currency, and balances in **transactions accounts** (checking accounts with banks and other financial institutions) in exchange for items sold, including labor services. The question remains, why are we willing to accept as payment something that has no intrinsic value? After all, you could not sell checks to

Liquidity
The degree to which an asset can be acquired or disposed of without much danger of any intervening loss in *nominal* value and with small transaction costs. Money is the most liquid asset.

Transactions accounts
Checking account balances in commercial banks and other types of financial institutions, such as credit unions and mutual savings banks; any accounts in financial institutions on which you can easily write checks without many restrictions.

Fiduciary monetary system
A system in which currency is issued by the government and its value is based uniquely on the public's faith that the currency represents command over goods and services.

anybody for use as a raw material in manufacturing. The reason is that in this country the payments arise from a **fiduciary monetary system.** This means that the value of the payments rests on the public's confidence that such payments can be exchanged for goods and services. *Fiduciary* comes from the Latin *fiducia,* which means "trust" or "confidence." In our fiduciary monetary system, money, in the form of currency or transactions accounts, is not convertible to a fixed quantity of gold, silver, or some other precious commodity. The paper money that people hold cannot be exchanged for a specified quantity of some specified commodity. The bills are just pieces of paper. Coins have a value stamped on them that is normally greater than the market value of the metal in them. Nevertheless, currency and transactions accounts are money because of their acceptability and predictability of value.

Acceptability

Transactions accounts and currency are money because they are accepted in exchange for goods and services. They are accepted because people have confidence that they can later be exchanged for other goods and services. This confidence is based on the knowledge that such exchanges have occurred in the past without problems. Even during a period of relatively rapid inflation, we would still be inclined to accept money in exchange for goods and services because it is so useful. Barter is a costly and time-consuming alternative.

Realize always that money is socially defined. Acceptability is not something that you can necessarily predict. For example, the U.S. government has tried to circulate types of money that were socially unacceptable. How many $2 bills have you seen lately? The answer is probably none. No one wanted to make room for $2 bills in register tills or billfolds.

Predictability of Value

The purchasing power of the dollar (its value) varies inversely with the price level. The more rapid the rate of increase of some price level index, such as the Consumer Price Index, the more rapid the decrease in the value, or purchasing power, of a dollar. Money still retains its usefulness even if its value—its purchasing power—is declining year in and year out, as in periods of inflation, because it still retains the characteristic of predictability of value. If you believe that the inflation rate is going to be around 10 percent next year, you know that any dollar you receive a year from now will have a purchasing power equal to 10 percent less than that same dollar this year. Thus you will not necessarily refuse to use money or accept it in exchange simply because you know that its value will decline by the rate of inflation next year.

CONCEPTS IN BRIEF

- Money is defined by its functions, which are as a medium of exchange, a unit of accounting or standard of value, a store of value or purchasing power, and a standard of deferred payment.

- Because money is a highly liquid asset, it can be disposed of without high transaction costs and with relative certainty as to its value.

- The United States has a fiduciary monetary system—our money is not convertible into a fixed quantity of a commodity such as gold or silver.

- Money is accepted in exchange for goods and services because people have confidence that it can later be exchanged for other goods and services. Another reason for this is that it has a predictable value.

DEFINING THE U.S. MONEY SUPPLY

Money is important. Changes in the total **money supply**—the amount of money in circulation—and changes in the rate at which the money supply increases or decreases affect important economic variables, such as the rate of inflation, interest rates, employment, and the equilibrium level of real national income. Although there is widespread agreement among economists that money is indeed important, they have never agreed on how to define or measure it. There are two approaches to defining and measuring money: the **transactions approach,** which stresses the role of money as a medium of exchange, and the **liquidity approach,** which stresses the role of money as a temporary store of value.

Money supply
The amount of money in circulation.

Transactions approach
A method of measuring the money supply by looking at money as a medium of exchange.

Liquidity approach
A method of measuring the money supply by looking at money as a temporary store of value.

The Transactions Approach to Measuring Money: M1

Using the transactions approach to measuring money, the money supply consists of the following:

1. Currency
2. Checkable (transaction) deposits
3. Traveler's checks

The official designation of the money supply, including currency, checkable deposits, and traveler's checks not issued by banks is **M1.** The various elements of M1 for a typical year are presented in panel (a) of Figure 15-2.

M1
The money supply, taken as the total value of currency plus checkable deposits plus traveler's checks not issued by banks.

Currency. Currency includes coins minted by the U.S. Treasury and paper currency, usually in the form of Federal Reserve notes, issued by the Federal Reserve banks (to be discussed shortly). Although nowhere near as important as checkable deposits as a percent-

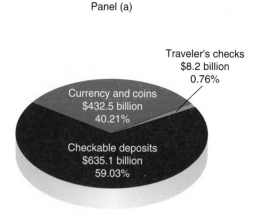

Panel (a)

Traveler's checks
$8.2 billion
0.76%

Currency and coins
$432.5 billion
40.21%

Checkable deposits
$635.1 billion
59.03%

M1 = $1,075.8 billion

Panel (b)

Overnight repurchase agreement
and Eurodollars
$389.6 billion
9.5%

Small time
deposits at all
depository
institutions
$2,003.3 billion
48.9%

M1 =
$1,075.8 billion
26.3%

Retail money market mutual fund shares
$627.4 billion
15.3%

M2 = $4,096.1 billion

FIGURE 15-2

Composition of the U.S. M1 and M2 Money Supply, 1998
Panel (a) shows the M1 money supply, of which the greatest component is checkable deposits (over 65 percent). M2 consists of M1 plus three other components, the most important of which is small time deposits at all depository institutions (over 50 percent).

Sources: Federal Reserve Bulletin; Economic Indicators, various issues. Data are for 1998.

age of the money supply, currency has increased in significance in the United States. One of the major reasons for the increased use of currency in the U.S. economy is the growing number of illegal transactions, especially illegal drug transactions.

POLICY EXAMPLE
Should the Penny and the Dollar Bill Be Eliminated?

The U.S. Mint started making the penny over 200 years ago. When first put into circulation, the penny could be exchanged for coffee, a loaf of bread, and many other goods. Today, you can buy virtually nothing with one penny. The American government spends millions of dollars a year minting pennies because Americans lose them, throw them out, or just keep them at home. On average, Americans have almost $10 worth of pennies in each household.

The Bureau of Engraving and Printing also spends over $300 million a year printing $1 bills.

Some members of Congress have proposed that the dollar bill be phased out and replaced with a coin. After all, few industrialized countries have a bill that is worth so little. Indeed, in the 1980s and 1990s, Australia, Canada, France, Japan, New Zealand, Norway, Spain, and the United Kingdom each replaced its lowest denomination bills with coins. The British, for example, replaced the one-pound note with a one-pound coin (worth about $1.60). Although coins cost more to produce, they last 30 years compared to a bill, which lasts only 17 months. On a per-year basis, dollar bills cost 10 times more than dollar coins would to keep in circulation.

Not everyone is in favor of replacing dollars with coins, however. There is a social cost to be incurred by carrying around bulky, heavy change. Paper is lighter and often more convenient, although not in vending machines, to be sure.

FOR CRITICAL ANALYSIS: In 1979, the Susan B. Anthony dollar coin was introduced. It flopped. Can you guess why? ●

Checkable Deposits. Most major transactions today are done with checks. The convenience and safety of using checks has made checking accounts the most important component of the money supply. For example, in 1998 it is estimated that currency transactions accounted for only .5 percent of the *dollar* amount of all transactions. The rest (excluding barter) involved checks. Checks are a way of transferring the ownership of deposits in financial institutions. They are normally acceptable as a medium of exchange. The financial institutions that offer **checkable deposits** are numerous and include virtually all **thrift institutions**—mutual savings banks, savings and loan associations (S&Ls), and credit unions. Regular banks, called commercial banks, used to be the only financial institutions that could offer checkable deposits.

Traveler's Checks. **Traveler's checks** are paid for by the purchaser at the time of transfer. The total quantity of traveler's checks outstanding issued by institutions other than banks is part of the M1 money supply.[1] American Express, Citibank, Cook's, and other institutions issue traveler's checks.

Checkable deposits
Any deposits in a thrift institution or a commercial bank on which a check may be written.

Thrift institutions
Financial institutions that receive most of their funds from the savings of the public; they include mutual savings banks, savings and loan associations, and credit unions.

Traveler's checks
Financial instruments purchased from a bank or a nonbanking organization and signed during purchase that can be used as cash upon a second signature by the purchaser.

---

[1]Banks place the funds that are to be used to redeem traveler's checks in a special deposit account, and they are therefore already counted as checkable accounts. Nonbank issuers, however, do not place these funds in checkable accounts. Improvements in data collection have made it possible to estimate the total amount of nonbank traveler's checks, and since June 1981 they have been included in M1.

INTERNATIONAL EXAMPLE
Greenbacks Abroad

For years, estimates of the M1 money supply have seemed at odds with the amount of dollars that are printed each year. Of the almost $400 billion in currency and coins circulating outside the banking system, over 85 percent could not be accounted for. University of Wisconsin economist Edgar L. Feige discovered that fully 45 percent is held abroad. Indeed, the dollar is a de facto currency in many developing countries. Feige further discovered that U.S. citizens admit to hoarding another 12 percent of the missing currency and businesses another 10 percent. The underground economy accounts for between 4 and 6 percent.

FOR CRITICAL ANALYSIS: Foreigners hold lots of our currency. Why don't we generally hold any of their currency? ●

What About Credit Cards?

Even though a large percentage of transactions are accomplished by using a plastic credit card, we do not consider the credit card itself money. Remember the functions of money. A credit card is not a unit of accounting, a store of value, or a standard of deferred payment. The use of your credit card is really a loan to you by the issuer of the card, be it a bank, a retail store, a gas company, or American Express. The proceeds of the loan are paid to the business that sold you something. You must pay back the loan to the issuer of the credit card, either when you get your statement or with interest throughout the year if you don't pay off your balance. (We ignore those with credit card debt who become "deadbeats.") It is not a store of value. Credit cards *defer* rather than complete transactions that ultimately involve the use of money.

A relative newcomer, the *debit card* automatically withdraws money from a transactions account. When you use your debit card to purchase something, you are giving an instruction to your bank to transfer money directly from your bank account to the store's bank account. If the store in which you are shopping has a direct electronic link to the bank, that transfer may be made instantaneously. Use of a debit card does not create a loan. A debit card is therefore not a new type of "money."

The Liquidity Approach to Measuring Money: M2

The liquidity approach to defining and measuring the U.S. money supply involves taking into account not only the most liquid assets that people use as money, which are already included in the definition of M1, but also other assets that are highly liquid—that is, that can be converted into money quickly without loss of nominal dollar value and without much cost. Any (non-M1) assets that come under this definition have been called **near monies.** Thus the liquidity approach to the definition of the money supply will include M1 plus near monies. Also consider that the liquidity approach views money as a temporary store of value and thus includes all of M1 plus all near monies. Panel (b) of Figure 15-2 on page 324 shows the components of **M2**—money as a temporary store of value. We examine each of these components in turn.

Savings Deposits. **Savings deposits** in all **depository institutions** (such as commercial banks, mutual savings banks, savings and loan associations, and credit unions) are part of the M2 money supply. A savings deposit is distinguishable from a time deposit because savings funds may be withdrawn without payment of a penalty. Funds are fully protected against loss in their nominal value. There are two types of savings deposits, statement and passbook.

Near monies
Assets that are almost money. They have a high degree of liquidity; they can be easily converted into money without loss in value. Time deposits and short-term U.S. government securities are examples.

M2
M1 plus (1) savings and small-denomination time deposits at all depository institutions, (2) overnight repurchase agreements at commercial banks, (3) overnight Eurodollars held by U.S. residents other than banks at Caribbean branches of member banks, (4) balances in retail money market mutual funds, and (5) money market deposit accounts (MMDAs).

Savings deposits
Interest-earning funds that can be withdrawn at any time without payment of a penalty.

Depository institutions
Financial institutions that accept deposits from savers and lend those deposits out at interest.

1. *Statement savings deposit.* A statement savings deposit is similar to a checking account because the owner (depositor) receives a monthly statement or record of the deposits and withdrawals and the interest earned during the month. Deposits and withdrawals from a statement savings account can be made by mail.
2. *Passbook savings account.* A passbook savings account requires that the owner present a physical passbook at the time of each deposit or withdrawal. Deposits, withdrawals, and interest are recorded in the passbook.

Time Deposits. A basic distinction has always been made between a checkable deposit, which is a checking account, and a **time deposit,** which theoretically requires notice of withdrawal and on which the financial institution pays the depositor interest. The name indicates that there is an agreed period during which the funds must be left in the financial institution. If they are withdrawn prior to the end of that period, a penalty may be applied. The distinction between checkable and time deposits has been blurred over time, but it is still used in the official definition of the money supply.

Small-Denomination Time Deposits. Time deposits include savings certificates and small **certificates of deposit (CDs).** To be included in the M2 definition of the money supply, such time deposits must be less than $100,000—hence the name *small-denomination time deposits.* The owner of a savings certificate is given a receipt indicating the amount deposited, the interest rate to be paid, and the maturity date. A CD is an actual certificate that indicates the date of issue, its maturity date, and other relevant contractual matters.

A variety of small-denomination time deposits are available from depository institutions, ranging in maturities from one month to 10 years.

Money Market Deposit Accounts (MMDAs). Since 1982, banks and thrift institutions have offered **money market deposit accounts (MMDAs),** which usually require a minimum balance and set limits on the number of monthly transactions (deposits and withdrawals by check).

Overnight Repurchase Agreements at Commercial Banks (REPOs, or RPs). A **repurchase agreement (REPO, or RP)** is made by a bank to sell Treasury or federal agency securities to its customers, coupled with an agreement to repurchase them at a price that includes accumulated interest. REPOs fill a gap in that depository institutions are not yet allowed to offer to businesses interest-bearing commercial checking accounts. Therefore, REPOs can be thought of as a financial innovation that bypasses regulation because businesses can deposit their excess cash in REPOs instead of leaving it in non-interest-bearing commercial checking accounts.

Overnight Eurodollars. **Eurodollar deposits** are dollar-denominated deposits in foreign commercial banks and in foreign branches of U.S. banks. *Dollar-denominated* simply means that although the deposit might be held at a Caribbean commercial bank, its value is stated in terms of U.S. dollars rather than in terms of the local currency. The term *Eurodollar* is inaccurate because banks outside continental Europe participate in the so-called Eurodollar market and also because banks in some countries issue deposits denominated in German marks, Swiss francs, British sterling, and Dutch guilders.

Money Market Mutual Fund Balances. Many individuals keep part of their assets in the form of shares in **money market mutual funds.** These retail mutual funds invest only in short-term credit instruments. The majority of these money market funds allow check-writing privileges, provided that the size of the check exceeds some minimum.

Time deposit
A deposit in a financial institution that requires notice of intent to withdraw or must be left for an agreed period. Withdrawal of funds prior to the end of the agreed period may result in a penalty.

Certificate of deposit (CD)
A time deposit with a fixed maturity date offered by banks and other financial institutions.

Money market deposit accounts (MMDAs)
Accounts issued by banks yielding a market rate of interest with a minimum balance requirement and a limit on transactions. They have no minimum maturity.

Repurchase agreement (REPO, or RP)
An agreement made by a bank to sell Treasury or federal agency securities to its customers, coupled with an agreement to repurchase them at a price that includes accumulated interest.

Eurodollar deposits
Deposits denominated in U.S. dollars but held in banks outside the United States, often in overseas branches of U.S. banks.

Money market mutual funds
Funds of investment companies that obtain funds from the public that are held in common and used to acquire short-maturity credit instruments, such as certificates of deposit and securities sold by the U.S. government.

M2 and Other Money Supply Definitions. When all of these assets are added together, the result is M2. The composition of M2 is given in panel (b) of Figure 15-2 (page 324).

Economists and researchers have come up with even broader definitions of money than M2.[2] More assets are simply added to the definition. Just remember that there is no one best definition of the money supply. For different purposes, different definitions are appropriate. If we want to use a definition that seems to correlate best with economic activity on an economywide basis, M2 is probably best.

THE U.S. BANKING STRUCTURE

The United States's banking system consists of a **central bank** called the Federal Reserve System, or **the Fed.** In addition, there are a large number of commercial banks, which are privately owned, profit-seeking institutions, and thrift institutions (savings and loan associations, mutual savings banks, and credit unions).

Financial Intermediaries: Sources and Uses of Funds

The financial institutions in our banking system are all in the same business—transferring funds from savers to investors. This process has become known as **financial intermediation,** and its participants are called **financial intermediaries.** Savers lend funds through financial intermediaries (banks, savings and loans, etc.) to borrowers such as businesses, governments, and home buyers. The process of financial intermediation is illustrated in Figure 15-3.

Central bank
A banker's bank, usually an official institution that also serves as a country's treasury's bank. Central banks normally regulate commercial banks.

The Fed
The Federal Reserve System; the central bank of the United States.

Financial intermediation
The process by which financial institutions accept savings from businesses, households, and governments and lend the savings to other businesses, households, and governments.

Financial intermediaries
Institutions that transfer funds between ultimate lenders (savers) and ultimate borrowers.

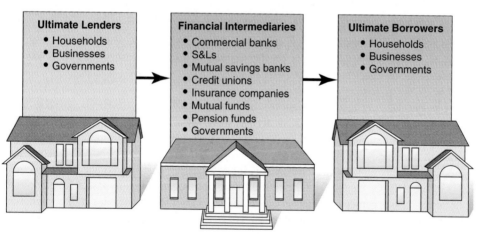

Ultimate Lenders
- Households
- Businesses
- Governments

Financial Intermediaries
- Commercial banks
- S&Ls
- Mutual savings banks
- Credit unions
- Insurance companies
- Mutual funds
- Pension funds
- Governments

Ultimate Borrowers
- Households
- Businesses
- Governments

FIGURE 15-3

The Process of Financial Intermediation
The process of financial intermediation is depicted here. Note that ultimate lenders and ultimate borrowers are the same economic units—households, businesses, and governments—but not necessarily the same individuals. Whereas individual households can be net lenders or borrowers, households as an economic unit are net lenders. Specific businesses or governments similarly can be net lenders or borrowers; as economic units, both are net borrowers.

---

[2]They include M3, which is equal to M2 plus large-denomination time deposits and REPOs (in amounts over $100,000) issued by commercial banks and thrift institutions, Eurodollars held by U.S. residents and foreign branches of U.S. banks worldwide and all banking offices in the United Kingdom and Canada, and the balances in both taxable and tax-exempt institution-only money market mutual funds. An even broader definition is called L, for liquidity. It is defined as M3 plus nonbank public holdings of U.S. savings bonds, short-term Treasury securities, commercial paper, and bankers' acceptances.

TABLE 15-2
Financial Intermediaries and Their Assets and Liabilities

Financial Intermediary	Assets	Liabilities
Commercial banks	Car loans and other consumer debt, business loans, government securities, home mortgages	Transactions accounts, savings deposits, various other time deposits, money market deposit accounts
Savings and loan associations	Home mortgages, some consumer and business debt	Savings and loan shares, transactions accounts, various time deposits, money market deposit accounts
Mutual savings banks	Home mortgages, some consumer and business debt	Transactions accounts, savings accounts, various time deposits, money market deposit accounts
Credit unions	Consumer debt, long-term mortgage loans	Credit union shares, transactions accounts
Insurance companies	Mortgages, stocks, bonds, real estate	Insurance contracts, annuities, pension plans
Pension and retirement funds	Stocks, bonds, mortgages, time deposits	Pension plans
Money market mutual funds	Short-term credit instruments such as large-bank CDs, Treasury bills, and high-grade commercial paper	Fund shares with limited checking privileges

Liabilities
Amounts owed; the legal claims against a business or household by nonowners.

Assets
Amounts owned; all items to which a business or household holds legal claim.

Each financial intermediary in the U.S. system has its own primary source of funds, which are called **liabilities.** When you deposit $100 in your checking account in the bank, the bank creates a liability—it owes you $100—in exchange for the funds deposited. A commercial bank gets its funds from checking and savings accounts; an insurance company gets its funds from insurance policy premiums.

Each financial intermediary normally has a different primary use of its **assets.** For example, a credit union usually makes small consumer loans, whereas a mutual savings bank makes mainly home mortgage loans. Table 15-2 lists the assets and liabilities of financial intermediaries. Be aware, though, that the distinction between different financial institutions is becoming more and more blurred. As the laws and regulations change, there will be less need to make any distinction. All may ultimately be treated simply as financial intermediaries.

CONCEPTS IN BRIEF

- The money supply can be defined in a variety of ways, depending on whether we use the transactions approach or the liquidity approach. Using the transactions approach, the money supply consists of currency, checkable deposits, and traveler's checks. This is called M1.

- Checkable deposits (transactions accounts) are any deposits in financial institutions on which the deposit owner can write checks.

- Credit cards are not part of the money supply, for they simply defer transactions that ultimately involve the use of money.

- When we add savings deposits, time deposits, small-denomination time deposits (certificates of deposit), money market deposit accounts, overnight REPOs, overnight Eurodollars, and retail money market mutual fund balances to M1, we obtain the measure known as M2.

- Financial intermediaries transfer funds from ultimate lenders (savers) to ultimate borrowers. This process of financial intermediation is undertaken by commercial banks, savings and loan associations, mutual savings banks, credit unions, insurance companies, mutual funds, pension funds, and governments.

THE FEDERAL RESERVE SYSTEM

The Federal Reserve System is the most important regulatory agency in our monetary system and is usually considered the monetary authority. Our central bank was established by the Federal Reserve Act, signed on December 23, 1913, by President Woodrow Wilson. The act was the outgrowth of recommendations from the National Monetary Commission, which had been authorized by the Aldridge-Vreeland Act of 1908. Basically, the commission had attempted to find a way to counter the periodic financial panics that had occurred in our country. The Federal Reserve System was established to aid and supervise banks and also to provide banking services for the U.S. Treasury.

Organization of the Federal Reserve System

Figure 15-4 shows how the Federal Reserve is organized. It is run by the Board of Governors, composed of seven full-time members appointed by the nation's president with the approval of the Senate. The 12 Federal Reserve district banks have a total of 25 branches. The boundaries of the 12 federal reserve districts and the cities in which a Federal Reserve bank is located are shown in Figure 15-5 on page 332. The Federal Open Market Committee (FOMC) determines monetary policy actions for the Fed. This committee is composed of the members of the Board of Governors, the president of the New York Federal Reserve Bank, and representatives of four other reserve banks, rotated periodically. The FOMC determines the future growth of the money supply and other important variables.

Depository Institutions

The banks and other depository institutions—all financial institutions that accept deposits—that comprise our monetary system consist of approximately 10,000 commercial banks, 2,100 savings and loan associations, 12,000 credit unions, and 500 mutual savings banks. No one financial institution dominates the marketplace. For example, the largest bank holds only 6 percent of total banking system deposits. All depository institutions, including member and nonmember commercial banks, as well as savings and loan associations, credit unions, and mutual savings banks, may purchase services from the Federal Reserve System on an equal basis. Also, almost all depository institutions are required to keep a certain percentage of their deposits in reserve at the Federal Reserve district banks or as vault cash. This percentage depends on the bank's volume of business. (For further discussion, see Chapter 16.)

Functions of the Federal Reserve System

Here we will present in detail what the Federal Reserve does in this country.

1. *The Fed supplies the economy with fiduciary currency.* The Federal Reserve banks must supply the economy with paper currency called Federal Reserve notes. For example,

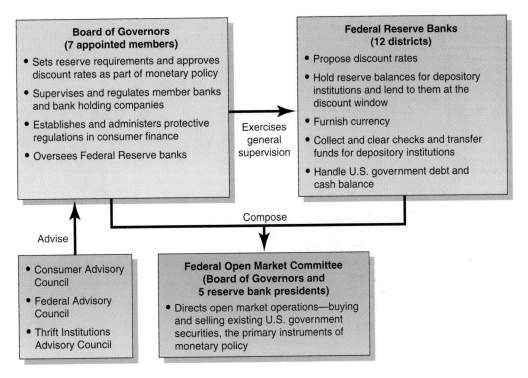

FIGURE 15-4

Organization of the Federal Reserve System

The 12 Federal Reserve district banks are headed by 12 separate presidents. The main authority of the Fed resides with the Board of Governors of the Federal Reserve System, whose seven members are appointed for 14-year terms by the president and confirmed by the Senate. Open market operations are carried out through the Federal Open Market Committee (FOMC), consisting of the seven members of the Board of Governors plus five presidents of the district banks (always including the president of the New York bank, with the others rotating).

Source: Board of Governors of the Federal Reserve System, *The Federal Reserve System: Purposes and Functions,* 7th ed. (Washington, D.C., 1984), p. 5.

at Christmastime, when there is an abnormally large number of currency transactions, more paper currency is desired. Commercial banks find this out as deposit holders withdraw large amounts of cash from their accounts. Commercial banks then turn to the Federal Reserve banks to replenish vault cash. Hence the Federal Reserve banks must have on hand a sufficient amount of cash to accommodate the demands for paper currency at different times of the year. Note that even though all Federal Reserve notes are printed at the Bureau of Engraving and Printing in Washington, D.C., each note is assigned a code indicating from which of the 12 Federal Reserve banks it "originated."

2. *The Fed provides a system for check collection and clearing.* The Federal Reserve System has established a clearing mechanism for checks. Suppose that John Smith in Chicago writes a check to Jill Jones, who lives in San Francisco. When Jill receives the check in the mail, she deposits it at her commercial bank. Her bank then deposits the check in the Federal Reserve Bank of San Francisco. In turn, the Federal Reserve Bank of San Francisco sends the check to the Federal Reserve Bank of Chicago. The Chicago Fed then sends the check to John Smith's commercial bank, where the amount of the check is deducted from John's account. The schematic diagram in Figure 15-6 on page 333 illustrates this check-clearing process. All member banks and

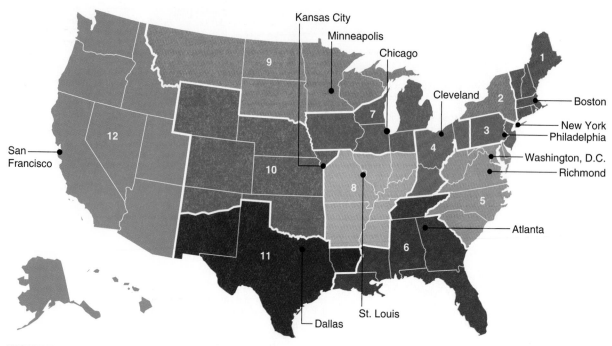

FIGURE 15-5

The Federal Reserve System
The Federal Reserve System is divided into 12 districts, each served by one of the Federal Reserve district banks, located in the cities indicated. The Board of Governors meets in Washington, D.C.

depository institutions in a particular Federal Reserve district can send deposited checks to one location—their district bank—thereby reducing the cost of check clearing. (The Fed's check collection and clearing operations compete with private clearinghouses. Since the Fed began charging for these services, some of this business has shifted back to the private sector.)

3. *The Fed holds depository institutions' reserves.* The 12 Federal Reserve district banks hold the reserves (other than vault cash) of depository institutions. As you will see in Chapter 16, depository institutions are required by law to keep a certain percentage of their deposits in reserves. Even if they weren't required to do so by law, they would still wish to keep some reserves. Depository institutions act just like other businesses. A firm would not try to operate with a zero balance in its checking account, would it? It would keep a positive balance on hand from which it could draw for expected and unexpected transactions. So, too, would a depository institution desire to have reserves in its banker's bank (the Federal Reserve) on which it could draw funds needed for expected and unexpected transactions.

4. *The Fed acts as the government's fiscal agent.* The Federal Reserve is the banker and fiscal agent for the federal government. The government, as we are all aware, collects large sums of money through taxation. The government also spends and distributes equally large sums. Consequently, the U.S. Treasury has a checking account with the Federal Reserve. Thus the Fed acts as the government's banker, along with commercial banks that hold government deposits. The Fed also helps the government collect certain tax revenues and aids in the purchase and sale of government securities.

Exercise 15.2
Visit www.econtoday.com for more about the Fed.

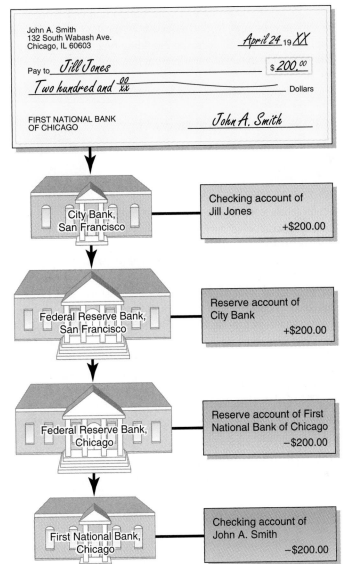

FIGURE 15-6
How a Check Clears
The check-clearing process for an out-of-town check normally involves four steps, including two with Federal Reserve district banks.

5. *The Fed supervises member banks.* The Fed (along with the Comptroller of the Currency and the Federal Deposit Insurance Corporation) is the supervisor and regulator of depository institutions. (All banks are regulated by some agency. No bank, savings and loan association, or credit union in the United States is unregulated.) The Fed will periodically and without warning examine member commercial banks to see what kinds of loans have been made, what has been used to back the loans, and who has received them. Whenever such an examination indicates that a member bank is not conforming to current banking rules and standards, the Fed can exert pressure on the bank to alter its banking practices.

6. *The Fed acts as the "lender of last resort."* As our central bank, the Fed stands ready to temporarily assist any part of the banking system that is in trouble. In this sense, it acts as a lender of last resort to depository institutions that it has decided should not fail.

7. *The Fed regulates the money supply.* Perhaps the Fed's most important task is its ability to regulate the nation's money supply. To understand how the Fed manages the money supply, we must examine more closely its reserve-holding function and the way in which depository institutions aid in expansion and contraction of the money supply. We will do this in Chapter 16.

FORCED INTO ELECTRONIC BANKING BY THE GOVERNMENT

The federal government is making cyberbanking, or at least a small part of it, a reality for millions of Americans. In an attempt to save on transaction costs, it is trying to force all recipients of federal funds to receive payments electronically, rather than by paper checks. For example, it is attempting to force military contractors who receive millions of dollars, as well as Social Security recipients who receive only thousands of dollars, to have those deposits made directly into their bank accounts. The goal is to eliminate all paper checks, at an estimated savings of over $500 million during the period 1999 to 2004.

Consider that the federal government makes over 850 million individual payments a year. Until recently, about half were made with paper checks, which cost 42 cents each to process, compared to electronic direct deposits, which cost only 2 cents. To achieve some of these savings, the federal government is turning to the E-Pay network of Visa U.S.A. Companies that receive federal payments must install software that they obtain from Visa. When many companies have the same software, they will surely start settling private transactions via the electronic payment system. Until then, though, small businesses that deal with the government will be at a disadvantage. Electronic transfers for businesses require detailed data about the services covered by the payment. Many small businesses do not have the software to complete all this information. Small banks also do not have systems in place to handle electronic data interchange.

FOR CRITICAL ANALYSIS: Many poorer individuals do not have bank accounts but instead use check-cashing outlets. What will happen to the demand for such outlets as the federal government forces individuals to accept direct deposits? ●

CONCEPTS IN BRIEF

- The central bank in the United States is the Federal Reserve System, which was established on December 13, 1913.

- There are 12 Federal Reserve district banks, with 25 branches. The Federal Reserve is run by the Board of Governors in Washington, D.C.

- The Fed has control over virtually all depository institutions in the United States, including commercial banks, savings and loan associations, credit unions, and mutual savings banks. Most must keep a certain percentage of their deposits on reserve with the Fed.

- The functions of the Federal Reserve are to supply fiduciary currency, provide for check collection and clearing, hold depository institution reserves, act as the government's fiscal agent, supervise member banks, act as the lender of last resort, and regulate the supply of money.

Security Risks and Money Laundering On-Line

Because of the risk that cash obtained through drug sales will be confiscated, as in the above photo, drug traffickers usually want to launder their profits quickly. How does the Internet help them?

Visit www.econtoday.com for an Internet Activity that expands your understanding of these concepts.

The age of cyberbanking is here. Cyberbanking involves doing your banking on-line over the Internet. Some banks, such as Citibank, give you special software that allows you to dial directly into that bank's system. This form of on-line banking does not use the Internet and, in principle, is more secure.

Many banks, such as Wells Fargo, are allowing customers to use the Internet to access their accounts. If you instruct your Web browser to enter an encrypted mode, you can be reasonably confident that no one else can gain access to your transaction.

What Does Cyberbanking Allow?

Cyberbanking allows you to pay your bills electronically (but usually for a fee) and to transfer funds among accounts, find out which checks have cleared, and learn your current balance. Most programs allow you to download transactions into a money management program, such as Intuit's Quicken or Microsoft Money.

The World of Digital Cash

Digital cash, or *e-cash*, is an alternative to using the traditional banking system. Instead of paper currency, accounts are debited and credited without cash or checks changing hands. Eventually people will be able to download funds to their PC or to palm-sized electronic wallets or to transfer money instantly to Internet merchants. As electronic commerce becomes more widespread, so does the problem of money laundering.

Digital Money Laundering

Tax evaders and drug traffickers, among others, need to move funds around the world without their actions being traced. This is known as money laundering. The Financial Action Task Force, a group of 26 countries fighting money laundering, believes that the speed, security, and anonymity of new Internet payment systems will lead to massive additional money laundering. Drug traffickers in particular will no longer need to smuggle currency across borders—they will be able to move funds through the Internet. Technology will permit anonymous transactions outside the regulated banking sector. All restrictions on the banking system to make money laundering riskier and costlier will be for naught. Even when digital cash enters the banking system, it will have already bounced among numerous intermediaries, making the funds hard to trace. By definition, e-cash will be heavily encrypted. Thus law enforcement authorities will not be able to reconstruct transactions, nor will private providers of e-cash. DigiCash, a major European electronic money provider, indicates that it cannot track how its customers spend their money.

FOR CRITICAL ANALYSIS

1. Currently, banks that transfer cash into digital money systems have a limit of a few hundred dollars per transfer. Is there any way for money launderers to overcome this constraint?

2. What do you think the most convenient use of digital money will be, particularly now that money is available on a "smart card," which has its own computer chip?

CHAPTER SUMMARY

1. The functions of money are as a medium of exchange, a unit of accounting (standard of value), a store of value or purchasing power, and a standard of deferred payment.

2. We have a fiduciary monetary system in the United States—our money, whether in the form of currency or checkable accounts, is not convertible into a fixed quantity of a commodity, such as gold or silver.

3. Our money is exchangeable for goods and services because it has acceptability: People have confidence that whatever money they receive can be exchanged for other goods and services later. Our money also has a predictable value.

4. There are numerous ways to define the U.S. money supply. One method is called the transactions approach, which stresses the role of money as a medium of exchange. The other method is the liquidity approach, which stresses the role of money as a temporary store of value.

5. The transactions approach generates the M1 definition of money, which includes currency, checkable deposits, and traveler's checks not issued by banks.

6. The liquidity approach generates the M2 definition of money, which includes M1 plus such near monies as savings deposits, overnight repurchase agreements, retail money market mutual fund balances, money market deposit accounts, and overnight Eurodollars.

7. Our central bank is the Federal Reserve System, which consists of 12 district banks with 25 branches. The governing body of the Federal Reserve System is the Board of Governors. The group that makes monetary policy decisions is the Federal Open Market Committee.

8. The basic functions of the Federal Reserve System are supplying the economy with fiduciary currency, providing a system for check collection and clearing, holding depository institutions' reserves, acting as the government's fiscal agent, supervising member banks, acting as a lender of last resort, and regulating the money supply.

DISCUSSION OF PREVIEW QUESTIONS

1. What is money?

Money is defined by its functions. Thus money is whatever is generally accepted for use as a medium of exchange, a unit of accounting, a store of value or purchasing power, and a standard of deferred payment. In various places in the world, throughout history, different items have performed these functions: wampum, gold, silver, cows, stones, paper, diamonds, salt, cigarettes, and many others.

2. What "backs" the U.S. dollar?

Some students think that the U.S. dollar is "backed" by gold, but alas (some experts say fortunately), this is not the case. The United States is presently on a fiduciary monetary standard, and as such the U.S. dollar is backed only by faith—the public's confidence that it can be exchanged for goods and services. This confidence comes from the fact that other people will accept the dollar in transactions because our government has declared it legal tender and

because, despite inflation, it still retains the characteristic of predictability of value.

3. What are the functions of the Federal Reserve System?

The Fed's most important function is to regulate the U.S. money supply, a topic covered in the next several chapters. The Fed also holds depository institutions' reserves, acts as the U.S. government's fiscal agent, supervises member banks, serves as a lender of last resort, clears checks, and supplies fiduciary currency to the public.

4. Who is involved in the process of transferring funds from savers to investors?

Financial intermediation involves the transfer of funds from savers to investors. The ultimate lenders are the savers—households, businesses, and governments, including the federal government and state and local governments. The ultimate borrowers are also households, businesses, and governments—the same economic units but not necessarily the same individuals. Between ultimate lenders and ultimate borrowers are financial intermediaries, including commercial banks, savings and loans, mutual savings banks, credit unions, insurance companies, mutual funds, pension funds, and governments.

PROBLEMS

(Answers to the odd-numbered problems appear at the back of the book.)

15-1. Consider each type of asset in terms of its potential use as a medium of exchange, a unit of accounting, and a store of value or purchasing power. Indicate which use is most appropriately associated with each asset.

   a. A painting by Renoir
   b. A 90-day U.S. Treasury bill
   c. A time deposit account with a savings and loan association in Reno, Nevada
   d. One share of IBM stock
   e. A $50 Federal Reserve note
   f. A MasterCard credit card
   g. A checkable account in a mutual savings bank in New England
   h. A lifetime pass to the Los Angeles Dodgers' home baseball games

15-2. The value of a dollar bill is the reciprocal of the price index. In 1983 the CPI had a value of 1; hence the value of a dollar in 1983 equaled $1. If the price index now is 2, what is the value of the dollar in 1983 prices? If the price index is 2.5?

15-3. What are the components of M2?

15-4. How have technological changes altered the form of money?

15-5. Elsa Lee can make several uses of her money. Indicate for each case whether her money is being used as a medium of exchange (E), a unit of accounting (A), a store of value (V), or a standard of deferred payment (P).

   a. Lee has accumulated $600 in her checking account at a depository institution.
   b. Lee decides to use this $600 to purchase a new washing machine and goes shopping to compare the prices being charged by different dealers for the machine she wishes to buy.

   c. Lee finds that the lowest price at which she can purchase the machine she wants is $498.50. She has the dealer deliver the machine and agrees to pay the dealer in 30 days.
   d. Thirty days later, Lee sends the dealer a check drawn on her checking account to pay for the washer.

15-6. Explain why a debit card is not a new form of money.

15-7. Consider a barter economy in which 10 goods and services are produced and exchanged. How many exchange rates exist in that economy, which does not use money?

15-8. Use the data in the table to compute M1.

Components	Amount ($ billions)
Currency outside of the Treasury, Federal Reserve banks, and vaults of depository institutions	193.2
Checkable accounts other than those owned by depository institutions, the U.S. government, foreign banks, and foreign institutions	541.9
Large time deposits, short-term REPOs, liabilities, and overnight Eurodollars	743.4
Nonbank public holdings of U.S. savings bonds	643.0
Nonbank traveler's checks	8.1

15-9. Cash and checks account for nearly 98 percent of the total *number* of all payments in the United States, but wire transfers account for over 82 percent of the dollar *value* of all payments in the United States. How can both situations be true simultaneously?

COMPUTER-ASSISTED INSTRUCTION

The key conceptual and institutional features of our monetary and banking systems are illuminated with the aid of real-world questions.

Complete problem and answer appear on disk.

INTERACTING WITH THE INTERNET

If you would like to read about security issues in cyberbanking, check out Wells Fargo's Web site at

wellsfargo.com/nav/security

You can find information on the Federal Reserve's function by going to the home page of the Federal Reserve Bank of San Francisco at

www.frbsf.org

Here are the Web sites for the various Federal Reserve banks:

Atlanta: **www.frbatlanta.org/**

Boston: **www.bos.frb.org**

Chicago: **www.frbchi.org**

Cleveland: **www.clev.frb.org**

Dallas: **www.dallasfed.org/fedhome.html**

Kansas City: **www.frbkc.org/contents.htm**

Minneapolis: **woodrow.mpls.frb.fed.us/**

New York: **www.ny.frb.org**

Philadelphia: **www.phil.frb.org**

Richmond: **www.Rich.FRB.org/**

St. Louis: **www.stls.frb.org/**

San Francisco: **www.frbsf.org/index2.html**

In the depths of the Great Depression, Americans learned firsthand what a banking crisis was all about. Before President Franklin D. Roosevelt declared a "banking holiday," over 5,000 banks had failed. Their customers were left high and dry. More recently, in the 1980s, saving and loan associations failed right and left. U.S. taxpayers bailed them out to the tune of hundreds of billions of dollars. During that crisis, no depositors lost any of their funds, but the economy suffered nonetheless. Some of the most recent banking crises involved the Asian countries of Japan, Thailand, and South Korea. What causes such crises, and how much do they cost each nation's economy? To understand this question fully, you need to know more about how money is created in an economy and what effect deposit insurance has on the way bankers behave.

PREVIEW QUESTIONS

1. What is a fractional reserve banking system?

2. What happens to the total money supply when a person deposits in one depository institution a check drawn on another depository institution?

3. What happens to the overall money supply when a person who sells a U.S. government security to the Federal Reserve places the proceeds in a depository institution?

4. How does the existence of deposit insurance affect a financial institution's choice of risky versus nonrisky assets?

Did You Know That . . . virtually overnight, Nick Leeson, a 27-year-old manager in the Singapore branch of Barings Bank, was able to inflict losses of several billion dollars on the institution? Barings was founded in 1762. In 1803, it helped the United States purchase the Louisiana Territory from France. It provided credit to the British government during the Napoleonic Wars (1803–1815). When Barings collapsed in 1995, it was bought by former competitors, thereby ending the life of one of the longest-running financial institutions in the world. Could the collapse of such an important bank lead to serious problems in the world's banking sector? A lot depends on whether the losses suffered by Barings's depositors would cause other banks to contract. That, in turn, depends on the relationship between deposits in different banks.

If you were to attend a luncheon of local bankers and ask the question, "Do you as bankers create money?" you would get a uniformly negative response. Bankers are certain that they do not create money. Indeed, no individual bank can create money. But along with the Federal Reserve System, depository institutions do create money; they determine the total deposits outstanding. In this chapter we will examine the **money multiplier process,** which explains how an injection of new money into the banking system leads to an eventual multiple expansion in the total money supply. We will also take a look at federal deposit insurance and its role in provoking the past crisis in the savings and loan industry.

LINKS BETWEEN CHANGES IN THE MONEY SUPPLY AND OTHER ECONOMIC VARIABLES

How fast the money supply grows or does not grow is important because no matter what model of the economy is used, theories link the money supply growth rate to economic growth or to business fluctuations. There is in fact a long-standing relationship between changes in the money supply and changes in GDP. Some economists use this historical evidence to argue that money is an important determinant of the level of economic activity in the economy.

Another key economic variable in our economy is the price level. At least one theory attributes changes in the rate of inflation to changes in the growth rate of money in circulation. Figure 16-1 shows the relationship between the rate of growth of the money supply and the inflation rate. There seems to be a loose, albeit consistent, direct relationship between changes in the money supply and changes in the rate of inflation. Increases in the money supply growth rate seem to lead to increases in the inflation rate, after a time lag.

THE ORIGINS OF FRACTIONAL RESERVE BANKING

As early as 1000 B.C., uncoined gold and silver were being used as money in Mesopotamia. Goldsmiths weighed and assessed the purity of those metals; later they started issuing paper notes indicating that the bearers held gold or silver of given weights and purity on deposit with the goldsmith. These notes could be transferred in exchange for goods and became the first paper currency. The gold and silver on deposit with the goldsmiths were the first bank deposits. Eventually, goldsmiths realized that the amount of gold and silver on deposit always exceeded the amount of gold and silver withdrawn—often by a predictable ratio. These goldsmiths started issuing to borrowers paper notes that exceeded in value the amount of gold and silver they actually kept on hand. They charged interest on these loans. This constituted the earliest form of what is now called **fractional reserve banking.** We know that goldsmiths operated this way in Delphi, Didyma, and Olympia in

Money multiplier process
The process by which an injection of new money into the banking system leads to a multiple expansion in the total money supply.

Fractional reserve banking
A system in which depository institutions hold reserves that are less than the amount of total deposits.

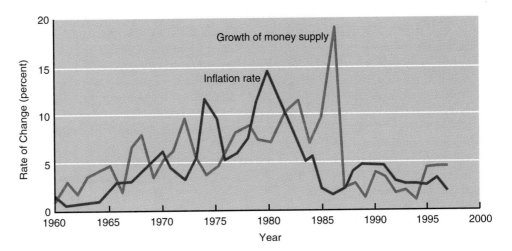

FIGURE 16-1

Money Supply Growth Versus the Inflation Rate
These time-series curves indicate a loose correspondence between money supply growth and the inflation rate. Actually, closer inspection reveals a direct relationship between changes in the growth rate of money and changes in the inflation rate *in a later period.* Increases in the rate of growth of money seem to lead to subsequent increases in the inflation rate; decreases in the rate of money growth seem to lead to subsequent reductions in the inflation rate.

Sources: Economic Report of the President; Federal Reserve Bulletin; Economic Indicators, various issues.

Greece as early as the seventh century B.C. In Athens, fractional reserve banking was well developed by the sixth century B.C.

In a fractional reserve banking system, banks do not keep sufficient reserves on hand to cover 100 percent of their depositors' accounts. And the reserves that are held by depository institutions in the United States are not kept in gold and silver, as they were with the early goldsmiths, but rather in the form of deposits on reserve with Federal Reserve district banks and in vault cash.

RESERVES

Reserves
In the U.S. Federal Reserve System, deposits held by Federal Reserve district banks for depository institutions, plus depository institutions' vault cash.

Depository institutions are required by the Fed to maintain a specified percentage of their customer deposits as **reserves.** Different types of depository institutions are required to hold different percentages of reserves. Also, within one type of depository institution, the larger the institution, the larger the reserve requirements. On checkable accounts, most depository institutions have to keep 10 percent as reserves.

Take a hypothetical example. If the required level of reserves is 10 percent and the bank[1] has $1 billion in customer checkable deposits, it must hold at least $100 million as reserves. These can be either deposits with the Federal Reserve district bank or vault cash. There are three distinguishable types of reserves: legal, required, and excess.

Legal reserves
Reserves that depository institutions are allowed by law to claim as reserves—for example, deposits held at Federal Reserve district banks and vault cash.

1. *Legal reserves.* For depository institutions, **legal reserves** constitute anything that the law permits them to claim as reserves. Today, that consists only of deposits held at the

---

[1]The term *bank* will be used interchangeably with the term *depository institution* in this chapter because distinctions among financial institutions are becoming less and less meaningful.

Federal Reserve district bank plus vault cash. Government securities, for example, are not legal reserves, even though the owners and managers of the depository institutions may consider them such because they can easily be turned into cash, should the need arise, to meet unusually large net withdrawals by customers.

2. *Required reserves.* **Required reserves** are the *minimum* amount of legal reserves—vault cash plus deposits with the Fed—that a depository institution must have to back its checkable deposits. They are expressed as a ratio of required reserves to total checkable deposits (banks need hold no reserves on noncheckable deposits). The **required reserve ratio** is currently 10 percent.

3. *Excess reserves.* Depository institutions often hold reserves in excess of what is required by law. This difference between actual (legal) reserves and required reserves is called **excess reserves.** (Excess reserves can be negative, but they rarely are. Negative excess reserves indicate that depository institutions do not have sufficient reserves to meet their required reserves. When this happens, they borrow from other depository institutions or from a Federal Reserve district bank, sell assets such as securities, or call in loans.) Excess reserves are an important potential determinant of the rate of growth of the money supply, for as we shall see, it is only to the extent that depository institutions have excess reserves that they can make new loans. Because reserves produce no income, profit-seeking financial institutions have an incentive to minimize excess reserves. They use them either to purchase income-producing securities or to make loans with which they earn income through interest payments received. In equation form, we can define excess reserves in this way:

$$\text{Excess reserves} = \text{legal reserves} - \text{required reserves}$$

In the analysis that follows, we examine the relationship between the level of reserves and the size of the money supply. This analysis implies that factors influencing the level of the reserves of the banking system as a whole will ultimately affect the level of the money supply, other things held constant. We show first that when someone deposits in one depository institution a check that is written on another depository institution, the two depository institutions involved are individually affected, but the overall money supply does not change. Then we show that when someone deposits in a depository institution a check that is written on the Fed, a multiple expansion in the money supply results.

Required reserves
The value of reserves that a depository institution must hold in the form of vault cash or deposits with the Fed.

Required reserve ratio
The percentage of total deposits that the Fed requires depository institutions to hold in the form of vault cash or deposits with the Fed.

Excess reserves
The difference between legal reserves and required reserves.

CONCEPTS IN BRIEF

- Ours is a fractional reserve banking system in which depository institutions must hold only a percentage of their deposits as reserves, either on deposit with a Federal Reserve district bank or as vault cash.

- Required reserves are usually expressed as a ratio, in percentage terms, of legal reserves to total deposits.

THE RELATIONSHIP BETWEEN RESERVES AND TOTAL DEPOSITS

To show the relationship between reserves and depository institution deposits, we first analyze a single bank (existing alongside many others). A single bank is able to make new loans to its customers only to the extent that it has reserves above the level legally required to cover the new deposits. When an individual bank has no excess reserves, it cannot make loans.

How a Single Bank Reacts to an Increase in Reserves

Balance sheet
A statement of the assets and liabilities of any business entity, including financial institutions and the Federal Reserve System. Assets are what is owned; liabilities are what is owed.

To examine the **balance sheet** of a single bank after its reserves are increased, the following assumptions are made:

1. The required reserve ratio is 10 percent for all checkable deposits; that is, the federal government requires that an amount equal to 10 percent of all checkable deposits be held in reserve in a Federal Reserve district bank or in vault cash.
2. Checkable deposits are the bank's only liabilities; reserves at a Federal Reserve district bank and loans are the bank's only assets. Loans are promises made by customers to repay some amount in the future; that is, they are IOUs and as such are assets to the bank.
3. An individual bank can lend all it wants at current market interest rates.
4. Every time a loan is made to an individual (consumer or business), all the proceeds from the loan are put into a checkable account; no cash (currency or coins) is withdrawn.
5. Depository institutions seek to keep their excess reserves at a zero level because reserves at the Federal Reserve district bank do not earn interest. (Depository institutions are run to make profits; we assume that all depository institutions wish to convert excess reserves that do not pay interest into interest-bearing loans.)

Look at the simplified initial position of the bank in Balance Sheet 16-1. Liabilities consist of $1 million in checkable deposits. Assets consist of $100,000 in reserves, which you can see are required reserves in the form of vault cash or deposits in the institution's reserve account at the Federal Reserve district branch, and $900,000 in loans to customers. Total assets of $1 million equal total liabilities of $1 million. With a 10 percent reserve requirement and $1 million in checkable deposits, the bank has the actual required reserves of $100,000 and no excess reserves. The simplifying assumption here is that the bank has a zero **net worth.** A depository institution rarely has a net worth of more than a small percentage of its total assets.

Net worth
The difference between assets and liabilities.

BALANCE SHEET 16-1
Bank 1

ASSETS			LIABILITIES	
Total reserves		$100,000	Checkable deposits	$1,000,000
Required reserves	$100,000			
Excess reserves	0			
Loans		900,000		
Total		$1,000,000	Total	$1,000,000

Assume that a *new* depositor writes a $100,000 check drawn on another depository institution and deposits it in Bank 1. Checkable deposits in Bank 1 immediately increase by $100,000, bringing the total to $1.1 million. Once the check clears, total reserves of Bank 1 increase to $200,000. A $1.1 million total in checkable deposits means that required reserves will have to be 10 percent of $1.1 million, or $110,000. Bank 1 now has excess reserves equal to $200,000 minus $110,000, or $90,000. This is shown in Balance Sheet 16-2.

BALANCE SHEET 16-2
Bank 1

ASSETS			LIABILITIES	
Total reserves		$200,000	Checkable deposits	$1,100,000
Required reserves	$110,000			
Excess reserves	90,000			
Loans		900,000		
Total		$1,100,000	Total	$1,100,000

Look at excess reserves in Balance Sheet 16-2. Excess reserves were zero before the $100,000 deposit, and now they are $90,000—that's $90,000 worth of assets not earning any income. By assumption, Bank 1 will now lend out this entire $90,000 in excess reserves in order to obtain interest income. Loans will increase to $990,000. The borrowers who receive the new loans will not leave them on deposit in Bank 1. After all, they borrow money to spend it. As they spend it by writing checks that are deposited in other banks, actual reserves will fall to $110,000 (as required), and excess reserves will again become zero, as indicated in Balance Sheet 16-3.

ASSETS			LIABILITIES	
Total reserves		$110,000	Checkable deposits	$1,100,000
Required reserves	$110,000			
Excess reserves	0			
Loans		990,000		
Total		$1,100,000	Total	$1,100,000

BALANCE SHEET 16-3
Bank 1

In this example, a person deposited an additional $100,000 check drawn on another bank. That $100,000 became part of the reserves of Bank 1. Because that deposit immediately created excess reserves in Bank 1, further loans were possible for Bank 1. The excess reserves were lent out to earn interest. A bank will not lend more than its excess reserves because, by law, it must hold a certain amount of required reserves.

Effect on the Money Supply. A look at the balance sheets for Bank 1 might give the impression that the money supply increased because of the new customer's $100,000 deposit. Remember, though, that the deposit was a check written on *another* bank. Therefore, the other bank suffered a *decline* in its checkable deposits and its reserves. While total assets and liabilities in Bank 1 have increased by $100,000, they have *decreased* in the other bank by $100,000. The *total* amount of money and credit in the economy is unaffected by the transfer of funds from one depository institution to another.

Each individual depository institution can create new loans (and deposits) only to the extent that it has excess reserves. In our example, Bank 1 had $90,000 of excess reserves after the deposit of the $100,000. But the bank on which the check was written found that its excess reserves were now a *negative* $90,000 (assuming that it had zero excess reserves previously). That bank now has fewer reserves than required by law. It will have to call in loans or sell assets to make actual reserves meet required reserves.

The thing to remember is that new reserves are not created when checks written on one bank are deposited in another bank. The Federal Reserve System can, however, create new reserves; that is the subject of the next section.

THE FED'S DIRECT EFFECT ON THE OVERALL LEVEL OF RESERVES

Now we shall examine the Fed's direct effect on the level of reserves. An explanation of how a change in the level of reserves causes a multiple change in the total money supply follows. Consider the Federal Open Market Committee (FOMC), whose decisions essentially determine the level of reserves in the monetary system.

Federal Open Market Committee

Open market operations
The purchase and sale of existing U.S. government securities (such as bonds) in the open private market by the Federal Reserve System.

Open market operations are the purchase and sale of *existing* U.S. government securities in the open market (the private secondary U.S. securities market) by the FOMC in order to change the money supply. If the FOMC decides that the Fed should buy or sell bonds, it instructs the New York Federal Reserve Bank trading desk to do so.[2]

A Sample Transaction

Assume that the trading desk at the New York Fed has received an order from the FOMC to purchase $100,000 worth of U.S. government securities.[3] The Fed pays for these securities by writing a check on itself for $100,000. This check is given to the bond dealer in exchange for the $100,000 worth of bonds. The bond dealer deposits the $100,000 check in its checkable account at a bank, which then sends the $100,000 check back to the Federal Reserve. When the Fed receives the check, it adds $100,000 to the reserve account of the bank that sent it the check. The Fed has created $100,000 of reserves. The Fed can create reserves because it has the ability to "write up" (add to) the reserve accounts of depository institutions whenever it buys U.S. securities. When the Fed buys a U.S. government security in the open market, it initially expands total reserves and the money supply by the amount of the purchase.

Using Balance Sheets. Consider the balance sheets of the Fed and of the depository institution, such as a typical bank, receiving the check. Balance Sheet 16-4 shows the results for the Fed after the bond purchase and for the bank after the bond dealer deposits the $100,000 check.[4] The Fed's balance sheet (which here reflects only account *changes*) shows that after the purchase, the Fed's assets have increased by $100,000 in the form of U.S. government securities. Liabilities have also increased by $100,000 in the form of an increase in the reserve account of the bank. The balance sheet for the bank shows an increase in assets of $100,000 in the form of reserves with its Federal Reserve district bank. The bank also has an increase in its liabilities in the form of $100,000 in the checkable account of the bond dealer; this is an immediate $100,000 increase in the money supply.

BALANCE SHEET 16-4

Balance Sheets for the Fed and the Bank When a U.S. Government Security Is Purchased by the Fed, Showing Changes in Assets and Liabilities

The Fed		Bank	
ASSETS	LIABILITIES	ASSETS	LIABILITIES
+$100,000 U.S. government securities	+$100,000 depository institution's reserves	+$100,000 reserves	+$100,000 checkable deposit owned by bond dealer

---

[2] Actually, the Fed usually deals in Treasury bills that have a maturity date of one year or less.

[3] In practice, the trading desk is never given a specific dollar amount to purchase or to sell. The account manager uses personal discretion in determining what amount should be purchased or sold in order to satisfy the FOMC's latest directive. For expositional purposes, assume nonetheless that the account manager is directed to make a specific transaction.

[4] Strictly speaking, the balance sheets that we are showing should be called the *consolidated balance sheets* for the 12 Federal Reserve district banks. We will simply refer to these banks as the Fed, however.

Sale of a $100,000 U.S. Government Security by the Fed

The process is reversed when the account manager at the New York Fed trading desk sells a U.S. government security from the Fed's portfolio. When the individual or institution buying the security from the Fed writes a check for $100,000, the Fed reduces the reserves of the bank on which the check was written. The $100,000 sale of the U.S. government security leads to a reduction in reserves in the banking system.

Using Balance Sheets Again. Balance Sheet 16-5 shows the results for the sale of a U.S. government security by the Fed. When the $100,000 check goes to the Fed, the Fed reduces by $100,000 the reserve account of the bank on which the check is written. The Fed's assets are also reduced by $100,000 because it no longer owns the U.S. government security. The bank's liabilities are reduced by $100,000 when that amount is deducted from the account of the bond purchaser, and the money supply is thereby reduced by that amount. The bank's assets are also reduced by $100,000 because the Fed has reduced its reserves by that amount.

The Fed		Bank	
ASSETS	LIABILITIES	ASSETS	LIABILITIES
−$100,000 U.S. government securities	−$100,000 depository institution's reserves	−$100,000 reserves	−$100,000 checkable deposit balances

BALANCE SHEET 16-5

Balance Sheets After the Fed Has Sold $100,000 of U.S. Government Securities, Showing Changes Only

CONCEPTS IN BRIEF

- If a check is written on one depository institution and deposited in another, there is no change in total deposits or in the total money supply. No new reserves have been created.
- The Federal Reserve, through its Federal Open Market Committee (FOMC), can directly increase depository institutions' reserves by purchasing U.S. government securities in the open market; it can decrease depository institutions' reserves by selling U.S. government securities in the open market.

MONEY EXPANSION BY THE BANKING SYSTEM

Consider now the entire banking system. For practical purposes, we can look at all depository institutions taken as a whole. To understand how money is created, we must understand how depository institutions respond to Fed actions that increase reserves in the entire system.

Fed Purchases of U.S. Government Securities

Assume that the Fed purchases a $100,000 U.S. government security from a bond dealer. The bond dealer deposits the $100,000 check in Bank 1 (which started out in the position depicted in Balance Sheet 16-1 on page 343). The check, however, is not written on another depository institution; rather, it is written on the Fed itself.

Look at the balance sheet for Bank 1 shown in Balance Sheet 16-6. It is the same as Balance Sheet 16-2. Reserves have been increased by $100,000 to $200,000, and checkable deposits have also been increased by $100,000. Because required reserves on $1.1 million of checkable deposits are only $110,000, there is $90,000 in excess reserves.

BALANCE SHEET 16-6
Bank 1

ASSETS			LIABILITIES	
Total reserves		$200,000	Checkable deposits	$1,100,000
Required reserves	$110,000			
Excess reserves	90,000			
Loans		900,000		
Total		$1,100,000	Total	$1,100,000

Effect on the Money Supply. The major difference between this example and the one given previously is that here the money supply has increased by $100,000 immediately. Why? Because checkable deposits held by the public—the bond dealers are members of the public—are part of the money supply, *and no other bank has lost reserves.* Thus the purchase of a $100,000 U.S. government security by the Federal Reserve from the public (a bond dealer or a bank) increases the money supply immediately by $100,000.

Not the End of the Process. The process of money creation does not stop here. Look again at Balance Sheet 16-6. Bank 1 has excess reserves of $90,000. No other depository institution (or combination of depository institutions) has negative excess reserves of $90,000 as a result of the Fed's bond purchase. (Remember, the Fed simply created the money to pay for the bond purchase.)

Bank 1 will not wish to hold non-interest-bearing excess reserves. It will expand its loans by creating deposits equal to $90,000. This is shown in Balance Sheet 16-7, which is exactly like Balance Sheet 16-3, except there has been no corresponding reduction in loans at any other depository institution.

BALANCE SHEET 16-7
Bank 1

ASSETS			LIABILITIES	
Total reserves		$110,000	Checkable deposits	$1,100,000
Required reserves	$110,000			
Excess reserves	0			
Loans		990,000		
Total		$1,100,000	Total	$1,100,000

The individuals who have received the $90,000 of new loans will spend (write checks on) these funds, which will then be deposited in other banks. To make this example simple, assume that the $90,000 in excess reserves was lent to a single firm for the purpose of buying a Burger King franchise. After the firm buys the franchise, Burger King deposits the

$90,000 check in its account at Bank 2. For the sake of simplicity, ignore the previous assets and liabilities in Bank 2 and concentrate only on the balance sheet *changes* resulting from this new deposit, as shown in Balance Sheet 16-8. A plus sign indicates that the entry has increased, and a minus sign indicates that the entry has decreased. For the depository institution, Bank 2, the $90,000 deposit, after the check has been sent to the Fed, becomes an increase in reserves (assets) as well as an increase in checkable deposits (liabilities) and hence the money supply. Because the reserve requirement is 10 percent, or $9,000, Bank 2 will have excess reserves of $81,000. But, of course, excess reserves are not income-producing, so Bank 2 will reduce them to zero by making loans of $81,000 (which will earn interest income) by creating deposits for borrowers equal to $81,000. This is shown in Balance Sheet 16-9.

ASSETS			LIABILITIES	
Total reserves		+$90,000	New checkable deposits	+$90,000
Required reserves	$9,000			
Excess reserves	+81,000			
Total		+$90,000	Total	+$90,000

BALANCE SHEET 16-8
Bank 2 (Changes Only)

ASSETS			LIABILITIES	
Total reserves		$9,000	Checkable deposits	$90,000
Required reserves	$9,000			
Excess reserves	0			
Loans		+81,000		
Total		$90,000	Total	$90,000

BALANCE SHEET 16-9
Bank 2 (Changes Only)

Remember that in this example, the original $100,000 deposit was a check issued by a Federal Reserve bank to the bond dealer. That $100,000 constituted an immediate increase in the money supply of $100,000 when deposited in the bond dealer's checkable account. The deposit creation process (in addition to the original $100,000) occurs because of the fractional reserve banking system, coupled with the desire of depository institutions to maintain a minimum level of excess reserves.

Continuation of the Deposit Creation Process. Assume that the company that has received the $81,000 loan from Bank 2 wants to buy into an oil-drilling firm. This oil-drilling firm has an account at Bank 3. Look at Bank 3's simplified account in Balance Sheet 16-10, where, again, only changes in the assets and liabilities are shown. When the firm borrowing from Bank 2 pays the $81,000 to the oil-drilling firm's owner, the owner deposits the check in Bank 3; checkable deposits and the money supply increase by $81,000. Total reserves of Bank 3 rise by that amount when the check is sent to the Fed.

ASSETS			LIABILITIES	
Total reserves		+$81,000	New checkable deposits	+$81,000
Required reserves	$8,100			
Excess reserves	+72,900			
Total		+$81,000	Total	+$81,000

BALANCE SHEET 16-10
Bank 3 (Changes Only)

Because the reserve requirement is 10 percent, required reserves rise by $8,100, and excess reserves are therefore $72,900. Bank 3 will want to lend those non-interest-earning assets (excess reserves). When it does, loans (in the form of created checkable deposits) will increase by $72,900. This bank's total reserves will fall to $8,100, and excess reserves become zero as the oil-drilling firm's manager writes checks on the new deposit. This is shown in Balance Sheet 16-11.

BALANCE SHEET 16-11

Bank 3 (Changes Only)

ASSETS			LIABILITIES	
Total reserves		$8,100	Checkable deposits	$81,000
Required reserves	$8,100			
Excess reserves	0			
Loans		+72,900		
Total		$81,000	Total	$81,000

Progression to Other Banks. This process continues to Banks 4, 5, 6, and so forth. Each bank obtains smaller and smaller increases in deposits because 10 percent of each deposit must be held in reserves; therefore, each succeeding depository institution makes correspondingly smaller loans. Table 16-1 shows the new deposits, possible loans, and required reserves for the remaining depository institutions in the system.

Effect on Total Deposits. In this simple example, deposits increased initially by the $100,000 that the Fed paid the bond dealer in exchange for a bond. They were further increased by a $90,000 deposit in Bank 2, and they were again increased by an $81,000 deposit in Bank 3. Eventually, total deposits will increase by $1 million, as shown in Table 16-1. The money multiplier process is portrayed graphically in Figure 16-2 on page 350.

Increase in Overall Reserves

Even with fractional reserve banking, if there are zero excess reserves, deposits cannot expand unless overall reserves are increased. The original new deposit in Bank 1, in our

TABLE 16-1

Maximum Money Creation with 10 Percent Required Reserves
This table shows the maximum new loans plus investments that banks can make, given the Fed's deposit of a $100,000 check in Bank 1. The required reserve ratio is 10 percent. We assume that all excess reserves in each bank are used for new loans or investments.

Bank	New Deposits (new reserves)	New Required Reserves	Maximum New Loans plus Investments (excess reserves)
1	$100,000 (from Fed)	$10,000	$90,000
2	90,000	9,000	81,000
3	81,000	8,100	72,900
4	72,900	7,290	65,610
.	.	.	.
.	.	.	.
.	.	.	.
All other banks	656,100	65,610	590,490
Totals	$1,000,000	$100,000	$900,000

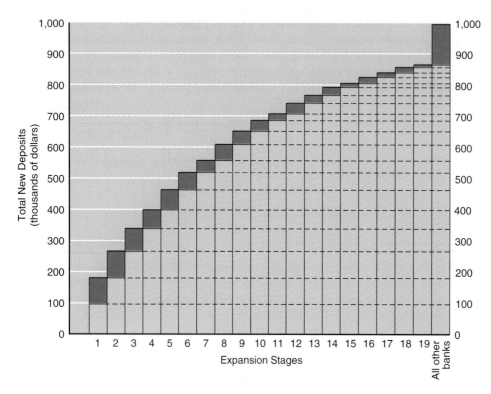

FIGURE 16-2

The Multiple Expansion in the Money Supply Due to $100,000 in New Reserves When the Required Reserve Ratio is 10 Percent

The banks are all aligned in decreasing order of new deposits created. Bank 1 receives the $100,000 in new reserves and lends out $90,000. Bank 2 receives the $90,000 and lends out $81,000. The process continues through banks 3 to 19 and then the rest of the banking system. Ultimately, assuming no leakages, the $100,000 of new reserves results in an increase in the money supply of $1,000,000, or 10 times the new reserves, because the required reserve ratio is 10 percent.

example, was in the form of a check written on a Federal Reserve district bank. It therefore represented new reserves to the banking system. Had that check been written on Bank 3, by contrast, nothing would have happened to the total amount of checkable deposits; there would have been no change in the total money supply. To repeat: Checks written on banks within the system represent assets and liabilities that simply cancel each other out. Only when excess reserves are created by the Federal Reserve System can the money supply increase.

In our example, the depository institutions use their excess reserves to make loans. It is not important how they put the money back into the system. If they bought certificates of deposit or any other security, the analysis would be the same because the party they bought those securities from would receive a check from the purchasing depository institution. The recipient of the check would then deposit it into his or her own depository institution. The deposit expansion process would be the same as we have already outlined.

You should be able to work through the foregoing example to show the reverse process when there is a decrease in reserves because the Fed sells a $100,000 U.S. government security. The result is a multiple contraction of deposits and therefore of the total money supply in circulation.

CONCEPTS IN BRIEF

- When reserves are increased by the Fed through a purchase of U.S. government securities, the result is a multiple expansion of deposits and therefore of the supply of money.

- When the Fed reduces the banking system's reserves by selling U.S. government securities, the result is a multiple contraction of deposits and therefore of the money supply.

THE MONEY MULTIPLIER

In the example just given, a $100,000 increase in excess reserves generated by the Fed's purchase of a security yielded a $1 million increase in total deposits; deposits increased by a multiple of 10 times the initial $100,000 increase in overall reserves. Conversely, a $100,000 decrease in excess reserves generated by the Fed's sale of a security will yield a $1 million decrease in total deposits; they will decrease by a multiple of 10 times the initial $100,000 decrease in overall reserves. We can now make a generalization about the extent to which the money supply will change when the banking system's reserves are increased or decreased. If we assume that no excess reserves are kept and that all loan proceeds are deposited in depository institutions in the system, the following equation applies:

$$\text{Potential money multiplier} = \frac{1}{\text{required reserve ratio}}$$

Money multiplier
The reciprocal of the required reserve ratio, assuming no leakages into currency and no excess reserves. It is equal to 1 divided by the required reserve ratio.

The **money multiplier** gives the *maximum* potential change in the money supply due to a change in reserves. The actual change in the money supply—currency plus checkable account balances—will be equal to the following:

$$\text{Actual change in money supply} = \text{actual money multiplier} \times \text{change in excess reserves}$$

Now we examine why there is a difference between the *potential* money multiplier—1/required reserve ratio—and the actual multiplier.

Forces That Reduce the Money Multiplier

We made a number of simplifying assumptions to come up with the potential money multiplier. In the real world, the actual money multiplier is considerably smaller. Several factors account for this.

Leakages. The entire loan (check) from one bank is not always deposited in another bank. At least two leakages can occur:

- *Currency drains.* When deposits increase, the public may want to hold more currency. Currency that is kept in a person's wallet remains outside the banking system and cannot be held by banks as reserves from which to make loans. The greater the amount of cash leakage, the smaller the actual money multiplier.
- *Excess reserves.* Depository institutions may wish to maintain excess reserves. Depository institutions do not, in fact, always keep excess reserves at zero. To the extent that they want to keep positive excess reserves, the money multiplier will be smaller. A bank receiving $1 million in new deposits might, in our example with the 10 percent required reserve, keep more than $100,000 as reserves. The greater the excess reserves, the smaller the actual money multiplier. Empirically, the currency drain is more significant than the effect of excess reserves.

Real-World Money Multipliers. The required reserve ratio determines the maximum potential money multiplier because the reciprocal of the required reserve ratio tells us what that is. The maximum is never attained for the money supply as a whole because of currency drains and excess reserves. Also, each definition of the money supply, M1 or M2, will yield different results for money multipliers. For several decades, the M1 multiplier has varied between 2.5 and 3.0. The M2 multiplier, however, has shown a trend upward, ranging from 6.5 at the beginning of the 1960s to over 12 in the 1990s.

WAYS IN WHICH THE FEDERAL RESERVE CHANGES THE MONEY SUPPLY

As we have just seen, the Fed can change the money supply by directly changing reserves available to the banking system. It does this by engaging in open market operations. To repeat: The purchase of a U.S. government security by the Fed results in an increase in reserves and leads to a multiple expansion in the money supply. A sale of a U.S. government security by the Fed results in a decrease in reserves and leads to a multiple contraction in the money supply.

The Fed changes the money supply in two other ways, both of which will have multiplier effects similar to those outlined earlier in this chapter.

Borrowed Reserves and the Discount Rate

If a depository institution wants to increase its loans but has no excess reserves, it can borrow reserves. One place it can borrow reserves is from the Fed itself. The depository institution goes to the Federal Reserve and asks for a loan of a certain amount of reserves. The Fed charges these institutions for any reserves that it lends them. The interest rate that the Fed charges used to be called the *rediscount rate* but is now called the **discount rate.** In most other English-speaking countries, it is called the *bank rate.* When newspapers report that the Fed has decreased the discount rate from 6 to 5 percent, you know that the Fed has decreased its charge for lending reserves to depository institutions. Borrowing from the Fed increases reserves and thereby enhances the ability of the depository institution to engage in deposit creation, thus increasing the money supply.

Often the Federal Reserve System makes changes in the discount rate not necessarily to encourage or discourage depository institutions from borrowing from the Fed but rather as a signal to the banking system and financial markets that there has been a change in the Fed's monetary policy. We discuss monetary policy in more detail in Chapter 17.

Depository institutions actually do not often go to the Fed to borrow reserves because the Fed will not lend them all they want. Indeed, the Fed can even refuse to lend reserves when the depository institutions need the reserves to make their reserve accounts meet legal requirements. There are, however, alternative sources for the banks to tap when they want to expand their reserves or when they need reserves to meet a requirement. The primary source is the **federal funds market.** The federal funds market is an interbank market in reserves, with one bank borrowing the excess reserves of another. The generic term *federal funds market* refers to the borrowing or lending (purchase or sale) of reserve funds repaid within the same 24-hour period.

Depository institutions that borrow in the federal funds market pay the **federal funds rate.** Because the federal funds rate is a ready measure of the price that banks must pay to raise funds, the Federal Reserve often uses it as a yardstick by which to measure the effects of its policies. Consequently, the federal funds rate is a closely watched indicator of the Fed's anticipated intentions.

Discount rate
The interest rate that the Federal Reserve charges for reserves that it lends to depository institutions. It is sometimes referred to as the rediscount rate or, in Canada and England, as the bank rate.

Federal funds market
A private market (made up mostly of banks) in which banks can borrow reserves from other banks that want to lend them. Federal funds are usually lent for overnight use.

Federal funds rate
The interest rate that depository institutions pay to borrow reserves in the interbank federal funds market.

Reserve Requirement Changes

Another method by which the Fed can alter the money supply is by changing reserve requirements. Earlier we assumed that reserve requirements were given. Actually, these requirements are set by the Fed within limits established by Congress. Reserve requirements are set according to the net amount of checkable deposits in a given bank. Fed reserve requirements were initially imposed only on member banks, but now they are imposed on all depository institutions.

What would a change in reserve requirements from 10 to 20 percent do (if there were no excess reserves)? We already discovered that the maximum money multiplier was the reciprocal of the required reserve ratio. If reserve requirements are 10 percent, the maximum money multiplier would be the reciprocal of $\frac{1}{10}$, or 10 (assuming no leakages). If, for some reason, the Fed decided to increase reserve requirements to 20 percent, the maximum money multiplier would equal the reciprocal of $\frac{1}{5}$, or 5. The maximum money multiplier is therefore inversely related to the required reserve ratio. If the Fed decides to increase reserve requirements, there will be a decrease in the maximum money multiplier. With any given level of legal reserves already in existence, the money supply will therefore contract.

Notice the difference between this method and the first method the Federal Reserve has for changing the total money supply in circulation. When the Fed makes open market purchases or sales of bonds, it directly alters reserves. When the Fed alters reserve *requirements,* however, it does not change reserves as we have defined them. When the Fed lowers reserve requirements, it "liberates" a certain portion of required reserves and converts them into excess reserves, which the banks can then lend out. An increase in total deposits and in the money supply will result. In contrast, if the Fed increases reserve requirements, it reduces excess reserves and causes banks to contract their deposits, thereby decreasing the money supply.

Open market operations allow the Federal Reserve to control the money supply much more precisely than changes in reserve requirements do, and they also allow the Fed to reverse itself quickly. In contrast, a small change in reserve requirements can result in a very large change in the money supply. That is why the Federal Reserve does not change reserve requirements very often.

POLICY EXAMPLE
Changing Reserve Requirements and the Tax on Banks

Changing reserve requirements is a policy decision that the Federal Reserve does not make casually. But over the past two decades, the Fed has reduced reserve requirements as a way to reduce the implicit tax on banks. Realize that reserves held by banks do not earn interest; therefore, the cost of holding reserves is the interest forgone, which can be considered a tax on banks. Obviously, banks would hold some cautionary reserves even if the Fed did not require them. But the Fed has probably caused them to hold more than they would have otherwise. That is how they have been taxed. This decreased as reserve requirements fell from 18 percent in 1974 to 10 percent in 1992, where they are today.

FOR CRITICAL ANALYSIS: How has the reduction of the reserve requirements affected the sensitivity of the money supply to changes in Federal Reserve open market operations? •

CONCEPTS IN BRIEF

- The maximum money multiplier is equal to the reciprocal of the required reserve ratio.

- The actual multiplier is much less than the maximum money multiplier because of currency drains and excess reserves voluntarily held by banks.

- The Fed changes the money supply in three ways: (1) It can change reserves and hence the money supply through open market operations in which it buys and sells existing U.S. government securities. Open market operations are the primary form of monetary policy. (2) It can encourage changes in reserves by changing the discount rate. (3) It can change the amount of deposits created from reserves by changing reserve requirements.

DEPOSIT INSURANCE AND FLAWED BANK REGULATION

When businesses fail, they create hardships for creditors, owners, workers, and customers. But when a depository institution fails, an even greater hardship results because many individuals and businesses depend on the safety and security of banks. Figure 16-3 indicates that during the 1920s, an average of about 600 banks failed each year. In the 1930s, during

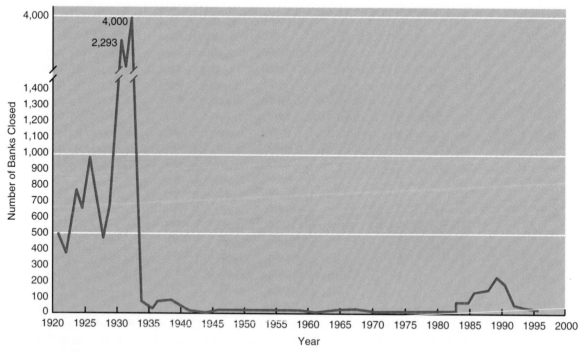

FIGURE 16-3

Commercial Bank Closings

During the Great Depression, a tremendous number of commercial banks were closed. Federal deposit insurance was created in 1933. Thereafter, bank closures were few until around 1984. Failures peaked at over 200 in 1989 and are now fewer than a dozen per year.

Source: Federal Deposit Insurance Corporation.

Federal Deposit Insurance Corporation (FDIC)

A government agency that insures the deposits held in member banks; all members of the Fed and other banks that qualify can join.

the Great Depression, that average soared to 2,000 failures each year. In 1933, at the height of such bank failures, the **Federal Deposit Insurance Corporation (FDIC)** was founded to insure the funds of depositors and remove the reason for ruinous runs on banks. In 1934, the Federal Savings and Loan Insurance Corporation (FSLIC) was installed to insure deposits in savings and loan associations and mutual savings banks. In 1971, the National Credit Union Share Insurance Fund (NCUSIF) was created to insure deposits in credit unions. In 1989, the FSLIC was dissolved and the Savings Association Insurance Fund (SAIF) was established to protect the deposits of those institutions.

As can be seen in Figure 16-3, a tremendous drop in bank failure rates occurred after the passage of the early federal legislation. The long period from 1935 until the 1980s was relatively quiet: From World War II to 1984, fewer than nine banks failed per year. From 1985 until the beginning of 1993, however, 1,065 commercial banks failed—an annual average of nearly 120 bank failures per year, more than 10 times the average for the preceding years! We will examine the reasons shortly. But first we need to understand how deposit insurance works.

The Need for Deposit Insurance

Bank runs

Attempts by many of a bank's depositors to convert checkable and time deposits into currency out of fear for the bank's solvency.

The FDIC, FSLIC, and NCUSIF were established to mitigate the primary cause of bank failures, **bank runs**—the simultaneous rush of depositors to convert their demand deposits or time deposits into currency.

Consider the following scenario. A bank begins to look shaky; its assets may not seem sufficient to cover its liabilities. If the bank has no deposit insurance, depositors in this bank (and any banks associated with it) will all want to withdraw their money from the bank at the same time. Their concern is that this shaky bank will not have enough money to return their deposits to them in the form of currency. Indeed, this is what happens in a bank failure when insurance doesn't exist. Just as with the failure of a regular business, the creditors of the bank may not all get paid, or if they do, they will get paid less than 100 percent of what they are owed. Depositors are creditors of a bank because their funds are on loan to the bank. In a fractional reserve banking system, banks do not hold 100 percent of their depositors' money in the form of reserves. Consequently, all depositors cannot withdraw all their money simultaneously. It would be desirable to assure depositors that they can have their deposits converted into cash when they wish, no matter how serious the financial situation of the bank.

The FDIC (and later the FSLIC, NCUSIF, and SAIF) provided this assurance. By insuring deposits, the FDIC bolstered depositors' trust in the banking system and provided depositors with the incentive to leave their deposits with the bank, even in the face of widespread talk of bank failures. In 1933, it was sufficient for the FDIC to cover each account up to $2,500. The current maximum is $100,000.

How Deposit Insurance Causes Increased Risk Taking by Bank Managers

Exercise 16.1
Visit www.econtoday.com for more about banks' health.

Until very recently, all insured depository institutions paid the same small fee for coverage. (In 1996, the fee was reduced to zero for most banks.) The fee that they paid was completely unrelated to how risky their assets were. A depository institution that made loans only to General Motors and Microsoft Corporation paid the same deposit insurance premium as another depository institution that made loans (at higher interest rates) only to the governments of developing countries that were teetering on the brink of financial collapse.

Although deposit insurance premiums for a while were adjusted somewhat in response to the riskiness of a depository institution's assets, they never reflected all of the relative risk. This can be considered a flaw in the deposit insurance scheme. The result is that bank managers have an incentive to invest in more assets of higher yield, and therefore higher risk, than they would if there were no deposit insurance. Thus the premium rate is artificially low, permitting institution managers to obtain deposits at less than market price (because depositors will accept a lower interest payment on insured deposits); and even if the institution's portfolio becomes riskier, its deposit insurance premium rarely rises by much. Consequently, depository institution managers can increase their net interest margin by using lower-cost insured deposits to purchase higher-yield, higher-risk assets. The gains to risk taking accrue to the managers and stockholders of the depository institutions; the losses go to the deposit insurer (and, as we will see, ultimately to taxpayers).

To combat the inherent flaws in the financial institution industry and in the deposit insurance system, a vast regulatory apparatus was installed. The FDIC was given regulatory powers to offset the risk-taking temptations to depository institution managers; those powers included the ability to require higher capital investment; the ability to regulate, examine, and supervise bank affairs; and the ability to enforce its decisions. Still higher capital requirements were imposed in the early 1990s, but the basic flaws in the system remain.

The financial industry has been organized so as to protect firms from the rigors of competition; market discipline on the behavior of financial institutions was replaced by regulatory discipline. In many respects, the system worked well until 1982. No small saver had lost a penny of insured money since federal deposit insurance was established. (Today, a few smaller banks are allowed to fail and some of their bigger depositors don't get all of their deposits back.) Furthermore, there have been no true bank runs on federally insured institutions. Nevertheless, as the 1990s began, the number of depository institution closures and insolvencies increased to record post-Depression highs, though the situation has greatly improved since then.

Exercise 16.2
Visit www.econtoday.com for more about alternatives to banks.

Deposit Insurance, Adverse Selection, and Moral Hazard

When financial transactions take place, one party often does not have all the knowledge needed about the other party to make correct decisions. This is known as the problem of **asymmetric information.** For example, borrowers generally know more than lenders about the returns and risks associated with the investment projects they intend to undertake.

Adverse Selection. **Adverse selection** arises when there is asymmetric information before a transaction takes place. In financial markets, it often occurs because individuals and firms that are worse credit risks than they appear to be are the ones most willing to borrow at any given interest rate. This willingness makes them likely to be selected by lenders, yet their inferior ability to repay (relative to the interest rate being charged) means that loans to them more often yield adverse outcomes for lenders (default). The potential risks of adverse selection make lenders less likely to lend to anyone and more inclined to charge higher interest rates when they do lend.

Adverse selection is often a problem when insurance is involved because people or firms that are relatively poor risks are sometimes able to disguise that fact from insurers. It is instructive to examine the way this works with the deposit insurance provided by the FDIC. Deposit insurance shields depositors from the potential adverse effects of risky

Asymmetric information
Information possessed by one side of a transaction but not the other. The side with more information will be at an advantage.

Adverse selection
A problem created by asymmetric information prior to a transaction. Individuals who are the most undesirable from the other party's point of view end up being the ones who are most likely to want to engage in a particular financial transaction, such as borrowing.

decisions and so makes depositors willing to accept riskier investment strategies by their banks. Clearly, this encourages more high-flying, risk-loving entrepreneurs to become managers of banks. Moreover, because depositors have so little incentive to monitor the activities of insured banks, it is also likely that the insurance actually encourages outright crooks—embezzlers and con artists—to enter the industry. The consequences for the FDIC—and often for the taxpayer—are larger losses.

Moral hazard

A situation in which, after a transaction has taken place, one of the parties to the transaction has an incentive to engage in behavior that will be undesirable from the other party's point of view.

Moral Hazard. **Moral hazard** arises as the result of information asymmetry after a transaction has occurred. In financial markets, lenders face the hazard that borrowers may engage in activities that are contrary to the lender's interest and thus might be said to be immoral from the lender's perspective. For example, because lenders do not share in the profits of business ventures, they generally want borrowers to agree to invest prudently. Yet once the loan has been made, borrower-investors have an incentive to invest in high-risk, high-return projects because they are able to keep all of the extra profits if the projects succeed. Such behavior subjects the lender to greater hazards than are being compensated for under the terms of the loan agreement.

Moral hazard is also an important phenomenon in the presence of insurance contracts, such as the deposit insurance provided by the FDIC. Insured depositors know that they will not suffer losses if their bank fails. Hence they have little incentive to monitor their bank's investment activities or to punish their bank by withdrawing their funds if the bank assumes too much risk. Thus insured banks have incentives to take on more risks than they otherwise would—and with those risks come higher losses for the FDIC and for taxpayers.

THINKING CRITICALLY ABOUT THE MEDIA

Bailouts That Cost Taxpayers Billions

During the savings and loan crisis in the United States in the late 1980s and early 1990s, the media bombarded us with inflated figures of how much the U.S. taxpayer was paying to bail out S&Ls. The same sorts of numbers are being bandied about for the potential bailout of banks in Japan. Although technically not inaccurate, such stories fail to point out that such bailouts always occur *after the fact.* The $200 billion or so lost by U.S. savings and loans had already occurred by the time of the bailout. That is to say, the U.S. economy had already seen a $200 billion reduction in its wealth because of bad investments by S&Ls. The same is now true for the Japanese economy. The investments made by Japanese banks that turned sour will not magically increase in value if the Japanese government decides to use taxpayers' money to bail out the banks. Banking rescue plans as such are simply a determination of who will bear losses that have already occurred.

The Results of Moral Hazard: America's Savings and Loan Debacle. For a variety of reasons, by the mid-1980s, the savings and loan industry in the United States was facing disaster. What was occurring at that time was a perfect example of the perverse incentives that occur when government-provided deposit insurance exists. Depository institution managers undertake riskier actions than they otherwise would because of the existence of deposit insurance. Moreover, because of the existence of deposit insurance, depositors in savings and loan associations and other depository institutions have little incentive to investigate the financial dealings and stability of those institutions. After all, deposits are guaranteed by an agency of the federal government, so why worry? Hence there has been little incentive for households and firms to monitor depository institutions or even to diversify their deposits across institutions. From an S&L manager's point of view, as long as deposit insurance protected depositors, the manager could feel confident to "go for the gold." One result was the increased amount of high-risk, high-yielding assets purchased by many savings and loan associations.

The first year of the S&L crisis, 135 institutions failed. Over the next two years, another 600 went bankrupt. By the end of the crisis, 1,500 thrift institutions had gone under. Politicians chose to solve the crisis by passing the Financial Institutions Reform, Recovery and Enforcement Act (FIRREA), popularly known as the Thrift Bailout Act of 1989. The estimated cost to American taxpayers was about $200 billion.

POLICY EXAMPLE
Moral Hazard in the Banking Industry

After the costly savings and loan association bailout, Congress decided to do something. It passed the Federal Deposit Insurance Corporation Improvement Act in 1991. Part of the act was an attempt to eliminate the moral hazard problem of depositors' being guaranteed full repayment of all funds deposited in American financial institutions. In principle, deposits were insured only up to $100,000; nevertheless, in practice, all depositors of the more than 1,000 financial institutions that failed in the 1980s received $1 for every $1 deposited. So the latest legislation specifically states that uninsured depositors—those with more than $100,000 in one account at a financial institution—cannot receive protection if doing so would increase the costs to the Federal Deposit Insurance Corporation.

Congress, though, included an escape clause. Uninsured depositors can still be bailed out if the their bank's failure poses a risk to the entire banking system. While it is true that such a bailout would require the approval of the secretary of the Treasury, the Federal Reserve Board of Governors, and the directors of the FDIC, nonetheless this loophole indicates a "too big to fail" incentive structure within our banking system. Hence the moral hazard problem inherent in deposit insurance still remains for our largest banks. After all, if all its deposits are implicitly fully insured, any bank has an incentive to take on more risk. Bank managers in our largest banks know that they are in fact too big to fail. If they get into trouble, the FDIC will bail them out. Also, there is no deductible, as there is in auto and health insurance. When you have a deductible in your auto insurance policy, you have an incentive to drive more carefully. There is no such incentive in the management of risk in a large bank in the United States. Indeed, bank managers have a perverse incentive to take on more risk, for more risk means higher rates of return. Managers know that if their risky investments do not pay off, their depositors will not suffer—the U.S. taxpayer will bail them out.

It is no surprise that financial institutions have been engaged in a major merger war. The bigger they get, the more certain they are that the FDIC will never let them fail. Consequently, they can take on riskier investments, thereby offering their depositors and investors higher rates of return.

FOR CRITICAL ANALYSIS: If you had more than $100,000 in funds, how would you decide in which bank to deposit them? •

CONCEPTS IN BRIEF

- Federal deposit insurance was created in 1933 when the Federal Deposit Insurance Corporation (FDIC) was founded. In 1934, the Federal Savings and Loan Insurance Corporation (FSLIC) was founded to insure deposits in savings and loan associations and mutual savings banks.

- The FSLIC was dissolved in 1989; deposits remain protected by the Savings Association Insurance Fund (SAIF).

- Deposit insurance was designed to prevent bank runs in which individual demand deposit and savings deposit holders attempt to turn their deposits into currency. Since the advent of federal deposit insurance, there have been no true bank runs at federally insured banks.

- Because of the way deposit insurance is set up in the United States, it encourages bank managers to invest in riskier assets to make higher rates of returns.

Bank crises can cause panics severe enough to require police intervention, as happened in Venezuela in 1994. Such scenes rarely occur in the United States, where depositors are almost certain they will never lose any of their funds.

Banking Crises Around the World

CONCEPTS APPLIED:

MORAL HAZARD, ADVERSE SELECTION, ASYMMETRIC INFORMATION, INCENTIVES

Visit www.econtoday.com for an Internet Activity that expands your understanding of these concepts.

You learned in this chapter that the savings and loan bailout in the 1980s cost the American taxpayer at least $200 billion. That constituted at the time about 2 to 3 percent of one year's GDP. As it turns out, America's banking crisis is small potatoes compared to recent banking crises in other countries, at least in percentage terms.

The World of Banking Crises

Table 16-2 shows the estimated losses in various countries' banking crises expressed as a percentage of their GDP. At the head of the list is Argentina, whose banking crises cost its economy 55 percent of one year's GDP between 1980 and 1982.

The Usual Cause: Perverse Incentives

Most modern banking crises occur for the same reason we had a savings and loan crisis in the 1980s. The governments of virtually all the countries listed in Table 16-2 created perverse incentives for bank managers. For example, during the mid-1990s, Japanese banks held problem loans equal to about $1 trillion, or a quarter of Japan's GDP. The Japanese authorities nonetheless continued to allow banks to lend problem debtors sufficient funds to cover unpaid interest.

A perverse incentive for governments to act the way they do involves the International Monetary Fund (IMF), which serves as an international "bailout" organization. When Thailand's banking system got into trouble, the IMF came to the rescue. The same was true with South Korea, where the IMF pledged a $57 billion bailout. As long as governments believe that the IMF will bail them out when they fail to put reins on their own countries' banks, these perverse incentives will continue to cause banking crises.

TABLE 16-2

Estimated Cost of Banking Crises Around the World Since 1980

Country	Crisis Period	Estimated Loss (percentage of one year's GDP)
Argentina	1980–1982	55
Chile	1981–1983	41
Israel	1977–1983	30
Ivory Coast	1988–1991	25
Venezuela	1994–1995	18
Benin	1988–1990	17
Senegal	1988–1991	17
Spain	1977–1985	17
Mauritania	1984–1993	15
Hungary	1995	10
Japan	1990s	10
South Korea	1997	10
Tanzania	1987–1995	10
Thailand	1997	10

Sources: Institute of International Economics and author's estimates.

FOR CRITICAL ANALYSIS

1. What does the information presented here tell you about whether or not we will see future banking crises throughout the world?

2. If a country's government chooses to bail out its banking system, who pays?

CHAPTER SUMMARY

1. All depository institutions are required to maintain reserves, which consist of deposits in Federal Reserve district banks plus vault cash. The Federal Reserve requires that certain reserve ratios be maintained, depending on the size of the bank and the types of deposits it has.

2. When depository institutions have more reserves than are required, they are said to have excess reserves.

3. The Federal Reserve can control the money supply through open market operations—by buying and selling U.S. government securities.

4. When the Fed buys a bond, it pays for the bond by writing a check on itself. This creates additional reserves for the banking system. The result will be an increase in the money supply that is a multiple of the value of the bond purchased by the Fed. If the Fed sells a bond, it reduces reserves in the banking system. The result will be a decrease in the money supply that is a multiple of the value of the bond sold by the Fed.

5. Single depository institutions that have no excess reserves cannot alter the money supply.

6. The banking system as a whole can change the money supply pursuant to a change in reserves brought about by a Federal Reserve purchase or sale of government bonds. The Fed can also change the money supply by changing the discount rate or the required reserve ratio.

7. The maximum money multiplier is equal to the reciprocal of the required reserve ratio.

8. The actual money multiplier will be less than the maximum because of leakages—currency drains and excess reserve holdings of some banks.

9. The Federal Deposit Insurance Corporation was created in 1933 to insure commercial bank deposits. Because of the existence of federal deposit insurance, the probability of a run on the banking system, even if a significant number of depository institutions were to fail, is quite small.

10. A major flaw in the deposit insurance system has been the relatively low price for the insurance irrespective of risk. Moral hazard under the current federal deposit insurance system has led to overly risky and fraudulent behavior on the part of numerous depository institution managers. One result was the savings and loan crisis of the late 1980s and early 1990s.

DISCUSSION OF PREVIEW QUESTIONS

1. What is a fractional reserve banking system?

A fractional reserve banking system is one in which the reserves kept by the depository institutions are only a fraction of total deposits owned by the public. In general, depository institutions accept funds from the public and offer their depositors interest or other services. In turn the depository institutions lend out some of these deposits and earn interest. Because at any given time new deposits are coming in while people are drawing down on old deposits, prudent banking does not require a 100 percent reserve-deposit ratio. Because U.S. depository institutions keep less than 100 percent of their total deposits in the form of reserves, we refer to our banking structure as a *fractional* reserve system.

2. What happens to the total money supply when a person deposits in one depository institution a check drawn on another depository institution?

Nothing; the total money supply is unaffected. A transfer of checks from one depository institution to another does not generate any excess reserves in the banking system; hence there will be no overall deposit (and therefore money) creation. Suppose that Gerald Wong deposits in Bank A a $1,000 check that he received for services rendered to Lisa Romano, who deals with Bank B. Wong deposits a $1,000 check in Bank A, drawn on Bank B. Note that Bank A experiences an increase in total deposits and reserves and can increase its lending. However, just the opposite happens to Bank B: It experiences a reduction in deposits and reserves and must curtail its lending. There will be no net change in excess reserves; hence no net change in deposit creation and therefore no net change in the money supply occurs.

3. What happens to the overall money supply when a person who sells a U.S. government security to the Federal Reserve places the proceeds in a depository institution?

Assume that Wong now sells a $1,000 bond to the Fed and in exchange receives a check for $1,000, which he deposits in Bank A. Wong has received a $1,000 checkable deposit (which is money) in exchange for a $1,000 bond (which is not money); the money supply has just increased by $1,000. Furthermore, Bank A has now increased its reserves by $1,000; of this, $900 is excess reserves (assuming a 10 percent required reserve ratio). We stress that this increase in excess reserves for Bank A is *not* offset elsewhere in the banking institution; hence a net increase in excess reserves has occurred. Bank A may well lend all $900 (create $900 in checkable deposits for borrowers), thereby increasing the overall money supply by another $900; the total change

so far is $1,900. There is no need for the process to end here, because the people who borrowed $900 from Bank A will now spend this $900 on goods or services provided by people who may well deal with Bank B—which receives $900 in deposits and reserves and now has $720 in excess reserves that it can lend. And so the process of deposit and money creation continues.

4. How does the existence of deposit insurance affect a financial institution's choice of risky versus non-risky assets?

The best way to answer this question is with an analogy. Assume that you are given $1 million to gamble in Las Vegas. In situation 1, you share equally with your benefactor in losses and in gains. In situation 2, your benefactor lets you share in the gains (at less than 100 percent) but incurs all losses. Will your behavior be any different in situation 1 than in situation 2 while you are in Las Vegas? The answer is, of course, yes. In situation 1, you will be much more careful—you will choose games of chance that offer less risk but lower potential payoffs. In situation 2, you might as well try to break the bank. At the roulette wheel, rather than going for odd or even or red or black, you might as well bet your benefactor's money on single numbers or groups of numbers or zero or double zero because if you hit it, you stand to gain a lot, but if you don't, you stand to lose nothing. Situation 2 is analogous to that of today's managers in depository institutions—it is a situation that involves moral hazard. When times get tough and business is bad, they have had a tendency to "go for broke." They bought risky but high-yielding assets, such as dubious real estate loans, loans at high interest rates to developing countries, and oil development loans. For those whose bets didn't pay off, the federal government has bailed out all the depositors. The few whose bets did pay off look like heroes.

PROBLEMS

(Answers to the odd-numbered problems appear at the back of the book.)

16-1. Bank 1 has received a deposit of $1 million. Assuming that the banks retain no excess reserves, answer the following questions.

a. The reserve requirement is 25 percent. Fill in the blanks in the following table on the next page. What is the money multiplier?
b. Now the reserve requirement is 5 percent. Fill in the blanks in a similar table. What is the money multiplier?

Multiple Deposit Creation			
Bank	Deposits	Reserves	Loans
Bank 1	$1,000,000	$ _____	$ _____
Bank 2	_____	_____	_____
Bank 3	_____	_____	_____
Bank 4	_____	_____	_____
Bank 5	_____	_____	_____
All other banks	_____	_____	_____
Totals	_____	_____	_____

16-2. Arrange the following items on the proper side of a bank's balance sheet.

   a. Checkable deposits
   b. Vault cash
   c. Time deposits
   d. Deposits with the Federal Reserve district bank
   e. Loans to private businesses
   f. Loans to households
   g. Holdings of U.S. government, state, and municipal bonds
   h. Borrowings from other banks

ASSETS	LIABILITIES

16-3. If the required reserve ratio is 10 percent, what will be the maximum change in the money supply in each of the following situations?

   a. Theola Smith deposits in Bank 2 a check drawn on Bank 3.
   b. Smith buys a $5,000 U.S. government bond from the Fed by drawing down on her checking account.
   c. Smith sells a $10,000 U.S. government bond to the Fed and deposits the $10,000 in Bank 3.
   d. Smith finds $1,000 in coins and paper currency buried in her backyard and deposits it in her checking account.

   e. Smith writes a $1,000 check on her own account and takes $1,000 in currency and buries it in her backyard.

16-4. The Fed purchases a $1 million government security from Sandro Mondrone, who deposits the proceeds in Bank 1. Use balance sheets to show the immediate effects of this transaction on the Fed and on Bank 1.

16-5. Continuing the example from Problem 16-4:

   a. Indicate Bank 1's position more precisely if required reserves equal 5 percent of checkable deposits.
   b. By how much can Bank 1 increase its lending?

16-6. Assume a required reserve ratio of 8 percent. A check for $60,000 is drawn on an account in Bank B and deposited in a checkable deposit in Bank A.

   a. How much have the excess reserves of Bank A increased?
   b. How much in the form of new loans is Bank A now able to extend to borrowers?
   c. By how much have reserves of Bank B decreased?
   d. By how much have excess reserves of Bank B decreased?
   e. The money supply has increased by how much?

16-7. Assume that the required reserve ratio is 15 percent and that the Fed sells $3 million worth of government securities to a customer who pays with a check drawn on the Second National Bank.

   a. The excess reserves of the Second National Bank have changed by how much?
   b. By how much has the money supply changed?
   c. What is the maximum change in the money supply that can result from this sale?

16-8. Examine the following balance sheet of B Bank.

B Bank

ASSETS		LIABILITIES	
Total reserves	$ 50	Checkable deposits	$200
Loans	100	Capital stock	200
U.S. government			
securities	50		
Property	200		

Assume that the required reserve ratio is 10 percent.

a. Calculate the excess reserves of B Bank.

b. How much money can B Bank lend out?

c. If B Bank lends the money in part (b) of this problem, what are the new values for total reserves? For checkable deposits? For loans?

d. What is the maximum expansion of the money supply if B Bank lends the amount suggested in part (b) of this problem?

16-9. Assume a 5 percent required reserve ratio, zero excess reserves, no currency leakage, and a ready loan demand. The Fed buys a $1 million Treasury bill from a depository institution.

a. What is the maximum money multiplier?

b. By how much will total deposits rise?

16-10. The year is A.D. 2310. Residents of an earth colony on Titan, the largest moon of the planet Saturn, use checkable deposits at financial institutions as the only form of money. Depository institutions on Titan wish to hold 10 percent of deposits as excess reserves at all times. There are no other deposits in the banking system. If the banking system on Titan has $300 million in reserves and the total quantity of money is $1.5 billion, what is the required reserve ratio set by the Titan colony's central bank?

COMPUTER-ASSISTED INSTRUCTION

What happens to the money supply (and to the value of bank deposits) when the Fed purchases a $100,000 government security on the open market? Step-by-step calculations using balance sheets show how bank deposits (money) rise with each transaction. In the process, the mechanics of the bank deposit and money supply expansion process are revealed.

Complete problem and answer appear on disk.

INTERACTING WITH THE INTERNET

You do not have to go to a bank to get a loan anymore. You can go to many other financial services institutions. For example, examine the following Web site to see what banking services are offered by the Prudential Insurance Company:

www.prudential.com/

Material on the FDIC, for depositors and for others interested in the system, can be found at

www.fdic.gov/

It covers virtually all portions of this agency's activities.

For useful information on the NCUSIF, go to

ncua.gov/about/NCUSIF.html

To find out what the Office of Thrift Supervision is doing, go to

www.ots.treas.gov

Find out about the "too big to fail" policy problem with current deposit insurance by going to

woodrow.mpls.frb.fed.us/pubs/region/97-09/gs-fixFDICIA.html

CHAPTER 17

MONETARY POLICY

"It's as good as gold." That familiar cliché has been misleading for at least a decade. Had you invested $100 in a mutual fund made up of the Standard & Poor's 500-stock index 10 years ago, today you would have approximately $350. If you had put $100 into gold 10 years ago, today it would be worth $70. Nonetheless, central banks around the world hold about 1.1 billion ounces of gold as reserves. Also, gold has played a major role in the history of money and monetary policy. Back in 1973, the United States officially separated its monetary policy from gold. There still continue to be proposals to make gold a prominent centerpiece of U.S. monetary policy. Some people argue that our currency should be convertible into gold. Does this make sense? To find out if it does, you need to know more about how monetary policy works in the United States.

PREVIEW QUESTIONS

1. What is the demand for money curve, and how is it related to the interest rate?

2. Why is the price of existing bonds inversely related to the interest rate?

3. How do the supply of and demand for money determine the interest rate?

4. What is a monetarist?

Did You Know That... the chair of the Board of Governors of the Federal Reserve System is often considered the second most important person after the president? Indeed, if the head of the Fed is seated next to the first lady while the president is delivering the State of the Union message, the media try to puzzle out what that might mean. Why is the head of the Fed considered so important? Because the Fed chair, along with the other members of the Federal Open Market Committee, determine monetary policy in the United States. A strongly worded public statement by the head of the Federal Reserve can cause instant gyrations in our financial markets and sometimes in those in the rest of the world.

This chapter deals with monetary policy—the Fed's changing of the supply of money (or the rate at which it grows) in order to achieve national economic goals. When you were introduced to aggregate demand in Chapter 10, you discovered that the position of the aggregate demand curve is determined by the willingness of firms, individuals, governments, and foreigners to purchase domestically produced goods and services. Monetary policy works in a variety of ways to change this willingness, both directly and indirectly.

Think about monetary policy in an intuitive way: An increase in the money supply adds to the amount of money that firms and individuals have on hand and so increases the amount that they wish to spend. The result is an increase in aggregate demand. A decrease in the money supply reduces the amount of money that people have on hand to spend and so decreases aggregate demand.

WHAT'S SO SPECIAL ABOUT MONEY?

By definition, monetary policy has to do, in the main, with money. But what is so special about money? Money is the product of a "social contract" in which we all agree to do two things:

1. Express all prices in terms of a common unit of account, which in the United States we call the dollar
2. Use a specific medium of exchange for market transactions

These two features of money distinguish it from all other goods in the economy. As a practical matter, money is involved on one side of every nonbarter transaction in the economy—and trillions of them occur every year. What this means is that something that changes the amount of money in circulation will have some effect on many transactions and thus on elements of GDP. If something affects the number of snowmobiles in existence, probably only the snowmobile market will be altered. But something that affects the amount of money in existence is going to affect *all* markets.

Holding Money

All of us engage in a flow of transactions. We buy and sell things all of our lives. But because we use money—dollars—as our medium of exchange, all *flows* of nonbarter transactions involve a *stock* of money. We can restate this as follows:

To use money, one must hold money.

Given that everybody must hold money, we can now talk about the *demand* to hold it. People do not demand to hold money just to look at pictures of past presidents. They hold it to be able to use it to buy goods and services.

The Demand for Money: What People Wish to Hold

People have a certain motivation that causes them to want to hold money balances. Individuals and firms could try to have zero non-interest-bearing money balances. But life is inconvenient without a ready supply of money balances. There is a demand for money by the public, motivated by several factors.

The Transactions Demand. The main reason why people hold money is that money can be used to purchase goods and services. People are paid at specific intervals (once a week, once a month, and so on), but they wish to make purchases more or less continuously. To free themselves from making expenditures on goods and services only on payday, people find it beneficial to hold money. The benefit they receive is convenience: They willingly forgo interest earnings in order to avoid the inconvenience and expense of cashing in such nonmoney assets as bonds every time they wish to make a purchase.

Thus people hold money to make regular, *expected* expenditures under the **transactions demand.** As national income rises, the community will want to hold more money. Suppose that national income rises due exclusively to price level increases. If people are making the same volume of physical purchases but the goods and services cost more due to higher prices, people will want to hold more money.

Transactions demand
Holding money as a medium of exchange to make payments. The level varies directly with nominal national income.

The Precautionary Demand. The transactions demand involves money held to make *expected* expenditures; people hold money for the **precautionary demand** to make *unexpected* purchases or to meet emergencies. It is not unreasonable to maintain that as the price level or real national income rises, people will want to hold more money. In effect, when people hold money for the precautionary demand, they incur a cost in forgone interest earnings that is offset by the benefit that the precautionary balance provides. Nonetheless, the higher the rate of interest, the lower the money balances people wish to hold for the precautionary demand.

Precautionary demand
Holding money to meet unplanned expenditures and emergencies.

The Asset Demand. Remember that one of the functions of money is a store of value. People can hold money balances as a store of value, or they can hold bonds or stocks or other interest-earning assets. The desire to hold money as a store of value leads to the **asset demand** for money. People choose to hold money rather than other assets for two reasons: its liquidity and the lack of risk. Moreover, if deflation is expected, holding money balances makes sense.

The disadvantage of holding money balances as an asset, of course, is the interest earnings forgone. Each individual or business decides how much money to hold as an asset by looking at the opportunity cost of holding money. The higher the interest rate—which is our proxy for the opportunity cost of holding money—the lower the money balances people will want to hold as assets. Conversely, the lower the interest rate offered on alternative assets, the higher the money balances people will want to hold as assets.

Asset demand
Holding money as a store of value instead of other assets such as certificates of deposit, corporate bonds, and stocks.

The Demand for Money Curve

Assume that transactions demand for money is fixed, given a certain level of income. That leaves the precautionary and asset demands for money, both determined by the opportunity cost of holding money. If we assume that the interest rate represents the cost of holding money balances, we can graph the relationship between the interest rate and the quantity of money demanded. In Figure 17-1, the demand for money curve shows a familiar downward slope. The horizontal axis measures the quantity of money demanded, and the vertical axis is the interest rate. In this sense, the interest rate is the price of holding money. At a higher price, a lower quantity of money is demanded, and vice versa.

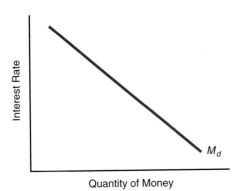

FIGURE 17-1

The Demand for Money Curve
If we use the interest rate as a proxy for the opportunity cost of holding money balances, the demand for money curve, M_d, is downward-sloping, similar to other demand curves.

Imagine two scenarios. In the first one, you can earn 20 percent a year if you put your cash into purchases of U.S. government securities. In the other scenario, you can earn 1 percent if you put your cash into purchases of U.S. government securities. If you have $1,000 average cash balances in a non-interest-bearing checking account, in the second scenario over a one-year period, your opportunity cost would be 1 percent of $1,000, or $10. In the first scenario, your opportunity cost would be 20 percent of $1,000, or $200. Under which scenario would you hold more cash?

INTERNATIONAL EXAMPLE
The Choice Between Cash and Savings Accounts in Colombia

In countries with high inflation rates, nominal interest rates are also high. Remember from Chapter 7 that the nominal interest rate equals the real interest rate plus the expected rate of inflation. Colombia is one country that has consistently high rates of inflation. Consequently, its depository institutions usually offer high nominal interest rates to attract people's cash. In Ciudad, Bolívar, about an hour from Bogotá, the Caja Social de Ahorros (Social Savings Bank) services a low-income area of about a million people. This depository institution was started by a Jesuit priest and continues to be overseen by a board of directors appointed by the Jesuits. On passbook savings accounts, it pays 19 percent. This sounds high, but not compared to Colombia's 22 percent annual inflation. Thus its 10,000 depositors are willing to accept a *negative* real rate of interest of 3 percent. Why? In the first place, if they kept their cash as cash, they would suffer a 22 percent reduction in purchasing power every year. In the second place, the Caja Social keeps its low-income clients' money safe in a high-crime area.

FOR CRITICAL ANALYSIS: Why are nominal interest rates higher when a country experiences inflation? •

CONCEPTS IN BRIEF

- To use money, people must hold money. Therefore, they have a demand for money balances.

- The determinants of the demand for money balances are the transactions demand, the precautionary demand, and the asset demand.

- Because holding money carries with it an opportunity cost—the interest income forgone—the demand for money curve showing the relationship between money balances and the interest rate slopes downward.

EFFECTS OF AN INCREASE IN THE MONEY SUPPLY

To understand how monetary policy works in its simplest form, we are going to run an experiment in which you increase the money supply in a very direct way. Assume that the government has given you hundreds of millions of dollars in just-printed bills that you load into a helicopter. You then go around the country, dropping the money out of the window. People pick it up and put it in their billfolds. Some deposit the money in their checking accounts. The first thing that happens is that they have too much money—not in the sense that they want to throw it away but rather in relation to other things that they own. There are a variety of ways to dispose of this "new" money.

Direct Effect

The simplest thing that people can do when they have excess money balances is to go out and spend it on goods and services. Here we have a direct impact on aggregate demand. Aggregate demand rises because with an increase in the money supply at any given price level, people now want to purchase more output of real goods and services.

Indirect Effect

Not everybody will necessarily spend the newfound money on real output. Some people may wish to deposit some or all of this excess cash in banks. The recipient banks now discover that they have higher reserves than they need to hold. As you learned in Chapter 16, one thing that banks can do to get interest-earning assets is to lend out the excess reserves. But banks cannot induce people to borrow more money than they were borrowing before unless the banks lower the interest rate that they charge on loans. This lower interest rate encourages people to take out those loans. Businesses will therefore engage in new investment with the money loaned. Individuals will engage in more consumption of such durable goods as housing, autos, and home entertainment centers. Either way, the increased loans have created a rise in aggregate demand. More people will be involved in more spending, even those who did not pick up any of the money that was originally dropped out of your helicopter.

Graphing the Effects of an Expansionary Monetary Policy

We have now established the existence of both the direct and indirect effects on aggregate demand when there is an expansion in the money supply. Look at Figure 17-2. We start out in long-run and short-run equilibrium with long-run aggregate supply at *LRAS,* short-run aggregate supply at $SRAS_1$, and aggregate demand at AD_1. All three intersect at $7 trillion of real GDP at a price level of 120, at point E_1. Because of the direct and indirect effects of the increase in the money supply, aggregate demand shifts outward to the right to AD_2. At price level 120, there is an excess demand for real goods and services equal to the horizontal distance between E_1 and A. This horizontal distance shown here is $500 billion. The excess demand for goods and services must be matched, dollar for dollar, by the corresponding excess supply of money (excess liquidity). It is this excess supply of money that has caused the aggregate demand curve to shift outward to AD_2.

In the short run, something has to give. Here the excess demand for real output induces a move to point E_2. The price level rises to 130 at an output rate of $7.25 trillion per year. In the long run, though, expectations are revised upward, and input prices are revised accordingly. Therefore, the short-run aggregate supply curve, $SRAS_1$, begins to shift

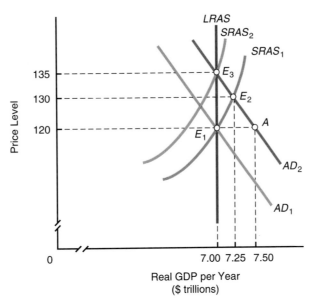

FIGURE 17-2

The Effects of Expansionary Monetary Policy

If we start with equilibrium at E_1, an increase in the money supply will cause the aggregate demand curve to shift to AD_2. There is an excess quantity of real goods and services demanded. The price level increases so that we move to E_2 at an output rate of $7.25 trillion per year and a price level of 130. But input owners revise their expectations of prices upward, and $SRAS_1$ shifts to $SRAS_2$. The new long-run equilibrium is at E_3 at the long-run aggregate supply of $7 trillion of real GDP per year and a price level of 135.

upward vertically to $SRAS_2$. Long-run equilibrium occurs at E_3, and the ultimate effect is a rise in the price level.

CONCEPTS IN BRIEF

- The direct effect of an increase in the money supply arises because people desire to spend more on real goods and services when they have excess money balances.

- The indirect effect of an increase in the money supply works through a lowering of the interest rates, which encourages businesses to make new investments with the money loaned to them. Individuals will also engage in more consumption (on consumer durables) because of lower interest rates.

MONETARY POLICY IN THE REAL WORLD

Of course, monetary policy does not consist of dropping dollar bills from a helicopter. Nonetheless, it is true that the Fed seeks to alter consumption, investment, and aggregate demand as a whole by altering the rate of growth of the money supply. The Fed uses three tools as part of its policymaking action: open market operations, discount rate changes, and reserve requirement changes.

Open Market Operations

The Fed changes the amount of reserves in the system by its purchases and sales of government bonds issued by the U.S. Treasury. To understand how the Fed does so, you must first start out in an equilibrium in which everybody, including the holders of bonds, is satisfied with the current situation. There is some equilibrium level of interest rate (and bond prices) outstanding. Now if the Fed wants to conduct open market operations, it must somehow induce individuals, businesses, and foreigners to hold more or fewer U.S. Treasury bonds. The inducement must be in the form of making people better off. So if the Fed

Panel (a)
Fed Sells

Panel (b)
Fed Buys

FIGURE 17-3

Determining the Price of Bonds
In panel (a), the Fed offers more bonds for sale. The price drops from P_1 to P_2. In panel (b), the Fed purchases bonds. This is the equivalent of a reduction in the supply of bonds available for private investors to hold. The price of bonds must rise from P_1 to P_3 to clear the market.

wants to buy bonds, it is going to have to offer to buy them at a higher price than exists in the marketplace. If the Fed wants to sell bonds, it is going to have to offer them at a lower price than exists in the marketplace. Thus an open market operation must cause a change in the price of bonds.

Graphing the Sale of Bonds. The Fed sells some of the bonds in its portfolio. This is shown in panel (a) of Figure 17-3. Notice that the supply of bonds is shown here as a vertical line with respect to price. The demand for bonds is downward-sloping. If the Fed offers more bonds for sale, it shifts the supply curve from S_1 to S_2. It cannot induce people to buy the extra bonds at the original price of P_1, so it must lower the price to P_2.

The Fed's Purchase of Bonds. The opposite occurs when the Fed purchases bonds. In panel (b) of Figure 17-3, the original supply curve is S_1. The new supply curve of outstanding bonds will end up being S_3 because of the Fed's purchases of bonds. You can view this purchase of bonds as a reduction in the stock of bonds available for private investors to hold. To get people to give up these bonds, the Fed must offer them a more attractive price. The price will rise from P_1 to P_3.

Relationship Between the Price of Existing Bonds and the Rate of Interest. There is an inverse relationship between the price of existing bonds and the rate of interest. Assume that the average yield on bonds is 5 percent. You decide to purchase a bond. A local corporation agrees to sell you a bond that will pay you $50 a year forever. What is the price you are willing to pay for it? $1,000. Why? Because $50 divided by $1,000 equals 5 percent. You purchase the bond. The next year something happens in the economy. For whatever reason, you can go out and obtain bonds that have effective yields of 10 percent. That is to say, the prevailing interest rate in the economy is now 10 percent. What has happened to the market price of the existing bond that you own, the one you purchased the year before? It will have fallen. If you try to sell it for $1,000, you will discover that no investors will buy it from you. Why should they when they can obtain $50 a year from someone else by paying only $500? Indeed, unless you offer your bond for sale at a price of $500, no buyers will be forthcoming. Hence an increase in the prevailing interest rate in the economy has caused the market value of your existing bond to fall.

The important point to be understood is this:

The market price of existing bonds (and all fixed-income assets) is inversely related to the rate of interest prevailing in the economy.

Contractionary Monetary Policy: Effects on Aggregate Demand, the Price Level, and Real GDP. Consider contractionary monetary policy by the Fed. When the Fed engages in contractionary monetary policy, it increases its sales of U.S. government bonds. Remember that when it does so, bond prices will fall. But lowering the price of bonds is the same thing as raising the interest rate on existing bonds. In any event, let's assume that the Fed sells bonds exclusively to banks. (This is not quite accurate because it actually deals with a small number of bond dealers.) The banks that purchase the bonds from the Fed do so with reserves. This puts banks too close to not being able to meet their reserve requirements. They replenish their reserves by reducing their lending. The way they ration available money among potential borrowers is by raising the rate of interest they charge on loans. Some borrowers, deeming the new rate too high, will eliminate themselves from the market. (The interest rate in the economy will have already gone up a bit anyway because of the initial sale of bonds to the banks.) Consequently, some borrowers who otherwise would have borrowed in order to spend no longer will do so at the higher rate of interest. The aggregate demand curve shifts from AD_1 to AD_2 in Figure 17-4. The initial equilibrium was at point E_1 with a price level of 120 and real GDP of $7 trillion per year. AD_1, $SRAS_1$, and $LRAS$ all intersect at point E_1. Now that the Fed has sold bonds, the aggregate demand curve shifts to AD_2. In the short run, we move along $SRAS_1$ to point E_2, at which the price level has dropped to 110 and real GDP has decreased to $6.5 trillion per year.

In the long run, in a fully adjusting economy, expectations adjust and so do factor (input) prices. All of the shock is absorbed in a lower price level as $SRAS_1$ moves to $SRAS_2$. The new equilibrium is at E_3, again at $7 trillion real GDP per year but at a lower price level of 100.

Expansionary Monetary Policy: Effect of a Purchase of Bonds. The Fed engages in expansionary monetary policy by purchasing bonds. Remember that for the Fed to purchase bonds, it must bid up the price it pays for bonds. That means that the interest rate on existing bonds will go down. In any event, the Fed buys the bonds from banks, which now have more reserves. Flush with excess reserves, the banks seek ways to lend them out. To induce customers to borrow more, the banks will cut interest rates even further. People who thought they were not going to be able to buy a new car, house, or whatever now find themselves able to do so. Their spending rises.

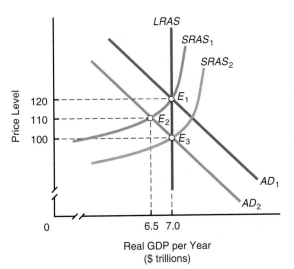

FIGURE 17-4

Contractionary Monetary Policy via Open Market Sales
If we start out in long-run and short-run equilibrium at point E_1, contractionary monetary policy by open market sales will shift aggregate demand to AD_2. The new short-run equilibrium will be at E_2. This is at a lower price level, however. Input owners will revise their expectations downward, and $SRAS_1$ will shift to $SRAS_2$. The new long-run equilibrium will be at E_3.

The graph of expansionary monetary policy was presented in Figure 17-2 on page 369; it is the opposite case to Figure 17-4.

A Real-World Caveat. Contractionary monetary policy has involved a reduction in the money supply with a consequent decline in the price level (deflation). In the real world of policymaking, contractionary monetary policy normally involves reducing the *rate of growth* of the money supply, thereby reducing the rate of increase in the price level (inflation). Similarly, real-world expansionary monetary policy typically involves increasing the rate of growth of the money supply. To show this in our diagrams, we would have to change them from static to dynamic, with a considerable amount of increased complexity.

Changes in the Discount Rate

When it was founded, the most important tool in the Fed's monetary policy kit was changes in the discount rate, discussed in Chapter 16. The Fed originally relied on the discount rate to carry out monetary policy because it had no power over reserve requirements. More important, its initial portfolio of government bonds was practically nonexistent and hence insufficient to conduct open market operations. Furthermore, the Fed did not really understand open market operations and what it could do with them until the mid-1930s. But as it has come increasingly to rely on open market operations, the Fed has used the discount rate less frequently as a tool of monetary policy—especially since the end of World War II.

Exercise 17.1

Visit www.econtoday.com for more about monetary policy.

Increasing the Discount Rate. Recall that the discount rate is the interest rate the Fed charges depository institutions when they borrow reserves directly from the Fed. An increase in the discount rate increases the cost of funds. In other words, depository institutions that seek loans from the Fed are now charged a higher price for those loans. That means that the price of one of their major lending inputs—the cost of money—has just gone up. Depository institutions pass at least part of this increased cost on to their borrowing customers by raising the interest rates they charge on loans.

Decreasing the Discount Rate. A reduction in the discount rate lowers depository institutions' cost of funds. It enables them to lower the rates they charge their customers for borrowing. People who thought they were not able to manage to purchase consumer durables, for example, now find themselves able to do so. The aggregate demand curve shifts outward as shown in Figure 17-2 on page 369, just as it did with expansionary open market operations (the purchase of bonds). In the short run, real output may increase without too much increase in the price index. Ultimately, though, all of the increase in demand is translated into a higher price level with output returning to its long-run equilibrium.

Changes in Reserve Requirements

Although the Fed rarely uses changes in reserve requirements as a form of monetary policy, most recently it did so in 1992, when it decreased reserve requirements on checkable deposits to 10 percent. In any event, here is how changes in reserve requirements affect the economy.

An Increase in the Required Reserve Ratio. If the Fed increases reserve requirements, this makes it more expensive for banks to meet their reserve requirements. They must replenish their reserves by reducing their lending. They induce potential borrowers not to borrow so much by raising the interest rates they charge on the loans they offer. Therefore, some borrowers who would have borrowed to purchase goods and service will no longer do so. The aggregate demand curve shifts from AD_1 to AD_2 as in Figure 17-4 on page 371. In the short run, both the price index and real GDP fall. In the long run, as expectations adjust and so do input prices, all of the shock is absorbed in a lower price level.

A Decrease in the Required Reserve Ratio. When the Fed decreases reserve requirements, as it did in 1992, some depository institutions attempt to lend their excess reserves out. To induce customers to borrow more, depository institutions cut interest rates. Individuals and firms that thought they would be unable to make new purchases now find themselves able to do so, and their spending increases. The aggregate demand curve shifts outward from AD_1 to AD_2 as in Figure 17-2 on page 369. In the short run, output increases and the price index rises moderately. In the long run, changes in expectations and input costs cause the short-run aggregate supply curve to shift so that the increase in aggregate demand is simply translated into a higher price level. (Recall from Chapter 16 that any change in the required reserve ratio changes the money multiplier.)

CONCEPTS IN BRIEF

- Monetary policy consists of open market operations, discount rate changes, and reserve requirement changes.

- When the Fed sells bonds, it must offer them at a lower price. When the Fed buys bonds, it must pay a higher price.

- There is an inverse relationship between the prevailing rate of interest in the economy and the market price of existing bonds.

- If we start out in long-run and short-run equilibrium, contractionary monetary policy first leads to a decrease in aggregate demand, resulting in a reduction in real GDP and in the price level. Eventually, though, the short-run aggregate supply curve shifts downward, and the new equilibrium is at *LRAS* but at an even lower price level. Expansionary monetary policy works the opposite way.

OPEN ECONOMY TRANSMISSION OF MONETARY POLICY

So far we have discussed monetary policy in a closed economy. When we move to an open economy, in which there is international trade and the international purchase and sale of all assets including dollars and other currencies, monetary policy becomes more complex. Consider first the effect on exports of any type of monetary policy.

The Net Export Effect

When we examined fiscal policy, we pointed out that deficit financing can lead to higher interest rates. Higher (real, after-tax) interest rates do something in the foreign sector— they attract foreign financial investment. More people want to purchase U.S. government securities, for example. But to purchase U.S. assets, people first have to obtain U.S. dollars. This means that the demand for dollars goes up in foreign exchange markets. The international price of the dollar therefore rises. This is called an *appreciation* of the dollar, and it tends to reduce net exports because it makes our exports more expensive in terms of foreign currency and imports cheaper in terms of dollars. Foreigners demand fewer of our goods and services, and we demand more of theirs. In this way, expansionary fiscal policy that creates deficit spending financed by U.S. government borrowing can lead to a reduction in net exports.

But what about expansionary monetary policy? If expansionary monetary policy reduces real, after-tax U.S. interest rates, there will be a positive net export effect because foreigners will want fewer U.S. financial instruments, demanding fewer dollars and thereby causing the international price of the dollar to fall. This makes our exports cheaper for the rest of the world, which then demands a larger quantity of our exports. It also means that foreign goods and services are more expensive in the United States, so we therefore demand fewer imports. We come up with two conclusions:

1. Expansionary fiscal policy may cause international flows of financial capital (responding to interest rate *increases*) to offset its effectiveness to some extent. The net export effect is in the opposite direction of fiscal policy.
2. Expansionary monetary policy may cause interest rates to fall. Such a fall will induce international outflows of financial capital, thereby lowering the value of the dollar and making American goods more attractive. The net export effect of expansionary monetary policy will be in the same direction as the monetary policy effect.

Contractionary Monetary Policy

Now assume that the economy is experiencing inflation and the Federal Reserve wants to contract monetary policy. In so doing, it may cause interest rates to rise. Rising interest rates will cause financial capital to flow into the United States. The demand for dollars will increase, and their international price will go up. Foreign goods will now look cheaper to Americans, and imports will rise. Foreigners will not want our exports as much, and exports will fall. The result will be a deterioration in our international trade balance. Again, the international consequences reinforce the domestic consequences of monetary policy.

Globalization of International Money Markets

On a broader level, the Fed's ability to control the rate of growth of the money supply may be hampered as U.S. money markets become less isolated. With the push of a computer button, millions or even billions of dollars can change hands halfway around the world. In the world dollar market, the Fed finds an increasing number of dollars coming from *private* institutions. If the Fed reduces the growth of the money supply, individuals and firms in the United States can increasingly obtain dollars from other sources. People in the United States who want more liquidity can obtain their dollars from foreigners or can even obtain foreign currencies and convert them into dollars in the world dollar market. Indeed, it is possible that as world markets become increasingly integrated, U.S. residents may someday conduct transactions in *foreign* currencies.

MONETARY POLICY DURING PERIODS OF UNDERUTILIZED RESOURCES

If the national economy is operating at an equilibrium output level that is below that given by the long-run aggregate supply curve, monetary policy (like fiscal policy) can generate increases in the equilibrium level of real GDP per year up to a long-run equilibrium on

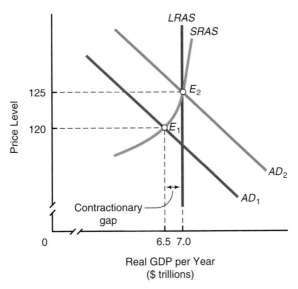

FIGURE 17-5

Expansionary Monetary Policy with Underutilized Resources
If we start out with equilibrium at E_1, expansionary monetary policy will shift AD_1 to AD_2. The new equilibrium will be at E_2.

LRAS. In Figure 17-5, you see initial aggregate demand as AD_1. It intersects *SRAS* at E_1, at an output rate of $6.5 trillion of real GDP per year and a price level of 120. There is a contractionary gap of $500 billion. That is the difference between *LRAS* and the current equilibrium. The Fed can engage in expansionary monetary policy, the direct and indirect effects of which will cause AD_1 to shift to AD_2. The new equilibrium is at E_2, at an output rate of $7 trillion of real GDP per year and a price level of 125. Note that expansionary monetary policy gets the economy to its *LRAS* sooner than otherwise.

CONCEPTS IN BRIEF

- Monetary policy in an open economy has repercussions for net exports.

- If expansionary monetary policy reduces U.S. interest rates, there is a positive net export effect because foreigners will demand fewer U.S. financial instruments, thereby demanding fewer dollars and hence causing the international price of the dollar to fall. This makes our exports cheaper for the rest of the world.

- Expansionary monetary policy during periods of underutilized resources can cause the equilibrium level of real GDP to increase (sooner than it otherwise would) to the rate of real output consistent with the vertical long-run aggregate supply curve.

MONETARY POLICY AND INFLATION

Most theories of inflation relate to the short run. The price index in the short run can fluctuate because of events such as oil price shocks, labor union strikes, or discoveries of large amounts of new natural resources. In the long run, however, empirical studies show a relatively stable relationship between excessive growth in the money supply and inflation.

Simple supply and demand can explain why the price level rises when the money supply is increased. Suppose that a major oil discovery is made, and the supply of oil increases dramatically relative to the demand for oil. The relative price of oil will fall; now it will take more units of oil to exchange for specific quantities of non-oil products. Similarly, if the supply of money rises relative to the demand for money, it will take more units of money to purchase specific quantities of goods and services. That is merely another way of stating that the price level has increased or that the purchasing power of money has fallen. In fact, the classical economists referred to inflation as a situation in which more money is chasing the same quantity of goods and services.

The Equation of Exchange and the Quantity Theory

A simple way to show the relationship between changes in the quantity of money in circulation and the price level is through the **equation of exchange,** developed by Irving Fisher:

$$M_s V \equiv PQ$$

where

$M_s =$ actual money balances held by the nonbanking public
$V =$ **income velocity of money,** or the number of times, on average, each monetary unit is spent on final goods and services
$P =$ price level or price index
$Q =$ real national output (real GDP)

Consider a numerical example involving a one-commodity economy. Assume that in this economy the total money supply, M_s, is $100; the quantity of output, Q, is 50 units of a good; and the average price, P, of this output is $10 per unit. Using the equation of exchange,

$$M_s V \equiv PQ$$

$$\$100V \equiv \$10 \times 50$$

$$\$100V \equiv \$500$$

$$V \equiv 5$$

Thus each dollar is spent an average of five times a year.

The Equation of Exchange as an Identity. The equation of exchange must always be true—it is an *accounting identity.* The equation of exchange states that the total amount of money spent on final output, $M_s V$, is equal to the total amount of money *received* for final output, PQ. Thus a given flow of money can be seen from either the buyers' side or the producers' side. The value of goods purchased is equal to the value of goods sold.

If Q represents real national output and P is the price level, PQ equals the dollar value of national output, or *nominal* national income. Thus

$$M_s V \equiv PQ \equiv Y$$

The Crude Quantity Theory of Money and Prices. If we now make some assumptions about different variables in the equation of exchange, we come up with the simplified theory of why prices change, called the **crude quantity theory of money and prices.** If you assume that the velocity of money, V, is constant and that real national output, Q, is basically stable, the simple equation of exchange tells you that a change in the money supply can lead only to a proportionate change in the price level. Continue with

Equation of exchange
The formula indicating that the number of monetary units times the number of times each unit is spent on final goods and services is identical to the price level times output (or nominal national income).

Income velocity of money
The number of times per year a dollar is spent on final goods and services; equal to GDP divided by the money supply.

Crude quantity theory of money and prices
The belief that changes in the money supply lead to proportional changes in the price level.

Pity Those Poor Printing Presses

An examination of stories about hyperinflation throughout the world over the past several decades yields one common media statement: "Prices are increasing so fast that the money printing presses can't keep up with the inflation." What is wrong with this statement is that the order of causation is reversed. Hyperinflation is caused by an excessive growth in the money supply—hyperactive money printing presses, if you will. Countries that have experienced hyperinflation have typically had governments that resorted to printing excessive amounts of currency. Indeed, economists have hundreds of years of empirical evidence to validate such a statement, the media notwithstanding.

our numerical example. Q is 50 units of the good. V equals 5. If the money supply increases to 200, the only thing that can happen is that the price index, P, has to go up from 10 to 20. Otherwise the equation is no longer in balance.

INTERNATIONAL EXAMPLE
Inflation and Money Growth Throughout the World

Is there much evidence that the rate of inflation is closely linked to the rate of monetary growth? The answer seems to be that in the long run there is a clear correlation between the two. Look at Figure 17-6. On the horizontal axis, in ratio form, is the rate of growth of the money supply. On the vertical axis is the annual rate of inflation (again, based on a ratio scale). As you can see, if you were to draw a line through the average of the points, it would slope upward: Faster monetary growth leads to a higher rate of inflation throughout different countries. This relationship appears to hold in the United States also. Decades of relatively high money supply growth are consistent with relatively higher rates of inflation and vice versa in the United States.

FOR CRITICAL ANALYSIS: Do the data shown in Figure 17-6 "prove" the crude quantity theory of money and prices? •

Empirical Verification. There is considerable evidence of the empirical validity of the relationship between excessive monetary growth and high rates of inflation. Look back at Figure 16-1 on page 341. There you see the loose correspondence between money supply growth and the rate of inflation in the United States from 1960 to the present.

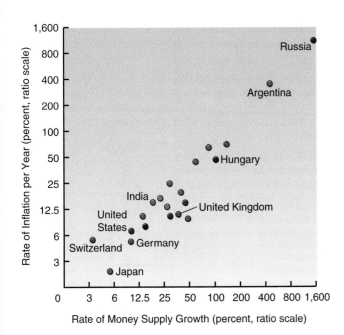

FIGURE 17-6
International Relationship Between Money Supply Growth Rates and Rates of Inflation

If we plot rates of inflation and rates of monetary growth for different countries, we come up with a scatter diagram that shows an obvious direct relationship. If you were to draw a line through the "average" of the points in this figure, it would be upward-sloping, showing that an increase in the rate of growth of the money supply leads to an increase in the rate of inflation.

Source: International Monetary Fund. Data are for latest available periods.

CONCEPTS IN BRIEF

- The equation of exchange states that the expenditures by some people will equal income receipts by others, or $M_sV \equiv PQ$ (money supply times velocity equals nominal national income).

- Viewed as an accounting identity, the equation of exchange is always correct, because the amount of money spent on final output must equal the total amount of money received for final output.

- The crude quantity theory of money and prices states that a change in the money supply will bring about an equiproportional change in the price level.

MONETARY POLICY IN ACTION: THE TRANSMISSION MECHANISM

At the start of this chapter, we talked about the direct and indirect effects of monetary policy. The direct effect is simply that an increase in the money supply causes people to have excess money balances. To get rid of these excess money balances, they increase their expenditures. The indirect effect occurs because some people have decided to purchase interest-bearing assets with their excess money balances. This causes the price of such assets—bonds—to go up. Because of the inverse relationship between the price of existing bonds and the interest rate, the interest rate in the economy falls. This lower interest rate induces people and businesses to spend more than they otherwise would have spent.

The Keynesian Transmission Mechanism

One school of economists believes that the indirect effect of monetary policy is the more important. This group, typically called Keynesian because of its belief in Keynes's work, asserts that the main effect of monetary policy occurs through changes in the interest rate. The Keynesian money transmission mechanism is shown in Figure 17-7. There you see that the money supply changes the interest rate, which in turn changes the desired rate of investment. This transmission mechanism can be seen explicitly in Figure 17-8. In panel (a), you see that an increase in the money supply reduces the interest rate. This reduction in the interest rate causes desired investment expenditures to increase from I_1 to I_2 in panel (b). This increase in investment shifts aggregate demand outward from AD_1 to AD_2 in panel (c).

The Monetarists' View of Money Supply Changes. Monetarists, economists who believe in a modern quantity theory of money and prices, contend that monetary policy works its way more directly into the economy. They believe that changes in the money supply lead to changes in nominal GDP in the same direction. An increase in the money supply because of expansionary open market operations (purchases of bonds) by the Fed leads the public to have larger money holdings than desired. This excess quantity of

Monetarists
Macroeconomists who believe that inflation is always caused by excessive monetary growth and that changes in the money supply affect aggregate demand both directly and indirectly.

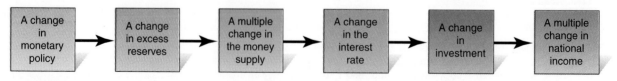

FIGURE 17-7
The Keynesian Money Transmission Mechanism

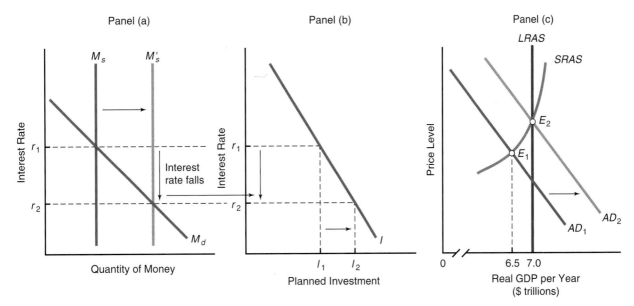

FIGURE 17-8

Adding Monetary Policy to the Keynesian Model

In panel (a), we show a demand for money function, M_d. It slopes downward to show that at lower rates of interest, a larger quantity of money will be demanded. The money supply is given initially as M_s, so the equilibrium rate of interest will be r_1. At this rate of interest, we see from the planned investment schedule given in panel (b) that the quantity of planned investment demanded per year will be I_1. After the shift in the money supply to M'_s, the resulting increase in investment from I_1 to I_2 shifts the aggregate demand curve in panel (c) outward from AD_1 to AD_2. Equilibrium moves from E_1 to E_2, at $7 trillion real GDP per year.

money demanded induces the public to buy more of everything, especially more durable goods such as cars, stereos, and houses. If the economy is starting out at its long-run equilibrium rate of output, there can only be a short-run increase in real GDP. Ultimately, though, the public cannot buy more of everything; it simply bids up prices so that the price level rises.

Monetarists' Criticism of Monetary Policy. The monetarists' belief that monetary policy works through changes in desired spending does not mean that they consider such policy an appropriate government stabilization tool. According to the monetarists, although monetary policy can affect real GDP (and employment) in the short run, the length of time required before money supply changes take effect is so long and variable that such policy is difficult to conduct. For example, an expansionary monetary policy to counteract a contractionary gap may not take effect for a year and a half, by which time inflation may be a problem. At that point, the expansionary monetary policy will end up making the then current inflation worse. Monetarists therefore see monetary policy as a *destabilizing* force in the economy.

Monetary rule

A monetary policy that incorporates a rule specifying the annual rate of growth of some monetary aggregate.

According to the monetarists, therefore, policymakers should follow a **monetary rule:** Increase the money supply *smoothly* at a rate consistent with the economy's long-run average growth rate. *Smoothly* is an important word here. Increasing the money supply at 20 percent per year half the time and decreasing it at 17 percent per year the other half of the time would average out to about a 3 percent increase, but the results would be disastrous, say the monetarists. Instead of permitting the Fed to use its discretion in setting monetary policy, monetarists would force it to follow a rule such as "Increase the money supply smoothly at 3.5 percent per year" or "Abolish the Fed and replace it with a computer program allowing for a steady rise in the money supply."

FED TARGET CHOICE: INTEREST RATES OR MONEY SUPPLY?

Money supply and interest rate targets cannot be pursued simultaneously. Interest rate targets force the Fed to abandon control over the money supply; money stock growth targets force the Fed to allow interest rates to fluctuate.

Figure 17-9 shows the relationship between the total demand for money and the supply of money. Note that in the short run (in the sense that nominal national income is fixed), the demand for money is constant; short-run money supply changes leave the demand for money curve unaltered. In the short run, the Fed can choose either a particular interest rate (r_e or r_1) or a particular money supply (M_s or M'_s).

If the Fed wants interest rate r_e, it must select money supply M_s; if it desires a lower interest rate in the short run, it must increase the money supply. Thus by targeting an interest rate, the Fed must relinquish control of the money supply. Conversely, if the Fed wants to target the money supply at, say, M'_s, it must allow the interest rate to fall to r_1.

Consider now the case in which the Fed wants to maintain the present level of interest rates. If actual market interest rates in the future rise persistently above the present (desired) rates, the Fed will be continuously forced to increase the money supply. The initial increase in the money supply will only temporarily lower interest rates. The increased money stock eventually will induce inflation, and inflationary premiums will be included in nominal interest rates. To pursue its low-interest-rate policy, the Fed must *again* increase the money stock because interest rates are still rising. Note that to attempt to maintain an interest rate target (stable interest rates), the Fed must abandon an independent money stock target. Symmetrical reasoning indicates that by setting growth rate targets at M_s or M'_s, the Fed must allow short-run fluctuations in interest rates when the economy experiences a contraction or an expansion.

INTERNET EXERCISE

Exercise 17.2
Visit www.econtoday.com for more about changing interest rates.

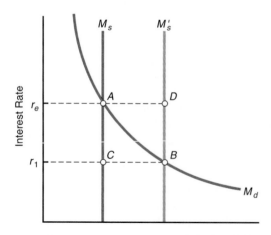

Quantity of Money Supplied and Demanded

FIGURE 17-9

Choosing a Monetary Policy Target
The Fed, in the short run, can select an interest rate or a money supply target but not both. It cannot, for example, choose r_e and M'_s; if it selects r_e, it must accept M_s; if it selects M'_s, it must allow the interest rate to fall to r_1. The Fed can obtain point A or B. It cannot get to point C or D. It must therefore choose one target or the other.

But which should the Fed target, interest rates or monetary aggregates? (And which interest rate or which money stock?) It is generally agreed that the answer depends on the source of instability in the economy. If the source of instability is variations in private or public spending, monetary aggregate (money supply) targets should be set and pursued. However, if the source of instability is an unstable demand for (or perhaps supply of) money, interest rate targets are preferred.

One perennial critic of the Federal Reserve, Milton Friedman, argues that no matter what, "I believe that the idea that a central bank can target interest rates is utterly false. Interest rates are partly a real magnitude, partly a nominal magnitude. The Federal Reserve cannot target real interest rates and has done great damage by trying to do so." Here Friedman is referring to the concept of the nominal rate of interest being comprised of the real interest rate plus the future expected inflation rate.

INTERNATIONAL POLICY EXAMPLE
Targeting the Rate of Inflation in Other Countries

Rather than targeting interest rates or the rate of growth of the money supply, the central banks of New Zealand, Canada, and Britain have targeted the rate of inflation. Consider New Zealand, which started inflation targeting in 1990. It aimed to cut inflation to less than 2 percent by the beginning of 1993. The rate of inflation did stay below 2 percent from mid-1991 until recently (with a brief time above 2 percent both in 1995 and 1996). Canada started its experiment a few months earlier. Its rate of inflation has stayed almost always below 2 percent ever since. Britain started inflation targeting in 1992. Its inflation rate has been around 3 percent ever since. Among the main benefits of this type of monetary policy, according to economists Frederick Mishkin and Adam Posen, who studied those three countries, are that monetary policy is more transparent, it is more coherent, and policymakers are more accountable.

FOR CRITICAL ANALYSIS: Why do you think policymakers in the three countries mentioned do not use a rate of inflation of zero as a target? ●

CONCEPTS IN BRIEF

- In the Keynesian model, monetary transmission operates through a change in the interest rates, which changes investment, causing a multiple change in the equilibrium level of national income.

- Monetarists believe that changes in the money supply lead to changes in nominal GDP in the same direction. The effect is both direct and indirect, however, as individuals spend their excess money balances on cars, stereos, houses, and a variety of many other things.

- Monetarists, among others, argue in favor of a monetary rule—increasing the money supply smoothly at a rate consistent with the economy's long-run average growth rate. Monetarists do not believe in discretionary monetary (or fiscal) policy.

- The Fed can choose to stabilize interest rates or to change the money supply but not both.

Central banks still hold over a billion ounces of gold as reserves. In spite of its long history as a reserve commodity, gold's real market value has not held up well in the 1990s. Why do central banks still hold gold?

Restore the Gold Standard—or Sell Off All the Gold?

CONCEPTS APPLIED:

RESERVES, MONEY, MONETARY POLICY, MONEY SUPPLY, INFLATION, CENTRAL BANKING

Visit www.econtoday.com for an Internet Activity that expands your understanding of these concepts.

They call them hard-money advocates or "gold bugs"—individuals who believe there is a role for gold in our monetary policy. Specifically, gold advocates argue that we should enhance the role of gold in monetary policy to help maintain the purchasing power of our money.

Does the Convertibility of Cash into Gold Guarantee Stable Prices?

One of the main arguments for including gold in our monetary policy is that in so doing, we would presumably have more stable prices. Do the data bear this out? Consider the period from 1934 to 1968, when the price of gold in the United States was fixed at $35 an ounce. During those years, wholesale prices increased approximately threefold. By contrast, between 1968 and 1997, the price of gold was allowed to float, and it increased almost three times as much as the Consumer Price Index. Thus the lesson of the past is that the real price of gold is far from stable. Furthermore, short-term movements in gold prices have been much more erratic than movements in the general price level.

Gold Prices Go Down

At the beginning of 1998, the price of gold reached a 13-year low when it fell below $290 an ounce. As a store of value, gold has not been particularly effective. As we pointed out at the start of this chapter, investing in gold 10 years ago relative to investing in the stock market would have left you one-fifth as wealthy.

Central Banks React

In 1997, central banks sold about 30 million ounces of gold, or approximately 2 percent of gold stocks. Some economists argue that all gold held by central banks should be sold. The United States has 20 percent of the 1.1 billion ounces of gold held in central bank vaults. Keeping such reserves simply wastes resources. A Federal Reserve study argued that a complete sell-off by central banks would result in a net gain in economic welfare of almost $400 billion. Where would the benefit come from? First, such a sell-off would satisfy the demand for gold for jewelry and the semiconductor industry for years to come. Consequently, fewer resources would be devoted to mining gold. Second, central banks would stop holding non-interest-earning gold reserves and invest the proceeds instead in interest-earning assets.

To be sure, some companies would be hurt by the sell-off of central bank gold reserves. In particular, at, say, $250 an ounce, 90 percent of South Africa's gold mines would be working at a loss. Consequently, everyone with investments in South African gold mines would end up losing wealth. Tens of thousands of miners in South Africa would become unemployed also.

FOR CRITICAL ANALYSIS
1. "Gold has a 2,500-year history." Does this make any difference in our analysis of the role of gold in monetary policy?
2. In recent years, what has been the effective rate of return to central banks for holding gold reserves?

CHAPTER SUMMARY

1. The determinants of the demand for money balances are the transactions demand, the precautionary demand, and the asset demand.

2. Because holding money carries an opportunity cost—the interest income forgone—the demand for money curve showing the relationship between money balances and the interest rate slopes downward.

3. The direct effect of an increase in the money supply occurs through people desiring to spend more on real goods and services when they have excess money balances. The indirect effect of an increase in the money supply works through a lowering of the interest rate, thereby encouraging businesses to make new investments with the money loaned to them. Individuals will also engage in more consumption because of lower interest rates.

4. When the Fed sells bonds, it must offer them at a lower price. When the Fed buys bonds, it must pay a higher price. There is an inverse relationship between the prevailing rate of interest in the economy and the market price of existing bonds.

5. If we start out in long-run and short-run equilibrium, contractionary monetary policy initially leads to a decrease in aggregate demand, resulting in a reduction in real GDP and in the price level. Eventually, though, the short-run aggregate supply curve shifts downward, and the new equilibrium is at *LRAS* but at an even lower price level. Expansionary monetary policy works the opposite way if we are starting out in both long-run and short-run equilibrium. The end result is simply a higher price level rather than a change in the equilibrium level of real GDP per year.

6. If expansionary monetary policy reduces U.S. interest rates, there is a positive net export effect because

foreigners will demand fewer U.S. financial instruments, thereby demanding fewer dollars, causing the international price of the dollar to fall. This makes our exports cheaper for the rest of the world.

7. Expansionary monetary policy during periods of underutilized resources can cause the equilibrium level of real GDP to increase up to that rate of real output consistent with the vertical long-run aggregate supply curve.

8. The equation of exchange states that the expenditures by some people will equal income receipts by others: $M_sV \equiv PQ$ (money supply times velocity equals nominal national income). Viewed as an accounting identity, the equation of exchange is always correct because the amount of money spent on final output must equal the total amount of money received for final output.

9. The crude quantity theory of money and prices states that a change in the money supply will bring about a proportional change in the price level.

10. In the Keynesian model, monetary transmission operates through a change in the interest rates, which changes investment, causing a multiple change in national income.

11. Monetarists believe that changes in the money supply lead to changes in nominal GDP in the same direction. The effect is direct and indirect because individuals have excess money balances that they spend on cars, stereos, houses, and other things. Monetarists, among others, argue in favor of a monetary rule—increasing the money supply smoothly at a rate consistent with the economy's long-run growth rate. Monetarists do not believe in discretionary monetary (or fiscal) policy.

DISCUSSION OF PREVIEW QUESTIONS

1. **What is the demand for money curve, and how is it related to the interest rate?**

Three types of demands—transactions, precautionary, and asset—motivate people to hold money, and each type provides benefits to money holders. Because people get paid at discrete intervals but want to make expenditures more or less continuously, they find it convenient to hold a stock of money (transactions

demand); the benefit they receive is *convenience.* People also desire a pool of readily available purchasing power in order to meet emergencies (precautionary demand); the benefit is a measure of *security.* Finally, money is an asset; it is a means of storing value or wealth. At certain times money becomes a superior form of wealth—superior to other asset forms (bonds, stocks, real estate, and the like) that are risky. Asset demand money holders receive the benefit of *liquidity*. There is an opportunity cost to holding money (especially the narrow form of money, M1). The opportunity cost is forgone interest. The demand for money curve shows an inverse relationship between the interest rate and desired money holdings. As the interest rate falls, the opportunity cost of holding money falls concomitantly; people are more and more disposed to avail themselves of the benefits of holding money as the cost of doing so falls.

2. Why is the price of existing bonds inversely related to the interest rate?

Suppose that you know nothing about some faraway planet except that a bond (or an investment project) there yields $100 per year forever. Can you determine whether that bond or investment project will have a high price; that is, will it be "valuable"? No, you can't; you would have to know what the interest rate was on that planet. If interest rates are very, very low, say, one-thousandth of 1 percent, that bond or investment would be very valuable indeed. This is because the interest rate summarizes the opportunity cost for investment projects or bonds; if interest rates are very low, a given amount of money can earn very little annually, but if interest rates are very high, a given amount of money can earn a great deal annually. Thus $100 per year looks good (high) or bad (low) depending on whether prevailing interest rates are low or high, respectively. The nature of a bond is such that it yields a given and known stream of revenues (nominal dollar amounts) over time. This given revenue stream will be priced relatively high if interest rates are relatively low and will command a low price if interest rates are high. In short, an inverse relationship exists between the price (market value) of an existing bond and the prevailing economywide interest rate.

3. How do the supply of and demand for money determine the interest rate?

The accompanying graph depicts the total supply and demand for money in an economy. To demonstrate that given these supply and demand schedules for money, the equilibrium interest rate will eventually be established at i_e, we must rule out all other possible interest rates. Thus let i_2 represent any interest rates below i_e. At i_2, the group wants to hold more money than is actually available ($M_d = 300 > M_s = 200$), and a shortage of liquidity exists. People

become more liquid (hold more cash) by selling bonds (converting bonds, which are nonmoney, into money). As many people try to become more liquid, they attempt to sell many bonds. This forces bond prices down and interest rates up. These same conditions exist at all interest rates below i_e. Similarly, at all interest rates above i_e (i_1 in particular), $M_s > M_d$, and the group will be holding more money than it wants to hold to meet the three money-holding motives demands. Hence many people will buy bonds (to rid themselves of the opportunity cost of holding money), forcing bond prices up—and interest rates down toward i_e. At i_e, $M_d = M_s = 200$, and the group is voluntarily holding the available money supply.

4. What is a monetarist?

Monetarists are economists who maintain that changes in the money supply are the *primary* influence on the levels of employment, output, and prices. They maintain that there is little theoretical or empirical evidence to indicate the effectiveness of fiscal policy. Moreover, they maintain that monetary policy is not desirable either. This is because the time lag between changes in the money supply and changes in these macroeconomic variables is too long and imprecise and that control of the money supply is not independent of politics. Consequently, present-day monetarists suggest that the government get out of the stabilization business; governments should use neither fiscal nor monetary policy. Instead, monetarists say governments should raise taxes and make expenditures only for pressing social matters (national defense, welfare, and so on), and monetary authorities should be commanded to increase the money supply at some constant and predetermined rate.

PROBLEMS

(Answers to the odd-numbered problems appear at the back of the book.)

17-1. Briefly outline the Keynesian monetary transmission mechanism.

17-2. The equation that indicates the value (price) right now of a nonmaturing bond (called a consol) is $V = R/i$, where V is the present value, R is the annual net income generated from the bond, and i is the going interest rate.

    a. Assume that a bond promises the holder \$1,000 per year forever. If the interest rate is 10 percent, what is the bond worth now (V)?

    b. Continuing part (a), what happens to the value of the bond (V) if interest rates rise to 20 percent? What if they fall to 5 percent?

    c. Suppose that there were an indestructible machine that was expected to generate \$2,000 per year in revenues but costs \$1,000 per year to maintain—forever. How would that machine be priced relative to the bond described in part (a)?

17-3. Show in the form of a chart the processes by which the Fed can reduce inflationary pressures by raising the discount rate.

17-4. Assume that $M = \$300$ billion, $P = \$1.72$, and $Q = 900$ billion units per year. What is the income velocity of money?

17-5. Briefly outline expansionary monetary policy according to a monetarist.

COMPUTER-ASSISTED INSTRUCTION

The basic comparative statics implications of changes in monetary policy are demonstrated with extensive use of graphics. An additional series of questions illustrates the operation of the basic tools of the Federal Reserve System.

Complete problem and answer appear on disk.

INTERACTING WITH THE INTERNET

You may want to check out the actions of the Federal Open Market Committee (FOMC), which is the part of the Fed and is most responsible for monetary policy. Go to

www.bog.frb.fed.us/fomc

You can find out more about monetary policy by accessing the home page of the Federal Reserve Bank of Minneapolis at

woodrow.mpls.frb.fed.us/info/policy/

In particular, examine the documents *What Is the FMOC?* and *Understanding Open Market Operations.* You can go directly to the minutes of the FOMC by typing **fomcmin/index.html** at the end of the URL given above.

If you have Windows installed on your computer, you can download a monetary and fiscal policy interactive computer simulation at

www.frbsf.org/econedu/curriculum/interdl.html

MONETARY POLICY:
A KEYNESIAN PERSPECTIVE

According to the traditional Keynesian approach to monetary policy, changes in the money supply can affect the level of aggregate demand only through their effect on interest rates. Moreover, interest rate changes act on aggregate demand solely by changing the level of investment spending. Finally, the traditional Keynesian approach argues that there exist plausible circumstances under which monetary policy may have little or no effect on aggregate demand.

Figure D-1 measures real national income along the horizontal axis and total planned expenditures (aggregate demand) along the vertical axis. The components of aggregate demand are consumption *(C),* investment *(I),* government spending *(G),* and net exports *(X).* The height of the schedule labeled $C + I + G + X$ shows total planned expenditures (aggregate demand) as a function of income. This schedule slopes upward because consumption depends positively on income. Everywhere along the line labeled $Y = C + I + G + X$, planned spending equals income. At point Y^*, where the $C + I + G + X$ line intersects this 45-degree reference line, planned spending is consistent with income. At any income less than Y^*, spending exceeds income, so income and thus spending will tend to rise. At any level of income greater than Y^*, planned spending is less than income, so income and thus spending will tend to decline. Given the determinants of *C, I, G,* and *X,* total spending (aggregate demand) will be Y^*.

INCREASING THE MONEY SUPPLY

According to the Keynesian approach, an increase in the money supply pushes interest rates down. This reduces the cost of borrowing and thus induces firms to increase the level of investment spending from *I* to *I'.* As a result, the $C + I + G + X$ line shifts upward in Figure D-1 by the full amount of the rise in investment spending, thus yielding the line $C + I' + G + X$. The rise in investment spending causes income to rise, which in turn

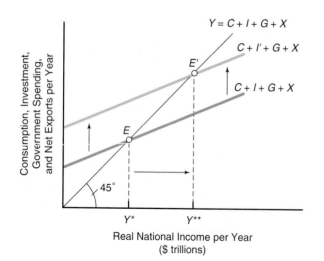

FIGURE D-1

An Increase in the Money Supply
An increase in the money supply increases income by lowering interest rates and thus increasing investment from *I* to *I'.*

causes consumption spending to rise, which further increases income. Ultimately, aggregate demand rises to Y^{**}, where spending again equals income. A key conclusion of the Keynesian analysis is that total spending rises by *more* than the original rise in investment spending because consumption spending depends positively on income.

DECREASING THE MONEY SUPPLY

Not surprisingly, contractionary monetary policy works in exactly the reverse manner. A reduction in the money supply pushes interest rates up, which increases the cost of borrowing. Firms respond by reducing their investment spending, and this starts income downward. Consumers react to the lower income by scaling back on their consumption spending, which further depresses income. Thus the ultimate decline in income is larger than the initial drop in investment spending. Indeed, because the change in income is a multiple of the change in investment, Keynesians note that changes in investment spending (similar to changes in government spending) have a *multiplier* effect on the economy.

ARGUMENTS AGAINST MONETARY POLICY

It might be thought that this multiplier effect would make monetary policy a potent tool in the Keynesian arsenal, particularly when it comes to getting the economy out of a recession. In fact, however, many traditional Keynesians argue that monetary policy is likely to be relatively ineffective as a recession fighter. According to their line of reasoning, although monetary policy has the potential to reduce interest rates, changes in the money supply have little actual impact on interest rates. Instead, during recessions, people try to build up as much as they can in liquid assets to protect themselves from risks of unemployment and other losses of income. When the monetary authorities increase the money supply, individuals are willing to allow most of it to accumulate in their bank accounts. This desire for increased liquidity thus prevents interest rates from falling very much, which in turn means that there will be virtually no change in investment spending and thus little change in aggregate demand.

PROBLEMS

D-1. Assume that the following conditions exist:

a. All banks are fully loaned up—there are no excess reserves, and desired excess reserves are always zero.

b. The money multiplier is 3.

c. The planned investment schedule is such that at a 10 percent rate of interest, investment is $200 billion; at 9 percent, investment is $225 billion.

d. The investment multiplier is 3.

e. The initial equilibrium level of national income is $2 trillion.

f. The equilibrium rate of interest is 10 percent.

Now the Fed engages in expansionary monetary policy. It buys $1 billion worth of bonds, which increases the money supply, which in turn lowers the market rate of interest by 1 percent. Indicate by how much the money supply increased, and then trace out the numerical consequences of the associated reduction in interest rates on all the other variables mentioned.

CHAPTER 18

ISSUES IN STABILIZATION POLICY

As the 1990s come to a close, the U.S. economy is booming. In early 1998, the unemployment rate reached its lowest level in a quarter of a century, 4.6 percent. The reverse has occurred in Europe. The European Union's strongest nation, Germany, experienced unemployment rates in excess of 12 percent, the highest since before World War II. The French unemployment rate has remained above 12 percent for several years; unemployment is even higher in Spain. In short, while the U.S. economy has continued to add jobs—sometimes at the rate of 400,000 a month—virtually no private-sector jobs have been created in most countries on the "old" continent in the past 10 years. How can we explain this anomaly? Are American policymakers better or smarter? If not, how can we explain so much job creation in the United States? To understand this issue better, we must know something about stabilization policy.

PREVIEW QUESTIONS

1. What does the rational expectations hypothesis say about people's forecasting errors?

2. How do the new classical economists view economic policy?

3. What does the real business cycle theory say about the causes of recession?

4. How does the new Keynesian economics explain the stickiness of wages and prices?

**Active (discretionary)
policymaking**

All actions on the part of monetary and fiscal policymakers
that are undertaken in response
to or in anticipation of some
change in the overall economy.

**Passive (nondiscretionary)
policymaking**

Policymaking that is carried out
in response to a rule. It is therefore not in response to an actual or potential change in overall
economic activity.

Exercise 18.1

Visit www.econtoday.com for more
about the unemployment rate.

Did You Know That . . . since the recession that started in November 1948 until today, Congress, usually at the behest of the president, has passed at least a dozen bills aimed at fighting recession with fiscal policy? In the mid-1990s, in one 17-month period, the Fed increased short-term interest rates seven times and cut them once. And over a longer period, the Fed has even changed its basic operating targets.

ACTIVE VERSUS PASSIVE POLICYMAKING

All of these actions constitute part of what is called **active (discretionary) policymaking.** At the other extreme is **passive (nondiscretionary) policymaking,** in which there is no deliberate stabilization policy at all. You have already been introduced to one nondiscretionary policymaking idea in Chapter 17—the *monetary rule,* by which the money supply is allowed to increase at a fixed rate per year. In the fiscal arena, passive (nondiscretionary) policy might be simply to balance the federal budget over the business cycle. Recall from Chapter 13 that there are numerous time lags between when the national economy enters into a recession or a boom and when that event becomes known, acted on, and sensed by the economy. Proponents of passive policy argue strongly that such time lags often render short-term stabilization policy ineffective, or worse, procyclical.

To take a stand on this debate concerning active versus passive policymaking, you first need to know what the potential trade-offs are that policymakers believe they face. Then you need to see what the data actually show. The most important policy trade-off appears to be between price stability and unemployment. Before exploring that trade-off, we need first to look at the economy's natural, or long-run, rate of unemployment.

THE NATURAL RATE OF UNEMPLOYMENT

Recall from Chapter 7 that there are different types of unemployment: frictional, cyclical, seasonal, and structural. Frictional unemployment arises because individuals take the time to search for the best job opportunities. Except when the economy is in a recession or a depression, much unemployment is of this type.

Note that we did not say that frictional unemployment was the *sole* form of unemployment during normal times. There is also *wait unemployment,* caused by a variety of "rigidities" throughout the economy. Wait unemployment results from factors such as these:

1. Union activity that sets wages above the equilibrium level and also restricts the mobility of labor
2. Government-imposed licensing arrangements that restrict entry into specific occupations or professions
3. Government-imposed minimum wage laws and other laws that require all workers to be paid union wage rates on government contract jobs
4. Welfare and unemployment insurance benefits that reduce incentives to work

In each case, these factors reduce individuals' abilities or incentives to choose employment rather than unemployment.

As an example, consider the effect of unemployment insurance benefits on the probability of an unemployed person's finding a job. When unemployment benefits run out, according to economists Lawrence Katz and Bruce Meyer, the probability of an unemployed person's finding a job doubles. The conclusion is that unemployed workers are more serious about finding a job when they are no longer receiving such benefits.

Frictional and wait unemployment both exist even when the economy is in long-run equilibrium—they are a natural consequence of costly information (the need to conduct a job search) and the existence of rigidities such as those noted. Because these two types of unemployment are a natural consequence of imperfect information and rigidities, they are related to what economists call the **natural rate of unemployment.** It is defined as the rate of unemployment that would exist in the long run after everyone in the economy fully adjusted to any changes that have occurred. Recall that national output tends to return to the level implied by the long-run aggregate supply curve *(LRAS)*. Thus whatever rate of unemployment the economy tends to return to can be called the natural rate of unemployment.

Natural rate of unemployment

The rate of unemployment that is estimated to prevail in long-run macroeconomic equilibrium, when all workers and employers have fully adjusted to any changes in the economy.

EXAMPLE
The U.S. Natural Rate of Unemployment

At the end of World War II, the unemployment rate was below 4 percent. By the early 1990s, it was above 6 percent. These two endpoints for half a cycle of unemployment rates prove nothing by themselves. But look at Figure 18-1. There you see not only what has happened to the unemployment rate over that same time period but an esti-

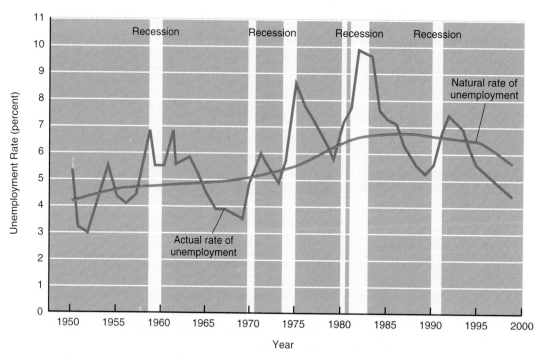

FIGURE 18-1

Estimated U.S. Natural Rate of Unemployment

As you can see in this figure, the actual rate of unemployment has varied widely in the United States in the second half of the twentieth century. If we estimate the natural rate of unemployment by averaging unemployment rates from five years earlier to five years later at each point in time, we get the heavy solid line so labeled. It rose from the 1950s until the mid-1980s and seems to be gradually descending since then. (Post-1991 natural rate is approximated.)

Sources: Economic Report of the President; Economic Indicators, various issues.

mate of the natural rate of unemployment. The solid line labeled "Natural rate of unemployment" is estimated by averaging unemployment rates from five years earlier to five years later at each point in time. This computation reveals that until about 1983, the natural rate of unemployment was rising. But since then, a downward trend appears to have taken hold.

FOR CRITICAL ANALYSIS: Of the four factors listed on page 389 that create wait unemployment, which do you think explained the gradual trend upward in the natural rate of unemployment since World War II until the 1990s in the United States? •

Departures from the Natural Rate of Unemployment

Even though the unemployment rate has a strong tendency to stay at and return to the natural rate, it is possible for fiscal and monetary policy to move the actual unemployment rate away from the natural rate, at least in the short run. Deviations of the actual unemployment rate from the natural rate are called *cyclical unemployment* because they are observed over the course of nationwide business fluctuations. During recessions, the overall unemployment rate exceeds the natural rate; cyclical unemployment is positive. During periods of economic booms, the overall unemployment rate can go below the natural rate; at such times, cyclical unemployment is in essence negative.

To see how departures from the natural rate of unemployment can occur, let's consider two examples. Referring to Figure 18-2, we begin in equilibrium at point *E*, with the associated price level P_1 and real GDP per year of level Q_1.

The Impact of Expansionary Policy. Now imagine that the government decides to use fiscal or monetary policy to stimulate the economy. Further suppose, for reasons that will soon become clear, that this policy surprises decision makers throughout the economy in the sense that they did not anticipate that the policy would occur. The aggregate demand curve shifts from AD_1 to AD_2 in Figure 18-2, so both the price level and real GDP rise to P_2 and Q_2, respectively. In the labor market, individuals would find that conditions had

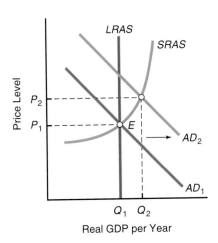

FIGURE 18-2

Impact of an Increase in Aggregate Demand on Output and Unemployment

If the economy is operating at *E*, it is in both short-run and long-run equilibrium. Here the actual rate of unemployment is equal to the natural rate of unemployment. Subsequent to expansionary monetary or fiscal policy, the aggregate demand curve shifts outward to AD_2. The price level rises to P_2; real GDP per year increases to Q_2. The unemployment rate will fall to below the natural rate of unemployment.

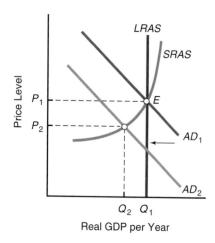

FIGURE 18-3

Impact of a Decline in Aggregate Demand on Output and Unemployment

Starting from equilibrium at E, a decline in aggregate demand to AD_2 leads to a lower price level, P_2, and real GDP declines to Q_2. The unemployment rate will rise above the natural rate of unemployment.

improved markedly relative to what they expected. Firms seeking to expand output will want to hire more workers. To accomplish this, they will recruit more actively and possibly ask workers to work overtime, so that individuals in the labor market will find more job openings and more possible hours they can work. Consequently, as you learned in Chapter 7, the average duration of unemployment will fall so that the unemployment rate falls. This unexpected increase in aggregate demand simultaneously causes the price level to rise to P_2 and the unemployment rate to fall.

The Consequences of Contractionary Policy. Instead of expansionary policy, the government could have decided to engage in contractionary (or deflationary) policy. As shown in Figure 18-3, the sequence of events would have been in the opposite direction of those in Figure 18-2. Again, beginning from an initial equilibrium E, an unanticipated reduction in aggregate demand puts downward pressure on both prices and real GDP; the price level falls to P_2, and real GDP declines to Q_2. Fewer firms will be hiring, and those that are hiring will offer fewer overtime possibilities. Individuals looking for jobs will find that it takes longer than predicted. As a result, unemployed individuals will remain unemployed longer. The average duration of unemployment will rise, and so, too, will the rate of unemployment. The unexpected decrease in aggregate demand simultaneously causes the price level to fall to P_2 and the unemployment rate to rise.

The Phillips Curve: The Trade-Off?

Let's recap what we have just observed. An *unexpected* increase in aggregate demand causes the price level to rise and the unemployment rate to fall. Conversely, an *unexpected* decrease in aggregate demand causes the price level to fall and the unemployment rate to rise. Moreover, although not shown explicitly in either diagram, two additional points are true:

1. The greater the unexpected increase in aggregate demand, the greater the amount of inflation that results, and the lower the unemployment rate.

2. The greater the unexpected decrease in aggregate demand, the greater the deflation that results, and the higher the unemployment rate.

The Negative Relationship Between Inflation and Unemployment. Figure 18-4 summarizes these findings. The inflation rate (*not* the price level) is measured along the vertical axis, and the unemployment rate is measured along the horizontal axis. Point *A* shows an initial starting point, with the unemployment rate at the natural rate, U^*. Note that as a matter of convenience, we are starting from an equilibrium in which the price level is stable (the inflation rate is zero). Unexpected increases in aggregate demand cause the price level to rise—the inflation rate becomes positive—and cause the unemployment rate to fall. Thus the economy moves up to the left from *A* to *B*. Conversely, unexpected decreases in aggregate demand cause the price level to fall and the unemployment rate to rise above the natural rate—the economy moves from point *A* to point *C*. If we look at both increases and decreases in aggregate demand, we see that high inflation rates tend to be associated with low unemployment rates (as at *B*) and that low (or negative) inflation rates tend to be accompanied by high unemployment rates (as at *C*).

Is There a Trade-Off? The apparent negative relationship between the inflation rate and the unemployment rate shown in Figure 18-4 has come to be called the **Phillips curve,** after A. W. Phillips, who discovered that a similar relationship existed historically in Great Britain. Although Phillips presented his findings only as an empirical regularity, economists quickly came to view the relationship as representing a *trade-off* between inflation and unemployment. In particular, policymakers believed they could *choose* alternative combinations of unemployment and inflation (or worse, that the trade-off was inevitable because you could not get more of one without giving up the other). Thus it seemed that a government that disliked unemployment could select a point like *B* in Figure 18-4, with a positive inflation rate but a relatively low unemployment rate. Conversely, a government that feared inflation could choose a stable price level at *A,* but only at the expense of a higher associated unemployment rate. Indeed, the Phillips curve seemed to suggest that it was possible for policymakers to fine-tune the economy by selecting the policies that would produce the exact mix of unemployment and inflation that suited current government objectives. As it turned out, matters are not so simple.

Phillips curve
A curve showing the relationship between unemployment and changes in wages or prices. It was long thought to reflect a trade-off between unemployment and inflation.

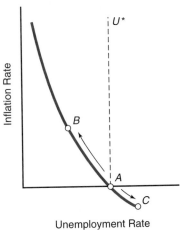

FIGURE 18-4

The Phillips Curve
Unanticipated changes in aggregate demand produce a negative relationship between the inflation rate and unemployment. U^* is the natural rate of unemployment.

The NAIRU. If we accept that a trade-off exists between the rate of inflation and the rate of unemployment, then the notion of "noninflationary" rates of unemployment seems appropriate. In fact, some economists have proposed what they call the **nonaccelerating inflation rate of unemployment (NAIRU).** If the Phillips curve trade-off exists and if the NAIRU can be estimated, that estimate will define the short-run trade-off between the rate of unemployment and the rate of inflation. Economists who have estimated the NAIRU for the world's 24 richest industrial countries claim that it has been steadily rising since the 1960s. Critics of the NAIRU concept argue that inflationary expectations must be taken into account.

Nonaccelerating inflation rate of unemployment (NAIRU)

The rate of unemployment below which the rate of inflation tends to rise and above which the rate of inflation tends to fall.

The Importance of Expectations

The reduction in unemployment that takes place as the economy moves from A to B in Figure 18-4 occurs because the wage offers encountered by unemployed workers are unexpectedly high. As far as the workers are concerned, these higher *nominal* wages appear, at least initially, to be increases in *real* wages; it is this fact that induces them to reduce their duration of search. This is a sensible way for the workers to view the world if aggregate demand fluctuates up and down at random, with no systematic or predictable variation one way or another. But if policymakers attempt to exploit the apparent trade-off in the Phillips curve, according to some macroeconomists, aggregate demand will no longer move up and down in an *unpredictable* way.

The Effects of an Unanticipated Policy. Consider Figure 18-5, for example. If the Federal Reserve attempts to reduce the unemployment rate to U_1, it must increase the money supply enough to produce an inflation rate of π_1. If this is a one-shot affair in which the money supply is first increased and then held constant, the inflation rate will temporarily rise to π_1 and the unemployment rate will temporarily fall to U_1; but as soon as the money supply stops growing, the inflation rate will return to zero and unemploy-

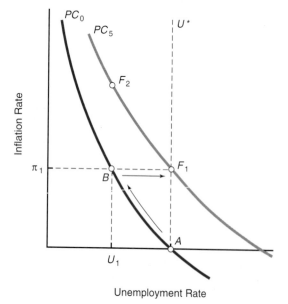

FIGURE 18-5

A Shift in the Phillips Curve
When there is a change in the expected inflation rate, the Phillips curve *(PC)* shifts to incorporate the new expectations. PC_0 shows expectations of zero inflation; PC_5 reflects an expected inflation rate of 5 percent.

ment will return to U^*, its natural rate. Thus a one-shot increase in the money supply will move the economy from point A to point B, and the economy will move of its own accord back to A.

If the authorities wish to prevent the unemployment rate from returning to U^*, some macroeconomists argue that the Federal Reserve must keep the money supply growing fast enough to keep the inflation rate up at π_1. But if the Fed does this, all of the economic participants in the economy—workers and job seekers included—will come to *expect* that inflation rate to continue. This, in turn, will change their expectations about wages. For example, suppose that π_1 equals 5 percent per year. When the expected inflation rate was zero, a 5 percent rise in nominal wages meant a 5 percent expected rise in real wages, and this was sufficient to induce some individuals to take jobs rather than remain unemployed. It was this perception of a rise in real wages that reduced search duration and caused the unemployment rate to drop from U^* to U_1. But if the expected inflation rate becomes 5 percent, a 5 percent rise in nominal wages means *no* rise in *real* wages. Once workers come to expect the higher inflation rate, rising nominal wages will no longer be sufficient to entice them out of unemployment. As a result, as the *expected* inflation rate moves up from 0 percent to 5 percent, the unemployment rate will move up also.

The Role of Expected Inflation. In terms of Figure 18-5, as authorities initially increase aggregate demand, the economy moves from point A to point B. If the authorities continue the stimulus in an effort to keep the unemployment rate down, workers' expectations will adjust, causing the unemployment rate to rise. In this second stage, the economy moves from B to point F_1: The unemployment rate returns to the natural rate, U^*, but the inflation rate is now π_1 instead of zero. Once the adjustment of expectations has taken place, any further changes in policy will have to take place along a curve such as PC_5, say, a movement from F_1 to F_2. This new schedule is also a Phillips curve, differing from the first, PC_0, in that the actual inflation rate consistent with any given unemployment rate is higher because the expected inflation rate is higher.

Not surprisingly, when economic policymakers found that economic participants engaged in such adjustment behavior, they were both surprised and dismayed. If decision makers can adjust their expectations to conform with fiscal and monetary policies, then policymakers cannot choose a permanently lower unemployment rate of U_1, even if they are willing to tolerate an inflation rate of π_1. Instead, the policymakers would end up with an unchanged unemployment rate in the long run, at the expense of a permanently higher inflation rate.

Initially, however, there did seem to be a small consolation, for it appeared that in the short run—before expectations adjusted—the unemployment rate could be *temporarily* reduced from U^* to U_1, even though eventually it would return to the natural rate. If an important national election were approaching, it might be possible to stimulate the economy long enough to get the unemployment rate low enough to assure reelection. However, policymakers came to learn that not even this was likely to be a sure thing.

The U.S. Experience with the Phillips Curve

In separate articles in 1968, Milton Friedman and E. S. Phelps published pioneering studies suggesting that the apparent trade-off suggested by the Phillips curve could not be exploited by policymakers. Friedman and Phelps both argued that any attempt to reduce unemployment by inflating the economy would soon be thwarted by economic participants'

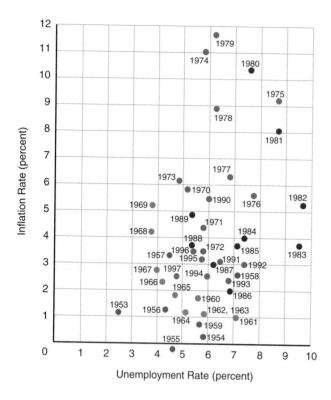

FIGURE 18-6

The Phillips Curve: Theory Versus Data

If you plot points representing the rate of inflation and the rate of unemployment for the United States from 1953 to the present, there does not appear to be any Phillips curve trade-off between the two variables.

Sources: Economic Report of the President; Economic Indicators, various issues.

incorporating the new higher inflation rate into their expectations. The Friedman-Phelps research thus implies that for any given unemployment rate, *any* inflation rate is possible, depending on the actions of policymakers. As reflected in Figure 18-6, the propositions of Friedman and Phelps were to prove remarkably accurate.

When we examine the data for unemployment and inflation in the United States over the past half century, we see virtually no clear relationship between them. Although there seemed to have been a Phillips curve trade-off between unemployment and inflation from the mid-1950s to the mid-1960s, apparently once people in the economy realized what was happening, they started revising their forecasts accordingly. So, once policymakers attempted to exploit the Phillips curve, the apparent trade-off between unemployment and inflation disappeared.

INTERNATIONAL POLICY EXAMPLE
Can European Policymakers Exploit the Phillips Curve?

Although the data for the United States seem clear—policymakers cannot exploit the Phillips curve trade-off—what about Europe? It appears that European policymakers cannot exploit the trade-off either. As Figure 18-7 shows, the unemployment rate in Europe remained almost constant from 1967 to 1974 in spite of a skyrocketing inflation rate.

If one believes in the Phillips curve analysis, there seems to be little hope today for European policymakers to reduce their double-digit unemployment rates. More complete research was conducted by two British economists, David Blanchslower and Andrew Oswald, who spent five years analyzing numerous data points across 12 countries. Their conclusion was that there is no relationship between inflation and unemployment.

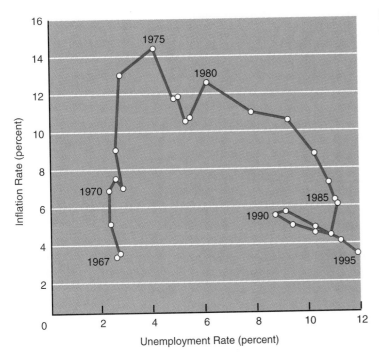

FIGURE 18-7

**Relationship Between Inflation and
Unemployment in Europe**
If we examine the so-called Philips curve trade-off in
Europe since 1967, there does not appear to be any
long-run stable relationship between the rate of infla-
tion and the rate of unemployment.

Source: David Blanchslower and Andrew Oswald.

FOR CRITICAL ANALYSIS: How do the data in Figure 18-6 and Figure 18-7 support
the proponents of a monetary rule? ●

CONCEPTS IN BRIEF

• The natural rate of unemployment is the rate that exists in long-run equilibrium, when
workers' expectations are consistent with actual conditions.

• Departures from the natural rate of unemployment can occur when individuals encounter unanticipated changes in fiscal or monetary policy; an unexpected rise in aggregate demand will reduce unemployment below the natural rate, whereas an unanticipated decrease in aggregate demand will push unemployment above the natural
rate.

• The Phillips curve exhibits a negative relationship between the inflation rate and the
unemployment rate that can be observed when there are *unanticipated* changes in
aggregate demand.

• It was originally believed that the Phillips curve represented a trade-off between inflation and unemployment. In fact, no trade-off exists because workers' expectations
adjust to any systematic attempts to reduce unemployment below the natural rate.

RATIONAL EXPECTATIONS AND THE NEW
CLASSICAL MODEL

You already know that economists assume that economic participants act *as though* they
were rational and calculating. We think of firms that rationally maximize profits when they
choose today's rate of output and consumers who rationally maximize utility when they
choose how much of what goods to consume today. One of the pivotal features of current

macro policy research is the assumption that rationality also applies to the way that economic participants think about the future as well as the present. This relationship was developed by Robert Lucas, who won the Nobel Prize in 1995 for his work. In particular, there is widespread agreement among a growing group of macroeconomics researchers that the **rational expectations hypothesis** extends our understanding of the behavior of the macroeconomy. There are two key elements to this hypothesis:

1. Individuals base their forecasts (or expectations) about the future values of economic variables on all available past and current information.
2. These expectations incorporate individuals' understanding about how the economy operates, including the operation of monetary and fiscal policy.

In essence, the rational expectations hypothesis assumes that Abraham Lincoln was correct when he stated, "It is true that you may fool all the people some of the time; you can even fool some of the people all of the time; but you can't fool *all* of the people *all* of the time."

If we further assume that there is pure competition in all markets and that all prices and wages are flexible, we obtain the **new classical model** (referred to in Chapter 13 when discussing the Ricardian equivalence theorem). To see how rational expectations operate within the context of this model, let's take a simple example of the economy's response to a change in monetary policy.

Rational expectations hypothesis
A theory stating that people combine the effects of past policy changes on important economic variables with their own judgment about the future effects of current and future policy changes.

New classical model
A modern version of the classical model in which wages and prices are flexible, there is pure competition in all markets, and the rational expectations hypothesis is assumed to be working.

The New Classical Model

Consider Figure 18-8, which shows the long-run aggregate supply curve (*LRAS*) for the economy, as well as the initial aggregate demand curve (AD_1) and the short-run aggregate supply curve ($SRAS_1$). The money supply is initially given by $M = M_1$, and the price level and real GDP are shown by P_1 and Q_1, respectively. Thus point A represents the initial equilibrium.

Suppose now that the money supply is unexpectedly increased to M_2, thereby causing the aggregate demand curve to shift outward to AD_2. Given the location of the short-run aggregate supply curve, this increase in aggregate demand will cause output and the price

FIGURE 18-8

Response to an Unanticipated Rise in Aggregate Demand
Unanticipated changes in aggregate demand have real effects. In this case, the rise in demand causes real output to rise from Q_1 to Q_2.

level to rise to Q_2 and P_2, respectively. The new short-run equilibrium is at B. Because output is *above* the long-run equilibrium level of Q_1, unemployment must be below long-run levels (the natural rate), and so workers will soon respond to the higher price level by demanding higher nominal wages. This will cause the short-run aggregate supply curve to shift upward vertically, moving the economy to the new long-run equilibrium at C. The price level thus continues its rise to P_3, even as real GDP declines back down to Q_1 (and unemployment returns to the natural rate). So as we have seen before, even though an increase in the money supply can raise output and lower unemployment in the short run, it has no effect on either variable in the long run.

The Response to Anticipated Policy. Now let's look at this disturbance with the perspective given by the rational expectations hypothesis, as it is embedded in the new classical model. Suppose that workers (and other input owners) know ahead of time that this increase in the money supply is about to take place. Assume also that they know when it is going to occur and understand that its ultimate effect will be to push the price level from P_1 to P_3. Will workers wait until after the price level has increased to insist that their nominal wages go up? The rational expectations hypothesis says that they will not. Instead, they will go to employers and insist on nominal wages that move upward in step with the higher prices. From the workers' perspective, this is the only way to protect their real wages from declining due to the anticipated increase in the money supply.

The Policy Irrelevance Proposition. As long as economic participants behave in this manner, when we draw the *SRAS* curve, we must be explicit about the nature of their expectations. This we have done in Figure 18-9. In the initial equilibrium, the short-run aggregate supply curve is labeled to show that the expected money supply (M_e) and the actual money supply (M_1) are equal ($M_e = M_1$). Similarly, when the money supply changes in a way that is anticipated by economic participants, the aggregate supply curve shifts to reflect this expected change in the money supply. The new short-run aggregate supply

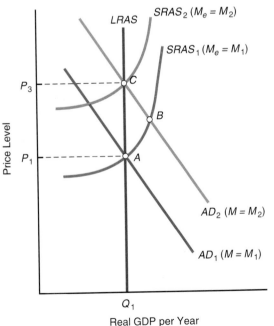

FIGURE 18-9

Effects of an Anticipated Rise in Aggregate Demand
When policy is fully anticipated, a rise in the money supply causes a rise in the price level from P_1 to P_3, with no change in real output.

curve is labeled ($M_e = M_2$) to reveal this. According to the rational expectations hypothesis, the short-run aggregate supply will shift upward *simultaneously* with the rise in aggregate demand. As a result, the economy will move directly from point A to point C in Figure 18-9 without passing through B: The *only* response to the rise in the money supply is a rise in the price level from P_1 to P_3; neither output nor unemployment changes at all. This conclusion—that fully anticipated monetary policy is irrelevant in determining the levels of real variables—is called the **policy irrelevance proposition:**

> Under the assumption of rational expectations on the part of decision makers in the economy, anticipated monetary policy cannot alter either the rate of unemployment or the level of real GDP. Regardless of the nature of the anticipated policy, the unemployment rate will equal the natural rate, and real GDP will be determined solely by the economy's long-run aggregate supply curve.

Policy irrelevance proposition
The new classical and rational expectations conclusion that policy actions have no real effects in the short run if the policy actions are anticipated and none in the long run even if the policy actions are unanticipated.

What Must People Know? There are two important matters to keep in mind when considering this proposition. First, our discussion has assumed that economic participants know in advance exactly what the change in monetary policy is going to be and precisely when it is going to occur. In fact, the Federal Reserve does not announce exactly what the future course of monetary policy (down to the last dollar) is going to be. Instead, the Fed tries to keep most of its plans secret, announcing only in general terms what policy actions are intended for the future. It is tempting to conclude that because the Fed's intended policies are not freely available, they are not available at all. But such a conclusion would be wrong. Economic participants have great incentives to learn how to predict the future behavior of the monetary authorities, just as businesses try to forecast consumer behavior and college students do their best to forecast what their next economics exam will look like. Even if the economic participants are not perfect at forecasting the course of policy, they are likely to come a lot closer than they would in total ignorance. The policy irrelevance proposition really assumes only that *people don't persistently make the same mistakes in forecasting the future.*

What Happens If People Don't Know Everything? This brings us to our second point. Once we accept the fact that people are not perfect in their ability to predict the future, the possibility emerges that some policy actions will have systematic effects that look much like the movements A to B to C in Figure 18-8. For example, just as other economic participants sometimes make mistakes, it is likely that the Federal Reserve sometimes make mistakes—meaning that the money supply may change in ways that even the Fed does not predict. And even if the Fed always accomplished every policy action it intended, there is no guarantee that other economic participants would fully forecast those actions. What happens if the Fed makes a mistake or if firms and workers misjudge the future course of policy? Matters will look much as they do in panel (a) of Figure 18-10, which shows the effects of an unanticipated increase in the money supply. Economic participants expect the money supply to be M_0, but the actual money supply turns out to be M_1. Because $M_1 > M_0$, aggregate demand shifts relative to aggre-

THINKING CRITICALLY ABOUT THE MEDIA

High Interest Rates and "Tight" Monetary Policy

The media often report changes in interest rates to indicate changes in monetary policy, whether they are referring to the United States or any other country. The problem with such analyses is that they fail to distinguish between real and nominal interest rates. Normally, a high interest rate is evidence that a country's central bank has been pursuing *loose* monetary policy in the past rather than tight monetary policy now. Why? Because in the long run, consistent increases in the rate of growth of the money supply lead to a higher rate of inflation. A higher rate of inflation normally leads to expectations of inflation and therefore higher *nominal* interest rates. After all, the nominal interest rate is equal to the real rate of interest plus the expected rate of inflation. In the long run, evidence shows that monetary authorities have little effect on an economy's real rate of interest.

FIGURE 18-10

Effects of an Unanticipated Rise in Aggregate Demand
Even with rational expectations, an unanticipated change in demand can affect output in the short run.

gate supply. The result is a rise in real output (real GDP) in the short run from Q_1 to Q_2; corresponding to this rise in real output will be an increase in employment and hence a fall in the unemployment rate. So even under the rational expectations hypothesis, monetary policy *can* have an effect on real variables in the short run, but only if the policy is unsystematic and therefore unanticipated.

In the long run, this effect on real variables will disappear because people will figure out that the Fed either accidentally increased the money supply or intentionally increased it in a way that somehow fooled individuals. Either way, people's expectations will soon be revised so that the short-run aggregate supply curve will shift upward. As shown in panel (b) of Figure 18-10, real GDP will return to long-run levels, meaning that so will the employment and unemployment rates.

The Policy Dilemma

Perhaps the most striking and disturbing feature of the new classical model is that it seems to suggest that only mistakes can have real effects. If the Federal Reserve always does what it intends to do and if other economic participants always correctly anticipate the Fed's actions, monetary policy will affect only the price level and nominal input prices. It appears that only if the Fed makes a mistake in executing monetary policy or people err in anticipating that policy will changes in the money supply cause fluctuations in real output and employment. If this reasoning is correct, the Fed is effectively precluded from using monetary policy in any rational way to lower the unemployment rate or to raise the level of real

GDP. This is because fully anticipated changes in the money supply will lead to exactly off-setting changes in prices and hence no real effects. Many economists were disturbed at the prospect that if the economy happened to enter a recessionary period, policymakers would be powerless to push real GDP and unemployment back to long-run levels. As a result, they asked the question, In light of the rational expectations hypothesis, is it *ever* possible for systematic policy to have predictable real effects on the economy? The answer has led to even more developments in the way we think about macroeconomics.

CONCEPTS IN BRIEF

- The rational expectations hypothesis assumes that individuals' forecasts incorporate all available information, including an understanding of government policy and its effects on the economy.
- The new classical economics assumes that the rational expectations hypothesis is valid and also that there is pure competition and that all prices and wages are flexible.
- The policy irrelevance proposition says that under the assumptions of the new classical model, fully anticipated monetary policy cannot alter either the rate of unemployment or the level of real GDP.
- The new classical model implies that policies can alter real economic variables only if the policies are unsystematic and therefore unanticipated, otherwise people learn and defeat the desired policy goals.

REAL BUSINESS CYCLE THEORY

The modern extension of new classical theory involves reexamining the first principles that assume fully flexible prices.

The Distinction Between Real and Monetary Shocks

The research of the new business cycle theorists differs importantly from that of new classical theorists in that business cycle theorists seek to determine whether real, as opposed to purely monetary, forces might help explain aggregate economic fluctuations. An important stimulus for the development of **real business cycle theory,** as it has come to be known, was the economic turmoil of the 1970s. During that decade, world economies were staggered by two major disruptions to the supply of oil. The first occurred in 1973, the second in 1979. In both episodes, members of the Organization of Petroleum Exporting Countries (OPEC) reduced the amount of oil they were willing to supply and raised the price at which they offered it for sale. Each time, the price level rose sharply in the United States, and real GDP declined. Thus each episode produced a period of "stagflation"—real economic stagnation combined with high inflation. Figure 18-11 illustrates the pattern of events.

We begin at point E_1 with the economy in both short- and long-run equilibrium, with the associated supply curves, $SRAS_1$ and $LRAS_1$. Initially, the level of real GDP is Q_1, and the price level is P_1. Because the economy is in long-run equilibrium, the unemployment rate must be at the natural rate.

A reduction in the supply of oil, as occurred in 1973 and 1979, causes the $SRAS$ curve to shift to the left to $SRAS_2$ because fewer goods will be available for sale due to the reduced supplies. If the reduction in oil supplies is (or is believed to be) permanent, the

Real business cycle theory
An extension and modification of the theories of the new classical economists of the 1970s and 1980s, in which money is neutral and only real, supply-side factors matter in influencing labor employment and real output.

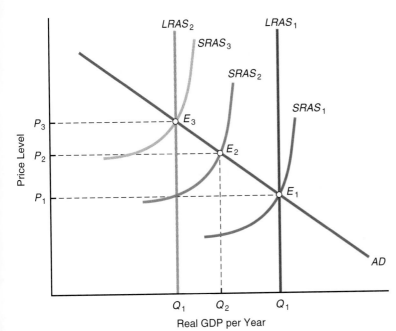

FIGURE 18-11

Effects of a Reduction in the Supply of Resources

The position of the *LRAS* depends on our endowments of all types of resources. Hence a reduction in the supply of one of those resources, such as oil, causes a reduction—an inward shift—in the aggregate supply curve. In addition, there is a rise in the equilibrium price level and a fall in the equilibrium rate of real GDP per year (output).

LRAS shifts to the left also. This assumption is reflected in Figure 18-11, where $LRAS_2$ shows the new long-run aggregate supply curve associated with the lowered output of oil.

In the short run, two adjustments begin to occur simultaneously. First, the prices of oil and petroleum-based products begin to rise, so that the overall price level rises to P_2. Second, the higher costs of production occasioned by the rise in oil prices induce firms to cut back production, so total output falls to Q_2 in the short run. The new temporary short-run equilibrium occurs at E_2, with a higher price level (P_2) and a lower level of real GDP (Q_2).

Impact on the Labor Market

If we were to focus on the labor market while this adjustment from E_1 to E_2 was taking place, we would find two developments occurring. The rise in the price level pushes the real wage rate downward, even as the scaled-back production plans of firms induce them to reduce the amount of labor inputs they are using. So not only does the real wage rate fall, but the level of employment declines as well. On both counts, workers are made worse off due to the reduction in the supply of oil.

Now this is not the full story, because owners of nonoil inputs (such as labor) who are willing to put up with reduced real payments in the short run simply will not tolerate them in the long run. Thus, for example, some workers who were willing to continue working at lower wages in the short run will eventually decide to retire, switch from full-time work to part-time employment, or drop out of the labor force altogether. In effect, there is a reduction in the supply of nonoil inputs, reflected in an upward shift in the *SRAS* from $SRAS_2$ to $SRAS_3$. This puts additional upward pressure on the price level and exerts a downward force on real GDP. The final long-run equilibrium thus occurs at point E_3, with the price level at P_3 and real GDP at Q_3. (In principle, because the oil supply shock has had no long-term effect on labor markets, the natural rate of unemployment does not change when equilibrium moves from E_1 to E_3.)

Generalizing the Theory

Naturally, the focus of real business cycle theory goes well beyond the simple "oil shock" that we have discussed here, for it encompasses all types of real disturbances, including technological changes and shifts in the composition of the labor force. Moreover, a complete treatment of real shocks to the economy is typically much more complex than we have allowed for in our discussion. For example, an oil shock such as is shown in Figure 18-11 would likely also have effects on the real wealth of Americans, causing a reduction in aggregate demand as well as aggregate supply. Nevertheless, our simple example still manages to capture the flavor of the theory.

It is clear that real business cycle theory has improved our understanding of the economy's behavior, but there is also agreement among economists that it alone is incapable of explaining all of the facets of business cycles that we observe. For example, it is difficult to imagine a real disturbance that could possibly account for the Great Depression in this country, when real income fell more than 30 percent and the unemployment rate rose to 25 percent. Moreover, real business cycle theory continues to assume that prices are perfectly flexible and so fails to explain a great deal of the apparent rigidity of prices throughout the economy.

NEW KEYNESIAN ECONOMICS

Although the new classical and real business cycle theories both embody pure competition and flexible prices, a body of research called the **new Keynesian economics** drops both of these assumptions. The new Keynesian economists do not believe that market-clearing models of the economy can explain business cycles. Consequently, they argue that macroeconomics models must contain the "sticky" wages and prices assumption that Keynes outlined in his major work. Thus the new Keynesian research has as its goal a refinement of the theory of aggregate supply that explains how wages and prices behave in the short run. There are several such theories. The first one relates to the cost of changing prices.

New Keynesian economics
Economic models based on the idea that demand creates its own supply as a result of various possible government fiscal and monetary coordination failures.

Small-Menu Cost Theory

If prices do not respond to demand changes, two conditions must be true: Someone must be consciously deciding not to change prices, and that decision must be in the decision maker's self-interest. One combination of facts that is consistent with this scenario is the **small-menu cost theory,** which supposes that much of the economy is characterized by imperfect competition and that it is costly for firms to change their prices in response to changes in demand. The costs associated with changing prices are called *menu costs,* and they include the costs of renegotiating contracts, printing price lists (such as menus), and informing customers of price changes.

Many such costs may not be very large in magnitude; that is why they are called *small-menu costs.* Some of the costs of changing prices, however, such as those incurred in bringing together business managers from points around the nation or the world for meetings on price changes or renegotiating deals with customers, may be significant.

Firms in different industries have different cost structures. Such differences explain diverse small-menu costs. Therefore, the extent to which firms hold their prices constant in the face of changes in demand for their products will vary across industries. Not all prices will be rigid. Nonetheless, new Keynesian theorists argue that many—even most—firms'

Small-menu cost theory
A hypothesis that it is costly for firms to change prices in response to demand changes because of the cost of renegotiating contracts, printing price lists, and so on.

Exercise 18.2
Visit www.econtoday.com for more about the CPI.

prices are sticky for relatively long time intervals. As a result, the aggregate level of prices could be very nearly rigid because of small-menu costs.

Although most economists agree that such costs exist, there is considerably less agreement on whether they are sufficient to explain the extent of price rigidity that is observed.

Efficiency Wage Theory

Efficiency wage theory
The hypothesis that the productivity of workers depends on the level of the real wage rate.

An alternative approach within the new Keynesian framework is called the **efficiency wage theory.** It proposes that worker productivity actually *depends on* the wages that workers are paid, rather than being independent of wages, as is assumed in other theories. According to this theory, higher real wages encourage workers to work harder, improve their efficiency, increase morale, and raise their loyalty to the firm. Across the board, then, higher wages tend to increase workers' productivity, which in turn discourages firms from cutting real wages because of the damaging effect that such an action would have on productivity and profitability. Under highly competitive conditions, there will generally be an optimal wage—called the *efficiency wage*—that the firm should continue paying, even in the face of large fluctuations in the demand for its output.

The efficiency wage theory model is a rather simple idea, but it is somewhat revolutionary. All of the models of the labor market adopted by traditional classical, traditional Keynesian, monetarist, new classical, and new Keynesian theorists alike do not consider such real-wage effects on worker productivity.

There are significant, valid elements in the efficiency wage theory, but its importance in understanding national business fluctuations remains uncertain. For example, although the theory explains rigid real wages, it does not explain rigid prices. Moreover, the theory ignores the fact that firms can (and apparently do) rely on a host of incentives other than wages to encourage their workers to be loyal, efficient, and productive.

EXAMPLE
Henry Ford and the Efficiency Wage Model

One of the most clear-cut examples of the efficiency wage model involved the Ford Motor Company. When nominal wage rates were about $2 to $3 a day in 1914 (about $30 in today's dollars and with no benefits such as health insurance), Henry Ford ordered his managers to start paying workers $5 a day. Ford later argued that the increase in wages was a "cost-cutting" move. The evidence bears him out. Absenteeism dropped by over 70 percent. Moreover, labor turnover virtually disappeared. Consequently, Ford's managers had to spend less time training new workers.

FOR CRITICAL ANALYSIS: What alternative ways do managers have to provide incentives to their workers to become more efficient? ●

Effect of Aggregate Demand Changes on Output and Employment in the Long Run

Some new Keynesian economists argue that a reduction in aggregate demand that causes a recession may affect output and employment even in the long run. They point out that workers who are fired or laid off may lose job skills during their period of unemployment. Consequently, they will have a more difficult time finding new employment later.

Furthermore, those who remain unemployed over long periods of time may change their attitudes toward work. They may even have a reduced desire to find employment later on. For these reasons and others, a recession could permanently raise the amount of frictional unemployment.

As yet, little research has been done to quantify this theory.

MACROECONOMIC MODELS AND THEIR IMPLICATIONS FOR STABILIZATION POLICY

Although it is impossible to compare accurately and completely every single detail of the various macroeconomic approaches we have examined, it is useful to summarize and contrast some of their key aspects. Table 18-1 presents features of our five key models: tradi-

TABLE 18-1

A Comparison of Macroeconomic Models

Issue	Macroeconomic Model				
	Traditional Classical	Traditional Keynesian	New Classical	New Keynesian	Modern Monetarist
Stability of capitalism	Yes	No	Yes	Yes, but can be enhanced by policy	Yes
Price-wage flexibility	Yes	No	Yes	Yes, but imperfect	Yes, but some restraints
Belief in natural rate of employment hypothesis	Yes	No	Yes	Yes	Yes
Factors sensitive to interest rate	Saving, consumption, investment	Demand for money	Saving, consumption, investment	Saving, consumption, investment	Saving, consumption, investment
View of the velocity of money	Stable	Unstable	No consensus	No consensus	Stable
Effect of changes in money supply on economy	Changes aggregate demand	Changes interest rates, which change investment and real output	No effect on real variables if anticipated	Changes aggregate demand	Directly changes aggregate demand
Effects of fiscal policy on the economy	Not applicable	Multiplier changes in aggregate demand and output	Generally ineffective*	Changes aggregate demand	Ineffective unless money supply changes also
Causes of inflation	Excess money growth	Excess real aggregate demand	Excess money growth	Excess money growth	Excess money growth
Stabilization policy	Unnecessary	Fiscal policy necessary and effective; monetary policy ineffective	Too difficult to conduct	Both fiscal and monetary policy may be useful	Too difficult to conduct

*Some fiscal policies affect relative prices (interest rates) and so many have real effects on economy.

tional classical, traditional Keynesian, new (modern) classical, new (modern) Keynesian, and modern monetarist. Realize when examining the table that we are painting with a broad brush.

STABILIZATION POLICY AND THE NEW GROWTH THEORISTS

Recall from Chapter 9 that there is a group of economists who support what is now called new growth theory. In this theory, real wealth creation comes from innovation, which is part of new technology. Such new growth theorists as Paul Romer of the University of California at Berkeley and Robert Barro of Harvard repeatedly point out that small differences in annual rates of growth over a few decades make a tremendous difference in the standard of living of each individual. Indeed, they argue that short-run monetary and fiscal stabilization policies are in fact beside the point. To them, the Keynesian emphasis on the business cycle appears to be a strange fixation.

If what really matters is the underlying growth rate rather than the business cycle around it, then any efforts to fine-tune the economy are perhaps misguided. Actually, according to the new growth theorists, one of the processes underlying the business cycle is that of discovery and innovation. This process generates long-run improvements in the standard of living. It determines in large part how steep the slope is over a long-run upward trend. The little wiggles—business cycles—take on less importance. The federal government should not be concerned with them.

Does that mean that government policy has no place in our economy? The answer from the new growth theorists is that the government does have a place, but it has little to do with discretionary changes in taxes or spending or monetary growth rates. Rather, it has to do with speeding up the pace of innovation. It also has to do with government's devising policies that promote new technology. One of these policies might be to strengthen patent protection. In any event, the new growth theorists would probably agree with economists who argue in favor of passive nondiscretionary stabilization policy.

In sum, stabilization policy analysis is really about the costs and benefits of getting the economy to where it *eventually* will go anyway—to its long-run aggregate supply curve (*LRAS*). According to the new growth theorists, the costs outweigh the benefits so that short-run stabilization policy should not be the main macroeconomic activity of the federal government. It is economic growth that shifts *LRAS* rightward. Government macroeconomic policy should focus, according to the new growth theorists, solely on this issue.

CONCEPTS IN BRIEF

- Real business cycle theory holds that even if all prices and wages are perfectly flexible, real shocks to the economy (such as technological change and changes in the supplies of factors of production) can cause national business fluctuations.

- The new Keynesian economics explains why various features of the economy, such as small-menu costs and wage rates that affect productivity, make it possible for monetary shocks to cause real effects.

- Although there remain significant differences between the classical and Keynesian branches of macroeconomics, the rivalry between them is an important source of innovation that helps improve our understanding of the economy.

- New growth theorists in general reject the efficacy of short-run discretionary stabilization policies and argue, in contrast, that the federal government should focus its policy efforts on fostering a climate that will generate higher economic growth rates.

More than 11 percent of the European labor force is without jobs. How might reduced wage inequality in Europe contribute to higher employment rates there?

Is There a Trade-off Between Labor Market Flexibility and Unemployment?

CONCEPTS APPLIED:

UNEMPLOYMENT, NATURAL RATE OF UNEMPLOY-
MENT, LABOR-MARKET RIGIDITIES, EFFICIENCY WAGES

Visit www.econtoday.com for an Internet Activity that expands your understanding of these concepts.

When continental Europeans (the European Union minus the United Kingdom) are asked to justify their more than 11 percent average unemployment rate versus less than 5 percent in the United States, they usually make the following statement: "You may have less unemployment in the United States, but we have less inequality of income." They are correct. As it turns out, the data show a strong reverse correlation between wage inequality and unemployment. Here is how the theory goes.

The Necessity of Flexible Labor Markets

With increased global competition, low-wage workers in developing countries compete more with low-wage workers in developed countries. The latter still have relatively higher wages. Thus only with flexible labor markets can low-skilled workers in developed countries keep their jobs—they must accept lower wages. Indeed, this is what happened in the United States. In the 1980s and 1990s, a typical American male worker toward the top of the income ladder earned 3.2 times as much as his counterpart toward the bottom of the wage ladder. By the year 2000, that ratio will increase to 4.4. A similar ratio in continental Europe during the same time period will be unchanged or actually fall. In Germany, it is only 2.2.

An International Comparison of Wage Inequality and Unemployment

Figure 18-12 shows that wage inequality has increased in the United States, the United Kingdom, and New Zealand. And the unemployment rate during the period studied fell in those three nations. Conversely, during the same period, wage inequality in France and Germany decreased, and unemployment increased.

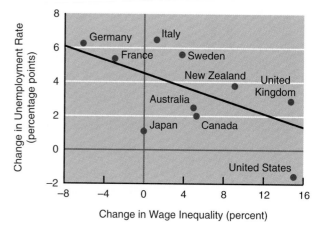

FIGURE 18-12

Wage Inequality Versus Unemployment, 1980–1995
Source: Organization of Economic Cooperation and Development.

There is more. Not only is there less flexibility in wages in Europe than in the United States, but there are generous unemployment benefits and a relatively high cost in firing someone. A typical low-skilled, middle-aged male is eight times more likely to lose his job in the United States than in France. In contrast, hirings per worker in the United States are six times greater than in France.

FOR CRITICAL ANALYSIS

1. If the data are so obvious, why don't European policymakers reduce labor market rigidities?

2. Most continental European countries have relatively high minimum wage rates. How does this relate to the issue discussed here?

CHAPTER SUMMARY

1. The natural rate of unemployment is the rate that exists in long-run equilibrium, when workers' expectations are consistent with actual conditions. Departures from the natural rate of unemployment can occur when individuals are surprised by unanticipated changes in fiscal or monetary policy.

2. The Phillips curve shows a negative relationship between the inflation rate and the unemployment rate that can be observed when there are unanticipated changes in aggregate demand. It was originally believed that the Phillips curve represented a trade-off between inflation and unemployment. In fact, no trade-off exists because workers' expectations adjust to systematic attempts to reduce unemployment below its natural rate.

3. The rational expectations hypothesis assumes that individuals' forecasts incorporate all available information, including an understanding of government policy and its effects on the economy. The new classical economics assumes that the rational expectations hypothesis is valid and also that there is pure competition and that all prices and wages are flexible.

4. The policy irrelevance proposition says that under the assumptions of the new classical model, anticipated monetary policy cannot alter either the rate of unemployment or the level of real GDP. Thus according to the new classical model, policies can alter real economic variables only if the policies are unsystematic and therefore unanticipated; such policies cannot affect output and employment systematically.

5. Real business cycle theory holds that even if all prices and wages are perfectly flexible, real shocks to the economy (such as technological change and changes in the supplies of factors of production) can cause national business fluctuations.

6. The new Keynesian economics explains why various features of the economy, such as small-menu costs and wage rates that affect productivity, make it possible for monetary shocks to cause real effects.

DISCUSSION OF PREVIEW QUESTIONS

1. What does the rational expectations hypothesis say about people's forecasting errors?

The simplest version of the rational expectations hypothesis simply says that people do not persistently make the same mistakes in forecasting the future. More generally, the hypothesis says that individuals base their forecasts about the future values of economic variables on the basis of all available past and current information and that these forecasts incorporate individuals' understanding about how the economy operates, including the operation of monetary and fiscal policy. As a result, people's forecasting errors are completely unpredictable over time and thus cannot be used by policymakers in formulating policy.

2. How do the new classical economists view economic policy?

The new classical economists assume that the rational expectations hypothesis is valid and also that there is pure competition and that all prices and wages are flexible. As a result, they say, anticipated monetary policy cannot alter either the rate of unemployment or the level of real GDP. Regardless of the nature of the anticipated policy, the unemployment rate will equal the natural rate, and real GDP will be determined solely by the economy's long-run aggregate supply curve. This conclusion is called the policy irrelevance theorem.

3. What does the real business cycle theory say about the causes of recession?

Real business cycle theory shows that even if all prices and wages are perfectly flexible, real shocks to the economy (such as technological change and changes in the supplies of factors of production) can cause national business fluctuations. One example of such real shocks is the type of oil shock that hit the United States economy during the 1970s.

4. How does the new Keynesian economics explain the stickiness of wages and prices?
Generally, a combination of factors is cited, including the existence of contracts, small-menu costs, and efficiency wages. The key point is that there are a variety of rational reasons that economic participants have for entering into agreements that fix either nominal or real relative prices (including wages). Given the existence of such agreements, as well as the existence of costs of changing prices of all types, monetary policy can have real effects on the economy by changing aggregate demand.

PROBLEMS

(Answers to the odd-numbered problems appear at the back of the book.)

18-1. Answer the following questions based on the accompanying graph.

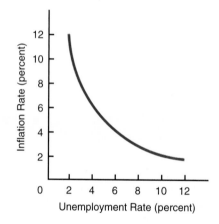

a. If we regard this curve as showing a trade-off between inflation and unemployment, how much unemployment will it "cost" to reduce inflation to 2 percent per year?
b. What might cause this curve to shift upward?
c. Why do economists argue that there is generally no useable trade-off between unemployment and inflation?

18-2. The natural rate of unemployment is a function of a variety of factors, including wage and price rigidities and interferences with labor mobility. Give some examples of such rigidities and interferences.

18-3. How does the existence of contracts, small-menu costs, and efficiency wages affect the amount of discretion available to policymakers?

18-4. Explain how the average duration of unemployment may be different for a given rate of unemployment.

18-5. What effect does the average duration of unemployment have on the rate of unemployment if we hold constant the variables you used to explain Problem 18-4?

18-6. What is meant by an optimal duration of unemployment? What may affect such an optimal duration of unemployment?

18-7. If both employers and workers incorrectly perceive the rate of inflation to the same extent, would the Phillips curve still be expected to be negatively sloped?

18-8. Unemployment is arbitrarily defined. What differences do different definitions have with respect to policy?

COMPUTER-ASSISTED INSTRUCTION

This session focuses on changes in the unemployment rate to illustrate the views of the new classical economists, the real business cycle theorists, and the new Keynesian economists.

Complete problem and answer appear on disk.

PART 6

DIMENSIONS OF MICROECONOMICS

"One person's meat is another person's poison." That familiar saying can be translated into economic terms as follows: The utility, or satisfaction, that some other individual derives from consuming a good or service cannot be measured by how *you* value that particular good or service. Consider the satisfaction that smokers derive from the act of inhaling smoke that includes tars and nicotine. Such an activity is, in the long run, harmful to most people who engage in it. Nonetheless, smoking continues. But the government has decided to "do something about it." It has tentatively assessed tobacco companies billions of dollars in fines. Many states have raised taxes on cigarettes. What group of Americans will be most affected by a higher price for cigarettes? Before we answer that question, we want to consider the theory of consumer choice.

PREVIEW QUESTIONS

1. What is the law of diminishing marginal utility?
2. How does a consumer maximize total utility?
3. What happens to consumer optimum when price changes?
4. How can the law of diminishing marginal utility account for the law of demand?

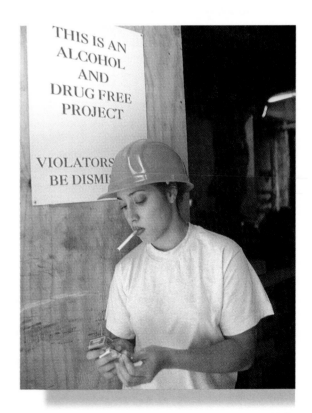

Did You Know That . . . in a typical year, an American family spends about 15 percent of its income on food and about the same on housing? Within individual families, however, these relative percentages may be quite different. Some families devote much higher percentages of their income to housing than others. What determines how much each family spends on different items in their budget? One explanation is simply tastes—the values that family members place on different items on which they can spend their income. The saying "You can't argue with tastes" suggests that different individuals have different preferences for how to allocate their limited incomes. Although there is no real theory of what determines people's tastes, we can examine some of the behavior that underlies how consumers react to changes in the prices of the goods and services that they purchase. Recall from Chapter 3 that people generally purchase less at higher prices than at lower prices. This is called the law of demand.

Because the law of demand is important, its derivation is useful because it allows us to arrange the relevant variables, such as price, income, and tastes, in such a way as to understand the real world better and even perhaps generate predictions about it. One way of deriving the law of demand involves an analysis of the logic of consumer choice in a world of limited resources. In this chapter, therefore, we discuss what is called *utility analysis.*

UTILITY THEORY

When you buy something, you do so because of the satisfaction you expect to receive from having and using that good. For everything that you like to have, the more you have of it, the higher the level of satisfaction you receive. Another term that can be used for satisfaction is **utility,** or want-satisfying power. This property is common to all goods that are desired. The concept of utility is purely subjective, however. There is no way that you or I can measure the amount of utility that a consumer might be able to obtain from a particular good, for utility does not imply "useful" or "utilitarian" or "practical." For this reason, there can be no accurate scientific assessment of the utility that someone might receive by consuming a frozen dinner or a movie relative to the utility that another person might receive from that same good or service. Nevertheless, we can infer whether a person receives more utility from consuming one good versus another by that person's behavior. For example, if an individual buys more coffee than tea (when both tea and coffee are priced equally), we are able to say that the individual receives more utility from consuming coffee than from consuming tea.

The utility that individuals receive from consuming a good depends on their tastes and preferences. These tastes and preferences are normally assumed to be given and stable for a given individual. An individual's tastes determine how much utility that individual derives from consuming a good, and this in turn determines how that individual allocates his or her income. People spend a greater proportion of their incomes on goods they like. But we cannot explain why tastes are different between individuals. For example, we cannot explain why some people like yogurt but others do not.

We can analyze in terms of utility the way consumers decide what to buy, just as physicists have analyzed some of their problems in terms of what they call force. No physicist has ever seen a unit of force, and no economist has ever seen a unit of utility. In both cases, however, these concepts have proved useful for analysis.

Throughout this chapter, we will be discussing **utility analysis,** which is the analysis of consumer decision making based on utility maximization.

Utility
The want-satisfying power of a good or service.

Utility analysis
The analysis of consumer decision making based on utility maximization.

Utility and Utils

Economists once believed that utility could be measured. In fact, there is a philosophical school of thought based on utility theory called *utilitarianism,* developed by the English philosopher Jeremy Bentham (1748–1832). Bentham held that society should seek the greatest happiness for the greatest number. He sought to apply an arithmetic formula for measuring happiness. He and his followers developed the notion of measurable utility and invented the **util** to measure it. For the moment, we will also assume that we can measure satisfaction using this representative unit. Our assumption will allow us to quantify the way we examine consumer behavior.[1] Thus the first chocolate bar that you eat might yield you 4 utils of satisfaction; the first peanut cluster, 6 utils; and so on. Today, no one really believes that we can actually measure utils, but the ideas forthcoming from such analysis will prove useful in our understanding of the way in which consumers choose among alternatives.

Util
A representative unit by which utility is measured.

Total and Marginal Utility

Consider the satisfaction, or utility, that you receive each time that you rent and watch a video on your VCR. To make the example straightforward, let's say that there are hundreds of videos to choose from each year and that each of them is of the same quality. Let's say that you normally rent one video per week. You could, of course, rent two, or three, or four per week. Presumably, each time you rent another video per week, you will get additional satisfaction, or utility. The question, though, that we must ask is, given that you are already renting one per week, will the next one rented that week give you the same amount of additional utility?

That additional, or incremental, utility is called **marginal utility,** where *marginal,* as before, means "incremental" or "additional." (Marginal changes also refer to decreases, in which cases we talk about *decremental* changes.) The concept of marginality is important in economics because we make decisions at the margin. At any particular point, we compare additional (marginal) benefits with additional (marginal) costs.

Marginal utility
The change in total utility due to a one-unit change in the quantity of a good or service consumed.

Applying Marginal Analysis to Utility

The specific example presented in Figure 19-1 on page 416 will clarify the distinction between total utility and marginal utility. The table in panel (a) shows the total utility and the marginal utility of watching videos each week. Marginal utility is the difference between total utility derived from one level of consumption and total utility derived from another level of consumption. A simple formula for marginal utility is this:

$$\text{Marginal utility} = \frac{\text{change in total utility}}{\text{change in number of units consumed}}$$

In our example, when a person has already watched two videos in one week and then watches another, total utility increases from 16 utils to 19. Therefore, the marginal utility (of watching one more video after already having watched two in one week) is equal to 3 utils.

---

[1]What follows is typically called *cardinal utility analysis* by economists. It requires cardinal measurement. Numbers such as 1, 2, and 3 are cardinals. We know that 2 is exactly twice as many as 1 and that 3 is exactly three times as many as 1. You will see in Appendix E at the end of this chapter a type of consumer behavior analysis that requires only *ordinal* measurement of utility, meaning ranked or ordered. *First, second,* and *third* are ordinal numbers; nothing can be said about their exact size relationships. We can only talk about their importance relative to each other. Temperature, for example, is an ordinal ranking. One hundred degrees Celsius is not twice as warm as 50 degrees Celsius. All we can say is that 100 degrees Celsius is warmer than 50 degrees Celsius.

Panel (a)

(1) Number of Videos Watched per Week	(2) Total Utility (utils per week)	(3) Marginal Utility (utils per week)
0	0	
		10 (10 − 0)
1	10	
		6 (16 − 10)
2	16	
		3 (19 − 16)
3	19	
		1 (20 − 19)
4	20	
		0 (20 − 20)
5	20	
		−2 (18 − 20)
6	18	

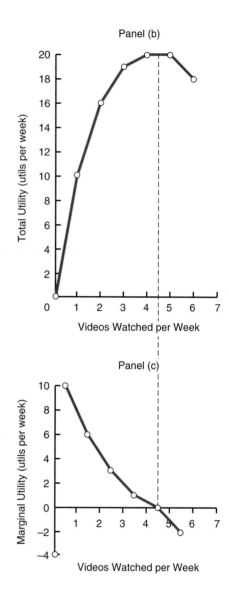

FIGURE 19-1

Total and Marginal Utility of Watching Videos

If we were able to assign specific values to the utility derived from watching videos each week, we could obtain a marginal utility schedule similar in pattern to the one shown in panel (a). In column 1 is the number of videos watched per week; in column 2, the total utility derived from each quantity; and in column 3, the marginal utility derived from each additional quantity, which is defined as the change in total utility due to a change of one unit of watching videos per week. Total utility from panel (a) is plotted in panel (b). Marginal utility is plotted in panel (c), where you see that it reaches zero where total utility hits its maximum at between 4 and 5 units.

GRAPHIC ANALYSIS

We can transfer the information in panel (a) onto a graph, as we do in panels (b) and (c) of Figure 19-1. Total utility, which is represented in column 2 of panel (a), is transferred to panel (b).

Total utility continues to rise until four videos are watched per week. This measure of utility remains at 20 utils through the fifth video, and at the sixth video per week it falls to 18 utils; we assume that at some quantity consumed per unit time period, boredom sets in. This is shown in panel (b).

Marginal Utility

If you look carefully at panels (b) and (c) of Figure 19-1, the notion of marginal utility becomes very clear. In economics, the term *marginal* always refers to a change in the total. The marginal utility of watching three videos per week instead of two videos per week is the increment in total utility and is equal to 3 utils per week. All of the points in panel (c) are taken from column 3 of the table in panel (a). Notice that marginal utility falls throughout the graph. A special point occurs after four videos are watched per week because the total utility curve in panel (b) is unchanged after the consumption of the fourth video. That means that the consumer receives no additional (marginal) utility from watching the fifth video. This is shown in panel (c) as *zero* marginal utility. After that point, marginal utility becomes negative.

In our example, when marginal utility becomes negative, it means that the consumer is fed up with watching videos and would require some form of compensation to watch any more. When marginal utility is negative, an additional unit consumed actually lowers total utility by becoming a nuisance. Rarely does a consumer face a situation of negative marginal utility. Whenever this point is reached, goods become in effect "bads." A rational consumer will stop consuming at the point at which marginal utility becomes negative, even if the good is free.

Exercise 19.1

Visit www.econtoday.com for more about chocolate's marginal utility.

CONCEPTS IN BRIEF

- Utility is defined as want-satisfying power; it is a power common to all desired goods and services.

- We arbitrarily measure utility in units called utils.

- It is important to distinguish between total utility and marginal utility. Total utility is the total satisfaction derived from the consumption of a given quantity of a good or service. Marginal utility is the *change* in total utility due to a one-unit change in the consumption of the good or service.

Diminishing marginal utility
The principle that as more of any good or service is consumed, its extra benefit declines. Otherwise stated, increases in total utility from the consumption of a good or service become smaller and smaller as more is consumed during a given time period.

DIMINISHING MARGINAL UTILITY

Notice that in panel (c) of Figure 19-1, marginal utility is continuously declining. This property has been named the principle of **diminishing marginal utility.** There is no way that we can prove diminishing marginal utility; nonetheless, economists and others have for years believed strongly in the notion. Diminishing marginal utility has even been called a law. This supposed law concerns a psychological, or subjective, utility that you receive as you consume more and more of a particular good. Stated formally, the law is as follows:

> **As an individual consumes more of a particular commodity, the total level of utility, or satisfaction, derived from that consumption usually increases. Eventually, however, the *rate* at which it increases diminishes as more is consumed.**

Take a hungry individual at a dinner table. The first serving is greatly appreciated, and the individual derives a substantial amount of utility from it. The second serving does not have quite as much impact as the first one, and the third serving is likely to be even less satisfying. This individual experiences diminishing marginal utility of food until he or she stops eating, and this is true for most people. All-you-can-eat restaurants count on this fact; a second helping of ribs may provide some marginal utility, but the third helping would have only a little or even negative marginal utility. The fall in the marginal utility of other goods is even more dramatic.

Consider for a moment the opposite possibility—increasing marginal utility. Under such a situation, the marginal utility after consuming, say, one hamburger would increase. The second hamburger would be more valuable to you, and the third would be even more valuable yet. If increasing marginal utility existed, each of us would consume only one good or service! Rather than observing that "variety is the spice of life," we would see that monotony in consumption was preferred. We do not observe this, and therefore we have great confidence in the concept of diminishing marginal utility.

Consider an example that may affect you or someone you know—having a birthday on or within a few days of December 25. Even if you receive exactly the same number of presents that you would have if your birthday were six months later, your total level of utility, or satisfaction, from your presents will be lower. Why? Because of diminishing marginal utility. Let's say that your relatives and friends all give you compact discs. The total utility you receive from, say, 20 CDs on December 25 is less than if you received 10 in December and 10 on your birthday several months later.

EXAMPLE
Newspaper Vending Machines Versus Candy Vending Machines

Have you ever noticed that newspaper vending machines nearly everywhere in the United States allow you to put in the correct change, lift up the door, and take as many newspapers as you want? Contrast this type of vending machine with candy machines. They are completely locked at all times. You must designate the candy that you wish, normally by using some type of keypad. The candy then drops down to a place where you reach to retrieve it but from which you cannot grab any other candy. The difference between these two types of vending machines is explained by diminishing marginal utility. Newspaper companies dispense newspapers from coin-operated boxes that allow dishonest people to take more copies than they pay for. What would a dishonest person do with more than one copy of a newspaper, however? The marginal utility of a second newspaper is normally zero. The benefit of storing excessive newspapers is usually nil because yesterday's news has no value. But the same analysis does not hold for candy. The marginal utility of a second candy bar is certainly less than the first, but it is normally not zero. Moreover, one can store candy for relatively long periods of time at relatively low cost. Consequently, food vending machine companies have to worry about dishonest users of their machines and must make their machines much more theftproof than newspaper companies do.

FOR CRITICAL ANALYSIS: *Can you think of a circumstance under which a substantial number of newspaper purchasers might be inclined to take more than one newspaper out of a vending machine?* ●

OPTIMIZING CONSUMPTION CHOICES

Consumer optimum
A choice of a set of goods and services that maximizes the level of satisfaction for each consumer, subject to limited income.

Every consumer has a limited income. Choices must be made. When a consumer has made all of his or her choices about what to buy and in what quantities, and when the total level of satisfaction, or utility, from that set of choices is as great as it can be, we say that the consumer has *optimized.* When the consumer has attained an optimum consumption set of goods and services, we say that he or she has reached **consumer optimum.**[2]

Consider a simple two-good example. The consumer has to choose between spending income on the rental of videos at $5 each and on purchasing deluxe hamburgers at $3 each. Let's say that the last dollar spent on hamburgers yields 3 utils of utility but the last dollar spent on video rentals yields 10 utils. Wouldn't this consumer increase total utility if some dollars were taken away from hamburger consumption and allocated to video rentals? The answer is yes. Given diminishing marginal utility, more dollars spent on video rentals will reduce marginal utility per last dollar spent, whereas fewer dollars spent on hamburger consumption will increase marginal utility per last dollar spent. The optimum—where total utility is maximized—might occur when the satisfaction per last dollar spent on both hamburgers and video rentals per week is equal for the two goods. Thus the amount of goods consumed depends on the prices of the goods, the income of the consumers, and the marginal utility derived from each good.

Table 19-1 presents information on utility derived from consuming various quantities of videos and hamburgers. Columns 4 and 8 show the marginal utility per dollar spent on

TABLE 19-1
Total and Marginal Utility from Consuming Videos and Hamburgers on an Income of $26

(1) Videos per Period	(2) Total Utility of Videos per Period (utils)	(3) Marginal Utility (utils) MU_v	(4) Marginal Utility per Dollar Spent (MU_v/P_v) (price = $5)	(5) Hamburgers per Period	(6) Total Utility of Hamburgers per Period (utils)	(7) Marginal Utility (utils) MU_h	(8) Marginal Utility per Dollar Spent (MU_h/P_h) (price = $3)
0	0.0	—	—	0	0	—	—
1	50.0	50.0	10.0	1	25	25	8.3
2	95.0	45.0	9.0	2	47	22	7.3
3	135.0	40.0	8.0	3	65	18	6.0
4	171.5	36.5	7.3	4	80	15	5.0
5	200.0	28.5	5.7	5	89	9	3.0

---

[2]Optimization typically refers to individual decision-making processes. When we deal with many individuals interacting in the marketplace, we talk in terms of an equilibrium in the marketplace. Generally speaking, equilibrium is a property of markets rather than of individual decision making.

videos and hamburgers, respectively. If the prices of both goods are zero, individuals will consume each as long as their respective marginal utility is positive (at least five units of each and probably much more). It is also true that a consumer with infinite income will continue consuming goods until the marginal utility of each is equal to zero. When the price is zero or the consumer's income is infinite, there is no effective constraint on consumption.

Consumer optimum is attained when the marginal utility of the last dollar spent on each good yields the same utility and income is completely exhausted. The individual's income is $26. From columns 4 and 8 of Table 19-1, maximum equal marginal utilities occur at the consumption level of four videos and two hamburgers (the marginal utility per dollar spent equals 7.3). Notice that the marginal utility per dollar spent for both goods is also (approximately) equal at the consumption level of three videos and one hamburger, but here total income is not completely exhausted. Likewise, the marginal utility per dollar spent is (approximately) equal at five videos and three hamburgers, but the expenditures necessary for that level of consumption exceed the individual's income.

Table 19-2 shows the steps taken to arrive at consumer optimum. The first video would yield a marginal utility per dollar of 10, while the first hamburger would yield a marginal utility of only 8.3 per dollar. Because it yields the higher marginal utility per dollar, the video is purchased. This leaves $21 of income. The second video yields a higher marginal utility per dollar (9, versus 8.3 for hamburgers), so it is also purchased, leaving an unspent income of $16. At the third purchase, the first hamburger now yields a higher marginal utility per dollar than the next video (8.3 versus 8), so the first hamburger is purchased. This leaves income of $13 to spend. The process continues until all income is exhausted and the marginal utility per dollar spent is equal for both goods.

To restate, consumer optimum requires the following:

A consumer's money income should be allocated so that the last dollar spent on each good purchased yields the same amount of marginal utility (when all income is spent).

Exercise 19.2
Visit www.econtoday.com for more about making choices.

TABLE 19-2

Steps to Consumer Optimum

In each purchase situation described here, the consumer always purchases the good with the higher marginal utility per dollar spent (MU/P). For example, at the time of the third purchase, the marginal utility per last dollar spent on videos is 8, but it is 8.3 for hamburgers, and $16 of income remains, so the next purchase will be a hamburger. Here $P_v = \$5$ and $P_h = \$3$.

	Choices					
	Videos		Hamburgers			
Purchase	Unit	(MU_v/P_v)	Unit	($MU_h/(P_h)$)	Buying Decision	Remaining Income
1	First	10.0	First	8.3	First video	$26 − $5 = $21
2	Second	9.0	First	8.3	Second video	$21 − $5 = $16
3	Third	8.0	First	8.3	First hamburger	$16 − $3 = $13
4	Third	8.0	Second	7.3	Third video	$13 − $5 = $ 8
5	Fourth	7.3	Second	7.3	Fourth video and second hamburger	$ 8 − $5 = $ 3 $ 3 − $3 = $ 0

A Little Math

We can state the rule of consumer optimum in algebraic terms by examining the ratio of marginal utilities and prices of individual products. This is sometimes called the *rule of equal marginal utilities per dollar spent* on a basket of goods. The rule simply states that a consumer maximizes personal satisfaction when allocating money income in such a way that the last dollars spent on good A, good B, good C, and so on, yield equal amounts of marginal utility. Marginal utility (*MU*) from good A is indicated by *MU* of good A. For good B, it is *MU* of good B. Our algebraic formulation of this rule, therefore, becomes

$$\frac{MU \text{ of good A}}{\text{price of good A}} = \frac{MU \text{ of good B}}{\text{price of good B}} = \cdots = \frac{MU \text{ of good Z}}{\text{price of good Z}}$$

The letters A, B, . . . , Z indicate the various goods and services that the consumer might purchase.

We know, then, that the marginal utility of good A divided by the price of good A must equal the marginal utility of any other good divided by its price in order for the consumer to maximize utility. Note, though, that the application of the rule of equal marginal utility per dollar spent is not an explicit or conscious act on the part of consumers. Rather, this is a model of consumer optimum.

HOW A PRICE CHANGE AFFECTS CONSUMER OPTIMUM

Consumption decisions are summarized in the law of demand, which states that the amount purchased is inversely related to price. We can now see why by using the law of diminishing marginal utility.

Purchase decisions are made such that the value of the marginal utility of the last unit purchased and consumed is just equal to the price that had to be paid. No consumer will, when optimizing, buy 10 units of a good per unit time period when the personal valuation placed on the tenth unit is less than the price of the tenth unit.

If we start out at consumer optimum and then observe a price decrease, we can predict that consumers will respond to the price decrease by consuming more. Why? Because before the price change, the marginal utility of the last unit was about equal to the price paid for the last unit. Now, with a lower price, it is possible to consume more than before and still not have the marginal utility be less than the price, because the price has fallen. If the law of diminishing marginal utility holds, the purchase and consumption of additional units will cause marginal utility to fall. Eventually it will fall to the point at which it is equal to the price of the final good consumed. The limit to this increase in consumption is given by the law of diminishing marginal utility. At some point, the marginal utility of an additional unit will be less than what the person would have to give up (price) for that additional unit, and the person will stop buying.

A hypothetical demand curve for video rentals per week for a typical consumer is presented in Figure 19-2 on page 422. At a rental price of $5 per video, the marginal utility of the last video rented per week is MU_1. At a rental price of $4 per video per week, the marginal utility is represented by MU_2. Because of the law of diminishing marginal utility—with the consumption of more videos, the marginal utility of the last unit of these additional videos is lower—MU_2 must be less than MU_1. What has happened is that at a lower price, the number of video rentals per week increased from two to three; marginal utility must have fallen. At a higher consumption rate, the marginal utility falls to meet the lower price for video rentals per week.

FIGURE 19-2

Video Rental Prices and Marginal Utility
The rate of video rentals per week will increase as long as the marginal utility per last video rental per week exceeds the cost of that rental. A reduction in price from $5 to $4 per video rental causes consumers to increase consumption until marginal utility falls from MU_1 to MU_2 (because of the law of diminishing marginal utility).

The Substitution Effect

What is happening as the price of video rental falls is that consumers are substituting the now relatively cheaper video rentals for other goods and services, such as restaurant meals and live concerts. We call this the **substitution effect** of a change in price of a good because it occurs when consumers substitute relatively cheaper goods for relatively more expensive ones.

We assume that people desire a variety of goods and pursue a variety of goals. That means that few, if any, goods are irreplaceable in meeting demand. We are generally able to substitute one product for another to satisfy demand. This is commonly referred to as the **principle of substitution.**

Let's assume now that there are several goods, not exactly the same, and perhaps even very different from one another, but all serving basically the same purpose. If the relative price of one particular good falls, we will most likely substitute in favor of the lower-priced good and against the other similar goods that we might have been purchasing. Conversely, if the price of that good rises relative to the price of the other similar goods, we will substitute in favor of them and not buy as much of the now higher-priced good.

If the price of some item that you purchase goes down while your money income and all other prices stay the same, your ability to purchase goods goes up. That is to say that your effective **purchasing power** is increased, even though your money income has stayed the same. If you purchase 20 gallons of gas a week at $1.20 per gallon, your total outlay for gas is $24. If the price goes down by 50 percent, to 60 cents a gallon, you would have to spend only $12 a week to purchase the same number of gallons of gas. If your money income and the prices of other goods remain the same, it would be possible for you to continue purchasing 20 gallons of gas a week *and* to purchase more of other goods. You will feel richer and will indeed probably purchase more of a number of goods, including perhaps even more gasoline.

The converse will also be true. When the price of one good you are purchasing goes up, without any other change in prices or income, the purchasing power of your income will drop. You will have to reduce your purchases of either the now higher-priced good or other goods (or a combination).

In general, this **real-income effect** is usually quite small. After all, unless we consider broad categories, such as housing or food, a change in the price of one particular item that

Substitution effect
The tendency of people to substitute cheaper commodities for more expensive commodities.

Principle of substitution
The principle that consumers and producers shift away from goods and resources that become relatively higher priced in favor of goods and resources that are now relatively lower priced.

Purchasing power
The value of money for buying goods and services. If your money income stays the same but the price of one good that you are buying goes up, your effective purchasing power falls and vice versa.

Real-income effect
The change in people's purchasing power that occurs when, other things being constant, the price of one good that they purchase changes. When that price goes up, real income, or purchasing power, falls, and when that price goes down, real income increases.

we purchase will have a relatively small effect on our total purchasing power. Thus we expect the substitution effect usually to be more important than the real-income effect in causing us to purchase more of goods that have become cheaper and less of goods that have become more expensive.

THE DEMAND CURVE REVISITED

Linking the "law" of diminishing marginal utility and the rule of equal marginal utilities per dollar gives us a negative relationship between the quantity demanded of a good or service and its price. As the relative price of video rentals goes up, for example, the quantity demanded will fall; and as the relative price of video rentals goes down, the quantity demanded will rise. Figure 19-2 shows this demand curve for video rentals. As the price of video rentals falls, the consumer can maximize total utility only by renting more videos, and vice versa. In other words, the relationship between price and quantity desired is simply a downward-sloping demand curve. Note, though, that this downward-sloping demand curve (the law of demand) is derived under the assumption of constant tastes and incomes. You must remember that we are keeping these important determining variables constant when we simply look at the relationship between price and quantity demanded.

Marginal Utility, Total Utility, and the Diamond-Water Paradox

Even though water is essential to life and diamonds are not, water is cheap and diamonds are dear. The economist Adam Smith in 1776 called this the "diamond-water paradox." The paradox is easily understood when we make the distinction between total utility and marginal utility. The total utility of water greatly exceeds the total utility derived from diamonds. What determines the price, though, is what happens on the margin. We have relatively few diamonds, so the marginal utility of the last diamond consumed is high. The opposite is true for water. Total utility does not determine what people are willing to pay for a unit of a particular commodity; marginal utility does. Look at the situation graphically in Figure 19-3. We show the demand curve for diamonds, labeled $D_{diamonds}$. The demand curve for water is labeled D_{water}. We plot quantity in terms of kilograms per unit time

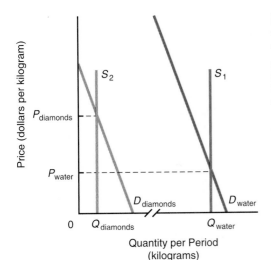

FIGURE 19-3

The Diamond-Water Paradox
We pick kilograms as a common unit of measurement for both water and diamonds. To demonstrate that the demand and supply of water is immense, we have put a break in the horizontal quantity axis. Although the demand for water is much greater than the demand for diamonds, the marginal valuation of water is given by the marginal value placed on the last unit of water consumed. To find that, we must know the supply of water, which is given as S_1. At that supply, the price of water is P_{water}. But the supply for diamonds is given by S_2. At that supply, the price of diamonds is $P_{diamonds}$. The total valuation that consumers place on water is tremendous relative to the total valuation consumers place on diamonds. What is important for price determination, however, is the marginal valuation, or the marginal utility received.

period on the horizontal axis. On the vertical axis we plot price in dollars per kilogram. We use kilograms as our common unit of measurement for water and for diamonds. We could just as well have used gallons, acre-feet, or liters.

Notice that the demand for water is many, many times the demand for diamonds (even though we really don't show this in the diagram). We draw the supply curve of water as S_1 at a quantity of Q_{water}. The supply curve for diamonds is given as S_2 at quantity $Q_{diamonds}$. At the intersection of the supply curve of water with the demand curve of water, the price per kilogram is P_{water}. The intersection of the supply curve of diamonds with the demand curve of diamonds is at $P_{diamonds}$. Notice that $P_{diamonds}$ exceeds P_{water}. Diamonds sell at a higher price than water.

Exercise 19.3
Visit www.econtoday.com for more about paying for nature.

INTERNATIONAL EXAMPLE
The World of Water in Saudi Arabia

The diamond-water paradox deals with the situation in which water, although necessary for life, may be much cheaper than some luxury item. In Saudi Arabia, as you might expect, the contrary can be true. A liter of water costs five times as much as a liter of gasoline, whereas a pair of custom-made British wool dress pants only costs $20. These relative prices are quite different from what we are used to seeing in America. Water costs next to nothing, a liter of gas about 40 cents, and custom-made wool pants at least $200. To understand what has happened in Saudi Arabia, simply substitute gasoline for water and water for diamonds in Figure 19-3.

FOR CRITICAL ANALYSIS: List some of the effects on human behavior that such a high relative price of water would cause. •

CONCEPTS IN BRIEF

• The law of diminishing marginal utility tells us that each successive marginal unit of a good consumed adds less extra utility.

• Each consumer with a limited income must make a choice about the basket of commodities to purchase; economic theory assumes that the consumer chooses the basket of commodities that yields optimum consumption. The consumer maximizes total utility by equating the marginal utility of the last dollar spent on one good with the marginal utility per last dollar spent on all other goods. That is the state of consumer optimum.

• To remain in consumer optimum, a price decrease requires an increase in consumption; a price increase requires a decrease in consumption.

• Each change in price has a substitution effect and a real-income effect. When price falls, the consumer substitutes in favor of the relatively cheaper good. When price falls, the consumer's real purchasing power increases, causing the consumer to purchase more of most goods. The opposite would occur when price increases. Assuming that the law of diminishing marginal utility holds, the demand curve must slope downward.

Despite the evidence on the negative effects of smoking, many Americans continue to smoke. Those who earn the lowest incomes smoke disproportionately more than those in higher income brackets. Consequently, who will bear the greatest burden of a significant increase in the price per pack of cigarettes?

Increased Cigarette Prices: Who Is Hit Hardest?

CONCEPTS APPLIED:

UTILITY, MARGINAL UTILITY, DEMAND, REVEALED PREFERENCES

 Visit www.econtoday.com for an Internet Activity that expands your understanding of these concepts.

There is little doubt that smoking leads to shortness of breath, emphysema, lung cancer, early death, and increased emotional pain to relatives of affected victims. But so far, at least for individuals over 18, smoking is a legal activity. Consequently, tobacco companies may sell cigarettes to any willing adult. For many decades, most people have known that smoking is harmful—as early as the 1920s, cigarettes were being referred to as "coffin nails." In any event, lawsuits against tobacco companies filed by sick smokers or their surviving relatives consistently failed in court. Enter the state governments. They decided to sue the tobacco companies on the basis of how much their Medicaid expenses increased from having to treat sick smokers. Rather than fight, the tobacco companies reached an agreement with the state governments. That agreement called for billions of dollars in "reparations" to be paid to various state governments each year.

Taxes, Too

Various state governments have imposed higher cigarette taxes in order to discourage smoking. As can be expected, the taxes are lowest in the tobacco-producing states. As can also be expected, cigarettes have been smuggled from low-tax states, such as Virginia, to high-tax states, such as New York.

The Effect of Higher Cigarette Prices

The tens and eventually hundreds of billions of dollars that the tobacco companies will pay out for any settlement will lead to higher cigarette prices. Which group of individuals is affected the most by higher cigarette prices? Look at Figure 19-4. The shaded area of the graph indicates the proportion of individuals in each income bracket who smoke. Poor individuals' revealed preferences show that they receive higher marginal utility from

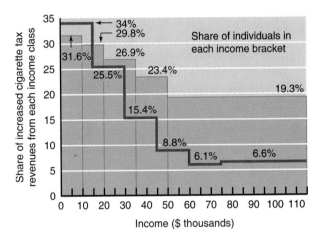

FIGURE 19-14

Who Will Pay the Higher Cigarette Prices
Lower-income earners smoke proportionately more than higher-income earners and will pay a disproportionately higher share of any tax on cigarettes.

Source: National Center for Health Statistics.

smoking than higher-income individuals. Whereas almost 32 percent of Americans earning $10,000 or less smoke, only about 19 percent of those earning above $50,000 smoke.

Now consider what will happen following a multibillion-dollar payment from tobacco companies to the government. The Tax Foundation in Washington, D.C., calculated that over a third of those dollars will be paid by 22 percent of Americans earning $15,000 or less. About 60 percent will be paid by the 45 percent of Americans earning below $30,000, as can be seen in the "stepladder" curve in the figure.

FOR CRITICAL ANALYSIS

1. If states save money because smokers die early, does that necessarily mean that we should subsidize smoking?

2. Why aren't cigarette smokers effectively fighting against higher cigarette taxes?

CHAPTER SUMMARY

1. As an individual consumes more of a particular commodity, the total level of utility, or satisfaction, derived from that consumption increases. However, the *rate* at which it increases diminishes as more is consumed. This is known as the law of diminishing marginal utility.

2. An individual reaches consumer optimum when the marginal utility per last dollar spent on each commodity consumed is equal to the marginal utility per dollar spent on every other good.

3. When the price of a particular commodity goes up, to get back into an optimum position, the consumer must reduce consumption of the now relatively more expensive commodity. As this consumer moves back up the marginal utility curve, marginal utility increases. A change in price has both a substitution effect and a real-income effect. As the price goes down, for example, the consumer substitutes in favor of the cheaper good, and also as the price goes down, real purchasing power increases, causing a general increase in consumer purchases of most goods and services.

4. It is possible to derive a downward-sloping demand curve by using the principle of diminishing marginal utility.

DISCUSSION OF PREVIEW QUESTIONS

1. **What is the law of diminishing marginal utility?**
The law of diminishing marginal utility states that as an individual consumes more and more units of a commodity per unit of time, eventually the extra benefit derived from consuming successive units will fall. Thus the fourth hamburger consumed in an eight-hour period yields less satisfaction than the third, and the third less than the second. The law is quite general and holds for almost any commodity.

2. **How does a consumer maximize total utility?**
This question deals with the maximization of utility derived not from the consumption of one commodity but from the consumption of all commodities that the individual wants, subject to an income constraint. The rule is that maximization of total utility requires that the last dollar spent on each commodity consumed by the individual have the same marginal utility. Stated differently, the consumer should purchase goods and services up to the point where the consumer's marginal utilities per dollar (marginal utility divided by price) for all commodities are equated and all income is spent (or saved for future spending). For example, assume that you are about to spend all of your income but discover that the marginal utility per dollar's worth for bread will be 10 utils and the marginal utility per dollar's worth of milk will be 30 utils. This means that the last dollar you are going to spend on bread will increase your total utility by 10, whereas the last dollar you are going to spend on milk will increase your total utility by 30. By spending one dollar more on milk and one dollar less on bread, you raise your total utility by about 20 utils, while your total dollar expenditures remain constant. This reallocation causes the marginal utility per dollar's worth of milk to fall and the marginal utility per dollar's worth of bread to rise. To maximize total utility, you will continue to buy more or less of each commodity until the marginal utilities per dollar's worth of all goods you consume are equated.

3. **What happens to consumer optimum when price changes?**
Assume that you have reached an optimum: The marginal utilities per dollar's worth for all the goods you purchase are equated. Assume that the last dollar spent on each of the commodities you purchase increases your total utility by 20 utils. Now suppose that the price of bread falls while all other prices remain constant. Because the price of bread has fallen, the last dollar spent on bread now has a higher marginal utility. This is true because at a lower price

for bread, a $1 bill can purchase a greater quantity of bread. This means that marginal utility per dollar's worth of bread now *exceeds* 20 utils, whereas the marginal utility per dollar's worth of each of the other goods you purchase still equals 20 utils. In short, you are no longer optimizing; your old pattern of expenditures does not maximize your total utility. You can now increase your total utility by purchasing more bread. Note that a reduction in the price of bread (other things held constant) leads to your purchasing more bread per unit of time.

4. How can the law of diminishing marginal utility account for the law of demand?

When a consumer is optimizing, total utility is maximized. An increase in expenditures on any specific commodity will necessarily lead to a reduction in expenditure on another commodity and a reduction in overall total utility. Why? Because of the law of diminishing marginal utility. For example, suppose that you are maximizing your overall total utility and that the marginal utility per dollar's worth of each commodity you purchase is 20 utils. Suppose that you experiment and spend another dollar on bread—and therefore spend one dollar less on milk. Your total utility must fall because you will receive less than 20 utils for the next dollar's worth of bread, and you lose 20 utils by spending a dollar less on milk. Thus, on net balance, you lose utility. We can see intuitively, then, that because you get less and less additional benefit from consuming more and more bread (or any other commodity), the price of bread (or any other commodity) *must fall* before you will voluntarily purchase more of it. That is how diminishing marginal utility helps explain the law of demand.

PROBLEMS

(Answers to the odd-numbered problems appear at the back of the book.)

19-1. Suppose that you are standing in the checkout line of a grocery store. You have 5 pounds of oranges and three ears of corn. A pound of oranges costs 30 cents; so does an ear of corn. You have $2.40 to spend. You are satisfied that you have reached the highest level of satisfaction, or total utility. Your sister comes along and tries to convince you that you have to put some of the corn back and replace it with oranges. From what you know about utility analysis, how would you explain this disagreement?

19-2. To increase marginal utility, the consumer must decrease consumption (other things being constant). This sounds paradoxical. Why is it a correct statement nonetheless?

19-3. Assume that Alice Warfield's marginal utility is 100 utils for the last hamburger she consumed. If the price of hamburgers is $1 apiece, what is Warfield's marginal utility per dollar's worth of hamburger? What is her marginal utility per dollar's worth if the price is 50 cents per hamburger? If the price is $2? How do we calculate marginal utility per dollar's worth of specific commodities?

19-4. A fall in the price of one good leads to more of that good being consumed, other things remaining constant. How might this increase in consumption be broken down?

19-5. Consider the accompanying table. Following the optimizing rule, how much of each good will be consumed?

Quantity of Good A	Marginal Utility of Good A	Price of Good A	Quantity of Good B	Marginal Utility of Good B	Price of Good B
100	15	$4.51	9	7	$1.69
101	12	4.51	10	5	1.69
102	8	4.51	11	3	1.69
103	6	4.51	12	2	1.69

19-6. If total utility is increasing as more is consumed, what is happening to marginal utility?

19-7. Yesterday you were consuming four eggs and two strips of bacon. Today you are consuming three eggs and three strips of bacon. Your tastes did not change overnight. What might have caused this change? Are you better or worse off?

19-8. The marginal utility of X is five times the marginal utility of Y, but the price of X is only four times the price of Y. How can this disequilibrium be remedied?

19-9. Look at the accompanying table; then answer the questions that follow.

Quantity of X Consumed	Total Utility (utils)
0	0
1	20
2	50
3	70
4	80

a. What is the marginal utility of consuming the first unit of X?
b. What is the marginal utility of consuming the fourth unit of X?
c. When does marginal utility start to diminish?

COMPUTER-ASSISTED INSTRUCTION

The consumer is optimizing when $MU_a/P_a = MU_b/P_b = \cdots = MU_z/P_z$. What does it mean if $MU_a/P_a > MU_b/P_b$? If $MU_a/P_a < MU_b/P_b$? How is a consumer likely to react to such inequalities? Why will the consumer's total utility increase on buying more or less of each good if an inequality exists? Specific calculations shed light on these questions.

Complete problem and answer appear on disk.

MORE ADVANCED CONSUMER CHOICE THEORY

It is possible to analyze consumer choice verbally, as we did for the most part in Chapter 19. The theory of diminishing marginal utility can be fairly well accepted on intuitive grounds and by introspection. If we want to be more formal and perhaps more elegant in our theorizing, however, we can translate our discussion into a graphic analysis with what we call indifference curves and the budget constraint. Here we discuss these terms and their relationship and demonstrate consumer equilibrium in geometric form.

ON BEING INDIFFERENT

What does it mean to be indifferent? It usually means that you don't care one way or the other about something—you are equally disposed to either of two alternatives. With this interpretation in mind, we will turn to two choices, video rentals and restaurant meals. In panel (a) of Figure E-1, we show several combinations of video rentals and restaurant meals per week that a representative consumer considers equally satisfactory. That is to say, for each combination, *A, B, C,* and *D,* this consumer will have exactly the same level of total utility.

The simple numerical example that we have used happens to concern video rentals and restaurant meals per week. This example is used to illustrate general features of indifference curves and related analytical tools that are necessary for deriving the demand curve. Obviously, we could have used any two commodities. Just remember that we are using a *specific* example to illustrate a *general* analysis.

We can plot these combinations graphically in panel (b) of Figure E-1, with restaurant meals per week on the horizontal axis and video rentals per week on the vertical axis. These are our consumer's indifference combinations—the consumer finds each combination as acceptable as the others. When we connect these combinations with a smooth curve, we obtain what is called the consumer's **indifference curve.** Along the indifference curve, every combination of the two goods in question yields the same level of satisfaction. Every point along the

Indifference curve
A curve composed of a set of consumption alternatives, each of which yields the same total amount of satisfaction.

FIGURE E-1

Combinations That Yield Equal Levels of Satisfaction
A, B, C, and *D* represent combinations of video rentals and restaurant meals per week that give an equal level of satisfaction to this consumer. In other words, the consumer is indifferent among these four combinations.

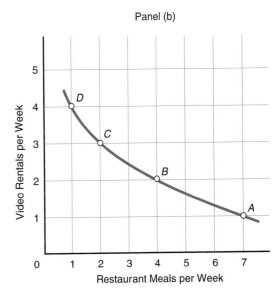

Panel (b)

Panel (a)

Combination	Video Rentals per Week	Restaurant Meals per Week
A	1	7
B	2	4
C	3	2
D	4	1

indifference curve is equally desirable to the consumer. For example, four video rentals per week and one restaurant meal per week will give our representative consumer exactly the same total satisfaction as two video rentals per week and four restaurant meals per week.

PROPERTIES OF INDIFFERENCE CURVES

Indifference curves have special properties relating to their slope and shape.

Downward Slope

The indifference curve shown in panel (b) of Figure E-1 slopes downward; that is, it has a negative slope. Now consider Figure E-2. Here we show two points, A and B. Point A represents four video rentals per week and two restaurant meals per week. Point B represents five video rentals per week and six restaurant meals per week. Clearly, B is always preferred to A because B represents more of everything. If B is always preferred to A, it is impossible for points A and B to be on the same indifference curve because the definition of the indifference curve is a set of combinations of two goods that are equally preferred.

Curvature

The indifference curve that we have drawn in panel (b) of Figure E-1 is special. Notice that it is curved. Why didn't we just draw a straight line, as we have usually done for a demand curve? To find out why we don't posit straight-line indifference curves, consider the implications. We show such a straight-line indifference curve in Figure E-3. Start at point A. The consumer has no restaurant meals and five video rentals per week. Now the consumer wishes to go to point B. He or she is willing to give up only one video rental in order to get one restaurant meal. Now let's assume that the consumer is at point C, consuming one video rental and four restaurant meals per week. If the consumer wants to go to point D, he or she is again willing to give up one video rental in order to get one more restaurant meal per week.

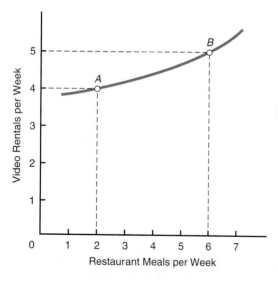

FIGURE E-2

Indifference Curves: Impossibility of an Upward Slope

Point B represents a consumption of more video rentals per week and more restaurant meals per week than point A. B is always preferred to A. Therefore, A and B cannot be on the same indifference curve, which is positively sloped, because an indifference curve shows *equally preferred* combinations of the two goods.

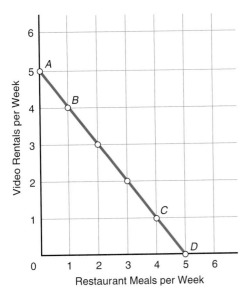

FIGURE E-3

Implications of a Straight-Line Indifference Curve

If the indifference curve is a straight line, the consumer will be willing to give up the same number of video rentals (one for one in this simple example) to get one more restaurant meal per week, whether the consumer has no restaurant meals or a lot of restaurant meals per week. For example, the consumer at point *A* has five video rentals and no restaurant meals per week. He or she is willing to give up one video rental in order to get one restaurant meal per week. At point *C*, however, the consumer has only one video rental and four restaurant meals per week. Because of the straight-line indifference curve, this consumer is willing to give up the last video rental in order to get one more restaurant meal per week, even though he or she already has four.

In other words, no matter how many videos the consumer rents, he or she is willing to give up one video rental to get one restaurant meal per week—which does not seem plausible. Doesn't it make sense to hypothesize that the more videos the consumer rents per week, the less he or she will value an *additional* video rental? Presumably, when the consumer has five video rentals and no restaurant meals per week, he or she should be willing to give up more than one video rental in order to get one restaurant meal. Therefore, a straight-line indifference curve as shown in Figure E-3 no longer seems plausible.

In mathematical jargon, an indifference curve is convex with respect to the origin. Let's look at this in panel (a) of Figure E-1. Starting with combination *A*, the consumer has one video rental but seven restaurant meals per week. To remain indifferent, the consumer would have to be willing to give up three restaurant meals to obtain one more video rental (as shown in combination *B*). However, to go from combination *C* to combination *D*, notice that the consumer would have to be willing to give up only one restaurant meal for an additional video rental per week. The quantity of the substitute considered acceptable changes as the rate of consumption of the original item changes.

Consequently the indifference curve in panel (b) of Figure E-1 will be convex when viewed from the origin.

THE MARGINAL RATE OF SUBSTITUTION

Instead of using marginal utility, we can talk in terms of the marginal rate of substitution between restaurant meals and video rentals per week. We can formally define the consumer's marginal rate of substitution as follows:

> **The marginal rate of substitution is equal to the change in the quantity of one good that just offsets a one-unit change in the consumption of another good, such that total satisfaction remains constant.**

We can see numerically what happens to the marginal rate of substitution in our example if we rearrange panel (a) of Figure E-1 into Table E-1. Here we show restaurant meals

(1) Combination	(2) Restaurant Meals Per Week	(3) Video Rentals Per Week	(4) Marginal Rate of Substitution of Restaurant Meals for Video Rentals
A	7	1	
			3:1
B	4	2	
			2:1
C	2	3	
			1:1
D	1	4	

TABLE E-1

Calculating the Marginal Rate of Substitution

As we move from combination A to combination B, we are still on the same indifference curve. To stay on that curve, the number of restaurant meals decreases by three and the number of video rentals increases by one. The marginal rate of substitution is 3:1. A three-unit decrease in restaurant meals requires an increase in one video rental to leave the consumer's total utility unaltered.

in the second column and video rentals in the third. Now we ask the question, What change in the consumption of video rentals per week will just compensate for a three-unit change in the consumption of restaurant meals per week and leave the consumer's total utility constant? The movement from A to B increases video rental consumption by one. Here the marginal rate of substitution is 3:1—a three-unit decrease in restaurant meals requires an increase of one video rental to leave the consumer's total utility unaltered. Thus the consumer values the three restaurant meals as the equivalent of one video rental. We do this for the rest of the table and find that as restaurant meals decrease further, the marginal rate of substitution goes from 3:1 to 1:1. The marginal rate of substitution of restaurant meals for video rentals per week falls as the consumer obtains more video rentals. That is, the consumer values successive units of video rentals less and less in terms of restaurant meals. The first video rental is valued at three restaurant meals; the last (fourth) video rental is valued at only one restaurant meal. The fact that the marginal rate of substitution falls is sometimes called the *law of substitution*.

In geometric language, the slope of the consumer's indifference curve (actually, the negative of the slope) measures the consumer's marginal rate of substitution. Notice that this marginal rate of substitution is purely subjective or psychological.

THE INDIFFERENCE MAP

Let's now consider the possibility of having both more video rentals *and* more restaurant meals per week. When we do this, we can no longer stay on the same indifference curve that we drew in Figure E-1. That indifference curve was drawn for equally satisfying combinations of video rentals and restaurant meals per week. If the individual can now attain more of both, a new indifference curve will have to be drawn, above and to the right of the one shown in panel (b) of Figure E-1. Alternatively, if the individual faces the possibility of having less of both video rentals and restaurant meals per week, an indifference curve will have to be drawn below and to the left of the one in panel (b) of Figure E-1. We can map out a whole set of indifference curves corresponding to these possibilities.

Figure E-4 shows three possible indifference curves. Indifference curves that are higher than others necessarily imply that for every given quantity of one good, more of the other good can be obtained on a higher indifference curve. Looked at another way, if one goes from curve I_1 to I_2, it is possible to consume the same number of restaurant meals *and* be able to rent more videos per week. This is shown as a movement from point A to point B in Figure E-4. We could do it the other way. When we move from a lower to a higher indif-

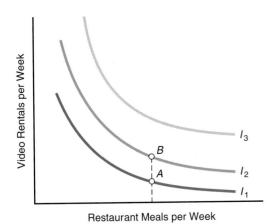

Video Rentals per Week

B

A

I_3

I_2

I_1

Restaurant Meals per Week

FIGURE E-4

A Set of Indifference Curves

An infinite number of indifference curves can be drawn. We show three possible ones. Realize that a higher indifference curve represents the possibility of higher rates of consumption of both goods. Hence a higher indifference curve is preferred to a lower one because more is preferred to less. Look at points A and B. Point B represents more video rentals than point A; therefore, bundles on indifference curve I_2 have to be preferred over bundles on I_1 because the number of restaurant meals per week is the same at points A and B.

ference curve, it is possible to rent the same number of videos *and* to consume more restaurant meals per week. Thus the higher a consumer is on the indifference map, the greater that consumer's total level of satisfaction.

THE BUDGET CONSTRAINT

Budget Constraint

All of the possible combinations of goods that can be purchased (at fixed prices) with a specific budget.

Our problem here is to find out how to maximize consumer satisfaction. To do so, we must consult not only our *preferences*—given by indifference curves—but also our *market opportunities*—given by our available income and prices, called our **budget constraint.** We might want more of everything, but for any given budget constraint, we have to make choices, or trade-offs, among possible goods. Everyone has a budget constraint; that is, everyone faces a limited consumption potential. How do we show this graphically? We must find the prices of the goods in question and determine the maximum consumption of each allowed by our budget. For example, let's assume that videos rent for $10 apiece and restaurant meals cost $20. Let's also assume that our representative consumer has a total budget of $60 per week. What is the maximum number of videos the consumer can rent? Six. And the maximum number of restaurant meals per week he or she can consume? Three. So now, as shown in Figure E-5, we have two points on our budget line, which is sometimes called the *consumption possibilities curve*. These anchor points of the budget line are obtained by dividing money income by the price of each product. The first point is at b on the vertical axis; the second, at b' on the horizontal axis. The budget line is linear because prices are given.

Any combination along line bb' is possible; in fact, any combination in the colored area is possible. We will assume, however, that the individual consumer completely uses up the available budget, and we will consider as possible only those points along bb'.

Slope of the Budget Constraint

The budget constraint is a line that slopes downward from left to right. The slope of that line has a special meaning. Look carefully at the budget line in Figure E-5. Remember from our discussion of graphs in Appendix A that we measure a negative slope by the ratio of the fall in Y over the run in X. In this case, Y is video rentals per week and X is restaurant meals per week. In Figure E-5, the fall in Y is -2 video rentals per week (a drop from 4 to 2) for a run in X of one restaurant meal per week (an increase from 1 to 2); therefore, the slope of

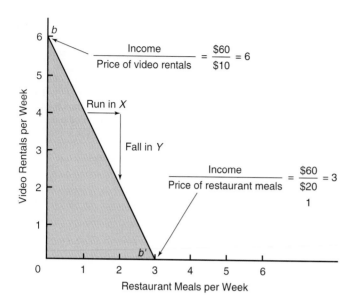

The Budget Constraint
The line *bb'* represents this individual's budget constraint. Assuming that video rentals cost $10 each, restaurant meals cost $20 each, and the individual has a budget of $60 per week, a maximum of six video rentals or three restaurant meals can be bought each week. These two extreme points are connected to form the budget constraint. All combinations within the colored area and on the budget constraint line are feasible.

the budget constraint is $-2/1$, or -2. This slope of the budget constraint represents the rate of exchange between video rentals and restaurant meals; it is the realistic rate of exchange, given their prices.

Now we are ready to determine how the consumer achieves the optimum consumption rate.

CONSUMER OPTIMUM REVISITED

Consumers will try to attain the highest level of total utility possible, given their budget constraints. How can this be shown graphically? We draw a set of indifference curves similar to those in Figure E-4, and we bring in reality—the budget constraint *bb'*. Both are drawn in Figure E-6. Because a higher level of total satisfaction is represented by a higher indifference curve, we know that the consumer will strive to be on the highest indifference

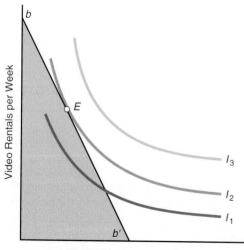

FIGURE E-6

Consumer Optimum
A consumer reaches an optimum when he or she ends up on the highest indifference curve possible, given a limited budget. This occurs at the tangency between an indifference curve and the budget constraint. In this diagram, the tangency is at *E*.

curve possible. However, the consumer cannot get to indifference curve I_3 because the budget will be exhausted before any combination of video rentals and restaurant meals represented on indifference curve I_3 is attained. This consumer can maximize total utility, subject to the budget constraint, only by being at point E on indifference curve I_2 because here the consumer's income is just being exhausted. Mathematically, point E is called the tangency point of the curve I_2 to the straight line bb'.

Consumer optimum is achieved when the marginal rate of substitution (which is subjective) is just equal to the feasible, or realistic, rate of exchange between video rentals and restaurant meals. This realistic rate is the ratio of the two prices of the goods involved. It is represented by the absolute value of the slope of the budget constraint. At point E, the point of tangency between indifference curve I_2 and budget constraint bb', the rate at which the consumer wishes to substitute video rentals for restaurant meals (the numerical value of slope of the indifference curve) is just equal to the rate at which the consumer *can* substitute video rentals for restaurant meals (the slope of the budget line).

EFFECTS OF CHANGES IN INCOME

A change in income will shift the budget constraint bb' in Figure E-6. Consider only increases in income and no changes in price. The budget constraint will shift outward. Each new budget line will be parallel to the original one because we are not allowing a change in the relative prices of video rentals and restaurant meals. We would now like to find out how an individual consumer responds to successive increases in income when relative prices remain constant. We do this in Figure E-7. We start out with an income that is represented by a budget line bb'. Consumer optimum is at point E, where the consumer attains the highest indifference curve I_1, given the budget constraint bb'. Now we let income increase. This is shown by a shift outward in the budget line to cc'. The consumer attains a new optimum at point E'. That is where a higher indifference curve, I_2, is reached. Again, the consumer's income is increased so that the new budget line is dd'. The new optimum now moves to E''. This is where indifference curve I_3 is reached. If we connect the three consumer optimum points, E, E', and E'', we have what is called an income-consumption curve. The **income-consumption curve** shows the optimum consumption points that would occur if income

Income-consumption curve
The set of optimum consumption points that would occur if income were increased, relative prices remaining constant.

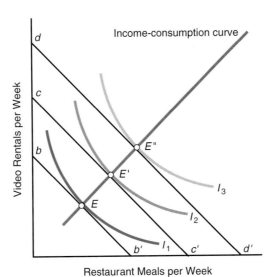

Restaurant Meals per Week

FIGURE E-7

Income-Consumption Curve
We start off with income sufficient to yield budget constraint bb'. The highest attainable indifference curve is I_1, which is just tangent to bb' at E. Next we increase income. The budget line moves outward to cc', which is parallel to bb'. The new highest indifference curve is I_2, which is just tangent to cc' at E'. We increase income again, which is represented by a shift in the budget line to dd'. The new tangency point of the highest indifference curve, I_3, with dd', is at point E''. When we connect these three points, we obtain the income-consumption curve.

Price-Consumption Curve
As we lower the price of restaurant meals, income measured in terms of restaurant meals per week increases. We show this by rotating the budget constraint from *bb'* to *bb''* and finally to *bb'''*. We then find the highest indifference curve that is attainable for each successive budget constraint. For budget constraint *bb'*, the highest indifference curve is l_1, which is tangent to *bb'* at point *E*. We do this for the next two budget constraints. When we connect the optimum points, *E, E'*, and *E''*, we derive the price-consumption curve, which shows the combinations of the two commodities that a consumer will purchase when money income and the price of one commodity remain constant while the other commodity's price changes.

for that consumer were increased continuously, holding the prices of video rentals and restaurant meals constant.

THE PRICE-CONSUMPTION CURVE

In Figure E-8, we hold money income and the price of video rentals constant while we lower the price of restaurant meals. As we keep lowering the price of restaurant meals, the quantity of meals that could be purchased if all income were spent on restaurant meals increases; thus the extreme points for the budget constraint keep moving outward to the right as the price of restaurant meals falls. In other words, the budget line rotates outward from *bb'* to *bb''* and *bb'''*. Each time the price of restaurant meals falls, a new budget line is formed. There has to be a new optimum point. We find it by locating on each new budget line the highest attainable indifference curve. This is shown at points *E, E'*, and *E''*. We see that as price decreases for restaurant meals, the consumer purchases more restaurant meals per week. We call the line connecting points *E, E'*, and *E''* the **price-consumption curve.** It connects the tangency points of the budget constraints and indifference curves, thus showing the amounts of two goods that a consumer will buy when money income and the price of one commodity are held constant while the price of the remaining good changes.

DERIVING THE DEMAND CURVE

We are now in a position to derive the demand curve using indifference curve analysis. In panel (a) of Figure E-9, we show what happens when the price of restaurant meals decreases, holding both the price of video rentals and income constant. If the price of restaurant meals decreases, the budget line rotates from *bb'* to *bb''*. The two optimum points are given by the tangency at the highest indifference curve that just touches those two budget lines. This is at *E* and *E'*. But those two points give us two price-quantity pairs. At point *E,* the price of restaurant meals is $20; the quantity demanded is 2. Thus we have one point that we can transfer to panel (b) of Figure E-9. At point *E'*, we have another price-quantity pair. The price has fallen to $10; the quantity demanded has increased to 5. We therefore transfer this other point to panel (b). When we connect these two points (and all the others in between), we derive the demand curve for restaurant meals; it slopes downward.

Price-consumption curve
The set of consumer optimum combinations of two goods that the consumer would choose as the price of one good changes, while money income and the price of the other good remain constant.

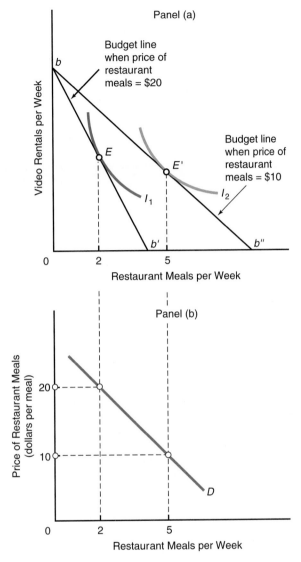

FIGURE E-9

Deriving the Demand Curve

In panel (a), we show the effects of a decrease in the price of restaurant meals from $20 to $10. At $20, the highest indifference curve touches the budget line bb' at point E. The quantity of restaurant meals consumed is two. We transfer this combination—price, $20; quantity demanded, 2—down to panel (b). Next we decrease the price of restaurant meals to $10. This generates a new budget line, or constraint, which is bb". Consumer optimum is now at E'. The optimum quantity of restaurant meals demanded at a price of $10 is five. We transfer this point—price, $10; quantity demanded, 5—down to panel (b). When we connect these two points, we have a demand curve, D, for restaurant meals.

APPENDIX SUMMARY

1. Along an indifference curve, the consumer experiences equal levels of satisfaction. That is to say, along any indifference curve, every combination of the two goods in question yields exactly the same level of satisfaction.

2. Indifference curves usually slope downward and are usually convex to the origin.

3. To measure the marginal rate of substitution, we find out how much of one good has to be given up in order to allow the consumer to consume one more unit of the other good while still remaining on the same indifference curve. The marginal rate of substitution falls as one moves down an indifference curve.

4. Indifference curves represent preferences. A budget constraint represents opportunities—how much can be purchased with a given level of income. Consumer optimum is obtained when the highest indifference curve is just tangent to the budget constraint line; at

that point, the consumer reaches the highest feasible indifference curve.

5. When income increases, the budget constraint shifts outward to the right, parallel to the previous budget constraint line.

6. As income increases, the consumer optimum moves up to higher and higher indifference curves. When

we connect those points with a line, we derive the income-consumption curve.

7. As the price of one good decreases, the budget line rotates. When we connect the tangency points of the highest indifference curves to these new budget lines, we derive the price-consumption curve.

PROBLEMS

(Answers to the odd-numbered problems appear at the back of the book.)

E-1. Suppose that a consumer prefers A to B and B to C but insists that she also prefers C to A. Explain the logical problem here.

E-2. Suppose that you are indifferent among the following three combinations of food (f) and drink (d): $1f$ and $10d$, $2f$ and $7d$, $3f$ and $2d$. Calculate the marginal rate of substitution in consumption between the two goods. Does the substitution of the third f imply a greater sacrifice of d than the second did?

E-3. Construct a budget line from the following information: nominal income of $100 per week; price of beef, P_b, $2 per pound; price of shelter, P_s, $20 per week; all income is spent on beef and shelter. Suppose that your money income remains constant, the price of beef doubles to $4 per pound, and the price of housing falls to $10 per week. Draw the new budget line. Are you now better off or worse off? What do you need to know before deciding?

E-4. Given the following three combinations of goods, $A = 3x + 4y$, $B = 4x + 6y$, and $C = 5x + 4y$, answer the following questions:

a. Is any one bundle preferred to the other two?

b. Could a consumer possibly find B and C to be equally acceptable? How about A and C?

E-5. Calculate the marginal rate of substitution of burritos for yogurt for the following consumer's indifference schedule:

Servings of Yogurt per Week	Burritos per Week
10	1
6	2
3	3
1	4

E-6. Assume that you are consuming only yogurt (Y) and gymnasium exercise (G). Each serving of yogurt costs $4, and each visit to the gym costs $8. Given your food and exercise budget, you consume 15 servings of yogurt and five visits to the gym each week. One day, the price of yogurt falls to $3 per serving and the price of gym visits increases to $10. Now you buy 20 servings of yogurt and four gym visits per week.

a. Draw the old and new budget constraints, and show the two equilibrium bundles of yogurt servings and visits to the gym.

b. What is your weekly budget for food and exercise?

E-7. Explain why each of the following statements is or is not consistent with our assumptions about consumer preferences.

a. I can't decide whether to go abroad this summer or to stay at home.

b. That is mine. You cannot have it. There is nothing you can do to make me change my mind.

c. I love hot pretzels with mustard at football games. If I had my way, I would never stop eating them.

CHAPTER 20

DEMAND AND SUPPLY ELASTICITY

Europeans living in major cities have used subways most of their lives, whereas most Americans have never used the subway. The reason, of course, is that few subway systems exist in America. The city with the most extensive subway system is New York. The New York City subway has rarely been known for its cleanliness or safety. Transit authorities in that city did, however, make a concerted effort to clean it up as well as to make it safer. Subway ridership reached its highest level in 21 years in November 1995. The very next month, however, ridership fell by nearly 4 million, compared to December a year earlier. What happened in New York City? To understand this issue, you need to know more about how people respond to changing prices.

PREVIEW QUESTIONS

1. How is total revenue related to the price elasticity of demand?

2. What are the determinants of the price elasticity of demand?

3. What is the income elasticity of demand?

4. What is the price elasticity of supply?

Did **You Know That . . .** the government predicted it would raise $6 million per year in new revenues from a new 10 percent luxury tax on private airplane and yacht sales a few years ago, but it actually collected only $53,000? How can that be? The answer lies in understanding the relationship between the quantities that people demand at lower prices relative to the quantities that people demand at higher prices. The year during which the 10 percent luxury tax was imposed also saw expensive new yacht sales fall to almost nothing. Clearly, even rich people respond to rising prices, which in this case were caused by a new government tax.

It is not only the government that has to worry about how individuals respond to rising prices; it is perhaps even more important that all businesses take into account consumer response to changing prices. If McDonald's lowers its prices by 10 percent, will fast-food consumers respond by buying so many more Big Macs that the company's revenues will rise? At the other end of the spectrum, can Rolls Royce dealers "get away" with a 2 percent increase in prices? Otherwise stated, will Rolls Royce purchasers respond so little to the relatively small increase in price that the total revenues received for Rolls Royce sales will not fall and may actually rise? The only way to answer these questions is to know how responsive people in the real world will be to changes in prices. Economists have a special name for price responsiveness—*elasticity,* which is the subject of this chapter.

PRICE ELASTICITY

To begin to understand what elasticity is all about, just keep in mind that it means "responsiveness" or "stretchiness." Here we are concerned with the price elasticity of demand and the price elasticity of supply. We wish to know the extent to which a change in the price of, say, petroleum products will cause the quantity demanded and the quantity supplied to change, other things held constant. Let's restrict our discussion at first to the demand side.

Price Elasticity of Demand

We will formally define the **price elasticity of demand,** which we will label E_p, as follows:

$$E_p = \frac{\text{percentage change in quantity demanded}}{\text{percentage change in price}}$$

What will price elasticity of demand tell us? It will tell us the relative amount by which the quantity demanded will change in response to a change in the price of a particular good.

Consider an example in which a 10 percent rise in the price of oil leads to a reduction in quantity demanded of only 1 percent. Putting these numbers into the formula, we find that the price elasticity of demand for oil in this case equals the percentage change in quantity demanded divided by the percentage change in price, or

$$E_p = \frac{-1\%}{+10\%} = -.1$$

An elasticity of $-.1$ means that a 1 percent *increase* in the price would lead to a mere .1 percent *decrease* in the quantity demanded. If you were now told, in contrast, that the price elasticity of demand for oil was -1, you would know that a 1 percent increase in the price of oil would lead to a 1 percent decrease in the quantity demanded.

Relative Quantities Only. Notice that in our elasticity formula, we talk about *percentage* changes in quantity demanded divided by *percentage* changes in price. We are there-

Price elasticity of demand (E_p)
The responsiveness of the quantity demanded of a commodity to changes in its price; defined as the percentage change in quantity demanded divided by the percentage change in price.

fore not interested in the absolute changes, only in relative amounts. This means that it doesn't matter if we measure price changes in terms of cents, dollars, or hundreds of dollars. It also doesn't matter whether we measure quantity changes in ounces, grams, or pounds. The percentage change will be independent of the units chosen.

POLICY EXAMPLE
How Will a $1.50-per-Pack Tax Affect Your Smoking?

As part of his "war on tobacco," President Clinton announced a centerpiece $1.50-per-pack tax increase for cigarettes. He declared that he wanted to cut youth smoking in half by the year 2005. One researcher at the University of Illinois, Professor Frank Chaloup, had already estimated the price responsiveness of teens to cigarette price increases: a 10 percent increase in the price of cigarettes causes a 6.7 percent decrease in the number of teens who smoke. So a $1.50 tax hike, which would increase the average nationwide price of a pack of cigarettes by 80 percent, should lead to a reduction of more than 50 percent in teen smoking.

FOR CRITICAL ANALYSIS: When Canada increased tobacco taxes by more than 250 percent, bootlegging from abroad—especially the United States—became a serious problem. What does Canada's experience tell us about the proposed $1.50-per-pack increase in the U.S. tax on cigarettes? ●

Always Negative. The law of demand states that quantity demanded is *inversely* related to the relative price. An increase in the price of a good leads to a decrease in the quantity demanded. If a decrease in the relative price of a good should occur, the quantity demanded would increase by a certain percentage. The point is that price elasticity of demand will always be negative. By convention, *we will ignore the minus sign in our discussion from this point on.*

Basically, the greater the *absolute* price elasticity of demand (disregarding sign), the greater the demand responsiveness to relative price changes—a small change in price has a great impact on quantity demanded. The smaller the absolute price elasticity of demand, the smaller the demand responsiveness to relative price changes—a large change in price has little effect on quantity demanded.

CONCEPTS IN BRIEF

- Elasticity is a measure of the price responsiveness of the quantity demanded and quantity supplied.
- The price elasticity of demand is equal to the percentage change in quantity demanded divided by the percentage change in price.
- Price elasticity of demand is calculated in terms of percentage changes in quantity demanded and in price. Thus it is expressed as a unitless, dimensionless number.
- The law of demand states that quantity demanded and price are inversely related. Therefore, the price elasticity of demand is always negative, because an increase in price will lead to a decrease in quantity demanded and a decrease in price will lead to an increase in quantity demanded. By convention, we ignore the negative sign in discussions of the price elasticity of demand.

Calculating Elasticity

To calculate the price elasticity of demand, we have to compute percentage changes in quantity demanded and in relative price. To obtain the percentage change in quantity demanded, we divide the change in the quantity demanded by the original quantity demanded:

$$\frac{\text{Change in quantity demanded}}{\text{Original quantity demanded}}$$

To find the percentage change in price, we divide the change in price by the original price:

$$\frac{\text{Change in price}}{\text{Original price}}$$

There is an arithmetic problem, though, when we calculate percentage changes in this manner. The percentage change, say, from 2 to 3—50 percent—is not the same as the percentage change from 3 to 2—$33\frac{1}{3}$ percent. In other words, it makes a difference where you start. One way out of this dilemma is simply to use average values.

To compute the price elasticity of demand, we need to deal with the average change in quantity demanded caused by the average change in price. That means that we take the average of the two prices and the two quantities over the range we are considering and compare the change with these averages. For relatively small changes in price, the formula for computing the price elasticity of demand then becomes

$$E_p = \frac{\text{change in quantity}}{\text{sum of quantities}/2} \div \frac{\text{change in price}}{\text{sum of prices}/2}$$

We can rewrite this more simply if we do two things: (1) We can let Q_1 and Q_2 equal the two different quantities demanded before and after the price change and let P_1 and P_2 equal the two different prices. (2) Because we will be dividing a percentage by a percentage, we simply use the ratio, or the decimal form, of the percentages. Therefore,

$$E_p = \frac{\Delta Q}{(Q_1 + Q_2)/2} \div \frac{\Delta P}{(P_1 + P_2)/2}$$

where the Greek letter Δ stands for "change in."

INTERNATIONAL EXAMPLE
The Price Elasticity of Demand for Newspapers

Newspaper owners are always seeking to increase their paper's circulation, not because they want the revenue generated from the sales of the paper, but because the larger the circulation, the more the newspaper can charge for its advertising space. The source of most of a paper's revenues—and profits—comes from its advertisers.

One newspaper owner, Rupert Murdoch, ran an experiment to see how high he could boost sales of a particular newspaper by lowering its price. For one day, he lowered the price of the British daily paper *Today* from 25 pence to 10 pence. According to London's *Financial Times,* the sales of *Today* almost doubled that day, increasing the circulation from

590,000 to 1.05 million copies. We can estimate the price elasticity of demand for *Today* by using the formula presented earlier (under the assumption, of course, that all other things were held constant):

$$E_p = \frac{\Delta Q}{(Q_1 + Q_2)/2} \div \frac{\Delta P}{(P_1 + P_2)/2}$$

$$= \frac{1,050,000 - 590,000}{(590,000 + 1,050,000)/2} \div \frac{25 \text{ pence} - 10 \text{ pence}}{(10 \text{ pence} + 25 \text{ pence})/2}$$

$$= \frac{460,000}{820,000} \div \frac{15 \text{ pence}}{17.5 \text{ pence}} = .66$$

The price elasticity of demand of .66 means that a 1 percent decrease in price will lead to a .66 percent increase in quantity demanded.

FOR CRITICAL ANALYSIS: Would the estimated price elasticity of the Today *newspaper have been different if we had* not *used the average-values formula? How?* ●

PRICE ELASTICITY RANGES

We have names for the varying ranges of price elasticities, depending on whether a 1 percent change in price elicits more or less than a 1 percent change in the quantity demanded.

Elastic demand
A demand relationship in which a given percentage change in price will result in a larger percentage change in quantity demanded. Total expenditures and price changes are inversely related in the elastic region of the demand curve.

Unit elasticity of demand
A demand relationship in which the quantity demanded changes exactly in proportion to the change in price. Total expenditures are invariant to price changes in the unit-elastic region of the demand curve.

Inelastic demand
A demand relationship in which a given percentage change in price will result in a less than proportionate percentage change in the quantity demanded. Total expenditures and price are directly related in the inelastic region of the demand curve.

1. *Elastic demand.* We say that a good has an **elastic demand** whenever the price elasticity of demand is greater than 1. A 1 percent change in price causes a greater than a 1 percent change in the quantity demanded.
2. *Unit elasticity of demand.* In a situation of **unit elasticity of demand,** a 1 percent change in price causes a response of exactly a 1 percent change in the quantity demanded.
3. *Inelastic demand.* In a situation of **inelastic demand,** a 1 percent change in price causes a response of less than a 1 percent change in the quantity demanded. The most extreme inelastic demand is *perfectly inelastic;* no matter what the price, the quantity demanded remains the same, so the price elasticity of demand is zero.

When we say that a commodity's demand is elastic, we are indicating that consumers are relatively responsive to changes in price. When we say that a commodity's demand is inelastic, we are indicating that its consumers are relatively unresponsive to price changes. When economists say that demand is inelastic, it does not mean that quantity demanded is totally unresponsive to price changes. Remember, the law of demand suggests that there will be some responsiveness in quantity demanded to a price change. The question is how much. That's what elasticity attempts to determine.

Extreme Elasticities

There are two extremes in price elasticities of demand. One extreme represents total unresponsiveness of quantity demanded to price changes, which is referred to as

FIGURE 20-1

Extreme Price Elasticities

In panel (a), we show complete price unresponsiveness. The demand curve is vertical at the quantity of 8 million units per year. This means that the price elasticity of demand is zero. In panel (b), we show complete price responsiveness. At a price of 30 cents, in this example, consumers will demand an unlimited quantity of the particular good in question. This is a case of infinite price elasticity of demand.

perfectly inelastic demand, or zero elasticity. The other represents total responsiveness, which is referred to as, infinitely, or **perfectly elastic demand.**

We show perfect inelasticity in panel (a) of Figure 20-1. Notice that the quantity demanded per year is 8 million units, no matter what the price. Hence for any percentage price change, the quantity demanded will remain the same, and thus the change in the quantity demanded will be zero. Look back at our formula for computing elasticity. If the change in the quantity demanded is zero, the numerator is also zero, and a nonzero number divided into zero results in an answer of zero too. Hence there is perfect inelasticity. At the opposite extreme is the situation depicted in panel (b) of Figure 20-1. Here we show that at a price of 30 cents, an unlimited quantity will be demanded. At a price that is only slightly above 30 cents, no quantity will be demanded. There is complete, or infinite, responsiveness here, and hence we call the demand schedule in panel (b) infinitely elastic.

Perfectly inelastic demand
A demand that exhibits zero responsiveness to price changes; no matter what the price is, the quantity demanded remains the same.

Perfectly elastic demand
A demand that has the characteristic that even the slightest increase in price will lead to zero quantity demanded.

CONCEPTS IN BRIEF

- One extreme elasticity occurs when a demand curve is vertical. It has zero price elasticity of demand; it is completely inelastic.

- Another extreme elasticity occurs when a demand curve is horizontal. It has completely elastic demand; its price elasticity of demand is infinite.

ELASTICITY AND TOTAL REVENUES

Suppose that you are in charge of the pricing decision for a cellular telephone service company. How would you know when it is best to raise or not to raise prices? The answer depends in part on the effect of your pricing decision on total revenues, or the total receipts of your company. (The rest of the equation is, of course, your cost structure, a subject we examine in Chapter 22.) It is commonly thought that the way to increase total receipts is to increase price per unit. But is this always the case? Is it possible that a rise in price per unit could lead to a decrease in total revenues? The answers to these questions depend on the price elasticity of demand.

Let's look at Figure 20-2 on page 446. In panel (a), column 1 shows the price of cellular telephone service in dollars per minute, and column 2 represents billions of minutes per year. In column 3, we multiply column 1 times column 2 to derive total revenue because total revenue is always equal to the number of units (quantity) sold times the price per unit, and in column 4, we calculate values of elasticity. Notice what happens to total revenues throughout the schedule. They rise steadily as the price rises from 10 cents to 50 cents per minute; but when the price rises further to 60 cents per minute, total revenues remain constant at $3 billion. At prices per minute higher than 60 cents, total revenues fall as price increases. Indeed, if prices are above 60 cents per minute, total revenues can be increased only by *cutting* prices, not by raising them.

Labeling Elasticity

The relationship between price and quantity on the demand schedule is given in columns 1 and 2 of panel (a) in Figure 20-2. In panel (b), the demand curve, *D,* representing that schedule is drawn. In panel (c), the total revenue curve representing the data in column 3 is drawn. Notice first the level of these curves at small quantities. The demand curve is at a maximum height, but total revenue is zero, which makes sense according to this demand schedule—at a price of $1.10 and above, no units will be purchased, and therefore total revenue will be zero. As price is lowered, we travel down the demand curve, and total revenues increase until price is 60 cents per minute, remain constant from 60 cents to 50 cents per minute, and then fall at lower unit prices. Corresponding to those three sections, demand is elastic, unit-elastic, and inelastic. Hence we have three relationships among the three types of price elasticity and total revenues.

1. *Elastic demand.* A negative relationship exists between small changes in price and changes in total revenues. That is to say, if price is lowered, total revenues will rise when the firm faces demand that is elastic, and if it raises price, total revenues will fall. Consider another example. If the price of Diet Coke were raised by 25 percent and the price of all other soft drinks remained constant, the quantity demanded of Diet Coke would probably fall dramatically. The decrease in quantity demanded due to the increase in the price of Diet Coke would lead in this example to a reduction in the total revenues of the Coca-Cola Company. Therefore, if demand is elastic, price and total revenues will move in *opposite* directions.
2. *Unit-elastic demand.* Changes in price do not change total revenues. When the firm is facing demand that is unit-elastic, if it increases price, total revenues will not change; if it decreases price, total revenues will not change either.
3. *Inelastic demand.* A positive relationship exists between changes in price and total revenues. When the firm is facing demand that is inelastic, if it raises price, total revenues will go up; if it lowers price, total revenues will fall. Consider another example. You have just invented a cure for the common cold that has been approved by the Food and Drug Administration for sale to the public. You are not sure what price you should charge, so you start out with a price of $1 per pill. You sell 20 million pills at that price over a year. The next year, you decide to raise the price by 25 percent, to $1.25. The number of pills you sell drops to 18 million per year. The price increase of 25 percent

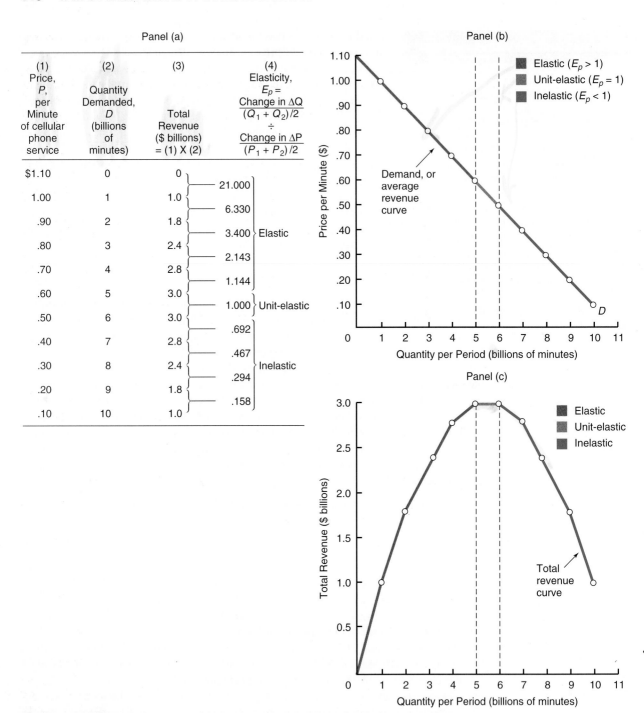

Panel (a)

(1) Price, P, per Minute of cellular phone service	(2) Quantity Demanded, D (billions of minutes)	(3) Total Revenue ($ billions) = (1) X (2)	(4) Elasticity, $E_p = \dfrac{\text{Change in } \Delta Q}{(Q_1 + Q_2)/2} \div \dfrac{\text{Change in } \Delta P}{(P_1 + P_2)/2}$
$1.10	0	0	
			21.000
1.00	1	1.0	
			6.330
.90	2	1.8	
			3.400 Elastic
.80	3	2.4	
			2.143
.70	4	2.8	
			1.144
.60	5	3.0	
			1.000 Unit-elastic
.50	6	3.0	
			.692
.40	7	2.8	
			.467
.30	8	2.4	Inelastic
			.294
.20	9	1.8	
			.158
.10	10	1.0	

FIGURE 20-2

The Relationship Between Price Elasticity of Demand and Total Revenues for Cellular Phone Service

In panel (a), we show the elastic, unit-elastic, and inelastic sections of the demand schedule according to whether a reduction in price increases total revenues, causes them to remain constant, or causes them to decrease, respectively. In panel (b), we show these regions graphically on the demand curve. In panel (c), we show them on the total revenue curve.

has led to a 10 percent decrease in quantity demanded. Your total revenues, however, will rise to $22.5 million because of the price increase. We therefore conclude that if demand is inelastic, price and total revenues move in the *same* direction.

The elastic, unit-elastic, and inelastic areas of the demand curve are shown in Figure 20-2. For prices from $1.10 per minute of cellular phone time to 60 cents per minute, as price decreases, total revenues rise from zero to $3 billion. Demand is price-elastic. When price changes from 60 cents to 50 cents, however, total revenues remain constant at $3 billion; demand is unit-elastic. Finally, when price falls from 50 cents to 10 cents, total revenues decrease from $3 billion to $1 billion; demand is inelastic. In panels (b) and (c) of Figure 20-2, we have labeled the sections of the demand curve accordingly, and we have also shown how total revenues first rise, then remain constant, and finally fall.

The relationship between price elasticity of demand and total revenues brings together some important microeconomic concepts. Total revenues, as we have noted, are the product of price per unit times number of units sold. The law of demand states that along a given demand curve, price and quantity changes will move in opposite directions: One increases as the other decreases. Consequently, what happens to the product of price times quantity depends on which of the opposing changes exerts a greater force on total revenues. But this is just what price elasticity of demand is designed to measure—responsiveness of quantity demanded to a change in price. The relationship between price elasticity of demand and total revenues is summarized in Table 20-1.

TABLE 20-1

Relationship Between Price Elasticity of Demand and Total Revenues

Price Elasticity of Demand		Effect of Price Change on Total Revenues (TR)	
		Price Decrease	Price Increase
Inelastic	$(E_p < 1)$	TR ↓	TR ↑
Unit-elastic	$(E_p = 1)$	No change in TR	No change in TR
Elastic	$(E_p > 1)$	TR ↑	TR ↓

INTERNATIONAL EXAMPLE
A Pricing Decision at Disneyland Paris

Several years after it opened with great fanfare, the $4 billion investment in Disneyland Paris (formerly called EuroDisney) was in trouble. In an attempt to improve profits (actually, decrease losses), Disney management decided to lower prices starting in the summer of 1995. Entrance fees during peak periods (April 1 to October 1) dropped from 250 francs (about $50) to 195 francs (about $40). Was this 22 percent reduction in ticket prices a good management strategy for Disney officials? That depends in part on what happened to total revenues. As it turned out, park attendance increased by 700,000 visitors. Thus total revenues increased by more than 22 percent, indicating that the demand for Disneyland Paris is elastic in the price range between $40 to $50.

FOR CRITICAL ANALYSIS: What other factors may have affected attendance at Disneyland Paris? ●

CONCEPTS IN BRIEF

- Price elasticity of demand is related to total revenues (and total consumer expenditures).
- When demand is *elastic*, the change in price elicits a change in total revenues (and total consumer expenditures) in the direction opposite that of the price change.
- When demand is *unit-elastic*, a change in price elicits no change in total revenues (or in total consumer expenditures).
- When demand is *inelastic*, a change in price elicits a change in total revenues (and in consumer expenditures) in the same direction as the price change.

Exercise 20.1
Visit www.econtoday.com for more about food price elasticity.

DETERMINANTS OF THE PRICE ELASTICITY OF DEMAND

We have learned how to calculate the price elasticity of demand. We know that theoretically, it ranges numerically from zero, completely inelastic, to infinity, completely elastic. What we would like to do now is come up with a list of the determinants of the price elasticity of demand. The price elasticity of demand for a particular commodity at any price depends, at a minimum, on the following:

1. The existence, number, and quality of substitutes
2. The percentage of a consumer's total budget devoted to purchases of that commodity
3. The length of time allowed for adjustment to changes in the price of the commodity

Existence of Substitutes

The closer the substitutes for a particular commodity and the more substitutes there are, the greater will be its price elasticity of demand. At the limit, if there is a perfect substitute, the elasticity of demand for the commodity will be infinity. Thus even the slightest increase in the commodity's price will cause an enormous reduction in the quantity demanded: quantity demanded will fall to zero. We are really talking about two goods that the consumer believes are exactly alike and equally desirable, like dollar bills whose only difference is serial numbers. When we talk about less extreme examples, we can only speak in terms of the number and the similarity of substitutes that are available. Thus we will find that the more narrowly we define a good, the closer and greater will be the number of substitutes available. For example, the demand for a Diet Coke may be highly elastic because consumers can switch to Diet Pepsi. The demand for diet drinks in general, however, is relatively less elastic because there are fewer substitutes.

Share of Budget

We know that the greater the percentage of a total budget spent on the commodity, the greater the person's price elasticity of demand for that commodity. The demand for pepper is thought to be very inelastic merely because individuals spend so little on it relative to their total budgets. In contrast, the demand for things such as transportation and housing is thought to be far more elastic because they occupy a large part of people's budgets—changes in their prices cannot be ignored so easily without sacrificing a lot of other alternative goods that could be purchased.

Consider a numerical example. A household earns $40,000 a year. It purchases $4 of pepper per year and $4,000 of transportation services. Now consider the spending power of this family when the price of pepper and the price of transportation both go up by 100 percent. If the household buys the same amount of pepper, it will now spend $8. It will thus have to reduce other expenditures by $4. This $4 represents only .01 percent of the entire household budget. By contrast, a doubling of transportation costs requires that the family spend $8,000, or $4,000 more on transportation, if it is to purchase the same quantity. That increased expenditure on transportation of $4,000 represents 10 percent of total expenditures that must be switched from other purchases. We would therefore predict that the household will react differently to the doubling of prices for pepper than it will for transportation. It will buy almost the same amount of pepper but will spend significantly less on transportation.

Time for Adjustment

Exercise 20.2
Visit www.econtoday.com for more about demand for wine.

When the price of a commodity changes and that price change persists, more people will learn about it. Further, consumers will be better able to revise their consumption patterns the longer the time period they have to do so. And in fact, the longer the time they do take, the less costly it will be for them to engage in this revision of consumption patterns. Consider a price decrease. The longer the price decrease persists, the greater will be the number of new uses that consumers will discover for the particular commodity, and the greater will be the number of new users of that particular commodity.

It is possible to make a very strong statement about the relationship between the price elasticity of demand and the time allowed for adjustment:

The longer any price change persists, the greater the elasticity of demand, other things held constant. Elasticity of demand is greater in the long run than in the short run.

Let's take an example. Suppose that the price of electricity goes up 50 percent. How do you adjust in the short run? You can turn the lights off more often, you can stop using the stereo as much as you do, and so on. Otherwise it's very difficult to cut back on your consumption of electricity. In the long run, though, you can devise methods to reduce your consumption. Instead of using electric heaters, the next time you have a house built you will install gas heaters. Instead of using an electric stove, the next time you move you will have a gas stove installed. You will purchase fluorescent bulbs because they use less electricity. The more time you have to think about it, the more ways you will find to cut your electricity consumption. We would expect, therefore, that the short-run demand curve for electricity would be relatively inelastic (in the price range around P_e), as demonstrated by D_1 in Figure 20-3 on page 450. However, the long-run demand curve may exhibit much more elasticity (in the neighborhood of P_e), as demonstrated by D_3. Indeed, we can think of an entire family of demand curves such as those depicted in that figure. The short-run demand curve is for the period when there is no time for adjustment. As more time is allowed, the demand curve goes first to D_2 and then all the way to D_3. Thus in the neighborhood of P_e, elasticity differs for each of these curves. It is greater for the less steep curves (but, slope alone does not measure elasticity for the entire curve).

How to Define the Short Run and the Long Run. We've mentioned the short run and the long run. Is the short run one week, two weeks, one month, two months? Is the long run three years, four years, five years? The answer is that there is no single answer. What we mean by the long run is the period of time necessary for consumers to make a full adjustment to a given price change, all other things held constant. In the case of the demand for electricity, the long run will be however long it takes consumers to switch over to cheaper sources of heating, to buy houses that are more energy-efficient, to purchase manufactured appliances that are more energy-efficient, and so on. The long-run elasticity of

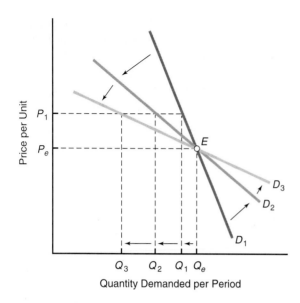

FIGURE 20-3

Short-Run and Long-Run Price Elasticity of Demand

Consider an equilibrium situation in which the market price is P_e and the quantity demanded is Q_e. Then there is a price increase to P_1. In the short run, as evidenced by the demand curve D_1, we move from equilibrium quantity demanded, Q_e, to Q_1. After more time is allowed for adjustment, the demand curve rotates at original price P_e to D_2. Quantity demanded falls again, now to Q_2. After even more time is allowed for adjustment, the demand curve rotates at price P_e to D_3. At the higher price P_1, in the long run, the quantity demanded falls all the way to Q_3.

demand for electricity therefore relates to a period of at least several years. The short run—by default—is any period less than the long run.

EXAMPLE
What Do Real-World Price Elasticities of Demand Look Like?

In Table 20-2, we present demand elasticities for selected goods. None of them is zero, and the largest is 3.8—a far cry from infinity. Remember that even though we are leaving off the negative sign, there is an inverse relationship between price and quantity demanded,

TABLE 20-2

Demand Elasticity for Selected Goods

Here are estimated demand elasticities for selected goods. All of them are negative, although we omit the minus sign. We have given some estimates of the long-run price elasticities of demand. The long run is associated with the time necessary for consumers to adjust fully to any given price change.

Category	Estimated Elasticity	
	Short Run	Long Run
Lamb	2.65	—
Bread	.15	—
Tires and related items	.8	1.2
Auto repair and related services	1.4	2.4
Radio and television repair	.5	3.8
Legitimate theater and opera	.2	.31
Motion pictures	.87	3.7
Foreign travel by U.S. residents	.1	1.8
Taxicabs	.6	—
Local public transportation	.6	1.2
Intercity bus	.2	2.2
Electricity	.1	1.8
Jewelry and watches	.4	.6

and the minus sign is understood. Also remember that these elasticities represent averages over given price ranges. Choosing different price ranges would yield different elasticity estimates for these goods.

Economists have consistently found that estimated price elasticities of demand are greater in the long run than in the short run, as seen in Table 20-2. There you see, for example, in the far-right column that the long-run price elasticity of demand for tires and related items is 1.2, whereas the estimate for the short run is .8. Throughout the table, you see that all estimates of long-run price elasticities of demand exceed their short-run counterparts.

FOR CRITICAL ANALYSIS: Explain the intuitive reasoning behind the difference between long-run and short-run price elasticity of demand. ●

CROSS PRICE ELASTICITY OF DEMAND

In Chapter 3, we discussed the effect of a change in the price of one good on the demand for a related good. We defined substitutes and complements in terms of whether a reduction in the price of one caused a decrease or an increase, respectively, in the demand for the other. If the price of compact discs is held constant, the amount of CDs demanded (at any price) will certainly be influenced by the price of a close substitute such as audiocassettes. If the price of stereo speakers is held constant, the amount of stereo speakers demanded (at any price) will certainly be affected by changes in the price of stereo amplifiers.

What we now need to do is come up with a numerical measure of the price responsiveness of demand to the prices of related goods. This is called the **cross price elasticity of demand (E_xy),** which is defined as the percentage change in the demand for one good (a shift in the demand curve) divided by the percentage change in the price of the related good. In equation form, the cross price elasticity of demand for good X with good Y is

> **Cross price elasticity of demand (E_xy)**
> The percentage change in the demand for one good (holding its price constant) divided by the percentage change in the price of a related good.

$$E_{xy} = \frac{\text{percentage change in demand for good X}}{\text{percentage change in price of good Y}}$$

Alternatively, the cross price elasticity of demand for good Y with good X would use the percentage change in the demand for good Y as the numerator and the percentage change in the price of good X as the denominator.

When two goods are substitutes, the cross price elasticity of demand will be positive. For example, when the price of margarine goes up, the demand for butter will rise too as consumers shift away from the now relatively more expensive margarine to butter. A producer of margarine could benefit from a numerical estimate of the cross price elasticity of demand between butter and margarine. For example, if the price of butter went up by 10 percent and the margarine producer knew that the cross price elasticity of demand was 1, the margarine producer could estimate that the demand for margarine would also go up by 10 percent at any given price. Plans for increasing margarine production could then be made.

When two related goods are complements, the cross price elasticity of demand will be negative (and we will not disregard the minus sign). For example, when the price of stereo amplifiers goes up, the demand for stereo speakers will fall. This is because as prices of amplifiers increase, the quantity of amplifiers demanded will naturally decrease. Because amplifiers and stereo speakers are often used together, the demand for speakers is likely to fall. Any manufacturer of stereo speakers must take this into account in making production plans.

If goods are completely unrelated, their cross price elasticity of demand will be zero.

Exercise 20.3
Visit www.econtoday.com for more about cross price elasticity.

LIBRARIES VERSUS THE INTERNET

A significant portion of property taxes in the United States goes for public libraries. Some policymakers argue that there is no longer any reason to subsidize public libraries. Fewer and fewer people are using libraries. Their substitute is the Internet. Anyone can use a variety of popular search engines to find out just about anything electronically. Furthermore, encyclopedias and other information sources are available on inexpensive CD-ROMs. On-line information services are also relatively cheap. Indeed, as the price of such services has fallen, the demand for traditional library services has decreased. No one has yet calculated the exact cross price elasticity of demand for traditional library services, but we know that the decrease in usage of such libraries has been significant.

FOR CRITICAL ANALYSIS: Compare your cost of using the library with the cost of using on-line information services. ●

INCOME ELASTICITY OF DEMAND

In Chapter 3, we discussed the determinants of demand. One of those determinants was income. Briefly, we can apply our understanding of elasticity to the relationship between changes in income and changes in demand. We measure the responsiveness of quantity demanded to income changes by the **income elasticity of demand (E_i):**

$$E_i = \frac{\text{percentage change in demand}}{\text{percentage change in income}}$$

holding relative price constant.

Income elasticity of demand refers to a *horizontal shift* in the demand curve in response to changes in income, whereas price elasticity of demand refers to a movement *along* the curve in response to price changes. Thus income elasticity of demand is calculated at a given price, and price elasticity of demand is calculated at a given income.

A simple example will demonstrate how income elasticity of demand can be computed. Table 20-3 gives the relevant data. The product in question is compact discs. We assume that the price of compact discs remains constant relative to other prices. In period 1, six CDs per month are purchased. Income per month is $400. In period 2, monthly income increases to $600, and the quantity of CDs demanded per month is increased to eight. We can apply the following calculation:

$$E_i = \frac{(8 - 6)/6}{(600 - 400)/400} = \frac{1/3}{1/2} = \frac{2}{3} = .667$$

Hence measured income elasticity of demand for CDs for the individual represented in this example is .667. Note that this holds only for the move from six CDs to eight CDs purchased per month. If the situation were reversed, with income decreasing from $600 to

Income elasticity of demand (E_i)
The percentage change in demand for any good, holding its price constant, divided by the percentage change in income; the responsiveness of demand to changes in income, holding the good's relative price constant.

TABLE 20-3 **How Income Affects Quantity of CDs Demanded**	Period	Number of CDs Demanded per Month	Income per Month
	1	6	$400
	2	8	600

$400 per month and CDs purchased dropping from eight to six CDs per month, the calculation becomes

$$E_i = \frac{(6-8)/8}{(400-600)/600} = \frac{-2/8}{-1/3} = \frac{-1/4}{-1/3} = \frac{3}{4} = .75$$

In this case, the measured income elasticity of demand is equal to .75.

To get the same income elasticity of demand over the same range of values regardless of direction of change (increase or decrease), we can use the same formula that we used in computing the price elasticity of demand. When doing so, we have:

$$E_i = \frac{\text{change in quantity}}{\text{sum of quantities}/2} \div \frac{\text{change in income}}{\text{sum of incomes}/2}$$

You have just been introduced to three types of elasticities. Two of them—the price elasticity of demand (E_p), and income elasticity (E_i)—are the two most important factors in influencing the quantity demanded for most goods. Reasonably accurate estimates of these can go a long way toward making accurate forecasts of demand for goods or services.

EXAMPLE
Traffic Fatalities, Rising Incomes, and Alcohol Consumption

Economist Christopher Ruhm of the National Bureau of Economic Research discovered that the income elasticity of demand for alcoholic beverages is significant. He found that over a 14-year period, a $1,250 rise in real per capita personal income (expressed in 1996 dollars) increased alcoholic beverage consumption by 1.2 percent. There were also resulting increases in traffic fatalities.

FOR CRITICAL ANALYSIS: A common view is that people turn to drink in times of economic distress. What do the data tell us? •

CONCEPTS IN BRIEF

- Some determinants of price elasticity of demand are (1) the existence, number, and quality of substitutes, (2) the share of the total budget spent on the good in question, and (3) the length of time allowed for adjustment to a change in prices.

- Cross elasticity of demand measures one good's demand responsiveness to another's price changes. For substitutes, it is positive; for complements, it is negative.

- Income elasticity of demand tells you by what percentage demand will change for a particular percentage change in income.

ELASTICITY OF SUPPLY

Price elasticity of supply (E_s)
The responsiveness of the quantity supplied of a commodity to a change in its price; the percentage change in quantity supplied divided by the percentage change in price.

The **price elasticity of supply (E_s)** is defined similarly to the price elasticity of demand. Supply elasticities are generally positive; this is because at higher prices, larger quantities will generally be forthcoming from suppliers. The definition of the price elasticity of supply is as follows:

$$E_s = \frac{\text{percentage change in quantity supplied}}{\text{percentage change in price}}$$

Classifying Supply Elasticities

Just as with demand, there are different types of supply elasticities. They are similar in definition to the types of demand elasticities.

If a 1 percent increase in price elicits a greater than 1 percent increase in the quantity supplied, we say that at the particular price in question on the supply schedule, *supply is elastic*. The most extreme elastic supply is called **perfectly elastic supply**—the slightest reduction in price will cause quantity supplied to fall to zero.

If, conversely, a 1 percent increase in price elicits a less than 1 percent increase in the quantity supplied, we refer to that as an *inelastic supply*. The most extreme inelastic supply is called **perfectly inelastic supply**—no matter what the price, the quantity supplied remains the same.

If the percentage change in the quantity supplied is just equal to the percentage change in the price, we call this *unit-elastic supply*.

We show in Figure 20-4 two supply schedules, *S* and *S'*. You can tell at a glance, without reading the labels, which one is infinitely elastic and which one is perfectly inelastic. As you might expect, most supply schedules exhibit elasticities that are somewhere between zero and infinity.

Perfectly elastic supply
A supply characterized by a reduction in quantity supplied to zero when there is the slightest decrease in price.

Perfectly inelastic supply
A supply for which quantity supplied remains constant, no matter what happens to price.

Price Elasticity of Supply and Length of Time for Adjustment

We pointed out earlier that the longer the time period allowed for adjustment, the greater the price elasticity of demand. It turns out that the same proposition applies to supply. The longer the time for adjustment, the more elastic the supply curve. Consider why this is true:

1. The longer the time allowed for adjustment, the more firms are able to figure out ways to increase (or decrease) production in an industry.
2. The longer the time allowed for adjustment, the more resources can flow into (or out of) an industry through expansion (or contraction) of existing firms.

FIGURE 20-4

The Extremes in Supply Curves
Here we have drawn two extremes of supply schedules: *S* is a perfectly elastic supply curve; *S'* is a perfectly inelastic one. In the former, an unlimited quantity will be supplied at price P_1. In the latter, no matter what the price, the quantity supplied will be Q_1. An example of *S'* might be the supply curve for fresh fish on the morning the boats come in.

FIGURE 20-5

Short-Run and Long-Run Price Elasticity of Supply
Consider a situation in which the price is P_e and the quantity supplied is Q_e. In the immediate run, we hypothesize a vertical supply curve, S_1. With the price increase to P_1, therefore, there will be no change in the short run in quantity supplied; it will remain at Q_e. Given some time for adjustment, the supply curve will rotate to S_2. The new amount supplied will increase to Q_1. The long-run supply curve is shown by S_3. The amount supplied again increases to Q_2.

We therefore talk about short-run and long-run price elasticities of supply. The short run is defined as the time period during which full adjustment has not yet taken place. The long run is the time period during which firms have been able to adjust fully to the change in price.

Consider an increase in the price of housing. In the immediate run, when there is no time allowed for any adjustment, the amount of housing offered for rent or for sale is perfectly inelastic. However, as more time is allowed for adjustment, current owners of the housing stock can find ways to increase the amount of housing they will offer for rent from given buildings. The owner of a large house can decide, for example, to have two children move into one room so that a "new" extra bedroom can be rented out. This can also be done by the owner of a large house who decides to move into an apartment and rent each floor of the house to a separate family. Thus the quantity of housing supplied will increase. With more time, landlords will find it profitable to build new rental units.

We can show a whole set of supply curves similar to the ones we generated for demand. As Figure 20-5 shows, when nothing can be done in the immediate run, the supply curve is vertical, S_1. As more time is allowed for adjustment, the supply curve rotates to S_2 and then to S_3, becoming more elastic as it rotates.

INTERNATIONAL EXAMPLE
French Truffle Production Takes a Nosedive

Some of the best truffles in the world come from the seven *départements* (counties) in the middle of France that make up the Périgord region. Black truffles are often called "black diamonds" because they are so expensive and also because they have a faceted skin. Their official name is *Tuber melanosporum*. Ranging in size from that of a hazelnut to that of a baseball, truffles are sliced fine and used in cooking as a pungent addition to many refined dishes. Their prices range from $250 to $500 a pound wholesale to as much as $1,000 a pound retail. Yet things are not well in the French truffle industry. The Chinese have started exporting their version of truffles, considered inferior by the French

456 PART 6 • DIMENSIONS OF MICROECONOMICS

but popular nonetheless in the open market. The average price for French-grown truffles in 1996 dropped by 30 percent. Many French farmers, fed up with lower prices, are simply giving up on truffles. That same year, French production decreased by 25 percent. Hence the estimated short-run price elasticity of supply was .83. (Why?)

FOR CRITICAL ANALYSIS: There is a company in the United States that will sell you trees inoculated with the truffle organism so that you can "grow your own." How will this affect the price of truffles and thus French production? •

CONCEPTS IN BRIEF

- Price elasticity of supply is calculated by dividing the percentage change in quantity supplied by the percentage change in price.

- Usually, price elasticities of supply are positive—higher prices yield larger quantities supplied.

- Long-run supply curves are more elastic than short-run supply curves because the longer the time allowed, the more resources can flow into or out of an industry when price changes.

When New York transit authorities raised subway fares a few years ago, ridership dropped immediately. Is there a difference between short-run and long-run responses to price increases?

Mass Transit Riders Respond to Higher Prices

CONCEPTS APPLIED:
PRICE ELASTICITY OF DEMAND, LONG RUN, SHORT RUN, REAL PRICES

Visit www.econtoday.com for an Internet Activity that expands your understanding of these concepts.

Early in the 1990s, the New York City Transit Authority started to experience increased ridership. The subway system had previously suffered from a series of brutal killings and had become, according to some riders, filthy. Homeless people had taken over some seats, and the trains did not run on schedule. Roving gangs of youths terrorized riders. Graffiti was everywhere. The lighting was dim on most of the platforms, lending a sinister feeling to the waiting areas.

Ridership had started a long decline more than two decades earlier, in 1970. Then there were 1.3 billion riders a year. By 1991, ridership had dropped to 995 million. But from 1992 through 1995, subway ridership increased by 9.7 percent (with the biggest rise on weekends), due to improved service and better security, plus a growing local economy.

The Effects of a Fare Increase

In December 1995, the Transit Authority raised subway fares by 25 cents to $1.50. Ridership dropped, relative to the previous December by 4.3 percent. Let's figure out the *short-run* price elasticity of demand. The original price was $1.25, and the increase was 25 cents, or 20 percent. So using the simplest price elasticity of demand formula, the short-run price elasticity of demand for ridership on the New York subway system is

$$E_p = \frac{\text{percentage change in quantity demand}}{\text{percentage change in price}} = \frac{4.3\%}{20\%} = .215$$

Thus at the original price of $1.25, the short-run price elasticity of demand for subway ridership in New York City was inelastic.

What about the *long-run* price elasticity of demand? Historically, similar drop-offs in ridership have occurred virtually every time there has been a fare increase in the system. Most ridership drop-offs, however, were temporary. In other words, it appears that the long-run price elasticity of demand is even less than the short-run price elasticity of demand. There is a problem with this analysis, however. It ignores inflation. For the most part, fares on New York City's subway have simply kept up with inflation. That means that in the long run, the real price of using the subway in New York City has not risen by much at all, so accurately measuring the long-run elasticity of demand is not feasible.

The Bus System Is Affected Also

At the same time that subway prices rose, so did New York bus prices. An identical price increase led to an 11 percent reduction in bus riders compared to the previous December. The short-run price elasticity of demand for bus ridership turned out to be .55 (using the same simple price elasticity of demand formula).

We cannot accurately estimate the long-run price elasticity of demand without correcting all fare increases for inflation. Corrected for inflation, bus fares have not changed over the years.

457

FOR CRITICAL ANALYSIS

1. Assume that the 4.3 percent ridership decline for the subway system was derived using the last formula on page 442. Recalculate the short-run price elasticity of demand using the average-change formula for the price change.

2. Even though the real (inflation-corrected) price of subway fares has changed little, people react in the short run to a nominal increase in price. Why?

CHAPTER SUMMARY

1. Price elasticity of demand is a measure of the percentage change in quantity demanded relative to the percentage change in price, given income, the prices of other goods, and time. Because of the law of demand, price elasticity of demand is always negative.

2. We classify demand as *elastic* if a 1 percent change in price leads to a more than 1 percent change in quantity demanded, *unit-elastic* if it leads to exactly a 1 percent change in quantity demanded, and *inelastic* if it leads to less than a 1 percent change in quantity demanded.

3. When facing a perfectly elastic demand, the slightest increase in price leads to zero quantity demanded; when facing a perfectly inelastic demand, no matter what the price, the quantity demanded remains unchanged. Perfect inelasticity means absolutely no price responsiveness.

4. Price elasticity of demand falls as we move down a straight-line demand curve. It goes from infinity to zero. Elasticity and slope are not equivalent; for example, the slope of a straight-line curve is always constant, whereas elasticity changes as we move along a linear curve. A vertical demand curve is perfectly inelastic; a horizontal demand curve is perfectly elastic.

5. Price elasticity of demand depends on (a) the existence, number, and quality of substitutes, (b) the share of total budget accounted for by the commodity, and (c) the length of time allowed for adjustment to changes in price of the commodity.

6. Cross price elasticity of demand measures the responsiveness of the demand for one product, either a substitute or a complement, to changes in the price of another product. When the cross price elasticity of demand is negative, the two commodities under study are complements; when the cross price elasticity of demand is positive, they are substitutes.

7. Income elasticity of demand is given by the percentage change in demand divided by the percentage change in income, given relative price.

8. Price elasticity of supply is given by the percentage change in quantity supplied divided by the percentage change in price. The greater the time allowed for adjustment, the greater the price elasticity of supply.

DISCUSSION OF PREVIEW QUESTIONS

1. How is total revenue related to the price elasticity of demand?

Total revenue is defined as price times quantity demanded; because price changes lead to changes in quantity demanded, total revenue and elasticity are intimately related. If, over the price range in question, demand is inelastic, this means that buyers are relatively unresponsive to price changes. Intuitively, then, we know that if price rises and quantity demanded does not fall by much, total revenue will rise. Conversely, if price falls and quantity demanded rises only slightly, total revenue will fall. If, over the price range in question, demand is elastic, buyers will be quite responsive to price changes. We can tell intuitively that if price rises and quantity demanded falls greatly, total revenue will fall. Similarly, if price falls and quantity demanded rises greatly, total revenue will rise. Finally, if we are in the range of unit elasticity, given percentage changes in price will lead to equal percentage changes in quantity. Thus total revenue remains unaffected in the unit-elasticity range.

2. **What are the determinants of the price elasticity of demand?**

Three major determinants of price elasticity of demand are (a) the existence, number, and quality of substitutes, (b) the share of the total budget that the commodity represents, and (c) the length of time buyers have to react to price changes. Clearly, the more substitutes and the better they are, the greater will be the price elasticity of demand. Therefore, the price elasticity of demand rises as we consider the commodities "fruit," then "oranges," then "Sunkist oranges"; more and better substitutes exist for a specific brand of oranges than for the fruit group. Also, when a commodity takes up a small percentage of the consumer budget (other things being constant), we expect the price elasticity of demand to be lower, compared with items important to a budget. Presumably, buyers will have a greater incentive to shop around and seek substitutes for high-cost items than

for low-cost items. Finally, for a given percentage change in price, quantity responsiveness (and therefore elasticity) will increase with the time period allowed for adjustment. With the passage of time, buyers are better able to find and use substitutes.

3. **What is the income elasticity of demand?**

Income elasticity of demand refers to the responsiveness of buyers to income changes, given relative price. Technically, income elasticity of demand is defined as the percentage change in demand divided by the percentage change in income. The resulting measure is referred to as being income-elastic, unit-elastic, or income-inelastic, depending on whether or not it is greater than, equal to, or less than 1.

4. **What is the price elasticity of supply?**

Price elasticity of supply refers to the responsiveness of sellers to changes in price. Technically, price elasticity of supply is defined as the percentage change in quantity supplied divided by the percentage change in price. The resulting measure can be greater than, equal to, or less than the number 1—referred to as elastic, unit-elastic, and inelastic price, respectively. The longer the adjustment time, the greater the quantity responsiveness of sellers to given price changes (and hence the greater the price elasticity of supply).

PROBLEMS

(Answers to the odd-numbered problems appear at the back of the book.)

20-1. Use the following hypothetical demand schedule for tea to answer the questions.

Quantity Demanded per Week (ounces)	Price per Ounce	Elasticity
1,000	$ 5	
800	10	
600	15	
400	20	
200	25	

a. Using the demand schedule, determine the elasticity of demand for each price change. (Example: When price changes from $5 to $10, quantity demanded changes from 1,000 to 800 ounces, so the elasticity of demand, using average values, is $\frac{1}{3}$, or .33.)

b. The data given in the demand schedule would plot as a straight-line demand curve. Why is demand more elastic the higher the price?

20-2. Calculate the price elasticity of demand for the product in the table on the next page using average values for the prices and quantities in your formula. Over the price range in question, is this demand schedule inelastic, unit-elastic, or elastic? Is total revenue greater at the lower price or the higher price?

Price per Unit	Quantity Demanded
$4	22
6	18

20-3. Calculate the income elasticity of demand for the product in the following table, using average values for incomes and quantities.

Quantity of VCRs per Year	Per Capita Annual Group Income
1,000	$15,000
2,000	20,000

  a. Is the demand for this product income-elastic or income-inelastic?
  b. Would you consider this commodity a luxury or a necessity?

20-4. Can any demand curve possibly be perfectly inelastic ($E_p = 0$) regardless of price? Explain.

20-5. A new mobile home park charges nothing whatsoever for water used by its inhabitants. Consumption is 100,000 gallons per month. The decision is then made to charge according to how much each mobile home owner uses, at a rate of $10 per 1,000 gallons. Consumption declines to 50,000 gallons per month. What is the difficulty here in accurately estimating the price elasticity of the demand for water by these residents?

20-6. Which of the following cross elasticities of demand would you expect to be positive and which to be negative?

  a. Tennis balls and tennis racquets
  b. Tennis balls and golf balls
  c. Dental services and toothpaste
  d. Dental services and candy
  e. Liquor and ice cubes
  f. Liquor and cocaine

20-7. Suppose that the price of salt rises from 15 cents to 17 cents a pound. The quantity demanded decreases from 525 pounds to 475 pounds per month, and the quantity supplied increases from 525 pounds to 600 pounds per month. (Use averages in calculating elasticities.)

  a. Calculate the price elasticity of demand (E_p) for salt.
  b. Is the demand for salt price-elastic or price-inelastic?
  c. Calculate the elasticity of supply (E_s) for salt.
  d. Is the supply for salt price-elastic or price-inelastic?

20-8. Suppose that an automobile dealer cuts his car prices by 15 percent. He then finds that his car sales revenues have increased by 10 percent.

  a. What can you say about the price elasticity of demand for cars?
  b. What will happen to the dealer's total revenue?

20-9. For any given relative price, would you think that the demand for canal transportation was more or less elastic in 1840 than in 1880? How about the demand for Pony Express messengers before and after the transcontinental telegraph? The demand for rail transportation before and after the Model T Ford? The demand for transatlantic cable-laying equipment before and after communications satellites? The demand for slide rules before and after introduction of the pocket-sized calculator? Why?

COMPUTER-ASSISTED INSTRUCTION

Given a (linear) demand schedule, can you demonstrate that the price elasticity of demand falls as price falls? This problem requires specific calculations of the price elasticity of demand at various prices.

Complete problem and answer appear on disk.

CHAPTER 21

THE FINANCIAL ENVIRONMENT OF BUSINESS

You have probably heard about the stock market crash of 1929, which preceded the Great Depression. You may even have heard about the stock market crash of 1987, which did not precede anything of note in the overall economy. Then there was a stock market minicrash of 1997. Do these periodic stock market crashes tell you to avoid placing your accumulated savings in the stock market? You have to do *something* with your savings. Fortunately, your choices among alternative allocations are virtually unlimited. In addition to stocks, you can invest in corporate bonds, tax-free state and municipal bonds, taxable U.S. Treasury bonds, diamonds, precious metals, real estate, art—the list is long indeed. Before you determine what is the best choice for your savings, you need to know more about the financial environment of business.

PREVIEW QUESTIONS

1. What are the main organizational forms that firms take, and what are their advantages and disadvantages?
2. What are corporations' primary sources of financial capital?
3. What are the major differences between stocks and bonds?
4. Is there a world market for U.S. government securities?

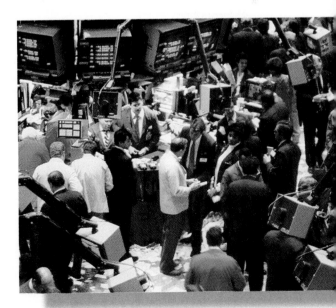

Did You Know That . . . every year in the United States, over 2 million new businesses are started? Although most of these involve individuals going into business for themselves, many entrepreneurs raise large sums of money from investors to get under way. These companies turn to financial markets to raise money. They seek **financial capital.**

You've been introduced to the term *physical capital* as one of the five factors of production. In that context, capital consists of the goods that do not directly satisfy human wants but are used to make other goods. *Financial capital* is the money that is made available to purchase capital goods.

Different types of businesses are able to raise financial capital in different ways. Your first step in understanding the firm's financial environment is therefore to understand the way firms are organized.

THE LEGAL ORGANIZATION OF FIRMS

We all know that firms differ from one another. Some sell frozen yogurt, others make automobiles; some advertise, some do not; some have annual sales of a few thousand dollars, others have sales in the billions of dollars. The list of differences is probably endless. Yet for all this diversity, the basic organization of *all* firms can be thought of in terms of a few simple structures, the most important of which are the proprietorship, the partnership, and the corporation.

Proprietorships

The most common form of business organization is the **proprietorship;** as shown in Table 21-1, more than 74 percent of all firms in the United States are proprietorships. Each is owned by a single individual who makes the business decisions, receives all the profits, and is legally responsible for all the debts of the firm. Although proprietorships are numerous, generally they are rather small businesses, with annual sales typically under $50,000. For this reason, even though there are more than 10 million proprietorships in the United States, they account for only about 6 percent of all business revenues.

Advantages of Proprietorships. Proprietorships offer several advantages as a form of business organization. First, they are *easy to form and to dissolve.* In the simplest case, all one must do to start a business is to start working; to dissolve the firm, one simply stops working. Even a more complicated proposition, such as starting a restaurant or a small retail shop, involves only meeting broadly defined health and zoning rules and the payment of a modest business license fee to the local government. To go out of business, one simply

Financial capital
Money used to purchase capital goods such as buildings and equipment.

Proprietorship
A business owned by one individual who makes the business decisions, receives all the profits, and is legally responsible for all the debts of the firm.

TABLE 21-1
Forms of Business Organization

Type of Firm	Percentage of U.S. Firms	Average Size (annual sales in dollars)	Percentage of Total Business Revenues
Proprietorship	74.5	47,766	5.7
Partnership	6.9	427,111	4.8
Corporation	18.6	2,979,571	89.5

Sources: U.S. Bureau of the Census; *1998 Statistical Abstract.*

locks the front door. The second advantage of the proprietorship is that *all decision-making power resides with the sole proprietor.* The owner decides what and how much will be offered for sale, what the hours of operation will be, and who will perform what tasks. No partners, shareholders, or board of directors need be consulted. The third advantage is that its *profit is taxed only once.* All profit is treated by law as the net income of the proprietor and as such is subject only to personal income taxation.

Disadvantages of Proprietorships. The most important disadvantage of a proprietorship is that the proprietor faces **unlimited liability** *for the debts of the firm.* This means that the owner is personally responsible for all of the firm's debts. Thus the owner's personal assets—home, car, savings account, coin collection—can be subject to seizure by the firm's creditors. The second disadvantage is that it has *limited ability to raise funds,* to expand the business or even simply to help it survive bad times. Because the success of a proprietorship depends so heavily on the good judgment and hard work of but one person—the owner—many lenders are reluctant to lend large sums to a proprietorship. Thus much of the financing of proprietorships often comes from the personal funds of the owner, which helps explain why proprietorships are usually small. The third disadvantage of proprietorships is that they normally *end with the death of the proprietor.* This, of course, creates added uncertainty for prospective lenders or employees, for a freak accident or sudden illness can turn a prosperous firm into a bittersweet memory.

Partnerships

The second important form of business organization is the **partnership.** As shown in Table 21-1, partnerships are far less numerous than proprietorships but tend to be significantly larger, with average sales about eight times greater. A partnership differs from a proprietorship chiefly in that there are two or more co-owners, called partners. They share the responsibilities of operating the firm and its profits, and they are *each* legally responsible for *all* of the debts incurred by the firm. In this sense, a partnership may be viewed as a proprietorship with more than one owner. The partners may contribute equal or different amounts of financial capital to the firm, may have widely different operating responsibilities, and may share the profits in any way they see fit. Not surprisingly, partnerships share many of the advantages and disadvantages of proprietorships.

Advantages of Partnerships. The first advantage of a partnership is that it is *easy to form.* In fact, it is almost as easy as forming a proprietorship, except that it requires two or more participants. Second, partnerships, like proprietorships, often help *reduce the costs of monitoring job performance.* This is particularly true when interpersonal skills are important for successful performance and in lines of business where, even after the fact, it is difficult to measure performance objectively. Thus attorneys and physicians often organize themselves as partnerships. Similarly, in professions such as these, a spectacular success may consist of a greatly reduced jail term for a client or greatly delayed death for a patient. In such circumstances, each partner has far more incentive to monitor his or her own work performance than he or she would as an employee, because the partner shares in the profits of the firm. A third advantage of the partnership is that it *permits more effective specialization* in occupations where, for legal or other reasons, the multiple talents required for success are unlikely to be uniform across individuals. Finally, partnerships share with proprietorships the advantage that the income of the partnership is treated as personal income and thus is subject only to personal taxation.

Unlimited liability
A legal concept whereby the personal assets of the owner of a firm can be seized to pay off the firm's debts.

Partnership
A business owned by two or more co-owners, or partners, who share the responsibilities and the profits of the firm and are individually liable for all of the debts of the partnership.

Exercise 21.1
Visit www.econtoday.com for more about business organizations.

Disadvantages of Partnerships. Not surprisingly, partnerships also have their disadvantages. First, the *partners each have unlimited liability*. Thus the personal assets of *each* partner are at risk due to debts incurred on behalf of the partnership by *any* of the partners. One partner's poor business judgment may impose substantial losses on all the other partners, a problem the sole proprietor need not worry about. Second, *decision making is generally more costly* in a partnership than in a proprietorship; there are more people involved in making decisions, and they may have differences of opinion that must be resolved before action is possible. Finally, *dissolution of the partnership is generally necessary* when a partner dies or voluntarily withdraws or when one or more partners wish to remove someone from the partnership. As with proprietorships, this creates potential uncertainty for creditors and employees.

Corporations

A **corporation** is a legal entity that may conduct business in its own name just as an individual does. The owners of a corporation are called *shareholders* because they own shares of the profits earned by the firm. By law, shareholders enjoy **limited liability,** which means that if the corporation incurs debts that it cannot pay, creditors have no recourse to the shareholders' personal property. As shown in Table 21-1, corporations are far less numerous than proprietorships, but because of their large size, they are responsible for over 90 percent of all business revenues in the United States. Many, such as Microsoft, IBM, AT&T, and Exxon, are so large that their annual sales are measured in billions of dollars and their names are household words.

Advantages of Corporations. The fact that corporations conduct most of the nation's business suggests that the corporation offers significant advantages as a form of business organization. Perhaps the greatest of these is that the owners of a corporation (the shareholders) enjoy *limited liability*. The liability of shareholders is limited to the value of their shares. The second advantage arises because the law treats it as a legal entity in and of itself; thus the corporation *continues to exist* even if one or more owners of the corporation cease to be owners. A third advantage of the corporation stems from the first two: Corporations are well positioned for *raising large sums of financial capital*. People are able to buy ownership shares or lend money to the corporation knowing that their liability is limited to the amount of money they invest and confident that the corporation's existence does not depend on the life of any one of the firm's owners.

Disadvantages of Corporations. The chief disadvantage of the corporation is the fact that corporate income is subject to *double taxation*. The profits of the corporation are subject first to corporate taxation. Then, if any of the after-tax profits are distributed to shareholders as **dividends,** such payments are treated as personal income to the shareholders and subject to personal taxation. The combined effect is that owners of corporations pay about twice as much in taxes on corporate income as they do on other forms of income.

A second disadvantage of the corporation is that corporations are potentially subject to problems associated with the *separation of ownership and control*. Specifically, it is commonplace for the owners (shareholders) of corporations to have little, if anything, to do with the actual management of the firm. Instead, these tasks are handled by professional managers who may have little or no ownership interest in the firm. The objective of the shareholders is presumably to maximize the value of their holdings. Unless their sole compensation is in the form of shares of stock in the corporation, however, the objective of the managers may differ from this. For example, managers may choose to have more luxurious

Corporation
A legal entity that may conduct business in its own name just as an individual does; the owners of a corporation, called shareholders, own shares of the firm's profits and enjoy the protection of limited liability.

Limited liability
A legal concept whereby the responsibility, or liability, of the owners of a corporation is limited to the value of the shares in the firm that they own.

Dividends
Portion of a corporation's profits paid to its owners (shareholders).

offices than are needed for the efficient operation of the firm. If there are costs to the shareholders in preventing such behavior, the result may be that the market value of the firm is not maximized.

In principle, such problems could arise with a partnership or a proprietorship if the owner or partners hired a manager to take care of day-to-day operations. Nevertheless, the separation of ownership and control is widely regarded as a more important problem for corporations; their attractiveness as a means of raising financial capital from many investors makes them subject to higher costs of agreement among owners with respect to penalties for managers who fail to maximize the value of the firm.

CONCEPTS IN BRIEF

- Proprietorships are the most common form of business organization, comprising more than 74 percent of all firms. Each is owned by a single individual who makes all business decisions, receives all the profits, and has unlimited liability for the firm's debts.

- Partnerships are much like proprietorships, except that two or more individuals, or partners, share the decisions and the profits of the firm. In addition, each partner has unlimited liability for the debts of the firms.

- Corporations are responsible for the largest share of business revenues. The owners, called shareholders, share in the firm's profits but normally have little responsibility for the firm's day-to-day operations. They enjoy limited liability for the debts of the firm.

METHODS OF CORPORATE FINANCING

When the Dutch East India Company was founded in 1602, it raised financial capital by selling shares of its expected future profits to investors. The investors thus became the owners of the company, and their ownership shares eventually became known as "shares of stock," or simply *stocks*. The company also issued notes of indebtedness, which involved borrowing money in return for interest on the funds, plus eventual repayment of the principal amount borrowed. In modern parlance, these notes of indebtedness are called *bonds*. As the company prospered over time, some of its revenues were used to pay lenders the interest and principal owed them; of the profits that remained, some were paid to shareholders in the form of dividends, and some were retained by the company for reinvestment in further enterprises. The methods of financing used by the Dutch East India Company nearly four centuries ago—stocks, bonds, and reinvestment—remain the principal methods of financing for today's corporations.

Share of stock

A legal claim to a share of a corporation's future profits; if it is *common stock*, it incorporates certain voting rights regarding major policy decisions of the corporation; if it is *preferred stock*, its owners are accorded preferential treatment in the payment of dividends.

A **share of stock** in a corporation is simply a legal claim to a share of the corporation's future profits. If there are 100,000 shares of stock in a company and you own 1,000 of them, you own the right to 1 percent of that company's future profits. If the stock you own is *common stock*, you also have the right to vote on major policy decisions affecting the company, such as the selection of the corporation's board of directors. Your 1,000 shares would entitle you to cast 1 percent of the votes on such issues. If the stock you own is *preferred stock*, you also own a share of the future profits of the corporation, but you do *not* have regular voting rights. You do, however, get something in return for giving up your voting rights: preferential treatment in the payment of dividends. Specifically, the owners of preferred stock generally must receive at least a certain amount of dividends in each period before the owners of common stock can receive *any* dividends.

A **bond** is a legal claim against a firm, entitling the owner of the bond to receive a fixed annual *coupon* payment, plus a lump-sum payment at the maturity date of the bond.[1] Bonds are issued in return for funds lent to the firm; the coupon payments represent interest on the amount borrowed by the firm, and the lump-sum payment at maturity of the bond generally equals the amount originally borrowed by the firm. Bonds are *not* claims to the future profits of the firm; legally, bondholders are to be paid whether the firm prospers or not. To help ensure this, bondholders generally must receive their coupon payments each year, and any principal that is due, before *any* shareholders can receive dividend payments.

You can see a comparison of stocks and bonds in Table 21-2.

Reinvestment takes place when the firm uses some of its profits to purchase new capital equipment rather than paying the money out as dividends to shareholders. Although sales of stock are an important source of financing for new firms, reinvestment and borrowing are the principal means of financing for existing firms. Indeed, reinvestment by established firms is such an important source of financing that it dominates the other two sources of corporate finance, amounting to roughly 75 percent of new financial capital for corporations in recent years. Also, small businesses, which are the source of much current growth, usually cannot rely on the stock market to raise investment funds.

Primary and Secondary Financial Markets

Both businesses and investors engage in financial transactions in primary and secondary financial markets.

Primary Markets. If you have ever heard of a "new issue," you are familiar with one aspect of a primary securities market. A **primary market** is one in which newly issued

Bond
A legal claim against a firm, usually entitling the owner of the bond to receive a fixed annual coupon payment, plus a lump-sum payment at the bond's maturity date. Bonds are issued in return for funds lent to the firm.

Reinvestment
Profits (or depreciation reserves) used to purchase new capital equipment.

Primary market
A financial market in which newly issued securities are bought and sold.

TABLE 21-2		
The Difference Between Stocks and Bonds	Stocks	Bonds
	1. Stocks represent ownership.	1. Bonds represent debt.
	2. Common stocks do not have a fixed dividend rate.	2. Interest on bonds must always be paid, whether or not any profit is earned.
	3. Stockholders can elect a board of directors, which controls the corporation.	3. Bondholders usually have no voice in or control over management of the corporation.
	4. Stocks do not have a maturity date; the corporation does not usually repay the stockholder.	4. Bonds have a maturity date on which the bondholder is to be repaid the face value of the bond.
	5. All corporations issue or offer to sell stocks. This is the usual definition of a corporation.	5. Corporations need not issue bonds.
	6. Stockholders have a claim against the property and income of a corporation after all creditors' claims have been met.	6. Bondholders have a claim against the property and income of a corporation that must be met before the claims of stockholders.

---

[1]Coupon payments on bonds get their name from the fact that bonds once had coupons attached to them when they were issued. Each year, the owner would clip a coupon off the bond and send it to the issuing firm in return for that year's interest on the bond.

securities are bought and sold. A company that is raising money for the first time goes to the primary market, usually to sell stocks. Corporations can also sell newly issued bonds in primary securities markets. Sometimes you may read about large corporations, such as General Motors, issuing new bonds.

Secondary market
A financial market in which previously issued securities are bought and sold.

Secondary Markets. A **secondary market** is one in which existing securities are exchanged. When you read about what happened on the stock market today, that is information about a secondary market. Secondary markets are important to primary markets because they make stocks and bonds sold in primary markets more liquid. Most of the activities of stockbrokers involve dealings for investors in secondary market transactions. The stockbroker is an intermediary (middleman) who brings together buyers and sellers of various stocks and bonds. In return for the broker's services, which include executing market exchanges for buyers and sellers, the broker receives a commission, or brokerage fee.

THE MARKETS FOR STOCKS AND BONDS

Economists often refer to the "market for wheat" or the "market for labor." For stocks and bonds, there really are markets—centralized, physical locations where exchange takes place. By far the largest and most prestigious of these are the New York Stock Exchange (NYSE) and the New York Bond Exchange, both located in New York City. Numerous other stock and bond markets, or exchanges, are located throughout the United States and in various financial capitals of the world, such as London and Tokyo. Although the exact process by which exchanges are conducted in these markets varies slightly from one to another, the process used on the NYSE is representative of the principles involved.[2]

More than 2,500 stocks are traded on the NYSE, which is sometimes called the "Big Board." Leading brokerage firms—about 600 of them—own seats on the NYSE. These seats, which are actually rights to buy and sell stocks on the floor of the Big Board, are themselves regularly exchanged. In recent years, their value has fluctuated between $350,000 and $1 million each. These prices reflect the fact that stock trades on the NYSE are ultimately handled by the firms owning these seats, and the firms earn commissions on each trade. As trading volume rises, as it did during the 1980s, the value of the seats rises.

The Theory of Efficient Markets

At any point in time, there are tens of thousands, even millions of persons looking for any bit of information that will enable them to forecast correctly the future prices of stocks. Responding to any information that seems useful, these people try to buy low and sell high. The result is that all publicly available information that might be used to forecast stock prices gets taken into account by those with access to the information and the knowledge and ability to learn from it, leaving no

---

[2]A number of stocks and bonds are traded in so-called over-the-counter (OTC) markets, which, although not physically centralized, otherwise operate in much the same way as the NYSE and so are not treated separately in this text.

forecastable profit opportunities. And because so many people are involved in this process, it occurs quite swiftly. Indeed, there is some evidence that *all* information entering the market is fully incorporated into stock prices within less than a minute of its arrival. One view of the stock market is that most public information you will obtain will prove to have little value.

The result of this process is that stock prices tend to follow a *random walk,* which is to say that the best forecast of tomorrow's price is today's price. This is called the **random walk theory.** Although large values of the random component of stock price changes are less likely than small values, nothing else about the magnitude or direction of a stock price change can be predicted. Indeed, the random component of stock prices exhibits behavior much like what would occur if you rolled two dice and subtracted 7 from the resulting score. On average, the dice will show a total of 7, so after you subtract 7, the average result will be zero. It is true that rolling a 12 or a 2 (resulting in a net score of +5 or −5) is less likely than rolling an 8 or a 6 (yielding a net score of +1 or −1). Nevertheless, positive and negative net scores are equally likely, and the expected net score is zero.

Random walk theory
The theory that there are no predictable trends in security prices that can be used to "get rich quick."

Inside Information

Isn't there any way to "beat the market"? The answer is yes—but normally only if you have **inside information** that is not available to the public. Suppose that your best friend is in charge of new product development at the country's largest software firm, Microsoft Corporation. Your friend tells you that the company's smartest programmer has just come up with major new software that millions of computer users will want to buy. No one but your friend and the programmer—and now you—is aware of this. You could indeed make money using this information by purchasing shares of Microsoft and then selling them (at a higher price) as soon as the new product is publicly announced. There is one problem: Stock trading based on inside information such as this is illegal, punishable by substantial fines and even imprisonment. So unless you happen to have a stronger than average desire for a long vacation in a federal prison, you might be better off investing in Microsoft after the new program is publicly announced.

Inside information
Information that is not available to the general public about what is happening in a corporation.

EXAMPLE
How to Read the Financial Press: Stock Prices

Table 21-3, reproduced from the *Wall Street Journal,* contains information about the stocks of four companies. Across the top of the financial page are a series of column headings. Under the heading "Stock" we find the name of the company—in the second row, for example, is Eastman Kodak, the photographic materials firm. The two columns to the left of the company's name show the highest and lowest prices at which shares of that company's stock traded during the past 52 weeks. These prices are typically quoted in dollars and eighths of dollars.

Immediately to the right of the company's name you will find the company's *symbol* on the NYSE. This symbol (omitted by some newspapers) is simply the unique identifier used by the exchange when it reports information about the stock. For example, the designation EK is used by the exchange as the unique identifier for the firm Eastman Kodak.

The last four columns of information for each firm summarize the behavior of the firm's stock price on the latest trading day. On this particular day, the highest price at which Kodak stock traded was $59.00, the lowest price was $56.5625, and the last (or closing) price at which it traded was $58.00 per share. The *net change* in the price of Kodak stock

TABLE 21-3
Reading Stock Quotes

52 Weeks Hi	Lo	Stock	Sym	Div	Yld %	PE	Vol 100s	Hi	Lo	Close	Net Chg
$65\frac{3}{8}$	$50\frac{3}{4}$	Eastman Chm	EMN	1.76	3.0	14	2348	$58\frac{13}{16}$	$57\frac{1}{4}$	$57\frac{3}{4}$	$-\frac{3}{4}$
$94\frac{3}{4}$	$53\frac{5}{16}$	EKodak	EK	1.76	3.0	21	22451	59	$56\frac{9}{16}$	58	...
$103\frac{3}{8}$	$66\frac{3}{4}$	Eaton	ETN	1.76	2.0	20	3124	$90\frac{11}{16}$	$89\frac{1}{16}$	$90\frac{1}{16}$	$-1\frac{1}{4}$
$37\frac{13}{16}$	$20\frac{7}{8}$	Eaton/Vance	EV	48f	1.3	17	271	$36\frac{1}{16}$	$35\frac{7}{8}$	$35\frac{15}{16}$	$-\frac{1}{16}$

The summary of stock market information presented on the financial pages of many newspapers reveals the following:

52 Weeks Hi/Lo: The highest and lowest prices, in dollars per share, of the stock during the previous 52 weeks.
Stock: The name of the company (frequently abbreviated).
Sym: Highly abbreviated name of the company, as it appears on the stock exchange ticker tape.
Div: Dividend paid, in dollars per share.
Yld %: Yield in percent per year; the dividend divided by the price of the stock.
PE: Price-earnings ratio; the price of the stock divided by the earnings (profits) per share of the company.
Vol 100s: Number of shares traded during the day, in hundreds of shares.
Hi: Highest price at which the stock traded that day.
Lo: Lowest price at which the stock traded that day.
Close: Last price at which the stock traded that day.
Net Chg: Net change in the stock's price from the previous day's closing price.

was zero, which means that it *closed* the day at a price per share equal to the price at which it closed the day before.

The dividend column, headed "Div," shows the annual dividend (in dollars and cents) that the company has paid over the preceding year on each share of its stock. In Kodak's case, this amounts to $1.76 a share. If the dividend is divided by the closing price of the stock ($1.76 ÷ $58.00), the result is 3.0 percent, which is shown in the yield percentage ("Yld %") column for Kodak. In a sense, the company is paying interest on the stock at a rate of about 3.0 percent. At first glance, this seems like an absurdly low amount; after all, at the time this issue of the *Wall Street Journal* was printed, ordinary checking accounts were paying about 4.0 percent. The reason people tolerate this seemingly low yield on Kodak (or any other stock) is that they expect that the price of the stock will rise over time, yielding capital gains.

The column heading "PE" stands for *price-earnings ratio.* To obtain the entries for this column, the firm's total earnings (profits) for the year are divided by the number of the firm's shares in existence to give the earnings per share. When the price of the stock is divided by the earnings per share, the result is the price-earnings ratio.

The column to the right of the PE ratio shows the total *volume* of the shares of the stock traded that day, measured in hundreds of shares.

FOR CRITICAL ANALYSIS: Is there necessarily any relationship between the net change in a stock's price and how many shares have been sold on a particular day? ●

CONCEPTS IN BRIEF

• Many economists believe that asset markets, especially the stock market, are efficient, meaning that one cannot make a higher than normal rate of return without having inside information (information that the general public does not possess).

• Stock prices normally follow a random walk, meaning that you cannot predict changes in future stock prices based on information about stock price behavior in the past.

Exercise 21.2
Visit www.econtoday.com for more about the stock market.

GLOBAL CAPITAL MARKETS

Financial institutions in the United States are tied to the rest of the world via their lending capacities. In addition, integration of all financial markets is increasing. Indeed, recent changes in world finance have been nothing short of remarkable. Distinctions among financial institutions and between financial institutions and nonfinancial institutions have blurred. As the legal barriers that have preserved such distinctions are dismantled, multinational corporations offering a wide array of financial services are becoming dominant worldwide.

Globalizing Financial Markets

The globalization of financial markets is not entirely new. U.S. banks developed worldwide branch networks in the 1960s and 1970s for loans, check clearing, and foreign exchange (currency) trading. Also in the 1970s, firms dealing in U.S. securities (stocks and bonds) expanded their operations in London (on the Eurobond market) and then into other financial centers, including Tokyo. Similarly, foreign firms invaded U.S. shores: first the banks, then securities firms. The "big four" Japanese securities firms now have offices in New York and London.

Money and capital markets today are truly international. Markets for U.S. government securities, interbank lending and borrowing, foreign exchange trading, and common stocks are now trading continuously, in vast quantities, around the clock and around the world.

The World Market for U.S. Government Debt. Trading for U.S. government securities has been described as "the world's fastest-growing 24-hour market." This market was made possible by (1) sophisticated communications and computer technology, (2) deregulation of financial markets in foreign countries to permit such trading, (3) U.S. legislation in 1984 to enable foreign investors to buy U.S. government securities tax-free, and (4) huge annual U.S. government budget deficits, which have poured a steady stream of tradable debt into the world markets.

Other Globalized Markets. Foreign exchange—the buying and selling of foreign currencies—became a 24-hour, worldwide market in the 1970s. Instruments tied to government bonds, foreign exchange, stock market indexes, and commodities (grains, metals, oil) are now traded increasingly in financial futures markets in all the world's major centers of commerce. Most financial firms are coming to the conclusion that to survive as a force in any one of the world's leading financial markets, a firm must have a significant presence in all of them. It is predicted that by the turn of the twenty-first century, between 30 and 50 financial institutions will be at the centers of world finance—New York, London, Tokyo, and Frankfurt—and they will be competing in all those markets to do business with the world's major corporations and portfolio managers. Today, major corporate borrowers throughout the world can choose to borrow from a wide variety of lenders, also located throughout the world. Borrowing on the international capital markets was estimated at $850 billion for the year 1996 for the 24 leading industrialized nations, according to the Organization for Economic Cooperation and Development (OECD).

CONCEPTS IN BRIEF

- Financial markets throughout the world have become increasingly integrated, leading to a global financial market. Interbank lending and borrowing, foreign exchange trading, and common stock sales now occur virtually 24 hours a day throughout the world.
- Many U.S. government or government-guaranteed securities trade 24 hours a day.

PROBLEMS IN CORPORATE GOVERNANCE

Many corporations issue stock to raise financial capital that they will use to fund expansion or modernization. The decision to raise capital in this way is ordinarily made not by the owners of the corporation—the holders of its stock—but by the company's managers. This **separation of ownership and control** in corporations leads to incentive problems. Managers may not act in the best interest of shareholders. Further incentive problems arise when corporations borrow money in financial markets. These corporate governance problems have to do with information that is not the same for everyone.

Asymmetric Information: The Perils of Adverse Selection and Moral Hazard

If you invest in a corporation, you give purchasing power to the managers of that corporation. Those managers have much more information about what is happening to the corporation and its future than you do. The inequality of information between the two parties is called **asymmetric information.** If asymmetric information exists before a transaction takes place, we have a circumstance of **adverse selection.** In financial markets, adverse selection occurs because borrowers who are the worst credit risks (and thus likely to yield the most adverse outcomes) are the ones most likely to seek, and perhaps to receive, loans.

Consider two firms seeking to borrow funds by selling bonds. Suppose that one of the firms, the Dynamic Corporation, is pursuing a project with a small chance of yielding large profits and a large chance of bankruptcy. The other firm, the Reliable Company, intends to invest in a project that is guaranteed to yield the competitive rate of return, thereby ensuring repayment of its debts. Because Dynamic knows the chance is high that it will go bankrupt and never have to pay its debts, it can offer a high interest rate on the bonds it issues. Unless prospective bond purchasers can distinguish perfectly between the two firms' projects, they will select the high-yielding bonds offered by Dynamic and refuse to buy the low-yielding bonds offered by Reliable. Firms like Reliable will be unable to get funding, yet lenders will lose money on firms like Dynamic. Adverse selection thus makes investors less likely to lend to anyone and more inclined to charge higher interest rates when they do lend.

Moral hazard occurs as a result of asymmetric information *after* a transaction occurs. To continue with our example of the Dynamic Corporation, once the firm has sold the bonds, it must choose among alternative strategies in executing its project. Lenders face the hazard that Dynamic may choose strategies contrary to the lenders' well-being and thus immoral from their perspective. Because bondholders are entitled to a fixed amount regardless of the firm's profits, Dynamic has an incentive to select strategies offering a small chance of high profits, thereby enabling the owners to keep the largest amount after paying

Separation of ownership and control

The situation that exists in corporations in which the owners (shareholders) are not the people who control the operation of the corporation (managers). The goals of these two groups are often different.

Asymmetric information

Information possessed by one side of a transaction but not the other. The side with more information will be at an advantage.

Adverse selection

The circumstance that arises in financial markets when borrowers who are the worst credit risks are the ones most likely to seek loans.

Moral hazard

A problem that occurs because of asymmetric information *after* a transaction occurs. In financial markets, a person to whom money has been lent may indulge in more risky behavior, thereby increasing the probability of default on the debt.

bondholders. Such strategies are also the riskiest—ones that make it more likely that lenders will not be repaid—so the presence of moral hazard makes lenders less likely to lend to anyone and more inclined to charge higher interest rates when they do lend.

EXAMPLE
Explaining the Success of at Least One Multibillionaire

Multibillionaires are special, and Warren Buffett is one of them. He initially invested $100 and ended up with Berkshire Hathaway, a company with businesses in insurance, candy manufacturing, and newspaper publishing, among others. The company's market value is over $20 billion, though Buffett doesn't own it all. His technique has been an attempt to eliminate the asymmetry problem that is associated with the separation of ownership and control. Buffett invests large sums of money only in businesses that he understands thoroughly. He pays special attention to what management does with excess cash that cannot be properly reinvested inside the corporation. For that is where managers can easily divert funds in ways that do not serve shareholders' best interests. One way of obtaining more information than a typical investor in the companies in which he invests, Buffett has discovered, is becoming a member of the board of directors and befriending the chief executive. He has done so in every enterprise in which he has invested heavily. As a result, he has profited handsomely from his ability to reduce information costs.

FOR CRITICAL ANALYSIS: Is it possible for the average investor to avoid the asymmetric information problem when making an investment decision? •

The Principal-Agent Problem

A type of moral hazard problem that occurs within firms is called the **principal-agent problem.** The shareholders who own a firm are referred to as *principals,* and the managers who operate the firm are the *agents* of the owners. When the managers do not own all of a firm (as is usually the case), a separation of ownership and control exists, and if the stockholders have less information about the firm's opportunities and risks than the managers do (as is also usually the case), the managers may act in their own self-interests rather than in the interests of the shareholders.

> **Principal-agent problem**
> The conflict of interest that occurs when agents—managers of firms—pursue their own objectives to the detriment of the goals of the firms' principals, or owners.

Consider, for example, the choice between two investment projects, one of which involves an enormous amount of work but also promises high profits, while the other requires little effort and promises small returns. Because the managers must do all the work while the shareholders receive all the profits, the managers' incentives are different from those of the shareholders. In this case, the presence of moral hazard will induce the managers to choose the "good life," the easy but low-yielding project—an outcome that fails to maximize the economic value of the firm.

Solving Principal-Agent and Moral Hazard Problems

The dangers associated with asymmetric information are well known to participants in financial markets, who regularly undertake vigorous steps to minimize its costly conse-

Collateral
An asset pledged to guarantee the repayment of a loan.

Incentive-compatible contract
A loan contract under which a significant amount of the borrower's assets are at risk, providing an incentive for the borrower to look after the lender's interests.

quences. For example, research companies such as Standard & Poor's gather financial data and other information about corporations and sell the information to their subscribers. When even this is insufficient to eliminate the dangers of adverse selection, lenders often require that borrowers post **collateral**—assets that the borrower will forfeit in the event that repayment of a debt is not made. A variant of this strategy, designed to reduce moral hazard problems, is called the **incentive-compatible contract:** Lenders make sure that borrowers have a large amount of their own assets at risk so that the incentives of the borrower are compatible with the interests of the lender. Although measures such as these cannot eliminate the losses caused by asymmetric information, they reduce them below what would otherwise be the case.

EXAMPLE
Making Executives Own a Share of the Company

One way to minimize the principal-agent problem is to require that executives own stock in the companies for which they work. An increasing number of corporations are requiring directors and top management to own shares of stock. By the mid-1990s, almost 20 percent of companies surveyed by *Fortune* prepared "guidelines" specifying the amount of stock that executives must own. These include Black & Decker, Union Pacific, and US West. Usually executives are told that they must buy over a period of five years an amount ranging from one to four times their annual salaries.

Do shareholders benefit from top management's owning "a piece of the rock"? One study indicated that companies in which the chief executives had significant ownership experienced a 4 percent higher annual rate of return over a five-year period than similar companies that did not require executives to own stock.

FOR CRITICAL ANALYSIS: Is there any way you can use this information to determine in which corporations you should invest? ●

CONCEPTS IN BRIEF

- When two parties to a transaction have different amounts of information, we call this asymmetric information. Whenever asymmetric information occurs before a transaction takes place, it can result in adverse selection. Adverse selection causes borrowers who are the worst credit risks to be the ones most likely to seek loans.

- When asymmetric information occurs after a transaction, this can cause moral hazard. Lenders often face the hazard that borrowers will choose more risky actions after borrowers have taken out loans.

- The separation of ownership and control in today's large corporations can give rise to the principal-agent problem, whereby the agents (managers) may have interests that differ from those of the principals (shareholders).

- Several methods exist for solving the principal-agent and moral hazard problems. They include requiring lenders to post collateral and devising incentive-compatible contracts in which borrowers have a large amount of their own assets at risk.

The stock market crashed in 1929 and again in 1987, when it lost more than 20 percent of its value in one day. Does that mean investing in stocks is too risky?

The Truth About Investing in Stocks

CONCEPTS APPLIED:

LONG RUN, SHORT RUN, INFLATION, STOCKS VERSUS BONDS, EQUITY VERSUS DEBT, RISK-INVESTED YIELDS

Visit www.econtoday.com for an Internet Activity that expands your understanding of these concepts.

The boom market during most of the 1990s seemed to indicate that stocks were the way to go. After all, anybody who invested in a broad range of stocks—through a mutual fund, for example—would have seen his or her wealth increase rather dramatically. As single years go, nothing beats the percentage rate of return that investors in the stock market obtained in 1933. During that one-year period, stocks increased in value by 54 percent! But the market has done well at other times, too. For the five-year period from 1950 to 1954, for example, the annual compounded rate of return for holding stocks was 24 percent. A $10,000 stock market investment in 1950 would have been worth almost $30,000 at the end of 1954. Consider an even longer period, 1942 to 1961. A $10,000 investment during that period would have grown to $220,542.

Sounds great, doesn't it? There is one problem with such analyses. It has to do with selectively choosing the time period. Consider that if you had invested $1,000 in the stock market at the beginning of 1931, by January 1, 1932, that $1,000 would have been worth only $570. If you had started your investing in 1929 with $10,000, twenty years later, at the end of 1948, you would have had only $18,440.

Although the 84 percent rise in the value of your savings in the last example might sound good, it brings us to two serious long-run problems. The first has to do with inflation; the other has to do with taxes.

Correcting for Inflation and Taxes

Inflation is important because it reduces the purchasing power of your savings. You need to know how much you can purchase in real terms when making historical comparisons. Figure 21-1 contains several curves. The top curve shows the long-run average total return that is *inflation-*

adjusted from 1801 until 1998. This long-run "real" rate of return turns out to be an annualized corrected rate of 6.6 percent—not bad. But when you take taxes into account, assuming that you are in the highest marginal tax bracket starting in 1913 when income taxes were introduced, your after-tax real inflation-adjusted annualized rate of return drops to 2.4 percent. So you can beat inflation by investing in the stock market in the long run, but taxes tend to beat you down.

The Demographics of U.S. Stock Market Investors

Who owns stocks in the United States? As it turns out, a considerable number of Americans own stocks, either directly or indirectly through pension plans. More than one household in four owns stocks and mutual funds shares directly. An even greater number own stocks indirectly through their pension plans. Whereas in 1962 the wealthiest 2.5 percent of U.S. households owned 75 percent of publicly traded stocks, today the wealthiest 2 percent of U.S. households hold less than 20 percent of publicly traded stocks. The median household income of shareholders of publicly traded stock is below $60,000.

What About Bonds?

In the investing world, risk and rate of return are positively correlated. Because there is so much variation in what happens to stock prices, you would expect that the rate of return for investing in the stock market has to be higher than in bonds, which are more stable. Look at the three curves in Figure 21-1 that show corporate and Treasury bonds, inflation-adjusted but before taxes; municipal bonds, inflation-adjusted (they are nontaxable); and corporate and Treasury bonds, inflation-adjusted after taxes.

FIGURE 21-1

Stocks Are the Best Investment—but Are They Really So Good?
Stocks are clearly a better investment than any type of bonds, at least in the long run. Here you see what happened to $1 invested at the beginning of the 1800s, depending on whether it was invested in stocks or in taxable or nontaxable bonds. Almost 200 years later, that $1 would have compounded to about $530,000 (corrected for inflation) if left in the stock market, but after taking account of taxes, it would have only been about $24,000. That's still better than nontaxable bonds ($415) or taxable bonds (after taxes only $75).

Sources: Jeremy J. Siegel and author's estimates

After accounting for inflation, $1 invested in 1801 in municipal bonds would have yielded after inflation about $415 in 1998. Corporate and Treasury bonds after inflation and after taxes would have yielded only about $75. The graph shows you that in the long run, stocks are better than bonds. Moreover, for any 30-year period from 1801 to the present, stocks have outperformed bonds. And since 1926, for any 20-year holding period, stocks have outperformed bonds 98 percent of the time.

Art Is Up Too

Recent art auctions have yielded record sums for paintings by well-known artists, leading some commentators to argue that they are superior assets in which to invest. Economic theory nonetheless implies that total returns, adjusted for risk, should be about the same over the long run for all investments. Art objects include a psychic or consumption benefit from owning and viewing them. Therefore, one should expect that the real (financial) rate of return for art objects will be lower than the rate of return on financial assets.

According to economists Bruno Frey and Werner Pommerehne, this is exactly the case. They examined the auction prices of quality paintings by over 300 of the world's best-known painters for a 350-year period. They found that the real rate of return on paintings was 1.5 percent per year. During that same time period, the real rate of return on government bonds was 3 percent per year, or double the financial return on paintings. In the period since 1950, the real rate of return on paintings has increased slightly to 1.7 percent a year, but the real rate of return on bonds was higher still, at about 2.5 percent per year.

FOR CRITICAL ANALYSIS

1. The government provides for numerous types of savings programs that allow individuals to accumulate assets tax-free, only to pay taxes when they take out funds after retirement. How do such plans affect our analysis with respect to stock market returns?
2. Our analysis notwithstanding, are there some individuals who should invest mainly in bonds? Why?

CHAPTER SUMMARY

1. Proprietorships are the most common form of business organization, comprising more than 74 percent of all firms. Each is owned by a single individual who makes all business decisions, receives all the profits, and has unlimited liability for the firm's debts.

2. Partnerships are much like proprietorships, except that two or more individuals, or partners, share the decisions and the profits of the firm; each partner has unlimited liability for the debts of the firm.

3. Corporations are responsible for the largest share of business revenues. The owners, called shareholders, share in the firm's profits but normally have little responsibility for the firm's day-to-day operations. Owners of corporations enjoy limited liability for the debts of the firm.

4. When two parties to a transaction have different amounts of information, we call this asymmetric information. Whenever asymmetric information occurs before a transaction takes place, it can result in adverse selection. Adverse selection causes borrowers who are the worst credit risks to be the ones most likely to seek loans.

5. When asymmetric information occurs after a transaction, this can cause moral hazard. Lenders often face the hazard that borrowers will choose more risky actions after borrowers have taken out loans.

6. The separation of ownership and control in today's large corporation has led to the principal-agent problem, whereby the agents (managers) may have interests that differ from those of the principals (shareholders).

7. Several methods exist for solving the principal-agent and moral hazard problems, including requiring lenders to post collateral and devising incentive-compatible contracts in which borrowers have a large amount of their own assets at risk.

DISCUSSION OF PREVIEW QUESTIONS

1. **What are the main organizational forms that firms take, and what are their advantages and disadvantages?**

The primary organizational forms businesses take are the proprietorship, the partnership, and the corporation. The proprietorship is owned by a single person, the proprietor, who makes the business decisions, is entitled to all the profits, and is subject to unlimited liability—that is, is personally responsible for all debts incurred by the firm. The partnership differs from the proprietorship chiefly in that there are two or more owners, called partners. They share the responsibility for decision making, share the firm's profits, and individually bear unlimited liability for the firm's debts. The net income, or profits, of both proprietorships and partnerships is subject only to personal income taxes. Both types of firms legally cease to exist when the proprietor or a partner gives up ownership or dies. The corporation differs from proprietorships and partnerships in three important dimensions. Owners of corporations enjoy limited liability; that is, their responsibility for the debts of the corporation is limited to the value of their ownership shares. In addition, the income from corporations is subject to double taxation—corporate taxation when income is earned by the corporation and personal taxation when after-tax profits are paid as dividends to the owners. Finally, corporations do not legally cease to exist due to a change of ownership or the death of an owner.

2. **What are corporations' primary sources of financial capital?**

The main sources of financial capital for corporations are stocks, bonds, and reinvestment of profits. Stocks are ownership shares, promising a share of profits, sold to investors. Common stocks also embody voting rights regarding the major decisions of the firm; preferred stocks typically have no voting rights but enjoy priority status in the payment of dividends. Bonds are notes of indebtedness, issued in return for the loan of money. They typically promise to pay interest in the form of annual coupon payments, plus repayment of the original principal amount upon maturity. Bondholders are generally promised payment before any payment of dividends to shareholders, and for this reason bonds are less risky than stocks. Reinvestment involves the purchase of assets by the firm, using retained profits or depreciation reserves it has set aside for this purpose. No new stocks or bonds are issued in the course of reinvestment, although its value is fully reflected in the price of existing shares of stock.

3. What are the major differences between stocks and bonds?

Stocks represent ownership in a corporation. They are called equity capital. Bonds represent the debt of a corporation. They are part of the debt capital of a corporation. Bond owners normally receive a fixed interest payment on a regular basis, whereas owners of stock are not normally guaranteed any dividends. If a corporation goes out of business, bondholders have first priority on whatever value still exists in the entity. Owners of stock get whatever is left over. Finally, if the corporation is very successful, owners of stock can reap the increases in the market value of their shares of stock. In contrast, the market value of corporate bonds is not so closely tied to the profits of a corporation but is rather influenced by how interest rates are changing in the economy in general.

4. Is there a world market for U.S. government securities?

Trading in U.S. government securities is one of the fastest-growing 24-hour markets in the world, thanks to sophisticated communications and computer technology. The deregulation of financial markets in foreign countries now permits much more of such trading. Also, since 1984, the United States has allowed foreign investors to buy U.S. government securities tax-free.

PROBLEMS

(Answers to the odd-numbered problems appear at the back of the book.)

21-1. Suppose that federal tax policy were changed to exempt the first $10,000 in dividends each year from personal taxation. How would this affect the choice of organizational form for businesses?

21-2. How would the change in corporate tax policy mentioned in Problem 21-1 affect the method of financing that corporations use?

*21-3. Consider a firm that wishes to borrow $10,000 for one year. Suppose that there is a 20 percent chance that this firm will go out of business before the end of the year (repaying none of its debts) and an 80 percent chance that it will survive and repay all of its debts. If potential lenders can earn 10 percent per year by lending to other firms that are certain to repay their debts, what rate of interest will the risky firm have to offer if it is to be able to borrow the $10,000?

21-4. Should the government guarantee junk bonds to make sure that the buyers of these bonds do not lose money? What would happen if the government did this?

---

*This problem is optional; albegra is required.

COMPUTER-ASSISTED INSTRUCTION

Key determinants of the prices of shares of corporate stock are illustrated using numerical problems.

Complete problem and answer appear on disk.

INTERACTING WITH THE INTERNET

An excellent tool for learning about the functioning of financial markets is the Iowa Electronic Markets. It is a registered market that runs on the Internet and is designed to teach the fundamentals of trading in financial markets. To make the learning "real," participants risk their own funds (you can invest quite small amounts). There are two types of markets: political ones, based on the outcome of elections, and financial ones. See

www.biz.uiowa.edu/iem/

One service that provides financial information, some of it free, is QuoteCom at

www.quote.com

The American Stock Exchange can be reached at

www.amex.com

The New York Stock Exchange is at

www.nyse.com

NASDAQ can be found at

www.nasdaq.com

The Chicago Mercantile Exchange is at

www.cme.com

And the London International Financial Futures and Options Exchange can be reached at

www.liffe.com/

Not all exchanges offer complete pricing information, but they generally do have extensive material on themselves.

For information and discussion groups, go to StockMaster at

www.stockmaster.com

You can find out more about sole proprietorship, partnerships, and corporations at the following Web site:

www.comerica.com/smallbiz/workshop/bizstruc.html

You can find out more about how the stock market works by going to

tqd.advanced.org/3088/

When you start on the EduStock welcome page, choose *Stock Market* from the menu.

PART 7

MARKET STRUCTURE, RESOURCE ALLOCATION, AND REGULATION

CHAPTER 22

THE FIRM: COST AND OUTPUT DETERMINATION

By the time you read this, about 50 percent of American households will have access to the Internet. If you are one of them, you are connected through an Internet service provider, or ISP. There are many ISPs in America. They include AT&T, MCI, Sprint, and America Online (AOL). They also include literally thousands of smaller local companies. A few years ago, AOL followed the trend set by many smaller ISPs by declaring that instead of paying by the hour, its customers could have unlimited access to the Internet for $19.95 a month. AOL settled a class action lawsuit as a result of access problems resulting from charging a flat monthly fee pricing structure. To understand what these lawsuits are about and how people responded to a change in the pricing structure of Internet access, you need to know about the cost curves that individual businesses face.

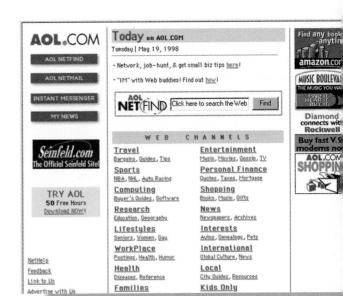

Did **You Know That** . . . there are more than 25 steps in the process of manufacturing a simple lead pencil? In the production of an automobile, there are literally thousands. At each step, the manufacturer can have the job done by workers or machines or some combination of the two. The manufacturer must also figure out how much to produce each month. Should a new machine be bought that can replace 10 workers? Should more workers be hired, or should the existing workers be paid overtime? If the price of aluminum is rising, should the company try to make do with plastic? What you will learn about in this chapter is how producers can select the best combination of inputs for any given output that is desired.

Before we look at the firm's costs, we need to define a firm.

THE FIRM

We define a business, or **firm,** as follows:

> **A firm is an organization that brings together factors of production—labor, land, physical capital, human capital, and entrepreneurial skill—to produce a product or service that it hopes can be sold at a profit.**

A typical firm will have an organizational structure consisting of an entrepreneur, managers, and workers. The entrepreneur is the person who takes the risks, mainly of losing his or her personal wealth. In compensation, the entrepreneur will get any profits that are made. Recall from Chapter 2 that entrepreneurs take the initiative in combining land, labor, and capital to produce a good or a service. Entrepreneurs are the ones who innovate in the form of new production and new products. The entrepreneur also decides whom to hire to manage the firm. Some economists maintain that the true quality of an entrepreneur becomes evident with his or her selection of managers. Managers, in turn, decide who should be hired and fired and how the business generally should be set up. The workers ultimately use the other inputs to produce the products or services that are being sold by the firm. Workers and managers are paid contractual wages. They receive a specified amount of income for a specified time period. Entrepreneurs are not paid contractual wages. They receive no reward specified in advance. The entrepreneurs make profits if there are any, for profits accrue to those who are willing to take risks. (Because the entrepreneur gets only what is left over after all expenses are paid, he or she is often referred to as a *residual claimant.* The entrepreneur lays claim to the residual—whatever is left.)

Profit and Costs

Most people think of profit as the difference between the amount of revenues a business takes in and the amount it spends for wages, materials, and so on. In a bookkeeping sense, the following formula could be used:

$$\text{Accounting profits} = \text{total revenues} - \text{explicit costs}$$

where **explicit costs** are expenses that the business managers must take account of because they must actually be paid out by the firm. This definition of profit is known as **accounting profit.** It is appropriate when used by accountants to determine a firm's taxable income. Economists are more interested in how firm managers react not just to changes in explicit costs but also to changes in **implicit costs,** defined as expenses that business managers do not have to pay out of pocket but are costs to the firm nonetheless because they represent an opportunity cost. These are noncash costs—they do not involve any direct cash outlay by the firm and must therefore be measured by the alternative cost principle. That is to say,

Chapter Outline

Firm
A business organization that employs resources to produce goods or services for profit. A firm normally owns and operates at least one plant in order to produce.

Explicit costs
Costs that business managers must take account of because they must be paid; examples are wages, taxes, and rent.

Accounting profit
Total revenues minus total explicit costs.

Implicit costs
Expenses that managers do not have to pay out of pocket and hence do not normally explicitly calculate, such as the opportunity cost of factors of production that are owned; examples are owner-provided capital and owner-provided labor.

they are measured by what the resources (land, capital) currently used in producing a particular good or service could earn in other uses. Economists therefore use the full opportunity cost of all resources as the figure to subtract from revenues to obtain a definition of profit. Another definition of implicit cost is therefore the opportunity cost of using factors that a producer does not buy or hire but already owns.

Opportunity Cost of Capital

Normal rate of return
The amount that must be paid to an investor to induce investment in a business; also known as the *opportunity cost of capital.*

Firms enter or remain in an industry if they earn, at minimum, a **normal rate of return.** People will not invest their wealth in a business unless they obtain a positive normal (competitive) rate of return—that is, unless their invested wealth pays off. Any business wishing to attract capital must expect to pay at least the same rate of return on that capital as all other businesses (of similar risk) are willing to pay. Put another way, when a firm requires the use of a resource in producing a particular product, it must bid against alternative users of that resource. Thus the firm must offer a price that is at least as much as other users are offering to pay. For example, if individuals can invest their wealth in almost any publishing firm and get a rate of return of 10 percent per year, each firm in the publishing industry must *expect* to pay 10 percent as the normal rate of return to present and future investors. This 10 percent is a *cost to the firm,* the **opportunity cost of capital.** The opportunity cost of capital is the amount of income, or yield, that could have been earned by investing in the next-best alternative. Capital will not stay in firms or industries in which the expected rate of return falls below its opportunity cost, that is, what could be earned elsewhere. If a firm owns some capital equipment, it can either use it or lease it and earn a return. If the firm uses the equipment for production, part of the cost of using that equipment is the forgone revenue that the firm could have earned had it leased out that equipment.

Opportunity cost of capital
The normal rate of return, or the available return on the next-best alternative investment. Economists consider this a cost of production, and it is included in our cost examples.

Opportunity Cost of Owner-Provided Labor and Capital

Single-owner proprietorships often grossly exaggerate their profit rates because they understate the opportunity cost of the labor that the proprietor provides to the business. Here we are referring to the opportunity cost of labor. For example, you may know people who run small grocery stores. These people will sit down at the end of the year and figure out what their "profits" are. They will add up all their sales and subtract what they had to pay to other workers, what they had to pay to their suppliers, what they had to pay in taxes, and so on. The end result they will call "profit." They normally will not, however, have figured into their costs the salary that they could have made if they had worked for somebody else in a similar type of job. By working for themselves, they become residual claimants—they receive what is left after all explicit costs have been accounted for. However, part of the costs should include the salary the owner-operator could have received working for someone else.

Consider a simple example of a skilled auto mechanic working 14 hours a day at his own service station, six days a week. Compare this situation to how much he could earn as a trucking company mechanic 84 hours a week. This self-employed auto mechanic might have an opportunity cost of about $20 an hour. For his 84-hour week in his own service station, he is forfeiting $1,680. Unless his service station shows accounting profits of more than that per week, he is losing money in an economic sense.

Another way of looking at the opportunity cost of running a business is that opportunity cost consists of all explicit and implicit costs. Accountants only take account of explicit costs. Therefore, accounting profit ends up being the residual after only explicit costs are subtracted from total revenues.

This same analysis can apply to owner-provided capital, such as land or buildings. The fact that the owner owns the building or the land with which he or she operates a business does not mean that it is "free." Rather, use of the building and land still has an opportunity cost—the value of the next-best alternative use for those assets.

Accounting Profits Versus Economic Profits

The term *profits* in economics means the income that entrepreneurs earn, over and above all costs including their own opportunity cost of time, plus the opportunity cost of the capital they have invested in their business. Profits can be regarded as total revenues minus total costs—which is how accountants think of them—but we must now include *all* costs. Our definition of **economic profits** will be the following:

$$\text{Economic profits} = \text{total revenues} - \text{total opportunity cost of all inputs used}$$

or

$$\text{Economic profits} = \text{total revenues} - (\text{explicit} + \text{implicit costs})$$

Remember that implicit costs include a normal rate of return on invested capital. We show this relationship in Figure 22-1.

The Goal of the Firm: Profit Maximization

When we examined the theory of consumer demand, utility (or satisfaction) maximization by the individual provided the basis for the analysis. In the theory of the firm and production, *profit maximization* is the underlying hypothesis of our predictive theory. The goal of the firm is to maximize economic profits, and the firm is expected to try to make the positive difference between total revenues and total costs as large as it can.

Economic profits
Total revenues minus total opportunity costs of all inputs used, or the total of all implicit and explicit costs.

THINKING CRITICALLY ABOUT THE MEDIA

Profits Increase by $500 Million!

Headlines like the one on this box make great eyecatchers in a newspaper. But without any other information, being told what the *absolute* profits of some company, such as General Motors or Exxon, are is meaningless. If the total reported yearly profits of Exxon are, say, $1 billion, that can mean that Exxon is doing well or doing abysmally. If the total investment in Exxon is $10 billion, then $1 billion in reported profits represents a 10 percent rate of return. If the investment in Exxon is $50 billion, in contrast, then $1 billion in profits represents only a 2 percent rate of return on investment, which could be considered terrible. Don't be fooled by "huge profits" headlines.

FIGURE 22-1

Simplified View of Economic and Accounting Profit
We see on the right column that accounting profit is the difference between total revenues and total explicit accounting costs. Conversely, we see on the left column that economic profit is equal to total revenues minus economic costs. Economic costs equal explicit accounting costs plus all implicit costs, including a normal rate of return on invested capital.

Exercise 22.1

Visit www.econtoday.com for more about starting a business.

Our justification for assuming profit maximization by firms is similar to our belief in utility maximization by individuals. To obtain labor, capital, and other resources required to produce commodities, firms must first obtain financing from investors. In general, investors are indifferent about the details of how a firm uses the money they provide. They are most interested in the earnings on this money and the risk of obtaining lower returns or losing the money they have invested. Firms that can provide relatively higher risk-corrected returns will therefore have an advantage in obtaining the financing needed to continue or expand production. Over time we would expect a policy of profit maximization to become the dominant mode of behavior for firms that survive.

CONCEPTS IN BRIEF

- Accounting profits differ from economic profits. Economic profits are defined as total revenues minus total costs, where costs include the full opportunity cost of all of the factors of production plus all other implicit costs.

- Single-owner proprietorships often fail to consider the opportunity cost of the labor services provided by the owner.

- The full opportunity cost of capital invested in a business is generally not included as a cost when accounting profits are calculated. Thus accounting profits often overstate economic profits.

- We assume throughout these chapters that the goal of the firm is to maximize economic profits.

SHORT RUN VERSUS LONG RUN

In Chapter 20, we discussed short-run and long-run price elasticities of supply and demand. For consumers, the long run meant the time period during which all adjustments to a change in price could be made, and anything shorter than that was considered the short run. For suppliers, the long run was the time in which all adjustments could be made, and anything shorter than that was the short run.

Now that we are discussing firms only, we will maintain a similar distinction between the short and the long run, but we will be more specific. In the theory of the firm, the **short run** is defined as any time period that is so short that there is at least one input, such as current **plant size,** that the firm cannot alter.[1] In other words, during the short run, a firm makes do with whatever big machines and factory size it already has, no matter how much more it wants to produce because of increased demand for its product. We consider the plant and heavy equipment, the size or amount of which cannot be varied in the short run, as fixed resources. In agriculture and in some other businesses, land may be a fixed resource.

There are, of course, variable resources that the firm can alter when it wants to change its rate of production. These are called *variable inputs* or *variable factors of production.* Typically, the variable inputs of a firm are its labor and its purchases of raw materials. In the short run, in response to changes in demand, the firm can, by definition, vary only its variable inputs.

The **long run** can now be considered the period of time in which *all* inputs can be varied. Specifically, in the long run, the firm can alter its plant size. How long is the long run? That depends on each individual industry. For Wendy's or McDonald's, the long run may be four

Short run
The time period when at least one input, such as plant size, cannot be changed.

Plant size
The physical size of the factories that a firm owns and operates to produce its output. Plant size can be defined by square footage, maximum physical capacity, and other physical measures.

Long run
The time period in which all factors of production can be varied.

---

[1]There can be many short runs but only one long run. For ease of analysis, in this section we simplify the case to one short run and talk about short-run costs.

or five months, because that is the time it takes to add new franchises. For a steel company, the long run may be several years, because that's how long it takes to plan and build a new plant. An electric utility might need over a decade to build a new plant, for example.

Short run and *long run* in our discussion are in fact management planning terms that apply to decisions made by managers. The firm can operate only in the short run in the sense that decisions must be made in the present. The same analysis applies to your own behavior. You may have many long-run plans about graduate school, vacations, and the like, but you always operate in the short run—you make decisions every day about what you do every day.

THE RELATIONSHIP BETWEEN OUTPUT AND INPUTS

A firm takes numerous inputs, combines them using a technological production process, and ends up with an output. There are, of course, a great many factors of production, or inputs. We classify production inputs into two broad categories (ignoring land)—labor and capital. The relationship between output and these two inputs is as follows:

Output per time period = some function of capital and labor inputs

In simple math, the production relationship can be written $Q = f(K, L)$, where Q = output per time period, K = capital, and L = labor.

We have used the word *production* but have not defined it. **Production** is any process by which resources are transformed into goods or services. Production includes not only making things but also transporting them, retailing, repackaging them, and so on. Notice that if we know that production occurs, we do not necessarily know the value of the output. The production relationship tells nothing about the worth or value of the inputs or the output.

Production
Any activity that results in the conversion of resources into products that can be used in consumption.

INTERNATIONAL EXAMPLE
Europeans Use More Capital

Since 1970, the 15 nations of the European Union (EU) have increased their total annual output of goods and services about as much as the United States. But over this same time period, the EU has dramatically increased the amount of capital relative to the amount of labor it uses in its production processes. Business managers in the EU have substituted capital for labor much more than in the United States because the cost of labor (wages corrected for inflation) has increased by almost 60 percent in the EU but by only 15 percent in the United States.

FOR CRITICAL ANALYSIS: *How does a firm decide when to buy more machines?* ●

The Production Function: A Numerical Example

The relationship between maximum physical output and the quantity of capital and labor used in the production process is sometimes called a **production function.** The production function is a technological relationship between inputs and output. Firms that are inefficient or wasteful in their use of capital and labor will obtain less output than the production function in theory will show. No firm can obtain more output than the production function shows, however. The production function specifies the maximum possible output that can be produced with a given amount of inputs. It also specifies the minimum amount of inputs necessary to produce a given level of output. The production function depends on the tech-

Production function
The relationship between inputs and output. A production function is a technological, not an economic, relationship.

nology available to the firm. It follows that an improvement in technology that allows the firm to produce more output with the same amount of inputs (or the same output with fewer inputs) results in a new production function.

Look at panel (a) of Figure 22-2. It shows a production function relating total output in column 2 to the quantity of labor measured in workers in column 1. When there are zero

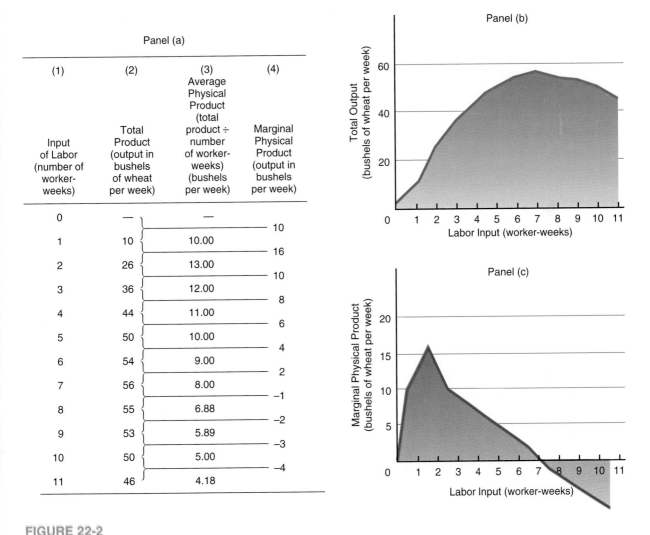

Panel (a)

(1) Input of Labor (number of worker- weeks)	(2) Total Product (output in bushels of wheat per week)	(3) Average Physical Product (total product ÷ number of worker- weeks) (bushels per week)	(4) Marginal Physical Product (output in bushels per week)
0	—	—	
			10
1	10	10.00	
			16
2	26	13.00	
			10
3	36	12.00	
			8
4	44	11.00	
			6
5	50	10.00	
			4
6	54	9.00	
			2
7	56	8.00	
			−1
8	55	6.88	
			−2
9	53	5.89	
			−3
10	50	5.00	
			−4
11	46	4.18	

FIGURE 22-2

Diminishing Returns, the Production Function, and Marginal Product:
A Hypothetical Case

Marginal product is the addition to the total product that results when one additional worker is hired. Thus the marginal product of the fourth worker is eight bushels of wheat. With four workers, 44 bushels are produced, but with three workers, only 36 are produced; the difference is 8. In panel (b), we plot the numbers from columns 1 and 2 of panel (a). In panel (c), we plot the numbers from columns 1 and 4 of panel (a). When we go from 0 to 1, marginal product is 10. When we go from one worker to two workers, marginal product increases to 16. After two workers, marginal product declines, but it is still positive. Total product (output) reaches its peak at seven workers, so after seven workers marginal product is negative. When we move from seven to eight workers, marginal product becomes −1 bushel.

workers per week of input, there is no output. When there are 5 workers per week of input (given the capital stock), there is a total output of 50 bushels per week. (Ignore for the moment the rest of that panel.) Panel (b) of Figure 22-2 shows this particular hypothetical production function graphically. Note again that it relates to the short run and that it is for an individual firm.

Panel (b) shows a total physical product curve, or the maximum amount of physical output that is possible when we add successive equal-sized units of labor while holding all other inputs constant. The graph of the production function in panel (b) is not a straight line. In fact, it peaks at 7 workers per week and starts to go down. To understand why it starts to go down with an individual firm in the short run, we have to analyze in detail the **law of diminishing (marginal) returns.**

But before that, let's examine the meaning of columns 3 and 4 of panel (a) of Figure 22-2—that is, average and marginal physical product.

Average and Physical Marginal Product

The definition of **average physical product** is straightforward: It is the total product divided by the number of workers expressed in output per week. You can see in column 3 of panel (a) of Figure 22-2 that the average physical product of labor first rises and then steadily falls after two workers are hired.

Remember that *marginal* means "additional." Hence the **marginal physical product** of labor is the change in total product that occurs when a worker joins an existing production process. (The term *physical* here emphasizes the fact that we are measuring in terms of physical units of production, not in dollar terms.) It is also the *change* in total product that occurs when that worker quits or is laid off an existing production process. The marginal physical product of labor therefore refers to the *change in output caused by a one-unit change in the labor input.* (Marginal physical product is also referred to as *marginal productivity* and *marginal return.*)

DIMINISHING MARGINAL RETURNS

The concept of diminishing marginal returns—also known as diminishing marginal product—applies to many situations. If you put a seat belt across your lap, a certain amount of safety is obtained. If you add another seat belt over your shoulder, some additional safety is obtained, but less than when the first belt was secured. When you add a third seat belt over the other shoulder, the amount of *additional* safety obtained is even smaller.

The same analysis holds for firms in their use of productive inputs. When the returns from hiring more workers are diminishing, it does not necessarily mean that more workers won't be hired. In fact, workers will be hired until the returns, in terms of the *value* of the *extra* output produced, are equal to the additional wages that have to be paid for those workers to produce the extra output. Before we get into that decision-making process, let's demonstrate that diminishing returns can be represented graphically and can be used in our analysis of the firm.

Measuring Diminishing Returns

How do we measure diminishing returns? First, we limit the analysis to only one variable factor of production (or input)—let's say the factor is labor. Every other factor of produc-

Law of diminishing (marginal) returns
The observation that after some point, successive equal-sized increases in a variable factor of production, such as labor, added to fixed factors of production, will result in smaller increases in output.

Average physical product
Total product divided by the variable input.

Marginal physical product
The physical output that is due to the addition of one more unit of a variable factor of production; the change in total product occurring when a variable input is increased and all other inputs are held constant; also called *marginal productivity* or *marginal return.*

tion, such as machines, must be held constant. Only in this way can we calculate the marginal returns from using more workers and know when we reach the point of diminishing marginal returns.

The marginal productivity of labor may increase rapidly at the very beginning. A firm starts with no workers, only machines. The firm then hires one worker, who finds it difficult to get the work started. But when the firm hires more workers, each is able to *specialize,* and the marginal productivity of those additional workers may actually be greater than it was with the previous few workers. Beyond some point, however, diminishing returns must set in, *not* because new workers are less qualified, but because each worker has (on average) fewer machines with which to work (remember, all other inputs are fixed). In fact, eventually the firm will become so crowded that workers will start to get in each other's way. At that point, total production declines and marginal physical product becomes negative.

Using these ideas, we can define the law of diminishing returns as follows:

> **As successive equal increases in a variable factor of production are added to fixed factors of production, there will be a point beyond which the extra, or marginal, product that can be attributed to each additional unit of the variable factor of production will decline.**

Note that the law of diminishing returns is a statement about the *physical* relationships between inputs and outputs that we have observed in many firms. If the law of diminishing returns were not a fairly accurate statement about the world, what would stop firms from hiring additional workers forever?

An Example of the Law of Diminishing Returns

Agriculture provides an example of the law of diminishing returns. With a fixed amount of land, fertilizer, and tractors, the addition of more farm workers eventually yields decreasing increases in output. After a while, when all the tractors are being used, additional farm workers will have to start farming manually. They obviously won't be as productive as the first farm workers who manned the tractors. The marginal physical product of an additional farm worker, given a specified amount of capital, must eventually be less than that for the previous workers.

A hypothetical set of numbers illustrating the law of diminishing marginal returns is presented in panel (a) of Figure 22-2. The numbers are presented graphically in panel (c). Marginal productivity (returns from adding more workers) first increases, then decreases, and finally becomes negative.

When one worker is hired, total output goes from 0 to 10. Thus marginal physical product is 10 bushels of wheat per week. When the second worker is hired, total product goes from 10 to 26 bushels of wheat per week. Marginal physical product therefore increases to 16 bushels of wheat per week. When a third worker is hired, total product again increases, from 26 to 36 bushels of wheat per week. This represents a marginal physical product of only 10 bushels of wheat per week. Therefore, the point of diminishing marginal returns occurs after two workers are hired.

Notice that after 7 workers per week, marginal physical product becomes negative. That means that the hiring of an eighth worker would create a situation that reduces total product. Sometimes this is called the *point of saturation,* indicating that given the amount of fixed inputs, there is no further positive use for more of the variable input. We have entered the region of negative marginal returns.

CONCEPTS IN BRIEF

- The technological relationship between output and input is called the production function. It relates output per time period to the several inputs, such as capital and labor.

- After some rate of output, the firm generally experiences diminishing marginal returns.

- The law of diminishing returns states that if all factors of production are held constant except one, equal increments in that one variable factor will eventually yield decreasing increments in output.

SHORT-RUN COSTS TO THE FIRM

You will see that costs are the extension of the production ideas just presented. Let's consider the costs the firm faces in the short run. To make this example simple, assume that there are only two factors of production, capital and labor. Our definition of the short run will be the time during which capital is fixed but labor is variable.

In the short run, a firm incurs certain types of costs. We label all costs incurred **total costs.** Then we break total costs down into total fixed costs and total variable costs, which we will explain shortly. Therefore,

Total costs
The sum of total fixed costs and total variable costs.

$$\text{Total costs (TC)} = \text{total fixed costs (TFC)} + \text{total variable costs (TVC)}$$

Remember that these total costs include both explicit and implicit costs, including the normal rate of return on investment.

After we have looked at the elements of total costs, we will find out how to compute average and marginal costs.

Total Fixed Costs

Let's look at an ongoing business such as Compaq Computer. The decision makers in that corporate giant can look around and see big machines, thousands of parts, huge buildings, and a multitude of other components of plant and equipment that have already been bought and are in place. Compaq has to take account of the technological obsolescence of this equipment, no matter how many computers it produces. The payments on the loans taken out to buy the equipment will all be exactly the same. The opportunity costs of any land that Compaq owns will all be exactly the same. These costs are more or less the same for Compaq no matter how many computers it produces.

We also have to point out that the opportunity cost (or normal rate of return) of capital must be included along with other costs. Remember that we are dealing in the short run, during which capital is fixed. If investors in Compaq Computer have already put $100 million into a new factory addition, the opportunity cost of that capital invested is now, in essence, a *fixed cost.* Why? Because in the short run, nothing can be done about that cost; the investment has already been made. This leads us to a very straightforward definition of fixed costs: All costs that do not vary—that is, all costs that do not depend on the rate of production—are called **fixed costs.**

Let's now take as an example the fixed costs incurred by an assembler of pocket calculators. This firm's total fixed costs will equal the cost of the rent on its equipment and the insurance it has to pay. We see in panel (a) of Figure 22-3 that total fixed costs per day are $10. In panel (b), these total fixed costs are represented by the horizontal line at $10 per day. They are invariant to changes in the output of calculators per day—no matter how many are produced, fixed costs will remain at $10 per day.

Fixed costs
Costs that do not vary with output. Fixed costs include such things as rent on a building. These costs are fixed for a certain period of time; in the long run, they are variable.

Panel (a)

(1) Total Output (Q/day)	(2) Total Fixed Costs (TFC)	(3) Total Variable Costs (TVC)	(4) Total Costs (TC) (4) = (2) + (3)	(5) Average Fixed Costs (AFC) (5) = (2) ÷ (1)	(6) Average Variable Costs (AVC) (6) = (3) ÷ (1)	(7) Average Total Costs (ATC) (7) = (4) ÷ (1)	(8) Total Costs (TC) (4)	(9) Marginal Cost (MC) (9) = change in (8) / change in (1)
0	$10	$ 0	$10	—	—	—	$10	
1	10	5	15	$10.00	$5.00	$15.00	15	$5
2	10	8	18	5.00	4.00	9.00	18	3
3	10	10	20	3.33	3.33	6.67	20	2
4	10	11	21	2.50	2.75	5.25	21	1
5	10	13	23	2.00	2.60	4.60	23	2
6	10	16	26	1.67	2.67	4.33	26	3
7	10	20	30	1.43	2.86	4.28	30	4
8	10	25	35	1.25	3.13	4.38	35	5
9	10	31	41	1.11	3.44	4.56	41	6
10	10	38	48	1.00	3.80	4.80	48	7
11	10	46	56	.91	4.18	5.09	56	8

Panel (b)

Panel (c)

FIGURE 22-3

Cost of Production: An Example

In panel (a), the derivation of columns 4 through 9 are given in parentheses in each column heading. For example, column 6, average variable costs, is derived by dividing column 3, total variable costs, by column 1, total output per day. Note that marginal cost (MC) in panel (c) intersects average variable costs (AVC) at the latter's minimum point. Also, MC intersects average total costs (ATC) at that latter's minimum point. It is a little more difficult to see that MC equals AVC and ATC at their respective minimum points in panel (a) because we are using discrete one-unit changes. You can see, though, that the marginal cost of going from 4 units per day to 5 units per day is $2 and increases to $3 when we move to 6 units per day. Somewhere in the middle it equals AVC of $2.60, which is in fact the minimum average variable cost. The same analysis holds for ATC, which hits minimum at 7 units per day at $4.28 per unit. MC goes from $4 to $5 and just equals ATC somewhere in between.

Total Variable Costs

Total **variable costs** are costs whose magnitude varies with the rate of production. One obvious variable cost is wages. The more the firm produces, the more labor it has to hire; therefore, the more wages it has to pay. Another variable cost is parts. In the assembly of calculators, for example, microchips must be bought. The more calculators that are made, the more chips must be bought. Part of the rate of depreciation (the rate of wear and tear) on machines that are used in the assembly process can also be considered a variable cost if depreciation depends partly on how long and how intensively the machines are used. Total variable costs are given in panel (a) of Figure 22-3 in column 3. These are translated into the total variable cost curve in panel (b). Notice that the total variable cost curve lies below the total cost curve by the vertical distance of $10. This vertical distance represents, of course, total fixed costs.

Variable costs
Costs that vary with the rate of production. They include wages paid to workers and purchases of materials.

Short-Run Average Cost Curves

In panel (b) of Figure 22-3 we see total costs, total variable costs, and total fixed costs. Now we want to look at average cost. The average cost concept is one in which we are measuring cost per unit of output. It is a matter of simple arithmetic to figure the averages of these three cost concepts. We can define them as follows:

$$\text{Average total costs (ATC)} = \frac{\text{total costs (TC)}}{\text{output } (Q)}$$

$$\text{Average variable costs (AVC)} = \frac{\text{total variable costs (TVC)}}{\text{output } (Q)}$$

$$\text{Average fixed costs (AFC)} = \frac{\text{total fixed costs (TFC)}}{\text{output } (Q)}$$

Exercise 22.2
Visit www.econtoday.com for more about different costs.

The arithmetic is done in columns 5, 6, and 7 in panel (a) of Figure 22-3. The numerical results are translated into a graphical format in panel (c). Because total costs (TC) equal variable costs (TVC) plus fixed costs (TFC), the difference between average total costs (ATC) and average variable costs (AVC) will always be identical to average fixed costs (AFC). That means that average total costs and average variable costs move together as output expands.

Now let's see what we can observe about the three average cost curves in Figure 22-3.

Average Fixed Costs (AFC). **Average fixed costs** continue to fall throughout the output range. In fact, if we were to continue the diagram farther to the right, we would find that average fixed costs would get closer and closer to the horizontal axis. That is because total fixed costs remain constant. As we divide this fixed number by a larger and larger number of units of output, the resulting AFC has to become smaller and smaller. In business, this is called "spreading the overhead."

Average fixed costs
Total fixed costs divided by the number of units produced.

Average Variable Costs (AVC). We assume a particular form of the curve for **average variable costs.** The form that it takes is U-shaped: First it falls; then it starts to rise. It is possible for the AVC curve to take other shapes in the long run.

Average variable costs
Total variable costs divided by the number of units produced.

Average Total Costs (ATC). This curve has a shape similar to that of the AVC curve. However, it falls even more dramatically in the beginning and rises more slowly after it has reached a minimum point. It falls and then rises because **average total costs** are the

Average total costs
Total costs divided by the number of units produced; sometimes called *average per-unit total costs.*

summation of the AFC curve and the AVC curve. Thus when AFC and AVC are both falling, ATC must fall too. At some point, however, AVC starts to increase while AFC continues to fall. Once the increase in the AVC curve outweighs the decrease in the AFC curve, the ATC curve will start to increase and will develop its familiar U shape.

Marginal Cost

We have stated repeatedly that the basis of decisions is always on the margin—movement in economics is always determined at the margin. This dictum also holds true within the firm. Firms, according to the analysis we use to predict their behavior, are very interested in their **marginal costs.** Because the term *marginal* means "additional" or "incremental" (or "decremental," too) here, marginal costs refer to costs that result from a one-unit change in the production rate. For example, if the production of 10 calculators per day costs a firm $48 and the production of 11 calculators costs it $56 per day, the marginal cost of producing the eleventh calculator per day is $8.

Marginal costs
The change in total costs due to a one-unit change in production rate.

Marginal costs can be measured by using the formula

$$\text{Marginal cost} = \frac{\text{change in total cost}}{\text{change in output}}$$

We show the marginal costs of calculator production per day in column 9 of panel (a) in Figure 22-3, calculated according to the formula just given. In our example, we have changed output by one unit every time, so we can ignore variations in the denominator in that particular formula.

This marginal cost schedule is shown graphically in panel (c) of Figure 22-3. Just like average variable costs and average total costs, marginal costs first fall and then rise. The U shape of the marginal cost curve is a result of increasing and then diminishing marginal returns. At lower levels of output, the marginal cost curve declines. The reasoning is that as marginal physical product increases with each addition of output, the marginal cost of this last unit of output must fall. Conversely, when diminishing marginal returns set in, marginal physical product decreases (and eventually becomes negative); it follows that the marginal cost of the last unit must rise. These relationships are clearly reflected in the geometry of panels (b) and (c) of Figure 22-3.

In summary:

> As long as marginal physical product rises, marginal cost will fall, and when marginal physical product starts to fall (after reaching the point of diminishing marginal returns), marginal cost will begin to rise.

POLICY EXAMPLE
Can "Three Strikes" Laws Reduce Crime?

Crime and violence have been the top concern of Americans for at least a decade. At both the federal and the state level, politicians have responded with a variety of policies aimed at reducing crime. One popular new law has been labeled "three strikes and you're out." A defendant with a prior conviction for two serious or violent offenses faces mandatory life imprisonment for a third offense.

Such legislation has dramatically affected the marginal cost of violence and murder to potential criminal defendants who have already been convicted of two felonies. Here is what one career criminal, Frank Schweickert, said in a *New York Times* interview: "Before, if I was doing a robbery and getting chased by cops, I'd lay my gun down. . . . But now you are talking about a life sentence. Why isn't it worth doing whatever it takes to get away? If that meant shooting a cop, if that meant shooting a store clerk, if that meant shooting someone innocent in my way, well, they'd have gotten shot. Because what is the worst thing that could happen to me: life imprisonment? If I'm getting a murder sentence anyway, I might as well do whatever it takes to maybe get away." In other words, the "three strikes" legislation has reduced the marginal cost of murder committed while engaging in a criminal activity after two prior felony convictions to zero.

FOR CRITICAL ANALYSIS: Do criminals subject to the new legislation have to understand the concept of marginal cost in order for our theory to predict well? Explain. ●

The Relationship Between Average and Marginal Costs

Let us now examine the relationship between average costs and marginal costs. There is always a definite relationship between averages and marginals. Consider the example of 10 football players with an average weight of 200 pounds. An eleventh player is added. His weight is 250 pounds. That represents the marginal weight. What happens now to the average weight of the team? It must increase. Thus when the marginal player weighs more than the average, the average must increase. Likewise, if the marginal player weighs less than 200 pounds, the average weight will decrease.

There is a similar relationship between average variable costs and marginal costs. When marginal costs are less than average costs, the latter must fall. Conversely, when marginal costs are greater than average costs, the latter must rise. When you think about it, the relationship makes sense. The only way for average variable costs to fall is for the extra cost of the marginal unit produced to be less than the average variable cost of all the preceding units. For example, if the average variable cost for two units of production is $4.00 a unit, the only way for the average variable cost of three units to be less than that of two units is for the variable costs attributable to the last unit—the marginal cost—to be less than the average of the past units. In this particular case, if average variable cost falls to $3.33 a unit, total variable cost for the three units would be three times $3.33, or almost exactly $10.00. Total variable cost for two units is two times $4.00, or $8.00. The marginal cost is therefore $10.00 minus $8.00, or $2.00, which is less than the average variable cost of $3.33.

A similar type of computation can be carried out for rising average variable costs. The only way for average variable costs to rise is for the average variable cost of additional units to be more than that for units already produced. But the incremental cost is the marginal cost. In this particular case, the marginal costs have to be higher than the average variable costs.

There is also a relationship between marginal costs and average total costs. Remember that average total cost is equal to total cost divided by the number of units produced. Remember also that marginal cost does not include any fixed costs. Fixed costs are, by definition, fixed and cannot influence marginal costs. Our example can therefore be repeated substituting *average total cost* for *average variable cost*.

These rising and falling relationships can be seen in Figure 22-3, where MC intersects AVC and ATC at their respective minimum points.

Minimum Cost Points

At what rate of output of calculators per day does our representative firm experience the minimum average total costs? Column 7 in panel (a) of Figure 22-3 shows that the minimum average total cost is $4.28, which occurs at an output rate of seven calculators per day.

We can also find this minimum cost by finding the point in panel (c) of Figure 22-3 at which the marginal cost curve intersects the average total cost curve. This should not be surprising. When marginal cost is below average total cost, average total cost falls. When marginal cost is above average total cost, average total cost rises. At the point where average total cost is neither falling nor rising, marginal cost must then be equal to average total cost. When we represent this graphically, the marginal cost curve will intersect the average total cost curve at the latter's minimum.

The same analysis applies to the intersection of the marginal cost curve and the average variable cost curve. When are average variable costs at a minimum? According to panel (a) of Figure 22-3, average variable costs are at a minimum of $2.60 at an output rate of five calculators per day. This is where the marginal cost curve intersects the average variable cost curve in panel (c) of Figure 22-3.

CONCEPTS IN BRIEF

- Total costs equal total fixed costs plus total variable costs.
- Fixed costs are those that do not vary with the rate of production; variable costs are those that do vary with the rate of production.
- Average total costs equal total costs divided by output (ATC = TC/Q).
- Average variable costs equal total variable costs divided by output (AVC = TVC/Q).
- Average fixed costs equal total fixed costs divided by output (AFC = TFC/Q).
- Marginal cost equals the change in total cost divided by the change in output (MC = ΔTC/ΔQ).
- The marginal cost curve intersects the minimum point of the average total cost curve and the minimum point of the average variable cost curve.

THE RELATIONSHIP BETWEEN DIMINISHING MARGINAL RETURNS AND COST CURVES

There is a unique relationship between output and the shape of the various cost curves we have drawn. Let's consider specifically the relationship between marginal cost and the example of diminishing marginal physical returns in panel (a) of Figure 22-4 on page 496. It turns out that if wage rates are constant, the shape of the marginal cost curve in panel (d) of Figure 22-4 is both a reflection of and a consequence of the law of diminishing returns. Let's assume that each unit of labor can be purchased at a constant price. Further assume that labor is the only variable input. We see that as more workers are hired, marginal physical product first rises and then falls after the point at which diminishing returns are encountered. Thus the marginal cost of each extra unit of output will first fall as long as marginal physical product is rising, and then it will rise as long as marginal physical product is falling. Recall that marginal cost is defined as

$$MC = \frac{\text{change in total cost}}{\text{change in output}}$$

Because the price of labor is assumed to be constant, the change in total cost is simply the constant price of labor, W (we are increasing labor by only one unit). The change in output

Panel (a)

(1) Labor Input	(2) Total Product (number of pairs sold)	(3) Average Physical Product (pairs per salesperson) (3) = (2) ÷ (1)	(4) Marginal Physical Product	(5) Average Variable Cost (5) = W ($100) ÷ (3)	(6) Marginal Cost (6) = W ($100) ÷ (4)
0	0	—	—	—	—
1	50	50	50	$2.00	$2.00
2	110	55	60	1.80	1.70
3	180	60	70	1.70	1.40
4	240	60	60	1.70	1.70
5	290	58	50	1.70	2.00
6	330	55	40	1.80	2.50
7	360	51	30	2.00	3.30

FIGURE 22-4

The Relationship Between Physical Output and Costs

As the number of salespeople increases, the total number of pairs of shoes sold rises, as shown in panels (a) and (b). In panel (c), marginal product (MP) first rises and then falls. Average product (AP) follows. The mirror image of panel (c) is shown in panel (d), in which MC and AVC first fall and then rise.

is simply the marginal physical product (MPP) of the one-unit increase in labor. Therefore, we see that

$$\text{Marginal cost} = \frac{W}{\text{MPP}}$$

This means that initially, when there are increasing returns, marginal cost falls (we are dividing W by increasingly larger numbers), and later, when diminishing returns set in and marginal physical product is falling, marginal cost must increase (we are dividing W by smaller numbers). As marginal physical product increases, marginal cost decreases, and as marginal physical product decreases, marginal cost must increase. Thus when marginal physical product reaches its maximum, marginal cost necessarily reaches its minimum. To illustrate this, let's return to Figure 22-2 on page 487 and consider specifically panel (a). Assume that a worker is paid $100 a week. When we go from zero labor input to one unit, output increases by 10 bushels of wheat. Each of those 10 bushels of wheat has a marginal cost of $10. Now the second unit of labor is hired, and it too costs $100 per week. Output increases by 16. Thus the marginal cost is $100 ÷ 16 = $6.25. We continue the experiment. We see that the next unit of labor yields only 10 additional bushels of wheat, so marginal cost starts to rise again back to $10. The following unit of labor increases marginal physical product by only 8, so marginal cost becomes $100 ÷ 8 = $12.50.

All of the foregoing can be restated in relatively straightforward terms:

Firms' short-run cost curves are a reflection of the law of diminishing marginal returns. Given any constant price of the variable input, marginal costs decline as long as the marginal product of the variable resource is rising. At the point at which diminishing marginal returns begin, marginal costs begin to rise as the marginal product of the variable input begins to decline.

The result is a marginal cost curve that slopes down, hits a minimum, and then slopes up. The average total cost curve and average variable cost curve are of course affected. They will have their familiar U shape in the short run. Again, to see this, recall that

$$\text{AVC} = \frac{\text{total variable costs}}{\text{total output}}$$

As we move from zero labor input to one unit in panel (a) of Figure 22-2, output increases from zero to 10 bushels. The total variable costs are the price per worker, W ($100), times the number of workers (1). Because the average product of one worker (column 3) is 10, we can write the total product, 10, as the average product, 10, times the number of workers, 1. Thus we see that

$$\text{AVC} = \frac{\$100 \times 1}{10 \times 1} = \frac{\$100}{10} = \frac{W}{\text{AP}}$$

From column 3 in panel (a) of Figure 22-2 we see that the average product increases, reaches a maximum, and then declines. Because AVC = W/AP, average variable cost decreases as average product increases and increases as average product decreases. AVC reaches its minimum when average product reaches its maximum. Furthermore, because ATC = AVC + AFC, the average total cost curve inherits the relationship between the average variable cost and diminishing returns.

To illustrate, consider a shoe store that employs salespeople to sell shoes. Panel (a) of Figure 22-4 presents in column 2 the total number of pairs of shoes sold as the number of salespeople increases. Notice that the total product first increases at an increasing rate and later increases at a decreasing rate. This is reflected in column 4, which shows that the marginal physical product increases at first and then falls. The average physical product too first rises and then falls. The marginal and average physical products are graphed in panel (c) of Figure 22-4. Our immediate interest here is the average variable and marginal costs. Because we can define average variable cost as $100/AP (assuming that the wage paid is constant at $100), as the average product rises from 50 to 55 to 60 pairs of shoes sold, the average variable cost falls from $2.00 to $1.82 to $1.67. Conversely, as average product falls from 60 to 50, average variable cost rises from $1.67 to $2.00. Likewise, because marginal cost can also be defined as W/MPP, we see that as marginal physical product rises from 50 to 70, marginal cost falls from $2.00 to $1.43. As marginal physical product falls to 30, marginal cost rises to $3.33. These relationships are also expressed in panels (b), (c), and (d) of Figure 22-4.

LONG-RUN COST CURVES

The long run is defined as a time period during which full adjustment can be made to any change in the economic environment. Thus in the long run, *all* factors of production are variable. Long-run curves are sometimes called *planning curves,* and the long run is sometimes called the **planning horizon.** We start out our analysis of long-run cost curves by considering a single firm contemplating the construction of a single plant. The firm has three alternative plant sizes from which to choose on the planning horizon. Each particular plant size generates its own short-run average total cost curve. Now that we are talking about the difference between long-run and short-run cost curves, we will label all short-run curves with an S and long-run curves with an L; short-run average (total) costs will be labeled SAC, and long-run average cost curves will be labeled LAC.

Panel (a) of Figure 22-5 shows three short-run average cost curves for three successively larger plants. Which is the optimal size to build? That depends on the anticipated normal,

Planning horizon
The long run, during which all inputs are variable.

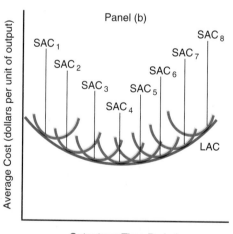

FIGURE 22-5

Preferable Plant Size and the Long-Run Average Cost Curve

If the anticipated permanent rate of output per unit time period is Q_1, the optimal plant to build would be the one corresponding to SAC$_1$ in panel (a) because average costs are lower. However, if the permanent rate of output increases to Q_2, it will be more profitable to have a plant size corresponding to SAC$_2$. Unit costs fall to C_3.

If we draw all the possible short-run average cost curves that correspond to different plant sizes and then draw the envelope (a curve tangent to each member of a set of curves) to these various curves, SAC$_1$–SAC$_8$, we obtain the long-run average cost curve, or the planning curve, as shown in panel (b).

sustained (permanent) rate of output per time period. Assume for a moment that the anticipated normal, sustained rate is Q_1. If a plant of size 1 is built, the average costs will be C_1. If a plant of size 2 is built, we see on SAC_2 that the average costs will be C_2, which is greater than C_1. Thus if the anticipated rate of output is Q_1, the appropriate plant size is the one from which SAC_1 was derived.

However, if the anticipated permanent rate of output per time period goes from Q_1 to Q_2 and a plant of size 1 had been decided on, average costs would be C_4. If a plant of size 2 had been decided on, average costs would be C_3, which is clearly less than C_4.

In choosing the appropriate plant size for a single-plant firm during the planning horizon, the firm will pick the size whose short-run average cost curve generates an average cost that is lowest for the expected rate of output.

Long-Run Average Cost Curve

Long-run average cost curve
The locus of points representing the minimum unit cost of producing any given rate of output, given current technology and resource prices.

Planning curve
The long-run average cost curve.

If we now assume that the entrepreneur faces an infinite number of choices of plant sizes in the long run, we can conceive of an infinite number of SAC curves similar to the three in panel (a) of Figure 22-5. We are not able, of course, to draw an infinite number; we have drawn quite a few, however, in panel (b) of Figure 22-5. We then draw the "envelope" to all these various short-run average cost curves. The resulting envelope is the **long-run average cost curve.** This long-run average cost curve is sometimes called the **planning curve,** for it represents the various average costs attainable at the planning stage of the firm's decision making. It represents the locus (path) of points giving the least unit cost of producing any given rate of output. Note that the LAC curve is *not* tangent to each individual SAC curve at the latter's minimum points. This is true only at the minimum point of the LAC curve. Then and only then are minimum long-run average costs equal to minimum short-run average costs.

WHY THE LONG-RUN AVERAGE COST CURVE IS U-SHAPED

Economies of scale
Decreases in long-run average costs resulting from increases in output.

Constant returns to scale
No change in long-run average costs when output increases.

Diseconomies of scale
Increases in long-run average costs that occur as output increases.

Notice that the long-run average cost curve, LAC, in panel (b) of Figure 22-5 is U-shaped, similar to the U shape of the short-run average cost curve developed earlier in this chapter. The reason behind the U shape of the two curves is not the same, however. The short-run average cost curve is U-shaped because of the law of diminishing marginal returns. But the law cannot apply to the long run, because in the long run, all factors of production are variable; there is no point of diminishing marginal returns because there is no fixed factor of production. Why, then, do we see the U shape in the long-run average cost curve? The reasoning has to do with economies of scale, constant returns to scale, and diseconomies of scale. When the firm is experiencing **economies of scale,** the long-run average cost curve slopes downward—an increase in scale and production leads to a fall in unit costs. When the firm is experiencing **constant returns to scale,** the long-run average cost curve is at its minimum point, such that an increase in scale and production does not change unit costs. When the firm is experiencing **diseconomies of scale,** the long-run average cost curve slopes upward—an increase in scale and production increases unit costs. These three sections of the long-run average cost curves are broken up into panels (a), (b), and (c) in Figure 22-6 on page 500.

Reasons for Economies of Scale

We shall examine three of the many reasons why a firm might be expected to experience economies of scale: specialization, the dimensional factor, and improved productive equipment.

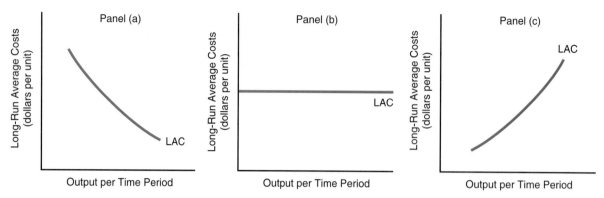

FIGURE 22-6

Economies of Scale, Constant Returns to Scale, and Diseconomies of Scale Shown with the Long-Run Average Cost Curve
Long-run average cost curves will fall when there are economies of scale, as shown in panel (a). They will be constant (flat) when the firm is experiencing constant returns to scale, as shown in panel (b). They will rise when the firm is experiencing diseconomies of scale, as shown in panel (c).

Specialization. As a firm's scale of operation increases, the opportunities for specialization in the use of resource inputs also increase. This is sometimes called *increased division of tasks* or *operations*. Gains from such division of labor or increased specialization are well known. When we consider managerial staffs, we also find that larger enterprises may be able to put together more highly specialized staffs.

Dimensional Factor. Large-scale firms often require proportionately less input per unit of output simply because certain inputs do not have to be physically doubled in order to double the output. Consider the cost of storage of oil. The cost of storage is basically related to the cost of steel that goes into building the storage container; however, the amount of steel required goes up less than in proportion to the volume (storage capacity) of the container (because the volume of a container increases more than proportionately with its surface area).

Improved Productive Equipment. The larger the scale of the enterprise, the more the firm is able to take advantage of larger-volume (output capacity) types of machinery. Small-scale operations may not be able profitably to use large-volume machines that can be more efficient per unit of output. Also, smaller firms often cannot use technologically more advanced machinery because they are unable to spread out the high cost of such sophisticated equipment over a large output.

For any of these reasons, the firm may experience economies of scale, which means that equal percentage increases in output result in a decrease in average cost. Thus output can double, but total costs will less than double; hence average cost falls. Note that the factors listed for causing economies of scale are all *internal* to the firm; they do not depend on what other firms are doing or what is happening in the economy.

DISSEMINATING IDEAS VIA THE INTERNET

Numerous economic studies have shown that the production of many goods that we consume have constant unit costs once production is under way. Otherwise stated, the production of most goods appears to look like panel (b) in Figure 22-6. Ideas, in contrast, often have exceedingly high costs for the first "unit" of knowledge. Once that first unit is produced, though, both the marginal and average costs for production of additional units is essentially zero. Numerous costs are involved in producing the ideas for new technology. Once those ideas are produced, they can be disseminated electronically on the Internet to everybody in the world at relatively small additional cost.

FOR CRITICAL ANALYSIS: Draw the appropriate long-run average cost curve for ideas. ●

Why a Firm Might Experience Diseconomies of Scale

One of the basic reasons that a firm can expect to run into diseconomies of scale is that there are limits to the efficient functioning of management. Moreover, as more workers are hired, a more than proportionate increase in managers and staff people may be needed, and this could cause increased costs per unit. This is so because larger levels of output imply successively larger *plant* size, which in turn implies successively larger *firm* size. Thus as the level of output increases, more people must be hired, and the firm gets bigger. However, as this happens, the support, supervisory, and administrative staff and the general paperwork of the firm all increase. As the layers of supervision grow, the costs of information and communication grow more than proportionately; hence the average unit cost will start to increase.

Some observers of corporate giants claim that many of them are experiencing some diseconomies of scale today. Witness the problems that General Motors and IBM had in the early 1990s. Some analysts say that the financial problems that they have experienced are at least partly a function of their size relative to their smaller, more flexible competitors, who can make decisions more quickly and then take advantage of changing market conditions more rapidly. This seems to be particularly true with IBM. It apparently adapted very slowly to the fact that the large mainframe computer business was declining as micro- and mini-computers became more and more powerful.

MINIMUM EFFICIENT SCALE

Economists and statisticians have obtained actual data on the relationship between changes in all inputs and changes in average cost. It turns out that for many industries, the long-run average cost curve does not resemble that shown in panel (b) of Figure 22-5. Rather, it more closely resembles Figure 22-7 on page 502. What you can observe there is a small portion of declining long-run average costs (economies of scale) and then a wide range of outputs over which the firm experiences relatively constant economies of scale. At the output rate when economies of scale end and constant economies of scale start, the **minimum efficient scale (MES)** for the firm is encountered. It occurs at point *A*. (The point is, of course, approximate. The more smoothly the curve declines into its flat portion, the more approximate will be our estimate of the MES.) The minimum efficient scale will always be the lowest rate of output at which long-run average costs are minimized. In any industry with a long-run average cost curve similar to the one in Figure 22-7, larger firms will have no cost-saving advantage over smaller firms as long as the smaller firms have at least obtained the minimum efficient scale at point *A*.

Among its uses, the minimum efficient scale gives us a rough measure of the degree of competition in an industry. If the MES is small relative to industry demand, the degree of competition in that industry is likely to be high because there is room for many efficiently

Minimum efficient scale (MES)
The lowest rate of output per unit time at which long-run average costs for a particular firm are at a minimum.

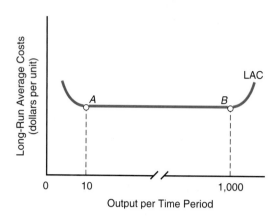

FIGURE 22-7

Minimum Efficient Scale
This long-run average cost curve reaches a minimum point at *A*. After that point, long-run average costs remain horizontal, or constant, and then rise at some later rate of output. Point *A* is called the minimum efficient scale for the firm because that is the point at which it reaches minimum costs. It is the lowest rate of output at which the average long-run costs are minimized.

sized plants. Conversely, when the MES is large relative to industry demand, the degree of competition is likely to be small because there is room for a relatively small number of efficiently sized plants or firms. Looked at another way, if it takes a very large scale of plant to obtain minimum long-run average cost, the output of just a few of these very large firms can fully satisfy total market demand. This means that there isn't room for a large number of smaller plants if maximum efficiency is to be obtained in the industry.

CONCEPTS IN BRIEF

• The long run is often called the planning horizon. The long-run average cost curve is the planning curve. It is found by drawing a line tangent to one point on a series of short-run average cost curves, each corresponding to a different plant size.

• The firm can experience economies of scale, diseconomies of scale, and constant returns to scale, all according to whether the long-run average cost curve slopes downward, slopes upward, or is horizontal (flat). Economies of scale refer to what happens to average cost when all factors of production are increased.

• We observe economies of scale for a number of reasons, among which are specialization, improved productive equipment, and the dimensional factor, because large-scale firms require proportionately less input per unit of output. The firm may experience diseconomies of scale primarily because of limits to the efficient functioning of management.

• The minimum efficient scale occurs at the lowest rate of output at which long-run average costs are minimized.

America Online, in an attempt to compete more aggressively, switched to zero-marginal-cost pricing a few years ago. What do you predict would be the effect on the quantity of AOL Internet access services demanded?

Zero Marginal Cost Pricing: The Case of Internet Access

CONCEPTS APPLIED:

FIXED COST, MARGINAL COST, FLAT-RATE PRICING, PEAK-LOAD (CONGESTION) PRICING

Visit www.econtoday.com for an Internet Activity that expands your understanding of these concepts.

People respond to incentives. That was made astonishingly clear by the customer reaction to America Online's decision a few years ago to allow its customers unlimited access to the Internet for a flat rate of just $19.95 per month. Until then, AOL had based its access fee on the number of hours its customers spent logged on. But such marginal cost pricing had become uncompetitive and so was slated to disappear. The result could have been predicted by any student of beginning economics. Flat-rate pricing encourages more use. A flat monthly price means that once you pay the "entry fee," that fee becomes a fixed cost. The marginal cost of additional use becomes zero; all users respond accordingly.

Graphic Analysis

Figure 22-8 shows the demand curve for hours on the Internet as a function of price charged per hour. At $1 per hour, the quantity Q_1 is demanded. With the flat-rate pricing system, the price per unit is always zero after the flat-rate fee is paid. The marginal cost curve is coincident with the horizontal axis and is actually the supply curve of hours on the Internet. The quantity demanded increases dramatically to Q_2. The monthly fixed cost of $19.95 (not shown on the graph, which measures hours of Internet use per month) has no impact on Internet use. People respond to marginal costs, not sunk costs.

The Problems at AOL

With a zero marginal cost, people tend to log on and stay on much longer than in the previous metered pricing system used by AOL. Under the old system, fees were assessed by the hour after a minimum monthly threshold, typically about five hours, was reached, so many users

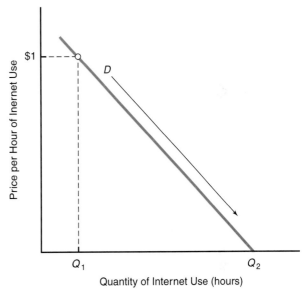

FIGURE 22-8

The Result of Eliminating Marginal Cost Pricing for Internet Use

Not surprisingly, when America Online switched its Internet access charges to a flat fee per month, the effective price for any use of the Internet became zero. Quantity demanded increased dramatically.

kept their on-line time below that minimum. Once the flat-fee pricing system went into effect, AOL's 8 million subscribers immediately began experiencing traffic jams. Many were forced to wait until the wee hours of the morning to access their e-mail and to get onto the Internet and the World Wide Web. Some could not log on for days. Many states' attorneys general brought suit against AOL for misrepresentation, fraud, and other "crimes." America Online promised to add equipment to reduce the jams. It also agreed to give rebates to dissatisfied customers.

Role of the Phone Companies

The flat-fee pricing system for Internet access would not create so much additional use if customers had to pay metered rates for local phone usage. Indeed, in Europe, there are numerous similar flat-fee Internet access pricing plans, but virtually all the phone companies in Europe charge on a per-minute basis for local phone use. Consequently, Internet customers in Europe use the Internet many fewer hours per month than customers in the United States do. In the United States, the phone companies do not usually charge for additional hours of local phone usage, so many U.S. users of the Internet, including corporations, log on and stay on. Users of popular "broadcast"-style data services, such as Pointcast, tend to leave their computers connected 24 hours a day. Yet these users pay no more than the price of a single local call and in some cases nothing at all if their local phone company charges a flat fee per month per phone line.

The ISPs' Dilemma

Most Internet service providers enroll 10 to 30 times more customers than their leased phone lines can accommodate at one time. That is fine as long as the typical customer does not spend a lot of time on-line. But when many users stay logged on, busy signals result. Then the ISP can keep its customers happy only if it leases more phone lines, but that drives costs up. To make a profit, the ISP then has to charge a higher flat rate.

Charge More for More Use?

There is a simple solution to the problem—charge a higher rate to users who log on for longer hours. Alternatively, companies can charge "premium" rates and offer premium services, such as immediate access even during peak periods. Of course, those who do not pay for the premium service may be cut off. For example, Concentric Network Corporation in Cupertino, California, has a standard $19.95-per-month plan but also a so-called consumer plan for $39.95 a month. If you pay for the premium service, you get priority access to the network. Such tiered pricing will probably grow as more and more people become heavy users of the Internet.

FOR CRITICAL ANALYSIS
1. Describe any similarities you see between restaurants that offer "all you can eat" meals for a fixed price and Internet service provider flat-rate pricing schemes.
2. Can you think of other flat-fee pricing systems that exist for goods or services that you might buy?

CHAPTER SUMMARY

1. It is important in economics to distinguish between accounting profits and economic profits. Accounting profits are equal to total revenues minus total explicit costs. Economic profits are equal to total revenues minus total opportunity costs of all factors of production.
2. The short run for the firm is defined as the period during which plant size cannot be altered. The long run is the period during which all factors of production can be varied.
3. Fixed costs are costs that cannot be altered in the short run. Fixed costs are associated with assets that the firm owns that cannot be profitably transferred to another use. Variable costs are associated with input costs that vary as the rate of output varies. Wages are a good example of a variable cost.
4. There are definitional relationships between average, total, and marginal costs:

$$ATC = \frac{TC}{Q}$$

$$AVC = \frac{TVC}{Q}$$

$$AFC = \frac{TFC}{Q}$$

$$MC = \frac{\text{change in TC}}{\text{change in } Q}$$

5. When marginal costs are less than average costs, average costs are falling. When marginal costs are greater than average costs, average costs are rising. The marginal cost curve intersects the average variable cost curve and the average total cost curve at their minimum points.

6. When we hold constant all factors of production except one, an increase in that factor will lead to a change in total physical product. That is how we derive the total physical product curve. The marginal physical product curve is derived from looking at the change in total physical product.
7. After some output rate, firms enter the region of diminishing marginal returns, or diminishing marginal physical product. In other words, after some point, each increment of the variable input will yield a smaller and smaller increment in total output.
8. Given a constant wage rate, the marginal cost curve is the mirror image of the marginal physical product curve. Thus because of the law of diminishing marginal returns, marginal costs will eventually rise.
9. We derive the long-run average cost curve by connecting a smooth line that is just tangent to all of the short-run average cost curves. This long-run average cost curve is sometimes called the planning curve.
10. It is possible for a firm to experience economies of scale, constant returns to scale, or diseconomies of scale, in which case a proportionate increase in *all* inputs will lead, respectively, to decreasing, constant, or increasing average costs. Firms may experience economies of scale because of specialization, the dimensional factor, and the ability to purchase improved productive equipment. Firms may experience diseconomies of scale because of the limitations of efficient management.
11. The long-run average cost curve will be downward-sloping, horizontal, or upward-sloping, depending on whether there are economics of scale, constant returns to scale, or diseconomies of scale.
12. Minimum efficient scale occurs at the lowest rate of output at which long-run average costs are minimized.

DISCUSSION OF PREVIEW QUESTIONS

1. How does the economist's definition of profit differ from the accountant's?

The accountant defines total profits as total revenues minus total costs; the economist defines total profits as total revenues minus total opportunity costs of all inputs used. In other words, the economist takes into account implicit as well as explicit costs; the economist's definition stresses that an opportunity cost exists for all inputs used in the production process. Specifically, the economist estimates the opportunity cost for invested capital, the owner's time, inventories on hand, and so on. Because the economist's definition of costs is more inclusive, accounting profits will exceed economic profits; economic profits exist only when all the opportunity costs are taken into account.

2. What distinguishes the long run from the short run?

The short run is defined as any time period when there is at least one factor of production that a firm cannot vary; in the long run, *all* factors of production can be varied by the firm. Because each industry is likely to be unique in its ability to vary all inputs, the long run differs from industry to industry. Presumably the long run is a lot shorter (in absolute time periods) for firms in the carpentry or plumbing industry than for firms in the automobile or steel industry. In most economic models, labor is usually assumed to be the variable input in the short run, whereas capital is considered to be fixed in the short run; this assumption is fairly descriptive of the real-world situation.

3. How does the law of diminishing marginal returns account for an *eventually* increasing marginal cost curve for a firm in the short run?

Assume that labor is the only variable factor of production. *Eventually,* the law of diminishing returns comes into play (prior to this point, specialization benefits might increase the marginal product of labor), and the marginal product of labor falls. That is, beyond the point of diminishing returns, extra laborers contribute less to total product than immediately preceding laborers do, per unit of time. In effect, this means that if output is to be increased by equal amounts (or equal "batches"), more and more labor time will be required due to its lower marginal product. Later units of output, which are physically identical to earlier units of output, embody more labor time. If wages are constant, later units, which require more worker-hours, have a higher marginal cost. We conclude that beyond the point of diminishing returns, the marginal cost of output rises for the firm in the short run. Prior to the point of diminishing returns, the marginal cost curve falls, due to rising marginal product of labor.

4. Why is the short-run average total cost curve U-shaped?

Average total cost (ATC) equals the sum of average fixed costs (AFC) and average variable costs (AVC); that is, ATC = AFC + AVC. The AFC curve continuously falls because it is derived by dividing a constant number (total fixed costs) by larger and larger numbers (output levels). It falls rapidly at first, then slowly. The AVC curve falls during the early output stages because the benefits of specialization cause the marginal physical product of labor to rise and the marginal cost of output to fall; beyond the point of diminishing returns, the marginal physical product of labor falls, eventually forcing marginal cost to rise above AVC, and therefore AVC rises too. As we go from zero output to higher and higher output levels per unit of time, AFC and AVC both initially fall; therefore, ATC falls too. At some point beyond the point of diminishing marginal returns, AVC rises and outweighs the now slowly falling AFC curve; the net result is that somewhere beyond the point of diminishing marginal returns, the ATC curve rises. Because the ATC curve falls at low output levels and rises at higher output levels, we describe it as U-shaped. Of course, it doesn't look exactly like a *U,* but it is close enough.

PROBLEMS

(Answers to the odd-numbered problems appear at the back of the book.)

22-1. "Now that I have paid off my van, it won't cost me anything except for the running expenses, such as gas, oil, and tune-ups, when I use it." What is wrong with this reasoning?

22-2. Examine this table.

Units of Labor (per eight-hour day)	Marginal Product of Labor (per eight-hour day)
1	2
2	4
3	6
.	.
.	.
.	.
12	20
13	10
14	5
15	3
16	2

a. Suppose that this firm wants to increase output over the short run. How much labor time is required to produce the first unit? The second and third? Do the fourth, fifth, and sixth units of output require more or less labor time than the earlier units?

b. Suppose that we have hired 11 laborers and now want to increase the short-run output in batches of 20. To produce the first batch of 20 (beyond the eleventh laborer), how many labor hours are required? What will the next batch of 20 cost, in labor hours? Do additional batches of 20 cost more or less than earlier batches (beyond the eleventh laborer)?

c. What do parts (a) and (b) imply about the relationship between the marginal product of labor and labor time embodied in equal increments of output?

22-3. Refer to the table in Problem 22-2. Assume that wage rates equal $1 per eight-hour day.

a. By hiring the twelfth unit of labor, what was the cost to the firm of this first batch of 20?

b. What was the marginal cost of output in that range? (Hint: If 20 units cost $1, what did *one* unit cost?)

c. What will the next batch of 10 cost the firm?

d. What is the marginal cost of output over that range?

e. What is happening to the marginal cost of output?

f. How are the marginal product of labor and the marginal cost of output related?

22-4. Your school's basketball team had a foul-shooting average of .800 (80 out of 100) before last night's game, during which they shot 5 for 10 at the foul line.

a. What was their marginal performance last night?

b. What happened to the team's foul-shooting average?

c. Suppose that their foul shooting in the next game is 6 for 10. What is happening to their marginal performance?

d. Now what is the team average foul-shooting percentage?

22-5. Define long-run average total cost. In light of the fact that businesses are operated day to day in the short run, of what use is the concept of long-run average total cost to the entrepreneur?

22-6. A recent college graduate turns down a $20,000-per-year job offer in order to open his own business. He borrows $150,000 to purchase equipment. Total sales during his first year are $250,000. Total labor costs for the first year are $160,000, and raw material costs are equal to $50,000. He pays $15,000 interest on the loan per year. Estimate the economic profit of this business for the first year.

22-7. Examine this table.

Output (units)	Average Fixed Cost	Total Cost
0	—	$200
5	$40	300
10	20	380
20	10	420
40	5	520

a. Find the average variable cost at each level of production.

b. What is the marginal cost of increasing output from 10 to 20 units? From 20 to 40 units?

c. Find the average total cost at each level of production.

22-8. You are given the following graph.

a. At what output level is AVC at a minimum?
b. At what output level is ATC at a minimum?
c. At what output level is MC at a minimum?
d. At what output level do the AVC and MC curves intersect?
e. At what output level do the ATC and MC curves intersect?

22-9. Fill in the missing values for marginal, average, and total product in the following table. Assume that capital and labor are the only two inputs in the production function and that capital is held fixed.

Units of Labor	Total Product	Marginal Product	Average Product
6	120	—	20
7	147	___	21
8	___	23	___
9	___	___	20

CHAPTER 23

PERFECT COMPETITION

Few Americans today would say that competition does not exist in the U.S. marketplace. But how much competition is there really? In the world of perfect competition, which you will read about in this chapter, there are so many suppliers of a particular good or service that above-competitive profits cannot exist for long. Is that true of big corporations in this country? Or have many corporations managed to avoid serious competition? To answer this question, you need to learn about the model of perfect competition and its assumptions.

PREVIEW QUESTIONS

1. How much will a perfect competitor produce in the short run?

2. What is the perfectly competitive firm's short-run supply curve?

3. Can a perfectly competitive firm earn economic profits?

4. Why is the perfectly competitive market structure considered economically efficient?

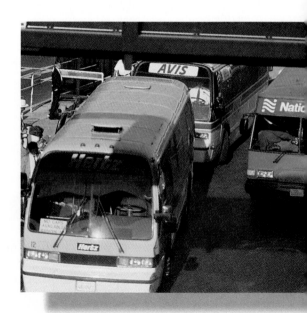

Perfect competition
A market structure in which the
decisions of individual buyers
and sellers have no effect on
market price.

Perfectly competitive firm
A firm that is such a small part
of the total industry that it cannot affect the price of the product it sells.

Price taker
A competitive firm that must
take the price of its product as
given because the firm cannot
influence its price.

Did You Know That . . . in the United States, there are tens of thousands of copy shops? There are also several thousand desktop publishing companies offering their services. The number of companies wanting to sell only Web site development is much smaller but growing. The number of companies offering to write software applications is somewhere in between, but that is only in the United States. Today, because of the cheapness and rapidity of modern telecommunications, much of the software code that goes in today's computer applications programs produced by American companies is written in India and elsewhere.

Competition is the word that applies to all of these situations. As used in common speech, *competition* simply means "rivalry." In perfectly competitive situations, individual buyers and sellers cannot affect the market price—it is determined by the market forces of demand and supply. In this chapter we examine what has become known as perfect competition.

CHARACTERISTICS OF A PERFECTLY COMPETITIVE MARKET STRUCTURE

We are interested in studying how a firm acting within a perfectly competitive market structure makes decisions about how much to produce. In a situation of **perfect competition,** each firm is such a small part that it cannot affect the price of the product in question. That means that each **perfectly competitive firm** in the industry is a **price taker**—the firm takes price as a given, something determined *outside* the individual firm.

This definition of a competitive firm is obviously idealized, for in one sense the individual firm *has* to set prices. How can we ever have a situation in which firms regard prices as set by forces outside their control? The answer is that even though every firm sets its own prices, a firm in a perfectly competitive situation will find that it will eventually have no customers at all if it sets its price above the competitive price. The best example is in agriculture. Although the individual farmer can set any price for a bushel of wheat, if that price doesn't coincide with the market price of a bushel of similar-quality wheat, no one will purchase the wheat at a higher price; nor would the farmer be inclined to reduce revenues by selling below the market price.

Let's examine the reasons why a firm in a perfectly competitive industry ends up being a price taker.

1. *There must be a large number of buyers and sellers.* When this is the case, no one buyer or one seller has any influence on price.
2. *The product sold by the firms in the industry must be homogeneous.* The product sold by each firm in the industry must be a perfect substitute for the product sold by each other firm. Buyers must be able to choose from a large number of sellers of a product that the buyers believe to be the same.
3. *Any firm can enter or leave the industry without serious impediments.* Firms in a competitive industry cannot be hampered in their ability to get resources or relocate resources. They move labor and capital in pursuit of profit-making opportunities to whatever business venture gives them their highest expected rate of return on their investment.
4. *Both buyers and sellers have equal information.* Consumers have to be able to find out about lower prices charged by competing firms. Firms have to be able to find out about cost-saving innovations in order to lower production costs and prices, and they have to be able to learn about profitable opportunities in other industries.

INTERNATIONAL EXAMPLE
The Global Coal Market

A good real-world example of perfect competition is the market for coal. Coal is a fossil fuel that started as luxurious vegetation growing in the swamps that covered much of the world about 300 million years ago. Today, coal is found in nearly every region of the world, although the most commercially important deposits are in Asia, Australia, Europe, and North America. Great Britain led the world in coal production until about a century ago.

Throughout the world, coal is produced in literally thousands of different mines. The purchasers of coal, such as steel mills and electric utility generating companies, constantly keep track of the prices of coal output throughout the world. If the price of coal goes up, there are literally thousands of known untapped coal deposits that can be developed. If the price of coal drops, coal mines can be closed. So the market for coal probably conforms as closely as possible to the assumptions underlining the model of perfect competition.

FOR CRITICAL ANALYSIS: There are actually several different grades of coal. Does this seriously violate assumption 2 for a perfectly competitive industry? ●

THE DEMAND CURVE OF THE PERFECT COMPETITOR

When we discussed substitutes in Chapter 20, we pointed out that the more substitutes there were and the more similar they were to the commodity in question, the greater was the price elasticity of demand. Here we assume for the perfectly competitive firm that it is producing a homogeneous commodity that has perfect substitutes. That means that if the individual firm raises its price one penny, it will lose all of its business. This, then, is how we characterize the demand schedule for a perfectly competitive firm: It is the going market price as determined by the forces of market supply and market demand—that is, where the market demand curve intersects the market supply curve. The single-firm demand curve in a perfectly competitive industry is perfectly elastic at the going market price. Remember that with a perfectly elastic demand curve, any increase in price leads to zero quantity demanded.

We show the market demand and supply curves in panel (a) of Figure 23-1. Their intersection occurs at the price of $5. The commodity in question is computer diskettes, and assume for the purposes of this exposition that all diskettes are perfect substitutes for all

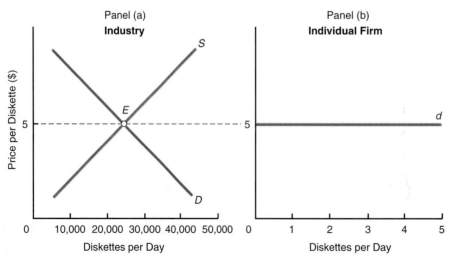

FIGURE 23-1

The Demand Curve for a Diskette Producer
At $5—where market demand, *D*, and market supply, *S*, intersect—the individual firm faces a perfectly elastic demand curve, *d*. If it raises its price even one penny, it will sell no diskettes at all. Notice the difference in the quantities of diskettes represented on the horizontal axis of panels (a) and (b).

others. At the going market price of $5 apiece, a hypothetical individual demand curve for a diskette producer who sells a very, very small part of total industry production is shown in panel (b). At the market price, this firm can sell all the output it wants. At the market price of $5 each, which is where the demand curve for the individual producer lies, consumer demand for the diskettes of that one producer is perfectly elastic. This can be seen by noting that if the firm raises its price, consumers, who are assumed to know that this supplier is charging more than other producers, will buy elsewhere, and the producer in question will have no sales at all. Thus the demand curve for that producer is perfectly elastic. We label the individual producer's demand curve *d,* whereas the *market* demand curve is always labeled *D.*

HOW MUCH SHOULD THE PERFECT COMPETITOR PRODUCE?

As we have shown, a perfect competitor has to accept the price of the product as a given. If the firm raises its price, it sells nothing; if it lowers its price, it makes less money per unit sold than it otherwise could. The firm has one decision left: How much should it produce? We will apply our model of the firm to this question to come up with an answer. We'll use the *profit-maximization model,* which assumes that firms attempt to maximize their total profits—the positive difference between total revenues and total costs.

Total Revenues

Total revenues
The price per unit times the total quantity sold.

Every firm has to consider its *total revenues,* or TR. **Total revenues** are defined as the quantity sold multiplied by the price. (They are the same as total receipts from the sale of output.) The perfect competitor must take the price as a given.

Look at Figure 23-2 on page 512. Much of the information in panel (a) comes from panel (a) of Figure 22-3, but we have added some essential columns for our analysis. Column 3 is the market price, *P,* of $5 per diskette, which is also equal to average revenue (AR) because

$$AR = \frac{TR}{Q} = \frac{PQ}{Q} = P$$

where *Q* stands for quantity. If we assume that all units sell for the same price, it becomes apparent that another name for the demand curve is the *average revenue curve* (this is true regardless of the type of market structure under consideration).

Column 4 shows the total revenues, or TR, as equal to the market price, *P,* times the total output in sales per day, or *Q.* Thus TR = *PQ.* We are assuming that the market supply and demand schedules intersect at a price of $5 and that this price holds for all the firm's production. We are also assuming that because our diskette maker is a small part of the market, it can sell all that it produces at that price. Thus panel (b) of Figure 23-2 shows the total revenue curve as a straight green line. For every unit of sales, total revenue is increased by $5.

Comparing Total Costs with Total Revenues

Total costs are given in column 2 of panel (a) of Figure 23-2 and plotted in panel (b). Remember, the firm's costs always include a normal rate of

Panel (a)

(1) Total Output and Sales per Day (Q)	(2) Total Costs (TC)*	(3) Market Price (P)	(4) Total Revenue (TR) (4) = (3) x (1)	(5) Total Profit (TR – TC) (5) = (4) – (2)	(6) Average Total Cost (ATC) (6) = (2) ÷ (1)*	(7) Average Variable Cost (AVC)*	(8) Marginal Cost (MC) (8) = $\frac{\text{Change in (2)}^*}{\text{Change in (1)}}$	(9) Marginal Revenue (MR) (9) = $\frac{\text{Change in (4)}}{\text{Change in (1)}}$
0	$10	$5	$ 0	–$10	—	—		
1	15	5	5	– 10	$15.00	$5.00	$5	$5
2	18	5	10	– 8	9.00	4.00	3	5
3	20	5	15	– 5	6.67	3.33	2	5
4	21	5	20	– 1	5.25	2.75	1	5
5	23	5	25	2	4.60	2.60	2	5
6	26	5	30	4	4.33	2.67	3	5
7	30	5	35	5	4.28	2.86	4	5
8	35	5	40	5	4.38	3.12	5	5
9	41	5	45	4	4.56	3.44	6	5
10	48	5	50	2	4.80	3.80	7	5
11	56	5	55	– 1	5.09	4.18	8	5

*From Figure 22-3.

FIGURE 23-2

Profit Maximization

Profit maximization occurs where marginal revenue equals marginal cost. Panel (a) indicates that this point occurs at a rate of sales of between seven and eight diskettes per day.

In panel (b), we find maximum profits where total revenues exceed total costs by the largest amount. This occurs at a rate of production and sales per day of seven or eight diskettes.

In panel (c), the marginal cost curve, MC, intersects the marginal revenue curve at a rate of output and sales of somewhere between seven and eight diskettes per day.

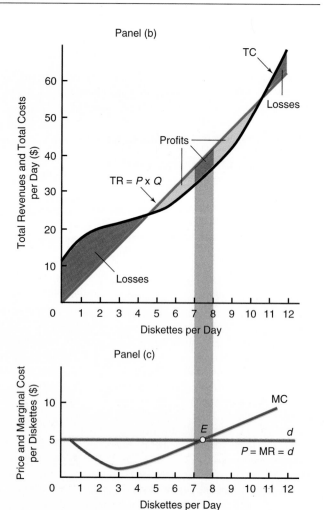

Panel (b)

Panel (c)

return on investment. So whenever we refer to total costs, we are talking not about accounting costs but about economic costs. When the total cost curve is above the total revenue curve, the firm is experiencing losses. When it is below the total revenue curve, the firm is making profits.

By comparing total costs with total revenues, we can figure out the number of diskettes the individual competitive firm should produce per day. Our analysis rests on the assumption that the firm will attempt to maximize total profits. In panel (a) of Figure 23-2, we see that total profits reach a maximum at a production rate of either seven or eight diskettes per day. We can see this graphically in panel (b) of the figure. The firm will maximize profits where the total revenue curve exceeds the total curve by the greatest amount. That occurs at a rate of output and sales of either seven or eight diskettes per day; this rate is called the **profit-maximizing rate of production.** (If output were continuously divisible or we were dealing with extremely large numbers of diskettes, we would get a unique profit-maximizing output.)

We can also find this profit-maximizing rate of production for the individual competitive firm by looking at marginal revenues and marginal costs.

Profit-maximizing rate of production
The rate of production that maximizes total profits, or the difference between total revenues and total costs; also, the rate of production at which marginal revenue equals marginal cost.

USING MARGINAL ANALYSIS TO DETERMINE THE PROFIT-MAXIMIZING RATE OF PRODUCTION

It is possible—indeed, preferred—to use marginal analysis to determine the profit-maximizing rate of production. We end up with the same results derived in a different manner, one that focuses more on where decisions are really made—on the margin. Managers examine changes in costs and relate them to changes in revenues. In fact, we almost always compare changes in cost with changes in benefits, where change is occurring at the margin, whether it be with respect to how much more or less to produce, how many more workers to hire or fire, or how much more to study or not study.

Marginal revenue represents the change in total revenues attributable to changing production by one unit of the product in question. Hence a more formal definition of marginal revenue is

Marginal revenue
The change in total revenues resulting from a change in output (and sale) of one unit of the product in question.

$$\text{Marginal revenue} = \frac{\text{change in total revenues}}{\text{change in output}}$$

In a perfectly competitive market, the marginal revenue curve is exactly equivalent to the price line or the individual firm's demand curve because the firm can sell all of its output (production) at the market price. Thus in Figure 23-1, the demand curve, d, for the individual producer is at a price of $5—the price line is coincident with the demand curve. But so is the marginal revenue curve, for marginal revenue in this case also equals $5.

The marginal revenue curve for our competitive diskette producer is shown as a line at $5 in panel (c) of Figure 23-2. Notice again that the marginal revenue curve is equal to the price line, which is equal to the individual firm's demand, or average revenue, curve, d.

When Are Profits Maximized?

Now we add the marginal cost curve, MC, taken from column 8 in panel (a) of Figure 23-2. As shown in panel (c) of that figure, the marginal cost curve first falls and then starts to rise because of the law of diminishing returns, eventually intersecting the marginal revenue curve and then rising above it. Notice that the numbers for both the marginal cost schedule, column 8 in panel (a), and the marginal revenue schedule, column 9 in panel (a), are printed *between* the rows on which the quantities appear. This indicates that we are looking at a *change* between one rate of output and the next.

In panel (c), the marginal cost curve intersects the marginal revenue curve somewhere between seven and eight diskettes per day. The firm has an incentive to produce and sell until the amount of the additional revenue received from selling one more diskette just equals the additional costs incurred for producing and selling that diskette. This is how the firm maximizes profit. Whenever marginal cost is less than marginal revenue, the firm will always make more profit by increasing production.

Now consider the possibility of producing at an output rate of 10 diskettes per day. The marginal cost curve at that output rate is higher than the marginal revenue (or d) curve. The firm would be spending more to produce that additional output than it would be receiving in revenues; it would be foolish to continue producing at this rate.

But how much should it produce? It should produce at point E, where the marginal cost curve intersects the marginal revenue curve from below.[1] The firm should continue production until the cost of increasing output by one more unit is just equal to the revenues obtainable from that extra unit. This is a fundamental rule in economics:

> **Profit maximization normally occurs at the rate of output at which marginal revenue equals marginal cost.**

For a perfectly competitive firm, this is at the intersection of the demand schedule, d, and the marginal cost curve, MC. When MR exceeds MC, each additional unit of output adds more to total revenues than to total costs, causing losses to decrease or profits to increase. When MC is greater than MR, each unit produced adds more to total cost than to total revenues, causing profits to decrease or losses to increase. Therefore, profit maximization occurs when MC equals MR. In our particular example, our profit-maximizing, perfectly competitive diskette producer will produce at a rate of either seven or eight diskettes a day. (If we were dealing with a very large rate of output, we would come up with an exact profit-maximizing rate.)

Exercise 23.2
Visit www.econtoday.com for more about product pricing.

CONCEPTS IN BRIEF

- Four fundamental characteristics of the market in perfect competition are (1) a large number of buyers and sellers, (2) a homogeneous product, (3) unrestrained exit from and entry into the industry by other firms, and (4) good information in the hands of both buyers and sellers.

- A perfectly competitive firm is a price taker. It has no control over price and consequently has to take price as a given, but it can sell all that it wants at the going market price.

- The demand curve for a perfect competitor is a line at the going market price. The demand curve is also the perfect competitor's marginal revenue curve because marginal revenue is defined as the change in total revenue due to a one-unit change in output.

- Profit is maximized at the rate of output where the positive difference between total revenues and total costs is the greatest. This is the same level of output at which marginal revenue equals marginal cost. The perfectly competitive firm produces at an output rate at which marginal cost equals the price per unit of output, because MR ≡ P.

---

[1]The marginal cost curve, MC, also cuts the marginal revenue curve, d, from above at an output rate of less than 1 in this example. This intersection should be ignored because it is irrelevant to the firm's decisions.

SHORT-RUN PROFITS

To find what our competitive individual diskette producer is making in terms of profits in the short run, we have to add the average total cost curve to panel (c) of Figure 23-2. We take the information from column 6 in panel (a) and add it to panel (c) to get Figure 23-3. Again the profit-maximizing rate of output is between seven and eight diskettes per day. If we have production and sales of seven diskettes per day, total revenues will be $35 a day. Total costs will be $30 a day, leaving a profit of $5 a day. If the rate of output in sales is eight diskettes per day, total revenues will be $40 and total costs will be $35, again leaving a profit of $5 a day. In Figure 23-3, the lower boundary of the rectangle labeled "Profits" is determined by the intersection of the profit-maximizing quantity line represented by vertical dashes and the average total cost curve. Why? Because the ATC curve gives us the cost per unit, whereas the price ($5), represented by *d,* gives us the revenue per unit, or average revenue. The difference is profit per unit. So the height of the rectangular box representing profits equals profit per unit, the length equals the amount of units produced, and when we multiply these two quantities, we get total profits. Note, as pointed out earlier, that we are talking about *economic profits* because a normal rate of return on investment is included in the average total cost curve, ATC.

It is certainly possible, also, for the competitive firm to make short-run losses. We give an example in Figure 23-4 on page 516, where we show the firm's demand curve shifting from d_1 to d_2. The going market price has fallen from $5 to $3 per diskette because of changes in market supply or demand conditions (or both). The firm will always do the best it can by producing where marginal revenue equals marginal cost. We see in Figure 23-4 that the marginal revenue (d_2) curve is intersected (from below) by the marginal cost curve at an output rate of about $5\frac{1}{2}$ diskettes per day. The firm is clearly not making profits because average total costs at that output rate are greater than the price of $3 per diskette. The losses are shown in the shaded area. By producing where marginal revenue equals marginal cost, however, the firm is minimizing its losses; that is, losses would be greater at any other output.

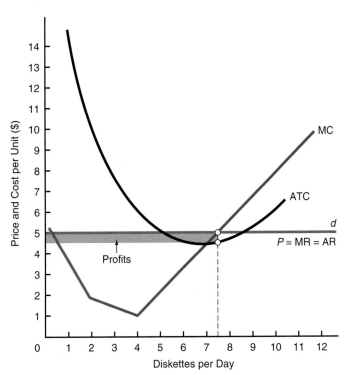

FIGURE 23-3

Measuring Total Profits
Profits are represented by the shaded area. The height of the profit rectangle is given by the difference between average total costs and price ($5), where price is also equal to average revenue. This is found by the vertical difference between the ATC curve and the price, or average revenue, line *d,* at the profit-maximizing rate of output of between seven and eight diskettes per day.

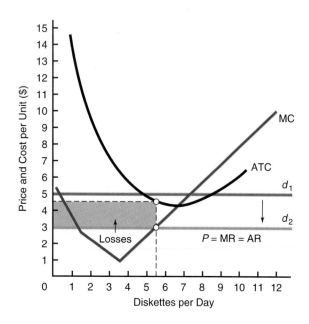

FIGURE 23-4

Minimization of Short-Run Losses

In cases in which average total costs exceed the average revenue, or price (and price is greater than or equal to average variable cost), profit maximization is equivalent to loss minimization. This again occurs where marginal cost equals marginal revenue. Losses are shown in the shaded area.

THE SHORT-RUN SHUTDOWN PRICE

In Figure 23-4, the firm is sustaining economic losses. Will it go out of business? In the long run it will, but surprisingly, in the short run the firm will not go out of business, for as long as the loss from staying in business is less than the loss from shutting down, the firm will continue to produce. A firm *goes out of business* when the owners sell its assets to someone else. A firm temporarily *shuts down* when it stops producing, but it still is in business.

Now how can we tell when the firm is sustaining economic losses in the short run and it is still worthwhile not to shut down? The firm must compare the cost of producing (while incurring losses) with the cost of closing down. The cost of staying in production in the short run is given by the total *variable* cost. Looking at the problem on a per-unit basis, as long as average variable cost (AVC) is covered by average revenues (price), the firm is better off continuing to produce. If average variable costs are exceeded even a little bit by the price of the product, staying in production produces some revenues in excess of variable costs that can be applied toward covering fixed costs.

A simple example will demonstrate this situation. The price of a product is $8, and average total costs equal $9 at an output of 100. In this example, average total costs are broken up into average variable costs of $7 and average fixed costs of $2. Total revenues, then, equal $8 × 100, or $800, and total costs equal $9 × 100, or $900. Total losses therefore equal $100. However, this does not mean that the firm will shut down. After all, if it does shut down, it still has fixed costs to pay. And in this case, because average fixed costs equal $2 at an output of 100, the fixed costs are $200. Thus the firm has losses of $100 if it continues to produce, but it has losses of $200 (the fixed costs) if it shuts down. The logic is fairly straightforward:

> As long as the price per unit sold exceeds the average *variable* cost per unit produced, the firm will be covering at least part of the opportunity cost of the investment in the business—that is, part of its fixed costs.

Calculating the Short-Run Break-Even Price

Look at demand curve d_1 in Figure 23-5. It just touches the minimum point of the average total cost curve, which, as you will remember, is exactly where the marginal cost curve

FIGURE 23-5
Short-Run Shutdown and Break-Even Prices
We can find the short-run break-even price and the short-run shut-down price by comparing price with average total costs and average variable costs. If the demand curve is d_1, profit maximization occurs at output E_1, where MC equals marginal revenue (the d curve). Because the ATC curve includes all relevant opportunity costs, point E_1 is the break-even point, and zero economic profits are being made. The firm is earning a normal rate of return. If the demand curve falls to d_2, profit maximization (loss minimization) occurs at the intersection of MC and MR (the d_2 curve), or E_2. Below this price, it does not pay for the firm to continue in operation because its average variable costs are not covered by the price of the product.

intersects the average total cost curve. At that price, which is about $4.30, the firm will be making exactly zero short-run economic profits. That price is called the **short-run break-even price,** and point E_1 therefore occurs at the short-run break-even price for a competitive firm. It is the point at which marginal revenue, marginal cost, and average total cost are all equal (that is, at which $P = MC$ and $P = ATC$). The break-even price is the one that yields zero short-run economic profits or losses.

Calculating the Short-Run Shutdown Price

Short-run break-even price
The price at which a firm's total revenues equal its total costs. At the break-even price, the firm is just making a normal rate of return on its capital investment. (It is covering its explicit and implicit costs.)

To calculate the firm's shutdown price, we must introduce the average variable cost (AVC) to our graph. In Figure 23-5, we have plotted the AVC values from column 7 in panel (a) of Figure 23-2. For the moment, consider two possible demand curves, d_1 and d_2, which are also the firm's respective marginal revenue curves. Therefore, if demand is d_1, the firm will produce at E_1, where that curve intersects the marginal cost curve. If demand falls to d_2, the firm will produce at E_2. The special feature of the hypothetical demand curve, d_2, is that it just touches the average variable cost curve at the latter's minimum point, which is also where the marginal cost curve intersects it. This price is the **short-run shutdown price.**

Short-run shutdown price
The price that just covers average variable costs. It occurs just below the intersection of the marginal cost curve and the average variable cost curve.

Why? Below this price, the firm would be paying out more in variable costs than it is receiving in revenues from the sale of its product. Each unit it sold would add to its losses. Clearly, the way to avoid incurring these additional losses, if price falls below the shutdown point, is in fact to shut down operations.

The intersection of the price line, the marginal cost curve, and the average variable cost curve is labeled E_2. The resulting short-run shutdown price is valid only for the short run because, of course, in the long run the firm will not stay in business at a yield less than a normal rate of return and hence at least zero economic profits.

THE MEANING OF ZERO ECONOMIC PROFITS

The fact that we labeled point E_1 in Figure 23-5 the break-even point may have disturbed you. At point E_1, price is just equal to average total cost. If this is the case, why would a firm continue to produce if it were making no profits whatsoever? If we again make the distinction between accounting profits and economic profits, then at that price the firm has zero economic profits but positive accounting profits. Recall that accounting profits are total revenues minus total explicit costs. What is ignored in such accounting is the reward offered to investors—the opportunity cost of capital—plus all other implicit costs.

In economic analysis, the average total cost curve includes the full opportunity cost of capital. Indeed, the average total cost curve includes the opportunity cost of *all* factors of production used in the production process. At the short-run break-even price, economic profits are, by definition, zero. Accounting profits at that price are not, however, equal to zero; they are positive. Consider an example. A baseball bat manufacturer sells bats at some price. The owners of the firm have supplied all the funds in the business. They have borrowed no money from anyone else, and they explicitly pay the full opportunity cost to all factors of production, including any managerial labor that they themselves contribute to the business. Their salaries show up as a cost in the books and are equal to what they could have earned in the next-best alternative occupation. At the end of the year, the owners find that after they subtract all explicit costs from total revenues, they have earned $100,000. Let's say that their investment was $1 million. Thus the rate of return on that investment is 10 percent per year. We will assume that this turns out to be equal to the rate of return that, on average, all other baseball bat manufacturers make in the industry.

This $100,000, or 10 percent rate of return, is actually, then, a competitive, or normal, rate of return on invested capital in that industry or in other industries with similar risks. If the owners had made only $50,000, or 5 percent on their investment, they would have been able to make higher profits by leaving the industry. The 10 percent rate of return is the opportunity cost of capital. Accountants show it as a profit; economists call it a cost. We include that cost in the average total cost curve, similar to the one shown in Figure 23-5. At the short-run break-even price, average total cost, including this opportunity cost of capital, will just equal that price. The firm will be making zero economic profits but a 10 percent *accounting* rate of return.

Now we are ready to derive the firm's supply curve.

THE PERFECT COMPETITOR'S SHORT-RUN SUPPLY CURVE

What does the supply curve for the individual firm look like? Actually, we have been looking at it all along. We know that when the price of diskettes is $5, the firm will supply seven or eight of them per day. If the price falls to $3, the firm will supply five or six diskettes per day. And if the price falls below $3, the firm will shut down in the short run. Hence in Figure 23-6, the firm's supply curve is the marginal cost curve above the short-run shutdown point. This is shown as the solid part of the marginal cost curve. ***The definition, then, of the individual firm's supply curve in a competitive industry is its marginal cost curve equal to and above the point of intersection with the average variable cost curve.***

The Short-Run Industry Supply Curve

In Chapter 3, we indicated that the market supply curve was the summation of individual supply curves. At the beginning of this chapter, we drew a market supply curve in Figure 23-1. Now we want to derive more precisely a market, or industry, supply curve to reflect individual producer behavior in that industry. First we must ask, What is an industry? It is merely a collection of firms producing a particular product. Therefore, we have a way to figure out the total supply curve of any industry: We add the quantities that each firm will

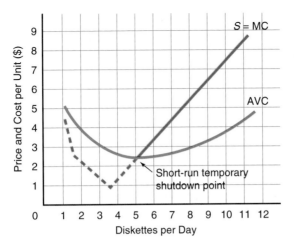

FIGURE 23-6

The Individual Firm's Short-Run Supply Curve
The individual firm's supply curve is the portion of its marginal cost curve above the minimum point on the average variable cost curve.

supply at every possible price. In other words, we sum the individual supply curves of all the competitive firms *horizontally*. The individual supply curves, as we just saw, are simply the marginal cost curves of each firm.

Consider doing this for a hypothetical world in which there are only two diskette producers in the industry, firm A and firm B. These two firms' marginal cost curves are given in panels (a) and (b) of Figure 23-7. The marginal cost curves for the two separate firms are presented as MC_A in panel (a) and MC_B in panel (b). Those two marginal cost curves are drawn only for prices above the minimum average variable cost for each respective firm. Hence we are not including any of the marginal cost curves below minimum average variable cost. In panel (a), for firm A, at price P_1, the quantity supplied would be q_{A1}. At price P_2, the quantity supplied would be q_{A2}. In panel (b), we see the two different quantities that

FIGURE 23-7

Deriving the Industry Supply Curve
Marginal cost curves above average minimum variable cost are presented in panels (a) and (b) for firms A and B. We horizontally sum the two quantities supplied, q_{A1} and q_{B1}, at price P_1. This gives us point *F* in panel (c). We do the same thing for the quantities at price P_2. This gives us point *G*. When we connect those points, we have the industry supply curve, *S,* which is the horizontal summation of the firms' marginal cost curves above their respective average minimum costs.

would be supplied by firm B corresponding to those two prices. Now for price P_1 we add horizontally the quantity of q_{A1} and q_{B1}. This gives us one point, F, for our short-run **industry supply curve**, S. We obtain the other point, G, by doing the same horizontal adding of quantities at P_2. When we connect points F and G, we obtain industry supply curve S, which is also marked ΣMC, indicating that it is the horizontal summation of the marginal cost curves (above the respective minimum average variable cost of each firm).[2] Because the law of diminishing returns makes marginal cost curves rise, the short-run supply curve of a perfectly competitive industry must be upward-sloping.

Industry supply curve
The locus of points showing the minimum prices at which given quantities will be forthcoming; also called the *market supply curve*.

Factors That Influence the Industry Supply Curve

As you have just seen, the industry supply curve is the horizontal summation of all of the individual firms' marginal cost curves above their respective minimum average variable cost points. This means that anything that affects the marginal cost curves of the firm will influence the industry supply curve. Therefore, the individual factors that will influence the supply schedule in a competitive industry can be summarized as the factors that cause the variable costs of production to change. These are factors that affect the individual marginal cost curves, such as changes in the individual firm's productivity, in factor costs (wages paid to labor, prices of raw materials, etc.), in taxes, and in anything else that would influence the individual firm's marginal cost curve.

All of these are *ceteris paribus* conditions of supply. Because they affect the position of the marginal cost curve for the individual firm, they affect the position of the industry supply curve. A change in any of these will shift the market supply curve.

CONCEPTS IN BRIEF

- Short-run average profits or average losses are determined by comparing average total costs with price (average revenue) at the profit-maximizing rate of output. In the short run, the perfectly competitive firm can make economic profits or economic losses.

- The competitive firm's short-run break-even output occurs at the minimum point on its average total cost curve, which is where the marginal cost curve intersects the average total cost curve.

- The competitive firm's short-run shutdown output is at the minimum point on its average variable cost curve, which is also where the marginal cost curve intersects the average variable cost curve. Shutdown will occur if price falls below average variable cost.

- The firm will continue production at a price that exceeds average variable costs even though the full opportunity cost of capital is not being met; at least some revenues are going toward paying fixed costs.

- At the short-run break-even price, the firm is making zero economic profits, which means that it is just making a normal rate of return in that industry.

- The firm's short-run supply curve is the portion of its marginal cost curve equal to or above minimum average variable costs. The industry short-run supply curve is a horizontal summation of the individual firms' marginal cost curves above their respective minimum average variable costs.

---

[2] The capital Greek sigma, Σ, is the symbol for summation.

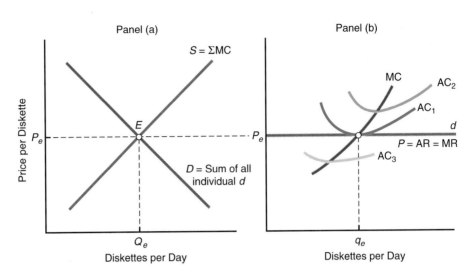

COMPETITIVE PRICE DETERMINATION

How is the market, or "going," price established in a competitive market? This price is established by the interaction of all the suppliers (firms) and all the demanders. The market demand schedule, D, in panel (a) of Figure 23-8 represents the demand schedule for the entire industry, and the supply schedule, S, represents the supply schedule for the entire industry. Price P_e is established by the forces of supply and demand at the intersection of D and the short-run industry supply curve, S. Even though each individual firm has no control or effect on the price of its product in a competitive industry, the interaction of *all* the producers and buyers determines the price at which the product will be sold. We say that the price P_e and the quantity Q_e in panel (a) of Figure 23-8 constitute the competitive solution to the pricing-quantity problem in that particular industry. It is the equilibrium where quantity demanded equals quantity supplied, and both suppliers and demanders are maximizing. The resulting individual firm demand curve, d, is shown in panel (b) of Figure 23-8 at the price P_e.

In a purely competitive industry, the individual producer takes price as a given and chooses the output level that maximizes profits. (This is also the equilibrium level of output from the producer's standpoint.) We see in panel (b) of Figure 23-8 that this is at q_e. If the producer's average costs are given by AC_1, q_e is also the short-run break-even output (see Figure 23-5); if its average costs are given by AC_2, at q_e, AC exceeds price (average revenue), and the firm is incurring losses. Alternatively, if average costs are given by AC_3, the firm will be making economic profits at q_e. In the former case, we would expect, over time, that people will cease production (exit the industry), causing supply to shift inward, whereas in the latter case, we would expect people to enter the industry to take advantage of the economic profits, thereby causing supply to shift outward. We now turn to these long-run considerations.

THE LONG-RUN INDUSTRY SITUATION: EXIT AND ENTRY

In the long run in a competitive situation, firms will be making zero economic profits. In the long run, we surmise that firms in perfect competition will tend to have average total cost curves that just touch the price (marginal revenue) curve, or individual demand curve d. How does this occur? It is through an adjustment process that depends on economic profits and losses.

Exit and Entry of Firms

Go back and look at Figures 23-3 and 23-4. The existence of either profits or losses is a signal to owners of capital both within and outside the industry. If the industry is characterized by firms showing economic profits as represented in Figure 23-3, this will signal owners of capital elsewhere in the economy that they, too, should enter this industry. If, by contrast, there are firms in the industry like the ones suffering economic losses represented in Figure 23-4, this signals resource owners outside the industry to stay out. It also signals resource owners within the industry not to reinvest and if possible to leave the industry. It is in this sense that we say that profits direct resources to their highest-valued use. In the long run, capital will flow into industries in which profitability is highest and will flow out of industries in which profitability is lowest.

The price system therefore allocates capital according to the relative expected rates of return on alternative investments. Entry restrictions will thereby hinder economic efficiency, and thus welfare, by not allowing resources to flow to their highest-valued use. Similarly, exit restrictions (such as plant closing laws) will act to trap resources (temporarily) in sectors in which their value is below that in alternative uses. Such laws will also inhibit the ability of firms to respond to changes in the domestic and international marketplace; yet to judge their desirability, we must weigh these factors against the costs to employees and local economies from such sudden economic disruptions.

Not every industry presents an immediate source of opportunity for every firm. In a brief period of time, it may be impossible for a firm that produces tractors to switch to the production of computers, even if there are very large profits to be made. Over the long run, however, we would expect to see such a change, whether or not the tractor producers want to change over to another product. In a market economy, investors supply firms in the more profitable industry with more investment funds, which they take from firms in less profitable industries. (Also, profits give existing firms internal investment funds for expansion.) Consequently, resources needed in the production of more profitable goods, such as labor, will be bid away from lower-valued opportunities. Investors and other suppliers of resources respond to market **signals** about their highest-valued opportunities.

Market adjustment to changes in demand will occur regardless of the wishes of the managers of firms in less profitable markets. They can either attempt to adjust their product line to respond to the new demands, be replaced by managers who are more responsive to new conditions, or see their firms go bankrupt as they find themselves unable to replace worn-out plant and equipment.

In addition, when we say that in a competitive long-run equilibrium situation firms will be making zero economic profits, we must realize that at a particular point in time it would be pure coincidence for a firm to be making *exactly* zero economic profits. Real-world information is not as precise as the curves we use to simplify our analysis. Things change all the time in a dynamic world, and firms, even in a very competitive situation, may for many reasons not be making exactly zero economic profits. We say that there is a *tendency* toward that equilibrium position, but firms are adjusting all the time to changes in their cost curves and in their individual demand curves.

Signals
Compact ways of conveying to economic decision makers information needed to make decisions. A true signal not only conveys information but also provides the incentive to react appropriately. Economic profits and economic losses are such signals.

EXAMPLE
Who Really Shops at Club Warehouses?

One of the most pervasive competitive innovations in retailing in the United States has been the club warehouse phenomenon. These now ubiquitous retail outlets were first developed by San Diego's Sol Price. He started the Price Club chain in 1976.

Since then, entry into the club warehouse business has been aggressive. It is dominated today by Wal-Mart-owned Sam's Club and PriceCostco, the successor to the original Price Club. Smaller club warehouse chains, such as B.J.'s (a subsidiary of Waban, Inc.), dominate regional markets.

One interesting aspect of club warehouses involves who shops there and their reasons for doing so. One might assume at first glance that poorer American families would patronize club warehouses more heavily because of the their lower prices. The reality is just the opposite—the average family shopping at a club warehouse has above-average income. What accounts for that? A club warehouse stocks only a few branded goods in each product category. In essence, the club warehouse has done each customer's comparison shopping and obtained the best terms from the vendors. Individuals who have a relatively higher opportunity cost of time (usually those who make higher incomes) find this a value-added service.

FOR CRITICAL ANALYSIS: *Why do you think the club warehouse market is dominated by a few large firms?* ●

Long-Run Industry Supply Curves

In panel (a) of Figure 23-8, we drew the summation of all of the portions of the individual firms' marginal cost curve above each firm's respective minimum average variable costs as the upward-sloping supply curve of the entire industry. We should be aware, however, that a relatively steep upward-sloping supply curve may be appropriate only in the short run. After all, one of the prerequisites of a competitive industry is free entry.

Long-run industry supply curve
A market supply curve showing the relationship between price and quantities forthcoming after firms have been allowed the time to enter into or exit from an industry, depending on whether there have been positive or negative economic profits.

Remember that our definition of the long run is a period of time in which adjustments can be made. The **long-run industry supply curve** is a supply curve showing the relationship between quantities supplied by the entire industry at different prices after firms have been allowed to either enter or leave the industry, depending on whether there have been positive or negative economic profits. Also, the long-run industry supply curve is drawn under the assumption that entry and exit have been completed.

The long-run industry supply curve can take one of three shapes, depending on whether input costs stay constant, increase, or decrease as the number of firms in the industry changes. In Chapter 22, we assumed that input prices remained constant to the firm regardless of the firm's rate of output. When we look at the entire industry, when all firms are expanding and new firms are entering, they may simultaneously bid up input prices.

Constant-cost industry
An industry whose total output can be increased without an increase in long-run per-unit costs; an industry whose long-run supply curve is horizontal.

Constant-Cost Industries. In principle, there are small enough industries that use such a small percentage of the total supply of inputs necessary for their production that firms can enter the industry without bidding up input prices. In such a situation, we are dealing with a **constant-cost industry.** Its long-run industry supply curve is therefore horizontal and is represented by S_L in panel (a) of Figure 23-9 on page 524.

We can work through the case in which constant costs prevail. We start out in panel (a) with demand curve D_1 and supply curve S_1. The equilibrium price is P_1. Market demand shifts rightward to D_2. In the short run, the equilibrium price rises to D_2. This generates positive economic profits for existing firms in the industry. Such economic profits induce capital to flow into the industry. The existing firms expand and/or new firms enter. The short-run supply curve shifts outward to S_2. The new intersection with the new demand curve is at E_3. The new equilibrium price is again P_1. The long-run supply curve is obtained by connecting the intersections of the corresponding pairs of demand and supply curves, E_1 and E_3. Labeled S_L, it is horizontal; its slope is zero. In a constant-cost industry, long-run

FIGURE 23-9

Constant-Cost, Increasing-Cost, and Decreasing-Cost Industries

In panel (a), we show a situation in which the demand curve shifts from D_1 to D_2. Price increases from P_1 to P_2; however, in time the short-run supply curve shifts outward because positive profits are being earned, and the equilibrium shifts from E_2 to E_3. The market clearing price is again P_1. If we connect points such as E_1 and E_3, we come up with the long-run supply curve S_L. This is a constant-cost industry. In panel (b), costs are increasing for the industry, and therefore the long-run supply curve slopes upward and long-run prices rise from P_1 to P_2. In panel (c), costs are decreasing for the industry as it expands, and therefore the long-run supply curve slopes downward such that long-run prices decline from P_1 to P_2.

supply is perfectly elastic. Any shift in demand is eventually met by an equal shift in supply so that the long-run price is constant at P_1.

Retail trade is often given as an example of such an industry because output can be expanded or contracted without affecting input prices. Banking is another example.

Increasing-Cost Industries. In an **increasing-cost industry,** expansion by existing firms and the addition of new firms cause the price of inputs specialized within that industry to be bid up. As costs of production rise, the ATC curve and the firms' MC curve shift upward, causing short-run supply curves (each firm's marginal cost curve) to shift upward. The result is a long-run industry supply curve that slopes upward, as represented by S_L in panel (b) of Figure 23-9. Examples are residential construction and coal mining—both use specialized inputs that cannot be obtained in ever-increasing quantities without causing their prices to rise.

Increasing-cost industry
An industry in which an increase in industry output is accompanied by an increase in long-run per-unit costs, such that the long-run industry supply curve slopes upward.

Decreasing-Cost Industries. An expansion in the number of firms in an industry can lead to a reduction in input costs and a downward shift in the ATC and MC curves. When this occurs, the long-run industry supply curve will slope downward. An example is given in panel (c) of Figure 23-9. This is a **decreasing-cost industry.**

LONG-RUN EQUILIBRIUM

In the long run, the firm can change the scale of its plant, adjusting its plant size in such a way that it has no further incentive to change. It will do so until profits are maximized. Figure 23-10 shows the long-run equilibrium of the perfectly competitive firm. Given a price

Decreasing-cost industry
An industry in which an increase in output leads to a reduction in long-run per-unit costs, such that the long-run industry supply curve slopes downward.

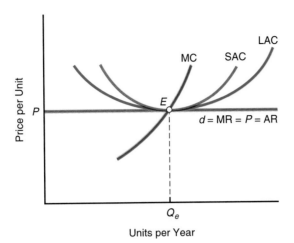

FIGURE 23-10
Long-Run Firm Competitive Equilibrium
In the long run, the firm operates where price, marginal revenue, marginal cost, short-run minimum average cost, and long-run minimum average cost are all equal. This occurs at point *E*.

of P and a marginal cost curve, MC, the firm produces at output Q_e. Because profits must be zero in the long run, the firm's short-run average costs (SAC) must equal P at Q_e, which occurs at minimum SAC. In addition, because we are in long-run equilibrium, any economies of scale must be exhausted so that we are on the minimum point of the long-run average cost curve (LAC). In other words, the long-run equilibrium position is where "everything is equal," which is at point E in Figure 23-10. There, *price* equals *marginal revenue* equals *marginal cost* equals *average cost* (minimum, short-run, and long-run).

Perfect Competition and Minimum Average Total Cost

Look again at Figure 23-10. In long-run equilibrium, the perfectly competitive firm finds itself producing at output rate Q_e. At that rate of output, the price is just equal to the minimum long-run average cost as well as the minimum short-run average cost. In this sense, perfect competition results in the production of goods and services using the least costly combination of resources. This is an important attribute of a perfectly competitive long-run equilibrium, particularly when we wish to compare the market structure of perfect competition with other market structures that are less than perfectly competitive. We will examine these other market structures in later chapters.

COMPETITIVE PRICING: MARGINAL COST PRICING

In a perfectly competitive industry, each firm produces where its marginal cost curve intersects its marginal revenue (d) curve from below. Thus perfectly competitive firms always sell their goods at a price that just equals marginal cost. This represents an optimal pricing situation because the price that consumers pay reflects the opportunity cost to society of producing the good. Recall that marginal cost is the amount that a firm must spend to purchase the additional resources needed to expand output by one unit. Given competitive markets, the amount paid for a resource will be the same in all of its alternative uses. Thus MC reflects relative resource input use; that is, if the MC of good 1 is twice the MC of good 2, one more unit of good 1 requires twice the resource input of one more unit of good 2. Because under perfect competition, price equals marginal cost, the consumer, in determining allocation of income on purchases on the basis of relative prices, is actually allocating income on the basis of relative resource input use.

Marginal Cost Pricing

The competitive firm produces up to the point at which the market price just equals the marginal cost. Herein lies the element of the optimal nature of a competitive solution. It is called **marginal cost pricing.** The competitive firm sells its product at a price that just equals the cost to society—the opportunity cost—for that is what the marginal cost curve represents. (But note here that it is the self-interest of firm owners that causes price to equal marginal social cost.) In other words, the marginal benefit to consumers, given by the price that they are willing to pay for the last unit of the good purchased, just equals the marginal cost to society of producing the last unit. (If the marginal benefit exceeds the marginal cost $(P > \text{MC})$, too little is being produced in that people value additional units more than the cost to society of producing them; if $P < \text{MC}$, the opposite is true.)

When an individual pays a price equal to the marginal cost of production, the cost to the user of that product is equal to the sacrifice or cost to society of producing that quantity of that good as opposed to more of some other good. (We are assuming that all marginal social costs are accounted for.) The competitive solution, then, is called *efficient,* in the economic sense of the word. Economic efficiency means that it is impossible to increase the output of any good without lowering the *value* of the total output produced in the economy. No juggling of resources, such as labor and capital, will result in an output that is higher in total value than the value of all of the goods and services already being produced. In an efficient situation, it is impossible to make one person better off without making someone else worse off. All resources are used in the most advantageous way possible, and society therefore enjoys an efficient allocation of productive resources. All goods and services are sold at their opportunity cost, and marginal cost pricing prevails throughout.

Marginal cost pricing
A system of pricing in which the price charged is equal to the opportunity cost to society of producing one more unit of the good or service in question. The opportunity cost is the marginal cost to society.

Market Failure

Although perfect competition does offer many desirable results, situations arise when perfectly competitive markets cannot efficiently allocate resources. Either too many or too few resources are used in the production of a good or service. These situations are instances of **market failure.** Externalities and public goods are examples. For reasons discussed in later chapters, perfectly competitive markets cannot efficiently allocate resources in these situations, and alternative allocation mechanisms are called for. Finally, the rate of innovation by perfectly competitive firms may be socially suboptimal, and the distribution of income may differ from what our normative judgment indicates. In all cases, alternative market structures, or government intervention, *may* improve the economic outcome.

Market failure
A situation in which an unrestrained market operation leads to either too few or too many resources going to a specific economic activity.

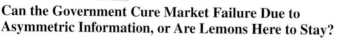 **POLICY EXAMPLE**
Can the Government Cure Market Failure Due to Asymmetric Information, or Are Lemons Here to Stay?

One kind of market failure may occur when assumption 4 with respect to perfect competition is violated. Specifically, if information is not the same for buyers and sellers, markets may be dominated by low-quality products. This is a situation of asymmetric information.

Lemons problem
The situation in which consumers, who do not know details about the quality of a product, are willing to pay no more than the price of a low-quality product, even if a higher-quality product at a higher price exists.

Exercise 23.3
Visit www.econtoday.com for more about lemon laws.

It has been called the **lemons problem** because cars, particularly used cars, that turn out to be "bad deals" are called lemons. The potential buyer of a used car has relatively little information about the true quality of the car—its motor, transmission, brakes, and so on. The only way the buyer can find out is to purchase the car and use it for a time. In contrast, the seller usually has much greater information about the quality of the car, for the seller has been using it for some time. The owner of the used car knows whether or not it is a lemon. In situations like this, with asymmetric information between buyer and seller, buyers typically tend to want to pay only a price that reflects the lower quality of the used car in the market, not a price that reflects the higher value of a truly good used car.

From the car seller's point of view, given that the price of used cars will tend to reflect average qualities, all of the owners of known lemons will want to put their cars up for sale. The owners of high-quality used cars will be more reluctant to do so. The logical result of this adverse selection is a disproportionate number of lemons on the used car market and consequently relatively fewer sales than would exist if information were symmetric.

So lemons will be overpriced and great-running used cars will be underpriced. Is there room for government policy to improve this market? Because the government has no better information than used-car buyers, it cannot provide any improved information. What the government has done, though, is require mileage certificates on all used cars and the disclosure of major defects and work that has been performed on them. What the market has done is use brand names both for cars and for firms that sell used cars. Additionally, used-car retailers offer extended warranties.

FOR CRITICAL ANALYSIS: If used-car dealers depend on repeat customers, is the lemons problem reduced or eliminated? ●

CONCEPTS IN BRIEF

- The competitive price is determined by the intersection of the market demand curve and the market supply curve; the market supply curve is equal to the horizontal summation of the portions of the individual marginal cost curves above their respective minimum average variable costs.

- In the long run, competitive firms make zero economic profits because of entry and exit of firms into and out of the industry whenever there are industrywide economic profits or economic losses.

- A constant-cost industry will have a horizontal long-run supply curve. An increasing-cost industry will have a upward-sloping long-run supply curve. A decreasing-cost industry will have a downward-sloping long-run supply curve.

- In the long run, a competitive firm produces where price, marginal revenue, marginal cost, short-run minimum average cost, and long-run minimum average cost are all equal.

- Competitive pricing is essentially marginal cost pricing, and therefore the competitive solution is called efficient because marginal cost represents the social opportunity cost of producing one more unit of the good; when consumers face a price equal to the full opportunity cost of the product they are buying, their purchasing decisions will lead to an efficient use of available resources.

Airport waiting areas for rental-car shuttles are a micro-cosm of the U.S. economy. Intense competition exists at all levels and may explain why average corporate after-tax profits, as a percentage of total revenues, have fallen steadily.

Have "Greedy" Corporations Been Able to Avoid Serious Competition?

CONCEPTS APPLIED:
COMPETITION, PERFECT COMPETITION, PROFITS, ECONOMIC PROFITS

Visit www.econtoday.com for an Internet Activity that expands your understanding of these concepts.

There are plenty of politicians who believe that "greedy" corporations are keeping wages down while generating record corporate profits. Of course, we would expect to hear this argument from organized labor and even from the average employee. But this seems to be the accepted dogma from many parts of our society. When the stock market is booming, it is usually because corporations are doing well. Thus the bull market of much of the 1990s seemed to be prima facie evidence that U.S. corporations are more avaricious than ever.

The Economic Meaning of *Greed*

The word *greed* really has no analytical use in economics. Our models all assume that everyone—individuals and businesses—act *as if they were maximizing either utility or profits*. If the directors and management of corporations were not practicing profit maximization, competitive pressures would presumably force the value of their stocks to fall. The result would be takeovers by investors or other companies that were more in tune with profit maximization.

Absolute Versus Relative Profits

When judging how well corporations have done financially over time, two factors are important: past rates of inflation and the relative size of the firm. The news that corporations have earned record profits does not tell us anything about the rate of return to investment or even earnings expressed as a percentage of revenues. The absolute dollar amount of profits for large corporations is by definition much larger than it was 20 or 40 years ago, for two reasons: Corporations have much greater total revenues today, and there has been a lot of inflation. In sum,

whether one corporation makes $10 million in profits and another makes $2 billion in profits tells us very little.

What the Data Show

Figure 23-11 shows profits of corporations after taxes expressed as a percentage of total revenues. During the 1990s, such after-tax profits averaged around 6 percent of revenues, compared to 8 percent in the 1970s, 9 percent in the 1960s, and more than 10 percent in the 1950s. One of the reasons the ratio of after-tax profits to total revenues has fallen is that corporations are investing more in short-lived equipment, such as computers. Even so, Figure 23-11 appears to indicate that if anything, competition has become more fierce in America's corporate world. This is probably due to deregulation in industries such as telephones, banking, airlines, and trucking. In addition, global competition is intensifying.

Are Workers Suffering?

The share of corporate revenues going to employees has remained about the same since World War II. According to the Commerce Department, in the decade of the 1990s, corporations paid out about 65 percent of revenues to employees in wages and fringe benefits. That is actually more than corporations paid out in the 1950s and 1960s. One of the reasons that workers may think, nonetheless, that they are not getting their "fair share" is that compensation has been increasingly paid out in benefits rather than in take-home pay. In the 1950s, employee benefits were 4.4 percent of corporate revenues, whereas today they are approaching 12 percent of corporate revenues.

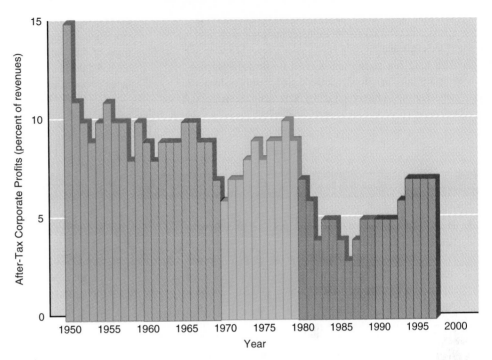

FIGURE 23-11

Declining Relative After-Tax Corporate Profits
The graph shows the ratio of corporate after-tax profits to total revenues. As you can see, this ratio is falling.

Source: U.S. Department of Commerce.

FOR CRITICAL ANALYSIS

1. What is a corporation anyway? Can such an entity be greedy?

2. How might corporate overexpansion—such as too many Borders bookstores in one city—lead to lower after-tax corporate profits as a percentage of revenues?

CHAPTER SUMMARY

1. We define a competitive situation as one in which individual firms cannot affect the price of the product they produce. This is usually when the firm is very small relative to the entire industry. A firm in a perfectly competitive situation is called a price taker; it must take price as a given.

2. The firm's total revenues will equal the price of the product times the quantity sold. Because the competitive firm can sell all it wants at the same price (the "going" price), total revenues equal the going price times the quantity the firm decides to sell.

3. The firm maximizes profits when marginal cost equals marginal revenue. The marginal revenue to the firm is represented by its own perfectly elastic demand curve. This is because marginal revenue is defined as the change in total revenues due to a change in output and sales by one unit. But the competitive firm can sell all it wants at the same price; therefore,

its marginal revenue will equal the price, which will equal its average revenue.

4. A perfectly competitive firm ends up in the long run making zero economic profits. However, it still makes a normal, or competitive, rate of return because that is the opportunity cost of capital. The competitive rate of return on investment is included in the costs as we have defined them for the firm.

5. The firm will always produce along its marginal cost curve unless the price falls below average variable costs; this would be the shutdown price. It occurs at the intersection of the average variable cost curve and the marginal cost curve. Below that price, it is not profitable to stay in production because variable costs will not be completely covered by revenues.

6. The supply curve of the firm is exactly equal to its marginal cost curve above the shutdown price. The supply curve of the industry is equal to the horizontal

summation of all the supply curves of the individual firms. This is a short-run industry supply curve, and it slopes upward.

7. The long-run supply curve will be upward-sloping, horizontal, or downward-sloping, depending on whether the industry is facing increasing, constant, or decreasing costs. The industry may have an upward-sloping long-run supply curve if it faces diseconomies of scale or increasing costs. The industry may have a downward-sloping long-run supply curve if it faces economies of scale or decreasing costs.

DISCUSSION OF PREVIEW QUESTIONS

1. **How much will a perfect competitor produce in the short run?**

   A perfect competitor will produce at the profit-maximizing rate of output; it will maximize the positive difference between total revenues and total costs. Another way of viewing this process is through analyzing marginal revenue (MR) and marginal cost (MC). The firm can maximize total profits by producing all outputs for which MR exceeds MC. Thus if MR > MC, the firm will produce the unit in question; if MR < MC, the firm will not produce the unit in question. If MC > MR, the extra cost of producing that unit is greater than the extra revenue that the firm can earn by selling it; producing a unit for which MC > MR leads to a reduction in total profits or an increase in total losses. In short, the perfect competitor will produce up to the output rate at which MR = MC; by doing so, it will have produced all units for which MR > MC, and it will be maximizing total profits.

2. **What is the perfectly competitive firm's short-run supply curve?**

   A supply curve indicates the various quantities per unit of time that will be offered, voluntarily, at different prices, other things being constant. Under perfect competition, price (P) equals marginal revenue (MR), and because the profit-maximizing output occurs where $P = MC$, it follows that any price above MC will induce more output until MC is driven up to equal that price. Thus the marginal cost curve is the firm's short-run supply schedule. We qualify this to note that because the firm has a shutdown point at the minimum average variable cost point, the technical short-run supply curve is the firm's marginal cost curve *above* the minimum average variable cost point.

3. **Can a perfectly competitive firm earn economic profits?**

   In the short run, yes; in the long run, no. Though it is possible for a perfectly competitive firm to earn profits in the short run, our assumption of free (unfettered but not costless) entry forces us to conclude that any positive economic (abnormal) profits will be bid away. This will happen because excess profits induce entry into the industry, which amounts to an increase in industry supply. Given demand, an increase in supply will cause market price to fall, thereby shifting the individual firm's demand curve downward. This process continues until economic profits equal zero; free entry allows new entrants to compete away economic profits.

4. **Why is the perfectly competitive market structure considered economically efficient?**

   The perfectly competitive market structure is considered economically efficient for two reasons: In the long run, economic profits are zero, and price equals marginal cost. We discuss each in turn. Profits are a signal; if economic profits are positive, the signal is that society wants *more* of this good; if economic profits are negative, this means that society wants *less* of this good; when economic profits are zero, just the "right" quantity of resources is being allocated to the production of a good. Also, the marginal cost of a good represents the social opportunity cost of producing one more unit of that good; the price of a good represents society's marginal valuation of that commodity. When price equals marginal cost, the value to society of the last unit produced (its price) is just offset by what society had to give up in order to get it (its marginal cost). Because under perfect competition, long-run economic profits equal zero and price equals marginal cost, an efficient allocation of resources exists.

PROBLEMS

(Answers to the odd-numbered problems appear at the back of the book.)

23-1. In the accompanying table, we list cost figures for a hypothetical firm. We assume that the firm is selling in a perfectly competitive market. Fill in all the blanks.

Output (units)	Fixed Cost	Average Fixed Cost (AFC)	Variable Cost	Average Variable Cost (AVC)	Total Cost	Average Total Cost (ATC)	Marginal Cost (MC)
1	$100	$_____	$40	$_____	$_____	$_____	$_____
2	100	_____	70	_____	_____	_____	_____
3	100	_____	120	_____	_____	_____	_____
4	100	_____	180	_____	_____	_____	_____
5	100	_____	250	_____	_____	_____	_____
6	100	_____	330	_____	_____	_____	_____

a. How low would the market price of its output have to go before the firm would shut down in the short run?

b. What is the price of its output at which the firm would just break even in the short run? (This is the same price below which the firm would go out of business in the long run.) What output would the firm produce at that price?

c. If the price of its output were $76, what rate of output would the firm produce, and how much profit would it earn?

23-2. Consider the accompanying graph. Then answer the questions.

a. Which demand curve indicates that the firm is earning normal profits?

b. Which demand curve indicates that the firm is earning abnormal profits?

c. Which demand curve indicates that the firm is indifferent between shutting down and producing?

d. Which curve is the firm's supply curve?

e. Below which price will the firm shut down?

23-3. In a perfectly competitive market, what is the difference between the demand the industry faces and the demand an individual firm faces?

23-4. Why might a firm continue to produce in the short run, even though the going price is less than its average total cost?

23-5. A firm in a perfectly competitive industry has total revenue of $200,000 per year when producing 2,000 units of output per year.

a. Find the firm's average revenue.

b. Find the firm's marginal revenue.

c. Assuming that the firm is maximizing profits, what is the firm's marginal cost?

d. If the firm is at long-run equilibrium, what are its short-run average costs?

23-6. The accompanying graph is for firm J. Study it; then answer the questions.

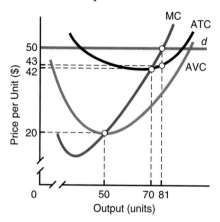

a. How many units will firm J sell in order to maximize profits?

b. What is firm J's total profit from selling the amount of output in part (a)?

c. At what price will firm J shut down in the short run?

d. If the cost curves shown represent production at the optimal long-run plant size, at what price will firm J shut down in the long run?

23-7. You have a friend who earns $25,000 a year working for a collection agency. In a savings and loan account she has $200,000 that she inherited. She is earning 6 percent per year on that money. She quits her job and buys a car wash with the $200,000. At the end of one year, she shows you her tax return. It indicates that the car wash had a pretax profit of $40,000. "What do you think about that?" she remarks. What is your answer?

COMPUTER-ASSISTED INSTRUCTION

Why do perfect competitors choose to produce at an output rate at which MR equals MC? What are the consequences for them if they fail to follow this rule?

Complete problem and answer appear on disk.

INTERACTING WITH THE INTERNET

For more information on the two largest club warehouses, go to

www.costco.com (PriceCostco)

www.samsclub.com (Sam's Club)

To investigate the international coal market, try some of the following Web addresses:

www.eia.doe.gov/historic.html

www.dri.mcgraw-hill.com/energy/eu0297.htm

www.globalcoal.com

CHAPTER 24

MONOPOLY

If you have traveled in the United States, you know that you are charged different prices in different cities for the same service from a taxicab. That is, the price per constant-quality unit of taxicab services differs across the United States. There is something else you might notice is different in the world of taxicabs in various cities: In some cities, you can always find a taxicab, whereas in others, it is often difficult to find one. In a competitive market with free entry and exit into the taxicab business, you would expect that the price per constant-quality unit of taxicab services would be about the same throughout the United States, as would the availability of taxicabs. Therein lies the problem—in many cities, it is not easy to enter the taxicab business. Indeed, in some cities, it is virtually impossible to start a new taxicab company unless you are willing to pay handsomely for the right to do so. To understand the motivation behind and consequences of closing a market to easy entry, you need to know about the theory of monopoly.

PREVIEW QUESTIONS

1. For the monopolist, marginal revenue is less than selling price. Why?

2. What is the profit-maximizing rate of output for the monopolist?

3. What are some common misconceptions about monopolists?

4. What is the cost to society of monopoly?

Did You Know That . . . the Central Selling Organization (CSO), a marketing group based in London, sells about 80 percent of the world's rough-cut diamonds each year, collecting handling fees of about 12 percent? The CSO is owned by South Africa's De Beers, the world's largest diamond mining company, controlled by Harry Oppenheimer. In any given year, the CSO sells between $4 and $5 billion in diamonds, making around $400 million a year in profits. It spends relatively little each year on advertising—"A diamond is forever." For all intents and purposes, there is one seller of rough-cut diamonds in the world, and you can be certain that the principal seller attempts to extract the maximum amount of profit possible under the circumstances.

Single sellers of goods and services exist all around you. The company that sells food in your school cafeteria has most probably been granted the exclusive right to do so by your college or university. The ski resort that offers you food at the top of the mountain does not allow anyone else to open a restaurant next to it. When you run a business that is the only one of its type in a particular location, you can usually charge a higher price per constant-quality unit than when there is intense competition. In this chapter you will read more about situations in which competition is restricted. We call these situations *monopoly*.

DEFINITION OF A MONOPOLIST

The word *monopoly* probably brings to mind notions of a business that gouges the consumer, sells faulty products, gets unconscionably rich, and other negative thoughts. But if we are to succeed in analyzing and predicting the behavior of noncompetitive firms, we will have to be more objective in our definition. Although most monopolies in the United States are relatively large, our definition will be equally applicable to small businesses: A **monopolist** is the *single supplier* of a good or service for which there is no close substitute.

In a monopoly market structure, the firm (the monopolist) and the industry are one and the same. Occasionally there may be a problem in identifying an industry and therefore determining if a monopoly exists. For example, should we think of aluminum and steel as separate industries, or should we define the industry in terms of basic metals? Our answer depends on the extent to which aluminum and steel can be substituted in the production of a wide range of products.

As we shall see in this chapter, a seller prefers to have a monopoly than to face competitors. In general, we think of monopoly prices as being higher than prices under perfect competition and of monopoly profits as being higher than profits under perfect competition (which are, in the long run, merely equivalent to a normal rate of return). How does a firm obtain a monopoly in an industry? Basically, there must be *barriers to entry* that enable firms to receive monopoly profits in the long run. Barriers to entry are restrictions on who can start a business or who can stay in a business.

Monopolist
A single supplier that comprises its entire industry for a good or service for which there is no close substitute.

BARRIERS TO ENTRY

For any amount of monopoly power to continue to exist in the long run, the market must be closed to entry in some way. Either legal means or certain aspects of the industry's technical or cost structure may prevent entry. We will discuss several of the barriers to entry that have allowed firms to reap monopoly profits in the long run (even if they are not pure monopolists in the technical sense).

Ownership of Resources Without Close Substitutes

Preventing a newcomer from entering an industry is often difficult. Indeed, some economists contend that no monopoly acting without government support has been able to prevent entry into the industry unless that monopoly has had the control of some essential natural resource. Consider the possibility of one firm's owning the entire supply of a raw material input that is essential to the production of a particular commodity. The exclusive ownership of such a vital resource serves as a barrier to entry until an alternative source of the raw material input is found or an alternative technology not requiring the raw material in question is developed. A good example of control over a vital input is the Aluminum Company of America (Alcoa), a firm that prior to World War II controlled the world's bauxite, the essential raw material in the production of aluminum. Such a situation is rare, though, and is ordinarily temporary.

Problems in Raising Adequate Capital

Certain industries require a large initial capital investment. The firms already in the industry can, according to some economists, obtain monopoly profits in the long run because no competitors can raise the large amount of capital needed to enter the industry. This is called the "imperfect" capital market argument employed to explain long-run, relatively high rates of return in certain industries. These industries are generally ones in which large fixed costs must be incurred merely to start production. Their fixed costs are generally for expensive machines necessary to the production process.

EXAMPLE
"Intel Inside"

Many observers of today's high-stakes high-technology world argue that the world's largest manufacturer of microprocessors, Intel, is a monopoly. They point out that to compete effectively with Intel, a potential adversary would have to invest billions of dollars. Intel provides the critical microprocessor chip that goes into the majority of the world's personal computers. Each new generation of microprocessor quickly becomes the industry standard for all IBM-compatible personal computers. Apple computers for years used a Motorola-made chip. In an attempt to fight back against Intel, Apple, Motorola, and IBM formed an alliance that did develop the Power PC microprocessor. So far, though, it has not made serious inroads into Intel's market. A few companies have attempted to clone Intel's chips, but they have not been very successful for both legal and technical reasons.

FOR CRITICAL ANALYSIS: Intel spends billions of dollars developing each new generation of microprocessor. Would it spend more or less if it had a smaller share of the microprocessor market? ●

Economies of Scale

Sometimes it is not profitable for more than one firm to exist in an industry. This is so if one firm would have to produce such a large quantity in order to realize lower unit costs that there would not be sufficient demand to warrant a second producer of the same product. Such a situation may arise because of a phenomenon we discussed in Chapter 22, economies of scale. When economies of scale exist, total costs increase less than proportionately to the increase in output. That is, proportional increases in output yield proportionately smaller

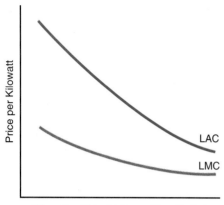

FIGURE 24-1

The Cost Curves That Might Lead to a Natural Monopoly: The Case of Electricity
Whenever long-run average costs are falling, so, too, will be long-run marginal costs. Also, long-run marginal costs (LMC) will always be below long-run average costs (LAC). A natural monopoly might arise in such a situation. The first firm to establish the low unit cost capacity would be able to take advantage of the lower average total cost curve. This firm would drive out all rivals by charging a lower price than the others could sustain at their higher average costs.

increases in total costs, and per-unit costs drop. The advantage in economies of scale lies in the fact that larger firms (with larger output) have lower costs that enable them to charge lower prices, and that drives smaller firms out of business.

When economies of scale occur over a wide range of outputs, a **natural monopoly** may develop. The natural monopoly is the firm that first takes advantage of persistent declining long-run average costs as scale increases. The natural monopolist is able to underprice its competitors and eventually force all of them out of the market.

In Figure 24-1, we have drawn a downward-sloping long-run average cost curve (LAC). Recall that when average costs are falling, marginal costs are less than average costs. We can apply the same analysis in the long run. When the long-run average cost curve (LAC) is falling, the long-run marginal cost curve (LMC) will be below the LAC.

In our example, long-run average costs are falling over such a large range of production rates that we would expect only one firm to survive in such an industry. That firm would be the natural monopolist. It would be the first one to take advantage of the decreasing average costs; that is, it would construct the large-scale facilities first. As its average costs fell, it would lower prices and get an increasingly larger share of the market. Once that firm had driven all other firms out of the industry, it would set its price to maximize profits.

Natural monopoly
A monopoly that arises from the peculiar production characteristics in an industry. It usually arises when there are large economies of scale relative to the industry's demand such that one firm can produce at a lower average cost than can be achieved by multiple firms.

Legal or Governmental Restrictions

Governments and legislatures can also erect barriers to entry. These include licenses, franchises, patents, tariffs, and specific regulations that tend to limit entry.

Licenses, Franchises, and Certificates of Convenience. In many industries, it is illegal to enter without a government license, or a "certificate of convenience and public necessity." For example, in many states you cannot form an electrical utility to compete with the electrical utility already operating in your area. You would first have to obtain a certificate of convenience and public necessity from the appropriate authority, which is usually the state's public utility commission. However, public utility commissions rarely, if ever, issue a certificate to a group of investors who want to compete directly in the same geographic area with an existing electrical utility; hence entry into the industry in a particular geographic area is prohibited, and long-run monopoly profits could conceivably be earned by the electrical utility already serving the area.

To enter interstate (and also many intrastate) markets for pipelines, television and radio broadcasting, and transmission of natural gas, to cite a few such industries, it is often necessary to obtain similar permits. Because these franchises or licenses are restricted, long-run monopoly profits might be earned by the firms already in the industry.

THE DWINDLING MONOPOLY POWER OF THE U.S. POSTAL SERVICE

CYBERSPACE EXAMPLE

In 1789, the Constitution gave Congress the power to "establish Post Offices and Post Roads." By 1792, the notion of a United States government monopoly on mail transportation was firmly established. In 1835, Congress passed definitive legislation called the Private Express Statutes to prevent any competition with the U.S. Post Office. Penalties for owners of vehicles that normally transported individuals employed as private letter carriers were spelled out. Today, the U.S. Postal Service (USPS) still maintains its monopoly on first-class mail. The USPS has always argued that because it is a natural monopoly, with large economies of scale, low-cost mail delivery is possible only with its coverage of the entire U.S. market. But entrepreneurialism and technology have eroded that argument, to the point that the concept of a USPS monopoly is losing its significance. United Parcel Service (UPS), Federal Express (FedEx), Airborne Express, DHL, and other private parcel carriers further chipped away at the USPS's monopoly. The fax machine became a player, too. And the Internet has virtually eliminated any remaining monopoly power that the USPS had, with half the businesses and households in the United States now communicating via e-mail. More than 6 billion e-mail messages are sent each year—and that's just within U.S. borders.

FOR CRITICAL ANALYSIS: In what ways might the USPS slow down the erosion of its monopoly position? ●

Patents. A patent is issued to an inventor to provide protection from having the invention copied or stolen for a period of 17 years. Suppose that engineers working for Ford Motor Company discover a way to build an engine that requires half the parts of a regular engine and weighs only half as much. If Ford is successful in obtaining a patent on this discovery, it can (in principle) prevent others from copying it. The patent holder has a monopoly. However, it is the patent holder's responsibility to defend the patent. That means that Ford—like other patent owners—must expend resources to prevent others from imitating its invention. If in fact the costs of enforcing a particular patent are greater than the benefits, the patent may not bestow any monopoly profits on its owner. The policing costs would be just too high.

Exercise 24.1
Visit www.econtoday.com for more about Coca-Cola.

EXAMPLE
Patents as Intellectual Property

A patent may bestow on its owner a monopoly for a given time period. So, too, may copyrights. Trademarks don't actually bestow monopoly power, but they do in certain cases have extreme value. Coca-Cola can exploit its trademark by licensing it for clothes and paraphernalia. So, too, can Harley-Davidson. Both of those companies have done so. Copyrights, trademarks, patents, and the like are all part of what is known as intellectual property. Songs, music, computer programs, and designs are all intellectual property. Indeed, some economists believe that the world value of intellectual property now exceeds the value of physical property, such as real estate, buildings, and equipment. Not surprisingly, in the corporate world, when a business buys another business, the acquiring company's lawyers have to worry a great deal about the acquired company's intellectual property portfolio. What intellectual property rights in terms of patents, trademarks, and copyrights does the soon-to-be-acquired company actually own?

FOR CRITICAL ANALYSIS: *Why doesn't the ownership of a well-known trademark bestow true monopoly power on its owner?* ●

Tariffs. **Tariffs** are special taxes that are imposed on certain imported goods. Tariffs have the effect of making imports relatively more expensive than their domestic counterparts so that consumers switch to the relatively cheaper domestically made products. If the tariffs are high enough, imports become overpriced, and domestic producers gain monopoly advantage as the sole suppliers. Many countries have tried this protectionist strategy by using high tariffs to shut out foreign competitors.

Tariffs
Taxes on imported goods.

Regulations. During much of the twentieth century, government regulation of the American economy has increased, especially along the dimensions of safety and quality. For example, pharmaceutical quality-control regulations enforced by the Food and Drug Administration may require that each pharmaceutical company install a $2 million computerized testing machine that requires elaborate monitoring and maintenance. Presumably, this large fixed cost can be spread over a larger number of units of output by larger firms than by smaller firms, thereby putting the smaller firms at a competitive disadvantage. It will also deter entry to the extent that the scale of operation of a potential entrant must be sufficiently large to cover the average fixed costs of the required equipment. We examine regulation in more detail in Chapter 26.

Cartels

"Being the only game in town" is preferable because such a monopoly position normally allows the monopolist to charge higher prices and make greater profits. Not surprisingly, manufacturers and sellers have often attempted to form an organization (which often is international) that acts as one. This is called a **cartel.** Cartels are an attempt by their members to earn higher than competitive profits. They set common prices and output quotas for their members. The key to the success of a cartel is keeping one member from competing against other members by expanding production and thereby lowering price. Apparently, one of the most successful international cartels ever was the Organization of Petroleum Exporting Countries (OPEC), an association of the world's largest oil-producing countries, including Saudi Arabia, which at times has accounted for a significant percentage of the world's crude oil output. OPEC effectively organized a significant cutback on the production of crude oil in the wake of the so-called Yom Kippur War in the Middle East in 1973. Within one year, the spot price of crude oil jumped from $2.12 to $7.61 per barrel on the world market. By the early 1980s, the price had risen to over $30.

Most cartels have not as much success.

Cartel
An association of producers in an industry that agree to set common prices and output quotas to prevent competition.

INTERNATIONAL EXAMPLE
"We're Just Trying to Keep the Market Stable"

The stated goal of most international cartels is keeping markets "stable." In reality, cartel members are seeking higher prices (and profits) for their product. But to achieve their aims, the producing countries have to be willing to withhold some of their production from the world market. In this way, the world price of a commodity does not fall if world production increases.

Nowhere are international cartels as prevalent as in the market for commodities. The International Coffee Organization lasted 30 years until the United States pulled out; it was succeeded by the Association of Coffee Producing Countries. Cocoa has the International Cocoa Organization. There is even an ostrich cartel called the Little Karoo Agricultural Cooperative.

The U.S. government has at times sanctioned the equivalent of a cartel. A meeting in Washington, D.C., involving executives from a dozen global aluminum producers and government officials representing the United States, the European Union, and four other nations ultimately resulted in an agreement by all those attending to reduce aluminum production. All such reductions were voluntary except by Russia. In exchange for cutting primary aluminum production by 500,000 tons over a two-year period, Russia received the promise of $250 million of U.S. taxpayers' money for equity investments. U.S. government officials claim that "the markets are still open" nonetheless.

FOR CRITICAL ANALYSIS: The price of gasoline today (corrected for inflation) is about 50 percent of what it was in 1984. What does that tell you about the long-run effectiveness of global cartels? •

CONCEPTS IN BRIEF

• A monopolist is defined as a single seller of a product or a good for which there is no good close substitute.

• To maintain a monopoly, there must be barriers to entry. Barriers to entry include ownership of resources without close substitutes; large capital requirements in order to enter the industry; economies of scale; legally required licenses, franchises, and certificates of convenience; patents; tariffs; and safety and quality regulations.

THE DEMAND CURVE A MONOPOLIST FACES

A *pure monopolist* is the sole supplier of *one* product, good, or service. A pure monopolist faces a demand curve that is the demand curve for the entire market for that good.

The monopolist faces the industry demand curve because the monopolist is the entire industry.

Because the monopolist faces the industry demand curve, which is by definition downward-sloping, its decision-making process with respect to how much to produce is not the same as for a perfect competitor. When a monopolist changes output, it does not automatically receive the same price per unit that it did before the change.

Profits to Be Made from Increasing Production

How do firms benefit from changing production rates? What happens to price in each case? Let's first review the situation among perfect competitors.

Marginal Revenue for the Perfect Competitor. Recall that a competitive firm has a perfectly elastic demand curve. That is because the competitive firm is such a small part of the market that it cannot influence the price of its product. It is a *price taker.* If the forces of supply and demand establish that the price per constant-quality pair of shoes is $50, the individual firm can sell all the pairs of shoes it wants to produce at $50 per pair. The average revenue is $50, the price is $50, and the marginal revenue is also $50.

Let us again define marginal revenue:

Marginal revenue equals the change in total revenue due to a one-unit change in the quantity produced and sold.

In the case of a competitive industry, each time a single firm changes production by one unit, total revenue changes by the going price, and price is always the same. Marginal revenue never changes; it always equals price, or average revenue. Average revenue was defined as total revenue divided by quantity demanded, or

$$\text{Average revenue} = \frac{\text{TR}}{Q} = \frac{PQ}{Q} = P$$

Marginal Revenue for the Monopolist. What about a monopoly firm? Because a monopoly is the entire industry, the monopoly firm's demand curve is the market demand curve. The market demand curve slopes downward, just like the other demand curves that we have seen. Therefore, to sell more of a particular product, given the industry demand curve, the monopoly firm must lower the price. Thus the monopoly firm moves *down* the demand curve. If all buyers are to be charged the same price, the monopoly must lower the price on all units sold in order to sell more. It cannot just lower the price on the *last* unit sold in any given time period in order to sell a larger quantity.

Put yourself in the shoes of a monopoly ferryboat owner. You have a government-bestowed franchise, and no one can compete with you. Your ferryboat goes between two islands. If you are charging $1 per crossing, a certain quantity of your services will be demanded. Let's say that you are ferrying 100 people a day each way at that price. If you decide that you would like to ferry more individuals, you must lower your price to all individuals—you must move *down* the existing demand curve for ferrying services. To calculate the marginal revenue of your change in price, you must first calculate the total revenues you received at $1 per passenger per crossing and then calculate the total revenues you would receive at, say, 90 cents per passenger per crossing.

It is sometimes useful to compare monopoly markets with perfectly competitive markets. The only way the monopolist can increase sales is by getting consumers to spend more of their incomes on the monopolist's product and less on all other products combined. Thus the monopolist is constrained by the entire market demand curve for its product. We see this in Figure 24-2, which compares the demand curves of the perfect competitor and the monopolist.

Panel (a)

Price per Unit

d

q

Demand If Individual Supplier Is in
Perfect Competition

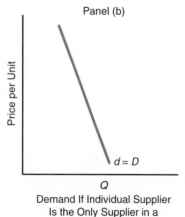

Panel (b)

Price per Unit

d = D

Q

Demand If Individual Supplier
Is the Only Supplier in a
Pure Monopoly

FIGURE 24-2

Demand Curves for the Perfect Competitor and the Monopolist
The perfect competitor in panel (a) faces a perfectly elastic demand curve, *d*. The monopolist in panel (b) faces the entire industry demand curve, which slopes downward.

Here we see the fundamental difference between the monopolist and the competitor. The competitor doesn't have to worry about lowering price to sell more. In a purely competitive situation, the competitive firm accounts for such a small part of the market that it can sell its entire output, whatever that may be, at the same price. The monopolist cannot. The more the monopolist wants to sell, the lower the price it has to charge on the last unit (and on *all* units put on the market for sale). Obviously, the extra revenues the monopolist receives from selling one more unit are going to be smaller than the extra revenues received from selling the next-to-last unit. The monopolist has to lower the price on the last unit to sell it because it is facing a downward-sloping demand curve and the only way to move down the demand curve is to lower the price on all units.

The Monopolist's Marginal Revenue: Less than Price

An essential point is that for the monopolist, marginal revenue is always less than price. To understand why, look at Figure 24-3, which shows a unit increase in sales due to a reduction in the price of a commodity from P_1 to P_2. After all, the only way that sales can increase, given a downward-sloping demand curve, is for the price to fall. Price P_2 is the price received for the last unit. Thus price P_2 times the last unit sold represents what is received from the last unit sold. That is equal to the vertical column (area A). Area A is one unit wide by P_2 high.

But price times the last unit sold is *not* the addition to *total* revenues received from selling that last unit. Why? Because price had to be reduced on all previous units sold (Q) in order to sell the larger quantity $Q + 1$. The reduction in price is represented by the vertical distance from P_1 to P_2 on the vertical axis. We must therefore subtract area B from area A to come up with the *change* in total revenues due to a one-unit increase in sales. Clearly, the change in total revenues—that is, marginal revenue—must be less than price because marginal revenue is always the difference between areas A and B in Figure 24-3. For example, if the initial price is $8 and quantity demanded is 3, to increase quantity to 4 units, it is necessary to decrease price to $7, not just for the fourth unit, but on all three previous units as well. Thus at a price of $7, marginal revenue is $7 − $3 = $4 because there is a $1 per unit price reduction on three previous units. Hence marginal revenue, $4, is less than price, $7.

MR = area A − area B

FIGURE 24-3

Marginal Revenue: Always Less than Price
The price received for the last unit sold is equal to P_2. The revenues received from selling this last unit are equal to P_2 times one unit, or the area of the vertical column. However, if a single price is being charged for all units, total revenues do not go up by the amount of the area represented by that column. The price had to be reduced on all the previous Q units that were being sold at price P_1. Thus we must subtract area B—the rectangle between P_1 and P_2 from the origin to Q—from area A in order to derive marginal revenue. Marginal revenue is therefore always less than price.

ELASTICITY AND MONOPOLY

The monopolist faces a downward-sloping demand curve (its average revenue curve). That means that it cannot charge just *any* price with no changes in quantity (a common misconception) because, depending on the price charged, a different quantity will be demanded.

Earlier we defined a monopolist as the single seller of a well-defined good or service with no *close* substitute. This does not mean, however, that the demand curve for a monopoly is vertical or exhibits zero price elasticity of demand. (Indeed, as we shall see, the profit-maximizing monopolist will never operate in a price range in which demand is inelastic.) After all, consumers have limited incomes and alternative wants. The downward slope of a monopolist's demand curve occurs because individuals compare the marginal satisfaction they will receive to the cost of the commodity to be purchased. Take the example of telephone service. Even if miraculously there were absolutely no substitute whatsoever for telephone service, the market demand curve would still slope downward. At lower prices, people will add more phones and separate lines for different family members.

Furthermore, the demand curve for telephone service slopes downward because there are at least several *imperfect* substitutes, such as letters, telegrams, in-person conversations, and CB and VHF-FM radios. Thus even though we defined a monopolist as a single seller of a commodity with no *close* substitute, we can talk about the range of *imperfect* substitutes. The more such imperfect substitutes there are, the more elastic will be the monopolist's demand curve, all other things held constant.

CONCEPTS IN BRIEF

- The monopolist estimates its marginal revenue curve, where marginal revenue is defined as the change in total revenues due to a one-unit change in quantity sold.

- For the perfect competitor, price equals marginal revenue equals average revenue. For the monopolist, price is always greater than marginal revenue. For the monopolist, marginal revenue is always less than price because price must be reduced on all units to sell more.

- The price elasticity of demand for the monopolist depends on the number and similarity of substitutes. The more numerous and more similar the substitutes, the greater the price elasticity of demand of the monopolist's demand curve.

COSTS AND MONOPOLY PROFIT MAXIMIZATION

To find out the rate of output at which the perfect competitor would maximize profits, we had to add cost data. We will do the same thing now for the monopolist. We assume that profit maximization is the goal of the pure monopolist, just as for the perfect competitor. The perfect competitor, however, has only to decide on the profit-maximizing rate of output because price was given. The competitor is a price taker. For the pure monopolist, we must seek a profit-maximizing *price-output combination* because the monopolist is a **price searcher.** We can determine this profit-maximizing price-output combination with either of two equivalent approaches—by looking at total revenues and total costs or by looking at marginal revenues and marginal costs. We shall examine both approaches.

Price searcher
A firm that must determine the price-output combination that maximizes profit because it faces a downward-sloping demand curve.

The Total Revenues–Total Costs Approach

We show hypothetical demand (rate of output and price per unit), revenues, costs, and other data in panel (a) of Figure 24-4. In column 3, we see total revenues for our hypothetical

Panel (a)

(1) Output (units)	(2) Price per Unit	(3) Total Revenues (TR) (3) = (2) x (1)	(4) Total Costs (TC)	(5) Total Profit (5) = (3) − (4)	(6) Marginal Cost (MC)	(7) Marginal Revenue (MR)
0	$8.00	$ .00	$10.00	−$10.00		
					$4.00	$7.80
1	7.80	7.80	14.00	− 6.20		
					3.50	7.40
2	7.60	15.20	17.50	− 2.30		
					3.25	7.00
3	7.40	22.20	20.75	1.45		
					3.05	6.60
4	7.20	28.80	23.80	5.00		
					2.90	6.20
5	7.00	35.00	26.70	8.30		
					2.80	5.80
6	6.80	40.80	29.50	11.30		
					2.75	5.40
7	6.60	46.20	32.25	13.95		
					2.85	5.00
8	6.40	51.20	35.10	16.10		
					3.20	4.60
9	6.20	55.80	38.30	17.50		
					4.00	4.20
10	6.00	60.00	42.30	17.70		
					6.00	3.80
11	5.80	63.80	48.30	15.50		
					9.00	3.40
12	5.60	67.20	57.30	9.90		

Panel (b)

Panel (c)

FIGURE 24-4

Monopoly Costs, Revenues, and Profits

In panel (a), we give hypothetical demand (rate of output and price per unit), revenues, costs, and other relevant data. As shown in panel (b), the monopolist maximizes profits where the positive differ-ence between TR and TC is greatest. This is at an output rate of between 9 and 10. Put another way, profit maximization occurs where marginal revenue equals marginal cost, as shown in panel (c). This is at the same output rate of between 9 and 10. (The MC curve must cut the MR curve from below.)

monopolist, and in column 4, we see total costs. We can transfer these two columns to panel (b). The only difference between the total revenue and total cost diagram in panel (b) and the one we showed for a perfect competitor in Chapter 23 is that the total revenue line is no longer straight. Rather, it curves. For any given demand curve, in order to sell more, the monopolist must lower the price. Thus, the basic difference between a monopolist and a perfect competitor has to do with the demand curve for the two types of firms. Monopoly market power is derived from facing a downward-sloping demand curve.

Profit maximization involves maximizing the positive difference between total revenues and total costs. This occurs at an output rate of between 9 and 10 units.

The Marginal Revenue–Marginal Cost Approach

Profit maximization will also occur where marginal revenue equals marginal cost. This is as true for a monopolist as it is for a perfect competitor (but the monopolist will charge a higher price). When we transfer marginal cost and marginal revenue information from columns 6 and 7 in panel (a) of Figure 24-4 to panel (c), we see that marginal revenue equals marginal cost at an output rate of between 9 and 10 units. Profit maximization occurs at the same output as in panel (b).

Why Produce Where Marginal Revenue Equals Marginal Cost? If the monopolist goes past the point where marginal revenue equals marginal cost, marginal cost will exceed marginal revenue. That is, the incremental cost of producing any more units will exceed the incremental revenue. It just wouldn't be worthwhile, as was true also in perfect competition. But if the monopolist produces less than that, it is also not making maximum profits. Look at output rate Q_1 in Figure 24-5. Here the monopolist's marginal revenue is at A, but marginal cost is at B. Marginal revenue exceeds marginal cost on the last unit sold; the profit for that *particular* unit, Q_1, is equal to the vertical difference between A

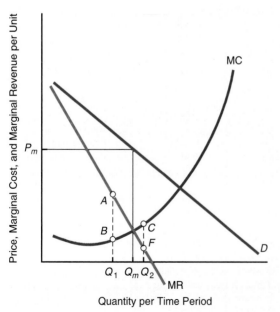

FIGURE 24-5

Maximizing Profits
The profit-maximizing production rate is Q_m, and the profit-maximizing price is P_m. The monopolist would be unwise to produce at the rate Q_1 because here marginal revenue would be Q_1A and marginal costs would be Q_1B. Marginal revenue exceeds marginal cost. The firm will keep producing until the point Q_m, where marginal revenue just equals marginal cost. It would be foolish to produce at the rate Q_2, for here marginal cost exceeds marginal revenue. It behooves the monopolist to cut production back to Q_m.

Price Increases Everywhere

Almost daily, stories appear in the media about price increases. They are usually presented as specific decisions by specific companies: "Ford announced a 3.2 percent increase in car prices" or "USX announced a 4.3 percent increase in its price of steel." One gets the impression that virtually all businesses in America raise prices whenever they want. Nothing could be further from the truth. Business pricing decisions depend on changes in cost and in demand. Just because individual firms have to have a price list does not mean that those prices are arbitrary. Even a monopolist faces a demand curve that is not perfectly inelastic.

and B, or the difference between marginal revenue and marginal cost. The monopolist would be foolish to stop at output rate Q_1 because if output is expanded, marginal revenue will still exceed marginal cost, and therefore total profits will rise. In fact, the profit-maximizing monopolist will continue to expand output and sales until marginal revenue equals marginal cost, which is at output rate Q_m. The monopolist won't produce at rate Q_2 because here, as we see, marginal costs are C and marginal revenues are F. The difference between C and F represents the *reduction* in total profits from producing that additional unit. Total profits will rise as the monopolist reduces its rate of output back toward Q_m.

What Price to Charge for Output?

How does the monopolist set prices? We know the quantity is set at the point at which marginal revenue equals marginal cost. The monopolist then finds out how much can be charged—how much the market will bear—for that particular quantity, Q_m, in Figure 24-5. We know that the demand curve is defined as showing the *maximum* price for which a given quantity can be sold. That means that our monopolist knows that to sell Q_m, it can charge only P_m because that is the price at which that specific quantity, Q_m, is demanded. This price is found by drawing a vertical line from the quantity, Q_m, to the market demand curve. Where that line hits the market demand curve, the price is determined. We find that price by drawing a horizontal line from the demand curve over to the price axis; that gives us the profit-maximizing price, P_m.

In our detailed numerical example, at a profit-maximizing rate of output of a little less than 10 in Figure 24-4, the firm can charge a maximum price of about \$6 and still sell all the goods produced, all at the same price.

The basic procedure for finding the profit-maximizing short-run price-quantity combination for the monopolist is first to determine the profit-maximizing rate of output, by either the total revenue–total cost method or the marginal revenue–marginal cost method, and then to determine by use of the demand curve, D, the maximum price that can be charged to sell that output.

Don't get the impression that just because we are able to draw an exact demand curve in Figure 24-4 and Figure 24-5, real-world monopolists have such perfect information. The process of price searching by a less than perfect competitor is just that—a process. A monopolist can only estimate the actual demand curve and therefore can only make an educated guess when it sets its profit-maximizing price. This is not a problem for the perfect competitor because price is given already by the intersection of market demand and market supply. The monopolist, in contrast, reaches the profit-maximizing output-price combination by trial and error.

CALCULATING MONOPOLY PROFIT

We have talked about the monopolist's profit, but we have yet to indicate how much profit the monopolist makes. We have actually shown total profits in column 5 of panel (a) in Figure 24-4. We can also find total profits by adding an average total cost curve to panel (c) of

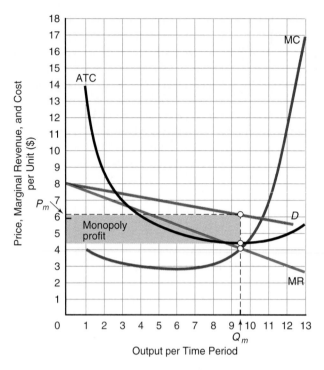

FIGURE 24-6

Monopoly Profit
We find monopoly profit by subtracting total costs from total revenues at an output rate of almost 10, labeled Q_m, which is the profit-maximizing rate of output for the monopolist. The profit-maximizing price is therefore about $6 and is labeled P_m. Monopoly profit is given by the shaded area, which is equal to total revenues (P × Q) minus total costs (ATC × Q). This diagram is similar to panel (c) of Figure 24-4, with the short-run average total cost curve (ATC) added.

that figure. We do that in Figure 24-6. When we add the average total cost curve, we find that the profit that a monopolist makes is equal to the shaded area [or total revenues minus total costs (ATC × Q)]. Given the demand curve and a uniform pricing system (i.e., all units sold at the same price), there is no way for a monopolist to make greater profits than those shown by the shaded area. The monopolist is maximizing profits where marginal cost equals marginal revenue. If the monopolist produces less than that, it will be forfeiting some profits. If the monopolist produces more than that, it will be forfeiting some profits.

The same is true of a perfect competitor. The competitor produces where marginal revenues equal marginal costs because it produces at the point where the marginal cost curve intersects the perfectly elastic firm demand curve. The perfectly elastic firm demand curve represents the marginal revenue curve for the pure competitor, for the same average revenues are obtained on all the units sold. Perfect competitors maximize profits at MR = MC, as do pure monopolists. But the perfect competitor makes no true economic profits in the long run; rather, all it makes is a normal, competitive rate of return.

In Chapter 23, we talked about companies experiencing short-run economic profits because they had, for example, invented something new. Competition, though, gradually eroded those higher than normal profits. The fact that a firm experiences higher than normal profits today does not mean that it has a monopoly forever. Try as companies may, keeping competitors away is never easy.

No Guarantee of Profits

The term *monopoly* conjures up the notion of a greedy firm ripping off the public and making exorbitant profits. However, the mere existence of a monopoly does not guarantee high

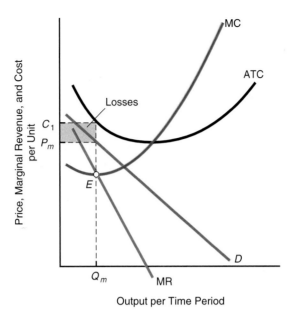

FIGURE 24-7

Monopolies: Not Always Profitable

Some monopolists face the situation shown here. The average total cost curve, ATC, is everywhere above the average revenue, or demand, curve, D. In the short run, the monopolist will produce where MC = MR at point E. Output Q_m will be sold at price P_m, but cost per unit is C_1. Losses are the shaded rectangle. Eventually, the monopolist will go out of business.

profits. Numerous monopolies have gone bankrupt. Figure 24-7 shows the monopolist's demand curve as D and the resultant marginal revenue curve as MR. It does not matter at what rate of output this particular monopolist operates; total costs cannot be covered. Look at the position of the average total cost curve. It lies everywhere above D (the average revenue curve). Thus there is no price-output combination that will allow the monopolist even to cover costs, much less earn profits. This monopolist will, in the short run, suffer economic losses as shown by the shaded area. The graph in Figure 24-7 depicts a situation for millions of typical monopolies that exist; they are called inventions. The owner of a patented invention or discovery has a pure legal monopoly, but the demand and cost curves may be such that production is not profitable. Every year at inventors' conventions, one can see many inventions that have never been put into production because they were deemed "uneconomic" by potential producers and users.

CONCEPTS IN BRIEF

• The basic difference between a monopolist and a perfect competitor is that a monopolist faces a downward-sloping demand curve, and therefore marginal revenue is less than price.

• The monopolist must choose the profit-maximizing price-output combination—the output at which marginal revenue equals marginal cost and the highest price possible as given by the demand curve for that particular output rate.

• Monopoly short-run profits are found by looking at average total costs compared to price per unit. This difference multiplied by quantity sold at that price determines monopoly profit.

• A monopolist does not necessarily earn a profit. If the average total cost curve lies entirely above the demand curve for a monopoly, production will not be profitable.

ON MAKING HIGHER PROFITS: PRICE DISCRIMINATION

In a perfectly competitive market, each buyer is charged the same price for every unit of the particular commodity (corrected for differential transportation charges). Because the product is homogeneous and we also assume full knowledge on the part of the buyers, a difference in price cannot exist. Any seller of the product who tried to charge a price higher than the going market price would find that no one would purchase it from that seller.

In this chapter we have assumed until now that the monopolist charged all consumers the same price for all units. A monopolist, however, may be able to charge different people different prices or different unit prices for successive units sought by a given buyer. When there is no cost difference, either one or a combination of these strategies is called **price discrimination.** A firm will engage in price discrimination whenever feasible to increase profits. A price-discriminating firm is able to charge some customers more than other customers.

It must be made clear at the outset that charging different prices to different people or for different units that reflect differences in the cost of service to those particular people does not amount to price discrimination. This is **price differentiation:** differences in price that reflect differences in marginal cost.

We can also say that a uniform price does not necessarily indicate an absence of price discrimination. Charging all customers the same price when production costs vary by customer is actually a case of price discrimination.

Price discrimination
Selling a given product at more than one price, with the price difference being unrelated to differences in cost.

Price differentiation
Establishing different prices for similar products to reflect differences in marginal cost in providing those commodities to different groups of buyers.

Necessary Conditions for Price Discrimination

Four conditions are necessary for price discrimination to exist:

1. The firm must face a downward-sloping demand curve.
2. The firm must be able to separate markets at a reasonable cost.
3. The buyers in the various markets must have different price elasticities of demand.
4. The firm must be able to prevent resale of the product or service.

For example, charging students a lower price than nonstudents for a movie can be done relatively easily. The cost of checking student IDs is apparently not significant. Also, it is fairly easy to make sure that students do not resell their tickets to nonstudents.

EXAMPLE
Cheaper Airfares for Some, Really Expensive Fares for Others

First-class airfares are often stunningly higher than coach class—far higher than any additional marginal cost warrants. This is a good example of price discrimination. And even in coach class, there may be fare differences of 800 percent. All coach passengers are packed in like sardines, so why the difference in price among them? The answer is again price discrimination, but this time it is based on how badly a person wants to fly. If you are a businessperson who is called to a meeting for the next day, you want to fly very badly. The fact that your company will not allow you to fly first class will not save you from having to pay, say, $2,000 to fly round-trip from Cincinnati to Los Angeles, particularly if you do not stay over on a Saturday. The Saturday stay-over requirement for low fares neatly differentiates individuals who must travel from those who have the time to stay over—people on business trips versus people on leisure trips. If you have a relatively high price elasticity of demand, you will also want to take advantage of low fares

FIGURE 24-8
Toward Perfect Price Discrimination
What the airlines attempt to do by dividing any particular round-trip fare into "buckets" is to price-discriminate as finely as possible. Here we show the airlines setting seven different prices for the same round trip. Those who pay price P_7 are the ones who are the last to ask for a reservation. Those who pay price P_1 are the ones who planned furthest in advance or happened to hit it lucky when seats were added to the low-fare bucket.

that require 7 days', 14 days', or longer advance purchase. The more price-sensitive you are, the more you will pay attention to such cheap-fare requirements, and the lower will be the fare you are likely to pay.

Airlines, with sophisticated computer programs performing what is known as yield management, are also able to change prices constantly. Such programs allow them to project relatively precisely how many last-minute business travelers are going to pay full fare to get on a flight. Computerized yield management works so well because of a mathematical formula that Bell Laboratories patented in 1988. It allows rapid calculations on fare problems with thousands of variables. The airlines compare historical databases on ridership with what is happening in terms of bookings right now. A typical flight will be divided into seven fare "buckets" that may have a differential of as much as 800 percent. The yield management computers constantly adjust the number of seats available in each bucket. When advance bookings are few, more seats are added to the low-fare buckets. When advance bookings are above normal, more seats are added to the highest-fare buckets. The result is lower fares for many and much higher fares for a few. In essence, the airlines are attempting to hit every "price point" on the demand curve for airline travel, as is shown in Figure 24-8.

FOR CRITICAL ANALYSIS: Assuming that the Bell Laboratories mathematical formula had been available 20 years ago, why couldn't airlines have used it then? ●

THE SOCIAL COST OF MONOPOLIES

Let's run a little experiment. We will start with a purely competitive industry with numerous firms, each one unable to affect the price of its product. The supply curve of the industry is equal to the horizontal sum of the marginal cost curves of the individual producers above their respective minimum average variable costs. In panel (a) of Figure 24-9 on page 550, we show the market demand curve and the market supply curve in a perfectly competitive situation. The competitive price in equilibrium is equal to P_e, and the equilibrium quantity at that price is equal to Q_e. Each individual competitor faces a demand curve (not shown) that is coincident with the price line P_e. No individual supplier faces the market demand curve, D.

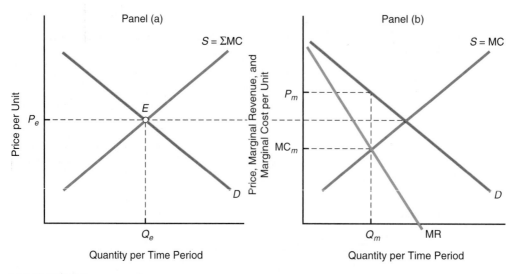

FIGURE 24-9

The Effects of Monopolizing an Industry
In panel (a), we show a competitive situation in which equilibrium is established at the intersection of D and S at point E. The equilibrium price would be P_e, and the equilibrium quantity would be Q_e. Each individual competitive producer faces a demand curve that is a horizontal line at the market clearing price, P_e. What happens if the industry is suddenly monopolized? We assume that the costs stay the same; the only thing that changes is that the monopolist now faces the entire downward-sloping demand curve. In panel (b), we draw the marginal revenue curve. Marginal cost is S because that is the horizontal summation of all the individual marginal cost curves. The monopolist therefore produces at Q_m and charges price P_m. P_m in panel (b) is higher than P_e in panel (a), and Q_m is less than Q_e. We see, then, that a monopolist charges a higher price and produces less than an industry in a competitive situation.

Now let's assume that a monopolist comes in and buys up every single competitor in the industry. In so doing, we'll assume that the monopolist does not affect any of the marginal cost curves or demand. We can therefore redraw D and S in panel (b) of Figure 24-9, exactly the same as in panel (a).

How does this monopolist decide how much to charge and how much to produce? If the monopolist is profit-maximizing, it is going to look at the marginal revenue curve and produce at the output where marginal revenue equals marginal cost. But what is the marginal cost curve in panel (b) of Figure 24-9? It is merely S because we said that S was equal to the horizontal summation of the portions of the individual marginal cost curves above each firm's respective minimum average variable cost. The monopolist therefore produces quantity Q_m and sells it at price P_m. Notice that Q_m is less than Q_e and that P_m is greater than P_e. A monopolist therefore produces a smaller quantity and sells it at a higher price. This is the reason usually given when economists criticize monopolists. Monopolists raise the price and restrict production, compared to a competitive situation. For a monopolist's product, consumers are forced to pay a price that exceeds the marginal cost of production. Resources are misallocated in such a situation—too few resources are being used in the monopolist's industry, and too many are used elsewhere.

Notice from Figure 24-9 that by setting $MR = MC$, the monopolist produces at a rate of output where $P > MC$ (compare P_m to MC_m). The marginal cost of a commodity (MC) represents what society had to give up in order to obtain the last unit produced. Price, by contrast, represents what buyers are willing to pay to acquire that last unit. Thus the price of a good represents society's valuation of the last unit produced. The monopoly outcome of $P > MC$ means that the value to society of the last unit produced is greater than its cost (MC); hence not enough of the good is being produced. As we have pointed out before, these differences between monopoly and competition arise not because of differences in costs but rather because of differences in the demand curves the individual firms face. The monopolist has monopoly power because it faces a downward-sloping demand curve. The individual perfect competitor faces a perfectly elastic demand curve.

Before we leave the topic of the cost to society of monopolies, we must repeat that our analysis is based on a heroic assumption. That assumption is that the monopolization of the perfectly competitive industry does not change the cost structure. If monopolization results in higher marginal cost, the cost to society is even greater. Conversely, if monopolization results in cost savings, the cost, if any, to society is less than we infer from our analysis. Indeed, we could have presented a hypothetical example in which monopolization led to such a dramatic reduction in average cost that society actually benefited. Such a situation is a possibility in industries in which economies of scale exist for a very great range of outputs.

CONCEPTS IN BRIEF

- Four conditions are necessary for price discrimination: (1) The firm must face a downward-sloping demand curve, (2) the firm must be able to distinguish markets, (3) buyers in different markets must have different price elasticities of demand, and (4) resale of the product or service must be preventable.

- A monopolist can make higher profits if it can price-discriminate. Price discrimination requires that two or more identifiable classes of buyers exist whose price elasticities of demand for the product or service are different and that these two classes of buyers can be distinguished at little cost.

- Price differentiation should not be confused with price discrimination. The former occurs when differences in price reflect differences in marginal cost.

- Monopoly results in a lower quantity being sold because the price is higher than it would be in an ideal perfectly competitive industry in which the cost curves were essentially the same as the monopolist's.

Finding a cab in New York City is not always easy. The city has severely restricted the number of licensed cabs. If you bought the right to operate a cab, would you expect to make a higher than normal rate of return on your investment?

Today's Hot Investment: A License to Operate a Taxi

CONCEPTS APPLIED:

MARKET POWER, MONOPOLY, ENTRY, COMPETITION, GOVERNMENT RESTRICTIONS

Visit www.econtoday.com for an Internet Activity that expands your understanding of these concepts.

One of the most important barriers to entry in certain markets is government restrictions. Even as it touts the importance of unfettered competition, government often supports special-interest groups by setting legal restrictions on entry. The taxicab business is one such example. Often the local government decides how many taxi "medallions" it will permit to exist. The most flagrant example of such government creation of monopoly involves New York City.

"Hey Buddy, Can You Spare $237,000?"

In a recent year, the right to operate a taxi in New York City was valued at $237,000. Why so high? Because New York City issued 11,787 licenses to operate taxis during the Great Depression—and then kept the number fixed for 60 years. Not until May 1996 did the city decide to auction off 53 new medallions. The 53 "lucky" bidders for those new medallions paid an average of $177,000. By 1998, they could have resold their licenses for $237,000. For six decades, medallions have been sold on the open market. Their price has increased about 18 percent a year, making them a better long-term investment than corporate stocks, which increased 10.9 percent per year over the same period.

Why Pay So Much for a Monopoly Right?

People who wish to buy medallions have to figure out how much they are really worth. The owner can use or lease the medallion by the day or the week. Many medal-

lion owners make their drivers supply the cars and the insurance. After all expenses are considered, a medallion owner can figure on making $20,000 to $30,000 a year. Most new purchasers of medallions take out a ten-year loan from a taxi industry credit union. The medallion is the collateral.

Does Competition Still Exist?

Because there are so few taxis relative to the population in New York City, you can expect competition to arise, even if it is illegal. Vans called *jitneys* operate illegally in many of New York's boroughs. The jitneys compete with taxis, as well as with the subway and buses. Many such vans are run by individuals who have applied for approval from the Taxi and Limousine Commission, only to be turned down by the City Council. Today, there are thousands of illegal van drivers in Brooklyn and Queens dodging the police. Many of them have banded together through a network of CB radios in order to avoid police cars.

One has to wonder about why such onerous restrictions on entry into the transportation business can last so long. The simple answer involves the "clout" that existing monopoly owners have within the political process that governs the regulation of taxicabs. (See Chapter 32 for more on special-interest groups.)

FOR CRITICAL ANALYSIS
1. Could you make a monopoly rate of return by buying a medallion?
2. What arguments might the city council use to justify refusing to license jitneys?

CHAPTER SUMMARY

1. We formally define a monopolist as the single supplier of a product or service with no close substitute. A monopolist faces the entire industry demand curve because the monopolist *is* the industry. Pure monopolists are rare.

2. A monopolist can usually remain a monopolist only if other firms are prevented from entering the industry and sharing in the monopoly profits. One barrier to entry is government restrictions. Patents are another.

3. A monopoly could arise because of firm economies of scale, which are defined as a situation in which an increase in output leads to a more than proportionate decrease in average total costs. If this were the case, average total costs would be falling as production increased. The first company to produce a great deal and take advantage of firm economies of scale could conceivably lower price and drive everyone else out of the industry. This would be a natural monopolist.

4. Health and quality regulations can be a barrier to entry because the increased fixed costs put smaller firms at a competitive disadvantage.

5. The marginal revenue that a monopolist receives is defined in the same way as the marginal revenue that a competitor receives. Nevertheless, because the monopolist faces the industry demand curve, it must lower price to increase sales, not only on the last unit sold, but also on all the preceding units. The monopolist's marginal revenue is therefore equal to the price received on the last unit sold minus the reduction in price on all the previous units times the number of previous units sold.

6. The profit-maximizing price that the monopolist charges is the maximum price that it can get away with while still selling everything produced up to the point where marginal revenue equals marginal cost.

We find this price by extending a vertical line from the intersection of the marginal revenue curve and the marginal cost curve up to the demand curve and then over to the vertical axis, which measures price.

7. Total profits are total revenues minus total costs. Total revenues are equal to the price of the product (the profit-maximizing price) times the quantity produced (the quantity found at the intersection of the marginal revenue and marginal cost curves). Total costs are equal to the quantity produced times average total costs. The difference between these total costs and total revenues is profits.

8. It can be shown that a competitive industry, if monopolized, will end up charging a higher price for its product but supplying a lower quantity of it. That is why monopolies are considered "bad" in an economic analysis. The monopolist will restrict production and increase price.

9. If a monopolist can effectively separate demanders into groups according to their demand elasticities, it can become a price-discriminating monopolist. (Resale between groups that were charged different prices must be prevented.) Price discrimination should not be confused with price differentiation, which occurs when differences in price reflect differences in marginal cost.

10. Four conditions are necessary for price discrimination to exist: (1) The firm must face a downward-sloping demand curve, (2) the firm must be able to distinguish markets, (3) buyers in different markets must have different price elasticities of demand, and (4) the firm must be able to prevent resale of the product.

11. Monopoly involves costs to society because the higher price leads to a reduction in output and consumption of the monopolized good.

DISCUSSION OF PREVIEW QUESTIONS

1. **For the monopolist, marginal revenue is less than selling price. Why?**

In the perfectly competitive model, the firm's selling price equals its marginal revenue (MR) because the firm can sell all it wants to sell at the going market price. This is not the case for the monopolist, which, as the sole supplier, faces the (downward-sloping) demand curve for the product. Thus the monopolist can sell more only by lowering price on all units sold per time period, assuming that it can't discriminate on price. Thus the monopolist's marginal revenue will equal price (which it gains from selling one more unit) *minus* the revenue that it loses from selling previously produced units at a lower price.

2. **What is the profit-maximizing rate of output for the monopolist?**

A monopolist will produce up to the point where marginal cost (MC) equals marginal revenue (MR). For example, if the output rate for the monopolist at which MR = MC is 80,000 units per week and MR is falling while MC is rising, any output beyond 80,000 units will have MC > MR; to produce units beyond 80,000 units will lower total profits. To produce at a rate less than 80,000 units per week would mean that not all the outputs at which MR > MC will be produced; hence total profits would not be maximized. Total profits are maximized at the output rate where MR = MC because all outputs for which MR > MC will be produced.

3. **What are some common misconceptions about monopolists?**

Many people think that a monopolist charges the highest price possible. This is untrue; the monopolist tries to maximize *total profits,* not price. The monopolist produces where MR = MC and *then* charges the highest price consistent with that output rate. Note that a monopolist can't charge any price *and* sell any amount; it must choose a price and have the amount

that it can sell be determined by the demand curve, or it must choose an output rate (where MR = MC) and have selling price determined by where that quantity intersects the demand curve. Another common misconception is that a monopolist must earn economic profits. This is not the case. To take an extreme example, if the monopolist's average cost curve lies above the demand curve, the monopolist will be suffering economic losses.

4. **What is the cost to society of monopoly?**

Because barriers to entry exist under monopoly, a monopolist could theoretically earn economic profits in the long run. Because profits are a signal that society wants more resources in that area, a misallocation of resources could exist; not enough resources flow to production of the monopolized commodity. Also, because the monopolist's selling price (P) exceeds its marginal revenue (MR) and the profit-maximizing output rate is where MR = MC (marginal cost), $P >$ MR = MC, or simply $P >$ MC (unlike under the perfectly competitive market structure, where $P =$ MC). The marginal cost of the commodity reflects what society had to give up in order to get the last unit produced, and price is what buyers have to pay in order to get it. Because $P >$ MC under monopoly, buyers must pay *more* to get this commodity than they must give up in order to get it; hence not enough of this commodity is produced. In short, under monopoly, price is higher and output is less than under perfect competition.

PROBLEMS

(Answers to the odd-numbered problems appear at the back of the book.)

24-1. Use the graph to answer the questions.

Quantity per Time Period

a. Suppose that a monopolist faces ATC_1. Define the rectangle that shows the monopolist's total costs at output rate Q. Also define the rectangle showing total revenue. Is the monopolist showing an economic loss, break-even (normal profit), or an economic profit? What is the significance of the MC = MR output?

b. Suppose that the monopolist faces ATC_2. Define the rectangle that shows the monopolist's total costs at output rate Q. Also define the rectangle showing total revenue. Is the monopolist showing an economic loss, break-even (normal profit), or an economic profit? What is the significance of the MC = MR output?

c. Suppose that the monopolist faces ATC_3. Define the rectangle that shows the monopolist's total costs at output rate Q. Also define the rectangle showing total revenue. Is the monopolist showing an economic loss, break-even (normal profit), or an economic profit? What is the significance of the MC = MR output?

24-2. Suppose that a monopolist faces the following demand schedule. Compute marginal revenue.

Price	Quantity Demanded	Marginal Revenue
$1,000	1	$_____
920	2	_____
840	3	_____
760	4	_____
680	5	_____
600	6	_____
520	7	_____
440	8	_____
350	9	_____
260	10	_____

24-3. State the necessary conditions for price discrimination. Then discuss how they might apply to the medical services of a physician.

24-4. In the text, we indicated that a monopolist will produce at the rate of output at which MR = MC and will then charge the highest price consistent with that output level. What conditions would exist if the monopolist charged a lower price? A higher price?

24-5. Summarize the relationship between price elasticity of demand and marginal revenue.

24-6. Explain why a monopolist will never set a price (and produce the corresponding output) at which the demand is price-inelastic.

24-7. Examine the revenue and cost figures for a monopoly firm in the table at the bottom of the page.
   a. Fill in the empty columns.
   b. At what rate(s) of output would the firm operate at a loss?
   c. At what rate(s) of output would the firm break even?
   d. At what rate(s) of output would the firm be maximizing its profits, and what would those profits be?

24-8. Answer the questions based on the accompanying graph for a monopolist.

   a. If this firm is a profit maximizer, how much output will it produce?
   b. At what price will the firm sell its output?
   c. How much profit or loss will this firm realize?
   d. ATC is at its minimum at what cost per unit?

Price	Quantity Demanded	Total Revenue	Marginal Revenue	Total Cost	Marginal Cost	Profit or Loss
$20	0	$_____	$_____	$ 4	$_____	$_____
16	1	_____	_____	10	_____	_____
12	2	_____	_____	14	_____	_____
10	3	_____	_____	20	_____	_____
7	4	_____	_____	28	_____	_____
4	5	_____	_____	40	_____	_____
0	6	_____	_____	54	_____	_____

24-9. Examine this information for a monopoly product.

Price	Quantity
$10.00	1,000
8.00	2,000
6.00	3,000
4.00	4,000
2.00	5,000
.50	6,000

    a. Calculate total revenue.
    b. Calculate marginal revenue.

    c. What is the maximum output that the producer of this product would ever produce?
    d. Why would this firm never produce more than the output amount in part (c)?

24-10. Suppose that a single-price monopolist and a comparable perfectly competitive industry experience a cost increase that causes average and marginal cost curves to shift upward by 10 percent. Will the resulting increase in market price be greater or less for the monopolist than for the perfectly competitive industry?

COMPUTER-ASSISTED INSTRUCTION

Monopolists follow the rule of producing at a quantity at which MR = MC, yet the outcome differs somewhat from that under competition. Here we find out why, and we explore the consequences for the monopolist if it deviates from this rule.

Complete problem and answer appear on disk.

INTERACTING WITH THE INTERNET

Find out about the Intel Corporation at

www.intel.com

Visit the U.S. Postal Service at

www.usps.com

CHAPTER 25

MONOPOLISTIC COMPETITION, OLIGOPOLY, AND STRATEGIC BEHAVIOR

The business world is a terribly competitive place, at least for most firms. Every firm would like to be a monopoly, but few achieve that status. Most firms are in either highly competitive industries or ones that face enough competition at home and abroad to prevent them from earning higher-than-competitive rates of return in the long run. In any event, decisions made by one company may affect many other companies, including suppliers, makers of complementary items, and manufacturers of substitutes. Can business decision making be thought of as a game? Further, in today's changing business world, can cooperation be a substitute for competition? These are questions about strategic behavior, the main focus of this chapter.

PREVIEW QUESTIONS

1. What are the characteristics of the monopolistically competitive market structure?

2. How does the monopolistic competitor determine the equilibrium price-output combination?

3. How does the monopolistically competitive market structure differ from that of perfect competition?

4. What are the characteristics of the oligopolistic market structure?

Did You Know That . . . the so-called father of the modern department store, John Wanamaker, once said, "Half the money I spend on advertising is wasted. The trouble is, I don't know which half"? Obviously, American businesses do not know either, for they continue to advertise more each year. Total advertising expenditures amount to billions of dollars every year. The number of ads popping up on the Internet's World Wide Web shows that American businesses will leave no stone unturned in their quest to let people know about their existence, what they have to sell, how they sell it, where it can be bought, and at what price.

Advertising did not show up in our analysis of perfect competition. Nonetheless, it plays a large role in industries that cannot be described as perfectly competitive but cannot be described as pure monopolies either. A combination of consumers' preferences for variety and competition among producers has led to similar but *differentiated* products in the marketplace. This situation has been described as *monopolistic competition,* the subject of the first part of this chapter. In the second part of the chapter, we look at how firms that are neither perfect competitors nor pure monopolists make strategic decisions. Such decisions do not exist for pure monopolists, who do not have to worry about actual competitors. And clearly, perfect competitors cannot make any strategic decisions, for they must take the market price as given. We call firms that have the ability to make strategic decisions *oligopolies,* which we will define more formally later in this chapter.

MONOPOLISTIC COMPETITION

In the 1920s and 1930s, economists became increasingly aware that there were many industries for which both the perfectly competitive model and the pure monopoly model did not apply and did not seem to yield very accurate predictions. Theoretical and empirical research was instituted to develop some sort of middle ground. Two separately developed models of **monopolistic competition** resulted. At Harvard, Edward Chamberlin published *The Theory of Monopolistic Competition* in 1933. The same year, Britain's Joan Robinson published *The Economics of Imperfect Competition.* In this chapter we will outline the theory as presented by Chamberlin.

Chamberlin defined monopolistic competition as a market structure in which there is a relatively large number of producers offering similar but differentiated products. Monopolistic competition therefore has the following features:

1. Significant numbers of sellers in a highly competitive market
2. Differentiated products
3. Sales promotion and advertising
4. Easy entry of new firms in the long run

Even a cursory look at the American economy leads to the conclusion that monopolistic competition is the dominant form of market structure in the United States. Indeed, that is true of all developed economies.

Monopolistic competition
A market situation in which a large number of firms produce similar but not identical products. Entry into the industry is relatively easy.

Number of Firms

In a perfectly competitive situation, there is an extremely large number of firms; in pure monopoly, there is only one. In monopolistic competition, there is a large number of firms, but not as many as in perfect competition. This fact has several important implications for a monopolistically competitive industry.

1. *Small share of market.* With so many firms, each firm has a relatively small share of the total market. Thus it has only a very small amount of control over the market clearing price.
2. *Lack of collusion.* With so many firms, it is very difficult for all of them to get together to collude—to cooperate in setting a pure monopoly price (and output). Price rigging in a monopolistically competitive industry is virtually impossible. Also, barriers to entry are minor, and the flow of new firms into the industry makes collusive agreements less likely. The large number of firms makes the monitoring and detection of cheating very costly and extremely difficult. This difficulty is compounded by differentiated products and high rates of innovation; collusive agreements are easier for a homogeneous product than for heterogeneous ones.
3. *Independence.* Because there are so many firms, each one acts independently of the others. No firm attempts to take into account the reaction of all of its rival firms—that would be impossible with so many rivals. Rivals' reactions to output and price changes are largely ignored.

Product Differentiation

Product differentiation
The distinguishing of products by brand name, color, and other minor attributes. Product differentiation occurs in other than perfectly competitive markets in which products are, in theory, homogeneous, such as wheat or corn.

Perhaps the most important feature of the monopolistically competitive market is **product differentiation.** We can say that each individual manufacturer of a product has an absolute monopoly over its own product, which is slightly differentiated from other similar products. This means that the firm has some control over the price it charges. Unlike the perfectly competitive firm, it faces a downward-sloping demand curve.

Consider the abundance of brand names for toothpaste, soap, gasoline, vitamins, shampoo, and most other consumer goods and a great many services. We are not obliged to buy just one type of television set, just one type of jeans, or just one type of footwear. There are usually a number of similar but differentiated products from which to choose. One reason is that the greater a firm's success at product differentiation, the greater the firm's pricing options.

Each separate differentiated product has numerous similar substitutes. This clearly has an impact on the price elasticity of demand for the individual firm. Recall that one determinant of price elasticity of demand is the availability of substitutes: The greater the number of substitutes available, other things being equal, the greater the price elasticity of demand. If the consumer has a vast array of alternatives that are just about as good as the product under study, a relatively small increase in the price of that product will lead many consumers to switch to one of the many close substitutes. Thus the ability of a firm to raise the price above the price of *close* substitutes is very small. The result of this is that even though the demand curve slopes downward, it does so only slightly. In other words, it is relatively elastic (over that price range) compared to a monopolist's demand curve. In the extreme case, with perfect competition, the substitutes are perfect because we are dealing with only one particular undifferentiated product. In that case, the individual firm has a perfectly elastic demand curve.

Exercise 25.1
Visit www.econtoday.com for more about the candy market.

Ease of Entry

For any current monopolistic competitor, potential competition is always lurking in the background. The easier—that is, the less costly—entry is, the more a current monopolistic competitor must worry about losing business.

A good example of a monopolistically competitive industry is the computer software industry. Many small firms provide different programs for many applications. The fixed capital costs required to enter this industry are small; all you need are skilled programmers. In addition, there are few legal restrictions. The firms in this industry also engage in extensive advertising in over 150 computer publications.

Sales Promotion and Advertising

Monopolistic competition differs from perfect competition in that no individual firm in a perfectly competitive market will advertise. A perfectly competitive firm, by definition, can sell all that it wants to sell at the going market price anyway. Why, then, would it spend even one penny on advertising? Furthermore, by definition, the perfect competitor is selling a product that is identical to the product that all other firms in the industry are selling. Any advertisement that induces consumers to buy more of that product will, in effect, be helping all the competitors, too. A perfect competitor therefore cannot be expected to incur any advertising costs (except for all firms in an industry collectively agreeing to advertise to urge the public to buy more beef or drink more milk).

But because the monopolistic competitor has at least *some* monopoly power, advertising may result in increased profits. Advertising is used to increase demand and to differentiate one's product. How much advertising should be undertaken? It should be carried to the point at which the additional revenue from one more dollar of advertising just equals that one dollar of marginal cost.

Advertising as Signaling Behavior. Recall from Chapter 23 that signals are compact gestures or actions that convey information. For example, high profits in an industry are signals that resources should flow to that industry. Individual companies can explicitly engage in signaling behavior. They do so by establishing brand names or trademarks, and then promoting them heavily. This is a signal to prospective consumers that this is a company that plans to stay in business. Before the modern age of advertising, banks in America faced a problem of signaling their soundness. They chose to make the bank building large, imposing, and constructed out of marble and granite. Stone communicated permanence. The effect was to give the bank's customers confidence that they were not doing business with a fly-by-night operation.

When Dell Computer advertises its brand name heavily, it incurs substantial costs. The only way it can recoup those costs is by selling lots of Dell computers over a long period of time. Thus heavy advertising of its brand name is a signal to personal computer buyers that Dell is interested in each customer's repeat business.

But what about advertising that does not seem to convey any information, not even about price? What good is an advertisement for, say, Wal-Mart that simply states, "We give you value that you can count on"?

EXAMPLE
Can Advertising Lead to Efficiency?

Advertising budgets by major retailers may just seem like an added expense, not a step on the road to economic efficiency. According to research by economists Kyle Bagwell of Northwestern University and Garey Ramey of the University of California at San Diego, just the opposite is true. When retailers advertise heavily, they increase the number of shoppers that come to their store. Such increased traffic allows retailers to offer a wider selection of goods, to invest in cost-reduction technology (such as computerized inventory and satellite communications), and to exploit manufacturers' quantity discounts. Such cost reductions can help explain the success of Wal-Mart, Circuit City, and Home Depot. Consequently, Bagwell and Ramey conclude that advertising can help promote efficiency even if it provides no "hard" information. Advertising signals to consumers where they can find big-company, low-priced, high-variety stores.

FOR CRITICAL ANALYSIS: Which is true, then: "We are bigger because we are better" or "We are better because we are bigger"? •

CONCEPTS IN BRIEF

- Monopolistic competition is a market structure that lies between pure monopoly and perfect competition.

- A monopolistically competitive market structure has (1) a large number of sellers, (2) differentiated products, (3) advertising, and (4) easy entry of firms in the long run.

- Because of the large number of firms, each has a small share of the market, making collusion difficult; the firms are independent.

PRICE AND OUTPUT FOR THE MONOPOLISTIC COMPETITOR

Now that we are aware of the assumptions underlying the monopolistic competition model, we can analyze the price and output behavior of each firm in a monopolistically competitive industry. We assume in the analysis that follows that the desired product type and quality have been chosen. We further assume that the budget and the type of promotional activity have already been chosen and do not change.

The Individual Firm's Demand and Cost Curves

Because the individual firm is not a perfect competitor, its demand curve slopes downward, as is shown in all three panels of Figure 25-1 on page 562. Hence it faces a marginal revenue curve that is also downward-sloping and below the demand curve. To find the profit-maximizing rate of output and the profit-maximizing price, we go to the output where the marginal cost curve intersects the marginal revenue curve from below. That gives us the profit-maximizing output rate. Then we draw a vertical line up to the demand curve. That gives us the price that can be charged to sell exactly that quantity produced. This is what we have done in Figure 25-1. In each panel, a marginal cost curve intersects the marginal revenue curve at E. The profit-maximizing rate of output is q_e, and the profit-maximizing price is P.

Short-Run Equilibrium

In the short run, it is possible for a monopolistic competitor to make economic profits—profits over and above the normal rate of return or beyond what is necessary to keep that firm in that industry. We show such a situation in panel (a) of Figure 25-1. The average total

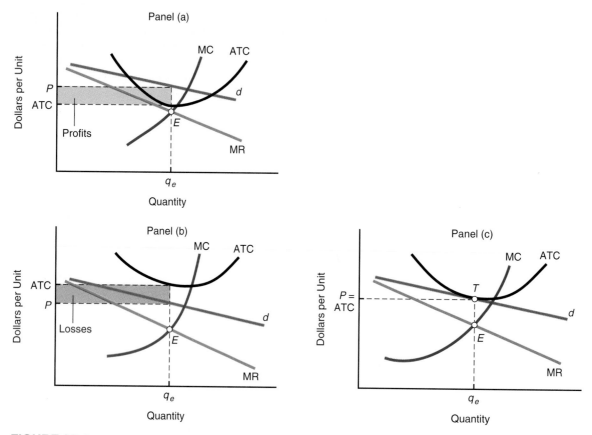

FIGURE 25-1

Short-Run and Long-Run Equilibrium with Monopolistic Competition

In panel (a), the typical monopolistic competitor is shown making economic profits. If that were the situation, there would be entry into the industry, forcing the demand curve for the individual monopolistic competitor leftward. Eventually, firms would find themselves in the situation depicted in panel (c), where zero economic profits are being made. In panel (b), the typical firm is in a monopolistically competitive industry making economic losses. If that were the case, firms would leave the industry. Each remaining firm's demand curve would shift outward to the right. Eventually, the typical firm would find itself in the situation depicted in panel (c).

cost curve is drawn in below the demand curve, d, at the profit-maximizing rate of output, q_e. Economic profits are shown by the shaded rectangle in that panel.

Losses in the short run are clearly also possible. They are presented in panel (b) of Figure 25-1. Here the average total cost curve lies everywhere above the individual firm's demand curve, d. The losses are marked as the shaded rectangle.

Just as with any market structure or any firm, in the short run it is possible to observe either economic profits or economic losses. (In the long run such is not the case with monopolistic competition, however.) In either case, the price does not equal marginal cost but rather is above it. Therefore, there is some misallocation of resources, a topic that we will discuss later in this chapter.

The Long Run: Zero Economic Profits

The long run is where the similarity between perfect competition and monopolistic competition becomes more obvious. In the long run, because so many firms produce substitutes for the product in question, any economic profits will disappear with competition. They will be reduced to zero either through entry by new firms seeing a chance to make a higher rate of return than elsewhere or by changes in product quality and advertising outlays by existing firms in the industry. (Profitable products will be imitated by other firms.) As for economic losses in the short run, they will disappear in the long run because the firms that suffer them will leave the industry. They will go into another business where the expected rate of return is at least normal. Panels (a) and (b) of Figure 25-1 therefore represent only short-run situations for a monopolistically competitive firm. In the long run, the average total cost curve will just touch the individual firm's demand curve *d* at the particular price that is profit-maximizing for that particular firm. This is shown in panel (c) of Figure 25-1.

A word of warning: This is an idealized, long-run equilibrium situation for each firm in the industry. It does not mean that even in the long run we will observe every single firm in a monopolistically competitive industry making *exactly* zero economic profits or *just* a normal rate of return. We live in a dynamic world. All we are saying is that if this model is correct, the rate of return will *tend toward* normal—economic profits will *tend toward* zero.

COMPARING PERFECT COMPETITION WITH MONOPOLISTIC COMPETITION

If both the monopolistic competitor and the perfect competitor make zero economic profits in the long run, how are they different? The answer lies in the fact that the demand curve for the individual perfect competitor is perfectly elastic. Such is not the case for the individual monopolistic competitor; its demand curve is less than perfectly elastic. This firm has some control over price. Price elasticity of demand is not infinite.

We see the two situations in Figure 25-2 on page 564. Both panels show average total costs just touching the respective demand curves at the particular price at which the firm is selling the product. Notice, however, that the perfect competitor's average total costs are at a minimum. This is not the case with the monopolistic competitor. The equilibrium rate of output is to the left of the minimum point on the average total cost curve where price is greater than marginal cost. The monopolistic competitor cannot expand output to the point of minimum costs without lowering price, and then marginal cost would exceed marginal revenue. A monopolistic competitor at profit maximization charges a price that exceeds marginal cost. In this respect it is similar to the monopolist.

It has consequently been argued that monopolistic competition involves waste because minimum average total costs are not achieved and price exceeds marginal cost. There are too many firms, each with excess capacity, producing too little output. According to critics of monopolistic competition, society's resources are being wasted.

Chamberlin had an answer to this criticism. He contended that the difference between the average cost of production for a monopolistically competitive firm in an open market and the minimum average total cost represented what he called the cost of producing

FIGURE 25-2

Comparison of the Perfect Competitor with the Monopolistic Competitor

In panel (a), the perfectly competitive firm has zero economic profits in the long run. The price is set equal to marginal cost, and the price is P_1. The firm's demand curve is just tangent to the minimum point on its average total cost curve, which means that the firm is operating at an optimum rate of production. With the monopolistically competitive firm in panel (b), there are also zero economic profits in the long run. The price is greater than marginal cost; the monopolistically competitive firm does not find itself at the minimum point on its average total cost curve. It is operating at a rate of output to the left of the minimum point on the ATC curve.

"differentness." Chamberlin did not consider this difference in cost between perfect competition and monopolistic competition a waste. In fact, he argued that it is rational for consumers to have a taste for differentiation; consumers willingly accept the resultant increased production costs in return for choice and variety of output.

CONCEPTS IN BRIEF

- In the short run, it is possible for monopolistically competitive firms to make economic profits or economic losses.

- In the long run, monopolistically competitive firms will make zero economic profits—that is, they will make a normal rate of return.

- Because the monopolistic competitor faces a downward-sloping demand curve, it does not produce at the minimum point on its average total cost curve. Hence we say that a monopolistic competitor has higher average total costs per unit than a perfect competitor would have.

- Chamberlin argued that the difference between the average cost of production for a monopolistically competitive firm and the minimum average total cost at which a competitive firm would produce is the cost of producing "differentness."

OLIGOPOLY

There is another market structure that we have yet to discuss, and it is an important one indeed. It involves a situation in which a few large firms dominate an entire industry. They are not competitive in the sense that we have used the term; they are not even monopolistically competitive. And because there are several of them, a pure monopoly does not exist. We call such a situation an **oligopoly,** which consists of a small number of interdependent sellers. Each firm in the industry knows that other firms will react to its changes in prices, quantities, and qualities. An oligopoly market structure can exist for either a homogeneous or a differentiated product.

Oligopoly
A market situation in which there are very few sellers. Each seller knows that the other sellers will react to its changes in prices and quantities.

Characteristics of Oligopoly

Oligopoly is characterized by the small number of interdependent firms that constitute the entire market.

Small Number of Firms. How many is "a small number of firms"? More than two but less than 100? The question is not easy to answer. Basically, though, oligopoly exists when a handful of firms dominate the industry enough to set prices. The top few firms in the industry account for an overwhelming percentage of total industry output.

Oligopolies usually involve three to five big companies dominating the industry. Between World War II and the 1970s, the U.S. automobile industry was dominated by three firms—General Motors, Chrysler, and Ford. Chewing-gum manufacturing and coin-operated amusement games are dominated by four large firms.

Interdependence. All markets and all firms are, in a sense, interdependent. But only when a few large firms dominate an industry does the question of **strategic dependence** of one on the others' actions arise. The firms must recognize that they are interdependent. Any action on the part of one firm with respect to output, price, quality, or product differentiation will cause a reaction on the part of other firms. A model of such mutual interdependence is difficult to build, but examples are not hard to find in the real world. Oligopolists in the cigarette industry, for example, are constantly reacting to each other.

Strategic dependence
A situation in which one firm's actions with respect to price, quality, advertising, and related changes may be strategically countered by the reactions of one or more other firms in the industry. Such dependence can exist only when there are a limited number of major firms in an industry.

Recall that in the model of perfect competition, each firm ignores the reactions of other firms because each firm is able to sell all that it wants at the going market price. At the other extreme, the pure monopolist does not have to worry about the reaction of current rivals because there are none. In an oligopolistic market structure, the managers of firms are like generals in a war: *They must attempt to predict the reaction of rival firms.* It is a strategic game.

Why Oligopoly Occurs

Why are some industries dominated by a few large firms? What causes an industry that might otherwise be competitive to tend toward oligopoly? We can provide some partial answers here.

Economies of Scale. Perhaps the strongest reason that has been offered for the existence of oligopoly is economies of scale. Recall that economies of scale are defined as a situation in which a doubling of output results in less than a doubling of total costs. When economies of scale exist, the firm's average total cost curve will slope downward as the firm produces more and more output. Average total cost can be reduced by continuing to expand the scale of operation. Smaller firms in such a situation will have a tendency to be inefficient. Their average total costs will be greater than those incurred by a large firm. Little by little, they will go out of business or be absorbed into the larger firm.

Barriers to Entry. It is possible that certain barriers to entry have prevented more competition in oligopolistic industries. They include legal barriers, such as patents, and control and ownership over critical supplies. Indeed, we can find periods in the past when firms maintained market power because they were able not only to erect a barrier to entry but also to keep it in place year after year. In principle, the chemical, electronics, and aluminum industries have been at one time or another either monopolistic or oligopolistic because of the ownership of patents and the control of strategic inputs by specific firms.

Oligopoly by Merger. Another reason that oligopolistic market structures may sometimes develop is that firms merge. A merger is the joining of two or more firms under single ownership or control. The merged firm naturally becomes larger, enjoys greater economies of scale as output increases, and may ultimately have a greater ability to control the market price for its product.

There are two types of mergers, horizontal and vertical. A **horizontal merger** involves firms selling a similar product. If two shoe manufacturing firms merge, that is a horizontal merger. If a group of firms, all producing steel, merge into one, that is also a horizontal merger. A **vertical merger** occurs when one firm merges with either a firm from which it purchases an input or a firm to which it sells its output. Vertical mergers occur, for example, when a coal-using electrical utility purchases a coal-mining firm or when a shoe manufacturer purchases retail shoe outlets. (Obviously, vertical mergers cannot create oligopoly as we have defined it.)

We have been talking about oligopoly in a theoretical manner until now. It is time to look at the actual picture of oligopolies in the United States.

> **THINKING CRITICALLY ABOUT THE MEDIA**
>
> **The "Big Three"**
>
> Media references to the automobile industry often make mention of "Detroit" or the "Big Three," referring to Ford, General Motors, and Chrysler. Indeed, the "Big Three" do account for about 90 percent of the value of total *domestic* shipments of motor vehicles. Thus it would seem that automobile manufacturing is a classic case of an oligopoly. Thirty years ago that was true; today it is not. The "Big Three" can no longer concern themselves merely with one another's reactions; they now have to worry about Toyota, Nissan, BMW, and a dozen other foreign competitors. Imports now account for almost 30 percent of total new car sales in the United States. The "Big Three" would love to be pure oligopolists in the U.S. market again, but increasing world trade has made that impossible.

Horizontal merger
The joining of firms that are producing or selling a similar product.

Vertical merger
The joining of a firm with another to which it sells an output or from which it buys an input.

Measuring Industry Concentration

As we have stated, oligopoly is a situation in which a few interdependent firms control a large part of total output in an industry. This has been called *industry concentration.* Before we show the concentration statistics in the United States, let's determine how industry concentration can be measured.

Concentration Ratio. The most popular way to compute industry concentration is to determine the percentage of total sales or production accounted for by the top four or top eight firms in an industry. This gives the four- or eight-firm **concentration ratio.** An example of an industry with 25 firms is given in Table 25-1. We can see in that table that the four largest firms account for almost 90 percent of total output in the hypothetical industry. That is an example of an oligopoly.

U.S. Concentration Ratios. Table 25-2 shows the four-firm *domestic* concentration ratios for various industries. Is there any way that we can show or determine which indus-

Concentration ratio
The percentage of all sales contributed by the leading four or leading eight firms in an industry; sometimes called the *industry concentration ratio.*

TABLE 25-1

Computing the Four-Firm Concentration Ratio

Firm	Annual Sales ($ Millions)		
1	150		
2	100	= 400	Total number of Firms in industry = 25
3	80		
4	70		
5 through 25	50		
Total	450		

Four-firm concentration ratio $= \dfrac{400}{450} = 88.9\%$

tries to classify as oligopolistic? There is no definite answer. If we arbitrarily picked a four-firm concentration ratio of 75 percent, we could indicate that tobacco products, soft drinks, breakfast cereals, and domestic motor vehicles were oligopolistic. But we would always be dealing with an arbitrary definition.

The concept of an industry is necessarily arbitrary. As a consequence, concentration ratios rise as we narrow the definition of an industry and fall as we broaden it. Thus we must be certain that we are satisfied with the measurement of the industry under study before we jump to conclusions about whether the industry is too concentrated as evidenced by a high measured concentration ratio.

Oligopoly, Efficiency, and Resource Allocation

Although oligopoly is not the dominant form of market structure in the United States, oligopolistic industries do exist. To the extent that oligopolies have market power, they lead to resource misallocations, just as monopolies do. Oligopolies charge prices that exceed marginal cost. But what about oligopolies that occur because of economies of scale? One could argue that consumers end up paying lower prices than if the industry were composed of numerous smaller firms.

TABLE 25-2

Four-Firm Domestic Concentration Ratios for Selected U.S. Industries

Industry	Percentage of Value of Total Domestic Shipments Accounted For by the Top Four Firms
Domestic motor vehicles	90
Breakfast cereals	87
Soft drinks	85
Tobacco products	82
Primary aluminum	74
Transportation equipment	52
Petroleum and coal products	30
Printing and publishing	7

Source: U.S. Bureau of the Census.

All in all, there is no definite evidence of serious resource misallocation in the United States because of oligopolies. In any event, the more U.S. firms face competition from the rest of the world, the less any current oligopoly will be able to exercise market power.

CONCEPTS IN BRIEF

- An oligopoly is a market situation in which there are a small number of interdependent sellers.

- Oligopoly may result from (1) economies of scale, (2) barriers to entry, and (3) mergers.

- Horizontal mergers involve the joining of firms selling a similar product.

- Vertical mergers involve the merging of one firm either with the supplier of an input or the purchaser of its output.

- Industry concentration can be measured by the percentage of total sales accounted for by the top four or top eight firms.

STRATEGIC BEHAVIOR AND GAME THEORY

At this point, we should be able to show oligopoly price and output determination in the way we showed it for perfect competition, pure monopoly, and monopolistic competition, but we cannot. Whenever there are relatively few firms competing in an industry, each can and does react to the price, quantity, quality, and product innovations that the others undertake. In other words, each oligopolist has a **reaction function.** Oligopolistic competitors are interdependent. Consequently, the decision makers in such firms must employ strategies. And we must be able to model their strategic behavior if we wish to predict how prices and outputs are determined in oligopolistic market structures. In general, we can think of reactions of other firms to one firm's actions as part of a *game* that is played by all firms in the industry. Not surprisingly, economists have developed **game theory** models to describe firms' rational interactions. Game theory is the analytical framework in which two or more individuals, companies, or nations compete for certain payoffs that depend on the strategy that the others employ. Poker is such a game situation because it involves a strategy of bluffing.

Some Basic Notions About Game Theory

Games can be either cooperative or noncooperative. If firms get together to collude or form a cartel, that is considered a **cooperative game.** Whenever it is too costly for firms to negotiate such collusive agreements and to enforce them, they are in a **noncooperative game** situation. Most strategic behavior in the marketplace would be described as a noncooperative game.

Games can be classified by whether the payoffs are negative, zero, or positive. A **zero-sum game** is one in which one player's losses are offset by another player's gains; at any time, sum totals are zero. If two retailers have an absolutely fixed total number of customers, the customers that one retailer wins over are exactly equal to the customers that the other retailer loses. A **negative-sum game** is one in which players as a group lose at the end of the game (although one perhaps by more than the other, and it's possible for one or more

Reaction function
The manner in which one oligopolist reacts to a change in price, output, or quality made by another oligopolist in the industry.

Game theory
A way of describing the various possible outcomes in any situation involving two or more interacting individuals when those individuals are aware of the interactive nature of their situation and plan accordingly. The plans made by these individuals are known as *game strategies.*

Cooperative game
A game in which the players explicitly collude to make themselves better off. As applied to firms, it involves companies colluding in order to make higher than competitive rates of return.

Noncooperative game
A game in which the players neither negotiate nor collude in any way. As applied to firms in an industry, this is the common situation in which there are relatively few firms and each has some ability to change price.

Zero-sum game
A game in which any gains within the group are exactly offset by equal losses by the end of the game.

Negative-sum game
A game in which players as a group lose at the end of the game.

Positive-sum game
A game in which players as a group are better off at the end of the game.

Strategy
Any rule that is used to make a choice, such as "Always pick heads"; any potential choice that can be made by players in a game.

Dominant strategies
Strategies that always yield the highest benefit. Regardless of what other players do, a dominant strategy will yield the most benefit for the player using it.

Prisoners' dilemma
A famous strategic game in which two prisoners have a choice between confessing and not confessing to a crime. If neither confesses, they serve a minimum sentence. If both confess, they serve a maximum sentence. If one confesses and the other doesn't, the one who confesses goes free. The dominant strategy is always to confess.

Payoff matrix
A matrix of outcomes, or consequences, of the strategies available to the players in a game.

players to win). A **positive-sum game** is one in which players as a group end up better off. Some economists describe all voluntary exchanges as positive-sum games. After an exchange, both the buyer and the seller are better off than they were prior to the exchange.

Strategies in Noncooperative Games. Players, such as decision makers in oligopolistic firms, have to devise a **strategy,** which is defined as a rule used to make a choice. The goal of the decision maker is of course to devise a strategy that is more successful than alternative strategies. Whenever a firm's decision makers can come up with certain strategies that are generally successful no matter what actions competitors take, these are called **dominant strategies.** The dominant strategy always yields the unique best action for the decision maker no matter what action the other "players" undertake. Relatively few business decision makers over a long period of time have successfully devised dominant strategies. We know this by observation: Few firms in oligopolistic industries have maintained relatively high profits consistently over time.

EXAMPLE
The Prisoners' Dilemma

One real-world example of game theory occurs when two people involved in a bank robbery are caught. What should they do when questioned by police? The result has been called the **prisoners' dilemma.** The two suspects, Sam and Carol, are interrogated separately and given various alternatives (they cannot communicate with each other). The interrogator indicates to Sam and Carol the following:

1. If both confess to the bank robbery, they will both go to jail for five years.
2. If neither confesses, they will each be given a sentence of two years on a lesser charge.
3. If one prisoner turns state's evidence and confesses, that prisoner goes free and the other one, who did not confess, will serve 10 years on bank robbery charges.

You can see the prisoners' alternatives in the **payoff matrix** in Figure 25-3. The two possibilities for each prisoner are "confess" and "don't confess." There are four possibilities:

1. Both confess.
2. Neither confesses.
3. Sam confesses (turns state's evidence) but Carol doesn't.
4. Carol confesses (turns state's evidence) but Sam doesn't.

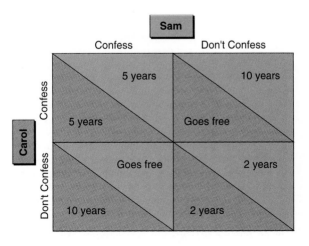

FIGURE 25-3

The Prisoners' Dilemma Payoff Matrix
Regardless of what the other prisoner does, each person is better off if he or she confesses. So confessing is the dominant strategy and each ends up behind bars for five years.

In Figure 25-3, all of Sam's possible outcomes are shown on the upper half of each rectangle, and all of Carol's possible outcomes are shown on the lower half.

By looking at the payoff matrix, you can see that if Carol confesses, Sam's best strategy is to confess also—he'll get only 5 years instead of 10. Conversely, if Sam confesses, Carol's best strategy is also to confess—she'll get 5 years instead of 10. Now let's say that Sam is being interrogated and Carol doesn't confess. Sam's best strategy is still to confess, because then he goes free instead of serving two years. Conversely, if Carol is being interrogated, her best strategy is still to confess even if Sam hasn't. She'll go free instead of serving 10 years. To confess is a dominant strategy for Sam. To confess is also a dominant strategy for Carol. The situation is exactly symmetrical. So this is the prisoners' dilemma. The prisoners know that both prisoners will be better off if neither confesses. Yet it is in each individual prisoner's interest to confess, even though the *collective* outcome of each prisoner's pursuing his or her own interest is inferior for both.

FOR CRITICAL ANALYSIS: Can you apply the prisoners' dilemma to the firms in a two-firm industry that agree to split the market? (Hint: Think about the payoff to cheating on the market-splitting agreement.) ●

Applying Game Theory to Pricing Strategies

We can apply game strategy to two firms—oligopolists—that have to decide on their pricing strategy. Each can choose either a high or a low price. Their payoff matrix is shown in Figure 25-4. If they each choose high prices, they can each make $6 million, but if they each choose low prices, they will only make $4 million each. If one sets a high price and the other a low one, the low-priced firm will make $8 million, but the high-priced firm will only make $2 million. As in the prisoners' dilemma, in the absence of collusion, they will end up choosing low prices.

Opportunistic Behavior

In the prisoners' dilemma, it was clear that cooperative behavior—both parties standing firm without admitting to anything—leads to the best outcome for both players. But each prisoner (player) stands to gain by cheating. Such action is called **opportunistic behavior.** Our daily economic activities involve the equivalent of the prisoners' dilemma all the time. We

Opportunistic behavior
Actions that ignore the possible long-run benefits of cooperation and focus solely on short-run gains.

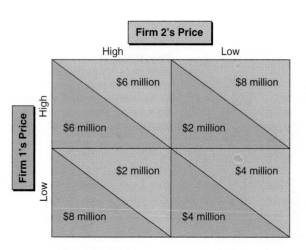

FIGURE 25-4

Game Theory and Pricing Strategies

This payoff matrix shows that if both oligopolists choose a high price, each makes $6 million. If they both choose a low price, each makes $4 million. If one chooses a low price and the other doesn't, the low-priced firm will make $8 million. Unless they collude, however, they will end up at the low-priced solution.

could engage in opportunistic behavior. You could write a check for a purchase knowing that it is going to bounce because you have just closed that bank account. When you agree to perform a specific task for pay, you could perform your work in a substandard way. When you go to buy an item, the seller might be able to cheat you by selling you a defective item.

In short, if all of us—sellers and buyers—engaged in opportunistic behavior all of the time, we would always end up in the bottom right-hand box of the prisoners' dilemma payoff matrix in Figure 25-3. We would constantly be acting in a world of noncooperative behavior. That is not the world in which most of us live, however. Why not? Because most of us engage in *repeat transactions.* Manufacturers would like us to keep purchasing their products. Sellers would like us to keep coming back to their stores. As a seller of labor services, each of us would like to keep our jobs, get promotions, or be hired away by another firm at a higher wage rate. We engage in a **tit-for-tat strategic behavior.** In tit-for-tat strategy, manufacturers and sellers continue to guarantee their merchandise, in spite of cheating by a small percentage of consumers.

Tit-for-tat strategic behavior
In game theory, cooperation that continues so long as the other players continue to cooperate.

INTERNATIONAL EXAMPLE
Russia's Opportunistic Behavior

Companies are not the only entities that can engage in opportunistic behavior. Nations can do so, too, particularly regarding how they act toward international agencies. A good example concerns Russia and the International Monetary Fund (IMF). The IMF routinely offers loans to developing countries. (More recently, it has offered large loans to countries that have suffered foreign exchange crises.) After Russia became an independent country at the beginning of the 1990s, it sought massive loans from the West. The West responded through the IMF, among other agencies. Typically, though, the IMF imposes a new economic "discipline" on the recipient nations. It might require, as a condition for the loan, that the recipient government reduce its rate of inflation, reduce its deficit, reduce government spending, improve its legal system, and so on. That is the tack the IMF took when it loaned Russia $10 billion. Russian officials signed the agreement promising a range of free-market reforms as well as curbs on the rate of inflation and government spending. When Russia's president, Boris Yeltsin, was up for reelection, the government flouted the agreement, but the IMF did not stop sending the money. Why? Because Western nations were desperate to have Yeltsin reelected. He and his fellow government officials acted opportunistically toward the IMF because they knew they could get away with it.

FOR CRITICAL ANALYSIS: Why might a foreign government engage in more opportunistic behavior with the IMF than it would with private lending institutions? ●

PRICE RIGIDITY AND THE KINKED DEMAND CURVE

Let's hypothesize that the decision makers in an oligopolistic firm assume that rivals will react in the following way: They will match all price decreases (in order not to be undersold) but not price increases (because they want to capture more business). There is no collusion. The implications of this reaction function are rigid prices and a kinked demand curve.

Nature of the Kinked Demand Curve

In Figure 25-5, we draw a kinked demand curve, which is implicit in the assumption that oligopolists match price decreases but not price increases. We start off at a given price of

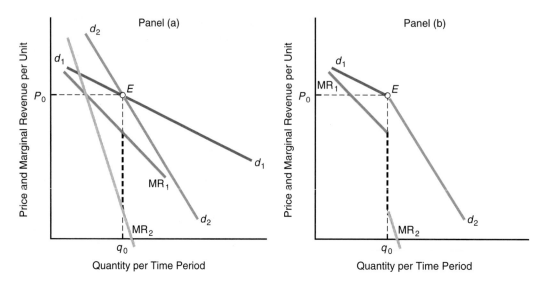

FIGURE 25-5

The Kinked Demand Curve

If the oligopolist firm assumes that rivals will not match price changes, it faces demand curve d_1d_1 and marginal revenue curve MR_1. If it assumes that rivals will match price changes, it faces demand curve d_2d_2 and marginal revenue curve MR_2. If the oligopolist believes that rivals will not react to price increases but will react to price decreases, at prices above P_0 it faces demand curve d_1d_1 and at prices below P_0 it faces the other demand curve, d_2d_2. The overall demand curve will therefore have a kink, as is seen in panel (b) at price P_0. The marginal revenue curve will have a vertical break, as shown by the dashed line in panel (b).

P_0 and assume that the quantity demanded at the price for this individual oligopolist is q_0. The starting price of P_0 is usually the stable market price. If the oligopolist assumes that rivals will not react, it faces demand curve d_1d_1 with marginal revenue curve MR_1. Conversely, if it assumes that rivals will react, it faces demand curve d_2d_2 with marginal revenue curve MR_2. More than likely, the oligopoly firm will assume that if it lowers price, rivals will react by matching that reduction to avoid losing their respective shares of the market. The oligopolist that initially lowers its price will not greatly increase its quantity demanded. So when it lowers its price, it believes that it will face demand curve d_2d_2. But if it increases price above P_0, rivals will probably not follow suit. Thus a higher price than P_0 will cause quantity demanded to decrease rapidly. The demand schedule to the left of and above point E will be relatively elastic, as represented by d_1d_1. At prices above P_0, the relevant demand curve is d_1d_1, whereas below price P_0, the relevant demand curve will be d_2d_2. Consequently, at point E there will be a *kink* in the resulting demand curve. This is shown in panel (b) of Figure 25-5, where the demand curve is labeled d_1d_2. The resulting marginal revenue curve is labeled MR_1MR_2. It has a discontinuous portion, or gap, represented by the boldfaced dashed vertical lines in both panels.

Price Rigidity

The kinked demand curve analysis may help explain why price changes might be infrequent in an oligopolistic industry without collusion. Each oligopolist can see only harm in a price change: If price is increased, the oligopolist will lose many of its customers to rivals who do not raise their prices. That is to say, the oligopolist moves up from point E along demand curve d_1 in panel (b) of Figure 25-5. However, if an oligopolist lowers its price, given that rivals will lower their prices too, its sales will not increase very much. Moving down from point E in panel (b) of Figure 25-5, we see that the demand curve is relatively inelastic. If the elasticity is less than 1, total revenues will fall rather than rise with the lowering of price. Given that the production of a larger output will increase total costs, the oligopolist's profits will fall. The lowering of price by the oligopolist might start a *price war* in which its rival firms will charge an even lower price.

The theoretical reason for price inflexibility under the kinked demand curve model has to do with the discontinuous portion of the marginal revenue curve shown in panel (b) of Figure 25-5, which we reproduce in Figure 25-6. Assume that marginal cost is represented by MC. The profit-maximizing rate of output is q_0, which can be sold at a price of P_0. Now assume that the marginal cost curve rises to MC′. What will happen to the profit-maximizing rate of output? Nothing. Both quantity and price will remain the same for this oligopolist.

Remember that the profit-maximizing rate of output is where marginal revenue equals marginal cost. The shift in the marginal cost curve to MC′ does not change the profit-maximizing rate of output in Figure 25-6 because MC′ still cuts the marginal revenue curve in the latter's discontinuous portion. Thus the equality between marginal revenue and marginal cost still holds at output rate q_0 even when the marginal cost curve shifts upward. What will happen when marginal costs fall to MC‴? Nothing. This oligopolist will continue to produce at a rate of output q_0 and charge a price of P_0. Whenever the marginal cost curve cuts the discontinuous portion of the marginal revenue curve, fluctuations (within limits) in marginal cost will not affect output or price because the profit-maximizing condition MR = MC will hold. The result is that even when firms in an oligopolistic industry such as this experience increases or decreases in costs, their prices do not change as long as MC cuts MR in the discontinuous portion. Hence prices are seen to be rigid in oligopolistic industries if oligopolists react the way we assume they do in this model.

FIGURE 25-6

Changes in Cost May Not Alter the Profit-Maximizing Price and Output

As long as the marginal cost curve intersects the marginal revenue curve in the latter's discontinuous portion, the profit-maximizing price P_0 (and output q_0) will remain unchanged even with changes in MC. (However, the firm's rate of profit will change.)

Criticisms of the Kinked Demand Curve

One of the criticisms directed against the kinked demand curve is that we have no idea how the existing price, P_0, came to be. If every oligopolistic firm faced a kinked demand curve, it would not pay for it to change prices. The problem is that the kinked demand curve does not show us how demand and supply originally determine the going price of an oligopolist's product.

As far as the evidence goes, it is not encouraging. Oligopoly prices do not appear to be as rigid, particularly in the upward direction, as the kinked demand curve theory implies. During the 1970s and early 1980s, when prices in the economy were rising overall, oligopolistic producers increased their prices frequently. Evidence of price changes during the Great Depression showed that oligopolies changed prices much more frequently than monopolies.

EXAMPLE
Do Pet Products Have Nine Lives?

H. J. Heinz's Pet Products Company knows all about the kinked demand curve. It makes 9-Lives cat food. To meet increased competition (at lower prices) from Nestlé, Quaker, Grand Metropolitan, and Mars, Heinz dropped prices by over 22 percent on the wholesale price of a case of 9-Lives. Finally, it had "had enough." It decided to buck the trend by *raising* prices. The result? A disaster, because none of Heinz's four major competitors increased their prices. Heinz's market share dropped from 23 percent to 15 percent almost overnight.

FOR CRITICAL ANALYSIS: *What does Heinz's experience with 9-Lives perhaps suggest about the price elasticity of demand for its product?* ●

CONCEPTS IN BRIEF

- Each oligopolist has a reaction function because oligopolistic competitors are interdependent. They must therefore engage in strategic behavior. One way to model this behavior is to use game theory.

- Games can be either cooperative or noncooperative. A cartel is cooperative. When a cartel breaks down and its members start cheating, the industry becomes a noncooperative game. In a zero-sum game, one player's losses are exactly offset by another player's gains. In a negative-sum game, all players collectively lose, perhaps one more than the others. In a positive-sum game, the players as a group end up better off.

- Decision makers in oligopolistic firms must devise a strategy. A dominant strategy is one that is generally successful no matter what actions competitors take.

- The kinked demand curve oligopoly model predicts that major shifts in marginal cost will cause any change in industry price.

STRATEGIC BEHAVIOR WITH IMPLICIT COLLUSION: A MODEL OF PRICE LEADERSHIP

What if oligopolists do not actually collude to raise prices and share markets but do so implicitly? There are no formal cartel arrangements and no formal meetings. Nonetheless, there is *tacit collusion*. One example of this is the model of **price leadership.**

Price leadership
A practice in many oligopolistic industries in which the largest firm publishes its price list ahead of its competitors, who then match those announced prices. Also called *parallel pricing*.

In this model, the basic assumption is that the dominant firm, usually the biggest, sets the price and allows other firms to sell all they can at that price. The dominant firm then sells the rest. The dominant firm always makes the first move in a price leadership model. By definition, price leadership requires that one firm be the leader. Because of laws against collusion, firms in an industry cannot communicate this directly. That is why it is often natural for the largest firm to become the price leader. In the automobile industry during the period of General Motors' dominance (until the 1980s), that company was traditionally the price leader. At various times in the breakfast food industry, Kellogg was the price leader. Some observers have argued that Harvard University was the price leader among Ivy League schools. In the banking industry, various dominant banks have been price leaders in announcing changes in the prime rate, the interest rate charged on loans offered to the best credit risks. One day a large New York–based bank, such as Chase Manhattan, would announce an increase or decrease in its prime rate. Five or six hours later, all other banks would announce the same change in their prime rate.

Price Wars

Price war
A pricing campaign designed to drive competing firms out of a market by repeatedly cutting prices.

Price leadership may not always work. If the price leader ends up much better off than the firms that follow, the followers may in fact not set prices according to those set by the dominant firm. The result may be a **price war.** The dominant firm lowers its prices a little bit, but the other firms lower theirs even more. Price wars have occurred in many industries. Supermarkets within a given locale often engage in price wars, especially during holiday periods. One may offer turkeys at so much per pound on Wednesday; competing stores cut their price on turkeys on Thursday, so the first store cuts its price even more on Friday. We see price wars virtually every year in the airline industry.

EXAMPLE
Cigarette Price Wars

Price wars occur commonly between long-distance telephone companies, between airlines, and between the makers of cigarettes, soft drinks, computer disc drives, diapers, frozen dinners, and personal computer hardware and software. They do not always lead to the desired result for the company that started the price war. Consider the case of Philip Morris, which cut the price of Marlboro cigarettes by 40 cents a pack to about $1.80. Its main competitor, RJR Nabisco, matched the price cut for Camels. Philip Morris claimed victory because Marlboro's market share increased from 22.1 percent to 27.3 percent. But the domestic operating profits for both companies plummeted in the process; so, too, did the trading value of their stocks. According to business consultants Mike Marn and Robert Garda of the McKinsey Company, the reason is that most companies are unable to offset lower prices with higher volume because variable costs do not start falling until sales increase by about 20 percent. When Philip Morris cut its prices by 18 percent, unit sales increased by only 12.5 percent and profits fell by 25 percent.

FOR CRITICAL ANALYSIS: How do price wars fit into the tit-for-tat strategic behavior of game theory? ●

DETERRING ENTRY INTO AN INDUSTRY

Some economists believe that all decision making by existing firms in a stable industry involves some type of game playing. An important part of game playing does not have to do with how existing competitors might react to a decision by others. Rather, it has to do with how *potential* competitors might react. Strategic decision making requires that existing firms in an industry come up with strategies to deter entrance into that industry. One important way is, of course, to get a local, state, or federal government to restrict entry. Another way is to adopt certain pricing and investment strategies that may deter entry.

Increasing Entry Costs

One **entry deterrence strategy** is to raise the cost of entry by a new firm. The threat of a price war is one technique. To sustain a long price war, existing firms might invest in excess capacity so that they can expand output if necessary. When existing firms invest in excess capacity, they are signaling potential competitors that they will engage in a price war.

Another way that existing domestic firms can raise the entry cost of foreign firms is by getting the U.S. government to pass stringent environmental or health and safety standards. These typically raise costs more for foreign producers, often in developing countries, than for domestic producers.

Entry deterrence strategy
Any strategy undertaken by firms in an industry, either individually or together, with the intent or effect of raising the cost of entry into the industry by a new firm.

EXAMPLE
Should Hair Braiders Be Licensed?

Many service industries have raised entry costs by getting legislation passed that requires extensive training and licensing before someone can enter the industry. Physicians and lawyers are good examples. Less well known are the high entry costs imposed on individuals who wish to give therapeutic massages or trim and style hair. For example, in California, a license to style hair requires the expenditure of about $6,000 for 1,600 hours of cosmetology classes. Hairstylists in California spend about $600 million a year on classes and test administration fees.

Enter hair braiders, who are hairstylists for the African-American community. Individuals entering this business long assumed that because they use no chemicals, they would not be required to take extensive classes in the use of chemicals. But the California Barbering and Cosmetology Board has recently ruled otherwise. Given that there are about 10,000 hair braiders in America, this issue affects more than California. Currently, there are several lawsuits challenging the licensing requirement for hair braiders. Hair braiders offer a lower-cost alternative to regular beauty salons, and the latter are fighting to prevent this new competition.

FOR CRITICAL ANALYSIS: Besides currently licensed hairstylists, who else might favor required cosmetology licensing for hair braiders? ●

Limit-Pricing Strategies

If existing firms make it clear to potential competitors that the existing firms will not change their output rate after entry, this is a signal. It tells potential firms that the existing firm will simply lower its market price (moving down the firm demand curve) until it sells the same quantity as before the new entry came into the industry. The existing firms limit their price to be above competitive prices, but if there is a new entrant, the new limit price will be below the one at which the new firm can make a profit. This is called the **limit-pricing model.**

Limit-pricing model
A model that hypothesizes that a group of colluding sellers will set the highest common price that they believe they can charge without new firms seeking to enter that industry in search of relatively high profits.

Raising Customers' Switching Costs

If an existing firm can make it more costly for customers to switch from its product or service to a competitor's, the existing firm can deter entry. There are a host of ways in which existing firms can raise customers' switching costs. Makers of computer equipment have in the past produced operating systems and software that would not run on competitors' computers. Any customer wanting to change from one computer system to another faced a high switching cost.

CONCEPTS IN BRIEF

• One type of strategic behavior involving implicit collusion is price leadership. The dominant firm is assumed to set the price and then allows other firms to sell all that they want to sell at that price. Whatever is left over is sold by the dominant firm. The dominant firm always makes the first move in a price leadership model. If the nondominant firms decide to compete, they may start a price war.

• One strategic decision may be to attempt to raise the cost of entry of new firms into an industry. The threat of a price war is one technique. Another is to lobby the federal government to pass stringent environmental or health and safety standards in an attempt to keep out foreign competition.

• If existing firms limit prices to a level above competitive prices before entry but are willing to reduce it, this is called a limit-pricing model.

• Another way to raise the cost to new firms is to make it more costly for customers to switch from one product or service to a competitor's.

COMPARING MARKET STRUCTURES

Now that we have looked at perfect competition, pure monopoly, monopolistic competition, and oligopoly, we are in a position to compare the attributes of these four different market structures. We do this in summary form in Table 25-3, in which we compare the number of sellers, their ability to set price, and whether product differentiation exists, and we give some examples of each of the four market structures.

TABLE 25-3
Comparing Market Structures

Market Structure	Number of Sellers	Unrestricted Entry and Exit	Ability to Set Price	Long-Run Economic Profits Possible	Product Differentiation	Nonprice Competition	Examples
Perfect competition	Numerous	Yes	None	No	None	None	Agriculture, coal
Monopolistic competition	Many	Yes	Some	No	Considerable	Yes	Toothpaste, toilet paper, soap, retail trade
Oligopoly	Few	Partial	Some	Yes	Frequent	Yes	Cigarettes, steel
Pure monopoly	One	No (for entry)	Considerable	Yes	None (product is unique)	Yes	Electric company, local telephone company

The makers of Nintendo tried to make themselves indispensable by restricting software developers to only five games. How much bargaining power did developers have?

In the Game of Business, Does Cooperation Make Sense?

CONCEPTS APPLIED:

COMPETITION, STRATEGIC BEHAVIOR, OPPORTUNISTIC BEHAVIOR, COMPLEMENTS, GAME THEORY

Visit www.econtoday.com for an Internet Activity that expands your understanding of these concepts.

"It's a dog-eat-dog world." "If you can't take the heat, don't get close to the fire." The clichés that relate to the business world are myriad. Most of them are based on the need to compete fiercely, albeit ethically and legally, to get ahead or at least to avoid bankruptcy. To many of today's students of business administration and management, such language seems out of place, anachronistic. The budding manager of today learns about teamwork, strategic alliances, working in tandem with suppliers, and building trust and loyalty. An increasingly common approach in the business world today is the desire to create a "win-win" situation. In such a world, business feuds are considered detrimental for everyone.

Game Theory's Brainchild

Until game theory came along, most economists and business management theorists assumed that firms could behave as they wished without taking the actions of their rivals into account. This is probably still true for the perfect competitor and the pure monopolist. (Although even a pure monopolist has to worry about *potential* competition if it earns very high monopoly profits that are obvious to outsiders.)

As you learned in this chapter, game theory requires the players to consider a strategy based on what they think other players are planning to do. So the game theory view of management is that decision makers must always make predictions about rivals' reactive behavior.

Number of Players Affects Outcomes

In any type of strategic competition, the number of players can affect the outcome. Competition against only one other company is not the same as competition against 15 other companies. For example, when Holland Sweetener Company tried to break NutraSweet's monopoly in the American artificial sweetener market, this competitive foray ended up benefiting Coca-Cola and Pepsi. Holland did not get those two companies' contracts for sweetener. Instead, Coca-Cola and Pepsi used the threat of competition from Holland Sweetener to force NutraSweet to lower its prices—and then they stayed with NutraSweet.

The reverse of this situation occurred a few years ago when American Express wanted to purchase health care coverage for its workers. It organized a group of large companies, which also wanted lower-cost health care for their workforces, to ask jointly for bids from various health care providers. Looking at all the participating companies together, the contract was so huge that the competing health care providers got into a bidding war and ended up offering health care at a very low price.

Toward an Alternative Theory: "Coopetition"

According to Professors Adam Brandenburger of Harvard Business School and Barry Nalebuff of Yale School of Management, the blending of cooperation and competition—"coopetition"—is the best way for a firm's decision makers to maximize profits. These theorists argue that the time to cooperate is when the market is growing. Further, they say that in any market, it is important to cooperate with firms that produce products that are complementary to your own. Microsoft—a software producer—and Intel—a chip producer—have learned the benefit of cooperation.

Playing Hardball Works, Too

Sometimes, not allowing cooperation at all may be the best course of action for a company. When Nintendo was expanding in the video game business, it focused on one particular strategically competitive tactic. It restricted software developers to making only five games each. It then shipped fewer games to its retailers than they asked for. Finally, it did much of its development in-house. Under those circumstances, its suppliers and its retailers had little bargaining power. Not many companies find themselves in a position to pursue this strategy, though.

But Playing Hardball Can Also Backfire

Staying tough doesn't always work. Just ask the shareholders of Apple Computer, Inc. Apple developed an intuitive, user-friendly operating system many years ago. Its main competitor was Microsoft's MS-DOS system, which most novices could not use easily. Apple and Microsoft chose two separate strategies, and the results were quite different.

Apple did not open up its operating system's architecture so that clones could be made. Thus anyone who wanted the easier-to-use Macintosh computer with its simple operating system had to buy a computer manufactured by Apple. Apple's profit margins were relatively high, so initially it made lots of money.

Microsoft opened up its MS-DOS architecture to everyone to use. Clones of the industry-standard IBM PC were developed and eventually became much cheaper than Apple's Macintosh computers. As a result, little by little, Apple lost market share. The world is now dominated by the Microsoft operating system, whereas the easier-to-use Mac operating system is dying out in the marketplace.

FOR CRITICAL ANALYSIS

1. The McKenzie consulting firm is offering practice sessions in game theory to the decision makers from large corporations. Which firms are more likely to send their executives to such practice sessions?
2. Today Apple's computers are competitively priced with all others. Why may it be too late anyway?

CHAPTER SUMMARY

1. Numerous market situations lie between the extremes of pure competition and pure monopoly. Monopolistic competition and oligopoly are two of these situations.
2. Monopolistic competition is a theory developed by Edward Chamberlin of Harvard University in 1933. It refers to a market composed of specific product groups in which the different companies involved have slight monopoly powers because each has a product slightly different from the others. Examples of product groups might include the toothpaste and soap industries. The monopolistic competitor ends up with zero economic profits because there is free entry into the industry. However, according to Chamberlin, the monopolistic competitor does not produce where

price equals marginal costs and therefore does not produce at the minimum point on the average total cost curve.

3. Advertising occurs in industries in which the firms are not pure price takers. The basic goal of advertisers is to increase demand for their product.
4. In the short run, it is possible for a monopolistic competitor to make economic profits or economic losses. In the long run, monopolistic competitors make zero economic profits (that is, they make just the normal rate of return).
5. When we compare monopolistic competition with perfect competition, we find that the monopolistic competitor does not produce where average total costs are at a minimum, whereas the perfect competitor does.

6. Oligopoly is a market situation in which there are just a few firms. Each firm knows that its rivals will react to a change in price. Oligopolies are usually defined as industries in which the four-firm concentration ratio is relatively high.

7. Oligopolies are characterized by relatively high barriers to entry, interdependence, product differentiation, and growth through merger.

8. Each oligopolist has a reaction function because oligopolistic competitors are interdependent and must therefore engage in strategic behavior. One way to model this behavior is to use game theory.

9. Games can be either cooperative or noncooperative. A cartel is cooperative. When a cartel breaks down and its members start cheating, the industry becomes a noncooperative game. In a zero-sum game, one player's losses are exactly offset by another player's gains. In a negative-sum game, players as a group lose, perhaps one more than the others. In a positive-sum game, players as a group end up better off.

10. The kinked demand curve oligopoly model indicates that prices will be relatively rigid unless demand or cost conditions change substantially.

11. Price leadership is strategic behavior that involves implicit collusion. The dominant firm is assumed to set the price and then allows other firms to sell all that they want to sell at that price. Whatever is left over is sold by the dominant firm. The dominant firm always makes the first move. If the nondominant firms decide to compete, they may start a price war.

12. One strategic decision may be to attempt to raise the cost of entry of new firms into an industry. The threat of a price war is one technique. Another is to lobby the federal government to pass stringent environmental or health and safety standards in an attempt to keep out foreign competition. A third is to make it more costly for customers to switch from one product or service to a competitor's.

DISCUSSION OF PREVIEW QUESTIONS

1. What are the characteristics of the monopolistically competitive market structure?

The monopolistically competitive market structure lies between the extremes of monopoly and perfect competition, but closer to the latter. Under monopolistic competition, there are a large number of sellers, each with a small market share, acting independently of one another, producing a differentiated product. This product differentiation is advertised; advertising emphasizes product differences or, on occasion, "creates" differences.

2. How does the monopolistic competitor determine the equilibrium price-output combination?

The monopolistic competitor has some control over price; it faces a downward-sloping demand curve. The monopolistic competitor must lower price in order to increase sales; the marginal revenue curve for the monopolistic competitor is therefore downward-sloping. In equilibrium, the profit-maximizing rate of output will therefore be where the upward-sloping (increasing) marginal cost curve intersects the downward-sloping (decreasing) marginal revenue curve. The output rate being thus established, price is set at the corresponding market clearing level. Any other output rate would lead to a reduction in total profits.

3. How does the monopolistically competitive market structure differ from that of perfect competition?

Like the perfect competitor, the monopolistic competitor acts independently of its competitors and is able to earn economic profits only in the short run; competition from entrants eliminates long-run economic profits under both market structures. Yet an important difference exists in the two models: The perfect competitor faces a perfectly elastic demand curve, whereas the monopolistic competitor faces a downward-sloping demand curve. Because economic profits must equal zero in the long run, the demand (average revenue) curve must be tangent to the average total cost (ATC) curve in both models. Under perfect competition, a perfectly elastic demand curve can only be tangent to a U-shaped ATC curve at the latter's minimum point (where its slope is zero). Under monopolistic competition, the demand curve must be tangent to the firm's ATC somewhere to the *left* of the ATC's minimum point. Thus under perfect competition, long-run equilibrium will be at minimum ATC, whereas under monopolistic competition, long-run equilibrium will be at a higher ATC—and at a lower output rate.

4. What are the characteristics of the oligopolistic market structure?

Like the monopolistically competitive market structure, oligopoly lies between the extremes of perfect competition and monopoly. However, oligopoly is closer to being unique; under oligopoly, a small number of firms dominate the market, and the firms cannot act independently. An oligopolist must take into account the reactions of its rivals when it sets policy; this interdependence makes the oligopoly model unique. It also makes the price-output decision a complex one for the oligopolists—and hence for economists who analyze this market structure. It is believed that oligopolies emerge because great economies of scale, in conjunction with a limited market demand, allow the few largest to drive out competitors. Also, oligopolies may arise because of barriers to entry and mergers.

PROBLEMS

(Answers to the odd-numbered problems appear at the back of the book.)

25-1. Suppose that you own a monopolistically competitive firm that sells automobile tune-ups at a price of $25 each. You are currently selling 100 per week. As the owner-operator, you initiate an ad campaign on a local AM radio station. You promise to smooth out any ill-running car at a price of $25. The result is that you end up tuning 140 cars per week. What is the "marginal revenue" of this ad campaign? What additional information do you need to determine whether your profits have risen?

25-2. The graph depicts long-run equilibrium for a monopolistic competitor.

Quantity per Time Period

a. Which output rate represents equilibrium?
b. Which price represents equilibrium?
c. Which labeled point indicates that economic profits are zero?
d. Which labeled point indicates minimum ATC?
e. Is ATC at the equilibrium output rate above or at minimum ATC?
f. Is the equilibrium price greater than, less than, or equal to the marginal cost of producing at the equilibrium output rate?

25-3. The table indicates some information for industry A.

Firm	Annual Sales ($ millions)
1	200
2	150
3	100
4	75
5 through 30	300

a. What is the four-firm concentration ratio for this industry (with just 30 firms)?
b. Assume that industry A is the steel industry. What would happen to the concentration index if we redefined industry A as the cold rolled-steel industry? As the metals industry?

25-4. Explain how, in the long run, any economic profits will be eliminated in a monopolistically competitive industry.

25-5. Explain why an oligopolist's demand curve might be kinked.

25-6. The table on the following page gives some cost and demand data for an oligopolistic industry. There are five firms. Assume that each one faces the same long-run total cost curve and that each firm knows that any change in price will be matched by all other firms in the industry.

a. Fill in the blanks.
b. What will the profit-maximizing rate of output be for each firm?
c. What price will be charged for this output?
d. What will the profits be for each of the five firms?

Price	Quantity Demanded	Total Revenue	Marginal Revenue	Quantity Demanded ÷ Number of Firms	Total Revenue ÷ Number of Firms	Marginal Revenue ÷ Number of Firms	Individual Firm Quantity Supplied	Long-Run Total Costs	Long-Run Marginal Costs
$20	5	$_____	$_____	_____	_____	_____	1	$20	$_____
18	10	_____	_____	_____	_____	_____	2	30	_____
16	15	_____	_____	_____	_____	_____	3	36	_____
14	20	_____	_____	_____	_____	_____	4	44	_____
12	25	_____	_____	_____	_____	_____	5	60	_____

25-7. Suppose that you run a movie theater. At your price of $5 per person, you sell 5,000 tickets per week. Without changing your price, you initiate a $1,000-per-week advertising campaign. Assuming that all your nonadvertising costs are totally unrelated to the number of weekly viewers you have, how much additional revenue must you generate to justify continuation of the ad campaign? How many more customers would this require?

25-8. Study the accompanying graph for a firm in an oligopolistic industry.

a. How much will this oligopolistic firm produce?
b. At what price will the firm sell this output?
c. How much can marginal cost vary without causing a change in price?

25-9. There are only two firms in an industry. They collude to share the market equally. They jointly set a monopoly price and split the quantity demanded at that price. Here are their options.

a. They continue to collude (no cheating) and make $10 million each in profits.
b. One firm cheats on the agreement, but the other firm doesn't. The firm that cheats makes $12 million a year in profit, whereas the firm that doesn't cheat makes $7 million in profit.
c. They both cheat and each one makes $6 million a year in profit.

Construct a payoff matrix for these two firms. How does this situation relate to the prisoners' dilemma?

COMPUTER-ASSISTED INSTRUCTION

Given a table with relevant information, can you determine an industry's four-firm concentration ratio? Does this ratio overstate or understate the true concentration of that industry? Specific calculations reveal some interesting answers about the usefulness of concentration ratios.

Complete problem and answer appear on disk.

REGULATION AND ANTITRUST POLICY

By now, most of you reading this text will have used a Web browser on the Internet. There are basically two competing Web browsers today: one developed by Netscape Communications Corporation, called Navigator, and the other developed by Microsoft Corporation, called Internet Explorer. A few years ago, when Netscape practically "owned" the Internet browser market, Microsoft decided to compete. The initial versions of Internet Explorer were not so good as Navigator. Little by little, though, Microsoft began to catch up, resulting in two browsers that are more or less equally easy to use and have similar features. Most of the world's computers use the Microsoft-owned Windows operating system. If Microsoft decided to "bundle" a new version of its Internet Explorer with its Windows operating system, could that destroy competition in the browser market? Before you answer this question, you need to know about regulation and antitrust policy.

PREVIEW QUESTIONS

1. What is a natural monopoly, and how does one arise?

2. If natural monopolies are required to price at marginal cost, what problem emerges?

3. What are some means of regulating a natural monopoly?

4. Why have economists been reevaluating the government's role as an economic regulator?

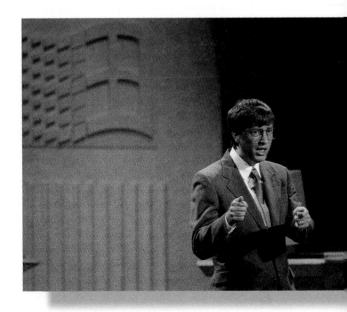

Did You Know That . . . each year about 70,000 pages of new or modified federal regulations are published? These regulations, found in the *Federal Register,* cover virtually every aspect of the way business can be conducted, products can be built, and services can be offered. In addition, every state and municipality publishes regulations relating to worker safety, restaurant cleanliness, and the number of lights needed in each room in a day-care center. There is no question about it, American business activities are highly regulated. Consequently, how regulators should act to increase economic efficiency and how they actually act are important topics for understanding our economy today. In addition to regulation, the government has one additional weapon to use in its attempts to prevent restraints of trade. It is called antitrust law, and it is the subject of the later part of this chapter.

Let's look first at how government might best regulate a single firm that has obtained a monopoly because of constantly falling long-run average costs, a situation known as a natural monopoly.

NATURAL MONOPOLIES REVISITED

You will recall from our discussion of natural monopolies in Chapter 24 that whenever a single firm has the ability to produce all of the industry's output at a lower per-unit cost than other firms attempting to produce less than total industry output, a natural monopoly arises. Natural gas and electric utilities are examples. Long-run average costs for those firms typically fall as output increases. In a natural monopoly, economies of large-scale production dominate, leading to a single-firm industry.

The Pricing and Output Decision of the Natural Monopolist

A monopolist (like any other firm) will set the output rate where marginal revenue is equal to marginal cost. We draw the market demand curve, D, and the revenue curve, MR, in panel (a) of Figure 26-1. The intersection of the marginal revenue curve and the marginal cost curve is at point A. The monopolist would therefore produce quantity Q_m and charge a price of P_m.

What do we know about a monopolist's solution to the price-quantity question? When compared to a competitive situation, we know that consumers end up paying more for the product, and consequently they purchase less of it than they would purchase under competition. The monopoly solution is economically inefficient from society's point of view; the price charged for the product is higher than the opportunity cost to society, and consequently there is a misallocation of resources. That is, the price does not equal the true marginal cost of producing the good because the true marginal cost is at the intersection A, not at price P_m.

Regulating the Natural Monopolist

Assume that the government wants the natural monopolist to produce at an output at which price equals marginal cost, so that the value of the satisfaction that individuals receive from the marginal unit purchased is just equal to the marginal cost to society. Where is that solution in panel (b) of Figure 26-1? It is at the intersection of the marginal cost curve and the demand curve, point B. Recall how we derived the competitive industry supply curve. We

Panel (a)

Panel (b)

FIGURE 26-1

Profit Maximization and Regulation Through Marginal Cost Pricing

The profit-maximizing natural monopolist here would produce at the point in panel (a) where marginal costs equal marginal revenue—that is, at point *A*, which gives the quantity of production Q_m. The price charged would be P_m. If a regulatory commission attempted to regulate natural monopolies so that price equaled long-run marginal cost, the commission would make the monopolist set production at the point where the marginal cost curve intersects the demand schedule. This is shown in panel (b). The quantity produced would be Q_1, and the price would be P_1. However, average costs at Q_1 are equal to AC_1. Losses would ensue, equal to the shaded area. It would be self-defeating for a regulatory commission to force a natural monopolist to produce at an output rate at which $MC = P$ without subsidizing some of its costs because losses would eventually drive the natural monopolist out of business.

looked at all of the upward-sloping portions of actual and potential firms' marginal cost curves above their respective average variable costs. We then summed all of these portions of the firms' supply curves; that gave us the industry supply curve. We assume that a regulatory commission forces the natural monopolist to engage in marginal cost pricing and hence to produce at quantity Q_1 and to sell the product at price P_1. How large will the monopolist's profits be? Profits, of course, are the *positive* difference between total revenues and total costs. In this case, total revenues equal P_1 times Q_1, and total costs equal average costs times the number of units produced. At Q_1, average cost is equal to AC_1. Average costs are higher than the price that the regulatory commission forces our natural monopolist to charge. Profits turn out to be losses and are equal to the shaded area in panel (b) of Figure 26-1. Thus regulation that forces a natural monopolist to produce and price as if it were in a competitive situation would also force that monopolist into negative profits, or losses. Obviously, the monopolist would rather go out of business than be subject to such regulation.

As a practical matter, then, regulators can't force a natural monopolist to engage in marginal cost pricing. Consequently, regulation of natural monopolies has often taken the form of allowing the regulated natural monopolist to set price where LAC intersects *D* in panel (b) of Figure 26-1. This is called *average cost pricing*. Average cost includes what the regulators deem a "fair" rate of return on investment.

...

POLICY EXAMPLE
Are Electric Utilities Still Natural Monopolies?

When we discussed natural monopolies, we used a few examples. Panel (a) of Figure 26-1 seems to apply to electric utilities quite well. Technology is changing that situation, however. Efficient high-voltage transmission lines now exist. This means that the market for electricity generation can transcend local and even national boundaries. There is no longer any reason to restrict entry or to regulate prices in electricity generation.

Competition in the electric utility market has already started in California. The Department of Energy predicted that the average retail price of electricity will fall by 6 to 22 percent in the next couple of years and by perhaps 28 percent by the year 2010. Such numbers are consistent with what occurred after competition was allowed in the sale of natural gas, interstate long-distance telephone services, airline travel, and railroad shipping. Some economists feel that price reductions will actually be much greater than this because of increased innovation in the industry.

Initially, competition in the electric utility market has proved to be somewhat confusing for retail customers. For example, nearly 200 companies registered to sell electricity in the newly competitive California market. Confusion such as this is likely in other states that are also allowing electricity competition, including Massachusetts, Maine, Pennsylvania, Illinois, Michigan, New Jersey, and Rhode Island.

FOR CRITICAL ANALYSIS: Is there really any true natural monopoly left in the world? ●

CONCEPTS IN BRIEF

- A natural monopoly arises when one firm can produce all of an industry's output at a lower per-unit cost than other firms.
- The first firm to take advantage of the declining long-run average cost curve can undercut the prices of all other sellers, forcing them out of business, thereby obtaining a natural monopoly.
- A natural monopolist allowed to maximize profit will set quantity where marginal revenue equals long-run marginal cost. Price is determined from the demand curve at that quantity.
- A natural monopolist that is forced to set price equal to long-run marginal cost will sustain losses.

Exercise 26.1
Visit www.econtoday.com for more about post offices.

REGULATION

The U.S. government began regulating social and economic activity early in the nation's history, but the amount of government regulation has increased in the twentieth century. There are three types of government regulation:

1. Regulation of natural monopolies
2. Regulation of inherently competitive industries
3. Regulation for public welfare across all industries, or so-called social regulation

For example, various state commissions regulate the rates and quality of service of electric power companies, which are considered natural monopolies. Trucking and interstate moving companies are inherently competitive industries but have nonetheless been made subject to government regulation in the past. And federal and state governments impose occupational, health, and safety rules on a wide variety of employers.

Objectives of Economic Regulation

Economic regulation is typically intended to control the prices that regulated enterprises are allowed to charge. Various public utility commissions throughout the United States regulate the rates (prices) of electrical utility companies and some telephone operating companies. This has usually been called rate regulation. The goal of rate regulation has, in principle, been the prevention of both monopoly profits and predatory competition.

Cost-of-service regulation
Regulation based on allowing prices to reflect only the actual cost of production and no monopoly profits.

Rate-of-return regulation
Regulation that seeks to keep the rate of return in the industry at a competitive level by not allowing excessive prices to be charged.

Two traditional methods of rate regulation have involved cost-of-service regulation and rate-of-return regulation. A regulatory commission using **cost-of-service regulation** allows the regulated companies to charge only prices that reflect the actual average cost of providing the services to the customer. In a somewhat similar vein, regulatory commissions using the **rate-of-return regulation** method allow regulated companies to set prices that ensure a normal, or competitive, rate of return on the investment in the business. We implied these two types of regulation when discussing panel (b) of Figure 26-1. If the long-run average cost curve in that figure includes a competitive rate of return on investment, regulating the price at AC_1 is an example of rate-of-return regulation.

A major problem with regulating monopolies concerns the quality of the service or product involved. Consider the many facets of telephone service: getting a dial tone, hearing other voices clearly, getting the operator to answer quickly, having out-of-order telephone lines repaired rapidly, putting through a long-distance call quickly and efficiently—the list goes on and on. But regulation of a telephone company usually dealt with the prices charged for telephone service. Of course, regulators were concerned with the quality of service, but how could that be measured? Indeed, it cannot be measured very easily. Therefore, it is extremely difficult for any type of regulation to be successful in regulating the *price per constant-quality unit.* Certainly, it is possible to regulate the price per unit, but we don't really know that the quality remains unchanged when the price is not allowed to rise "enough." Thus if regulation doesn't allow prices to rise, quality of service may be lowered, thereby raising the price per constant-quality unit.

POLICY EXAMPLE
Is There Any Reason Left to Regulate Phone Companies?

Long-distance phone service has been deregulated. Today, there may no longer be any rationale to regulate *any* type of phone service. Competition literally can be global in scope. Cellular phones can compete effectively with traditional wired telephone systems. Also, local telephone companies could be deregulated by simply allowing competitors access to each local grid if they pay a license fee for its use. Local telephone service could then be offered at unregulated but competitive rates. Also, given that it will soon be possible for electric companies to transmit phone and Internet communications through their grids, there truly will be no reason to regulate local phone service.

FOR CRITICAL ANALYSIS: Can the natural monopoly argument continue to apply to phone companies when cellular systems are available? •

Social Regulation

As mentioned, social regulation reflects concern for public welfare across all industries. In other words, regulation is focused on the impact of production on the environment and society, the working conditions under which goods and services are produced, and sometimes the physical attributes of goods. The aim is a better quality of life for all through a less polluted environment, better working conditions, and safer and better products. For example, the Food and Drug Administration (FDA) attempts to protect against impure and unsafe foods, drugs, cosmetics, and other potentially hazardous products; the Consumer Product Safety Commission (CPSC) specifies minimum standards for consumer products in an attempt to reduce "unreasonable" risks of injury; the Environmental Protection Agency (EPA) watches over the amount of pollutants released into the environment; the Occupational Safety and Health Administration (OSHA) attempts to protect workers against work-related injuries and illnesses; and the Equal Employment Opportunity Commission (EEOC) seeks to provide fair access to jobs.

Table 26-1 lists some major federal regulatory agencies and their areas of concern. Although most people agree with the idea behind such social regulation, many disagree on whether we have too much regulation—whether it costs us more than the benefits we receive. Some contend that the costs that firms incur in abiding by regulations run into the hundreds of billions of dollars per year. The result is higher production costs, which are then passed on to consumers. Also, the resources invested in complying with regulatory measures could be invested in other uses. Furthermore, extensive regulation may have an anticompetitive effect because it may represent a relatively greater burden for smaller firms than for larger ones.

But the *potential* benefits of more social regulation are many. For example, the water we drink in some cities is known to be contaminated with cancer-causing chemicals; air pollution from emissions and toxic wastes from production processes cause many illnesses. Some contaminated areas have been cleaned up, but many other problem areas remain.

The benefits of social regulation may not be easy to measure and may accrue to society for a long time. Furthermore, it is difficult to put a dollar value on safer working conditions

TABLE 26-1
Some Federal Regulatory Agencies

Agency	Jurisdiction	Date Formed	Major Regulatory Functions
Federal Communications Commission (FCC)	Product markets	1934	Regulates broadcasting, telephone, and other communication services.
Federal Trade Commission (FTC)	Product Markets	1914	Responsible for preventing businesses from engaging in unfair trade practices and in monopolistic actions, as well as protecting consumer rights.
Equal Employment Opportunity Commission (EEOC)	Labor markets	1964	Investigates complaints of discrimination based on race, religion, sex, or age in hiring, promotion, firing, wages, testing, and all other conditions of employment.
Securities and Exchange Commission (SEC)	Financial markets	1934	Regulates all public securities markets to promote full disclosure.
Environmental Protection Agency (EPA)	Environment	1970	Develops and enforces environmental standards for air, water, toxic waste, and noise.
Occupational Safety and Health Administration (OSHA)	Health and safety	1970	Regulates workplace safety and health conditions.

and a cleaner environment. In any case, the debate goes on. However, it should be pointed out that the controversy is generally not about whether we should have social regulation but about when and how it is being done and whether we take *all* of the costs and benefits into account. For example, is regulation best carried out by federal, state, or local authorities? Is a specific regulation economically justified through a complete cost-benefit analysis?

Creative Response and Feedback Effects: Results of Regulation

Creative response
Behavior on the part of a firm that allows it to comply with the letter of the law but violate the spirit, significantly lessening the law's effects.

Regulated firms commonly try to avoid the effects of regulation whenever they can. In other words, the firms engage in **creative response,** which is a response to a regulation that conforms to the letter of the law but undermines its spirit. Take state laws requiring male-female pay-equity: The wages of women must be on a par with those paid to males who are performing the same tasks. Employers that pay the same wages to both males and females are clearly not in violation of the law. However, wages are only one component of total employee compensation. Another component is fringe benefits, such as on-the-job training. Because on-the-job training is difficult to observe from outside the firm, employers could offer less on-the-job training to women and still not be in technical violation of pay-equity laws. This unobservable difference would mean that males were able to acquire skills that could raise their future income even though current wages among males and females were equal, in compliance with the law.

Individuals have a type of creative response that has been labeled a *feedback effect.* Regulation may alter individuals' behavior after the regulation has been put into effect. If regulation requires fluoridated water, then parents know that their children's teeth have significant protection against tooth decay. Consequently, the feedback effect on parents' behavior is that they may be less concerned about how many sweets their children eat.

EXAMPLE
The Effectiveness of Auto Safety Regulation

A good example of the feedback effect has to do with automotive safety regulation. Since the 1960s, the federal government has required automobile manufacturers to make cars increasingly safer. Some of the earlier requirements involved nonprotruding door handles, collapsible steering columns, and shatterproof glass. More recent requirements involve I-beams in the doors, better seat belts, and airbags. The desired result was fewer injuries and deaths for drivers involved in accidents. According to economist Sam Peltzman, however, due to the feedback effect, drivers have gradually started driving more recklessly. Automobiles with more safety features have been involved in a disproportionate number of accidents.

FOR CRITICAL ANALYSIS: The feedback effect has also been called the law of unintended consequences. Why? ●

EXPLAINING REGULATORS' BEHAVIOR

Regulation has usually been defended by contending that government regulatory agencies are needed to correct market imperfections. We are dealing with a nonmarket situation because regulators are paid by the government and their decisions are not determined or constrained by the market. A number of theories have been put forward to describe the behavior of regulators. These theories can help us understand how regulation has often harmed consumers through higher prices and less choice and benefited producers through higher profits and fewer competitive forces. Two of the best-known theories of regulatory behavior are the *capture hypothesis* and the *share-the-gains, share-the-pains theory.*

The Capture Hypothesis

It has been observed that with the passage of time, regulators often end up adopting the views of the regulated. According to the **capture hypothesis,**[1] no matter what the reason for a regulatory agency's having been set up, it will eventually be captured by the special interests of the industry that is being regulated. Consider the reasons.

Who knows best about the industry that is being regulated? The people already in the industry. Who, then, will be asked to regulate the industry? Again, people who have been in the industry. And people who used to be in the industry have allegiances and friendships with others in the industry.

Also consider that whenever regulatory hearings are held, the affected consumer groups will have much less information about the industry than the people already in the industry, the producers. Additionally, the cost to any one consumer to show up at a regulatory hearing to express concern about a change in the rate structure will certainly exceed any perceived benefit that that consumer could obtain from going to the rate-making hearing.

Because they have little incentive to do so, consumers and taxpayers will not be well organized, nor will they be greatly concerned with regulatory actions. But the special interests of the industry are going to be well organized and well defined. Political entrepreneurs within the regulatory agency see little payoff in supporting the views of consumers and taxpayers anyway. After all, few consumers understand the benefits deriving from regulatory agency actions. Moreover, how much could a consumer directly benefit someone who works in an agency? Regulators have the most incentive to support the position of a well-organized special-interest group within the industry that is being regulated.

Capture hypothesis
A theory of regulatory behavior that predicts that the regulators will eventually be captured by the special interests of the industry being regulated.

"Share the Gains, Share the Pains"

A somewhat different view of regulators' behavior is given in the **share-the-gains, share-the-pains theory.**[2] This theory looks at the specific aims of the regulators. It posits that a regulator simply wants to continue in the job. To do so, the regulator must obtain the approval of both the legislators who established and oversee the regulatory agency and the industry that is being regulated. A third group that must be taken into account is, of course, the customers of the industry.

Under the capture hypothesis, only the special interests of the industry being regulated had to be taken into account by the regulators. The share-the-gains, share-the-pains model contends that such a position is too risky because customers who are really hurt by improper regulation will complain to legislators, who might fire the regulators. Thus each regulator has to attach some weight to these three separate groups. What happens if there is an abrupt increase in fuel costs for electrical utilities? The capture theory would predict that regulators would relatively quickly allow for a rate increase in order to maintain the profits of the industry. The share-the-gains, share-the-pains theory, however, would predict that there will be an adjustment in rates, but not as quickly or as completely as the capture theory would predict. The regulatory agency is not completely captured by the industry; it has to take account of legislators and consumers.

Share-the-gains, share-the-pains theory
A theory of regulatory behavior in which the regulators must take account of the demands of three groups: legislators, who established and who oversee the regulatory agency; members of the regulated industry; and consumers of the regulated industry's products or services.

---

[1]See George Stigler, *The Citizen and the State: Essays on Regulation* (Chicago: University of Chicago Press, 1975).

[2]See Sam Peltzman, "Towards a More General Theory of Regulation," *Journal of Law and Economics,* 19 (1976), pp. 211–240.

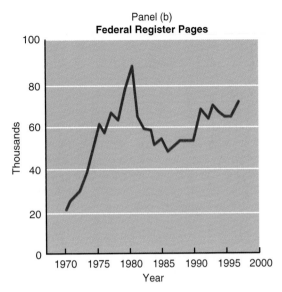

FIGURE 26-2

Regulation on the Rise

In panel (a), federal government regulatory spending is shown to exceed $16 billion per year today. State and local spending is not shown. In panel (b), the number of pages in the *Federal Register* per year has been rising since about 1990.

Sources: Institute for University Studies; *Federal Register,* various issues.

THE COSTS OF REGULATION

There is no truly accurate way to measure the costs of regulation. Panel (a) of Figure 26-2 shows regulatory spending in 1998 dollars. Except in the years 1981–1985, regulatory spending by federal agencies has increased. This is consistent with what has happened to the number of pages in the *Federal Register,* which publishes all the new federal regulatory rules; you can see that in panel (b). But actual direct costs to taxpayers are only a small part of the overall cost of regulation. Pharmaceutical-manufacturing safety standards raise the price of drugs. Automobile safety standards raise the price of cars. Environmental controls on manufacturing raise the price of manufactured goods. All of these increased prices add to the cost of regulation. According to economist Thomas Hopkins at the Rochester Institute of Technology, the economic cost of environmental and safety regulation exceeds $200 billion a year. When he adds the cost of all other kinds of regulations, he comes up with a grand total of over $600 billion a year, or about 8 percent of each year's total income in this country. Not surprisingly, the increasing cost of regulation on occasion has brought about cries for deregulation.

DEREGULATION

Deregulation
The elimination or phasing out of regulations on economic activity.

Regulation increased substantially during the 1970s. By the end of that decade, numerous proposals for **deregulation**—the removal of old regulations—had been made. Most deregulation proposals and actions since then have been aimed at industries in which price competition and entry competition by new firms continued to be thwarted by the regulators. The Air Deregulation Act of 1978 eliminated the Civil Aeronautics Board and allowed comptetition among the airlines themselves to control fares and routes flown. In 1980, the Interstate Commerce Commission's power over interstate trucking rates and routes was virtually eliminated, and the same occurred for buses in 1982. Savings account interest rates were deregulated in 1980. Railroad pricing was made more flexible during the same year.

Even prior to this spate of deregulatory acts by Congress, the Federal Communications Commission (FCC) had started in 1972 to deregulate the television broadcast industry. The result has been an increased number of channels, more direct satellite broadcasting, and more cable television transmissions. (Further deregulation occurred in 1996.) In 1975, the Securities and Exchange Commission (SEC) deregulated brokerage fees charged by brokers on the New York Stock Exchange.

Short-Run Versus Long-Run Effects of Deregulation

The short-run effects of deregulation are not the same as the long-run effects. In the short run, a regulated industry that becomes deregulated may experience numerous temporary adjustments. One is the inevitable shakeout of higher-cost producers with the concomitant removal of excess monopoly profits. Another is the sometimes dramatic displacement of workers who have labored long and hard in the formerly regulated industry. The level of service for some consumers may fall; for example, after the deregulation of the telephone industry, some aspects of telephone service decreased in quality. When airlines were deregulated, service to some small cities was eliminated or became more expensive. The power of unions in the formerly regulated industry may decrease. And bankruptcies may cause disruptions, particularly in the local economy where the headquarters of the formerly regulated firm are located.

Proponents of deregulation, or at least of less regulation, contend that there are long-run, permanent benefits. These include lower prices that are closer to marginal cost. Furthermore, fewer monopoly profits are made in the deregulated industry. Such proponents argue that deregulation has had positive *net* benefits.

Deregulation and Contestable Markets

A major argument in favor of deregulation is that when government-imposed barriers to entry are removed, competition will cause firms to enter markets that previously had only a few firms with market power due to those entry barriers. Potential competitors will become actual competitors, and prices will fall toward a competitive level. Recently, this argument has been bolstered by a relatively new model of efficient firm behavior that predicts competitive prices in spite of a lack of a large number of firms. This model is called the **theory of contestable markets.** Under the theory of contestable markets, most of the outcomes predicted by the theory of perfect competition will occur in certain industries with relatively few firms. Specifically, where the theory of contestable markets is applicable, the few firms may still produce the output at which price equals marginal cost in both the short run and the long run. These firms will receive zero economic profits in the long run.

Unconstrained and Relatively Costless Entry and Exit. For a market to be perfectly contestable, firms must be able to enter and leave the industry easily. Freedom of entry and exit implies an absence of nonprice constraints and of serious fixed costs associated with a potential competitor's decision to enter a contestable market. Such an absence of impor-

Exercise 26.2
Visit www.econtoday.com for more about deregulation.

Theory of contestable markets
A hypothesis concerning pricing behavior that holds that even though there are only a few firms in an industry, they are forced to price their products more or less competitively because of the ease of entry by outsiders. The key aspect of a contestable market is relatively costless entry into and exit from the industry.

tant fixed costs results if the firm need buy no specific durable inputs in order to enter, if it uses up all such inputs it does purchase, or if all of its specific durable inputs are salable upon exit without any losses beyond those normally incurred from depreciation. The important issue is whether or not a potential entrant can easily get his or her investment out at any time in the future.

The mathematical model of perfect contestability is complex, but the underlying logic is straightforward. As long as conditions for free entry prevail, any excess profits, or any inefficiencies on the part of incumbent firms, will serve as an inducement for potential entrants to enter. By entering, new firms can temporarily profit at no risk to themselves from the less than competitive situation in the industry. Once competitive conditions are again restored, these firms will leave the industry just as quickly.

Benefits of Contestable Markets. Contestable markets have several desirable characteristics. One has to do with profits. Profits that exceed the opportunity cost of capital will not exist in the long run because of freedom of entry, just as in a perfectly competitive industry. The elimination of "excess" profits can occur even with only a couple of firms in an industry. The threat of entry will cause them to expand output to eliminate excess profit.

Also, firms that have cost curves that are higher than those of the most efficient firms will find that they cannot compete. These firms will be replaced by entrants whose cost curves are consistent with the most efficient technology. In other words, in contestable markets, there will be no cost inefficiencies in the long run.

Rethinking Regulation Using Cost-Benefit Analysis

Rather than considering deregulation as the only solution to "too much" regulation, some economists argue that regulation should simply be put to a cost-benefit test. Specifically, the cost of existing and proposed regulations should be compared to the benefits. Unless it can be demonstrated that regulations generate net positive benefits (benefits greater than costs), such regulations should not be in effect.

CONCEPTS IN BRIEF

- It is difficult to regulate the price per constant-quality unit because it is difficult to measure all dimensions of quality.

- The capture hypothesis holds that regulatory agencies will eventually be captured by special interests of the industry. This is because consumers are a diffuse group who individually are not affected greatly by regulation, whereas industry groups are well focused and know that large amounts of potential profits are at stake and depend on the outcome of regulatory proceedings.

- In the share-the-gains, share-the-pains theory of regulation, regulators must take account of the interests of three groups: the industry, legislators, and consumers.

- The 1970s and 1980s were periods of deregulation during which formerly regulated industries became much more competitive. The short-run effects of deregulation in some industries were numerous bankruptcies and disrupted service. The long-run results in many deregulated industries included better service, more variety, and lower costs. One argument in favor of deregulation involves the theory of contestable markets—if entry and exit are relatively costless, the number of firms in an industry is irrelevant in terms of determining whether consumers pay competitive prices.

ANTITRUST POLICY

It is the expressed aim of our government to foster competition in the economy. To this end, numerous attempts have been made to legislate against business practices that seemingly destroy the competitive nature of the system. This is the general idea behind antitrust legislation: If the courts can prevent collusion among sellers of a product, monopoly prices will not result; there will be no restriction of output if the members of an industry are not allowed to join together in restraint of trade. Remember that the competitive solution to the price-quantity problem is one in which the price of the item produced is equal to its marginal social opportunity cost. Also, no *economic* profits are made in the long run.

The Sherman Antitrust Act of 1890

The Sherman Antitrust Act was passed in 1890. It was the first attempt by the federal government to control the growth of monopoly in the United States. The most important provisions of that act are as follows:

> *Section 1:* Every contract, combination in the form of trust or otherwise, or conspiracy, in restraint of trade or commerce among the several states, or with foreign nations, is hereby declared to be illegal.

> *Section 2:* Every person who shall monopolize, or attempt to monopolize, or combine or conspire with any other person or persons to monopolize any part of the trade or commerce . . . shall be guilty of a misdemeanor.[3]

Notice how vague this act really is. No definition is given for the terms *restraint of trade* or *monopolization.* Despite this vagueness, however, the act was used to prosecute the infamous Standard Oil trust of New Jersey. Standard Oil of New Jersey was charged with violations of Sections 1 and 2 of the Sherman Antitrust Act. This was in 1906, when Standard Oil controlled over 80 percent of the nation's oil-refining capacity. Among other things, Standard Oil was accused of both predatory price cutting to drive rivals out of business and obtaining preferential price treatment from the railroads for transporting Standard Oil products, thus allowing Standard to sell at lower prices.

Standard Oil was convicted in a district court. The company then appealed to the Supreme Court, which ruled that Standard's control of and power over the oil market created "a *prima facie* presumption of intent and purpose to maintain dominancy . . . not as a result from normal methods of industrial development, but by means of combination." Here the word *combination* meant taking over other businesses and obtaining preferential price treatment from railroads. The Supreme Court forced Standard Oil of New Jersey to break up into many smaller companies.

The Clayton Act of 1914

The Sherman Act was so vague that in 1914 a new law was passed to sharpen its antitrust provisions. This law was called the Clayton Act. It prohibited or limited a number of very specific business practices, which again were felt to be "unreasonable" attempts at restraining trade or commerce. Section 2 of that act made it illegal to "discriminate in price between different purchasers" except in cases in which the differences are due to actual dif-

---

[3] This is now a felony.

ferences in selling or transportation costs. Section 3 stated that producers cannot sell goods "on the condition, agreement or understanding that the . . . purchaser thereof shall not use or deal in the goods . . . of a competitor or competitors of the seller." And Section 7 provided that corporations cannot hold stock in another company if the effect "may be to substantially lessen competition."

The Federal Trade Commission Act of 1914 and Its 1938 Amendment

Exercise 26.3
Visit www.econtoday.com for more about the FTC.

The Federal Trade Commission Act was designed to stipulate acceptable competitive behavior. In particular, it was supposed to prevent cutthroat pricing—excessively aggressive competition, which would tend to eliminate too many competitors. One of the basic features of the act was the creation of the Federal Trade Commission (FTC), charged with the power to investigate unfair competitive practices. The FTC can do this on its own or at the request of firms that feel they have been wronged. It can issue cease and desist orders where "unfair methods of competition in commerce" are discovered. In 1938, the Wheeler-Lea Act amended the 1914 act. The amendment expressly prohibits "unfair or deceptive acts or practices in commerce." Pursuant to that act, the FTC engages in what it sees as a battle against false or misleading advertising, as well as the misrepresentation of goods and services for sale in the marketplace.

The Robinson-Patman Act of 1936

In 1936, Section 2 of the Clayton Act was amended by the Robinson-Patman Act. The Robinson-Patman Act was aimed at preventing producers from driving out smaller competitors by means of selected discriminatory price cuts. The act has often been referred to as the "Chain Store Act" because it was meant to protect *independent* retailers and wholesalers from "unfair discrimination" by chain stores.

The act was the natural outgrowth of increasing competition that independents faced when chain stores and mass distributors started to develop after World War I. The essential provisions of the act are as follows:

1. It was made illegal to pay brokerage fees unless an independent broker was employed.
2. It was made illegal to offer concessions, such as discounts, free advertising, or promotional allowances, to one buyer of a firm's product if the firm did not offer the same concessions to all buyers of that product.
3. Other forms of discrimination, such as quantity discounts, were also made illegal whenever they "substantially" lessened competition.
4. It was made illegal to charge lower prices in one location than in another or to sell at "unreasonably low prices" if such marketing techniques were designed to "destroy competition or eliminate a competitor."

POLICY EXAMPLE
Should Wal-Mart Be Forced to Raise Prices?

The issue of predatory pricing gained national prominence when three independent pharmacies filed suit against Wal-Mart in an Arkansas court. Independent retailers in small towns across the country have long accused Wal-Mart of selling goods below cost to drive them out of business. The three pharmacies that brought suit against

Wal-Mart claimed that it was engaging in predatory pricing by selling as many as 200 items below cost at its store in Conway, Arkansas. Wal-Mart responded that it makes its pricing decisions based on how much competition it faces: more competition, lower prices. Wal-Mart attorneys pointed out that when Wal-Mart entered the Conway business area, there were 12 pharmacies, all of which remain in existence today, plus two new ones. The number of pharmacists in the county increased from 38 to 58.

A local judge found Wal-Mart guilty; on appeal, Wal-Mart prevailed.

FOR CRITICAL ANALYSIS: Supermarkets routinely advertise "loss leaders" such as turkeys at Thanksgiving that are priced below cost. Is there any difference between spending on loss leaders and simply spending more on traditional types of advertising? ●

Exemptions from Antitrust Laws

Numerous laws exempt the following industries and business practices from antitrust legislation:

1. All labor unions
2. Public utilities—electric, gas, and telephone companies
3. Professional baseball
4. Cooperative activities among American exporters
5. Hospitals
6. Public transit and water systems
7. Suppliers of military equipment
8. Joint publishing arrangement in a single city by two or more newspapers

THE ENFORCEMENT OF ANTITRUST LAWS

Most antitrust enforcement today is based on the Sherman Act. The Supreme Court has defined the offense of **monopolization** as involving the following elements: "(1) the possession of monopoly power in the relevant market and (2) the willful acquisition or maintenance of that power, as distinguished from growth or development as a consequence of a superior product, business acumen, or historical accident."

Monopolization
The possession of monopoly power in the relevant market and the willful acquisition or maintenance of that power, as distinguished from growth or development as a consequence of a superior product, business acumen, or historical accident.

Monopoly Power and the Relevant Market

The Sherman Act does not define monopoly. Monopoly clearly is not a single entity. Also, monopoly is not a function of size alone. For example, a "mom and pop" grocery store located in an isolated desert town is a monopolist in at least one sense.

It is difficult to define and measure market power precisely. As a workable proxy, courts often look to the firm's percentage share of the "relevant market." This is the so-called **market share test.** A firm is generally considered to have monopoly power if its share of the relevant market is 70 percent or more. This is not an absolute dictum, however. It is only a loose rule of thumb; in some cases, a smaller share may be held to constitute monopoly power.

The relevant market consists of two elements: a relevant product market and a relevant geographic market. What should the relevant product market include? It must include all products produced by different firms that have identical attributes, such as sugar. Yet products that are not identical may sometimes be substituted for one another. Coffee may be substituted for tea, for example. In defining the relevant product market, the key issue is the degree of interchangeability between products. If one product is a sufficient substitute for another, the two products are considered to be part of the same product market.

Market share test
The percentage of a market that a particular firm controls, used as the primary measure of monopoly power.

The second component of the relevant market is the geographic boundaries of the market. For products that are sold nationwide, the geographic boundaries of the market encompass the entire United States. If a producer and its competitors sell in only a limited area (one in which customers have no access to other sources of the product), the geographic market is limited to that area. A national firm may thus compete in several distinct areas and have monopoly power in one area but not in another.

POLICY EXAMPLE
Should the FTC Be Allowed to Redefine the Relevant Market?

Recently, the FTC prevented the merger of Office Depot and Staples, both office supply superstore chains. To understand why the FTC opposed this proposed merger, let's consider the definition of a market. If it is office products, then firms sell such products in the following ways: (1) over the Internet, (2) via fax, (3) over the phone from different supply companies, (4) through salespeople from different suppliers who come directly to businesses, even very small ones, (5) from Wal-Mart and other general retail companies, (6) from small office supply retailers, (7) from club warehouses, such as PriceCostco, and (8) from office supply superstores. The total share of the national market for office supplies garnered by the superstores Staples and Office Depot accounts for between 4 and 5 percent.

The FTC, unable to stop the merger on the basis of a reasonable definition of the relevant market, developed a new definition—the sale of office supplies at office supply superstores! In other words, the FTC defined the market so that Office Depot and Staples would account for almost 100 percent of that market. Nowhere in the literature of antitrust does one find a definition of a market that depends on the way in which firms actually sell a good or service. The FTC nonetheless decided that Office Depot and Staples were not selling office supplies but rather a service called "one-stop shopping for office supplies." This is a strange definition coming from the Federal Trade Commission, an agency that purchases office supplies from 105 different vendors. There is also another problem, and it deals with what Office Depot and Staples actually sell. Office supplies account for about 40 percent of these two stores' sales. The other 60 percent includes cellular phones, computers, computer supplies, and furniture. They have no monopoly power in the sale of such items.

Perhaps the most important argument against the FTC's new definition of the relevant market has to do with e-commerce, the sale of goods over the Internet. Businesses, more than any other group of buyers, are using the Internet to make purchases. It is hard to imagine that Office Depot and Staples, as a merged company, could raise prices in a market in which price quotes are available at almost no cost at the click of a mouse.

FOR CRITICAL ANALYSIS: *Why do you imagine that the FTC decided to change the normal definition of the relevant market?* ●

CONCEPTS IN BRIEF

- The first national antitrust law was the Sherman Antitrust Act, passed in 1890, which made illegal every contract and combination in the form of a trust in restraint of trade.

- The Clayton Act made price discrimination and interlocking directorates illegal.

- The Federal Trade Commission Act of 1914 established the Federal Trade Commission. The Wheeler-Lea Act of 1938 amended the 1914 act to prohibit "unfair or deceptive acts or practices in commerce."

- The Robinson-Patman Act of 1936 was aimed at preventing large producers from driving out small competitors by means of selective discriminatory price cuts.

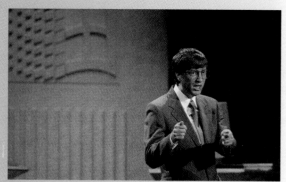

Microsoft CEO Bill Gates has had to defend himself in recent years against federal charges of attempting to monopolize the Internet browser market. Is it possible for any one company to have a monopoly in electronic commerce?

The Justice Department Goes After Microsoft Again

CONCEPTS APPLIED:

COMPETITION, MONOPOLY, MARKET POWER, ANTITRUST LAW

Visit www.econtoday.com for an Internet Activity that expands your understanding of these concepts.

Microsoft has been engaged in a head-to-head battle for dominance in the Internet browser market. As mentioned in the opening page of this chapter, its main competitor is Netscape Communications, which owns Navigator.

The Microsoft Plan

Microsoft was going to "bundle" the latest version of its browser, Internet Explorer, with the latest version of its industry-leading Windows operating system and with any future improvements to that system. What Microsoft was proposing to do was consistent with what has been observed in the software industry for years. Microsoft, Apple, IBM, Sun, Novell, and others have little by little included more features in each operating system they have offered. These included graphical user interface, type fonts, file compression features, networking, memory management, and other niceties.

Justice Says No

The Justice Department decided that Microsoft should unbundle its Internet browser program from its operating system. The court stated that "Microsoft's 'unfettered liberty' to impose its idea of what has been 'integrated' into its operating system stops at least at the point at which it would violate established antitrust law." The idea, of course, is that because Microsoft's dominant Windows operating system is in more than 80 percent of the world's computers, Microsoft can force computer manufacturers to whom it licenses that system to incorporate Microsoft's Internet Explorer Web browser.

Unlike monopolies, in the software and computer industry in general, prices have been falling for everything, including all Microsoft products. When one Justice Department official had this fact pointed out to him, he

stated that the Justice Department has to look to the future. In other words, the Justice Department believes that it can predict what will happen in the computer industry, and that is why it is trying to prevent Microsoft from bundling Internet Explorer with Windows.

Is the Justice Department Being Consistent?

While the Justice Department does not want Windows to include browsing capabilities, many of Microsoft's competitors are doing the equivalent. They are incorporating basic operating system services, such as the ability to print files and to run applications, into their own browsers, making them a type of operating system. If Microsoft's competitors can integrate an operating system into their browsers, why can't Microsoft integrate a browser into its operating system?

Could Microsoft Control Electronic Commerce?

An additional issue concerns electronic commerce. If Microsoft's Internet Explorer browser becomes the dominant one in the marketplace, could Microsoft then be able to monopolize travel, real estate, and banking services on the Internet? Perhaps not, for a browser is only a window; it's not the view. On the World Wide Web, the *content* is what people are after; how they get to that content is immaterial. Soon there will be hundreds of thousands of content providers on the Web selling travel, banking, and other services.

FOR CRITICAL ANALYSIS

1. How valid is the Justice Department's argument about looking to the future?
2. Why do most of the nation's computers use the Microsoft operating system today?

CHAPTER SUMMARY

1. Regulation may be applied to a natural monopoly, which arises when, for example, the average total cost curve falls over a very large range of production rates. In such a situation, only one firm can survive. It will be the firm that can expand production and sales faster than the others to take advantage of the falling average total costs. If regulation seeks to force the natural monopolist to produce at the point where the marginal cost curve (supply curve in the competitive case) intersects the demand curve, the natural monopolist will incur losses, because when average total costs are falling, marginal costs are below average total costs. The regulators face a dilemma.

2. There are several ways of regulating monopolies, the most common ones being on a cost-of-service basis or a rate-of-return basis. Under cost-of-service regulation, the regulated monopolies are allowed to charge prices that reflect only reasonable costs. Under rate-of-return regulation, the regulated monopolies are allowed to set rates so as to make a competitive rate of return for the equity shareholders. Supposedly, no monopoly profits can therefore be earned.

3. The capture hypothesis predicts that because of the diffuse interests of consumers as compared to the well-focused interests of industry members, regulators will eventually be captured by those whom they regulate.

4. The share-the-gains, share-the-pains theory predicts that regulators must take account not only of the desires of members of the industry but also of the wishes of legislators and consumers.

5. The 1970s and 1980s were periods of deregulation during which formerly regulated industries became much more competitive. The short-run effects of deregulation in some industries were numerous bankruptcies and disrupted service. The long-run results in many deregulated industries included better service, more variety, and lower costs.

6. One argument in favor of deregulation involves the theory of contestable markets—if entry and exit are relatively costless, the number of firms in an industry is irrelevant in terms of determining whether consumers pay competitive prices.

7. Some economists argue that all actual and proposed regulation be subject to strict cost-benefit analysis.

8. Antitrust legislation is designed to obviate the need for regulation. The major antitrust acts are the Sherman, Clayton, and Robinson-Patman acts.

DISCUSSION OF PREVIEW QUESTIONS

1. **What is a natural monopoly, and how does one arise?**
A natural monopoly is a situation in which the long-run average cost curve falls persistently as output expands. Thus the natural monopolist is a firm that by expanding is able to charge a price lower than its competitors can, thereby eliminating them. A natural monopolist arises due to tremendous economies of scale; expanding output causes ATC to fall.

2. **If natural monopolies are required to price at marginal cost, what problem emerges?**
We have noted in earlier chapters that efficiency requires that people pay the marginal cost for a good or a service. If regulators grant a firm monopoly privileges (recognizing it as a natural monopoly and regulating it to keep it in line) but force it to price at its marginal cost of production, a problem emerges. Because long-run ATC is persistently falling, it follows that long-run marginal cost must be below long-run ATC. Forcing a firm to charge a price equal to marginal cost implies that average revenue = price = marginal cost < average total cost (AR = P = MC < ATC). It follows that AR < ATC, and therefore the regulated natural monopolist would experience *negative* economic profits. In that case, it would shut down unless subsidized. In short, forcing a regulated natural monopolist to price at marginal cost

may be socially beneficial, but such a policy requires that the natural monopolist be subsidized to cover the resulting economic losses to the firm.

3. What are some means of regulating a natural monopoly?

Two important means of regulating a natural monopoly are cost of service and rate of return. Cost-of-service regulation aims at requiring a natural monopolist to price at levels that would result from a more competitive situation. In effect, the natural monopolist is required to charge the average cost of providing the service in question, thereby ensuring zero economic profits. The rate-of-return form of regulation in effect allows a natural monopolist to price at rates that permit it an *overall* "normal" rate of return, because the natural monopolist will remain in operation only if it earns at least a normal return on invested capital.

4. Why have economists been reevaluating the government's role as an economic regulator?

Presumably, regulation is an attempt to prevent monopoly abuses and to simulate a competitive market structure where one would not otherwise exist. Yet much academic research indicates that this is not the case; regulated industries apparently behave more like monopolies than the overall manufacturing sector does. Some analysts have claimed that the regulated firms sooner or later "capture" the regulatory agencies; before long, regulated industries have the protection and sanction of the regulatory bodies! Hence many economists favor deregulation—at least of the older variety of regulation, as existed in the airline, interstate transport, and communications industries. The consensus is less clear regarding regulation by the newer agencies such as the Environmental Protection Agency (EPA) and the Occupational Safety and Health Administration (OSHA).

PROBLEMS

(Answers to the odd-numbered problems appear at the back of the book.)

26-1. The accompanying graph depicts a situation for a monopolist.

Quantity per Time Period

  a. If this monopolist were required to price at marginal cost, what would the quantity and price be?
  b. What rectangle would indicate total economic losses if this monopolist were required to price at marginal cost?

26-2. "The elimination of all tariffs would dissipate more monopoly power than any other single government action." What do tariffs (taxes on imported goods only) have to do with monopoly power?

26-3. Assume that you are in charge of enforcing the Occupational Safety and Health Act. If you are not constrained to consider the costs of new regulations that increase worker health and safety, what *will* constrain your behavior, if anything? If you now must consider the costs of your new rules, how might you go about your job?

26-4. Would you expect to find more or less corruption of government officials in a regulatory agency that auctioned off "certificates of convenience" or in one that rationed them according to nonfinancial criteria? Why?

26-5. Why is the right of free entry insufficient to prevent sustained economic profits within a natural monopoly?

26-6. Suppose that you own the only natural mineral spring spa in your state. Why would we *not* expect to see the state government regulating the price you charge?

26-7. "Philosophically, I am vehemently opposed to government interference in the marketplace. As the owner of a liquor store, however, I can tell you that deregulation will be bad for the citizenry. You would not want a liquor store on every corner, would you?" Why would you predict that a liquor store owner would defend regulation of the liquor industry in this way?

26-8. The federal government brought an antitrust suit against IBM in 1982. Eventually the case was dismissed as being "without merit." In the beginning of the 1990s, IBM layed off thousands of its workers. What has happened since the time IBM was being prosecuted as a monopoly and today, when it is suffering hard financial times?

COMPUTER-ASSISTED INSTRUCTION

How do natural monopolies arise? This problem relates economies of scale and profit-maximizing behavior to the formation of natural monopolies.

INTERACTING WITH THE INTERNET

You can find the Federal Trade Commission (FTC) at

www.ftc.gov

To see what the antitrust division of the Department of Justice is doing, go to

www.usdoj.gov/atr/index.html

Find out what the Securities and Exchange Commission does by accessing it at

www.sec.gov

The Federal Communications Commission (FCC) home page is at

www.fcc.gov

PART 8

PRODUCTIVE FACTORS, POVERTY, THE ENVIRONMENT, AND INTEREST GROUPS

CHAPTER 27

LABOR DEMAND AND SUPPLY

One of the reasons that you are pursuing higher education is to increase your value to potential employers. Consequently, you can expect to be paid a higher salary than you would if you had only a high school diploma. President Clinton has said that "we are living in a world where what you earn is a function of what you learn." Historical data seem to reflect this view. Since the end of the 1970s, the wage premium that college graduates have enjoyed relative to other workers increased from 34 percent to over 50 percent. Some labor market researchers believe, however, that the wage differential will decline in the future. They point out that newly developed training software may reduce the value of a college education in the future. Before you can take a position on this issue, you need to understand the basic model of labor demand and supply.

PREVIEW QUESTIONS

1. When hiring labor, what general rule will be followed by employers who wish to maximize profits?
2. What is the profit-maximizing rate of employment for a perfectly competitive firm?
3. What is the profit-maximizing rate of employment for an imperfectly competitive firm?
4. How is an industry wage rate determined?

605

D id You Know That . . . the top 350 executives in America's biggest corporations are compensated, on the average, $2.5 million each, or about 60 times more than the median family income of a little over $40,000? Recently, the head of the Travelers Group, Sanford Weill, was paid almost $100 million in one year. You, in contrast, as a typical college student will probably make between $25,000 and $50,000 a year, or approximately one two-thousandth of Weill's annual salary. To comprehend why firms pay different employees such vastly different salaries, you must understand how the laws of demand and supply apply to labor.

A firm's demand for inputs can be studied in much the same manner as we studied the demand for output in different market situations. Again, various market situations will be examined. Our analysis will always end with the same commonsense conclusion: A firm will hire employees up to the point beyond which it isn't profitable to hire any more. It will hire employees to the point at which the marginal benefit of hiring a worker will just equal the marginal cost. Basically, in every profit-maximizing situation, it is most profitable to carry out an activity up to the point at which the marginal benefit equals the marginal cost. Remembering that guideline will help you in analyzing decision making at the firm level. We will start our analysis under the assumption that the market for input factors is perfectly competitive. We will further assume that the output market is perfectly competitive. This provides a benchmark against which to compare other situations in which labor markets or product markets are not perfectly competitive.

COMPETITION IN THE PRODUCT MARKET

Let's take as our example a compact disc (CD) manufacturing firm that is in competition with many companies selling the same kind of product. Assume that the laborers hired by our CD manufacturing firm do not need any special skills. This firm sells its product in a perfectly competitive market. A CD manufacturer also buys labor (its variable input) in a perfectly competitive market. A firm that hires labor under perfectly competitive conditions hires only a minuscule proportion of all the workers who are potentially available to the firm. By "potentially available" we mean all the workers in a given geographic area who possess the skills demanded by our perfect competitor. In such a market, it is always possible for the individual firm to pick up extra workers without having to offer a higher wage. Thus the supply of labor to the firm is perfectly elastic—that is, represented by a horizontal line at the going wage rate established by the forces of supply and demand in the entire labor market. The firm is a price taker in the labor market.

MARGINAL PHYSICAL PRODUCT

Look at panel (a) of Figure 27-1. In column 1, we show the number of workers per week that the firm can hire. In column 2, we show total physical product (TPP) per week, the total *physical* production that different quantities of the labor input (in combination with a fixed amount of other inputs) will generate in a week's time. In column 3, we show the additional output gained when a CD manufacturing company adds workers to its existing manufacturing facility. This column, the **marginal physical product (MPP) of labor,** represents the extra (additional) output attributed to employing additional units of the variable input factor. If this firm adds a seventh worker, the MPP is 118. The law of diminishing marginal returns predicts that additional units of a variable factor will, after some point, cause the MPP to decline, other things being held constant.

Marginal physical product (MPP) of labor
The change in output resulting from the addition of one more worker. The MPP of the worker equals the change in total output accounted for by hiring the worker, holding all other factors of production constant.

FIGURE 27-1

Marginal Revenue Product

In panel (a), column 4 shows marginal revenue product (MRP), which is the amount of additional revenue the firm receives for the sale of that additional output. Marginal revenue product is simply the amount of money the additional worker brings in—the combination of that worker's contribution to production and the revenue that that production will bring to the firm. For this perfectly competitive firm, marginal revenue is equal to the price of the product, or $6 per unit. At a weekly wage of $498, the profit-maximizing employer will pay for only 12 workers because then the marginal revenue product is just equal to the wage rate or weekly salary.

Panel (a)

(1) Labor Input (workers per week)	(2) Total Physical Product (TPP) CDs per Week	(3) Marginal Physical Product (MPP) CDs per Week	(4) Marginal Revenue (MR = P = $6 net) x MPP = Marginal Revenue Product (MRP) ($ per additional worker)	(5) Wage Rate ($ per week) = Marginal Factor Cost (MFC) = Change in Total Costs / Change in Labor
6	882			
		118	$708	$498
7	1,000			
		111	666	498
8	1,111			
		104	624	498
9	1,215			
		97	582	498
10	1,312			
		90	540	498
11	1,402			
		83	498	498
12	1,485			
		76	456	498
13	1,561			

In panel (b), we find the number of workers the firm will want to hire by observing the wage rate that is established by the forces of supply and demand in the entire labor market. We show that this employer is hiring labor in a perfectly competitive labor market and therefore faces a perfectly elastic supply curve represented by s at $498 per week. As in all other situations, we basically have a supply and demand model; in this example, the demand curve is represented by MRP, and the supply curve is s. Equilibrium occurs at their intersection.

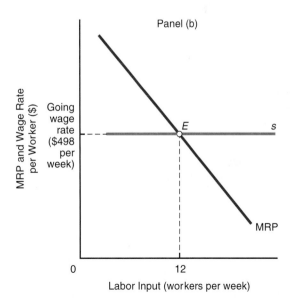

Why the Decline in MPP?

We are assuming all other nonlabor factors of production are held constant. So if our CD manufacturing firm wants to add one more worker to its production line, it has to crowd all the existing workers a little closer together because it does not increase its capital stock (the production equipment). Therefore, as we add more workers, each one has a smaller and smaller fraction of the available capital stock with which to work. If one worker uses one machine, adding another worker usually won't double the output because the machine can run only so fast and for so many hours per day. In other words, MPP declines because of the law of diminishing marginal returns.

Marginal Revenue Product

We now need to translate into a dollar value the physical product that results from hiring an additional worker. This is done by multiplying the marginal physical product by the marginal revenue of the firm. Because our CD firm is selling its product in a perfectly competitive market, marginal revenue is equal to the price of the product. If the seventh worker's MPP is 118 and the marginal revenue is $6 per CD, the **marginal revenue product (MRP)** is $708 (118 × $6). The MRP is shown in column 4 of panel (a) of Figure 27-1. *The marginal revenue product represents the worker's contribution to the firm's total revenues.*

When a firm operates in a competitive product market, the marginal physical product times the product price is also sometimes referred to as the *value of marginal product (VMP)*. Because price and marginal revenue are the same for a perfectly competitive firm, the VMP is also the MRP.

In column 5 of panel (a) of Figure 27-1, we show the wage rate, or *marginal factor cost,* of each worker. The marginal cost of workers is the extra cost incurred in employing that factor of production. We call that cost the **marginal factor cost (MFC).** Otherwise stated,

$$\text{Marginal factor cost} \equiv \frac{\text{change in total cost}}{\text{change in amount of resource used}}$$

Because each worker is paid the same competitively determined wage of $498 per week, the MFC is the same for all workers. And because the firm is buying labor in a perfectly competitive labor market, the wage rate of $498 per week really represents the firm's supply curve of labor. That curve is perfectly elastic because the firm can purchase all labor at the same wage rate, considering that it is a minuscule part of the entire labor-purchasing market. (Recall the definition of perfect competition.) We show this perfectly elastic supply curve as *s* in panel (b) of Figure 27-1.

Marginal revenue product (MRP)
The marginal physical product (MPP) times marginal revenue. The MRP gives the additional revenue obtained from a one-unit change in labor input.

Marginal factor cost (MFC)
The cost of using an additional unit of an input. For example, if a firm can hire all the workers it wants at the going wage rate, the marginal factor cost of labor is the wage rate.

EXAMPLE
Does Attractiveness Lead to Higher Marginal Revenue Product?

Economist Daniel Hamermesh of the University of Texas (Austin) and Jeff Biddle of Michigan State University discovered that "plain-looking" people earn 5 to 10 percent less than people of "average" looks, who in turn earn 5 percent less than those who are considered "good-looking." Surprisingly, their research showed that the "looks effect" on wages was greater for men than for women. This wage differential related to appearance is not, contrary to popular belief, evident only in modeling, acting, or working directly with the public. Looks seem to account for higher earnings in jobs such as bricklaying, factory work, and telemarketing.

According to Hamermesh and Biddle, part of the wage differential may be created by the fact that attractiveness leads to higher marginal revenue product. More attractive individuals may have higher self-esteem, which in turn causes them to be more productive on the job.

FOR CRITICAL ANALYSIS: What are some of the other possible reasons that more attractive people tend to earn more? ●

General Rule for Hiring

Virtually every optimizing rule in economics involves comparing marginal benefits with marginal cost. The general rule, therefore, for the hiring decision of a firm is this:

> **The firm hires workers up to the point at which the additional cost associated with hiring the last worker is equal to the additional revenue generated by that worker.**

In a perfectly competitive situation, this is the point at which the wage rate just equals the marginal revenue product. If the firm hired more workers, the additional wages would not be covered by additional increases in total revenue. If the firm hired fewer workers, it would be forfeiting the contributions that those workers could make to total profits.

Therefore, referring to columns 4 and 5 in panel (a) of Figure 27-1, we see that this firm would certainly employ the seventh worker, because the MRP is $708 while the MFC is only $498. The firm would continue to employ workers up to the point at which MFC = MRP because as workers are added, they contribute more to revenue than to cost.

The MRP Curve: Demand for Labor

We can also use panel (b) of Figure 27-1 to find how many workers our firm should hire. First, we draw a straight line across from the going wage rate, which is determined by demand and supply in the labor market. The straight line is labeled *s* to indicate that it is the supply curve of labor for the *individual* firm purchasing labor in a perfectly competitive labor market. That firm can purchase all the labor it wants of equal quality at $498 per worker. This perfectly elastic supply curve, *s,* intersects the marginal revenue product curve at 12 workers per week. At the intersection, *E,* the wage rate is equal to the marginal revenue product. Equilibrium for the firm is obtained when the firm's demand curve for labor, which turns out to be its MRP curve, intersects the firm's supply curve for labor, shown as *s*. The firm in our example would not hire the thirteenth worker, who will add only $456 to revenue but $498 to cost. If the price of labor should fall to, say, $456 per worker, it would become profitable for the firm to hire an additional worker; there is an increase in the quantity of labor demanded as the wage decreases.

DERIVED DEMAND

Derived demand
Input factor demand derived from demand for the final product being produced.

We have identified an individual firm's demand for labor curve as its MRP curve. Under conditions of perfect competition in both product and labor markets, MRP is determined by multiplying MPP times the product's price. This suggests that the demand for labor is a **derived demand.** That is to say that our CD firm does not want to purchase the services of labor just for the services themselves. Factors of production are rented or purchased not because they give any intrinsic satisfaction to the firms' owners but because they can be used to manufacture output that is expected to be sold for profit.

FIGURE 27-2

Demand for Labor, a Derived Demand

The demand for labor is derived from the demand for the final product being produced. Therefore, the marginal revenue product curve will shift whenever the price of the product changes. If we start with the marginal revenue product curve MRP at the going wage rate of $498 per week, 12 workers will be hired. If the price of CDs goes down, the marginal product curve will shift to MRP_1, and the number of workers hired will fall to 10. If the price of CDs goes up, the marginal revenue product curve will shift to MRP_2, and the number of workers hired will increase to 15.

We know that an increase in the market demand for a given product raises the product's price (all other things held constant), which in turn increases the marginal revenue product, or demand for the resource. Figure 27-2 illustrates the effective role played by changes in product demand in a perfectly competitive product market. The MRP curve shifts whenever there is a change in the price of the final product that the workers are making. If, for example, the market price of CDs goes down, the MRP curve will shift downward to the left from MRP_0 to MRP_1. We know that $MRP \equiv MPP \times MR$. If marginal revenue (here the output price) falls, so, too, does the demand for labor; at the same going wage rate, the firm will hire fewer workers. This is because at various levels of labor use, the marginal revenue product of labor falls so that at the initial equilibrium, the price of labor (here the MFC) becomes greater than MRP. Thus the firm would reduce the number of workers hired. Conversely, if the marginal revenue (output price) rises, the demand for labor will also rise, and the firm will want to hire more workers at each and every possible wage rate.

We just pointed out that $MRP \equiv MPP \times MR$. Clearly, then, a change in marginal productivity, or in the marginal physical product of labor, will shift the MRP curve. If the marginal productivity of labor decreases, the MRP curve, or demand curve, for labor will shift inward to the left. Again, this is because at every quantity of labor used, the MRP will be lower. A lower quantity of labor will be demanded at every possible wage rate.

THE MARKET DEMAND FOR LABOR

The downward-sloping portion of each individual firm's marginal revenue product curve is also its demand curve for the one variable factor of production—in our example, labor. When we go to the entire market for a particular type of labor in a particular industry, we find that quantity of labor demanded will vary as the wage rate changes. Given that the market demand curve for labor is made up of the individual firm demand curve for labor, we can safely assume that the market demand curve for labor will look like *D* in panel (b) of Figure 27-3: It will slope downward. That market demand curve for labor in the CD industry shows the quantities of labor demanded by all of the firms in the industry at various wage rates.

It is important to note that the market demand curve for labor is not a simple horizontal summation of the labor demand curves of all individual firms. Remember that the demand

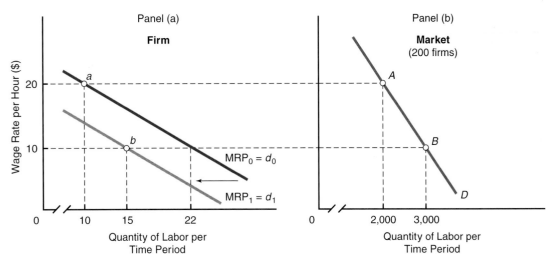

FIGURE 27-3

Derivation of the Market Demand Curve for Labor

The market demand curve for labor is not simply the horizontal summation of each individual firm's demand curve for labor. If wage rates fall from $20 to $10, all 200 firms will increase employment and therefore output, causing the price of the product to fall. This causes the marginal revenue product curve of each firm to shift inward, as from d_0 to d_1 in panel (a). The resulting market demand curve, D, in panel (b) is therefore less elastic than it would be if output price remained constant.

for labor is a derived demand. Even if we hold labor productivity constant, the demand for labor still depends on both the wage rate and the price of the final output. Assume that we start at a wage rate of $20 per hour and employment level 10 in panel (a) of Figure 27-3. If we sum all such employment levels—point a in panel (a)—across 200 firms, we get a market quantity demanded of 2,000—point A in panel (b)—at the wage rate of $20. A decrease in the wage rate to $10 per hour induces individual firms' employment level to increase toward a quantity demanded of 22. As all 200 firms simultaneously increase employment, however, there is a shift in the product supply curve such that output increases. Hence the price of the product must fall. The fall in the output price in turn causes a downward shift of each firm's MRP curve (d_0) to MRP_1 (d_1) in panel (a). Thus each firm's employment of labor increases to 15 rather than to 22 at the wage rate of $10 per hour. A summation of all such 200 employment levels gives us 3,000—point B—in panel (b).

DETERMINANTS OF DEMAND ELASTICITY FOR INPUTS

Just as we were able to discuss the price elasticity of demand for different commodities in Chapter 20, we can discuss the price elasticity of demand for inputs. The price elasticity of demand for labor is defined in a manner similar to the price elasticity of demand for goods: the percentage change in quantity demanded divided by the percentage change in the price of labor. When the numerical value of this ratio is less than 1, it is inelastic; when it is 1, unit-elastic; and when it is greater than 1, elastic.

There are four principal determinants of the price elasticity of demand for an input. The price elasticity of demand for a variable input will be greater:

1. The greater the price elasticity of demand for the final product
2. The easier it is for a particular variable input to be substituted for by other inputs

3. The larger the proportion of total costs accounted for by a particular variable input
4. The longer the time period being considered

Consider some examples. An individual radish farmer faces an extremely elastic demand for radishes, given the existence of many competing radish growers. If the farmer's laborers tried to obtain a significant wage increase, the farmer couldn't pass on the resultant higher costs to radish buyers. So any wage increase to the individual radish farmer would lead to a large reduction in the quantity of labor demanded.

Clearly, the easier it is for a producer to switch to using another factor of production, the more responsive that producer will be to an increase in an input's price. If plastic and aluminum can easily be substituted in the production of, say, car bumpers, then a price rise in aluminum will cause automakers to reduce greatly their quantity of aluminum demanded.

When a particular input's costs account for a very large share of total costs, any increase in that input's price will affect total costs relatively more. If labor costs are 80 percent of total costs, a company will cut back on employment more aggressively than if labor costs were only 8 percent of total costs, for any given wage increase.

Finally, over longer periods, firms have more time to figure out ways to economize on the use of inputs whose prices have gone up. Furthermore, over time, technological change will allow for easier substitution in favor of relatively cheaper inputs and against inputs whose prices went up. At first, a pay raise obtained by a strong telephone company union may not result in many layoffs, but over time, the telephone company will use new technology to replace many of the now more expensive workers.

CONCEPTS IN BRIEF

- The change in total output due to a one-unit change in one variable input, holding all other inputs constant, is called the marginal physical product (MPP). When we multiply marginal physical product times marginal revenue, we obtain the marginal revenue product (MRP).

- A firm will hire workers up to the point at which the additional cost of hiring one more worker is equal to the additional revenues generated. For the individual firm, therefore, its MRP of labor curve is also its demand for labor curve.

- The demand for labor is a derived demand, derived from the demand for final output. Therefore, if the price of final output changes, this will cause a shift in the MRP curve (which is also the firm's demand for labor curve).

- Input price elasticity of demand depends on final product elasticity, the ease of other input substitution, the relative importance of the input's cost in total costs, and the time allowed for adjustment.

WAGE DETERMINATION

Having developed the demand curve for labor (and all other variable inputs) in a particular industry, let's turn to the labor supply curve. By adding supply to the analysis, we can come up with the equilibrium wage rate that workers earn in an industry. We can think in terms of a supply curve for labor that slopes upward in a particular industry. At higher wage rates, more workers will want to enter that particular industry. The individual firm, however, does not face the entire *market* supply curve. Rather, in a perfectly competitive case, the indi-

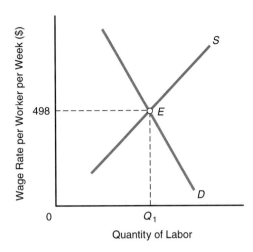

FIGURE 27-4

The Equilibrium Wage Rate and the CD Industry
The industry demand curve for labor is *D*. We put in a hypothetical upward-sloping labor supply curve for the CD industry, *S*. The intersection is at point *E*, giving an equilibrium wage rate of $498 per week and an equilibrium quantity of labor demanded of Q_1. At a price above $498 per week, there will be an excess quantity of workers supplied. At a price below $498 per week, there will be an excess quantity of workers demanded.

vidual firm is such a small part of the market that it can hire all the workers that it wants at the going wage rate. We say, therefore, that the industry faces an upward-sloping supply curve but that the individual *firm* faces a perfectly elastic supply curve for labor.

The demand curve for labor in the CD industry is *D* in Figure 27-4, and the supply curve of labor is *S*. The equilibrium wage rate of $498 a week is established at the intersection of the two curves. The quantity of workers both supplied and demanded at that rate is Q_1. If for some reason the wage rate fell to $400 a week, in our hypothetical example, there would be an excess number of workers demanded at that wage rate. Conversely, if the wage rate rose to $600 a week, there would be an excess quantity of workers supplied at that wage rate.

We have just found the equilibrium wage rate for the entire CD industry. The individual firm must take that equilibrium wage rate as given in the competitive model used here because the individual firm is a very small part of the total demand for labor. Thus each firm purchasing labor in a perfectly competitive market can purchase all of the input it wants at the going market price.

Exercise 27.1
Visit www.econtoday.com for more about labor markets.

POLICY EXAMPLE
Should the Minimum Wage Be Raised to Help Young People?

The equilibrium wage rate model shown in Figure 27-4 does not apply when the government sets a minimum wage rate below which employers are not allowed to pay workers and workers are not allowed to offer their services. Recall from Chapter 4 that in general, a minimum wage (if set above equilibrium) creates an excess quantity of labor supplied (a surplus) at that legal minimum. Thus young people probably would not be helped by an increase in minimum wages. Look at Figure 27-5 on page 614. There you see the unemployment rate for young people ages 16 to 19. As the minimum wage was raised starting in 1990, so did the rate of unemployment increase for young people. It started falling again only around 1992. Why? In part because what is important is the real, inflation-corrected minimum wage rate. In real terms, the minimum wage dropped to its lowest point in 45 years in 1989. Then it rose until 1992 and started falling again, exactly coincident with the reduction in the unemployment rate for young people. So to answer the policy question, raising the minimum wage probably would not help young people as a group, although it might help some young people who retain their jobs at the higher wage rate.

FIGURE 27-5

Teenage Unemployment and the Real Minimum Wage

Although the nominal minimum wage trends up, the real (inflation-corrected) minimum wage reached its peak in the late 1960s. The teenage unemployment rate is closely correlated with changes in the *real* minimum wage.

Source: U.S. Department of Labor, Bureau of Labor Statistics.

FOR CRITICAL ANALYSIS: Why are young people most affected by changes in the minimum wage? (Hint: Which workers have the lowest MRP?) ●

ALTERNATIVE THEORIES OF WAGE DETERMINATION: EFFICIENCY WAGES AND INSIDERS VERSUS OUTSIDERS

The relatively straightforward analysis of the supply and demand of labor just presented may not fully explain the equilibrium level of wages under certain circumstances. There are two important alternative theories of wage determination that may apply to at least some parts of the economy. We analyze those two theories now.

Efficiency Wages

Let's say that in the CD industry, employers can hire as many workers as they want at the equilibrium weekly wage rate of $498. Associated with that weekly wage rate is a specified amount of employment in each firm. Within each firm, though, there is turnover. Some workers quit to go on to other jobs. Turnover costs are significant. Workers have to be trained. What if a firm, even though it could hire workers at $498 a week, offered employment at $600 a week? Several things might occur. First, current employees would have less desire to look elsewhere to find better jobs. There would be less turnover. Second, those workers who applied for openings might be of higher quality, being attracted by the higher wage rate. Third, workers on the job might actually become more productive because they do not want to lose their jobs. They know that alternative competitive wages are $498 a week.

The higher-than-competitive wage rates offered by such a firm have been designated **efficiency wages.** The underlying assumption is that firms operate more efficiently if they pay their workers a higher wage rate.

Efficiency wages

Wages set above competitive levels to increase labor productivity and profits by enhancing the efficiency of the firm through lower turnover, ease of attracting higher-quality workers, and better efforts by workers.

Insiders and Outsiders

A related view of the labor market involves the notion of insiders within a firm. The insiders are those current employees who have the "inside track" and can maintain their positions because the firm would have to incur costs to replace them. These employee insiders are therefore able to exercise some control over the terms under which new employees (outsiders) are hired by the firm. They keep other potential workers out by not allowing them to offer themselves for work at a lower real wage rate than that being earned by the insiders. As pointed out earlier, the costs of hiring and firing workers are significant. Indeed, the cost of firing one worker may sometimes be relatively high: termination wages, retraining payments, and litigation if the worker believes termination was unjustified. All such costs might contribute to the development of insider-dominated labor markets. They contain significant barriers to entry by outsiders.

Insider-outsider theory
A theory of labor markets in which workers who are already employed have an influence on wage bargaining in such a way that outsiders who are willing to work for lower real wages cannot get a job.

So the **insider-outsider theory** predicts that wages may remain higher than the standard supply and demand model would predict even though outsiders are willing to work at lower real wages.

EXAMPLE
Competing for the Boss's Job

Although efficiency wage theory and the insider-outsider theory may explain wages that are somewhat above a competitive level, they have a harder time explaining really big differences in wages within a firm's management structure. CEOs tend to make many times more than vice-presidents do. Senior vice-presidents often make double what a regular vice-president makes. According to one theory, corporations create these big salary differentials, *not* in an attempt to reward the recipients, but rather to create a structure of powerful incentives to get people in the organization to work harder. Pay is based on *relative* performance, relative to one's peers within the management organization. The pay of a vice-president is not what motivates that vice-president; it is the pay of the CEO, to whose job the vice-president aspires. Economists Edward Lazer of Stanford University and Sherwin Rosen of the University of Chicago call this concept *tournament theory*. They argue that vice-presidents and others under them are involved in a series of tournaments. The winner of each tournament moves up to the next higher level. All aspire to the highest level, that of the CEO.

FOR CRITICAL ANALYSIS: If luck plays an unusually large role in a vice-president's rise to the top, will the pay differential between vice-presidents and the CEO have to be relatively large or small compared to a situation in which luck is not important? •

SHIFTS IN THE MARKET DEMAND FOR AND SUPPLY OF LABOR

Just as we discussed shifts in the supply curve and the demand curve for various products in Chapter 3, we can discuss the effects of shifts in supply and demand in labor markets.

Reasons for Labor Demand Curve Shifts

Many factors can cause the demand curve for labor to shift. We have already discussed a number of them. Clearly, because the demand for labor or any other variable input is a derived demand, the labor demand curve will shift if there is a shift in the demand for the final product. There are two other important determinants of the position of the demand curve for labor: changes in labor's productivity and changes in the price of related factors of production (substitutes and complements).

Changes in Demand for Final Product. The demand for labor or any other variable input is derived from the demand for the final product. The marginal revenue product is equal to marginal physical product times marginal revenue. Therefore, any change in the price of the final product will change MRP. This happened when we derived the market demand for labor. The general rule of thumb is as follows:

A change in the demand for the final product that labor (or any other variable input) is producing will shift the market demand curve for labor in the same direction.

Changes in Labor Productivity. The second part of the MRP equation is MPP, which relates to labor productivity. We can surmise, then, that, other things being equal,

A change in labor productivity will shift the market labor demand curve in the same direction.

Labor productivity can increase because labor has more capital or land to work with, because of technological improvements, or because labor's quality has improved. Such considerations explain why the real standard of living of workers in the United States is higher than in most countries. American workers generally work with a larger capital stock, have more natural resources, are in better physical condition, and are better trained than workers in many countries. Hence the demand for labor in America is, other things held constant, greater. Conversely, labor is relatively scarcer in the United States than it is in many other countries. One result of relatively greater demand and relatively smaller supply is a relatively higher wage rate.

EXAMPLE
Does It Pay to Go to College?

One way to increase labor productivity is to increase skill level. One way to do that, of course, is to go to college. Is there a big payoff? According to a recent study of identical twins carried out by economists Orley Ashenfelter and Alan Krueger, the answer is a resounding yes. They studied the earning patterns of more than 250 identical twins. In this manner, they were able to hold constant heredity, early home life, and so on. They focused on differences in the number of years of schooling. They discovered that each additional year of schooling increased wages almost 16 percent. Four years of college yielded a 67 percent increase in monthly wages compared to no college.

Some economists believe that a college degree is part of **labor market signaling.** Employers do not have much information about the future productivity of job applicants. Typically, the only way to find out is to observe someone working. Employers attempt to reduce the number of bad choices that they might make by using a job applicant's amount of higher education as a signal. According to the labor market signaling theory, even if higher education does not change productivity, it acts as an effective signal of greater individual abilities.

Labor market signaling
The process by which a potential worker's acquisition of credentials, such as a degree, is used by the employer to predict future productivity.

FOR CRITICAL ANALYSIS: Why does studying identical twins' earnings hold constant many of the factors that can determine differences in wages? ●

Change in the Price of Related Factors. Labor is not the only resource used. Some resources are substitutes and some are complements. If we hold output constant, we have the following general rule:

A change in the price of a substitute input will cause the demand for labor to change in the same direction. This is typically called the *substitution effect.*

Note, however, that if the cost of production falls sufficiently, the firm will find it more profitable to produce and sell a larger output. If this so-called *output effect* is great enough, it will override the substitution effect just mentioned, and the firm will end up employing not only more of the relatively cheaper variable input but also more labor. This is exactly what happened for many years in the American automobile industry. Auto companies employed more machinery (capital), but employment continued to increase in spite of rising wage rates. The reason: Markets were expanding and the marginal physical productivity of labor was rising faster than its wage rate.

With respect to complements, we are referring to inputs that must be used jointly. Assume now that capital and labor are complementary. In general, we predict the following:

> **A change in the price of a complementary input will cause the demand for labor to change in the opposite direction.**

If the cost of machines goes up but they must be used with labor, fewer machines will be purchased and therefore fewer workers will be used.

Determinants of the Supply of Labor

Exercise 27.3
Visit www.econtoday.com for more about immigration.

There are a number of reasons why labor supply curves will shift in a particular industry. For example, if wage rates for factory workers in the CD industry remain constant while wages for factory workers in the computer industry go up dramatically, the supply curve of factory workers in the CD industry will shift inward to the left as these workers shift to the computer industry.

Changes in working conditions in an industry can also affect its labor supply curve. If employers in the CD industry discover a new production technique that makes working conditions much more pleasant, the supply curve of labor to the CD industry will shift outward to the right.

Job flexibility also determines the position of the labor supply curve. For example, in an industry in which workers are allowed more flexibility, such as the ability to work at home via computer, the workers are likely to work more hours. That is to say, their supply curve will shift outward to the right. Some industries in which firms offer *job sharing,* particularly to people raising families, have found that the supply curve of labor has shifted outward to the right.

CONCEPTS IN BRIEF

- The individual competitive firm faces a perfectly elastic supply curve—it can buy all the labor it wants at the going market wage rate. The industry supply curve of labor slopes upward.

- By plotting an industrywide supply curve for labor and an industrywide demand curve for labor on the same coordinate system, we obtain the equilibrium wage rate in this industry.

- Efficiency wage theory predicts that wages paid above market wages may lead to high productivity because of lower turnover rates and better work effort by existing workers.

- The labor demand curve can shift because (1) the demand for the final product shifts, (2) labor productivity changes, or (3) the price of a related (substitute or complementary) factor of production changes.

MONOPOLY IN THE PRODUCT MARKET

So far we've considered only a perfectly competitive situation, both in selling the final product and in buying factors of production. We will continue our assumption that the firm purchases its factors of production in a perfectly competitive factor market. Now, however, we will assume that the firm sells its product in an *imperfectly* competitive output market. In other words, we are considering the output market structures of monopoly, oligopoly, and monopolistic competition. In all such cases, the firm, be it a monopolist, an oligopolist, or a monopolistic competitor, faces a downward-sloping demand curve for its product. Throughout the rest of this chapter, we will simply refer to a monopoly output situation for ease of analysis. The analysis holds for all industry structures that are less than perfectly competitive. In any event, the fact that our firm now faces a downward-sloping demand curve for its product means that if it wants to sell more of its product (at a uniform price), it has to lower the price, *not just on the last unit, but on all preceding units.* The *marginal revenue* received from selling an additional unit is continuously falling (and is less than price) as the firm attempts to sell more and more. This is certainly different from our earlier discussions in this chapter in which the firm could sell all it wanted at a constant price. Why? Because the firm we discussed until now was a perfect competitor.

Constructing the Monopolist's Input Demand Curve

In reconstructing our demand schedule for an input, we must account for the facts that (1) the marginal *physical* product falls because of the law of diminishing returns as more workers are added and (2) the price (and marginal revenue) received for the product sold also falls as more is produced and sold. That is, for the monopolist, we have to account for both the diminishing marginal physical product and the diminishing marginal revenue. Marginal revenue is always less than price for the monopolist. The marginal revenue curve is always below the downward-sloping demand curve.

Marginal revenue for the perfect competitor is equal to the price of the product because all units can be sold at the going market price. In our CD example, we assumed that the perfect competitor could sell all it wanted at $6 per compact disc. A one-unit change in sales always led to a $6 change in total revenues. Hence marginal revenue was always equal to $6 for that perfect competitor.

The monopolist, however, cannot simply calculate marginal revenue by looking at the price of the product. To sell the additional output from an additional unit of input, the monopolist has to cut prices on all previous units of output. As output is increasing, then, marginal revenue is falling. The underlying concept is, of course, the same for both the perfect competitor and the monopolist. We are asking exactly the same question in both cases: When an additional worker is hired, what is the benefit? In either case, the benefit is obviously the change in total revenues due to the one-unit change in the variable input, labor. In our discussion of the perfect competitor, we were able simply to look at the marginal physical product and multiply it by the *constant* per-unit price of the product because the price of the product never changed (for the perfect competitor, $P = \text{MR}$).

A single monopolist ends up hiring fewer workers than all of the competitive firms added together. To see this, we must calculate the marginal revenue product for the monopolist. To make it simple, we will look at it as simply the change in total revenues due to a one-unit change in the labor input for a monopolist. This is what we do in panel (a) of Figure 27-6, which shows the change in total revenues. Column 6, headed "Marginal Revenue

Panel (a)

(1) Labor Input (workers per week)	(2) Total Physical Product (TPP) CDs per week	(3) Marginal Physical Product (MPP) CDs per week	(4) Price of Product (P)	(5) Total Revenue (TR) = (2) x (4)	(6) Marginal Revenue Product (MRP$_m$) = Change in (5) / Change in (1)
7	1,000		$8.00	$ 8,000.00	
		111			$665.80
8	1,111		7.80	8,665.80	
		104			568.20
9	1,215		7.60	9,234.00	
		97			474.80
10	1,312		7.40	9,708.80	
		90			385.60
11	1,402		7.20	10,094.40	
		83			300.60
12	1,485		7.00	10,395.00	
		76			219.80
13	1,561		6.80	10,614.80	

FIGURE 27-6

A Monopolist's Marginal Revenue Product

The monopolist hires just enough workers to make marginal revenue product equal to the going wage rate. If the going wage rate is $498 per week, as shown by the labor supply curve, s, the monopolist would want to hire between 9 and 10 workers per week. That is the profit-maximizing amount of labor. The MRP curve for the perfect competitor from Figure 27-1 is also plotted (MRP$_c$). The monopolist's MRP curve will always be less elastic than it would be if marginal revenue were constant.

Product," gives the monopolistic firm a quantitative notion of how profitable additional workers and additional production actually are. The marginal revenue product curve for this monopolist has been plotted in panel (b) of the figure. To emphasize the steeper slope of the monopolist's MRP curve, MRP$_m$, the MRP curve for the perfect competitor in Figure 27-1, labeled MRP$_c$, has been plotted on the same graph.

Why does MRP$_m$ represent the monopolist's input demand curve? As always, our profit-maximizing monopolist will continue to hire labor as long as additional profits result. Profits are made as long as the additional cost of more workers is outweighed by the additional revenues made from selling the output of those workers. When the wage rate equals these additional revenues, the monopolist stops hiring. That is, it stops hiring when the wage rate is equal to the marginal revenue product because additional workers would add more to cost than to revenue.

Why the Monopolist Hires Fewer Workers

Because we have used the same numbers as in Figure 27-1, we can see that the monopolist hires fewer worker-weeks than the perfect competitor. That is to say, if we could magically change the CD industry in our example from one in which there is perfect competition in the output market to one in which there is monopoly in the output market, the amount of employment would fall. Why? Because the monopolist must take account of the declining product price that must be charged in order to sell a larger number of CDs. Remember that every firm hires up to the point at which marginal benefit equals marginal cost. The marginal benefit to the monopolist of hiring an additional worker is not simply the additional output times the price of the product. Rather, the monopolist faces a reduction in the price charged on all units sold in order to be able to sell more. So the monopolist ends up hiring fewer workers than all of the perfect competitors taken together, assuming that all other factors remain the same for the two hypothetical examples. But this should not come as a surprise. In considering product markets, by implication we saw that a monopolized CD industry would produce less output than a competitive one. Therefore, the monopolized CD industry would want fewer workers.

OTHER FACTORS OF PRODUCTION

The analysis in this chapter has been given in terms of the demand for the variable input labor. The same analysis holds for any other variable factor input. We could have talked about the demand for fertilizer or the demand for the services of tractors by a farmer instead of the demand for labor and reached the same conclusions. The entrepreneur will hire or buy any variable input up to the point at which its price equals the marginal revenue product.

A further question remains: How much of each variable factor should the firm use when all the variable factors are combined to produce the product? We can answer this question by looking at either the profit-maximizing side of the question or the cost-minimizing side.[1]

Profit Maximization Revisited

If a firm wants to maximize profits, how much of each factor should be hired (or bought)? As we just saw, the firm will never hire a factor of production unless the marginal benefit from hiring that factor is at least equal to the marginal cost. What is the marginal benefit? As we have pointed out several times, the marginal benefit is the change in total revenues due to a one-unit change in use of the variable input. What is the marginal cost? In the case of a firm buying in a competitive market, it is the price of the variable factor—the wage rate if we are referring to labor.

---

[1]Many economic problems involving maximization of profit or other economic variables have *duals,* or precise restatements, in terms of *minimization* rather than maximization. The problem "How do we maximize our output, given fixed resources?" for example, is the dual of the problem "How do we minimize our cost, given fixed output?" Noneconomists sometimes confuse their discussions of economic issues by mistakenly believing that a problem and its dual are two problems rather than one. Asking, for example, "How can we maximize our profits while minimizing our costs?" makes about as much sense as asking, "How can we cross the street while getting to the other side?"

The profit-maximizing combination of resources for the firm will be where, in a perfectly competitive situation,

MRP of labor = price of labor (wage rate)
MRP of land = price of land (rental rate per unit)
MRP of capital = price of capital (cost per unit of service)

Alternatively, we can express this profit-maximizing rule as

$$\frac{\text{MRP of labor}}{\text{Price of labor}} = \frac{\text{MRP of land}}{\text{price of land}} = \frac{\text{MRP of capital}}{\text{price of capital}}$$

The marginal revenue product of each of a firm's resources must be exactly equal to its price. If the MRP of labor were $20 and its price were only $15, the firm would be underemploying labor.

Cost Minimization

From the cost minimization point of view, how can the firm minimize its total costs for a given output? Assume that you are an entrepreneur attempting to minimize costs. Consider a hypothetical situation in which if you spend $1 more on labor, you would get 20 more units of output, but if you spend $1 more on machines, you would get only 10 more units of output. What would you want to do in such a situation? Most likely you would wish to hire more workers or sell off some of your machines, for you are not getting as much output per last dollar spent on machines as you are per last dollar spent on labor. You would want to employ factors of production so that the marginal products per last dollar spent on each are equal. Thus the least-cost, or cost minimization, rule will be as follows:

To minimize total costs for a particular rate of production, the firm will hire factors of production up to the point at which the marginal physical product per last dollar spent on each factor of production is equalized.

That is,

$$\frac{\text{MPP of labor}}{\text{Price of labor (wage rate)}} = \frac{\text{MPP of capital}}{\text{price of capital (cost per unit of service)}} = \frac{\text{MPP of land}}{\text{price of land (rental rate per unit)}}$$

All we are saying here is that the profit-maximizing firm will always use *all* resources in such combinations that cost will be minimized for any given output rate. This is commonly called the *least-cost combination of resources*. There is an exact relationship between the profit-maximizing combination of resources and the least-cost combination of resources. In other words, either rule can be used to yield the same cost-minimizing rate of use of each variable resource.[2]

---

[2] This can be proved as follows: Profit maximization requires that the price of every input must equal that input's marginal revenue product (the general case). Let i be the input. Then $P_i = \text{MRP}_i$. But MRP_i is equal to marginal revenue times marginal physical product of the input. Therefore, $P_i = \text{MR} \times \text{MPP}_i$. If we divide both sides by MPP_i, we get $P_i/\text{MPP}_i = \text{MR}$. If we take the reciprocal, we obtain $\text{MPP}_i/P_i = 1/\text{MR}$. That is another way of stating our cost minimization rule.

INTERNATIONAL EXAMPLE
Why Are European Businesses Using More Robots and Fewer Workers than U.S. Businesses?

What a strange world we live in, you might say. European countries are experiencing the highest levels of unemployment since the Great Depression. Typical unemployment rates exceed 10 percent throughout the European Union; they are near 13 percent in France and Italy and well over 15 percent in Spain. Compare this with the below 5 percent unemployment rate in the United States, and you can tell that Europe is in trouble. One would expect, therefore, that European firms could easily replace capital with labor and that there would be general pressure toward lower wages. The opposite has occurred. For example, in Germany, department stores use robots in shoe storerooms to seek out the shoes that a salesperson wants. In Denmark, milk warehouses have gone robotic. All in all, the market for automated systems in Europe has grown by more than 10 percent a year, a much greater rate than in the United States. The reason is that businesses in Europe have figured out that it is cheaper to use robots than people. In Germany, an industrial robot costs about $10 an hour to operate. An industrial worker may cost as much as $37 an hour. And while compensation to workers has continued to rise in Germany and elsewhere since the early 1990s, the operating costs of robots have fallen.

There are many reasons why wages remain so high in spite of massive unemployment in Europe. First of all, minimum wages there may be as much as 50 percent higher than in the United States. And social security contributions that employers have to pay for each worker often equal or even exceed the wages that the worker takes home. In addition, a firm must pay significant severance penalties if it fires a worker. Finally, many workers will not take low-paying jobs in some European countries because they are actually better off receiving unemployment and welfare benefits.

FOR CRITICAL ANALYSIS: Why have robots not taken over many jobs in the United States? ●

CONCEPTS IN BRIEF

- When a firm sells its output in a monopoly market, marginal revenue is less than price.

- Just as the MRP is the perfectly competitive firm's input demand curve, the MRP is also the monopolist's demand curve.

- For a less than perfectly competitive firm, the profit-maximizing combination of factors will occur where each factor is used up to the point where its MRP is equal to its unit price.

- To minimize total costs for a given output, the profit-maximizing firm will hire each factor of production up to the point where the marginal physical product per last dollar spent on each factor is equal to the marginal physical product per last dollar spent on each of the other factors of production.

This worker is being taught how to use a computerized training program which will reduce her learning time by a significant amount. Who may be hurt by such software?

Software May Be Reducing the Skill Levels Required for Many White-Collar Jobs

CONCEPTS APPLIED:
INPUT SUBSTITUTES, DEMAND FOR LABOR, VALUE OF MARGINAL PRODUCT, DERIVED DEMAND

Visit www.econtoday.com for an Internet Activity that expands your understanding of these concepts.

Let's say that you are a high school graduate but have not yet completed college. You answer a help-wanted ad from a local large corporation. When you interview for the job, the prospective employer does not ask you about any previous experience. Rather, the manager simply asks whether you would like a job selling a very complicated product. You say that you would love it, but you do not have any special training. The interviewer responds that you do not need it, for the company has a computerized training program that will teach you everything you need to know. You might end up making a lot more income than you ever thought you would.

Training Software: The Key to Expanding Job Opportunities

The scenario just outlined is not so far-fetched. In the early 1990s, a new type of software, known as electronic performance support systems, or EPSS, was developed. What sets this software apart is that it can automate many job-related mental skills as well as provide quick instructions to help users make human judgments that are still necessary for many jobs.

EPSS software was first used in blue-collar jobs. Chrysler mechanics use it to diagnose car troubles. Another use for EPSS software is in clerical jobs. Avis Rental Car Company's agents use it for navigating through paperwork and pricing decisions for leasing cars. Another field that is now making extensive use of EPSS software is the travel industry. Much of the specialized knowledge that travel agents have always had to learn in order to make plane reservations by computer is now irrelevant. All they need to use is the EPSS-based program.

Reduced Training Time and Fewer Needed Skills

In essence, the new EPSS software reduces the skill levels needed for many jobs. In addition, it reduces training time. A good example is the securities industry. The National Association of Securities Dealers (NASD) has reduced the training time required to conduct an audit of a securities firm. If you have ever used some of the household finance software, such as Quicken, produced by Intuit, you have an idea of how EPSS programs can make a difficult task seem simple. The program uses step-by-step instructions on the information and procedures that are needed to perform a securities firm audit. The results? Whereas it used to take 30 months to train a fully competent securities firm auditor, it now takes about 12.

A Boon to Less Skilled Workers

Clearly, if the new software can train someone with little experience, more highly trained workers have a smaller advantage than before. Lexus Car Company, for example, provides interactive training both in the technical features of its cars and in techniques for selling them. It has not shied away from hiring individuals with no previous sales or automobile experience, for it has found that the EPSS program it uses can make them into quality salespeople in short order.

The Rand Corporation of Santa Monica, California, has even developed an EPSS program to train some of the high-priced consultants who work for the big accounting firms, such as Price Waterhouse. Once this program is completed, it will offer all Price Waterhouse consultants—

experienced or not—information on companies and markets. This information typically takes years for an individual consultant to develop.

Smaller Premium for Experience

A possible result of EPSS systems is a reduction in the wage differentials that experienced workers currently earn. If a junior worker can obtain all the information quickly that the experienced worker has taken years to acquire, the experienced worker will not be significantly more valuable to the firm. If pay is a function of performance, the newly hired employee may quickly catch up with "old hands."

Increased Substitution of Software for Labor

While the computer revolution increases the use of labor in one sector of the economy, at the same time it may reduce employment in other sectors. In particular, accounting software (capital) is replacing certified public

accountants (labor) at an increasing rate. Accounting software has become more widespread, less costly, easier to use, and more sophisticated during the past several years. Nonetheless, the number of certified accountants has risen virtually every year since 1970. Given stable demand, we might predict that the relative salaries of CPAs should therefore fall in the future (all other things held constant).

The same analysis holds for attorneys. Legal software has proliferated, become more sophisticated yet easier to use, and dropped in price. Consequently, paralegals are now able to do many of the jobs that lawyers used to do. Not surprisingly, the paralegal profession is expanding rapidly, while the growth in the number of attorneys is starting to slow down.

FOR CRITICAL ANALYSIS
1. Computers have been around for a long time, so why has it taken so long for EPSS systems to be developed?
2. What do you predict will happen to the so-called higher education premium over the next decade?

CHAPTER SUMMARY

1. In a competitive situation in which the firm is a very small part of the entire product and labor market, the firm will want to hire workers up to the point at which the marginal revenue product just equals the going wage rate.
2. The marginal revenue product curve for the individual competitive firm is the input demand curve. The competitive firm hires up to the point at which the wage rate equals the MRP.
3. The summation of all the MRP curves does not equal the market demand curve for labor. The market demand curve for labor is less elastic than the sum of the MRP curves because as more workers are hired,

output is increased and the price of the product must fall, lowering the MRP.
4. The demand for labor is derived from the demand for the product produced.
5. The elasticity of demand for an input is a function of several determinants, including the elasticity of demand for the final product. Moreover, the price elasticity of demand for a variable input will usually be larger in the long run than it is in the short run because there is time for adjustment.
6. The firm buying labor in a perfectly competitive labor market faces a perfectly elastic supply curve at the going wage rate because the firm can hire all it

wants at that wage rate. The industry supply curve of labor slopes upward.

7. Efficiency wage theory predicts that wages paid above market wages may lead to high productivity because of lower turnover rates and better work effort by existing workers.

8. The demand curve for labor will shift if (a) the demand for final product shifts, (b) labor productivity changes, or (c) the price of a substitute or a complementary factor of production changes.

9. The MRP curve is also the monopolist's input demand curve. Because marginal revenue is less than the price of the product for a monopolist, the monopolist's input demand curve is steeper.

10. A firm minimizes total costs by equating the ratio of marginal physical product of labor divided by the price of labor with the ratio of marginal physical product of machines to the price of capital with all other such ratios for all the different factors of production. This is the mirror of profit maximization.

DISCUSSION OF PREVIEW QUESTIONS

1. **When hiring labor, what general rule will be followed by employers who wish to maximize profits?**
Employers who wish to maximize total profits will hire labor (or any other factor of production) up to the point at which the marginal cost of doing so equals the marginal benefit, MB. In that way, they will have used up all instances in which the marginal benefit of hiring labor exceeds the marginal cost, MC, of hiring labor. If MB > MC, they will hire more labor; if MB < MC, they will hire less; when MB = MC, they will be maximizing total profits.

2. **What is the profit-maximizing rate of employment for a perfectly competitive firm?**
The perfectly competitive firm will accept prevailing wage rates; it can hire as much labor as it wishes at the going rate. It follows that the MC of hiring labor to the perfectly competitive firm is a constant that is equal to the prevailing wage rate; MC = W, where W is the market wage rate. The MB of hiring labor is the value of the marginal product of an additional unit of labor. The perfectly competitive firm will maximize total profits by hiring labor up to the point at which it drives the MRP down to equal the constant wage rate: MRP = W. This is also how the firm minimizes costs for a given output.

3. **What is the profit-maximizing rate of employment for an imperfectly competitive firm?**
For an imperfectly competitive firm, P > MR. Thus in the short run the marginal benefit of hiring addi-

tional units of labor falls for two reasons: (a) The law of diminishing returns causes marginal physical product to diminish, and (b) to increase sales, price must fall—on previously produced units as well as the new one. Thus the MB of hiring labor equals the *marginal revenue* times the marginal physical product of labor: MB = MRP = MR × MPP.

By assumption, the imperfectly competitive firm is a competitor in the input markets, so in hiring labor it (like the perfect competitor) faces a constant marginal cost equal to the going wage rate; MC = W for the imperfectly competitive firm too. What about the profit-maximizing rate of employment for the imperfectly competitive firm? It hires up to the point at which it drives down the marginal revenue product of labor (MRP = MR × MPP) until it equals the going wage rate; MRP = W is the equilibrium condition in this model.

4. **How is an industry wage rate determined?**
Wage rates are a price; they are the price of labor. As such, wage rates are determined like all prices, by the forces of supply and demand. The market, or industry, wage rate will be determined by the point of intersection of the industry supply of labor curve and the industry demand for labor curve. At the point of intersection, the quantity of labor supplied equals the quantity of labor demanded, and equilibrium exists; both buyers and sellers are able to realize their intentions.

PROBLEMS

(Answers to the odd-numbered problems appear at the back of the book.)

27-1. Assume that the product in the table is sold by a perfectly competitive firm for $2 per unit.

    a. Use the information in the table to derive a demand schedule for labor.

    b. What is the most that this firm would be willing to pay each worker if five workers were hired?

    c. If the going salary for this quality labor is $200 per week, how many workers will be hired?

Quantity of Labor	Total Product per Week	MPP	MRP
1	250	_____	$ _____
2	450	_____	_____
3	600	_____	_____
4	700	_____	_____
5	750	_____	_____
6	750	_____	_____

27-2. The table presents some production function data for a firm in which the only variable input is capital; the labor input is fixed. First fill in the other columns. What quantity of capital will the firm use if the price of capital is $90 per machine-week? If the price of capital is $300 per machine-week, what quantity of capital will the firm use? Explain.

27-3. The accompanying graph indicates labor supply and demand in the construction industry.

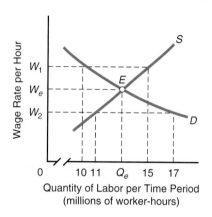

    a. When wage rates are W_1 per hour, how many worker-hours do workers intend to offer per unit?

    b. How much do businesses intend to buy at this wage rate?

    c. Which group can realize its intentions, and which can't?

    d. What forces will be set in motion at wage rate W_1, given a free market for labor?

27-4. Using the graph in Problem 27-3, answer the following questions.

    a. At wage rate W_2, how many worker-hours do workers intend to offer?

Quantity of Capital (machine-weeks)	Total Product per Week	Marginal Product of Capital per Week	Marginal Revenue (product price) per Unit	Marginal Revenue Product per Week
0	0	_____	$10	$ _____
1	25	_____	10	_____
2	45	_____	10	_____
3	60	_____	10	_____
4	70	_____	10	_____
5	75	_____	10	_____

b. At W_2, how many worker-hours do businesses intend to purchase?

c. Which group can realize its intentions, and which can't?

d. What forces will be set in motion at W_2 if a free market for labor exists in this industry?

e. What will the equilibrium wage rate be?

27-5. The price elasticity of demand for the final output product directly affects the elasticity of demand for the input factor. Why?

27-6. Suppose that you are seeking to maximize output for a given outlay. If the marginal physical product of input x is 10 and that of input y is 20, and the prices of the two inputs are $3 and $7, respectively, how should you alter your input mix in order to increase output and profit?

27-7. Suppose that you are a monopolist and labor is the only variable input you employ. You are currently producing 150 units of output and selling them for $20 apiece. You are considering the possibility of hiring an additional full-time employee. You estimate that daily output would increase to 160 units if you hired this additional person and that you

would be able to sell all of those units at a price of $19 each. What is the MRP of labor (per worker-day)? Assuming that you take the price of labor as a given, what is the maximum daily wage that would make it in your interest to hire this additional employee?

27-8. When there is only one variable input, how does a monopoly seller's demand for that input differ from that of a perfectly competitive seller?

27-9. Assume that you have graduated from college. You decide to look for a job rather than go for further schooling. Indicate how the following criteria might affect the salary that you will receive and the type of job you may end up taking after you graduate.

a. You want to stay near your family, so you do not consider moving out of your immediate geographic area to find a job.

b. You look only for jobs that allow you to apply the knowledge and skills you have learned in your college major.

c. You now live in the city but decide that you will only work in a rural area.

COMPUTER-ASSISTED INSTRUCTION

We explore the foundations of the demand for and the supply of labor, along the way demonstrating the consequences of the minimum wage.

Complete problem and answer appear on disk.

INTERACTING WITH THE INTERNET

For more information on the minimum wage, go to

www.dol.gov/dol/esa/public/minwage/q-a.htm

You can access the minimum wage hotline at

www.dir.ca.gov/DIR/Labor_law/DLSE/Rights/Minimum_Wage.html

CHAPTER 28

UNIONS AND LABOR MARKET MONOPOLY POWER

The average worker in America does not belong to a labor union. Indeed, as you will read in this chapter, labor unions have been losing much of their importance in the U.S. labor market. Nonetheless, some labor unions still have enough clout to bring at least part of the American economy to a halt. This is exactly what happened a few years ago when the Teamsters union called for a strike of its workers against United Parcel Service (UPS). That strike was a success, according to many commentators. Was it in fact a successful strike? And if so, did its success portend the revival of the American labor movement? Before you answer these questions, you need to know about monopoly power in the market for labor.

PREVIEW QUESTIONS

1. What are the major types of unions?
2. What do unions seek to maximize?
3. Do unions help workers?
4. What is a monopsonist, and how does one determine its profit-maximizing employment rate?

LOCAL 804
AFFILIATED WITH THE
INTERNATIONAL BROTHERHOOD
OF TEAMSTERS

Labor unions
Worker organizations that seek
to secure economic improvements for their members; they
also seek to improve the safety,
health, and other benefits
(such as job security) of their
members.

Craft unions
Labor unions composed of
workers who engage in a particular trade or skill, such as
baking, carpentry, or plumbing.

Collective bargaining
Bargaining between the management of a company or of a
group of companies and the
management of a union or a
group of unions for the purpose
of setting a mutually agreeable
contract on wages, fringe benefits, and working conditions for
all employees in all the unions
involved.

Did **You Know That . . .** in 1971, some 2.5 million workers were involved in strikes, but in the past few years, fewer than 250,000 have been involved? More than 12 times the number of workdays were lost to strikes in the 1950s than are lost to them today. The labor landscape has been changing in the United States. That does not mean that concerted activity on the part of groups of workers is insignificant in our economy, though. Some workers are able to earn more than they would in a competitive labor market because they have obtained a type of monopoly power. These are members of effective **labor unions,** workers' organizations that seek to secure economic improvements for their members. In forming unions, a certain monopoly element enters into the supply of labor equation. That is because we can no longer talk about a perfectly competitive labor supply situation when active and effective unions bargain as a single entity with management. The entire supply of a particular group of workers is controlled by a single source. Later in the chapter, we will examine the converse—a single employer who is the sole user of a particular group of workers.

THE AMERICAN LABOR MOVEMENT

The American labor movement started with local **craft unions.** These were groups of workers in individual trades, such as shoemaking, printing, or baking. Initially, in the United States, laborers struggled for the right to band together to bargain as a unit. In the years between the Civil War and the Great Depression (1861–1930s), the Knights of Labor, an organized group of both skilled and unskilled workers, demanded an eight-hour workday, equal pay for women and men, and the replacement of free enterprise with the socialist system. In 1886, a dissident group from the Knights of Labor formed the American Federation of Labor (AFL) under the leadership of Samuel Gompers. Until World War I, the government supported business's opposition to unions by offering the use of police personnel to break strikes. During World War I, the image of the unions improved and membership increased to more than 5 million. But after the war, the government decided to stop protecting labor's right to organize. Membership began to fall.

Then came the Great Depression. Franklin Roosevelt's National Industrial Recovery Act of 1933 gave labor the federal right to bargain collectively, but that act was declared unconstitutional. The 1935 National Labor Relations Act (NLRA), otherwise known as the Wagner Act, took its place. The NLRA guaranteed workers the right to start unions, to engage in **collective bargaining** (bargaining between management and representatives of all union members), and to be members in any union that was started.

INTERNATIONAL EXAMPLE
European Merchant Guilds, the Original Craft Unions

The origin of today's modern craft unions is found in a type of association that flourished in continental Europe and England during the Middle Ages. Around the eleventh century, merchants started traveling from market to market in a caravan to protect themselves from bandits. The members of the caravan elected a leader whose rules they pledged to obey. The name of such a caravan was *Gilde* in the Germanic countries of Europe. When the members of the caravan returned home, they frequently stayed in close association. They soon found it beneficial to seek exclusive rights to a particular trade from a feudal lord or, later, from the city government itself. Soon merchant guilds obtained a monopoly over an industry and its related commerce in a city. It supervised the crafts and the wholesale and retail selling of commodities manufactured in that city. Nonmember merchants were not allowed to sell goods at retail and were subject to many restrictions from which members of the guild were exempt.

FOR CRITICAL ANALYSIS: Analyze the medieval guild in terms of the insider-outsider theory presented in Chapter 27. ●

Industrial Unions

In 1938, the Congress of Industrial Organizations (CIO) was formed by John L. Lewis, the president of the United Mine Workers. Prior to the formation of the CIO, most labor organizations were craft unions. The CIO was composed of **industrial unions** such as the Knights of Labor—unions with membership from an entire industry such as steel or automobiles. In 1955, the CIO and the AFL merged. Organized labor's failure to grow at a continuing rapid rate caused leadership in both associations to seek the merger.

Three important industrial unions declared in the summer of 1995 that they, too, planned to merge. By the beginning of the twenty-first century, the United Auto Workers, the United Steelworkers of America, and the International Association of Machinists will have formed a single industrial union with nearly 2 million members.

Congressional Control over Labor Unions

Since the Great Depression, Congress has occasionally altered the relationship between labor and management through significant legislation. One of the most important pieces of legislation was the Taft-Hartley Act of 1947 (the Labor Management Relations Act). Among other things, it allows individual states to pass their own **right-to-work laws.** A right-to-work law makes it illegal for union membership to be a requirement for continued employment in any establishment.

More specifically, the act makes a **closed shop** illegal; a closed shop requires union membership before employment can be obtained. A **union shop,** however, is legal; a union shop does not require membership as a prerequisite for employment, but it can, and usually does, require that workers join the union after a specified amount of time on the job. (Even a union shop is illegal in states with right-to-work laws.)

Jurisdictional disputes, sympathy strikes, and secondary boycotts are made illegal by this act as well. A **jurisdictional dispute** involves two or more unions fighting (and striking) over which should have control in a particular jurisdiction. For example, should a carpenter working for a steel manufacturer be part of the steelworkers' union or the carpenters' union? A **sympathy strike** occurs when one union strikes in sympathy with another union's cause or strike. For example, if the retail clerks' union in an area is striking grocery stores, Teamsters may refuse to deliver products to those stores in sympathy with the retail clerks' demands for higher wages or better working conditions. A **secondary boycott** is the boycotting of a company that deals with a struck company. For example, if union workers strike a baking company, the boycotting of grocery stores that continue to sell that company's products is a secondary boycott. The secondary boycott brings pressure on third parties to force them to stop dealing with an employer who is being struck.

In general, the Taft-Hartley Act outlawed unfair labor practices of unions, such as make-work rules and forcing unwilling workers to join a particular union. Perhaps the most famous aspect of the Taft-Hartley Act is its provision that the president can obtain a court

Exercise 28.1
Visit www.econtoday.com for more about the AFL–CIO.

Industrial unions
Labor unions that consist of workers from a particular industry, such as automobile manufacturing or steel manufacturing.

Right-to-work laws
Laws that make it illegal to require union membership as a condition of continuing employment in a particular firm.

Closed shop
A business enterprise in which employees must belong to the union before they can be hired and must remain in the union after they are hired.

Union shop
A business enterprise that allows the hiring of nonunion members, conditional on their joining the union by some specified date after employment begins.

Jurisdictional dispute
A dispute involving two or more unions over which should have control of a particular jurisdiction, such as a particular craft or skill or a particular firm or industry.

Sympathy strike
A strike by a union in sympathy with another union's strike or cause.

Secondary boycott
A boycott of companies or products sold by companies that are dealing with a company being struck.

Exercise 28.2
Visit www.econtoday.com for more about the labor movement.

injunction that will stop a strike for an 80-day cooling-off period if the strike is expected to imperil the nation's safety or health.

The Current Status of Labor Unions

If you look at Figure 28-1, you can see that organized labor's heyday occurred from the 1940s through the 1970s. Since then, union membership has fallen almost every year. Currently, it is hovering around 15 percent of the civilian labor force. If you remove labor unions in the public sector—federal, state, and local government workers—private sector union membership in the United States is only about 11 percent of the civilian labor force.

Part of the explanation for the decline in union membership has to do with the shift away from manufacturing. Unions were always strongest in so-called blue-collar jobs. In 1948, workers in goods-producing industries, transportation, and utilities constituted 51.2 percent of private nonagricultural employment. Today that number is only 25 percent. Manufacturing jobs account for only 16 percent of all employment. In addition, persistent illegal immigration has weakened the power of unions. Much of the unskilled and typically nonunionized work in the United States is done by foreign-born workers, some of whom are undocumented. They are unlikely targets for union organizers.

FIGURE 28-1

Decline in Union Membership
Numerically, union membership in the United States has increased dramatically since the 1930s, but as a percentage of the labor force, union membership peaked around 1960 and has been falling ever since. Most recently, the absolute number of union members has also diminished.

Sources: L. Davis et al., *American Economic Growth* (New York: HarperCollins, 1972), p. 220; U.S. Department of Labor, Bureau of Labor Statistics. 1996 data estimated.

The deregulation of certain industries has also led to a decline in unionism. More intense competition in formally regulated industries, such as the airlines, has led to a movement toward nonunionized labor. Finally, increased labor force participation by women has led to a decline in union importance. Women have traditionally been less inclined to join unions than their male counterparts.

INTERNATIONAL EXAMPLE
Europe's Management-Labor Councils

Unionization rates are much higher in the European Union (EU) than in the United States, averaging 48 percent. Perhaps more important, most EU countries have institutionalized the concept of *management-labor councils*. In Germany, legislation dating back to the early 1950s created such councils, requiring that management and labor reach decisions jointly and unanimously. German management-labor councils use up a significant amount of management time. At H. C. Asmussen, a small German distilling company with 300 workers, there are five work councils, some of which meet weekly.

On a pan-European basis, an EU directive has forced 1,500 of the European Union's largest companies to set up Europe-wide worker-management consultative committees. In the United States, no such legislation exists, although there is a management desire to create more "quality circles" (to improve quality and to reduce costs) that involve workers and management. These are often used as a threat to unions or even a substitute for them. In fact, some American unions have succeeded in getting the federal government, through the National Labor Relations Board, to disband such quality circles.

FOR CRITICAL ANALYSIS: Why do you think American unions might be against quality circles involving management and workers? ●

CONCEPTS IN BRIEF

- The American Federation of Labor (AFL), composed of craft unions, was formed in 1886 under the leadership of Samuel Gompers. Membership increased until after World War I, at which time the government temporarily stopped protecting labor's right to organize.

- During the Great Depression, legislation was passed that allowed for collective bargaining. The National Labor Relations Act of 1935 guaranteed workers the right to start unions. The Congress of Industrial Organizations (CIO), composed of industrial unions, was formed during the Great Depression.

UNIONS AND COLLECTIVE BARGAINING CONTRACTS

Unions can be regarded as setters of minimum wages. Through collective bargaining, unions establish minimum wages below which no individual worker can offer his or her services. Each year, collective bargaining contracts covering wages as well as working conditions and fringe benefits for about 8 million workers are negotiated. Union negotiators act as agents for all members of the bargaining unit. They bargain with management about the provisions of a labor contract. Once union representatives believe that they have an acceptable collective contract, they will submit it to a vote of the union members. If approved by the members, the contract sets wage rates, maximum workdays, working conditions, fringe benefits, and other matters, usually for the next two or three years. Typically, collective bargaining contracts between management and the union apply also to nonunion members who are employed by the firm or the industry.

Strike: The Ultimate Bargaining Tool

Whenever union-management negotiations break down, union negotiators may turn to their ultimate bargaining tool, the threat or the reality of a strike. The first recorded strike in U.S. history occurred shortly after the Revolutionary War, when Philadelphia printers walked out in 1786 over a demand for a weekly minimum wage of $6. Strikes make headlines, but in only 4 percent of all labor-management disputes does a strike occur before the contract is signed. In the other 96 percent of cases, contracts are signed without much public fanfare.

The purpose of a strike is to impose costs on recalcitrant management to force its acceptance of the union's proposed contract terms. Strikes disrupt production and interfere with a company's or an industry's ability to sell goods and services. The strike works both ways, though. Workers draw no wages while on strike (they may be partly compensated out of union strike funds). Striking union workers may also be eligible to draw state unemployment benefits.

The impact of a strike is closely related to the ability of striking unions to prevent nonstriking (and perhaps nonunion) employees from continuing to work for the targeted company or industry. Therefore, steps are usually taken to prevent others from working for the employer. **Strikebreakers** can effectively destroy whatever bargaining power rests behind a strike. Numerous methods have been used to prevent strikebreakers from breaking strikes. Violence has been known to erupt, almost always in connection with attempts to prevent strikebreaking.

Strikebreakers
Temporary or permanent workers hired by a company to replace union members who are striking.

EXAMPLE
Strikes in Professional Sports

Twice in the past two decades, professional baseball players have gone on strike. In 1994, virtually the entire season was lost. At the start of the following season, professional baseball team owners hired replacement players at much lower salaries. The same action was taken by professional football team owners during the NFL strike in 1987. For three games, substitute football players, alongside regular team players who "crossed the picket line," courageously attempted to play professional football. The results were not quite what fans were used to seeing—and therein lies the rub. Compare this situation with one in which a shoemaking factory suffers a strike. Strikebreakers (substitute "players") can learn the strikers' jobs relatively quickly; the skills involved are not too difficult. But in professional sports, it is hard, if not impossible, to duplicate the skills of the best players. Therefore, professional league players are not so easily replaced. Moreover, current professional sports management cannot figure out ways to automate sports as, say, the telephone industry has done in order to weaken the power of unions in that industry.

FOR CRITICAL ANALYSIS: *Who benefited from the strikes in professional football and professional baseball?* •

UNION GOALS

We have already pointed out that one of the goals of unions is to set minimum wages. In many situations, any wage rate set higher than a competitive market clearing wage rate will reduce total employment in that market. This can be seen in Figure 28-2. We have a competitive market for labor. The market demand curve is D, and the market supply curve is S. The market clearing wage rate will be W_e; the equilibrium quantity of labor will be Q_e. If the union establishes by collective bargaining a minimum wage rate that exceeds W_e, an excess quantity of labor will be supplied (assuming no change in the labor demand schedule). If the minimum wage established by union collective bargaining is W_U, the quantity supplied would be Q_S; the quantity demanded would be Q_D. The difference is the excess quantity supplied, or surplus. Hence the following point becomes clear:

> **One of the major roles of a union that establishes a wage rate above the market clearing wage rate is to ration available jobs among the excess number of workers who wish to work in unionized industries.**

Note also that the surplus of labor is equivalent to a shortage of jobs at wage rates above equilibrium.

The union may use a system of seniority, a lengthening of the apprenticeship period to discourage potential members from joining, and other such rationing methods. This has the effect of shifting the supply of labor curve to the left in order to support the higher wage, W_U.

There is a trade-off here that any union's leadership must face: Higher wages inevitably mean a reduction in total employment, as more persons are seeking a smaller number of positions. (Moreover, at higher wages, more workers will seek to enter the industry, thereby adding to the surplus that occurs because of the union contract.) Facing higher wages, management may replace part of the workforce with machinery.

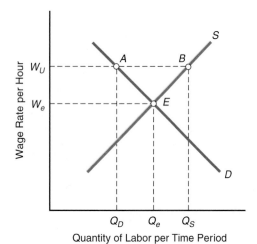

FIGURE 28-2

Unions Must Ration Jobs
If the union succeeds in obtaining wage rate W_U, the quantity of labor demanded will be Q_D, but the quantity of labor supplied will be Q_S. The union must ration a limited number of jobs to a greater number of workers; the surplus of labor is equivalent to a shortage of jobs at that wage rate.

Union Strategies

If we view unions as monopoly sellers of a service, we can identify three different wage and employment strategies that they use: ensuring employment for all members of the union, maximizing aggregate income workers, and maximizing wage rates for some workers.

Employing All Members in the Union. Assume that the union has Q_1 workers. If it faces a labor demand curve such as D in Figure 28-3, the only way it can "sell" all of those workers' services is to accept a wage rate of W_1. This is similar to any other demand curve. The demand curve tells the maximum price that can be charged to sell any particular quantity of a good or service. Here the service happens to be labor.

Maximizing Member Income. If the union is interested in maximizing the gross income of its members, it will normally want a smaller membership than Q_1—namely, Q_2 workers, all employed and paid a wage rate of W_2. The aggregate income to all members of the union is represented by the wages of only the ones who work. Total income earned by union members is maximized where the price elasticity of demand is numerically equal to 1. That occurs where marginal revenue equals zero. In Figure 28-3, marginal revenue equals zero at a quantity of labor Q_2. So we know that if the union obtains a wage rate equal to W_2, and therefore Q_2 workers are demanded, the total income to the union membership will be maximized. In other words, $Q_2 \times W_2$ (the shaded area) will be greater than any other combination of wage rates and quantities of union workers demanded. It is, for example, greater than $Q_1 \times W_1$. Note that in this situation, if the union started out with Q_1 members, there would be $Q_1 - Q_2$ members out of *union* work at the wage rate W_2. (Those out of union work either remain unemployed or go to other industries, which has a depressing effect on wages in nonunion industries due to the increase in supply of nonunion workers there.)

Maximizing Wage Rates for Certain Workers. Assume that the union wants to maximize the wage rates for some of its workers—perhaps those with the most seniority. If it wanted to keep a quantity of Q_3 workers employed, it would seek to obtain a wage rate of W_3. This would require deciding which workers should be unemployed and which workers should work and for how long each week or each year they should be employed.

FIGURE 28-3

What Do Unions Maximize?
Assume that the union wants to employ all its Q_1 members. It will attempt to get wage rate W_1. If the union wants to maximize total wage receipts (income), it will do so at wage rate W_2, where the elasticity of the demand for labor is equal to 1. (The shaded area represents the maximum total income that the union would earn at W_2.) If the union wants to maximize the wage rate for a given number of workers, say, Q_3, it will set the wage rate at W_3.

Limiting Entry over Time

One way to raise wage rates without specifically setting wages is for unions to limit the size of their membership to the size of their employed workforce when the union was first organized. No workers are put out of work at the time the union is formed. Over time, as the demand for labor in the industry increases, there is no net increase in union membership, so larger wage increases are obtained than would otherwise be the case. We see this in Figure 28-4. Union members freeze entry into their union, thereby obtaining a wage rate of $16 per hour instead of allowing a wage rate of $15 per hour with no restriction on labor supply.

Altering the Demand for Union Labor

Another way in which unions can increase wages is to shift the demand curve for labor outward to the right. This approach compares favorably with the supply restriction approach because it increases both wage rates and employment level. The demand for union labor can be increased by increasing worker productivity, increasing the demand for union-made goods, and decreasing the demand for non-union-made goods.

Increasing Worker Productivity. Supporters of unions have argued that unions provide a good system of industrial jurisprudence. The presence of unions may induce workers to feel that they are working in fair and just circumstances. If so, they work harder, increasing labor productivity. Productivity is also increased when unions resolve differences and reduce conflicts between workers and management, thereby providing a smoother administrative environment.

Increasing Demand for Union-Made Goods. Because the demand for labor is a derived demand, a rise in the demand for products produced by union labor will increase the demand for union labor itself. One way in which unions attempt to increase the demand for union labor–produced products is by advertising "Look for the union label."

Decreasing the Demand for Non-Union-Made Goods. When the demand for goods that are competing with (or are substitutes for) union-made goods is reduced, consumers

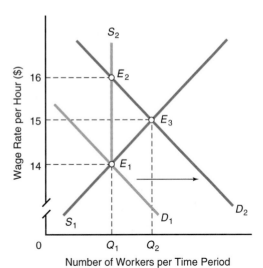

FIGURE 28-4

Restricting Supply over Time
When the union was formed, it didn't affect wage rates or employment, which remained at $14 and Q_1 (the equilibrium wage rate and quantity). However, as demand increased—that is, as the demand schedule shifted outward to D_2 from D_1—the union restricted membership to its original level of Q_1. The new supply curve is S_1S_2, which intersects D_2 at E_2, or at a wage rate of $16. Without the union, equilibrium would be at E_3 with a wage rate of $15 and employment of Q_2.

shift to union-made goods, increasing the demand. A good example is when various unions campaign against imports; restrictions on imported cars are supported by the United Auto Workers as strongly as the Textile Workers Unions support restrictions on imported textile goods. The result is greater demand for goods "made in the USA," which in turn presumably increases the demand for American union (and nonunion) labor.

HAVE UNIONS RAISED WAGES?

We have seen that unions are able to raise the wages of their members if they are successful at limiting the supply of labor in a particular industry. They are also able to raise wages above what wages would otherwise be to the extent that they can shift the demand for union labor outward to the right. This can be done using the methods we have just discussed, including collective bargaining agreements that require specified workers for any given job—for example, by requiring a pilot, a copilot, and an engineer in the cockpit of a jet airplane even if an engineer is not needed on short flights. Economists have done extensive research to determine the actual increase in union wages relative to nonunion wages. They have found that in certain industries, such as construction, and in certain occupations, such as commercial airline pilot, the union wage differential can be 50 percent or more. That is to say, unions have been able in some industries and occupations to raise wage rates 50 percent or more above what they would be in the absence of unions.

In addition, the union wage differential appears to increase during recessions. This is because unions often, through collective bargaining, have longer-term contracts than nonunion workers so that they do not have to renegotiate wage rates, even when overall demand in the economy falls.

On average, unions appear to be able to raise the wage rates of their members relative to nonunion members by 10 to 20 percent. Note, though, that when unions increase wages beyond what productivity increases would permit, some union members will be laid off. A redistribution of income from low- to high-seniority union workers is not equivalent to higher wages for *all* union members.

CAN UNIONS INCREASE PRODUCTIVITY?

A traditional view of union behavior is that unions decrease productivity by artificially shifting the demand curve for union labor outward through excessive staffing and make-work requirements. For example, some economists have traditionally felt that unions tend to bargain for excessive use of workers, as when requiring an engineer on all flights. This is referred to as **featherbedding.** Many painters' unions, for example, resisted the use of paint sprayers and required that their members use only brushes. They even specified the maximum width of the brush. Moreover, whenever a union strikes, productivity drops, and this reduction in productivity in one sector of the economy can spill over into other sectors.

Featherbedding
Any practice that forces employers to use more labor than they would otherwise or to use existing labor in an inefficient manner.

This traditional view against unions has recently been countered by a view that unions can actually increase productivity. The new labor economists contend that unions act as a collective voice for their members. In the absence of a collective voice, any dissatisfied worker either simply remains at a job and works in a disgruntled manner or quits. But unions, as a collective voice, can listen to worker grievances on an individual basis and then apply pressure on the employer to change working conditions and other things. The individual worker does not run the risk of being singled out by the employer and harassed. Also, the individual worker doesn't have to spend time trying to convince the employer that some change in the working arrangement should be made. Given that unions provide this collective voice, worker turnover in unionized industries should be less, and this should contribute to productivity. Indeed, there is strong evidence that worker turnover is reduced when unions are present. Of course, this evidence may also be consistent with the fact that wage rates are so attractive to union members that they will not quit unless working conditions become truly intolerable.

THE BENEFITS OF LABOR UNIONS

It should by now be clear that there are two opposing views about unions. One portrays them as monopolies whose main effect is to raise the wage rate of high-seniority members at the expense of low-seniority members. The other contends that they can increase labor productivity through a variety of means. Harvard economists Richard B. Freeman and James L. Medoff argue that the truth is somewhere in between. They came up with the following conclusions:

1. Unionism probably raises social efficiency, thereby contradicting the traditional monopoly interpretation of what unions do. Even though unionism reduces employment in the unionized sector, it does permit labor to develop and implement workplace practices that are more valuable to workers. In some settings, unionism is associated with increased productivity.
2. Unions appear to reduce wage inequality.
3. Unions seem to reduce profits.
4. Internally, unions provide a political voice for all workers, and unions have been effective in promoting general social legislation.
5. Unions tend to increase the stability of the workforce by providing services, such as arbitration proceedings and grievance procedures.

Freeman and Medoff take a positive view of unionism. But their critics point out that they may have overlooked the fact that many of the benefits that unions provide do not require that unions engage in restrictive labor practices, such as the closed shop. Unions could still do positive things for workers without restricting the labor market.

CONCEPTS IN BRIEF

- When unions raise wage rates above market clearing prices, they face the problem of rationing a restricted number of jobs to a more than willing supply of workers.

- Unions may pursue any one of three goals: (1) to employ all members in the union, (2) to maximize total income of the union's workers, or (3) to maximize wages for certain, usually high-seniority, workers.

- Unions can increase the wage rate of members by engaging in practices that shift the union labor supply curve inward or shift the demand curve for union labor outward (or both).

- Some economists believe that unions can increase productivity by acting as a collective voice for their members, thereby freeing members from the task of convincing their employers that some change in working arrangements should be made. Unions may reduce turnover, thus improving productivity.

MONOPSONY: A BUYER'S MONOPOLY

Let's assume that a firm is a perfect competitor in the product market. The firm cannot alter the price of the product it sells, and it faces a perfectly elastic demand curve for its product. We also assume that the firm is the only buyer of a particular input. Although this situation may not occur often, it is useful to consider. Let's think in terms of a factory town, like those dominated by textile mills or in the mining industry. One company not only hires the workers but also owns the businesses in the community, owns the apartments that workers live in, and hires the clerks, waiters, and all other personnel. This buyer of labor is called a **monopsonist,** the single buyer.

Monopsonist
A single buyer.

What does an upward-sloping supply curve mean to a monopsonist in terms of the costs of hiring extra workers? It means that if the monopsonist wants to hire more workers, it has to offer higher wages. Our monopsonist firm cannot hire all the labor it wants at the going wage rate. If it wants to hire more workers, it has to raise wage rates, including the wage of all its current workers (assuming a non-wage-discriminating monopsonist). It therefore has to take account of these increased costs when deciding how many more workers to hire.

EXAMPLE
Monopsony in College Sports

How many times have you read stories about colleges and universities violating National Collegiate Athletic Association (NCAA) rules? If you keep up with the sports press, these stories about alleged violations occur every year. About 600 four-year colleges and universities belong to the NCAA, which controls more than 20 sports. In effect, the NCAA operates an intercollegiate cartel that is dominated by universities that operate big-time athletic programs. It operates as a cartel with monopsony (and monopoly) power in four ways:

1. It regulates the number of student athletes that universities can recruit.
2. It often fixes the prices that the university charges for tickets to important intercollegiate sporting events.
3. It sets the prices (wages) and the conditions under which the universities can recruit these student athletes.
4. It enforces its regulations and rules with sanctions and penalties.

The NCAA rules and regulations expressly prohibit bidding for college athletes in an overt manner. Rather, the NCAA requires that all athletes be paid the same for tuition, fees, room, board, and books. Moreover, the NCAA limits the number of athletic scholarships that can be given by a particular university. These rules are ostensibly to prevent the richest universities from "hiring" the best student athletes.

Not surprisingly, from the very beginning of the NCAA, individual universities and colleges have attempted to cheat on the rules in order to attract better athletes. The original agreement among the colleges was to pay no wages. Almost immediately after this agreement was put into effect, colleges switched to offering athletic scholarships, jobs, free room and board, travel expenses, and other enticements. It was not unusual for athletes to be paid $10 an hour to rake leaves when the going wage rate for such work was only $5 an hour. Finally, the NCAA had to agree to permit wages up to a certain amount per year.

If all universities had to offer exactly the same money wages and fringe benefits, the academically less distinguished colleges in metropolitan areas (with a large potential number of ticket-buying fans) would have the most inducement to violate the NCAA agreements (to compensate for the lower market value of their degrees). They would figure out all sorts of techniques to get the best student athletes. Indeed, such schools have in fact cheated more than other universities and colleges, and their violations have been detected and punished with a greater relative frequency than those of other colleges and universities.

FOR CRITICAL ANALYSIS: College and university administrators argue that the NCAA rules are necessary to "keep business out of higher education." How can one argue that college athletics is related to academics? ●

Exercise 28.3
Visit www.econtoday.com for more about sports stars.

Marginal Factor Cost

The monopsonist faces an upward-sloping supply curve of the input in question because as the only buyer, it faces the entire market supply curve. Each time the monopsonist buyer of labor, for example, wishes to hire more workers, it must raise wage rates. Thus the marginal cost of another unit of labor is rising. In fact, the marginal cost of increasing its workforce will always be greater than the wage rate. This is because in the situation in which the monopsonist pays the same wage rate to everyone in order to obtain another unit of labor, the higher wage rate has to be offered not only to the last worker but also to all its other workers. We call the additional cost to the monopsonist of hiring one more worker the marginal factor cost (MFC).

The marginal factor cost for the last worker is therefore his or her wages plus the increase in the wages of all other existing workers. As we pointed out in Chapter 27, marginal factor cost is equal to the change in total variable cost due to a one-unit change in the one variable factor of production—in this case, labor. In Chapter 27, marginal factor cost was simply the competitive wage rate because the employer could hire all workers at the same wage rate.

Derivation of a Marginal Factor Cost Curve

Panel (a) of Figure 28-5 shows the quantity of labor purchased, the wage rate per hour, the total cost of the quantity of labor purchased per hour, and the marginal factor cost per hour for the additional labor bought.

We translate the columns from panel (a) to the graph in panel (b) of the figure. We show the supply curve as *S,* which is taken from columns 1 and 2. (Note that this is the same as the *average* factor cost curve; hence you can view Figure 28-5 as showing the relationship between average factor cost and marginal factor cost.) The marginal factor cost curve (MFC) is taken from columns 1 and 4. The MFC curve must be above the supply curve whenever the supply curve is upward-sloping. If the supply curve is upward-sloping, the firm must pay a higher wage rate in order to attract a larger amount of labor. This higher wage rate must be paid to all workers; thus the increase in total costs due to an increase in the labor input will exceed the wage rate. Note that in a perfectly competitive input market, the supply curve is perfectly elastic and the marginal factor cost curve is identical to the supply curve.

Employment and Wages Under Monopsony

To determine the number of workers that a monopsonist desires to hire, we compare the marginal benefit to the marginal cost of each hiring decision. The marginal cost is the mar-

Panel (a)

(1) Quantity of Labor Supplied to Management	(2) Required Hourly Wage Rate	(3) Total Wage Bill (3) = (1) x (2)	(4) Marginal Factor Cost $(MFC) = \frac{Change\ in\ (3)}{Change\ in\ (1)}$
0	—	—	
			$1.00
1	$1.00	$1.00	
			3.00
2	2.00	4.00	
			3.20
3	2.40	7.20	
			4.00
4	2.80	11.20	
			6.80
5	3.60	18.00	
			7.20
6	4.20	25.20	

FIGURE 28-5

Derivation of a Marginal Factor Cost Curve

The supply curve, *S*, in panel (b) is taken from columns 1 and 2 of panel (a). The marginal factor cost curve (MFC) is taken from columns 1 and 4. It is the increase in the total wage bill resulting from a one-unit increase in labor input.

Panel (b)

ginal factor cost curve, and the marginal benefit is the marginal revenue product curve. In Figure 28-6 on page 642, we assume competition in the output market and monopsony in the input market. A monopsonist finds its profit-maximizing quantity of labor demanded at *E,* where the marginal revenue product is just equal to the marginal factor cost.

How much is the firm going to pay these workers? In a nonmonopsonistic situation it would face a given wage rate in the labor market, but because it is a monopsonist, it faces the entire supply curve, *S*.

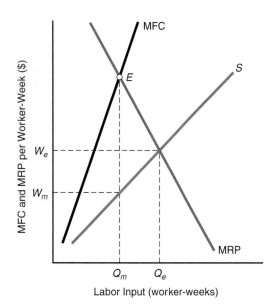

FIGURE 28-6

Marginal Factor Cost Curve for a Monopsonist

The monopsonist firm looks at a marginal cost curve, MFC, that slopes upward and is above its labor supply curve, S. The marginal benefit of hiring additional workers is given by the firm's MRP curve. The intersection of MFC with MRP, at point E, determines the number of workers hired. The firm hires Q_m workers but has to pay them only W_m in order to attract them. Compare this with the competitive solution, in which the wage rate would have to be W_e and the quantity of labor would be Q_e.

A monopsonist faces an *upward-sloping* supply curve for labor. Firms do not usually face the market supply curve; most firms can hire all the workers they want at the going wage rate and thus usually face a perfectly elastic supply curve for each factor of production. The market supply curve, however, slopes upward.

The monopsonist therefore sets the wage rate so that it will get exactly the quantity, Q_m, supplied to it by its "captive" labor force. We find that wage rate is W_m. There is no reason to pay the workers any more than W_m because at that wage rate, the firm can get exactly the quantity it wants. The actual quantity used is established at the intersection of the marginal factor cost curve and the marginal revenue product curve for labor—that is, at the point at which the marginal revenue from expanding employment just equals the marginal cost of doing so.

Notice that the profit-maximizing wage rate paid to workers (W_m) is lower than the marginal revenue product. That is to say that workers are paid a wage that is less than their contribution to the monopsonist's revenues. This is sometimes referred to as **monopsonistic exploitation** of labor. The monopsonist is able to do this because each individual worker has little power in bargaining for a higher wage. The organization of workers into a union, though, creates a monopoly supplier of labor, which gives the union some power to bargain for higher wages.

What happens when a monopsonist meets a monopolist? This is the situation called **bilateral monopoly,** defined as a market structure in which a single buyer faces a single seller. An example is a state education employer facing a single teachers' union in the labor market. Another example is a professional players' union facing an organized group of team owners. Such bilateral monopoly situations have indeed occurred in professional baseball and football. To analyze bilateral monopoly, we would have to look at the interaction of both sides, buyer and seller. The price outcome turns out to be indeterminate.

Monopsonistic exploitation
Exploitation due to monopsony power. It leads to a price for the variable input that is less than its marginal revenue product. Monopsonistic exploitation is the difference between marginal revenue product and the wage rate.

Bilateral monopoly
A market structure consisting of a monopolist and a monopsonist.

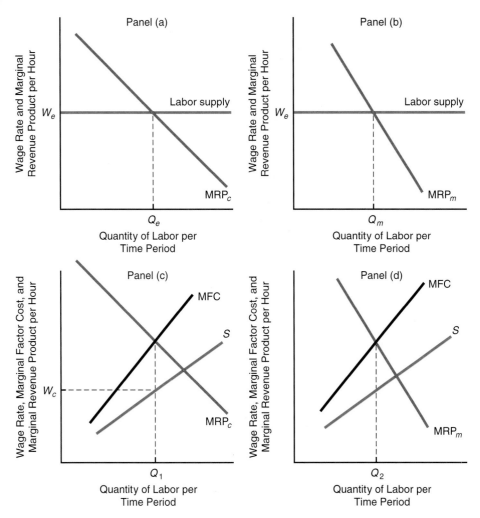

FIGURE 28-7
Summary of Pricing and Employment Under Various Market Conditions
In panel (a), the firm operates in perfect competition in both input and output markets. It purchases labor up to the point where the going rate W_e is equal to MRP_c. It hires quantity Q_e of labor. In panel (b), the firm is a perfect competitor in the input market but has a monopoly in the output market. It purchases labor up to the point where W_e is equal to MRP_m. It hires a smaller quantity of labor, Q_m, than in panel (a). In panel (c), the firm is a monopsonist in the input market and a perfect competitor in the output market. It hires labor up to the point where $MFC = MRP_c$. It will hire quantity Q_1 and pay wage rate W_c. Panel (d) shows bilateral monopoly. The wage outcome is indeterminate.

We have studied the pricing of labor in various situations, including perfect competition in both the output and input markets and monopoly in both the output and input markets. Figure 28-7 shows four possible situations graphically.

CONCEPTS IN BRIEF

• A monopsonist is a single buyer. The monopsonist faces an upward-sloping supply curve of labor.

• Because the monopsonist faces an upward-sloping supply curve of labor, the marginal factor cost of increasing the labor input by one unit is greater than the wage rate. Thus the marginal factor cost curve always lies above the supply curve.

• A monopsonist will hire workers up to the point at which marginal factor cost equals marginal revenue product. Then the monopsonist will find what minimal wage is necessary to attract that number of workers. This is taken from the supply curve.

This UPS striker went back to work after the Teamsters Union won its desired contract. In spite of this labor victory, union membership continues to fall in the United States.

LOCAL 804
AFFILIATED WITH THE
INTERNATIONAL BROTHERHOOD
OF TEAMSTERS

Are We Seeing a Rebirth of the American Labor Movement?

CONCEPTS APPLIED:

MONOPOLY, STRIKES, LABOR UNIONS, PRODUCTIVITY, UNION STRATEGIES

Visit www.econtoday.com for an Internet Activity that expands your understanding of these concepts.

You have seen in this chapter that the percentage of the labor force that is unionized has been in steady decline. Figure 28-8 shows that the number of labor strikes since World War II reached its peak in about 1953 and peaked twice again in the late 1960s and mid-1970s but has been declining ever since. The decline in the number of strikes mirrors the decline in private-sector membership in labor unions.

The Teamsters Enter the Fray

In 1997, the Teamsters struck United Parcel Service of America, Inc. (UPS). For a painful several weeks, mail-order companies, college book publishers, and hundreds of thousands of other firms scrambled to replace UPS shipments with an alternative. Federal Express and Airborne Express in particular gained handsomely from the Teamsters strike against UPS. UPS ultimately settled with the union. That settlement was declared a victory for the Teamsters as well as for organized labor. But was it really a victory?

What the UPS Drivers Really Won

A complete analysis of the UPS strike requires examining the average worker's lost income and comparing it with

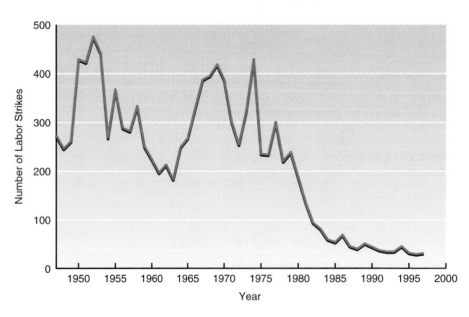

FIGURE 28-8

The Declining Number of Labor Strikes
Since about 1974, the number of labor walkouts each year has declined steadily. The power of unions seems to be on the wane.

Source: U.S. Bureau of Labor Statistics.

the present value of future wage increases. The Economic Policy Foundation estimated that the lost income for a typical UPS worker was about $1,850. The foundation calculated that it would take the average full-time UPS employee five years to come out ahead, compared to where he or she would have been had the union accepted the company's last offer before the strike. Further, the average part-time worker may earn *less* income over the life of the contract than if the union had accepted the company's final offer.

Why Strikes That Seem Irrational May Not Be So

It appears as if few strikes really earn very much for workers. It also appears that UPS may not have gained very much by holding out. Indeed, according to Professor David Lipsky of Cornell University, few strikes are ever justified on a financial basis for either side. So are they irrational? Not necessarily, for strikes might be necessary on occasion to establish bargaining credibility for future contract negotiations. After all, if a company knew that its workers' union would never strike, it would continue to make smaller and smaller offers for future contracts. If a union knew that a company would always cave in to avoid a strike, it would ask for larger and larger compensation increases in future contract demands.

Was UPS the Right Company to Strike?

One wonders if perhaps the UPS strike was not really in the best interest of members of the Teamsters union. Before the strike, UPS was already paying its full-time employees almost twice the national average wage rate. Its almost completely unskilled part-time workers were earning an average of $11 an hour with a full range of benefits. Indeed, UPS is one of the few companies (Starbucks is another) that provides full benefits to part-time workers. Part-time workers, because of fixed medical insurance and other fringe benefits, are actually a relatively expensive source of labor for UPS. UPS uses so many part-timers because it needs temporary employment during certain times of the year, such as Christmas.

It also needs thousands of workers for only a few hours each day when its planes arrive at and depart from its hubs. A majority of part-time workers at UPS are homemakers and college students who do not want to work full time.

Will the Teamsters' Victory Hurt Industrial Workers?

The Teamsters have long been at odds with other parts of organized labor. The Teamsters are basically transport workers. Transportation costs, such as trucking and railroads, are an additional cost of production, raising the price of the product to consumers and reducing quantity demanded. Hence higher wages for transportation workers typically lead to lower wages for industrial workers. Thus the Teamsters have always been on the outs with the rest of labor. Any victory that the Teamsters had in the UPS strike will be felt, perhaps not obviously, by workers in manufacturing. The products they make now will cost more to be shipped.

The Public Support for Strikers Is Growing

During the UPS strike, the public was squarely behind the striking workers. According to a Gallup poll at the time, 55 percent of the public was in favor of the workers. An examination of polls going back 60 years shows that public opinion about strikers was often far more negative. In the late 1930s, the public was sympathetic to strikers only about 33 percent of the time. Since the late 1980s, however, strikers have routinely received support from over 50 percent of Americans polled. For example, when Eastern Airlines' workers went out on strike in 1989, a Gallup poll received responses favoring the strikers from 57 percent of the people questioned.

FOR CRITICAL ANALYSIS

1. Former Secretary of Labor Robert Reich, after hearing of the Teamsters' victory in the UPS strike, hailed it as a "watershed" event in union history. What do you think he meant?
2. Is it ever possible for a strike to benefit both parties?

CHAPTER SUMMARY

1. The American labor movement started with local craft unions but was very small until the twentieth century. Important organizations in the history of labor in the United States are the Knights of Labor, the American Federation of Labor, and the Congress of Industrial Organizations.

2. The Great Depression facilitated passage of the National Industrial Recovery Act. This act established the right of labor to bargain collectively. It was later supplanted by the Wagner Act.

3. Unions raise union wage rates relative to nonunion wages. The union wage differential increases during recessions because of the longer-term nature of union collective bargaining contracts.

4. Because unions act as a collective voice for individual employees, they may increase productivity by reducing the time that employees spend trying to alter unproductive working arrangements. Unions may also increase productivity by reducing turnover.

5. Monopsony is a situation in which there is only one buyer of a particular input. The single buyer faces an upward-sloping supply curve and must therefore pay higher wage rates to attract additional workers. The single buyer faces a marginal factor cost curve that is upward-sloping and above the supply curve. The buyer hires workers up to the point at which the marginal revenue product equals the marginal factor cost. Then the labor buyer will find out how low a wage rate can be paid to get that many workers.

6. When a single buyer faces a single seller, a situation of bilateral monopsony exists.

DISCUSSION OF PREVIEW QUESTIONS

1. What are the major types of unions?

The earliest, and one of the most important forms today, is the craft union, which is an organization of skilled laborers. Another major type is the industrial union, in which all or most laborers in an industry, such as the steelworkers or mineworkers, unite.

2. What do unions seek to maximize?

Unions do not have unlimited power; in the United States, the rules that have evolved declare that unions can set wage rates *or* the number of laborers who will be employed, but not both. Consequently, a trade-off exists for union leaders: If they maximize wages, some members will become unemployed; if they maximize employment, wages will be relatively low. Union leaders often decide to maximize wages for a given number of workers—presumably the higher-seniority workers. Each union reaches its own decision as to how to resolve the trade-off.

3. Do unions help workers?

If unions are to be considered effective, they must increase real wage rates *above* productivity increas-es; after all, market forces will increase real wage rates at the rate of productivity change. Yet if real wage rates are increased more rapidly than the rate of productivity increases, unions will cause reduced employment; hence some laborers will be helped (those who retain their jobs at above-productivity wage levels), and some will be hurt (those who lose their jobs). The evidence is that unions are neither a necessary nor a sufficient condition for high real wages. Wages in the United States were relatively high before the U.S. labor movement. Moreover, labor's overall share of national income has not changed significantly since the 1930s, although *union* labor's share may have increased relative to nonunion labor's share.

4. What is a monopsonist, and how does one determine its profit-maximizing employment rate?

A monopsonist is a single buyer. A monopsonist hires labor up to the point at which the marginal benefit of doing so equals the marginal cost of doing so. The marginal benefit of hiring labor is labor's marginal revenue product: MB = MRP of labor. The marginal cost of hiring labor must reflect the fact that the monopsonist faces the industry labor supply schedule; hence the monopsonist must increase wage rates in order to hire more labor. Of course, it must increase wage rates for all the labor that it hires, not just the marginal laborer. Thus the MC of hiring labor for a monopsonist (the marginal factor cost, MFC)

will be greater than the wage rate. Since the profit-maximizing employment rate is generally where MB = MC, the monopsonist will hire labor up to the point where MRP = MFC. It then pays the lowest wage rate required to attract that quantity of labor. This wage rate will be below the MRP of labor.

PROBLEMS

(Answers to the odd-numbered problems appear at the back of the book.)

28-1. The accompanying graph indicates a monopsonistic firm that is also a perfect competitor in the product market.

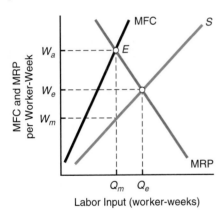

Labor Input (worker-weeks)

a. What does MRP stand for?
b. Which is the supply of labor curve?
c. How many laborers will this firm voluntarily hire?
d. Given the profit-maximizing employment rate, what is the lowest wage rate that this firm can offer to get this quantity of labor?

28-2. Does a perfectly competitive firm have to worry about the impact of its own demand for labor on the going wage rate?

28-3. Give examples of perfectly competitive sellers having monopsony power in the input market.

28-4. Suppose that you operate a firm that sells its output in a perfectly competitive market. However, you are the only employer in your island economy. You are currently employing 10 full-time employees at a wage rate of $50 per person per day, and you are producing 100 units of output per day. Labor is your only variable input. The market price of your output is $8 per unit. You estimate that daily output would rise to 108 units per day if you increased your workforce to 11 people. To attract the eleventh worker, you would have to pay a wage rate of $52 to all employees. Should you expand your workforce?

28-5. Imagine yourself managing a plant that is a monopsony buyer of its sole input and is also the monopoly seller of its output. You are currently employing 30 people, producing 20 units of output per day, and selling them for $100 apiece. Your current wage rate is $60 per day. You estimate that you would have to raise your wage scale for all workers to $61 per day in order to attract one more person to your firm. The 31 employees would be able to produce 21 units of output per day, which you would be able to sell at $99.50 apiece. Should you hire the thirty-first employee?

28-6. If a union, in its collective bargaining, sets a wage rate that maximizes total union members' income, will all union members be employed? Explain your answer.

28-7. Why will a union never want to bargain collectively for a wage rate that would exist with perfect competition in the labor market?

28-8. "The states that have right-to-work laws deprive workers from enjoying the full benefits of unions." What arguments can be used to support this statement? To deny its validity?

28-9. The marginal factor cost curve faced by a firm buying an input in a perfectly competitive market is identical to its supply curve for that input. Why is this not true for a monopsonist? Explain your answer.

COMPUTER-ASSISTED INSTRUCTION

How does the behavior of monopsonists differ from the behavior of competitive purchasers of labor? What are the consequences of these differences?

Complete problem and answer appear on disk.

INTERACTING WITH THE INTERNET

The AFL-CIO has a substantial amount of material on the organization and issues important to it at

www.aflcio.org/

You can learn about the World Confederation of Labour at

www.cmt-wcl.org/

If you want to read about the activities of one of our most effective monopsonies, go to

www.ncaa.org/

CHAPTER 29

RENT, INTEREST, AND PROFITS

We all continually make decisions in which we compare a cost today with the resulting future benefit. If you choose to jog on a regular basis, there is a cost involved: You give up doing some alternative that may be more pleasurable but has only immediate benefits, such reading a novel. You choose to jog regularly because of the long-term benefit—you will look and feel better or your risk of heart disease might decrease. The same type of calculation applies to many other activities, such as going to the gym regularly. For some people, though, no matter how hard they work out, run, or diet, they still have high cholesterol. There are drugs that can reduce these people's cholesterol levels. Health-maintenance organizations (HMOs) thus face an important policy decision: Should they provide such people with cholesterol-lowering drugs to reduce the probability of heart disease? Before you can understand how such a policy question must be analyzed, you need to learn about interest and present value, as well as rent and profits.

1. What is rent?
2. What is interest?
3. What is the economic function of interest rates?
4. What is the economic function of profits?

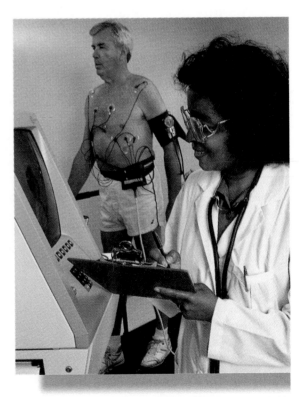

Did You Know That . . . in America, presumably one of the most industrialized countries in the world today, compensation for labor services makes up over 70 percent of national income every year? But what about the other 30 percent? It consists of compensation to the owners of the other factors of production that you read about in Part 1: land, capital, and entrepreneurship. Somebody owns the real estate downtown for which the monthly commercial rents are higher for one square foot than you might pay to rent a whole apartment. Land, obviously, is a factor of production, and it has a market clearing price. Businesses also have to use capital. Compensation for that capital is interest, and it, too, has a market clearing level. Finally, some of you may have entrepreneurial ability that you offer to the marketplace. Your compensation is called profit. In this chapter you will also learn about the sources and functions of profit.

RENT

When you hear the term *rent,* you are accustomed to having it mean the payment made to property owners for the use of land or apartments. The term *rent* has a different meaning in economics. **Economic rent** is payment to the owner of a resource in excess of its opportunity cost—the payment that would be necessary to call forth production of that amount of the resource. Economists originally used the term *rent* to designate payment for the use of land. What was thought to be important about land was that its supply is completely inelastic. Hence the supply curve for land is a vertical line; no matter what the prevailing market price for land, the quantity supplied will remain the same.

Economic rent
A payment for the use of any resource over and above its opportunity cost.

Determining Land Rent

The concept of economic rent is associated with the British economist David Ricardo (1772–1823). He looked at two plots of land on which grain was growing, one of which happened to be more fertile than the other. The owners of these two plots sold the grain that came from their land, but the one who owned the more fertile land grew more grain and therefore made more profits. According to Ricardo, the owner of the fertile land was receiving economic rents that were due not to the landowner's hard work or ingenuity but rather to an accident of nature. Ricardo asked his readers to imagine another scenario, that of walking up a hill that starts out flat with no rocks and then becomes steeper and rockier. The value of the land falls as one walks up the hill. If a different person owns the top of the hill than the bottom, the highland owner will receive very little in payment from, say, a farmer who wants to cultivate land for wheat production.

Here is how Ricardo analyzed economic rent for land. He first simplified his model by assuming that all land is equally productive. Then Ricardo assumed that the quantity of land in a country is *fixed.* Graphically, then, in terms of supply and demand, we draw the supply curve of land vertically (zero price elasticity). In Figure 29-1, the supply curve of land is represented by S. If the demand curve is D_1, it intersects the supply curve, S, at price P_1. The entire amount of revenues obtained, $P_1 \times Q_1$, is labeled "Economic rent." If the demand for land increased to D_2, the equilibrium price would rise to P_2. Additions to economic rent are labeled "More economic rent." Notice that the quantity of land remains insensitive to the change in price. Another way of stating this is that the supply curve is perfectly inelastic.

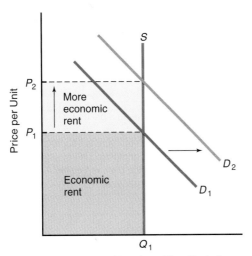

FIGURE 29-1

Economic Rent

If indeed the supply curve of land were completely price-inelastic in the long run, it would be depicted by S. At the quantity in existence, Q_1, any and all revenues are economic rent. If demand is D_1, the price will be P_1; if demand is D_2, price will rise to P_2. Economic rent would be $P_1 \times Q_1$ and $P_2 \times Q_1$, respectively.

ECONOMIC RENT TO LABOR

Land and natural resources are not the only factors of production to which the analysis of economic rent can be applied. In fact, the analysis is probably more often applicable to labor. Here is a list of people who provide different labor services, some of whom probably receive large amounts of economic rent:

Professional sports superstars
Rock stars
Movie stars
World-class models
Successful inventors and innovators
World-famous opera stars

Just apply the definition of economic rent to the phenomenal earnings that these people make. They would undoubtedly work for much, much less than they earn. Therefore, much of their earnings constitutes economic rent (but not all, as we shall see). Economic rent occurs because specific resources cannot be replicated exactly. No one can duplicate today's most highly paid entertainment figures, and therefore they receive economic rent.

Economic Rent and the Allocation of Resources

If an extremely highly paid movie star would make the same number of movies at half his or her current annual earnings, does that mean that 50 percent of his or her income is unnecessary? To answer the question, consider first why the superstar gets such a high income. The answer can be found in Figure 29-1. Substitute *entertainment activities of the superstars* for the word *land*. The high "price" received by the superstar is due to the demand for his or her services. If Kevin Costner announces that he will work for a measly $1 million a movie and do two movies a year, how is he going to know which production

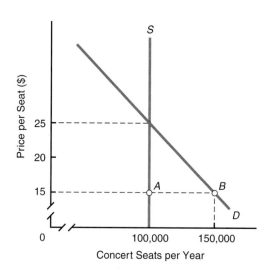

FIGURE 29-2

The Allocative Function of Rent
If the performer agrees to give five concerts a year "at any price" and there are 20,000 seats in each concert hall, the supply curve of concerts, S, is vertical at 100,000 seats per year. The demand curve is given by D. The performer wants a price of only $15 to be charged. At that price, the quantity of seats demanded per year is 150,000. The excess quantity demanded is equal to the horizontal distance between points A and B, or 50,000 seats per year.

company values his services the most highly? Costner and other movie stars let the market decide where their resources should be used. In this sense, we can say the following:

Economic rent allocates resources to their highest-valued use.

Otherwise stated, economic rent directs resources to the people who can most efficiently use them.

A common counterexample involves rock stars who claim that their tickets are over-priced. Consequently, they agree to perform, say, five concerts with all tickets being sold at the same price, $15. Assume that a star performs these concerts in halls with 20,000 seats. A total of 100,000 individuals per year will be able to see this particular performer. This is represented by point A in Figure 29-2. By assumption, this performer is still receiving some economic rent because we are assuming that the supply curve of concerts is vertical at 100,000 seats per year. At a price per ticket of $15, however, the annual quantity of seats demanded will be 150,000, represented by point B. The difference between points A and B is the excess quantity of tickets demanded at the below-market-clearing price of $15 a seat. The *additional* economic rent that could be earned by this performer by charging the clearing price of $25 per seat in this graph would serve as the rationing device that would make the quantity demanded equal to the quantity supplied.

In such situations, which are fairly common, part of the economic rent that could have been earned is dissipated—it is captured, for example, by radio station owners in the form of promotional gains when they are allowed to give away a certain number of tickets on the air (even if they have to pay $15 per ticket) because the tickets are worth $25. Ticket hold-ers who resell tickets at higher prices ("scalpers") also capture part of the rent. Conceiv-ably, at 100,000 seats per year, this performer could charge the market clearing price of $25 per ticket and give away to charity the portion of the economic rent ($10 per ticket) that would be dissipated. In such a manner, the performer could make sure that the recipients of the rent are worthy in his or her own esteem.

EXAMPLE
Do Entertainment Superstars Make Super Economic Rents?

Superstars certainly do well financially. Table 29-1 shows the earnings of selected individuals in the entertainment industry as estimated by *Forbes* magazine. Earn-ings are totaled for a two-year period. How much of these earnings can be called economic

TABLE 29-1
Superstar Earnings

Name	Occupation	Earnings (two years, millions of dollars)
Steven Spielberg	Director, producer, studio owner	313
George Lucas	Producer	241
Oprah Winfrey	Talk show host	201
Michael Crichton	Writer, producer	102
The Beatles	Rock group	98
Jerry Seinfeld	Actor, comedian	94
David Copperfield	Magician	85
Stephen King	Writer	84
Tom Cruise	Actor	82
Arnold Schwarzenegger	Actor	74

Source: Forbes, 1998.

rent? The question is not easy to answer, for an entertainment newcomer would almost certainly work for much less than he or she earns—thereby making high economic rents. The same cannot necessarily be said for entertainers who have been raking in millions for years. They probably have very high accumulated wealth and also a more jaded outlook about their work. It is therefore not clear how much they would work if they were not offered those huge sums of money.

FOR CRITICAL ANALYSIS: Even if some superstar entertainers would work for less, what forces cause them to make so much income anyway? ●

Taxing Away Economic Rent

Some people have argued in favor of imposing high taxes on economic rent. For example, drug companies that have developed *successful* patented drugs make large amounts of economic rent during the life of the patent. That is to say, the marginal cost of production is much less than the price charged. If the government taxed this economic rent completely, those successful drugs already on the market would in fact stay on the market. But there would be long-run consequences. Drug companies would invest fewer resources in discovering new successful drugs. So economic rent is typically a *short-run* phenomenon. In the long run, it constitutes a source of reward for risk taking in society. This is true not only in the drug business but also in entertainment and professional sports.

CONCEPTS IN BRIEF

- Economic rent is defined as payment for a factor of production that is completely inelastic in supply. It is payment for a resource over and above what is necessary to keep that resource in existence at its current level in the long run.

- Economic rent serves an allocative function by guiding available supply to the most efficient use.

Interest
The payment for current rather than future command over resources; the cost of obtaining credit. Also, the return paid to owners of capital.

INTEREST

The term **interest** is used to mean two different things: (1) the price paid by debtors to creditors for the use of loanable funds and (2) the market return earned by (nonfinancial) capital as a factor of production. Owners of capital, whether directly or indirectly, obtain interest income. Often businesses go to credit markets to obtain so-called money capital in order to invest in physical capital from which they hope to make a satisfactory return. In other words, in our complicated society, the production of capital goods often occurs because of the existence of credit markets in which borrowing and lending take place. For the moment, we will look only at the credit market.

Interest and Credit

When you obtain credit, you actually obtain money to have command over resources today. We can say, then, that interest is the payment for current rather than future command over resources. Thus interest is the payment for obtaining credit. If you borrow $100 from me, you have command over $100 worth of goods and services today. I no longer have that command. You promise to pay me back $100 plus interest at some future date. The interest that you pay is usually expressed as a percentage of the total loan calculated on an annual basis. If at the end of one year you pay me back $110, the annual interest is $10 ÷ $100, or 10 percent. When you go out into the marketplace to obtain credit, you will find that the interest rate charged differs greatly. A loan to buy a house (a mortgage) may cost you 7 to 10 percent annual interest. An installment loan to buy an automobile may cost you 9 to 14 percent annual interest. The federal government, when it wishes to obtain credit (issues U.S. Treasury securities), may have to pay only 3 to 8 percent annual interest. Variations in the rate of annual interest that must be paid for credit depend on the following factors.

1. *Length of loan.* In some (but not all) cases, the longer the loan will be outstanding, other things being equal, the greater will be the interest rate charged.
2. *Risk.* The greater the risk of nonrepayment of the loan, other things being equal, the greater the interest rate charged. Risk is assessed on the basis of the creditworthiness of the borrower and whether the borrower provides collateral for the loan. Collateral consists of any asset that will automatically become the property of the lender should the borrower fail to comply with the loan agreement.
3. *Handling charges.* It takes resources to set up a loan. Papers have to be filled out and filed, credit references have to be checked, collateral has to be examined, and so on. The larger the amount of the loan, the smaller the handling (or administrative) charges as a percentage of the total loan. Therefore, we would predict that, other things being equal, the larger the loan, the lower the interest rate.

What Determines Interest Rates?

The overall level of interest rates can be described as the price paid for loanable funds. As with all commodities, price is determined by the interaction of supply and demand. Let's first look at the supply of loanable funds and then at the demand for them.

The Supply of Loanable Funds. The supply of loanable funds (credit available) depends on individuals' willingness to save.[1] When you save, you exchange rights to current consumption for rights to future consumption. The more current consumption you give up, the more valuable is a marginal unit of present consumption in comparison with future consumption.

Recall from our discussion of diminishing marginal utility that the more of something you have, the less you value an additional unit. Conversely, the less of something you have, the more you value an additional unit. Thus when you give up current consumption of a

---

[1]Actually, the supply of loanable funds also depends on business and government saving and on the behavior of the monetary authorities and the banking system. For simplicity of discussion, we ignore these components here.

good—that is, have less of it—you value an additional unit more. The more you save today, the more utility you attach to your last unit of today's consumption. So to be induced to save more—to consume less—you have to be offered a bigger and bigger reward to match the marginal utility of current consumption you will give up by saving. Because of this, if society wants to induce people to save more, it must offer a higher rate of interest. Hence we expect that the supply curve of loanable funds will slope upward. At higher rates of interest, savers will be willing to offer more current consumption to borrowers, other things being constant.[2] When the income of individuals increases or when there is a change in individual preferences toward more saving, the supply curve of loanable funds will shift outward to the right, and vice versa.

The Demand for Loanable Funds. There are three major sources of the demand for loanable funds:

1. Households that want loanable funds for the purchase of services and nondurable goods, as well as consumer durables such as automobiles and homes
2. Businesses that want loanable funds to make investments
3. Governments that want loanable funds, usually to cover deficits—the excess of government spending over tax revenues

We will ignore the government's demand for loanable funds and consider only consumers and businesses.

Loans are taken out both by consumers and by businesses. It is useful for us to separate the motives underlying the demand for loans by these two groups of individuals. We will therefore treat consumption loans and investment loans separately. In the discussion that follows, we will assume that there is no inflation—that is, that there is no persistent increase in the overall level of prices.

Consumer Demand for Loanable Funds. In general, consumers demand loanable funds because they tend to prefer earlier consumption to later consumption. That is to say, people subjectively value goods obtained immediately more than the same goods of the same quality obtained later on. Consider that sometimes an individual household's present income falls below the average income level expected over a lifetime. Individuals may go to the credit market to borrow whenever they perceive a temporary dip in their current income—assuming that they expect their income to go back to normal later on. Furthermore, by borrowing, they can spread out purchases more evenly during their lifetimes. In so doing, they're able to increase their lifetime total utility.

Consumers' demand for loanable funds will be inversely related to the cost of borrowing—the rate of interest. Why? For the same reason that all demand curves slope downward: A higher rate of interest means a higher cost of borrowing, and a higher cost of borrowing must be weighed against alternative uses of limited income. At higher costs of borrowing, consumers will forgo current consumption.

POLICY EXAMPLE
Should Rent-to-Own Stores Be Regulated?

A growing number of consumers are implicitly borrowing money by dealing with rent-to-own stores that offer them television sets and refrigerators for low weekly payments. At the end of a very long period, they end up owning the item. For example, a consumer can rent a television for $12 a week and at the end of 91 weeks will own it.

---

[2]A complete discussion would include the income effect: At higher interest rates, households receive a higher yield on savings, permitting them to save less to achieve any given target.

Some investigators claim that because the TV is worth only $125 new, consumers are paying over 300 percent annual interest. The U.S. Public Interest Research Group found many cases in which refrigerators with a cash price of $350 ended up costing $1,172 to a customer buying them from a rent-to-own store. Pennsylvania passed legislation to put in an 18 percent cap on the implicit annual interest rate. Because the number of rent-to-own stores nationwide has increased from 3,000 in 1983 to almost 9,000 today, empirically we know that a consumer demand exists for their services. Typically, the people who use them do not qualify for normal consumer credit. That is why they end up paying such implicitly high interest rates.

FOR CRITICAL ANALYSIS: What do you think happened to the growth in rent-to-own stores after the Pennsylvania legislation was passed? •

Business Demand for Loanable Funds. Businesses demand loanable funds to make investments that they believe will increase productivity or profit. Whenever a business believes that by making an investment, it can increase revenues (net of other costs) by more than the cost of capital, it will make the investment. Businesses compare the interest rate they must pay in the loanable funds market with the interest rate they think they can earn by investing. This comparison helps them decide whether to invest.

In any event, we hypothesize that the demand curve for loanable funds by firms for investment purposes will be negatively sloped. At higher interest rates, fewer investment projects will make economic sense to businesses because the cost of capital (loanable funds) will exceed the net revenues derivable from the capital investment. Conversely, at lower rates of interest, more investment projects will be undertaken because the cost of capital will be less than the expected rate of return on the capital investment.

The Equilibrium Rate of Interest

When we add together the demand for loanable funds by households and businesses (and government in more complex models), we obtain a demand curve for loanable funds, as given in Figure 29-3. The supply curve is *S*. The equilibrium rate of interest is i_e.

Exercise 29.1
Visit www.econtoday.com for more about interest rates.

FIGURE 29-3

The Supply of and Demand for Loanable Funds

We draw *D* as the demand curve for all loanable funds by households and businesses (and governments). It slopes downward. *S* is the supply curve of credit, or loanable funds. It slopes upward. The intersection of *S* and *D* gives the equilibrium rate of interest at i_e.

Annual Interest Rate

i_e

Quantity of Credit, or Loanable Funds,
per Time Period

INTERNATIONAL EXAMPLE
One Consequence of Privatizing Italian Banks: Loan Sharking

Until 1994, almost all Italian banks were government-owned, and loans usually were decided on political grounds. When the Italian government got out of some of the banking business, though, the newly privatized bank loan officers lacked the skills and experience necessary to judge whether a potential borrower was a good or a bad credit risk. Consequently, during this interim period after privatization, many small businesspersons in Italy were turned away when they sought loans. Bank loan officers steered them to "loan sharks." Many such lenders operate in violation of Italian law and end up charging borrowers 300 to 500 percent per year, well above the posted "equilibrium" interest rate at the nation's biggest banks.

FOR CRITICAL ANALYSIS: Who typically ends up agreeing to the high interest rates charged by loan sharks? ●

Real Versus Nominal Interest Rates

Nominal rate of interest
The market rate of interest expressed in today's dollars.

We have been assuming that there is no inflation. In a world of inflation—a persistent rise in an average of all prices—the **nominal rate of interest** will be higher than it would be in a world with no inflation. Basically, nominal, or market, rates of interest rise to take account of the anticipated rate of inflation. If, for example, there is no inflation and no inflation is expected, the nominal rate of interest might be 5 percent for home mortgages. If the rate of inflation goes to 10 percent a year and stays there, everybody will anticipate that inflation rate. The nominal rate of interest will rise to about 15 percent to take account of the anticipated rate of inflation. If the interest rate did not rise to 15 percent, the interest earned at 5 percent would be worth less in the future because inflation would have eroded its purchasing power. We can therefore say that the nominal, or market, rate of interest is approximately equal to the real rate of interest plus the anticipated rate of inflation, or

$$i_n = i_r + \text{anticipated rate of inflation}$$

Real rate of interest
The nominal rate of interest minus the anticipated rate of inflation.

where i_n equals the nominal rate of interest and i_r equals the real rate of interest. In short, you can expect to see high nominal rates of interest in periods of high or rising inflation rates. The **real rate of interest** may not necessarily be high, though. We must first correct the nominal rate of interest for the anticipated rate of inflation before determining whether the real interest rate is in fact higher than normal.

The Allocative Role of Interest

Back in Chapters 4 and 6, we talked about the price system and the role that prices play in the allocation of resources. Interest is a price that allocates loanable funds (credit) to consumers and to businesses. Within the business sector, interest allocates loanable funds to different firms and therefore to different investment projects. Investment, or capital, projects with rates of return higher than the market rate of interest in the credit market will be undertaken, given an unrestricted market for loanable funds. For example, if the expected rate of return on the purchase of a new factory in some industry is 15 percent and loanable funds can be acquired for 11 percent, the investment project may proceed. If, however, that same project had an expected rate of return of only 9 percent, it would not be undertaken. In sum, the interest rate allocates loanable funds to industries whose investments yield the highest returns—where resources will be the most productive.

It is important to realize that the interest rate performs the function of allocating money capital (loanable funds) and that this ultimately allocates real physical capital to various firms for investment projects.

Interest Rates and Present Value

Businesses make investments in which they often incur large costs today but don't make any profits until some time in the future. Somehow they have to be able to compare their investment cost today with a stream of future profits. How can they relate present cost to future benefits?

Interest rates are used to link the present with the future. After all, if you have to pay $110 at the end of the year when you borrow $100, that 10 percent interest rate gives you a measure of the premium on the earlier availability of goods and services. If you want to have things today, you have to pay the 10 percent interest rate in order to have current purchasing power.

The question could be put this way: What is the present value (the value today) of $110 that you could receive one year from now? That depends on the market rate of interest, or the rate of interest that you could earn in some appropriate savings institution, such as in a savings account. To make the arithmetic simple, let's assume that the rate of interest is 10 percent. Now you can figure out the **present value** of $110 to be received one year from now. You figure it out by asking the question, How much money must I put aside today at the market interest rate of 10 percent to receive $110 one year from now? Mathematically, we represent this equation as

$$(1 + .1)PV_1 = \$110$$

where PV_1 is the sum that you must set aside now.

Let's solve this simple equation to obtain PV_1:

$$PV_1 = \frac{\$110}{1.1} = \$100$$

That is to say, $100 will accumulate to $110 at the end of one year with a market rate of interest of 10 percent. Thus the present value of $110 one year from now, using a rate of interest of 10 percent, is $100. The formula for present value of any sums to be received one year from now thus becomes

$$PV_1 = \frac{FV_1}{1 + i}$$

where

PV_1 = present value of a sum one year hence
FV_1 = future sum of money paid or received one year hence
i = market rate of interest

Present Values for More Distant Periods. The present-value formula for figuring out today's worth of dollars to be received at a future date can now easily be seen. How much would have to be put in the same savings account today to have $110 two years from now if the account pays a rate of 10 percent per year compounded annually?

After one year, the sum that would have to be set aside, which we will call PV_2, would have grown to $PV_2 \times 1.1$. This amount during the second year would increase to $PV_2 \times 1.1 \times 1.1$, or $PV_2 \times (1.1)^2$. To find the PV_2 that would grow to $110 over two years, let

$$PV_2 \times (1.1)^2 = \$110$$

Present value
The value of a future amount expressed in today's dollars; the most that someone would pay today to receive a certain sum at some point in the future.

TABLE 29-2

Present Value of a Future Dollar

This table shows how much a dollar received at the end of a certain number of years in the future is worth today. For example, at 5 percent a year, a dollar to be received 20 years in the future is worth 37.7 cents; if received in 50 years, it isn't even worth a dime today. To find out how much $10,000 would be worth a certain number of years from now, just multiply the figures in the table by 10,000. For example, $10,000 received at the end of 10 years discounted at a 5 percent rate of interest would have a present value of $6,140.

Year	Compounded Annual Interest Rate				
	3%	5%	8%	10%	20%
1	.971	.952	.926	.909	.833
2	.943	.907	.857	.826	.694
3	.915	.864	.794	.751	.578
4	.889	.823	.735	.683	.482
5	.863	.784	.681	.620	.402
6	.838	.746	.630	.564	.335
7	.813	.711	.583	.513	.279
8	.789	.677	.540	.466	.233
9	.766	.645	.500	.424	.194
10	.744	.614	.463	.385	.162
15	.642	.481	.315	.239	.0649
20	.554	.377	.215	.148	.0261
25	.478	.295	.146	.0923	.0105
30	.412	.231	.0994	.0573	.00421
40	.307	.142	.0460	.0221	.000680
50	.228	.087	.0213	.00852	.000109

and solve for PV_2:

$$PV_2 = \frac{\$110}{(1.1)^2} = \$90.91$$

Thus the present value of $110 to be paid or received two years hence, discounted at an interest rate of 10 percent per year compounded annually, is equal to $90.91. In other words, $90.91 put into a savings account yielding 10 percent per year compounded interest would accumulate to $110 in two years.

The General Formula for Discounting. The general formula for **discounting** becomes

$$PV_t = \frac{FV_t}{(1 + i)^t}$$

Discounting
The method by which the present value of a future sum or a future stream of sums is obtained.

where t refers to the number of periods in the future the money is to be paid or received.

Table 29-2 gives the present value of $1 to be received in future years at various interest rates. The interest rate used to derive the present value is called the **rate of discount.**

Rate of discount
The rate of interest used to discount future sums back to present value.

POLICY EXAMPLE
Should the "Pre-Death" Business Be Regulated?

Many Americans with terminal illnesses have life insurance policies which they would like to sell in order to use the proceeds while they are alive. To satisfy this demand, viatical ("provisions for a journey") companies make a present value calculation to determine how much they will pay to the person who is going to die. A terminally ill person with a life insurance policy may have an expected life of, say, four years. If the life insurance policy is sold to a viatical business, the latter must estimate the present value of receiving the payoff from the life insurance policy in four years. The company also has to determine an appropriate discount rate. The viatical business, which started around 1988, has enjoyed profits of around 20 percent a year. Cries in favor of state regulation of the business are now heard virtually everywhere. After all, dying people may be too willing to sell their life insurance policies at a low price because they do not have enough information. Already, state insurance commissioners have agreed that terminally ill patients with six months to live should be paid at least 80 percent of the face value of their policies.

FOR CRITICAL ANALYSIS: What alternatives do terminally ill life insurance policy holders have? (Hint: How could they use the policy as collateral?) ●

CONCEPTS IN BRIEF

- Interest is the price paid for the use of capital. It is also the cost of obtaining credit. In the credit market, the rate of interest paid depends on the length of the loan, the risk, and the handling charges, among other things.

- The interest rate is determined by the intersection of the supply curve of credit, or loanable funds, and the demand curve for credit, or loanable funds. The major sources for the demand for loanable funds are households, businesses, and governments.

- Nominal, or market, interest rates include a factor to take account of the anticipated rate of inflation. Therefore, during periods of high anticipated inflation, nominal interest rates will be relatively high.

- Payments received or costs incurred in the future are worth less than those received or incurred today. The present value of any future sum is lower the farther it occurs in the future and the greater the discount rate used.

Exercise 29.2
Visit www.econtoday.com for more about the lottery.

PROFITS

In Chapter 2, we identified entrepreneurship, or entrepreneurial talent, as a factor of production. Profit is the reward that this factor earns. You may recall that entrepreneurship involves engaging in the risk of starting new businesses. In a sense, then, nothing can be produced without an input of entrepreneurial skills.

Until now, we have been able to talk about the demand for and supply of labor, land, and capital. We can't talk as easily about the demand for and supply of entrepreneurship. For one thing, we have no way to quantify entrepreneurship. What measure should we use? We do know that entrepreneurship exists. We cannot, however, easily present a supply and demand analysis to show the market clearing price per unit of entrepreneurship. We must use a different approach, focusing on the reward for entrepreneurship—profit. First we will determine what profit is *not*. Then we will examine the sources of true, or economic, profit. Finally, we will look at the functions of profits in a market system.

Distinguishing Between Economic Profit and Business, or Accounting, Profit

In our discussion of rent, we had to make a distinction between the common notions of rent and the economist's concept of economic rent. We must do the same thing when we refer to profit. We always have to distinguish between **economic profit** and **accounting profit.** The accountant calculates profit for a business as the difference between total explicit revenues and total explicit costs. Consider an extreme example. You are given a large farm as part of your inheritance. All of the land, fertilizer, seed, machinery, and tools has been fully paid for by your deceased relative. You take over the farm and work on it diligently with

Economic profit
The difference between total revenues and the opportunity cost of all factors of production.

Accounting profit
Total revenues minus total explicit costs.

half a dozen workers. At the end of the year, you sell the output for $1 million. Your accountant then subtracts your actual ("explicit") expenses, mainly the wages you paid.

The difference is called profit, but it is not economic profit. Why? Because no accounting was taken of the *implicit* costs of using the land, seed, tools, and machinery. The only explicit cost considered was the workers' wages. But as long as the land could be rented out, the seed could be sold, and the tools and machinery could be leased, there was an opportunity cost to using them. To derive the economic profit that you might have earned last year from the farm, you must subtract from total revenues the full opportunity cost of all factors of production used (which will include both implicit and explicit costs).

In summary, then, accounting profit is used mainly to define taxable income and, as such, may include some returns to both the owner's labor and capital. Economic profit, by contrast, represents a return over and above the opportunity cost of all resources (including a normal return on the owner's entrepreneurial abilities).

When viewed in this light, it is possible for economic profit to be negative, even if accounting profit is positive. Turning to our farming example again, what if the opportunity cost of using all of the resources turned out to be $1.1 million? The economic profit would have been −$100,000. You would have suffered economic losses.

In sum, the businessperson's accounting definition and the economist's economic definition of profit usually do not coincide. Economic profit is a residual. It is whatever remains after all economic, or opportunity, costs have been taken into account.

Explanations of Economic Profit

Alternative explanations of profit are numerous. Let us examine a few of them: restrictions on entry, innovation, and reward for bearing uninsurable risks.

Restrictions on Entry. We pointed out in Chapter 24 that monopoly profits—a special form of economic profits—are possible when there are barriers to entry, and these profits are often called monopoly rents by economists. Entry restrictions exist in many industries, including taxicabs, cable television franchises, and prescription drugs and eyeglasses. Basically, monopoly profits are built into the value of the business that owns the particular right to have the monopoly.

Innovation. A number of economists have maintained that economic profits are created by innovation, which is defined as the creation of a new organizational strategy, a new marketing strategy, or a new product. This source of economic profit was popularized by Harvard economics professor Joseph Schumpeter (1883–1950). The innovator creates new economic profit opportunities through innovation. The successful innovator obtains a temporary monopoly position, garnering temporary economic profits. When other firms catch up, those temporary economic profits disappear.

Reward for Bearing Uninsurable Risks

There are risks in life, including those involved in any business venture. Many of these risks can be insured, however. You can insure against the risk of losing your house to fire, flood, hurricane, or earthquake. You can do the same if you own a business. You can insure against the risk of theft also. Insurance companies are willing to sell you such insurance because they can predict relatively accurately what percentage of a class of insured assets will suffer losses each year. They charge each insured person or business enough to pay for those fully anticipated losses and to make a normal rate of return.

But there are risks that cannot be insured. If you and a group of your friends get together and pool your resources to start a new business, no amount of statistical calculations can accurately predict whether your business will still be running a year from now or 10 years from now. Consequently, you can't, when you start your business, buy insurance against losing money, bad management, miscalculations about the size of the market, aggressive competition by big corporations, and the like. Entrepreneurs therefore incur uninsurable risks. According to a theory of profits advanced by economist Frank H. Knight (1885–1973), this is the origin of economic profit.

The Function of Economic Profit

In a market economy, the expectation of profits induces firms to discover new products, new production techniques, and new marketing techniques—literally all the new ways to make higher profits. Profits in this sense spur innovation and investment.

Profits also cause resources to move from lower-valued to higher-valued uses. Prices and sales are dictated by the consumer. If the demand curve is close to the origin, there will be few sales and few profits, if any. The lack of profits therefore means that there is insufficient demand to cover the opportunity cost of production. In the quest for higher profits, businesses will take resources out of areas in which either accounting losses or lower than normal rates of return are being made and put them into areas in which there is an expectation of higher profits. The profit reward is an inducement for an industry to expand when demand and supply conditions warrant it. Conversely, the existence of economic losses indicates that resources in the particular industry are not valued as highly as they might be elsewhere. These resources therefore move out of that industry, or at least no further resources are invested in it. Therefore, resources follow the businessperson's quest for higher profits. Profits allocate resources, just as wages and interest do.

CONCEPTS IN BRIEF

- Profit is the reward for entrepreneurial talent, a factor of production.

- It is necessary to distinguish between accounting profit and economic profit. Accounting profit is measured by the difference between total revenues and all explicit costs. Economic profit is measured by the difference between total revenues and the total of all opportunity costs of all factors of production.

- Theories of why profits exist include restriction on entry, innovation, and payment to entrepreneurs for taking uninsurable risks.

- The function of profits in a market economy is to allocate scarce resources. Resources will flow to wherever profits are highest.

HMOs and managed health care organizations must make choices about how much to spend on preventive care. Why can't HMOs simply "spend whatever they need" to prevent illness and premature death?

Should HMOs Provide Cholesterol-Reducing Drugs?

CONCEPTS APPLIED:

COSTS, BENEFITS, PRESENT VALUE, SCARCITY, TRADE-OFFS, OPPORTUNITY COST

Visit www.econtoday.com for an Internet Activity that expands your understanding of these concepts.

Individuals with higher-than-average cholesterol have an increased risk of heart disease. Reduction in fatty foods, alcohol, and nicotine, plus increased exercise, can help most individuals reduce their cholesterol levels. Some individuals can do all of these things and still be plagued with high cholesterol.

Cholesterol-Reducing Drugs

There are cholesterol-lowering compounds called statins. These drugs appear to be effective in helping to prevent heart disease, but they are expensive. A typical 50-year-old male with high cholesterol would require about $700 of these drugs per year for the rest of his life. That ends up being a significant outlay for just one HMO patient. And if you add up all of the potential recipients of such heart-disease-reducing drugs, the tab would come to billions of dollars per year.

Present Value and the Cost-Benefit Analysis

HMOs have to make a decision by looking at the present value of a stream of costs that starts today, versus the present value of an anticipated benefit—less heart disease and fewer hospital and medical expenses—at some time in the future. The issue then becomes at what point the financial burden—the present value of higher current costs—outweighs the expected gain—the present value of reduced future costs. Should HMOs target only high-risk individuals with such medications? Or should they extend such medications to other individuals? Heart disease is the costliest health problem by a large margin: a million Americans die annually from coronary artery disease. Some 800,000 patients a year undergo bypass surgery or other surgical procedures to reopen blocked arteries. The American Heart Association estimates that we are spending over 12 percent of our total yearly health care bill on heart disease.

Statins seem to be a natural for HMOs to reduce astronomical health care costs. Nonetheless, surveys show that only one-fourth of high-risk individuals are taking these drugs. One of the problems is that it takes at least two years of statin use in an HMO before the savings from prevented medical procedures start to show up. But HMOs face an annual member turnover of 15 percent or more. Some HMOs do not want to invest in expensive statins only to have such patients leave the HMO before it realizes the economic benefits.

FOR CRITICAL ANALYSIS

1. What are the ethical issues involved in prescribing preventive drugs for people at risk of heart disease?
2. How should HMOs decide these issues?

CHAPTER SUMMARY

1. Resources that have a fixed supply are paid what is called economic rent. We therefore define economic rent as the payment over and above what is necessary to keep a resource of constant quality and quantity in supply at its current level.

2. Resource owners (including labor owners) of factors with inelastic supply earn economic rent because competition among potential users of those resources bids up the price offered.

3. Interest can be defined as the payment for command over resources today rather than in the future. Interest is typically seen as the payment for credit, but it can also be considered the payment for the use of capital. Interest charged depends on length of loan, risk, and handling charges.

4. The equilibrium rate of interest is determined by the intersection of the demand for credit, or loanable funds, and the supply of credit, or loanable funds.

5. The nominal rate of interest includes a factor that takes account of the anticipated rate of inflation. In periods of high anticipated inflation, nominal, or market, interest rates will be high. Real interest rates may not actually be higher, however, because they are defined as the nominal rate of interest minus the anticipated rate of inflation.

6. The present value of any sum in the future is less than that same sum today. Present value decreases as the sum is paid or obtained further and further in the future and as the rate of discount increases.

7. Frank Knight believed that profit was a payment to entrepreneurs for undertaking risks that are uninsurable. Other reasons why profit exists include restrictions on entry and reward for innovation.

DISCUSSION OF PREVIEW QUESTIONS

1. What is rent?

Rent is payment for the use of land. Economists have long played with the notion that land is completely inelastic in supply, although this is a debatable issue and depends on various definitions. Modern economists now refer to a payment to any factor of production that is in excess of opportunity cost as economic rent. For instance, from society's point of view, the total supply of land is fixed. Also, athletes and entertainers presumably earn economic rent: Beyond some "normal" income, the opportunity cost to superstars of performing is zero; hence "abnormal" income is not necessary to induce them to perform. Note that we usually discuss positively sloped supply schedules indicating that higher relative prices are necessary to induce increased quantity supplied. This is not the case with economic rent.

2. What is interest?

On the most obvious level, interest is a payment for the use of money. On another level, interest can be considered payment for obtaining credit; by borrowing, people (consumers or businesses) obtain command over resources now rather than in the future. Those who wish to make purchases now instead of later are allowed to do so even if they do not currently earn purchasing power. They do so by borrowing, and interest is the price they must pay for the privilege of making expenditures now instead of later.

3. What is the economic function of interest rates?

Interest rates are the price of credit, and like all prices, interest rates play an allocative role. That is, interest is a rationing device. We have said that interest is the price of credit; this credit is allocated to the households and businesses that are willing to pay the highest price (interest rate). Such is the rationing function of credit. On a more fundamental level, we can see that something other than scarce loanable funds is allocated. After all, businesses don't borrow money simply for the privilege of paying interest! The key to understanding what *physical* resources are being allocated is to follow the money: On what do businesses spend this borrowed money? The answer is for the most part, capital goods. Thus the interest rate plays the crucial role of allocating scarce capital goods; the firms that are willing to pay the highest interest rates will be the ones that will be able to purchase the most scarce capital goods. Firms putting capital to the most profitable uses will be able to pay the highest interest rates (and be most acceptable to lenders) and will therefore receive disproportionately greater quantities of new capital. Interest rates help bring about this capital rationing scheme in a market economy.

4. What is the economic function of profits?

Profit is the return on entrepreneurial talent or the price paid to risk takers. Profits also play a rationing role in society. Profits (in conjunction with interest rates) perform the all-important function of deciding which industries (and which firms within an industry) expand and which are forced to contract. Profitable firms can reinvest profits (and offer to pay higher interest rates), while unprofitable firms are forced to contract or go bankrupt. In short, businesses' quests for profits assure that scarce resources flow from less profitable to more profitable uses; profits help society decide which firms are to expand and which are to contract.

PROBLEMS

(Answers to the odd-numbered problems appear at the back of the book.)

29-1. "All revenues obtained by the Italian government from Renaissance art museums are economic rent." Is this statement true or false, and why?

29-2. Some people argue that the extraordinary earnings of entertainment and sports superstars are not economic rent at all but merely the cost of ensuring that a steady stream of would-be stars and starlets continues to flow into the sports and entertainment fields. How would the argument go?

29-3. "If employers paid marginal revenue product (MRP) to each of their inputs, there would be no profits left over." Is this statement true or false, and why?

29-4. The accompanying graph shows the supply of and demand for land. The vertical axis is the price per year received by landowners for permitting the land to be used by farmers.

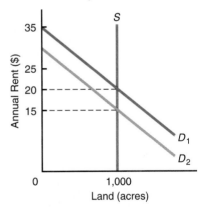

a. Assume that the demand curve for land is D_1. How much economic rent is received by landowners?

b. Now assume that the demand curve for land falls to D_2. How much economic rent is received now?

29-5. The graph shows the demand for and supply of loanable funds.

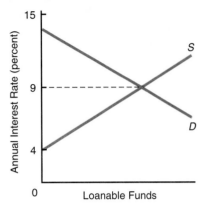

a. What is the equilibrium interest rate?

b. If the supply of loanable funds decreases, what will happen to the equilibrium interest rate?

c. If anticipated inflation is 4 percent for the year, what is the real equilibrium interest rate?

29-6. Make a list of risks that you might face in your life that you believe are insurable. Now make a list of risks that you believe are uninsurable. What is the general distinction between these lists?

29-7. Why do you think that the interest rate you have to pay on an automobile loan is greater than what you have to pay for a loan on a house? Why is the interest rate charged for a loan to purchase a used car usually more than for a loan to purchase a new car?

29-8. At the beginning of the 1980s, virtually all interest rates were much higher than they are in the 1990s. What do you think the major difference is between these two periods that might have caused interest rates to fall so dramatically?

29-9. Assume that everybody has perfect information about all events in the future. What would you expect to happen to economic profits in such a world?

COMPUTER-ASSISTED INSTRUCTION

We explore the many implications of the fact that differently dated goods are fundamentally different commodities.

Complete problem and answer appear on disk.

You have heard of the baby boom generation, the millions of Americans born after World War II, between 1946 and 1964. You may be the offspring of baby boomer parents. The baby boom generation represents a time bomb for all taxpayers. In the next 30 years, the number of Americans aged 65 and over will double. Today they number about 35 million; by 2030, they will be 68 million. Over the same period, the population aged 20 to 64 will increase by only about 20 percent. Therein lies the problem: You, as a member of that working-age population, will probably be expected to pay an increasingly large share in taxes to cover baby boomers' Social Security and Medicare benefits. To understand more about Social Security and Medicare, you need to learn about the issues of income distribution, poverty, and health care.

Distribution of income
The way income is allocated
among the population.

Did You Know That . . . the most recent Internal Revenue Service (IRS) survey
indicates that if your household makes about $75,000 or more in a one-year period, it
is in the top 10 percent of income tax filers? If your income exceeds $95,000, you are in the
top 5 percent of income earners, and if it exceeds $200,000, you are in the top 1 percent.
Yet at the same time, there are more than 34 million people officially defined as living
below the poverty line. Why do some people earn more income than others? Why is the
distribution of income the way it is? Economists have devised various theories to explain
this distribution. We will present some of these theories in this chapter. We will also present
some of the more obvious institutional reasons why income is not distributed equally in the
United States as well as what can be done about health care.

INCOME

Income provides each of us with the means of consuming and saving. Income can be derived from a payment for labor services or a payment for ownership of one of the other factors of production besides labor—land, physical capital, human capital, and entrepreneurship. In addition, individuals obtain spendable income from gifts and government transfers.
(Some individuals also obtain income by stealing, but we will not treat this matter here.)
Right now, let us examine how money income is distributed across classes of income earners within the United States.

Lorenz curve
A geometric representation of
the distribution of income. A
Lorenz curve that is perfectly
straight represents complete
income equality. The more
bowed a Lorenz curve, the
more unequally income is
distributed.

Measuring Income Distribution: The Lorenz Curve

We can represent the distribution of money income graphically with what is known as the
Lorenz curve, named after a U.S.-born statistician, Max Otto Lorenz, who proposed it in
1905. The Lorenz curve shows what portion of total money income is accounted for by different proportions of the nation's households. Look at Figure 30-1. On the horizontal axis,

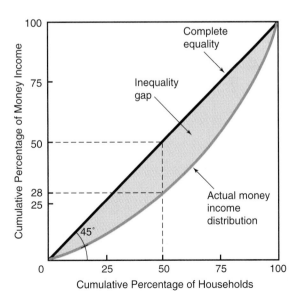

FIGURE 30-1

The Lorenz Curve
The horizontal axis measures the
cumulative percentage of households
from 0 to 100 percent. The vertical
axis measures the cumulative percentage of money income from 0 to
100. A straight line at a 45-degree
angle cuts the box in half and represents a line of complete income
equality, along which 25 percent of the
families get 25 percent of the money
income, 50 percent get 50 percent,
and so on. The Lorenz curve, showing
actual money income distribution, is
not a straight line but rather a curved
line as shown. The difference between
complete money income equality and
the Lorenz curve is the inequality gap.

we measure the *cumulative* percentage of households, lowest-income households first. Starting at the left corner, there are zero households; at the right corner, we have 100 percent of households; and in the middle, we have 50 percent of households. The vertical axis represents the cumulative percentage of money income. The 45-degree line represents complete equality: 50 percent of the households obtain 50 percent of total income, 60 percent of the households obtain 60 percent of total income, and so on. Of course, in no real-world situation is there such complete equality of income; no actual Lorenz curve would be a straight line. Rather, it would be some curved line, like the one labeled "Actual money income distribution" in Figure 30-1. For example, the bottom 50 percent of households in the United States receive about 28 percent of total money income.

In Figure 30-2, we again show the actual money income distribution Lorenz curve, and we also compare it to the distribution of money income in 1929. Since that year, the Lorenz curve has become less bowed; that is, it has moved closer to the line of complete equality.

Criticisms of the Lorenz Curve. In recent years, economists have placed less and less emphasis on the shape of the Lorenz curve as an indication of the degree of income inequality in a country. There are five basic reasons why the Lorenz curve has been criticized:

1. The Lorenz curve is typically presented in terms of the distribution of *money* income only. It does not include **income in kind,** such as government-provided food stamps, education, or housing aid, and goods or services produced and consumed in the home or on the farm.
2. The Lorenz curve does not account for differences in the size of households or the number of wage earners they contain.
3. It does not account for age differences. Even if all families in the United States had exactly the same *lifetime* incomes, chances are that young families would have lower incomes, middle-aged families would have relatively high incomes, and retired families would have low incomes. Because the Lorenz curve is drawn at a moment in time, it could never tell us anything about the inequality of *lifetime* income.
4. The Lorenz curve ordinarily reflects money income *before* taxes.
5. It does not measure unreported income from the underground economy, a substantial source of income for some individuals.

Exercise 30.1
Visit www.econtoday.com for more about U.S. residents.

Income in kind
Income received in the form of goods and services, such as housing or medical care; to be contrasted with money income, which is simply income in dollars, or general purchasing power, that can be used to buy *any* goods and services.

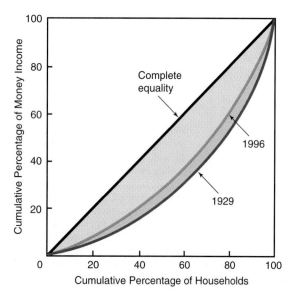

FIGURE 30-2

Lorenz Curves of Income Distribution, 1929 and 1996
Since 1929, the Lorenz curve has moved slightly inward toward the straight line of perfect income equality.
Source: U.S. Department of Commerce.

TABLE 30-1

Percentage Share of Money Income for Households Before Direct Taxes

Income Group	1996	1973	1960	1947
Lowest fifth	4.5	5.5	4.8	5.1
Second fifth	10.5	11.9	12.2	11.8
Third fifth	17.1	17.5	17.8	16.7
Fourth fifth	24.1	24.0	24.0	23.2
Highest fifth	43.9	41.1	41.3	43.3

Source: U.S. Bureau of the Census.
Note: Figures may not sum to 100 percent due to rounding.

Income Distribution in the United States

We could talk about the percentage of income earners within specific income classes—those earning between $20,001 and $30,000 per year, those earning between $30,001 and $40,000 per year, and so on. The problem with this type of analysis is that we live in a growing economy. Income, with some exceptions, is going up all the time. If we wish to make comparisons of the relative share of total income going to different income classes, we cannot look at specific amounts of money income. Instead, we talk about a distribution of income over five groups. Then we can talk about how much the bottom fifth (or quintile) makes compared with the top fifth, and so on. In Table 30-1, we see the percentage share of income for households before direct taxes. The table groups households according to whether they are in the lowest 20 percent of the income distribution, the second lowest 20 percent, and so on. We see that in 1996, the lowest 20 percent had a combined money income of 4.5 percent of the total money income of the entire population. This is a little less than the lowest 20 percent had at the end of World War II. Accordingly, the conclusion has been drawn that there have been only slight changes in the distribution of money income. Indeed, considering that the definition of money income used by the U.S. Bureau of the Census includes only wage and salary income, income from self-employment, interest and dividends, and such government transfer payments as Social Security and unemployment compensation, we have to agree that the distribution of money income has not changed. *Money* income, however, understates *total* income for individuals who receive in-kind transfers from the government in the form of food stamps, public housing, education, and so on. In particular, since World War II, the share of total income—money income plus in-kind benefits—going to the bottom 20 percent of households has probably more than doubled.

INTERNATIONAL EXAMPLE
Relative Income Inequality Throughout the Richest Countries

The United States wins again—it has, according to the World Bank, the greatest amount of income inequality of any of the major industrialized countries. Look at Figure 30-3 on page 670. There you see the ratio of income of the richest 20 percent of households to the poorest 20 percent of households. Should something be done about such income inequality?

Public attitudes toward the government's role in reducing income inequality differ dramatically in the United States and elsewhere. Whereas fewer than 30 percent of Americans believe that government should reduce income differentials, between 60 and 80 percent of Britons, Germans, Italians, and Austrians believe it is the government's job.

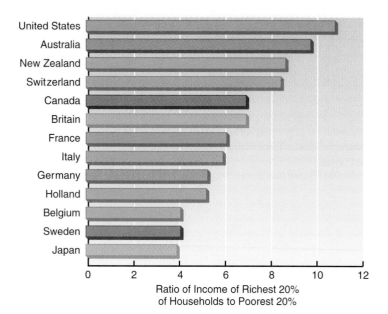

FIGURE 30-3

Relative Income Inequality in the World
The United States has greater income inequality than other developed countries.

Source: World Bank.

FOR CRITICAL ANALYSIS: Does it matter whether the same families stay in the lowest fifth of income earners over time? Otherwise stated, do we need to know anything about mobility across income groups? •

The Distribution of Wealth

We have been referring to the distribution of income in the United States. We must realize that income—a flow—can be viewed as a return on wealth (both human and nonhuman)—a stock. A discussion of the distribution of income in the United States is not the same thing as a discussion of the distribution of wealth. A complete concept of wealth would include tangible objects, such as buildings, machinery, land, cars, and houses—nonhuman wealth—as well as people who have skills, knowledge, initiative, talents, and so on—human wealth. The total of human and nonhuman wealth in the United States makes up our nation's capital stock. (Note that the terms *wealth* and *capital* are often used only with reference to nonhuman wealth.) The capital stock consists of anything that can generate utility to individuals in the future. A fresh ripe tomato is not part of our capital stock. It has to be eaten before it turns rotten, and once it has been eaten, it can no longer generate satisfaction.

Figure 30-4 shows that the richest 10 percent of U.S. households hold about two-thirds of all wealth. The problem with those data, gathered by the Federal Reserve System, is that they do not include many important assets. The first of these is workers' claims on private pension plans, which equal at least $4 trillion according to economist Lawrence B. Lindsey. If you add the value of these pensions, household wealth increases by almost a quarter, meaning that the majority of U.S. house-

---

THINKING CRITICALLY ABOUT THE MEDIA

Increasing Income Inequality and Working Spouses

The media have been having a field day pointing out that the United States has the greatest income inequality in the industrialized world. Underlying the statistics, though, is a little-known fact: Income inequality is measured with respect to *households*. No distinction is made between one- and two-earner households. If two $80,000-a-year lawyers marry, their household income is now $160,000, and they have moved into a higher income group. Not surprisingly, most single tax returns show smaller earnings than joint returns of married couples. In 1969, some 48 percent of working-age married couples had two earners; today that figure is 72 percent. Consequently, part of the reported increase in income inequality in the United States is simply due to an increase in the number of working spouses.

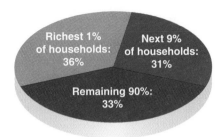

FIGURE 30-4
Measured Total Wealth Distribution
The top 10 percent of households have 67 percent of all measured wealth.
Source: Board of Governors of the Federal Reserve.

holds belong to the middle class. Also omitted is future Social Security liabilities, estimated at about $13 trillion. Again, most of this is "owned" by the middle class.

EXAMPLE
Are We Running to Stay in Place?

There are a lot of statistics around that can show that the typical working person in the United States has not experienced an increase in standard of living since 1970. If we correct take-home wages for inflation, that is an accurate statement. Indeed, the secretary of labor has frequently announced that real wages have actually *fallen* since 1973. There are at least two problems with such statements, though. The first concerns total compensation. Compensation of workers does not consist solely of wages. Whereas in 1970, nonsalary benefits (medical care, insurance, pension payments, and so on) amounted to 24 percent of wages, they now come to around 40 percent. Second, even if after-tax real wages have not increased, the typical American household is at least 20 percent better off than in 1970. Why? Because more households have a second breadwinner. Furthermore, fewer babies are being born, so expenses per household are lower.

One other piece of data is telling: Virtually every measure of consumption per capita is growing, year in and year out. Consequently, the majority of Americans continue to experience increases in their standard of living as measured by their actual purchases of goods and services.

FOR CRITICAL ANALYSIS: Why might an individual be most concerned about total compensation? ●

CONCEPTS IN BRIEF

- The Lorenz curve graphically represents the distribution of income. If it is a straight line, there is complete equality of income. The more it is bowed, the more inequality of income exists.

- The distribution of wealth is not the same as the distribution of income. Wealth includes assets such as houses, stocks, and bonds. Although the apparent distribution of wealth seems to be more concentrated at the top, the data used are not very accurate, and most summary statistics fail to take account of workers' claims on private and public pensions, which are substantial.

DETERMINANTS OF INCOME DIFFERENCES

We know that there are income differences—that is not in dispute. A more important question is why these differences in income occur, for if we know why income differences occur, perhaps we can change public policy, particularly with respect to helping people in the lowest income classes climb the income ladder. What is more, if we know the reasons for income differences, we can ascertain whether any of these determinants have changed over time. We will look at four income difference determinants: age, marginal productivity, inheritance, and discrimination.

Age

Age turns out to be a determinant of income because with age comes, usually, more education, more training, and more experience. It is not surprising that within every class of income earners, there seem to be regular cycles of earning behavior. Most individuals earn more when they are middle-aged than when they are younger or older. We call this the **age-earnings cycle.**

The Age-Earnings Cycle. Every occupation has its own age-earnings cycle, and every individual will probably experience some variation from the average. Nonetheless, we can characterize the typical age-earnings cycle graphically in Figure 30-5. Here we see that at age 18, income is relatively low. Income gradually rises until it peaks at about age 50. Then it falls until retirement, when it becomes zero (that is, currently earned income becomes zero, although retirement payments may then commence). The reason for such a regular cycle in earnings is fairly straightforward.

When individuals start working at a young age, they typically have no work-related experience. Their ability to produce is less than that of more seasoned workers—that is, their productivity is lower. As they become older, they obtain more training and accumulate more experience. Their productivity rises, and they are therefore paid more. They also generally start to work longer hours. As the age of 50 approaches, the productivity of individual workers usually peaks. So, too, do the number of hours per week that are worked. After this peak in the age-earnings cycle, the detrimental effects of aging—decreases in stamina, strength, reaction time, and the like—usually outweigh any increases in training

Age-earnings cycle
The regular earnings profile of an individual throughout his or her lifetime. The age-earnings cycle usually starts with a low income, builds gradually to a peak at around age 50, and then gradually curves down until it approaches zero at retirement.

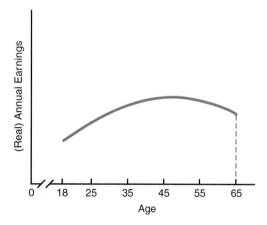

FIGURE 30-5

Typical Age-Earnings Profile
Within every class of income earners there is usually a typical age-earnings profile. Earnings are lowest when starting work at age 18, reach their peak at around age 50, and then taper off until retirement around age 65, when they become zero for most people. The rise in earnings up to age 50 is usually due to increased experience, longer working hours, and better training and schooling. (We abstract from economywide productivity changes that would shift the entire curve upward.)

or experience. Also, hours worked usually start to fall for older people. Finally, as a person reaches retirement, both productivity and hours worked diminish rather drastically.

Note that general increases in overall productivity for the entire workforce will result in an upward shift in the typical age-earnings profile given in Figure 30-5. Thus even at the end of the age-earnings cycle, when just about to retire, the worker would not receive a really low wage compared with the starting wage 45 years earlier. The wage would be higher due to factors that contribute to rising real wages for everyone, regardless of the stage in the age-earnings cycle.

Now we have some idea why specific individuals earn different incomes at different times in their lives, but we have yet to explain why different people are paid different amounts of money for their labor. One way to explain this is to recall the marginal productivity theory developed in Chapter 27.

Marginal Productivity

When trying to determine how many workers a firm would hire, we had to construct a marginal revenue product curve. We found that as more workers were hired, the marginal revenue product fell due to diminishing marginal returns. If the forces of demand and supply established a certain wage rate, workers would be hired until their marginal physical product times marginal revenue was equal to the going wage rate. Then the hiring would stop. This analysis suggests what workers can expect to be paid in the labor market: They can each expect to be paid their marginal revenue product (assuming that there are low-cost information flows and that the labor and product markets are competitive).

In a competitive situation, with mobility of labor resources (at least on the margin), workers who are being paid less than their marginal revenue product will be bid away to better employment opportunities. Either they will seek better employment themselves, or other employers will offer them a slightly higher wage rate. This process will continue until each worker is being paid his or her marginal revenue product.

You may balk at the suggestion that people are paid their marginal revenue product because you may personally know individuals whose MRP is more or less than what they are being paid. Such a situation may, in fact, exist because we do not live in a world of perfect information or in a world with perfectly competitive input and output markets. Employers cannot always seek out the most productive employees available. It takes resources to research the past records of potential employees, their training, their education, and their abilities. Nonetheless, competition creates a tendency toward equality of wages and MRP.

Determinants of Marginal Productivity.

If we accept marginal revenue product theory, we have a way to find out how people can earn higher incomes. If they can increase the value of their marginal physical product, they can expect to be paid more. Some of the determinants of marginal physical product are talent, education, experience, and training. Most of these are means by which marginal physical product can be increased. Let's examine them in greater detail.

Talent. This factor is the easiest to explain but difficult to acquire if you don't have it. Innate abilities and attributes can be very strong, if not overwhelming, determinants of a person's potential productivity. Strength, coordination, and mental alertness are facets of nonacquired human capital and thus have some bearing on the ability to earn income.

Someone who is extremely tall has a better chance of being a basketball player than someone who is short. A person born with a superior talent for abstract thinking has a better chance of making a relatively higher income as a mathematician or a physicist than someone who is not born with that talent.

Experience.   Additional experience at particular tasks is another way to increase productivity. Experience can be linked to the well-known *learning curve* that applies when the same task is done over and over. The worker repeating a task becomes more efficient: The worker can do the same task in less time or in the same amount of time but better. Take an example of a person going to work on an automobile assembly line. At first she is able to fasten only three bolts every two minutes. Then the worker becomes more adept and can fasten four bolts in the same time plus insert a rubber guard on the bumper. After a few more weeks, another task can be added. Experience allows this individual to improve her productivity. The more effectively people learn to do something, the quicker they can do it and the more efficient they are. Hence we would expect experience to lead to higher productivity. And we would expect people with more experience to be paid more than those with less experience. More experience, however, does not guarantee a higher wage rate. The *demand* for a person's services must also exist. Spending a long time to become a first-rate archer in modern society would probably add very little to a person's income. Experience has value only if the output is demanded by society.

Training.   Training is similar to experience but is more formal. Much of a person's increased productivity is due to on-the-job training. Many companies have training programs for new workers. On-the-job training is perhaps responsible for as much of an increase in productivity as is formal education beyond grade school.

EXAMPLE
Economists, Aging, and Productivity

Do the actions of professional economists fit the model that predicts a decrease in productivity after some peak at around age 50? Yes, according to University of Texas economist Daniel Hamermesh. One measure of productivity of economics professors is the number of articles they publish in professional journals. Whereas the over-50 economists constitute 30 percent of the profession, they contribute a mere 6 percent of the articles published in leading economics journals. Whereas 56 percent of economists between ages 36 and 50 submit articles on a regular basis, only 14 percent of economists over 50 do so.

FOR CRITICAL ANALYSIS: Why should we predict that an economist closer to retirement will submit fewer professional journal articles for publication than a younger economist? ●

Investment in Human Capital. Investment in human capital is just like investment in any other thing. If you invest in yourself by going to college, rather than going to work after high school and earning more current income, you will presumably be rewarded in the future with a higher income or a more interesting job (or both). This is exactly the motivation that underlies the decision of many college-bound students to obtain a formal higher education. Undoubtedly there would be students going to school even if the rate of return on formal education were zero or negative. But we do expect that the higher the rate of return on investing in ourselves, the more such investment there will be. U.S. Labor Department data demonstrate conclusively that, on average, high school graduates make more than grade school graduates and that college graduates make more than high school graduates. The estimated annual income of a full-time worker with four years of college in the late-1990s was about $55,000. That person's high school counterpart was estimated to earn only $31,000, which gives a "college premium" of about 57 percent. Generally, the rate of return on investment in human capital is on a par with the rate of return on investment in other areas.

To figure out the rate of return on an investment in a college education, we first have to figure out the marginal costs of going to school. The main cost is not what you have to pay for books, fees, and tuition but rather the income you forgo. *The main cost of education is the income forgone—the opportunity cost of not working.* In addition, the direct expenses of college must be paid for. Not all students forgo all income during their college years. Many work part time. Taking account of those who work part time and those who are supported by state tuition grants and other scholarships, the average rate of return on going to college is somewhere between 8 and 12 percent. This is not a bad rate. Of course, this type of computation does leave out all the consumption benefits you get from attending college. Also omitted from the calculations is the change in personality after going to college. You undoubtedly come out a different person. Most people who go through college feel that they have improved themselves both culturally and intellectually in addition to having increased their potential marginal revenue product so that they can make more income. How do we measure the benefit from expanding our horizons and our desire to experience different things in life? This is not easy to measure, and such nonmoney benefits from investing in human capital are not included in normal calculations.

Inheritance

It is not unusual to inherit cash, jewelry, stocks, bonds, homes, or other real estate. Yet only about 10 percent of income inequality in the United States can be traced to differences in wealth that was inherited. If for some reason the government confiscated all property that had been inherited, there would be very little measured change in the distribution of income in the United States. In any event, at both federal and state levels of taxation, substantial inheritance taxes are levied on the estates of relatively wealthy deceased Americans (although there are some legally valid ways to avoid certain estate taxes).

Discrimination

Economic discrimination occurs whenever workers with the same marginal revenue product receive unequal pay due to some noneconomic factor such as their race, sex, or age. Alternatively, it occurs when there is unequal access to labor markets. It is possible—and indeed quite obvious—that discrimination affects the distribution of income. Certain groups in our society are not paid wages at rates comparable to those received by other groups, even when we correct for productivity. Differences in income remain between whites and nonwhites and between men and women. For example, the median income of black families is about 60 percent that of white families. The median wage rate of women is about 70 percent that of men. Some people argue that all of these differences are due to discrimination against nonwhites and against women. We cannot simply accept *any* differences in income as due to discrimination, though. What we need to do is discover why differences in income between groups exist and then determine if factors other than discrimination in the labor market can explain them. The unexplained part of income differences can rightfully be considered the result of discrimination.

Access to Education. African Americans and other minorities have faced discrimination in the acquisition of human capital. The amount and quality of schooling offered black Americans has generally been inferior to that offered whites. Even if minorities attend school as long as whites, their scholastic achievement can be lower because they are typically allotted fewer school resources than their white counterparts. Nonwhite urban individuals are more likely to live in lower-income areas, which have fewer resources to allocate to education due to the lower tax base. One study showed that nonwhite urban males receive between 23 and 27 percent less income than white urban males because of lower-quality education. This would mean that even if employment discrimination were substantially reduced, we would still expect to see a difference between white and nonwhite income because of the low quality of schooling received by the nonwhites and the resulting lower level of productivity. We say, therefore, that among other things, African Americans and certain other minority groups, such as Hispanics, suffer from too small an investment in human capital. Even when this difference in human capital is taken into account, however, there still appears to be an income differential that cannot be explained. The unexplained income differential between whites and blacks is often attributed to discrimination in the labor market. Because no better explanation is offered, we will stick with the notion that discrimination in the labor market does indeed exist.

The Doctrine of Comparable Worth. Discrimination against women can occur because of barriers to entry in higher-paying occupations and because of discrimination in the acquisition of human capital, just as has occurred for African Americans. Consider the distribution of highest-paying and lowest-paying occupations. The lowest-paying jobs are dominated by females, both white and nonwhite. For example, the proportion of women in secretarial, clerical, janitorial, and food service jobs ranges from 70 percent (food service) to 97 percent (secretarial). Proponents of the **comparable-worth doctrine** feel that female secretaries, janitors, and food service workers should be making salaries comparable to those of male truck drivers or construction workers, assuming that the levels of skill and responsibility in these jobs are comparable. These advocates also believe that a comparable-worth policy would benefit the economy overall. They contend that adjusting the wages of workers in female-dominated jobs upward would create a move toward more efficient and less discriminatory labor markets.

THINKING CRITICALLY ABOUT THE MEDIA

Bad News—and Plenty of It

The media seem addicted to bad news, particularly with respect to the income and job gains of minorities and women. The reality is somewhat better, however. While it is still true that college-educated African-American males earn only 72 percent of what their white counterparts earn, 28 percent have executive, or administrative, or managerial jobs versus 30 percent of non-Hispanic whites. While it is still true that first-generation Hispanic immigrants have relatively low incomes, second-generation Mexican Americans earn almost identical wages to similarly educated non-Hispanic whites. Although women still earn less than men, in one generation they have gone from only low-level jobs to making up 40 percent of medical and law students, administrators, managers, executives, and Ph.D. candidates. Today, women make up almost 60 percent of public officials in America. Of course, the most elite jobs—senior managers in the top Fortune 500 companies—are still male-dominated. Consequently, many women are starting their own businesses.

The race and gender employment situation is not all roses, but it may not be as bad as the media tell us it is.

Comparable-worth doctrine The belief that women should receive the same wages as men if the levels of skill and responsibility in their jobs are equivalent.

THEORIES OF DESIRED INCOME DISTRIBUTION

We have talked about the factors affecting the distribution of income, but we have not yet mentioned the normative issue of how income *ought* to be distributed. This, of course, requires a value judgment. We are talking about the problem of economic justice. We can never completely resolve this problem because there are always going to be conflicting values. It is impossible to give all people what each thinks is just. Nonetheless, two particular normative standards for the distribution of income have been popular with economists. These are income distribution based on productivity and income distribution based on equality.

Productivity

The *productivity standard* for the distribution of income can be stated simply as "To each according to what he or she produces." This is also called the *contributive standard* because it is based on the principle of rewarding according to the contribution to society's total output. It is also sometimes referred to as the *merit standard* and is one of the oldest concepts of justice. People are rewarded according to merit, and merit is judged by one's ability to produce what is considered useful by society.

However, just as any standard is a value judgment, so is the productivity standard. It is rooted in the capitalist ethic and has been attacked vigorously by some economists and philosophers, including Karl Marx, who felt that people should be rewarded according to need and not according to productivity.

We measure a person's productive contribution in a capitalist system by the market value of that person's output. We have already referred to this as the marginal revenue product theory of wage determination.

Do not immediately jump to the conclusion that in a world of income distribution determined by productivity, society will necessarily allow the aged, the infirm, and the disabled to die of starvation because they are unproductive. In the United States today, the productivity standard is mixed with a standard based on people's "needs" so that the aged, the disabled, the involuntarily unemployed, the very young, and other unproductive (in the market sense of the word) members of the economy are provided for through private and public transfers.

Equality

The *egalitarian principle* of income distribution is simply "To each exactly the same." Everyone would have exactly the same amount of income. This criterion of income distribution has been debated as far back as biblical times. This system of income distribution has been considered equitable, meaning that presumably everybody is dealt with fairly and equally. There are problems, however, with an income distribution that is completely equal.

Some jobs are more unpleasant or more dangerous than others. Should the people undertaking these jobs be paid exactly the same as everyone else? Indeed, under an equal distribution of income, what incentive would there be for individuals to take risky, hazardous, or unpleasant jobs at all? What about overtime? Who would be willing to work overtime without additional pay? There is another problem: If everyone earned the same income, what incentive would there be for individuals to invest in their own human capital—a costly and time-consuming process?

Just consider the incentive structure within a corporation. Recall from Chapter 27 that much of the pay differential between, say, the CEO and all of the vice-presidents is meant to create competition among the vice-presidents for the CEO's job. The result is higher productivity. If all incomes were the same, much of this competition would disappear, and productivity would fall.

There is some evidence that differences in income lead to higher rates of economic growth. Future generations are therefore made better off. Elimination of income differences may reduce the rate of economic growth and cause future generations to be poorer than they otherwise might have been.

CONCEPTS IN BRIEF

- Most people follow an age-earnings cycle in which they earn relatively small incomes when they first start working, increase their incomes until about age 50, and then slowly experience a decrease in their real incomes as they approach retirement.

- If we accept the marginal revenue product theory of wages, workers can expect to be paid their marginal revenue product. However, full adjustment is never obtained, so some workers may be paid more or less than their MRP.

- Marginal physical productivity depends on talent, education, experience, and training.

- Going to school and receiving on-the-job training can be considered an investment in human capital. The main cost of education is the opportunity cost of not working.

- Discrimination is most easily observed in various groups' access to high-paying jobs and to quality education. Minorities and women are disproportionately underrepresented in high-paying jobs. Also, minorities sometimes do not receive access to higher education of the same quality offered to majority-group members.

- Proponents of the comparable-worth doctrine contend that disparate jobs can be compared by examining efforts, skill, and educational training and that wages should therefore be paid on the basis of this comparable worth.

- Two normative standards for income distribution are income distribution based on productivity and income distribution based on equality.

POVERTY AND ATTEMPTS TO ELIMINATE IT

Throughout the history of the world, mass poverty has been accepted as inevitable. However, this nation and others, particularly in the Western world, have sustained enough economic growth in the past several hundred years so that *mass* poverty can no longer be said to be a problem for these fortunate countries. As a matter of fact, the residual of poverty in the United States strikes us as bizarre, an anomaly. How can there still be so much poverty in a nation of such abundance? Having talked about the determinants of the distribution of income, we now have at least some ideas of why some people are destined to remain low-income earners throughout their lives.

There are methods of transferring income from the relatively well-to-do to the relatively poor, and as a nation we have been using them for a long time. Today, we have a vast array of welfare programs set up for the purpose of redistributing income. However, we know that these programs have not been entirely successful. Are there alternatives to our

FIGURE 30-6

Official Number of Poor in the United States

The number of individuals classified as poor fell steadily from 1959 through 1969. From 1970 to 1981, the number stayed about the same. It then increased during the 1981–1982 recession, dropped off for a while, and rose in the early 1990s and then leveled off.

Source: U.S. Department of Labor.

current welfare system? Is there a better method of helping the poor? Before we answer these questions, let's look at the concept of poverty in more detail and at the characteristics of the poor. Figure 30-6 shows that those classified as poor fell steadily from 1959 to 1969, then leveled off until the recession of 1981–1982. The number started to rise dramatically, fell back during the late 1980s, rose again after the recession in the early 1990s, and has been falling slowly since then.

INTERNATIONAL EXAMPLE
Poverty Rates in the European Union

For years, politicians throughout much of the European Union have proclaimed their unwillingness to adopt the more laissez-faire, "let the chips fall where they may" economic model that prevails in the United States. They are convinced that the result is too much poverty. But they were shocked to discover in an article published in the newspaper *Le Monde* in 1997 that the poverty rate for the European Union was more than 17 percent—fully 57 million people out of a population of 330 million. Whereas the poverty rate in the United States has hovered between 13 and 15 percent of the population since the 1970s, the rate in Europe has increased over the same period from 10 percent to the current 17 percent. One-third of the officially poor in the European Union work, one-third are retired, and one-third are unemployed.

FOR CRITICAL ANALYSIS: *What problems might there be in comparing poverty rates across nations?* •

Defining Poverty

The threshold income level, which is used to determine who falls into the poverty category, was originally based on the cost of a nutritionally adequate food plan designed by the U.S. Department of Agriculture for emergency or temporary use. The threshold was determined by multiplying the food plan cost by 3 on the assumption that food expenses comprise approximately one-third of a poor family's income. Annual revisions of the threshold level were based only on price changes in the food budget. In 1969, a federal interagency committee looked at the calculations of the threshold and decided to set new standards, with adjustments made on the basis of changes in the Consumer Price Index. For example, in 1996, the official poverty level for an urban family of four was around $16,000. It goes up each year to reflect whatever inflation has occurred.

Absolute Poverty

Because the low-income threshold is an absolute measure, we know that if it never changes in real terms, we will reduce poverty even if we do nothing. How can that be? The reasoning is straightforward. Real incomes in the United States have been growing at a compounded annual rate of almost 2 percent per capita for at least the past century and at about 2.5 percent since World War II. If we define the poverty line at a specific real level, more and more individuals will make incomes that exceed that poverty line. Thus in absolute terms, we will eliminate poverty (assuming continued per capita growth and no change in income distribution).

Relative Poverty

Be careful with this analysis, however. Poverty has generally been defined in relative terms; that is, it is defined in terms of the income levels of individuals or families relative to the rest of the population. As long as the distribution of income is not perfectly equal, there will always be some people who make less income than others, even if their relatively low income is high by historical standards. Thus in a relative sense, the problem of poverty will always exist, although it can be reduced. In any given year, for example, the absolute poverty level *officially* decided on by the U.S. government is far above the average income in many countries in the world.

Exercise 30.2
Visit www.econtoday.com for more about poverty.

Transfer Payments as Income

The official poverty level is based on pretax income, including cash but not in-kind subsidies—food stamps, housing vouchers, and the like. If we correct poverty levels for such benefits, the percentage of the population that is below the poverty line drops dramatically. Some economists argue that the way the official poverty level is calculated makes no sense in a nation that redistributed over $850 billion in cash and noncash transfers in 1998.

Furthermore, some of the nation's official poor partake in the informal, or underground, sectors of the economy without reporting their income from these sources. And some of the officially defined poor obtain benefits from owning their own home (40 percent of all poor households do own their own homes). Look at Figure 30-7 for two different views of what has happened to the relative position of this nation's poor. The graph shows the ratio of the top fifth of the nation's households to the bottom fifth of the nation's households. If we look only at measured income, it appears that the poor are getting relatively poorer compared to the rich (the top line). If we compare household spending (consumption), a different picture emerges. The nation's poorest households are in fact holding their own.

Attacks on Poverty: Major Income Maintenance Programs

There are a variety of income maintenance programs designed to help the poor. We examine a few of them here.

Social Security. For the retired, the unemployed, and the disabled, social insurance programs provide income payments in prescribed situations. The best known is Social Secu-

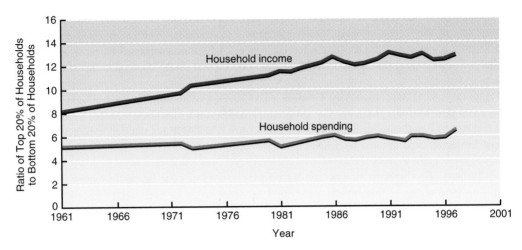

FIGURE 30-7

Relative Poverty: Comparing Household Incomes and Household Spending
This graph shows, on the vertical axis, the ratio of the top 20 percent of income-earning households to the bottom 20 percent. If measured household income is used, there appears to be increasing income inequality, particularly during the early to mid-1980s. If we look at household *spending*, though, inequality appears to remain constant.
Sources: U.S. Bureau of Labor Statistics; U.S. Bureau of the Census.

rity, which includes what has been called old-age, survivors', and disability insurance (OASDI). This is essentially a program of compulsory saving financed from compulsory payroll taxes levied on both employers and employees. Workers pay for Social Security while working and receive the benefits after retirement. The benefit payments are usually made to people who have reached retirement age. When the insured worker dies, benefits accrue to the survivors, including widows and children. Special benefits provide for disabled workers. Over 90 percent of all employed persons in the United States are covered by OASDI. Social Security was originally designed as a social insurance program that workers paid for themselves and under which they received benefits that varied with the size of past contributions. Today, it is simply an intergenerational income transfer that is only vaguely related to past earnings. It transfers income from Americans who work—the young through the middle-aged—to those who do not work—older retired persons.

In 1998, more than 49 million people were receiving OASDI checks averaging about $729 a month. Benefit payments from OASDI redistribute income to some degree. However, benefit payments are not based on recipient need. Participants' contributions give them the right to benefits even if they would be financially secure without them. Social Security is not really an insurance program because people are not guaranteed that the benefits they receive will be in line with the contributions they have made. It is not a personal savings account. The benefits are legislated by Congress. In the future, Congress may not be as sympathetic toward older people as it is today. It could (and probably will have to) legislate for lower real levels of benefits instead of higher ones.

Supplemental Security Income (SSI) and Temporary Assistance to Needy Families (TANF). Many people who are poor but do not qualify for Social Security benefits are assisted through other programs. The federally financed and administered Supplemental Security Income (SSI) program was instituted in 1974. The purpose of SSI is to establish a nationwide minimum income for the aged, the blind, and the disabled. SSI has become one of the fastest-growing transfer programs in America. Whereas in 1974 less than $8 billion was spent, the prediction for 1999 is $35.4 billion. Americans currently eligible for SSI include children and individuals claiming mental disabilities, including drug addicts and alcoholics.

Temporary Assistance to Needy Families (TANF) is a state-administered program, financed in part by federal grants. The program provides aid to families in need. TANF replaced Aid to Families with Dependant Children (AFDC). TANF is intended to be temporary. Projected expenditures for TANF are $21.4 billion in 1999.

Food Stamps. Food stamps are government-issued coupons that can be used to purchase food. The food stamp program was started in 1964, seemingly, in retrospect, mainly to shore up the nation's agricultural sector by increasing demand for food through retail channels. In 1964, some 367,000 Americans were receiving food stamps. In 1998, the estimate is over 28 million recipients. The annual cost has jumped from $860,000 to more than $30 billion. In 1998, almost one in every nine citizens (including children) was using food stamps. The food stamp program has become a major part of the welfare system in the United States. The program has also become a method of promoting better nutrition among the poor.

The Earned Income Tax Credit Program (EITC). In 1975, the EITC was created to provide rebates of Social Security taxes to low-income workers. Over one-fifth of all tax returns claim an earned-income tax credit. In some states, such as Mississippi, as well as the District of Columbia, nearly half of all families are eligible for EITC. The program works as follows: Households with a reported income of less than $25,300 (exclusive of welfare payments) receive EITC benefits up to $2,528. There is a catch, though. Those with earnings between $8,425 and $11,000 get a flat $2,528. But families earning between $11,000 and $25,300 get penalized 17.68 cents for every dollar they earn above $11,000. This constitutes a punitive tax. Thus the EITC discourages work by a low- or moderate-income earner more than it rewards work. In particular, it discourages low-income earners from taking on a second job. The General Accounting Office estimates that hours worked by working wives in EITC-beneficiary households have consequently decreased by 10 percent. The average EITC recipient works 1,300 hours compared to a normal work year of 2,000 hours.

No Apparent Reduction in Poverty Rates

In spite of the numerous programs in existence and the hundreds of billions of dollars transferred to the poor, the officially defined rate of poverty in the United States has shown no long-run tendency to decline. From 1945 until the early 1970s, the percentage of Americans in poverty fell steadily every year. It reached a low of around 11 percent in 1973, shot back up beyond 15 percent in 1983, fell steadily to 13.1 percent in 1990, and has stayed about that ever since. Why this has happened is a real puzzlement. Since the War on Poverty was launched under President Lyndon B. Johnson in 1965, nearly $4 trillion has been transferred to the poor, and yet more Americans are poor today than ever before. The Welfare Reform Act of 1996 put limits on people's use of welfare. The goal is now to get people off welfare and onto "workfare."

CONCEPTS IN BRIEF

• If poverty is defined in absolute terms, economic growth eventually decreases the number of officially defined poor. If poverty is defined relatively, however, we will never eliminate it.

• Major attacks on poverty have been social insurance programs in the form of Social Security, Supplemental Security Income, Aid to Families with Dependent Children, the earned-income tax credit, and food stamps.

• Although the relative lot of the poor measured by household income seems to have worsened, household spending by the bottom 20 percent of households compared to the top 20 percentile has shown little change since the 1960s.

HEALTH CARE

Exercise 30.3
Visit www.econtoday.com for more about health insurance.

It may seem strange to be reading about health care in a chapter on the distribution of income and poverty. Yet health care is in fact intimately related to those two topics. For example, sometimes people become poor because they do not have adequate health insurance (or have none at all), fall ill, and deplete all of their wealth on care. Moreover, sometimes individuals remain in certain jobs simply because their employer's health care package seems so good that they are afraid to change jobs and risk not being covered by health care insurance in the process. Finally, as you will see, much of the cause of the increased health care spending in America can be attributed to a change in the incentives that Americans face.

America's Health Care Situation

Spending for health care is estimated to account for 13 percent of the total annual income created in the U.S. economy. You can see from Figure 30-8 that in 1965, about 6 percent of annual income was spent on health care, but that percentage has been increasing ever since. Per capita spending on health care is greater in the United States than anywhere else in the world today. On a per capita basis, we spend more than twice as much as citizens of Luxembourg,

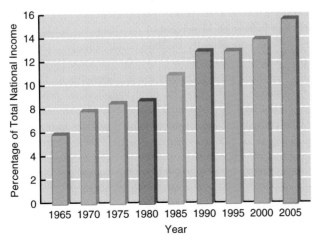

FIGURE 30-8

Percentage of Total National Income Spent on Health Care in the United States
Sources: U.S. Department of Commerce; U.S. Department of Health and Human Services; Deloitte and Touche LLP; VHA, Inc.

Austria, Australia, Japan, and Denmark. We spend almost three times as much on a per capita basis as citizens of Spain and Ireland.

Why Have Health Care Costs Risen So Much? There are numerous explanations for why health care costs have risen so much. At least one has to do with changing demographics: The U.S. population is getting older.

The Age–Health Care Expenditure Equation. The top 5 percent of health care users incur over 50 percent of all health costs. The bottom 70 percent of health care users account for only 10 percent of health care expenditures. Not surprisingly, the elderly make up most of the top users of health care services. Nursing home expenditures are made primarily by people older than 70. The use of hospitals is also dominated by the aged.

The U.S. population is aging steadily. More than 12 percent of the current 265 million Americans are over 65. It is estimated that by the year 2035, senior citizens will comprise about 22 percent of our population. This aging population stimulates the demand for health care. The elderly consume more than four times the per capita health care services that the rest of the population uses. In short, whatever the demand for health care services is today, it is likely to be considerably higher in the future as the U.S. population ages.

New Technologies. Another reason that health care costs have risen so dramatically is high technology. A CT (computerized tomography) scanner costs around $1 million. An MRI (magnetic resonance imaging) scanner can cost over $2 million. A PET (positron emission tomography) scanner costs around $4 million. All of these machines became increasingly available in the 1980s and 1990s and are desired throughout the country. Typical fees for procedures using them range from $300 to $500 for a CT scan to as high as $2,000 for a PET scan. The development of new technologies that help physicians and hospitals prolong human life is an ongoing process in an ever-advancing industry. New procedures at even higher prices can be expected in the future.

Third-Party Financing. Currently, government spending on health care constitutes over 40 percent of total health care spending (of which the *federal* government pays about 70 percent). Private insurance accounts for a little over 35 percent of payments for health care. The remainder—less than 20 percent—is paid directly by individuals. Figure 30-9 shows the change in the payment scheme for medical care in the United States since 1930. Medicare and Medicaid are the main sources of hospital and other medical benefits to 35 million Americans, most of whom are over 65. Medicaid—the joint state-federal program—provides long-term health care, particularly for people living in nursing homes. Medicare, Medicaid, and private insurance companies are considered **third parties** in the medical care equation. Caregivers and patients are the two primary parties. When third parties step in to pay for medical care, the quantity demanded for those services increases. For example, when Medicare and Medicaid went into effect in the 1960s, the volume of federal government–reimbursed medical services increased by more than 65 percent.

The availability of third-party payments for costly medical care has generated increases in the availability of hospital beds. Between 1974 and 1998, the number of hospital beds increased by over 50 percent. Present occupancy rates are only around 65 percent.

Third parties
Parties who are not directly involved in a given activity or transaction. For example, in the relationship between caregivers and patients, fees may be paid by third parties (insurance companies, government).

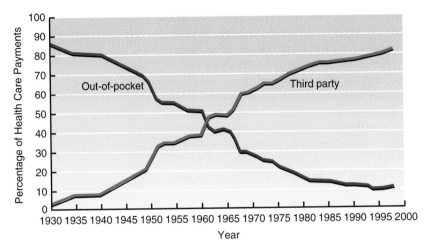

FIGURE 30-9

Third Party Versus Out-of-Pocket Health Care Payments
Out-of-pocket payments for health care services have been falling steadily since the 1930s. In contrast, third-party payments for health care have risen to the point that they account for over 80 percent of all such outlays today.

Sources: Health Care Financing Administration; U.S. Department of Health and Human Services.

Price, Quantity Demanded, and the Question of Moral Hazard. While some people may think that the demand for health care is insensitive to price changes, theory clearly indicates otherwise. Look at Figure 30-10. There you see a hypothetical demand curve for health care services. To the extent that third parties—whether government or private insurance—pay for health care, the out-of-pocket cost, or net price, to the individual will drop. In an extreme example, all medical expenses are paid for by third parties so that the price is zero in Figure 30-10 and the quantity demanded is many times what it would be at a higher price.

One of the issues here has to do with the problem of moral hazard. Consider two individuals with two different health insurance policies. The first policy pays for all medical expenses, but in the second the individual has to pay the first $1,000 a year (this amount is known as the *deductible*). Will the behavior of the two individuals be different? Generally, the answer is yes. The individual with no deductible may be more likely to seek treatment for health problems after they develop rather than try to avoid them and will generally expect medical attention on a more regular basis. In contrast, the individual who faces the first $1,000 of medical expenses each year will tend to engage in more wellness activities and will be less inclined to seek medical care for minor problems. The moral hazard here is that the individual with the zero deductible for medical care expenses may engage in a lifestyle that is less healthful than will the individual with the $1,000 deductible.

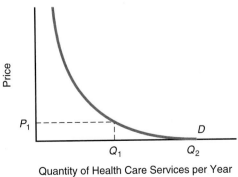

FIGURE 30-10

The Demand for Health Care Services
At price P_1, the quantity of health care services demanded per year would hypothetically be Q_1. If the price falls to zero (third-party payment with zero deductible), the quantity demanded expands to Q_2.

Moral Hazard as It Affects Physicians and Hospitals. The issue of moral hazard also has a direct effect on the behavior of physicians and hospital administrators. Due to third-party payments, patients rarely have to worry about the expense of operations and other medical procedures. As a consequence, both physicians and hospitals order more procedures. Physicians are typically reimbursed on the basis of medical procedures; thus they have no financial interest in trying to keep hospital costs down. Indeed, many have an incentive to raise costs.

Such actions are most evident with terminally ill patients. A physician may order a CT scan and other costly procedures for a terminally ill patient. The physician knows that Medicare or some other type of insurance will pay. Then the physician can charge a fee for analyzing the CT scan. Fully 30 percent of Medicare expenditures are for Americans who are in the last six months of their lives.

Rising Medicare expenditures are one of the most serious problems facing the federal government today. The number of beneficiaries has increased from 19.1 million in 1966 (first year of operation) to an estimated 40 million in 1996. Figure 30-11 shows that federal spending on Medicare has been growing at over 10 percent a year, adjusted for inflation.

Is National Health Insurance the Answer?

Proponents of a national health care system believe that the current system relies too heavily on private insurers. They argue in favor of a Canadian-style system. In Canada, the government sets the fees that are paid to each doctor for seeing a patient and prohibits private practice. The Canadian government also imposes a cap on the incomes that any doctor can receive in a given year. The Canadian federal government provides a specified amount of funding to hospitals, leaving it to them to decide how to allocate the funds. If we were to follow the Canadian model, the average American would receive fewer health services than at present. Hospital stays would be longer, but there would be fewer tests and procedures. Today, there is no discernible difference in infant mortality or life expectancy between the United States and Canada. If we switched to using the Canadian health care system model, we would hence not expect to see any change in those two statistics.

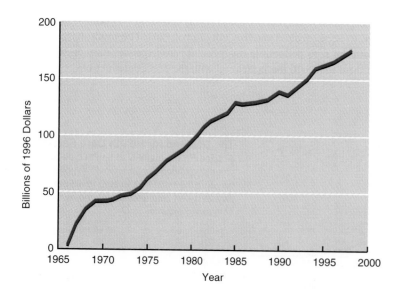

FIGURE 30-11

Federal Medicare Spending
Federal spending on Medicare has increased about 10 percent a year, after adjusting for inflation, since its inception in 1966.

Sources: Economic Report of the President; U.S. Bureau of Labor Statistics.

Alternatives to a national health care policy involve some type of national health insurance, perhaps offered only to people who qualify on the basis of low annual income. A number of politicians have offered variations on such a program. The over 20 million Americans who have no health insurance at some time during each year would certainly benefit. The share of annual national income that goes to health care expenditures would rise, however. Also, the federal budget deficit might increase by another $30 billion to $50 billion (or more) per year to pay for the program.

INTERNATIONAL EXAMPLE
Deterioration in the United Kingdom's National Health Care System

Many countries now have single-payer health care systems that in essence offer "free" universal health care. The United Kingdom's National Health Care Services (NHS) has been in existence since 1948. Once touted as one of the world's best national health care systems, both the system and the services it offers have deteriorated dramatically. In 1948, there were 10 hospital beds for every 1,000 people; today there are only 5 per 1,000. Since 1948, about 50 percent of that nation's hospitals have closed for "efficiency" reasons. The UK now has a lower hospital bed supply than any other Western European country except Portugal and Spain. Even its two most prestigious teaching hospitals are scheduled to close.

Because hospital bed space is limited, currently more than 1 million British subjects are on a waiting list for hospital admission. Many others who need medical care are not on the list because they are so discouraged by the long wait that they simply choose not to seek medical treatment. In some London hospitals, it is common for patients to wait more than 12 hours to see a doctor.

Despite all of the hospital closings and the decline in medical personnel, employment by the National Health Care system has skyrocketed. In 1948, there were .73 staff for each hospital bed; today there are 3.1. The additional staff do not deal directly with the treatment of patients, though. Rather they have become part of the NHS bureaucracy, which requires that a department or committee be established for every new area of medicine or research that develops. The NHS consists of a bureaucratic network unknown in the decentralized system in the United States.

FOR CRITICAL ANALYSIS: Why have so many hospitals been closed in the United Kingdom? •

Countering the Moral Hazard Problem: A Medical Savings Account

Medical savings accounts (MSAs)

A tax-exempt health care account to which individuals would pay into on a regular basis and from which medical care expenses could be paid.

As an alternative to completely changing the American health care industry, Congress has legislated an experiment in **medical savings accounts (MSAs).** Employers with 50 or fewer employees, as well as the self-employed and the uninsured, can set up a tax-free MSA. Eligible employees can make an annual tax-deductible contribution to an MSA up to a maximum of $2,250 for an individual and $4,500 for family. Money in the MSA accumulates tax-free, and distributions of MSA funds for medical expenses are also exempt. Any funds remaining in an MSA after an individual reaches age 65 can be withdrawn tax-free. Under current legislation, up to 750,000 employees can take advantage of the demonstration MSA program. The benefits can be impressive. A single person depositing $1,462.50 each year with no withdrawals will have $409,000 in the account after 40 years.

Combating Moral Hazard. A major benefit of an MSA is that the moral hazard problem is reduced. Individuals ultimately pay for their own minor medical expenses. They do not have the incentive to seek medical care as frequently for minor problems. In addition, they have an incentive to engage in wellness activities. Finally, for those using an MSA, the physician-patient relationship remains intact, for third parties (insurance companies or the government) do not intervene in paying or monitoring medical expenses. Patients with MSAs will not allow physicians to routinely order expensive tests for every minor ache or pain because they get to keep any money saved in the MSA.

Critics' Responses. Some critics argue that because individuals get to keep whatever they don't spend from their MSAs, they will forgo necessary visits to medical care facilities and may develop more serious medical problems as a consequence. Other critics argue that MSAs will sabotage managed care plans. Under managed care plans, deductibles are either reduced or eliminated completely. In exchange, managed health care plan participants are extremely limited in physician choice. Just the opposite would occur with MSAs—high deductibles and unlimited choice of physicians.

CYBERMEDICINE MAY REDUCE FUTURE MEDICAL COSTS

Cybermedicine, which is sometimes called *telemedicine*, involves using the Internet to send detailed digital X-rays, EKGs, and biopsy samples—reduced to computer data—to experts around the world. The use of the Internet to reach medical experts may eventually reduce medical costs. Individuals with rare diseases and medical problems will no longer have to travel to visit different experts. HMOs and managed care plans will be able to obtain second and third opinions about proposed surgery at minimal cost. Further, the Internet may eventually reduce the cost per constant-quality unit of medical care by spreading modern medical methods worldwide at a relatively low cost. Hundreds or thousands of doctors will be able to witness the latest in surgical and other procedures. Already, Massachusetts General Hospital, the Cleveland Clinic Foundation, Duke University Medical Center, and Johns Hopkins School of Medicine have formed a cybermedicine consortium called World-Care Limited in Cambridge, Massachusetts. Its goal is to spread modern medical techniques worldwide.

FOR CRITICAL ANALYSIS: Under what circumstances might cybermedicine actually increase the amount a nation's residents spend on medical care? •

CONCEPTS IN BRIEF

- Health care costs have risen because (1) our population has been getting older and the elderly use more health care services, (2) new technologies and medicine cost more, and (3) third-party financing—private and government-sponsored health insurance—reduces the incentive for individuals to reduce their spending on health care services.

- National health insurance has been proposed as an answer to our current problems, but it does little to alter the reasons why health care costs continue to rise.

- An alternative to a national health care program might be medical savings accounts, which allow individuals to set aside money that is tax exempt, to be used only for medical care. Whatever is left over becomes a type of retirement account.

The percentage of the U.S. population over age 65 is growing so fast that Medicare expenditures threaten to become a major impediment to a balanced federal budget.

Should You Worry About Possible Medicare Bankruptcy?

CONCEPTS APPLIED:

DEMAND, MORAL HAZARD, MEDICARE, THIRD-PARTY PAYMENTS

Visit www.econtoday.com for an Internet Activity that expands your understanding of these concepts.

The major way in which retirees' medical care is paid is through the federal government program called Medicare. During the program's first full year of operation in 1967, it cost a mere $2.5 billion (or about $11 billion in 1998 dollars). Medicare outlays have increased to an estimated $198 billion in 1998. Part of this increase in Medicare spending has been due to the increase in the population of Americans over 65 years old. Part has been due, as you read in the chapter, to more expensive medical technology. Another part results from the increase in the quantity of medical care demanded due to the dramatic reduction in the price that Medicare-covered patients must actually pay directly for medical services. There is a moral hazard issue here also. When the federal government pays for all medical care, some retired people do not engage in as many "wellness" activities as they would if they had to pay at least part of their initial medical payments each time they were sick.

Does It Matter If the Medicare Trust Fund Goes Bankrupt?

As Figure 30-12 shows, the Medicare Hospital Trust Fund is projected to go bankrupt sometime after the turn of the century. The fund's assets reached their peak in 1995 at $137 billion. Under current legislation, Medicare's hospital insurance is running deficits every year. This will continue. Currently, about 3.9 taxpayers support each beneficiary of Medicare's hospital insurance, but by the year 2030, there will be just 2.3 taxpayers per beneficiary. The baby boomers' Medicare hospital insurance benefits cannot possibly be paid out of the revenues raised at current Medicare tax rates.

Actually, though, Medicare's supposed bankruptcy is not really the issue, just as Social Security's supposed potential bankruptcy is not a real issue. Within the federal government itself, trust funds mean nothing in real terms. Medicare and Social Security taxes are not specifically earmarked or kept in separate accounts. In the federal government's budget, a dollar spent is simply a dollar spent, no matter where it is spent. Likewise, a dollar of revenue is just a dollar of revenue, no matter what kind of tax it comes from. The Medicare issue is simply this: What percentage of total federal government spending is going to go to pay for the medical expenses of the nation's retired population? On the funding side, the issue is, How much more can the federal government raise tax rates to cover increased Medicare (and Social Security) spending without "killing the goose that laid the golden egg"? Specifically, if Medicare spending continues to increase, how will it be paid for, and what will be the effect?

Congress Keeps Adding to Medicare Expenses

On the one hand, Congress has attempted to reduce Medicare expenses by pressuring medical care providers to keep their costs down. On the other hand, Congress continues to expand procedures covered by Medicare and the population that is eligible. For example, each year, Congress seems to add new benefits, most recently for mammograms, osteoporosis, and education in self-testing for diabetics. Also, Medicare payments to HMOs serving rural areas recently were increased. Under the Clinton administration, "kiddy care" was added (but not as part of Medicare per se). Finally, the Clinton administration proposed adding certain individuals who were not retired to the Medicare health insurance system, albeit for a monthly charge that most experts agree will not cover the additional expenses.

When all is said and done, however, these issues are swamped by the sheer size of the baby boom generation

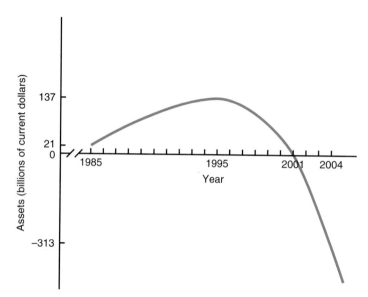

FIGURE 30-12

Rising Medicare Expenses Lead to a Depleted Medicare and Hospital Insurance Trust Fund
If current Medicare taxes stay the same, the Medicare Hospital Insurance Trust Fund will be depleted in the next few years and will accumulate deficits for years thereafter.

Source: Social Security Administration; Trustees of the Federal Hospital Insurance Trust Fund.

that is about to retire. This country is going to have an increasingly large post-65 population. The difference between current Medicare taxes and Medicare's hospital insurance payments—deficits—are projected to explode even before the baby boomers retire: $70 billion in 2003, almost $100 billion in 2005, and $115 billion in 2006. (The Federal Hospital Insurance Trust Fund trustees predict even greater deficits.)

The Bias in Medicare Spending

There is a strong bias in Medicare spending toward individuals in the last year of life. Nearly one-third of Medicare expenditures go to these individuals. Consequently, some critics of Medicare spending argue that longevity at any price should no longer be allowed. In other words, if as a society we wish to continue to provide medical insurance to retirees through the federal government, perhaps the government should limit its expenditures to only quality-enhancing medical care rather than longevity-enhancing medical care, at least for those over, say, some specific age such as 75. Britain, for example, does not allow kidney dialysis for people over a certain age. There are also restrictions on organ transplants for older people. In the United States there are none.

FOR CRITICAL ANALYSIS

1. "Life is priceless." How would the application of this philosophy change current medical spending in the United States?
2. Can you think of a way to reduce the moral hazard problem as it relates to Medicare health insurance? (Hint: Most eligible retirees pay almost nothing for most medical procedures.)

CHAPTER SUMMARY

1. We can represent the distribution of income graphically with a Lorenz curve. The extent to which the line is bowed from a straight line shows how unequal the distribution of income is.

2. The distribution of pretax money income in the United States has remained fairly constant since World War II. The lowest fifth of income earners still receive only about 5 percent of total pretax money

income, while the top fifth of income earners receive about 40 percent.

3. The distribution of wealth is not the same as the distribution of income. Wealth includes assets such as houses, stocks, and bonds. Though the apparent distribution of wealth seems to be more concentrated at the top, the data used are not very accurate, nor do most summary statistics take account of workers' claims on private and public pensions.

4. Most individuals face a particular age-earnings cycle. Earnings are lowest when starting out to work at age 18 to 24. They gradually rise and peak at about age 50, then fall until retirement age. They go up usually because of increased experience, increased training, and longer working hours.

5. The marginal productivity theory of the distribution of income indicates that workers can expect to be paid their marginal revenue product. The marginal physical product is determined largely by talent, education, experience, and training.

6. Discrimination is usually defined as a situation in which a certain group is paid a lower wage than other groups for the same work. It also exists in hiring and promotions.

7. One way to invest in your own human capital is to go to college. The investment usually pays off; the rate of return is somewhere between 8 and 12 percent.

8. A definition of poverty made in relative terms means that there will always be poor in our society because the distribution of income will never be exactly equal.

9. The major income maintenance programs are Social Security (OASDI), Aid to Families with Dependent Children (AFDC), Supplemental Security Income (SSI), and the Earned Income Tax Credit Program (EITC).

10. The costs of medical care have risen because the U.S. population has been getting older and the elderly use more health care services, new technologies and medicine cost more, and third-party financing (health insurance) lessens the incentive to reduce spending on health care services.

DISCUSSION OF PREVIEW QUESTIONS

1. **What is a Lorenz curve, and what does it measure?**
   A Lorenz curve indicates the portion of total money income accounted for by given proportions of a nation's households. It is a measure of income inequality that can be found by plotting the cumulative percentage of money income on the y axis and the percentage of households on the x axis. Two major problems with using the Lorenz curve to measure income equality are that it typically does not take into account income in kind, such as food stamps and housing aid, and that it does not account for differences in household size (and effort) or age. Adjustments for these would undoubtedly reduce the degree of measured income inequality in the United States.

2. **What has been happening to the distribution of income in the United States?**
   Since World War II, the distribution of *money* income has not changed significantly, but the distribution of *total* income—which includes in-kind government transfers—has changed a great deal. Since the 1960s, *total* income inequality has been reduced significantly. The fact that more (total) income equality has been achieved in the United States in recent years is of tremendous importance, yet few people seem to be aware of this fact.

3. **What is the difference between income and wealth?**
   Income is a *flow* concept and as such is measured per unit of time; we usually state that a person's income is X dollars *per year*. Wealth is a *stock* concept; as such, it is measured at a given point in time. We usually say that a person's wealth is $200,000 or $1 million. If people save out of a given income, it is possible for their wealth to be rising while their income is constant. Technically, a person's wealth may be defined as the value of his or her assets (human and

nonhuman) minus his or her liabilities (wealth being equivalent to net worth) at some point in time.

4. Why do people earn different incomes?
The major theory to account for income differentials in market economies is the marginal productivity theory. This theory says that laborers (as well as other resources) tend to be paid the value of their marginal revenue product. Laborers who are paid less than their MRP will go to other employers who will gladly pay them more (it will be profitable for them to do

so); laborers who are being paid more than their MRP may well lose their jobs (at least in the private sector). Thus productivity differences due to age, talent (intelligence, aptitudes, coordination), experience, and training can account for income differences. Of course, imperfect markets can potentially lead to income differences, at a given productivity, due to exploitation and discrimination. Income differences can also be accounted for by differences in nonhuman wealth—individuals can earn income on their property holdings.

PROBLEMS

(Answers to the odd-numbered problems appear at the back of the book.)

30-1. It is often observed that black Americans, on average, earn less than whites. What are some possible reasons for these differences?

30-2. The accompanying graph shows Lorenz curves for two countries.

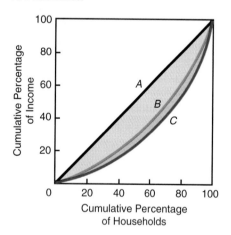

a. Which line indicates complete equality of income?
b. Which line indicates the most income inequality?
c. One country's "income inequality" is described by line *B*. Suppose that this country's income is to be adjusted for age and other variables such

that income on the *y* axis reflects *lifetime* income instead of income in a given year. Would the new, adjusted Lorenz curve move inward toward *A* or outward toward *C?*

30-3. What are two common normative standards of income distribution?

30-4. What does it mean when we say that some welfare recipients face a 120 percent marginal tax rate if they choose to go to work?

30-5. How might a program that truly made every household's income equal affect economy efficiency?

30-6. "Universal access" to health insurance has been a rallying cry for some people who wish to reform our current system. Under universal access, anyone who applies for insurance must be given it at the same rate that everybody else is paying. What might be some of the problems with such a system? (Hint: Would individuals want to join health insurance plans immediately or wait until they are sick with some long-term illness?)

30-7. What incentives do hospitals face when the federal and state governments pay for patients' health care? What incentives do government bureaucrats who work in the health care area face? What incentives do patients face when the government pays for their health care?

COMPUTER-ASSISTED INSTRUCTION

Many people believe that there is too much income inequality in the United States—that is, that the rich earn too much and the poor earn too little. This problem shows that the normal method of measuring income inequality is biased; it overstates true income inequality.

Complete problem and answer appear on disk.

INTERACTING WITH THE INTERNET

An excellent source for all sorts of statistics on the United States is the Census Bureau's site at

www.census.gov/

The holdings are quite extensive, so it may take a bit of effort to find what you want. Material includes the *Statistical Abstract of the United States,* providing details from the 1990 census, and the *County and City Data Book,* offering material on poverty. For nonmacroeconomic statistical material on the United States, you should check here first.

The Department of Health and Human Services is located at

www.os.dhhs.gov/

There you can find a number of links to its various agencies (such as the National Center for Health Statistics) and information about their programs.

For all the newest information on Medical Savings Accounts (MSAs) coming from Capitol Hill, go to

www.msanews.com/caphill.html

For general information and a whole lot more about Medicare, you can go to

www.hcfa.gov/medicare/medicare.htm

The Social Security Administration has its own Web page at

www.ssa.gov/

Recently, the founder of the CNN, Ted Turner, donated $1 billion (actually $100 million a year for ten years—he understands present value) to the United Nations. The purpose of the contribution was to help the UN fight global warming. Soon after the public announcement of the donation, Turner addressed a group of journalists on a summer day. He came into the room sweating. His first words were, "It's damn hot out there." The implication was that the extreme heat that day was a result of global warming. Is Turner right? If so, what is the best way to tackle the problem on a global scale? To answer these questions, you must learn about environmental economics. You will be looking at the costs and benefits of every action, including those already undertaken and those proposed to solve any problem of global dimension.

PREVIEW QUESTIONS

1. What is a negative externality?
2. How can poorly defined property rights create negative externalities?
3. If property rights are poorly defined, *must* negative externalities arise?
4. What is the optimal quantity of pollution?

Did You Know That . . . plants pollute? That's right, plants generate toxins as nature's attempt at protecting them from being eaten. Many of these toxins are known carcinogens. There are, for example, more known carcinogens in that cup of coffee you drink than in all of the pesticide residue on food that you consume in one year. Brussel sprouts, broccoli, mushrooms, potatoes, parsnips, and pears all contain natural carcinogens. When you think of pollution, nonetheless, you are probably thinking of smelly, foul, ugly air emanating from smokestacks across America, oil spills fouling pristine waters and killing wildlife, and other natural resources being ruined. Today, the American public, in general, appears to be willing to pay more to keep the environment "in good shape." But what does that mean?

As you might expect, after having read the previous chapters in this textbook, the economic way of thinking about the environment has a lot to do with costs. But of course your view of how to clean up the environment has a lot to do with costs also. Are you willing to give up driving your car in order to have a cleaner environment? Or would you pay $4 for a gallon of gas to help clean up the environment? In a phrase, how much of your current standard of living are you willing to give up to help the environment? The economic way of looking at ecological issues is often viewed as antienvironmental. But this is not so. Economists want to help citizens and policymakers opt for informed policies that have the maximum possible *net* benefits (benefits minus costs). As you will see, every decision in favor of "the environment" involves a trade-off.

PRIVATE VERSUS SOCIAL COSTS

Human actions often give rise to unwanted side effects—the destruction of our environment is one. Human actions generate pollutants that go into the air and the water. The question that is often asked is, Why can individuals and businesses continue to create pollution without necessarily paying directly for the negative consequences?

Until now, we've been dealing with situations in which the costs of an individual's actions are borne directly by the individual. When a business has to pay wages to workers, it knows exactly what its labor costs are. When it has to buy materials or build a plant, it knows quite well what these will cost. An individual who has to pay for car repairs or a theater ticket knows exactly what the cost will be. These costs are what we term *private costs.* **Private costs** are borne solely by the individuals who incur them. They are *internal* in the sense that the firm or household must explicitly take account of them.

What about a situation in which a business dumps the waste products from its production process into a nearby river or in which an individual litters a public park or beach? Obviously, a cost is involved in these actions. When the firm pollutes the water, people downstream suffer the consequences. They may not want to swim in or drink the polluted water. They may also be unable to catch as many fish as before because of the pollution. In the case of littering, the people who come along after our litterer has cluttered the park or the beach are the ones who bear the costs. The cost of these actions is borne by people other than those who commit the actions. The creator of the cost is not the sole bearer. The costs are not internalized by the individual or firm; they are external. When we add *external* costs to *internal,* or private, costs, we get **social costs.** Pollution problems—indeed, all problems pertaining to the environment—may be viewed as situations in which social costs exceed private costs. Because some economic participants don't pay the full social costs of their actions but rather only the smaller private costs, their actions are socially "unacceptable." In such situations in which there is a divergence between social and private costs, we

Private costs
Costs borne solely by the individuals who incur them. Also called *internal costs.*

Social costs
The full costs borne by society whenever a resource use occurs. Social costs can be measured by adding private, or internal, costs to external costs.

therefore see "too much" steel production, automobile driving, and beach littering, to pick only a few of the many possible examples.

The Costs of Polluted Air

Why is the air in cities so polluted from automobile exhaust fumes? When automobile drivers step into their cars, they bear only the private costs of driving. That is, they must pay for the gas, maintenance, depreciation, and insurance on their automobiles. However, they cause an additional cost, that of air pollution, which they are not forced to take account of when they make the decision to drive. Air pollution is a cost because it causes harm to individuals—burning eyes, respiratory ailments, and dirtier clothes, cars, and buildings. The air pollution created by automobile exhaust is a cost that individual operators of automobiles do not yet bear directly. The social cost of driving includes all the private costs plus at least the cost of air pollution, which society bears. Decisions made only on the basis of private costs lead to too much automobile driving or, alternatively, to too little money spent on the reduction of automobile pollution for a given amount of driving. Clean air is a scarce resource used by automobile drivers free of charge. They will use more of it than they would if they had to pay the full social costs.

EXTERNALITIES

When a private cost differs from a social cost, we say that there is an **externality** because individual decision makers are not paying (internalizing) all the costs. (We briefly covered this topic in Chapter 5.) Some of these costs remain external to the decision-making process. Remember that the full cost of using a scarce resource is borne one way or another by all who live in the society. That is, society must pay the full opportunity cost of any activity that uses scarce resources. The individual decision maker is the firm or the customer, and external costs and benefits will not enter into that individual's or firm's decision-making processes.

We might want to view the problem as it is presented in Figure 31-1. Here we have the market demand curve, D, for the product X and the supply curve, S_1, for product X. The

Externality
A situation in which a private cost diverges from a social cost; a situation in which the costs of an action are not fully borne by the two parties engaged in exchange or by an individual engaging in a scarce-resource-using activity. (Also applies to benefits.)

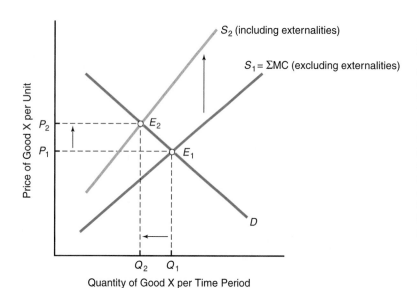

FIGURE 31-1

Reckoning with Full Social Costs
The supply curve, S_1, is equal to the horizontal summation (Σ) of the individual marginal cost curves above the respective minimum average variable costs of all the firms producing good X. These individual marginal cost curves include only internal, or private, costs. If the external costs were included and added to the private costs, we would have social costs. The supply curve would shift upward to S_2. In the uncorrected situation, the equilibrium price would be P_1 and the equilibrium quantity would be Q_1. In the corrected situation, the equilibrium price would rise to P_2 and the equilibrium quantity would fall to Q_2.

supply curve, S_1, includes only internal, or private, costs. The intersection of the demand and supply curves as drawn will be at price P_1 and quantity Q_1 (at E_1). However, we will assume that the production of good X involves externalities that the private firms did not take into account. Those externalities could be air pollution, water pollution, scenery destruction, or anything of that nature.

We know that the social costs of producing product X exceed the private costs. We show this by drawing curve S_2. It is above the original supply curve S_1 because it includes the full social costs of producing the product. If firms could be made to bear these costs, the price would be P_2 and the quantity Q_2 (at E_2). The inclusion of external costs in the decision-making process leads to a higher-priced product and a decline in quantity produced. Thus we see that when social costs are not being fully borne by the creators of those costs, the quantity produced is "excessive," because the price is too low.

CORRECTING FOR EXTERNALITIES

We can see here an easy method for reducing pollution and environmental degradation. Somehow the signals in the economy must be changed so that decision makers will take into account *all* the costs of their actions. In the case of automobile pollution, we might want to devise some method by which motorists are taxed according to the amount of pollution they cause. In the case of a firm, we might want to devise a system whereby businesses are taxed according to the amount of pollution for which they are responsible. In this manner, they would have an incentive to install pollution abatement equipment.

The Polluters' Choice

Facing an additional cost of polluting, firms will be induced to (1) install pollution abatement equipment or otherwise change production techniques so as to reduce the amount of pollution, (2) reduce pollution-causing activity, or (3) simply pay the price to pollute. The relative costs and benefits of each option for each polluter will determine which one or combination will be chosen. Allowing the choice is the efficient way to decide who pollutes and who doesn't. In principle, each polluter faces the full social cost of its actions and makes a production decision accordingly.

Is a Uniform Tax Appropriate?

It may not be appropriate to levy a *uniform* tax according to physical quantities of pollution. After all, we're talking about social costs. Such costs are not necessarily the same everywhere in the United States for the same action.

Essentially, we must establish the amount of the *economic damages* rather than the amount of the physical pollution. A polluting electrical plant in New York City will cause much more damage than the same plant in Remote, Montana. There are already innumerable demands on the air in New York City, so the pollution from smokestacks will not be cleansed away naturally. Millions of people will breathe the polluted air and thereby incur the costs of sore throats, sickness, emphysema, and even early death. Buildings will become dirtier faster because of the pollution, as will cars and clothes. A given quantity of pollution will cause more harm in concentrated urban environments than it will in less dense rural environments. If we were to establish some form of taxation to align private costs with social costs and to force people to internalize externalities, we would somehow have to come up with a measure of *economic* costs instead of *physical* quantities. But the tax, in any event, would fall on the private sector and modify private-sector economic agents' behavior. Therefore, because the economic cost for the same physical quantity of pollution would be different in different locations according to population density, the natural formation of mountains and rivers, and so forth, so-called optimal taxes on pollution would vary from location to location. (Nonetheless, a uniform tax might make sense when administrative costs, particularly the cost of ascertaining the actual economic costs, are relatively high.)

POLICY EXAMPLE
Should Car Antitheft Devices Be Subsidized?

Externalities exist for many activities. Consider the theft of automobiles. About 1.5 million cars are stolen in the United States every year. If you own an expensive car, you run a risk of having it stolen when you park on the street. Enter an antitheft device called Lojack, first used in 1986. A tiny transmitter is hidden in each Lojack-equipped car. When a car is stolen, in any of 20 major cities, the police can turn on the transmitter. About 95 percent of Lojack-equipped stolen cars are recovered and sustain less damage than other recovered stolen cars. Researchers Ian Ayres and S. D. Levitt of the National Bureau of Economic Research estimate that positive externalities are worth 15 times more than the benefit received by the Lojack-equipped car owner—when there are lots of Lojacks in the area, thieves leave the area, meaning that they don't steal non-Lojack-equipped cars either. One auto theft is eliminated annually for every three Lojacks installed in central cities.

FOR CRITICAL ANALYSIS: Who might want to subsidize Lojacks? ●

CONCEPTS IN BRIEF

- Private costs are costs that are borne directly by consumers and producers when they engage in any resource-using activity.
- Social costs are private costs plus any other costs that are external to the decision maker. For example, the social costs of driving include all the private costs plus any pollution and congestion caused.
- When private costs differ from social costs, externalities exist because individual decision makers are not internalizing all the costs that society is bearing.
- When social costs exceed private costs, we say that there are externalities.

POLLUTION

The term *pollution* is used quite loosely and can refer to a variety of by-products of any activity. Industrial pollution involves mainly air and water but can also include noise and such concepts as aesthetic pollution, as when a landscape is altered in a negative way. For the most part, we will be analyzing the most common forms, air and water pollution.

When asked how much pollution there should be in the economy, many people will respond, "None." But if we ask those same people how much starvation or deprivation of consumer products should exist in the economy, many will again say, "None." Growing and distributing food or producing consumer products creates pollution, however. In effect, therefore, there is no correct answer to how much pollution should be in an economy because when we ask how much pollution there *should* be, we are entering the realm of normative economics. We are asking people to express values. There is no way to disprove somebody's value system scientifically. One way we can approach a discussion of the "correct" amount of pollution would be to set up the same type of marginal analysis we used in our discussion of a firm's employment and output decisions. That is to say, we should pursue measures to reduce pollution only up to the point at which the marginal benefit from further reduction equals the marginal cost of further reduction.

Look at Figure 31-2. On the horizontal axis, we show the degree of cleanliness of the air. A vertical line is drawn at 100 percent cleanliness—the air cannot become any cleaner. Consider the benefits of obtaining a greater degree of air cleanliness. These benefits are represented by the marginal benefit curve, which slopes downward because of the law of diminishing marginal utility.

When the air is very dirty, the marginal benefit from air that is a little cleaner appears to be relatively high, as shown on the vertical axis. As the air becomes cleaner and cleaner, however, the marginal benefit of a little bit more air cleanliness falls.

Consider the marginal cost of pollution abatement—that is, the marginal cost of obtaining cleaner air. In the 1960s, automobiles had no pollution abatement devices. Eliminating only 20 percent of the pollutants emitted by internal-combustion engines entailed a relatively small cost per unit of pollution removed. The cost of eliminating the next 20 percent rose, though. Finally, as we now get to the upper limits of removal of pollutants from the emissions of internal-combustion engines, we find that the elimination of one more percentage point of the amount of pollutants becomes astronomically expensive. To go from 97 percent cleanliness to 98 percent cleanliness involves a marginal cost that is many times greater than going from 10 percent cleanliness to 11 percent cleanliness.

It is realistic, therefore, to draw the marginal cost of pollution abatement as an upward-sloping curve, as shown in Figure 31-2. (The marginal cost curve slopes up because of the law of diminishing returns.)

FIGURE 31-2

The Optimal Quantity of Air Pollution
As we attempt to get a greater degree of air cleanliness, the marginal cost rises until even the slightest attempt at increasing air cleanliness leads to a very high marginal cost, as can be seen at the upper right of the graph. Conversely, the marginal benefit curve slopes downward: The more pure air we have, the less we value an additional unit of pure air. Marginal cost and marginal benefit intersect at point E. The optimal degree of air cleanliness is something less than 100 percent at Q_0. The price that we should pay for the last unit of air cleanup is no greater than P_0, for that is where marginal cost equals marginal benefit.

The Optimal Quantity of Pollution

The **optimal quantity of pollution** is defined as the level of pollution at which the marginal benefit equals the marginal cost of obtaining clean air. This occurs at the intersection of the marginal benefit curve and the marginal cost curve in Figure 31-2, at point E, which is analytically exactly the same as for every other economic activity. If we increased pollution control by one more unit greater than Q_0, the marginal cost of that small increase in the degree of air cleanliness would be greater than the marginal benefit to society.

As is usually the case in economic analysis, the optimal quantity of just about anything occurs when marginal cost equals marginal benefit. That is, the optimal quantity of pollution occurs at the point at which the marginal cost of reducing (or abating) pollution is just equal to the marginal benefit of doing so. The marginal cost of pollution abatement rises as more and more abatement is achieved (as the environment becomes cleaner and cleaner, the *extra* cost of cleansing rises). The state of technology is such that early units of pollution abatement are easily achieved (at low cost), but attaining higher and higher levels of environmental quality becomes progressively more difficult (as the extra cost rises to prohibitive levels). At the same time, the marginal benefits of a cleaner and cleaner environment fall; the marginal benefit of pollution abatement declines as the concept of a cleaner and cleaner environment moves from human life-support requirements to recreation to beauty to a perfectly pure environment. The point at which the increasing marginal cost of pollution abatement equals the decreasing marginal benefit of pollution abatement defines the (theoretical) optimal quantity of pollution.

Recognizing that the optimal quantity of pollution is not zero becomes easier when we realize that it takes scarce resources to reduce pollution. It follows that a trade-off exists between producing a cleaner environment and producing other goods and services. In that sense, nature's ability to cleanse itself is a resource that can be analyzed like any other resource, and a cleaner environment must take its place with other societal wants.

Optimal quantity of pollution
The level of pollution for which the marginal benefit of one additional unit of clean air just equals the marginal cost of that additional unit of clean air.

Exercise 31.1
Visit www.econtoday.com for more about environmental protection.

CONCEPTS IN BRIEF

- The marginal cost of cleaning up the environment rises as we get closer to 100 percent cleanliness. Indeed, it rises at an increasing rate.
- The marginal benefit of environmental cleanliness falls as we have more of it.
- The optimal quantity of pollution is the quantity at which the marginal cost of cleanup equals the marginal benefit of cleanup.
- Pollution abatement is a trade-off. We trade off goods and services for cleaner air and water, and vice versa.

COMMON PROPERTY

In most cases, you do not have **private property rights**—exclusive ownership rights—to the air surrounding you, nor does anyone else. Air is a **common property**—nonexclusive—resource. Therein lies the crux of the problem. When no one owns a particular resource, no one has any incentive (conscience aside) to consider misuse of that resource. If one person decides not to pollute the air, there normally will be no significant effect on the total level of pollution. If one person decides not to pollute the ocean, there will still be approximately the same amount of ocean pollution—provided, of course, that the individual was previously responsible for only a small part of the total amount of ocean pollution.

Private property rights
Exclusive rights of ownership that allow the use, transfer, and exchange of property.

Common property
Property that is owned by everyone and therefore by no one. Air and water are examples of common property resources.

Basically, pollution occurs where we have poorly defined private property rights, as in air and common bodies of water. We do not, for example, have a visual pollution problem in people's attics. That is their own property, which they choose to keep as clean as they want, given their preferences for cleanliness as weighed against the costs of keeping the attic neat and tidy.

Where private property rights exist, individuals have legal recourse to any damages sustained through the misuse of their property. When private property rights are well defined, the use of property—that is, the use of resources—will generally involve contracting between the owners of those resources. If you own land, you might contract with another person who wants to use your land for raising cows. The contract would most likely be written in the form of a lease agreement.

INTERNATIONAL POLICY EXAMPLE
Dead Dogs in the Hills of Italy

Each September, about 110 miles north of Rome, a truffle hunt breaks out across 1,000 square miles of public land. Some 1,833 licensed "hunters" try their luck at finding truffles (a rare and hence expensive edible fungus), which grow wild on the buried roots of various trees. Truffle hunters use trained dogs to sniff out the hidden treasure. Each year, some of those dogs do not survive the truffle-hunting season. They are poisoned by bits of meat laced with strychnine—placed there by other truffle hunters seeking to reduce competition. In a recent year, more than 50 dogs died this way. The number of dogs poisoned turns out to be directly related to the market price of white Italian truffles. Several years ago, owing to a dry summer, the truffle crop dropped in half, the market price skyrocketed—and the number of dogs poisoned doubled from the previous year. Clearly, if the public land on which the truffles grow were not common property, the situation would be different.

FOR CRITICAL ANALYSIS: Assume that you owned all of the land in which Italian truffles grew. What system would you use for harvesting each year's crop? •

Voluntary Agreements and Transactions Costs

Is it possible for externalities to be internalized via voluntary agreement? Take a simple example. You live in a house with a nice view of a lake. The family living below you plants a tree. The tree grows so tall that it eventually starts to cut off your view. In most cities, no one has property rights to views; therefore, you cannot usually go to court to obtain relief. You do have the option of contracting with your neighbor, however.

Voluntary Agreements: Contracting. You have the option of paying your neighbors (contracting) to cut back the tree. You could start out with an offer of a small amount and keep going up until your neighbors agree or until you reach your limit. Your limit will equal the value you place on having an unobstructed view of the lake. Your neighbors will be willing if the payment is at least equal to the reduction in their intrinsic property value due to a stunted tree. Your offering the payment makes your neighbors aware of the social cost of their actions. The social cost here is equal to the care of the tree plus the cost suffered by you from an impeded view of the lake.

In essence, then, your offer of money income to your neighbors indicates to them that there is an opportunity cost to their actions. If they don't comply, they forfeit the money that you are offering them. The point here is that *opportunity cost always exists, whoever has property rights.* Therefore, we would expect under some circumstances that voluntary contracting will occur to internalize externalities.[1] The question is, When will voluntary agreements occur?

Transaction Costs. One major condition for the outcome just outlined above is that the **transaction costs**—all costs associated with making and enforcing agreements—must be low relative to the expected benefits of reaching an agreement. (We already looked at this topic briefly in Chapter 4.) If we expand our example to a much larger one such as air pollution, the transaction costs of numerous homeowners trying to reach agreements with the individuals and companies that create the pollution are relatively high. Consequently, we don't expect voluntary contracting to be an effective way to internalize the externality of air pollution.

Transaction costs
All costs associated with making, reaching, and enforcing agreements.

Changing Property Rights

In considering the problem of property rights, we can approach it by assuming that initially in a society, many property rights and many resources are not defined. But this situation does not cause a problem so long as no one cares to use the resources for which there are no property rights or so long as enough of these resources are available that people can have as much as they want at a zero price. Only when and if a use is found for a resource or the supply of a resource is inadequate at a zero price does a problem develop. The problem requires that something be done about deciding property rights. If not, the resource will be wasted and possibly even destroyed. Property rights can be assigned to individuals who will then assert control; or they may be assigned to government, which can maintain and preserve the resource, charge for its use, or implement some other rationing device. What we have seen with common property such as air and water is that governments have indeed attempted to take over the control of those resources so that they cannot be wasted or destroyed.

Another way of viewing the pollution problem is to argue that property rights are "sacred" and that there are property rights in every resource that exists. We can then say that each individual does not have the right to act on anything that is not his or her property. Hence no individual has the right to pollute because that amounts to using property that the individual does not specifically own.

Clearly, we must fill the gap between private costs and true social costs in situations in which we have to make up somehow for the fact that property rights are not well defined or assigned. There are three ways to fill this gap: taxation, subsidization, and regulation. Government is involved in all three. Unfortunately, government does not have perfect information and may not pick the appropriate tax, subsidy, or type of regulation. We also have to consider cases in which taxes are hard to enforce or subsidies are difficult to give out to "worthy" recipients. In such cases, outright prohibition of the polluting activity may be the optimal solution to a particular pollution problem. For example, if it is difficult to monitor the level of a particular type of pollution that even in small quantities can cause severe environmental damage, outright prohibition of such pollution may be the only alternative.

---

[1] This analysis is known as the *Coase theorem,* named after its originator, Ronald Coase, who demonstrated that negative or positive externalities do not necessarily require government intervention in situations in which property rights are defined and enforceable and transaction costs are relatively low.

Are There Alternatives to Pollution-Causing Resource Use?

Some people cannot understand why, if pollution is bad, we still use pollution-causing resources such as coal and oil to generate electricity. Why don't we forgo the use of such polluting resources and opt for one that apparently is pollution free, such as solar energy? Contrary to some people's beliefs, there is no nationwide or worldwide conspiracy to prevent us from shifting to solar power. The plain fact is that the cost of generating solar power in most circumstances is much higher than generating that same power through conventional means. We do not yet have the technology that allows us the luxury of driving solar-powered cars. Moreover, with current technology, the solar panels necessary to generate the electricity for the average town would cover massive sections of the countryside, and the manufacturing of those solar panels would itself generate pollution.

WILD SPECIES, COMMON PROPERTY, AND TRADE-OFFS

One of the most distressing common property problems concerns endangered species, usually in the wild. No one is too concerned about the quantity of dogs, cats, cattle, sheep, and horses. The reason is that virtually all of those species are private property. Spotted owls, bighorn mountain sheep, condors, and the like are typically common property. No one has a vested interest in making sure that they perpetuate in good health.

The federal government passed the Endangered Species Act in an attempt to prevent species from dying out. Initially, few individuals were affected by the rulings of the Interior Department with respect to which species were listed as endangered. Eventually, however, as more and more species were put on the endangered list, a trade-off became apparent. Nationwide, the trade-off was brought to the public's attention when the spotted owl was declared an endangered species in the Pacific Northwest. Ultimately, thousands of logging jobs were lost when the courts upheld the ban on logging in the areas presumed to be the spotted owl's natural habitat. Then another small bird, the marbled murrelet, was found in an ancient forest, causing the Pacific Lumber Company to cut back its logging practices. In 1995, the U.S. Supreme Court ruled that the federal government did have the right to regulate activities on private land in order to save endangered species.

The issues are not straightforward. Today, the earth has only .02 percent of all of the species that have ever lived. Every year, 1,000 to 3,000 new species are discovered and classified. Estimates of how many species are actually dying out vary from a high of 50,000 a year to a low of one every four years.

INTERNATIONAL POLICY EXAMPLE
Should Trading in Rhinoceros Horns Be Allowed?

Since 1977, the United Nations has banned international trade in rhino horns in order to save the species from extinction. The price for the illegal product has increased, and the amount of poaching of this once common species in Africa has skyrocketed—to the point that 90 percent of the world's rhinos have been lost. Some African countries have asked for the right to trade in rhino parts. They argue that they want to transfer ownership of rhinos to various tribes, which will then have an incentive to prevent poaching and to allow the rhino population to increase. The U.S. Humane Society and the U.S. Fish and Wildlife Service both continue to oppose the legalization of international trading in rhino products.

FOR CRITICAL ANALYSIS: Explain why protection of a species may require international trading in that species. •

CONCEPTS IN BRIEF

- A common property resource is one that no one owns—or, otherwise stated, that everyone owns.

- Common property exists when property rights are indefinite or nonexistent.

- When no property rights exist, pollution occurs because no one individual or firm has a sufficient economic incentive to care for the common property in question, be it air, water, or scenery.

- Private costs will not equal social costs when common property is at issue unless only a few individuals are involved and they are able to contract among themselves.

RECYCLING

As part of the overall ecology movement, there has been a major push to save scarce resources via recycling. **Recycling** involves reusing paper products, plastics, glass, and metals rather than putting them into solid waste dumps. Many cities have instituted mandatory recycling programs.

Recycling
The reuse of raw materials derived from manufactured products.

The benefits of recycling are straightforward. Fewer *natural* resources are used. But some economists argue that recycling does not necessarily save *total* resources. For example, recycling paper products may not necessarily save trees, according to A. Clark Wiseman, an economist for Resources for the Future in Washington, D.C. He argues that an increase in paper recycling will eventually lead to a reduction in the demand for virgin paper and thus for trees. Because most trees are planted specifically to produce paper, a reduction in the demand for trees will mean that certain land now used to grow trees will be put to other uses. The end result may be smaller rather than larger forests, a result that is probably not desired in the long run.

Recycling's Invisible Costs

The recycling of paper can also pollute. Used paper has ink on it that has to be removed during the recycling process. According to the National Wildlife Federation, the product of 100 tons of deinked (bleached) fiber generates 40 tons of sludge. This sludge has to be disposed of, usually in a landfill. A lot of recycled paper companies, however, are beginning to produce unbleached paper. In general, recycling does create waste that has to be disposed of.

There is also an issue involved in the use of resources. Recycling requires human effort. The labor resources involved in recycling are often many times more costly than the potential savings in scarce resources not used. That means that net resource use, counting all resources, may sometimes be greater with recycling than without it.

Exercise 31.2
Visit www.econtoday.com for more about recycling.

Landfills

One of the arguments in favor of recycling is to avoid a solid waste "crisis." Some people believe that we are running out of solid waste dump sites in the United States. This is perhaps true in and near major cities, and indeed the most populated areas of the country might ultimately benefit from recycling programs. In the rest of the United States, however, the data do not seem to indicate that we are running out of solid waste landfill sites. Throughout the United States, the disposal price per ton of city garbage has actually fallen. Prices vary, of course, for the 180 million tons of trash generated each year. In San Jose, California, it costs $10 a ton to dump, whereas in Morris County, New Jersey, it costs $131 a ton.

Currently, municipal governments can do three things with solid waste: burn it, bury it, or recycle it. The amount of solid waste dumped in landfills is dropping, even as total trash output rises. Consider, though, that the total garbage output of the United States for the entire twenty-first century could be put in a 30-square-mile landfill that is only 1,000 feet deep. Recycling to reduce solid waste disposal may end up costing society more resources simply because putting such waste into a landfill may be a less costly alternative.

INTERNATIONAL POLICY EXAMPLE
Can Citizens Recycle Too Much? The Case of Germany

Recycling is popular throughout the European Union, but the Germans have raised it to an art form. Germany has a law requiring that manufacturers or retailers take back their packaging or ensure that 80 percent of it is collected rather than thrown away. What is collected must be recycled or reused. The law covers about 40 percent of the country's garbage. The problem is that German consumers responded more enthusiastically than anticipated: So much plastic packaging has been collected that German recyclers do not have the capacity to use it all. Consequently, Germany has been exporting its recyclable waste to neighboring Belgium, France, and the Netherlands. France threatened to curb its imports of German recyclable trash. Belgium even argued in front of the European Parliament that Germany was engaging in unfair competition. In the meantime, the company in charge of recycling Germany's trash, Duales System Deutschland, is losing hundreds of millions of dollars a year. Considering that it costs $2,000 a ton to recycle plastic and that the price of petroleum (the main ingredient in plastic) is relatively low, the future of recycling in Germany does not look bright.

FOR CRITICAL ANALYSIS: How is it possible to recycle "too much"? •

THINKING CRITICALLY ABOUT THE MEDIA

We Are Running Out of Everything!

It is going to be a world with no more oil, natural gas, copper, or zinc. At least that is the impression one gets these days from the media. In reality, as Yale University economist William Nordhaus has discovered, the real (inflation-corrected) prices for most nonrenewable resources have fallen over the past 125 years. Real energy prices have dropped an average of 1.6 percent per year; major mineral prices have dropped 1.3 to 2.9 percent a year; even the price of land has dropped .8 percent per year. Unless supply and demand analysis is no longer valid, those numbers indicate that the supply of nonrenewable resources is increasing faster than the demand.

Should We Save Scarce Resources?

Periodically, the call for recycling focuses on the necessity of saving scarce resources because "we are running out." There is little evidence to back up this claim because virtually every natural resource has fallen in price (corrected for inflation) over the past several decades. In 1980, economist Julian Simon made a $1,000 bet with well-known environmentalist Paul Erlich. Simon bet $200 per resource that any five natural resources that Erlich picked would decline in price (corrected for inflation) by the end of the 1980s. Simon won. (When Simon asked Erlich to renew the bet for $20,000 for the 1990s, Erlich declined.) During the 1980s, the price of virtually every natural resource fell (corrected for inflation), and so did the price of every agricultural commodity. The same was true for every forest product. Though few people remember the dire predictions of the 1970s, many noneconomists throughout the world argued at that time that the world's oil reserves were vanishing. If this were true, the pretax, inflation-corrected price of gasoline would not be the same today as it was in the late 1940s (which it is).

In spite of predictions in the early 1980s by World Watch Institute president Lester Brown, real food prices did not rise. Indeed, the real price of food fell by more than 30 percent for the major agricultural commodities during the 1980s. A casual knowledge of supply and demand tells you that since demand for food did not decrease, supply must have increased faster than demand.

With respect to the forests, at least in the United States and Western Europe, there are more forests today than there were 100 years ago. In this country, the major problems of deforestation seem to be on land owned by the United States Forest Service for which private timber companies are paid almost $1 billion a year in subsidies to cut down trees.

EXAMPLE
Predicting Doom Sells Books

Since 1798, when Thomas Malthus wrote a pamphlet describing how population would outstrip the food supply, predictors of doom have made fortunes in the book market. In 1865, Stanley Jevons sold many copies of a book that predicted that Britain would run out of coal. Booklets were published by the U.S. Bureau of Mines in 1914 predicting that America would run out of oil by 1924. The U.S. Department of the Interior in 1939 and again in 1951 warned that Americans would run out of oil in 13 years. In 1972, the Club of Rome published a best-selling book, *Limits to Growth*. It predicted that we would run out of oil by the year 2000. In 1973, the World Watch Institute reiterated Malthus's prediction that the population would outstrip food production. Around that same time, such books as *The Population Bomb* became best-sellers, making predictions not too dissimilar to Malthus's.

On the environmental front, disaster has been predicted for hundreds of years, also. For example, the United Nations predicted in 1984 that the desert was claiming 50 million acres of land every year. Since that time, there has been no net advance of the desert at all. In 1992, Al Gore said that deforestation was occurring in the Amazon at a rate of 200 million acres a year. He was off by a factor of eight, but nobody seemed to mind.

The fact is, doom sells. Dispassionate economic analysis does not. After all, one can find numerous economists in the 1970s who predicted abundant food (which we have), cheap oil (corrected for inflation, oil sells for the price it did right after World War II), and copious minerals (virtually all real prices have fallen). The press tends to ignore such people even today.

FOR CRITICAL ANALYSIS: Why do you think predictions of doom sell so well but level-headed analyses do not? ●

CONCEPTS IN BRIEF

- Recycling involves reusing paper, glass, and other materials rather than putting them into solid waste dumps. Recycling does have a cost both in the resources used for recycling and in the pollution created during recycling, such as the sludge from deinking paper for reuse.

- Landfills are an alternative to recycling. Expansion of these solid waste disposal sites is outpacing demand increases.

- Resources may not be getting scarcer. The inflation-corrected price of most resources has been falling for decades.

Ted Turner meets with UN Secretary General Kofi Annan before announcing to the General Assembly his donation of $1 billion to be used exclusively to help fight global warming. What can the UN do with such funds?

The Real Issues Behind Global Warming

CONCEPTS APPLIED:
COSTS, BENEFITS, PRESENT VALUE, EXTERNALITIES

Visit www.econtoday.com for an Internet Activity that expands your understanding of these concepts.

Less than two decades ago, newsmagazines ran several years of articles on the "coming ice age." But today, we're worried about global warming—governments are ready to take drastic action to reduce so-called greenhouse gases, the cost of which may be in the trillions of dollars. The reality is that the earth has been experiencing a warming trend for the past 10,000 to 15,000 years—since the last ice age. Warm periods have alternated with ice ages for at least 2 million years; warming periods may last as long as 400,000 years.

Each year, humans release 6 billion tons of industrial carbon dioxide into the atmosphere. In contrast, 700 billion tons are released from geologic and biologic processes over which humans have no control. The latest major scientific study produced by the Intergovernmental Panel on Climate Change from the United Nations states that "none of the studies . . . have shown clear evidence that we can attribute the observed climate changes to the specific cause of increases in greenhouse gases." Nonetheless, President Clinton stated that "it is no longer a threat, but now a fact, that global warming is for real."

Looking at Costs and Benefits

Clearly, scientific debate continues on the issue of global warming. Let's look at the economics. If there is global warming and we do nothing, there are costs and benefits. If we do something, such as reduce greenhouse gases resulting from human activities, there are also costs and benefits. What are they?

Let's assume that the earth will warm by 2 degrees Celsius over the next century (that is far less, in fact, than what has actually occurred during various periods in the geologic past). There will be winners and losers. Much of the warming will be felt at night at higher latitudes, thereby extending growing seasons. The energy differential between polar and equatorial regions will decrease. On the cost side, some coastal areas may be affected by rising sea levels and warmer coastal waters, and some island populations may suffer.

Thus there are also costs and benefits for any policy to curtail global warming. Representatives of more than 100 countries who attended the Global Warming Summit in Kyoto, Japan, in December 1997 pledged that their nations would reduce greenhouse gases. Such a pledge, if carried out, may slow global warming, but it will carry a heavy price. Just in the United States, for example, reducing greenhouse gases to their 1990 levels would represent a loss to the economy of between 3 and 4 percent of total annual output—hundreds of billions of dollars. This would result from shutting down many electricity-generating and steelmaking plants that use coal.

FOR CRITICAL ANALYSIS

1. Any international treaty to reduce greenhouse gases must be approved by the Senate. Which groups in America will fight the hardest against approving such a treaty?
2. What are the arguments in favor of "doing something" about global warming, even if we are uncertain about its existence or severity?

CHAPTER SUMMARY

1. In some situations, there are social costs that do not equal private costs—that is, there are costs to society that exceed the cost to the individual. These costs may include air and water pollution, for which private individuals do not have to pay. Society, however, does bear the costs of these externalities. Few individuals or firms voluntarily consider social costs.

2. One way to analyze the problem of pollution is to look at it as an externality. Individual decision makers do not take account of the negative externalities they impose on the rest of society. In such a situation, they produce "too much" pollution and "too many" polluting goods.

3. It might be possible to ameliorate the situation by imposing a tax on polluters. The tax, however, should be dependent on the extent of the economic damages created rather than on the physical quantity of pollution. This tax will therefore be different for the same level of physical pollution in different parts of the country because the economic damage differs, depending on location, population density, and other factors.

4. The optimal quantity of pollution is the quantity at which the marginal cost of cleanup equals the mar-

ginal benefit of cleanup. Pollution abatement is a trade-off. We trade off goods and services for cleaner air and water, and vice versa.

5. Another way of looking at the externality problem is to realize that it involves the lack of definite property rights. No one owns common property resources such as air and water, and therefore no one takes account of the long-run pernicious effects of excessive pollution.

6. There are alternatives to pollution-causing resource use—for example, solar energy. We do not use solar energy because it is too expensive relative to conventional alternatives and because the creation of solar panels would generate pollution.

7. Recycling involves reusing paper, glass, and other materials rather than putting them into solid waste dumps. Recycling does have a cost both in the resources used for recycling and in the pollution created during recycling. Landfills are an alternative to recycling. These solid waste disposal sites are being expanded faster than the demand for them.

8. Resources may not be getting scarcer. The inflation-corrected price of most resources has been falling for decades.

DISCUSSION OF PREVIEW QUESTIONS

1. **What is a negative externality?**

   A negative externality exists if the social costs exceed the private costs of some activity; if parties not involved in that activity are adversely affected, negative externalities are said to exist. Pollution is an example of a negative externality; for example, transactions between automobile producers and users impose costs in the form of pollution on people who neither produce nor consume the autos.

2. **How can poorly defined property rights create negative externalities?**

   Nature's ability to cleanse itself can be considered a scarce resource, and as such, it behooves society to use this resource efficiently. However, if everyone owns natural resources, in effect *no one* owns them. Consequently, people will use natural resources, for good or for ill, as though they were free. Of course, excessive use of natural resources eventually impairs

nature's ability to cleanse itself; enter the concept of pollution (an accumulation of unwanted matter). Now the marginal cost to *private* polluters is still zero (or nearly zero), whereas the cost to society of using this (now scarce) resource is positive. In short, third parties are adversely affected when pollution results from the production and consumption of goods that lead to waste, which creates pollution.

3. **If property rights are poorly defined, *must* negative externalities arise?**

   No. If contracting costs are small and enforcement is relatively easy, voluntary contracts will arise and the full opportunity costs of actions will be accounted for. That is, when transaction costs are small, private and social costs will converge, as the parties affected contract with the parties creating the additional costs, and externalities will disappear. What is interesting is that regardless of how property rights are assigned, resources will be allocated in the same way. Of course, the specific assignment of property rights does affect the distribution of wealth, even though resource allocation is independent of the specific property right assignment; what is important for efficient resource allocation is that *someone* have property rights. It should be noted that, unfortunately, the main externalities, such as air and water pollution, are very complex, contracting costs are very high, and enforcement is difficult. As a consequence, free market solutions are not likely to emerge—indeed, they have not.

4. What is the optimal quantity of pollution?
The optimal quantity of pollution cannot be zero because at 100 percent cleanliness, the marginal cost

of pollution abatement would greatly exceed the marginal benefit. We would have too much pollution abatement; we would be using resources in a socially suboptimal manner. That means that the resources being used in pollution abatement would have a higher value elsewhere in society.

We live in a world of scarce resources. If the value we receive from spending one more dollar on cleaning up the environment is less than the value we would receive by spending that dollar on something else—such as cancer research—we are not allocating our resources efficiently if we still choose to spend that dollar on pollution abatement.

PROBLEMS

(Answers to the odd-numbered problems appear at the back of the book.)

31-1. Construct a typical supply and demand graph. Show the initial equilibrium price and quantity. Assume that the good causes negative externalities to third parties (persons not involved in the transactions). Revise the graph to compensate for that fact. How does the revised situation compare with the original?

31-2. Construct a second supply and demand graph for any product. Show the equilibrium price and quantity. Assuming that the good generates external benefits, modify the diagram to allow for them. Show the new equilibrium price and quantity. How does the revised situation compare with the original?

31-3. Suppose that polluters are to be charged by government agencies for the privilege of polluting.

  a. How should the price be set?
  b. Which firms will treat waste, and which will pay to pollute?
  c. Is it possible that some firms will be forced to close down because they now have to pay to pollute? Why might this result be good?
  d. If producers are charged to pollute, they will pass this cost on to buyers in the form of higher prices. Why might this be good?

31-4. Why has the free market not developed contractual arrangements to eliminate excess air pollution in major U.S. cities?

31-5. What is the problem with common property resources?

31-6. The accompanying graph shows external costs arising from the production of good Y.

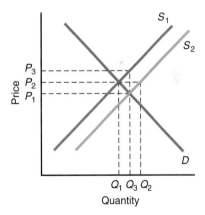

  a. Which curve includes only the private costs of producing good Y?
  b. Which supply curve includes the external costs of producing good Y?
  c. How much of good Y is produced and at what price?
  d. Who bears the cost of producing the amount of good Y in part (c)?
  e. If external costs are included, how much of good Y should be produced, and at what price should it be sold?

31-7.   The table shows the costs and benefits of removing air pollution.

Annual Units of Pollution	Annual Total Air Pollution Damage	Annual Total Costs of Air Pollution Reduction
0	$ 0	$410
1	30	260
2	70	160
3	150	80
4	270	20
5	430	0

a. Find the marginal benefits of pollution reduction.
b. Find the marginal costs of pollution reduction.
c. Assume that society is currently allowing 5 units of air pollution per year. If pollution is reduced to 3 units, what is the net gain or loss to society?
d. Suppose that all air pollution is eliminated. What would be the net gain or loss to society?
e. If air pollution were regulated efficiently, how many units of air pollution would be allowed each year?

31-8.   Examine this marginal cost and marginal benefit schedule for air cleanliness:

Quantity (%)	Marginal Benefit	Marginal Cost
0	$50,000	$ 5,000
20	45,000	10,000
40	35,000	15,000
60	25,000	25,000
80	10,000	40,000
100	0	∞

a. Graph the marginal benefit and marginal cost curves.
b. What is the optimal degree of air cleanliness?
c. How much will the optimal amount of air cleanliness cost?
d. What is the optimal amount of air pollution?
e. Would we want a level of zero pollution? Why or why not?

31-9.   Explain why it is possible to have too little pollution. What might government do to cause private individuals and businesses to generate too little pollution?

COMPUTER-ASSISTED INSTRUCTION

Environmental problems almost always involve externalities. You are asked to examine some of them in this exercise.

Complete problem and answer appear on disk.

INTERACTING WITH THE INTERNET

The Environmental Protection Agency (EPA) is located at

www.epa.gov/

It has general information about the agency and material on its programs, initiatives, rules, regulations, and legislation. It also has "Citizen Information," which describes the role individuals can play in environmental issues. An organization that takes an economist's view toward environmental issues is Resources for the Future at

www.rff.org/

So does the Political Economy Research Center (PERC) at

www.perc.org/

CHAPTER 32

PUBLIC CHOICE: The Economics of Interest Groups

During congressional hearings about Internal Revenue Service (IRS) abuse of American taxpayers, the public became privy to some shocking horror stories. Many infuriated politicians played on public outrage by calling for both the IRS and the current tax code to be abolished. In their place would be a simple tax system, such as a flat tax or a national sales tax. Gone would be the complex Internal Revenue Code and the unpardonable sins that the IRS visits on American taxpayers every year. Could a government agency such as the IRS really be abolished? Could we have a system that allowed most Americans to fill out a postcard or a simple electronic form? Before you try to answer these questions, you need to understand how interest groups operate in our system. This involves learning more about the theory of public choice.

1. What is the essence of the public-choice model?
2. Why can private choice indicate intensity of wants but public choice cannot?
3. How can logrolling enable legislators to indicate the intensity of their wants?
4. When do distributional coalitions emerge?

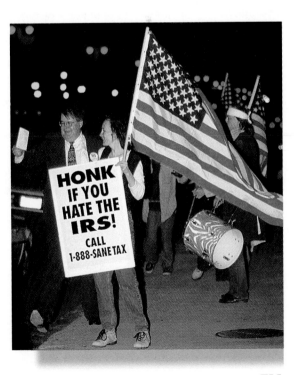

Did You Know That . . . more than 1,200 organizations whose names begin with the word *National* are listed in the Washington, D.C., telephone directory? Another 600 begin with the word *American* or *Americans*. At least 10,000 separate groups exist for the purpose of influencing government policies, and an estimated 80,000 persons are engaged in lobbying in the nation's capital at this very instant. Perhaps without realizing it, you have been introduced to a number of important **interest groups** in the last few chapters: unions, health care professionals, medical insurance companies, poverty workers, and environmentalists. What these diverse groups have in common is that they often seek to influence government legislation and change the flow of resources in our economy.

Another interest group that has had great success in influencing government is agriculture, to which you were first introduced in Chapter 4. Throughout this chapter, we will use agriculture as a key example to explain the economics of interest groups. This analysis can be subsumed under what economists call the *theory of public choice*.

COLLECTIVE DECISION MAKING: THE THEORY OF PUBLIC CHOICE

The public sector has a vast influence on the American economy. Yet the economic model used until now has applied only to the behavior of the private sector—firms and households. Such a model does not adequately explain the behavior of the public sector. We shall attempt to do so now.

Governments consist of individuals. No government actually thinks and acts; rather, government actions are the result of decision making by individuals in their roles as elected representatives, appointed officials, and salaried bureaucrats. Therefore, to understand how government works, we must examine the incentives for the people in government as well as those who would like to be in government—avowed candidates or would-be candidates for elective or appointed positions—and special-interest lobbyists attempting to get government to do something. At issue is the analysis of **collective decision making.** Collective decision making involves the actions of voters, politicians, political parties, interest groups, and many other groups and individuals. The analysis of collective decision making is usually called the **theory of public choice.** It has been given this name because it involves hypotheses about how choices are made in the public sector, as opposed to the private sector. The foundation of public-choice theory is the assumption that individuals will act within the political process to maximize their *individual* (not collective) well-being. In that sense, the theory is similar to our analysis of the market economy, in which we also assume that individuals are motivated by self-interest.

To understand public-choice theory, it is necessary to point out other similarities between the private market sector and the public, or government, sector; then we will look at the differences.

Similarities in Market and Public-Sector Decision Making

In addition to the similar assumption of self-interest being the motivating force in both sectors, there are other similarities.

Scarcity. At any given moment, the amount of resources is fixed. This means that for the private and the public sectors combined, there is a scarcity constraint. Everything that is

Interest group
Any group that seeks to cause government to change spending in a way that will benefit the group's members or to undertake any other action that will improve their lot. Also called a *special-interest group*.

Collective decision making
How voters, politicians, and other interested parties act and how these actions influence nonmarket decisions.

Theory of public choice
The study of collective decision making.

spent by all levels of government, plus everything that is spent by the private sector, must add up to the total income available at any point in time. Hence every government action has an opportunity cost, just as in the market sector.

Competition. Although we typically think of competition as a private market phenomenon, it is also present in collective action. Given the scarcity constraint government also faces, bureaucrats, appointed officials, and elected representatives will always be in competition for available government funds. Furthermore, the individuals within any government agency or institution will act as individuals do in the private sector: They will try to obtain higher wages, better working conditions, and higher job-level classifications. They will compete and act in their own, not society's, interest.

Similarity of Individuals. Contrary to popular belief, there are not two types of individuals, those who work in the private sector and those who work in the public sector; rather, individuals working in similar positions can be considered similar. The difference, as we shall see, is that the individuals in government face a different **incentive structure** than those in the private sector. For example, the costs and benefits of being efficient or inefficient differ when one goes from the private to the public sector.

Incentive structure
The system of rewards and punishments individuals face with respect to their own actions.

One approach to predicting government bureaucratic behavior is to ask what incentives bureaucrats face. Take the United States Postal Service as an example. The bureaucrats running that government corporation are human beings with IQs not dissimilar to those possessed by workers in similar positions at Microsoft or American Airlines. Yet the Postal Service does not function like either of these companies. The difference can be explained, at least in part, in terms of the incentives provided for managers in the two types of institutions. When the bureaucratic managers and workers at Microsoft make incorrect decisions, work slowly, produce shoddy products, and are generally "inefficient," the profitability of the company declines. The owners—millions of shareholders—express their displeasure by selling some of their shares of company stock. The market value, as tracked on the stock exchange, falls. But what about the U.S. Postal Service? If a manager, a worker, or a bureaucrat in the Postal Service gives shoddy service, there is no straightforward mechanism by which the organization's owners—the taxpayers—can express their dissatisfaction. Despite the Postal Service's status as a "government corporation," taxpayers as shareholders do not really own shares of stock in the organization that they can sell.

The key, then, to understanding purported inefficiency in the government bureaucracy is not found in an examination of people and personalities but rather in an examination of incentives and institutional arrangements.

Differences Between Market and Collective Decision Making

There are probably more dissimilarities between the market sector and the public sector than there are similarities.

Government, or political, goods
Goods (and services) provided by the public sector; they can be either private or public goods.

Government Goods at Zero Price. The majority of goods that governments produce are furnished to the ultimate consumers without direct money charge. **Government,** or **political, goods** can be either private goods or public goods. The fact that they are furnished to the ultimate consumer free of charge does *not* mean that the cost to society of those goods is zero, however; it only means that the price *charged* is zero. The full opportunity cost to society is the value of the resources used in the production of goods produced and provided by the government.

For example, none of us pays directly for each unit of consumption of defense or police protection. Rather, we pay for all these things indirectly through the taxes that support our governments—federal, state, and local. This special feature of government can be looked at in a different way. There is no longer a one-to-one relationship between the consumption of a government-provided good and the payment for that good. Consumers who pay taxes collectively pay for every political good, but the individual consumer may not be able to see the relationship between the taxes that he or she pays and the consumption of the good. Indeed, most taxpayers will find that their tax bill is the same whether or not they consume, or even like, government-provided goods.

Use of Force. All governments are able to engage in the legal use of force in their regulation of economic affairs. For example, governments can exercise the use of *expropriation,* which means that if you refuse to pay your taxes, your bank account and other assets may be seized by the Internal Revenue Service. In fact, you have no choice in the matter of paying taxes to governments. Collectively, we decide the total size of government through the political process, but individually we cannot determine how much service we pay for just for ourselves during any one year.

Voting Versus Spending. In the private market sector, a dollar voting system is in effect. This dollar voting system is not equivalent to the voting system in the public sector. There are, at minimum, three differences:

1. In a political system, one person gets one vote, whereas in the market system, the dollars one spends count as votes.
2. The political system is run by **majority rule,** whereas the market system is run by **proportional rule.**
3. The spending of dollars can indicate intensity of want, whereas because of the all-or-nothing nature of political voting, a vote cannot.

Majority rule
A collective decision-making system in which group decisions are made on the basis of 50.1 percent of the vote. In other words, whatever more than half of the electorate votes for, the entire electorate has to accept.

Proportional rule
A decision-making system in which actions are based on the proportion of the "votes" cast and are in proportion to them. In a market system, if 10 percent of the "dollar votes" are cast for blue cars, 10 percent of the output will be blue cars.

Ultimately, the main distinction between political votes and dollar votes here is that political outcomes may differ from economic outcomes. Remember that economic efficiency is a situation in which, given the prevailing distribution of income, consumers get the economic goods they want. There is no corresponding situation using political voting. Thus we can never assume that a political voting process will lead to the same decisions that a dollar voting process will lead to in the marketplace.

Indeed, consider the dilemma every voter faces. Usually a voter is not asked to decide on a single issue (although this happens); rather, a voter is asked to choose among candidates who present a large number of issues and state a position on each of them. Just consider the average U.S. senator who has to vote on several thousand different issues during a six-year term. When you vote for that senator, you are voting for a person who must make thousands of decisions during the next six years.

Political Participants: The Iron Triangle

In the private marketplace, we often focus on the behavior of the three key group participants: consumers, employees, and owners of businesses. In the political marketplace, these three groups correspond to constituents, bureaucrats, and members of Congress. As an example, let's consider the three groups that are involved in the agricultural industry. The principal constituents (consumers of Department of Agriculture subsidies and rules) are, of

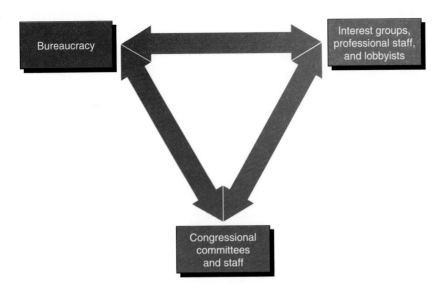

FIGURE 32-1
The Iron Triangle
The "iron triangle" is an alliance of mutual benefit among some unit within the bureaucracy, its interest or client group, and committees or subcommittees of Congress and their staff members.

course, the various interest groups that farmers have set up. These include the American Farm Bureau Federation, the National Cattlemen's Association, the National Milk Producers' Association, the Corn Growers' Association, and the Citrus Growers' Association.

The bureaucrats are within the Department of Agriculture, consisting of over 110,000 individuals who work directly for the federal government and many thousands more who work as contractors, subcontractors, or consultants to the department.

Finally, members of Congress in essence act as venture capitalists who provide the funding (via taxation) for agricultural spending programs and give overall directions to them. Within Congress, there are two major congressional committees concerned with agriculture: the House Committee on Agriculture and the Senate Committee on Agriculture, Nutrition, and Forestry. Each has seven subcommittees.

The relationship among these three groups has been said to form an "iron triangle," as shown in Figure 32-1.

EXAMPLE
Taking Over the Farm Bureaucracy

From 1933 until 1997, farmer-elected, farmer-member county committees, along with local employees of the Agricultural Department, both ran and received subsidies from the federal government. According to the Environmental Working Group in Washington, D.C., over 20 percent of county employees of the Agricultural Department received direct payments from the department as part of the farm program (to which you were first introduced in Chapter 4 using the example of price supports). The average member of the farmer-elected county committees received almost $40,000 a year, while county employees of the Agricultural Department received about $52,000 a year. As one example, county employees in agricultural department offices in Iowa during one 10-year period received $32 million in payments from the federal government, more than those in any other state.

FOR CRITICAL ANALYSIS: The way farm subsidies were given out has been compared to permitting welfare recipients to form neighborhood committees and run their own welfare programs, deciding how much each person should get every year. Is this analogy fair? ●

CONCEPTS IN BRIEF

- The theory of public choice analyzes how collective decision making is carried out in the public sector. It uses economic analysis to evaluate the operation of democratic government and assumes the self-interest of all political participants.

- Both the market sector and the public sector face scarcity, feature competition, and contain similar individuals.

- Collective decision making differs from market decision making in that many government, or political, goods are provided at zero price, collective action may involve the use of force, and political voting may lead to different results than dollar voting.

- The "iron triangle" of political participants is made up of constituents, bureaucrats, and members of Congress.

THE ECONOMICS OF INTEREST GROUPS: CONCENTRATION OF BENEFITS AND DISPERSION OF COSTS

Exercise 32.1
Visit www.econtoday.com for more about interest groups.

At the heart of how interest groups influence government in our democratic system is who benefits and who pays for government actions. By definition, interest groups represent relatively well defined groups of individuals or businesses that know what is in their own best interest. Whenever an interest group can obtain more government funding for its activities, its members experience increases in economic welfare. Taxpayers, in contrast, may end up *individually* paying very little for the concentrated benefits that go to the interest group. Thus the costs for many government actions are dispersed among all potential voters.

Distributional Coalitions

Concentrated groups in our democratic society succeed in transferring income to themselves from everybody else through what is known as **distributional coalitions.** These coalitions are small groups that gain much individually at the expense of many individuals who lose much collectively, but little individually, from the special privileges granted members of the coalition. Most collective action—action designed to influence public officials—takes place in small homogeneous groups rather than large diverse groups. Normally, individuals with a common interest will not voluntarily combine and act to further their common interest unless each individual has an incentive to participate in such collective action. Members of distributional coalitions have an incentive to act collectively to induce the median *legislator* to vote in a way that is not consistent with the interests of the median *constituent*.

Distributional coalitions
Associations such as cartels, unions, and cooperatives that are formed to gain special government privileges in order to redistribute wealth by taking small amounts from each of many people and giving large amounts to each of only a few.

EXAMPLE
Why Dairy Farmers Have Been Subsidized So Much

One clear-cut, tightly knit, homogeneous small group of individuals is dairy farmers. An examination of how much dairy farmers benefited in one state, Florida, is illustrative. In a recent year, Florida dairy farmers received $40.3 million in price support payments. Almost 100 percent went to 177 farmers. Each received an average payment in one year of $226,700. In the extreme, if the cost of these payments were borne solely by the residents of Florida, each resident in the state would pay $3.35. How much effort will the residents of Florida make—in other words, what is the value of the resources that they will spend—so as *not* to pay that $3.35 a year? At best they would pay $3.34. At worst, they would pay nothing—why should they take the effort? The 177 Florida dairy farmers, however, each have a great incentive to ensure that their payments from the federal government continue. The residents of the state have no incentive to try to stop these payments.

FOR CRITICAL ANALYSIS: There is a lobbying group aimed at helping the general public. It is called Common Cause. How much success do you think Common Cause can have? ●

Logrolling

Logrolling

The practice of exchanging political favors by elected representatives. Typically, one elected official agrees to vote for the policy of another official in exchange for the vote of the latter in favor of the former's desired policy.

Sometimes even lobbying or well-placed campaign contributions are not sufficient to get the programs that distributional coalitions want. In such cases, **logrolling** has been an effective tool. This practice involves an exchange of votes among legislators: Representative A votes for a program that benefits representative B's constituents in return for B's vote on a program that benefits A's constituents. One official may want the continuation of an army base in his hometown while another may want a new dam to be built in her home state, and so it goes. You vote for my army base, and I'll vote for your dam.

One of the major benefits of logrolling is that it allows an elected representative to demonstrate his or her *intensity* of preference, which presumably reflects the intensity of preferences of the constituents. For example, if a representative knows that it is extremely important for his constituents to keep the army base in his hometown, he may be willing to vote for a larger number of pet projects of other representatives to make sure that his pet project is passed. The problem, of course, is that typically—and our example fits perfectly—elected representatives care about geographic representation. *We have a geographically based political system.* The legislator has an incentive to represent local interests in the national legislature (Congress). The broader national issues typically suffer. National legislation becomes the vehicle for local support. The result is what is often known as "pork barrel" legislation that benefits very specific local areas.

EXAMPLE
Logrolling with Food Stamps

A classic example of logrolling as a device to facilitate the redistribution of wealth is found in government programs for "feeding the hungry." Legislators from rural farming regions and lawmakers representing low-income urban areas have forged an effective alliance to promote subsidized food distribution to the poor. Urban legislators get cheap food for their constituents, and rural legislators obtained a convenient means of disposing of the surpluses that were generated by past agricultural price supports.

Supporters of subsidized food distribution have been particularly successful in promoting and expanding the food stamp program. Indeed, according to the U.S. Senate Committee on Agriculture, the program "has been used in legislative strategy to entice urban legislators who might not otherwise support costly farm price support programs to do so in exchange for rural support for the food stamp program." This process began with the Food Stamp Act of 1964, which laid the foundation for the present-day system. In 1968, the timing of food stamp legislation was tied to the legislative cycle of the farm bill—presumably to facilitate enforcement of logrolling deals made between rural and urban legislators. In 1970, federal expenditures on food stamps were doubled, then doubled again in 1971. By this time, legislating against hunger had become a favorite activity in Congress, spurred by the rural-urban coalition of farm representatives and legislators from low-income districts.

FOR CRITICAL ANALYSIS: Why do legislators end up supporting welfare transfers in kind rather than in cash? Would recipients prefer cash or in-kind benefits? ●

CONCEPTS IN BRIEF

- Distributional coalitions, which are associations such as unions and farmers' cooperatives, are formed to gain special government privileges for their members. The members of these coalitions tend to gain a great deal individually, at the expense of the many, who lose much collectively but little individually.

- Logrolling is the exchange of votes among elected representatives, such as occurs when farm representatives agree to vote for food stamps for the poor in return for urban representatives' votes for farm subsidies.

THE ROLE OF BUREAUCRATS

Programs require people to operate them. This is manifested in government today in the form of well-established bureaucracies, in which **bureaucrats** (nonelected officials) work. Bureaucracies can exert great influence on matters concerning themselves—the amount of funding granted them and the activities in which they engage. In the political marketplace, well-organized bureaucracies can even influence the expression of public demand itself. In many cases, they organize the clientele (interest groups), coach that clientele on what is appropriate, and stick up for the "rights" of the clientele. Farm and welfare programs are good examples.

Bureaucrats
Nonelected government officials who are responsible for the day-to-day operation of government and the observance of its regulations and laws.

Gauging Bureaucratic Performance

It is tempting, but incorrect, to think of bureaucrats as mere "technocrats," executors of orders and channels of information, in this process. They have at least two incentives to make government programs larger and more resistant to attack than we might otherwise expect. First, society has decided that in general, government should not be run on a profit-making basis. Measures of performance other than bottom-line profits must be devised. In the private market, successful firms typically expand to serve more customers; although this growth is often incidental to the underlying profitability, the two frequently go hand in hand. In parallel, performance in government is often measured by the number of clients served, and rewards are distributed accordingly. As a result, bureaucrats have an incentive to expand the size of their clientele—not because it is more profitable (beneficial) to society but because that is how *bureaucrats'* rewards are structured.

In general, performance measures that are not based on long-run profitability are less effective at gauging true performance. This makes it potentially easier for the government bureaucrat to *appear* to perform well, collect rewards for measured performance, and then leave for greener pastures. To avoid this, a much larger proportion of the rewards given bureaucrats are valuable only as long as they continue being bureaucrats—large staffs, expensive offices, generous pensions, and the like. Instead of getting large current salaries (which can be saved for a rainy day), they get rewards that disappear if their jobs disappear. Naturally, this increases the incentives of bureaucrats to make sure that their jobs don't disappear.

Rational Ignorance

At this point you may well be wondering, How do these guys get away with it? The answer lies in *rational ignorance* on the part of voters, ignorance that is carefully cultivated by the members of distributional coalitions.

On most issues, there is little incentive for the individual voter to expend resources to determine how to vote. Moreover, the ordinary course of living provides most individuals with enough knowledge to decide whether they should invest in learning more about a given issue. For example, suppose that American voters were asked to decide if the sign marking the entrance to an obscure national park should be enlarged. Most voters would decide that the potential costs and benefits of this decision were negligible: The new sign is unlikely to be the size of the state of Rhode Island, and anybody who has even *heard* of the national park in question probably already has a pretty good idea of its location. Thus most voters would choose to remain rationally ignorant about the *exact* costs and benefits of enlarging the sign, implying that (1) many will choose not to vote at all and (2) those who do vote will simply flip a coin or cast their ballot based on some other, perhaps ideological, grounds.

Why Be Rationally Ignorant? For most political decisions, majority rule prevails. Only a coalition of voters representing slightly more than 50 percent of those who vote is needed. Whenever a vote is taken, the result is going to involve costs and benefits. Voters, then, must evaluate their share of the costs and benefits of any budgetary expenditure. Voters, however, are not perfectly informed. That is one of the crucial characteristics of the real world—information is a resource that is costly to obtain. Rational voters will, in fact, decide to remain at some level of ignorance about government programs because the benefits from obtaining more information may not be worth the cost, given each individual voter's extremely limited impact on the outcome of an election. For the same reason, voters will fail to inform themselves about taxes or other revenue sources to pay for proposed expenditures because they know that for any specific expenditure program, the cost to them individually will be small. At this point it might be useful to contrast this situation with what exists in the nonpolitical private market sector of the economy. In the private market sector, the individual chooses a mix of purchases and bears fully the direct and indirect consequences of this selection (ignoring for the moment the problem of externalities).

The Costs and Benefits of Voting. Voters' incentives to remain rationally ignorant about most issues are compounded by other factors. First, even if the *total* costs or benefits of a political decision are large, the costs or benefits to any *individual* voter are likely to be small. We saw this earlier with price support payments for Florida dairy farmers. Even though these payments cost Floridians as a group roughly $40 million, the cost to any individual in the state is unlikely to be much more than about $3.35. Because individual benefits (to non–dairy farmers) are unlikely to be much different, most Floridians will not bother to find out whether or not it is in their interest to favor price supports for milk (and the tax costs are actually spread among all Americans).

Why Not Vote the Rascals Out? Each time a legislator votes in favor of an interest group at the expense of the general public (and this happens almost all the time), it would seem that voters have an incentive to "vote the rascal out." The problem is that even if the legislator's constituents as a group suffer substantial costs due to dairy price supports, the loss suffered by any individual constituent is quite small. In the case of dairy price supports, few nonfarmer constituents are likely to vote against the legislator just because he or she voted in favor of dairy price supports. A constituent's vote on a legislative candidate depends on the entire *package* of positions adopted by the legislator; for nonfarmers, the issue of price supports is a trivial component of that package. Moreover, campaign contributions from farmers enable the legislator to inform constituents of his or her supportive votes on other issues of more importance to nonfarmers—education, perhaps, or child care. This typically more than offsets any votes lost due to the legislator's support for farm subsidies. Thus the activities of distributional coalitions (interest groups) create a gap between the self-interest of the median *legislator* and the self-interest of the median *constituent.* For this reason, farm subsidies and other special-interest legislation that might not be enacted if all citizens voted on the issue may still be enacted when only legislators vote.

THE ECONOMICS OF INTEREST GROUPS IN ACTION: MORE ON AGRICULTURE

The proportion of the U.S. population living on farms has dropped from 43.8 percent in 1880 to about 1.8 percent today. Although food is essential for life, citizens of the United States, a relatively wealthy nation, spend less than 10 percent of their incomes on food. The 1,925,000 farms in the United States are able to satisfy not only Americans' demand for food but also the demand by other countries' citizens in terms of food exports. The average farming family currently earns over $50,000 a year, of which $30,000 is from nonfarm activities. Each year, the federal government spends about $30,000 per farm on U.S. Department of Agriculture programs. You were introduced to one of those programs (phased out for the most part in 1996), price supports, in Chapter 4.

Exercise 32.2
Visit www.econtoday.com for more about agricultural subsidies.

The Economics and Politics of Price Supports

Traditionally, advocates of price supports argued that it was a method to guarantee a decent income for low-income farmers. More recently, it also was argued that the price support program helped keep small farmers in business, thus preventing agribusinesses from taking over all agricultural production. In fact, these political justifications made no economic sense.

Historically, the benefits of price support programs were skewed toward the owners of very large farms. The benefits of the price support programs were proportional to output:

Population Outgrowing Farmland

The media, without any critical comment, dutifully reported the outcome of several studies purporting to show that population is outgrowing farmland and therefore not everybody will have enough to eat in the not-too-distant future. One such report was generated by Population Action International. Another report with a similar conclusion was generated by the World Bank's Consultative Group on International Agricultural Research. Interestingly, economics was named the "dismal science" because the Reverend Thomas Malthus predicted the same thing in 1798. Just as his prediction was wildly off base, so, too, are those of the present-day Malthusians. Indeed, just the opposite has occurred: World food prices, corrected for inflation, have been following a general trend downward for the past 150 years. Because of improving technology, farm productivity has increased and continues to increase even faster than population.

Big farms with large incomes produce more output and therefore received more subsidies. The 15,000 largest farms in America account for more than 25 percent of all farm profits. The 125,000 largest farms obtain over 60 percent of all farm profits.

Price supports also failed to slow the move toward larger farms. Price support subsidies were made on a *per-bushel* basis, not on a *per-farm* basis. Thus the price support system provided no advantage to growing crops on small farms rather than large farms. If other factors make it more efficient to grow food on large farms, that is where it will be grown, whether there are price supports or not. Perhaps recognizing this, Congress responded by imposing upper limits on the total cash payment that any given farmer could receive. These limits, however, were easily and routinely avoided by the owners of large farms, who, for example, "leased" portions of their land to numerous tenants, each of whom qualified individually for the full allowable payment. Thus the limits had little practical impact.

There is one further point: *All* of the benefits derived from price support subsidies ultimately accrued to *landowners* on whose land price-supported crops could be grown. When price supports were announced and put into effect, the value of land rose to reflect the full value of the future price support subsidies. Thus the original landowners, rather than operators of farms, captured the benefit of the subsidies. Most of the benefits of the farm programs were capitalized into the value of the farmland. So much for helping the poor and the landless!

Acreage Restrictions

The politicians who introduced price supports realized that farmers would respond to higher prices with higher production and that the government would be stuck with the resulting surpluses. So from the beginning, *acreage restrictions* were imposed on farmers who participated in the price support programs. Farmers agreeing to acreage restrictions, or *acreage allotment programs,* as they are called, consented to reduce the number of acres they planted. There were no direct payments to the farmers for abiding by their acreage allotments; the program was merely the implicit entry fee for farmers who wished to take advantage of the price supports.

When the government required that land be removed from production, this caused a reduction in the supply of the crop. Nevertheless, if farmers were required to reduce the amount of land they used by, say, 20 percent, output at any given price did not fall by 20 percent because farmers withdrew their *least productive* land from use. Moreover, they figured out new ways of squeezing just a little more production from any given amount of land. They could still expand output by using other factors of production, such as fertilizer and machinery. To get any given level of output, they had to use more of these nonfixed inputs than they ordinarily would because they were not allowed to expand their usage of land. Thus the marginal cost of production was higher than it would have been in the absence of the acreage restriction.

The net effects of the acreage restrictions were thus twofold. First, crop surpluses were reduced but not eliminated. Second, the restrictions led to an inefficient use of resources, not from the standpoint of the farmers, for they produced at the lowest possible cost given the acreage restriction, but from the standpoint of society. Because the most efficient means of production (more land) was not permitted, more expensive inputs had to be used.

Target Prices and Deficiency Payments

Starting in 1973, government policy toward agriculture added a new twist: the **target price.** Target prices differed from price supports in that the government guaranteed that the farmer would *receive* at least the target price but permitted the price *paid* by consumers to fluctuate, depending on how much of the crop was produced. Instead of buying and storing commodities, the government simply sent a cash payment to farmers if the price paid by consumers was less than the target price. For example, if the target price for wheat was $4.50 per bushel and the price paid by consumers was $3.50, farmers received **deficiency payments** equal to the $1 difference multiplied by the number of bushels they sold on the open market. A deficiency payment, then, was simply another way to pay a subsidy to farmers without having the government actually purchase and store their crops.

The Freedom to Farm Act of 1996

For most crops, price supports, acreage restrictions, targets prices, and deficiency payments were eliminated in 1996. You can be sure, though, that farmers were not left out in the cold to battle the free market. Indeed, projected guaranteed federal government payments to farmers through the year 2002 actually exceed projected payments that would have occurred under the old agriculture subsidy programs. The new legislation also retains some "conservation" aspects, that is, paying some farmers to keep land as wildlife habitats. Additionally, price-support programs for sugar and peanuts were retained. So, in a nutshell, most farmers will be able to respond to worldwide market forces while at the same time receiving guaranteed subsidies for several years to come. Perhaps in the long run taxpayers and food consumers will be better off—provided of course that the old program isn't reinstituted after 2002.

Target price
A price set by the government for specific agricultural products. If the market clearing price was below the target price, a *deficiency payment*, equal to the difference between the market price and the target price, was given to farmers for each unit of the good they produce.

Deficiency payment
A direct subsidy paid to farmers equal to the amount of a crop they produced multiplied by the difference between the target price for that good and its market price.

Exercise 32.3
Visit www.econtoday.com for more about sugar prices.

CONCEPTS IN BRIEF

- Because price supports benefited farmers directly in proportion to the amount of farm goods they produce, owners of large farms received the bulk of the payments. Also, because the payments were tied to output and not farms, price supports did not help keep small farmers in business in preference to large farmers.

- The ultimate beneficiaries of price supports were the owners of farmland, for the price of this land rose whenever price supports were increased.

- Target prices were an attempt by the government to avoid the surpluses caused by price supports. The government set a target price, which it guaranteed that farmers would receive for their crops, but it allowed the market price to adjust to clear the market. If the market price was less than the target price, farmers received deficiency payments equal to the difference multiplied by the amount of the crop they produced.

- Target prices reduced surpluses, but they also made it more obvious that the government was making direct subsidy payments to farmers.

EUROPE'S AGRICULTURAL POLICY

While much of the world, including the United States, is moving away from complicated subsidy programs in agriculture, the European Union (a federation of 15 countries, sometimes called the EU) is not budging. Its Common Agricultural Policy (CAP) was developed between 1958 and 1962 and has not changed much since. It has all of the trappings of the former U.S. agricultural policy—minimum prices, government purchase of overproduction, government expenditures on storage, restrictions on cheaper foreign imports, and so on. European governments also subsidize exports of food products (which the U.S. government is still doing, too). The European Union has an annual budget of over $100 billion. About two-thirds of this budget is used up by the CAP.

The average family of four in Europe ends up paying $1,500 a year in artificially higher food prices. The average consumer pays in addition about $100 per person in taxes to subsidize farmers directly. The higher food price acts as a regressive tax, for poorer families spend a larger portion of their income on food. Remember from Chapter 5 that a regressive tax is one that in effect taxes low-income individuals at higher rates than higher-income individuals.

Other Results of Europe's Agricultural Policy

Some unseen, but important, additional results occur because of the CAP. Europe has slowly but surely reduced the amount of imports from the newly free Central European countries that are trying to liberalize their own markets. For example, currently Hungary can sell only about 6,000 tons of beef to the European Union each year. In the mid-1970s, it was allowed to sell over 100,000 tons. The EU dramatically restricts food imports from many other developing countries, thereby depriving those countries of opportunities to sell what they produce on their farms. Thus the CAP causes some of the poverty in developing countries, particularly those that rely on agricultural exports.

The environment in Europe is also affected negatively by the CAP. Artificially high agricultural prices cause many European farmers to damage the environment by destroying hedgerows and forests. They also use more chemical fertilizers. Why? Because they are paid their subsidies on the basis of their output, just like American farmers used to be. European farmers have an incentive to produce as much as they can, regardless of the consequences.

No Jobs Really Saved

Agricultural subsidies in Europe have been justified as a way of maintaining jobs in the agricultural sector. Ironically, in countries where farm subsidies are the most generous, the most agricultural jobs have been lost as a share of total employment. As a counterexample, consider New Zealand. It basically eliminated all of its farming sector's subsidies several years ago. In spite of dire predictions that the farming sector would be ruined, just the opposite has happened. On a lesser scale, the same has been true in Australia. These two low-subsidy, high-efficiency countries have done a much better job at keeping farmers at work than the European Union has.

One has to ask an important question here: If no agricultural jobs have been saved in the long run, why is there so much political support for keeping the Common Agricultural Policy alive in the European Union? The answer lies in the two words *long run*. The beneficiaries of agricultural subsidies in the EU aren't very interested in the long run. They can only see the costs to them in the short run of any reduction in their subsidies. So they have lobbied vigorously to keep the CAP in its present form. Consider that America's price support system was abandoned only after farmers were assured that over the following five years, they would receive a different set of subsidies that would leave them no worse off. Until some similar policy option occurs in the EU, its citizens will continue to pay higher prices for food.

The Estimated Benefits of Undistorted Agricultural Trade

In an open economy with undistorted agricultural trade, the industrially advanced economies would benefit—over and above the savings in reduced subsidies—to the tune of about $38 billion per year each. The major beneficiaries would be Japan, the European Union, and the United States. These numbers alone suggest that there must be pressure to open up world agricultural markets and to reduce farm subsidies. The future is not so rosy, however.

The cost of farming programs continues to be spread out among all consumers. Moreover, the cost per consumer in countries that become richer, all other things held constant, is falling. This is because food constitutes a declining share in the family budget as families get richer. Moreover, because of increases in farm productivity, the trend is toward lower (inflation-corrected) prices for food. Hence farmers can still maintain their relatively high subsidy levels while nonfarmers see food prices falling.

Perhaps more important, on the producer side, as the number of farmers decreases, the benefits of farm programs are more highly concentrated. This means that lobbying efforts become more efficient to undertake. In other words, as the number of farmers decreases, protection becomes relatively cheaper to obtain. Furthermore, the declining number of farmers and farms, particularly in the industrialized world, elicits a kind of sympathy. France is a particularly good example. Surveys continually show that the average French citizen believes that rural life would disappear without farm subsidies. And the French are apparently willing to continue paying those farm subsidies. Farm subsidies, though, in France and elsewhere, cannot stop the exodus from the farms. In France, for example, 3 percent of farmers and farmhands quit every year.

We can conclude that in spite of the pressures in an open economy to reduce farm subsidies throughout the world, they are not going to disappear overnight.

CONCEPTS IN BRIEF

- Voters may be rationally ignorant about many election issues because the cost of obtaining more information may outweigh the benefits of doing so. Distributional coalitions attempt to promote rational ignorance for their own benefit by hiding the true costs of the programs they favor.

- Bureaucrats often exert great influence on the course of policy because they are in charge of the day-to-day operation of current policy and provide much of the information needed to formulate future policy. Bureaucracies often organize their clientele, coach clients on what is appropriate, and stick up for their rights.

POLITICAL RENT SEEKING

Governments have the ability to bestow large monetary benefits on individuals and firms. Government can do this, for example, by picking one defense firm to become a monopoly supplier of a particular type of armament. In the past, the federal government has routinely given a monopoly to specific parts of the electromagnetic spectrum for radio and TV. In most states, the government makes it illegal for a competing electric company to go into business. In virtually all states, the government has made it illegal for individuals to practice law without a license, thereby restricting supply in the legal profession. The same is true for the medical profession.

In short, there are potentially large profits to be captured by getting the government to create a monopoly for you. We would expect, therefore, that individuals will expend resources to capture such profits. Indeed, an army of lawyers, business executives, and expert witnesses crowd the halls of Congress and the courtrooms, attempting to obtain government-bestowed monopolies, trying to prevent competition when a monopoly already exists, and engaging in various other endeavors that allow them to control a source of monopoly profits. Put yourself in the place of a monopolist who has been given monopoly power through some act of Congress. Let's say that you are making monopoly profits—profits over and above what you would make in a competitive industry—of $1 million per year. Wouldn't you be willing to spend a quarter of that million dollars a year on a lobbying effort to make sure that Congress does not change the law to allow competition in your industry? Indeed, you might spend considerably more than that to protect your $1 million annual monopoly profit. From a use-of-resources point of view, the resources that you spend in protecting your monopoly do not yield any true social product.

Of course, not all benefits from government action involve creating or maintaining monopolies. Rather, you have seen in this chapter that government actions can benefit industries through direct payments, such as agricultural subsidies. When interest groups make an attempt to influence and manipulate public policy for their own gain, they are engaged in what is known as **rent seeking.** This inelegant term comes from the economist's view of rent to which you were introduced in Chapter 29. Remember that economic rent is defined as the amount of payment to a resource over and above what is necessary to keep it in its current use and quality. Thus rent seeking involves individuals expending resources to capture economic rent that can be created by government actions. Part of the gains from getting government to benefit a particular interest group are therefore dissipated through rent-seeking activities. Those resources involve payments to lobbyists, lawyers, and accountants and occasionally direct bribes to politicians. Because the use of those resources is simply to obtain a *transfer* within society, we say that they are wasted and that inefficiency results. The problem is that in a democratic society, it is difficult to find a way around such inefficiencies. The First Amendment to the U.S. Constitution guarantees freedom of speech. By any measure, lobbying activities are speech.

Rent seeking
The use of resources in an attempt to get government to bestow a benefit on an interest group.

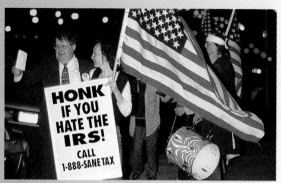

The federal agency everyone loves to hate is the IRS. The Internal Revenue Code is thousands of pages long and has become incomprehensible to the average taxpayer. Will the IRS ever be abolished?

CONCEPTS APPLIED:
INTEREST GROUPS, COALITIONS, SUBSIDIES, REGRESSIVE TAX

Visit www.econtoday.com for an Internet Activity that expands your understanding of these concepts.

L et there be no doubt about it, the IRS has treated some taxpayers unjustly. And the Internal Revenue Code has become more complicated than ever since the Tax Relief Act of 1997, passed by Congress and signed by President Clinton, added 832 pages to the code's existing 9,400 pages. So critics of both the IRS and the tax code have a strong argument for replacing them with a simple system of virtually no deductions and a flat tax rate or a national sales tax. Nevertheless, no such changes are likely anytime soon.

Interest Groups Guarantee Tax Complexity

The higher tax rates are, the more benefit an interest group can obtain by getting Congress to create a tax loophole. Given that the highest marginal tax rate is now around 40 percent, many interest groups have succeeded in getting Congress to create special benefits for them. This is known as the action-reaction syndrome, which arises when any government passes a law. A new tax is the action, and the reaction comes from the people who are affected by the tax, who then lobby for another action on the part of the government, and so on.

Any tax reform will create gainers and losers. Let's see who the losers might be if we switch to a simplified tax system with no deductions.

Interest Groups Who Will Fight Tax Reform

If all deductions and credits would be swept away under a tax reform, the first groups that would lobby against the

idea are churches, universities, and hospitals, for most charitable donations are tax-deductible. As an interest group, such nonprofits would defend the charitable deduction. One study predicted that without this deduction, individual giving would drop by 30 percent. Consider also the almost 70 million American homeowners. Most of them get to deduct interest payments on mortgages, as well as local property taxes, from their taxable income. The real estate industry and the mortgage industry would fight against removing these valuable deductions. Without them, housing prices might drop 10 to 15 percent.

There is also a large group of tax lawyers and accountants who would find their business vanish overnight if tax simplification were really enacted. They, too, form an interest group that might fight such reform.

Do Interest Groups Always Win?

The restaurant industry as an interest group fought against a reduction in the tax deductibility of business restaurant meals. It lost. Hence not every interest group succeeds in wooing Congress. True tax simplification, however, would involve so many interest groups that it is hard to imagine such reform ever occurring.

Consider the example of the Tax Reform Act of 1986, which initially simplified our federal tax system. Multiple marginal tax rates were reduced to just a few. The top marginal tax rate for high income earners dropped to 28 percent. But the simplified system didn't last long. So-called technical corrections started to be added almost immediately. More and higher marginal rates were added in 1990 and again in 1993. In 1997, almost a thousand more pages were added to the code. It's still safe to plan a career as a tax lawyer or accountant.

FOR CRITICAL ANALYSIS

1. What other groups would lose out if the federal tax system were greatly simplified?

2. Who would be the major beneficiaries of tax simplification? Why?

CHAPTER SUMMARY

1. Public-choice economics examines motives behind political entrepreneurs and the outcomes of political actions. Public-choice theory predicts that participants in the political marketplace, such as politicians, act so as to maximize their own self-interest rather than the public interest.

2. The market sector and the public sector both face scarcity, feature competition, and contain similar individuals. They differ in that many government, or political, goods are provided at zero price, collective action may involve the use of force, and political voting can lead to different results than dollar voting.

3. Distributional coalitions, which are associations such as unions and farmers' cooperatives, are formed to gain special government privileges for their members. The members of these coalitions tend to gain a great deal individually, at the expense of the many, who lose much collectively but little individually. Distributional coalitions have played a major role in the growth of government in the twentieth century.

4. Logrolling is the exchange of votes among elected representatives, such as occurs when farm representatives agree to vote for food stamps for the poor in return for urban representatives' votes for farm subsidies.

5. Bureaucrats often exert great influence on the course of policy because they are in charge of the day-to-day operation of current policy and provide much of the

information needed to formulate future policy. Bureaucracies often organize their clientele, coach clients on what is appropriate, and stick up for their rights.

6. Voters may be rationally ignorant about many election issues because the cost of obtaining more information may outweigh the benefits of doing so. Distributional coalitions attempt to promote rational ignorance for their own benefit by hiding the costs of the programs they favor.

7. Because price supports were tied to the volume of production, richer farmers received the bulk of the subsidies that resulted from price supports. Also, because price supports were paid without regard to the size of farms, they generally did not help keep smaller farmers in business.

8. Acreage restrictions were an attempt to reduce surpluses by requiring farmers to stop cultivating part of their land in return for price support subsidies. When they participated in acreage restriction programs, farmers put aside their least productive land and increased the use of nonland inputs on the remaining land in cultivation. These practices tended to offset the surplus-reducing intent of these programs.

9. Target prices avoided surpluses by making deficiency payments to farmers to make up for the difference between the government-established target price and the market clearing price.

DISCUSSION OF PREVIEW QUESTIONS

1. What is the essence of the public-choice model?
The essence of the public-choice model is that politicians, bureaucrats, and voters will act so as to maximize *their own* self-interest (or economic well-being) rather than the community's. In other words, because such people are human, they are subject to the same

motivations and drives as the rest of us. They will usually make decisions in terms of what benefits them, not society as a whole. Such an assumption permits economists to apply economic maximization principles to voters, candidates, elected officials, and policymakers.

2. Why can private choice indicate intensity of wants but public choice cannot?

If Ronald loves pasta, he can freely spend a high percentage of his income on it. The fact that he does spend a high percentage of his income on pasta and a zero percentage of his income on rice indicates the intensity of his wants. He can allocate his "dollar votes" in such a way as to reveal his preferences—and maximize his utility. In a "one-person, one-vote" situation, however, Ronald has only *one* vote. He must choose among different candidates, each of whom offers a platform of many publicly provided goods. Ronald's vote "buys" both the services he wants and the services he does not want.

3. How can logrolling enable legislators to indicate the intensity of their wants?

Logrolling is a procedure in which legislators can trade votes. If your legislator is in an oil-producing

state, she presumably has an intense desire to vote for bills that promote the interests of the oil industry. Legislators, however, also have only one vote per bill. By trading her vote on issues that she (and her constituents) are not concerned with, she can induce other legislators to vote for the pro-oil bill. Such vote trading, in effect, gives her more than one vote on this bill—and no vote on other bills.

4. When do distributional coalitions emerge?

Distributional coalitions emerge when it is possible for a small group to benefit hugely at the expense of a large group that pays *individually* relatively small amounts. For example, assume that 10,000 honey producers value government price supports at $100 million; assume also that the cost of the program to the rest of society is about 1 cent per person in taxes and 2 cents per pound more in the price for honey. Honey producers will find it profitable to form a distributional coalition, which will contribute to a politician's campaign for election or reelection. Taxpayers and honey consumers will not find it beneficial to form a counterforce to that distributional coalition.

PROBLEMS

(Answers to the odd-numbered problems appear at the back of the book.)

32-1. The existence of information and transactions costs has many implications in economics. What are some of these implications in the context of issues discussed in this chapter?

32-2. Suppose that a government program that subsidizes a certain group in America ends up generating $200,000 per year in additional income to each member of the group. The average income in America for a family of four is about $45,000 per year, and the official poverty line is much less than that. How could you explain the continued success of such a program? Under what circumstances might such a program be terminated?

32-3. A favorite presidential campaign theme in recent years has been to reduce the size, complexity, and

bureaucratic nature of the federal government. Nonetheless, the size of the federal government, however measured, continues to increase. Use the theory of public choice to explain why.

32-4. Civics textbooks often claim that voting is one of the most precious and important responsibilities of citizens living in a democracy. Yet if it is raining hard on election day, the percentage of eligible voters that actually votes usually falls. What does this tell you about the public's view of its voting responsibility?

32-5. Term limits have been declared unconstitutional at the federal level, yet many states impose term limits on their state legislatures. Use the theory of public choice to explain how such term limits might change the relationship among the participants in the political marketplace.

32-6. Suppose that you see a distinct problem in our country that needs solving. You decide to run for office and learn everything you can about the problem so that you are an expert in how government can solve it. You don't know much else about other problems or issues. How successful might you be in your campaign to be a "niche" politician? Explain.

32-7. Some people maintain that unless farmers are subsidized, many will leave the farms, a small number of farms will take over the industry (creating an oligopolistic market structure), and prices will rise correspondingly. Currently, about 1.9 million farms are in existence in the United States, and 20 percent of these farms account for 80 percent of the value of total farm output.

    a. What is the number of farms accounting for this 80 percent of output?

    b. In light of this fact, is it likely that an oligopoly, defined as a market structure with only a few firms accounting for most production and sales, will arise in the agricultural industry in the United States?

32-8. Farmers are usually required to put aside some land to take part in government programs. The objective is for farm output to be reduced. How might this objective not be achieved?

32-9. Explain how the theory of public choice predicts the persistence of agricultural subsidies in the face of a declining farm population.

32-10. Assume that farmers are poor. What is the difference between a general income redistribution program that would give poor farmers income directly and a farming subsidy program that pays them so much per unit of farm product output?

32-11. Outline what would occur if Congress eliminated all farm subsidies tomorrow. How would these events change if Congress instead indicated that it would eliminate all farm programs in 20 years?

COMPUTER-ASSISTED INSTRUCTION

Some people contend that we have had enormous food surpluses in the United States because our farmers are so efficient that they can produce more than we can eat. If that is so, how did this situation come about? Analyzing it requires the proper interpretation of graphs. Analysis reveals that food surpluses are due not to efficiency but to government price supports above the equilibrium.

Complete problem and answer appear on disk.

INTERACTING WITH THE INTERNET

You can find out about what the U.S. Department of Agriculture is doing by going to

www.usda.gov/

You can get a complete listing of the USDA's marketing programs at

www.ams.usda.gov/progserv.htm

You may especially enjoy reading about the dairy program, which is defined as one that assists "the dairy industry by providing stability and orderliness in the dairy marketplace, while at the same time assuring the availability of an abundant supply of high-quality milk and dairy products for U.S. consumers." Go to

www.ams.usda.gov/dairy/

You can also go to the "Economic Research Service" home page to get the "official source for economic analysis and information on agriculture, food, natural resources, and rural America"

www.econ.ag.gov/

You can find out about the European Union's agricultural policy by going to

www.europa.eu.int/pol/agr/en/info.htm

You can get continuing information on the flat tax by accessing House Majority Leader Dick Armey's flat tax page at

www.flattax.house.gov/

The Senate has a flat tax page, too:

www.senate.gov/~jec/fltxrept.html

CHAPTER 33
COMPARATIVE ADVANTAGE AND THE OPEN ECONOMY

When you drive in any city in the United States, you cannot help but see the evidence of international trade. The names of foreign car companies are posted at auto dealerships. Foreign cars—about 30 percent of all new cars sold in the United States—are everywhere. Moreover, when you go into an American department store, many electronic goods, branded with names that you know, come from companies in Japan or South Korea. The citizens of foreign countries are also seeing the evidence of world trade. Europeans drive some imported cars. Asians and Europeans, when they go to buy computers, will find U.S. brands, such as Apple, Compaq, Dell, Gateway, and IBM. In general, though, the average foreign consumer does not seem overwhelmed by imported American products. Nonetheless, there has been a constant stream of articles in the foreign press about how American culture is being forced on the rest of the world. How can this be happening? To understand this issue better, you must first learn about the various elements of international trade, as well as the arguments for and against free trade.

PREVIEW QUESTIONS

1. Is international trade important to the United States?
2. What is the relationship between imports and exports?
3. What is the ultimate effect of a restriction on imports?
4. What are some arguments against free trade?

Did You Know That... Boeing's latest airplane and the world's largest twin-engine jetliner, the 777, is made in Everett, Washington, but its parts come from 13 other countries, including Australia (rudder and elevators), Brazil (wingtips and dorsal fins), France (landing gears), Ireland (landing gear doors), Italy (wing outboard flaps), and Great Britain (flight computers and engines)? Japan provides 20 percent of the structure, including most of the fuselage.

The story of the Boeing 777 is repeated in the automobile industry. Parts from literally all over the world end up in cars "made in America." The running shoes you buy, the sheets you sleep on, and the clothes you put on your back are often wholly or partly produced outside the United States. Clearly, international trade today affects you whether you are aware of it or not. We are entering an age of a truly global economy. Learning about international trade is simply learning about everyday life.

THE WORLDWIDE IMPORTANCE OF INTERNATIONAL TRADE

Look at panel (a) of Figure 33-1. Since the end of World War II, world output of goods and services (world gross domestic product, or GDP) has increased almost every year until the present, when it is almost six times what it was. Look at the top line in panel (a). World trade has increased to almost 13 times what it was in 1950.

The United States figured prominently in this expansion of world trade. In panel (b) of Figure 33-1, you see imports and exports expressed as a percentage of total annual yearly

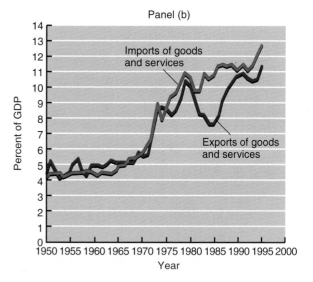

FIGURE 33-1

The Growth of World Trade

In panel (a), you can see the growth in world trade in relative terms because we use an index of 100 to represent real world trade in 1950. By the mid-1990s, that index had increased to over 1,300. At the same time, the index of world GDP (annual world income) had gone up to only around 600. World trade is clearly on the rise: Both imports and exports, expressed as a percentage of annual national income (GDP) in panel (b), have been rising.

Sources: Steven Husted and Michael Melvin, *International Economics,* 3d ed. (New York: HarperCollins, 1995), p. 11, used with permission; *International Trade;* Federal Reserve System; and U.S. Department of Commerce.

income (GDP). Whereas imports added up to barely 4 percent of annual national income in 1950, today they account for over 12 percent. International trade has definitely become more important to the economy of the United States.

INTERNATIONAL EXAMPLE
The Importance of International Trade in Various Countries

Whereas both imports and exports in the United States each account for more than 10 percent of total annual national income, in some countries the figure is much greater (see Table 33-1).

Another way to understand the worldwide importance of international trade is to look at trade flows on the world map in Figure 33-2 on page 736.

TABLE 33-1

Importance of Imports in Selected Countries

Country	Imports as a Percentage of Annual National Income
Luxembourg	95.0
Netherlands	58.0
Norway	30.0
Canada	23.5
Germany	23.0
United Kingdom	21.0
China	19.0
France	18.4
Japan	6.8

Source: International Monetary Fund.

FOR CRITICAL ANALYSIS: The yearly volume of imports in Hong Kong exceeds Hong Kong's total national income by several times. How is that possible? (Hint: Is there another reason to import a good besides wanting to consume it?) •

Exercise 33.1
Visit www.econtoday.com for more about trading with Taiwan.

WHY WE TRADE: COMPARATIVE ADVANTAGE AND EXHAUSTING MUTUAL GAINS FROM EXCHANGE

You have already been introduced to the concept of specialization and mutual gains from trade in Chapter 2. These concepts are worth repeating because they are essential to understanding why the world is better off because of more international trade. The best way to understand the gains from trade among nations is first to understand the output gains from specialization between individuals.

The Output Gains from Specialization

Suppose that a creative advertising specialist can come up with two pages of ad copy (written words) an hour or generate one computerized art rendering per hour. At the same time, a computer artist can write one page of ad copy per hour or complete one computerized art

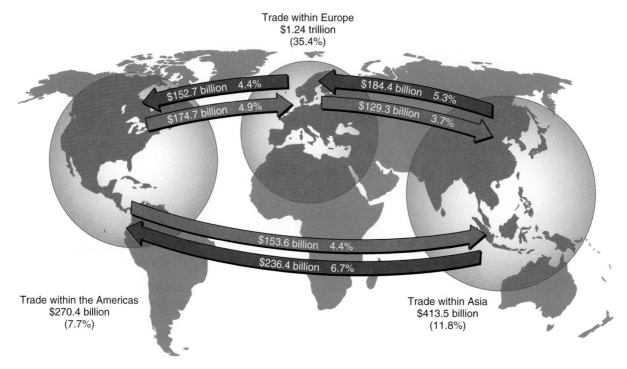

FIGURE 33-2

World Trade Flows

International merchandise trade amounts to over $3 trillion worldwide. The percentage figures show the proportion of trade flowing in the various directions.

Source: World Trade Organization (data are for 1995).

rendering per hour. Here the ad specialist can come up with more pages of ad copy per hour than the computer specialist and seemingly is just as good as the computer specialist at doing computerized art renderings. Is there any reason for the creative specialist and the computer specialist to "trade"? The answer is yes, because such trading will lead to higher output.

Consider the scenario of no trading. Assume that during each eight-hour day, the ad specialist and the computer whiz devote half of their day to writing ad copy and half to computerized art rendering. The ad specialist would create eight pages of ad copy (4 hours × 2) and four computerized art renderings (4 × 1). During that same period, the computer specialist would create four pages of ad copy (4 × 1) and four computerized art renderings (4 × 1). Each day, the combined output for the ad specialist and the computer specialist would be 12 pages of ad copy and eight computerized art renderings.

If the ad specialist specialized only in writing ad copy and the computer whiz specialized only in creating computerized art renderings, their combined output would rise to 16 pages of ad copy (8 × 2) and eight computerized art renderings (8 × 1). Overall, production would increase by four pages of ad copy per day.

The creative advertising employee has a comparative advantage in writing ad copy, and the computer specialist has a comparative advantage in doing computerized art renderings. **Comparative advantage** involves the ability to produce something at a lower opportunity cost compared to other producers, as we pointed out in Chapter 2.

Comparative advantage
The ability to produce a good or service at a lower opportunity cost compared to other producers.

TABLE 33-2
Comparative Costs of Production

Product	United States (worker-days)	France (worker-days)
Wine (1 liter)	1	1
Beer (1 liter)	1	2

Specialization Among Nations

To demonstrate the concept of comparative advantage for nations, let's take the example of France and the United States. In Table 33-2, we show the comparative costs of production of wine and beer in terms of worker-days. This is a simple two-country, two-commodity world in which we assume that labor is the only factor of production. As you can see from the table, in the United States, it takes one worker-day to produce 1 liter of wine, and the same is true for 1 liter of beer. In France, it takes one worker-day to produce 1 liter of wine but two worker-days for 1 liter of beer. In this sense, Americans appear to be just as good at producing wine as the French and actually have an **absolute advantage** in producing beer.

Absolute advantage
The ability to produce more output from given inputs of resources than other producers can.

Trade will still take place, however, which may seem paradoxical. How can trade take place if we can produce both goods at least as cheaply as the French can? Why don't we just produce both ourselves? To understand why, let's assume first that there is no trade and no specialization and that the workforce in each country consists of 200 workers. These 200 workers are divided equally in the production of wine and beer. We see in Table 33-3 that 100 liters of wine and 100 liters of beer are produced per day in the United States. In France, 100 liters of wine and 50 liters of beer are produced per day. The total daily world production in our two-country world is 200 liters of wine and 150 liters of beer.

Now the countries specialize. What can France produce more cheaply? Look at the comparative costs of production expressed in worker-days in Table 33-2. What is the cost of producing 1 liter more of wine? One worker-day. What is the cost of producing 1 liter more of beer? Two worker-days. We can say, then, that in France the opportunity cost of producing wine is less than that of producing beer. France will specialize in the activity that has the lower opportunity cost. In other words, France will specialize in its comparative advantage, which is the production of wine.

According to Table 33-4 on page 738, after specialization, the United States produces 200 liters of beer and France produces 200 liters of wine. Notice that the total world production per day has gone up from 200 liters of wine and 150 liters of beer to 200 liters of wine and 200 liters of beer per day. This was done without any increased use of resources. The gain, 50 "free" liters of beer, results from a more efficient allocation of resources worldwide. World output is greater when countries specialize in producing the goods in

TABLE 33-3
Daily World Output Before Specialization
It is assumed that 200 workers are available in each country.

Product	United States		France		World Output (liters)
	Workers	Output (liters)	Workers	Output (liters)	
Wine	100	100	100	100	200
Beer	100	100	100	50	150

Product	United States		France		World Output (liters)
	Workers	Output (liters)	Workers	Output (liters)	
Wine	—	—	200	200	200
Beer	200	200	—	—	200

TABLE 33-4

Daily World Output After Specialization
It is assumed that 200 workers are available in each country.

which they have a comparative advantage and then engage in foreign trade. Another way of looking at this is to consider the choice between two ways of producing a good. Obviously, each country would choose the less costly production process. One way of "producing" a good is to import it, so if in fact the imported good is cheaper than the domestically produced good, we will "produce" it by importing it. Not everybody, of course, is better off when free trade occurs. In our example, U.S. wine makers and French beer makers are worse off because those two *domestic* industries have disappeared.

Some people are worried that the United States (or any country, for that matter) might someday "run out of exports" because of overaggressive foreign competition. The analysis of comparative advantage tells us the contrary. No matter how much other countries compete for our business, the United States (or any other country) will always have a comparative advantage in something that it can export. In 10 or 20 years, that something may not be what we export today, but it will be exportable nonetheless because we will have a comparative advantage in producing it.

Other Benefits from International Trade: The Transmission of Ideas

Beyond the fact that comparative advantage generally results in an overall increase in the output of goods produced and consumed, there is another benefit to international trade. International trade bestows benefits on countries through the international transmission of ideas. According to economic historians, international trade has been the principal means by which new goods, services, and processes have spread around the world. For example, coffee was initially grown in Arabia near the Red Sea. Around A.D. 675, it began to be roasted and consumed as a beverage. Eventually, it was exported to other parts of the world, and the Dutch started cultivating it in their colonies during the seventeenth century and the French in the eighteenth century. The lowly potato is native to the Peruvian Andes. In the sixteenth century, it was brought to Europe by Spanish explorers. Thereafter, its cultivation and consumption spread rapidly. It became part of the American agricultural scene in the early eighteenth century.

All of the *intellectual property* that has been introduced throughout the world is a result of international trade. This includes new music, such as rock and roll in the 1950s and hip-hop and grunge in the 1990s. It includes the software applications that are common for computer users everywhere.

New processes have been transmitted through international trade. One of those involves the Japanese manufacturing innovation which emphasized redesigning the system rather than running the existing system in the best possible way. Inventories were reduced to just-in-time levels by reengineering machine setup methods. Just-in-time inventory control is now common in American factories.

INTERNET EXERCISE

Exercise 33.2
Visit www.econtoday.com for more about Korea.

INTERNATIONAL EXAMPLE
International Trade and the Alphabet

Even the alphabetic system of writing that appears to be the source of most alphabets in the world today was spread through international trade. According to some scholars, the Phoenicians, who lived on the long, narrow strip of Mediterranean coast north of Israel from the ninth century B.C. to around 300 B.C., created the first true alphabet. Presumably, they developed the alphabet to keep international trading records on their ships rather than having to take along highly trained scribes.

FOR CRITICAL ANALYSIS: Before alphabets were used, how might have people communicated in written form? •

THE RELATIONSHIP BETWEEN IMPORTS AND EXPORTS

The basic proposition in understanding all of international trade is this:

In the long run, imports are paid for by exports.[1]

The reason that imports are ultimately paid for by exports is that foreigners want something in exchange for the goods that are shipped to the United States. For the most part, they want goods made in the United States. From this truism comes a remarkable corollary:

Any restriction of imports ultimately reduces exports.

This is a shocking revelation to many people who want to restrict foreign competition to protect domestic jobs. Although it is possible to protect certain U.S. jobs by restricting foreign competition, it is impossible to make *everyone* better off by imposing import restrictions. Why? Because ultimately such restrictions lead to a reduction in employment in the export industries of the nation.

Think of exports as simply another way of producing goods. International trade is merely an economic activity like all others; it is a production process that transforms exports into imports.

INTERNATIONAL EXAMPLE
The Importation of Priests into Spain

Imports affect not only goods but also services and the movement of labor. In Spain, some 3,000 priests retire each year, but barely 250 young men are ordained to replace them. Over 70 percent of the priests in Spain are now over the age of 50. The Spanish church estimates that by 2005, the number of priests will have fallen to half the 20,441 who were active in Spain in 1990. The Spanish church has had to seek young seminarians from Latin America under what it calls Operation Moses. It is currently subsidizing the travel and training of an increasing number of young Latin Americans to take over where native Spaniards have been before.

FOR CRITICAL ANALYSIS: How might the Spanish Catholic church induce more native Spaniards to become priests? •

---

[1]We have to modify this rule by adding that in the short run, imports can also be paid for by the sale (or export) of real and financial assets, such as land, stocks, and bonds, or through an extension of credit from other countries.

INTERNATIONAL COMPETITIVENESS

"The United States is falling behind." "We need to stay competitive internationally." These and similar statements are often heard in government circles when the subject of international trade comes up. There are two problems with this issue. The first has to do with a simple definition. What does "global competitiveness" really mean? When one company competes against another, it is in competition. Is the United States like one big corporation, in competition with other countries? Certainly not. The standard of living in each country is almost solely a function of how well the economy functions *within that country,* not relative to other countries.

Another problem arises with respect to the real world. According to the Institute for Management Development in Lausanne, Switzerland, the United States continues to lead the pack in world competitiveness, ahead of Japan, Hong Kong, Germany, and the rest of the European Union. According to the report, America's top-class ranking is due to the rapid U.S. economic recovery from its 1990–1991 recession, widespread entrepreneurship, and a decade of economic restructuring. Other factors include America's sophisticated financial system and large investments in scientific research.

CONCEPTS IN BRIEF

- Countries can be better off materially if they specialize in producing goods for which they have a comparative advantage.

- It is important to distinguish between absolute and comparative advantage; the former refers to the ability to produce a unit of output with fewer physical units of input; the latter refers to producing output that has the lowest opportunity cost for a nation.

- Different nations will always have different comparative advantages because of differing opportunity costs due to different resource mixes.

ARGUMENTS AGAINST FREE TRADE

Numerous arguments are raised against free trade. They mainly point out the costs of trade; they do not consider the benefits or the possible alternatives for reducing the costs of free trade while still reaping benefits.

The Infant Industry Argument

A nation may feel that if a particular industry were allowed to develop domestically, it could eventually become efficient enough to compete effectively in the world market. Therefore, if some restrictions were placed on imports, domestic producers would be given the time needed to develop their efficiency to the point where they would be able to compete in the domestic market without any restrictions on imports. In graphic terminology, we would expect that if the protected industry truly does experience improvements in production techniques or technological breakthroughs toward greater efficiency in the future, the supply

Infant industry argument
The contention that tariffs should be imposed to protect from import competition an industry that is trying to get started. Presumably, after the industry becomes technologically efficient, the tariff can be lifted.

curve will shift outward to the right so that the domestic industry can produce larger quantities of each and every price. This **infant industry argument** has some merit in the short run and has been used to protect a number of industries in their infancy around the world. Such a policy can be abused, however. Often the protective import-restricting arrangements remain even after the infant has matured. If other countries can still produce more cheaply, the people who benefit from this type of situation are obviously the stockholders (and specialized factors of production that will earn economic rents) in the industry that is still being protected from world competition. The people who lose out are the consumers, who must pay a price higher than the world price for the product in question. In any event, it is very difficult to know beforehand which industries will eventually survive. In other words, we cannot predict very well the specific infant industries that should be protected. Note that when we talk about which industry "should be" protected, we are in the realm of normative economics. We are making a value judgment, a subjective statement of what *ought to be*.

 EXAMPLE
An Infant Industry Blossoms Due to Protection from Foreign Imports: The Case of Marijuana

Marijuana was made illegal in the United States in the 1930s, but just as for many other outlawed drugs, a market for it remained. Until about 25 years ago, virtually all the marijuana consumed in the United States was imported. Today, earnings from the burgeoning and increasingly high-tech "pot" industry are estimated at $35 billion a year, making it the nation's biggest cash crop (compared to corn at $15 billion). Starting with President Richard Nixon in the 1970s, the federal government has in effect ended up protecting the domestic marijuana industry from imports by declaring a war on drugs. Given virtually no foreign competition, the American marijuana industry expanded and invested millions in developing both more productive and more potent seeds as well as more efficient growing technologies. Domestic marijuana growers now dominate the high end of a market in which consumers pay $300 to $500 an ounce for a reengineered home-grown product. New growing technologies allow domestic producers, using high-intensity sodium lights, carbon dioxide, and advances in genetics, to produce a kilogram of the potent sinsemilla variety every two months in a space no bigger than a phone booth.

FOR CRITICAL ANALYSIS: What has spurred domestic producers to develop highly productive indoor growing methods? ●

Countering Foreign Subsidies and Dumping

Another strong argument against unrestricted foreign trade has to do with countering other nations' subsidies to their own producers. When a foreign government subsidizes its producers, our producers claim that they cannot compete fairly with these subsidized foreigners. To the extent that such subsidies fluctuate, it can be argued that unrestricted free trade will seriously disrupt domestic producers. They will not know when foreign governments are going to subsidize their producers and when they are not. Our competing industries will be expanding and contracting too frequently.

Dumping
Selling a good or a service abroad at a price below its cost of production or below the price charged in the home market.

The phenomenon called *dumping* is also used as an argument against unrestricted trade. **Dumping** occurs when a producer sells its products abroad at a price below its cost of production or below the price that is charged in the home market. Although cries of dumping against foreign producers are often heard, they typically occur only when the foreign nation is in the throes of a serious recession. The foreign producer does not want to slow down its production at home. Because it anticipates an end to the recession and doesn't want to hold large inventories, it dumps its products abroad at prices below its costs. This does, in fact, disrupt international trade. It also creates instability in domestic production and therefore may impair commercial well-being at home.

POLICY EXAMPLE
Are America's Antidumping Laws Fair?

The International Trade Administration (ITA) is supposed to render fair and impartial judgment on American companies' dumping complaints. Its track record is far from fair, however. Over 95 percent of cases have been decided against foreign firms. When an American company wants to block foreign competition, it can go to the ITA. For example, when the American supercomputer company Cray Research lost out to a subsidiary of NEC of Japan in bidding to supply a five-year leasing contract on a weather-simulating supercomputer, it went to the ITA. It claimed that NEC was selling the weather supercomputer for about 20 percent of its cost, thereby "dumping" in the U.S. market. The ITA agreed. The U.S. government now imposes tariffs of between 173 and 454 percent on all supercomputers imported from Japan. The result is that Cray no longer faces any competition from the Japanese. During the four-week investigation of NEC, the ITA required NEC to respond to an almost 200-page questionnaire written in English.

FOR CRITICAL ANALYSIS: Who loses because of the ITA's behavior? ●

Protecting American Jobs

Perhaps the argument used most often against free trade is that unrestrained competition from other countries will eliminate American jobs because other countries have lower-cost labor than we do. (Less restrictive environmental standards in other countries might also lower their costs relative to ours.) This is a compelling argument, particularly for politicians from areas that might be threatened by foreign competition. For example, a representative from an area with shoe factories would certainly be upset about the possibility of constituents' losing their jobs because of competition from lower-priced shoe manufacturers in Brazil and Italy. But of course this argument against free trade is equally applicable to trade between the states.

Economists David Gould, G. L. Woodbridge, and Roy Ruffin examined the data on the relationship between increases in imports and the rate of unemployment. Their conclusion was that there is no causal link between the two. Indeed, in half the cases they studied, when imports increased, unemployment fell.

Another issue has to do with the cost of protecting American jobs by restricting international trade. The Institute for International Economics examined just the restrictions on foreign textiles and apparel goods. U.S. consumers pay $9 billion a year more to protect jobs in those industries. That comes out to $50,000 a year for each job saved in an industry in which the average job pays only $20,000 a year. Similar studies have yielded similar results: Restrictions on the imports of Japanese cars have cost $160,000 *per year* for every job saved in the auto industry. Every

---

THINKING CRITICALLY ABOUT THE MEDIA

Unfair Competition from Low-Wage Countries

Protectionists are able to get the media to carry stories about how low-wage countries are stealing American jobs. The facts are exactly the opposite. The highest-labor-cost country in the world is Germany, and it is also the largest exporter in the world. The United States, Japan, France, and the United Kingdom also have relatively high labor costs, and they, too, are some of the world's biggest exporters. If the low-wage myth were true, the United States would never be able to compete with, say, Mexican labor. Yet the reality is that the United States exports much more to Mexico than it imports. Finally, both the World Bank and the Organization for Economic Cooperation and Development have done exhaustive studies on the issue. Their conclusion is that there is no evidence that trade with low-wage countries results in large-scale job losses to industrial countries. The real competition for American manufacturing comes from high-wage countries, such as Germany and Japan.

job preserved in the glass industry has cost $200,000 each and every year. Every job preserved in the U.S. steel industry has cost an astounding $750,000 per year.

In the long run, the industries that have had the most protection—textiles, clothing, and iron and steel—have seen the most dramatic reductions in employment in the United States.

CONCEPTS IN BRIEF

- The infant industry argument against free trade contends that new industries should be protected against world competition so that they can become technologically efficient in the long run.

- Unrestricted foreign trade may allow foreign governments to subsidize exports or foreign producers to engage in dumping—selling products in other countries below their cost of production. To the extent that foreign export subsidies and dumping create more instability in domestic production, they may impair our well-being.

WAYS TO RESTRICT FOREIGN TRADE

There are many ways in which international trade can be stopped or at least stifled. These include quotas and taxes (the latter are usually called *tariffs* when applied to internationally traded items). Let's talk first about quotas.

Quotas

Quota system
A government-imposed restriction on the quantity of a specific good that another country is allowed to sell in the United States. In other words, quotas are restrictions on imports. These restrictions are usually applied to one or several specific countries.

Under the **quota system,** individual countries or groups of foreign producers are restricted to a certain amount of trade. An import quota specifies the maximum amount of a commodity that may be imported during a specified period of time. For example, the government might not allow more than 50 million barrels of foreign crude oil to enter the United States in a particular year.

Consider the example of quotas on textiles. Figure 33-3 presents the demand and the supply curves for imported textiles. In an unrestricted import market, the equilibrium quantity

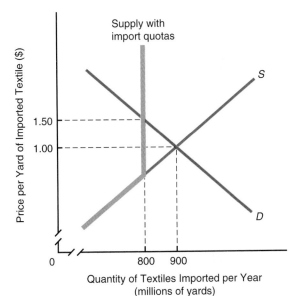

FIGURE 33-3

The Effect of Quotas on Textile Imports
Without restrictions, 900 million yards of textiles would be imported each year into the United States at the world price of $1.00 per yard. If the federal government imposes a quota of only 800 million yards, the effective supply curve becomes vertical at that quantity. It intersects the demand curve at the new equilibrium price of $1.50 per yard.

imported is 900 million yards at a price of $1 per yard (expressed in constant-quality units). When an import quota is imposed, the supply curve is no longer *S*. Rather, the supply curve becomes vertical at some amount less than the equilibrium quantity—here, 800 million yards per year. The price to the American consumer increases from $1.00 to $1.50. The domestic suppliers of textiles obviously benefit by an increase in revenues because they can now charge a higher price.

INTERNATIONAL EXAMPLE
Health Disputes in Trade: A Type of Quota

Governments, including our own, have figured out that they can impose implicit quotas on imports by claiming health concerns. Whenever a government convincingly claims that an imported product poses a health problem to its citizens, it can restrict imports of that product. The result is a benefit to domestic producers of goods that compete with the imported product.

Consider some examples. When "mad cow disease" was discovered in British cattle, the French and the rest of Europe imposed a ban on the importation of British beef. At the time of the ban, there was scant scientific evidence that the bovine disease had any effect on humans. French farmers were ecstatic at the ban. Around the same time, Russia prohibited the importation of frozen U.S. chickens. It used a vaguely worded concern about salmonella as its reason. And the ban on imports of American beef into the European Union was justified for many years over concern there that U.S. cattle farmers used hormones. In the United States, we have been able to keep out Mexican avocados because of concerns over fruit flies. California avocado growers have been the main beneficiaries.

FOR CRITICAL ANALYSIS: How do market forces tend to minimize food-related health concerns? •

Voluntary Quotas. Quotas do not have to be explicit and defined by law. They can be "voluntary." Such a quota is called a **voluntary restraint agreement (VRA)**. In the early 1980s, the United States asked Japan voluntarily to restrain its exports to the United States. The Japanese government did so, limiting itself to exporting 2.8 million Japanese automobiles. Today, there are VRAs on machine tools and textiles.

The opposite of a VRA is a **voluntary import expansion (VIE)**. Under a VIE, a foreign government agrees to have its companies import more foreign goods from another country. The United States almost started a major international trade war with Japan in 1995 over just such an issue. The U.S. government wanted Japanese automobile manufacturers voluntarily to increase their imports of U.S.-made automobile parts.

Voluntary restraint agreement (VRA)
An official agreement with another country that "voluntarily" restricts the quantity of its exports to the United States.

Voluntary import expansion (VIE)
An official agreement with another country in which it agrees to import more from the United States.

Tariffs

We can analyze tariffs by using standard supply and demand diagrams. Let's use as our commodity laptop computers, some of which are made in Japan and some of which are made domestically. In panel (a) of Figure 33-4, you see the demand and supply of Japanese laptops. The equilibrium price is $1,000 per constant-quality unit, and the equilibrium quantity is 10 million per year. In panel (b), you see the same equilibrium price of $1,000, and the *domestic* equilibrium quantity is 5 million units per year.

Now a tariff of $500 is imposed on all imported Japanese laptops. The supply curve shifts upward by $500 to S_2. For purchasers of Japanese laptops, the price increases to

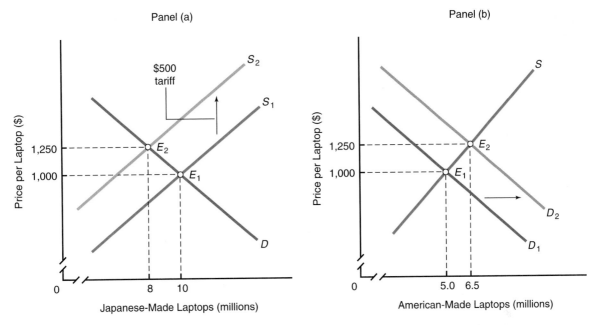

FIGURE 33-4

The Effect of a Tariff on Japanese-Made Laptop Computers
Without a tariff, the United States buys 10 million Japanese laptops per year at an average price of $1,000, as shown in panel (a). American producers sell 5 million domestically made laptops, also at $1,000 each, as shown in panel (b). A $500-per-laptop tariff will shift the Japanese import supply curve to S_2 in panel (a), so that the new equilibrium is at E_2, with price $1,250 and quantity sold reduced to 8 million per year. The demand curve for American-made laptops (for which there is no tariff) shifts to D_2 in panel (b). Sales increase to 6.5 million per year.

$1,250. The quantity demanded falls to 8 million per year. In panel (b), you see that at the higher price of imported Japanese laptops, the demand curve for American-made laptops shifts outward to the right to D_2. The equilibrium price increases to $1,250, but the equilibrium quantity increases to 6.5 million units per year. So the tariff benefits domestic laptop producers because it increases the demand for their products due to the higher price of a close substitute, Japanese laptops. This causes a redistribution of income from American consumers of laptops to American producers of laptops.

Tariffs in the United States.   In Figure 33-5 on page 746, we see that tariffs on all imported goods have varied widely. The highest rates in the twentieth century occurred with the passage of the Smoot-Hawley Tariff in 1930.

POLICY EXAMPLE
Did the Smoot-Hawley Tariff Worsen the Great Depression?

By 1930, the unemployment rate had almost doubled in a year. Congress and President Hoover wanted to do something that would help stimulate U.S. production and reduce unemployment. The result was the Smoot-Hawley Tariff, which set tariff schedules for over 20,000 products, raising duties on imports by an average of 52 percent. This attempt to improve the domestic economy at the expense of foreign economies backfired. Each trading partner of the United States in turn imposed its own high tariffs, including the United Kingdom, the Netherlands, France, and Switzerland. The result was a massive reduction in international trade by an incredible 64 percent in three years. Some believe that the ensuing world Great Depression was partially caused by such tariffs.

FOR CRITICAL ANALYSIS: The Smoot-Hawley Tariff has been labeled a "beggar thy neighbor" policy. Explain why. ●

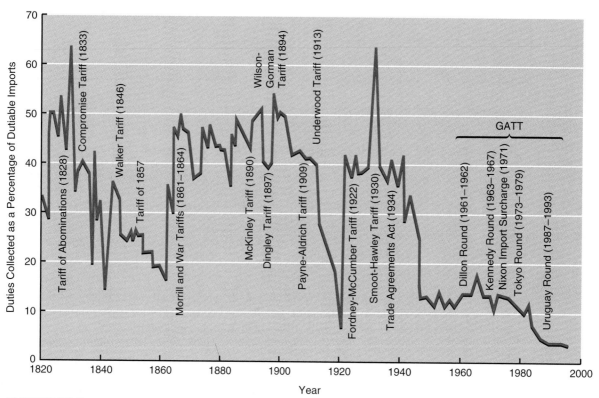

FIGURE 33-5

Tariff Rates in the United States Since 1820

Tariff rates in the United States have bounced around like a football; indeed, in Congress, tariffs are a political football. Import-competing industries prefer high tariffs. In the twentieth century, the highest tariff we have had was the Smoot-Hawley Tariff of 1930, which was almost as high as the "tariff of abominations" in 1828.

Source: U.S. Department of Commerce.

Current Tariff Laws. The Trade Expansion Act of 1962 gave the president the authority to reduce tariffs by up to 50 percent. Subsequently, tariffs were reduced by about 35 percent. In 1974, the Trade Reform Act allowed the president to reduce tariffs further. In 1984, the Trade and Tariff Act resulted in the lowest tariff rates ever. All such trade agreement obligations of the United States are carried out under the auspices of the **General Agreement on Tariffs and Trade (GATT),** which was signed in 1947. Member nations of GATT account for more than 85 percent of world trade. As you can see in Figure 33-5, there have been a number of rounds of negotiations to reduce tariffs since the early 1960s. The latest round was called the Uruguay Round because that is where the meetings were held.

General Agreement on Tariffs and Trade (GATT)
An international agreement established in 1947 to further world trade by reducing barriers and tariffs.

The World Trade Organization (WTO)

The Uruguay Round of the General Agreement on Tariffs and Trade (GATT) was ratified by 117 nations at the end of 1993. A year later, in a special session of Congress, the entire treaty was ratified. On January 1, 1995, the new **World Trade Organization (WTO)** replaced GATT. As of 1998, the WTO had 132 member nations, plus 32 observer governments, all but two of which have applied for membership. WTO decisions have concerned such topics as the European Union's "banana wars," in which the EU's policies were determined to favor unfairly many former European colonies in Africa, the Caribbean, and the Pacific at the expense of banana-exporting countries in Latin America. Now those former colonies no longer have a privileged position in European markets.

World Trade Organization (WTO)
The successor organization to GATT, it handles all trade disputes among its 132 member nations.

On a larger scale, the WTO fostered the most important and far-reaching global trade agreement ever covering financial institutions, including banks, insurers, and investment companies. The more than 100 signatories to this new treaty have legally committed themselves to giving foreigners more freedom to own and operate companies in virtually all segments of the financial services industry.

CONCEPTS IN BRIEF

- One means of restricting foreign trade is a quota system. Beneficiaries of quotas are the importers who get the quota rights and the domestic producers of the restricted good.

- Another means of restricting imports is a tariff, which is a tax on imports only. An import tariff benefits import-competing industries and harms consumers by raising prices.

- The main international institution created to improve trade among nations is the General Agreement on Tariffs and Trade (GATT). The latest round of trade talks under GATT, the Uruguay Round, led to the creation of the World Trade Organization.

今世紀最大の陰謀ミステリー。

ケヴィン・コスナー

オリヴァーストーン監督作品

JFK

Nowhere is American culture more pervasive than in the film industry. Although American movies account for a small share of American exports, they spread American culture worldwide.

Is American Culture More Pervasive than It Used to Be?

CONCEPTS APPLIED:

INTERNATIONAL TRADE, EXPORTS, IMPORTS, GOODS, SERVICES

Visit www.econtoday.com for an Internet Activity that expands your understanding of these concepts.

International trade, expressed as a percentage of yearly total national income in the United States, has been rising since the 1950s. This mirrors a worldwide trend—world output has been growing at an annual rate of 3.5 percent, and world trade has been growing at almost double that rate over the past 10 years.

Why Trade Has Been Growing

At least two forces having been driving the increased flows of goods and funds: (1) trade liberalization—reduced trade barriers due to such agreements as NAFTA and the WTO—and (2) rapidly falling computing and communication costs, which together have sharply reduced some of the natural barriers of time and space that separate national markets. Consider panel (a) of Figure 33-6. There you see how the price of a three-minute telephone call from New York to London in constant 1998 dollars has fallen. But this does not explain the domination of American culture worldwide.

The Export of American Services

The fact that Americans can talk more cheaply to the rest of the world and vice versa does not explain the spread of American culture. Cheaper international telephone calls are, however, indicative of a major shift in American trade. Trade involves both goods and services, and over the past two decades, the United States has been exporting a larger and larger amount of services. That accounts for much of the expansion of American culture.

Foreign tourism in the United States now amounts to about $80 billion of service exports a year. When foreign-

ers visit the United States, they are buying service exports, such as the use of hotel rooms. Obviously, the more tourists who come to the United States, the more likely that foreign residents will learn about American culture and may take some of our culture back to their home countries.

More important, the sale of intellectual property in the form of American movies and TV programs has skyrocketed. Foreign sales account for over half of our film industry's $25 billion box office revenues. Less impressive, but similar, numbers have risen in the American music business. The sale of U.S. intellectual property abroad is perhaps the single most important factor in spreading American culture.

The United States is also exporting each year more than $20 billion of the services of many of its professionals, such as engineers, architects, accountants, investment bankers, and marketing specialists. Finally, foreign students constitute over 3 percent of all U.S. college students. When they go back to their own countries, they take with them a strong dose of American culture.

Panel (b) of Figure 33-6 shows the recent trend in the export of services versus the export of goods. In the past two decades, exports of services have grown twice as rapidly as exports of goods.

FOR CRITICAL ANALYSIS

1. What are some foreign influences on American culture?
2. French law requires that 40 percent of radio and TV be of French origin. Portrayed as a law to preserve French culture, how does this restriction affect foreign trade?

Panel (a)

Panel (b)

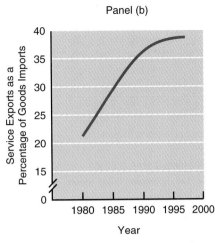

FIGURE 33-6

Cheaper International Phone Calls and the Increased Export of Services
In panel (a), you can see that the price of a three-minute call between London and New York, expressed in 1998 dollars, has fallen dramatically. In panel (b), the percentage of export services relative to goods exports has been growing steadily.
Sources: World Bank; U.S. Department of Commerce.

CHAPTER SUMMARY

1. It is important to distinguish between absolute and comparative advantage. A person or country that can do everything "better" (with higher labor productivity) than every other person or country has an absolute advantage in everything. Nevertheless, trade will still be advantageous if people will specialize in the things that they do *relatively* best, exploiting their respective comparative advantage.

2. Along with the gains, there are costs from trade. Certain industries and their employees may be hurt if trade is opened up.

3. An import quota restricts the quantity of imports coming into the country. It therefore raises the price. Consumers always lose.

4. When governments impose "voluntary" quotas, they are called voluntary restraint agreements (VRAs).

5. An import tariff raises the domestic price of foreign produced goods. It therefore allows domestic producers to raise their own prices. The result is a higher price to consumers, a lower quantity of imports, and a lower volume of international trade.

6. The main international institution created to improve trade among nations was the General Agreement on Tariffs and Trade (GATT), replaced in 1993 by the World Trade Organization (WTO).

DISCUSSION OF PREVIEW QUESTIONS

1. **Is international trade important to the United States?**
The direct impact of international trade on the United States, as measured by the ratio of exports to GDP, is relatively small compared with many other nations. Yet it is hard to imagine what life would be like without international trade. Initially, many prices would rise rapidly, but eventually domestic production would begin on many goods we presently import. However, consider life without imports of coffee, tea, bananas, and foreign wines, motorcycles, automobiles, televisions, VCRs, and hundreds of other goods from food and clothing to electronics—not to mention vital imports such as bauxite, chromium, cobalt, nickel, platinum, and tin.

2. **What is the relationship between imports and exports?**
Because foreigners eventually want real goods and services as payment for the real goods and services they export to other countries, ultimately each country pays for its imports with its exports. Hence on a worldwide basis, the value of imports must equal the value of exports.

3. **What is the ultimate effect of a restriction on imports?**

   Because each country must pay for its imports with its exports, any restriction on imports must ultimately lead to a reduction in exports. So even though restrictions on imports because of tariffs or quotas may benefit workers and business owners in the protected domestic industry, such protection will harm workers and business owners in the export sector in general.

4. **What are some arguments against free trade?**

   The infant industry argument maintains that new industries developing domestically need protection from foreign competitors until they are mature enough themselves to compete with foreigners, at which time protection will be removed. One problem with this argument is that it is difficult to tell when maturity has been reached, and domestic industries will fight against weaning. Moreover, this argument is hardly relevant to most U.S. industries. It is also alleged (and is true to a large extent) that free trade leads to instability for specific domestic industries as comparative advantage changes in a dynamic world. Nations that have traditionally held a comparative advantage in the production of some goods occasionally lose that advantage (while gaining others). Regional hardships are a result, and protection of domestic jobs is demanded.

PROBLEMS

(Answers to the odd-numbered problems appear at the back of the book.)

33-1. Examine the hypothetical table of worker-hours required to produce caviar and wheat in the United States and in Russia.

Product	United States	Russia
Caviar (ounce)	6 worker-hours	9 worker-hours
Wheat (bushel)	3 worker-hours	6 worker-hours

   a. What is the opportunity cost to the United States of producing one ounce of caviar per time period? What is the opportunity cost to the United States of producing one bushel of wheat?

   b. What is the opportunity cost to Russia of producing one ounce of caviar per time period? What is the opportunity cost to Russia of producing one bushel of wheat?

   c. The United States has a comparative advantage in what? Russia has a comparative advantage in what?

33-2. Study the hypothetical table of worker-hours required to produce coffee and beans in Colombia and Turkey.

Product	Colombia	Turkey
Coffee (pound)	2 worker-hours	1 worker-hour
Beans (pound)	6 worker-hours	2 worker-hours

   a. What is the opportunity cost to Colombia of producing one pound of coffee? One pound of beans?

   b. What is the opportunity cost to Turkey of producing one pound of coffee? One pound of beans?

   c. Colombia has a comparative advantage in what? Turkey has a comparative advantage in what?

33-3. Assume that the United States can produce *everything* with fewer labor-hours than any other country on earth. Even under this extreme assumption, why would the United States still trade with other countries?

33-4. Examine the hypothetical table of worker-hours required to produce cheese and cloth in two countries, A and B.

Product	Country A	Country B
Cheese (pound)	$\frac{2}{3}$ worker-hours	2 worker-hours
Cloth (yard)	$\frac{1}{2}$ worker-hours	1 worker-hour

a. What is the opportunity cost to country A of producing one pound of cheese? One yard of cloth?

b. What is the opportunity cost to country B of producing one pound of cheese? One yard of cloth?

c. Country A has a comparative advantage in what?

d. Country B has a comparative advantage in what?

33-5. The use of tariffs and quotas to restrict imports results in higher prices and is successful in reducing imports. In what way is using a tariff different from using a quota?

33-6. Two countries, Austral Land and Boreal Land, have the following production opportunities shown in the graphs.

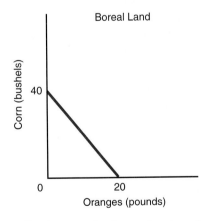

a. Who has an absolute advantage in corn? In oranges?

b. Who has a comparative advantage in corn? In oranges?

c. Should Boreal Land export at all? If so, which good should it export?

d. What is Austral Land's opportunity cost of oranges in terms of corn? What is Boreal Land's opportunity cost of corn in terms of oranges?

33-7. The accompanying graph gives the supply and demand for grapes. S and D are the United States' supply and demand curves, respectively. Assume that the world price of grapes is 50 cents per pound.

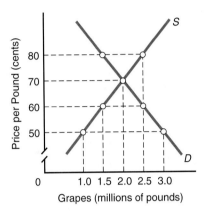

a. How many pounds are produced domestically? How many pounds are imported?

b. Suppose that the United States imposes a 10-cent-per-pound tariff. How many pounds would now be produced domestically? How many pounds would be imported? What are the U.S. government's revenues?

c. Suppose now that the government imposes a 20-cent-per-pound tariff. What price can domestic growers now receive for their grapes? How many pounds will domestic growers produce? How many pounds will be imported? What are government revenues?

33-8. If free trade is so obviously beneficial, why are there so many restrictions on international trade? (Hint: Review the theory presented in Chapter 32.)

33-9. Explain why an increase in taxes on imports (tariffs) will reduce exports.

33-10. Assume that a country with whom the United States is trading imposes restrictions on U.S.-made imports into that country. Will the United States be better off by simultaneously imposing restrictions on the other country's imports into the United States? Why or why not?

COMPUTER-ASSISTED INSTRUCTION

We show that the combination of specialization and exchange is the next best thing to a free lunch.

Complete problem and answer appear on disk.

INTERACTING WITH THE INTERNET

You can access all of the activities of the World Trade Organization (WTO) at

www.wto.org

If you are interested in the rules of international trade, go to

www.un.or.at/uncitral/

You can go to the home page of Michigan State University's Center for International Business Education and Research to access a wide variety of international business resources on the Web. Visit them at

ciber.bus.msu.edu/busres/statinfo.htm

You can get information on trade patterns in every region of the world by accessing the CIA's *World Fact Book* at

www.odci.gov/cia/publications/factbook/index.html

If you are interested in taking a closer look at world trade patterns, go to the World Trade Analyzer at

www.tradecompass.com/trade_analyzer/

CHAPTER 34

EXCHANGE RATES AND THE BALANCE OF PAYMENTS

In the past, if you traveled to any of the 15 countries of the European Union, you would have had to exchange dollars for each country's national currency. By the time you read this, in at least some of those 15 countries, you may have to exchange your dollars only once for a new currency called the *euro*. If all of the European Union's members agreed on a single currency, they would represent an economy 18 percent larger than that of the United States. Does this mean that the almighty dollar will lose its preeminence in world financial markets? Before you can answer such a question, you need to know more about international financial transactions and the determinants of foreign exchange rates.

PREVIEW QUESTIONS

1. What is the difference between the balance of trade and the balance of payments?
2. What is a foreign exchange rate?
3. What is a flexible exchange rate system?
4. What is the gold standard?

Did You Know That . . . every day, around the clock, over $1 trillion of foreign currencies are traded? Along with that trading come news headlines, such as "The dollar weakened today," "The dollar is clearly overvalued," "The dollar is under attack," and "Members of the Group of Seven agreed to prevent the dollar from rising." If you are confused by such newspaper headlines, join the crowd. Surprisingly, though, if you regard the dollar, the pound, the deutsche mark, the yen, and the franc as assets that are subject to the laws of supply and demand, the world of international finance can be quickly demystified. Perhaps the first step is to examine the meaning of the terms used with respect to America's international financial transactions during any one-year period.

THE BALANCE OF PAYMENTS AND INTERNATIONAL CAPITAL MOVEMENTS

Governments typically keep track of each year's economic activities by calculating the gross domestic product—the total of expenditures on all newly produced final domestic goods and services—and its components. In the world of international trade also, a summary information system has been developed. It relates to the balance of trade and the balance of payments. The **balance of trade** refers specifically to exports and imports of *goods and services* as discussed in Chapter 33. When international trade is in balance, the value of exports equals the value of imports.

The **balance of payments** is a more general concept that expresses the total of all economic transactions between two nations, usually for a period of one year. Each country's balance of payments summarizes information about that country's exports, imports, earnings by domestic residents on assets located abroad, earnings on domestic assets owned by foreign residents, international capital movements, and official transactions by central banks and governments. In essence, then, the balance of payments is a record of all the transactions between households, firms, and government of one country and the rest of the world. Any transaction that leads to a *payment* by a country's residents (or government) is a deficit item, identified by a negative sign (−) when we examine the actual numbers that might be in Table 34-1. Any transaction that leads to a *receipt* by a country's residents (or government) is a surplus item and is identified by a plus sign (+) when actual numbers are considered. Table 34-1 gives a listing of the surplus and deficit items on international accounts.

Balance of trade
The value of goods and services bought and sold in the world market.

Balance of payments
A summary record of a country's economic transactions with foreign residents and governments over a year.

TABLE 34-1
Surplus (+) and Deficit (−) Items on the International Accounts

Surplus Items (+)	Deficit Items (−)
Exports of merchandise	Imports of merchandise
Private and governmental gifts from foreigners	Private and governmental gifts to foreigners
Foreign use of domestically owned transportation	Use of foreign-owned transportation
Foreign tourists' expenditures in this country	Tourism expenditures abroad
Foreign military spending in this country	Military spending abroad
Interest and dividend receipts from foreigners	Interest and dividends paid to foreigners
Sales of domestic assets to foreigners	Purchases of foreign assets
Funds deposited in this country by foreigners	Funds placed in foreign depository institutions
Sales of gold to foreigners	Purchases of gold from foreigners
Sales of domestic currency to foreigners	Purchases of foreign currency

Accounting Identities

Accounting identities
Statements that certain numerical measurements are equal by accepted definition (for example, "assets equal liabilities plus stockholders' equity").

Accounting identities—definitions of equivalent values—exist for financial institutions and other businesses. We begin with simple accounting identities that must hold for families and then go on to describe international accounting identities.

If a family unit is spending more than its current income, such a situation necessarily implies that the family unit must be doing one of the following:

1. Drawing down its wealth. The family must reduce its money holdings, or it must sell stocks, bonds, or other assets.
2. Borrowing.
3. Receiving gifts from friends or relatives.
4. Receiving public transfers from a government, which obtained the funds by taxing others. (A transfer is a payment, in money or in goods or services, made without receiving goods or services in return.)

In effect, we can use this information to derive an identity: If a family unit is currently spending more than it is earning, it must draw on previously acquired wealth, borrow, or receive either private or public aid. Similarly, an identity exists for a family unit that is currently spending less than it is earning: It must increase its wealth by increasing its money holdings or by lending and acquiring other financial assets, or it must pay taxes or bestow gifts on others. When we consider businesses and governments, each unit in each group faces its own identities or constraints; thus, net lending by households must equal net borrowing by businesses and governments.

Even though our individual family unit's accounts must balance, in the sense that the identity discussed previously must hold, sometimes the item that brings about the balance cannot continue indefinitely. *If family expenditures exceed family income and this situation is financed by borrowing, the household may be considered to be in disequilibrium because such a situation cannot continue indefinitely.* If such a deficit is financed by drawing on previously accumulated assets, the family may also be in disequilibrium because it cannot continue indefinitely to draw on its wealth; eventually, it will become impossible for that family to continue such a lifestyle. (Of course, if the family members are retired, they may well be in equilibrium by drawing on previously acquired assets to finance current deficits; this example illustrates that it is necessary to understand circumstances fully before pronouncing an economic unit in disequilibrium.)

Individual households, businesses, and governments, as well as the entire group of households, businesses, and governments, must eventually reach equilibrium. Certain economic adjustment mechanisms have evolved to ensure equilibrium. Deficit households must eventually increase their incomes or decrease their expenditures. They will find that they have to pay higher interest rates if they wish to borrow to finance their deficits. Eventually their credit sources will dry up, and they will be forced into equilibrium. Businesses, on occasion, must lower costs and/or prices—or go bankrupt—to reach equilibrium.

When nations trade or interact, certain identities or constraints must also hold. Nations buy goods from people in other nations; they also lend to and present gifts to people in other nations. If a nation interacts with others, an accounting identity ensures a balance (but not an equilibrium, as will soon become clear). Let's look at the three categories of balance of payments transactions: current account transactions, capital account transactions, and official reserve account transactions.

Current Account Transactions

During any designated period, all payments and gifts that are related to the purchase or sale of both goods and services constitute the current account in international trade. The three major types of current account transactions are the exchange of merchandise goods, the exchange of services, and unilateral transfers.

Merchandise Trade Transactions. The largest portion of any nation's balance of payments current account is typically the importing and exporting of merchandise goods. During 1998, for example, as can be seen in lines 1 and 2 of Table 34-2, the United States exported $679.0 billion of merchandise and imported $907.3 billion. The balance of merchandise trade is defined as the difference between the value of merchandise exports and the value of merchandise imports. For 1998, the United States had a balance of merchandise trade deficit because the value of its merchandise imports exceeded the value of its merchandise exports. This deficit amounted to $228.3. billion (line 3).

Service Exports and Imports. The balance of (merchandise) trade has to do with tangible items—you can feel them, touch them, and see them. Service exports and imports have to do with invisible or intangible items that are bought and sold, such as shipping, insurance, tourist expenditures, and banking services. Also, income earned by foreigners on U.S. investments and income earned by Americans on foreign investments are part of service imports and exports. As can be seen in lines 4 and 5 of Table 34-2, in 1998, service exports were $256.7 bil-

> **THINKING CRITICALLY ABOUT THE MEDIA**
>
> ### Perhaps the Trade Situation Isn't So Bad After All
>
> Virtually every month, there appears a spate of articles and TV sound bites about America's trade deficit. The official numbers may be in error, however, for they ignore the multinational nature of modern firms. American international trade figures exclude sales in other countries for subsidiaries of American-owned companies. Because of a host of other problems, some government economists believe that they are underestimating the value of U.S. exports by as much as 10 percent. Economist Paul Krugman of Stanford University agrees. When he added up the value of world exports and compared it with the value of world imports, he found that the planet Earth had a trade deficit of $100 billion! Perhaps we are trading with aliens and don't know it.

TABLE 34-2

U.S. Balance of Payments Account, 1998 Figures are Billions of Dollars.

Current Account		
(1) Exports of goods	+679.0	
(2) Imports of goods	−907.3	
(3) Balance of trade		−228.3
(4) Exports of services	+256.7	
(5) Imports of services	−175.7	
(6) Balance of services		+81.0
(7) Balance on goods and services [(3) + (6)]		−147.3
(8) Net unilateral transfers	−41.1	
(9) Balance on current account		−188.4
Capital Account		
(10) U.S. capital going abroad	−451.7	
(11) Foreign capital coming into the United States	+657.8[a]	
(12) Balance on capital account [(10) + (11)]		+206.1
(13) Balance on current account plus balance on capital account [(9) + (12)]		−17.7
(14) Official transactions		+17.7
(15) Total (balance)		$00.00

Sources: U.S. Department of Commerce, Bureau of Economic Analysis; U.S. Department of the Treasury.
[a]Includes a $54 billion statistical discrepancy, probably unaccounted capital inflows, many of which relate to the illegal drug trade.

Exercise 34.1
Visit www.econtoday.com for more
about balance of trade.

lion and service imports were $175.7 billion. Thus the balance of services was about $81.0 billion in 1998 (line 6). Exports constitute receipts or inflows into the United States and are positive; imports constitute payments abroad or outflows of money and are negative.

When we combine the balance of merchandise trade with the balance of services, we obtain a balance on goods and services equal to −$147.3 billion in 1998 (line 7).

Unilateral Transfers. Americans give gifts to relatives and others abroad. The federal government grants gifts to foreign nations. Foreigners give gifts to Americans, and some foreign governments have granted money to the U.S. government. In the current account, we see that net unilateral transfers—the total amount of gifts given by Americans minus the total amount received by Americans from abroad—came to −$41.1 billion in 1998 (line 8). The fact that there is a minus sign before the number for unilateral transfers means that Americans gave more to foreigners than foreigners gave to Americans.

Balancing the Current Account. The balance on current account tracks the value of a country's exports of goods and services (including military receipts plus income on investments abroad) and transfer payments (private and government) relative to the value of that country's import of goods and services (including military payments) and transfer payments (private and government). In 1998, it was a *negative* $188.4 billion.

If exports exceed imports, a current account surplus is said to exist; if imports exceed exports, a current account deficit is said to exist. A current account deficit means that we are importing more than we are exporting. Such a deficit must be paid for by the export of money or money equivalent, which means a capital account surplus.

Capital Account Transactions

In world markets, it is possible to buy and sell not only goods and services but also real and financial assets. This is what the capital accounts are concerned with in international transactions. Capital account transactions occur because of foreign investments—either foreigners investing in the United States or Americans investing in other countries. The purchase of shares of stock on the London stock market by an American causes an outflow of funds. The building of a Japanese automobile factory in the United States causes an inflow of funds. Any time foreigners buy U.S. government securities, that is an inflow of funds. Any time Americans buy foreign government securities, there is an outflow of funds. Loans to and from foreigners cause outflows and inflows.

Line 10 of Table 34-2 indicates that in 1998, the value of private and government capital going out of the United States was −$451.7 billion, and line 11 shows that the value of private and government capital coming into the United States (including a statistical discrepancy) was $657.8 billion. U.S. capital going abroad constitutes payments or outflows and is therefore negative. Foreign capital coming into the United States constitutes receipts or inflows and is therefore positive. Thus there was a positive net capital movement of $206.1 billion into the United States (line 12). This is also called the balance on capital account.

There is a relationship between the current account and the capital account, assuming no interventions by the central banks of nations. *The current account and the capital account must sum to zero. Stated differently, the current account deficit equals the capital account surplus. Any nation experiencing a current account deficit, such as the United States, must also be running a capital account surplus.*

POLICY EXAMPLE
Should the United States Worry About Its Continuing Trade Deficit?

Look at the current account line at the bottom of Figure 34-1. On a current account basis, the United States has been "in the red" for years. Some people believe that trade deficits are bad and should be reduced. Further, they believe that maintaining a trade deficit creates an untenable foreign debt burden for Americans. It is true that total indebtedness to foreigners increased from nothing in 1987 to almost $1 trillion in 1999. This is not surprising, for every year that we have a current account deficit, Americans must borrow more from foreigners to finance extra spending at home. The real question is, should we be worried?

The simple answer is probably not. First of all, the trade deficit enables us to increase domestic investment and consumption over and above what we could do without the trade deficit. More important, foreigners cannot invest in the United States *unless* there is a current account deficit. Look at the top line in Figure 34-1, where you see the capital account, which mirrors the current account. Most of the so-called increased net foreign debt is not really debt but rather investments in equity and in real assets that foreigners have made in the United States. They obviously believe strongly in the stability and soundness of our

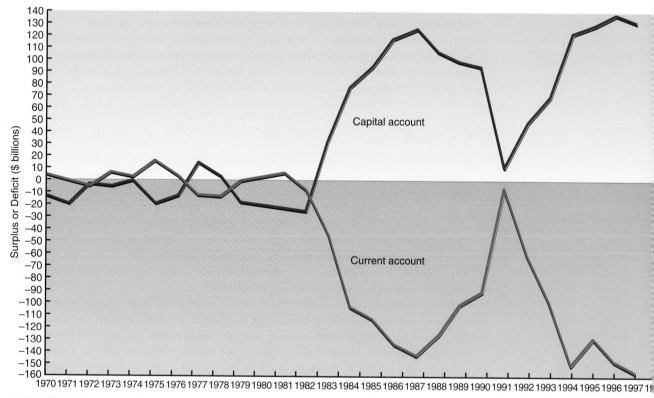

FIGURE 34-1

The Relationship Between the Current Account and the Capital Account
To some extent, the capital account is the mirror image of the current account. We can see this in the years since 1970. When the current account was in surplus, the capital account was in deficit. When the current account was in deficit, the capital account was in surplus. Indeed, virtually the only time foreigners can invest in America is when the current account is in deficit.

Sources: International Monetary Fund; *Economic Indicators.*

economy. If we want continued foreign investment here, we have to expect continued current account deficits.

FOR CRITICAL ANALYSIS: Politicians are still worried about trade deficits. Why? ●

Official Reserve Account Transactions

The third type of balance of payments transaction concerns official reserve assets, which consist of the following:

1. Foreign currencies
2. Gold
3. **Special drawing rights (SDRs),** which are reserve assets that the International Monetary Fund created to be used by countries to settle international payment obligations
4. The reserve position in the International Monetary Fund
5. Financial assets held by an official agency, such as the U.S. Treasury Department

Special drawing rights (SDRs)
Reserve assets created by the International Monetary Fund that countries can use to settle international payments.

To consider how official reserve account transactions occur, look again at Table 34-2. The surplus in our capital account was +$206.1 billion. But the deficit in our current account was −$188.4 billion, so we had a net deficit on the combined accounts (line 13) of −$17.7 billion. In other words, the United States obtained less in foreign money in all its international transactions than it used. How is this deficiency made up? By our central bank drawing down its existing balances of foreign monies, or the +$17.7 billion in official transactions shown on line 14 in Table 34-2. You might ask why there is a plus sign on line 14. The answer is because this represents a *supply* (an inflow) of foreign exchange into our international transactions.

The balance (line 15) in Table 34-2 is zero, as it must be with double-entry bookkeeping. Our balance of payments deficit is measured by the official transactions figure on line 14. (This does not mean we are in equilibrium, though.)

What Affects the Balance of Payments?

A major factor affecting our balance of payments is our rate of inflation relative to that of our trading partners. Assume that the rate of inflation in the United States and in France is equal. All of a sudden, our inflation rate increases. The French will find that American products are becoming more expensive, and we will export fewer of them to France. Americans will find French products relatively cheaper, and we will import more. The converse will occur if our rate of inflation suddenly falls relative to that of France. All other things held constant, whenever our rate of inflation exceeds that of our trading partners, we expect to see a "worsening" of our balance of trade and payments. Conversely, when our rate of inflation is less than that of our trading partners, other things being constant, we expect to see an "improvement" in our balance of trade and payments.

Another important factor that sometimes influences our balance of payments is our relative political stability. Political instability causes *capital flight:* Owners of capital in countries anticipating or experiencing political instability will often move assets to countries that are politically stable, such as the United States. Hence our balance of payments is likely to improve whenever political instability looms in other nations in the world.

CONCEPTS IN BRIEF

- The balance of payments reflects the value of all transactions in international trade, including goods, services, financial assets, and gifts.

- The merchandise trade balance gives us the difference between exports and imports of tangible items. Merchandise trade transactions are represented by exports and imports of tangible items.

- Service exports and imports relate to the trade of intangible items, such as shipping, insurance, and tourist expenditures. They include income earned by foreigners on U.S. investments and income earned by Americans on foreign investments.

- Unilateral transfers involve international private gifts and federal government grants or gifts to foreign nations.

- When we add the balance of merchandise trade plus the balance of services and take account of net unilateral transfers, we come up with the balance on current account, which is a summary statistic taking into account the three transactions that form the current account transactions.

- There are also capital account transactions that relate to the buying and selling of financial and real assets. Foreign capital is always entering the United States, and American capital is always flowing abroad. The difference is called the balance on capital account.

- Another type of balance of payments transaction concerns the official reserve assets of individual countries, or what is often simply called official transactions. By standard accounting convention, official transactions are exactly equal to but opposite in sign to the balance of payments of the United States.

- Our balance of trade can be affected by our relative rate of inflation and by political instability elsewhere compared to the stability that exists in the United States.

DETERMINING FOREIGN EXCHANGE RATES

When you buy foreign products, such as French wine, you have dollars with which to pay the French winemaker. The French winemaker, however, cannot pay workers in dollars. The workers are French, they live in France, and they must have francs to buy goods and services in that country. There must therefore be some way of exchanging dollars for the francs that the winemaker will accept. That exchange occurs in a **foreign exchange market,** which in this case specializes in exchanging francs and dollars. (When you obtain foreign currencies at a bank or an airport currency exchange, you are participating in the foreign exchange market.)

Foreign exchange market
The market for buying and selling foreign currencies.

The particular exchange rate between francs and dollars that would prevail depends on the current demand for and supply of francs and dollars. In a sense, then, our analysis of the exchange rate between dollars and francs will be familiar, for we have used supply and demand throughout this book. If it costs you 20 cents to buy one franc, that is the **foreign exchange rate** determined by the current demand for and supply of francs in the foreign exchange market. The French person going to the foreign exchange market would need five francs to buy one dollar. (Our numbers are, of course, hypothetical.)

Foreign exchange rate
The price of one currency in terms of another.

We will continue our example in which the only two countries in the world are France and the United States. Now let's consider what determines the demand for and supply of foreign currency in the foreign exchange market.

Demand for and Supply of Foreign Currency

You wish to buy some French Bordeaux wine. To do so, you must have French francs. You go to the foreign exchange market (or your American bank). Your desire to buy the French wine therefore causes you to offer (supply) dollars to the foreign exchange market. Your demand for French francs is equivalent to your supply of American dollars to the foreign exchange market. Indeed:

> **Every U.S. transaction concerning the importation of foreign goods constitutes a supply of dollars and a demand for some foreign currency, and the opposite is true for export transactions.**

In this case, this import transaction constitutes a demand for French francs.

In our example, we will assume that only two goods are being traded, French wine and American jeans. The American demand for French wine creates a supply of dollars and a demand for francs in the foreign exchange market. Similarly, the French demand for American jeans creates a supply of francs and a demand for dollars in the foreign exchange market. In the situation of **flexible exchange rates,** the supply of and demand for dollars and francs in the foreign exchange market will determine the equilibrium foreign exchange rate. The equilibrium exchange rate will tell us how many francs a dollar can be exchanged for—that is, the dollar price of francs—or how many dollars (or fractions of a dollar) a franc can be exchanged for—the franc price of dollars.

Flexible exchange rates
Exchange rates that are allowed to fluctuate in the open market in response to changes in supply and demand. Sometimes called *floating exchange rates.*

The Equilibrium Foreign Exchange Rate

To determine the equilibrium foreign exchange rate, we have to find out what determines the demand for and supply of foreign exchange. We will ignore for the moment any speculative aspect of buying foreign exchange; that is, we assume that there are no individuals who wish to buy francs simply because they think that their price will go up in the future.

The idea of an exchange rate is no different from the idea of paying a certain price for something you want to buy. If you like coffee, you know you have to pay about 75 cents a cup. If the price went up to $2.50, you would probably buy fewer cups. If the price went down to 5 cents, you might buy more. In other words, the demand curve for cups of coffee, expressed in terms of dollars, slopes downward following the law of demand. The demand curve for francs slopes downward also, and we will see why.

Demand Schedule for French Francs. Let's think more closely about the demand schedule for francs. Let's say that it costs you 20 cents to purchase one franc; that is the exchange rate between dollars and francs. If tomorrow you had to pay 25 cents for the same franc, the exchange rate would have changed. Looking at such an increase with respect to the franc, we would say that there has been an **appreciation** in the value of the franc in the foreign exchange market. But this increase in the value of the franc means that there has been a **depreciation** in the value of the dollar in the foreign exchange market. The dollar used to buy five francs; tomorrow, the dollar will be able to buy only four francs at a price of 25 cents per franc. If the dollar price of francs rises, you will probably demand fewer francs. Why? The answer lies in looking at the reason you demand francs in the first place.

> **Appreciation**
> An increase in the value of a currency in terms of other currencies.
>
> **Depreciation**
> A decrease in the value of a currency in terms of other currencies.

You demand francs in order to buy French wine. Your demand curve for French wine, we will assume, follows the law of demand and therefore slopes downward. If it costs you more American dollars to buy the same quantity of French wine, presumably you will not buy the same quantity; your quantity demanded will be less. We say that your demand for French francs is *derived from* your demand for French wine. In panel (a) of Figure 34-2, we present the hypothetical demand schedule for French wine in the United States by a representative wine drinker. In panel (b), we show graphically the American demand curve for French wine in terms of American dollars taken from panel (a).

Let us assume that the price per liter of French wine in France is 20 francs. Given that price, we can find the number of francs required to purchase up to 4 liters of French wine. That information is given in panel (c) of Figure 34-2. If one liter requires 20 francs, 4 liters require 80 francs. Now we have enough information to determine the derived demand curve for French francs. If one franc costs 20 cents, a bottle of wine would cost $4 (20 francs per bottle × 20 cents per franc = $4 per bottle). At $4 per bottle, the typical representative American wine drinker would, we see from panel (a) of Figure 34-2, demand 4 liters. From panel (c) we see that 80 francs would be demanded to buy the 4 liters of wine. We show this quantity demanded in panel (d). In panel (e), we draw the derived demand curve for francs. Now consider what happens if the price of francs goes up to 30 cents. A bottle of French wine costing 20 francs in France would now cost $6. From panel (a) we see that at $6 per liter, 3 liters will be imported from France into the United States by our representative domestic wine drinker. From panel (c) we see that 3 liters would require 60 francs to be purchased; thus in panels (d) and (e) we see that at a price of one franc per 30 cents, the quantity demanded will be 60 francs. We continue similar calculations all the way up to a price of 50 cents per franc. At that price a bottle of French wine costing 20 francs in France would cost $10, and our representative wine drinker would import only one bottle.

Downward-Sloping Derived Demand. As can be expected, as the price of francs falls, the quantity demanded will rise. The only difference here from the standard demand analysis developed in Chapter 3 and used throughout this text is that the demand for francs is derived from the demand for a final product—French wine in our example.

Supply of French Francs. The supply of French francs is a derived supply in that it is derived from a French person's demand for American jeans. We could go through an example similar to the one for wine to come up with a supply schedule of French francs in France. It slopes upward. Obviously, the French want dollars in order to purchase American goods. In principle, the French will be willing to supply more francs when the dollar price of francs goes up because they can then buy more American goods with the same quantity of francs; that is, the franc would be worth more in exchange for American goods than when the dollar price for francs was lower. Let's take an example. Suppose a pair of jeans in the United States costs $10. If the exchange rate is 25 cents for one franc, the French have to come up with 40 francs (= $10 at 25 cents per franc) to buy one pair of

Panel (a)
Demand Schedule for French Wine in the United States per Week

Price per Liter	Quantity Demanded (liters)
$10	1
8	2
6	3
4	4

Panel (b)
American Demand Curve for French Wine

Panel (c)
Francs Required to Purchase Quantity Demanded (at P = 20 francs per liter)

Quantity Demanded	Francs Required
1	20
2	40
3	60
4	80

Panel (d)
Derived Demand Schedule for Francs in the United States with Which to Pay for Imports of Wine

Dollar Price of One Franc	Dollar Price of Wine	Quantity of Wine Demanded (liters)	Quantity of Francs Demanded per Week
$ .50	$10	1	20
.40	8	2	40
.30	6	3	60
.20	4	4	80

FIGURE 34-2

Deriving the Demand for French Francs

In panel (a), we show the demand schedule for French wine in the United States, expressed in terms of dollars per liter. In panel (b), we show the demand curve, *D,* which slopes downward. In panel (c), we show the number of francs required to purchase up to 4 liters of wine. If the price per liter of wine in France is 20 francs, we can now find the quantity of francs needed to pay for the various quantities demanded. In panel (d), we see the derived demand for francs in the United States in order to purchase the various quantities of wine given in panel (a). The resultant demand curve, D_1, is shown in panel (e). It is the American derived demand for francs.

Panel (e)
American Derived Demand for Francs

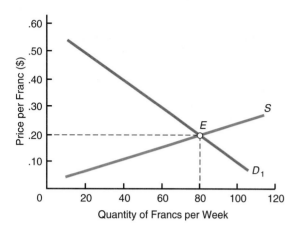

FIGURE 34-3

The Equilibrium Exchange Rate for Two Individuals
The derived demand curve for French francs is taken from panel (e) of Figure 34-2. The derived supply curve, *S,* results from the representative French purchaser of American jeans, who supplies francs to the foreign exchange market when demanding U.S. dollars in order to buy American jeans. D_1 and *S* intersect at *E.* The equilibrium exchange rate is 20 cents per franc.

jeans. If, however, the exchange rate goes up to 50 cents for one franc, the French must come up with only 20 francs (= $10 at 50 cents per franc) to buy a pair of American jeans. At a lower price (in francs) of American jeans, the French will demand a larger quantity. In other words, as the price of French francs goes up in terms of dollars, the quantity of American jeans demanded will go up, and hence the quantity of French francs supplied will go up. Therefore, the supply schedule of foreign currency (francs) will slope upward.[1]

We could easily work through a detailed numerical example to show that the supply curve of French francs slopes upward. Rather than do that, we will simply draw it as upward-sloping in Figure 34-3. In our hypothetical example, assuming that there is only one wine drinker in America and one demander of jeans in France, the equilibrium exchange rate will be set at 20 cents per franc, or 5 francs to one dollar. Let us now look at the aggregate demand for and supply of French francs. We take all demanders of French wine and all demanders of American jeans and put their demands for and supplies of francs together into one diagram. Thus we are showing an aggregate version of the demand for and supply of French francs. The horizontal axis in Figure 34-4 represents a quantity of foreign exchange—the number of francs per year. The vertical axis represents the exchange rate—the price of foreign currency (francs) expressed in dollars (per franc). Thus at the foreign currency price of 25 cents per franc, you know that it will cost you 25 cents to buy one franc. At the foreign currency price of 20 cents per franc, you know that it will cost you 20 cents to buy one franc. The equilibrium is again established at 20 cents for one franc. This equilibrium is not established because Americans like to buy francs or because the French like to buy dollars. Rather, the equilibrium exchange rate depends on how many pairs of jeans the French want and how much French wine the Americans want (given their respective incomes, their tastes, and the relative price of wine and jeans).[2]

A Shift in Demand. Assume that a successful advertising campaign by American wine importers has caused the American demand (curve) for French wine to double. Americans

---

[1]Actually, the supply schedule of foreign currency will be upward-sloping if we assume that the demand for American imported jeans on the part of the French is price-elastic. If the demand schedule for jeans is price-inelastic, the supply schedule will be negatively sloped. In the case of unit elasticity of demand, the supply schedule for francs will be a vertical line. Throughout the rest of this chapter, we will assume that demand is price-elastic. Remember that the price elasticity of demand tells us whether or not total expenditures by jeans purchasers in France will rise or fall when the French franc drops in value. In the long run, it is quite realistic to think that the price elasticity of demand for imports is numerically greater than 1 anyway.

[2]Remember that we are dealing with a two-country world in which we are considering only the exchange of American jeans and French wine. In the real world, more than just goods and services are exchanged among countries. Some Americans buy French financial assets; some French buy American financial assets. We are ignoring such transactions for the moment.

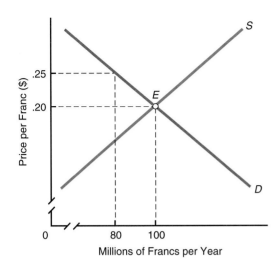

FIGURE 34-4

Aggregate Demand for and Supply of French Francs
The aggregate supply curve for French francs results from the total French demand for American jeans. The demand curve, *D*, slopes downward like most demand curves, and the supply curve, *S*, slopes upward. The foreign exchange price, or the U.S. dollar price of francs, is given on the vertical axis. The number of francs, in millions, is represented on the horizontal axis. If the foreign exchange rate is 25 cents—that is, if it takes 25 cents to buy one franc—Americans will demand 80 million francs. The equilibrium exchange rate is at the intersection of *D* and *S*. The equilibrium exchange rate is 20 cents. At this point, 100 million French francs are both demanded and supplied each year.

demand twice as much wine at all prices. Their demand curve for French wine has shifted outward to the right.

The increased demand for French wine can be translated into an increased demand for francs. All Americans clamoring for bottles of French wine will supply more dollars to the foreign exchange market while demanding more French francs to pay for the wine. Figure 34-5 presents a new demand schedule, D_2, for French francs; this demand schedule is to the right of and outward from the original demand schedule. If the French do not change their desire for American jeans, the supply schedule for French francs will remain stable. A new equilibrium will be established at a higher exchange rate. In our particular example, the new equilibrium is established at an exchange rate of 30 cents per franc. It now takes 30 cents to buy one French franc, whereas it took 20 cents before. This is translated as an increase in the price of French wine to Americans and as a decrease in the price of American jeans to the French. (Otherwise stated, there has been a decline in the foreign exchange value of the dollar.)

A Shift in Supply. We just assumed that Americans' preference for French wine had shifted. Because the demand for French francs is a derived demand by Americans for

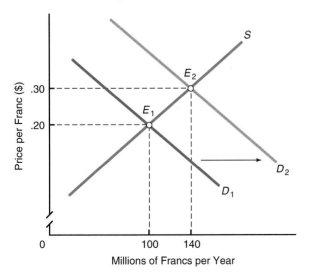

FIGURE 34-5

A Shift in the Demand Schedule
The demand schedule for French wine shifts to the right, causing the derived demand schedule for francs to shift to the right also. We have shown this as a shift from D_1 to D_2. We have assumed that the French supply schedule for francs has remained stable—that is, French demand for American jeans has remained constant. The old equilibrium foreign exchange rate was 20 cents. The new equilibrium exchange rate will be E_2; it will now cost 30 cents to buy one franc. The higher price of francs will be translated into a higher U.S. dollar price for French wine and a lower French franc price for American jeans.

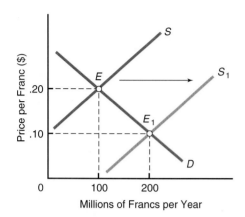

FIGURE 34-6

A Shift in the Supply of French Francs
There has been a shift in the supply curve for French francs. The new equilibrium will occur at E_1, meaning that 10 cents, rather than 20 cents, will now buy one franc. After the exchange rate adjustment, the amount of francs demanded and supplied will increase to 200 million per year.

French wine, it has caused a shift in the demand curve for francs. Alternatively, assume that the supply curve of French francs shifts outward to the right. This may occur for many reasons, the most probable one being a relative rise in the French price level. For example, if the price of all French-made clothes went up 100 percent in francs, American jeans would become relatively cheaper. That would mean that French people would want to buy more American jeans. But remember that when they want to buy more American jeans, they supply more francs to the foreign exchange market. Thus we see in Figure 34-6 that the supply curve of French francs moves from S to S_1. In the absence of restrictions—that is, in a system of flexible exchange rates—the new equilibrium exchange rate will be one franc equals 10 cents, or $1 equals 10 francs. The quantity of francs demanded and supplied will increase from 100 million per year to 200 million per year. We say, then, that in a flexible international exchange rate system, shifts in the demand for and supply of foreign currencies will cause changes in the equilibrium foreign exchange rates. Those rates will remain in effect until supply or demand shifts.

Market Determinants of Exchange Rates

The foreign exchange market is affected by many other changes in market variables in addition to changes in relative price levels, including these:

1. *Changes in real interest rates.* If the United States interest rate, corrected for people's expectations of inflation, abruptly increases relative to the rest of the world, international investors elsewhere will increase their demand for dollar-denominated assets, thereby increasing the demand for dollars in foreign exchange markets. An increased demand for dollars in foreign exchange markets, other things held constant, will cause the dollar to appreciate and other currencies to depreciate.
2. *Changes in productivity.* Whenever one country's productivity increases relative to another's, the former country will become more price competitive in world markets. The demand for its exports will increase, and so, too, will the demand for its currency.
3. *Changes in product preferences.* If Germany's citizens suddenly develop a taste for American-made automobiles, this will increase the derived demand for American dollars in foreign exchange markets.
4. *Perceptions of economic stability.* As already mentioned, if the United States looks economically and politically more stable relative to other countries, more foreigners will want to put their savings into U.S. assets than in their own domestic assets. This will increase the demand for dollars.

CONCEPTS IN BRIEF

- The foreign exchange rate is the rate at which one country's currency can be exchanged for another's.
- The demand for foreign exchange is a derived demand; it is derived from the demand for foreign goods and services (and financial assets). The supply of foreign exchange is derived from foreigners' demands for our goods and services.
- In general, the demand curve of foreign exchange slopes downward and the supply curve of foreign exchange slopes upward. The equilibrium foreign exchange rate occurs at the intersection of the demand and supply curves for a currency.
- A shift in the demand for foreign goods will result in a shift in the demand for foreign exchange. The equilibrium foreign exchange rate will change. A shift in the supply of foreign currency will also cause a change in the equilibrium exchange rate.

THE GOLD STANDARD AND THE INTERNATIONAL MONETARY FUND

The current system of more or less freely floating exchange rates is a recent development. We have had, in the past, periods of a gold standard, fixed exchange rates under the International Monetary Fund, and variants of these two.

The Gold Standard

Gold standard

An international monetary system in which nations fix their exchange rates in terms of gold. All currencies are fixed in terms of all others, and any balance of payments deficits or surpluses can be made up by shipments of gold.

Until the 1930s, many nations were on a **gold standard.** The values of their currencies were tied directly to gold.[3] Nations operating under this gold standard agreed to redeem their currencies for a fixed amount of gold at the request of any holder of that currency. Although gold was not necessarily the means of exchange for world trade, it was the unit to which all currencies under the gold standard were pegged. And because all currencies in the system were linked to gold, exchange rates between those currencies were fixed. Indeed, the gold standard has been offered as the prototype of a fixed exchange rate system. The heyday of the gold standard was from about 1870 to 1914. England had been on such a standard as far back as the 1820s.

There turns out to be a relationship between the balance of payments and changes in domestic money supplies throughout the world. Under a gold standard, the international financial market reached equilibrium through the effect of gold flows on each country's money supply. When a nation suffered a deficit in its balance of payments, more gold would flow out than in. Because the domestic money supply was based on gold, an outflow of gold to foreigners caused an automatic reduction in the domestic money supply. This caused several things to happen. Interest rates rose, thereby attracting foreign capital and improving the balance of payments. At the same time, the reduction in the money supply was equivalent to a restrictive monetary policy, which caused national output and prices to fall. Imports were discouraged and exports were encouraged, thereby again improving the balance of payments.

---

[3] This is a simplification. Most nations were on a *specie metal standard* using gold, silver, copper, and other precious metals as money. Nations operating under this standard agreed to redeem their currencies for a fixed exchange rate.

Two problems that plagued the gold standard were that no nation had control of its domestic monetary policy and that the world's commerce was at the mercy of gold discoveries.

POLICY EXAMPLE
Should We Go Back to the Gold Standard?

In the past several decades, the United States has consistently run a current account deficit. The dollar has become weaker. We have had inflation. We have had recessions. Some economists and politicians argue that we should return to the gold standard. The United States actually operated under two gold standards. From 1879 to 1933, the dollar was defined as 32.22 grains of gold, yielding a gold price of $20.671835 an ounce. During that time period, general prices more than doubled during World War I, there was a major depression in 1920–1921, and the Great Depression occurred. The second gold standard prevailed from 1933 to 1971, when the price of gold was pegged at $35 an ounce. A dollar was defined as 13.714286 grains of gold. During that time period, general prices quadrupled.

Clearly, a gold standard guarantees neither stable prices nor economic stability.

FOR CRITICAL ANALYSIS: Why does no country today operate on a gold standard? •

Bretton Woods and the International Monetary Fund

In 1944, as World War II was ending, representatives from the world's capitalist countries met in Bretton Woods, New Hampshire, to create a new international payment system to replace the gold standard, which had collapsed during the 1930s. The Bretton Woods Agreement Act was signed on July 31, 1945, by President Harry Truman. It created a new permanent institution, the **International Monetary Fund (IMF),** to administer the agreement and to lend to member countries in balance of payments deficit. The arrangements thus provided are now called the old IMF system or the Bretton Woods system.

Each member nation was assigned an IMF contribution quota determined by its international trade volume and national income. Twenty-five percent of the quota was contributed in gold or U.S. dollars and 75 percent in its own currency. At the time, the IMF therefore consisted of a pool of gold, dollars, and other major currencies.

Member governments were then obligated to intervene to maintain the values of their currencies in foreign exchange markets within 1 percent of the declared **par value**—the officially determined value. The United States, which owned most of the world's gold stock, was similarly obligated to maintain gold prices within a 1 percent margin of the official rate of $35 an ounce. Except for a transitional arrangement permitting a one-time adjustment of up to 10 percent in par value, members could alter exchange rates thereafter only with the approval of the IMF. The agreement stated that such approval would be given only if the country's balance of payments was in *fundamental disequilibrium,* a term that has never been officially defined.

Special Drawing Rights. In 1967, the IMF created a new type of international money, *special drawing rights (SDRs).* SDRs are exchanged only between monetary authorities (central banks). Their existence temporarily changed the IMF into a world central bank. The IMF creates SDRs the same way that the Federal Reserve can create dollars. The IMF allocates SDRs to member nations in accordance with their quotas. Currently, the SDR's

International Monetary Fund (IMF)
An institution set up to manage the international monetary system, established in 1945 under the Bretton Woods Agreement Act, which established fixed exchange rates for the world's currencies.

Par value
The legally established value of the monetary unit of one country in terms of that of another.

Exercise 34.2
Visit www.econtoday.com for more about the IMF.

value is determined by making one SDR equal to a bundle of currencies. In reality, the SDR rises or falls in terms of the dollar.

End of the Old IMF. On August 15, 1971, President Richard Nixon suspended the convertibility of the dollar into gold. On December 18, 1971, we officially devalued the dollar against the currencies of 14 major industrial nations. Finally, on March 16, 1973, the finance ministers of the European Economic Community (now the EU) announced that they would let their currencies float against the dollar, something Japan had already begun doing with its yen. Since 1973, the United States and most other trading countries have had either freely floating exchange rates or managed ("dirty") floating exchange rates.

THE DIRTY FLOAT AND MANAGED EXCHANGE RATES

Dirty float
A system between flexible and fixed exchange rates in which central banks occasionally enter foreign exchange markets to influence rates.

The United States went off the Bretton Woods system in 1973, but it has nonetheless tried to keep certain elements of that system in play. We have occasionally engaged in what is called a **dirty float,** or management of flexible exchange rates. The management of flexible exchange rates has usually come about through international policy cooperation. For example, the Group of Five (G-5) nations—France, Germany, Japan, the United Kingdom, and the United States—and the Group of Seven (G-7) nations—the G-5 nations plus Italy and Canada—have for some time shared information on their policy objectives and procedures. They do this through regular meetings between economic policy secretaries, ministers, and staff members. One of their principal objectives has been to "smooth out" foreign exchange rates. Initially, the G-5 attempted to push the value of the dollar downward to help correct U.S. trade deficits and reduce Japanese foreign trade surpluses. What the five nations agreed to do was supply dollars in foreign exchange markets. This increased supply would reduce the dollar's value.

Is it possible for these groups to "manage" foreign exchange rates? Some economists do not think so. For example, economists Michael Bordo and Anna Schwartz studied the foreign exchange intervention actions coordinated by the Federal Reserve and the U.S. Treasury for the second half of the 1980s. Besides showing that such interventions were sporadic and variable, Bordo and Schwartz came to an even more compelling conclusion: Exchange rate interventions were trivial relative to the total trading of foreign exchange on a daily basis. For example, in April 1989, total foreign exchange trading amounted to $129 billion per day, yet the American central bank purchased only $100 million in deutsche marks and yen during that entire month (and did so on a single day). For all of 1989, Fed purchases of marks and yen were only $17.7 billion, or the equivalent of less than 14 percent of the amount of an average *day's* trading in April of that year. Their conclusion is that neither the American central bank nor the central banks of the other G-7 nations can influence exchange rates in the long run.

CONCEPTS IN BRIEF

- The International Monetary Fund was developed after World War II as an institution to maintain fixed exchange rates in the world. Since 1973, however, fixed exchange rates have disappeared in most major trading countries.

- A dirty float occurs in a flexible exchange rate system whenever central banks intervene to influence exchange rates.

In May 1998, 11 of the 15 European Union members qualified to join "Euroland," in which a new currency, the euro, will replace all their individual national currencies by the year 2002.

Will the Euro Put an End to Dollar Dominance?

CONCEPTS APPLIED:
FOREIGN EXCHANGE, FOREIGN EXCHANGE RESERVES, KEY CURRENCY

Visit www.econtoday.com for an Internet Activity that expands your understanding of these concepts.

Since World War II, the U.S. dollar has been the currency of choice in international financial transactions, accounting for over 50 percent of global private financial wealth. Almost 70 percent of world trade is invoiced in dollars, as is 75 percent of international bank lending. But Figure 34-7 shows what has happened to official foreign exchange reserves throughout the world that are held in dollars. In 1973, the dollar constituted 76 percent of official reserves; today, it accounts for only 64 percent. Some analysts have predicted that the euro will weaken America by replacing the dollar as a reserve currency.

Implications of a Dollar in Less Demand

Suppose that the euro became a key currency. U.S. residents could still borrow in dollars, but perhaps they might have to pay a higher interest rate. Even if oil prices were quoted in euros instead of dollars, that would not change the real price of oil to anybody. The reality is that even if the dollar were deposed by the euro in international financial transactions, there would be no serious repercussions in the United States.

Why the Euro Probably Will Not Depose the Dollar

Consider that the dollar constitutes over 60 percent of official reserves throughout the world, yet the United States accounts for only about 23 percent of world output and one-sixth of world exports. Consider also that in the past 30 years, the dollar's value relative to the yen and the mark has dropped by about 50 percent. Nonetheless, the yen and the mark have been unable to push the dollar aside as the key international currency.

Now consider truly international markets for oil, metals, and other basic commodities. Buyers and sellers exist throughout the world. Because of the extreme distances, a single unit for commercial transactions is necessary, and it has to be one on which everyone can agree. Some economists argue that there is room for only one international "language" in financial transactions, and that language is the dollar.

Further, consider the position of the United States as the promoter and sponsor of virtually all important global

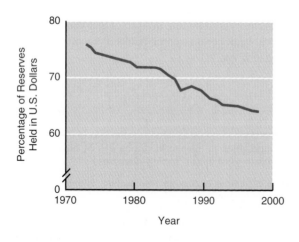

FIGURE 34-7

The Declining Share of Dollar Reserves

Central banks outside the United States now hold a smaller percentage of dollar reserves than they did 20 years ago.

Source: International Monetary Fund.

economic institutions, such as the International Monetary Fund, the World Trade Organization, and the World Bank. Moreover, consider that U.S. Treasury debt is essentially free from default. U.S. government debt serves as the reference of creditworthiness for virtually the entire international system. Thus the relative size of the U.S. economy in the world market is not the sole determinant of whether the dollar will remain the key reserve currency in the world. Equally important is that the dollar is the safest asset in the existing world economic system. At most, then, we can expect that the euro will provide an alternative to the dollar in special circumstances.

A Further Problem: Euro Vulnerability

Some U.S. economists, including Federal Reserve Chairman Alan Greenspan, have accepted that the euro will come into being, but they have serious doubts about its sustainability. Currency speculator George Soros even predicted that a single currency will bear the brunt of European anger over high unemployment rates there. The European Commission understands the vulnerability of the euro and has tried to protect it from speculative attack. In 1997, it announced that from January 1999 onward, the currencies of all its members would be expressed in euros. Until 2002, the German mark, French franc, Italian lira, and Spanish peseta will be regarded as subdivisions of a euro. These subdivisions—defined in terms of euro cents—were supposedly irrevocably fixed during 1998. What this all means is that no one can benefit by selling

lire to buy marks, for example, because they would simply be selling euros to buy euros and end up with the same quantity at the end of the transaction.

A Bigger EU Role in International Finance

In spite of doubts about the euro's long-term sustainability, European finance ministers are arguing that the European Union should take a bigger role in international finance. There is a question about how the euro zone should be represented in the Group of Seven or the International Monetary Fund because a problem that exists, at least for the next couple of years. Britain, Sweden, Denmark, and Greece have indicated that they will not immediately adopt the euro. They do not want the euro zone to have an increased say in international financial institutions such as the IMF.

If this all sounds somewhat confusing and contradictory, it has to be by its very nature. The states within the United States have had a uniform currency since 1863. The merging of 15 nations' currencies into one has never been tried. Problems are bound to arise.

FOR CRITICAL ANALYSIS
1. What might happen to the retail foreign exchange businesses throughout Europe once the euro takes hold?
2. Does it matter whether the dollar remains the key international currency?

CHAPTER SUMMARY

1. The balance of merchandise trade is defined as the value of goods bought and sold in the world market, usually during the period of one year. The balance of payments is a more inclusive concept that includes the value of all transactions in the world market.
2. Americans purchase financial assets in other countries, and foreigners purchase American financial assets, such as stocks or bonds. The buying and selling of foreign financial assets has the same effect on the balance of payments as the buying and selling of goods and services.
3. Our balance of trade and payments can be affected by our relative rate of inflation and by political instability elsewhere compared to the stability that exists in the United States.

4. Market determinants of exchange rates are changes in real interest rates (interest rates corrected for inflation), changes in productivity, changes in product preferences, and perceptions of economic stability.
5. To transact business internationally, it is necessary to convert domestic currencies into other currencies. This is done via the foreign exchange market. If we were trading with France only, French producers would want to be paid in francs because they must pay their workers in francs. American producers would want to be paid in dollars because American workers are paid in dollars.
6. An American's desire for French wine is expressed in terms of a supply of dollars, which is in turn a demand for French francs in the foreign exchange market. The opposite situation arises when the

French wish to buy American jeans. Their demand for jeans creates a demand for American dollars and a supply of French francs. We put the demand and supply schedules together to find the equilibrium foreign exchange rate. The demand schedule for foreign exchange is a derived demand—it is derived from Americans' demand for foreign products.

7. With no government intervention, a market clearing equilibrium foreign exchange rate will emerge. After a shift in demand or supply, the exchange rate will change so that it will again clear the market.

8. If Americans increase their demand for French wine, the demand curve for French wine shifts to the right. The derived demand for francs also shifts to the right. The supply schedule of francs, however, remains stable because the French demand for American jeans has remained constant. The shifted demand schedule intersects the stable supply schedule at a higher price (the foreign exchange rate increases). This is an appreciation of the value of French francs (a depreciation of the value of the dollar against the franc).

9. In a managed exchange rate system (a "dirty float"), central banks occasionally intervene in foreign exchange markets to influence exchange rates.

10. Under a gold standard, movement of gold across countries changes domestic money supplies, causing price levels to change and to correct balance of payments imbalances.

11. In 1945, the International Monetary Fund (IMF) was created to maintain fixed exchange rates throughout the world. This system was abandoned in 1973.

DISCUSSION OF PREVIEW QUESTIONS

1. What is the difference between the balance of trade and the balance of payments?

The balance of trade is defined as the difference between the value of exports and the value of imports. If the value of exports exceeds the value of imports, a trade surplus exists; if the value of exports is less than the value of imports, a trade deficit exists; if export and import values are equal, we refer to this situation as a trade balance. The balance of payments is more general and takes into account the value of *all* international transactions. Thus the balance of payments identifies not only goods and services transactions among nations but also investments (financial and nonfinancial) and gifts (private and public). When the value of all these transactions is such that one nation is sending more to other nations than it is receiving in return, a balance of payments deficit exists. A payments surplus and payments balance are self-explanatory.

2. What is a foreign exchange rate?

We know that nations trade with one another; they buy and sell goods, make and receive financial and nonfinancial investments, and give and receive gifts. However, nations have different currencies. People who sell to, invest in, or receive gifts from the United States ultimately want their own currency so that they can use the money domestically. Similarly, U.S. residents who sell in, invest in, or receive gifts from people in other countries ultimately want U.S. dollars to spend in the United States. Because most people ultimately want to end up with their own currencies, foreign exchange markets have evolved to enable people to sell one currency for other currencies. A foreign exchange rate, then, is the rate at which one country's currency can be exchanged for another's. For example, the exchange rate between the United Kingdom (U.K.) and the United States might dictate that one pound sterling is equivalent to $1.50; alternately stated, the U.S. dollar is worth .667 pound sterling.

3. What is a flexible exchange rate system?

A flexible exchange rate system is an international monetary system in which foreign exchange rates are allowed to fluctuate to reflect changes in the supply of and demand for international currencies. Say that the United States and the U.K. are in payments balance at the exchange rate of one pound sterling to U.S. $1.50. The U.S. demand for sterling is derived from private and government desires to buy British goods, to invest in the U.K., or to send gifts to the British people and is *inversely* related to the number of dollars it takes to buy one pound. Conversely, the supply of sterling is derived from the U.K.'s private and governmental desires to buy U.S. goods and services, to invest in the United States, and to send gifts to U.S. residents. The supply of sterling is *directly* related to the number of dollars one pound is worth. The intersection of the supply and demand curves for sterling determines the market foreign exchange rate of dollars per pound. In a system of flexible exchange rates, shifts in the supply or demand curves will lead to changes in the foreign exchange rates between nations.

4. What is the gold standard?

The gold standard is an international monetary system in which each nation values its currency unit at a specific quantity of gold. Under such a standard, exchange rates are fixed in terms of each other. For example, the U.S. dollar was originally backed by one-twentieth of an ounce of gold, and the British valued their coins (or paper backed by gold) at one-quarter of an ounce of gold; the British monetary unit was therefore worth five times the U.S. monetary unit. The resulting exchange rate was that one pound sterling was worth $5. The gold standard was, in matters of exchange rates, similar to the fixed exchange rate system. However, payment imbalances were automatically corrected by gold flows. For instance, if the United States had a payment deficit with the U.K. (which therefore had a payment surplus with the United States), gold would flow from the United States to the U.K. The result of these gold flows (which, in effect, are equivalent to money movements) would be to raise the price level in the U.K. and lower it in the United States. This would lead to an increase in U.S. exports and a decrease in U.S. imports and a corresponding increase in British imports and decrease in British exports. Thus, in the past, the gold standard brought nations into payment balance by altering price *levels* in each country. The current system of flexible exchange rates corrects payment imbalances leaving price levels unaltered; it changes *one* price—the exchange rate.

PROBLEMS

(Answers to the odd-numbered problems appear at the back of the book.)

34-1. In the graph, what can be said about the shift from D to D_1?

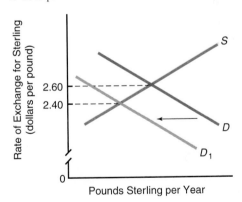

a. It could be caused by Britons demanding fewer U.S. products.
b. It is a result of increased U.S. demand for British goods.
c. It causes an appreciation of the dollar relative to the pound.
d. It causes an appreciation of the pound relative to the dollar.

34-2. If the rate of exchange between the pound and the dollar is $1.45 for one pound, and the United States then experiences severe inflation, we would expect the exchange rate (under a flexible rate system) to shift. What would be the new rate?

a. More than $1.45 for one pound
b. Less than $1.45 for one pound
c. More than one pound for $1.45
d. None of the above

34-3. The dollar, the pound sterling, and the deutsche mark are the currency units of the United States, the United Kingdom, and Germany, respectively. Suppose that these nations decide to go on a gold standard and define the value of their currencies in terms of gold as follows: $35 = 1 ounce of gold; 10 pounds sterling = 1 ounce of gold; and 100 marks = 1 ounce of gold. What would the exchange rate be between the dollar and the pound? Between the dollar and the mark? Between the mark and the pound?

34-4. Examine the following hypothetical data for U.S. international transactions, in billions of dollars.

Exports: goods, 165.8; services, 130.5
Imports: goods, −250.7; services, −99.3
Net unilateral transfers: −20.0

a. What is the balance of trade?
b. What is the balance on goods and services?
c. What is the balance on current account?

34-5. Maintenance of a fixed exchange rate system requires government intervention to keep exchange rates stable. What is the policy implication of this fact? (Hint: Think in terms of the money supply.)

34-6. Suppose that we have the following demand schedule for German beer in the United States per week:

Price per Case	Quantity Demanded (cases)
$40	2
32	4
24	6
16	8
8	10

a. If the price is 30 deutsche marks per case, how many marks are required to purchase each quantity demanded?

b. Now derive the demand schedule for marks per week in the United States to pay for German beer.

c. At a price of 80 cents per mark, how many cases of beer would be imported from Germany per week?

34-7. The accompanying graph shows the supply of and demand for pounds sterling.

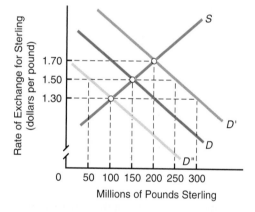

a. Assuming that the demand for sterling is represented by D, what is the dollar price of pounds? What is the equilibrium quantity?

b. Suppose that there is general inflation in the United States. Starting at D, which demand curve could represent this situation? If exchange rates are allowed to float freely, what would be the new dollar price of one pound sterling? What would be the equilibrium quantity?

c. Suppose that the inflation in part (b) occurs and the United States has the dollar price of one pound sterling fixed at $1.50. How would the Federal Reserve be able to accomplish this?

d. Now suppose that instead of inflation, there was general deflation in the United States. Which demand curve could represent this situation? How could the United States maintain a fixed price of $1.50 per pound sterling in this situation?

34-8. Which of the following will cause the yen to appreciate? Explain.

a. U.S. real incomes increase relative to Japanese real incomes.

b. It is expected that in the future the yen will depreciate relative to the dollar.

c. The U.S. inflation rate rises relative to the Japanese inflation rate.

d. The after-tax, risk-adjusted real interest rate in the United States rises relative to that in Japan.

e. U.S. tastes change in favor of Japanese-made goods.

COMPUTER-ASSISTED INSTRUCTION

Suppose that the United States and France have formed a two-country gold standard, and a balance of payments equilibrium exists. What happens if tastes change so that U.S. residents now prefer French goods more than they did previously, other things being constant? This problem shows how balance of payments equilibrium is restored under a gold standard, a specific fixed exchange rate system.

Complete problem and answer appear on disk.

INTERACTING WITH THE INTERNET

You can find out what the International Monetary Fund is doing by going to

www.imf.org

Information from the World Bank can be found easily at

www.worldbank.org

In the days before inexpensive cassette recorders, record companies did not have to worry about piracy. It was simply too expensive for bootleggers to copy records. Then the cassette recorder became so cheap that bootlegged versions of popular records were common. Many people made copies for friends, not for profit. Next, with the advent of relatively cheap compact disc reproduction, bootlegged CDs started to show up worldwide. Go to any flea market in many parts of the world, and you can find CDs of live performances by well-known recording artists. These are not copies of existing CDs but rather unauthorized performance reproductions, for which the artists get paid nothing. Now the digital world has added a new twist—massive copyright violations over the Internet—and with the possibility of perfect quality. How will artists and recording companies cope with the possible onslaught of massive bootlegging? Before you tackle this issue, you need to know a little more about the impact of the Internet on our economic system.

PREVIEW QUESTIONS

1. How does technological change affect the demand for labor?

2. What is the main reason the Internet may lead to increased efficiency?

3. If different tax jurisdictions each take "their piece" of an Internet transaction, what might be the long-run result?

4. Why does the software business seem to belie the traditional law of diminishing marginal returns?

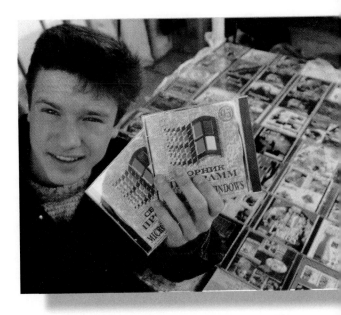

Did You Know That . . . the Internet has its origins in a 1966 U.S. Department of Defense program designed to provide a communications network for defense-related research that could survive a nuclear calamity? The program, called the Advanced Research Projects Agency Network, soon became the favorite form of communication for researchers and academics in non-defense-related fields. Then the National Science Foundation established a distributed network, which greatly increased the traffic. The current system is based on a common addressing system and communications **protocol** that was created in 1983. The world has never been the same.

In this chapter, you will explore the new world of **cybernomics**. You will find out about the growing world of electronic commerce, banking, and finance. In addition, you will find out about the changes it is bringing in the theory of the firm, monopoly, and labor markets.

A WORLD OF CONTINUOUS CHANGE

As with all technological changes, there are losers and winners. The cyberspace revolution is creating many winners and, of course, some losers. That is not new. Decades ago, when elevator control systems were automated, elevator operators lost their jobs. When optical character recognition systems were perfected, bank employees who manually sorted checks were laid off. As word processing systems have become easier to use, the demand for typing specialists has diminished. Technological change will almost always reduce the demand for traditional labor services, but at the same time it will increase the demand for new types of labor services. The fear of technological change has been around for centuries, as you can see in the following example.

INTERNATIONAL EXAMPLE
Luddites Unite Against Automated Textile Machinery

In the vicinity of Nottingham toward the end of 1811, an organized band of English craftsmen started riots with the aim of destroying the textile machines that were replacing them. The members of the band were called Luddites, named after an imaginary leader known as King Ludd. Bands of Luddites were generally masked and operated at night. They were often supported by the local townspeople—but certainly not by threatened employers. One employer, a man named Horsfall, ordered his supporters to open fire on a band of them in 1812. The Luddite movement eventually lost steam by 1817, when prosperity again reigned in England.

FOR CRITICAL ANALYSIS: What are some other technological changes that have created job losses? ●

The Age of Information

Let there be no mistake, the information age is here. What is one of the most important industries in the United States? The answer is information technology, or IT. Sales of the American computing and telecommunications industry have doubled during the 1990s, to exceed $1 trillion a year. IT is the largest American industry—ahead of food products, automotive manufacturing, and construction. The share of IT in American firms' total investment in equipment was a mere 7 percent in 1970 and is now about 45 percent. If you add software investment, current U.S. business spending on IT exceeds investment in tra-

Protocol
The data formatting system that permits computers to access each other and communicate.

Cybernomics
The application of economic analysis to human and technological activities related to the use of the Internet in all of its forms.

ditional machinery. Employment in the IT sector now accounts for around 6 million workers and is growing. The average IT worker earns wages that are about 60 to 70 percent greater than the average wage in the private sector. The American Electronics Association wants to call this the "new economy." This so-called new economy consists of high-tech companies that are generating new work practices and new challenges in public policy.

Household and Business Use of the Internet

Panel (a) of Figure 35-1 shows the rise in the percentage of households with a link to the Internet. At the beginning of the 1990s, the number was virtually zero; the estimate for the year 2005 is over 50 percent. In panel (b), you see average hours per week spent on-line per household connected to the Internet. At the beginning of the 1990s it was almost nothing, whereas today it is over eight hours per week.

For the moment, the greatest use of the Internet is electronic mail, or e-mail. U.S. businesses alone send about 10 billion e-mail messages a year, and that figure is likely to increase. The number of Internet hosts has increased from a few thousand in 1988 to about 20 million today. Worldwide, about 200 million global citizens are connected to the Net. Some estimates for the year 2030 put that number well over a billion.

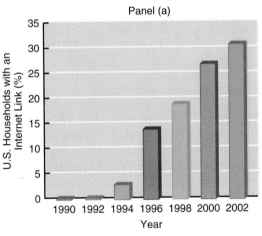

FIGURE 35-1

The Internet Invades America
Perhaps no other innovation has caught on so quickly in America. Not only are more people connecting to the Internet, but they are also using it more.

Source: Consumer Electronics Manufacturer's Association. Figures after 1998 are predictions.

EFFICIENCY, TRANSACTION COSTS, AND E-COMMERCE

In Chapter 4, you learned that individuals turn to markets because markets reduce the costs of exchange, which are called transaction costs. Remember that these are defined as the costs associated with finding out exactly what is being transacted, as well as the cost of enforcing contracts. Entrepreneurs since the beginning of time have attempted to make markets more efficient by figuring out ways to reduce transaction costs.

A big part of transaction costs is the cost of obtaining information. Buyers need information about sellers—their existence, the goods and services they offer, and the prices of those goods and services. A stroll through one's local mall may be a pastime for some, but it is a costly activity for all—time usually does not have a zero opportunity cost. The advent of mail-order shopping reduced transaction costs for many. It also introduced additional competition for retailers located in remote cities. After all, one no longer had to rely solely on the local camera store once camera ads from stores in New York City and elsewhere started appearing in nationally available print publications.

Exercise 35.1
Visit www.econtoday.com for more about e-commerce.

The Web as a Reducer of Transaction Costs

Enter the Internet and the World Wide Web. The existence of information about numerous goods and services, such as automobiles and cameras, via the Web simply means that transaction costs are being further reduced. This should make the market work more efficiently and should lead to less variation in price per constant-quality unit for any good offered for sale.

Business-to-Business E-Commerce

The first place that **e-commerce** has been extensively used is for the sale of goods between businesses. A good example is Cisco Systems, Inc., a major producer of Internet computer routers. It estimates that over 40 percent of its orders are already handled through the Internet—to the tune of about $5 billion a year. The benefits to Cisco by taking orders on-line are many: faster service for its customers, quicker production cycles, and savings on labor and printing charges. Cisco believes that it has reduced overall costs by more than $500 million a year by relying so heavily on e-commerce.

As can be expected, the first companies to take full advantage of the ease of ordering through the Internet have been those involved in information technology, particularly computers and computer parts. In any event, business-to-business Internet commerce is not highly visible, and this may explain why the government underestimated annual on-line sales for 1997 at $5 billion when they were probably closer to $25 billion. If current trends continue, e-commerce should account for almost $1 trillion of sales in the year 2002.

e-commerce
The use of the Internet in any manner that allows buyers and sellers to find each other. It can involve business selling directly to other businesses or business selling to retail customers. Both goods and services are involved in e-commerce.

"E-'Tailing"

While the growth rate in e-commerce at the retail level has been impressive, the total dollar volume is still a mere drop in the bucket compared to retail sales through normal retail outlets. An increasing proportion of Internet users are willing to purchase via the Net, but they do not do so on a regular basis. One issue that retail customers are concerned about is security. They worry that it is too easy for their credit card number to be stolen off the Net by individuals who wish to use it for fraudulent purposes. The real problem area, though, involves Internet merchants, particularly those selling software for immediate download, for these people have been the victims of cybercrimes much more than consumers who have had their credit cards "lifted" out of cyberspace.

Cybershopping Crooks. The ease of selling software over the Internet also makes it easy for cybershoppers to defraud Internet sellers of software provided on-line. Occasionally, CyberSource, the owner of the on-line retail source Software.Net, experiences more fraudulent sales than legitimate ones. Cybercrooks use someone else's credit card number to order the software. CyberSource downloads the software almost instantaneously. By the time the seller discovers the fraud, the buyer has a copy of the software and can resell it.

On-line software sellers have struck back. They have developed a computer model that looks at 150 factors to calculate the risk of fraud for any particular purchase. Any on-line company can pay 50 cents to have a pending credit card request run through the model. There is also an ever more complete name-fraud database that can be used as a reference point.

Better Encryption. Encryption systems—software systems that prevent anyone else from obtaining information provided on-line—are getting better all the time. Both Netscape's Navigator and Microsoft's Internet Explorer browsers have built-in encryption systems. On-line retailers are developing even better ones. Given the demand for a system that is totally secure, we can predict that concerns over losing a credit card number in cyberspace will virtually disappear over time. In any event, even current encryption systems are much more secure than a telephone conversation with a mail-order company operator to whom you give your credit card number in order to have goods shipped to you.

Using Intelligent Shopping Agents

Intelligent shopping agents
Computer programs that an individual or business user of the Internet can instruct to carry out a specific task, such as looking for the lowest-priced car of a particular make and model. The agent then searches the Internet (usually just the World Wide Web) and may even purchase the product when the best price has been found.

Intelligent shopping agents are software programs that search the Web to find a specific item that you specify. Using these agents saves the time you might have to spend searching all potential sites through your broswer. Suppose that you wanted to order a pair of pants. An intelligent shopping agent would ask you for essential descriptions and then go searching on the Web.

A new software program called XML—for "extensible markup language"—will assist intelligent shopping agents. Preparing a Web home page in XML makes the Web site smart enough to tell other machines what is inside in great detail. In essence, XML puts "tags" on Web pages that describe bits of information. Each group of on-line businesses—travel, stocks and bonds, and so on—will have its own set of agreed-on tags. This will allow searching intelligent shopping agents to "flip through" all of the Web sources for a particular item more easily.

Suppose that you are considering the purchase of some airline tickets in the middle of a fare price war. You are not sure how low the tickets prices are going to go. In the near future, you will be able to tell your intelligent shopping agent to keep looking for a lower fare as the airlines change prices on a daily basis. When the agent finds the best price, it can automatically order the tickets on your behalf.

The development of XML along with better intelligent shopping agents is crucial for the most efficient utilization of the Web. Currently, there are over 450,000 commercial sites selling products on-line, and the number is sure to increase rapidly. In the meantime, certain search engines, such as Excite, offer services to compare listed prices from various cyberstores for a desired product.

The Trend Away From Mass Merchandising

Electronic retailing may reverse the trend toward mass merchandising that we have seen over the past 50 years. This reversal has already taken place in the computer industry. Computer mail-order pioneer Dell does not even start the production of a computer until the customer selects all the features—size of hard drive, amount of memory, processor speed, modem speed, and so on. Over 10 percent of Dell's orders are now through the Internet. Dell asks the customer each feature it wants and gives a menu. Apple is doing the same thing on a full selection of its latest computers. Levi Strauss and Company has a customized jeans site on the Internet—a type of on-line fitting room. A similar plan has been put forth by Custom Foot, a large shoe retailer.

BUYING A CAR ON THE NET

They said it could never be done—selling cars in cyberspace. After all, the thinking went, before purchasing such an expensive item, consumers would want to "kick the tires." For most consumers, that is still true. But a growing number now use the Internet to search for the best price on exactly the car they want. And many more have discovered that the most painless way to start looking for a car is on the Net. You can go to Microsoft's CarPoint site at **www.carpoint.msn.com**. You will even find videos that display car interiors. This allows you to take a look at all your options in order to narrow your choices. You can go to Kelley Blue Book at **www.kbb.com** to get exact dealer invoice prices including destination charges. This tells you what the dealer paid for the basic car wholesale. All you have to do is add the prices of optional equipment that you want. These prices are also available at the Kelley Web site. (From the total price listed, you should deduct about 3 percent, which is what the dealer gets from the manufacturer when the car is sold—this is known as the "holdback.")

Once you know what you want, you can start shopping for the actual car via the numerous Web sites for dealers throughout the country. Some dealers are making more than 10 percent of their total sales via the Web. You can also use an on-line car-buying service that processes orders and forwards them to dealers. Detroit's Big Three—Chrysler, General Motors, and Ford—now have their own on-line selling sites.

FOR CRITICAL ANALYSIS: *Car dealers argue that on-line auto shopping will destroy customer bonds. Why should this matter?* ●

The Advent of the Internet Shopping Mall

Perhaps the wave of the future in Internet retail shopping is the equivalent of today's shopping mall. The biggest player in on-line shopping malls is netMarket.com. Sales for 1997 were $1.2 billion, and the company anticipates that its sales will more than double every year into the foreseeable future. The netMarket site sells everything from books and videos to cars, travel, CDs, and kitchen appliances. Within the next several years, netMarket will sell about 95 percent of the goods purchased by a typical household. The on-line firm netMarket is like a club warehouse, for it charges a $49 annual fee. In effect, though, netMarket is not a mall. Rather, it's a megastore that uses the best specialized retailers' efficiencies and discounts. Unlike the typical megastore, such as Wal-Mart or a club warehouse, such as PriceCostco, on-line megastores carry no inventory. They simply pass the orders on electronically to distributors or manufacturers, who then ship the goods from their own warehouses directly to the buyers.

Exercise 35.2
Visit www.econtoday.com for more about an e-commerce shopping mall.

Reduction in the Demand for Retail Space

If more shopping will be done over the Internet in the future, less shopping will be done in traditional retail outlets. Even in those retail outlets that exist, customization may be the order of the day because of new digital scanning and manufacturing systems. The Levi's store in Manhattan allows customers to be scanned electronically to order perfectly fitting jeans. There are a few stores where customers' feet are scanned electronically for custom-made shoes. If more consumers opt for such custom-made items, retail stores will carry much smaller inventories, keeping on hand only samples or computerized images.

The result will be a reduced demand for commercial retail space. Moreover, there will be a reduced demand for trucking to haul inventory, for electricity to light and heat retail space, and for the paper that is used for all the ordering.

CONCEPTS IN BRIEF

- Extensive use of the Web will lead to greater efficiency through a reduction in transaction costs.

- Most e-commerce is between businesses today.

- Retail business will expand as better encryption methods are used for protecting credit card numbers.

- Internet retailing requires no inventory costs for "malls" that simply send orders to other companies for fulfillment.

- If more Internet retailing occurs, the demand for traditional retail space will decrease over time.

THE INCREASING IMPORTANCE OF BRANDS

Brands have value because they indicate to potential purchasers of a branded item that a strong and successful company stands behind it. Successful companies typically have well-recognized brands—think of Microsoft, IBM, Levi's, Mercedes Benz, Sony, Nike. In the world of e-commerce, cybershoppers will increasingly look for branded items to satisfy their purchase desires. Why? Because there will be no salesperson extolling the virtues of a perhaps lower-priced but less well known item.

Brands Created on the Net

That does not rule out new brands' establishing themselves on the Net. A case in point is Amazon.com. The most successful virtual bookseller, Amazon.com didn't even exist before it went on-line. Nonetheless, it has established its brand name as a reputable place to purchase books. Amazon offers incentives to other Web site owners to link with it. If you link your Web site to Amazon, you get a 3 to 8 percent commission on each book purchase made by anyone who follows that link and buys that book from Amazon. Because Amazon orders only books that customers have agreed to buy, the return rate is less than one-quarter of 1 percent, versus 30 to 40 percent for the industry overall.

Reputation on the Web is crucial for success. Jeff Bezos, CEO of the company, makes it clear: "This is the Web. If people feel mistreated by us, they don't tell five people—they tell 5,000."

SELLING CDS ON-LINE

While Amazon.com and Barnes & Noble are busily selling books on-line, the music industry has had a slower start. According to Juniper Communications, on-line music purchases represent less than a half a percent of the U.S. industry's $13 billion total sales. Some small companies are nonetheless doing well. Internet Underground Music Archive at **www.iuma.com** started in business by selling CDs of bands that were not yet under contract. Today, it carries over 1,000 bands, gets a quarter of a million "hits" (visitors to its site) a day, and is selling CDs at the rate of $1 million a day. The on-line CD purchaser gets a sample song before purchase and also typically spends less than at a regular retail CD store. Many minor artists are starting their own Web sites to publicize their works and sell them, too.

The real future in on-line CD sales will begin when Web surfers can quickly and easily download entire albums in digital quality onto blank CDs.

FOR CRITICAL ANALYSIS: Who will be affected most by the digital on-line downloading of CDs? ●

Marketing and Advertising on the Net

If you are marketing a product and you have 20 potential purchasers, you can use the phone to call them. If you want to reach 20 million potential purchasers, you take out a TV ad during the Super Bowl. What do you do if you want to reach 10,000 people? Typically, you engage in direct-mail advertising, at a cost of 50 cents to $1 per person targeted. But now you've got the Internet. In principle, the Net makes it easier to reach more finely targeted audiences and to communicate with them. Consider an example. You are using the search engine InfoSeek, and you enter the keyword "airline tickets." When you do so, a banner ad for American Express's travel services will appear on top of the resulting list of potential Web sites.

The key difference between a similar-looking ad on a TV screen and one on your computer is important—you can click on the one on your computer for an instant response. For TV advertising (and space ads in newspapers and magazines, too), there is no way of really knowing how many people's behavior is truly changed. With Internet advertising, all you have to do is count the number of "click-throughs." If American Express finds out that its travel service ad on InfoSeek has only a 1 percent click-through rate, it will rethink that particular type of advertising.

The future of Internet advertising is impressive. America Online already has more "viewers" than any single cable television network and more "readers" than most popular magazines. As Internet service providers, browsers, home pages, and the like attract larger and larger audiences, the potential for more extensive advertising is dramatic. Currently, Internet advertising revenues represent only a few percent of the annual $35 billion spent on television advertising. But that proportion will change.

TAXES AND THE INTERNET

The United States has some 30,000 tax jurisdictions. In addition to the 50 states, there are thousands of municipalities as well as other taxing districts. Not surprisingly, many of these tax jurisdictions are looking covetously at e-commerce. It represents a potential boon as sales of products and services on the Internet grow. But there is a big potential problem: taxation confusion.

A single Internet transaction does not just go from one entity to another. The nature of the Internet is such that servers may be located virtually anywhere in the world, and the transaction from one end point to the other may be routed through half a dozen servers in numerous tax jurisdictions. Virtually every tax jurisdiction in the United States has different fees and regulations. If all jurisdictions started imposing their tax structures on every Internet transaction, the result would be total confusion. This chaos would inhibit firms from getting involved in electronic commerce and would slow the growth of the use of the Internet.

A bill is in Congress, a draft of the Internet Tax Freedom Act. The bill proposes a five-year moratorium on any new taxes and regulations in cyberspace. The underlying reasoning is simple: A uniform policy must be developed for on-line transactions to ward off confusion. Governors and mayors are fighting vigorously against enactment of the Internet Tax Freedom Act. They want to be able to tax Internet sales. Under current law, the Constitution has been interpreted as prohibiting the states from taxing interstate commerce. They can tax the activities only of companies that have a physical presence in the same state as the consumer. What if states argued that Internet and on-line service providers, such as America Online, are really just acting as independent agents of any company doing business on the Internet? If this interpretation were to be accepted by the courts, every company selling anything over the Internet would have a taxable telecommunications nexus in every state in the union and could owe dozens of taxes on each transaction.

Even if we assume that uniformity of taxation does not apply to transactions on the Net, the market will still punish governments that attempt to apply relatively high taxes on cybertransactions. When Tacoma, Washington, decided to subject on-line service providers to its 6 percent telecommunications tax, the companies immediately threatened to move elsewhere. The city reversed its decision.

CYBERSPACE EXAMPLE — AVOIDING TAXES BY SETTING UP OFFSHORE

If you are willing to break the law, you can set up an Internet business in a Caribbean tax haven. One such place is Anguilla. All you have to do is send your name, phone number, e-mail address, and a proposed Web address for your business to **www.offshore.com.ai**. You will have a Web site set up, and an Anguillan lawyer will register your corporation. You can open a corporate bank account with the Anguillan branch of Barclays Bank or the local National Bank of Anguilla. You can transfer the $1,500 fee using DigiCash, Inc.'s e-cash—which is untraceable. Anguilla does not impose any taxes on your venture. It does not cooperate with the U.S. Internal Revenue Service, either. You can get a corporate credit card and spend your money anywhere you want. Remember, though, that as a citizen or legal resident of the United States, you owe federal income taxes on your worldwide income. On Schedule B of your tax form 1040, there is a box to check if you have an offshore bank account. If you do not check it when you have such an account, you have committed a felony.

FOR CRITICAL ANALYSIS: What types of businesses would individuals seeking to avoid taxes most likely set up on an offshore Web site? •

CONCEPTS IN BRIEF

- Brands can be established on the Web itself.
- The Internet allows for a better way of reaching more finely tuned groups of potential customers. It is cheaper and perhaps even more effective than traditional direct-mail marketing methods.
- Because any Internet transaction may pass through numerous jurisdictions, confusion may reign for e-commerce unless a uniform taxing policy is adopted.

E-TRADING AND CAPITAL MARKETS

Gone are the days when all stock market transactions had to be run through a licensed broker. The Internet has transformed the industry—from two angles. First, anybody can trade on-line from virtually anywhere in the world for as little as $8 a trade no matter what the size of the transaction. Second, small companies can now find financing through the Internet.

On-Line Trading

A few years ago, on-line trading seemed to be a fantasy. You had to call your broker, usually at a full-service brokerage firm, and pay hundreds or sometimes thousands of dollars in commissions, depending on the number of shares you bought or sold. Discount brokers then entered the fray. Commissions were slashed to half or less. Now on-line retail brokerage firms offer commission rates that "can't be beat." One of the first and biggest is E*Trade. You can buy or sell 200 shares of a $20 stock on-line and pay less than $15 in commissions. You can buy or sell 3,000 shares of a $10 stock and pay less than $75.

Fierce Competition

During the first half of 1998, average daily on-line financial trades increased by more than 50 percent over the previous six months. Currently, there are about 3.5 million on-line investing accounts. Forester Research, Inc., of Cambridge, Massachusetts, predicts 15 million by the year 2002.

Datek Securities, Ameritrade, and Suretrade offer a fixed-price commission. The commission prices are incredibly low compared to what people were paying just a few short years ago—in fact, none of those companies charges more than $10 a trade.

The bright future of on-line trading does not bode well for the future of regular retail securities brokers in the industry. The demand for their services should shift leftward through time.

Seeking Capital on the Web

For very small firms, it has always been difficult, if not impossible, to obtain public financing for expansion. The costs of reaching potential investors, filing with the various state and federal regulatory agencies, and dealing with all the other red tape have been just too great.

In 1996, the U.S. Small Business Administration, working with the federal Securities and Exchange Commission (SEC), helped privately financed Angel Capital Electronic Network launch its first Internet site (**ace-net.sr.unh.edu/**). The goal of this Web site is to have small business entrepreneurs provide information to investors about promising small businesses that wish to raise from $250,000 to $5 million in equity financing.

On-Line IPOs. What's more, it is now possible to go public on the Internet—to sell initial shares of stock to the public directly, as you can see in the following example.

GOING PUBLIC VIA THE NET

History was made when Spring Street Brewing Company became the first company to conduct an initial public offering (IPO) over the Internet in 1995. In March 1996, the company again made history when the SEC allowed Spring Street to trade its shares via its Web site without registering as a broker-dealer—provided that the company modified its program. Among other things, the SEC required Spring Street, which had been directly processing the funds received from buyers, to use an independent agent, such as a bank or escrow agent, to receive such funds.

FOR CRITICAL ANALYSIS: Why would the SEC give up control over public offerings? •

Advantages of Using the Web. According to the government, going public via the normal route takes about 900 hours, most of it devoted to preparing a prospectus prior to the sale of stock. It also involves hiring specialized lawyers and using an underwriter, who takes 10 percent of the IPO as a fee. The alternative is to buy a computer program called CapScape, which automates the process of compiling the offer documents. Then the shares can be sold directly to investors over the Internet.

Who will ultimately benefit from Internet IPOs? Small businesses. Who will lose? Lawyers, accountants, and financiers who specialize in raising money for small companies. The demand for their services should drop over time.

$500 MILLION OF BONDS THROUGH THE INTERNET?

One of the first major uses of the Internet in the capital market was to aid General Motors Acceptance Corporation (GMAC) in selling $500 million of bonds. It used Chicago Corporation, a regional investment bank, to get the job done. What Chicago did was unusual, though. It used a Web-based bulletin board called Direct Access Notes. Investors were able to download the prospectus for the bond offering and an interactive bond calculator. GMAC also developed a multimedia "dog and pony show" for its Web site. This allowed more investors to view the road show personally than would have otherwise. They bought bonds directly off of Chicago's Web site. Investors even participated in chat room discussions about the bond offering.

FOR CRITICAL ANALYSIS: Who benefits most from such Internet activities? •

CONCEPTS IN BRIEF

- The buying and selling of securities has become much cheaper with the advent of e-trading. Commissions are less than they used to be, and stock traders can access markets directly from their home cheaply and easily via their computers.

- The capital market for small firms may become more efficient with the new possibility of raising funds on the Internet.

THE MICRO THEORY OF BUSINESS BEHAVIOR WITH THE INTERNET ADDED

The theory of the way firms make decisions discussed in this textbook was developed well before the Internet became even a pipe dream. How has the advent of the Internet changed the theory of the firm? To understand the answers to this question we look at several areas, including pricing and cost of entry.

Pricing

In a competitive market, the perfect competitor has no control over price—the perfect competitor is a *price taker.* The market price simply equals the price at which the market demand curve intersects the market supply curve. A firm with any market power, however, is a *price setter.* The profit-maximizing price occurs at the quantity at which marginal revenue equals marginal cost, with the price being read off the market demand curve.

Marginal Cost for Software. Consider the issue of marginal cost. Once a software program is developed, the marginal cost of providing one more unit to the world via Internet transmission is very close to zero. Moreover, this marginal cost is probably constant over all of the potential demanders throughout the entire world (at least with respect to the cost incurred by the offering firm). What, then, is the correct pricing decision for a software company that can provide millions of users with its product at a virtually zero marginal cost? You will find the answer in Figure 35-2.

Such a pricing strategy cannot, however, provide revenues to compensate for the initial development costs of the program. So some software providers have come up with different ways to obtain revenues, even while "selling" their programs at a zero price. Microsoft Corporation has offered its Internet Explorer at no charge for years now. It obtains revenues from the advertising that it sells on the Explorer pages. Netscape went one step further at the beginning of 1998 and opened up its entire Navigator program free to the world. Anybody can modify Navigator now to suit a particular environment. The share of Netscape's total revenues from its Navigator browser program had already fallen to 13 percent when it made this policy change. The other 87 percent was obtained from the development of corporate intranets and the like.

Many software firms have offered their programs free of charge simply to "capture" the names of users to whom it might later sell upgraded versions. This is true, for example, of the free e-mail program Eudora. Some accounting software has also been given away free. The best-known example among game players is Doom. The first few levels of the game are given away free on the Net. Once "hooked," though, players pay extra to get to more difficult levels. Several million copies have now been sold.

No Traditional Law of Diminishing Returns. Recall from Chapter 22 the law of diminishing marginal returns. Also remember that a firm's short-run cost curves are a reflection of the law of diminishing marginal returns. When diminishing marginal returns begin, marginal cost begins to rise.

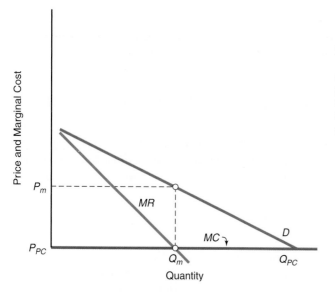

FIGURE 35-2

Pricing When Marginal Cost Equals Zero
For a monopolist, MR = MC at quantity Q_m. The monopoly price would be P_m. For a perfect competitor, MR = MC = 0, so price would be P_{PC} (=0) and quantity would be Q_{PC}.

Software production, now that the Internet exists, does not appear to follow this traditional rule. Once a program has been written, any number of copies can be sent out via the Internet at very little cost, and the cost does not increase with the number of copies. Software companies can cheaply capture a significant market share by giving away a program and then selling follow-up products (upgrades, add-ons, manuals) at higher prices.

Cost of Entry

One thing the Internet has certainly done is reduce the cost of entry, at least for companies willing to sell goods via the Internet. Amazon.com has no inventory, only an Internet site, programmers, and a small staff. Numerous CD retailers on the Internet carry no inventories. The megamalls on the Internet carry no inventories. Entry and operating costs cover simply development of the software retailing programs, paying for the server, and other relatively modest outlays.

CYBERSPACE EXAMPLE   YOUR BUSINESS ON THE NET FOR $25,000

If you have an existing retail business, you can set up on the Net for an initial investment of $25,000. The offer to do so was announced by Pandesic at the beginning of 1998. For the $25,000 fee, a small to midsized company can obtain everything it needs to put its business on the Net— and do so in less than six weeks. This includes computer hardware (a server) plus software programs to handle finance, shipping, and inventory. In addition, however, once the retailer is on the Net and up and running, Pandesic takes a fee of 1 to 6 percent of monthly sales. In return, Pandesic provides all of the installation, training, upgrades, and maintenance of the system. This approach has been taken by Thin Blue Line, Inc., a small mountain-bike maker in Canada that has stormed the U.S. market via its Web site.

FOR CRITICAL ANALYSIS: To make a profit, what else must a company do besides get on the Net? •

The Global Connection

One thing is certain: Because anybody can set up an e-commerce site from anywhere in the world, the Internet is easing entry into any retailing or wholesaling business. Moreover, foreigners can operate Internet sites just as U.S. citizens can. Thus worldwide competition is a given on the Internet. Software that can be downloaded from anywhere is a clear example.

CONCEPTS IN BRIEF

- Pricing decisions for software products that can be downloaded off of the Internet are difficult. The marginal cost becomes zero, but a product given away doesn't yield revenues to pay for its development.

- Some firms have succeeded by giving away their programs but charging for upgrades and updated versions.

- The Internet is leading to lower costs of entry, especially in retailing.

This young man is proud of his bootlegged CDs. If unauthorized copies of CDs can be downloaded easily from the Internet, how will this affect the sales of legally produced copies?

CONCEPTS APPLIED:
COPYRIGHT, INTELLECTUAL PROPERTY, MONOPOLY, LAW OF DEMAND, MARGINAL COST

Visit www.econtoday.com for an Internet Activity that expands your understanding of these concepts.

The first legal copyright protection can be found in a statute passed in Britain in 1709. Later, in 1787, the following phrase was included in the U.S. Constitution: "Congress shall have Power . . . To promote the Progress of Science and useful Arts, by securing for limited Times to Authors and Inventors the exclusive Rights to their respective Writings and Discoveries."

Currently, copyright laws are governed by the Copyright Act of 1976, as amended. No law, whether in the United States or elsewhere, has been very effective against the bootlegging of *intellectual property*—any creation whose source is a person's intellect, as opposed to physical property. The International Federation of the Phonographic Industry (IFPI) estimates that one-fifth of all sales of recorded music are of pirated copies. For CDs, that group estimates that one in three sales is pirated.

First Things First: The Law of Demand

The pirating of recorded music is widespread and worldwide. There have even been diplomatic flaps over it in China. The United States has repeatedly asked the Chinese government to close down the numerous illegal bootlegged-CD factories in that country. Recently, CD bootlegging has become a huge industry in Hong Kong.

There is a problem with the IFPI estimates, nonetheless. When estimating what legitimate CD sales would be in the absence of pirating, the IFPI assumes that pirated copies displace legitimate copies one for one, even though the pirated copies have much lower prices than legitimate copies. This assumption is a clear violation of the law of demand. In fact, there will be a larger quantity demanded at a lower price. Thus the lower-priced pirated copies of recorded music induce purchasers to buy more of them. If pirated copies did not exist, we could not predict that legal sales of CDs would simply replace them

one for one. But pirated copies do exist, inflating potential sales estimates.

This same analysis can apply to pirated copies of software. The Business Software Alliance estimates that at least half the global market for software is pirated products. That does not mean, though, that if no pirating occurred, the sales of software would double. Remember the law of demand.

Altruists on the Internet

There has been a major change in pirating with the advent of the Internet. When you purchase a bootlegged CD, the group that produced the pirated version did so to make a profit. In contrast, many Internet devotees offer downloadable copies of software and recorded music at no charge. In other words, organized profit-seeking gangs are not always involved here. Such anarchy on the Internet may have serious long-term repercussions. People invest in producing high-quality intellectual property, be it software programs or recorded music, because they expect to be paid. The more unauthorized copies of such intellectual properties that people distribute on the Internet for free, the lower the payoff to investing in the development of such property. Without ways to reduce the bootlegging of intellectual property (for one can never prevent it completely), there will certainly be a decrease in the growth of investment of people's time, effort, and creative energy in the development of software, recorded music, and other intellectual property.

How to Survive Internet Copying

It used to be that a copy of a record was of lower quality than the original. A copy of a CD on cassette has a poorer sound quality than the CD. But the same cannot be said of digital copying on the Internet. Zeros and ones copy just as well through cyberspace as they do in a sophisticated studio setup.

There are ways, though, for intellectual property owners to improve their chances of retaining direct sales of their products. They can provide more "goodies" along with legally sold CDs in the standard plastic jewel box—the words to the songs, better liner notes, perhaps contests and drawings, and so on. Software providers have already learned that by offering more useful instructional packages with legally purchased programs, they are able to encourage potential buyers to shy away from bootlegged copies.

Finally, a technological breakthrough will help recording companies track down bootleggers. It is a type of "watermarking" system imbedded in the digital information stored on a compact disc. It allows investigators to determine whether a CD was obtained legally or illegally.

Perhaps the extreme concern over the fate of recording artists in the digital Internet world is much ado about nothing. After all, when the Grateful Dead were touring, they allowed anybody to "bootleg" their live sessions. In the process, they created a cult of fans who could identify a particular concert in a particular city on a given date simply upon hearing the opening bars of a "bootlegged" CD or tape. The result was increased interest in purchasing other Grateful Dead recordings and paraphernalia.

FOR CRITICAL ANALYSIS

1. Is there any way to police the downloading of copyrighted material on the Internet?
2. Most people have at least once copied a computer program or a CD. Is this always bad for the copyright owner of such material?

CHAPTER SUMMARY

1. The twenty-first century is dawning on the age of information. The use of the Internet by businesses has mushroomed, and billions of e-mail messages are sent each year. In the home, the number of households connected to the Internet may be over 50 percent by 2005.

2. The rising use of the Internet allows for a reduction in transaction costs. Relatively inexpensive programs for searching for the lowest price on the Web will lead to less variation in the price per constant-quality unit for any given item.

3. The greatest volume of transactions on the Web is between businesses. Retailing on the Web is taking longer to establish itself, in part because of fears that credit card numbers can be stolen in cyberspace. Better encryption programs will ultimately resolve this problem.

4. Increased acceptance of Web shopping will lead to a reduction in the demand for retail space.

5. In the past, the purchase and sale of securities had to be done through a licensed retail securities broker. Today, securities transactions can be done on the Internet for relatively very low commissions per trade.

6. Capital can be raised directly through the Internet, without a costly registration process and without an expensive underwriter.

7. Pricing is a problem for software sold on the Web because once the software is produced, it can be distributed at very little cost to literally millions of potential users.

8. Because the Internet has made it easier and cheaper to go into retailing, the cost of entry has fallen. Also, foreign competition now exists that was too expensive to consider before.

DISCUSSION OF PREVIEW QUESTIONS

1. How does technological change affect the demand for labor?

Though technological change undoubtedly reduces the demand for more traditional labor services, that is never the end of the story. Individuals who provide

such services are thrown out of work, but at the same time (or perhaps after a time lag), new types of labor services are demanded. Who could have imagined 20 years ago the types of labor services now demanded for Web design, Web marketing, and the like?

2. What is the main reason the Internet may lead to increased efficiency?

The Internet can be viewed as a giant ongoing process that reduces transaction costs. The more quickly buyers can locate sellers, the more efficient our economy becomes. The more competition occurs, even from other parts of the world, the more efficient our economy becomes.

3. If different tax jurisdictions each take "their piece" of an Internet transaction, what might be the long-run result?

To enter the e-commerce world, businesses have to know what they are in for. If they can never tell when,

for example, a city government may try to tax an Internet transaction, they may be reluctant to move forward. Because Internet transactions go through many servers in many jurisdictions, too many taxes on a single transaction will hamper the growth of e-commerce.

4. Why does the software business seem to belie the traditional law of diminishing marginal returns?

Generally, after the production of an ever-increasing number of an item, its marginal cost starts to rise, due to diminishing marginal returns. For software production, an increasing number of copies can be distributed on the Internet without any significant rising marginal cost.

PROBLEMS

(The answer to Problem 35-1 appears at the back of the book.)

35-1. Imagine that you are selling a new word processing program that you have decided to give away free of charge on the Internet. How can you make a profit?

35-2. Assume that you got a great Web designer to make you a terrific-looking home page for your new business. Does this necessarily mean that you can stay in business?

INTERACTING WITH THE INTERNET

You can look at some alternative e-commerce shopping malls at

www.shopping.com

www.my-world.de

You can visit the Small Business Administration on-line at

www.sbaonline.sba.gov/

You can obtain information on on-line trading of stock and bonds from numerous sources. Try some of the following:

www.dljdirect.com/

www.wallstreete.com/

www.etrade.com/

www.eschwab.com/

www.suretrade.com

www.ameritrade.com

If you want to participate in an on-line auction, you can find a long list of possible cites for many categories of products at:

www.internetauctionlist.com/

You can scan thousands of classified ads, by category, if you access:

www.classifieds2000.com/

For on-line job searching, there are many cites which offer everything from career advice to actual want ads. One of the most often used is:

www.careermosaic.com/

Try also any of the following:

www.jobbankusa.com

www.doleta.gov/programs/onet/

www.online-jobs.com/

You can learn more about e-commerce from a monthly on-line publication called *E-Business*. Go to:

www.hp.com/Ebusiness/main1.html

CHAPTER 1

1-1. A large number of possible factors might affect the probability of death, including age, occupation, diet, and current health. Thus one model would show that the older someone is, the greater is the probability of dying within the next five years; another would show that the riskier the occupation, other things being equal, the greater the probability of dying within five years; and so forth.

1-3. a. We should observe younger drivers to be more frequently involved in traffic accidents than older persons.
      b. Slower monetary expansion should be associated with less inflation.
      c. Professional basketball players receiving smaller salaries should be observed to have done less well in their high school studies.
      d. Employees being promoted rapidly should have lower rates of absenteeism than those being promoted more slowly.

1-5. The decreasing relative attractiveness of mail communication has no doubt decreased students' demand for writing skills. Whether or not the influence has been a significant one is a subject for empirical research. As for the direction of causation, it may well be running both ways. Cheaper nonwritten forms of communication may decrease the demand for writing skills. Lower levels of writing skills probably further increase the demand for audio and video communications media.

1-7. a. Normative, involving a value judgment about what should be
      b. Positive, for it is a statement of what has actually occurred
      c. Positive, for it is a statement of what actually is
      d. Normative, involving a value judgment about what should be

CHAPTER 2

2-1. The law of increasing relative cost does seem to hold because of the principle that some resources may be more suited to one productive use than to another. In moving from butter to guns, the economy will first transfer those resources most easily sacrificed by the butter sector, holding on to the very specialized (to butter) factors until the last. Thus different factor intensities will lead to increasing relative costs.

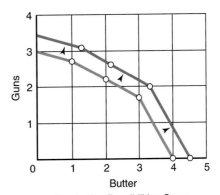

Production Possibilities Curve
for Guns and Butter
(before and after 10 percent growth)

2-3. a. Neither, because each can produce the same total number of jackets per time period (2 jackets per hour)
      b. Neither, because each has the same cost of producing ties ($\frac{2}{3}$ jacket per tie)
      c. No, because with equal costs of production, there are no gains from specialization
      d. Output will be the same as if they did not specialize (16 jackets per day and 24 ties per day)

2-5. a. Only the extra expense of lunch in a restaurant, above what lunch at home would have cost, is part of the cost of going to the game.

b. This is part of the cost of going to the game because you would not have incurred it if you had watched the game on TV at home.

c. This is part of the cost of going to the game because you would not have incurred it if you had watched the game on TV at home.

2-7. For most people, air is probably not an economic good because most of us would not pay simply to have a larger volume of the air we are currently breathing. But for almost everyone, *clean* air is an economic good because most of us would be willing to give something up to have cleaner air.

APPENDIX A

A-1.

y	x
12	4
9	3
6	2
3	1
0	0
−3	−1
−6	−2
−9	−3
−12	−4

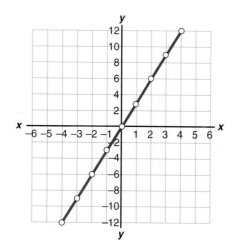

CHAPTER 3

3-1. The equilibrium price is $30. The quantity supplied and demanded is about 10.5 million skateboards per year.

3-3. a. The demand curve for vitamin C will shift outward to the right because the product has taken on a desirable new quality.

b. The demand curve for teachers will shift inward to the left because the substitute good, the interactive educational CD-ROM, is now a lower-cost alternative. (Change in the price of a substitute)

c. The demand curve for beer will shift outward to the right because the price of a complementary good—pretzels—has decreased. Is it any wonder that tavern owners often give pretzels away? (Change in the price of a complement)

3-5. As the graph indicates, demand doesn't change, supply decreases, the equilibrium price of oranges rises, and the equilibrium quantity falls.

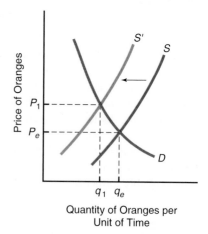

3-7. The speaker has learned well the definition of a surplus but has overlooked one point. The "surpluses" that result from the above-equilibrium minimum prices don't go begging; the excess quantities supplied are in effect purchased by the

Department of Agriculture. In that sense, they are not surpluses at all. When one includes the quantity that is demanded by the Department of Agriculture, along with the quantities being purchased by private purchasers at the support price, the quantity demanded will equal the quantity supplied, and there will be an equilibrium of sorts.

3-9. As the graph illustrates, rain consumers are not willing to pay a positive price to have nature's bounty increased. Thus the equilibrium quantity is 200 centimeters per year (the amount supplied freely by nature), and the equilibrium price is zero (the amount that consumers will pay for an additional unit, given that nature is already producing 200 centimeters per year).

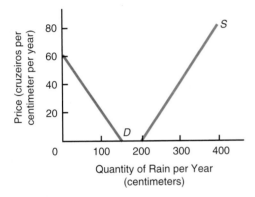

CHAPTER 4

4-1. a. The demand curve will shift to the right (increase).
   b. The supply curve will shift to the right (increase).
   c. Because the price floor, or minimum price, is below the equilibrium price of 50 cents, there will be no effect on price or quantity.
   d. Because the price floor is now greater than the equilibrium price, there will be a surplus at the new price of 75 cents.
   e. Assuming that grapefruits are a substitute for oranges, the demand curve for oranges will shift to the right (increase).
   f. Assuming that oranges are a normal good, the demand curve will shift to the left (decrease).

4-3. The "equilibrium" price is $40 per calculator, and the equilibrium quantity is zero calculators per year. This is so because at a price of $40, the quantity demanded—zero—is equal to the quantity supplied—also zero. None will be produced or bought because the highest price that any consumer is willing to pay for even a single calculator ($30) is below the lowest price at which any producer is willing to produce even one calculator ($50).

4-5. The equilibrium price is $4 per crate, and the equilibrium quantity is 50 million crates per year. At $2 per crate, the quantity demanded is 90 million crates per year and the quantity supplied is 10. This is called a shortage, or excess quantity demanded. The excess quantity demanded is 80 million crates per year. At $5 per crate, the quantity demanded is 20 million crates per year and the quantity supplied is 80 million crates. This is called a surplus, or excess quantity supplied. The excess quantity supplied is 60 million crates per year.

4-7. As shown in the graph, if the equilibrium price of oranges is 10 cents, a price floor of 15 cents will result in a surplus equal to $Q_s - Q_d$. A price floor of 5 cents per orange will have no effect, however, because it is below the equilibrium price and thus does not prevent suppliers and demanders from doing what they want to do—produce and consume Q_e oranges at 10 cents each.

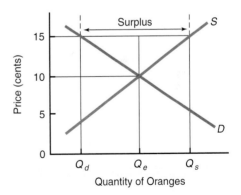

CHAPTER 5

5-1. The marginal tax rate on the first $3,000 of taxable income is 0 percent because no taxes are imposed until $5,000 is earned. The marginal rate on $10,000 is 20 percent, as it is on $100,000 and all other amounts above the $5,000 level, because for each additional dollar earned after $5,000, 20 cents will be taxed away. The average tax rate, which is the tax amount divided by the pretax income, is 0 for $3,000, 10 percent for $10,000, and 19 percent for $100,000. The average tax rate will *approach* a maximum of 20 percent as income increases. It cannot reach *exactly* 20 percent because of the untaxed $5,000 at the beginning. Such is the nature of a *degressive* tax system.

5-3. Mr. Smith pays nothing on his first $1,500 of income, 14 percent ($70) on the $500 of earnings between $1,500 and $2,000, and 20 percent ($100) on the $500 that he earns above $2,000. Thus Mr. Smith has a total tax bill of $170 on an income of $2,500; his average tax rate is 6.8 percent, and his marginal tax rate is 20 percent.

5-5. Among the ideas that have been proposed is that a good tax system should meet the requirements of equity, efficiency, and ease of administration. Equity means that each person should pay a "fair share." The efficiency requirement is that the tax system should minimize interferences with economic decisions. Ease of administration means that the tax system should not be excessively costly to administer and that it should be understandable to the taxpayer. Even though the U.S. tax system was not designed through a master plan, these ideas have had their influence on the American system.

5-7. There are both public good and private good aspects to police protection. When an officer patrols the neighborhood in a police car, criminals are deterred from burglarizing every home in the neighborhood; this is a public good aspect of police protection because the protection afforded one person is simultaneously afforded all of the neighbors. But when an officer spends time arresting the person who broke into Mr. Smith's home, that is time the officer cannot spend arresting the person who broke into Ms. Jones's home; this is the private good aspect of police protection, for when these services are provided Mr. Smith, Ms. Jones is excluded from simultaneously using those services.

5-9. a. If you give and everyone else does also, you account for 1 percent. If you are the only one who gives, you account for 100 percent. If you give nothing, you account for 0 percent, regardless of what others give.
b. In principle, your contribution matters whatever the level of participation. But as a practical matter, if participation is near 100 percent, the absence of your contribution may have little practical effect.
c. There is no free ride. If you do not make your contribution, total contributions will be lower,

and the quality of the services provided will be lower.

5-11. Strictly speaking, probably all the items except national defense should go into the column labeled "Private Goods," either because residents *could* be excluded from consuming them or because one person's consumption reduces the amount available for other individuals. As a practical matter, however, there are several goods on the list (public television, elementary education, and the museum) for which full exclusion generally does not take place and/or consumption by one person reduces the amount that other persons can consume by only a small amount.

CHAPTER 6

6-1. On the supply side, all of the industries responsible for automobile inputs would have to be considered. This would include steel (and coke and coal), glass, tires (and rubber), plastics, railroads (and thus steel again), aluminum (and electricity), and manufacturers of stereos, hubcaps, and air conditioners, to name a few. On the demand side, you would have to take into account industries involving complements (such as oil, gasoline, concrete, and asphalt) and substitutes (including bicycles, motorcycles, buses, and walking shoes). Moreover, resource allocation decisions regarding labor and the other inputs, complements, and substitutes for these goods must also be made.

6-3. a. Profit equals total revenue minus total cost. Because revenue is fixed (at $172), if the firm wishes to maximize profit, this is equivalent to minimizing costs. To find total costs, simply multiply the price of each input by the amount of the input that must be used for each technique.

Costs of A = ($10)(7) + ($2)(6) + ($15)(2) + ($8)(1) = $120
Costs of B = ($10)(4) + ($2)(7) + ($15)(6) + ($8)(3) = $168
Costs of C = ($10)(1) + ($2)(18) + ($15)(3) + ($8)(2) = $107

Because C has the lowest costs, it yields the highest profits, and thus it will be used.
b. Profit equals $172 − $107 = $65.
c. Each technique's costs rise by the increase in the price of labor multiplied by the amount of

labor used by that technique. Because technique A uses the least amount of labor, its costs rise the least, and it thus becomes the lowest-cost technique at $132. (The new cost of B is $182, and the new cost of C is $143.) Hence technique A will be used, resulting in profits of $172 − $132 = $40.

6-5. a. In the market system, the techniques that yield the highest (positive) profits will be used.
  b. Profit equals total revenue minus total cost. Because revenue from 100 units is fixed (at $100), if the firm wishes to maximize profit, this is equivalent to minimizing costs. To find total costs, simply multiply the price of each input by the amount of the input that must be used for each technique.

Costs of A = ($10)(6) + ($8)(5) = $100
Costs of B = ($10)(5) + ($8)(6) = $98
Costs of C = ($10)(4) + ($8)(7) = $96

Because technique C has the lowest costs, it also yields the highest profits ($100 − $96 = $4).
  c. Following the same methods yields these costs: A = $98, B = $100, and C = $102. Technique A will be used because it is the most profitable.
  d. The profits from using technique A to produce 100 units of X are $100 − $98 = $2.

CHAPTER 7

7-1. Although your boss gave you a raise of $1,200 ($30,000 × .04), you are not $1,200 better off after taxes. You are now in the 28 percent marginal tax bracket. You must pay .28 × $1,200 in additional taxes, or $336. That leaves you with an additional $864 in take-home pay. That is how much better off you are because of the raise.

7-3. a. 5 percent
  b. One month
  c. 5 percent
  d. 10 percent
  e. In this example, the unemployment rate doubled, but it is not obvious that the economy has gotten sicker or that workers are worse off.

7-5. a. The nominal rate of interest is composed of the real rate of interest plus the anticipated rate of inflation. If the current rate of inflation is zero and people anticipate that there will continue to be no inflation, the real rate of interest equals the nominal rate of interest—in this example, 12 percent.
  b. If the nominal rate of interest stays at 12 percent while the rate of inflation goes to 13 percent, and if that rate is anticipated to last, the real rate of interest drops to a *negative* 1 percent! Lending money at 12 percent would not normally be advisable in such a situation.

7-7. a. 10, 9, 8, 7, 6, 5, 4, 3
  b. 8.0, 8.3, 9.4, 10.9, 12.0, 13.8, 16.0

CHAPTER 8

8-1. a. GDP = $950; NDP = $900; NI = $875
  b. GDP = $825
  c. The value of depreciation exceeding gross private investment implies that the total capital stock of the country is declining. This would likely decrease future productivity because capital is a productive resource.

8-3. a. Coal; $2
  b. $3. Auto manufacturers took something worth $5 and transformed it into an auto that they sold for $8.
  c. $9 because intermediate goods are *not* counted.
  d. $9, resulting from adding the value added at each stage. Note that in this economy, which produces only autos, the earnings and the income approaches both yield a GDP estimate of $9.

8-5. a. It falls.
  b. It is unchanged because illegal transactions are not measured anyway.
  c. It rises.

8-7. a. Nominal GDP for 1992 = ($4)(10) + ($12)(20) + ($6)(5) + ($25)(10) = $560. Nominal GDP for 1997 = ($8)(12) + ($36)(15) + ($10)(15) + ($30)(12) = $1,146.
  b. Real GDP for 1992 = $560. Real GDP for 1997 = ($4)(12) + ($12)(15) + ($6)(15) + ($25)(12) = $618.

CHAPTER 9

9-1. Point *B* is associated with the highest feasible growth rate. Capital goods implicitly represent future consumption, and point *B* has the highest feasible ratio of capital goods to current consumption (and thus the highest ratio of future consumption to current consumption).

9-3.   a. *M*
      b. *K*

CHAPTER 10

10-1. At P_1, the quantity of *AS* exceeds the quantity of *AD;* therefore, a surplus of real national income (output) exists. At that price level, suppliers are willing to produce more than buyers want to purchase; in this surplus situation, producers find their inventories rising involuntarily, and they find it profitable to reduce prices and output. At P_2, the quantity of *AD* exceeds the quantity of *AS,* and a shortage exists. At that price level, buyers want more than producers are willing to produce, and buyers, competing for goods and services, will bid the price level upward. A higher price level induces an increase in the quantity of *AS* and a decrease in the quantity of *AD*. Only at P_e does the quantity of *AS* equal the quantity of *AD;* at P_e, equilibrium exists.

10-3. The long-run aggregate supply curve is vertical at the point representing the maximum potential output possible. Prices can vary, but output cannot. In the short run, some increase in the level of output is possible with prices rising. This is possible because of the existence of some excess capacity, as well as flexibility in the nature and intensity of work. Therefore, the positively sloped portion of the aggregate supply curve constitutes the short-run aggregate supply curve.

10-5. a. The price level increases.
      b. National output decreases.

CHAPTER 11

11-1. If the interest rate is higher than equilibrium, desired saving exceeds desired investment. Those who desire investment funds from savers will offer to pay lower rates of interest. Savers, in competition with each other, will be willing to accept lower rates of interest. The interest rate will be bid down, which will simultaneously decrease the quantity of saving desired and increase the quantity of investment desired.

11-3. Equilibrium starts out at E_1 with the price level at 100 and equilibrium real GDP at Q_0. When AD_1 shifts to AD_2, the end result is that the equilibrium

is at E_1 with the same equilibrium level of real GDP per year but a price level of only 90. The equilibrium level of real GDP is supply-determined.

CHAPTER 12

12-1.

Disposable Income	Consumption	Saving
$ 500	$510	$−10
600	600	0
700	690	10
800	780	20
900	870	30
1,000	960	40

a.

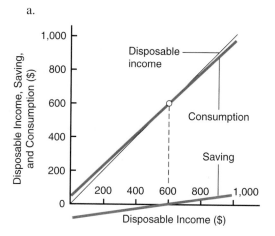

b. The marginal propensity to consume is .9; the marginal propensity to save is .1.

c.

Disposable Income	Average Propensity to Consume	Average Propensity to Save
$ 500	1.0200	−.0200
600	1.0000	0
700	.9857	.0142
800	.9750	.0250
900	.9667	.0333
1,000	.9600	.0400

12-3. Stock: a, c; Flow: b, d, e, f, g

12-5.

Real National Income	Consumption Expenditures	Saving	Investment	APC	APS	MPC	MPS
$1,000	$1,100	$-100	$100	1.1	-.1	.9	.1
2,000	2,000	0	100	1.0	.0	.9	.1
3,000	2,900	100	100	.967	.033	.9	.1
4,000	3,800	200	100	.950	.050	.9	.1
5,000	4,700	300	100	.940	.060	.9	.1
6,000	5,600	400	100	.933	.067	.9	.1

a.

b.

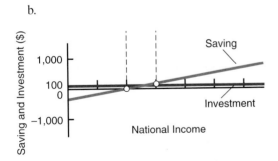

c. The multiplier effect from the inclusion of investment is to raise equilibrium national income by $1,000 over the equilibrium level it would otherwise have reached.
d. The value of the multiplier is 10.
e. The equilibrium level of national income without investment is $2,000; with investment, it is $3,000.

f. Equilibrium income will rise by $1,000.
g. Equilibrium income will again rise by $1,000 to $4,000.

12-7. a. Multiplier = 10
b. Multiplier = 3.33
c. Multiplier = 6.67
d. Multiplier = 2.86

CHAPTER 13

13-1. Discretionary fiscal policy is policy in which the levels of government spending and taxes change as a result of a deliberate decision by the government. *Example:* A change in the structure of tax rates, a change in government expenditures not associated with a change in government revenues.

    Automatic stabilizers cause the level of government spending or taxes to change as a result of endogenous changes in a variable such as income, other than changes due to deliberate decisions of the government. *Example:* Government revenues increasing from taxes during an economic expansion.

13-3. Consumers must not regard current budget deficits as equivalent to higher future taxes and current budget surpluses as equivalent to lower future taxes. For example, if consumers regard a $1 million deficit as imposing an equivalent amount of new taxes on them in the future, they will increase current saving so as to be in a position to pay the higher future taxes. As a result, current consumption will decline, and at least some and possibly all of the stabilizing effect of the deficit will be wiped out.

APPENDIX B

B-1. a. The marginal propensity to consume is equal to $1 - MPS$, or $\frac{6}{7}$.

b. Investment or government spending must increase by $50 billion.

c. The government would have to cut taxes by $58.33 billion.

B-3. a. Aggregate demand will shift downward by $500; therefore, national income will fall by $5,000.

b. Aggregate demand will shift upward by $.9(\$500) = \$450$; therefore, national income will rise by $4,500.

CHAPTER 14

14-1. The federal budget deficit is the difference between federal spending and federal taxes—in this case, $300 billion.

14-3. Ultimately, all government debt must be repaid by means of taxation. (The government cannot forever "repay" its debt by issuing more debt because ultimately the public debt would exceed the wealth of the entire nation!) Thus when the government adds to the debt, it is simultaneously adding to future taxes that must be equivalent in present value to the added debt.

14-5. Some observers say that the true burden of government is the real value of the resources it uses. Changing the way the books are kept leaves this burden unchanged. Moreover, neither current nor future taxes would be affected by this accounting change, so no one's tax liability would be altered. In brief, the change will have no real consequences. The net public debt equals the gross public debt *minus* the portion held by government agencies (what the government owes to itself).

CHAPTER 15

15-1. a. The painting by Renoir would have the greatest advantage as a store of value, for works of art have generally appreciated over time. As a medium of exchange or a unit of accounting, it would be deficient because of its high and sometimes variable value and the limited market for its exchange.

b. A 90-day U.S. Treasury bill also has a good store of value; it is guaranteed by the government and it will pay some interest. Of course, to the extent that the money to be returned for the matured bill is an imperfect store of value, so will be the bill. A 90-day bill will not vary much in value over its life because the redemption date is not far off and there is a ready market for its exchange; thus it is a serviceable medium of exchange and unit of accounting. But the large denominations in which these bills are issued detract from the latter functions.

c. It is important to distinguish between the balances in a time deposit account and the account itself. The account is a relationship between depositor and bank. The money in the account will have the attributes of money, qualified by the increased return that interest pays, the "notice" risk of withdrawal, and the solvency of the savings and loan association in Reno.

d. There are significant transactions costs in exchanging one share of IBM stock, and its value can be volatile in the short run, making it an imperfect medium of exchange and unit of accounting. Its qualities as a store of value depend on the health of the company and the economy in which it operates.

e. A $50 Federal Reserve note is cash, and its qualities will correspond accordingly. Of course, its denomination is a multiple of the common unit of our account, which is $1.

f. A MasterCard, like the savings account, indicates the existence of a relationship. Its transferability is severely limited, and its value depends on the terms of the credit agreement. (There is probably an illegal market for Master-Cards, in which they assume an independent value for exchange, although they probably lack most of the advantages of a store of value or unit of accounting.)

g. Because it is negotiable, a checkable account could be a useful medium of exchange, as long as its size does not restrict the available market too strongly. The only limits on its qualities as a store of value are the reliability of the bank and the value of the money into which it can be converted. Because the value is determined by the size of an anticipated transaction, there is no real independent unit of accounting to be measured by the checkable account.

h. Assuming that the pass is for the lifetime of the Dodgers and not for an owner who could not trade the pass, the ticket would be like many other nonmoney goods. Its money qualities would depend on the market available for its exchange and the value taken on by the good in the market. The fortunes of the Dodgers, the Los Angeles consumers' taste for baseball, and other demand determinants would affect the three monetary qualities of a lifetime pass.

15-3. M2 consists of the values of M1 plus overnight repurchase agreements (REPOs), overnight Euro-dollars, money market mutual funds, savings deposits, and small-denomination time deposits.

15-5. a. V
b. A
c. P
d. E

15-7. If there are n goods, the number of exchange rates will be $n(n - 1)/2$. In this case, $n = 10$, so the number of exchange rates will be $10(10 - 1)/2 = 90/2 = 45$.

15-9. The *number* of payments and the *value* of the payments are two different concepts. Specifically, the value of the payments must equal the average size of the payments, multiplied by the number of payments. Consider this example: A family of four buys a secondhand Rolls-Royce for $99,900, using a wire transfer to pay for it. To celebrate the purchase, the family goes out and has lunch, each family member using cash to pay for his or her own lunch. Each person's lunch costs $25, for a total of $100. There are five transactions (one car plus four lunches), so cash accounts for $4/5 = 80$ percent of the *number* of transactions. Yet there is $100,000 worth of transactions, so the wire transfer accounts for $99,000/$100,000 = 99.9$ percent of the *value* of the transactions.

CHAPTER 16

16-1. a. Multiple Deposit Creation

Bank	Deposits	Reserves	Loans
Bank 1	$1,000,000	$ 250,000	$ 750,000
Bank 2	750,000	187,500	562,500
Bank 3	562,500	140,625	421,875
Bank 4	421,875	105,469	316,406
Bank 5	316,406	79,102	237,304
All other banks	949,219	237,304	711,915
Totals	4,000,000	1,000,000	3,000,000

The money multiplier is 4.

b. Multiple Deposit Creation

Bank	Deposits	Reserves	Loans
Bank 1	$ 1,000,000	$ 50,000	$ 950,000
Bank 2	950,000	47,500	902,500
Bank 3	902,500	45,125	857,375
Bank 4	857,375	42,869	814,506
Bank 5	814,506	40,725	773,781
All other banks	15,475,619	773,781	14,701,838
Totals	20,000,000	1,000,000	19,000,000

The money multiplier is 20.

16-3. a. No change.
b. The money supply decreases by $50,000.
c. The money supply rises by $100,000.
d. This is a little tricky. If the Fed had been "keeping track" of currency, the $1,000 currency buried in Smith's backyard is accounted for; therefore, the money supply will rise by $9,000 because the Fed did not have to "create" the $1,000 already in existence.
e. The money supply will decrease by $9,000; see (d).

16-5. a.

ASSETS		LIABILITIES	
Total reserves	+$1,000,000	Demand deposits	+$1,000,000
Required reserves ($50,000) + excess reserves ($950,000)			
Total	+$1,000,000	Total	+$1,000,000

b. Bank 1 can increase its lending by $950,000.

16-7. a. The bank's excess reserves have decreased by $2,550,000.
   b. The money supply has decreased by $3 million.
   c. The money supply can decrease by as much as $20 million.

16-9. a. The maximum money multiplier will be 1/r where r = reserve ratio. In this case, r = .05, so the multiplier is 1/.05 = 20.
   b. Deposits will rise by an amount equal to the multiplier times the initial change in reserves. In this case, the rise will be equal to $1 million $\times$ 20 = $20 million.

CHAPTER 17

17-1. A change in monetary policy leads to a change in interest rates, which leads to a change in investment. This, then, through the multiplier process, leads to a change in income.

17-3.

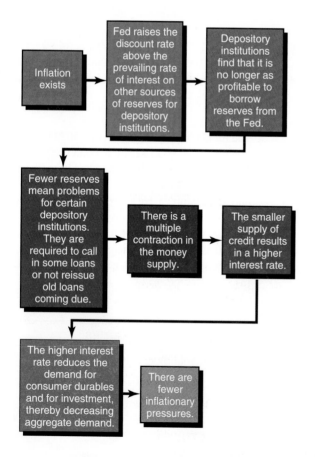

APPENDIX D

D-1. By its purchase of $1 billion in bonds, the Fed increased excess reserves by $1 billion. This ultimately caused a $3 billion increase in the money supply after full multiple expansion. The 1 percent drop in the interest rate, from 10 to 9 percent, caused investment to rise by $25 billion, from $200 billion to $225 billion. An investment multiplier of 3 indicates that equilibrium national income rose by $75 billion to $2,075 trillion.

CHAPTER 18

18-1. a. 10 percent
   b. A rise in the expected rate of inflation will cause the curve to shift upward by the amount of the rise.
   c. Because the systematic policies that attempt to exploit the seeming trade-off will be incorporated into workers' and firms' expectations. As a result, the expected inflation rate will move in lockstep with the actual rate (excepting random errors), so that the unemployment rate will not change when the inflation rate changes.

18-3. The existence of contracts, small-menu costs, and efficiency wages will increase the amount of discretion available to policymakers because all of these will tend to slow the adjustment of wages to changes in expectations.

18-5. A rise in the duration of unemployment will tend to raise the average unemployment rate because each unemployed person will be counted as unemployed more times over any given time period.

17-5. a. An expansionary open market operation (purchase of bonds) means that (b) the public has larger money holdings than desired. (c) This excess quantity of money demanded induces the public to buy more of everything, especially more durable goods. So (d) if the economy is starting out at its long-run equilibrium rate of output, there can only be a short-run increase in real GDP. Hence (e) ultimately, the public cannot buy more of everything, so it simply bids up prices, such that the price level rises.

18-7. Yes. It is precisely the fact both employers and workers incorrectly perceive a change in nominal demand as a change in real demand that generates the negatively sloping Phillips curve.

CHAPTER 19

19-1. For you, the marginal utility of the fifth pound of oranges is equal to the marginal utility of the third ear of corn. Apparently, your sister's tastes differ from yours—for her, the marginal utilities are not equal. For her, corn's marginal utility is too low, while that of oranges is too high—that's why she wants you to get rid of some of the corn (raising its marginal utility). She would have you do this until marginal utilities, for her, were equal. If you follow her suggestions, you will end up with a market basket that maximizes *her* utility subject to the constraint of *your* income. Is it any wonder that shopping from someone else's list is a frustrating task?

19-3. Her marginal utility is 100 at $1,200 at 50 cents, and 50 at $2. To calculate marginal utility per dollar, divide marginal utility by price per unit.

19-5. Optimum satisfaction is reached when marginal utilities per dollar of both goods are equal. This occurs at 102 units of A and 11 units of B. (Marginal utility per dollar is 1.77.)

19-7. Either your income or the relative price of eggs and bacon must have changed. Without more information, you can't make any judgments about whether you are better or worse off.

19-9. a. 20
b. 10
c. With consumption of the third unit of X

APPENDIX E

E-1. The problem here is that such preferences are inconsistent (*intransitive* is the word that economists use). If this consumer's tastes really are this way, then when confronted with a choice among A, B, and C, she will be horribly confused because A is preferred to B, which is preferred to C, which is preferred to A, which is preferred to B, which is preferred to C, and so on forever. Economists generally assume that preferences are consistent (or *transitive*): If A is preferred to B and B is preferred

to C, then A is preferred to C. Regardless of what people may *say* about their preferences, the assumption of transitivity seems to do quite well in predicting what people actually do.

E-3. With an income of $100 and the original prices, you could have consumed *either* 50 pounds of beef *or* 5 units of shelter *or* any linear combination shown by the budget line labeled "Original" on the graph below. With the same income but the new prices, you can now consume 25 pounds of beef or 10 units of shelter or any linear combination shown by the line labeled "New budget." Without information about your preferences, there is no way to tell whether you are better off or worse off. Draw a few indifference curves on the diagram. You will find that if you are a "shelter lover" (your indifference curves are relatively steep), the decline in the relative price of shelter will tend to make you better off. Conversely, if you are a "beef lover" (your indifference curves are relatively flat), the rise in the relative price of beef will make you worse off.

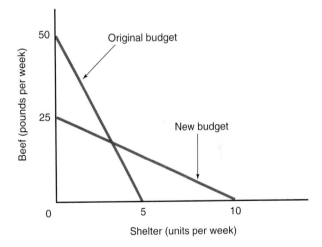

E-5. The first burrito is substituted at a rate of 10 servings of yogurt per burrito; the second burrito is substituted at a rate of 4:1; the third at a rate of 3:1; and the fourth at a rate of 2:1.

E-7. a. This person is simply indifferent between going or staying, an attitude that is perfectly consistent with our assumptions about consumer preferences.
b. This statement denies the law of substitution and so is inconsistent with our assumptions about preferences.

c. If we interpret "if I had my way" to mean "if I had an unlimited budget," this statement simply says that there is nonsatiation for these goods for this consumer—which is perfectly consistent with our assumptions about preferences.

CHAPTER 20

20-1. a.

Quantity Demanded per Week (ounces)	Price per Ounce	Elasticity
1,000	$ 5	
800	10	$\frac{1}{3}$, or .33
600	15	$\frac{5}{7}$, or .714
400	20	$\frac{7}{5}$, or 1.4
200	25	$\frac{9}{3}$, or 3

b. There are several ways to explain why elasticity is greater at higher prices on a linear curve. At higher prices, a given price change will result in a smaller percentage price change. The smaller resulting denominator of the elasticity ratio leads to a larger overall ratio. Similarly, as prices rise, quantities fall, thereby implying greater percentage quantity changes for a given absolute quantity change, and a larger numerator. Alternatively, the sizes of total revenue changes first increase and then decrease as price is lowered throughout a linear demand curve, thus implying declining elasticity.

20-3. a. Using averages in the elasticity equation, the income elasticity of demand for VCRs is .6666 ÷ .2857 = 2.33. It is income-elastic.
b. It is presumably a luxury good.

20-5. The problem is with the denominator, percentage change in P. Because the initial price was zero, any increase in price is of infinite percentage. However, if we take the average elasticity over a segment, there will be no problem. P will become the average of P_1 ($= 0$) and P_2 ($= 10$), or $(P_1 + P_2)/2 = 5$.

20-7. a. $E_p = \dfrac{50}{(475 + 525)/2} \div \dfrac{.02}{(.15 + .17)/2} = .8$

b. Demand is price-inelastic.

c. $E_s = \dfrac{75}{(525 + 600)/2} \div \dfrac{.02}{(.15 + .17)/2} = 1.067$

d. Supply is price-elastic (but only slightly so).

20-9. In each case, "before" is before the development of an acceptable substitute for the good in question, and "after" is after the development of that substitute. For example, between 1840 and 1880, the railroad emerged as a good substitute for canal transportation. In general, the better the substitutes for a good, the greater the price elasticity of demand for that good. Thus in each case we would expect the price elasticity of demand to be higher after the emergence of the substitute.

CHAPTER 21

21-1. Taxation of corporate dividend income can be thought of as a tax on the corporate form of organization. Increasing the amount of dividends exempt from taxes thus amounts to reducing taxes on dividends and hence reducing the tax on the corporate form of organization. As a result, more firms would choose to incorporate, and fewer would choose to be proprietorships or partnerships.

21-3. For simplicity, assume that potential lenders care only about the expected value of their lending decisions. If $10,000 is lent to a risk-free borrower at 10 percent interest, the borrower is certain to have ($10,000)(1 + .10) = $11,000 one year from now. If a loan is made to the risky firm, the borrower has a 20 percent chance of ending up with nothing and an 80 percent chance of repayment in full. Hence the amount the borrower expects to end up with is $E = (.20)(0) + (.80)($10,000)(1 + R)$, where R is the rate of interest charged to the risky firm. We seek the value of R that makes E equal to $11,000 because that will make the lender equally well off whether lending to the risk-free borrower or to the risky borrower. Thus we solve $11,000 = 0 + ($8,000)(1 + R)$ so that at a rate of interest $R = 37.5$ percent, the risky firm will be able to borrow the $10,000.

CHAPTER 22

22-1. The opportunity cost of continuing to possess the van is being ignored. For example, if the van could be sold without much problem for $10,000 and you could earn 10 percent per year by investing that $10,000 in something else, the opportunity cost of keeping the van is $1,000 per year.

22-3. a. $1
 b. 5 cents
 c. $1
 d. 10 cents
 e. It is rising.
 f. When the marginal product of labor is rising, the marginal cost of output falls; when the marginal product of labor is falling, the marginal cost of output rises.

22-5. The long-run average costs represent the points that give the least unit cost of producing any given rate of output. The concept is important when one must decide which scale of operations to adopt. Such a decision usually takes the form of deciding what size "plant" to construct.

22-7. a.

Output	AVC
0	$ 0
5	20
10	18
20	11
40	8

b. The marginal cost is $40 when increasing output from 10 to 20 units and $100 when increasing from 20 to 40.

c.

Output	ATC
0	$ 0
5	60
10	38
20	21
40	13

22-9.

Units of Labor	Total Product	Marginal Product	Average Product
6	120	—	20
7	147	27	21
8	170	23	21.25
9	180	10	20

CHAPTER 23

23-1.

Output (units)	Fixed Cost	AFC	Variable Cost	AVC	Total Cost	ATC	MC
1	$100	$100.00	$ 40	$40	$140	$140.00	$40
2	100	50.00	70	35	170	85.00	30
3	100	33.33	120	40	220	73.33	50
4	100	25.00	180	45	280	70.00	60
5	100	20.00	250	50	350	70.00	70
6	100	16.67	330	55	430	71.67	80

a. The price would have to drop below $35 before the firm would shut down in the short run.

b. $70 is the short-run break-even point for the firm. The output at this price would be 5 units per period.

c. At a price of $76, the firm would produce 5 units and earn a profit of $30 ($6 per unit over 5 units).

23-3. The industry demand curve is negatively sloped; it is relevant insofar as its interaction with the industry supply curve (ΣMC) determines the product price. The demand the individual firm faces, however, is infinitely elastic (horizontal) at the current market price.

23-5. a. $100
 b. $100
 c. $100
 d. $100

23-7. For simplicity, assume that your friend computed her "profit" the way many small businesses do: She ignored the opportunity cost of her time and her money. Instead of operating the car wash, she could have earned $25,000 at the collection agency plus $12,000 ($200,000 × 6 percent) on her savings. Thus the opportunity cost to her of operating the car wash was $37,000. Subtracting this amount from the $40,000 yields $3,000, which is her actual profit, over and above opportunity costs. You would tell her she really isn't making such great profits.

CHAPTER 24

24-1. a. The rectangle that shows total costs under ATC_1 is $0WCQ$. Total revenue is shown by $0XBQ$. This monopolist is in an economic profit situa-

tion. MC = MR is the output at which profit— the difference between total cost and total revenue—is maximized.
 b. With ATC_2, the rectangle showing total costs is $0XBQ$. The same rectangle, $0XBQ$, gives total revenue. This monopolist is breaking even. MC = MR shows the only quantity that does not cause losses.
 c. Under ATC_3, total costs are represented by rectangle $0YAQ$, total revenue by $0XBQ$. Here the monopolist is operating at an economic loss, which is minimized by producing where MC = MR.

24-3. Four conditions are necessary: (1) market power, (2) ability to separate markets at a reasonable cost, (3) differing price elasticities of demand, and (4) ability to prevent resale.

24-5. If E_p is numerically greater than 1 (elastic), marginal revenue is positive; a decrease in price will result in more total revenues. If E_p is numerically equal to 1 (unit-elastic), marginal revenue is 0; a change in price will not affect total revenues at all. If E_p is numerically less than 1 (inelastic), marginal revenue is negative; a decrease in price will result in less total revenues.

24-7. a.

Price	Quantity Demanded	Total Revenue	Marginal Revenue	Total Cost	Marginal Cost	Profit or Loss
$20	0	$ 0	—	$ 4	—	$−4
16	1	16	$ 16	10	$ 6	6
12	2	24	8	14	4	10
10	3	30	6	20	6	10
7	4	28	−2	28	8	0
4	5	20	−8	40	12	−20
0	6	0	−20	54	14	−54

b. The firm would operate at a loss if it produced 0, 5, or 6 units.
 c. The firm would break even at a rate of output of 4 units.
 d. The firm would maximize its profits by producing either 2 or 3 units. At either of those two outputs, it would be earning a profit of $10.

24-9. a. TR = $10,000, $16,000, $18,000, $16,000, $10,000, $3,000
 b. MR = $6,000, $2,000, −$2,000, −$6,000, −$7,000
 c. 3,000 units
 d. A profit-maximizing firm always sets MR = MC, and at any output level greater than 3,000,

MR is negative. Naturally, MC can never be negative, thus ensuring that output levels where MR is negative are impossible for a profit-maximizing firm.

CHAPTER 25

25-1. The marginal revenue of this ad campaign is $1,000. There was an addition of 40 cars per week at $25 per car. To determine whether profits have risen, we would have to know how much additional cost was incurred in the tuning of these cars, as well as the cost of the advertisement itself.

25-3. a. Approximately 64 percent ($525 million ÷ $825 million).
   b. The ratio would rise as the industry is more narrowly defined and fall as it is more broadly defined. Because an "industry" is arbitrarily defined, concentration ratios may be misleading.

25-5. The kink arises from the assumptions of the model. It is assumed that if any one firm raises its price, none of the others will follow. Consequently, a maverick firm's price increase will result in a drastic decrease in its total revenue. Conversely, the model assumes that any price decrease will be matched by all rivals. For this reason, the quantity demanded will probably not increase enough to cover increased costs. And profit will probably be less. Under these assumptions, it is in no individual firm's interest to "rock the boat."

25-7. The advertising campaign must increase weekly ticket revenues by at least $1,000 per week or it will be discontinued. This will require an additional 200 movie viewers each week.

25-9. The payoff matrix looks like this:

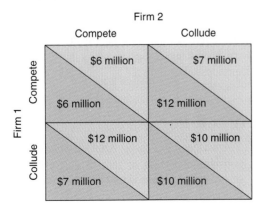

This situation parallels that of the prisoners' dilemma in that it is in the firms' *collective* interest to collude but in their *individual* interests to compete. If the possibility for collusion is a one-time-only arrangement, we have exactly the circumstances of the classic prisoners' dilemma, in which the dominant strategy is to compete, resulting in profits of $6 million for each firm. (This sounds good until you remember that each is *losing* $4 million relative to the joint maximum possible with collusion!) If this is a repeating game and if each firm can observe the behavior of its rival, it may be possible for the firms to overcome their dilemma and reach the joint maximum—for example, by employing the "tit for tat" strategy discussed in the text.

CHAPTER 26

26-1. a. Quantity produced would be Q_b, and price would be P_c.
   b. Losses would equal the rectangle P_bBCP_c.

26-3. There will still be political pressure from Congress if you enforce new regulations that dramatically increase the costs and hence the prices of products. Thus you can simply do anything you feel like concerning new rules in the workplace. If you must now consider costs, you might want to estimate the impact each new rule has on the unit cost of each product affected. You would compare the total costs thus incurred because of the new rule with the estimated benefits to the community in terms of higher levels of worker safety and health.

26-5. By definition, a natural monopolist's costs are lower than those of potential entrants. Hence although other firms may be free to enter, they are unlikely to do so. The natural monopolist can thus earn economic profits equal to the difference between its costs and its potential rivals' costs.

26-7. Liquor store owners do not like to compete any more than anyone else does. Nevertheless, simply telling the truth about this distaste is unlikely to garner them much political support in favor of restricting entry into their industry. What the liquor store owners seek is an argument that what is good for them is also good for you, and many people probably find the idea of a liquor store next door distasteful.

CHAPTER 27

27-1.

Quantity of Labor	Total Product per Week	MPP	MRP
1	250	250	$500
2	450	200	400
3	600	150	300
4	700	100	200
5	750	50	100
6	750	0	0

a. Demand schedule for labor:

Weekly Wage	Laborers Demanded per Week
$500	1
400	2
300	3
200	4
100	5

b. $100 each

c. Four

27-3. a. 15 million worker-hours per time period

b. 10 million per time period

c. Buyers can get all the labor they want at W_1; laborers can't sell all they want to sell at W_1.

d. Because a surplus of labor exists, the unemployed will offer to work for less, and industry wage rates will fall toward W_e.

27-5. Suppose that the demand for the output product is highly elastic. Even a relatively small increase in the price of the input factor, which correspondingly raises the price of the output product, will cause a large decrease in the quantity of output demanded and therefore in the employment of the input.

27-7. The MRP of labor is $40 per worker-day ($3,040 less $3,000, divided by a change in labor input of one worker-day). The maximum wage that would still make it worthwhile to hire this additional employee would be $39.99 per day. If the going market wage is above that figure, you will not expand output.

27-9. Imposing limitations such as these implicitly reduces the ability of employers to compete for your services. Thus you can expect to receive a lower wage and to work in a less desirable job.

CHAPTER 28

28-1. a. Marginal revenue product

b. S

c. Q_m

d. W_m

28-3. Some examples would be Coors beer in Golden, Colorado; Bethlehem Steel in Bethlehem, Pennsylvania; Winnebago Corporation in Forest City, Iowa; and many coal-mining companies in towns in West Virginia. As long as your example is one of an employer that is dominant in its local labor market selling in fairly competitive markets, you are correct.

28-5. No, you should not. The MRP when you employ 31 people is $89.50 ($99.50 in revenue from selling the twenty-first unit, less $10 forgone in selling the first 20 units for 50 cents less than originally). The MFC is $91 ($61 to attract the twenty-first employee to your firm, plus the additional $1 per day to each of the original 20 employees). Because MFC exceeds MRP, you should not expand output.

28-7. Because the union acts in the interests of its members and the competitive wage is lower than the highest wage the union can obtain for its members.

28-9. The monopsonist's decisions about how much to purchase influence the price of the good it is buying. As a result, the marginal factor cost curve facing a monopsonist lies above the average factor cost curve (which is the supply curve of the industry producing the good being purchased by the monopsonist).

CHAPTER 29

29-1. The statement is false. Although there may be a substantial portion of rent in the revenues from these museums, we would have to assume that the museums are absolutely costless to keep in their current use in order to make the statement that *all* revenues are economic rent. The most obvious expenses of keeping the museums operating are the costs of maintenance: cleaning, lighting, and other overhead costs. But these may be minor compared to the opportunity cost involved in keeping the museum *as a museum.* The buildings might make ideal government office buildings. They may be on land that would be extremely valuable if sold on the private real estate market. If there are any such alternative uses, the value of these uses must be subtracted from the current revenues in order to arrive at the true level of economic rent. Forgoing these alternative opportunities is as much a cost of operating the museum as the monthly utility bill.

29-3. The statement is false. Because a firm utilizes an input only to the point that the input's MRP is equal to its price, and marginal product is declining, it follows that all the intramarginal (up-to-the-marginal) units are producing more value than they are being paid. This differential is used to compensate for other factor inputs. The residual, if any, would be profits.

29-5. a. 9 percent
b. The equilibrium interest rate will increase.
c. 5 percent

29-7. In each case, the asset that qualifies the borrower for a lower interest rate is better collateral (or security) for the lender and thus reduces both the chances of default and the lender's losses in the event that default does occur.

29-9. They would be reduced but not necessarily eliminated (because, for example, economic profits due to entry restrictions might still persist).

CHAPTER 30

30-1. Whites might invest more in human capital; blacks might receive less and lower-quality education and/or training; blacks in the workforce may, on average, be younger; discrimination may exist.

30-3. Productivity and equality.

30-5. Such a program would drastically reduce efficiency. It would eliminate individuals' incentives to maximize the economic value of resources because they would receive no reward for doing so. It

would also eliminate their incentive to minimize production costs because there would be no penalty for failing to do so.

30-7. When governments pay for health care, hospitals have reduced incentives to operate efficiently because they are less likely to be penalized for being inefficient. Bureaucrats are less likely to provide the services that patients want at the lowest cost because the rewards from doing so are diminished when the government (rather than the patient) pays for the services. Finally, because the patient is not directly footing the bill, the patient has less incentive to choose wisely (that is, in a manner that equates the true marginal benefits and costs) when choosing health care.

CHAPTER 31

31-1. When the external costs are added to the supply curve (which is itself the sum of marginal costs of the industry), the total (private plus public) marginal costs of production are above the private supply schedule. At quantity Q_1 in the graph below, marginal costs to society are greater than the value attached to the marginal unit. The demand curve is below the social supply curve. To bring marginal cost and marginal benefit back into line, thus promoting an economically efficient allocation of resources, quantity would have to be reduced to Q_2 and price raised to P_2.

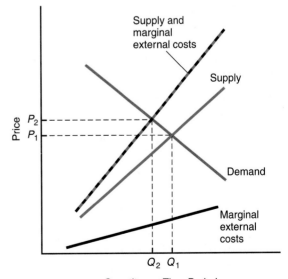

31-3. a. The price of polluting should be set according to the marginal economic damage imposed by polluters; this means that similar quantities of pollution will cost polluters different prices in different parts of the country; pollution will be more costly in New York City than in a small town in the Midwest.

b. Firms that find it cheaper to treat will do so; firms that find it cheaper to pay to pollute will pollute.

c. Yes, some firms will be forced to shut down due to increased costs; this is efficient, as the true costs to society of their operations were not paid by them and their customers; they were able to remain in business only by imposing costs on third parties.

d. This might be good because now the people who are using the resources will be forced to pay for them instead of imposing costs on others. Those who are *not* using these products were, in effect, subsidizing lower prices to those who were. This new solution seems more fair and is certainly efficient.

31-5. Everyone owns them and nobody owns them. Consequently, there is no incentive for any user to be concerned with the future value of the resource in question. This is perhaps most clearly observable in the behavior of fishing boat owners. The goal of each boat owner is to harvest fish as long as marginal private cost is less than the going price of such fish. The opportunity cost of depleting the stock of fish does not affect the decisions of the proprietor. In light of the nonownership of the fish, any single boat operator would be foolish to behave otherwise.

31-7.

Annual Units of Pollution	a. Marginal Benefits	b. Marginal Costs
0	—	—
1	$ 30	$150
2	40	100
3	80	80
4	120	60
5	160	20

a. The net gain is $(430 - 150) - 80 = 200$.
b. The net gain is $430 - 410 = 20$.

c. The optimal level is between 2 and 3 units, or where marginal benefit equals marginal cost.

31-9. The economically efficient amount of pollution occurs at a level at which the marginal costs of reducing it further would just exceed any benefits from that reduction. If pollution is reduced below this point, we would be better off with more pollution. The government might directly require firms or individuals to generate too little pollution (for example, through inappropriate environmental regulations), or it might establish pollution fees, fines, or taxes that overstate the damages done by the pollution and thus induce firms or individuals to reduce pollution too much.

CHAPTER 32

32-1. The existence of these costs implies the notion of rational ignorance, so that individuals choose not to be informed about certain issues because the cost of being informed is high relative to any benefit forthcoming from the state of the issue. This also contributes to the growth of special-interest groups because individuals have no strong economic incentive to act against them.

32-3. Legislators find themselves in a situation much like a prisoners' dilemma (see Chapter 25): They have a collective incentive to act in the best interests of society as a whole but individual incentives to act in the interests of their own constituents or other narrow special interests. The favors handed out by legislators could, in principle, come in the form of either lower taxes or higher spending. As a practical matter, it is usually easier to disguise higher spending as something socially beneficial for which the recipient is uniquely qualified. Hence spending (and thus the size of the government) tends to increase. (Clearly there is some limit to this process, for the government cannot be larger than the economy as a whole. Nevertheless, the limit does not appear to be in sight.)

32-5. Currently, lobbyists are paid to influence state legislators, the benefits of which may redound to those seeking the political favors for many years, given that often state legislators stay in office for many years. Under a system of term limits, each legislator's time in office is definitely terminated after, for example, 12 years. Thus, using the theory of public choice, we predict that fewer resources will be used to influence each legislator in those states that have term limits. The reason is that the potential payoff will last a shorter time period. More newly elected legislators will have to be influenced under term limits, so fewer resources will go toward influencing each legislator individually, all other things held constant.

32-7. a. 20 percent of 1.9 million is 380,000 farms.
 b. Oligopoly seems highly unlikely in this industry in the foreseeable future—there are simply too many firms.

32-9. One of the trickiest things about handing out subsidies is that everybody wants to receive them but not everyone can receive them (at least not after netting out the taxes used to pay for them). Farmers are uniquely positioned to be the recipients of subsidies because of the natural limiting factor—farmland—that constrains their numbers.

32-11. The demand for farmland would fall, resulting in lower prices for such land and a diversion of some of it to other uses, possibly including residential neighborhoods or national parks. The demand for other farm resources—including the labor of farmers—would also fall, inducing some of these resources to move into alternative occupations as well. The price of food would fall, reducing malnutrition but also possibly increasing obesity. Imports of some crops (such as sugar) would rise sharply, while production of goods that use foodstuffs as inputs would also rise. These (and many other) effects would be greatly dampened today if the change in policy were not to take place until 20 years from now—partly because the present value of distant events is small and partly because Congress would have plenty of opportunities over 20 years to reverse itself.

CHAPTER 33

33-1. a. The opportunity cost to the United States of producing one ounce of caviar is two bushels of wheat. The six hours that were needed to make the caviar could have been used to grow two bushels. The opportunity cost of producing one bushel of wheat is $\frac{1}{2}$ ounce of caviar.

 b. The opportunity cost to Russia of producing one ounce of caviar is $1\frac{1}{2}$ bushels of wheat. The opportunity cost of producing a bushel of wheat in Russia is $\frac{2}{3}$ ounce of caviar.
 c. The United States has a comparative advantage in wheat because it has a lower opportunity cost in terms of caviar. Russia has a comparative advantage in caviar. Less wheat is forgone to produce an ounce of caviar in Russia.

33-3. The assumption given in the question is equivalent to the United States' having an absolute advantage in the production of all goods and services. But the basis of world trade lies in differences in *comparative* advantage. As long as other countries have a lower opportunity cost in producing some goods and services, the United States will benefit from international trade.

33-5. Tariffs yield government revenues; quotas do not.

33-7. a. One million pounds are produced and 2 million pounds are imported.
 b. With a 10-cent tariff, 1.5 million pounds would be produced and 1 million pounds would be imported. Government revenues would amount to ($2.5 million − $1.5 million) × $.10 = $100,000.
 c. With a 20-cent tariff, domestic growers can receive 70 cents per pound. They will produce 2 million pounds, and no grapes will be imported, in which case government revenues are zero.

33-9. Consider trade between the United States and Canada. The United States purchases timber from Canada, and Canada purchases computers from the United States. Ultimately, the Canadians pay for U.S.-made computers with the timber that they sell here. If the United States imposes a tax on Canadian timber and thus reduces the amount of timber that the Canadians are able to sell to the United States, the necessary result is that the Canadians will be able to buy fewer American computers. American exports of computers will decline as a result of the reduction in American imports of timber.

CHAPTER 34

34-1. The answer is (c). A declining dollar price of the pound implies an increasing pound price of the dollar—appreciation of the dollar. (a) is incorrect because an increase in demand for U.S. products would affect the supply of pounds and the demand for dollars, whereas here we are dealing with the demand for pounds. (b) explains a phenomenon that would have just the opposite result as that shown in the graph: An increased U.S. demand for British goods would lead to an increase in the demand for the pound, not a decrease as shown. (d) is incorrect because the pound depreciates.

34-3. One pound equals $3.50; $1 equals .2857 pound. One mark equals 35 cents; $1 equals 2.857 marks. One mark equals .1 pound; one pound equals 10 marks.

34-5. To maintain the exchange rate, domestic policy variables such as the money supply are also affected. Suppose that the government plans an expansive monetary policy to encourage output growth. A balance of payments deficit leads the government to buy up dollars, which in turn leads to a contraction in the domestic money supply. Therefore, in order to maintain the expansionary monetary policy, the government would have to expand the money supply in larger magnitudes than it would without the balance of payments deficits with a fixed exchange rate system.

34-7. a. The dollar price of pounds is $1.50. The equilibrium quantity is 150 million.

b. Curve D' describes this situation. The new dollar price of pounds would be $1.70, and the equilibrium quantity would be 200 million.
c. At a price of $1.50 per pound, 250 million pounds sterling would be demanded and only 150 million would be supplied, so the Fed would have to supply an extra 100 million to American buyers of British goods or British exporters.
d. Curve D'' describes this situation. 150 million pounds sterling would be supplied at a price of $1.50, but only 50 million pounds would be demanded. Therefore, the Fed would have to buy up 100 million pounds sterling.

CHAPTER 35

35-1. You could do what the makers of popular game Doom did: You could offer a more complete version of your word processing program for a fee. You could use the e-mail addresses of everyone who downloaded your free program to form the basis of a new marketing campaign to sell related items, such as self-improvement CD-ROMs. You could, of course, sell everyone a new, updated version of your program every year for some low price, such as $15.

Absolute advantage The ability to produce a good or service at an "absolutely" lower cost, usually measured in units of labor or resource input required to produce one unit of the good or service. *Can also be viewed as* the ability to produce more output from given inputs of resources than other producers can.

Accounting identities Statements that certain numerical measurements are equal by accepted definition (for example, "assets equal liabilities plus stockholders' equity").

Accounting profit Total revenues minus total explicit costs.

Action time lag The time required between recognizing an economic problem and putting policy into effect. The action time lag is short for monetary policy but quite long for fiscal policy, which requires congressional approval.

Active (discretionary) policymaking All actions on the part of monetary and fiscal policymakers that are undertaken in response to or in anticipation of some change in the overall economy.

Adverse selection A problem created by asymmetric information prior to a transaction. Individuals who are the most undesirable from the other party's point of view end up being the ones who are most likely to want to engage in a particular financial transaction, such as borrowing. *Can also be viewed as* the circumstance that arises in financial markets when borrowers who are the worst credit risks are the ones most likely to seek loans.

Age-earnings cycle The regular earnings profile of an individual throughout his or her lifetime. The age-earnings cycle usually starts with a low income, builds gradually to a peak at around age 50, and then gradually curves down until it approaches zero at retirement.

Aggregate demand The total of all planned expenditures for the entire economy.

Aggregate demand curve A curve showing planned purchase rates for all goods and services in the economy at various price levels, all other things held constant.

Aggregate demand shock

Any shock that causes the aggregate demand curve to shift inward or outward.

Aggregates Total amounts or quantities; aggregate demand, for example, is total planned expenditures throughout a nation.

Aggregate supply The total of all planned production for the entire economy.

Aggregate supply shock Any shock that causes the aggregate supply curve to shift inward or outward.

Anticipated inflation The inflation rate that we believe will occur; when it does, we are in a situation of fully anticipated inflation.

Antitrust legislation Laws that restrict the formation of monopolies and regulate certain anticompetitive business practices.

Appreciation An increase in the value of a currency in terms of other currencies.

Asset demand Holding money as a store of value instead of other assets such as certificates of deposit, corporate bonds, and stocks.

Assets Amounts owned; all items to which a business or household holds legal claim.

Asymmetric information Information possessed by one side of a transaction but not the other. The side with more information will be at an advantage.

Automatic, or built-in, stabilizers Special provisions of the tax law that cause changes in the economy without the action of Congress and the president. Examples are the progressive income tax system and unemployment compensation.

Autonomous consumption The part of consumption that is independent of (does not depend on) the level of disposable income. Changes in autonomous consumption shift the consumption function.

Average fixed costs Total fixed costs divided by the number of units produced.

Average physical product Total product divided by the variable input.

Average propensity to consume (APC) Consumption divided by disposable income; for any given level of income, the proportion of total disposable income that is consumed.

Average propensity to save (APS) Saving divided by disposable income; for any given level of income, the proportion of total disposable income that is saved.

Average tax rate The total tax payment divided by total income. It is the proportion of total income paid in taxes.

Average total costs Total costs divided by the number of units produced; sometimes called *average per-unit total costs.*

Average variable costs Total variable costs divided by the number of units produced.

Balance of payments A summary record of a country's economic transactions with foreign residents and governments over a year.

Balance of trade The value of goods and services bought and sold in the world market.

Balance sheet A statement of the assets and liabilities of any business entity, including financial institutions and the Federal Reserve System. Assets are what is owned; liabilities are what is owed.

Bank runs Attempts by many of a bank's depositors to convert checkable and time deposits into currency out of fear for the bank's solvency.

Barter The direct exchange of goods and services for other goods and services without the use of money.

Base year The year that is chosen as the point of reference for comparison of prices in other years.

Bilateral monopoly A market structure consisting of a monopolist and a monopsonist.

Black market A market in which goods are traded at prices above their legal maximum prices or in which illegal goods are sold.

Bond A legal claim against a firm, usually entitling the owner of the bond to receive a fixed annual coupon payment, plus a lump-sum payment at the bond's maturity date. Bonds are issued in return for funds lent to the firm.

Budget constraint All of the possible combinations of goods that can be purchased (at fixed prices) with a specific budget.

Bureaucrats Nonelected government officials who are responsible for the day-to-day operation of government and the observance of its regulations and laws.

Business fluctuations The ups and downs in overall business activity, as evidenced by changes in national income, employment, and the price level.

Capital consumption allowance Another name for depreciation, the amount that businesses would have to save in order to take care of the deterioration of machines and other equipment.

Capital gain The positive difference between the purchase price and the sale price of an asset. If a share of stock is bought for $5 and then sold for $15, the capital gain is $10.

Capital goods Producer durables; nonconsumable goods that firms use to make other goods.

Capitalism An economic system in which individuals own productive resources; these individuals can use the resources in whatever manner they choose, subject to common protective legal restrictions.

Capital loss The negative difference between the purchase price and the sale price of an asset.

Capture hypothesis A theory of regulatory behavior that predicts that the regulators will eventually be captured by the special interests of the industry being regulated.

Cartel An association of producers in an industry that agree to set common prices and output quotas to prevent competition.

Central bank A banker's bank, usually an official institution that also serves as a country's treasury's bank. Central banks normally regulate commercial banks.

Certificate of deposit (CD) A time deposit with a fixed maturity date offered by banks and other financial institutions.

Ceteris paribus **[KAY-ter-us PEAR-uh-bus] assumption** The assumption that nothing changes except the factor or factors being studied.

Checkable deposits Any deposits in a thrift institution or a commercial bank on which a check may be written.

Closed shop A business enterprise in which employees must belong to the union before they can be hired and must remain in the union after they are hired.

Collateral An asset pledged to guarantee the repayment of a loan.

Collective bargaining Bargaining between the management of a company or of a group of companies and the management of a union or a group of unions for the purpose of setting a mutually agreeable contract on wages, fringe benefits, and working conditions for all employees in all the unions involved.

Collective decision making How voters, politicians, and other interested parties act and how these actions influence nonmarket decisions.

Common property Property that is owned by everyone and therefore by no one. Air and water are examples of common property resources.

Communism In its purest form, an economic system in which the state has disappeared and individuals contribute to the economy according to their productivity and are given income according to their needs.

Comparable-worth doctrine The belief that women should receive the same wages as men if the levels of skill and responsibility in their jobs are equivalent.

Comparative advantage The ability to produce a good or service at a lower opportunity cost compared to other producers.

Complements Two goods are complements if both are used together for consumption or enjoyment—for example, coffee and cream. The more you buy of one, the more you buy of the other. For complements, a change in the price of one causes an opposite shift in the demand for the other.

Concentration ratio The percentage of all sales contributed by the leading four or leading eight firms in an industry; sometimes called the *industry concentration ratio.*

Constant-cost industry An industry whose total output can be increased without an increase in long-run per-unit costs; an industry whose long-run supply curve is horizontal.

Constant dollars Dollars expressed in terms of real purchasing power using a particular year as the base or standard of comparison, in contrast to current dollars.

Constant returns to scale No change in long-run average costs when output increases.

Consumer optimum A choice of a set of goods and services that maximizes the level of satisfaction for each consumer, subject to limited income.

Consumer Price Index (CPI) A statistical measure of a weighted average of prices of a specified set of goods and services purchased by wage earners in urban areas.

Consumption The use of goods and services for personal satisfaction. *Can also be viewed as* spending on new goods and services out of a household's current income. Whatever is not consumed is saved. Consumption includes such things as buying food and going to a concert.

Consumption function The relationship between amount consumed and disposable income. A consumption function tells us how much people plan to consume at various levels of disposable income.

Consumption goods Goods bought by households to use up, such as food, clothing, and movies.

Contraction A business fluctuation during which the pace of national economic activity is slowing down.

Contractionary gap The gap that exists whenever the equilibrium level of real national income per year is less than the full-employment level as shown by the position of the long-run aggregate supply curve.

Cooperative game A game in which the players explicity collude to make themselves better off. As applied to firms, it involves companies colluding in order to make higher than competitive rates of return.

Corporation A legal entity that may conduct business in its own name just as an individual does; the owners of a corporation, called shareholders, own shares of the firm's profits and enjoy the protection of limited liability.

Cost-of-living adjustments (COLAs) Clauses in contracts that allow for increases in specified nominal values to take account of changes in the cost of living.

Cost-of-service regulation Regulation based on allowing prices to reflect only the actual cost of production and no monopoly profits.

Cost-push inflation Inflation caused by a continually decreasing short-run aggregate supply curve.

Craft unions Labor unions composed of workers who engage in a particular trade or skill, such as baking, carpentry, or plumbing.

Creative response Behavior on the part of a firm that allows it to comply with the letter of the law but violate the spirit, significantly lessening the law's effects.

Cross price elasticity of demand (E_{xy}) The percentage change in the demand for one good (holding its price constant) divided by the percentage change in the price of a related good.

Crowding-out effect The tendency of expansionary fiscal policy to cause a decrease in planned investment or planned consumption in the private sector; this decrease normally results from the rise in interest rates.

Crude quantity theory of money and prices The belief that changes in the money supply lead to proportional changes in the price level.

Cybernomics The application of economic analysis to human and technological activities related to the use of the Internet in all of its forms.

Cyclical unemployment Unemployment resulting from business recessions that occur when aggregate (total) demand is insufficient to create full employment.

Decreasing-cost industry An industry in which an increase in output leads to a reduction in long-run per-unit costs, such that the long-run industry supply curve slopes downward.

Deficiency payment A direct subsidy paid to farmers equal to the amount of a crop they produce multiplied by the difference between the target price for that good and its market price.

Deflation The situation in which the average of all prices of goods and services in an economy is falling.

Demand A schedule of how much of a good or service people will purchase at any price during a specified time period, other things being constant.

Demand curve A graphical representation of the demand schedule; a negatively sloped line showing the inverse relationship between the price and the quantity demanded (other things being equal).

Demand-pull inflation Inflation caused by increases in aggregate demand not matched by increases in aggregate supply.

Demerit good A good that has been deemed socially undesirable through the political process. Heroin is an example.

Dependent variable A variable whose value changes according to changes in the value of one or more independent variables.

Depository institutions Financial institutions that accept deposits from savers and lend those deposits out at interest.

Depreciation Reduction in the value of capital goods over a one-year period due to physical wear and tear and also to obsolescence; also called *capital consumption allowance. Can also be viewed as a decrease in the value of a currency in terms of other currencies.*

Depression An extremely severe recession.

Deregulation The elimination or phasing out of regulations on economic activity.

Derived demand Input factor demand derived from demand for the final product being produced.

Diminishing marginal utility The principle that as more of any good or service is consumed, its extra benefit declines. Otherwise stated, increases in total utility from the consumption of a good or service become smaller and smaller as more is consumed during a given time period.

Direct expenditure offsets Actions on the part of the private sector in spending money that offset government fiscal policy actions. Any increase in government spending in an area that competes with the private sector will have some direct expenditure offset.

Direct relationship A relationship between two variables that is positive, meaning that an increase in one variable is associated with an increase in the other and a decrease in one variable is associated with a decrease in the other.

Dirty float A system between flexible and fixed exchange rates in which central banks occasionally enter foreign exchange markets to influence rates.

Discounting The method by which the present value of a future sum or a future stream of sums is obtained.

Discount rate The interest rate that the Federal Reserve charges for reserves that it lends to depository institutions. It is sometimes referred to as the rediscount rate or, in Canada and England, as the bank rate.

Discouraged workers Individuals who have stopped looking for a job because they are convinced that they will not find a suitable one. Typically, they become convinced after unsuccessfully searching for a job.

Diseconomies of scale Increases in long-run average costs that occur as output increases.

Disposable personal income (DPI) Personal income after personal income taxes have been paid.

Dissaving Negative saving; a situation in which spending exceeds income. Dissaving can occur when a household is able to borrow or use up existing owned assets.

Distributional coalitions Associations such as cartels, unions, and cooperatives that are formed to gain special government privileges in order to redistribute wealth by taking small amounts from each of many people and giving large amounts to each of only a few.

Distribution of income The way income is allocated among the population.

Dividends Portion of a corporation's profits paid to its owners (shareholders).

Division of labor The segregation of a resource into different specific tasks; for example, one automobile worker puts on bumpers, another doors, and so on.

Dominant strategies Strategies that always yield the highest benefit. Regardless of what other players do, a dominant strategy will yield the most benefit for the player using it.

Dumping Selling a good or a service abroad at a price below its cost of production or below the price charged in the home market.

Durable consumer goods Consumer goods that have a life span of more than three years.

E-commerce The use of the Internet in any manner that allows buyers and sellers to find each other. It can involve business selling directly to other businesses or business selling to retail customers. Both goods and services are involved in e-commerce.

Economic goods Goods that are scarce, for which the quantity demanded exceeds the quantity supplied at a zero price.

Economic growth Increases in per capita real GDP measured by its rate of change per year.

Economic profits Total revenues minus total opportunity costs of all inputs used, or the total of all implicit and explicit costs. *Can also be viewed as the difference between total revenues and the opportunity cost of all factors of production.*

Economic rent A payment for the use of any resource over and above its opportunity cost.

Economics The study of how people allocate their limited resources to satisfy their unlimited wants.

Economic system The institutional means through which resources are used to satisfy human wants.

Economies of scale Decreases in long-run average costs resulting from increases in output.

Effect time lag The time that elapses between the onset of policy and the results of that policy.

Efficiency The case in which a given level of inputs is used to produce the maximum output possible. Alternatively, the situation in which a given output is produced at minimum cost.

Efficiency wages Wages set above competitive levels to increase labor productivity and profits by enhancing the efficiency of the firm through lower turnover, ease of attracting higher-quality workers, and better efforts by workers.

Efficiency wage theory The hypothesis that the productivity of workers depends on the level of the real wage rate.

Effluent fee A charge to a polluter that gives the right to discharge into the air or water a certain amount of pollution. Also called a *pollution tax*.

Elastic demand A demand relationship in which a given percentage change in price will result in a larger percentage change in quantity demanded. Total expenditures are invariant to price changes in the unit's elastic portion of the demand curve.

Empirical Relying on real-world data in evaluating the usefulness of a model.

Endowments The various resources in an economy, including both physical resources and such human resources as ingenuity and management skills.

Entitlements Guaranteed benefits under a government program such as Social Security, Medicare, or Medicaid.

Entrepreneurship The factor of production involving human resources that perform the functions of raising capital, organizing, managing, assembling other factors of production, and making basic business policy decisions. The entrepreneur is a risk taker.

Entry deterrence strategy Any strategy undertaken by firms in an industry, either individually or together, with the intent or effect of raising the cost of entry into the industry by a new firm.

Equation of exchange The formula indicating that the number of monetary units times the number of times each unit is spent on final goods and services is identical to the price level times output (or nominal national income).

Equilibrium The situation when quantity supplied equals quantity demanded at a particular price.

Eurodollar deposits Deposits denominated in U.S. dollars but held in banks outside the United States, often in overseas branches of U.S. banks.

Excess reserves The difference between legal reserves and required reserves.

Exclusion principle The principle that no one can be excluded from the benefits of a public good, even if that person hasn't paid for it.

Expansion A business fluctuation in which overall business activity is rising at a more rapid rate than previously or at a more rapid rate than the overall historical trend for the nation.

Expansionary gap The gap that exists whenever the equilibrium level of real national income per year is greater than the full-employment level as shown by the position of the long-run aggregate supply curve.

Expenditure approach A way of computing national income by adding up the dollar value at current market prices of all final goods and services.

Explicit costs Costs that business managers must take account of because they must be paid; examples are wages, taxes, and rent.

Externality A consequence of an economic activity that spills over to affect third parties. Pollution is an externality. *Can also be viewed as* a situation in which a private cost diverges from a social cost; a situation in which the costs of an action are not fully borne by the two parties engaged in exchange or by an individual engaging in a scarce-resource-using activity. (Also applies to benefits.)

Featherbedding Any practice that forces employers to use more labor than they would otherwise or to use existing labor in an inefficient manner.

The Fed The Federal Reserve System; the central bank of the United States.

Federal Deposit Insurance Corporation (FDIC) A government agency that insures the deposits held in member banks; all members of the Fed and other banks that qualify can join.

Federal funds market A private market (made up mostly of banks) in which banks can borrow reserves from other banks that want to lend them. Federal funds are usually lent for overnight use.

Federal funds rate The interest rate that depository institutions pay to borrow reserves in the interbank federal funds market.

Fiduciary monetary system A system in which currency is issued by the government and its value is based uniquely on the public's faith that the currency represents command over goods and services.

Final goods and services Goods and services that are at their final stage of production and will not be transformed into yet other goods or services. For example, wheat is normally not a final good because usually it is used to make bread, which is a final good.

Financial capital Money used to purchase capital goods such as buildings and equipment.

Financial intermediaries Institutions that transfer funds between ultimate lenders (savers) and ultimate borrowers.

Financial intermediation The process by which financial institutions accept savings from businesses, households, and governments and lend the savings to other businesses, households, and governments.

Firm A business organization that employs resources to produce goods or services for profit. A firm normally owns and operates at least one plant in order to produce.

Fiscal policy The discretionary changing of government expenditures and/or taxes in order to achieve national economic goals, such as high employment with price stability.

Fixed costs Costs that do not vary with output. Fixed costs include such things as rent on a building. These costs are fixed for a certain period of time; in the long run, they are variable.

Fixed investment Purchases by businesses of newly produced producer durables, or capital goods, such as production machinery and office equipment.

Flexible exchange rates Exchange rates that are allowed to fluctuate in the open market in response to changes in supply and demand. Sometimes called *floating exchange rates.*

Flow A quantity measured per unit of time; something that occurs over time, such as the income you make per week or per year or the number of individuals who are fired every month.

Foreign exchange market The market for buying and selling foreign currencies.

Foreign exchange rate The price of one currency in terms of another.

45-degree reference line The line along which planned real expenditures equal real national income per year.

Fractional reserve banking A system in which depository institutions hold reserves that are less than the amount of total deposits.

Free-rider problem A problem that arises when individuals presume that others will pay for public goods so that, individually, they can escape paying for their portion without causing a reduction in production.

Frictional unemployment Unemployment due to the fact that workers must search for appropriate job offers. This takes time, and so they remain temporarily ("frictionally") unemployed.

Full employment As presented by the Council of Economic Advisers, an arbitrary level of unemployment that corresponds to "normal" friction in the labor market. In 1986, the council declared that 6.5 percent unemployment was full employment. Today, it is around 5.5 percent.

Game theory A way of describing the various possible outcomes in any situation involving two or more interacting individuals when those individuals are aware of the interactive nature of their situation and plan accordingly.

The plans made by these individuals are known as *game strategies.*

GDP deflator A price index measuring the changes in prices of all new goods and services produced in the economy.

General Agreement on Tariffs and Trade (GATT) An international agreement established in 1947 to further world trade by reducing barriers and tariffs.

Gold standard An international monetary system in which nations fix their exchange rates in terms of gold. All currencies are fixed in terms of all others, and any balance of payments deficits or surpluses can be made up by shipments of gold.

Goods All things from which individuals derive satisfaction or happiness.

Government, or political, goods Goods (and services) provided by the public sector; they can be either private or public goods.

Gross domestic income (GDI) The sum of all income—wages, interest, rent, and profits—paid to the four factors of production.

Gross domestic product (GDP) The total market value of all final goods and services produced by factors of production located within a nation's borders.

Gross private domestic investment The creation of capital goods, such as factories and machines, that can yield production and hence consumption in the future. Also included in this definition are changes in business inventories and repairs made to machines or buildings.

Gross public debt All federal government debt irrespective of who owns it.

Horizontal merger The joining of firms that are producing or selling a similar product.

Human capital The accumulated training and education of workers.

Hyperinflation Extremely rapid rise of the average of all prices in an economy.

Implicit costs Expenses that managers do not have to pay out of pocket and hence do not normally explicitly calculate, such as the opportunity cost of factors of production that are owned; examples are owner-provided capital and owner-provided labor.

Import quota A physical supply restriction on imports of a particular good, such as sugar. Foreign exporters are unable to sell in the United States more than the quantity specified in the import quota.

Incentive-compatible contract A loan contract under which a significant amount of the borrower's assets are at risk, providing an incentive for the borrower to look after the lender's interests.

Incentives Rewards for engaging in a particular activity.

Incentive structure The motivational rewards and costs that individuals face in any given situation. Each economic system has its own incentive structure. The incentive structure is different under a system of private property than under a system of government-owned property, for example. *Can also be viewed as* the system of rewards and punishments individuals face with respect to their own actions.

Income approach A way of measuring national income by adding up all components of national income, including wages, interest, rent, and profits.

Income-consumption curve The set of optimum consumption points that would occur if income were increased, relative prices remaining constant.

Income elasticity of demand (E_i) The percentage change in demand for any good, holding its price constant, divided by the percentage change in income; the responsiveness of the demand to changes in income, holding the good's relative price constant.

Income in kind Income received in the form of goods and services, such as housing or medical care; to be contrasted with money income, which is simply income in dollars, or general purchasing power, that can be used to buy *any* goods and services.

Income velocity of money The number of times per year a dollar is spent on final goods and services; equal to GDP divided by the money supply.

Increasing-cost industry An industry in which an increase in industry output is accompanied by an increase in long-run per-unit costs, such that the long-run industry supply curve slopes upward.

Independent variable A variable whose value is determined independently of, or outside, the equation under study.

Indifference curve A curve composed of a set of consumption alternatives, each of which yields the same total amount of satisfaction.

Indirect business taxes All business taxes except the tax on corporate profits. Indirect business taxes include sales and business property taxes.

Industrial unions Labor unions that consist of workers from a particular industry, such as automobile manufacturing or steel manufacturing.

Industry supply curve The locus of points showing the minimum prices at which given quantities will be forthcoming; also called the *market supply curve*.

Inefficient point Any point below the production possibilities curve at which resources are being used inefficiently.

Inelastic demand A demand relationship in which a given percentage change in price will result in a less than proportionate percentage change in the quantity demanded. Total expenditures and price are directly related in the inelastic region of the demand curve.

Infant industry argument The contention that tariffs should be imposed to protect from import competition an industry that is trying to get started. Presumably, after the industry becomes technologically efficient, the tariff can be lifted.

Inferior goods Goods for which demand falls as income rises.

Inflation The situation in which the average of all prices of goods and services in an economy is rising.

Innovation Transforming an invention into something that is useful to humans.

Inside information Information that is not available to the general public about what is happening in a corporation.

Insider-outsider theory A theory of labor markets in which workers who are already employed have an influence on wage bargaining in such a way that outsiders who are willing to work for lower real wages cannot get a job.

Intelligent shopping agents Computer programs that an individual or business user of the Internet can instruct to carry out a specific task, such as looking for the lowest-priced car of a particular make and model. The agent then searches the Internet (usually just the World Wide Web) and may even purchase the product when the best price has been found.

Interest The payment for current rather than future command over resources; the cost of obtaining credit. Also, the return paid to owners of capital.

Interest group Any group that seeks to cause government to change spending in a way that will benefit the group's members or to undertake any other action that will improve their lot. Also called a *special-interest group*.

Interest rate effect One of the reasons that the aggregate demand curve slopes down is because higher price levels indirectly increase the interest rate, which in turn causes businesses and consumers to reduce desired spending due to the higher cost of borrowing.

Intermediate goods Goods used up entirely in the production of final goods.

International Monetary Fund (IMF) An institution set up to manage the international monetary system, established in 1945 under the Bretton Woods Agreement Act, which established fixed exchange rates for the world's currencies.

Inventory investment Changes in the stocks of finished goods and goods in process, as well as changes in the raw materials that businesses keep on hand. Whenever inventories are decreasing, inventory investment is negative; whenever they are increasing, inventory investment is positive.

Inverse relationship A relationship between two variables that is negative, meaning that an increase in one variable is associated with a decrease in the other and a decrease in one variable is associated with an increase in the other.

Investment Any use of today's resources to expand tomorrow's production or consumption. *Can also be viewed as* the spending by businesses on things such as machines and buildings, which can be used to produce goods and services in the future. The investment part of total income is the portion that will be used in the process of producing goods in the future.

Job leaver An individual in the labor force who quits voluntarily.

Job loser An individual in the labor force who was employed and whose employment was involuntarily terminated or who was laid off.

Jurisdictional dispute A dispute involving two or more unions over which should have control of a particular jurisdiction, such as a particular craft or skill or a particular firm or industry.

Keynesian short-run aggregate supply curve The horizontal portion of the aggregate supply curve in which there is unemployment and unused capacity in the economy.

Labor Productive contributions of humans who work, involving both mental and physical activities.

Labor force Individuals aged 16 years or older who either have jobs or are looking and available for jobs; the number of employed plus the number of unemployed.

Labor force participation rate
The percentage of noninstitutionalized working-age individuals who are employed or seeking employment.

Labor market signaling   The process by which a potential worker's acquisition of credentials, such as a degree, is used by the employer to predict future productivity.

Labor productivity   Total real domestic output (real GDP) divided by the number of workers (output per worker).

Labor unions   Worker organizations that seek to secure economic improvements for their members; they also seek to improve the safety, health, and other benefits (such as job security) of their members.

Laissez-faire   French for "leave [it] alone"; applied to an economic system in which the government minimizes its interference with economy.

Land   The natural resources that are available from nature. Land as a resource includes location, original fertility and mineral deposits, topography, climate, water, and vegetation.

Law of demand   The observation that there is a negative, or inverse, relationship between the price of any good or service and the quantity demanded, holding other factors constant.

Law of diminishing (marginal) returns   The observation that after some point, successive equal-sized increases in a variable factor of production, such as labor, added to fixed factors of production, will result in smaller increases in output.

Law of increasing relative cost   The observation that the opportunity cost of additional units of a good generally increases as society attempts to produce more of that good. This accounts for the bowed-out shape of the production possibilities curve.

Law of supply   The observation that the higher the price of a good, the more of that good sellers will make

available over a specified time period, other things being equal.

Least-cost combination   The level of input use that produces a given level of output at minimum cost.

Legal reserves   Reserves that depository institutions are allowed by law to claim as reserves—for example, deposits held at Federal Reserve district banks and vault cash.

Lemons problem   The situation in which consumers, who do not know details about the quality of a product, are willing to pay no more than the price of a low-quality product, even if a higher-quality product at a higher price exists.

Liabilities   Amounts owed; the legal claims against a business or household by nonowners.

Limited liability   A legal concept whereby the responsibility, or liability, of the owners of a corporation is limited to the value of the shares in the firm that they own.

Limit-pricing model   A model that hypothesizes that a group of colluding sellers will set the highest common price that they believe they can charge without new firms seeking to enter that industry in search of relatively high profits.

Liquidity   The degree to which an asset can be acquired or disposed of without much danger of any intervening loss in *nominal* value and with small transaction costs. Money is the most liquid asset.

Liquidity approach   A method of measuring the money supply by looking at money as a temporary store of value.

Logrolling   The practice of exchanging political favors by elected representatives. Typically, one elected official agrees to vote for the policy of another official in exchange for the vote of the latter in favor of the former's desired policy.

Long run   The time period in which all factors of production can be varied.

Long-run aggregate supply curve   A vertical line representing real output of goods and services based on full information and after full adjustment has occurred. *Can also be viewed as* representing the real output of the economy under conditions of full employment—the full-employment level of real GDP.

Long-run average cost curve   The locus of points representing the minimum unit cost of producing any given rate of output, given current technology and resource prices.

Long-run industry supply curve   A market supply curve showing the relationship between price and quantities forthcoming after firms have been allowed the time to enter into or exit from an industry, depending on whether there have been positive or negative economic profits.

Lorenz curve   A geometric representation of the distribution of income. A Lorenz curve that is perfectly straight represents perfect income equality. The more bowed a Lorenz curve, the more unequally income is distributed.

Lump-sum tax   A tax that does not depend on income or the circumstances of the taxpayer. An example is a $1,000 tax that every family must pay, irrespective of its economic situation.

M1   The money supply, taken as the total value of currency plus checkable deposits plus traveler's checks not issued by banks.

M2   M1 plus (1) savings and small-denomination time deposits at all depository institutions, (2) overnight repurchase agreements at commercial banks, (3) overnight Eurodollars held by U.S. residents other than banks at Caribbean branches of member banks, (4) balances in retail money market mutual funds, and (5) money market deposit accounts (MMDAs).

Macroeconomics   The study of the behavior of the economy as a whole, including such economywide phenomena as changes in unemployment, the general price level, and national income.

Majority rule A collective decision-making system in which group decisions are made on the basis of 50.1 percent of the vote. In other words, whatever more than half of the electorate votes for, the entire electorate has to accept.

Marginal cost pricing A system of pricing in which the price charged is equal to the opportunity cost to society of producing one more unit of the good or service in question. The opportunity cost is the marginal cost to society.

Marginal costs The change in total costs due to a one-unit change in production rate.

Marginal factor cost (MFC) The cost of using an additional unit of an input. For example, if a firm can hire all the workers it wants at the going wage rate, the marginal factor cost of labor is the wage rate.

Marginal physical product The physical output that is due to the addition of one more unit of a variable factor of production; the change in total product occurring when a variable input is increased and all other inputs are held constant; also called *marginal productivity* or *marginal return*.

Marginal physical product (MPP) of labor The change in output resulting from the addition of one more worker. The MPP of the worker equals the change in total output accounted for by hiring the worker, holding all other factors of production constant.

Marginal propensity to consume (MPC) The ratio of the change in consumption to the change in disposable income. A marginal propensity to consume of .8 tells us that an additional $100 in take-home pay will lead to an additional $80 consumed.

Marginal propensity to save (MPS) The ratio of the change in saving to the change in disposable income. A marginal propensity to save of .2 indicates that out of an additional $100 in take-home pay, $20 will be saved. Whatever is not saved is consumed. The marginal propensity to save plus the marginal propensity

to consume must always equal 1, by definition.

Marginal revenue The change in total revenues resulting from a change in output (and sale) of one unit of the product in question.

Marginal revenue product (MRP) The marginal physical product (MPP) times marginal revenue. The MRP gives the additional revenue obtained from a one-unit change in labor input.

Marginal tax rate The change in the tax payment divided by the change in income, or the percentage of additional dollars that must be paid in taxes. The marginal tax rate is applied to the highest tax bracket of taxable income reached.

Marginal utility The change in total utility due to a one-unit change in the quantity of a good or service consumed.

Market All of the arrangements that individuals have for exchanging with one another. Thus we can speak of the labor market, the automobile market, and the credit market.

Market clearing, or **equilibrium, price** The price that clears the market, at which quantity demanded equals quantity supplied; the price where the demand curve intersects the supply curve.

Market demand The demand of all consumers in the marketplace for a particular good or service. The summing at each price of the quantity demanded by each individual.

Market failure A situation in which an unrestrained market economy leads to too few or too many resources going to a specific economic activity.

Market share test The percentage of a market that a particular firm controls, used as the primary measure of monopoly power.

Medical savings accounts (MSAs) A tax-exempt health care account to which individuals would pay into on a regular basis and from which medical care expenses could be paid.

Medium of exchange Any asset that sellers will accept as payment.

Merit good A good that has been deemed socially desirable through the political process. Museums are an example.

Microeconomics The study of decision making undertaken by individuals (or households) and by firms.

Minimum efficient scale (MES) The lowest rate of output per unit time at which long-run average costs for a particular firm are at a minimum.

Minimum wage A wage floor, legislated by government, setting the lowest hourly rate that firms may legally pay workers.

Mixed economy An economic system in which decisions about how resources should be used are made partly by the private sector and partly by the government, or the public sector.

Models, or **theories** Simplified representations of the real world used as the basis for predictions or explanations.

Monetarists Macroeconomists who believe that inflation is always caused by excessive monetary growth and that changes in the money supply directly affect aggregate demand both directly and indirectly.

Monetary rule A monetary policy that incorporates a rule specifying the annual rate of growth of some monetary aggregate.

Money Any medium that is universally accepted in an economy both by sellers of goods and services as payment for those goods and services and by creditors as payment for debts.

Money illusion Reacting to changes in money prices rather than relative prices. If a worker whose wages double when the price level also doubles thinks he or she is better off, the worker is suffering from money illusion.

Money market deposit accounts (MMDAs) Accounts issued by banks yielding a market rate of interest with a minimum balance requirement and a limit on transactions. They have no minimum maturity.

Money market mutual funds Funds of investment companies that obtain funds from the public that are held in common and used to acquire short-maturity credit instruments, such as certificates of deposit and securities sold by the U.S. government.

Money multiplier The reciprocal of the required reserve ratio, assuming no leakages into currency and no excess reserves. It is equal to 1 divided by the required reserve ratio.

Money multiplier process The process by which an injection of new money into the banking system leads to a multiple expansion in the total money supply.

Money price The price that we observe today, expressed in today's dollars. Also called the *absolute, nominal,* or *current price.*

Money supply The amount of money in circulation.

Monopolist A single supplier that comprises its entire industry for a good or service for which there is no close substitute.

Monopolistic competition A market situation in which a large number of firms produce similar but not identical products. Entry into the industry is relatively easy.

Monopolization The possession of monopoly power in the relevant market and the willful acquisition or maintenance of that power, as distinguished from growth or development as a consequence of a superior product, business acumen, or historical accident.

Monopoly A firm that has great control over the price of a good. In the extreme case, a monopoly is the only seller of a good or service.

Monopsonist A single buyer.

Monopsonistic exploitation Exploitation due to monopsony power. It

leads to a price for the variable input that is less than its marginal revenue product. Monopsonistic exploitation is the difference between marginal revenue product and the wage rate.

Moral hazard A situation in which, after a transaction has taken place, one of the parties to the transaction has an incentive to engage in behavior that will be undesirable from the other party's point of view. *Can also be viewed as* a problem that occurs because of asymmetric information *after* a transaction occurs. In financial markets, a person to whom money has been lent may indulge in more risky behavior, thereby increasing the probability of default on the debt.

Multiplier The ratio of the change in the equilibrium level of real national income to the change in autonomous expenditures; the number by which a change in autonomous investment or autonomous consumption, for example, is multiplied to get the change in the equilibrium level of real national income.

National income accounting A measurement system used to estimate national income and its components; one approach to measuring an economy's aggregate performance.

National income (NI) The total of all factor payments to resource owners. It can be obtained by subtracting indirect business taxes from NDP.

Natural monopoly A monopoly that arises from the peculiar production characteristics in an industry. It usually arises when there are large economies of scale relative to the industry's demand such that one firm can produce at a lower average cost than can be achieved by multiple firms.

Natural rate of unemployment The rate of unemployment that is estimated to prevail in long-run macroeconomic equilibrium, when all workers and employers have fully adjusted to any changes in the economy.

Near monies Assets that are almost money. They have a high degree of liq-

uidity; they can be easily converted into money without loss in value. Time deposits and short-term U.S. government securities are examples.

Negative-sum game A game in which all players are worse off at the end of the game.

Net domestic product (NDP) GDP minus depreciation.

Net investment Gross private domestic investment minus an estimate of the wear and tear on the existing capital stock. Net investment therefore measures the change in capital stock over a one-year period.

Net public debt Gross public debt minus all government interagency borrowing.

Net worth The difference between assets and liabilities.

New classical model A modern version of the classical model in which wages and prices are flexible, there is pure competition in all markets, and the rational expectations hypothesis is assumed to be working.

New entrant An individual who has never held a full-time job lasting two weeks or longer but is now in the labor force.

New growth theory A relatively modern theory of economic growth that examines the factors that determine why technology, research, innovation, and the like are undertaken and how they interact.

New Keynesian economics Economic models based on the idea that demand creates its own supply as a result of various possible government fiscal and monetary coordination failures.

Nominal rate of interest The market rate of interest expressed in today's dollars.

Nominal values The values of variables such as GDP and investment expressed in current dollars, also called *money values;* measurement in terms of the actual market prices at which goods are sold.

Nonaccelerating inflation rate of unemployment (NAIRU) The rate of unemployment below which the rate of inflation tends to rise and above which the rate of inflation tends to fall.

Noncooperative game A game in which the players neither negotiate nor collude in any way. As applied to firms in an industry, this is the common situation in which there are relatively few firms and each has some ability to change price.

Nondurable consumer goods Consumer goods that are used up within three years.

Nonincome expense items The total of indirect business taxes and depreciation.

Nonprice rationing devices All methods used to ration scarce goods that are price controlled. Whenever the price system is not allowed to work, nonprice rationing devices will evolve to ration the affected goods and services.

Normal goods Goods for which demand rises as income rises. Most goods are considered normal.

Normal rate of return The amount that must be paid to an investor to induce investment in a business; also known as the *opportunity cost of capital*.

Normative economics Analysis involving value judgments about economic policies; relates to whether things are good or bad. A statement of *what ought to be*.

Number line A line that can be divided into segments of equal length, each associated with a number.

Oligopoly A market situation in which there are very few sellers. Each seller knows that the other sellers will react to its changes in prices and quantities.

Open economy effect One of the reasons that the aggregate demand curve slopes downward is because higher price levels result in foreigners' desiring to buy fewer American-made goods while Americans now desire more foreign-made goods, thereby reducing net exports, which is equivalent to a reduction in the amount of real goods and services purchased in the United States.

Open market operations The purchase and sale of existing U.S. government securities (such as bonds) in the open private market by the Federal Reserve System.

Opportunistic behavior Actions that ignore the possible long-run benefits of cooperation and focus solely on short-run gains.

Opportunity cost The highest-valued, next-best alternative that must be sacrificed to attain something or to satisfy a want.

Opportunity cost of capital The normal rate of return, or the available return on the next-best alternative investment. Economists consider this a cost of production, and it is included in our cost examples.

Optimal quantity of pollution The level of pollution for which the marginal benefit of one additional unit of clean air just equals the marginal cost of that additional unit of clean air.

Origin The intersection of the *y* axis and the *x* axis in a graph.

Partnership A business owned by two or more co-owners, or partners, who share the responsibilities and the profits of the firm and are individually liable for all of the debts of the partnership.

Par value The legally established value of the monetary unit of one country in terms of that of another.

Passive (nondiscretionary) policymaking Policymaking that is carried out in response to a rule. It is therefore not in response to an actual or potential change in overall economic activity.

Patent A government protection that gives an inventor the exclusive right to make, use, or sell an invention for a limited period of time (currently, 17 years).

Payoff matrix A matrix of outcomes, or consequences, of the strategies available to the players in a game.

Perfect competition A market structure in which the decisions of individual buyers and sellers have no effect on market price.

Perfectly competitive firm A firm that is such a small part of the total industry that it cannot affect the price of the product it sells.

Perfectly elastic demand A demand that has the characteristic that even the slightest increase in price will lead to zero quantity demanded.

Perfectly elastic supply A supply characterized by a reduction in quantity supplied to zero when there is the slightest decrease in price.

Perfectly inelastic demand A demand that exhibits zero responsiveness to price changes; no matter what the price is, the quantity demanded remains the same.

Perfectly inelastic supply A supply for which quantity supplied remains constant, no matter what happens to price.

Personal income (PI) The amount of income that households actually receive before they pay personal income taxes.

Phillips curve A curve showing the relationship between unemployment and changes in wages or prices. It was long thought to reflect a trade-off between unemployment and inflation.

Physical capital All manufactured resources, including buildings, equipment, machines, and improvements to land that is used for production.

Planning curve The long-run average cost curve.

Planning horizon The long run, during which all inputs are variable.

Plant size The physical size of the factories that a firm owns and operates to produce its output. Plant size can be defined by square footage, maximum physical capacity, and other physical measures.

Policy irrelevance proposition The new classical and rational expectations conclusion that policy actions have no real effects in the short run if the policy actions are anticipated and none in the long run even if the policy actions are unanticipated.

Positive economics Analysis that is strictly limited to making either purely descriptive statements or scientific predictions; for example, "If A, then B." A statement of *what is*.

Positive-sum game A game in which players as a group are better off at the end of the game.

Precautionary demand Holding money to meet unplanned expenditures and emergencies.

Present value The value of a future amount expressed in today's dollars; the most that someone would pay today to receive a certain sum at some point in the future.

Price ceiling A legal maximum price that may be charged for a particular good or service.

Price-consumption curve The set of consumer optimum combinations of two goods that the consumer would choose as the price of one good changes, while money income and the price of the other good remain constant.

Price controls Government-mandated minimum or maximum prices that may be charged for goods and services.

Price differentiation Establishing different prices for similar products to reflect differences in marginal cost in providing those commodities to different groups of buyers.

Price discrimination Selling a given product at more than one price, with the price difference being unrelated to differences in cost.

Price elasticity of demand (E_p) The responsiveness of the quantity de-

manded of a commodity to changes in its price; defined as the percentage change in quantity demanded divided by the percentage change in price.

Price elasticity of supply (E_s) The responsiveness of the quantity supplied of a commodity to a change in its price; the percentage change in quantity supplied divided by the percentage change in price.

Price floor A legal minimum price below which a good or service may not be sold. Legal minimum wages are an example.

Price index The cost of today's market basket of goods expressed as a percentage of the cost of the same market basket during a base year.

Price leadership A practice in many oligopolistic industries in which the largest firm publishes its price list ahead of its competitors, who then match those announced prices. Also called *parallel pricing*.

Price searcher A firm that must determine the price-output combination that maximizes profit because it faces a downward-sloping demand curve.

Price system An economic system in which relative prices are constantly changing to reflect changes in supply and demand for different commodities. The prices of those commodities are signals to everyone within the system as to what is relatively scarce and what is relatively abundant.

Price taker A competitive firm that must take the price of its product as given because the firm cannot influence its price.

Price war A pricing campaign designed to drive competing firms out of a market by repeatedly cutting prices.

Primary market A financial market in which newly issued securities are bought and sold.

Principal-agent problem The conflict of interest that occurs when agents—managers of firms—pursue

their own objectives to the detriment of the goals of the firms' principals, or owners.

Principle of rival consumption The recognition that individuals are rivals in consuming private goods because one person's consumption reduces the amount available for others to consume.

Principle of substitution The principle that consumers and producers shift away from goods and resources that become relatively higher priced in favor of goods and resources that are now relatively lower priced.

Prisoners' dilemma A famous strategic game in which two prisoners have a choice between confessing and not confessing to a crime. If neither confesses, they serve a minimum sentence. If both confess, they serve a maximum sentence. If one confesses and the other doesn't, the one who confesses goes free. The dominant strategy is always to confess.

Private costs Costs borne solely by the individuals who incur them. Also called *internal costs*.

Private goods Goods that can be consumed by only one individual at a time. Private goods are subject to the principle of rival consumption.

Private property rights Exclusive rights of ownership that allow the use, transfer, and exchange of property.

Privatization The sale or transfer of state-owned property and businesses to the private sector, in part or in whole. Also refers to *contracting out*—letting private business take over government-provided services such as trash collection.

Producer durables, or **capital goods** Durable goods having an expected service life of more than three years that are used by businesses to produce other goods and services.

Producer Price Index (PPI) A statistical measure of a weighted average of prices of commodities that firms purchase from other firms.

Product differentiation The distinguishing of products by brand name, color, and other minor attributes. Product differentiation occurs in other than perfectly competitive markets in which products are, in theory, homogeneous, such as wheat or corn.

Production Any activity that results in the conversion of resources into products that can be used in consumption.

Production function The relationship between inputs and output. A production function is a technological, not an economic, relationship.

Production possibilities curve (PPC) A curve representing all possible combinations of total output that could be produced assuming (1) a fixed amount of productive resources of a given quality and (2) the efficient use of those resources.

Profit-maximizing rate of production The rate of production that maximizes total profits, or the difference between total revenues and total costs; also, the rate of production at which marginal revenue equals marginal cost.

Progressive taxation A tax system in which as income increases, a higher percentage of the additional income is taxed. The marginal tax rate exceeds the average tax rate as income rises.

Property rights The rights of an owner to use and to exchange property.

Proportional rule A decision-making system in which actions are based on the proportion of the "votes" cast and are in proportion to them. In a market system, if 10 percent of the "dollar votes" are cast for blue cars, 10 percent of the output will be blue cars.

Proportional taxation A tax system in which regardless of an individual's income, the tax bill comprises exactly the same proportion. Also called a *flat-rate tax.*

Proprietorship A business owned by one individual who makes the business decisions, receives all the profits, and is legally responsible for all the debts of the firm.

Protocol The data formatting system that permits computers to access each other and communicate.

Public debt The total value of all outstanding federal government securities.

Public goods Goods to which the principle of rival consumption does not apply; they can be jointly consumed by many individuals simultaneously at no additional cost and with no reduction in quality or quantity.

Purchasing power The value of money for buying goods and services. If your money income stays the same but the price of one good that you are buying goes up, your effective purchasing power falls, and vice versa.

Purchasing power parity Adjustment in exchange rate conversions that takes into account differences in the true cost of living across countries.

Quota system A government-imposed restriction on the quantity of a specific good that another country is allowed to sell in the United States. In other words, quotas are restrictions on imports. These restrictions are usually applied to one or several specific countries.

Random walk theory The theory there are no predictable trends in security prices that can be used to "get rich quick."

Rate of discount The rate of interest used to discount future sums back to present value.

Rate-of-return regulation Regulation that seeks to keep the rate of return in the industry at a competitive level by not allowing excessive prices to be charged.

Rational expectations hypothesis A theory stating that people combine the effects of past policy changes on important economic variables with their own judgment about the future effects of current and future policy changes.

Rationality assumption The assumption that people do not intentionally make decisions that would leave them worse off.

Reaction function The manner in which one oligopolist reacts to a change in price, output, or quality made by another oligopolist in the industry.

Real-balance effect The change in the real value of money balances when the price level changes, all other things held constant. Also called the *wealth effect.*

Real business cycle theory An extension and modification of the theories of the new classical economists of the 1970s and 1980s, in which money is neutral and only real, supply-side factors matter in influencing labor employment and real output.

Real-income effect The change in people's purchasing power that occurs when, other things being constant, the price of one good that they purchase changes. When that price goes up, real income, or purchasing power, falls, and when that price goes down, real income increases.

Real rate of interest The nominal rate of interest minus the anticipated rate of inflation.

Real values Measurement of economic values after adjustments have been made for changes in the average of prices between years.

Recession A period of time during which the rate of growth of business activity is consistently less than its long-term trend or is negative.

Recognition time lag The time required to gather information about the current state of the economy.

Recycling The reuse of raw materials derived from manufactured products.

Reentrant An individual who used to work full time but left the labor force and has now reentered it looking for a job.

Regressive taxation A tax system in which as more dollars are earned, the percentage of tax paid on them falls. The marginal tax rate is less than the average tax rate as income rises.

Reinvestment Profits (or depreciation reserves) used to purchase new capital equipment.

Relative price The price of one commodity divided by the price of another commodity; the number of units of one commodity that must be sacrificed to purchase one unit of another commodity.

Rent control The placement of price ceilings on rents in particular cities.

Rent seeking The use of resources in an attempt to get government to bestow a benefit on an interest group.

Repricing, or menu, cost of inflation The cost associated with recalculating prices and printing new price lists when there is inflation.

Repurchase agreement (REPO, or RP) An agreement made by a bank to sell Treasury or federal agency securities to its customers, coupled with an agreement to repurchase them at a price that includes accumulated interest.

Required reserve ratio The percentage of total deposits that the Fed requires depository institutions to hold in the form of vault cash or deposits with the Fed.

Required reserves The value of reserves that a depository institution must hold in the form of vault cash or deposits with the Fed.

Reserves In the U.S. Federal Reserve System, deposits held by Federal Reserve district banks for depository institutions, plus depository institutions' vault cash.

Resource allocation The assignment of resources to specific uses by determining what will be produced, how it will be produced, and for whom it will be produced.

Resources Things used to produce other things to satisfy people's wants.

Retained earnings Earnings that a corporation saves, or retains, for investment in other productive activities; earnings that are not distributed to stockholders.

Ricardian equivalence theorem The proposition that an increase in the government budget deficit has no effect on aggregate demand.

Right-to-work laws Laws that make it illegal to require union membership as a condition of continuing employment in a particular firm.

Saving The act of not consuming all of one's current income. Whatever is not consumed out of spendable income is, by definition, saved. *Saving* is an action measured over time (a flow), whereas *savings* are a stock, an accumulation resulting from the act of saving in the past.

Savings deposits Interest-earning funds that can be withdrawn at any time without payment of a penalty.

Say's law A dictum of economist J. B. Say that supply creates its own demand; producing goods and services generates the means and the willingness to purchase other goods and services.

Scarcity A situation in which the ingredients for producing the things that people desire are insufficient to satisfy all wants.

Seasonal unemployment Unemployment resulting from the seasonal pattern of work in specific industries. It is usually due to seasonal fluctuations in demand or to changing weather conditions, rendering work difficult, if not impossible, as in the agriculture, construction, and tourist industries.

Secondary boycott A boycott of companies or products sold by companies that are dealing with a company being struck.

Secondary market A financial market in which previously issued securities are bought and sold.

Separation of ownership and control The situation that exists in corporations in which the owners (shareholders) are not the people who control the operation of the corporation (managers). The goals of these two groups are often different.

Services Mental or physical labor or help purchased by consumers. Examples are the assistance of doctors, lawyers, dentists, repair personnel, housecleaners, educators, retailers, and wholesalers; things purchased or used by consumers that do not have physical characteristics.

Share of stock A legal claim to a share of a corporation's future profits; if it is *common stock,* it incorporates certain voting rights regarding major policy decisions of the corporation; if it is *preferred stock,* its owners are accorded preferential treatment in the payment of dividends.

Share-the-gains, share-the-pains theory A theory of regulatory behavior in which the regulators must take account of the demands of three groups: legislators, who established and who oversee the regulatory agency; members of the regulated industry; and consumers of the regulated industry's products or services.

Shortage A situation in which quantity demanded is greater than quantity supplied at a price below the market clearing price.

Short run The time period when at least one input, such as plant size, cannot be changed.

Short-run aggregate supply curve The relationship between aggregate supply and the price level in the short run, all other things held constant; the curve is normally positively sloped.

Short-run break-even price The price at which a firm's total revenues equal its total costs. At the break-even price, the firm is just making a normal rate of return on its capital investment. (It is covering its explicit and implicit costs.)

Short-run shutdown price The price that just covers average variable costs. It occurs just below the intersection of the marginal cost curve and the average variable cost curve.

Signals Compact ways of conveying to economic decision makers information needed to make decisions. A true signal not only conveys information but also provides the incentive to react appropriately. Economic profits and economic losses are such signals.

Slope The change in the y value divided by the corresponding change in the x value of a curve; the "incline" of the curve.

Small-menu cost theory A hypothesis that it is costly for firms to change prices in response to demand changes because of the cost of renegotiating contracts, printing price lists, and so on.

Social costs The full costs borne by society whenever a resource use occurs. Social costs can be measured by adding private, or internal, costs to external costs.

Socialism An economic system in which the state owns the major share of productive resources except labor. Socialism also usually involves the redistribution of income.

Special drawing rights (SDRs) Reserve assets created by the International Monetary Fund that countries can use to settle international payments.

Specialization The division of productive activities among persons and regions so that no one individual or one area is totally self-sufficient. An individual may specialize, for example, in law or medicine. A nation may specialize in the production of coffee, computers, or cameras.

Standard of deferred payment A property of an asset that makes it desirable for use as a means of settling debts maturing in the future; an essential property of money.

Stock The quantity of something, measured at a given point in time—for example, an inventory of goods or a bank account. Stocks are defined independently of time, although they are assessed at a point in time.

Store of value The ability to hold value over time; a necessary property of money.

Strategic dependence A situation in which one firm's actions with respect to price, quality, advertising, and related changes may be strategically countered by the reactions of one or more other firms in the industry. Such dependence can exist only when there are a limited number of major firms in an industry.

Strategy Any rule that is used to make a choice, such as "Always pick heads"; any potential choice that can be made by players in a game.

Strikebreakers Temporary or permanent workers hired by a company to replace union members who are striking.

Structural unemployment Unemployment resulting from fundamental changes in the structure of the economy. It occurs, for example, when the demand for a product falls drastically so that workers specializing in the production of that product find themselves out of work.

Subsidy A negative tax; a payment to a producer from the government, usually in the form of a cash grant.

Substitutes Two goods are substitutes when either one can be used for consumption to satisfy a similar want—for example, coffee and tea. The more you buy of one, the less you buy of the other. For substitutes, the change in the price of one causes a shift in demand for the other in the same direction as the price change.

Substitution effect The tendency of people to substitute cheaper commodities for more expensive commodities.

Supply A schedule showing the relationship between price and quantity supplied for a specified period of time, other things being equal.

Supply curve The graphical representation of the supply schedule; a line (curve) showing the supply schedule, which generally slopes upward (has a positive slope), other things being equal.

Supply-side economics The notion that creating incentives for individuals and firms to increase productivity will cause the aggregate supply curve to shift outward.

Surplus A situation in which quantity supplied is greater than quantity demanded at a price above the market clearing price.

Sympathy strike A strike by a union in sympathy with another union's strike or cause.

Target price A price set by the government for specific agricultural products. If the market clearing price is below the target price, a *deficiency payment*, equal to the difference between the market price and the target price, is given to farmers for each unit of the good they produce.

Tariffs Taxes on imported goods.

Tax bracket A specified interval of income to which a specific and unique marginal tax rate is applied.

Tax incidence The distribution of tax burdens among various groups in society.

Technology Society's pool of applied knowledge concerning how goods and services can be produced.

Terms of exchange The terms under which trading takes place. Usually the terms of exchange are equal to the price at which a good is traded.

Theory of contestable markets A hypothesis concerning pricing behavior that holds that even though there are only a few firms in an industry, they are forced to price their products more or less competitively because of the ease of entry by outsiders. The key aspect of a contestable market is relatively costless entry into and exit from the industry.

Theory of public choice The study of collective decision making.

Third parties   Parties who are not directly involved in a given activity or transaction. For example, in the relationship between caregivers and patients, fees may be paid by third parties (insurance companies, government).

Thrift institutions   Financial institutions that receive most of their funds from the savings of the public; they include mutual savings banks, savings and loan associations, and credit unions

Time deposit   A deposit in a financial institution that requires notice of intent to withdraw or must be left for an agreed period. Withdrawal of funds prior to the end of the agreed period may result in a penalty.

Tit-for-tat strategic behavior   In game theory, cooperation that continues so long as the other players continue to cooperate.

Total costs   The sum of total fixed costs and total variable costs.

Total income   The yearly amount earned by the nation's resources (factors of production). Total income therefore includes wages, rent, interest payments, and profits that are received, respectively, by workers, landowners, capital owners, and entrepreneurs.

Total revenues   The price per unit times the total quantity sold.

Transaction costs   All of the costs associated with exchanging, including the informational costs of finding out price and quality, service record, and durability of a product, plus the cost of contracting and enforcing that contract.

Transactions accounts   Checking account balances in commercial banks and other types of financial institutions, such as credit unions and mutual savings banks; any accounts in financial institutions on which you can easily write checks without many restrictions.

Transactions approach   A method of measuring the money supply by looking at money as a medium of exchange.

Transactions demand   Holding money as a medium of exchange to make payments. The level varies directly with nominal national income.

Transfer payments   Money payments made by governments to individuals for which in return no services or goods are concurrently rendered. Examples are welfare, Social Security, and unemployment insurance benefits.

Transfers in kind   Payments that are in the form of actual goods and services, such as food stamps, low-cost public housing, and medical care, and for which in return no goods or services are rendered concurrently.

Traveler's checks   Financial instruments purchased from a bank or a non-banking organization and signed during purchase that can be used as cash upon a second signature by the purchaser.

Unanticipated inflation   Inflation at a rate that comes as a surprise, either higher or lower than the rate anticipated.

Unemployment   The total number of adults (aged 16 years or older) who are willing and able to work and who are actively looking for work but have not found a job.

Union shop   A business enterprise that allows the hiring of nonunion members, conditional on their joining the union by some specified date after employment begins.

Unit elasticity of demand   A demand relationship in which the quantity demanded changes exactly in proportion to the change in price. Total expenditures are invariant to price changes in the unit-elastic portion of the demand curve.

Unit of accounting   A measure by which prices are expressed; the common denominator of the price system; a central property of money.

Unlimited liability   A legal concept whereby the personal assets of the owner of a firm can be seized to pay off the firm's debts.

Util   A representative unit by which utility is measured.

Utility   The want-satisfying power of a good or service.

Utility analysis   The analysis of consumer decision making based on utility maximization.

Value added   The dollar value of an industry's sales minus the value of intermediate goods (for example, raw materials and parts) used in production.

Variable costs   Costs that vary with the rate of production. They include wages paid to workers and purchases of materials.

Vertical merger   The joining of a firm with another to which it sells an output or from which it buys an input.

Voluntary exchange   An act of trading, done on a voluntary basis, in which both parties to the trade are subjectively better off after the exchange.

Voluntary import expansion (VIE)   An official agreement with another country in which it agrees to import more from the United States.

Voluntary restraint agreement (VRA)   An official agreement with another country that "voluntarily" restricts the quantity of its exports to the United States.

Wait unemployment   Unemployment that is caused by wage rigidities resulting from minimum wages, unions, and other factors.

Wants   What people would buy if their incomes were unlimited.

Wealth   The stock of assets owned by a person, household, firm, or nation. For a household, wealth can consist of a house, cars, personal belongings, bank accounts, and cash.

World Trade Organization (WTO)   The successor organization to GATT, it handles all trade disputes among its 132 member nations.

x axis   The horizontal axis in a graph.

y axis   The vertical axis in a graph.

Zero-sum game   A game in which any gains within the group are exactly offset by equal losses by the end of the game.

MACROECONOMIC PRINCIPLES

COST OF HOLDING MONEY

The cost of holding money (its opportunity cost) is measured by the alternative interest yield obtainable by holding some other asset.

POLICY IRRELEVANCE PROPOSITION

Under the assumption of rational expectations on the part of decision makers in the economy, anticipated monetary policy cannot alter either the rate of unemployment or the level of real GDP. Regardless of the nature of the anticipated policy, the unemployment rate will equal the natural rate, and real GDP will be determined solely by the economy's long-run aggregate supply curve.

NATURAL RATE OF UNEMPLOYMENT

The natural rate of unemployment is the rate of unemployment that exists when workers and employers correctly anticipate the rate of inflation.

EQUATION OF EXCHANGE

$$M_s V = PQ$$

where M_s = actual money balances held by the nonbanking public
V = income velocity of money, or the number of times, on average, each monetary unit is spent on final goods and services
P = price level or price index
Q = real national output (real GDP)

MONEY MULTIPLIER

The reciprocal of the required reserve ratio, assuming no leakages into currency and no excess reserves, is the money multiplier.

$$\text{Money multiplier} = \frac{1}{\text{required reserve ratio}}$$

DEFINITION OF MONEY SUPPLY

M1 = currency + checkable accounts + traveler's checks

M2 = M1 +
1. Savings and small-denomination time deposits at all depository institutions
2. Overnight repurchase agreements at commercial banks
3. Overnight Eurodollars issued to U.S. residents by foreign branches of U.S. banks worldwide
4. Balances in money market mutual funds
5. Money market deposit accounts (MMDAs)

RELATIONSHIP BETWEEN IMPORTS AND EXPORTS

In the long run, imports are paid for by exports.

Therefore, any restriction of imports ultimately reduces exports.

MICROECONOMIC PRINCIPLES

OPPORTUNITY COST

In economics, cost is always a forgone opportunity.

LAW OF DEMAND

When the price of a good goes up, people buy less of it, *other things being equal.*

MOVEMENT ALONG, VERSUS SHIFT IN, A CURVE

If the relative price changes, we *move along* a curve–there is a change in quantity demanded and/or supplied. If something else changes, we *shift* a curve–there is a change in demand and/or supply.

INCOME ELASTICITY OF DEMAND

$$\text{Income elasticity of demand} = \frac{\text{percentage change in demand for a good}}{\text{percentage change in income}}$$

LAW OF DIMINISHING RETURNS

As successive equal increases in a variable factor of production, such as labor, are added to other fixed factors of production, such as capital, there will be a point beyond which the extra, or marginal, product that can be attributed to each additional unit of the variable factor of production will decline.

SUPPLY

At higher prices, a larger quantity will generally be supplied than at lower prices, *all other things held constant.*

Or stated otherwise:

At lower prices, a smaller quantity will generally be supplied than at higher prices, *all other things held constant.*

PROFITS

$$\text{Accounting profits} = \text{total revenues} - \text{total costs}$$

$$\text{Economic profits} = \text{total revenues} - \text{total opportunity cost of all inputs used}$$

ELASTICITY OF DEMAND

$$E_p = \frac{\text{percentage change in quantity demanded}}{\text{percentage change in price}}$$

ELASTICITY OF SUPPLY

$$E_s = \frac{\text{percentage change in quantity supplied}}{\text{percentage change in price}}$$

MONOPSONY AND MONOPOLY

		Output Market Structure	
		Perfect Competition	**Monopoly**
Input Market Structure	**Perfect Competition**	$\text{MC} = \text{MR} = P$ $W = \text{MFC} = \text{MRP}_c$	$\text{MC} = \text{MR}(< P)$ $W = \text{MFC} = \text{MRP}_m\,(< \text{MRP}_c)$
	Monopsony	$\text{MC} = \text{MR} = P$ $W < \text{MFC} = \text{MRP}_c$	$\text{MC} = \text{MR}(< P)$ $W < \text{MFC} = \text{MRP}_m\,(< \text{MRP}_c)$